FOUNDATIONS
OF
DOGMATICS

FOUNDATIONS
OF
DOGMATICS

by
OTTO WEBER

Translated and annotated by
DARRELL L. GUDER

VOLUME I

GRAND RAPIDS, MICHIGAN
WILLIAM B. EERDMANS PUBLISHING COMPANY

Translated from the German edition, *Grundlagen der Dogmatik*, I
Copyright 1955 by Verlag der Buchhandlung des Erziehungsvereins,
Neukirchen: Kreis Moers.

Library of Congress Cataloging in Publication Data
Weber, Otto, 1902-1966.
Foundations of dogmatics.

Translation of: Grundlagen der Dogmatik.
Includes indexes.
1.Theology, Doctrinal. 2. Theology, Doctrinal—
History. I. Title.
BT75.2.W413 1981   230   81-7852
ISBN 0-8028-3554-6   AACR2

Translator's Preface

Since its appearance in Germany, Professor Weber's *Grundlagen* has served generations of theological students as the basic textbook in dogmatics, as well as a valuable reference work. I hope that English-speaking students will find it just as useful, and I have sought to make the translation with that goal in mind. In addition to the translation of the German text, I have provided translations of all material in Latin or other languages used in the original in the German edition. The technical Latin terms are given in parentheses with their English equivalents in quotation marks; they are also indexed in Latin (the index of *termini*), which reference aid will help the student to recognize and use Latin terms which appear frequently in theological works.

With the needs of the English-speaking student in mind, special care has been given to the bibliographical entries. There is a vast amount of theological literature in German which will never be translated into English. All such citations have been expanded into full bibliographical entries, particularly for the scholar who would look to research a theme further. Subtitles of German works have been included, since they customarily give the reader a clear concept of the contents of the book. Whenever a work has been translated, I have used the English edition for quotations and page references, rather than the German original. Commonly used abbreviations for these works are found in the list of abbreviations. Where it has not been possible to find a work, I have indicated this with the abbreviation "n.l." (not located).

Books which appeared before 1800 can seldom be given a full bibliographical entry, since very few of them have been reissued. In those instances, I have simply given Professor Weber's entry with whatever additional bibliographical information could be found. In some instances, the English translation of a cited work did not convey the point Weber was making, and thus a retranslation was necessary. If the English translation appeared a long time after the original German work was published, I have included the German publication date in parentheses with a "g."

Consistency in the translation of theological terms and concepts has been a further goal of the project. The German term *Kirche* has been consistently translated "Church," and the term *Gemeinde* is rendered "Community." Any other terminological problems will be explained in translator's footnotes.

Bibliographical entries are made anew the first time a work is cited within a chapter, and thereafter within the chapter with either *op. cit.* or a short version of the title.

Professor Weber resorted extensively to italics in the German original. In this edition, I have attempted to render his accents and emphases without as much use of italics, since we use italics for foreign terms, whereas German does not. In some cases, italics for emphasis were necessary, but I have been sparing in their use.

Suggestions for the improvement of the translation or information on bibliographical annotation will be very much appreciated and will be taken into account should a further edition ever prove possible.

There are many who should be thanked for their special support in completing this project. First of all, I would like to thank Eerdmans Publishing Company for the initial commission and the grant for a sabbatical to complete the major part of the translation. The president and the editor-in-chief of this distinguished publishing house have been cooperative, encouraging, and exceedingly patient with me, particularly as the annotation and bibliographical project took much longer than originally intended. Further, I would like to mention a group of Scottish clergy whose original attempt at the translation of the two volumes, although incomplete, was often quite helpful to me. I am also grateful to my colleagues in the mission of Young Life who have graciously allowed me the time and opportunity to finish this project after I joined the Training Department of this mission.

Special mention must be given to the following libraries and their staffs, all of whom provided assistance in a uniformly gracious manner: Fuller Theological Seminary, Pasadena, CA; Luther-Northwestern Theological Seminary, St. Paul, MN; St. John's University, Collegeville, MN; Dubuque Theological Seminary, Dubuque, IA; *Bibliothek des Oberkirchenrats*, Stuttgart, Germany; Tutt Library of Colorado College, Colorado Springs, CO; Iliff Theological Seminary, Denver, CO; St. Thomas Seminary, Denver, CO.

Finally, I have been privileged to have the assistance of several graduate and undergraduate students who have devoted many hours to searching out references and completing bibliographical entries: Mr. Michael Douglas, Ludwigsburg, Germany; Mrs. Michael Hassell, Colorado Springs, CO; Mr. William C. Lee, Berlin, Germany; Mr. T. J. McGinty, Colorado Springs, CO; Miss Barbara Thompson, Pasadena, CA. To all of them I extend my hearty thanks.

It would be in the spirit of Otto Weber, who was a master teacher of the Christian faith, for me to dedicate the translation of this work to four Germans, all of whom have been my teachers in the Christian faith, both in their theological discipline and through the personal relationships which we have developed:

Rev. Dr. Helmut Frik, Consistory of the Church of Württemberg, Stuttgart;

†Prof. Dr. Leonhard Goppelt, formerly Professor in the Theological Faculties of the universities of Hamburg and Munich;

Prof. Dr. Hans-Joachim Kraus, formerly Professor at the University of Hamburg Theology Faculty, now Professor of Reformed Theology at the University of Göttingen;

Prof. Dr. Helmut Thielicke, Professor Emeritus of the Theology Faculty of the University of Hamburg.

DARRELL L. GUDER

Foreword

These two volumes are the final result of my initial endeavor to provide the students in my lectures the written materials they required. The inclusion of much of this detailed material is extraordinarily burdensome for lectures, and therefore it is presumably desirable to delegate this task to the printed exposition.

In the presentation and development of this material, however, I have not been able to remain neutral, nor do I believe that this is really possible.

In this fashion a textbook has evolved which, as its title says, describes the "Foundations of Dogmatics." Its purpose is to examine critically the chief elements of dogmatics at the most important points. My own position is stated briefly and, as much as possible, in continual dialogue with the "fathers and brethren"; frequently, my own thinking takes only the form of a critical commentary. This method seems to me to be appropriate not only for didactic reasons. Although dogmatics certainly is subject to a given criterion which is beyond all questioning, it is equally subject to the process of dialogue and discussion with the fathers and brethren, a process which is also subordinate to the given criterion. Dogmatics neither starts anew at a given point in time, nor does it commence with the destruction of what has gone before in history; it begins with critical respect for what has gone before.

I hope to be able to show that listening to the fathers and brethren, while this happens in bondage to the Word of God, makes us free for the contemporary questions. If I see things correctly, the deepest tension under which the work of dogmatics is done today is based on the unbalanced antithesis between a one-sided theology of the incarnation and a one-sided theology of the cross. This antithesis can only be overcome if the one-sided approaches which produce it are eliminated. If this book can contribute something to the present discussion, such a contribution, details apart, lies in the comprehensively undertaken attempt to move beyond this antithesis—even if this is not always immediately obvious. I may assume it to be well known that I am indebted in my work to none of my theological contemporaries so deeply as I am to Karl Barth, and this is shown in numerous references. Barth himself often stated that "Barthians" were not congenial to him, and I believe that I, at any rate, cannot be mistaken for one.

Göttingen, at Pentecost, 1954   Otto Weber

Contents

Abbreviations

AE   Martin Luther, *Luther's Works*, ed. J. Pelikan and H. Lehmann (St. Louis: Concordia, 1955–) (AE—American Edition).

ANF   *The Ante-Nicene Fathers*, ed. Roberts and Donaldson (Buffalo: The Christian Literature Publishing Company, 1884–86).

ANW   *Ancient Christian Writers*, ed. J. Quasten and J. C. Plumpe (Westminster, MD: Newman Press, 1949).

BekSchr   *Die Bekenntnisschriften der evangelisch-lutherischen Kirche*, ed. E. Wolf (Göttingen: Vandenhoeck and Ruprecht, 1967).

CD   Karl Barth, *Church Dogmatics*, ed. G. W. Bromiley and T. F. Torrance (Edinburgh: T. & T. Clark, 1936–69; New York: Scribner, 1955–1962).

ChrF   F. Schleiermacher, *The Christian Faith*, tr. Mackintosh and Stewart (Edinburgh: T. & T. Clark, 1928; New York: Harper & Row, 1963).

CR   *Corpus Reformatorum*, ed. W. Baum, E. Cunitz, and E. Reuss (Braunschweig: Schwetschke, 1863). (See also Zwingli, *CR*, below.)

CSEL   *Corpus Scriptorum ecclesiasticorum latinorum* (Vienna: 1886ff.)

DchrWahrheit   Paul Althaus, *Die christliche Wahrheit; Lehrbuch der Dogmatik* (2 vols.; Gütersloh: Bertelsmann, 1949).

Denzinger   H. Denzinger, *The Sources of Catholic Dogma*, tr. R. J. Deferrari (from 30th ed.; St. Louis: Herder, 1957).

Dogmatics, I-III   Emil Brunner, *The Christian Doctrine of God, Dogmatics I*, tr. O. Wyon (Philadelphia: Westminster Press, 1950); *The Christian Doctrine of Creation and Redemption, Dogmatics II*, tr. O. Wyon (Philadelphia: Westminster Press, 1962); *The Christian Doctrine of the Church, Faith and the Consummation, Dogmatics III*, tr. D. Cairns and T. H. L. Parker (Philadelphia: Westminster Press, 1962).

EKL   *Evangelisches Kirchen-Lexikon*, ed. H. Brunotte and O. Weber (Göttingen: Vandenhoeck and Ruprecht, 1956).

ET   English translation.

EvTheol   *Evangelische Theologie* (German theological journal).

f   French (reference to the publication date of French edition cited in Weber).

FC   *The Fathers of the Church*, ed. R. J. Deferrari *et al*. (New York: Fathers of the Church, Inc., 1957; Washington, D.C.: The Catholic University of America Press, 1964).

g   German (reference to publication date of German edition cited in Weber).

GBWW   *Great Books of the Western World.*

GCS   *Die griechischen christlichen Schriftsteller der ersten drei Jahrhunderte* (Leipzig: J. C. Hinrichs, 1897ff.).

Heppe-Bizer   Heinrich, Heppe, *Reformed Dogmatics; Set Out and Illustrated from the Sources*, rev. and ed. Ernst Bizer, tr. G. T. Thomson (London: Allen & Unwin Ltd., 1950).

Institutes   John Calvin, *Institutes of the Christian Religion*, tr. F. Battles, vols. XX and XXI of the *LCC*, always cited from the *LCC* without volume numbers.

Jacobs   *The Book of Concord; or The Symbolical Books of the Evangelical Church*, tr. and ed. H. E. Jacobs (Philadelphia: The United Lutheran Publication House, 1911).

LCC   *Library of Christian Classics*, ed. J. Baillie, J. T. McNeill, and H. P. van Dusen (Philadelphia: Westminster Press, 1953ff.).

Migne, *PG*   *Patrologia Graeca* and *Patrologia Latina*, ed. J. B. Migne
Migne, *PL*   (Paris: 1844ff.).

n.l.   not located; indicates that the work cited has not been located and therefore a complete bibliographical entry has not been possible.

NPNF   *Nicene and Post-Nicene Fathers*, ed. P. Schaff (1st series; Grand Rapids: Eerdmans, 1956 [1887ff.]; 2nd series; New York: The Christian Literature Company, 1890ff.); the first series is not specially noted; vols. from the second series are marked 2nd ser.

RE   *Realencyklopädie für protestantische Theologie und Kirche*, founded by J. J. Herzog, 3rd ed. prepared by A. Hauck, 21 vols. (1898–1908), index in 1909, supplement in 2 vols. (1913); articles cited by Weber which are found in *SH* are cited here only in the latter work; citations from *RE* are therefore German articles not translated into the American edition or so strongly edited in *SH* as not to be usable for Weber's purposes.

RGG   *Religion in Geschichte und Gegenwart*; none of Professor Weber's citations is in the third edition now in use, but in the second or first editions, as noted.

Schaff   P. Schaff, *The Creeds of Christendom* (3 vols.; Grand Rapids: Baker Book House, 1969).

Schmid   H. Schmid, *The Doctrinal Theology of the Evangelical Lutheran Church, Verified from the Original Sources*, tr. C. A. Hay and H. E. Jacobs (Philadelphia: Lutheran Publication Society, 1889).

SH   *The New Schaff-Herzog Encyclopedia of Religious Knowledge*,
         ed. S. M. Jackson, based upon *RE* (3rd ed., repr. of 1907 ed.;
         Grand Rapids: Baker Book House, 1977); translations of ar-
         ticles from *RE* are cited in this encyclopedia.

STh   Thomas Aquinas, *Summa Theologica*, tr. Fathers of the Eng-
         lish Dominican Province (3 vols.; New York: Benziger Press,
         1947–48).

Stupperich *Melanchthons Werke in Auswahl*, ed. Robert Stupperich (7
         vols. in 9; Gütersloh: Bertelsmann, 1951–53, Gerd Mohn, 1963–
         75).

TDNT   R. Kittel *et al.*, *Theological Dictionary of the New Testament*,
         tr. and ed. G. W. Bromiley (Grand Rapids: Eerdmans, 1964ff.).

ThLZ   *Theologische Literatur Zeitung* (theological journal, Leipzig).

ThR   *Theologische Rundschau* (theological journal).

TR   Translator.

WA   *Weimarer Ausgabe*, the standard German edition of Luther's
         works.

ZNW   *Zeitschrift für die neutestamentliche Wissenschaft und die Kunde
         des Urchristentums* (theological journal).

ZsysTh   *Zeitschrift für systematische Theologie* (theological journal,
         Berlin).

ZThK   *Zeitschrift für Theologie und Kirche* (theological journal,
         Tübingen).

Zwingli, CR Citations of Zwingli in *Corpus Reformatorum* give the *CR* vol-
         ume number and then a second number in parentheses; this
         latter number refers to the volume in *Zwingli's Sämtliche Werke*,
         ed. E. Egli and G. Finsler (Berlin: Schwetschke, 1905).

ZZ   *Zwischen den Zeiten* (theological journal published by Karl
         Barth and others during the late 20's and early 30's).

PART ONE

Introduction

I. The Questionableness and Necessity of Christian Doctrine

A. FAITH IN CHRIST AND CHRISTIAN DOCTRINE

1. METHODOLOGICAL CONSIDERATIONS

The opening sections of almost every more recent exposition of dogmatics, often called "prolegomena," discuss the concept, task, subject, and method of dogmatic work. It was not always thought to be necessary to begin with such preliminary reflections. But they have always been implied: the dogmatician must clarify what he is doing, and why he can and ought to be doing it.

Now such a beginning is not only difficult; in the case of dogmatics, it is decidedly dangerous. The first consideration might be something like this: If I want to define a particular area of human intellectual endeavor more precisely, then I must mark off its boundaries. That means that within the (presumed) totality of thought or of its objects I must look for the particular "place" which dogmatics occupies, and further, I must identify the roads that lead to this "place." In the realm of the so-called exact sciences this task is relatively easy, since it can always demonstrate its object with empirical means or simply assume that everyone agrees about its object. It is clearly not that simple with dogmatics. To be sure, everyone expects that Christian dogmatics will talk about God. But God is not an object which can be assumed to be universally known. And how is a "place" to be assigned to him as the "object" of dogmatics within the totality of the discernible or the real? Not only the sceptic, the agnostic, or perhaps the atheist will protest at this point. Here the very proclamation of the Church puts in a protest. A god who is merely one component part of the perceivable whole is not the God to whom the Church bears witness and in whom the Christian believes. Thus with our first steps we come up against a difficult problem, indeed, the crucial problem.

a. The Ontological Order of Things. This problem has not always been viewed with equal clarity. In particular, it did not exist as long as dogmatics and indeed all theology considered itself completely integrated into an all-embracing ontology, as the center of that system, that is, into one single concept or one comprehensive doctrine of being and its articulated unity. The most impressive attempt to do dogmatics on the basis of ontology is to be found in Scholasticism. For Scholasticism, the problem of dogmatics could scarcely arise, and if it did, then as nothing more than an illustration of the whole problem of scientific knowledge. God was, as it were, the peak of the mighty pyramid of being with which all thought and knowledge dealt on the basis of this presupposed ontology. Specifically Christian knowledge only had to build upon this basis, since it itself contributed fundamental insights which were peculiarly its own. Accents could then be variously placed, but in general this ontology provided the guarantee that the work of dogmatics rested upon a scientific foundation which was almost universally acknowledged.

Medieval ontology has now disintegrated. But the "modern" thought which has taken its place has not wholly broken off all ties to it. Indeed, at the height of German Idealism, in such thinkers as Hegel, Schelling, and Schleiermacher, there were new attempts made to develop a comprehensive philosophy of being. They have their central perspective in the "I" or the "We," or at least in the human. It is understandable that, based on this new ontology, a fresh attempt could be made to assign a place to dogmatics—both for its theme and for its method—within the totality of human knowledge and its themes. The ways by which this was done need not be detailed here: the most impressive attempts were made with speculative dogmatics on the one hand (e.g., Daub) and with speculative-empirical dogmatics on the other (Schleiermacher and along with him many other dogmaticians of the 19th century). Dogmatics now sought to find its actual theme by deriving itself from the "idea," from "religion," from "piety," or from anthropology or ethics (both of which merge in Schleiermacher), and it adjusted its methods correspondingly. The "prolegomena" to dogmatics now became much more extensive. The presupposed ontology was by no means generally accepted by all thinkers as was the case in the Middle Ages; now it had to be established and secured and dogmatics integrated into it with great care. To the degree to which idealistic ontology was modified or replaced by the new philosophies of value, life, or finally of existence, dogmatics too was forced to make severe modifications if it wanted further to define its "place" from within the framework of a presupposed totality. The most clearly influential form of this is evident today wherever dogmatic statements are either derived from human self-understanding or at least closely related to it.

b. Predogmatic Prolegomena? Wherever dogmatics arises out of a presupposed ontology, or from an otherwise assumed totality of human experience, human self-understanding, or human behavior, its "prolegomena" (or whatever corresponds to them either implicitly or explicitly) are regarded as *predogmatic*. For Schleiermacher, for example, it is self-evident that since "the preliminary process of defining a science cannot belong to the science itself, it follows that none of the propositions [which appear in the "Introduction" to his dogmatics] can itself have a dogmatic character."[1] This thesis admits that dogmatics, if it is indeed a task of Christian theology, cannot possibly *exhaust* itself in the reception of ethical, anthropological, or other extratheological insights of knowledge. Any

---

1. Schleiermacher, *ChrF*, §1, 1, I, p. 2.

dogmatics which so defines its position is thereby forced at some point to make a leap. Certainly this point is the doctrine of the person of Jesus Christ—Jesus Christ does not occur in a general ontology.

However, the attempt to find an approach for dogmatics by relating it to a given general doctrine of being or knowledge or existence already contains in point of fact a substantial dogmatic position. It is impossible to begin in this fashion and then later on to abandon this beginning completely. The history of dogmatics shows that such an approach, instead of being predogmatic, becomes, on the contrary, virtually characteristic for the whole dogmatic scheme which is developed. The *starting* point of every dogmatics is implicitly given in its *central* point. There are no real *pro*-legomena to dogmatics.[2]

It should now be clear why we regarded the introduction to dogmatics as fraught with danger. The danger consists in the fact that every step that is taken here has its unavoidable and necessary consequences for the dogmatics which follows. This danger is heightened by the provisional tone of introductory remarks which easily conceals their essentially dogmatic nature. This can lead to an almost unnoticed alienation of dogmatics. There is no dogmatic system which can be protected from this danger in advance. But the effort to avoid it is required of all dogmatics.

c. A Self-contained Dogmatics? If, then, the introduction to dogmatics is itself unavoidably dogmatic, then a new danger seems to arise from the other side. Under these circumstances dogmatics seems to be a self-contained structure of thought about whose "place," boundaries, and methodology decisions can be made only on the basis of such criteria as are inherent in the structure itself. Will it not thereby turn out to be a system merely revolving dialectically around itself, an intellectual mythologoumenon which need never submit itself to any criterion which is outside of its sphere? Must it not thereby become an arcane system of knowledge, accessible only to the initiated? Does it not in this way become a bastion which certainly cannot be captured from without, but which also permits no further sorties outside its walls? In that case, can it even be called *Christian* anymore? Such counter-questions are raised primarily by those who would link dogmatics up with a general system of knowledge or would relate its theme to absolute being. Nonetheless, these questions are by no means to be set aside.

d. The Question of a Criterion. As we have seen, dogmatics is not in fact accessible exclusively from *outside* itself, since all the possible approaches are themselves already dogmatic in nature. Nor, on the other hand, can it be *self-contained*. That would mean nothing less than that dogmatics were mistress of its

---

2. This has been made clear by K. Barth (first in *Christliche Dogmatik im Entwurf; Die Lehre vom Worte Gottes* [Munich: Kaiser, 1927], I, 17, and then especially in *CD*, I,1, p. 45). The premise is likewise generally valid for philosophy that the definition of the concept and method of philosophy already is philosophy in a notable sense (cf. the still valuable essay by W. Windelband, "Was ist Philosophie?" *Präludien; Aufsätze und Reden zur Philosophie und ihrer Geschichte* (2 vols.; Tübingen: J. C. B. Mohr [P. Siebeck], 1924), I, 1ff.

own criterion or criteria, that it carried within itself the truth which is being sought, and thus it would move unhesitatingly into the place which according to Christian proclamation is reserved for the triune God alone.

Therefore dogmatics must face this question: Whence is it determined and defined? It cannot be self-determining. It cannot be determined by man. Whence then is it determined? Wherein lies its criterion?

The nearest answer would be the *Church*. Dogmatics gets its name (first used in the 17th century) from "dogma," and dogma is an activity of the Church. No less a person than Schleiermacher propounded the thesis that dogmatics as a "theological discipline" "pertains solely to the Christian Church,"[3] and contemporary dogmatics in particular has entirely adopted this thesis in its own way.[4]

Our present study takes no other view. Nevertheless, it is not possible to look for the criteria or the criterion of dogmatics in the Church alone, for the Church is as little autonomous as is dogmatics. It is as impossible for the Church as it is for dogmatics to be submitted to criteria which might be advanced from the world or from men. Like dogmatics, the Church cannot be its own master; that dogmatics cannot be its own master follows directly from the fact that it is a "function" of the Church.

The Church, its dogma, and the dogmatics conducted within its bounds are all subject to the same, identical criterion.

It would now be natural to elaborate the "prolegomena" to dogmatics in such a way that the quest for this criterion would be its essential contents. In doing so, one would have to bear in mind from the beginning that the search for this criterion is already dogmatics in the full sense of the word. The "prolegomena" would thus present an outline of the dogmatic system—"the *first* things to be said" would be discussed. This was Karl Barth's approach, and his "Prolegomena"[5] became a complete dogmatic design surpassing in weight and compass most of the more recent presentations.

My work cannot adopt such an approach. If the criterion of a dogmatics is the Word of God, as Karl Barth maintains and as will be shown in this study, then the theological development of this insight requires in fact a dogmatics *in nuce*. But the point of our whole presentation is to be nothing other than such a dogmatics *in nuce*. It would not be in keeping with the didactic purpose of this book to preface it with anything more than a short discussion of the introductory questions which obviously arise. In doing this, the question of the criterion will continually be dealt with implicitly, until it is discussed explicitly at its proper place.

---

3. Schleiermacher (*ChrF*, 2, Thesis, I, p. 3) says that his dogmatics "entirely disclaims the task of establishing on a foundation of general principles a Doctrine of God . . ." (*ibid.*). This, however, does not prevent him from deriving the "conception of 'Church' in general" "from Ethics," which he then defines as the "speculative presentation of Reason, in the whole range of its activity, which runs parallel to natural science" (*op. cit.*, p. 5, Postscript 2).

4. Cf. K. Barth, *CD*, I,1: "Dogmatics is a theological discipline. But theology is a function of the church" (p. 1), and E. Brunner, *Dogmatics*, I: "Thus if dogmatics is anything at all, it is *a function of the Church*" (p. 3).

5. *CD*, I,1 and I,2.

2. THE PROBLEM OF CHRISTIAN DOCTRINE

a. Dogmatics Is Doctrine.[6] Dogmatics is not the only form in which Christian doctrine—teaching in the Church—occurs. The most original form of Christian teaching is preaching.[7] Another form is dogma, which is essentially related to preaching. In contrast to both of these, dogmatics is secondary in a sense still to be discussed, and it is also methodologically independent of both.

That Christian doctrine should exist is by no means undisputed. This is also true of preaching to the extent that it "teaches." But it is particularly true of dogma and dogmatics. The fact that the legitimacy of dogmatics and dogma is disputed will be assumed for the moment. We shall have to deal later with the most frequently adduced arguments for this.

What is of immediate importance for us is the prevailing attitude, constantly advocated in the last two centuries, that the existence of Christian *doctrine* cannot be reconciled with the nature of Christian *faith*. This attitude has at first glance much to recommend itself—so much that we ought to take the antithesis it posits as the starting point for our considerations here.

b. Faith as Faith in Christ. Christian faith is essentially faith in Christ. That can be presupposed as generally accepted. What it means in detail is a matter of manifold controversy, and it requires a more detailed discussion. But one further thing may be presupposed, namely, that Christian faith, in that it is faith in Christ, is in any event an attitude and a relationship to the *person* of Jesus Christ. This means, *first*, that faith is not directed toward objective issues primarily but only insofar as it encounters the person of Jesus Christ himself in these issues. Faith as obedience, trust, and self-surrender is a way of relating to a Thou, not to an It, to a person, not to an objective issue or fact. *Secondly*, faith, as faith in Jesus Christ, is never directly oriented toward propositions, however true, or views, however correct. To be sure, it always has to do with objective issues, just as it has to do with propositions, as we must shortly take into account. But it does not direct itself at these in a straight line. It is therefore not faith "in Christianity" or "in" a dogma. It deals continually with propositions and views because it has to do with Jesus Christ as person. It is indeed proper that the person-oriented confession, "*credo*" (I believe), should then be secondarily related to a "creed," to a confession of faith formulated by the Church, just as it is true that faith is

---

6. In this section, Professor Weber uses the term "doctrine" (*Lehre*) in its original sense of "teaching"—TR.

7. In the older usage of the Church, "doctrine" always meant "preaching." Augustine's famous work, *De doctrina christiana*, is a hermeneutic and a homiletic, not a dogmatics (or rather only a dogmatics insofar as relevant hermeneutics and homiletics are always dogmatics). This understanding persists up through the Augsburg Confession, Article VII: the agreement "concerning the doctrine of the Gospel" refers clearly back to the phrase "in which the Gospel is rightly taught" or "purely preached," and the German text speaks in both cases of "preaching," not of "doctrine" which is separated from preaching. To be sure, the translation of *doctrina evangelii* (doctrine of the Gospel) continues, "in order that preaching may be done in unanimity according to the *pure understanding* of the Gospel." The distinction is beginning to emerge: dogma is beginning to precede preaching once again, but in another way as before (Schaff, III, 3ff.).

also "regarding something as true."[8] But the truth which conquers us in faith is God's own truth; it is God himself in his Word, in Jesus Christ.

Thirdly: just as in faith I have to do with the person of Jesus Christ, I am also a person myself in doing so. Precisely because faith in its literal sense is a man's self-surrender, it is an act of the person. The general tendency today is to express this by interpreting faith as *decision*, which can be misunderstood. It means that in believing I risk my self. Faith, therefore, is not submission before the force of facts or acceptance of stronger arguments. It happens in such a way that its opposite seems at least as "possible" as it is itself: it is a "risk." It is risk because it is not merely an act of the intellect or the will but an act of the whole man, of the man as "I," as a person. Here I am unquestionably "I myself," unprotected and unsecured. Here no protective wall of my past, my profession, or my possessions surrounds me; here, every conceivable defense has become ineffective. Of course, this does not mean that the "world" in which I exist has disappeared for me. But my believing is not based upon this world; rather, my faith redirects me toward this world.

A *fourth* point might be added: faith is *temporal*. The category of decision is time. In today's favored parlance, faith happens *hic et nunc*, here and now. It deals, not with something timeless, but with time, and it does not lift us out of our time but radically sets our existence within time. This, of course, does not mean that our existence in faith would become a particular temporal point.[9] Rather, it becomes historical in a particular sense, namely, that the person of Jesus Christ meets us in history, in his history, in the history of his *Church*, and in *our* history. Yet this happens in such a way that we, in believing in Jesus Christ, do not mean by that a substratum of history or a meaning of history, but rather time, which as such is God's time for us, time in which eternity happens, without our being able to speculate about it after the fact.

c. *"Doctrine."* When we now turn to the phenomenon of Christian *doctrine*, bearing in mind what we have discussed, it is not necessary to elaborate at length the tension which arises. For clearly doctrine consists of propositions which have factual or abstract (but still fact-oriented) contents as their theme.

"Proposition" means here a judgment that man, by virtue of his reason, makes in the form of valid statements about a set of circumstances or a person— i.e., statements that claim to be true within the particular realm of reality to which they belong. The realms of reality and the appropriate form for the statements considered to be true within their bounds are diverse:[10] the truth of a philosophical proposition has a different structure from that of a physical or a historical one.

---

8. See, for example, the Heidelberg Catechism answer to Question 21 (Schaff, III, 313).

9. See my essay, "Die Treue Gottes und die Kontinuität der menschlichen Existenz," in the special edition of the journal *Evangelische Theologie* for E. Wolf (1952), pp. 131ff.

10. Customarily we particularly differentiate between the (natural) sciences and the arts. Regarding this problem, note especially Heinrich Rickert, *Science and History; A Critique of Positivist Epistemology*, tr. G. Reisman, ed. A. Goddard (Princeton: Van Nostrand, 1962 [g1899]); *Die Grenzen der naturwissenschaftlichen Begriffsbildung; eine logische Einleitung in die historischen Wissenschaften* (5th ed.; Tübingen: Mohr, 1929).

But if we formulate doctrinal propositions at all, we always do so intending to posit such propositions as will have validity not only for one individual but for all people, not only for one particular time but for all time. We can then surely admit that by and large we have not achieved our purpose of setting forth propositions of universal validity, and perhaps we shall never reach it. However, the purpose as such remains. Customarily we apply the term "pure" to such scientific insights and cognitive methods as are fundamentally unaffected by the tangential and accidental, and therefore able to make the most emphatic claim to universal validity. Since the beginning of the Enlightenment, pure mathematics has served as the model of all pure sciences, and mathematical propositions as the ideal type of all propositions. The mathematical proposition is basically independent of the tangential and accidental nature of its theme. Since it is not tied down to any objects, mathematics in particular evades the criterion of the practical applicability of its propositions; it stands over against the world of objects with sovereign freedom in every direction, with the freedom of a sovereign who does not need this world of objects but gives it its law, which is nothing else than the law of pure reason, whose validity is all-embracing. The mathematical proposition, and every proposition of another science derived in analogy to mathematics, is an assertion of reason—this assertion gains its validity through the medium of thought, which in turn is established by reason. In essence, this assertion is an expression of the eternity of reason, projected into time.

Seen in this fashion, it is impossible to make such a proposition into the object of a personal decision. A purely descriptive or analytical proposition, which itself is only the precursor of and material for the actual doctrine (which seeks to state eternal truth), does not call for decision, but only for verification. For its part, the "pure" proposition is dependent upon "pure" proof, which in the last resort depends upon unprovable axioms, which by virtue of their inherent self-evidence need no syllogistic derivation. But neither the proof nor the self-evident axiom behind it needs or is capable of an act of decision. Any proposition which required that a decision be made would no longer be a doctrinal proposition as we have defined it.

It is, however, true that the view of doctrine and doctrinal propositions which we have been assuming until now has in fact been in the process of disintegration for a long time. Positivism and relativism have impugned the majesty of the doctrinal proposition. Moreover, their campaign has been primarily directed against the divinity of God and the truth of revelation. It does not make room for those methods of Christian proclamation which reject the form of doctrine anyway; it rules them out just as it dethrones the majesty of the doctrinal proposition. For this reason, theology has no cause to welcome a would-be ally here. In addition, it has become apparent that positivism and relativism have developed into the pacemakers of a despotism of thought and action which threatens the very fabric of our culture. If there is something regal in the doctrinal proposition, there is something tyrannical in relativism. It makes relativity an absolute, because for relativism there is nothing there to which relativity relates; it is the tyranny of thought without a center—and it must deny that there is a center in order to be able to exist itself as relativism.

Next to the doctrinal proposition which follows the analogy of mathematics, there is also the *historical* proposition, in the broadest sense of the term. But as soon as it appears as a value judgment and not merely as a judgment of fact, it has the character of a historical-*philosophical* judgment, which is as keenly and structurally antithetical to faith in Christ as was the mathematical proposition. To illustrate this, let us hypothetically presuppose that there could be such a thing as "the doctrine of a person." If we understand "doctrine" as "the establishment of facts," this would be valid: history "teaches" us who Caesar or Napoleon was. But what would the outcome be if such a doctrine attempted to define the value or significance of a person? Then, doubtless, the *doctrine* would either have to deal with the concept of "person" in general, or else, if it had a definite, historical person in mind, it would have to divest him of his concrete nature and his uniqueness and understand him rather as a manifestation of something universal, timeless, and abiding, in order to be able to arrive at general propositions of any kind. The very center of Christian doctrine, however, has always been the doctrine of Jesus Christ. Assuming it were some special kind of doctrine, it could only proceed by making Jesus Christ the paradigm of a general doctrine of "person," or else the (perhaps highest or absolute) expression of the timeless (and in some sense divine) idea which lies behind him and manifests itself in him. It would then manifestly be doing exactly the opposite of what faith does.

d. Christian Doctrine in Analogy to Other Doctrine. If Christian doctrine were only a special instance or one manifestation of doctrine in general, then, as we have shown up until now, a contradiction would have to be made between it and faith in Christ, and this contradiction would place the very existence of Christian doctrine in question.

This is by no means a merely hypothetical consideration. Since the beginning of the explicit formulation of Christian doctrine, there has been a persistent tendency to develop it in analogy to whatever had currently emerged as doctrine in general. This trend can be observed in the early Apologists. It becomes dominant with victorious power in Origen, to some degree even in Augustine, and comprehensively in Scholasticism and Protestant Orthodoxy. It does not form the heart of our dogmatic tradition, but it is always an operative factor and not seldom determinative. The antithesis to the nature of faith in Christ which then emerges is, in the nature of things, overlooked. And this all the more so when, to all appearances, the propositions which are set forth are usually "orthodox." To mention the most frequent form of the phenomenon we are discussing, who can take exception when the Bible is made into the epitome of divinely revealed doctrinal truths (salvation-truths), when faith appears as the obedient or self-evidently rational acceptance of these truths, and when the Church is supposed to be the guardian of these truths or the fellowship of discerning believers? One thing ought to be clear: the person of Jesus Christ must occupy a rather odd position in this sort of conception, regardless of how central he may be. Jesus Christ is either made into one doctrinal truth among others (and thus is no longer himself the truth), or he is made into the most outstanding, perhaps the only, bearer or herald of the truths which are involved. Faith in Christ is now faith either in the sense that it has among other points a definite conception of Jesus Christ as its doctrinal theme, or else that it makes the "historical" Jesus into its originator. From a historical point of view, Orthodoxy and Rationalism are shown to be closely related to one another, in spite of all their differences.

Wherever Christian doctrine appears in analogy to whatever other doctrine is currently being maintained, two essential consequences are unavoidable:

First of all, faith—either as obedience or as rational insight or as a combination of both—moves away from the center of Christian existence. It can now become (as it did for long periods in the Middle Ages) one pious achievement among others, whereby it then retreats before love, which then develops faith into a worthwhile form (*fides caritate formata*—faith formed by love). Or it is considered to be an attitude that must be surpassed by what is genuinely Christian: thus in Origen, and not alone in him, the pneumatic is more than the pistic, the enlightened one has a higher place than the mere believer, or "practical Christianity" is valued more highly than faith. The precondition for a great deal of Enthusiasm and of Christian ethicism is a concept of faith which has been tainted by reason, which then necessarily must be contrasted with something higher, something which really does belong to the essence of faith.

Secondly, Christian doctrine thus understood becomes a world view, a *philosophia christiana*. There is something originally and essentially Christian in this tendency: since Christian doctrine as a statement about God can never be limited within the created world, Christian doctrine (as we have just described it) must of necessity embrace the whole of reality, and hence must enter into competition with any other attempt to interpret this whole comprehensively. If Christian doctrine is understood as analogous to some other existing doctrine, then it must become a comprehensive exposition of information about God and the world, which means that it is a philosophy with supernatural foundations. But if this happens, then Christian doctrine becomes a way of achieving mastery over the world (and thereby mastery over and understanding of the self), to be sure, supposedly Christian in intent and persuasion. This means that—the children of darkness being once again wiser than the children of light—imperceptibly but inevitably Christian doctrine falls into line with whatever is the prevailing form of self-interpretation and world mastery; in other words, it submits to the currently dominant philosophy. It is characteristic of Christian world views that they easily lose their "Christian" aspect, although certainly their originators intend them to have it. Nowhere can this be seen more clearly than in the Middle Ages. In our current situation the question arises whether the predominance here and there of existential philosophy in theology is not in fact transforming theology into a world view again—a world view which, to be sure, is newly conceived and is influenced by Christian thought (Kierkegaard!). Indeed, the predominance of existentialism in theology may be the result of the fact that Christian doctrine was already transformed into a world view in a very special sense.

e. Faith's Connectedness with History. How difficult a problem it is to try to understand Christian doctrine in analogy with the general concept of "doctrine" as otherwise accepted is shown most clearly by this observation: within the framework of doctrine as generally understood, it is impossible to make any allowances for the specific and exclusive relationship of faith to a very *special* history. Paul Althaus[11] has shown that in the Aristotelian concept of science, history has no place, because, for Aristotle, science is always a matter of "concept-definition and proof." Under the influence of Aristotelian thinking, theology has always had a difficult time classifying the specific historicity of Christian proclamation scientifically, but it has never shrunk from the task nor forgotten completely what it was dealing with. In more recent times, especially since Hegel, it might have seemed easier to take into consideration scientifically the specific historicity of the Christian message. However, modern thought actually leaves no possibility open for the proposition that God deals with us only in concrete revelational events, that we cannot forge beyond the concrete event into the realm of the eternally valid, but rather we must stop intellectually and existentially at the boundaries of this concrete event. To illustrate, Hegel agrees with Lessing that history receives its dignity from the universal which manifests itself in history, or (for Lessing) whose self-manifestation in historical "accidence" is the core of the problem itself. Nevertheless, Christian doctrine is always essentially historical reporting. It is not even "interpretation" of history, if by "interpretation" we mean the understanding of concrete history from a perspective outside of it. It is a "witness" to this history, a history which has happened, but which has happened *for us* and which has manifested itself *to us*. To that extent it is *interpretation*—but, as it were, interpretation from within, interpretation based upon an encounter, an encounter to which we bring no effective categories of interpretation, and in which we receive instead of categories of interpretation the revelation and self-communication of God. Since it reaches us from this source, Christian doctrine falls outside the framework of all other possible "doctrine" as commonly understood. Hence it cannot possibly have to do with the universal, the timeless, or the impersonal. It must necessarily deal with the particular, with time, with the personal.

3. THE NECESSITY OF CHRISTIAN DOCTRINE

Christian doctrine cannot be doctrine in the usual sense of the term. That was the result of our preliminary discussion. It was an open question whether doctrine in the former sense is meaningful at all.[12] We were primarily concerned with a phenomenological comparison.

On the other hand, we had to leave unanswered for the time being the question of whether and how Christian doctrine can be possible at all, if it does not follow the analogy of other doctrine.

Before we pursue this question further, though, we must deal with another one: Is that which we have hypothetically assumed to be possible really necessary, and if so, why?

---

11. *Die Prinzipien der deutschen reformierten Dogmatik im Zeitalter der aristotelischen Scholastik* (Leipzig: Deichert, 1914; Darmstadt: Wissenschaftliche Buchgesellschaft, 1967), pp. 241f.

12. See the radical criticism in Eberhard Grisebach, *Gegenwart*; *Eine kritische Ethik* (Halle: Niemeyer, 1928).

a. No Basis in General Criteria. From the perspective of the "general" concept of science, it is certainly necessary to research and describe the concepts which motivate a cultural force as influential as the Christian Church. Therefore, some description of the so-called "essence of Christianity" must find its place within the totality of scientific endeavors. For the same obvious reasons, a similar description of the "essence of Islam" is required. In terms of general science, however, only the necessity of a science of religion can be demonstrated. To anticipate a point, theology certainly would not seek to deny that such a thing as the science of religion should exist; on the contrary, it would be in theology's interest that such a discipline could exist and could deal with "Christianity." Just as it is certain that "Christianity" is not identical with Christ, nor with revelation, nor with the salvation-event, nor with the Christian Church, it is equally certain that one aspect of the "essence" of the revelation-event is that, as a historical event and quite apart from revelation as such, it is not concealed but available to historical perception. "Christianity" is the "religion" which is not absolutely identical with but is still subordinate to revelation, in that the revelational event is also a historical and interpersonal occurrence. Thus "Christianity" is the inherent misunderstanding which can never be separated from revelation.

The necessity of *Christian doctrine* is, however, not to be demonstrated on the basis of general intellectual concepts. This would still hold true even if the "general" concept of science were not "secularized," that is, if it had not already *a priori* excluded the possibility of God as a genuine counterpart to man and his world. Even if there was a Christian concept of science—and there is such a thing[13]—and even if this concept were to receive general recognition, at least within so-called European culture—which it does not—the conclusion could never be drawn based upon such a *general* concept of science (regardless of how "Christian" it might be) that Christian doctrine is necessary as a scientific interpretation of what is *absolutely unique*, which stands in its uniqueness over against everything general, universal, and given, namely, the revelational event and the witness to that event. A Christian doctrine whose necessity could be demonstrated on the basis of some general criteria (even if they were Christian) would have to be characterized by the generality, timelessness, and impersonality which are the implicit or explicit presuppositions of all such "general" criteria. The unique cannot be derived as a necessary consequence of what is not unique. (The reverse question is whether or not the "general" can be derived from the absolutely unique, that is, whether or not there can exist a view of general science which derives from the perception of revelation.)

---

13. Recently work has been done on this problem, especially in Holland, based on the theology of Abraham Kuyper. See especially D. H. T. Vollenhoven, *De Noodzakelijkheid eener Christelijke Logica* (n.1.; 1932); H. Dooyeweerd, *De crisis der humanistische staatsleer in het licht eener calvinistische kosmologie en kennistheorie* (Amsterdam: N.v. Boekhandel W. ten Have, 1931); and H. Dooyeweerd, *A New Critique of Theoretical Thought*, tr. D. H. Freeman and W. S. Young (4 vols.; Amsterdam: H. J. Paris; Philadelphia: Presbyterian and Reformed, 1953–58). See also the unpublished dissertation of E. E. Rosenboom, *Die Idee einer christlichen Universität im theologischen Denken von Abraham Kuyper* (1950), with its comprehensive evaluation.

b. Preliminary Thesis. The fact that Christian doctrine is necessary can only be established by the nature of the revelation-event, or better, by the faith which responds to that event. In our discussion up until now, which has been necessarily of a preliminary character, we have interpreted faith as faith in Christ, and thus as "personal," temporal, and related to history. This led us to the conclusion that *doctrine* as it is customarily understood (outside the Christian Church) can hardly be made to harmonize with the nature of faith and the revelation to which faith responds. Now we shall have to assert and demonstrate the opposite, that Christian doctrine does possess the character of *necessity* because doctrine alone is able to maintain a firm hold upon the "personality" which inheres in the faith (*this* personality and no other!) and the historical connectedness of faith (again, *this* and no other). Only when Christian doctrine exists and is continually attempted anew, can faith in Christ be understood as what it is.

The thesis just stated can best be substantiated by considering the objections which are raised against the endeavor of Christian doctrine, and especially against dogma and dogmatics. It remains to be seen whether these objections do not in fact reveal the very points at which the necessity of Christian doctrine arises, rather than contradicting that necessity.

1) **"Practical Christianity."** One objection could arise from an understanding of Christianity as the piety or life-style which Jesus of Nazareth lived, taught, and realized. This objection is based upon the "practical" character of Christian piety, and it opposes all Christian doctrine as being a perversion of Christianity into theory. In its original form this point of view is as good as dead in theology. But it is still prevalent in many circles: there is a widespread feeling of mistrust, a feeling that everything "dogmatic" could destroy any willingness for practical action.

As long as Christianity is understood, as was formerly done, as the form of piety and the life-style brought to us by Jesus, it is obvious that Jesus Christ is to be distinguished completely from his "doctrine" and from the exemplary character of his life. What is important is not he himself but what he accomplished in word and deed. Of course, he may be emphatically celebrated as the "divine teacher," but his personal identity is not the decisive thing. To be a Christian can mean nothing other than to live *as* he lived and *as* he taught. Undeniably he has as a *person* no significance for the Christian life. We are to be much more concerned with that which was represented in him and that toward which he was directing us. He has fundamentally no more significance for Christian piety than does Pythagoras for the theorem named after him. Nobody accepts this theorem on the authority of Pythagoras; in fact, it is irrelevant for the theorem and its validity whether Pythagoras ever lived or had any connection with it. The pioneer, however highly he may be esteemed as such, is always of only secondary importance compared with what he discovered, and after him, his discovery lives on, totally independent of his person. The honor we owe the pioneer is not shown to his person but is revealed in what we do with his discovery. If Jesus of Nazareth is the author, the bringer, and the pattern of a "devout Christian life," then there is definitely *no* personal relationship with him. Rather, the issue at stake is what he stood for, a specific kind of piety, a definite moral style of behavior. That means, plainly put, that we are dealing here with an impersonal, nonhistorical, ultimately timeless religio-moralistic *doctrinairianism*. A doctrine, Jesus' own doctrine, perhaps in a developed form as elaborated by other great spirits of "Christianity," takes the place of the person, a fundamental universal takes the place of the unique, the timeless takes the place of the temporal.

This objection to dogma and dogmatics as just outlined is seldom found in its pure form. One can say that its pure form already had disappeared by the beginning of the 19th century with the emergence of Romanticism and the Hegelian concept of history. It is widely acknowledged that we are not just the trustees of history but also the beneficiaries. It is the concept of the creative source which has constantly appeared and which essentially altered the conception outlined above. There are historical "personalities" who are more than pioneers of something: they participate in the nature of that which they discover. They cannot then rationally be separated from that which they pass on to us. But the source which reveals itself in them is still understood as the Universal (as in the young Schleiermacher) or as the Absolute Spirit (as in Hegel) or as the nameless One, but never as personal, as the Thou in relationship to the I. Thus, the creative source may emerge *in* the "personalities," and not just in their pioneering and yet mediating discoveries or findings, but it nevertheless can never be identical with a historical figure as such. If we try to understand Jesus of Nazareth as such a personality, then we can perhaps credit him with creative originality. But faith *in* him remains just as impossible as it was under the presuppositions of rational-nonhistorical moralism. At most I can believe in "something" *in* him, and this "faith" can in fact be nothing other than letting our own actions be determined by this source, by referring back to it historically and by relating it to the religious and moral situation in the present. However, that means that we have not advanced much beyond the position described previously; the rejection of Christian doctrine in favor of a personality defined by Christ means in fact that there can be no such thing as faith in Jesus Christ himself. The relationship which we might develop with him is certainly not a personal one, and the faith, to what extent that is even of interest anymore, is not really faith in Christ.

To sum up: the rejection of Christian doctrine based on the assumptions of "practical Christianity" or upon the idea of a Christ-determined personality is founded upon an understanding of the Christian faith which is not personal, and therefore ultimately not temporal and historical. Usually, a pronounced doctrinairianism is the background for such approaches. Thus, rejection of "dogmatic Christianity" really amounts to the advocacy of a counter-dogma.

It might be added that this counter-dogma also appears where Christian doctrine is rejected on the basis of the assumptions of modern philosophy, as is especially the case with Eberhard Grisebach[14] and (at least for the time being)

---

14. *Op. cit.*, pp. 199ff., and p. 596, the table of terms.

with Wilhelm Kamlah.[15] In modern philosophy we are dealing largely with intellectual concepts which were derived from theology;[16] such concepts of Christian provenance, when separated from faith in Christ, then mold themselves by inner necessity into counter-dogma, which then categorizes all Christian doctrine as "passe,"[17] as figurative, as a hardened position based upon the authority of now anonymous figures.

2) **Inwardness.** A second objection to the development of Christian doctrine is based upon the point of view that piety is something so delicate, inward, and ineffable that dogma, dogmatics, or even theology in general could not possibly be anything but caricature and perversion. How can that which is most personal of all be forced into intellectual formulae? How can the ineffable be conceptually dismembered and logically categorized? This is fundamentally the objection raised by *mysticism*. Its ultimate roots may be traced back to Neo-Platonism, indeed to Plato's view of the divine as the *apoion* (neutral, without quality or attributes). Now it could well be said here, for better or poorer reasons, that this objection has always been basically foreign to theology, and especially so today. Yet this objection does express what fills countless Christians with deep distrust of anything dogmatic, even though they are not nor would want to be mystics or Neo-Platonists. Moreover, it is just a short step from this objection to what was just described as the position of contemporary philosophers: the peculiar kind of objectivity which is part and parcel of Christian doctrine must appear as a contradiction to the repeated challenge of philosophy, the challenge to bold personal decision, to openness to the future, to grasping existence at the present moment.

The problem of mysticism is not to be discussed here in detail. The question with which we must deal here is whether the thesis advanced either openly or unconsciously and tacitly can in any sense be said to characterize relevantly faith in Christ—the thesis that piety is the inexpressible, the ever present, that which pertains to the moment and to that which authenticates itself as the deepest depth of the individual, a thesis, therefore, which excludes in principle doctrinal statements. This question must be firmly answered in the negative. Piety, interpreted in this mystical fashion, does not include person, time, or history, all of which faith in Christ always includes. Rather, it refers to the super-temporal and super-personal ground of all being, or if time, person, and the present are mentioned, then to absolutized time, to conceptualized and memorialized person, to pure and non-dimensional contemporaneity.[18] All mysticism places little value on the

---

15. *Christentum und Selbstbehauptung, historische und philosophische Untersuchungen zur Entstehung des Christentums und zu Augustins "Bürgerschaft Gottes"* (Frankfurt/Main: Klostermann, 1940); cf. in this regard R. Bultmann, "New Testament and Mythology," in H. W. Bartsch, ed., *Kerygma and Myth; A Theological Debate*, tr. R. H. Fuller (London: S.P.C.K., 1953), I, 27ff.

16. Kierkegaard has had the greatest influence here: central concepts such as "existence" and "decision," and more indirectly "the present," are all characteristic of the influence of Kierkegaard's theological and philosophical protest against Hegel.

17. As in Grisebach, *op. cit.*, p. 596.

18. See my essay, "Die Treue Gottes und die Kontinuität der menschlichen Existenz," in the special edition of the journal *Evangelische Theologie* for E. Wolf (1952), pp. 131ff.

"word"—it wants to know nothing of the word which addresses and challenges us, and therefore it can say nothing about the answering word of man.[19]

As far as we have seen up until now, the rejection of Christian doctrine is clearly *not* based upon an accurate understanding of the Christian faith as faith in Christ. This rejection is not characterized by a personal, temporal, historical faith, but is either the product of an impersonal, religio-moralistic doctrinairianism or the expression of a subjectivism which seeks truth in the depth of the innermost soul or in the absolutized present moment. It could then be conjectured, on the other hand, that Christian doctrine as such is not so much the critical questioning of the personal, historical, temporal character of faith as it is the expression of such faith. At the moment, however, that is nothing more than mere conjecture.

3) **The Biblicistic Objection.** The most serious objection to the pursuit of Christian doctrine is based upon the authoritative position of Holy Scripture within the Church. Only in discussing this objection can we test the validity of the conjecture which has been made.

No one will dispute the fact that the Christian faith is dependent upon the Bible. With good reason the Reformation churches have understood the authority of Holy Scripture as *unique* authority (*sola scriptura*—Scripture alone). What is meant by this must be discussed later.[20] At any rate, the protest of the Reformation is directed against any attempt to admit or establish the authority of *tradition* or *reason* side by side with the authority of Holy Scripture. But that being the case, an important question arises. Must not the authority ascribed to a dogma actually mean that *tradition*, now as Evangelical[21] tradition, has reentered the scene and claimed a place of its own? And along with *tradition* has not *reason* now laid claim to its own authority alongside of, if not over, Scripture? Why should we not be satisfied with the authority of Scripture alone, and why does not the interpretation of Scripture stand alone rather than share its position with dogmatics, as it must in the Protestant churches? Has not the Church suffered as a result of this? Has not dogma proven itself to be a straitjacket, and has not dogmatics been explosively destructive in its predilection for fine distinctions and its overemphasis upon logic? How can the conceptual intellectualization of dogmatics and dogma stand up against the candor and simplicity of the biblical witnesses?

This objection appears in Evangelical churches sometimes as the more instinctive defense mechanism of simple biblical piety against the conceptual apparatus of the "theologians," and other times as more deliberate, well-thought-through "Biblicism." It is directed against the confessional cleavage that supposedly has its origins not in the Bible but in dogmatics; against the domination of theologians which is supposed to be so arranged that authority is rendered not

---

19. E. Brunner was definitely right with his antithesis *Die Mystik und das Wort* (Tübingen: Mohr, 1928²), which he formulated in his interpretation of Schleiermacher. His interpretation of Schleiermacher is not, however, to be discussed here.

20. See p. 271.

21. The term "Evangelical" means "Protestant" in German usage and should be understood in this sense throughout the translation—TR.

to Scripture, which is available to everyone, but only to dogma, which is comprehensible only to the few; against the bitter infighting of theologians which, it is asserted, must arise when the living word of Scripture has been transformed into dead terminology. In short, all Christian doctrine is seriously suspect of being something basically irrelevant and even unchristian.

The thesis of the unique authority of Holy Scripture in the Church is an axiom: it cannot be established from some other source, but rather it is the expression of a fact which establishes everything else. The doctrine of Holy Scripture cannot establish why Scripture possesses unique authority; it can only explain what this unique authority means.

Obviously, to say that Scripture is uniquely authoritative does not mean that, for Christians, Scripture has taken over *God's* place. "Biblical faith" is, strictly speaking, not faith "in" the Bible but faith in the God who reveals himself to us through the biblical witness. We honor the Bible only when we honor its *witness*. We believe the Bible only when we believe *in* the Word of *God* which sounds through it. In that this is so, Christian faith again demonstrates that it is "personal" in its dependence upon the Bible. The Bible is the "Word of God" because it bears witness to the one "Word of God," Jesus Christ.[22] "Bible faith" which has not perceived this witness would not be the Christian faith.

However, our statement that the Bible is the Word of God and the proposition that this Word is one Word and therefore cannot simply be equated with a large number of words—these are statements which are "dogmatic" theses, although they are based on the Bible. That means that they are the result of searching Scripture for its "essence," and they are not, for example, the summary of historical repetitions of the factual contents of Holy Scripture. Every statement about the authority of the Bible, whether it takes the above-mentioned form or some other, is inevitably a dogmatic proposition. This must be briefly explained.

c. The Bible and Christian Doctrine. Holy Scripture presents itself to us as a historically developed multiplicity of documents in very different forms, differing contents (by no means always harmonious or even convergent), dating from many different periods. What we perceive is an extremely diverse choir of voices. These voices can be heard as such by everyone: not only by the unguarded ear of the "simple Bible reader" but also by the trained ear of the historian. Both can try to harmonize the many voices heard into a unity. For the historian, this unity is a definite course of history: he can use the biblical documents as resource materials for a particular history of ideas, or religion, or devotion, or the cultic. Whether or not such an undertaking will result in a relatively coherent pattern must remain an open question. But one thing is certain: on the basis of these presuppositions the unity or totality which is said to confront us in Scripture could only be a substratum. It would be as if we were to say that we find here, in and through all of the variety, certain fundamental aspects of the same religion; the substratum "religion" would be the unity and totality which could be found. That the Word of God really encounters us in this choir of voices, and to what

---

22. Barmen Declaration, Thesis 1.

extent it does, is something that history cannot tell us. At the very most, it can state that the claim to be or to speak God's Word is also sounding in the midst of this choir—but it cannot deal with this claim; it must assign it to the general substratum "religion." Normally, history regards those things as incidental which for the Church and for faith are essential. The question of what is essential cannot be answered historically.

This holds true even when it is admitted that the biblical texts are not only to be noted but rather that they challenge the reader to take a position. This position could be the "yes" of the historian to the value of his source, the "yes" of the aesthete to the powerful impressiveness of a human self-revelation, the "yes" of the thinker to the intellectual depth of this or that statement—in short, the pronouncement of "yes" or "no" (even conditionally) could be based on any number of possible value scales. This is continually happening. But every "yes" or "no" expressed in this fashion would be absolutely different from the "yes" of faith or the "no" of unbelief. What is, then, that essential thing which is capable of calling forth the "yes" of faith or the "no" of unbelief? Again, this question cannot be answered directly "from the sources" nor indirectly through the introduction of a system of values.

d. The Authoritative in the Bible. At this point we confront the issue of ultimate authority or validity. What is valid and authoritative cannot be "proven" in its authority. The task of a proof is to take a conjectured thesis and subject it to examination by our standards and our irrefutable past experience, in order to see if it will stand. What has thus been proven is no longer capable of *decision*: no one can or should want to decide about something which can be proven. The *authoritative* and *valid*, however, is in its very nature something which requires a decision (without being dependent upon that decision, of course). How then can Scripture, which we encounter as literature, as the self-manifestation of long-dead men, and which can thereby certainly not be proven to be "authoritative," nevertheless be authoritative and valid for faith; how can it call forth the qualified "no" of unbelief which is ignited by its very claim to be authoritative? These functions of Scripture are not directly deducible from the words themselves.

The problem is complicated even more when we admit that there are many statements in the Bible whose plain contents require not just acknowledgment nor respect, but *obedience*. Let us assume that someone is willing to subject himself to this claim; he now encounters a variety of claims for his obedience. There is the claim of the law, including the requirement that certain sacrifices be brought in certain ways, that certain holidays be celebrated, and other precise cultic regulations be followed. On the other hand, there is the Pauline statement which is directed against the very requirement of circumcision, which in the same Bible is insisted upon for the covenant partners of God (Galatians versus Genesis 17). Or there is Jesus' saying about the Sabbath which stands in opposition to the unconditional Sabbath commandment of the Old Testament. What is authoritative and valid here? To be sure, *Christianity* has always, apart from exceptions, answered that in such cases the New Testament witness is authoritative and valid. But why? If this decision, once made and constantly repeated, is not to be looked upon as an arbitrary act, then it must be measured against some criterion. This criterion is provided by the contents of the Bible only when they are made the subject of a *decision*; for example, Luther's famous (and controversial) decision expressed in the words "what promotes Christ" (*Was Christum treibet*). What this decision means and how it is based cannot be determined by means of a pure "Biblicism." The Bible itself forces us to the *dogmatic* question.

It becomes clear that the Bible does this when we are to preach about the biblical witness upon the basis of a specific biblical text. For preaching is not the communication of bygone human words or their historical, aesthetic, or intellectual reproduction, but rather the proclamation of the Word of God. In view of the variety within the given biblical witness and the "contingency" of the regularly assigned selected preaching text, how can the sermon be the One Word of God? Must not preaching either be the mere communication of information or be based upon the expectation that somehow the One Word of God will "descend from above"—beyond all thought—or else not "descend from above"? Can preaching be orderly, in the proper sense "rational," relevant utterance? And since that is certainly supposed to be the case, what is then the authoritative thing about the text in its larger context, that which speaks to us and is to be spoken by us today, yesterday, and tomorrow?

e. The Necessity of Christian Doctrine in View of the Biblicistic Objection. In regard to the two first-mentioned objections to Christian doctrine, we came to the supposition that Christian doctrine, instead of running counter to the personal, historical, and temporal nature of faith in Christ, could perhaps have the opposite effect and protect them. In the case of the third and weightiest objection, which we have now discussed, this conjecture could be said to become a firm and positive *insight*. Without the endeavor of Christian doctrine, the Bible must become for us an unintelligible, benumbingly contradictory multiformity within which every element claims a hearing and obedience to the same degree as every other element. This must mean that the One Word is replaced by the multiplicity of words, and the One Truth by the multiplicity of truths; the necessary result is not the preservation but the disintegration of the proper, effective authority of the Bible. For the Bible certainly has no authority at all if its authoritative claim is submerged in a mass of individual claims which possibly are mutually exclusive. The Bible is authoritative only when, *in* the variety of voices, the One Voice is heard—the Voice of the One who is heard by the believing Community.[23] There is no personal faith in a multiplicity as such. In that Christian doctrine seeks the One—and seeks him in the *Bible*—its knowledge about faith is very vitally faith in *Christ*.

It should be added that "Biblicism," that stream of theology which in appealing to the Bible assumes a critical attitude toward dogma and dogmatics, is itself a dogmatics. The *dogmatic* conception of federal-theological Biblicism, or of Swabian, Menken's, or Beck's Biblicism, is easily recognized. As such, it should be taken very seriously and can provide a fruitful means for the critical exami-

---

23. The German term *Gemeinde* is translated regularly as "Community" or "believing Community" in order to distinguish it from *Kirche* (Church)—TR.

nation of other, more familiar conceptions. Indeed, the less-thought-through Biblicism which is dominant in many of the most serious groups of the Church reveals readily that there are "dogmatic" fundamental principles underlying it. Biblicism *is* itself a form of Christian *doctrine*.

f. The Task of Christian Doctrine and the Believing Community. On the basis of the foregoing considerations, the task of Christian doctrine may best be described with Calvin's concept of *interpretation*[24]—a concept, incidentally, which he used in the controversy with a biblicistic denial of the doctrine of the Trinity. Christian doctrine is the interpretation of the witness of Holy Scripture, coming from the witness of the believing Community. In its witness, the Community confesses that it has heard the *Word of God* in Scripture, and it proclaims what it has heard. Without going into greater detail at this early stage, this concept implies the following: First of all, Christian doctrine does not possess some sort of new and secondary criterion apart from Scripture; rather, it depends upon the criterion which is perceptible in Scripture itself. Secondly, all Christian doctrine is qualified by the fact that there is a listening and proclaiming Community, and this Community lives by the One Word. Thirdly, this Word is neither the property of the Community nor of the dogmatician; it is something which must be sought again and again in Scripture.

Christian doctrine is a function of the *Church*, of the *Community*. If we spoke of the "personality" which inheres in the Christian faith, then we must now immediately add by way of explanation that this "personality" is not the "individuality" of the isolated individual together with his Bible. If we spoke of "historicity," then we must now interpret this by saying that the historicity and historical relationship of the Christian faith does not consist of a relationship to a "completed past" (K. Heim), but rather to a history which is taking place *now*, which frees and binds us *today* and *tomorrow*. Christ is our personal counterpart as our brother. He is the Christ of history in the present as his coming makes itself known. Christian doctrine is *Church* doctrine, even as it is the task assigned to the individual *in* the Church.

B. CHRISTIAN DOCTRINE AS A FUNCTION OF THE CHURCH

1. PROCLAMATION AND SELF-UNDERSTANDING

a. Transition. The necessity of Christian doctrine was demonstrated for us in our consideration of those arguments which are raised *against* it. Christian doctrine is necessary to prevent faith in Christ from developing into "Christianity." It is necessary to insure that faith remains recognizably personal, historical, and temporal. It is necessary so that faith does not dissolve into the timeless and universal, or conversely lose its relationship to history in favor of the absolutized

---

24. *Institutes*, I, xiii, 3, pp. 123f.

present. Finally, and above all, it is necessary because faith as "Bible faith" does not stand for truths but for the Truth, not for multiplicity but for the One Word of God.

It is only an extension of the lines already laid down when we now take into consideration the fact that Christian doctrine, however it is structured, is *Church* doctrine, that it is a work of the believing Community or an event within this Community. For it is precisely at this point that the personality, historicity, temporality, and concreteness which are characteristic of the Christian faith are to be seen. If faith were only an individual relationship or attitude toward Christ, then it could imply a Christ conceived as one's own idea. Faith is concrete and personal in that the relationship of the believer to Christ is at the same time a relationship to other concrete persons.

b. The Church's "Understanding" as an Act of Reception. The Church's existence is based upon the Word of God which is spoken to it, received and proclaimed by it. It *exists* in that it *receives*, and on the basis of its act of reception it *speaks* and *acts*. Its fellowship with Jesus Christ is not a given but a gift which it is always to expect anew. It initially takes on concrete form as a fellowship in the understanding of the Word of God. Its existence is not based upon the fact that it is such a fellowship;[25] rather, the Church exists upon the basis of the Word itself.[26] However, it only *has* the Word in that it *seeks* it and in its seeking and proclaiming *opens* itself to it. Under these circumstances, "understanding" has been the crucial problem of the Church's existence through all ages, even though the problem has assumed many forms: the understanding of the *Word* spoken to the Church and given to it as Scripture and simultaneously the self-understanding of the person who hears this Word and understands himself on the basis of this Word. The Word is not unrelated and existent per se, rather it is directed to *man*. The issue of man who understands the Word and then understands himself on the basis of the Word or in confrontation with the Word is the unavoidable one, even though it is indeed a secondary issue over against the question of the Word itself. All proclamation happens in the tension between the first definitive question and this second unavoidable one, which is in turn authoritatively defined by the first. For God's Word authoritatively applies to real man.

c. Human Self-understanding and the Church's Proclamation. The question now is, "Who is this real man?" Man is characterized by the fact that he tran-

---

25. E. Brunner, *The Misunderstanding of the Church*, tr. H. Knight (Philadelphia: Westminster, 1953), views ecclesiology in the tension between institution and communion of persons, and he opts for the latter. He is right in saying that the Church, since it does not possess its being as Church, is as *creatura verbi* ("creation of the Word"—Luther) always and primarily a host of questioning, waiting, understanding, and misunderstanding people who do all this *together* in fellowship. Wherever this form of the Church (noetically the primary form, in essence the secondary form) is neglected, the Word becomes a possession, and this must lead to a perverted institutionalism. Wherever, on the other hand, this form is separated from its relationship to the Word, that is, it is relativized, the Church becomes a school or a philosophical society.

26. K. Barth, *CD*, I,2, and elsewhere: Jesus Christ as the "Being of the Church."

scends himself, that is, he makes himself into the object of a "self-understanding."
He *exists* in that he "understands" himself in one fashion or another. This self-
understanding, which is usually unreflected and lacking all systematic order, finds
its articulated and definitive structure in the great philosophical systems, the formative "world views." When man, in his reflecting and structuring, relates the
reality around and contingent to him to himself, when he evaluates and shapes it,
then he is applying his self-understanding to the world. In this way, he "gains
control" of himself and of his world in his thinking and structuring. This can
happen both actively and passively, both confidently and skeptically. The decisive
thing is that man, in so doing, "posits" himself. The more comprehensive and
carefully thought-through his world view is, the more he gains control of himself
and his world in that world view. This still holds true when the world view and
the self-understanding behind it contain a definite view of a "highest being," of
a "god," which is usually the case even though this highest being often appears
in contemporary systems in the very effective disguise of "nothingness." This
elaborated world view and clarified self-understanding then begin to affect imperceptibly the broad course of human life which is never (or seldom) the subject
of systematic reflection. This influence often takes a long time to make itself felt,
but for that reason it is all the more effective. In short, man does indeed believe
that he knows who and what he is and what the state of his world is. Proclamation
now encounters a man who already "understands" himself in one way or another.
This is not meant merely noetically, for in this self-understanding man really
"possesses" himself. Hence his self-understanding is, as Paul says, the ground
and content of his "boast" or "boasting" (Rom. 2:17; 3:27; 4:2; 1 Cor. 1:29; 3:21;
5:6; etc.). He affirms himself in his self-understanding. Therefore, the "Word of
the cross" becomes folly to him or a "stumbling block." If proclamation is right
and if it becomes effective, a collision results: the proclaimed Word is experienced
as attack. There is, to be sure, another alternative: man can receive the Word
proclaimed to him into the given context of his self-understanding, can seek to
incorporate it as a deepening or improvement of what already was the theme of
his self-affirmation. This in turn deprives the Word of all its power and leads to
its transformation into a "new" world view or into the coronation of the view
already present.

   At this point a danger comes into view which threatens the very proclamation itself. We remember that proclamation is a wooing, exhorting Word, desirous of winning over the hearer (this is how Paul understands it; see 2 Cor. 5:11,
20). How natural then must it be for proclamation, as a human act, to "link itself
up" with what is already given and to encourage the very interpretation which
we just noted! How rapidly in the history of the early Church the Word of the
cross developed into a supernaturalistic coronation of what was already there, a
confirmation of man as he was and therefore as he understood himself, whether
Hellenistically or Gnostically. And conversely, how easy it is for the newly formulated antithesis or diastasis to appear as a new, supranatural world view in
competition with the previous ones, so that "boasting" now becomes "Christian"
boasting and the protection afforded by the given structure becomes "Christian"
securitas (security over against certitude). Proclamation would not be a human
activity if this danger were not essentially permanent.

d. The Beginning of Heresy. The appearance of this danger is identical with the constantly threatening temptation to *heresy*. Heresy is present *in nuce* wherever the Church in its proclamation makes a given or inherited human self-understanding into the criterion of the Word. Invariably this happens with the best of intentions: to mitigate the strangeness of the proclaimed Word, to make it easier for the listener to find access to the Word, to make it possible for the believer to exist in "his" world. We must state, in fact, that the Church's proclamation can never avoid this *danger*. By the very nature of things, it cannot do so if it desires to remain open to the world, and it has the most serious of reasons for being open. Nor can it escape the danger if it recognizes and makes the antithesis manifest; when the message is propounded antithetically or diastatically, it can become a substitute for the given world view and becomes itself a world view in the process. In any case, what happens is that the message appears either connectively and synthetically as the ultimate confirmation of already accepted value systems, or already established conceptual positions, or an already valid world view. The other alternative is that it appears antithetically and diastatically as the absolute transcending of all those, or as the needed completion of faulty systems, or as the rectification of already present error. In any event, it is man as he understands himself from his own point of view, man as such, who is the obvious or concealed criterion for the Word of God, or at least for the form of its presentation, to put it in a somewhat milder and more diluting form, as is often done. The fact is that man, as long as he continues to affirm himself with his own self-understanding, fails to find the meaning of his existence, overlooks his creatureliness and denies in unbelief that he only be truly man when he is man *coram Deo* (in the presence of God). In his unbelief he fails to see that he is subject to another criterion rather than being the measure of himself, and this other criterion deprives him of all autonomous securities. In many ways, all of this has been disregarded or passed over by the Church's proclamation—understandably, less in times of powerful and virulent opposition to this proclamation and more in times of comparative general agreement. To the extent, however, that man's understanding of himself or of the world overtly or covertly takes control in or over proclamation, heresy has made its appearance. By no means does it always look like a direct contradiction of Scripture. It can even make use of Scripture. In essence, it often appears as the pious, moralistic, or rationalistic autonomousness with which the Christian undertakes to use the Word of God as a *means* of improving what was already there, to gain mastery finally over the world or "life" both in thought and in action.

e. The Question of "Pure" Doctrine. In opposition to such autonomousness, Christian doctrine is the preservation of the *lordship* of the Word of God in the Church (it is this by its nature though certainly not as a phenomenon). Wherever in its dogma the Church endeavors to insure this preservation, it does so in opposition to itself; in a sense, in opposition to what would be the more likely tendency of its proclamation than "pure doctrine" and what would seem to offer greater chances of success for its proclamation. Wherever in dogmatics individual theologians are at work in the service of the Church, their endeavors can only be significant if they address the query to the Church of whether its proclamation is "right" proclamation, that is, whether it is really the proclamation of the Word of God or perhaps the mere use of the Word for a self-interpretation of Christian man, whether then it is in truth "service" of the Word or lordship over the Word. In short, the purpose of Christian doctrine is to submit the proclamation of the Church to the criterion of its *commission*. and thus to help it to be relevant to its mandate. Whether or not doctrine measures up to this purpose is another question. For dogma, and dogmatics too, are subject not only to the limitations of human powers of understanding but above all to the influence of the variously given self-understandings. Hence Christian doctrine is never equipped with better knowledge because of its special or official nature. Instead, it is the function by which the Church declares and respects its essential *subjection* to the criterion which defines it. Only when dogmatics fulfills this function is it meaningful and necessary.

2. THE LANGUAGE OF THE CHURCH

a. Language and Self-understanding. The Church's proclamation encounters us in the form of human speech. Even the lonely man, reading his Bible alone, is dependent upon the interpretive ministry of the Church, in that preaching has its effect.

The Church's speech happens in a concrete language, but there is no special Church language. Rather, the Church's proclamation always is couched in one of the available "worldly" languages. It would not be human address to human beings if this were not so.

Language, however, is not merely a technical means of communication nor a neutral vessel for any "content" whatever. It is primarily the manifestation of the *self-understanding* which dominates consciously or unconsciously in the grouping of those using a specific language. Language is not manufactured, it grows, and its growth is inextricably bound up with the history of the community using the language. It may very well be that the encounter of a language community (as, for example, in the case of Europe) with Christian proclamation leaves indelible traces in the language itself. Originally, however, all languages are "unbaptized."

In any event, Christian speech enters into a language area which has already been molded. This is demonstrated most clearly in the specific vocabulary of religion. Most languages contain words like "god," "faith," "sin," "grace," and "law." With all of these words, however, there is a kind of "pre-understanding" already present. This is shown most impressively in the biblical languages, and here most markedly in the Greek. Our "New Testament dictionaries" are remarkable documents for this—and also for the way in which they make the great difficulty clear which the emergence of the Christian message must mean in what is always going to be a *heathen* language. Now what is true of New Testament Greek is all the more true of all contemporary languages. One need only think of the difficulty inherent in the word "faith": is it merely a difference in the prepositional object when we speak of faith *in* Christ in a language community which once spoke of "faith in Germany" or still speaks of "faith in democracy" or "faith in the Christian West"? What then is "faith" supposed to be in Christian speech?[27] In a language realm which is also thoroughly steeped with the Christian idiom, the Church may not always sense the actual tension present—at great harm to its own cause. Certainly the translator of the Bible senses this tension—we are reminded of Luther's efforts in this regard and refer to his *Sendbrief vom Dolmetschen.*[28] The missionary senses this tension even more acutely. Is he able to "link up" with the religious terms of his foreign environment? Is it not possible that every connection he makes must be an *a priori* compromise of the cause he wishes to further? He must experience very often that every language decision he has made must necessarily result in misunderstandings.

What is true of vocabulary is all the more true of syntax (often, too, of grammar: e.g., the tenses in Hebrew). For it is in the shaping of the sentences that the train of thought is adequately expressed. It was not without reason that in the curriculum of the medieval university the budding scholar was made to study, among other things, grammar, rhetoric, and dialectic. These three belonged together, and together they formed what for that time can be called the "pre-understanding."[29]

b. The Church's Secret Language. On the other hand, Christian speech is under no circumstances a secret language.

To be sure, in the *public worship* of the Roman Catholic and the Orthodox churches a foreign language (i.e., one unfamiliar to the person not specially trained) has been maintained—Latin and Church Slavonic, respectively. However, *proclamation*, to the degree that it is at all vital, is always in the vernacular. When the Reformation made the use of the vernacular for all of worship the general practice—or if not the vernacular, at least a language understood by all participants—it removed the separation between the liturgy in a foreign tongue and the sermon in the known language, and thereby it shaped the whole service of worship around the proclamation. What led in fact to the conservation of a foreign language in the conduct of the "cultus"? The decisive factor might well have been that the "cultus" was understood as the representation and performance of a mystery whose foreignness and independence of the present, the language-community, and "pre-understanding" was sensed so strongly that the language no longer used in ordinary discourse seemed to be the appropriate vehicle for it. One gets the impression that there has been an analogous development in Evangelical churches in regard to the sermon: "pulpit-language" (as it has emerged in the German churches) has largely lost touch with spoken language—it is the "language of Canaan." What is the point of "translation" if the hearer is certainly not going to be able to grasp the *contents* in a "natural" fashion? Let us be clear about this, however: wherever one thinks or, more frequently, feels this way, a *dogmatic*

---

27. For much of what is here under discussion see Friso Melzer, *Unsere Sprache im Lichte der Christus-Offenbarung* (Tübingen: J. C. B. Mohr, 1946), especially pp. 259ff.

28. "On Translating: An Open Letter," AE, XXXV, 181–202.

29. How far rhetoric and dialectic can penetrate into theology may be observed especially in Melanchthon's *Loci*; see also W. Neuser, *Der Ansatz der Theologie Philipp Melanchthons (Beiträge zur Geschichte und Lehre der reformierten Kirche*, 9; Neukirchen: Buchhandlung des Erziehungsvereins, 1957).

decision has in fact already been made. The mystery of the Word of God has been transformed into the palpable mystery of unintelligible language. This way of thinking goes right down to the roots of theological thought. Nevertheless, we may in general assume that the basic proposition will be agreed to that Christian language (if the phrase may be permitted) is not a secret language. This necessarily means that this "Church" language must remain in dialogue with the language spoken elsewhere. And that means in turn that it is necessary to consider thoughtfully what, in truth, the essence of Christianity has to do with real man and what its relationship to man's self-understanding really is.

The language of the Church is, accordingly, always threatened by two dangers: the danger of making the Word of God subservient to the given self-understanding of man, and the danger of its becoming a secret language by disregarding this self-understanding. Both dangers are equally great, although they do not appear with equal acuteness at all times. It may be that today the second danger is really the more pressing.

c. *The Task of Christian Doctrine.* In view of this two-sided danger, the Church needs Christian doctrine as, so to speak, a grammar and syntax of Christian speech. It needs the organ which serves to summon it back from all kinds of self-understandings to the mandate with which it has been commissioned. But it needs the same organ to keep it from letting its mandate, in its notorious strangeness and proneness to mystery, become an *artificial*, fabricated, or recklessly contrived *rationalist* mystery, rather than seeing the mystery at the place where it is really supposed to be. The twofold inquiry that is imperative here—the key question about the "essential contents" and their subordinate, the question of "man"—is not ultimately the inquiry about something which could be said to be at the disposal of the Church or even the dogmatician in the Church. Rather, it leads to the decisive issue, which is only meaningful in that it is the inquiry into the Word of God. If we *had* this "essence" the way one otherwise has contents or things under control, then it would probably not be so difficult to "present" or to "translate" it. But the essence we mean is the essence that underlies us, and its nature is such that we only "have" it in baffled inquiry.[30]

---

30. The difference between the theological-linguistic philosophical conception of J. G. Herder and J. G. Hamann may well ultimately consist of the fact that Herder believes he has the "essence," whereas Hamann, on the contrary, does not. On Hamann, see James O'Flaherty, *Unity and Language: A Study in the Philosophy of Johann George Hamann* (Chapel Hill: University of North Carolina Press, 1952).

II. Dogma and Dogmatics

A. CONFESSION AND DOGMA

1. CONFESSION

In the preceding chapter we spoke quite generally about "Christian doctrine." It was scarcely more than implied in what form Christian doctrine occurs. Perhaps it has begun to become clear that we are concerned here with a threefold form. First of all, Christian doctrine occurs in preaching itself. This was what Augustine had in mind when he wrote *De doctrina christiana*, and preaching is what the confessional writings of the Reformation mean when they speak of doctrine. If Christian doctrine is fulfilling its task, then the sermon is the place where this is shown or not shown. Preaching is primarily, however, proclamation. It is constantly betraying whether it is being obedient to the criterion which obtains for the life and work of the Church, because the Church is derived from it. However, preaching is dependent upon the fact that the inquiry into this criterion takes place in other ways, out of responsibility for preaching. This leads us to the second form of Christian doctrine: the process just alluded to takes place in the consensus of the Church as the form of *dogma*. Now dogma is not law, but the manifestation of a spiritual and spiritually binding consensus. Hence it requires the work of individuals who, since it is not the criterion itself, examine and interpret it in light of the criterion it manifests, and who, since it is not a dead factor, try to understand it as a vital issue, to consider it critically, and to formulate it anew. This means that Christian doctrine takes as its third form that of *dogmatics*. Dogma and dogmatics are related to preaching. Of course, the sermon is something other than rhetorical dogma or verbalized dogmatics. However, it is dependent upon the guidance which dogma provides and the critical inquiry which is the business of dogmatics.

This programmatic outline must now be dealt with in detail. The point of departure must be dogma, which definitely is the superior instance over against dogmatics, although it is not to be uncritically accepted by dogmatics.

Dogma received its original and primary character in the *confession of faith*.

Therefore, our first step will be to inquire into the nature and the dogmatic significance of confession.[1]

a. Confession as Act. Let us note carefully that confession is not dogma; rather, it is the original form of dogma. In essence, confession is an *event*, not a document. In the New Testament, the verb *homologein* (to confess, to acknowledge) occurs much more frequently than the noun *homologia* (confession, acknowledgment), and the same is true of *martyrein* (to bear witness) in relation to *martyria* and *martyrion* (witness, testimony). But the nouns *homologia* and *martyria*, *martyrion* all designate, in fact, an act (see 2 Cor. 9:13 or 1 Tim. 6:13). This act does not possess any kind of autonomy; rather, it is a *response*. We might express it this way: In response to the fact that God has disclosed himself to man in Jesus Christ, man (or the believing Community representing man) ought to and is permitted to acknowledge God. Hence in the New Testament all confession is thankful, praising, self-committing *acceptance* of God's self-revelation in Jesus Christ. Thus confession finds its basic formulation in the statement, "Jesus Christ is Lord," which we encounter in Philippians 2:11 (and 1 Cor. 12:3), and which reflects its Aramaic form in 1 Corinthians 16:22, with the eschatological accent there as well as in Philippians 2.

In that this confession occurs, *Community* happens. The Community does not "have" its confession, as though it were of secondary importance; rather, the Community confesses, and it "exists" in its confessing. However, it does not exist by virtue of its confession, for confession is simply response, not Word, and the Community does not make Jesus into the Christ or the Lord. Instead, it lives by the very fact that it recognizes Jesus as all this and praises him for it. In the New Testament, confession appears with an eschatological aspect: it is the behavior which is appropriate to and anticipates the "last hour"; the Community does what "every tongue" should do (Phil. 2:11); in confession it is, so to speak, the advance guard of "every creature" (Rev. 5:13) and the repeater of the angels' words (Rev. 5:8ff.). In confession, the Community projects itself into the future, to him who is and who was and who is to come (Rev. 1:8). It abandons itself in its confession. Therefore, confession is the most inappropriate foundation conceivable for the Church to use to assert its position. By its very nature, confession is specifically "martyrdom."[2] On the other hand, the Community has its proper *freedom* in the obligatory confession, that is, its freedom from the "world," from its claims and promises.

b. Confession as Statement. Confession is, however, simultaneously act and statement. Even the so-called confession in deeds is a confession only by virtue of the statement conveyed by such deeds. "Jesus Christ is Lord" is certainly more than a doctrinal proposition, but it is *also* a doctrinal proposition: it says

---

1. See W. Betzendörfer, *Glauben und Wissen bei den grossen Denkern des Mittelalters* (Gotha: L. Klotz, 1931).
2. See H. F. von Campenhausen, *Die Idee des Martyriums in der Alten Kirche* (Göttingen: Vandenhoeck & Ruprecht, 1964[2]).

"something." To confess Jesus as the Christ and as the Lord means in any event to say something "dogmatic." In this sense, confession is the original form of dogma. It states something valid about the historical man Jesus of Nazareth, and thereby it rejects other nonvalid statements. By its very nature confession involves polemics: this man, and no other, is Christ the Lord. It is further clear that from the outset the necessity for interpretation was bound up with terms such as "Christ," "Lord," and "Son of God." The question was unavoidable regarding the reception of the Old Testament, and more indirectly the question of the relationship to the Hellenistic and Gnostic environment. To be sure, interpretation was not the only requirement: confession was originally oriented not primarily to the area of intellectual clarification, but was imbedded in the setting of the service of worship[3] and of the external struggle.[4] The necessity of interpretation was equally pressing for both of these areas, and it would not be wrong to regard the entire New Testament as a commentary on the confession, "Jesus Christ is Lord."

Confession as a statement can be understood as the brief summary in which the kerygma is put in its most pointed form.[5] In that it transmits "history," the kerygma is testimony to something which is found in no history as such and which can be limited to no one history. To put it in Johannine language, it is the manifestation of a paradox: "The Word became flesh." Insofar as dogma is taking on its own form in confession, this is *the* dogmatic thesis. The oldest summaries of the kerygma (1 Cor. 15; Phil. 2:6ff.; and 1 Cor. 11:23ff.) revolve around this paradox, which is the paradox of the cross and the resurrection.

c. The Ongoing Process of the Confession of Faith. Confession of faith is subject to change. The reason for this is obviously not the One who is the "theme" of confession and of the statement which is bound up with the confession. In terms of its central theme, the Church never has anything else to say except, "Jesus Christ is Lord." But this theme is neither a discursively gained doctrinal proposition which is open to better insights nor law engraved on stone tablets which must remain "untouched." This "theme" is a person, the person of the *Christus praesens* (the present Christ), who is no other than the "Christ of history." The Church, which confesses this Christ, does it in the "world," surrounded by the temptation which comes from the powers of the present age, from the self-understanding of man which obtrudes upon the Church and tries to assert

---

3. Special reference is made to this in Wilhelm Maurer, *Bekenntnis und Sakrament; ein Beitrag zur Entstehung der christlichen Konfessionen* (Berlin: A. Töpelmann, 1939).

4. More comprehensive than Maurer: O. Cullmann, *The Earliest Christian Confessions*, tr. J. K. S. Reid (London: Lutterworth, 1949). See also E. Stauffer, *New Testament Theology*, tr. J. Marsh (London: S.C.M., 1955), pp. 236ff.

5. The fact that the formulations of the confession (as the *regula fidei*—rule of faith) were subsumed within the so-called "arcane disciplines" or the Discipline of the Secret (the secrecy shrouding the liturgical acts of the Church, presumably from the 3rd to the 6th century—TR), which perhaps went back as far as the primitive Christian period, does not contradict this statment. The Rule of Faith was connected with baptism very early and thereby was attributed the character of a mystery. Of course, the kerygma was by its nature directed toward the public; it was the exterior aspect of the mystery. Proclamation would have had to come to a standstill if the mystery had absorbed the kerygma.

itself in it again and again—as heresy. This temptation comes simultaneously from "without" and from "within." Confession, in which the Church rediscovers its freedom, becomes thus its *defense* against heresy, in constantly changing forms. Since the confession always speaks the language of its age, and yet turns away from the self-understanding of man which determines this language in the very use of it, confession must retain the character of paradoxical speech (i.e., the nullification of a self-understanding by use of its own means of expression). The classical example of this is the Trinitarian dogma of the 4th century. It does not say more than "Jesus Christ is Lord," nor does it "fortify" this statement; rather it restates the issue anew, within the given linguistic framework, without any special securities, but with its thrust aimed both at heresy and at the threatening alienation of the Church from without.[6] Thus by its very nature it bears the character of the ongoing process of confession. There is nothing of a new discovery here—there never is. It is stating the "old" confession, but it is saying it in a new way. And it does this, not because a new age requires new means of expression (this would only be a criterion if what we wanted to say were a doctrinal proposition which in its eternal validity could and would have to assume the cloak of any age), but because new temptations attack the old Word then and now. This leads us to understand that each new confession does not abolish its precursors, but incorporates them. Thus, for example, the Reformation confessional statements expressly acknowledge the symbols of the ancient Church. The Church preserves its tradition in that it does not become fossilized in it.

The ongoing process of confession, as it appears in the old "symbols" or in the Reformation documents, is *declaratory*. The reason for this is not to be sought only in the declarative form of the old Rule of Faith, of the symbol of which Cyprian already knew,[7] but also in that the ongoing process of confession presupposes the original, summarizing, and fundamental confession, and certainly never replaces it. The confessional declaration is not the confession as such, but rather the ongoing process of that confession. Hence it is itself only binding insofar as it is bound to the original confession and thereby to Christ himself. It does contain the danger of misunderstanding, however, which arises whenever the declarative formulation, in perhaps something as comprehensive as a detailed document (for instance, the so-called Athanasian Creed, or in particular The Formula of Concord or The Canons of the Synod of Dort), is viewed as something in which we are supposed to believe.[8] That is to say, the declarative formulation can conceal the "personal" meaning which inheres in even the most differentiated of thematic statements. It can even claim to be the *Truth* which is really Christ alone. But then the heart of the Christian message gets lost.

The confessional declaration, which is what we usually have in mind when

---

6. On this see H. Berkhof, *Kirche und Kaiser; eine Untersuchung der Entstehung der byzantinischen und der theokratischen Staatsauffassung im 4. Jahrhundert*, tr. G. W. Locher (Zollikon: Evangelischer Verlag, 1947).

7. St. Cyprian, *Letters (FC*, vol. 51, Letter 69, pp. 244ff.); on the Rule of Faith see Tertullian, *The Prescription Against Heretics*, tr. P. Holmes (*ANF*, III, 13f., 243–67).

8. *Quicunque vult salvus esse* = "Whosoever wishes to be saved" (the Athanasian Creed)!

we talk about "confession," "confessional obligation," or "confessionally appropriate," can only be properly understood in relationship to the actual "theme" of the confession. This happens when it is confronted concretely with the testimony of *Scripture*, which is the criterion directly given for this. No confession can replace Scripture, and none can adequately reproduce its total breadth and fullness. What the confession can accomplish is simply to provide guidance to the right understanding of Scripture, which means the understanding which measures up to Christ. Scripture itself guards the confession from understanding itself as truth, where it really is no more than the reproduction of the understanding of Scripture which is given to the Church and which unites it. Conversely, the confession guards our understanding of Scripture from deteriorating into a pluralism with no center. However, this will only remain effective if, in turn, the confession is not misunderstood positivistically and pluralistically.

   d. Confession and Confessionalism.[9] It has only been in the last centuries that the term "confession" has gone through a change in meanings expressed in the somewhat ambiguous ways the term is used today. "Confession" is actually the Vulgate translation for *homologia*, and therefore means the same thing as "confession of faith" or "Bekenntnis" in German. The term itself was scarcely used in confessional formulae at first, although perhaps there is a trace of it behind Hebrews 3:1. Moreover, the many confessional formulations produced by the ancient Church are not called *confessiones*—the usual designation is *symbolum* (symbol). Indeed, the term "confession" seems to have been considerably narrowed down later; it is used simply for the confessional or penitential act (*confessio oris*, or oral confession). On the other hand, during the Reformation the term "confession" is used to designate documents in which the Reformation understanding of the Gospel is "confessed" (the Augsburg Confession, etc.). This use of the term is legitimate insofar as the Reformation confessional writings were in fact actual, factual confessions of faith, or were regarded as such. Yet the confessional documents were often documents of state law at the same time; in Germany, since the Peace of Augsburg (1555) the Augsburg Confession increasingly became such as its recognition became the decisive factor for the invocation of the rights which the Peace guaranteed the Lutheran imperial estates, or the estates "of the Augsburg Confession." Thus the emphasis of the term "confession" shifted more and more from its actual meaning into the area of the institutional and the formal. "Confession" became the specific document which governed the religious condition of a territory, or later, of a church or congregation. This in turn opened the way for another shift in meaning: since there already were territories of this or that "confession" regulated by imperial law (since 1648 the Reformed Churches were included in this, as they were excluded from the Peace of Augsburg), "confession" gradually developed into the designation of a church organization defined by one or several such documents. Thus, the "confes-

---

9. This section deals with the term *confession* as used to designate a confessional grouping or denomination. The distinction is easier in German since "Bekenntnis" means confession in the classical sense of "confession of faith," while "Konfession" means confessional grouping or denomination—TR.

sional churches" came into being and with them the idea that the Church is founded upon a confession. This idea was strongly expanded in the course of German Romanticism and the theology influenced by it. The "confessions" were seen to be morphological constructions whose "principle" needed to be researched and which presumably developed organically out of their "principles" like living plants. This is the concept of confession that is still held in many quarters today, at least in Germany. The impartial observer would scarcely realize what "confession" really means, that within the continuity of the Church in its history, it is primarily the act of responsive manifestation of faith in Jesus Christ. In fact, even the decisive function of the document itself is almost forgotten—it is conceivable that one could be "confessional" without regarding the confessional statements themselves as in any sense binding, perhaps without even knowing them. It ought to be clear that this is a case of mistaken development, although it is historically understandable. The Barmen Declaration of 1934 could have been regarded as a summons to examine carefully this development in the face of the actual confession of faith with which the various churches, coming from different "confessional" traditions, had been able to come together. Seen as whole, it cannot be said that this in fact did happen.

2. DOGMA

In the most original form known to us (Phil. 2:11), confession was in fact simultaneously dogma, that is, the forming of church doctrine by affirmation and negation. The circumstance in which we first encounter church dogma in its essential form as a confession is important for our understanding of dogma. Dogma as a statement is at the same time witness, although more indirectly, in that it is related to the public proclamation of Christ by his Community. It is not an isolated intellectual activity, such as the development of a principle[10] or the presentation of an ontic theme. It is open, as it were, to the past (to history), upward (to the present Christ), and to the future (to the coming Lord).

However, what is "dogma"—and what can it be legitimately in the context of a Christian dogmatics?

a. The Origin and Problematics of the Term. We can begin with the New Testament. Here, *dogma* means, first of all, "official ordinance" or "decree" (Luke 2:1; Acts 17:7; Heb. 11:23 in some MSS, and also Dan. 2:13 verbally); secondly, "Mosaic rule" (Eph. 2:15; Col. 2:14; probably also Col. 2:20 verbally); and thirdly, in one instance, an apostolic decree dealing with practical behavior (Acts 16:4). It is noteworthy that in all these instances the relationship to doctrine is lacking or appears only indirectly in the case of the third meaning. The usage of the term "dogma" for "church doctrine" has no roots in the New Testament.

Instead, it has its roots in the terminology of late Greek philosophy which used *dogma* to designate the official views of a particular philosophical school.[11]

---

10. See pp. 34ff.
11. See the article "*dogma*" in Kittel, *TDNT*, II, 230–32.

Christian theology took over this usage to the same degree that it fell under the influence of the Hellenistic spirit. Just as there was the dogma of the Stoics or the Cynics, there was the dogma of the Christians. Later,[12] this dogma assumed a position as the scientifically formulated way of expressing the Christian message, occupying a place next to the kerygma, which itself lacked such systematic formulations. This process was unmistakably connected to the transformation of the Church into both a sacral institution and a center of instruction, and it was also related to the view which held that *gnosis* (knowledge) surpassed mere *pistis* (faith). Thus, clearly, dogma became, on the one hand, the possession of those who were specially qualified (the gnostically enlightened or the rationally educated) and, on the other hand, something objective which, as tradition, did not need to be completely inflexible but which could never be really relevant.

All of these factors make it clear that great care is needed when we consider the origin of the term "dogma." Certainly theology is entitled, and often obliged, to use terms for the sake of proper interpretation which are not "biblical" (there are really no *purely* "biblical" terms); yet great caution is justified when a term is to be used which in its traditional form is decisively shaped by a fundamental understanding which cannot be Christian.

Nevertheless, a *legitimate* use for the term "dogma" can be found.

1) Church Dogma in Relation to Established Philosophical Views. The idea of binding force is always associated with the term "dogma." This association as such is not illegitimate, but it needs more precise definition. The determinative factor must be that the binding force of dogma be of a spiritual nature, and this can only be true when it is related to the binding force of the Word of God.

We begin by citing for comparison the concept of dogma as the official philosophy of a Christian school of thought. The binding force of a "school" position is relative in several directions. Above all, it is relative to *reason* as the acknowledged criterion for philosophy—whereby we may leave undiscussed the question of the ways reason has been and can be understood. No school position can persist over against a rational insight asserting itself, nor would it be meaningful to want to resist such an insight. Yet the diversity of school positions stems from the circumstance that rational insights lead to differing results. The very existence of contradictory philosophical schools is an argument against any palpable universal validity of rational insights. In addition, the ancient philosophical schools were to a certain extent sociological structures, not seldom virtual guilds or corporations, in some senses comparable with the later Christian confessions or the various traditions within Judaism. Thus, each particular dogma was to a degree the result of the pluralization of the truth. This has remained the hallmark of the history of human thought. Those insights shared by absolutely everyone would not be in need of "dogmatic" formulation. Thus, indirectly dogma always implies rejection. But this does not necessarily exclude the possibility that philo-

---

12. G. Kittel (*ibid.*, p. 232) names St. Basil the Great (*On the Holy Spirit*, tr. G. Lewis [*Christian Classics Series*; London: Religious Tract Society, 1889], IV, 27) as the first theologian for whom the Christian message is made up of the two parts, *ta dogmata* and *ta kerygmata*.

sophically conceived dogma—the ruling school's position—fundamentally re-
tains its relationship to reason. It is in principle refutable and alterable. Its historical-
sociological relativity is only the mirror of its fundamental relationship to reason.

There appears to be a formal analogy between Church dogma and philosophical dogma, since the former has only relative binding force like the latter.
But the relativity of Christian dogma is not in connection with reason (or self-
understanding) but with revelation. Revelation, however, is neither the surpassing
nor the annulment of reason, neither the divine announcement of a principle nor
the emergence of a rationality which had been concealed before or wrongly understood. It is so qualitatively different from all reason that it neither annuls nor
confirms reason. Revelation is an event in which the living God breaks through
the rationally objectivized selfhood of man, in which God as "the totally Other"
encounters man personally as the One who is very near to him. Since dogma is
relative to revelation, its relativity is not to something essentially accessible to
man, but to the One who encounters man solely as his opposite and thus as the
One who can be apprehended by him only in decision, that is, in faith. Decision,
however, is precisely what autonomous reason wants to make superfluous: to the
extent that rational insights are valid, they are *not* the objects of decision. Therefore, reason can never acknowledge revelation as revelation. Reason must relativ-
ize the revelational event from its own perspective, which could mean that it
derives from revelation those eternal truths which it can acknowledge, or that it
rejects revelation in principle because such eternal truths are lacking. At most it
can concede—with Lessing's *Education of the Human Race*—that revelation provides an anticipatory grasp of rational insights which otherwise could only have
been gained much later, or else—as many medieval thinkers held—revelation
could be understood as the supernatural pronouncement of "supernatural" truths
which served as the confirmation of the "natural" truths. In every instance, the
real and essential thing is reason, in a higher or lower sense, and revelation as an
event, as a *person*, is viewed in an instrumental or relative relationship to it.

Accordingly, dogma distinguishes itself in regard to its binding force from
every philosophical position in that it is not relative to reason or to rational insights
but rather to the *event* of revelation and thus always involves a decision. The most
concrete expression of this is the fact that the original structure of dogma is the
confession of faith.

2) **Dogma: Doctrinal Decision and Not Doctrinal Law.** We have stated that
dogma possesses its binding force in that it always involves decision. This can be
understood in two ways: first, dogma is itself the object of a doctrinal decision
of the Church; secondly, dogma continually becomes a new summons to make
this decision again. Both of these options are now to be examined.

First of all: "Dogma is the object of a doctrinal decision." The distinction
here from the classical positions of philosophy is obvious, for they are the result
of philosophical labor, and not the object of a decision. But dogma is so very
much the object of a decision that it is risked at the danger of placing one's
outward existence and personal objective correctness in jeopardy. It can plunge
the Church into extreme crises and has often done so. It can also materially err;
an infallible insurance against that would only be given if the Church itself had

revelation in its possession and needed simply to distribute and interpret it.[13] In other words, dogma is unconditional decision. When the Church makes this decision, it puts all other considerations aside and affirms only its subjection to the essential matter out of which and for which it exists. It is for this reason the decision in which the Church manifests its freedom, which can only be freedom based upon the Word of God. This signifies that dogma is binding in that the decision which produces dogma demonstrates that the absolute authority of the Word of God is believed and is at work. It is precisely as decision that dogma is binding.

It could appear that, as defined, the most essential aspect of dogma were its *positivity*, its character as a discretionary position. The model of such a position is civil law, and it will be necessary for us to compare this in its structure with dogma; this is justified by the linguistic usage of the New Testament.

Civil law is also relative—it is related to the circumstances of the age for which it is formulated, and to the essence of "justice" which it is supposed to serve but which as such is never attainable but can only be sought within the given situation and under the influence of certain forms of human self-understanding and certain constellations of power.

It can certainly happen that a legal expert might evaluate the regulations of valid laws critically or even reject them (from the standpoint of a sense of justice, or of their usefulness, or their practicability, etc.); yet he remains positively bound to the given law, and if he is a judge, he renders his judgments according to it. A conflict situation can arise where injustice is formally legalized. But there is an abundance of cases where this radicality is not present; there are better and poorer laws. In any event, the fundamental criticism of justice does not necessarily exclude its binding force.

This possible coincidence of legal validity and substantive criticism of the law (which can diverge radically in conflict situations) can occur in the realm of the state because the law deals with actions and omissions within given forms of conduct and relationships (e.g., a contract), but it does not deal with the interior conditions of man (e.g., attitudes or convictions). In my actions, under certain circumstances, I can or must submit to norms whose substantive legality I contest and whose alteration I quite possibly am pursuing actively, and the judge can and must base his judgments upon valid law even if he is critical of it.

It is quite clear that the Church's dogma has a totally different structure from civil law. Both are "positive." Both in their own ways are also relative. But it would be impossible to require of someone that he "acknowledge" a certain dogma in opposition to his own faith, merely because it was a positive ruling of the Church. To be sure, dogma is primarily related to actions such as preaching, teaching, etc. Yet it would be impossible to require someone to preach the contents of a dogma in contradiction to his own insights into the Word of God. The positivity of dogma does not produce "outer" binding force, such as civil law possesses, but an "inner" binding force. And while certainly dogma like law rests

---

13. Note the Roman Catholic concept of *depositum fidei* (deposit of faith), below, pp. 39ff.

upon decision, it is just as certain that, in contrast to law, dogma is oriented toward and dependent upon constantly new decisions; indeed, it is to be understood as a summons to these decisions.

To put it briefly, dogma is certainly a doctrinal decision but never doctrinal law.

3) Dogma as the Word of the Fathers. Nevertheless it must be added that the other aspect of the decision quality of dogma, its being a constant summons to make decisions anew, cannot mean the establishment of the authority of the pious subject in opposition to the doctrinal decisions of the Church. Dogma is the voice of the *Fathers*. No father can claim to have divine authority in regard to his son. However, in the very fact that dogma claims to have *no* authority of its own, it lays claims to the authority of the Word of God which it acknowledges and testifies to. Every individual is referred exclusively to this standard. However, this standard is not his private property but addresses him concretely in proclamation, and that means, within the Community of the Fathers and brethren. Therefore the individual will have to *listen* long and intently and practice obedience to the Word before he perhaps *speaks* and finally even "criticizes." The Church is not the sum of many pious individuals, but rather as the "assembly," as "the people of God," as "the body of Christ," it is the Community which precedes the individual in his faith. While quite certainly it is not infallible, it is just as certainly our "mother," without whom we would not be Christians. It is therefore not a discussion group but the place of concrete, though relative, authority. It is difficult but necessary to make clear that the Church, according to the Evangelical understanding, is by no means without authority. Where this is not clearly understood, it is easy to fall prey to the opinion that one must be Roman Catholic in order to avoid the dangers of subjectivism.

4) The Spiritual, Binding Force of Dogma. After all this has been said, what can be the meaning of "spiritual, binding force of dogma"?

It is not to be confused with the positive, binding force of the law nor with the changeable validity of philosophical positions which is based upon subjective rational apprehension. Dogma is not a collective philosophical position and it is not doctrinal law. Its spiritual, binding force rather is founded upon the fact that it is based upon a decision, made again and again, in which the Church knows itself to be summoned from its own erring ways and out of the dominion of every possible self-understanding and back to the Word of God—that is, in its form dogma is confession. This force manifests itself in that it is the word of the Fathers, the word of the Church which we do not form but which conforms us to itself. It has its spiritual qualification in the fact that dogma does not demand authority for itself but for the Word, and that it, therefore, is not the expansion of the Church's possessions, but—as a statement which affirms, negates, confirms, rejects, and even damns—the demonstration of the fact that the Church must reach out after the truth. It determines the boundary of dogmas as a boundary over against the criterion which controls it, not over against what we ourselves have to say or to think. It is also true of dogma that it does not live by having, but that by not having it really lives.

If then the criterion of dogma is the Word of God, then the concrete criterion which dogma must measure up to is the testimony of Scripture, examined from its central point. Since the central point of Scripture is witnessed to in Scripture, but not placed at our disposal, this means that the possibility of discussing the criterion does not mean that we can manage it in a positivistic or quantitative way. Dogma is to lead us to Scripture, but Scripture is the mistress of dogma.

B. THE TASK OF DOGMATICS

1. DOGMATICS AND DOGMA

a. The Name "Dogmatics." It will not be contested that dogmatics has something to do with dogma. But the name "dogmatics" is no proof of this, because it has not been used for very long as the designation of our discipline. Lukas Reinhart of Altorf (*Synopsis theologiae dogmaticae* [1659]) is often mentioned as the first person to use this term. Previously, apart from an abundance of various "dogmatic" tractates, other designations sufficed—witness the medieval *Summae*, Melanchthon's *Loci* as well as those of others, Calvin's *Institutes of the Christian Religion*, and the not infrequent works which speak simply of "theology" and offer a "compendium" or a "medulla" of it just as the great Scholastics once prepared their *Summae*. It can perhaps be said that the name "dogmatics" emerged first in the period when the relationship of dogmatics to dogma had begun to become a problem. But it was not generally accepted in that period, and in the 19th century, particularly since Schleiermacher's *The Christian Faith according to the Principles of the Evangelical Church* (1821), it has had to compete with the term "doctrine of the faith." In short, the name is of little importance. So little, that even works which deal with "dogma," like Adolf Schlatter's *Das christliche Dogma* (1911) (Christian Dogma) could take very little notice of already existing dogma. But, on the other hand, it has never been disputed that a relationship exists here. The question arises, "What kind of relationship?"

b. Reproductive or Productive Dogmatics? It may help toward clarification if we envisage two extreme possibilities. First of all, it could be assumed that dogmatics were the scientific treatment, that is, essentially the interpretation, of given dogma. The other option: it could be held to be the task of dogmatics to express, establish, and comprehend what is "Christian" anew, and in so doing to regard given dogma at the most as incidental, perhaps emphasized historically as an earlier solution of the same dogmatic task. In the first case, dogmatics would be the *reproduction* of dogma, and in the second it would be essentially the *production* of dogma.

c. Historical Reproduction. It cannot be denied that there is the task of presenting and interpreting dogma. Even on the basis of the most general concept of science it will appear necessary to research documents of such historical significance as the dogmatic accomplishments of the Christian Church. Who would even attempt to understand whole stretches of late classical, medieval, or early modern history without dealing scientifically with the Christian dogmas? It is equally incontrovertible that no dogmatics, no matter how "free of dogma" it may appear, can simply neglect the ancient documents.

It must be asked, though, whether a mere reproduction can suffice. And this question is already a *dogmatic* question.

One can respond positively to this question from two antithetical points of view. One can, on the one hand, build upon the assumption of "Neo-Protestantism" that given dogma is in principle only of historical significance. Then all of the care would be given to dogma which in the age of Historicism was devoted to the "merely-historical." The great accounts of the history of doctrine—above all, that of Harnack—are witnesses to this. The fundamental approach will then appear to be purely historical. Harnack summed it up in the thesis: "Dogmatic Christianity is therefore a definite stage in the history of the development of Christianity."[14] This historical judgment is unmistakably conditioned by a dogmatic one: "Christianity" cannot by its very nature be "dogmatic"; under the influence of the late classical period it can have gone through this developmental phase, but in its essence it is something different. Dogma is in any event a transformation, if not a deformation, and since the (supposed) demise of dogma, Christianity has not ceased to exist, but has found its way back to its very essence. The judgment that dogma is nothing other than historical matter is based upon another judgment which says that Christianity in essence is the conviction, attitude, or piety which Jesus Christ taught, exemplified, and perhaps fulfilled as its epitome. But this judgment is under no circumstances in conformity with the New Testament.

d. Dialectic Reproduction. The other option, a historical reproduction of dogma, would suffice if we were to assume that dogma were to contain directly the revelation, the Word of God itself. Such a view would, when taken in its most radical form, necessarily make the reproduction of dogma undesirable. For if the truth in all its inherent validity were contained directly and palpably in the Church's doctrinal decisions, then it would seem to be most appropriate to preserve simply the old dogma, perhaps to recite it in worship, whereas reproduction would be subject to the danger of introducing in the course of history some relativization or in the course of interpretation some misunderstanding. There may be groupings in the Eastern churches which, if they do not express this view overtly, in practice hold to it. In general, especially in European Catholicism, the direct revelational fullness of doctrine is asserted in such a way that this view is linked with the concept of the formal incompleteness of dogma. What is meant here is the concept of the *depositum fidei* (deposit of the faith) which holds sway in this thinking. This concept states that the Church has been left by the Apostles in Scripture and in the oral tradition a truth-filled legacy, both literary and nonliterary in form, which is *potential* dogma out of which *actual* formulated dogma is to be drawn

---

14. A. von Harnack, *History of Dogma*, tr. N. Buchanan (7 vols.; London: Williams & Norgate, 1894 [g1935⁵]), I, 16. This famous sentence then follows by way of explanation: "Dogma in its conception and development is a work of the Greek spirit on the soil of the Gospel" (p. 17).

like so much water out of a well. The result of this concept is that all dogma
heretofore contained infallible truths, because the Church is infallible in this regard, but that out of the potential store of truth *new* dogma can be developed. If
this were so, then there really could be a *profectus religionis*[15] (progress of religion), naturally only in the sense of formulation. Dogma would then be true
authority only to the degree that it were derived from the infallible formulating
and deciding activity of the Church and its teaching office, on the basis of the
depositum. The task of theology can then be to come to a deeper grasp of given
dogma by means of dialectic interpretation, that is, deeper than was possible for
preceding generations. Another function could be to advise and even to prepare
the Church's teaching office, to which theology is subject, about coming decisions—which alone could be the effect of an interpretation of already given dogma.
It is clear that basically a reproductive function of dogmatics is all that is admis-
sible here; however, since the means of reproduction is not, as was the case in
the first instance, historical and critical research, but rather dialectical interpretation, with the help of philosophy, there results a very broad scope in reality.
How broad it is can be seen in the labors of the great Scholastics and, in part,
of contemporary Roman Catholic dogmaticians, especially in France and Germany. It is not necessary to demonstrate that in this case a dogmatic judgment
holds sway, namely, a certain self-estimation of the Church. It is the thesis that
the Church is competent in matters of truth in the sense that truth inheres in the
Church by virtue of the fact that Jesus Christ indwells it. Our affirmation or
rejection of this thesis is not only decisive in regard to the question under discussion, but in regard to our total judgment of Roman Catholicism. According to
the Roman Catholic view, Jesus is the Lord *in* the Church and *through* the *Church*,
but not *over* the Church in the sense that he alone defines the word of the Church
through the apostolic witness and makes this word secondary to that witness. The
Reformation saw in the churchly claim to infallibility an attack upon the fact that
Jesus Christ alone and irreplaceably has been made our wisdom, our righteousness and sanctification and redemption (1 Cor. 1:30). That is, the Reformation
discovered the relationship between a false doctrine of justification (confusing the
righteousness of Christ with the righteousness of works) and a false ecclesiology
(merging Christ's lordship with the lordship of the Church, Christ's truth with *our*
truths). Whoever is in agreement with the Reformation in this decisive question
can certainly accord the Roman Catholic interpretation of dogma all due respect,
but must reject its basis categorically.

   e. Productive Dogmatics. The alternative position in regard to the problem
of "dogma and dogmatics"—it may easily appear to be the actual Protestant
position—is to understand dogmatics in some sense as the *production* of dogma,
or better, of scholastic opinion. It is not always easy to find this position in its
pure form. Even the conscious "dogma-producing" dogmatician will seek to link
himself with great predecessors or with the churchly tradition. A classical example

---

   15. See Vincent of Lerins, *Commonitorium*, tr. R. E. Morris (New York: Fathers of
the Church, 1949), I, 22f.; and in this regard, K. Barth, *CD*, I,1, p. 15.

is Schleiermacher's constant reference to the confessional writings, for he regarded himself as a theologian of the "Reformed School" and not without historical reason. But basically, virtually all of the neo-Protestant dogmatics proceeds
in a productive fashion. This is done either with an appeal to the direct relationship
of every Christian to Scripture which is an essential part of Protestantism or on
the basis of the view that the religious person as such has a direct relationship to
God or that the Christian has a direct relationship to revelation. In its extreme
instances, this produces a "biblicistic" dogmatics, conceived on the basis of pious
experience or of the pious Christian consciousness, but always based on "reason." It is difficult today to take a position in regard to this approach, since its
rejection has become so common: "undogmatic" or "dogma-free" Christianity
has been losing ground for over three decades. Nevertheless, we ought to be
cautioned by the fact that the dogmatic labors of the Fathers of the Church, seen
formally, could not have been reproduction of already extant dogma to a vast
extent. In addition, we ought to consider carefully the fact that contemporary
dogmatics, which on the whole draws our attention seriously to Church dogma,
is not conceivable without the results of the theological work of the 19th and early
20th centuries. One may think of Schleiermacher, of the Erlangen theology, of
Kähler, Schlatter, and among our contemporaries, Karl Heim! In contrast to a
return to dogma which unconsciously would be analogous to Roman Catholicism,
the assertion of a direct relationship to Scripture or to revelation, which was part
and parcel of that recent phase of theology, had to have great critical significance.
Nonetheless, this theology failed to see that dogmatics can only have such a direct
relationship as an event *in* the Church, within the hearing and responding Community. It was *in* the Church that the dogmatic labors of the Church Fathers were
so vital; in fact, we must add that the extent to which the dogmatic work of the
last century was fruitful (and it was far more fruitful than is generally acknowledged today) was due to the fact that it lived *in* the Church and by the continuing
existence of the Church! We will have to admit that the view under discussion is
right when it states that the mediatory position of the Church and of the dogma
for which it is responsible possesses absolutely no autonomous authority. But it
cannot be admitted that, therefore, every mediatory function could be abandoned
as though nothing had happened! In such a case, the autonomy of the individual
(in this instance, the dogmatician) would have replaced the autonomy of the
Church, particularly as conceived by the Roman Catholic Church. There have
been such consequences, and they are having their dangerous effect up to today:
churchly proclamation more or less divorced from the doctrine of the *Fathers*
ends up at the mercy of the *preachers* in reality, and they in turn, as students of
this or that dogmatician, divide up into schools. The end of all this must be the
deterioration of the Church into theological schools and the sacrifice of the congregations to their clergymen. The lordship of pious, or biblically informed, or
even enlightened individualism in the Church is always tyranny.

f. Critical Interpretation of Dogma as the Task of Dogmatics. Our discussion
of two extremely contradictory methods of structuring the relationship between
dogma and dogmatics made it necessary for us to raise fundamental questions
regarding the doctrine of the Church. The methodological decision is in every

instance a dogmatic one. This is naturally just as true of the solution which is now to be sought. It revolves around the thesis that dogmatics is neither reproduction of inherited dogma nor production of a dogmatic school position, but rather the *critical interpretation* of dogma in reference to its own criterion, that is, the inquiry about the Word of God witnessed to in Scripture in relationship to the dogma of the Church.

If we are going to discuss a critical interpretation of dogma, then we are assuming that the thesis of the infallibility of churchly doctrinal decisions is untenable. The churches that are molded by the Reformation are distinguished by the fact that they have relativized themselves, that is, they are aware that nothing can take the place of the lordship, truth, and righteousness of Jesus Christ. Any church which relinquished this insight, perhaps by asserting the infallibility of its Reformational confessional writings, would not have denied just a secondary element of the theology of the 16th century but would have denied its very existence as "true" Church, in the Reformation sense.

The necessity of a critical interpretation of dogma is evident along two lines: First, by its nature dogma is relative to the Word of God. It has authority not as an independent but as an obedient word. But it is a part of obedience that the ones obeying admit the limitations of their understanding. Dogma can, therefore, be wrong in its contents; it can be ambiguous, incomplete, or fragmentary. The necessity of examining dogma in light of its intended theme and the criterion which has been imposed upon it is emphasized by the observation that we do not possess one uniform dogma but a divergence of dogmas among themselves. Every concrete church is placed in question by every other church whose dogmas differ from its own. The finalization of developed dogma would mean the finalization of the schism which divides the churches. But no one church could agree to this. That in dogma one church may possibly designate another church as "false," may level the anathema or some condemnation upon it, only raises the question of the justification of such anathemas and condemnations. Whoever raises this question has taken a critical position in regard to the dogma or the "confession" of his own church fellowship and is thereby assisting it toward "ecumenical" openness.

Second, there is no guarantee that dogmatic decisions which were relevant in their time will retain this relevance in their unchanging formulations over against new temptations and attacks to which churchly proclamation is subjected. A dogma can become a blunt sword which is no longer able to sever anything. In view of the errors which threatened the German Church in 1933, no recitation or reproduction of the Apostles' Creed, no matter how seriously meant, or of the Reformation confessional writings, would have been of any use unless they were shifted into the context of a *new* doctrinal decision. Perseverance here could only mean the renewed search for the "right" doctrine. To be sure, wherever "right" doctrine was sought anew and new answers found, the old answers began to show a new and very impelling illuminative power. We observe the same thing in the way the Reformers interpreted and expounded the Apostles' Creed anew.

g. Dogmatics' Subjection to the Church and Its Freedom. The necessity of a critical interpretation of dogma, however, does not necessarily lead to the conclusion that dogmatics is something which should be done. For both the examination of dogma in light of its own criterion and the ongoing process of dogma in new doctrinal decisions are not actually the task of theology but of the Church itself. Dogmatics can perform its work, and in particular its critical work, in the service of the Church alone. This means, first, that just as dogmatics is by nature uncreative and is related to a given, its given is only in a relative sense dogma; in an absolute sense it is the Word of God to which dogma bears witness (right or mistaken witness!). Dogmatics manifests that the Church, in whose service it stands, does not live by dogma but by the Word of God, particularly in its dogmatic decisions. The very existence of dogmatics is the expression of the Church's need for self-criticism, for continual and renewed subjection to the criterion which is given to it. Secondly, dogmatics can only carry out its inquiry into the criterion of dogma as a service to the Church when it does this in *freedom*, which means in independence of the wishes of the Church, of the expectations which may move congregations, their preachers, and church administrations. Dogmatics laboring under orders would merely repeat what everyone was saying and that would be no service to the Church and its proclamation. Thirdly, it is a part of the freedom of dogmatics, if it is to be done as a service to the Church, that it not bind its work to other criteria than the one which is its theme; this requirement is all the more difficult to meet since dogmatics is constantly in dialogue with man (also outside the Church), who is endeavoring to identify his self-understanding or at least is defined by it. The Church must be careful of falling into a spirit of "knowing it all better" than man as described, since such a spirit would merely be the characteristic of a Church which insisted upon possessing the truth and which in so doing would lose the truth. Fourthly, in exposing itself to dangers to which it is constantly prone (the twofold danger of a profound irrelevance and man's inflexible rejection) and in seeking God's Word in these dangers, dogmatics—addressing itself to the present or future bearers of proclamation and leading and summoning them to participate in its quest—can perhaps pave the Church's way to future doctrinal decisions. Such doctrinal decisions are then decisions for the one and against the other dogmatics (it has always been so), and thus they never result from dogmatic work with any predictable certainty. Nevertheless, churchly dogma has always been a product of the work of dogmatics, or better, a product of the inquiry which dogmatics pursues. Dogmatics pursues the ongoing process of dogma provisionally, always open to a better way of doing it and always directing the question to the Church whether it, too, will be able to participate in the ongoing process in the same fashion. Dogmatics today places in question dogma that has developed, so that the Church tomorrow might be prepared for new decisions.

2. DOGMATICS AS SCIENCE

From the beginning, dogmatics has appeared on the scene as a science,[16] or as Karl Barth puts it, as "inquiry."[17] If one may regard the Apologists as its first

---

16. See F. Naville, "La Regina Scientiarum et sa place dans le système des sciences," *Revue de théologie et de philosophie* (1930). Also, Heinrich Scholz, "Was ist unter einer theologischen Aussage zu verstehen," in E. Wolf, ed., *Theologische Aufsätze Karl Barth zum 50. Geburtstag* (Munich: Kaiser, 1936), pp. 25ff.

17. *CD*, I,1, pp. 11ff.

precursors, then we may ascertain that they designated their endeavors quite unabashedly as "philosophy."[18] For centuries theology was the very science to which philosophy was subordinated, presumably as its ancillary.

a. The Dispute About the Scientific Character of Dogmatics. Dogmatics' claim to be a science not only confronts opposition among some representatives of scientific methodology,[19] it also awakens the mistrust of many Christians.

Whenever the doctrine of science reacts negatively, it always refers to one decisive point. It will always contend that all science deals with a generally accessible object or theme according to generally understandable methods and under the control of generally valid criteria in order to achieve results which also possess general validity and whose acceptance then is the moral duty of every rational person. Turning to dogmatics, it will then be said that it deals neither with a generally accessible object or theme nor with generally valid criteria, and therefore, even if it might make use of generally available methods, it cannot arrive at generally valid and binding results. Thus, the one or the other subsidiary element of this discipline, such as the historical research of Christian dogmas, could be regarded as possessing scientific character, but never the total discipline itself.

The problem which arises here is only in a certain respect the concept of science which has developed since the European Enlightenment. It would not be difficult to show that this understanding of science merely expresses the self-understanding of a specific epoch, and, moreover, that "thereby it has come about that individual sciences or a particular interpretation of reality such as the idealistic or the positivistic establishes itself as absolute."[20]

This concept of science, too, is conditioned by time: there is a style of science, just as there are architectural styles. Therefore, no concept of science can be accepted uncritically as normative. The modern concept of science is, in addition, in fact fundamentally a secularization of certain originally theological conceptions—like much of what is "modern." Its claim to be absolute is the secularized form of Scholastic absolutistic thought, which discovered the historical "contingency" of "revelation" and put it aside in favor of the eternally accessible. Scholasticism (and in part Protestant Orthodoxy) sought to move beyond the mere historical in revelation to the eternally valid, and this contingency, this underivable uniqueness of revelation has become the "accidental truth of history" which is contrasted to the "eternal truth of reason" as conclusively secondary, as something which always requires justification. The result is that the modern concept of science excludes the possibility of revelational events (although not the possibility of the conception of God as the pinnacle of an ontological system), and in doing so, it finds it very difficult to cope with the possibility of genuine,

---

18. Thus, e.g., Melito of Sardis (see Eusebius, *Ecclesiastical History* [*FC*, XIX, Book Four, Ch. 26, p. 264]) and Miltiades (*ibid.*, Book Five, Ch. 17, p. 321); cf. A. Harnack, *op. cit.*, II, 190ff.

19. The most significant protest even today was that uttered by Heinrich Scholz: "Wie ist eine evangelische Theologie als Wissenschaft moglich?" ("How is an evangelical theology possible as a science?"), *ZZ* (1931), pp. 8ff.

20. P. Althaus, *DchrWahrheit*, I, 15.

unpredictable history in any sense at all. "Science" can only deal with "the special case" as a manifestation of the general, and this must mean the demise of history. Thus, one could assert that theology really has no good reason to submit itself to the dictatorship of an alien doctrine of science. Moreover, the serious question must be raised today whether there is anything like a concept of science anymore which can lay claim to general validity. The profound decline of European common thought has hit the concept of science very hard and virtually dissolved it.

b. The "General" as the Core of the Problem. In spite of this, it is probably not quite so easy to ignore the protests of the general doctrine of science against dogmatics' claim to be a science. This protest is in fact nourished not just by the special views of the Enlightenment. Rather, it is based, in often varying forms, on the concept of the *general* and of *reason*, which comprehends what is generally valid in that it conforms to or is a part of that "universal" or "general." If we subtract all of the special features of the modern development, this simple proposition is the basic remainder: Science consists of the methodologically understandable comprehension of what is accessible to reason and that means, what is generally or universally valid. When Christian proclamation then rejects both the direct accessibility of the content of proclamation to reason and thereby the perceivable universal validity of its statements—to put it another way, when proclamation has to do with something special and beyond the realm of reason—then it appears to make a *science* of its theme impossible.

The problem as we have phrased it has often been sensed in theology. Even if the Apologists also appeared as "philosophers" and appealed to the *logos sōphrōn* (word of moderation), still none of them had any intention of denying that Christianity, in spite of its affinity to philosophy, was in truth something completely different from philosophy on account of its being based upon revelation. Both early and medieval theology, then, strenuously endeavored to understand revelation or the Revealer as the unveiling of the ultimate and generally valid truth which was also the business of science. The term "logos" makes this obvious. All of the impressive attempts to integrate the interpretation of revelation within the context of already given systems—available were Platonism, Aristotelianism, Neo-Platonism, and late Stoicism—led to the same conclusion: the God about whom the Church is talking is to be conceived of in analogy to the Highest and thus to the Most General, which was known in every system; he is the "Being of Beings," or the First Mover, or the World Mind. Within each of these systems Jesus Christ is understood always as the manifestation of the Highest and Most Universal or as the way to reach it. In short, dogmatics elevated the universal, being, the existing one, the cosmos, and the mind which fills it to theological themes and created for itself in the process the possibility of appearing as a science in the sense in which science was otherwise understood. To put it another way, theology was persuaded that the truth which the Church proclaimed was the one which philosophy was seeking, perhaps even in vain. Thus, theology entered on its own into science and prepared the way for its own elevation to the queen of the sciences in the Middle Ages. In that it permitted itself to be legitimized by science, it in turn legitimized science. In that it set aside a place for the suprarational, it permitted reason to guarantee this procedure, which in turn resulted in the theological confirmation of reason.

Was this the wrong way to have gone? It is not possible for us to answer with a simple "yes" or "no." For this way was taken in the total certainty that God as he has revealed himself in Jesus Christ really is the Lord of the world, that the truth which we encounter in Christ is really universally valid truth. The age in which the structure of early theology was drafted was the age of great Christian missionary activity. And theology was the expression of the Church's certainty about the truth in the forms of scientific thought then current. Looking beyond that period, however, no Christian theology can reject its claim that what it is saying is really true. In other words, it can never be the mere self-explanation of the historical phenomenon "Christianity" or "the Church." It addresses itself to everyone because it is persuaded that the Word of God is valid for everyone.

Nevertheless, a "no" must stand alongside the "yes." To be sure, God is the Lord of the world. But he is so in Christ. His lordship is not an ontological principle but a historical reality which has been inaugurated, is taking place, and is being consummated. It is directed to everyone because Jesus Christ is there for all. But the way in which he is there for all is such that at the same time he is this man, Jesus of Nazareth, in unpredictable uniqueness and personality, reducible to no principle, but one person in his vulnerability, one person whose cross is manifest but whose glory in the resurrection is still concealed. The universality of the lordship of God and of the truth which encounters us as God's truth in Jesus Christ is therefore actual only in proclamation which is addressed to all but which does not disclose itself as effective to all. But it is not something which can be proven to be universally valid, which is accessible and available and which merely needs to be discovered with the help of revelation because it is already there. As the content and theme of proclamation, it is also the object of announcement,[21] but not of rational demonstration. If, under these circumstances dogmatics' accounting of Christian doctrine is *scientific*, then it can only be so in that it refuses to deduce revelation from some universal truth or make it comprehensible on the basis of such a truth. It cannot buy its way into a "universal" or "general" system of science at the cost of eliminating the very uniqueness which is its source. On the other hand, it must view its very uniqueness as directed to all men, to the whole world, and express it this way.

c. Counterpositions to the Postulate of Universality. If, in opposition to all ontologism, the strict relationship of dogmatic statements to the uniqueness of the revelation-event is recognized, then the next step could be to look for analogies in the realm of reality accessible to our thinking or our experience, and even to postulate a category of the unique or particular as an alternative to the category

---

21. R. Rothe, *Zur Dogmatik* (Gotha: F. A. Perthes, 1863), writes on p. 54, "to the completeness of mankind's redemption" there also belongs "a complete process of becoming rational" on the part of the Gospel. In the context of his eschatology he envisages what one must term the eschatological limits of dogma: initially dogma can only exist with the presupposition that "it is not an obvious or truistic truth, not a universally evident insight of reason" (*loc. cit.*).

of the universal. Kierkegaard did this when, in opposition to Hegel's ontologism with its theological consequences, he worked out the category of the *individual*, of *existence*, as the only one suitable for the Christian faith. The same thing is done when, in going back to Rickert's and Windelband's discovery of the special scientific structure of the liberal arts or even more so to Dilthey's philosophy of life, the special nature of history is worked out and then the attempt is made to develop the method of theology in analogy to history's method. Finally, Karl Heim undertook a similar approach when he worked out the incoordinability of "dimensions" of differing kinds and illustrated by use of the I-Thou relationship that it required entirely different thought-forms than the I-It relationship. All of these approaches, which are not to be dealt with in greater detail here, share the same goal of finding a form of expression (and thus a category of understanding) within which the particular nature and the personality of Christian speech can function.

Here again it is not possible to say simply "yes" or "no" to these attempts. They are all right at the point where we faulted all of those intellectual movements oriented toward the "general" or toward "being." The classical theology of being, as it was inaugurated with the Alexandrians, must lead to weakening of the special nature of revelation as event. It is, however, this special nature which theology seeks to preserve in that it rejects all forms of ontologism. That is the important thing about this theology.

Yet, we cannot be satisfied with a "yes" here either. The first reason that we cannot is that the attempt to cover the special nature in some way as a category or "dimension" can scarcely have any other result than to produce the self-contradictory concept that there is a *general* category of the particular or special. But there can be no category to cover what is absolutely unique. Whoever goes this route will find it hard to avoid replacing general being with general person, the I-Thou relationship which can be found everywhere, or something like it—so that in effect one universality has been replaced by another. The second reason demonstrates this: the approaches being discussed are no less substantively bound to the philosophical conceptions to which they are near than the ontological approach already discussed. Again, the scientific right to speak and be heard is being bought at the price that the general thought system within which space for Christian discourse is to be set aside is being confirmed by the very act of making this space available. This is expressed especially in the way in which often the Christian faith's inherent orientation to *all* mankind and the *whole* world is set aside as unattainable in favor of an other-worldly personalism, thereby subjecting the doctrines of the creation and of eschatology to reinterpreted abbreviations.

d. Dogmatics as the Science of the Absolutely Unique. As a science, dogmatics is neither the generally accessible statement about the universal nor the generally accessible statement about the particular which can be worked out in general terms. It is the statement about the absolute uniqueness of God's revelation, which as *God's* revelation is valid for all mankind and should be proclaimed to all mankind. The scientific quality of dogmatics is totally dependent, therefore, upon the validity of an insight which is only gained in faith, that is, the insight that Jesus Christ is the Lord, that he is the truth. No generally accessible method can lead to this knowledge. But based upon this knowledge, dogmatics has its inherent right and its duty, arising out of faith itself, to present itself as a science. It can and it must express its uniqueness, which is the theme of its inquiry and its source as well, in such a way that it can be perceived as something which concerns all mankind. Thus, just like the oldest dogmatics, it is the analogy to missions in the area of thought.

We must now ask what that means.

1) **Terminology**. It means that dogmatics must seek to define the absolute uniqueness of the revelation-event, which is both the subject and source of its inquiry, in the realm of thought by means of the most precise delimitation. This delimitation, since dogmatics is dealing with the *absolutely* unique, is not the setting of boundaries within a given pattern of thought but the setting of boundaries over against every given pattern of thought. This delimitation can only be done in the realm of thought by means of terms or concepts, in the broadest sense. Therefore, dogmatics needs clear terminology in order to get its object precisely in focus.

2) **Clarity**. The absolute uniqueness of the revelation-event does not mean that it is related to an esoteric circle, nor that it is limited to a specially sacred realm or to particularly enlightened people. Rather, dogmatics must proceed from the fact that the One who encounters us in Jesus Christ as a person is the Creator and Lord of the world. Under no circumstances, then, can dogmatics be the carefully protected doctrinal possession of a secret sect, and it has never been that. On the contrary, it must speak openly and require proclamation to be public. It must therefore strive for clarity. Any ambiguity could betray the fact that in reality it was not speaking of the Lord of the world. Dogmatics must know that its clearest speech is not able to "mediate" its object. But never will it be permitted to use unclear, ambiguous speech, avoiding dialogue or making it impossible, and justify all this by appealing to the mystery of Christ and the mystery of the Holy Spirit.

3) **Freedom from a "Universal" View of Man**. Under these circumstances dogmatics raises a protest and an attack on an "admittedly 'heathen' general concept of science."[22] Since, in its inquiry, it derives from the One who desires to be the Lord of all mankind, it cannot ultimately *believe* in man's self-closure, which expresses itself in the current concept of science. In any event, it will always be motivated by faith in God instead of by the deception caused by a concept of science which has closed itself off from God.

4) **Freedom to Use "Alien" Concepts**. Dogmatics does not have a vocabulary at its disposal which it first created. It cannot even attempt to create its own vocabulary of concepts. Even the exclusive use of biblical terms would not alter this, for they are not by their nature "Christian" concepts—many of them also

---

22. K. Barth, *CD*, I,1, p. 10.

belong to the vocabulary of philosophy. It is unavoidable that dogmatics uses concepts which are alien to it. It is able to do this because it is interpretation.[23] It must do it because it does not seek to protect what it is inquiring about and discussing as though it were the secret doctrine in an esoteric circle, but rather it wants to make the revealed mystery understandable.

5) **Freedom from the Compulsion of a System.** This conceptual vocabulary, which dogmatics is free to use by virtue of its own proper theme, must also be used by dogmatics *in freedom*, also by virtue of its own proper theme. Dogmatics cannot tie itself down to one set of concepts. This means that it cannot permit its structure to be dictated to it by the given structure of any one philosophical system and thus it cannot find its own realm of expression limited by such a system. If this were to happen, then the self-understanding which is behind every philosophical system would become the criterion of dogmatics, and this would mean that substantive heresy would have emerged. Under these circumstances the conceptual vocabulary and together with it the logical structure of dogmatics will always seem to be "eclectic." To bind dogmatics logically into one system would be to integrate its message into an already given exclusive totality of interpretations of being and existence. In such a total system, God would then occupy the place which had been foreseen for him in the spirit of that system. This God could not be the One who revealed himself in Jesus Christ. The very nature of the theme of dogmatics necessitates this "eclectic" and consciously illogical character of the dogmatic use of concepts. If dogmatics' refusal to be locked into one single philosophical system is regarded as a criterion for its unscientific nature, which would mean that what we say about God would necessarily be forced into a human system by means of a decision motivated by a theory of science, which in turn would serve to make that human system into an absolute, then dogmatics— which cannot hinder such a process—would simply have to judge it impossible for it to claim to be a science on those terms. But this does not in turn mean that dogmatics could renounce the claim nor the task of doing its work scientifically. On the other hand, it does not require that it be acknowledged to be a science. Rather, it requires the scientific character which is appropriate to its task. If dogmatics corresponds in many regards to the process of missions, then here would be the analogy to persecution, where from outside its camp a rejection of dogmatics' scientific nature were to assert itself. The Church does not die in the course of persecution, and dogmatics does not become unscientific when it is not permitted to participate in many kinds of scientific labor. One thing it may not do: it may not remove itself from the sphere of scientific inquiry, declaration, and response.

6) **Methodological Consequences.** The methodological implications of what has just been discussed can be put briefly. Dogmatics proceeds scientifically in that it takes up its obligatory inquiry methodically. In doing so, it distinguishes itself from what Karl Barth meant with the term "irregular dogmatics"[24]: this is

---

23. See Calvin, *Institutes*, I, xiii, 3, pp. 123f.
24. K. Barth, *CD*, I,1, pp. 318ff.

the researching of the content which makes dogma into valid statements without resorting to a strict method—a procedure based upon the contingency of biblical proclamation which often has been responsible for indicating to more methodical dogmatics the way it should go. Nonetheless, dogmatics as inquiry or as research requires method. This need not be proven anymore. In addition, dogmatics is obligated to provide an accounting of the method it uses, for it would not be a science if it were not subject to some kind of controls. We scarcely need to state that these controls cannot mean that dogmatics should submit to something which is alien to its nature. But it must be able to say, about each of the conceptual steps it takes, for what reasons, on the basis of which axioms, in the course of which structural presuppositions, and in which logical form it is doing so. This implied "postulate of controllability" leads then to a further requirement that dogmatics, like every other science, must be oriented toward a totality. One cannot say more than that; more than that would be untrue of any science which knew its own limits. But this is certainly an irrevocable requirement. It is not really opposed by the circumstance that dogmatics can be expressed in the form of paradox. This can happen just as well in the area of philosophy. However, paradox is not an arbitrary act in the realm of thought, and it may not become the way of least resistance. Therefore, the paradoxical statement must also be provided with adequate reasons and be integrated into the total structure of dogmatics.

At this point, we have arrived at a fundamental issue of methodology, which must be dealt with separately: we are speaking of the question whether dogmatics can assume the form of a *system*. Can it be oriented toward a totality *without* becoming a "system"? But can it come to terms with the contingency, the unpredictability, of the revelation-event if it is a system?

3. THE STRUCTURE OF DOGMATICS

a. Dogmatics in the Context of Theology. Dogmatics is one direction of the work of theology. It is one direction of work, not a quantitatively definable element, for dogmatics cannot really function without exegesis and church history; it cannot think relevantly without a constant view to the practice of the Church, and it can distinguish itself from the other theological disciplines only in regard to the thrust of its own inquiry but not in regard to their common theme. The same is true of the other disciplines in their relationship to dogmatics: none of them can skirt the special questions raised by dogmatics. Every direction of theological work deals ultimately with the quest for the Word of God, for God in his Word: exegesis with the Word of God as the Word testified to in Scripture, church history with the Word heard and responded to by the Church in the course of its history, and practical theology with the Word which constantly must be stated anew in the reality of the Church. It is the particular task of dogmatics to inquire about the Word as the authoritative Word, as the criterion for all preaching, instruction, all fellowship or worship of the Church—which is the criterion toward which both exegesis and church history are leading with their own questions.[25]

It may be noted here that the term "theology" (originally a pagan term) meant for the Greeks first of all the poetry of the gods, then the interpretation of that poetry as conducted by (philosophical) science, and out of that source it then received the specific meaning of an intellectual, structured doctrine of God. Christian "theology" has molded this concept, first of all applying it to the doctrine of God as such, especially the doctrine of the Trinity, and then gradually expanding its meaning in the course of the Middle Ages to apply to the whole of "dogmatics." It has only been since the end of the 17th century that both exegesis and church history, which long were essential to the process of theology, were accorded the status of fully independent disciplines. And in the 19th century, since Schleiermacher's "Short Exposition of Theology Study" (1811), practical theology as a discipline has been added. It is not without significance that the division of theological disciplines still in use today was arrived at during a period in which theology as a whole had lost sight of its actual question. Thus, we can understand that this division meant a simultaneous methodological separation in the process of which exegesis thought it could derive its method (and more) from the methods of philology, church history its methods from general history, dogmatics (and ethics) the arrangements of its work from philosophy, and practical theology its definitive aspects increasingly from consideration of utility, usefulness, or aesthetics and rhetorics. To the degree that each of the disciplines ceased to understand itself as a special way of seeking out the Word of God, they all lost their center of orientation, and not only that, their relevant and appropriate method.

b. The Problem of the System. It is important for our considerations in this section that in this phase of the history of theology (and of the term itself), dogmatics together with ethics began to be designated with the title "systematic theology." The question whether this designation is appropriate leads to the further question whether a *system* can be the fitting structure for dogmatics.[26]

We understand by "system" the totality of an intellectual structure which is based upon a fundamental concept (a "principle") and which develops it logically and methodically. The presupposition is, accordingly, that the "principle" contains potentially the one and total content which is then explained in greater detail in the systematic exposition. This means in turn that in its exposition the system cannot contain elements which are not already given in the "principle." The "principle" is, therefore, the intellectual condensation of an all-embracing totality.

---

25. K. Barth, *CD*, I,1, p. 3, seems to be expressing the same thought: "Thus as Biblical theology, theology is the question as to the foundation, as practical theology it is the question as to the aim, as dogmatic theology it is the question as to the content, of the language peculiar to the Church." However, I cannot follow Barth when he relegates church history to the mere position of an auxiliary science.

26. The term and the phenomenon of a systematically constructed dogmatics is first found in Bartholomew Keckermann, *Systema SS. Theologiae*, appended to vol. II of the *Opera* (1614).

The decision about the possibility of a system must begin with the question as to whether there is such a "principle" and whether it can be grasped by man in such a way that his exposition of it can truly express the totality of the intended reality. Philosophy has, since the days of the pre-Socratic doctrinal poems and world interpretations, answered the question in the affirmative. The frequent titles of those interpretations of totality, *peri archōn* (On First Principles), show clearly what direction they are going. Anaximander sought the beginning (*archē*) in a nonempirical continuum, the *apeiron* (the infinite), and prepared the way therewith for the interpretations which held the empirical to be secondary to the nonempirical and ultimately strove toward an intellectual solution. This is the way that great Greek philosophy—Plato's and Aristotle's—continued along with such impressive logic. Systematic philosophy in the precise sense of the term (i.e., a philosophy which produces a system) has remained like this through all the centuries: the "principle," which contained the whole within itself, could then by the nature of things not be an element of the whole, but had to comprehend everything in itself and therefore would be open to empirical examination, but on the basis of its origins would be independent of it. The general result was that the "principle" evolved into the universal idea, that is, a conception of the whole in one single idea. However, this idea was a human one. In setting up such a "principle," a universal idea, the concept was generated that man is capable of grappling with the whole intellectually, or to put it another way, the whole is so constituted that it can be condensed to one human thought. Since the "idea" is always an expression of the self-understanding of man, this whole approach means then in fact that man, in that he understands himself, understands the whole. This means that the whole is at the disposal of man, that it is the world of man. This in turn makes it possible to understand that the so-structured system cannot in principle contain anything which is unpredictable; everything fits, without any exceptions. Even if a concept of God is found at the pinnacle of such a system, which is generally the case, this concept must fit into the system without any dislocation. The god of a system designed on the basis of a "principle" is in a profound sense always the god of man.

Theology cannot form systems in the sense that philosophical directions have done in such great numbers because it cannot get around Jesus Christ. It would have to ignore the historicity of Jesus Christ, or regard it as secondary, if it wanted to go that route. As a matter of fact, it has always had the absolute uniqueness and the unpredictable contingency of the person of Jesus Christ in view. Yet, it was not able to prevent steps being taken in the direction of a system—Origen was the first great example of this, but Irenaeus could also be mentioned. The only way it was possible to do this was to incorporate the person of Jesus Christ and the revelation-event into an already given interpretation of the whole, or to elevate them into a "principle" themselves.

The connection between a systematics based upon a universal principle and the reference to the special history of Jesus Christ was made possible because Hellenism provided the intellectual means of doing this—specifically with the concept of Logos. The concept that God was present in his revelation, that the Father was present in the Son, appeared to let itself be expressed appropriately with the help of the Logos concept, and all the more so in the context of Neo-

Platonism, with its manifold understandings of Being and God. Thus, a system was made possible within which both being and event found their proper places. The effects of this synthesis, arrived at in the late classical period, remained formative for theology for approximately a millennium. In later times, only one other system was to be conceived which in a similar fashion, although with completely different presuppositions and concepts, offered a synthesis of being and event and therefore seemed to dogmatics to be a new point of departure for a comprehensive systematization: the philosophy of Hegel.

c. Formal and Material Systematics. Since it is the task of dogmatics as a science to order its many statements into one context and to orient it toward a totality, it does need some kind of interconnecting structure. Just as there can be "irregular" dogmatics, a collection of aphorisms could well be of dogmatic significance. But this cannot be the approach of scientific dogmatics, and it never was. On the other hand, the form is not the decisive factor in determining whether a dogmatic scheme does in fact bear the character of a *system*. The decision is based upon the question as to whether or not the scheme has been conceived of on the basis of a *principle* or whether the historicity, unpredictability, and contingency of the revelation-event, which break through every principle, have been preserved. Even a dogmatics which does not appear to be a system, such as Melanchthon's *Loci communes* in its first editions, can possibly be very systematic. Yes, even a dogmatician like Karl Barth,[27] who expressly and with good reason rejects the admissibility of a system, is subject to the evaluation from his most penetrating critic that a "systematic compulsion"[28] dominates his work, that is, there are important sections of his work which appear only because they are implied in the systematic approach of the whole. Therefore, we must differentiate between material and formal systematics.

d. Formal and Material Systematics in the History of Dogmatics. This is all the truer because the designation of a dogmatic scheme as a "system" appears seldom in early Orthodoxy and more frequently in late Orthodoxy. As far as the earliest periods of the Church are concerned, we discover virtually no comprehensive outlines of dogmatics, in a formal sense. Origen's *peri archōn (On First Principles)* contains, for example, no developed soteriology in spite of the comprehensive title. Most of the dogmatic writings of the Eastern and the Western Church were tractates about individual dogmatic questions (especially on the doctrine of the Trinity and on Christology), or were polemic writings (such as Atha-

---

27. *CD*, I,2, pp. 861ff. "System" is defined as "a structure of principles, founded on the presupposition of a basic view of things, constructed with the help of various sources of knowledge and axioms, and self-contained and complete in itself." The most important counter-argument: "In dogmatic systems the presupposed basic view acquires inevitably the position and function which according to all our previous considerations can be ascribed only to the Word of God" (p. 862).

28. Hans Urs von Balthasar, *The Theology of Karl Barth*, tr. J. Drury (New York: Holt, Rinehart and Winston, 1971), pp. 181ff., especially pp. 198ff., with regard to the "straitened schematization" of the "Christological orientation."

nasius' discourses against the Arians or even the anti-Gnostic pamphlet by Irenaeus, *Adversus haereses* [*Against Heresies*]) or even learned catechisms (for instance, Gregory of Nyssa's *Catechetical Orations*). A theologian such as Augustine
did not really leave us a "dogmatics" in the actual sense of the word; his *Enchiridion ad Laurentium* (*Introductory Handbook, addressed to Laurentium*) is
only an introduction. None of these theologians can be accused of lacking a
material systematic. But they do not offer formally a system. The first one to
present a total dogmatic scheme was John of Damascus in his *pēgē gnōseos*
(*Fount of Wisdom*), which was actually more a collection than a system. In the
Middle Ages there was an analogy to John of Damascus in that the doctrinal
tradition of the ancient Church was presupposed as authoritative. This tradition
by its very nature did not form a system, since it was a variety resulting out of
the development in history. Therefore, it challenged interpretation—and as the
nearest available method they had to recognize very quickly the ancient and still
current science of dialectics, which divided the material up into thesis and antithesis and sought to come to conclusions by way of discourse on the terms and
concepts. The beginnings were again not comprehensive works but individual
tractates, as, for example, the inexhaustible and usually very brief writings of
Anselm of Canterbury. If we encounter here the dialogue, the original form of
dialectics, then it is not very far to the brilliant dialectics of Abelard (*Sic et non!*)
and then on to the equally brilliant summarization of the whole of tradition in
Peter Lombard's *Sententiarum libri IV* (the *Sentences*), which were fundamental
for the centuries thereafter. Peter Lombard was definitely a systematician, and
the arrangement of material in his work (Book I: The Trinity, Book II: Creation
and Sin, Book III: The Incarnation and the Virtues, Book IV: The Sacraments)
was formative far into the development of Protestant doctrine and remains influential up to today. The work of Peter Lombard formed the foundation for the
great *Summae* of the high Middle Ages, whose systematic basis was the incorporation of traditional theology into the intellectual structure of recently rediscovered (original) Aristotelianism (although usually under the strong influence of
Neo-Platonism). As far as its form is concerned, a *Summa* is not a system but
really nothing more than the summarization and compilation of the doctrinal matter in a certain interpretation. However, material systematics emerged more and
more clearly with time, in its most impressive form in the *Summa theologica* of
Thomas Aquinas. The fact that Scholasticism did not press beyond the form of
the *Summa* to a formal system was due primarily to its obligation to deal with the
disparate results of churchly tradition. Thus it was not free to conceive what it
could and wanted to—in this transformed form it was still aware of the contingency of the revelation-event: it was not the contingency of revelation itself but
rather the response to it given by the ancient Church.

Reformation and Orthodox theology could not simply take over the form of
the *Summa*, which was already deteriorating in the late Middle Ages, because
their relationship to the ancient Church tradition and to the latter's
Aristotelian–Neo-Platonic interpretation, the two structural elements, was fundamentally altered by the new encounter with Scripture, with Jesus Christ as its
center, although the relationship was certainly not totally broken off. The Reformation rediscovered the Word as event in its significance for the form of dog-

matics. This meant initially a decisive reduction of dogmatic content: what a small volume was Melanchthon's *Loci communes* in its first edition (1521) compared to the mighty *Summae* of the high Middle Ages! Whole sections and themes were simply deleted from the new point of view. Luther himself did not conceive any dogmatics at all; instead, he put what he wanted to say as a dogmatician in the form of tractates (especially *De servo arbitrio* [1525] [*On the Bondage of the Will*]), of commentaries (the most comprehensive was the great *Commentary on Galatians* of 1535), and of disputations. Proclamation, dogmatics, and exegesis move very close to one another, even in their form. Melanchthon did produce in the late edition of his *Loci praecipui theologici* (1559) a formally proper dogmatics, but he felt that he should use the historical order found in Scripture in writing his own work—an intention to which he did not remain entirely faithful.[29] Calvin, who based the first version of his *Institutes of the Christian Religion* (1536) on Luther's *Shorter Catechism*, finally worked up to a formal systematics in the great final form of his work (1559). The four books (The Knowledge of God the Creator, The Knowledge of God the Redeemer, The Way in Which We Receive the Grace of Christ, The External Means. . . .) are supposed to be based, according to Calvin, upon the four articles of the Apostles' Creed, whereby the formative influence of Peter Lombard can still be recognized. Orthodox dogmatics on the Lutheran side remained in the main, formally, in the tradition of Melanchthon and retained in general his "synthetic" method,[30] whereas on the Reformed side there was a plurality of forms and the method was somewhat less unified. On the whole, however, Reformed dogmatics were also more strongly "systematic" in their form. We shall have to deal with this presently.

Since the age of the Enlightenment, dogmatics have tended in general to appear materially and, increasingly, formally as a system. In the case of Rationalism this was a result of its approach, and of Supranaturalism a result of the integration of reason and revelation as prepared in Orthodoxy. In the case of 19th-century theology, it was a result on the one hand of the effects of speculative philosophy, on the other hand and more essentially because dogmatics then understood itself as the scientific expression of "Christianity" or of the "Christian consciousness" and liked to build upon a fundamental conception of the "Christian" which was then explicated in the system. The varying approaches diverged as broadly as the basic conception of what is really "Christian" can diverge.

e. Basic Forms of a Material Systematic. Since dogmatics' becoming a formal system is a more recent development, we must first ask what the basic forms of a material systematic are. This question will then lead us to the roots of *formal* systematics.

1) Ontology. The first basic form of systematizing dogmatics can be designated *ontological*[31] (or *cosmological*). It emerges as early as Origen and appears

---

29. See *Praefatio*, *CR*, XXI, 605ff.; Stupperich, II/1, pp. 169ff.
30. See below, pp. 58ff.
31. See H. E. Eisenhuth, *Ontologie und Theologie* (Göttingen: Vandenhoeck & Ruprecht, 1933).

almost continuously through the Middle Ages and the period of Orthodoxy up to and including the speculative dogmaticians of the school of Hegel. The ontological pattern is characterized by its regularly developing a definite concept of being with the appropriate concept of God or letting such a basic connection become obvious from the very beginning. Then, by means of this dominant concept of being, it regularly appears as an objectivistic system, transcending all experience, and it endeavors to incorporate the revelation-event into its pre-established ontology. The ontological systems used by dogmatics, all of which have been borrowed from the area of philosophy, share the feature that there is room in them for the event, just as they generally offer a great deal of room for maneuvering within their structures. However, their thinking is always oriented from the act of existence to being itself, from the event to the permanent, from time to timeless eternity. Thus ontological-systematic dogmatics often appear quite readily to be "theocentric," and their systems frequently begin with statements about the nature of God in which everything else is already implied or contained potentially. Ontologically formulated concepts of God generally are characterized by the most extreme abstractness; just as thinking tends strongly away from the concrete toward the abstract, and the conceptual possesses the higher truth in comparison with the mere event, so thought itself tends to move on from the concreteness of revelation to the abstract source of it.

Ontological systematics can be so strongly oriented toward abstractness only because it places so much confidence in *reason*. Its theocentricity is, therefore, simultaneously an expression of a certain self-evaluation of man. Of course, "reason" does not necessarily have to be the same thing as "understanding": very often ontological systems appear in connection with an ontological mysticism, and in the case of Scholasticism one can even speak of an intellectual mysticism. It would not be wise to speak here of an autonomous concept of reason; rather, we are dealing here with reason which has been enlightened by revelation and claimed by it. But one thing must not be overlooked: ontological systematics is always based on the fundamental assumption that revelation can be coordinated with human reason or with the capacity to reason. This does then mean that reason and revelation coexist in a synthetic relationship.

2) **Anthropology.** A second basic form of material systematics can be designated quite generally with the term "anthropological." Since an anthropological judgment is also part and parcel of the ontological systematics, as we just saw, these two basic forms are not mutually exclusive. Nevertheless, there is a certain readiness in anthropological systematics to do without the metaphysics of being. The most frequent type in this series results wherever the *ethical* question is made into the point of departure for a dogmatic system. A tendency in this direction can be observed in the early Church with the *Antiochians*. Then, the reserve of the earlier Western (Latin) theology in regard to ontology is based upon the preeminent position of the ethical. There is an unmistakable and similar current in late Scholasticism, more precisely in Occamism, and then very definitely in the theology of the Enlightenment, followed then by the school of Albrecht Ritschl, building upon Kant's philosophical foundations. It could be demonstrated that this current is still influential in contemporary theology; however, here the ethical

question has been expanded into the existential question. Another just as influential form of anthropological systematics is built upon religious *experience*; its originator was the Englishman William Ames (a resident of Holland), and its mightiest representative up to the present day was the Schleiermacher of the "doctrine of faith"[32] (which must be distinguished from the other trend in his thought, in which his philosophical ethics definitely stood for an ontological conception, but in such a way that both conceptions bore and conditioned each other).

Anthropological systematics can easily create the impression that it does greater justice to the event nature of revelation, by virtue of its point of departure, than do the ontological systems. It can, however, present itself as the mere self-explanation of the religious consciousness rooted in revelation. With the young Melanchthon, it can do without the discussion of the *mysteria divinitatis* (divine mysteries) and relate everything to the *beneficia Christi* (benefits of Christ). It can speak of God and of Christ in such a way that only the *pro nobis* (for us) comes into view, and thus it appears as pointed criticism of theological speculation and of "metaphysics" in theology; this was what Ritschl in particular did. Nonetheless, this is as much a systematics as was the case with ontology. With at least the same degree of energy the self-interpretation of man is absorbed into the dogmatic "principle." The fact that, together with ontology, "nature" often disappears from the purview of dogmatics is not the result of any material theological conclusion (in view of the message of God the Creator this would be hard to imagine) but is as a matter of fact the result of the effect of an ontological approach which puts the "outer world," "the morally neutral," aside because it is devalued in this system. Because anthropological systematics are also genuinely systematic, they are subject to the "compulsion of the system" just as is the ontological approach: those elements of biblical proclamation which cannot be fitted into the system are put aside and regarded as of little worth. This is often the case with the Old Testament in particular, which obviously would not let itself be incorporated into an anthropological system.

3) **Salvation-history.** Where the two first basic forms of dogmatic systematization are related to one another as thesis and antithesis, the third's relationship to both is one of incommensurability. We can best term it with a concept which first emerged in the 19th century: *salvation-history* (*Heilsgeschichte*). The basic issue at stake here is first found in the history of dogmatics in Irenaeus. It would be easy to assume that there were no systematic present there. For, to a great degree, we do not find here the points of connection to philosophy which were so easy to discover in the other two forms. And above all, there does not seem to be a "principle" at work here. Instead, the point of departure is the revelation-event, and—even in Irenaeus—careful attention is paid to the fact that its uniqueness must not be sacrificed to some presupposed universality. Nevertheless, salvation-historical systematics (not the salvation-historical aspect!) is in fact based upon a fundamental thought. To express it abstractly, it generally takes such a shape that the ultimately concrete element of the salvation-event becomes

---

32. The literal translation of the title of his great work, *The Christian Faith*—TR.

special history within a *special* sphere (usually the sacral sphere): the mystery becomes the arcanum, kerygma becomes the cultic myth, eschatology becomes the doctrine of "life" which in surpassing all other life as it moves into immortality issues forth from the mystery. The idea of a mystery which creates life in a special historical process looks completely different in the ancient setting in which Irenaeus stood than it does in the setting of Schelling's thought, which influenced the salvation-historical theology of the 19th century (namely, in Hofmann). The fullest expression of it is that of the Erlangen School, with its basic idea of the correlation of salvation-history and individual Christian experience. It must be emphasized that in all of these approaches Scripture plays a much more significant role than in ontological systematics. But it should also be clear that these are all examples of systematics, which means in this instance that, although the contingency of the revelation-event is taken into consideration, the historicity of the message of the revelation-event is not seen.

4) The Doctrine of Decrees. A special form of salvation-historical dogmatics was developed early in Reformed Orthodoxy, beginning with Theodore Beza: the Doctrine of the Decrees, that is, the application of the doctrine of the decrees of God as the principle and structural pattern of dogmatics. All of history is understood here as salvation-history since it is nothing other than the execution of an absolute decree which as such was concluded before history began. We are not going to investigate the origins of the Doctrine of Decrees here; in many respects they are to be sought in the view of history in Augustine's *City of God*, especially Books XI–XXII. It is noteworthy that the theology of decrees received a decidedly soteriological emphasis in the Federal Theology of Johannes Cocceius (1603–69), and in the teaching of Moyse Amyraut (1596–1664) it was transferred from an absolutistic pattern into time.[33] In the most broadly represented form, the theology of decrees was the most highly systematized structure which salvation-history thought achieved, and it achieved this because it began with the absolute and prehistorical decree, which was in fact ontological (theocentric-transcendent).

f. Synthetic and Analytic Method. We have briefly reviewed the most important basic forms of material systematics. However, the picture would be incomplete if we did not also look at an important methodological decision in the area of Orthodoxy, out of which the systematics of more recent theology has gradually grown. We mean here the problem of analytical method in opposition to synthetic. It was not a coincidence that the first theologian to introduce the term "system"[34]—Bartholomew Keckermann (1571/3–1609)—was also the first

33. Regarding Cocceius, see Gottlob Schrenk, *Gottesreich und Bund im älteren Protestantismus; vornehmlich bei Johannes Coccejus* (Gütersloh: C. Bertelsmann, 1923); and especially the very instructive remarks in K. Barth, *CD*, II,2, pp. 114f. Regarding Amyraut, see J. Moltmann, *Gnadenbund und Gnadenwahl* (Göttingen dissertation, 1951).
34. See O. Ritschl, *Dogmengeschichte des Protestantismus* (4 vols.; Leipzig: Hinrichs, 1908–27), III, 271; and O. Ritschl, *System und systematische Methode in der Geschichte des wissenschaftlichen Sprachgebrauchs und der philosophischen Methodologie* (Bonn: C. Georgi, 1906), pp. 26ff.

great representative of the analytic method in dogmatics.[35] We must briefly describe this approach and matter. The point of departure was the question whether theology is a theoretical science (a speculative or contemplative science) or, more like medicine, a practical science. Thomas Aquinas answered with the first option, albeit with reservations.[36] Luther, among others, favored the second option.[37] If the first form is accepted, then theology's most appropriate method is the deductive, which operates from the concept of God or from God's eternal decrees. This method has been called "synthetic" ever since Flacius (1520–75), because it does not build upon God's creative activity as the goal but leads up to it very gradually.[38] Keckermann, on the other hand, regarded theology as a practical science (an "operative discipline, . . . not contemplative").[39] As such, it ought to begin with the goal, with the process of salvation so to speak, and then demonstrate which subject is at work here and which means are being used. We see here the clear attempt, cloaked in Aristotelian thinking (!), to construct dogmatics soteriologically, that is, to structure it as prudent thought whose task it is to present clearly the way of salvation in logical and dialectical analysis. This then justifies the term which Keckermann introduced, *system*: it is a doctrinal structure which is designed from the very beginning with a specific goal in mind. This understanding of "system" is still present in our thought when we talk about "working on something systematically"—"systematically" means here "goal-oriented planning."

Keckermann, himself an Orthodox Reformed theologian of the Heidelberg persuasion, found few disciples among the Reformed for his method, one of the most obvious ones being Ludwig Crocius (1590–1659).[40] In general, the method which once emanated from Heidelberg was not received by the Reformed so much as by later Lutheranism, especially by Georg Calixtus (1586–1656) and the theology influenced by him.[41] It is in Calixtus that we find the weighty formulation, that the *finis internus* (internal end), which was the source of theology, is faith, which leads to the *finis externus* (external end), to blessedness. This means

---

35. The most significant investigation is in Paul Althaus, *Die Prinzipien der deutschen reformierten Dogmatik im Zeitalter der aristotelischen Scholastik* (Leipzig: Deichert, 1914; Darmstadt: Wissenschaftliche Buchgesellschaft, 1967), pp. 40ff. and 138ff.

36. *STh*, I,i,4, vol. I, p. 3: "Still [sacred doctrine] is speculative rather than practical, because it is more concerned with divine things than with human acts. . . ."

37. Thus in *Table Talk*: "True theology is practical, and its foundation is Christ, whose death is appropriated to us through faith" (*Table Talk*, Nr. 153 [AE, LIV, 22]; see also Nr. 644). Note the influence of Nominalism!

38. See Alexander Schweizer, *Glaubenslehre der evangelisch-reformierten Kirche, dargestellt und aus den Quellen belegt* (2 vols.; Zürich: Orell, Füssli, 1847), I, 97, with reference to Flacius' *Clavis Scripturae Sacrae*, Tract, 1 (1567).

39. See his *Systema Sacrosanctae Theologiae* (Geneva: 1611), I, 1. Regarding the whole complex, see P. Althaus, *op. cit.*, pp. 41ff.

40. Bohatec, writing in *Theologische Studien und Kritiken* (1908), p. 286, thought that he could trace the analytical method back to Calvin, and P. Althaus, who does not agree with him, does find tendencies toward the analytical method as early as Olevianus (1536–87), *De substantis foederis gratuiti . . .* (1585), and above all in the Heidelberg Catechism! See also H. E. Weber, *Der Einfluss der protestantischen Schulphilosophie auf die orthodoxe lutherische Dogmatik* (Leipzig: Deichert, 1908; repr. Darmstadt: Wissenschaftliche Buchgesellschaft, 1969), pp. 21ff.

41. G. Calixtus, *Epitome Theologiae* (1619).

that dogmatics now becomes the *doctrine of faith*: it is supposed to teach that which is of service to faith as the means to blessedness, and accordingly it selects what it requires from the traditional teaching of theology, and what is left over is for the use of the theologians alone.[42] At this point, the analytical method becomes the initial approach for both the Enlightened method, as well as the widely used methodology of the 19th century, including that of Schleiermacher. In addition, the system becomes in the process something completely different from what Keckermann once understood it to be: it becomes the explanation of the faith (which gradually evolves from the end to the foundation), and faith itself becomes the empirical *principle* of the system. From this point it is easy for the path to lead on to the anthropological pattern.

g. *Critique of Material Systematics.* Dogmatic systems have been written from many different viewpoints. The evaluation of the problem as to whether or not a dogmatic system is possible cannot be based upon the admissibility or inadmissibility of whatever aspects are dominant. For the aspects are a matter of dispute between the systems, so that deciding for one aspect can often mean that one is merely deciding against an opposing option. One could even admit that every fundamental aspect possesses some degree of relative correctness; that is certainly true of the anthropological and the salvation-historical approaches, and it is also true of the ontological approach in that it expresses the fact that the truth under examination in dogmatics is not just one truth, but the only truth, and therefore also the truth of philosophy—of course, in a completely different way than ontological systematics in general assert. The possibility of a genuine (material) systematics depends rather on another issue: whether or not it is possible to speak of man's possessing the power of truth, even if only receptively grounded. Whoever would assert this must then defend the thesis that the one truth of God, revealed to us in the person of Jesus Christ, can in its totality be so received by our "reason" that its reproduction in our statements is in itself a completed whole consisting of both the implicit wholeness, which inheres in the principle, and the explicit whole, which is in fact the closed system. Our *intelligere* (understanding, to use Anselm's famous term[43]) would have to be a parallel expression for the truth which is comprehended in faith (and which must then be totally comprehended in it). It is indeed true that our believing is comprehensive in nature, but for the reason that it derives from the faithfulness of God, which is certainly comprehensive—but that is the only reason! As far as our *knowledge* is concerned, 1 Corinthians 13:9 applies here as it does with all of the spiritual gifts—it is only "in part." The reason for this in Paul is that our "knowledge"—just as "prophetic speech"—is now on this side of the "consummation," this side of the Parousia, and is presently in the status of the "not yet." Systems will always have a tendency to ignore this character of the "not yet." They are based upon the firm givenness of a principle or of the object dealt with therein and then build upon the appropriateness of our thought in relationship to what actually "sur-

---

42. See O. Ritschl, *Dogmengeschichte des Protestantismus . . .*, IV, 389ff.
43. See K. Barth, *Fides Quaerens Intellectum: Anselm's Proof of the Existence of God in the Context of His Theological Scheme*, tr. I. W. Robertson (Richmond: John Knox Press, 1960).

passes knowledge" (Eph. 3:19). Dogmatics is limited by eschatology. *That* is the actual argument against systems. The epistemological argument, which states that our thinking never measures up to the object of dogmatic inquiry, must be understood from this fundamental polemic. If there were no appropriate human speech for dealing with the Word of God (and therefore no fitting human thought), then that would mean that there could not be genuine proclamation. And this, in turn, could only be said if one were to presuppose that there was no genuine entrance of God himself in the world of creation. The result of this would then be that all Christian discourse would be arbitrarily subject to our opinions and views, because it would be in every case inauthentic speech. But all of this cannot be said. Because there is such a thing as the incarnation, there is the possibility of obedient speech. Obedient speech, however, does not derive from its own inherent appropriateness for its object, nor from its given openness for it, but rather from *hearing* and *waiting*. Christian speech which is sure of its appropriateness, as it is in systems, is uneschatological and by its very structure not defined by obedience. There can be no system because God's truth is not given to us as a principle but as a person, and this in turn not as a person who would be the perfect expression of a principle but rather as the person about whom it is stated that he not only is and was, but that he is *coming*. The completion of all Christian thought is still before us, never already present. But the way in which it is before us is in that it is given to us as the promise and as the content of the Gospel: not as a gift which has passed us by but as a gift which is constantly contemporary in new ways as we hear and obey. A system can only exist under the secret presupposition that we effectively possess grace, and thus the most closed systematics of all was that of the Middle Ages which was built upon this presupposition. The Theology of the Word will always have to remain open. It cannot proceed in the closedness of a system.

h. Multiplicity and Unity of the Total Dogmatic Declaration. If, then, material systems are not possible, we must not conclude that dogmatics necessarily will be the opposite of a system, something like a collection of aphorisms or of individual tractates, and that it can be nothing more. The method much used since Melanchthon, that of putting together lists of theological *Loci* (Places, Citations),[44] is certainly not safe from the penetration of a material systematics, and above all is not meant as a disorderly listing of disparate teachings. There is absolutely no formal protection against the emergence of material systematics. But the formal system offers the least protection because it tends so strongly toward the material.

Two points of view will have important bearing for the structuring of a dogmatics. First, dogmatics deals with God's activity with man. This activity has many aspects because it is historical activity. Dogmatics does not deal with the

---

44. The term *Loci* (Gk. *topoi*) derives from ancient rhetorics and dialectics and via the latter (as with Melanchthon) was viewed in connection with the methods used in Scholasticism. The "local method" is therefore not unsystematic. See W. Neuser, *Der Ansatz der Theologie Philipp Melanchthons* (*Beiträge zur Geschichte und Lehre der reformierten Kirche*, 9; Neukirchen: Buchhandlung des Erziehungsvereins, 1957); and O. Ritschl, *System und systematische Methode. . . .*

idea which constantly underlies this activity, but rather with God in this activity. This is, properly understood, the meaning of Melanchthon's *"historica series"* ("historical sequence") or of Calvin's careful distinction between the knowledge of God in creation and the knowledge of God in redemption.[45] We conclude that dogmatics must make a wide variety of statements. Another necessary conclusion is that human thought is unavoidably discursive: we cannot desire to say everything at once. This multiplicity is, in a certain sense (which must always be more carefully examined), a sequence. Second, in and not behind its multiplicity, dogmatics deals with the inquiry about the one thing essential, that is, with the question of the Word of God. If the conclusion of the historicity of God's activity was the multiplicity and sequential nature of theological statements, then this second point of view leads to the conclusion that the multiplicity is always to be queried about the one thing essential, and that the sequence is never to be understood as a mere list of things. If only the first point were valid, then dogmatics would deteriorate and decay. If only the second were valid, then it would become a system. Only the connection of both points of view does justice to the object of dogmatics.

This means that the old "local method" is the most appropriate one but in such a way that within each area of doctrine the totality, the one thing which is the object of dogmatics, will be expressed in a methodically ordered way. To give an example, it would not be fitting to discuss both creation and the atonement in one context; it would be just as inappropriate to discuss the atonement before dealing with the creation, but it would be equally out of place to treat of creation without coming to the atonement, or to deal with the atonement without ever having touched upon creation.

The final reason for the necessity of holding onto the unity of God while differentiating within God's activity, that is, of never letting an absolute separation arise, is based upon the fact that God himself, as he reveals himself in history, is the One in such a way that he is always himself *in* his revelation. The reason for this is the fact that God is the triune God. Dogmatics will therefore always be seen, in all of its statements, under the dominant aspect of the doctrine of the Trinity. This can be expressed in that dogmatics is structured in a Trinitarian fashion.[46] But however it is structured, the Trinity must be clearly perceived as the central point.[47]

---

45. Melanchthon, *CR*, XXI, 605f.; Stupperich, II/1, pp. 169ff. Calvin's distinction is explained in the *Institutes*, I,ii,1, pp. 39–41.

46. This is the method of, e.g., Martin Rade, *Glaubenslehre* (3 vols.; Gotha: Leopold Klotz, 1924–27); also of T. Häring, *The Christian Faith: a System of Dogmatics*, tr. J. Dickie and G. Ferris (London and New York: Hodder and Stoughton, 1913 [g1906, 1912]).

47. H. Urs von Balthasar, *op. cit.*, p. 211, finds that in Barth and Thomas Aquinas the Trinity and the Church "do not play a central role in the shaping of their theologies." Whether or not this is true would have to be investigated more carefully. But Barth's approach is unmistakably Trinitarian. Yet one gains the impression that at times the basic Christological conception, instead of being incorporated into this approach, actually replaces it. This is then related to what one could call "the compulsion of the system," particularly in the doctrine of God's gracious election and the doctrine of evil (see my essay, "Die Lehre von der Erwählung," in Weber, Kreck, and Wolf, *Die Predigt von der Gnadenwahl* [*Theologische Existenz heute*, 28; Munich: Kaiser, 1951], pp. 34ff.).

4. DOGMATICS AND ETHICS

a. The Reasons for the Separation. For a long time it has been customary to deal with dogmatics separately from ethics. This can be justified on purely technical grounds,[48] perhaps by referring to the fact that ethics, if it is to be concrete, must examine an abundance of actual questions which are better handled by themselves. Still one must admit, in Schleiermacher's words, that "the Christian rules of life" are "no less propositions of faith" than "the actual dogmatic ones."[49]

Basically, dogmatics and ethics are not separated. This does not become visible, however, until we reach the phase where closed systems are to be found. As long as there were only dogmatic (theological) tractates, be they of very comprehensive content, it was entirely possible to have "dogmatic" treatises next to "ethical" ones (for example, the *Paedagogus* of Clement of Alexandria [c. 150–c. 215] or the numerous ethical writings of Tertullian [c. 160–c. 220]). The comprehensive presentations in the Middle Ages, especially the *Summae*, consist of dogmatics and ethics together (see section II,ii of Thomas's *Summa*).

The roots of the separation of ethics from the context of dogmatics can be observed very early, and they are regularly the result either of philosophical influences or of a conception of the "Christian life" which views this as independently examinable, describable, and explainable. "Christian life" as something which can be examined on its own is naturally compared to whatever else was present as a form of life and thus belonged to the field of endeavor of philosophical ethics.

This process of separation is not primarily a matter of scientific method, but rather it is rooted in the gradual dissociation of the life of the Christian person from the direct framework of the proclamation of Christ. The Christian way of life appears then as the confirmation of Christian truth (as superior to the essence of paganism as is this truth),[50] or it appears as the means of recognition that the Christian is on the road to perfection.[51] The term "ethics" first appears as the title of a written work when it is used for the monastic regulations of Basil (c. 330–79).[52] The "Christian life" is now becoming the preliminary stage to the "angelic life"! Alongside a contemplatively conceived dogmatics there is now an ascetic and perfectionist ethics! This doubling process can be traced back, as we said, to its roots in the 2nd century. It is precisely analogous to the other process

---

48. See Schleiermacher, *Brief Outline on the Study of Theology*, tr. T. N. Tice (Richmond: John Knox Press, 1966 [g1811, 1910]).

49. *Ibid.* Schleiermacher then proceeds to explain by saying, ". . . they are dealing with the same self-consciousness of Christian devotion as it reveals itself as a motive."

50. Justin Martyr (c. 100–c.165), "The First Apology," *Justin Martyr and Athenagoras (ANCL*, II, Chs. XV–XVII, pp. 18–22), and Aristides (2nd cent.), *Apology on behalf of the Christians*, tr. J. R. Harris (Cambridge, Eng.: The University Press, 1893), pp. 15–17. (See also R. Seeberg, ed., *Texte und Untersuchungen zur Geschichte der altchristlichen Literatur*, begründet von O. Gebhardt & A. Harnack [1894], pp. 56ff.)

51. So in Clement (c. 150–c. 215) and Origen (c. 185–c. 254), and then very generally in the estimation of marriage and the ideal of virginity, up to Athanasius (c. 296–373).

52. Basil calls the eighty rules of monastic communities *ēthika*, in his *Herewith begin the Morals* (*FC*, IX, 71ff.; Migne, *PG*, XXXI, 699ff.).

in which the development of the creed became subject to the dominant influence of ontological speculation. The moralization of ethics and the logification of dogmatics are two sides of the same thing.

This material doubling is not without its effect where, as is the case in the great *Summae* of the Middle Ages, there is no outward separation between dogmatics and ethics. To a degree, this separation did not appear because the Aristotelian legacy made the dissociation of what is to be believed (*credenda*) and what is to be done (*agenda*) difficult. The duality becomes very obvious in post-Tridentine Catholicism, especially in Jesuit "moral theology," which was influenced by the voluntarism of Occamistic Scholasticism. Even where the Jesuits were not accepted in substance, moral theology remained a discipline and the title of numerous works alongside of dogmatics.

In the tradition defined by the Reformation there was not much difference in what happened. To be sure, we find not even an implication of such a doubling in Luther and Calvin: a Theology of the Word could scarcely be divided into the *credenda* and the *agenda*. If the center of theology was discovered anew, then both faith and action had to be subordinated to it, although they were not equated, of course. Even the strict distinction between law and Gospel did not invalidate this, for it was just as strict an ordering of these elements to one another. Things changed, however, wherever Christian action again became the focus of independent interest—especially in light of "natural law"—and thus entered again into competition with "the natural." This first happened in Melanchthon, who did offer within his *Loci* an exposition of the decalogue,[53] but still very early wrote a philosophical ethics,[54] and then later developed this in the *Ethicae doctrinae elementa*,[55] which for a long time was the standard textbook. There are other early attempts to deal with ethics independently of dogmatics: on the Lutheran side as early as 1529 in the *De virtute christiana* by Thomas Venatorius of Nuremberg (1488–1551), and on the Reformed level the *Ethice christiana* by Lambert Daneau (Danaeus; 1530–95) in 1577. After that it was the practice for a long time to deal with ethics as a part of dogmatic presentations, or alternatively as the subject of special treatments, and occasionally as both by the same author.[56]

In more recent times, the division of dogmatics and ethics has become the general rule. There are certainly exceptions: Carl Immanuel Nitzsch's *System der christlichen Lehre* (1829), or H. H. Wendt's *System der christlichen Lehre* (2nd ed. 1920), or above all Martin Kähler's *Wissenschaft der christlichen Lehre* (1883 and thereafter)—in the last instance, this is the attempt to rediscover the Reformation's unity. In our day, Karl Barth has reestablished the old unity from new points of view and frequently given a carefully reasoned explanation for doing

---

53. *CR*, XXI, 688ff.; Stupperich, II/1, pp. 281ff.

54. *CR*, XVI, 21ff.; *Epitome philosophiae moralis* (1538). Even earlier: *Epitome ethices* (1532), in Heineck, "Die älteste Fassung von Melanchthons Ethik," *Philosophische Monatshefte* (*Archiv für systematische Philosophie und Soziologie* [Berlin: 1893], pp. 129ff.).

55. *CR*, XVI, 165ff.

56. Thus, as we have seen, in Melanchthon, or later, e.g., in William Ames (1576–1633), *The Marrow of Theology* (1656), tr. and ed. J. D. Eusden (Boston: Pilgrim Press, 1968), and *De conscientia* (1654); or in G. Calixtus (1586–1656), *Epitome theologiae* (1619) and the more influential *Epitome theologiae moralis* (1634).

so.[57] In particular, Barth has demonstrated that ethics dissociated from dogmatics has evidenced, since Richard Rothe (1799–1867) and Albrecht Ritschl (1822–89), a strong tendency to give ethics the methodological and essential priority over dogmatics. Ethics sets the framework (for Rothe it is speculative, for Ritschl it is anthropological) into which dogmatics must integrate itself. Ethics speaks of the human-Christian reality which dogmatics then merely deals with as an explanation of Church doctrine, that is, from one side only (as in Rothe), or investigates in order to find its roots (which is fundamentally Ritschl's approach). Wilhelm Herrmann has put most plainly what is at stake here: "In order to understand the Christian faith and the spiritual processes in which it unfolds itself, one must begin with the understanding of the moral."[58] The question could be raised whether this was not actually expressing what was the unconscious motivation already at work in Melanchthon—and we need only to replace the "moral" with "existence" in order to find ourselves in the middle of the contemporary problem.

 b. Evaluation. The question whether a substantive division of dogmatics and ethics is allowable depends upon the deeper question as to whether there can be an isolated discussion of human action, proceeding upon the basis of its own and special criteria.

 1) **Credenda-agenda = Believing-Doing.** A positive answer to this question could result, first, from the position that dogmatics deals with faith whereas ethics has to do with acting or doing. The tone is set here by the ancient distinction between *credenda* (what is to be believed) and *agenda* (what is to be done). This can mean that our view is directed to man as both believing and acting man. That means that dogmatics and ethics are essentially statements about man. This was done most clearly by Schleiermacher: "The formula of the dogmatic task is the question: What must *be*, because the religious form of self-consciousness, the religious frame of mind *is*? The formula of our ethical task is the question: What must *develop* out of the religious self-consciousness and through it, *because* the religious self-consciousness *is*."[59] Nonetheless Schleiermacher himself finds that under these circumstances dogmatics and ethics are merely two ways of looking at the same thing (namely, the religious self-consciousness), and it is only for dialectical reasons that we separate the "two final points of the religious frame of mind."[60] Schleiermacher's conception may be faced with the theological question which applies to his entire approach: Will not a theology which is based upon the religious self-consciousness of man (regardless of how it is set up) of necessity always return to its initial premise, and is it thus not actually the self-explication of man, analyzed and interpreted in great depth?

---

57. Barth's comprehensive reasons (*CD*, I,2, pp. 782ff., and II,2, pp. 543ff.), with which we agree.

58. W. Herrmann, *Ethik* (Tübingen and Leipzig: J. C. B. Mohr, 1935[5] [1901[1]]), p. 6.

59. Schleiermacher, *Christliche Sittenlehre in Vorlesungen* (1843 posthumously), *Bibl. theol. Klass.*, 37, I, p. 24, in *Sämtliche Werke* (30 vols.; Berlin: G. Reimer), I,12, p. 24.

60. *Op. cit.*, p. 25, in *Sämtliche Werke*, I,12, p. 24.

2) God's Work—Man's Work. Our question could (secondly) be answered affirmatively from the point of view that dogmatics deals in substance with *God's* work, and ethics conversely treats of *man's* activities. This was especially the approach of Albrecht Ritschl (1822–99) and Theodor Häring (1848–1928).[61] In the background there is a decisive intention of Reformation theology: we should make a sharp distinction between that which God does and does perfectly and that which is always the imperfect work of man, which can ultimately effect nothing. It is then concluded that this distinction can be preserved by understanding the Christian life as no more than the consequences of the gift of God with which dogmatics is dealing. Very early in the Reformation this was done here and there: we are reminded of the title of Thomas Venatorius' (c. 1488–1551) ethics, *De virtute christiana* (Of Christian Virtue [1529]), and then even of Melanchthon's view of the "third use of the law" (*tertius usus legis*). In view of all this, the question must be raised whether the distinction did not produce the very thing which they were seeking to avoid by making it. If dogmatics deals with God's gift and ethics with man's activity, then the latter, as much as one may try to avoid it, becomes the polar opposite to the former, and the result must be synergism (whether coarse or refined). Doctrine and life are then related to one another in analogy to God's gift and man's reception and utilization of that gift, but this is done as man's own activity. Is it not necessary that the attempt to relate dogmatics and ethics to each other as opposites in this fashion must be based upon the conception that the life of the Christian person contains in itself a capacity for examination, description, and realization quite apart from the Word of God and grace? And if this were so, then the gift of God would be the presupposition, but not the constitutive power for the Christian life. If, alternatively, God's Word and gift are the constitutive power for the life of the Christian, then the ethical question must always be the inquiry about God's Word and gift, and that means that it must be the dogmatic question.

3) Dogmatics and Ethics in Relationship to Man. Finally, the development of an ethics separated from dogmatics can be based upon the point of view that the material of theological ethics, the object placed in its purview, is, in distinction from dogmatics, already given. The reality within which the ethical question

---

61. A. Ritschl, *The Christian Doctrine of Justification and Reconciliation; the Positive Development of the Doctrine*, tr. H. R. Mackintosh and A. B. Macaulay (New York: Scribner's, 1900; repr. Clifton, N.J.: Reference Book Publishers, 1966), p. 14: It is true that dogmatics and ethics stand under the "constitutive influence" of both the "idea of redemption" and "the idea of the kingdom of God"; however, dogmatics "comprises all the presuppositions of Christianity under the form of 'Divine operation'; ethics, presupposing the former discipline, comprises the province of personal and social Christian life under the form of 'personal activity.' "

Theodor Häring, *The Ethics of the Christian Life*, tr. J. S. Hill (London: Williams & Norgate, 1909): Dogmatics and ethics constitute an internal unity in such a way that "doctrine shows us how the kingdom of God becomes to us an assured personal possession, as God's gift by faith in Christ," whereas ethics represents "how this faith is our incentive and motive power to co-operation in the task, implicit in the gift, of realising the 'kingdom of God' . . ." (p. 4).

emerges is the reality of human life *per se*. And this reality is conditioned by recognizable constant factors: "everywhere," for example, we find marriage, some kind of political order, and so on. It is equally indisputable that within human reality so viewed there are also requirements which take the form of norms, norms of a "moral" as well as legal nature. Even if theological ethics evaluates these constant factors and these normative requirements differently than would philosophical ethics, it still must deal with them. And is it not conceivable that ethics will conclude that they deserve the rank of secondary criteria in that it speaks of both the "law" and the "orders" (E. Brunner), or of the revealed law (*lex revelata*), the law of nature (*lex naturae*), and the natural right (*jus naturale*) (as did Melanchthon and many before and after him)? In fact, cannot the insight that the ethical question (at least this one!) is man's essential question lead to the conclusion that the "concept of a special theological ethics" should be "done away with as untenable," as it did for Wilhelm Herrmann?[62] It would obviously be just as possible to "do away" with the concept of Christian theology "as untenable"—for the question of God, whether everyone everywhere is confronted by it or not, is always the question of man as such, and the Church's answer to the question of God (out of which in fact the proper question can first be formulated) is always stated with the claim not to be an answer for a special kind of person, that is, for Christians, but really to be God's answer to all men. The circumstance that the ethical question is not a unique feature of Christendom does not justify making theological ethics autonomous, but rather it raises an important dogmatic problem: it points out the universality of God's commands, even though they are not thereby to be generalized. And the universality of divine commanding (which is only the reverse side of the universality of divine election in Jesus Christ) casts its light upon the universality of human existence, upon the remarkable constants within which that existence goes on, and upon the equally remarkable demands with which man is continuously although very differently confronted. But the light falls from the universality of God's commands! Any dogmatics or ethics which begins with man in general can never be really a dogmatics or an ethics, if it is true that in Jesus Christ man has been accepted by God. In addition, it has been seen that an ethics which begins with man "in general" will fail to grasp man because the "unity of the human race" is not an empirical given, but rather something which can only be recognized in faith in Jesus Christ.[63] "Man" is either an abstract which succumbs to the pluralities of races, classes, and world views, or he is recognized in the one man who is the Son of God!

   c. The Basis of Unity. To make ethics autonomous over against dogmatics would imply that there are special criteria available for ethics. But we cannot find

---

62. *Op. cit.*, p. 1. Nevertheless, Herrmann's work carries the divisions "Natural Life and Moral Thought" and "The Christian Moral Life." Herrmann is persuaded that "moral thought" brings man "of necessity onto the pathway of religion" (*op. cit.*, p. 93), and on the other hand, "the Christian faith as the consciousness of divine forgiveness" is also the "power to do good" (pp. 135ff.).

63. See pp. 469ff.

such criteria. Therefore ethics can only be an element of dogmatics. The positive reason for this is that dogmatics' inquiry about the Word of God as the criterion which is definitive for everything is true both of God and man, since the Word of God has become flesh, and since God in Jesus Christ is man's God. A dogmatics which were not ethics at the same time would have to become a theory about a god who existed as the essence of all existence or as the highest of all thoughts vast distances away from man, and the only organ of human receptivity which would correspond to such a god would be the intellect or the self-consciousness. But the Bible does not speak of such a god, and the Church does not proclaim such a one, and therefore dogmatics cannot have this kind of god in mind. To make ethics autonomous must mean that dogmatics is transferred to the realm of the intellectual, the purely mind-oriented, and in this sense the "theoretical." However, since the point of departure of dogmatics in its inquiry into the Word of God is the reality of the Word become flesh, it can never remain in the realm of abstraction or intellectuality; it can never pass by man whom God has received unto himself in Jesus Christ, and therefore it cannot be without its practical emphasis. To remove the practical side (which could include, next to ethics, special forms of asceticism and poimenics) would free dogmatics of a function which cannot be separated from it. And it would not be of any use to such an autonomous ethics. It would only seem to be the case that ethics were not "practical": even autonomous ethics would still be the theory of Christian action, but it would be a doubtful theory because Christian activity viewed in this kind of separation could not be grasped in its essence. Such an independent ethics would almost automatically be forced to seek out special criteria for this special Christian life (for instance, setting up love next to faith, or attempting to give the law authority next to the Gospel), and in doing that, it would tear asunder what must remain together.[64]

There is obviously nothing objectionable about the purely didactic, technical separation of these areas of content. Since there is no such thing as a pure "dogmatic" or a pure "ethical" statement, this separation will always consist of the fact that the special treatment of the ethical insights gained in dogmatics will always be dealt with technically as its own section. A dogmatics which does not speak of God's commandments is just as inconceivable as a dogmatics which does not deal with man, with sin, with forgiveness, with justification and sanctification.

---

64. Werner Elert, in *The Christian Ethos*, tr. Carl J. Schindler (Philadelphia: Muhlenberg Press, 1957), states on pp. 13–14 that dogmatics and ethics are not related to each other as "*credenda* and *agenda* or *docenda* (things to be taught) and *agenda*," but rather "it is like the contrast of *qualitas* (character) and *doctrina* (teachings) in a person." He adds, "There are ethical elements in the dogma which appear in the teachings of the church in precisely the same manner in which a man's moral code comes to light in what he says." One might assume that in light of this thesis he would integrate dogmatics and ethics into each other. But he does not do so. He states that ". . . dogma is not invalidated because it is occasionally preached by individuals without the Christian ethos . . ." (p. 15). The misfortune this represents would only be increased if one were to understand the "Christian ethos" merely "as part of the dogma." Therefore, dogmatics and ethics are supposed to be separated. This reasoning is not sufficient, for the ethicist, too, could possibly be "devoid of the Christian ethics," and he, too, would certainly have to deal with "dogma."

Since these statements cannot be made in utter abstraction, no dogmatics is imaginable which does not speak of the concrete reality within which man is man. But it is certainly possible to reproduce the very special concretions of the parenetic sections of the New Testament letters, as related to and conditioned by time as they are, in a presentation which is made by itself. But it may not become permanent in that kind of isolation. That would be in reality nothing more than the extraction of certain texts and themes from the totality of dogmatics, that is, of Christian doctrine.

PART TWO

On the History of Dogmatics

III. The Dogmatics of the Early Church

A. THE EAST

a. Preliminary Remarks. The newer studies of dogmatics in general offer no overview of the history of dogmatics. There are good reasons for this. First of all, the history of dogmatics, like the history of theology in general, is a special area of expertise which requires the combined labors of the dogmatician and the church historian. Secondly, this area of discipline is so vast that we are still lacking a truly comprehensive presentation of the history of theology or the history of dogmatics, and it is difficult to believe that it will soon be forthcoming. The attempt to incorporate the basic lines of a history of dogmatics into a presentation of dogmatics like this book will always be subject to attack. The danger that the reader would be tempted to come to unqualified conclusions through such an overview is just as great as the other danger that this overview could be confusingly superficial.

In spite of the fact that all of these dangers are clearly seen, the attempt is still being made to provide an introduction to the history of dogmatics. The reasons for this are both didactic and based upon a theological consideration. The didactic reasons are obvious: every account of dogmatics will, implicitly or explicitly, incorporate a great amount of historical material into its discussion, and it seems to be desirable that at one point in the account at least the opportunity is given to gain a view of this material in its historical context. It is certainly necessary to come to know the history of dogmatics as the history of its problem and its problems, to grasp the multiplicity of its methods, and to understand the relationship of dogmatics to dogma, to the Church and its proclamation, but also to philosophy, the development of ideas, and all of the most important points of juncture. But why is all of this theologically necessary? Because every dogmatic labor, to the extent that it takes place within the Church, stands in a tradition. This tradition has its major impact primarily on dogma. We have already discussed what dogmatics has to do with this. But alongside of that, there is the dogmatic work which leads up to dogma, away from dogma, and now and again passes over dogma, and this also has its own tradition. If dogma is not "propositional law" then there will certainly not be any obligatory nature in the tradition of dogmatics.

Just as the history of the Church is not a continuation of revelation *(continuatio revelationis)*, the history of dogmatics is not an effect of revelation. But it cannot be denied that we would not be seeking out the Word of God if others had not been doing it long before us. The way in which they were asking and answering cannot be of no importance to us. For the Church does not exist exclusively in a vertical dimension but exists also in a horizontal dimension, which derives from the vertical, from the proclaimed and believed Word, and thus is the horizontal existence of the *Church,* but as such must be taken very seriously. Seen this way, dogmatic work of the past is not just instructive and illuminating for us but is the work of the "fathers" which we certainly cannot accept uncritically but also may not abandon in disrespect. This is all the more true since the history of dogmatics does not proceed in a linear fashion: the temporal distance of an early dogmatician may mean in substance the most extreme vicinity—and vice versa. Therefore the encounter with the dogmatics of the past is never just a preoccupation with something earlier than we are which deserves our attention but may not be able to provide us any direct help, but rather the actualization of the knowledge that all dogmatic work takes place within the fellowship of the Church. Each new conception is not the removal of what has gone before, either in overcoming or surpassing it, but is a new approach to examining what has always been under examination, but now from another side. Therefore it must be able to justify itself in encounter with the questions and answers of the past. In the Church we are always students.

   b. The Timelessness and Timeliness of the Kerygma. The work of dogmatics is always related to the Church's dogma, but it does not always necessarily presuppose it. Formulated dogma is also a result of dogmatic work. But dogmatics always presupposes the kerygma.[1] Dogmatic work was the result of the Church's knowing its task, on the one hand, which was to proclaim the one kerygma, but having to carry out, on the other hand, this proclamation at a temporal and spatial distance from the kerygma, that is, at other times and in new areas.[2]

   If the knowledge that the kerygma is contingent and historical, because it is the proclamation of the person of Jesus Christ, had been lost in the Church, then the kerygma would easily have been transformed into a religious or theological doctrinal proposition which would then merely need to be applied to the most varying of possibilities. This perversion of the nature of the kerygma did however, in spite of all of the temptations to go in that direction, not happen, generally speaking. The remembrance of the historicity of the kerygma persisted. This

---

   1. Martin Kähler introduced the concept kerygma into the vocabulary of theology.
   2. Martin Werner, *The Formation of Christian Dogma: an Historical Study of its Problem,* tr. S. G. F. Brandon (New York: 1957 [g1941]), derives (in accordance with the general approach of his theology) the emergence of dogma from the reaction of the Church to the fact that the Parousia did not come. We are not going to discuss here the fundamental thesis of Werner's work. But one could counter this conclusion with the assertion that the early Church's mission, without which the emergence of Church dogmatics could not be understood, had its original motivation in eschatology itself. It is, however, correct that with the flagging of eschatology, or with its later incorporation into a salvation-history scheme, dogmatics shifted more and more into the sphere of intellectual reflection about pure being.

resulted then in the fact that the Church did not meet its changing situations with a timeless idea which undergirded it, but rather with a message which was indissolubly related to a specific time and history, but which did not appear as the object of a memory or a meditation on the past but as genuine presence. This produced the tension out of which dogmatics grew and has continually grown: the Church with its kerygma could neither close itself off to all temporality, to all of the human self-understandings which confronted it, nor could it be absolutely open to man, to the age, to self-understandings in such a way that it would compromise the concrete truth of the kerygma, that is, make it into one truth among many others. With either of these alternatives, the Church would have ceased to be the Church. Both of them have been its permanent danger. And yet, the power of the message has been great enough to prevent it from succumbing to this danger. The benchmarks for the most heated struggles and for the most significant victories of the message in both directions have been the great decisions in the history of dogma.

c. *The Points of Departure*. The dogmatic work of the early Church is characterized by the tensions which have just been broadly sketched. Two points of departure determined its early development: on the one hand, it was trying to open the kerygma of the Church for the "world" and keep it open, and yet on the other hand it could not but investigate the kerygma itself in its unconditionality. This in turn opened it up to the reverse danger that dogmatics would become a secret doctrine which would fit into a concept of the Church which was defined entirely by ritual. The dogmatic labors of the East, mostly written in Greek, are distinguished from those of the West by the stronger Eastern tendency toward speculation, toward the drafting of great cosmological schemes, toward a pure Gnosticism divorced from the "practice" of the Church. In the West the primary emphasis was upon the concrete, the earthly, and the human, and dogmatics there corresponded to a form of the Church in which from a very early date authority, order, and law had a greater significance than daring intellectual concepts.

d. *The Apologists*. If we have described the situation correctly, then the Apologists[3] are to be regarded as early dogmaticians, although they certainly were not that methodologically, and probably should be assigned to the "irregular" dogmatics, to use Barth's phrase. All of them, although they come from many and varying premises, endeavor to keep Christian proclamation open toward the "outside world"—Christian proclamation as they understand it. In that they are "defending," they are interpreting! And they interpret within the context of the Hellenistic thought which surrounded them, and occasionally, as with Justin, in the context of Jewish thought. The basic thrust of their "apologetic" procedure is characteristically different: in the one figure, the (Greek) philosophy appears as the preliminary stage, the preparation or precursor of Christian proclamation—this philosophy in its greatest representatives, those free of idolatry, and here

---

3. See the original sources in *FC, ANCL, ANW,* and *LCC*. On Justin, see his *Dialogue with Trypho*, in *Justin Martyr and Athenagoras (ANCL,* II, 85ff.).

Socrates is continually the ideal type just as he was in broad circles of Hellenism. In other figures, the apologetics is characterized by uncertainty, lacking knowledge of the truth, in short, by imperfection in every regard—in total contradiction to Christian proclamation in its complete perfection. The terminological material for both directions of apologetics is provided in part by the primarily Stoic critique of the mythological and philosophical traditions, and in part especially by the concept of the Logos,[4] as it had already been developed by classical Greek philosophy and then received by Hellenism, often under the influence of Gnosticism. It was generally the "popular philosophy" of which the first defenders of Christianity in the Hellenistic world made use, and it is only through this means that they view the classical philosophy of antiquity.

The difference in the basic thrust—both integrative continuation and rejective devaluation—ought not to keep us from seeing that there was still an ultimate common ground with the Apologists. They might, with Justin, discover that the *sperma tou logou* (germ or seed of the Logos) was already at work in the ancient Greeks,[5] the Logos which in truth and reality always was and is Jesus Christ. Or they might go the other way and see pagan philosophy, poetry, and life-style as under the dominion of demons and thus value them as worthless in their imperfection. But regardless of how they proceeded, their common presupposition was that Christianity is comparable to philosophy, that is, that it belongs to the identical category.[6] The attitude of the Apologists generally is determined by a confident assurance of victory. This then is transformed into the persuasion that the Christian faith reveals its superior power at the very point where the world up until then had reached its intellectual peak and was closest to eternally valid truth. If then truth there and here—the Logos there and the Logos of the Christian message—were all to be seen within one category, then this contained a decisive judgment about Christian proclamation, a dogmatic judgment which stated that the terminology of philosophy seemed appropriate for the interpretation of the essence of Christianity—it was really predestined to receive the Christian message. Once this assumption was accepted, then the direction of thought could either be the way of synthesis or the way of diastasis. But in both cases, the comparability was presupposed. And in both cases, the philosophy of the age provided adequate helps: synthesis could orient itself to the Stoics and was already well received by late Jewish apologetics, and diastasis could appeal to the Skeptics and the Cynics—the intellectual controversy of Hellenism with the Greek past had long been going on in this same dual direction. It is therefore not surprising that we find both basic thrusts of the controversy in the same Apologists;

---

4. See especially E. Nestle, *Vom Mythos zum Logos, die Selbstentfaltung des griechischen Denkens von Homer bis auf die Scholastik und Sokrates* (Stuttgart: Kröner, 1942; Aalen: Scientia Verlag, 1966).

5. "The Second Apology," *Justin Martyr and Athenagoras (ANCL*, II, Ch. VIII, p. 78).

6. "And yet the doctrine of the Christians can only be compared with philosophy. For, so far as this latter is genuine, it is also guided by the Logos; and, conversely, what the Christians teach concerning the Father of the world, the destiny of man . . . , has also been attested to by the wisest of the Greeks" (A. von Harnack, *History of Dogma*, tr. N. Buchanan [7 vols.; London: Williams & Norgate, 1896], II, 182f., speaking of Justin).

Justin can express himself very skeptically, but that which was absolutely different from anything else in primitive Christian proclamation, distinct from all human searching and asking, now becomes a diastasis within a categorical context, a long-term development with its consequences into the present age. Christian doctrine, as perfect truth, opposes all that is imperfect in both synthesis and diastasis.

In what we have just outlined, we have summarized the most consequential contribution of the Apologists to the development of a Christian dogmatics. We need not deal here with the details. But we must reject the misunderstanding which asserts that with the Apologists the Christian message was virtually betrayed to Hellenistic popular philosophy. It cannot be denied that the power of the kerygma was still alive in the Apologists. And it is equally undeniable that it was not their intention to conduct this controversy with the pagan world upon the level of thought alone; they were persuaded of the power of demons who still enslaved the pagans, and they were just as persuaded of the triumph of Jesus Christ over this power. When they are talking about it, they easily slip into the intellectual sphere of Gnosticism, or, as with Tertullian, into the stream of Montanism.[7]

e. The Alexandrians. The "regular" dogmatic work of the Church in the East developed out of Alexandria. Clement and Origen are its major proponents. Regarding the latter figure, we may state that the dogmatics of the East rapidly ascended to the summit of its possibilities in him. No other Eastern dogmatician would reach the greatness of Origen. It was nonetheless a dangerous greatness and reveals many of the dangers which in some fashion accompany all dogmatic work.

f. Gnosticism, Christian Gnosticism, Churchly Gnosticism. The Alexandrians[8] may be designated as theologians of the churchly Gnosticism. And this in a double sense. First of all, their work cannot be grasped without the "Christian Gnosticism" which they further develop ecclesiastically and even seek to surpass. And secondly, the concept of "knowledge," together with the fundamental concept of the Logos, is central to their thought. They are churchly Gnostics, in comparison to the extra-Christian Gnosticism of the day and to the controversy with the Christian Gnostics represented, for example, by the Valentinians. In that this is true, the Alexandrians maintained close contact with philosophy, with both the ancient Platonic and the contemporary philosophy: Origen was probably also a student of Ammonius Saccas (c. 175–242) and approaches in his philosophical views the Neo-Platonism which was then emerging.

---

7. Tertullian's role as an Apologist indicates that there were also apologetic endeavors in the West. In spite of that, our discussion of the Western dogmatics of the early Church will not even deal with the Apologists, because their dogmatic significance can be shown more clearly in the East than in the West.

8. Origen can only be called an Alexandrian with reservations since he spent long and decisive years outside the city, above all in Palestinian Caesarea—not voluntarily and not at peace with the Church of his home city.

Gnosticism[9] is basically an extra- and pre-Christian religious stream which originates in the Orient. The form in which it encounters early Christianity had already gone through the shaping medium of Hellenism. It is depicted as a redemption religion in which redemption happens through knowledge. This knowledge is the intellectual comprehension of a mystery; it is therefore supernatural knowledge. The mystery in turn is cosmic: it deals with the structure of all of reality in the manifold number of "aeons" which stretch from the lowest level of worthlessness up to the most supreme values, and it deals then, too, with the position of the human soul within this reality, divided into stages.

The soul in its present state, enslaved in the body, is subjected to cosmic powers (the so-called "Archons"), fate, death, inauthenticity. But it is the soul's destiny to regain its actual home. This is made possible in that (as many opinions hold) a redeemer figure out of the highest aeon condescends into the lowest in order to proclaim to the soul its actual authenticity and its true home and to make it possible to ascend there through knowledge. The redemptive event (knowledge, mystery cult, mystery community) is imbedded in a cosmic, even "supercosmic" event (H. Leisegang), just as all aspects of reality in this aeon are indissolubly related to similar aspects in the higher aeon (angels, spirits, constellations). The cosmic event with its redemption can be imagined more mythologically (as in the earlier periods) or more philosophically (theosophically) (as in the later periods). Participation in it is, in any event, only available to the possessor of knowledge, who as such is the elect one.

---

9. R. Reitzenstein, *Die hellenistischen Mysterienreligionen, nach ihren Grundgedanken und Wirkungen* (Stuttgart: Teubner, 1956 [g1927[3]]); H. Jonas, *The Gnostic Religion; the Message of the Alien God and the Beginnings of Christianity* (Boston: Beacon Press, 1958 [the English edition is a re-working of the German original of 1934]); H. Leisegang, *Die Gnosis* (Stuttgart: A. Kröner, 1955[4]); W. Bousset, *Hauptprobleme der Gnosis* (Göttingen: Vandenhoeck & Ruprecht, 1907, 1973); and the outline in *Kyrios Christos*, tr. J. E. Steely (Nashville: Abingdon, 1970 [g1913, 1935]), pp. 245ff.; as well as his article on "Gnosis" in G. Wissowa, *Pauly's Real-Enzyclopädie der classischen Altertumswissenschaften*, ed. W. Knoll (Stuttgart: Metzlersche Buchhandlung, 1912), VII, cols. 1502ff.; H. Leisegang, article on "Gnosis" I in *Religion in Geschichte und Gegenwart (RGG)*, 2nd ed., II, 1276ff.; G. Krüger, article on "Gnosticism," Schaff-Herzog, IV, 496–500; W. Anz, *Zur Frage nach dem Ursprung des Gnostizismus*, in *Texte und Untersuchungen zur Geschichte der altchristlichen Literatur*, begründet von O. von Gebhardt and A. Harnack, Nr. 15,4 (1897); F. C. Burkitt, *Church and Gnosis* (Cambridge: The University Press, 1932); H. Schlier, *Christus und die Kirche im Epheserbrief (Beiträge zur historischen Theologie*, 6; Tübingen: J. C. B. Mohr [Paul Siebeck], 1930); E. Käsemann, *Leib und Leib Christi, eine Untersuchung zur paulinischen Begrifflichkeit* (Tübingen: J. C. B. Mohr, 1933); E. Käsemann, *Das wandernde Gottesvolk, eine Untersuchung zum Hebräerbrief* (Göttingen: Vandenhoeck & Ruprecht, 1939, 1957); E. Haenchen, "Gab es eine vorchristliche Gnosis," *ZThK* (1952), pp. 123ff.; K. G. Kuhn, "Die Sektenschrift und die iranische Religion," *ZThK* (1952), pp. 296ff.; E. Haenchen, "Das Buch Baruch; Ein Beitrag zum Problem der christlichen Gnosis," *ZThK* (1953), pp. 123ff.; E. Peterson, "Der Hass wider das Fleisch; Versuchung und Fall durch die Gnosis," in *Wort und Wahrheit* (Vienna: 1952), pp. 5ff.

The tendency of some researchers to expand the concept of "Gnosticism" so that ultimately it includes Plato, and a certain pan-Gnosticism of the exegesis derived from Hellenism should have been corrected by the recently found Palestinian texts. For an understanding of early Church dogmatics, however, the outline of Gnosticism provided here is to be presupposed.

Christian Gnosticism, in the form in which Irenaeus (c. 130–c. 200) pre-supposed and characterized it in his polemical writing, and in the form in which Hippolytus (c. 170–c. 236) knew it and the Alexandrians integrated it in a churchly fashion and sought thereby to overcome it, was obviously made possible because Gnosticism believed in a redeemer figure.[10] What would be more logical than to identify this redeemer figure with the divine in Jesus Christ? Wherever this happened, the concrete historicity of Jesus, his normal humanity, would have had to appear to be secondary or even unreal; Christian Gnosticism was fundamentally "docetic." The human and earthly aspects of Jesus could only be understood as something inauthentic, even unreal, since they belonged to the lower sphere of reality which was enslaved in inauthenticity. Thus the Church necessarily had to be inauthentic and ultimately unreal in its outwardly perceivable form: it included there all the "mere" believers who had not yet penetrated the "knowledge" which alone could save, that is, the "pistics" who were not yet "gnostics"! Christian Gnosticism signified the transformation of the Church into a mystery community.

The theology of the Alexandrians, especially that of Origen, was intended to integrate Christian Gnosticism into the established Church, and in so doing to surpass and to overcome it.

g. Clement. Clement[11] (c. 150–c. 215) never wrote a dogmatics; however, his three major writings (each having an orderly inner structure) do reveal a position which can justly be called "dogmatic." If his *Protrepticus* was an appeal to become a Christian in the form and with the thinking of the earlier Apologies, then his *Paedagogus* (the first Christian "ethics") develops the structure of this Christian existence, and his *Stromateis*, a loose collection of individual exposi-tions, leads to the depths of Christian Gnosticism. He approaches the Greek tradition with the same sense of victory as did the Apologists, but he has left the phase of struggle behind and now, delighted and proud of his learning, believes that he can express Christian proclamation as the completion and surpassing of all that had been passed down. The identification of the Logos with the divine world reason which rules everywhere and with the divine nature of Jesus Christ begins to have wide-reaching consequences: what the Church believes and teaches should be done is in fact the essence of reason. Thought and action become lucid and clear wherever the Logos is understood. And it is understood not just by the "Gnostic," but also by the mere "believer." Clement seeks to reunite what Gnos-ticism had divorced: knowledge and faith, the Old and the New Testaments, the heavenly and the earthly. In this, he is a theologian and dogmatician "of the Church." But nevertheless he shares with Christian Gnosticism the strict distinc-tion between knowledge and faith, and the path of his thought proceeds from faith toward knowledge, to which he assigns a relative but very significant priority. The

---

10. W. Völker, ed., *Quellen zur Geschichte der christlichen Gnosis* (Tübingen: J. C. B. Mohr, 1932).

11. For editions of Clement, see the standard collections of Church Fathers, espe-cially *ANCL*, vols. II, IV, XII. There is a masterful introduction with an exciting overview in H. Lietzmann, *A History of the Early Church*, tr. B. L. Woolf (London: Lutterworth, 1961), I and II, 275–95.

actual dogmatics of the East is initially marked, therefore, in a way which is fraught with consequences and very disquieting.

h. Origen. Origen (c. 185–c. 254),[12] who is superior to all other theologians of the early Church by virtue of the comprehensiveness of his knowledge and of his wisdom, was the first writer of a "dogmatics" (*peri archōn* = *De principiis* = On First Principles), which can be more or less reconstructed on the basis of Rufinus' (c. 345–410) translation, the critical commentaries of Jerome (c. 342–420), and the partially preserved original text in Greek. He was, to a much greater extent than Clement, a biblical theologian—his valuable work on the text history of the Old Testament is certainly well known. He was at the same time a "middle" Platonian, deeply imbued with the unconditional priority of the idea over every kind of outward appearance, and thus with the actual spiritual "sense" of every biblical citation in relationship to its "mere" historical form and content. He is the theologian of the Logos in the complete sense of the word: of the Logos which is eternal world meaning and world content just as it is temporal incidence, or, in the language of the Church, God's uncreated Son as well as God's revelation in created reality. He is, as theologian of the Logos, also theologian of the Church (which is understood exclusively on the basis of the Logos), in which, as Adolf von Harnack put it, religion is " 'true' in its mythical form"[13] and therefore the mere believer *(pistic)* does grasp the same and total truth as the knower *(Gnostic)*—although the latter is ranked higher than the former.

That the first great dogmatics of the Church, those of Origen, began with a concept of God which was philosophically (Platonically) determined had far-reaching consequences. God per se is at the acme of the system. The center is then formed by the Logos, uncreated as is the Father and yet the mediator to the infinite variety of created worlds (Origen cannot imagine a "beginning" and always thinks from timelessness into the temporal). The created, or better, the reality which goes forth out of God, appears in an infinite series of levels or stages, and just as in Plato and the Gnostics, matter is the most worthless level. Of course, as a theologian of the Church, which Origen definitely desires to be, he understands the Logos in its union with Jesus. He is a theologian of the incarnation, not of the cross: the incarnation is the initial point for the redemptive process of leading man to a higher level, of freeing man from what is material and low. This means, in regard to knowledge, that man, in recognizing that the Logos is in Jesus Christ, recognizes God and knows the meaning of all of reality. In regard to religious behavior, this means that man, in recognizing the Logos, will be dissociated progressively from the lower things, and at the end all humanity

---

12. See the edition of the Maurist Charles de la Rue, *Opera Omnia* . . . (Paris: 1733–59); based upon that, the edition of C. H. E. Lommatzsch (Berlin: 1831–48) and Migne, *PG*, XI–XVII. New edition: *GCS* since 1899. English selection in *ANCL*, vol. X. An especially impressive introduction is von Harnack, "System of Origen," *op. cit.*, II, 332–80; see also, by the same author, the article in *RGG*, 2nd ed., IV, 780ff., as well as H. Lietzmann, *op. cit.*, I and II, 295–317. For older literature see E. Preuschen in Schaff-Herzog, VIII, 268–73, and for newer literature, see Harnack, *loc. cit.*

13. Harnack, *RGG*, 2nd ed., IV, 783.

will be released from the material and in the process of *apokatastasis* will be brought to the meaning of their existence. It is obvious that the doctrine of free will plays an important role in this approach: the effect of the Logos in man finds its point of contact in the free will.

Origen's hermeneutic method corresponds then to the "idealism" of the total scheme. This great theologian of the Bible is interested in the actual text and in its historical understanding only for the sake of the actual and spiritual sense. In this he is not only in agreement with Clement and very broadly with the Apologists, but particularly with Philo (c. 20 B.C.– c. 50 A.D.), who had a strong influence upon the Alexandrians. In Origen, the doctrine of the manifold meanings of Scripture belongs to the totality of a system: the literal understanding of Scripture (and of the Rule of Faith) corresponds to the level of the pistic and is therefore important, because the mere believer who only comprehends the mythical (to put it in Harnack's terms) still grasps the truth in that form; the Gnostic is, however, higher, in that he receives the Word behind the words, the pneumatic sense beyond the literal sense—the allegorical understanding of Scripture is the nobler and higher one.

i. The Effects of Origen's Theology. In the course of later dogmatic work, Origen could be taken as pointing in a variety of directions. In his theology he tried to relate Biblicism and cosmological-ontological speculation, Church membership and Gnosticism, historicity and timelessness, faith and knowledge, and the obvious two-sidedness of his concept of the Logos made it possible for him to do this. For him, the Logos was the uncreated self-reflection and self-expression of the Father and simultaneously the conveyor of meaning to creation; it was timeless and, in Jesus, historical at the same time. But what the great Alexandrians were able to keep integrated later separated. The originally Gnostic-timeless, cosmological-ontological element of his theology, as it was absorbed into the Church, and accepted by the Catholic Church which was then emerging, could become the dominant theme of a theology which viewed the earthly Church as the location of the eternal, now become temporal, and the clergy (whom Origen did not appear to hold in high regard) as the initiated guardians of knowledge *(gnosis)*. This was the situation in Alexandria later on. On the other hand, the biblicistic-ethical elements were able to assert their independence, resulting in a concept of the Logos which placed it at the summit of creation and gave to man the task to embark upon the ascending road, under the guidance of the Logos. For a time, Antioch was the center of this kind of thinking. In the one as in the other case, Origen was not being followed directly. It could even be said that the great Trinitarian and Christological controversies of the following ages[14] discharged the tensions which Origen had still been able to avoid. Nevertheless, other theological currents were having their effect alongside of the Alexandrian theology of the Logos, the strongest one being that of Irenaeus, whose dogmatic position was established before Origen's.

---

14. We are not going to deal with these controversies here, but see Part 4, pp. 347ff.

j. Irenaeus. Irenaeus (c. 130–c. 300),[15] although he was the Bishop of Lyon
from about 177 on and although his major work, the *Adversus haereses (Against
Heresies),* is available only in Latin translation except for a few small portions,
should still be counted with the dogmaticians of the East, from which
region he originally came. He is discussed here after the Alexandrians, although
they came later in time, because his theological conception leads toward the
consummation of the early Catholic Church, in a different fashion than with the
Alexandrians; the high regard with which he was held in the West bears this out.
However, it is not possible to understand the basic conception of Athanasius
without Irenaeus.

Whereas the Alexandrians were trying to integrate Gnosticism into the fabric of the Church, Irenaeus, in his longest writing, devotes himself to the struggle
against Gnostic systems, about which we derive our greatest amount of information from the first book of the *Adversus haereses*. But the struggle only draws
out the theologian in Irenaeus: he is not engaging in dialogue primarily with
Hellenic and Hellenistic paganism, as were most of the Alexandrians, but with
the heresy which had broken out within the Church; thus a new front of dogmatic
activity becomes visible. Certainly Irenaeus speaks about the Logos, but it is
very clear that his major dogmatic concern is directed more toward the term
"life," if we want to try to reduce him to a schematic pattern. He does not
confront heresy with daring intellectual concepts (he can even be scornful of
these), but rather with the reality of redemption experienced in the Church, in
which the mortality of man is victoriously overcome by the life which conquers
death. Divine life, superior to death, has been revealed in Christ; even the Old
Testament is a witness to this. This life is the actual miracle per se: in Jesus
Christ, God has become man, so that fallen man might become what Jesus Christ
is.[16] This is the concept of recapitulation through Christ which is implied and
which permeates all of Irenaeus' thought: fallen creation is restored to its true
created nature in that in Christ God descends to it (see Eph. 1:10), and ultimately
it is perfected. It is not surprising that Irenaeus understands salvation as a process
of healing and speaks especially of baptism and the eucharist as means of healing.
This raises the question whether or not this is a reassertion of Pauline thinking;
in any event, Irenaeus is closer to Paul than were the Alexandrians. What distinguishes him from Paul is the way in which he sees salvation as an object; one
could say that for him justification has become healing salvation. It is clear that
Irenaeus, from this point of view, was able to think in a highly developed sense
of salvation-history. And his interpretation of Scripture corresponds to this: it is

15. Irenaeus, *Writings (ANCL*, vols. VI and IX); the short writing, "Demonstration
of the Apostolic Preaching," discovered in 1904 in Armenian, can be found with a German
translation in *Texte und Untersuchungen zur Geschichte der altchristlichen Literatur*, begründet von O. von Gebhardt and A. Harnack (Leipzig: 1882ff.); for English translations
see the standard collections, especially A. Roberts and W. H. Rambault in *ANCL* and J. A.
Robinson in the S.P.C.K. edition, *Translations of Christian Literature* (1920); most important
monograph: G. N. Bonwetsch, *Die Theologie des Irenäus* (Gütersloh: C. Bertelsmann, 1925).
16. Irenaeus, *Against Heresies*, V, Preface, 55, ". . . who did, through His transcendent love, become what we are, that He might bring us to be even what He is Himself";
see in general *Against Heresies*, V, xiv, 91–94.

much less influenced by the allegorical method than is that of the Alexandrians, and much more by the idea of the unfolding of the divine gift of salvation in a process which is virtually one of growth. Wherever, in later times, dogmatics assumes the form of salvation-history, there the thinking of Irenaeus is having its effect, either consciously or unconsciously. At the same time, wherever Irenaeus tends to understand salvation as a "thing," he is the pacesetter of the sacralism and sacramentalism in both theology and the Church, and in that very sense he is a theologian of the Catholicism which was then emerging.

k. The Later Dogmatics of the East. Since Irenaeus' "Demonstration" is not to be looked upon as a comprehensive dogmatic outline, we must conclude that in spite of Irenaeus the Church of the East had in Origen alone a dogmatician who dealt with the totality of Christian doctrine. The dogmaticians of the centuries of struggle which began with Arianism and led to the gradual dying out of Christological controversies did not produce total systems but rather individual expositions or collections. One may judge that in their dogmatic approach they did not move beyond what Irenaeus and Origen had done and had, each in his own way, sought to draw together into a unity. The nearest thing to an attempt at a total approach would be the *Catechetical Orations* of Gregory of Nyssa (c. 330–c. 395).[17] But Athanasius (c. 296–373), who left his mark so firmly upon the 4th century, has left us in his work on the incarnation *(Oratio de incarnatione)* a Christology and with it a theology of the Trinity, but not a complete system.[18] This is even more true of the later theologians of the East. It was not until much later, when the West had long taken over leadership in the area of theology, that another comprehensive theology was produced in the East, based upon the renewal of Aristotelianism: the *Fount of Wisdom* of John of Damascus (c. 675–c. 749)[19] became the concluding dogmatics of the Eastern Church.

The actual achievement of Eastern dogmatics since the 4th century has consisted more in the great influence it has exercised over the Church's decisions and the dogmas of the age. The decision on the theology of the Trinity, dramatic in every way, was necessitated by the Hellenization and orientalization of the Gospel which had become traditional by then. This led by its own inner logic to the conclusion that the Logos became the very epitome of created reality, elevated into the sphere of the divine (this was the point of view of those who distorted Origen's position in a rationalistic way), or that it was the divine gift to the ideal man Jesus. In either case, faith *in* Jesus Christ would have to appear nonsensical. The intent of Trinitarian dogma was to understand the Logos strictly as God

---

17. Migne, *PG*, XLV, 9ff. and J. H. Scrawley, ed., *Cambridge Patristic Texts* (Cambridge: University Press, 1903, 1956).

18. "On the Incarnation" (*LCC*, III, 55ff.); see also W. Schneemelcher, "Athanasius von Alexandrien als Theologe und als Kirchenpolitiker," *ZNW*, XLIII (1950/51), 242ff., and the literature given there; in addition, see the usual histories of doctrine, especially von Harnack, *op. cit.*, III, 272ff.

19. The most important part of the *Fount of Wisdom* is the section on orthodox faith, "An Exact Exposition of the Orthodox Faith" (*NPNF*, IX, 1ff.). It is the third section of the whole work. The first two contain the philosophical foundations and a rebuttal of the heresies.

himself (this was the meaning of the term *homoousios* which was ultimately to carry the day) and God's nature as being in three and yet a unity ("three persons, one nature"). If the dissolution of the Christian kerygma had happened by means of the terminology of Hellenism, then its restoration was accomplished with the same terms, and that must mean that the formulae had to be paradoxical. Similarly paradoxical were the dogmatic decisions in the Christological controversy: based upon the presupposition that the divine "nature" of Jesus Christ really was understood as godly or deity, it was possible in terms of Hellenistic thought either to assume that this godliness could only be connected with but not united with the human, or alternatively, to assume that the godly nature absorbed the human into itself. In the Definition of Chalcedon the Church rejected both views and stood firm with the paradoxical formulations that the divine and human "natures" in Jesus Christ, to put it briefly, are both indivisible and unconfused, that is, that they are in inexpressible and unmistakable unity. It is not our intent to discuss the actual terms here. The important thing is that both the Hellenization and the orientalization of the Church's language were brought to a halt by the setting up of a genuine paradox which in truth proclaimed the breakthrough of the Christian mystery through the whole rich and seductive world of conceptual formulae.

B. THE WEST

a. General Characteristics. In terms of both contents and method, the foundations of dogmatics are the work of the Church of the East.

For a long time, the West produced nothing comparable to the Eastern legacy in reference to either the method or the foundations of dogmatic work. Nonetheless, while the East became essentially reproductive very early, and the Eastern churches (both orthodox and heretical) viewed it as their very nature to preserve the once-for-all established dogma and to maintain the traditional forms, the occidental Church and theology remained in constant movement, in spite of all regard for the tradition. As far as dogmatics is concerned, the major contribution was made by the Latin or Roman heritage. Western dogmaticians are not characterized so much by the daring sweep of their thought as by their clear sense of order, authority, and practical-ethical action. Thus their dogmatic labors are defined methodologically by their striving for clear terminology, and substantively by their concern to be "of the Church" and their orientation toward ethics. If we may designate the dogmatics of the East as the doctrine of knowledge and of salvation, then we would call that of the West (without implying that the above-mentioned were lacking) the doctrine of man in the Church—more precisely, of acting man in an acting Church. The West seems to be virtually inexhaustible in its powers of creation and structuring. In any event, dogmatics has been fundamentally formed by the Latin West for over a thousand years, even though its real foundations do certainly lie in the East. This is equally true of Protestantism, whose mutual bonds with the Roman Church ought never to be forgotten when emphasizing the distinctions. If the East raised all of the fundamental questions which have remained the task of dogmatics, then the West has structured the answers definitively—so very much so that Evangelical dogmatics simply cannot be done without knowledge of Augustine or the great Scholastics.

b. Tertullian. Tertullian (c. 160–c. 220)[20] is the first real European in our context, and it is said of him quite rightly that he structured the concepts and terms for later Latin theology, with which it has worked up to today. He is also the first of the dogmaticians who enjoyed a formal legal education (and jurisprudence has played understandably a far greater role for the theological thought of the West than for the East). He is very much in debt to tradition in his general approach, as is evident in his ethical tracts, in his polemical writings, and in the controversy with Gnosticism (especially in his work *Against Marcion*) and with the representatives of Gnostic Christology *(Against Praxeas)*—particularly the tradition of Asia Minor. He is not nearly as creative as Origen would be or Irenaeus was (a strong influence upon him), but he possessed an extraordinary ability to structure things and at the same time a confident sense for the way which the Christology and anthropology of the Church would later follow. He is definitely a Catholic theologian—in his thinking the Scripture as norm is joined by the Rule of Faith. This is true even though he became a Montanist due to his ethical rigorism and as such battled with the Church: even his conversion to Montanism was a result of his traditionalism. He found in the Montanist movement what he regarded as the original essence of the early and true Church. The most important thing for him was the practical, ethical aspect—like many of the Latins Tertullian was not overly interested in speculation. This is not to say that he totally lacked an overarching conception, but that he declared this to be fit within the framework of the salvation-history thinking of Irenaeus and lacked any reference to the bold system which Origen would present. This all goes along with the fact that he remained without any direct relationship to Platonism and in his philosophical conception was essentially indebted to the Stoics.

c. Cyprian, Lactantius, Pelagius. The dogmatics of the West did not follow in the path of the Montanists, but of the Church theologian, Tertullian. This is true of Cyprian (d. 258)[21] with the one reservation that he can scarcely be regarded as a "dogmatic" writer, with the exception of his *De ecclesiae catholicae unitate (On the One Catholic Church)*. Still he should be named here, because

---

20. His works are in Migne, *PL*, vols. I and II; English editions in *ANCL* and *ANF*. A comprehensive introduction: Nathan Bonwetsch's article in *RE*, 3rd ed., XIX, 537ff.; see also Schaff's article in *SH*, XI, 305ff. Of the newer literature, see especially Joseph Lortz, *Tertullian als Apologet*, I (Münster: Aschendorff, 1927-28); J. Klein, *Tertullian; Christliches Bewusstsein und sittliche Forderungen* (Düsseldorf: Mosella-Verlag, 1940); A. Kolping, *Sacramentum Tertullianeum; Untersuchung über die Anfänge des christlichen Gebrauchs der Vokabel Sacramentum* (Regensburg-Münster: Potsberg, 1948).

21. His works (numerous old editions in the preparation of which Roman Catholics, Anglicans, and Reformed competed) are most easily accessible in *CSEL*. III (3 vols.) and in Migne, *PL*, vols. IIIf.; in English, see *The Writings (ANCL* [1869, Scotland], vols. VIII and XIII, and *ANCL* [1886, America], vol. V); more recent general discussions: A. d'Alès, *La Théologie de St. Cyprien* (Paris: G. Beauchesne, 1922²); J. Boutet, *St. Cyprien, Eveque de Carthage et Martyr* (Aubanel Freres: Libraires-Editeurs, 1922).

Cyprian, following after Tertullian and preceding Augustine (all three were from North Africa), expanded the actual "catholic" understanding of the Church and of theology in this kind of Church. Lactantius (c. 240–c. 320)[22] deserves more mention since in his *Divinae Institutiones* he produced a "regular" dogmatics (and apologetics), although in terms of intellectual power it cannot begin to compete with the work of the Greeks; he also attained importance in his contributions to anthropology, similar to Tertullian, especially with his little writing, *De opificio Dei*.[23]

In many ways, Pelagius (*fl.* 405–18)[24] can be looked upon as the heir of the old Latin theology. His doctrine on the "freedom of the will" follows generally along the path already described by the Latins in the 4th century (and by the Greeks as well). He was something like a "dogmatician," but his work on the Trinity is lost. Yet those writings which still exist indicate that he was a theologian whose position had to be taken seriously—Augustine did not have an unworthy thinker as his chief protagonist!

d. Augustine. Whereas the dogmatic labors of the Eastern Church rapidly ascended to their high-water mark, Origen, who left to his successors little more to do than to preserve, expand upon, defend, and integrate into the Church what he had accomplished, the West required centuries until it reached its summit in the work of Augustine (d. 604/5). This high-water mark has seldom been reached again since, and in the abundance of its many aspects it is certainly unique. Dogmatics will never reach the end of the legacy of the great African; it would be possible to conceive of the whole history of post-Augustinian dogmatics of Europe as the history of its understanding of Augustine.

Obviously, we can deal here only with Augustine's significance for dogmatics, and that only in the broadest of outlines. In doing so, we shall concentrate upon the core of his work, for Augustine was primarily a teacher and as such he relied upon dogma as something given—Harnack can go so far as to say that, since Augustine, dogma is the "building material" for the "cathedral" of dog-

---

22. Lactantius has also been published very early and then later in numerous editions. See *CSEL*, vols. XIX and XXVII (1-2) as well as Migne, *PL*, vols. VIf. (which is inferior to the Viennese edition). M. E. Heinig, *Die Ethik des Lactantius* (Grimma: F. Bode, 1887 [Leipzig dissertation]); F. Marbach, *Die Psychologie des Firmianus Lactantius* (1889 [Jena dissertation]). Now: H. Karpp, *Probleme altchristlicher Anthropologie; biblische Anthropologie und philosophische Psychologie bei den Kirchenvätern des dritten Jahrhunderts* (*Beiträge zur Förderung christlicher Theologie*, 44,3; Gütersloh: Bertelsmann, 1950), pp. 132ff. English edition of Lactantius in *ANCL*, vols. XXI–XXII (1871). See also *FC*, vol. XLIX (1964), for Books I–VII of *The Divine Institutes*.

23. "On the Workmanship of God" (*ANCL*, XXII, 49–91).

24. The works of the Irish-Scottish monk have largely been lost. Remnants (reworked in the Church) can be found in Migne, *PL*, vol. XLVIII, and above all in A. Souter, "Pelagius's Exposition of Thirteen Epistles of St. Paul," in *Texts and Studies*, ed. J. A. Robinson (Cambridge: The University Press, 1922–31), vol. IX. Also important: F. Loofs, article on Pelagius and the Pelagian controversy in *SH*, VIII, 438–44, with exhaustive references to sources and literature.

matics.[25] Certainly Augustine's undeniable influence on dogma is secondary to his influence on dogmatics (other than with, e.g., Athanasius).

The first contribution which Augustine made to the work of dogmatics was his own drawing together of all the spiritual and churchly development which had preceded, and which he appropriated in a very independent fashion in the course of a complex life. As a young man, already deeply involved in the question of the origin and nature of evil, he was attracted to the dualism of Manichaeism, after Cicero's *Hortensius* had provided him the initial start toward questioning the meaning of earthly possessions or poverty. But he remained neither with the one nor the other. Both of the spiritual forces which first formed him led him toward interior self-examination, and the question which he finally directed to the Church was the question of this inner being which the world could not fulfill, Aristotle's problematics not solve, and the appeal of the Skeptics not deafen. At first the Church was not able to provide an answer which convinced him; even a powerful figure like Ambrose at first only fascinated the young African with his rhetoric—although he also relieved Augustine of much of the torturous problem of the Old Testament (which seemed so superficial for a man of such inward inclination) by means of allegorical interpretation. Before Augustine became a Christian, the Bishop of Hippo Regius, and Father of the Church, he absorbed Neo-Platonism, which reached him via Marius Victorinus; however, he did not receive it primarily as a cosmological system but as a philosophy of the spiritual and the soul. Then, in a rather sudden turn-around, he departed from it and entered upon the way of ascetic Christianity. How many worlds had he traversed before he made that decisive step, before the God encountered him who was not the epitome of a speculative thought construct but the one who gives himself in freedom! But everything which Augustine had been and had thought through— Platonism, Aristotelianism, Stoicism, Neo-Platonism, Manichaeism, but above all Neo-Platonism—remained an indelible part of him as a teacher of the Church, because he remained aware of the questions he had once struggled with as he now dealt with the answer, and he interpreted this answer on the basis of the questions which had once been his. It has remained highly significant for the European Church that its greatest dogmatician was able to view the Christian life from outside, so to speak, because he had come into it from outside. This is part of the most important and most influential contribution which Augustine made to the history of dogmatics.

However, it is almost of greater importance that Augustine embarked upon the full exposition of his theology in the struggle with two church movements which, each in its own way, have demonstrated a remarkable permanence on European soil: we are speaking of Donatism and Pelagianism. Both of them have what one might call an "activistic" tendency: Donatism strives toward the "pure" Church (at least with its clergy), and Pelagianism, which is originally ascetic, wants to remove the excuse of Christians that they cannot "avoid" sin. The Western world has frequently been shaken and (fruitfully) provoked by move-

---

25. A. von Harnack, *History of Dogma*, tr. Buchanan *et al.* (7 vols.; London: Williams & Norgate, 1896–99), V, 5, n. 1.

ments which were similar to these two classical ecclesiological and soteriological heresies. And it was the great legacy of Augustine which preserved the power to call the Church back to its true mandate whenever it was wasting itself in activism or setting about to transform the Gospel into law. And all of this, although Augustine himself was an ascetic! However, he was not one in order to become a Christian, but as a result of the fact that he was a Christian! And he was not an ascetic marked by the disquiet of one having to accomplish something, but by the peace and stillness of receptivity.

Deum et animam scire cupio (God and the soul, that is what I desire to know)[26]—this was the way that the young Augustine formulated the basic question of his piety and his thought. God and the soul—he could conceive of the two only in relationship to one another. The soul, which is created for God,[27] needs God. But Augustine knew the other side, that this soul, as it is, does not love God willingly. Therefore, the mystical and Neo-Platonic answer is not adequate, as it shows the soul how to proceed up to its origins and to pure existence. He became a Christian as it became clear to him that God, who is certainly pure, original, eternal Being, is not the goal of human endeavors but rather the One who overcomes the soul in the overwhelming power of his grace. This became clear to him in relationship to Jesus Christ. It was affirmed for him by the Church. He received it in faith. Thus Neo-Platonism, which remained systematically an influence, is set under a new sign. The question of God, the question of human existence, the question of truth—all of these lead up to the question of grace, which is the "fundamental notion of Augustinianism."[28]

It is significant both for the later course of dogmatics and for Augustine himself that he then appears in a dual and contradictory light, seen from the issue of grace.

e. The Reformation View of Augustine. The Reformers and the Orthodox, the Reformed almost more than the Lutherans, claimed Augustine as their great spokesman among all of the Church Fathers (without being totally uncritical of him). They did this especially in regard to the anti-Pelagian element of his doctrine of grace. Who else had contested as much as he, man's (active) capacity to receive grace, who else had emphasized the failure of free will (which otherwise was very much a part of his thinking) in relation to salvation, who else had grasped the power of "original sin" so thoroughly? In spite of all the Pelagian insistence upon nature and its possible virtue, he countered rigorously with his insistence upon grace alone. As the Reformers saw it, Paul was really understood here; here, thinking of his *De Spiritu et litera (On the Spirit and the Letter)* and its significance for the Reformers, the distinction between law and Gospel, between the letter and the spirit, was brought to full theological validity. Here man's arrogant and yet torturous way from below to above was cut off radically and God's honor protected against all human vanity! Here God's predestination was witnessed to

---

26. Augustine, *Soliloquies*, I, 7 (*NPNF,* VII, 539).
27. Augustine, *Confessions*, I, 1 (*NPNF,* I, 45).
28. Harnack, *op. cit.*, V, 203.

powerfully, and here was one who did not shrink back from the most horrifying consequences of the doctrine of election! Here the foundation of thought really was the freedom of divine grace as it is proclaimed in the Word and represented in the sacraments! And then the Reformed theologians specifically could continue: here, in the doctrine of the sacraments, God's gracious freedom was truly upheld in that the elements were understood merely as signs, the sacrament itself as the *verbum visibile* (visible Word), in short, the sacrament as a means and an instrument but not as effective in itself. In addition, the Reformers could, as they claimed the great African, appeal to the "Augustinian reactionary movements" of the Middle Ages, and this they did, particularly in regard to the doctrine of the sacraments. No one can be surprised that the dogmatic writings of the Reformers, especially those of Calvin, are well sprinkled with quotations from Augustine.

    f. The "Catholic" Understanding of Augustine. And yet, as much as Augustine was a Reformer of the Church and its doctrine in his age, and as much as the Reformation of the 16th century would not have been historically possible without the centuries of his influence, it is not simply the case that the African stood on the side of the Reformers alone. The Reformers quote in the way that was generally done in previous times: they lift out of the works of the Fathers individual sentences or passages without thinking through the total structure of the thought behind these quotations. The concept of the "personality" whose single major thought is then expressed in manifold utterances is part of a later age. Thus the Reformers could find in Augustine an echo and thereby a certain legitimation of their own insights without having to grapple with the fact that they would have to reject other statements by the same Father of the Church. Their Roman opponents proceeded in the same way and with the same right. One must ask whether or not the Catholics, in spite of their unequivocal rejection of decisive elements of Augustine's thought, were not relatively closer to the Father of the Church than were the Reformers. Certainly Augustine contested the active capability of man in his original sin to receive grace. But he established this incapability from two directions: on the one hand, on the basis of man's self-love which absolutely hinders his loving God and adhering to God; and on the other hand, man's natural and hereditary concupiscence (which Augustine did not fail to understand erotically). The Reformers could accept the first reason, but the second they actually could not. Further, it is certainly true that Augustine understood grace as a pure gift—but, just as original sin was a vice which resulted out of the genetic process, so grace was also a power, a supernatural gift, which was given to man in an incomprehensible fashion, as irresistible grace. Thus it was ultimately the extreme magnification of the natural and the effecting of a new ability which resided in the one so gifted. Thus, to put it in Lutheran terms, there emerges behind the "theology of the cross" a "theology of glory" (*theologia crucis* and *theologia gloriae*): the person transformed by grace, the person in the Church, in the sphere of grace of the sacraments, is now able by the power of "cooperating grace" (*gratia cooperans*) to do what man otherwise is incapable of. Salvation, which Augustine certainly did not understand as a process of healing as did many Greek Fathers, still became the origin of such a process. And the Church, whose holiness Augustine had so clearly seen as residing in grace in the struggle with

Donatism, and that means in the grace of the Word and the sacrament, now became an institution purveying grace. To be sure, it did so in such a fashion that its earthly form was always a body related to the heavenly, invisible, and incomprehensible reality of its *anima ecclesiae* (soul of the Church). And yet the body participates in the splendor of the soul by means of the grace at work in it and through it. And this paves the way for the thinking which dominates the Middle Ages: just as grace was a magnification and surpassing of nature, the Church was the comprehensive surpassing of the "earthly city"; the result had to be a two-leveled kind of thinking which found its greatest exposition in the great Scholastics: grace and nature, the city of God and the earthly city, are now ordered as two levels within the same being, one over the other (although that was not the way Augustine had described it). Eschatology, which Augustine had not forgotten, became a supernatural condition which would absorb the natural into itself by virtue of its inherent supernatural quality and would ultimately fill nature with grace! When, after receiving the shock which the Reformation had brought, Roman Catholicism was reflecting upon a new fundamental position (in Trent), it was again concepts of Augustine in new clothing which were used to counter the Reformation and its late medieval opponents. Augustine became once again, in the 16th century, the "destiny" of dogmatic thought and of the structures of the Church.

  g. The Later Latin Fathers. Compared to Augustine[29] the later Latin Fathers of the early Church are not very significant. Alongside the Greek writings of Dionysius the Pseudo-Areopagite, Boethius (c. 480–c. 524)[30] became important because he translated and commented on Aristotle and the Neo-Platonist Porphyry (c. 232–303). The actual dogmaticians of late Latin antiquity either defended Augustine, as did Fulgentius of Ruspe (468–533) and Caesarius of Arles (c. 470–542), or diluted his theology in the direction of what has been called Semi-Pelagianism since the post-Reformation period; this was done by John Cassian (c. 360–435) and Vincent of Lerins (d. before 450).

---

29. His works are published on the basis of the Maurist edition: Migne, *PL*, vols. XXXII–XLVII. There are many English editions, especially in *NPNF, FC, LCC*, and many others.
  The literature is too vast to be summarized. Overviews are found in the encyclopaedias, and very detailed in Harnack, *op. cit.*, V, 61ff. Newer and especially important publications: Erich Dinkler, *Die Anthropologie Augustins* (Stuttgart: Kohlhammer, 1934); H. Barth, *Die Freiheit der Entscheidung im Denken Augustins* (Basel: Helbing & Lichtenhahn, 1935); J. Barion, *Plotin und Augustin; Untersuchungen zum Gottesproblem* (Berlin: Junker & Dünnhaupt, 1935); W. Kamlah, *Christentum und Geschichtlichkeit; Untersuchungen zur Entstehung des Christentums und zu Augustins "Bürgerschaft Gottes"* (Stuttgart: Kohlhammer, 1951²); earlier: *Christentum und Selbstbehauptung; historische und philosophische Untersuchungen zur Entstehung des Christentums und zu Augustins "Bürgerschaft Gottes"* (Frankfurt/Main: Klostermann, 1940); D. Hofmann, *Der Kirchenbegriff des Hl. Augustinus; in seinen Grundlagen und in seiner Entwicklung* (Munich: Max Hueber, 1933); M. Grabmann and J. Mausbach, ed., *Aurelius Augustinus; Festschrift der Görres-Gesellschaft* (Cologne: Bachem, 1930).
  30. Migne, *PL*, vols. LXIIIf.

IV. The Dogmatics of the Middle Ages

a. Evaluation and Significance of the Middle Ages. The term "Middle Ages" was coined during the Renaissance. It bears a value judgment: the Middle Ages are the interim period between the antique blooming of humanity and the new age which the Renaissance viewed as then emerging. The later concept of the "Dark Ages" does not add much to this value judgment.

There are few in our time who would agree with this value judgment. The term "Middle Ages" has become a technical term: it is merely the designation of the period which begins with the collapse of classical antiquity and ends with the Renaissance, Humanism, the Reformation, and the Enlightenment. When this end in fact took place is much more difficult to determine in terms of the history of thought than it is in the special case of the history of dogmatics. From the perspective of the general history of ideas, it could be asked whether the breakthrough of the modern period did not begin until the Enlightenment of the 17th century.[1] For the history of dogmatics, Luther's emergence and that of the other Reformers is a profound turning point which was surpassed by no later figure or event.

There has recently been a general change in thought which has indicated that the Middle Ages are looked upon as the essence of clarity and coherence, as the youthful developmental phase of the European spirit, the epoch of wholeness, of the unity of thought and action. Protestantism, in contrast, appears as the collapse of this mighty structure, as the disintegration of unity, as extremism and impoverishment. This new value judgment can be regarded as a sign of "the end of the modern age"[2] or as the result of effective Roman Catholic propaganda. It is quite certainly about as relevant as the thesis of the "Dark Ages"! The most important of all questions for the history of dogmatics is being sounded here: Was what happened in the Reformation only the result of an intellectual process (which

---

1. E. Troeltsch, *Kultur der Gegenwart* (1906, 2nd ed. 1909; n.l.), I, 1, 4, and *Das Wesen des modernen Geistes*, in *Gesammelte Schriften* (Tübingen: J. C. B. Mohr, 1926, and Aalen: Scientia, 1961–66), IV, 297ff., purely a historical treatment; more general: K. Heussi, *Altertum, Mittelalter und Neuzeit in der Kirchengeschichte* (Tübingen: J. C. B. Mohr, 1921); see also H. Hoffmann, "Neuzeit . . . ," *RGG*, 2nd ed., IV, 524ff.

2. Romano Guardini, *The End of the Modern World; a Search for Orientation*, tr. J. Theman and H. Burke (New York: Sheed and Ward, 1956 [g1951³]).

then could easily be understood as a process of disintegration) or was it the return of the Church to the Word out of which it lives?

In any event, one must conclude that the dogmatics of the Reformation and the Orthodox periods cannot be understood without precise knowledge of the dogmatic work of the Middle Ages. For too long a time it has not been recognized that the Reformers grew up in the thought-forms of the Middle Ages. Is it not reasonable to assume that their theology in its dogmatic development would be more strongly influenced by their early conditioning than is often admitted? Walther Köhler has posed this question more emphatically than others, and he has undertaken to interpret the significant dogmatic divergencies like the communion controversy between Luther and Zwingli from their medieval roots.[3] Who really can understand the Reformers as dogmaticians without seeing them in the contexts that were already there, for example, Luther in the setting of late Occamism, Zwingli in the *via antiqua* (ancient way, as modified as it was), and Calvin in Realism (certainly conditioned by the effects of Duns Scotus)? Even the Evangelical theologian who as a matter of principle refuses to know anything about the Middle Ages will have to know something of this dark period if he wants to understand "his" Reformers.

b. Genuine Dogmatics? The dogmatics of the Middle Ages in Europe as well as in educationally and culturally superior Byzantium were characterized by the fact that this was a period of victory on the part of the Church. For the dogmatician of the Middle Ages paganism was either a matter of the past or a phenomenon on the margins of his world. This world as such had become "Christian."

We have already considered the fact that the necessity of Christian doctrine is in part based upon the way in which a "natural" self-understanding of man will encounter the proclamation of the Gospel either in opposition or with the claim that it be affirmed. One could be tempted to assume that such a "natural" self-understanding was totally lacking in the Middle Ages.

Superficially this assumption would be confirmed in that medieval dogmatics appears for the most part to be occupied with reworking the dogmatic legacy of the early Church as far as it was available in written form—which meant in particular to analyze it terminologically and dialectically. Abelard (1079–1142)[4]

---

3. See especially W. Köhler, *Zwingli und Luther; Ihr Streit über das Abendmahl nach seinen politischen und religiösen Beziehungen (Quellen zur Reformationsgeschichte*, 6; 2 vols., I: Leipzig: Heinsius, 1924; II: Gütersloh: Bertelsmann, 1953).

4. Abelard, *Opera*, ed. V. Cousin (2 vols.; Paris: A. Durand, 1849, 1859); and Migne, *PL*, vol. CLXXVIII; *Sic et non*, ed. E. L. T. Henke and G. S. Lindenkohl (Marburg: 1851). S. M. Deutsch, *Petrus Abelard; ein kritische Theologe des zwölften Jahrhunderts* (Leipzig: S. Hirzel, 1883).

On Abelard and the whole period of Scholasticism, see Martin Grabmann, *Geschichte der scholastischen Methode* (Basel: B. Schwabe, 1909–11, 1957); Arthur Michael Landgraf, *Einführung in die Geschichte der theologischen Literatur der Frühscholastik* (Regensburg: Gregorius-Verlag, 1948) and *Dogmengeschichte der Frühscholastik* (Regensburg: F. Pustet, 1952–56). On Abelard see especially M. Grabmann, *op. cit.*, II, 168ff.; A. M. Landgraf, *Einführung . . .*, pp. 62ff.

In regard to the dogmatic significance of Abelard, we refer to A. Ritschl's famous interpretation in *A Critical History of the Christian Doctrine of Justification and Reconciliation*, tr. J. S. Black (Edinburgh: Edmonston & Douglas, 1872).

in his work *Sic et non* brought together quotations from the Fathers, but he did not do so out of historical interest, nor in the intention of gleefully opposing the "yes" of the one Father to the "no" of the other, but rather to apply the dialectic method, that is, the intellectual endeavor which seeks to bring contradictions into agreement with each other *(concordantia discordantium)*. Peter Lombard (c. 1100–60)[5] concentrated this method so much in his four books of *Sentences* that his chief work became the normal dogmatic textbook of the Middle Ages. Would it not be safe to assume that in such dogmatic efforts the Christians were "alone in their own company," uninfluenced by any "alien" understanding of either self or of the world? And is not the whole schools-science of dogmatics, Scholasticism, basically pursuing this very approach?

This superficial impression is deceptive. The very well-known fact that the Middle Ages were shaken by the struggle of the most varying theological directions indicates that we are not dealing here with merely the formal and even formalistic reception of the legacy of the ancient Church, but rather that we have genuine dogmatics and real decisions before us. The "natural" self-understanding which medieval theology obviously would not find "outside" the Church has been integrated into the Church, and it would be a marvel if anything else were the case. Just as peoples of all kinds gathered within the medieval cathedrals, and just as their façades revealed not only Christian forms and emblems, so also the theology of the age, which is so often compared with the cathedrals, had room enough for man too, as he understood himself. This is what makes the dogmatics of the Middle Ages dramatic—it carries its partner as it were within itself. But it was not a dogmatic meditation lost in self-analysis.

c. The Problem of Universals. The most concrete expression of this is in the fact that medieval dogmatics are closely related to philosophy in a way which cannot be observed of any other complete epoch. The dogmaticians of this age are the philosophers of their day. As both philosophers and dogmaticians they stand in a specific tradition which was decisively molded by Plato, and then later, after his total work became known, by Aristotle—but continually in such a way that Neo-Platonism set the atmosphere within which the great predecessors were understood. However, the dogmaticians of the Middle Ages were not, as philosophers, mere reproducers. This they could not be because of the limitations of the materials which had been preserved for them, at least in the first centuries of the period. But for the most part they were much too lively to be only repeaters.

---

5. The *Sentences* have been given a fine edition by the Franciscans of Quaracchi (*Petri Lombardi Libri IV Sententiarum* [2 vols.; Ad Claras Aquas: Quaracchi, 1916]); the nearest best edition, Migne, *PL*, vol. CXCII, has been surpassed; however, Migne offers all of the other writings of Peter Lombard in *PL*, vols. CXCf. See also M. Grabmann, *op. cit.*, II, 359ff.; A. M. Landgraf, *Einführung*, pp. 93ff.; and J. N. Espenberger, *Die Philosophie des Petrus Lombardus* (Münster: Aschendorff, 1901).

The *Sentences* of Peter Lombard, written between 1148 and 1150, treat in Book 1 of the mystery of the Trinity, in 2 of the creation and of sin, in 3 of the incarnation of the Word, and in 4 of the doctrine of the signs or the sacraments. The Church Father quoted most extensively is Augustine, and aside from him especially Gregory the Great (c. 540–604) and Jerome (c. 342–420); there is very little reference to the dogmatics of the early Eastern Church, although there are references to Origen (c. 185–c. 254).

Thus, in their own way they did philosophy, and with the help of this philosophy they did their dogmatics (philosophy was regarded very early as "ancillary to theology"—an *ancilla theologiae*).[6]

The combination of theology and philosophy and the energy with which the Middle Ages sought to relate faith to thought led to the result that one philosophical problem became the very essence of the dominant theological directions: the problem of universals *(universalia)*. This problem, in which metaphysics, epistemology, and logic all are joined, is by no means the great issue of Scholasticism. But it was the catalyst for the historical differences which developed, and the Scholastic dogmaticians are usually grouped according to the solutions they found. What was at stake?[7] In terms of the literature involved, it concerns the interpretation of the introduction *(Isagoge)* to the *Categories* of Aristotle written by the Neo-Platonist Porphyry and commented on by Boethius. The issue itself: the reality of the general concepts contained in or presupposed by every judgmental proposition *(genus* and *species)*. The person making the judgment perceives with his senses, and what he perceives is always individual objects. If this person then utters a judgment, it combines concepts with whatever it was that he outwardly perceived. The conceptual and general components of his judgment are not given via the senses. The question is, then, what is the type and validity of this nonobjective component in the process of knowing?

d. Realism. Answers were already available from the period of antiquity. The first answer went back to Plato and was known to the early Middle Ages both through his *Timaeus* and especially through the mediation of the Neo-Platonists. It can be formulated with the thesis that what is truly real is only the nonobjective, nonsensible essences, the general concepts; the incidental or special forms, that which is available to the senses at any given time, is only of derived reality, and is based upon the nonobjective essence. This view, Realism, is obviously consequent Idealism. In the early Middle Ages, it was held especially by John Scotus Erigena (c. 810–c. 877),[8] and later by Anselm of Canterbury

---

6. C. Baeumker (*Kultur der Gegenwart*, in W. Wundt *et al.*, *Allgemeine Geschichte der Philosophie* [Leipzig: Taübner, 1913[2]], I, 5, p. 348) observes that Peter Damian (1007–72) was the one who coined the term.

7. Regarding the universals controversy, see especially (aside from M. Grabmann, *op. cit.*) Maurice de Wulf, *History of Medieval Philosophy*, tr. E. C. Messenger (2 vols.; New York: Dover Publications, 1952); I, 137ff. and *passim*; Windelband, Heimsoeth, ed., *A History of Philosophy*, tr. J. H. Tufts (2 vols.; New York: Harper, 1958), I, 287ff.; J. H. Löwe, *Der Kampf zwischen Nominalismus und Realismus im Mittelalter; sein Ursprung und sein Verlauf* (Prag: Kosmack & Neugebauer, 1876); J. Reiners, *Der aristotelische Idealismus in der Frühscholastik* (1907; n.l.), and *Der Nominalismus in der Frühscholastik; ein Beitrag zur Geschichte der Universalienfrage im Mittelalter* (Münster: Aschendorff, 1910); see also W. Betzendörfer, *Glauben und Wissen bei den grossen Denkern des Mittelalters* (Gotha: L. Klotz, 1931); Heinz Heimsoeth, *Die sechs grossen Themen der abendländischen Metaphysik und der Ausgang des Mittelalters* (Berlin-Steglitz: Junker & Dünnhaupt, 1934).

8. *Works*, ed. by H. J. Floss for Migne, *PL*, vol. CXXII; chief works: *De divisione naturae (On the Division of Nature)* and *Liber de praedestinatione (Book on Predestination)*. T. Christlieb, *Leben und Lehre des Johannes Scotus Erigena, in ihrem Zusammenhang mit der vorhergehenden und unter Angabe ihrer Berührungspuncte mit der neueren Philosophie und Theologie dargestellt* (Gotha: 1860); article by S. M. Deutsch in *SH*, X, 303–307; H. Dörries, *Zur Geschichte der Mystik; Erigena und der Neuplatonismus* (Tübingen: Mohr, 1925).

(c. 1033–1109) and William of Champeaux (c. 1070–1121). John Scotus Erigena is, of all these early figures, the one who integrated Neo-Platonism most thoroughly into Christian thought. The special and perceivable is for him established only through the general and the conceptual; it has therefore only derived being and occupies the very lowest level. Higher up in order is the concept, or rather, what manifests itself in the concept, original being. This in turn reaches its highest point in the being of God which is the foundation for everything and which itself is not founded by anything. The knowing spirit participates, as the one knowing, understanding, penetrating beyond the sensibly perceivable, in the original and divine being. It is only a short step from here to Pantheism: should not God be the concealed interior aspect of reality, which reveals itself only to thinking or contemplative knowledge? And does this not mean, as W. Windelband expressed it, that "God and the world . . . are one," in that "the same 'nature' *(physis)* . . . is, as creative unity, God, and as created plurality, the world?"[9] Scotus Erigena, who inaugurated the theological thinking of the Middle Ages, grasped at the most extreme of possibilities with a great sense of daring. But he did not fully realize them. And the other, later "Realists," Anselm being their chief, did everything they could to maintain the ontologism of their thinking in agreement with their faith. This meant that for them God, whom they called the *ens realissimum* (the most real being) and whose being sustained the being and existence of all creation, was actually not the summit of an ontological structure but primarily the God of man *(Deus homo)*. The creator of the "ontological proof of the existence of God"[10] is also the man who tried to answer the question *Cur Deus homo?* (why did God become man?); the theologian who understood God as the most real being *(ens realissimum)* also formulated the motto of Scholasticism according to which theology (in good Augustinian fashion) is nothing else than *fides quaerens intellectum*[11] (faith seeking understanding). Nevertheless, none of this prevented Realism from being ultimately mystical contemplation transformed into the realm of pure thought: just as the basic act of mysticism consists of penetrating from the plurality and disintegration, even the inauthenticity of the given to the depths of the one and unspeakable reality, for Realism the comprehension of plurality within a concept, the ordering of its elements within a universal, consists of reducing this plurality to its ontological authenticity, or the

---

9. Windelband(-Heimsoeth), *op. cit.*, I, 290.

10. The proof is found in the *Proslogium*, 2–4. Anselm's works are in Migne, *PL*, vols. CLVIIIf.; newest edition by F. S. Schmitt, *Opera Omnia* (Edinburgh: Nelson, 1946–61). Editions of single works: in the *Florilegium Patristicum, Cur Deus homo* (1920), *Proslogium*, and *Ep. De incarnatione Verbi* (1931) (regarding the latter work see A. Wilmart, *Le premier ouvrage de saint Anselme contre le trithéisme de Roscelin; Recherches de théologie ancienne et médiévale* [1931], III, 20–36; n.l.); further, Augustinus Daniels, Anselm's *Proslogion*, etc. in *Quellenbeiträge und Untersuchungen zur Geschichte der Gottesbeweise im 13. Jahrhundert, mit besonderer Berücksichtigung des Arguments im Proslogion des hl. Anselm* (Münster: Aschendorff, 1909); ET: *St. Anselm (Proslogium, Monologium; An Appendix in Behalf of the Fool by Gaunilon; and Cur Deus Homo)*, tr. S. N. Deane (La Salle, Ill: Open Court Publishing, 1944, 1962).

11. This was supposed to have been the title of Anselm's *Proslogium* as he intended it; see the foreword to the writing. Regarding the problem, see Karl Barth, *Fides quaerens intellectum, Anselm's Proof of the Existence of God in the Context of His Theological Scheme*, tr. I. W. Robertson (Richmond: John Knox Press, 1960 [g1931]).

derived being to its original being. Thinking becomes thereby intellectual mysticism. This is the only way to understand that for Realism the concept "being" contains the concept of value within itself: the higher "being" is the higher value.

e. Nominalism. In the same way that Realism represented a renewal of Platonism, in a Christian transformation, its opponent, Nominalism, represented the application of the logical, epistemological, and ontological thought of Aristotle. In its oldest form, it dealt primarily with his book *Categories*, for the complete Aristotle first became known to the High Middle Ages via the mediation and commentaries of the Spanish (Islamic and Jewish) philosophers. The term "Nominalism" has, first, a negative meaning in contradistinction to every form of Realism, in that the universals are never "substances." Only individual things are "substances." Its positive meaning states that the concepts which we use are the product of our spirit; they are (this is the most radical version) in truth merely names *(nomina)* which we use for those things which reveal certain mutual empirical characteristics. In its radical form Nominalism asserts that our thinking comprehension is exclusively our own concern and the concepts or "names" we select are exclusively our choice; the names are merely means to understanding and communication, and there is nothing essentially real before or behind the objects to which they correspond. The first great defender of Nominalism (comparable in reverse to John Scotus Erigena) was the most radical, and he thrust himself right into the middle of theology with his ideas: Roscellinus of Compiègne[12] (d. c. 1125) understood the Trinity in such a way that he encountered in the realm of experience the Father, the Son, and the Holy Ghost, and that he could see their unity only in the concept "God" which was voluntarily brought in—and this obviously led to the objection of Tritheism. This particular application of Nominalism disqualified its total intention in the area of the Church for a long time. But it was not able to abolish it completely. For it was not only the empirical factor which was on the side of of Nominalism (the only givens we have are individual objects). It also raised the claim, which was persuasive to the thinking individual, that the object of knowledge can be integrated in one's own activity into one's own formulated contexts. Nominalism sat well with the domineering tendency which inheres in all knowledge as a way of gaining control over the world, whereas Realism to all appearances emphasized the humility of the receiver (who then, of course, as the one who penetrates intellectually into the depths really asserts his superiority over the mere object). In the last analysis, both Realism and Nominalism are expressions of the proud self-consciousness of the thinker, who in Realism understood the being of being in things and in Nom-

---

12. His position is known to us almost exclusively through the polemics of his opponents (Anselm and William of Champeaux—see p. 95, n. 10). See also F. Picavet, *Roscelin, Philosophe et Théologien, d'après la Légende et d'après l'Histoire; sa Place dans l'Histoire générale et comparés des Philosophies médiévales* (Paris: Alcan, 1911); M. de Wulf, *op. cit.*, pp. 148–50. Roscellinus' doctrine of the Trinity was condemned in 1092 at the Council of Soissons.

inalism assigned grandly to all things their place and meaning. Both could have led to "Enlightenment,"[13] and both did.

f. Attempted Solutions in High Scholasticism. From a scientific point of view, neither Realism nor Nominalism could be upheld in its pure form; they remained marginal phenomena in medieval theology. Realism had to find out how the *ens realissimum*, the unity in the depth of all that exists, could manifest itself in such a manifold and contradictory reality; it could not ignore the fact that reality certainly allows no unimpeded reduction to the being of beings (how are the many things with their contradictory accidence to be derived from or lead back to one being?). But then Nominalism had to cope with the question whether the thinking intellect established its "names" *(nomina)* arbitrarily, or whether there were indications emanating from the objective world which led to this or that designation. The philosophy of the High Middle Ages, which by now possessed knowledge of the real Aristotle and could apply the commentaries of both Islamic and Jewish philosophers, evolved moderate forms of Realism and Nominalism, especially in the systems known as *Thomism* and *Scotism*.

g. Thomas Aquinas, c. 1225–74. Thomism is "Aristotelian Realism": it combines the mystical and the ontological elements of older Realism with Aristotelianism upon the basis of the fundamental view that the controversial universals are "before all things" *(ante rem)* in God, and also "in all things" *(in re)* by virtue of divine creation, and then "after all things" *(post rem)* in the process of knowing. Together with Plato and older Realism, the universals have priority over the objective world. But then, in agreement with Aristotle, they are simultaneously the product of what the objective world (as form) grants: existence, meaning, value, and knowability. Thus they are also concepts in the knowing subject, but not established arbitrarily—they are determined by the authentic reality of the objects and ultimately by the Creator. It is clear that in this approach as well the knowing process is, in the final analysis, similar to a mystical event. But it is even more important to see that between the Creator and the knowing subject the authentic and formative aspect of the things themselves intervenes, which as existing objects participate in the being of God: epistemology results in a thought-through ontology, on the basis of which the subject discovers in what is given (and thus what is objective) both the limits and the validity of his own knowledge. Ever since Erich Przywara,[14] the ontological pattern described here has been designated as the *analogia entis* (analogy of being). Briefly, it means that between the Creator and the creature (and, within the created world, between the object of knowledge and the subject himself—the knower) there is a relationship of

---

13. H. Reuter, *Geschichte der religiösen Aufklärung im Mittelalter vom Ende des achten bis zum Anfang des 14. Jahrhunderts* (2 vols.; Berlin, 1875–77; repr. Aalen: Scientia Verlag, 1963).

14. Erich Przywara, *Analogia entis (I), Metaphysik* (Munich: J. Kösel & F. Pustet, 1932; Einsiedeln: Johannes Verlag, 1952).

correspondence despite all of the differences, and this is based upon the participation of creation in the being of the Creator. This is the great synthesis which is established here, and it then has its effect upon all intellectual objects, especially upon theology. The qualitative distinction between Creator and creature is understood as a difference in being which is gradual and therefore makes the analogy of both possible. The qualitative distinction between nature and grace is also overcome by means of a graduated synthesis. The same thing happens in the area of ethics, if we remember how Thomas combines the four Aristotelian cardinal virtues (prudence, temperance, fortitude, and justice) with the three "theological" virtues (faith, hope, and charity). Thomism, which certainly can be interpreted in a variety of ways, depending upon whether the scale of gradation is read from top to bottom (as with Thomas himself) or from bottom to top, is unquestionably in its basic structure the purest expression of "Catholicism": everything has its proper place, everything is subsumed into the total system, and even the lowest elements derive glory and honor from the first and highest. In all this, Thomas himself,[15] who definitely thinks from the top down to the bottom, is in all his thought a true theologian, the greatest dogmatician of the Church since Augustine, whose steps he more consciously followed than many would assume. His philosophy is the result of his fundamental theological approach: God, who exists in and out of himself, who in his "pure activity" is subject to no other condition than to himself, the Triune One in the fullness of his name and perfection, is at the same time the Creator and the Establisher of all truth which his creation can come upon either through thought or contemplation. Are we to say that Thomas was doing a philosophy of faith? That would be difficult to assert, for one thing is absolutely firm in his thinking, and that is that God can also be known "naturally" because he is the Creator and Establisher of all truth—theologically integrated ontology remains ontology, and the nature surpassed by grace remains nature!

   h. Duns Scotus, c. 1264–1308. It is only with reservations that we may

---

15. The complete Latin edition known as the *Leonina* has been appearing in Rome since 1882. Standard edition of *Summa Theologica*, tr. Fathers of the English Dominican Province (3 vols.; New York: Benziger Bros., 1947–48); an abridged edition of this translation is in *GBWW*. See also Thomas Aquinas, *Summa Theologica* [die deutsche Thomas Ausgabe], tr. Dominicans and Benedictines of Germany and Austria (Salzburg: Anton Pustet, 1933–). His *Summa contra gentiles* ("philosophical Summa") is a kind of apologetics— ET: *On the Truth of the Catholic Faith; Summa contra Gentiles,* tr. A. C. Pegis *et al.* (5 vols.; Garden City: Doubleday, 1955). The vast older literature on Thomas is indexed in P. Mandonnet and J. Destrez, *Bibliographie thomiste* (Paris: J. Vrin, 1921, now 1960), and since then in *Bulletin Thomiste.*

   The divisions of the *Summa Theologica:* I. Of God; II, i. Of the Movement of Rational Creatures to God; II, ii. Of the Types of Man in Particular (Ethics); III. Of Christ (Christology and doctrine of the sacraments; the work ends abruptly in the doctrine of penitence; a supplement was added in later centuries). M. Grabmann has written a useful book, *Introduction to the Theological Summa of St. Thomas,* tr. J. S. Zybura (St. Louis: B. Herder, 1930).

regard the great protagonist of Thomas, the Franciscan Johannes Duns Scotus,[16] as his real opponent. Duns Scotus is not a Nominalist, as Roscellinus once was and as William of Occam would be. To be sure, the universals are for him concepts for the understanding of the objective world, and to be sure, he refuses to consider what rank they may have over or before the things themselves. But he is convinced that the concepts which are formed in our intellect are not established arbitrarily but are the result of an inner necessity in the objective order of things. Therefore, in many ways Duns Scotus can be viewed as closer to Thomas than to many of the earlier or later Nominalists. Nevertheless, the intellectual world of the great Scotsman is already "more modern" than that of Thomas. Where Thomas was still confident that he had proved many dogmas to be scientifically necessary, Duns Scotus is more reserved; he is concerned only with the scientific possibility of a dogma, for it is the will which then decides, and not as with Thomas the intellect primarily. The primacy of the will, which Duns Scotus upholds both in his concept of God and in his anthropology, implies that the world of faith is no longer without its own questions. Augustine and Anselm may be having their influence here, but the world in which Duns Scotus proclaimed the primacy of the will is already the world of the late Middle Ages, in the process of disintegration.

i. Other Scholastics of the High Middle Ages. It would be a most unfortunate abbreviation if we were to base our picture of the theological work of the Middle Ages solely upon the various positions taken in regard to the universals controversy. There were great theologians, particularly in High Scholasticism, who did not make significant contributions to this battle, but who, in their interpretation of the *Sentences* of Peter Lombard, left mighty theological works to history. Of these we would name, first of all, two Franciscans with particular emphasis because they both tended toward Realism while their Order later became the bastion of the Nominalistic directions. Alexander of Hales (c. 1170–1245), who became a Minorite later on in his career, left a comprehensive *Summa totius theologiae*,[17] and his student, Bonaventure (1223–74), wrote a strongly mystical commentary on the *Sentences* (under the profound influence of Dionysius the Pseudo-

---

16. The *Opera,* ed. F. Vives (26 vols.; Paris: 1891–95); now appearing: crit. ed. studio et cura Commissionis Scotisticae ad fidem codium editum, praeside C. Balic (Rome: 1950ff.); the chief work, *Commentaria Oxoniensia* on Peter Lombard's *Sentences,* has been edited by the Franciscans of Quaracchi (1912ff.). In English, see *Philosophical Writings,* ed. and tr. A. Walter (Edinburgh: Nelson, 1962); *God and Creatures; The Quodlibetal Questions,* tr. F. Alluntis and A. B. Wolter (Princeton: Princeton University Press, 1975). The best monograph on the theology of Duns Scotus: Reinhold Seeberg, *Die Theologie des Johannes Duns Scotus* (Leipzig: Dieterich, J. Weicher, 1900); P. Minges, *Das Verhältnis zwischen Glauben und Wissen, Theologie und Philosophie nach Duns Scotus* (Paderborn: F. Schöningh, 1908); W. Betzendörfer, *op. cit.*

17. The (incomplete) *Works* have received an exemplary edition: *Summa Theologica* (Ad Claras Aquas: 1924–48). See K. Heim, *Das Wesen der Gnade und ihr Verhältnis zu den natürlichen Funktionen bei Al. Halesius* (Leipzig: M. Heinsius Nachf., 1907).

Areopagite), and the delightful *Breviloquium*.[18] The Dominican Albertus Magnus (c. 1200–80) had greater influence than either of these: in Cologne he was the teacher of Thomas, had broader scientific interests than his student who was still superior to him, was a master in the area of medieval study and interpretation of nature, and most importantly, the author of a *Summa theologiae* which did remain incomplete.[19]

j. Exegesis and Mysticism. Since Anselm and Abelard, medieval dogmatics was Scholasticism, that is, school dogmatics, the reworking of the traditional teaching of the Church with the tools of dialectics and in the forms of philosophy. But this does not mean that theological work was limited to Scholastic dogmatics and ethics. The exegesis of the Middle Ages is far too frequently ignored, and it is important. To be sure, it was similar to its classic models in that it made use of the allegorical method (as, e.g., in the commentaries of Rupert of Deutz, c. 1070–1129 or 1135[20]) and often consisted of nothing more than collections of citations from the Fathers (e.g., the *Catena aurea* of St. Thomas[21]). Both are of dogmatic interest, however, particularly where allegorical exposition expresses a special view of history which we could call "salvation-historical." This is true of Rupert, and was the view most especially influenced by Augustine. More important is the fact that although the great Scholastics held to the distinction between the literal sense and the mystical sense, the former sense formed the basis for exposition. This was the approach taken by Nicholas of Lyra (c. 1270–1340), who was encouraged by the interpretive work of the Jewish scholar Solomon Rashi (1040–1105) in the Old Testament, in his great exegetical works, which were of considerable use to the Reformers.[22]

The extensive writings of mysticism stand next to the exegetical literature

---

18. We are again the debtors of the Franciscans of Quaracchi for an exemplary edition (1882–1902), *The Works of Bonaventure; Cardinal, Seraphic Doctor, and Saint,* tr. Jose de Vinck (Paterson, N.J.: St. Anthony Guild Press, 1960–). Bonaventure, who also was the biographer of St. Francis of Assisi, was relatively uninterested in philosophy; for him theology was information about the way of salvation, understood mystically and ultimately dependent upon illumination. He is not the greatest but the most likeable of the Scholastics.

19. *Opera,* ed. A. Borgnet (38 vols.; Paris: 1890–99); more recent, *Opera omnia,* ed. B. Geyer (Münster: Aschendorff, 1951–55). The most important works next to the incomplete *Summa theologiae* are his Commentary on the Areopagite, and the *Summa de creaturis.* Albertus Magnus is the only German among the great Scholastics—the first great Swabian among theologians. See G. von Hertling, *Albertus Magnus; Beiträge zu seiner Würdigung* (Köln: 1880; 2nd edition in *Beiträge zur Geschichte der Philosophie des Mittelalters* . . .[vol. XIV, Heft 5/6; Münster: 1914]).

20. *Opera* in Migne, *PL,* vols. CLXVII–CLXX; commentaries on Job, John's Gospel, the Apocalypse, Song of Songs, the twelve minor prophets. His chief work was *De Trinitate et operibus eius,* a mighty but very speculative "salvation-historical" concept. See W. Rocholl, *Rupert von Deutz* (1886); A. Hauck, *Kirchengeschichte Deutschlands* (Berlin: Akademie Verlag, 1954[8], 1958), IV, 432ff.

21. *Glossa continua; Catena aurea; Commentary on the Four Gospels,* tr. M. Patton (Oxford: Henry & Parker, 1864[2]).

22. A modern edition of Nicholas is needed! His *Postillae perpetuae* were frequently printed up to the 17th century, the last time being Antwerp, 1634.

and are more well known than the latter and probably than the actual Scholastic writings: the Christ mysticism of the argumentative Bernard of Clairvaux (1090–1153),[23] the metaphysics of being, reworked into mysticism by Meister Eckhart (c. 1260–1327),[24] and the sermons of Johann Tauler (c. 1300–61)[25]—we mention these three because they are all of importance for the history of dogmatic thought, but they are only a few of a great number.

    k. Late Middle Ages. The thought of the Middle Ages has often been compared to its cathedrals in regard to its breadth, boldness, and assured forcefulness. The mightiest expressions of this spirit also share with the cathedrals the fact that they remained largely incomplete. Was man attempting too much here? It is, in any event, significant that the unity of all thought, the synthesis of nature and grace, of knowledge and faith, of the world and God, which was intended by High Scholasticism and was documented in the *Summae*, did not last beyond the 13th century. With the beginning of the fall of medieval unity, the *Summae* also recede; Duns Scotus did not write a *Summa*, and the great representative of Nominalism in the 14th century, William of Occam (c. 1300–c. 1349), put his most important thoughts into a commentary on the *Sentences*, just as Duns Scotus did;[26] the "last Scholastic," Gabriel Biel (c. 1420–95), who followed Occam in substance, summarized and interpreted the Occamite commentary on the *Sentences* as his chief work.[27] This strong attachment to the customary textbook of medieval dog-

---

23. *Opera*, based on the edition of J. Mabillon, in Migne, *PL*, vols. CLXXXII–CLXXXV; A. Neander, *Der heilige Bernard und sein Zeitalter* (2 vols.; Berlin: 1813; Hamburg: Perthes, 1848[2]; Gotha: Perthes, 1889 [*Bibliothek theologischer Klassiker*, ET of 1st ed. in 1843]); E. Vacandrard, *La Vie de Saint-Bernhard* (1895; n.l.; GT 1897 and 1898); for further bibliography, see *SH*, II, 65f.

24. *Opera* (with supplementary studies), ed. J. Quint and J. Koch, 1935ff. (incomplete); *Opera latina* (Leipzig: 1934); *Meister Eckhart; A Modern Translation*, tr. R. B. Blakney (New York and London: Harper, 1957).

Meister Eckhart shows how minor the modifications need be in order to move from Dominican High Scholasticism to a mysticism which is ultimately beyond history.

25. See the edition by Ferdinand Vetter in *Deutsche Texte des Mittelalters* (1910), vol. XI; *The Sermons and Conferences of John Tauler of the Order of Preachers* . . ., tr. W. Elliott (Washington, D.C.: Apostolic Mission House, 1910); G. Siedel, *Die Mystik Taulers nebst einer Erörterung über den Begriff der Mystik* (Leipzig: J. C. Hinrich, 1911); A. V. Müller, *Luther und Tauler* (1918; n.l.); O. Scheel, *Taulers Mystik und Luthers reformatorische Entdeckung* (no publisher, 1920).

26. There is no newer edition of Occam, and a complete edition has not been attempted. A listing and study of his writing are found in A. G. Little, *The Grey Friars in Oxford* (Oxford: Oxford Historical Society, 1892). Important: E. Hochstetter, *Studien zur Metaphysik und Erkenntnislehre Wilhelms von Ockham* (Berlin and Leipzig: de Gruyter, 1927); E. Amann, *Dictionnaire de Théologie catholique* (Paris-VI: Libraire Letouzey et Ane, 1931); S. Riezler, *Die literarischen Widersacher der Päpste; zur Zeit Ludwig des Baiers* (Leipzig: 1874; repr. New York: B. Franklin, 1961); very comprehensive materials are to be found in the detailed dissertation of S. U. Zuidema, *De philosophie van Occam in zijn Commentar op de Sentenzien* (2 vols.; Hilversum: Schipper, 1936).

27. Gabriel Biel, *Epitome et Collectorium ex Occamo circa quattuor Sententiarum* (1495, 1501) (Frankfurt/Main: Minerva, 1965); see also C. Feckes, *Die Rechtfertigungslehre des Gabriel Biel und ihre Stellung innerhalb der nominalistischen Schule* (Münster: Münsterische Beiträge zur Theologie, 1925).

matics was not just a matter of the usual form of academic instruction but also
was related to the fact that with the gradual increase of the sense of criticism,
which tended to assign the decisions to the will, the sense of tradition also expanded. The late Middle Ages attempted criticism of both thought and action, but
there was no longer the self-confidence that could produce the great systems such
as the *Summae*. Thus the form of theological work reveals what was equally true
of its content: to the degree that the great unity was disintegrating, two forces
dominated the field, both tradition and the individual, who was contrasted to
tradition and still submitted to it but yet regarded this submission as an act of the
will and no longer thought that the intellect of faith *(intellectus fidei)* was possible.

We cannot conclude this overview without remembering that in the very
period of the declining Middle Ages other forces emerged which wanted to replace
the style of philosophy and theology which pure Nominalism had introduced (the
so-called *via moderna* or modern way) with an earlier form. These were the
proponents of the *via antiqua* (ancient way), who formally wanted nothing else
than a return to the old method. In terms of content, however, they were trying
to oppose the separation of faith and knowledge by attempting a new synthesis.[28]
There was no lack of such attempts in the whole period of the late Middle Ages,
especially among the Dominicans. They began to gain ground toward the end of
the epoch—and then they connected up with the beginnings of Humanism! In one
regard Humanism was more Thomist than Nominalist: like Thomas it was trying
to achieve a synthesis, it placed great trust in human knowing also for matters of
faith, and it resisted the acceptance of dogmatic theses on the basis of authority
alone.

The struggle of the two "ways" *(viae)* at the beginning of the 16th century
did not directly lead up to the Reformation, but the thinking of the Reformers was
not uninfluenced by it. It was of weighty significance that Luther was fundamentally an Occamist, whereas, for example, Zwingli revealed Thomist aspects and
Calvin, too, firmly rejected the fundamental theses of Nominalism, e.g., the thesis
of *Deus exlex* (God beyond or without law).

---

28. See primarily G. Ritter, *Die Heidelberger Universität; ein Stück deutscher Geschichte* (Heidelberg: G. Winter, 1936); Ritter, *Studien zur Spätscholastik (Sitzungsberichte
der Heidelberger Akademie)* (3 vols.; Heidelberg: C. Winter, 1921–27).

V. Dogmatics in the Age of the Reformation and of Orthodoxy

A. REFORMATION DOGMATICS

a. The Dogmatic Significance of the Reformation. As a movement within church history, the Reformation of the 16th century is primarily the exercise of the fundamental activity for all dogma, which is the concrete return of the Church to the Word of God which establishes its freedom and sets an end to its arbitrariness. The doctrine of justification and the self-understanding of the Church are indissolubly intertwined in the Church's dogma. The Middle Ages understood grace as a supernatural ontic given and then divided the righteousness of man between the free gift of God and personal activity of man (which also rested upon grace), and in the medieval understanding of the Church there was a division between the unique truth and lordship of Jesus Christ and the truth and lordship which emanated from men who were under grace. The necessary consequence of the widespread and dominant synthesis was that gaining salvation and remaining saved (if the language is permitted) were primarily based upon the saving activity of God but also upon the activity of man, either made possible by grace or incurring the after-effect of grace. The same synthesis led to a precisely analogous division in the understanding of the Church, of its regiment and its claim to truth. The common themes "faith *and* works," "Scripture *and* tradition," as easily misunderstood as they can be, highlight the situation which is our concern here. When the Reformation contested both of these "ands," it attacked the foundations of medieval dogmatics.

The Reformation was ignited not in regard to the concept of the Church but to the understanding of God's righteousness, and so it was only as a secondary effect that the Church's inherent authority over truth and the unconditional validity of its dogmas were subjected to questioning (for Luther, not until the Leipzig Disputation of 1519). Thus it is understandable that this essentially dogmatic movement produced neither a new dogmatic decision nor a new dogmatic system at first. It may have also been an effective factor that the dogmatic creativity of the preceding late Middle Ages had more or less atrophied; it was certainly a major factor that Luther so curtly rejected Aristotle for substantive theological reasons. He developed a negative reaction toward the theological self-glorification of "reason," although no other philosophers were available to him than those

103

who stood in his tradition. In any event, we are faced with the fact that the Reformation did not begin to produce effective dogmatic systems until its second phase.

b. Luther, 1483–1546. Luther left no writings which could be designated as dogmatics. His theology is found in his exegetical labors, such as the lectures on Romans, the great commentary on Galatians, his sermons, the many occasional and controversial pieces (particularly *De servo arbitrio*) and, with proper school form, in his disputations. It is difficult to imagine how Luther would have formulated his theology in a closed systematic presentation; he would have been hindered not only by his Occamistic past but also and chiefly by his dislike of systematizing reason. Based upon his fundamental insights, he is a theologian of the antithesis, especially the antithesis of law and Gospel, which is difficult to work into a system. So he became unquestionably the authoritative theologian of Protestantism—he is also the Reformer for the Reformed Churches!—without becoming its first academic dogmatician.[1] He is a Reformer without being the

---

1. Luther is cited here in the American edition (AE) of *Luther's Works*, ed. J. Pelikan and H. Lehmann (St. Louis: Concordia, 1955–   ); if a work is not there, other English editions are cited; the *Weimar Ausgabe (WA)* is cited only when no English translation has been found.

The theology of the Reformer has of course produced an incredibly vast amount of literature. Comprehensive treatments: Theodosius Harnack, *Luthers Theologie; mit besonderer Beziehung auf seine Versöhnungs- und Erlösungslehre* (1862, 1927) (2 vols.; Amsterdam: Rodopi, 1969); J. Köstlin, *The Theology of Luther in its Historical Development and Inner Harmony*, tr. C. E. Hay (2 vols.; Philadelphia: Lutheran Publishing Society, 1897); Reinhold Seeberg, *Text-Book of the History of Doctrines*, tr. C. E. Hay (2 vols. in 1; Grand Rapids: Baker Book House, 1952–58), II, 221–345; Karl Holl, *Gesammelte Aufsätze zur Kirchengeschichte* (3 vols.; I, "Luther," and additional essays in III, "Der Westen"; Tübingen: J. C. B. Mohr [Paul Siebeck], 1928–48; Darmstadt: Wissenschaftliche Buchgesellschaft, 1948–65); Erich Seeberg, *Luthers Theologie, Motive und Ideen; I, Die Gottesanschauung* (Göttingen: Vandenhoeck & Ruprecht, 1929); *II, Christus, Wirklichkeit und Urbild* (Stuttgart: Kohlhammer, 1937); Erich Seeberg, *Luthers Theologie in ihren Grundzügen* (Stuttgart: W. Kohlhammer, 1940, 1950²); Otto Ritschl, *Dogmengeschichte des Protestantismus* (4 vols.; Leipzig: Hinrichs, 1908–27), vol. II; Carl Stange, *Studien zur Theologie Luthers* (Gütersloh: Bertelsmann, 1928); more biographical: Otto Scheel, *Martin Luther; Vom Katholizismus zur Reformation* (Tübingen: J. C. B. Mohr, 1916–17¹, 1917², 1930); based upon the major writings: Paul Wernle, *Der evangelische Glaube nach den Hauptschriften der Reformatoren* (2 vols.; Tübingen: J. C. B. Mohr, 1918–19), vol. I; Johannes Gottschick, *Luthers Theologie* (from *ZThK*, Supplement; Tübingen: Mohr, 1914); Gerhard Ritter, *Luther; His Life and Work*, tr. J. Riches (London: Collins, 1963 [g1928]).

Of the newer specialized publications I would especially mention: Wilhelm Link, *Das Ringen Luthers um die Freiheit der Theologie von der Philosophie*, ed. E. Wolf and M. Mezger (München: Kaiser, 1955²)—almost a comprehensive exposition!; Gerhard Ebeling, *Ev. Evangelienauslegung; eine Untersuchung zu Luthers Hermeneutik* (Darmstadt: Wissenschaftliche Buchgesellschaft, 1962 [g1942]); Walther von Loewenich, *Luthers theologia crucis* (München: Kaiser, 1929¹, 1933², 1954⁴); Adolf Hamel, *Der junge Luther und Augustin; ihre Beziehungen in der Rechtfertigungslehre nach Luthers ersten Vorlesungen* (2 vols.; Gütersloh: Bertelsmann, 1934–35); Paul Althaus, *Paulus und Luther über den Menschen* (Gütersloh: C. Bertelsmann, 1938, 1951², 1958³, 1963⁴); Erich Vogelsang, *Die Anfänge von Luthers Christologie nach der ersten Psalmenvorlesung . . .* (Berlin and Leipzig: de Gruyter, 1929); Emanuel Hirsch, *Luthers Gottesanschauung* (Göttingen: Vandenhoeck

head of a school. This in itself is one of the reasons for his superiority, which even a man like Calvin acknowledged.

c. Melanchthon, 1497–1560. The first dogmatician of the Reformation is Melanchthon.[2] The influence of his work was equally great for both later Lutheran and Reformed dogmatics. It is well known that Luther jubilantly greeted his *Loci communes*, which first appeared in 1521 and finally, after many alterations and considerably weakened in impact, were concluded as the *Loci praecipui theologici* (1559).[3] Here was the thoughtful, school-like formulation which was not the kind of thing the Reformer would have done. And at the same time, the negative aspects can be seen here. Compared to the great *Summae* of the Middle Ages, Melanchthon wrote an almost diminutive little book, and even the final version was only an outline. The reduction of the basic theological issue to "salvation,"

& Ruprecht, 1918); Ernst Wolf, *Staupitz und Luther; ein Beitrag zur Theologie des Johannes von Staupitz und deren Bedeutung für Luthers theologischen Werdegang* (Leipzig: M. Heinsius Nachf., 1927); H. J. Iwand, *Rechtfertigungslehre und Christusglaube; eine Untersuchung zur Systematik der Rechtfertigungslehre Luthers in ihren Anfängen* (München: Kaiser [g1930[1], 1966[3]); H. J. Iwand, *Glaubensgerechtigkeit nach Luthers Lehre* (München: Kaiser, 1937[1], 1951[2], 1959[3]); Ernst Wolf, "Luthers Erbe?" *EvTheol* (1946), pp. 100ff., and the literature mentioned there; Wilfried Joest, *Gesetz und Freiheit; das Problem des Tertius usus legis bei Luther und die neutestamentliche Paranese* (Göttingen: Vandenhoeck & Ruprecht, 1952[1], 1956[2], 1961); G. Törnvall, *Geistliches und weltliches Regiment bei Luther; Studien zu Luthers Weltbild und Gesellschaftsverständnis* (München: C. Kaiser, 1947); G. Wingren, *Luther on Vocation,* tr. C. C. Rasmussen (Philadelphia: Muhlenberg Press, 1957); E. Wolf, *Peregrinatio; Studien zur reformatorischen Theologie und zum Kirchenproblem* (2 vols.; München: C. Kaiser, 1954–65).

The works mentioned open the way to the total theology of Luther via one of the individual problems.

2. His works are to be found in the *Corpus Reformatorum*, vols. I–XXVIII (1834ff.); Robert Stupperich, ed., *Melanchthons Werke in Auswahl* (5 vols.; Gütersloh: Bertelsmann, 1951f.—cited as Stupperich); *Loci Communes, 1521,* ed. T. Kolde (based on G. L. Plitt; Leipzig: Deichert, 1925); ET: *Loci communes theologici* (1521), tr. L. J. Satre (*LCC*, XIX, 3–154); *On Christian Doctrine; Loci Communes, 1555,* tr. and ed. C. L. Manschreck (New York: Oxford University Press, 1965); other translations and editions also available in English.

T. Herrlinger, *Die Theologie Melanchthons in ihrer geschichtlichen Entwicklung und im Zusammenhange mit der Lehrgeschichte und Culturbewegung der Reformation* (Gotha: Perthes, 1879); Hans Engelland, *Melanchthon, Glauben und Handeln* (München: C. Kaiser, 1931), with comprehensive bibliography; Ernst Troeltsch, *Vernunft und Offenbarung bei Joh. Gerhard und Phil. Melanchthon* (1891; n.l.); F. Hübner, *Natürliche Theologie und theokratische Schwärmerei bei Melanchthon* (Gütersloh: Bertelsmann, 1936); K. Hartfelder, *Philipp Melanchthon als Praeceptor Germaniae* (Berlin: Hofmann, 1889; Nieuwkoop: B. de Graff, 1964); W. Neuser, *Der Ansatz der Theologie Melanchthons (Beiträge zur Geschichte und Lehre der Reformierten Kirche;* Neukirchen: Buchhandlung des Erziehungsvereins, 1957); M. Köhler, *Melanchthon und der Islam; ein Beitrag zur Klärung des Verhältnisses zwischen Christentum und Fremdreligionen in der Reformationszeit* (Leipzig: L. Klotz, 1938); R. Nürnberger, *Kirche und weltliche Obrigkeit bei Melanchthon* (Würzburg: Triltsch, 1937).

3. ". . . Philip Melanchthon's *Commonplaces*—an unanswerable little book which in my judgment deserves not only to be immortalized, but even canonized," *The Bondage of the Will* (AE, XXXIII, 16). See also the enthusiastic judgment of Calvin regarding the later version in "Preface de la Somme de Melanchthon" (1546) (*CR*, IX, 847ff.). The *Commonplaces (Loci)* appeared in Geneva in 1546 in a French translation with the preface by Calvin just cited.

to the "consolation of the fearful conscience" *(consolatio perterrefactae conscientiae)*, thus the reduction of the stuff of dogmatics to the basic issues of free will, sin, law, Gospel, justification, faith, love, hope, and to a few questions on the doctrine of the sacraments and the doctrine of worldly authority—all of this, together with the famous statement about the benefits of Christ which were the only real issue at stake, has often enough been praised and is certainly impressive enough. However, when Melanchthon proceeded soteriologically in this way (a result of Luther's influence), he undertook to make a systematization of the soteriological approach, which means that he really began with anthropology. This means from the very onset that the great area of the doctrine of God (especially the Trinity), which had been worked on so much until then, was set aside at least at the beginning, and Christology was reduced to the doctrine of the "benefits" *(beneficia)*. Later on, when Melanchthon found reason to return to these older and traditional doctrinal issues, this meant that he remained essentially in the traditional molds when he dealt with them—the theology of the Orthodox age, influenced by him, reproduced in fact the old ontology because Melanchthon and his students did not succeed in penetrating this area with the new insights and knowledge of the Reformation. This resulted in turn in a superimposition of the traditional approach over the Reformation position, including Aristotle who ultimately was returned to full honors. This can be observed in Melanchthon at a number of points. Since he began anthropologically, he injected the ethical issue into theology as an independent theme, and in that he linked himself smoothly with previous tradition. He could not finally avoid combining Luther's thoughts on predestination and freedom systematically, thus leading back to the issue of free will. In that he systematically placed the law and the Gospel in relationship to one another, he had to reach the point of comprehending both in one category, and what resulted was again a return to previous tradition. If the Gospel was understood as a benefit directed toward man, then the law was also something which had to do with man, and so the concept of natural law *(lex naturalis)* asserted itself over Luther's understanding of the law as one side of the One Word of God. The anthropological approach becomes in the hands of the ethicist and rational thinker, Melanchthon, the principle of an ontology. The way this happens can be seen most clearly in regard to the understanding of faith. Certainly Melanchthon wanted to distinguish sharply between faith and works, together with Paul and Luther. However, in the course of his understanding justification exclusively as a forensic event, faith becomes the knowledge, affirmation, and trustful acceptance *(notitia, assensus,* and *fiducia)* of what is in itself the purely objective salvation-event. But this means that gradually only *fiducia*, trustful acceptance, remains the real miracle of faith: *notitia* and *assensus* are progressively assigned to the realm of reason and the will. This means that faith requires something else to be complete; if it is the affirming and trusting acceptance of the objective work of salvation, then it really leads man to point zero. Luther's insight that wherever there is forgiveness of sins there is also "life and blessedness" is something Melanchthon cannot quite uphold with his rationally established concept of faith. Therefore, the practice of the subjective condition of salvation, which is based upon faith and always rests upon it, becomes an independent problem, and to solve it both ethics and anthropology must be called upon. In this fashion, soteriology is located between the anthropologically controlled question of forgiveness and the anthropologically controlled question of Christian practice. Based upon this approach, it can be understood why Melanchthon softened his original rejection of the thesis of free will from one version of his *Loci* to another (second version in 1535, third in 1543) and finally went over to the opposite position; similarly he gradually diluted the radical irrationalism of Luther's doctrine of communion; thus he approached Roman doctrine in the one regard, and Reformed in the other. Most of his students found their way into the Reformed direction (the German-Reformed school, strongly represented in Heidelberg and Herborn and impressively expressed in the Heidelberg Catechism). In doing so, they accepted essential elements of the original legacy of Calvin and thus shifted Melanchthon's approach again in the direction of Luther. The most notable of the German-Reformed students of Melanchthon was Christoph Pezel (1539–1604).[4] Within the context of Lutheranism, Melanchthon's greatest student was Martin Chemnitz (1522–86),[5] the founder of actual Lutheran Orthodoxy; in every essential area he followed along in the footsteps of his master and thus imposed upon incipient Orthodoxy Melanchthon's molding influence.

d. Calvin, 1509–64. John Calvin produced the most significant dogmatics in the Reformation period (and for centuries thereafter) in his *Institutes of the Christian Religion*. Similar to Melanchthon's *Loci,* this work did not reach its final form until the end of a long history of development. The first version appeared in Basel in 1536, in every way the work of a well-educated French Lutheran, based in its structure and in part in its wording on Luther's *Smaller Catechism*. It was the work of a twenty-six-year-old man who could have been expected to pursue a brilliant literary career, but whose future did not seem to include the weighty burden of the completion of the Geneva Reformation. A few years later, after the first Genevan attempt had failed and Calvin had found refuge in Strasbourg in 1539, he rewrote the work as a textbook for use in instruction— it was originally conceived as an apology for French Protestantism—and in its new form it revealed more sharply the typical characteristics of his alert and incisive spirit. The final edition appeared in 1559 after many refinements and expansions. The four books (I. The Knowledge of God the Creator, II. The Knowledge of God the Redeemer in Christ, III. The Way in Which We Receive the Grace of Christ, IV. The External Means or Aids by Which God Invites Us . . .) are based upon the Apostles' Creed, which Calvin understood as being divided into four parts.

Calvin was no less significant a Humanist than was Melanchthon, but scholastically (more in the sense of the "ancient way"—*via antiqua*) he was much better and more comprehensively educated and was able to translate the Reformation view, in an original synthesis, into a total statement. In his earlier stages,

---

4. Pezel's chief work is the *Argumenta et objectiones de praecipuis articulis doctrinae christianae* (1580ff.), with frequent references to Melanchthon.

5. Chief work: *Examination of the Council of Trent*, tr. F. Kramer (St. Louis: Concordia, 1971-   ), vol. I; see also Hermann Hachfeld, *Martin Chemnitz nach seinem Leben und Wirken, insbesonders nach seinem Verhältnis zum Tridentinum* (Leipzig: Breitkopf & Härtel, 1867); G. Noth, *Grundzüge der Theologie des Martin Chemnitz* (Erlangen dissertation, 1930).

he appears as a dogmatician whose thoughts run along the lines of "Upper German Lutheranism" in the pattern of Bucer, while the contacts with Zwingli are only recognizable on the margins. After 1539 his own position emerges more clearly: methodologically a most unusual and broadly informed connection of biblical theology and Scholastic systematics transformed by the Reformation; in content a Reformation renewal of Augustine's anti-Pelagian theses especially evident in the doctrines of God, predestination, and the sacraments; then, an ecclesiology which penetrates everything and presses toward actualization—a "theology of the diagonal,"[6] for which we search in vain for a dominating "principle" because in fact it grapples successfully with the strongest of tensions and resolves them for those with a superficial view.[7]

---

6. See J. Bohatec, *Calvinstudien; Festschrift zum 400. Geburtstage Johann Calvins* (*"Elberfelder Calvinstudien"*) (Leipzig: R. Haupt, 1909), p. 353.

7. The *Opera* in *CR*, vols. XXIX–LXXXVII, usually counted as vols. I–LIX, as is done here. Citations not found in an English edition are cited in *CR* rather than in German editions. The *Institutes* are cited in the edition of *LCC*, vols. XX and XXI. The commentaries are found in the older (Scottish) translation published by Eerdmans, now being replaced by a modern translation published by the same house. Modern German edition of the works: Barth-Niesel, ed., *Opera Selecta* (München: C. Kaiser, 1936).

Most comprehensive treatment of Calvin's theology: Emile Doumergue, *Jean Calvin, les hommes et les choses de son temps* (7 vols.; Lausanne: G. Bridel, 1899–1927), especially vol. IV: *La pensée religieuse de Calvin* (1910), and vol. V: *La pensée ecclésiastique et la pensée politique de Calvin* (1917); F. Wendel, *Calvin; The Origins and Development of his Religious Thought*, tr. P. Mairet (New York: Harper & Row, 1963); Wilhelm Niesel, *The Theology of Calvin*, tr. H. Knight (Philadelphia: Westminster Press, 1956 [g1938]); August Lang, *Johannes Calvin; Ein Lebensbild* . . . (Leipzig: Verein für Reformationsgeschichte, 1909); Karl Holl, *Johannes Calvin; Rede zur Feier der 400. Wiederkehr des Geburtstages Calvins* (Tübingen: Mohr, 1909), much expanded in *Gesammelte Aufsätze* . . . , vol. III; J. Bohatec, ed., *op. cit.*

From the many monographs: J. Bohatec, *Calvin und das Recht* (Feudingen/Westfalen: Buchdruckerei & Verlagsanstalt GmbH, 1934); J. Bohatec, *Calvins Lehre von Staat und Kirche, mit besonderer Berücksichtigung des Organismusgedankens* (Breslau: M. & H. Marcus, 1937; Aalen: Scientia, 1961); Josef Bohatec, *Budé und Calvin; Studien zur Gedankenwelt des französischen Frühhumanismus* (Graz: H. Böhlaus Nachf., 1950); Karl B. Hundeshagen, *Beiträge zur Kirchenverfassungsgeschichte und Kirchenpolitik insbesonders des Protestantismus* (Wiesbaden: Niedner, 1864; Frankfurt/Main: Minerva, 1963), vol. I (important for the context of Calvin's theology); Peter Brunner, *Vom Glauben bei Calvin* (Tübingen: J. C. B. Mohr [Paul Siebeck], 1925); S. P. Dee, *Het Geloofsbegrip van Calvijn* (Kampen: J. H. Kok, 1918); Joachim Beckmann, *Vom Sakrament bei Calvin; Die Sakramentslehre Calvins in ihren Beziehungen zu Augustin* (Tübingen: J. C. B. Mohr [Paul Siebeck], 1926); Heinz Otten, *Calvins theologische Anschauung von der Prädestination* (München: C. Kaiser, 1938); Paul Jacobs, *Praedestination und Verantwortlichkeit bei Calvin* (Neukirchen: Buchhandlung des Erziehungsvereins, 1937; Darmstadt: Wissenschaftliche Buchgesellschaft, 1968); T. F. Torrance, *Calvin's Doctrine of Man* (London: Lutterworth Press, 1952; Grand Rapids: Eerdmans, 1957); Wilhelm Niesel, *Calvin's Lehre vom Abendmahl* (München: Kaiser, 1930, 1935); W. Kolfhaus, *Die Christusgemeinschaft bei Johannes Calvin* (Neukirchen: Buchhandlung des Erziehungsvereins, 1939); W. Kolfhaus, *Vom christlichen Leben nach Johannes Calvin* (Neukirchen: Neukirchener Verlag, 1949); Erwin Müllhaupt, *Die Predigt Calvins, ihre Geschichte, ihre Form, und ihre religiösen Grundgedanken* (Berlin: de Gruyter, 1931); T. H. L. Parker, *The Oracles of God; An Introduction to the Preaching of John Calvin* (London: Lutterworth, 1947); H. Quistorp, *Calvin's Doctrine of the Last Things*, tr. H. Knight (London: Lutterworth, 1955 [g1941]). We have mentioned here only those works which are of general significance.

e. The Reformation's Variety. The widespread tendency either to treat Calvin as Luther's greatest disciple or basically to see him in polarity to the Wittenberg Reformer is nourished by the erroneous opinion that the Reformation was something like a planned action which, aside from Zwingli, was carried out under Luther's leadership alone, and thus the criteria for the various elements of the Reformation are to be found in his theology. The dogmatic work of the Reformation age reveals a whole number of relatively independent directions which cannot all be derived from one common source. Even Luther and Melanchthon are mutually independent; Osiander (1498–1552)[8] and Johann Brenz (1499–1570)[9] each represent their own approach to things; Martin Bucer (1491–1551) is certainly unique, even in his connection of contraries,[10] and Calvin, who summarizes everything which he finds available, can certainly not be measured with an alien standard. The common thing for all of the men (and also for Zwingli[11] [1484–1531])

---

8. Especially important: *De unico mediatore Jesu Christo et justificatione fidei* (1551) *(Confession of the Only Mediator and of Justification by Faith)*. Most important monograph: E. Hirsch, *Die Theologie des Andreas Osiander und ihre geschichtlichen Vorraussetzungen* (Göttingen: Vandenhoeck & Ruprecht, 1919).

9. The most important writing is the so-called Swabian *Syngramma* (1526), the first significant document on the doctrine of ubiquity; also important is the Commentary on John (1530); the *Werke* are appearing at Tübingen: Mohr, 1970– ; W. Köhler, *Bibliographia Brentiana* (Berlin: C. A. Schwetschke, 1904; repr. Nieuwkoop: B. de Graaf, 1963); O. Fricke, *Die Christologie des Johann Brenz, im Zusammenhang mit der Lehre vom Abendmahl und der Rechtfertigung* (München: Kaiser, 1927).

10. Alongside Luther, Zwingli, and Calvin, Bucer deserves to be named as one of the trailblazing Reformers. Thus it is all the more unfortunate that an edition of his works is just now being prepared, R. Stupperich, ed. (Paris: 1960ff.). But shortly after his death the first volume of an edition appeared (*Tomus Anglicanus* [Basel: 1577]). This edition contains the work most appropriately regarded as "dogmatic": *De Regno Christi* (1551); see in regard to it W. Pauck, *Das Reich Gottes auf Erden; Utopie und Wirklichkeit, eine Untersuchung zu Butzers "De Regno Christi" und zur englischen Staatskirche des 16. Jahrhunderts* (Berlin: de Gruyter, 1928). The other important works are Bucer's commentaries: *Matthew* (1527), *Psalms* (1529ff.), and *Romans* (1536ff.).

Modern scientific research on Bucer begins with the biography by J. W. Baum, which also deals with Capito, *Capito und Butzer, Strassburgs Reformatoren* (Elbersfeld: R. L. Fridericks, 1860; reissued Nieuwkoop: B. deGraaf, 1967); see also A. Lang, *Der Evangelienkommentar Martin Butzers und die Grundzüge seiner Theologie* (Leipzig: Dietrich, 1900); R. Seeberg, *Textbook of the History of Doctrines . . .*, II, 347–426; Gustav Anrich, *Martin Bucer* (Strassburg: K. J. Trübner, 1914); J. Couvoisier, *La notion d'Église chez Bucer dans son Developpement historique* (dissertation, Geneve) (Paris: Imprimerie "Je Sers," 1933); W. Köhler, *Zwingli und Luther; Ihr Streit über das Abendmahl nach seinen politischen und religiösen Beziehungen* (Quellen zur Reformationsgeschichte, 6; vol. 1, Leipzig: Heinsius, 1924, vol. 2: Gütersloh: Bertelsmann, 1953); E. Bizer, *Studien zur Geschichte des Abendmahlsstreits im 16. Jahrhundert* (2nd ed.; Darmstadt: Wissenschaftliche Buchgesellschaft, 1962 [repr. of 1st ed., 1940]); W. Pauck's title mentioned above; A. Lang, *Puritanismus und Pietismus; Studien zu ihrer Entwicklung von M. Butzer bis zum Methodismus* (Neukirchen: Buchhandlung des Erziehungsvereins, 1941).

11. The *Opera* are in *CR*, LXXXVIIIff.; an older edition: *Sämtliche Werke*, ed. M. Schuler and J. Schulthess (Zürich: Schulthess, 1828–36); *Selected Works*, ed. S. M. Jackson (Philadelphia: University of Pennsylvania Press, 1972); see also selections in *LCC*, vol. XXIV.

A. Baur, *Zwinglis Theologie; Ihr Werden und ihr System* (2 vols.; Halle: Niemeyer, 1885, 1889 [basically a collection of materials]); G. Locher, *Die Theologie Huldrich Zwinglis*

was their point of departure, the "Reformation approach," and it was Luther's unique position to have found and established it. The variety of dogmatic directions and of practical forms of the Reformation really did not become a problem or the source of long-ranging conflicts until the Reformation movement began to feel a necessity, for internal and external (religious and legal) reasons, to find a unified line. It is a tragic thing that the divergencies which have not been overcome until today really grew out of these efforts to find unity, out of the efforts to form a pan-Protestant political alliance, out of Calvin's attempt to come to an understanding with Bullinger (1504–75)[12] in the communion issue (Consensus Tigurinus, 1549), and out of the endeavors of "Gnesio"-Lutherans (as they viewed themselves) to draw up an "Agreement" *(Konkordie)* of the Lutheran classes in doctrinal issues (The Formula of Concord, 1576). To put it another way, the justified variety of dogmatics became explosive when no common ground in the area of dogma was established; the result was that this variety led finally to the confessionalization of Church and dogmatics. Since Calvin, in the midst of the process whose tragic conclusion he would not live to see, sought more energetically to combine the unity of the Church with the variety of dogmatic directions and emerging confessions than did most of the German Lutherans, the "Reformed" dogmatics largely (although not exclusively) influenced by him tended to remain more differentiated than the "Lutheran." Reformed dogmatics could be influenced not only by Calvin, whose importance for many areas should not be overestimated, but also by the rigidity (and often the narrowness) of Theodore Beza's system (1519–1605),[13] by the biblicistic breadth of Bullinger's theology,[14] and

---

im Lichte seiner Christologie (Zürich: Zwingli-Verlag, 1952–   ).

For constant reference: *Zwingliana* (Zürich, since 1897); P. Wernle, *Der ev. Glaube nach den Hauptschriften der Reformatoren* (2 vols.; Tübingen: J. C. B. Mohr, 1918–19), especially vol. II; J. M. Usteri, *Ulrich Zwingli* (1883; n.l.); A. Rich, *Die Anfänge der Theologie H. Zwinglis* (Zürich: Zwingli Verlag, 1949); R. Pfister, *Das Problem der Erbsünde bei Zwingli* (Leipzig: M. Heinsius Nachf., 1939); W. Köhler, *Zwingli und Luther* . . .(see p. 109, n. 10); W. Köhler, *Huldrich Zwingli* (Leipzig: Koehler & Amelang, 1943[2], 1954); W. Köhler, *Das Buch der Reformation H. Zwinglis* . . . (München: E. Reinhardt, 1926); O. Farner, *Huldrich Zwingli* (4 vols.; Zürich: Zwingli-Verlag, 1943, 1946, 1954); Max Huber, *Natürliches Gotteserkenntnis; Ein Vergleich zwischen Thomas von Aquinas und Huldrych Zwingli* (Bern: Haupt, 1950); A. Farner, *Die Lehre von Kirche und Staat bei Zwingli* (Tübingen: J. C. B. Mohr [Paul Siebeck], 1930); J. Pollet, article on "Zwinglianisme," *Dictionnaire de Theologie catholique*, X (1950), 3745ff. All of these are significant monographs. Outdated: E. Zeller, *Das theologische System Zwinglis* (Tübingen: L. F. Fuss, 1853).

12. There is no edition of Bullinger [but see Fritz Büsser, ed., *Werke* (Zürich: Theologischer-Verlag, 1972–   )—TR]. Important for dogmatics is his *Confessio Helvetica posterior* (1566); see W. Hildebrandt and R. Zimmerman, *Bedeutung und Geschichte des Zweiten Helvetischen Bekenntnisses* (Zürich: Zwingli-Verlag, 1938), with further bibliography; also important are Bullinger's widely distributed *Decades, Sermonum Decades quinque, de potissimis Christianae religionis capitibus* (1522 and often); ET: *The Decades of Henry Bullinger*, tr. and ed. T. Harding (4 vols.; Cambridge: The University Press, 1849–52); and the *Catechesis* of 1559.

13. *Tractationes theologicae* (1570–82); see also J. W. Baum, *Theodor Beza, nach handschriftlichen Quellen dargestellt* (Leipzig: Weidmann, 1843–51); Eugène Choisy, *L'Etat chrétien à Genève au temps de Th. de Bèze* (Genève: C. Eggimann; Paris: Fischbacher, 1902).

14. See G. Schrenk, *Gottesreich und Bund im älteren Protestantismus, vornehmlich bei Johannes Coccejus* (Gütersloh: C. Bertelsmann, 1923).

above all by the effects of Melanchthon.[15] Alongside very rigid systems, based upon the predestination dogma now elevated to a "principle," there were very early independent and new approaches such as the Heidelberg-Herborn school[16] or the school of Saumur[17] or even the federal-theological direction which would soon emerge.[18] On the Lutheran side the differences in content remained minimal, although there could also be heated controversies on individual points. In addition, Lutheran dogmatics remained for a very long time an exclusively German affair, whereas Reformed dogmatics developed in the very differing intellectual atmospheres of western Germany and western Europe, and, especially on British soil, enjoyed a fully independent development.[19]

f. The Revitalization of Roman Catholic Dogmatics. In the controversy with the Reformation, the Roman Catholic world also experienced a new sense of vitality in the area of dogmatics. The dogmatic labors of highly qualified theologians desirous of inner-Catholic Reform, such as Johann Gropper (1503–59) with his *Enchiridion* (1538),[20] and above all Gasparo Contarini (1483–1542),[21] provided very important contributions for the conciliar decisions later formulated at Trent; then, the Jesuit Robert Bellarmine (1542–1621),[22] both a contemporary and opponent of early Protestant Orthodoxy, wrote his *Disputationes de controversiis Christianae fidei* (1586ff.) upon the basis of the Council of Trent;[23] his work pro-

---

15. Still important: H. Heppe, *Dogmatik des deutschen Protestantismus im 16. Jahrhundert* (3 vols.; Gotha: F. A. Perthes, 1857); W. Gass, *Geschichte der protestantischen Dogmatik in ihrem Zusammenhang mit der Theologie überhaupt* (4 vols.; Berlin: G. Reimer, 1854–67), vol. I.

16. See K. Bauer, *Aus der grossen Zeit der theologischen Fakultät zu Heidelberg* (Verein für Kirchengeschichte in der ev. Landeskirche Baden, Veröffentlichungen, 14; Lahr: Schauenburg, 1938, with much material).

17. J. Moltmann, *Gnadenbund und Gnadenwahl* (Göttingen dissertation, 1951); A. Schweizer, *Die protestantischen Centraldogmen in ihrer Entwicklung innerhalb der Kirche* (2 vols.; n.p., 1854–56), vol. II; H. E. Weber, *Reformation, Orthodoxie, und Rationalismus* (2 vols. in 3; Gütersloh: C. Bertelsmann, 1937–51; repr. Darmstadt: Wissenschaftliche Buchgesellschaft, 1966), vol. II.

18. See G. Schrenk, *op. cit.*, and E. Graf von Korff, *Die Anfänge der Foederaltheologie und ihre erste Ausgestaltung in Zürich und Holland* (Bonn dissertation) (Bonn: E. Eisele, 1908); G. Weth, *Die Heilsgeschichte; ihr universeller und ihr individueller Sinn in der offenbarungsgeschichtlichen Theologie des 19. Jahrhunderts* (München: Kaiser, 1931).

19. A. Lang, *Puritanismus und Pietismus* . . .; A. A. van Schelven, *Het Calvinisme gedurende zijn bloeitijd* (2 vols.; Amsterdam: W. ten Have, 1943–51), vol. II. Both works provide comprehensive bibliographies; Lang emphasizes and overestimates the influence of Bucer.

20. Regarding Gropper see now W. Lipgens, *Kardinal Johannes Gropper, 1503–1559, und die Anfänge der katholischen Reform in Deutschland* (Münster: Aschendorffsche Verlagsbuchhandlung, 1951).

21. H. Rückert, *Die Rechtfertigungslehre auf dem tridentinischen Konzil* (Bonn: Marcus & Weber, 1925) and *Die theologische Entwicklung Gasparo Contarinis* (Bonn: Marcus & Weber, 1926).

22. *Opera* (Cologne: 1620; Paris: 1870–74, 1875–91; Frankfurt/Main: 1965).

23. For the texts, see the selection in Denzinger, pp. 243ff., pars. 782ff., as well as many editions of the decrees and canons. See also H. Jedin, *A History of the Council of Trent*, tr. Dom E. Graf, O.S.B. (2 vols.; London: Thomas Nelson & Sons, 1957–61); H. Rückert, *Die Rechtfertigungslehre auf dem tridentinischen Konzil* (Bonn: Marcus & Weber, 1925); K. D. Schmidt, *Studien zur Geschichte des Konzils von Trient* (1925; n.l.).

vided ample material for controversies with evangelical dogmatics and interconfessional debates.[24] There was at that time much closer contact, even if it was not always friendly, between the dogmatics of both sides than one would usually imagine. This is true at least of central Europe, whereas Spain in this period experienced a virulent revival of Scholasticism.

B. ORTHODOX DOGMATICS

The Age of Orthodoxy coincides with the 17th century in terms of the history of evangelical dogmatics;[25] for the Church it lasts into the 18th century—new movements require decades before they begin to have their effect upon the life of the Church. On the other hand, philosophical approaches which are customarily assigned to the Enlightenment, above all Descartes' approach, were already influencing the Orthodoxy of the 17th century, especially the Reformed.

a. Orthodoxy and the Reformation. Orthodox dogmatics grew out of the dogmatics of the Reformation: not out of the Reformation itself, but out of the dogmatic work which was developed from it. With the second version of Melanchthon's *Loci*, the Antinomian Disputations of Luther, and the second edition of Calvin's *Institutes* in 1539, the decision was made which built the bridge between the Reformation and Orthodoxy; the Reformation became a dogmatic movement. This meant that it began to make use of the school theology of the previous ages both directly and in the development of its own school theology. This helps to explain why Luther's verdict against the autonomy of reason and his polemics

---

24. Chiefly Daniel Chamier, *Panstratia catholica* (1626); Martin Chemnitz's *Examen Concilii Tridentini* (1565ff.), preceded Bellarmine's work.

25. H. E. Weber, *Reformation, Orthodoxie, Rationalismus . . .*; Otto Ritschl, *Dogmengeschichte des Protestantismus . . .*; W. Gass, *Geschichte der protestantischen Dogmatik . . .* (vols. III and IV do not apply here).

Excerpts from Orthodox dogmatics can be found in H. Schmid, *The Doctrinal Theology of the Evangelical Lutheran Church, Verified from the Original Sources*, tr. C. A. Hay and H. E. Jacobs (Philadelphia: Lutheran Publication Society, 1889); Heinrich Heppe, *Reformed Dogmatics, Set Out and Illustrated from the Sources*, rev. and ed. Ernst Bizer, tr. G. T. Thomson (London: Allen & Unwin Ltd., 1950); A. Schweizer, *Die Glaubenslehre der evangelisch-reformierten Kirche, dargestellt und aus den Quellen belegt* (2 vols.; Zürich: Orell, Füssli, 1847); C. Hase, *Hutterus redivivus, oder Dogmatik der evangelischen-Lutherischen Kirche, ein Dogmatisches Repertorium für Studierende* (Leipzig: Breitkopf & Haertel, 1868).

An overview of Orthodox dogmatic literature is found in H. E. Weber, *op. cit.,* vol. II.

Useful newer editions: J. Gerhard, *Loci communes theologici* (1610ff.), ed. F. R. Frank (1885ff.); J. Wolleb, *Christianae theologiae Compendium* (1626), in J. W. Beardslee III, ed. and tr., *Reformed Dogmatics* (New York: Oxford University Press, 1965); L. Hutterus, *Compendium locorum theologicorum* (1610), A. Twesten, ed. (Berlin: Hertz, 1855); W. Trillhaas, ed. (Berlin: de Gruyter, 1961); ET: *Compend of Lutheran Theology,* tr. H. E. Jacobs and G. F. Speiker (Philadelphia: Lutheran Book Store, 1868).

German excerpts (Reformation and Orthodoxy) in E. Hirsch, *Hilfsbuch zum Studium der Dogmatik; Die Dogmatik der Reformatoren und der alt-evangelischen Lehrer quellenmässig belegt und verdeutscht* (Berlin: Walter de Gruyter, 1958, 1964).

against Aristotle lost their effectiveness. For if Reformation dogmatics was to proceed along the path of thoughtful analysis, then this meant that this would be done primarily with Aristotelian thought-forms, and it was not long before the high schools of Protestantism, under Melanchthon's influence, began to use Aristotle again; however, they did it with less zeal than in the Middle Ages because the decisive aspects of Reformation theology could not be adequately expressed in these thought-forms. The beginnings of non-Aristotelian philosophy which are found in the 16th century—the religiously defined empiricism of Petrus Ramus (1515–72)[26] and the older Italian Renaissance attempts at a new Platonism[27]— were accepted by Reformed Orthodoxy only in a very limited way.[28] In general, Orthodoxy was dominated by Aristotelianism. In this schoolroom, Orthodoxy learned how to analyze and subdivide material dialectically and conceptually, and here it gained its virulent natural theology, its pattern for the doctrine of the law, and so on.[29]

In spite of all this, nothing could be more incorrect than to understand the dogmatics of Orthodoxy merely as Protestant Aristotelianism. This would mean a misunderstanding of Orthodoxy's intention, which was to preserve the Reformation approach, which had become a tradition and a legacy, and to order everything conceptual in it. "The doctrine of justification remains the banner of Orthodoxy."[30] Thus, the Reformation standard of Scripture alone *(sola scriptura)* was firmly upheld by Orthodoxy and proved itself to be a strong wall of resistance against the disintegration of dogmatics into all kinds of general and rational prop-

---

26. Regarding Petrus Ramus: Paul Lobstein, *Petrus Ramus als Theologe; Ein Beitrag zur Geschichte der protestantischen Theologie* (Strassburg: 1878); on his influence upon William Ames, K. Reuter, *Wilhelm Amesius, der führende Theologe des erwachenden reformierten Pietismus* (Neukirchen: Neukirchener Verlag, 1940); ET: "William Ames, The Leading Theologian . . . ," tr. D. Horton, in Nethenus, Visscher, and Reuter, *William Ames* (Cambridge: Harvard Divinity School Library, 1965).

27. It is probable that the philosophy of Pico della Mirandola influenced Calvin. Important insights into the history of Italian spiritualism can be found in the textual edition of D. Cantimore and E. Feist, *Per la storia degli eretici italiana del secolo XVI in Europa* (Rome: Reale Academia d'Italia, 1937); also Cantimore, *Eretici italiani del Cinquecento* (Firenze: G. C. Sansom, 1939, 1967²); GT: *Italienische Haeretik er der Spätrenaissance,* tr. W. Kaegi (Basel: B. Schwabe, 1949). Otherwise see especially J. Bohatec, *Budé und Calvin. . . .*

28. The thesis of Platonic tendencies in Calvin (with a strong emphasis upon the influence of Erasmus) is advanced by M. Schulze, *Meditatio futurae vitae; Ihr Begriff und ihre herrschende Stellung im System Calvins* (Leipzig: Dieterich, T. Weicher, 1901); and *Calvins Jenseitschristentum* (1902; n.l.); a more careful approach: H. Quistorp, *op. cit.*

29. The philosophical foundations of Orthodoxy have been especially investigated in H. E. Weber, *Die philosophische Scholastik des deutschen Protestantismus im Zeitalter der Orthodoxie* (Leipzig: Quelle & Meyer, 1907) (Erlangen dissertation); H. E. Weber, *Der Einfluss der protestantischen Schulphilosophie auf die orthodoxe lutherische Dogmatik* (Leipzig: Deichert, 1908; repr. Darmstadt: Wissenschaftliche Buchgesellschaft, 1969); P. Althaus, *Die Prinzipienlehre der deutschen reformierten Dogmatik im Zeitalter der aristotelischen Scholastik* (Leipzig: Deichert, 1914; Darmstadt: Wissenschaftliche Buchgesellschaft, 1967); J. Bohatec, *Die cartesianische Scholastik, in der Philosophie und reformierten Dogmatik des 17. Jahrhunderts* (Leipzig: A. Deichert, 1912); regarding the whole setting see W. Dilthey, *Gesammelte Schriften II* (15 vols.; Leipzig: Teubner, 1914–58), vol. II (1913, 1929).

30. H. E. Weber, *Reformation, Orthodoxie, und Rationalismus . . . ,* II, xvii.

ositions. The event-character of the Word remained in view, and together with it the ultimate unpredictability of revelation. Orthodoxy also had to cope with the long-standing tension between being and event, general existence and "the most concrete of things" *(concretissimum)*. Certainly Orthodoxy favored in its thinking the elements of being and the universal, but it found it much harder than did Scholasticism to incorporate the event and the concrete into these, or even to neglect them totally. One effect of the Reformation approach ("God incarnate," "God over against us") was that Orthodoxy evidenced unusual breakthroughs of rationalistic, being-oriented thinking.

b. Confessional Divisions. Orthodoxy also differed from Scholasticism in that it occurred in a Church which was confessionally divided (the Eastern Schism had had little effect upon the course of Scholasticism). The Reformation had led up to a new and contradictory process of the formation of dogma: the conclusions are more or less marked by the Council of Trent, the Formula of Concord, and the Canons of Dort (although the last were only partially comparable to the others). The Church had become "confessional." In the German Empire the confessions were bound by imperial law with the territory. But the Peace of Augsburg did not protect the Reformed as such—they had to prove that they were "related to the Augsburg Confession," were followers of it. Outside the German Empire, Switzerland demonstrated a similar territorial enforcement of confessionality, which is no longer as total as it was. In the Netherlands there was a similar process among the Provinces. They differed in their confessions, although there was also a movement toward solidarity as a result of their common history over against the recession of Spanish authority. In Scandinavia, a relatively free Lutheranism ruled without any limitations. The two kingdoms on British soil found in the 17th century the form of political and ecclesiastical cooperation which was to remain permanent. In all instances we may state that the connection of confessions and territory was never a hindrance to theological encounters, either polemical or irenic, where the common presupposition was that there is only one Christian truth and that it therefore would be found either in one's own confession or in certain "fundamental articles" about which the Protestants at least were able to agree.[31] Under these circumstances, Orthodox dogmatics were "confessional"—in another sense among the Reformed than among most of the Lutherans, because of the former's confessionality generally being less consistent and cohesive. However, no dogmatician in any confession can avoid dealing with the questions of the other confessions. This leads of necessity to an ongoing mutual influence, or at least it keeps it alive. At some points Reformed Orthodoxy reveals medieval tendencies; the Lutheran is not uninfluenced by the newer Nom-

---

31. On the Fundamental Articles see especially H. Leube, *Calvinismus und Luthertum im Zeitalter der Orthodoxie* (Leipzig: Deichert, 1928; repr. Aalen: Scientia Verlag, 1966), vol. I; and O. Ritschl, *Dogmengeschichte . . .*, IV, 252ff. The first occurrence of the term *articuli fundamentales* is to the best of my knowledge in F. Junius, "Eirenicum," in *Opuscula theologica selecta, recognivit et praefatus est Abr. Kuyperus* (Amstelodami: Apud F. Muller et J. H. Kruyt; Neo-Eboraci: Apud B. Westermann, 1882). It was later in general usage.

inalism of some Jesuits (Molinism)—for example, in questions of providence or of the free will; Roman Catholic devotional literature begins to influence Protestant piety before the Pietist epoch. Fortunately, the confessionalism of dogmatics did not mean that the various directions were undisturbed by one another.

c. The Setting of the Time. In other regards, too, the history of Orthodox dogmatics should not be viewed as an undisturbed process. Later generations forget easily that High Orthodoxy in Germany coincided more or less with the Thirty Years' War; it was not the time for meditative isolation, and it is cause for admiration that in a time like that such monumental theological accomplishments were achieved at all. Yet even where the outer circumstances were somewhat more positive, as in the Netherlands or Switzerland, there was no lack of problems and challenges. Reformed Orthodoxy in these countries had to cope continually with opponents who were establishing a link between the Italian Spiritualism of the Renaissance and the Enlightenment then emerging in the West: Socinianism and Arminianism were the embracing movements for these groups, and they are still a very real presence in the West European churches.[32] In France, Arminianism's influence was coupled with pressures being exercised from outside, and England in the Orthodox Age was being shaken by the storms of a reform movement which coalesced with a revolution and departed from it in part, namely, Puritanism. Obviously the various dangers alluded to here lead to a variety of shapes of Orthodoxy. In the area of German Lutheranism, which saw itself endangered far more from outside than from within, these dangers had a stiffening effect, whereas the Reformed Orthodoxy of the West, which was related to Humanism in a special way deriving from its very sources, was not only forced by its inner protagonists to such hard decisions as the Canons of Dort (1618–19) or the Formula Consensus Helvetica (1675) but also loosened up in the process. In addition, exegesis was a stronger force in the Reformed world, and biblical philology celebrated its great triumphs[33] while raising highly uncomfortable questions for dogmatics. Finally, we must not overlook the fact that dogmatics never established dictatorial authority in the Church: both devotional literature and hymnody went largely their own, pre-Pietistic ways, with a certain amount of contact with Catholic asceticism, and from early on there was a tendency in preaching to give the "heart"—within the context of Orthodox possibilities, of course—what dogmatics seemed to be keeping from it. In the Netherlands, Pietism arose very early

---

32. See Delio Cantimori (p. 113, n. 27). On Socinianism especially O. Fock, *Der Sozinianismus nach seiner Stellung in der Gesamtentwicklung des christlichen Geistes, nach seinem historischen Verlauf und nach seinem Lehrbegriff* (Kiel: Schröder, 1847); J. C. van Slee, *Het Socinianisme in Nederland* (1912; n.l.).

Socinianism was especially widespread in Poland; see K. Völker, *Kirchengeschichte Polens* (Berlin: W. de Gruyter, 1930). Regarding Arminianism see especially A. Schweizer, *Die protestantischen Centraldogmen . . .*, II, 31ff.

33. The chief centers were Basel and Leiden; especially Basel, with the work of the Hebraists and Rabbinists J. Buxtorf, father and son (1564–1629 and 1599–1664); but also Leiden, with the Frenchman Joseph Justus Scaliger (1540–1609), and later Johann Jakob Wettstein (1693–1754), who was already critical in his approach.

within the Orthodox world,[34] and with his *Pia Desideria*, the very Orthodox Alsatian, Philipp Jakob Spener (1635–1705), penetrated into the realm of German Lutheranism. It was a highly changing world in which Orthodox thinking was being done, and the Orthodox theologians were constantly forced to struggle for the issues which were at stake. This often made them hard, even difficult to digest. It also resulted in Orthodoxy's losing contact with real man[35] and ultimately being unable to reach either his feelings or his intellect. But it would not be correct to say that this self-isolation was the general rule—it was a reaction to the struggle, but not the customary way of going about things.

The two characteristic marks of the dogmatic thought of Orthodoxy were (1) the interrelationship of reason and revelation, and (2) the formal principle of Scripture. The two are related to each other: both draw a boundary between the rational and the super-rational, but assume in regard to the super-rational that it is superior to or has priority over the rational within the same category of being. Both can be traced back to the Reformation. H. E. Weber has demonstrated that not just Melanchthon but all of the Reformation theologians were a part of this development, especially Matthias Flacius Illyricus (1520–75) and in some points Calvin, too.[36] We shall discuss briefly what is involved here.

d. Reason and Revelation. That God's revelation did not simply push aside reason was certainly a view of the Reformation. But it was also acknowledged that the "realm" to which reason belongs does not belong to the same category within which the "realm" of grace or revelation is found, but rather that there is a categorical distinction here. This insight can lead Luther to formulate theological statements in total paradox: in that "revelation" is expressed rationally, it destroys the structure of rationality which otherwise remains intact—for example, in the area of politics. This is probably one of the reasons for Luther's not having written a dogmatics as one would have expected.

However, the necessity for the appropriate expression of Reformation thought could not, in the polemical situation present, be discounted. The Reformation encountered a "system" already present, as much in disarray as it was, and had to encounter this system on its own terms. It had to provide evidence and to establish relationships; for evidence it had to demonstrate its criteria, and to establish relationships it had to make use of the apparatus of logic and dialectics. Luther himself felt this necessity—his enthusiasm for Melanchthon's *Loci communes* shows this. Beyond Melanchthon, and often in controversy with him, there were others who went in the same direction, especially Calvin. Mere polemics

---

34. Fundamental here is W. G. Goeters, *Die Vorbereitung des Pietismus, in der ref. Kirche d. Niederland bis. z. labadist. Krisis 1670* (Leipzig: J. C. Hinrichs, 1911).

35. See A. Tholuck, *Der Geist der lutherischen Theologen Wittenbergs im Verlaufe des 17. Jahrhunderts . . .* (Hamburg: F. & A. Perthes, 1852); *Das akademische Leben des 17. Jahrhunderts; Vorgeschichte des Rationalismus*, 1,1 (Halle: Anton, 1853ff.); *Das kirchliche Leben des 17. Jahrhunderts; Vorgeschichte des Rationalismus*, 2,1 2,2 (Berlin: Wiegand & Grieben, 1861ff.).

36. H. E. Weber, *Reformation, Orthodoxie, und Rationalismus . . .*, I,1 and I,2.

evolved into antithetical arguments. In addition, within the Reformation camp the well-known divergencies arose, not only those which later would result in "confessions," but also those associated with Osiander (1498–1552), Flacius (1520–75), and the Philippists. How were such encounters to be possible, how were the protagonists to make their respective positions clear if they did not present an orderly and all-embracing system? The controversies contributed not a little to the development of the "orthodox" system. It was not enough to posit paradox formulations, since everyone more or less agreed on what these formulations defined. Evangelical theology could also not be satisfied with the mere recapitulation of the Church's decisions—Church Positivism, which the heirs of Nominalism encouraged—because to do so would mean to give up the Reformation's rejection of the principle of tradition.

The rational elaboration of the Reformation position would probably not have happened if there had not been inner tendencies toward it in Reformation thought from a very early date.[37] These are found directly alongside the Reformation approach itself: If the "righteousness of God" (*justitia Dei*) was understood as the "righteousness of the Gospel" (*justitia evangelii*) in sharp contrast to any "righteousness of the law or of works" (*justitia legis* or *operum*), then the Pauline text itself would suggest that the genuine righteousness of God which alone justifies should be viewed as *imputed* righteousness; this in turn would suggest that the objectivity of the salvation-event be thought out in contrast to any "subjective" activity of man. But if the salvation-event is something objective, then it is as such open to objective-rational discourse: the objectivism of salvation results in its being capable of rationalization. The handiest pattern of objectification available was the juridical one: God's justifying activity takes place before his forum ("forensic") and consists of the "imputation of the merits of Christ" (*imputatio meriti Christi*), in the nonimputation of human sin, and in the mediate imputation of faith which grasps the "merit of Christ" (*meritum Christi*). Thus, the original Reformation concept of "in Christ" was transformed into a more manageable "by means of the merits of Christ" (*propter meritum Christi*), which was opposed to all human merit. However, this merit was not cut off from reason (which of course was bound to revelation) because it was an object. It could therefore be intellectually related to any other object, such as to sin as an object, to faith as "something possessed" (*habitus*), to the Church as an institution. This objectification was already beginning to happen in the age of the Reformation, and Orthodoxy only needed to keep building on it.

To be sure, it was not "natural" reason which was able to gain insight into the objective fact of salvation, but only reason illuminated by the Word of God. But it was still reason. And this meant that a boundary was being drawn: reason could be initially natural reason, without the Word of God and thus without knowledge of the objective facts of salvation—but still not ill-equipped to recognize them in light of the Word. Hypothetically, reason is found to be capable of being reason which is conditioned by salvation and related to salvation. Thus a continuum was posited: reason without revelation can make reliable judgments up

---

37. H. E. Weber, *op. cit.*, I,1 and I,2 *passim*.

to a certain point, and beyond this point the same reason can do so when guided by revelation. The point itself remained variable. But the continuity of reason persisted in its position. It is obvious that in this way the door was opened for the further question as to how much reason could comprehend the divine, the law, the nature of man and the world. In fact, the issue was now one of quantity! The question of natural theology, already raised by biblical texts, was now set forth as a result of the interior structure of theological thought itself.

The concept of the objective fact of salvation opened the door to Rationalism and finally permitted revelation to become the supernatural announcement of supernatural truths. On the other hand, it was precisely this rational "objectivism" which is characteristic of Orthodoxy which had to raise the issue of the subject of faith. It would be difficult to conceive of this subject as being exclusively governed by reason. The result was that the more strongly reason became the dominant ruler, the more loudly the appeal was sounded for a way of life which corresponded to faith, the call for a "new obedience" *(nova oboedientia)*, for the "practice of piety" *(praxis pietatis)*, up to and including the longed-for "mystical union" *(unio mystica)*. Ethicism and emotionalism join with formal Rationalism by means of an inner necessity as undeniable equivalents. The Reformers, proceeding upon the basis of the righteousness of Christ, had seen man and experienced him as a unity, but this unity was divided in the Age of Orthodoxy. This also made way for the incursion of Roman Catholic devotional literature, writings on prayer, etc.; the piety of the Orthodox period often revealed pre-Pietistic elements as early as the Thirty Years' War and even earlier in the Netherlands, not to speak of England, where Puritanism and Pietism scarcely can be differentiated.[38]

e. The Principle of Scripture. The Reformation approach was developed in and through Scripture. It could only be defended by means of the appeal to Scripture—in this regard, Luther's rejection of the infallibility of conciliar decisions at the Leipzig Disputation (1519) signified a very deep break. Thus, the Reformation theologians themselves were gradually forced to provide a systematic demonstration of their view that the Bible alone was authoritative in questions of faith. This happened in the first decades with a degree of hesitation. The reason is certainly not so much that interest was lacking in this problem but rather that[39] the late Middle Ages, building upon the foundation of the early Church, had produced a fully developed principle of Scripture. This "principle," together with its doctrine of inspiration, seems to be incomparably more "orthodox" than was Luther's view,[40] which looked upon Scripture from the position of law and Gos-

---

38. A. Lang, *op. cit.*

39. F. Kropatscheck, *Das Schriftprinzip der lutherischen Kirche; Geschichtliche und dogmatische Untersuchungen* (Leipzig: A. Deichert, 1904), I ("The Legacy of the Middle Ages").

40. There is a good introduction in P. Schempp, "Luther's Stellung zur Heiligen Schrift," in R. Widmann, ed., *Theologische Entwürfe* (Theologische Bücherei, 50; Munich: Kaiser, 1973 [1929]); see otherwise the treatments of Luther's theology.

pel, and equally more "orthodox" than Calvin's well-developed doctrine[41] with its strong emphasis upon the necessity of the "testimony of the Holy Spirit" *(testimonium Spiritus Sancti)*.

Orthodox theology made use generally of the medieval views. Thus, the Bible was transformed from the testimony which causes faith to a supranatural thing which could be rationally grasped as an objective means and fact of revelation. The corollary then was the gradual tendency to establish the authority of Scripture rationally: the external criteria (the antiquity of the biblical documents, the reliability of the historical reports, the absence of contradictions in the contents) became progressively more important. It must be said that a certain insecurity can be traced behind all of these efforts: the Catholic principle of tradition had its own influence in the midst of the Orthodox Age (Georg Calixtus [1586–1656]), while, on the other hand, doubts began to arise particularly out of the zealous philological labors of the Reformed (we think of Ludwig Capella [1585–1658] and also of Rudolf Wettstein [1614–84][42]); Orthodoxy responded with the thesis (already to be found in Flacius) of inspiration, including even the punctuation of the Masoretic texts (Formula Consensus Helvetica [1675]). The more that Orthodoxy tried to secure its position, the weaker it became; it found itself being continuously forced to retreat more and more from the reality of the living biblical Word testified to in proclamation to its supernatural origins and preservation, that is, to an "objective" fact which as such was objectively subject to attack.

f. The Effects of These Chief Characteristics. The consequences which follow for Orthodox dogmatics from these briefly sketched chief characteristics are obvious.

As soon as supranaturalism had established itself in theology, as soon as reason had been assigned the rôle of a continuum, and as soon as it became an indispensable means, it could very soon take over the additional role of a criterion. If the boundary between the "natural" and "supernatural" areas was within the same category, then this boundary could also be moved around. This is what happened in later Orthodoxy: the boundaries of the "natural" moved into those areas formerly reserved for the "supernatural," and then the Enlightenment pushed the boundaries so far that finally revelation was understood as superfluous or at most as the anticipation of what later on would be just as accessible to reason.

When Scripture became a supernatural "object" with supernatural characteristics, then these characteristics, since they had to be rationally recognizable, were subject to the controls of philology, which itself emerged strongly as a rational science in the 17th century and moved on to critical positions in the 18th century; such controls could have negative results. We need only to review the road between Rudolf Wettstein (1614–84) and Johann Jakob Wettstein (1693–1754)

---

41. *Institutes*, I, vi-ix, pp. 69–96; D. J. de Groot, *Calvijns opvatting over de inspiratie der Heilige Schrift* (Zutphen: N. V. Nauta, 1931); J. A. Cramer, *De Heilige Schrift bij Calvijn* (Utrecht: O. Oosthoek, 1926); H. Noltensmeier, *Reformatorische Einheit; das Schriftverständnis bei Luther und Calvin* (Graz: H. Böhlaus Nachf., 1953).

42. On Rudolf Wettstein, see Max Geiger, *Die Basler Kirche und Theologie im Zeitalter der Hochorthodoxie* (Zollikon: Evangelischer Verlag, 1952).

in order to see this clearly.[43] The combination of emerging historical and literary criticism with Orthodoxy's presuppositions and assertions led almost unavoidably to an objective rejection of Scripture or of those elements under fire. In that the scriptural "principle" had become in fact rational, it was now "rationally" refutable—the Enlightenment enters the scene! Potentially, in the form of Italian Spiritualism, it had long been there, and now it only needed to expand its positions, to take its Orthodox opponents at their word in order to win the day.

   g. *Differences Between Lutheran and Reformed Orthodoxy.* As we said, Orthodox dogmatics was confessionally determined. Its age can be called the "Confessional Age." This confessional determination did not mean, however, that the dogmatics of one "confession" would be noetically isolated from another. Everyone was well informed about everyone else in the 17th century. Still, the total direction of dogmatic work was really defined by the dogmatic decisions already made. The central orientation of Lutheran dogmatics is the doctrine of the salvation-event and the appropriation of salvation, of justification, and of faith; that of the Reformed generally (there is greater variety here) the doctrine of God's decrees and of their realization in salvation-history. They are not mutually exclusive: the Lutherans have their doctrine of predestination too, and the Reformed certainly do not neglect the doctrine of justification. But their thematic approach is different. And this leads to a separation in terms of contents: the usual Lutheran doctrine of predestination tends more and more to keep a space open for free will and to limit predestination to the faith which God knew of in advance in his "foreknowledge" (*praescientia*; this necessitated the very difficult attempts to distinguish between the knowledge and the will of God). Conversely, the Reformed doctrine of justification was built into their system of the doctrine of decrees, and reconciliation and justification appear as elements of the salvific act ordered and carried out by God for the benefit of the elect (which then necessitated the difficult consideration of the question whether Christ really had died for the sins of the whole world). It is clear that with the Lutherans, subjectivism, which was unavoidable as a counterweight to their system's objectivism, established itself above all in the act of appropriating salvation, in faith itself, so much so that finally a fully developed doctrine of the ("subjective") order of salvation *(ordo salutis)* appears, whereas on the Reformed side faith itself remained completely within the doctrine of decrees, and thus the activity of faith (if the term is permitted), that is, gratitude and new obedience, receives strong emphasis. We cannot deal with all of the details here; these references to the various themes will have to suffice, although it would require that we complete them by dealing with all of the relevant questions in order to arrive at truly clear positions.[44]

   h. *Lutheran Orthodoxy.* It is possible to distinguish rather roughly three

---

43. W. J. Leute, *Het leven en Werken van J. J. Wettstein* (n.l.; 1902).
   44. We must refer again here to the works of H. E. Weber and O. Ritschl as well as to W. Grass's *Geschichte der Dogmatik.* . . .

phases in the course of Lutheran Orthodoxy: Early Orthodoxy, beginning with the theologians of the Formula of Concord and dealing essentially with its problems; High Orthodoxy, whose most outstanding spokesman was Johann Gerhard of Jena (1582–1637) and which was somewhat removed from the actual situation of confessional conflict and moving on to the formulation of comprehensive systems; and Late Orthodoxy, in which the aspects of supranaturalism already developed now more clearly demonstrate their tendency toward rationalism.

Early Orthodoxy found its most important representatives in Martin Chemnitz (1522–86),[45] who remained the authoritative figure in Lower Saxony and who was very strongly influenced by Melanchthon, and in the Swabian Aegidius Hunnius (1550–1603),[46] who was active primarily in Marburg. The former's most significant accomplishment, aside from his keen and perceptive critique of Trent, was his Christology, which was the cause of heated controversies. It reduced the doctrine of ubiquity, originally developed by the Swabians, to the absolute minimum necessary for the Lutheran doctrine of communion, and it removed the ubiquity doctrine's tendency toward Gnosticism, which the Melanchthon disciple definitely felt to be there. Aegidius Hunnius, a virulent opponent of the Reformed in Hessia, established the predestination doctrine of Orthodox Lutheranism along the broad middle line where it remained, in opposition to the universalism of the Swiss theologian, the wandering Samuel Huber (1547–1624).

Moving toward High Orthodoxy, we see the controversial Swabian Leonhard Hutter (1563–1616), whose *Compendium locorum theologicorum*[47] became the major dogmatic textbook of Lutheranism in that period and replaced Melanchthon's *Loci*. Hutter is basically moderate in his dogmatic position. And this is all the more true of his superior student, Johann Gerhard (1582–1637), who presented the most comprehensive work of Lutheran Orthodoxy in his *Loci com-*

---

45. *Examination of the Council of Trent*, tr. F. Kramer (St. Louis: Concordia, 1971–   ), vol. I; otherwise especially important: *The Two Natures in Christ*, tr. J. A. O. Preus (St. Louis: Concordia, 1971 [g1578]); *Loci communes theologici* (1591 posthumously). Biography by Hermann Hachfeld, *Martin Chemnitz nach seinem Leben und Wirken, insbesondere nach seinem Verhältnis zum Tridentinum* (Leipzig: Breitkof & Härtel, 1867).

The question about the sense in which Christ possessed the characteristics of majesty in the so-called "status of emptying" *(in status exinanitionis)* (the special concern was his ubiquity) was initiated by Chemnitz in that he injected into the debate the distinction between the "status of emptiness" *(status exinanitionis)* and the "status of exaltation" *(status exaltationis)*. From 1619 on it was the subject of heated and fruitless controversies between the Giessen theologians (especially Balthasar Mentzer) and the Tübingen scholars (especially Lukas Osiander); the Giessen representatives, along the lines of Martin Chemnitz and directly influenced by Johannes Marbach, held to the concept of *kenosis* (emptying), while the Tübingen theologians wanted to have only *krypsis* (concealment, the factual nonimplementation of the characteristics of majesty).

46. *Opera* in Latin ed. of Helv. Gartius (1607ff.; n.l.).

47. Appeared 1610; ET: see p. 112, n. 25; his more comprehensive *Loci communes* (1619 posthumously) (they resemble Melanchthon's work). Twesten's German edition of the *Compendium* cited above includes excerpts from Wolleb and Pictet. Hutter can be seen as a controversial theologian especially in his *Concordia concors* (1614), in which he responded to the *Concordia discors* of R. Hospinian of Zürich (1607).

munes theologici,[48] almost a *Summa* of theology. Of the Wittenberg scholars of the same period we would mention Johannes Hülsemann[49] (1602–61), who was one of the chief opponents of Georg Calixtus (see below) and who in the course of that struggle was led to reintroduce the older problem of the "fundamental articles" *(articuli fundamentales)*.[50] At about the same time, Johann Conrad Dannhauer (1603–66)[51] of Strasbourg produced a rather well-developed version of what later would be called an "order of salvation" *(ordo salutis)*.

High Orthodoxy and even more strongly Late Orthodoxy are overshadowed by the "syncretistic" theology which emanated from Helmstedt. The leading theologian of Late Orthodoxy, Abraham Calovius of Wittenberg (1612–86),[52] even attempted to establish a new confession directed against the Helmstedtians (Consensus repetitus, printed in 1664). His contemporary in Wittenberg was Andreas Quenstedt (1617–88), related to him in thought and later even as his father-in-law, but less original; however, his *Theologia didactico-polemica*[53] can be regarded as the normative dogmatics of developed Lutheran Orthodoxy, along with the older and shorter textbook by Johann Friedrich König of Rostock (1619–64)[54] or the contemporary *Compendium theologiae positivae* of the moderate Johann Wilhelm Baier of Jena (1647–95).[55] As the last great accomplishment of Orthodoxy we mention the *Examen theologicum acroamaticum*, written at the beginning of the 18th century (1707) by David Hollaz (1648–1713); its date makes clear that it was already part of a new age.

The great mischief-maker in the realm of Lutheran Orthodoxy was Georg Calixtus of Helmstedt (1586–1656), who has already been mentioned in connec-

---

48. New edition of the *Loci* (1610–22), by E. Preuss (1863ff.) and F. R. Frank (1885). It is significant that Johann Gerhard also wrote devotional literature, e.g., an *Exercitium pietatis quotidianum* (1612), and also a *Disputatio de studio pietatis* (1624).
E. Troeltsch, *Vernunft und Offenbarung bei Johann Gerhard und Melanchthon, Gesammelte Schriften* (Tübingen: J. C. B. Mohr, 1912–25; repr.: Aalen: Scientia Verlag, 1961–66); R. Hupfeld, *Die Ethik Johann Gerhards; ein Beitrag zum Verständnis der lutherischen Ethik* (Berlin: Trowitzsch, 1908).
49. *Calvinismus irreconciliabilis* (1644; n.l.); see also M. Keller-Hüschemenger, *Das Problem der Fundamentalartikel bei Johannes Hülsemann in seinem theologiegeschichtlichen Zusammenhang (Beiträge zur Förderung christlicher Theologie*, 41/2; Gütersloh: Bertelsmann, 1939).
50. See p. 107, n.4; in later periods N. Hunnius should be mentioned; he used the concept of the fundamental articles polemically, contrary to its original meaning: *Diaskepsis theologica de fundamentali Dissensu doctrinae Evangelicae Lutheranae et Calvinae seu Reformatae* (1626).
51. *Hodosophia Christiana* (1649) (Argentorati: Spoor, 1666); see also H. Leube, *Die Reformideen in der deutschen lutherischen Kirche zur Zeit der Orthodoxie* (Leipzig: Dörfling & Franke, 1924). Dannhauer influenced Philipp Jakob Spener, who then participated in a later edition of the *Hodosophia* (see H. E. Weber, *op. cit.*, II, xx).
52. His home, Mohrungen, was the birthplace a century later of Johann Gottfried Herder. His twelve-volume *Systema locorum theologicorum* appeared in 1655–77, with a selection of excerpts in 1682 *(Theol. pos.)*.
53. Wittenberg, 1685.
54. First published in 1664 with the title *Theologia positiva acroamatica*.
55. First published 1686, new edition by E. Preuss, 1864; C. F. G. Walther, ed. (St. Louis: Concordia, 1879).

tion with his application of the analytical method[56] and also his separation of ethics from dogmatics, which he based on the view that ethics describes the life of the reborn person. But what disturbed his contemporaries most in this very unusual personality[57] was his endeavor to reconcile the confessional divisions theologically, an endeavor which was at least hypothetical but which became quite practical in his role at the Colloquy of Thorn in 1645. As a Humanist, a well-traveled man, a historian, and a traditionalist, he tried to demonstrate that the early Church had fully developed the essential and fundamental insights of Christianity and that compared to these the discrepancies of his age were only of secondary importance. This is the doctrine of the *Consensus quinquesaecularis* (theological agreement of the first five centuries), which later would be so influential, that is being presented here. It led to Calixtus and his Helmstedt followers being suspected of crypto-papism and alternatively of crypto-Calvinism—in reality he was just pursuing the traditionalist line already found in Melanchthon. He belongs to the group of traditionalist irenicists based upon Humanism, and thus he forms a bridge in the midst of the Orthodox Age between the 16th and the enlightened 18th centuries.

i. Reformed Orthodoxy.

i. Reformed Orthodoxy. Reformed Orthodoxy had to cope with many more "mischief-makers" than did Lutheran.

It had to struggle with the ongoing effects of Humanism and of the Italian Renaissance, as they were found in Socinianism and also in Arminianism and proved themselves constantly strong—there were times in the Netherlands when the Arminians could appear as the original bearers of the Reformed Church. In addition, Reformed Orthodoxy lacked a confessional document which uniformly bound all parties together on a mutual basis, this in spite of the significant effect which finally, at the heights of Orthodoxy, was achieved by the Canons of the Synod of Dort. Finally, Reformed Orthodoxy developed in very diverse political and cultural areas which were connected by highly active communication and contacts, but still each had its own unique characteristics. One thing they all did have in common: the inherited intellectual legacy including Humanism was not just integrated here, but was transformed. The result was that there were Reformed who showed an astonishing traditionalism and others who evidenced unusual, often discontinuous movement and variety in their actual theological work. Therefore, it is not possible to make a historical judgment about what really was "orthodox" in Reformed dogmatics without making some kind of dogmatic judgment. A dogmatician as controversial as Moyse Amyraut (1596–1664)[58] must be regarded as Orthodox, and based upon his thinking alone even an Arminian like

---

56. See pp. 58–60. It should be noted that J. Acontius also supported the analytical method (*De methodo* [1558]).

57. His biography, E. L. T. Henke, *Georg Calixtus und seine Zeit* (2 vols.; Halle: Buchhandlung des Waisenhauses, 1856); see also Weber, *op. cit.*, vol. II, and O. Ritschl, *op. cit.*, vol. IV, *passim*. Works by Calixtus include *Epitome Theologiae moralis* (1634) and *De pactis quae Deus cum hominibus iniit* (1654).

58. J. Moltmann, *op. cit.*; H. E. Weber, *op. cit.*, II, 128ff. Out of date: A. Schweizer, *Die Centraldogmen der reformierten Kirche . . .*, II, 225ff.

Simon Episcopius (1583–1643)[59] is very close to being an Orthodox, not to speak of Church theologians like Johannes Cocceius (1603–69), William Ames (1576–1633), even William Perkins (1558–1602) and Richard Baxter (1615–91), although Cocceius, Ames, and Baxter were subjected to severe opposition.

In spite of all this, we can determine that a certain constancy is to be found in the group which built its Orthodoxy as a predestinarian system. Theodore Beza (1519–1605) is the point of departure, more so than Calvin. It was the dogmaticians of this direction who prepared theologically the decisions of Dort, but in such a fashion that one of the most caustic of them, Francis Gomar of Groningen (1563–1641), lost out with his supralapsarianism to the decisions favoring infralapsarianism.[60] Those who were definite predestinarians included Samuel Des Marets (Maresius)[61] in Groningen (1599–1673), Johannes Maccovius (1588–1644) in Franeker,[62] and the Silesian who was active in Basel, Amandus Polman von Polansdorf, known as Polanus (1561–1610),[63] and then among the Huguenots the school of Sedan which like the Leiden faculty presented a common formulation of Orthodox predestinarianism.[64] The author of the best-liked Compendium in this period, Johannes Wolleb (1586–1629) of Basel, belongs in general in this group.[65] The structural peculiarities of the Orthodox system as they were outlined above are found in well-defined form only in this group, whose centers were Leiden, Groningen, Franeker, Utrecht, Basel, Geneva, and Sedan. Their most significant personality, comparable both in character and in greatness with Johann Gerhard, was Gisbert Voetius of Utrecht (1589–1676); he was an Orthodox dogmatician, a specialist in Church law, and a patron of pre-Pietistic piety movements, who did not deny that he was obligated to the Herborn theology (Wilhelm Zepper) for his chief work, and who connected the salvation-historical approach to predestinarianism.[66] One last proponent of extreme Orthodoxy was Johann Heinrich

---

59. *Opera theologica*, ed. S. Curcellaeus and in part A. Poelenburgh (Amstelodami: Blaev, 1650 and 1665); compare A. H. Hoentjens, *Simon Episcopius* (1899; n.l.).

60. *Works*, published in 3 vols. (fol., Amsterdam, 1644). Gomar was the most embittered of the opponents of Arminius. He was, incidentally, a student of Ursinus. See G. B. van Itterzon, *Franciscus Gomarus* ('s Gravenhage: M. Nijhoff, 1930).

61. A native of Picardy like Calvin, first active in France, then for decades in Groningen; see his *Collegium theologicum sive systema universalis Theologiae* (1645 and often thereafter).

62. Polish by birth (like John à Lasco); see his *Collegia theologica* (1623, 1631, 1641); *Loci communes* (1639); A. Kuyper, *Johannes Maccovius* (Leyden: 1899; n.l.). Maccovius opposed above all William Ames (*Medulla theologiae* [1628]; ET: *The Marrow of Theology*, tr. and ed. J. D. Eusden [Boston: Pilgrim Press, 1968]).

63. *Syntagma theologiae* (1624; n.l.).

64. *Thesaurus Theologiae Sedanensis* (1661); Leiden: *Synopsis purioris theologiae (1626)* (1652), new edition by H. Bavinck, *Synopsis purioris theologiae disputationibus* (Leiden Synopsis, 1626, 1652) (Lugduni Batavorum: Didericum Donner, 1881).

65. However, Wolleb shows more traces than the others in this circle of Covenant Theology.

66. *Selectae disputationes theologicae*, in *Reformed Dogmatics*, ed. and tr. J. W. Beardslee III (N.Y.: Oxford University Press, 1965); *Politica ecclesiastica* (1663ff.) (which contains the first instance of practical theology in our contemporary sense); see also A. C. Duker, *Gisbertus Voetius* (3 vols. in 4; Leiden: E. J. Brill, 1897–1914); and W. G. Goeters, *Die Vorbereitung des Pietismus, in der ref. Kirche d. Niederland bis z. labadist. Krisis 1670* (Leipzig: J. C. Hinrichs, 1911).

Heidegger (1633–98) of Zürich, the major author of the Formula Consensus Helvetica in 1675.

Probably more significant than the normal Orthodoxy already discussed were the special forms which developed on its margins. The most important source for this form was Heidelberg and along with it Herborn, and then Marburg and Bremen, all places where the Reformed movement was strongly influenced by Melanchthon; one could, with Heinrich Heppe,[67] call this grouping "German-Reformed" if there had not been very early similar developments and influences in the Netherlands, France, England, and finally Switzerland. Of course, the thinking here is also predestinarian. But the concept of the *covenant* is dominant. This means that the decrees of God are not understood so strongly as God's decisions per se but rather the historicity of their realization and the humanity of the covenant partner are seen more clearly. The whole emphasis is shifted from the Absolute to salvation-history and anthropology. That this can be done in a very "Orthodox" fashion is demonstrated by the *Explicationes Catecheseos* of Zacharias Ursinus (1534–83).[68] The degree to which the human element can receive its own importance in Christology can be seen in the very controversial view of Johannes Piscator (1546–1625) of Herborn that Christ actually accomplished reconciliation not by virtue of his "active obedience" *(oboedientia activa)*, to which he was obligated anyway through the incarnation, but only by virtue of his "passive obedience" *(oboedientia passiva)*. Other typical representatives of the Heidelberg-Herborn form of Orthodoxy were Johann Heinrich Alsted (1588–1638)[69] and Heinrich Alting (1583–1644).[70] The Melanchthonian legacy (and the anthropological element) produced in this group a strongly irenic attitude, which is first documented in the *Irenikon* of the Frenchman, Franciscus Junius (Francois du Jon,

---

67. *Die Dogmatik des deutschen Protestantismus im 16. Jahrhundert* . . .; *Kirchengeschichte beider Hessen* (Marburg: Sipmann'sche Buchhandlung [C. Kraatz], 1876). On the characteristics, see H. E. Weber, *op. cit.*, II, 158ff. J. Moltmann, *op. cit.* There is a study about the first great period of development in Heidelberg: K. Bauer, *Aus der grossen Zeit der theologischen Fakultät zu Heidelberg* (Verein für Kirchengeschichte in der ev. Landeskirche Baden, Veröffentlichungen, 14; Lahr: Schauenburg, 1938); regarding Herborn see H. Schlosser and W. Neuser, *Die Evangelische Kirche in Nassau-Oranien, 1530–1930* (Siegen: Kreissynode, 1931), I, 15ff. and J. H. Steubing, *Geschichte der Hohen Schule Herborn* (1823; n.l.). A comprehensive study of the whole and so unusually fruitful special type is lacking. We may mention now the book by W. Pixberg, *Die reformierten Schulordnungen* (1952; n.l.). Also helpful is O. V. Gierke, *Johannes Althusius; The Development of Political Theory*, tr. B. Freyd (New York: H. Fertig, 1966), and the essay on Althusius in Erik Wolf, *Grosse Rechtsdenker der deutschen Geistesgeschichte* (Tübingen: J. C. B. Mohr [P. Siebeck], 1939, 1944). We mention in passing that Amos Comenius also was a product of Herborn.

68. Z. Ursinus, *The Commentary on the Heidelberg Catechism*, tr. G. W. Williard (Grand Rapids: Eerdmans, 1956).

69. *Theologia didactica* (Hanover: C. Eifridi, 1618); *Theologia polemica* (Hanover: C. Eifridi, 1620); *Theologia naturalis* (Hanover: C. Eyfridi, 1623); *Encyclopaedia Biblica* (Frankfurt: B. Schmidt, 1625, 1630). Alsted developed a consequence of salvation-historical theology which later often appeared: Chiliasm (in 1694 the world was to end). Following his time in Herborn, he was active in Weissenburg in Siebenbürgen.

70. He was active in Herborn and Heidelberg, and later, after the Catholicization of the Palatinate, in Groningen. He was a thorough Biblicist and, like Alsted, a Ramist in philosophy. See his *Scripta theologicorum Heidelbergensium* (Amstelodami: J. Janssonum, 1646).

1545–1602),[71] and the most important work was that of David Pareus (1548–1622), who also was significant as a dogmatician.[72]

The Heidelberg-Herborn circle, closely connected with Zürich (Bullinger) in the one direction and with the Netherlands in the other (there were political relations between Herborn and Holland), influenced directly or indirectly two famous special developments: Federal Theology *(Föderaltheologie)* and the Theology of Saumur.

j. Federal Theology. Federal Theology,[73] which can be traced back to Zürich, Heidelberg, Herborn, and very strongly Bremen, was most importantly represented by Johannes Cocceius (1603–69; Johann Koch was his German name).[74] Its great accomplishment was to replace the view that God's decrees were carried out in an absolute fashion with a view of history unfolding in phases or stages; to put it another way, they connected the distinction between law and Gospel with the doctrine of decrees within a historical scheme. This led to the historicizing of the principle of Scripture. Federal Theology, which totally agreed with the broad Orthodox view of Scripture, made way in practice for a historical understanding of the Bible. In that it took up the Herborn approach and pursued the concept of the covenant even further, beyond the boundaries of theology, it helped to emphasize the concept of mutual obligation *(mutua obligatio)* as the essence of every legal relationship, thus indirectly preparing the way for the emergence of the modern concept of the state.

k. Amyraldism. The School of Saumur was introduced by the Scottish theologian John Cameron (c. 1579–1625), who earned his doctorate at Heidelberg and was active in France,[75] and its chief figure was the broadly educated Moyse Amyraut (Amyraldus [1596–1664]), who came to an alteration of the Orthodox doctrine of predestination as a result of the controversy with Arminianism,[76] not only by linking it up with the concept of the covenant but especially in the sense that he can actually speak of a "change in the counsels of God" *(mutatio consiliorum Dei)*. This means that he modifies the old concept of the "immutability of God" *(immutabilitas Dei)* and also sees the essence of the predestinarian problem not in the eternal decrees of God but in the puzzling dissimilarity of human behavior: God's first and original decree was in fact the salvation of all, because this decree is established in Christ—but it was the salvation of all *under the presupposition of faith*, which is not the faith of all. To put it pointedly, predes-

---

71. See p. 114, n. 31.

72. Born a Silesian like Ursinus and Polanus. His *Irenicum* appeared in 1614 and 1615. As a dogmatician, Pareus was a disciple of Ursinus, whose works he partially edited (see p. 125, n. 68).

73. The best presentation: G. Schrenk, *op. cit.* See also E. Graf von Korff, *op. cit.* For later periods see G. Weth, *op. cit.*

74. *Summa doctrinae de foedere* (1648); *Summa theologiae* (1662); bibliography in Schrenk, *op. cit.*, pp. 348ff.

75. *Works*, ed. F. Spanheim, Geneva (!) (1659).

76. *Brief traité de la prédestination* (1634); *Doctrinae Jo. Calvini de absoluto decreto defensio* (1641). See also J. Moltmann, *op. cit.*; the location of the literature is given there.

tination becomes election to faith. Such a view had to have many opponents, but from very early on, it found acceptance—for example, by Richard Baxter and his followers—and later it was positively received by a dogmatician of German Lutheran Pietism, Joachim Lange (1670–1744). It was a real blow for predestinarian Orthodoxy, because Amyraut was able to base his position firmly on Calvin, whom he restored to general notice—Beza's work had generally removed Calvin's from the focus of attention.

It is clear that with both the Cocceian and the Amyraldan Covenant Theology we are already on the threshold of a new age: in the midst of Reformed Orthodoxy, both Pietism and the Enlightenment begin to make themselves heard.

VI. Modern Dogmatics

A. THE ENLIGHTENMENT AND PIETISM IN DOGMATICS

a. The New Age. The trailblazers of the European Enlightenment were contemporaries of the Orthodox Epoch. Bacon's *Novum Organon* (1620), Descartes' *Discours de la methode* (1637), Hobbes' *Elements of Law natural and politic* (1640) and his *Leviathan* (1651), Spinoza's *Ethica more geometrico demonstrata* (1677 posthumously), Locke's *Essay Concerning Human Understanding* (1690) as well as the first great works of Leibniz (*De primae philosophiae emendatione* [1694]; *Système nouveau de la Nature* [1695]) all belong to the 17th century or lap over into the 18th century (as does Leibniz' *Monadologie* [1714]). Tolerant states such as the Netherlands, or England as it moves toward tolerance in the latter half of the century (since 1689), or Sweden, and gradually many royal courts in Germany, became centers of refuge for the new spirit in which the world was broadening and deepening itself in a way totally unforeseen by the late Renaissance (Galilei, Giordano Bruno). According to this spirit, man, as the bearer of reason or as the being capable of empirically controlling the world, stands autonomously in the midst of reality, which is steadily being relieved of all its wonders and mysteries. Therefore this spirit also seeks to free religion of all heteronomous necessity (e.g., Bacon, Cherbury, Spinoza, and most perfectly then in John Toland, *Christianity not mysterious* [1696]), which can never be more than merely externally binding (so Hobbes). As the natural world expands itself infinitely, the historical horizons are also broadened; the uniqueness of Christianity is put in question, even though it still appears to be the highest religion; the Orthodox order governing the relationship of the natural-rational and the supernatural-irrational is shifted in favor of the former; the infallibility of the Bible becomes doubtful—in fact, the whole approach of Orthodoxy, which still was centered upon soteriology, is now looked upon as old-fashioned, since the basic problem of man's life is the relationship of man to the world; the issue becomes ultimately that of the problem of providence connected with the ethical and political questions. This enormous transformation took place during the period of and in part directly before the eyes of the Orthodox theologians: with the Reformed leading, they were able partially at least to appropriate Cartesianism (e.g., the Duisburg School around Clauberg), whereas very

128

soon they were involved in battle with Spinoza; Spinoza, on the other hand, always active, was engaged in Church affairs and endeavored to lead the churches closer to each other.[1]

Orthodoxy did not produce the Enlightenment. It had its foundations in the Renaissance and in the gradual transformation of man's view of the world which had been emerging since Copernicus. But Orthodoxy prepared the way for rationalism as the preferred and characteristic thought structure of the Age of Enlightenment, especially theological Rationalism. In major representatives of Late Orthodoxy, especially in Samuel Werenfels (1657–1740),[2] Jean Alphonse Turrettini (1671–1737),[3] and Jean Frédéric Ostervald (1663–1747),[4] the outlines of what is going to come can be clearly recognized, in Ostervald connected to an obvious tendency toward Anglicanism which at the time was widely looked upon as the perfect amalgamation of tradition and rationality.

b. Late Orthodoxy Between Pietism and the Enlightenment. Theological Rationalism did not follow the course of the philosophical Enlightenment until the 18th century and the beginning of the 19th century, and then with a remarkable amount of hesitation. Theology responded to the Enlightenment at first with a kind of holding action in that it set new accents in traditional supranaturalism in favor of the "natural." In addition, theology was more directly confronted on German soil by Pietism than by the Enlightenment. And Pietism for its part arose at first in protest against the formalism of Orthodoxy. The response of Orthodoxy was not just negative; there was also a positive echo; Valentin Ernst Löscher (1673–1749) is a witness for both responses.[5] The Pietists' own dogmatic production was able generally to stay within the given framework; after all, both the doctrine of the "order of salvation" (*ordo salutis*) with its tendency toward "mystical union" (*unio mystica*) and the subjective element in Orthodoxy sketched out above had long been preparing the way for Pietism in German Lutheranism, not to mention the Netherlands and England. Of the Pietistic dogmaticians, Joachim

---

1. A comprehensive presentation, in fact a history of European thought in the last centuries: E. Hirsch, *Geschichte der neueren evangelischen Theologie* (5 vols.; Gütersloh: C. Bertelsmann, 1949–50).

2. *Disp. theologicae* (1675ff.); compare K. Barth, *EvTheol*, vol. III (1936).

3. *Opera* (4 vols.; New York: R. Carter, 1847–48), and *Institutio theologicae elencticae*, in *Reformed Dogmatics*, ed. and tr. J. W. Beardslee III (New York: Oxford University Press, 1965); P. Wernle, *Der schweizerische Protestantismus im 18. Jahrhundert* (3 vols.; Tübingen: J. C. B. Mohr, 1922–25); Eugène de Bude, *Vie de Jean Alphonse Turrettini, Théologien Genevois 1671–1737* (Lausanne: Bridel, 1880).

4. *Comp. theol. christ.* (1739); *Ethicae Christianae Comp.* (1739); David Durand, *La Vie de Jean Frederic Ostervald, pasteur de Neufchatel en Suisse* (Londres: To Payne et fils, 1778); Robert Gretillat, *Jean Frederic Ostervald 1663–1747* (Neuchatel: P. Attinger, 1904); see also J. J. von Allmen, *L'Église et ses Fonctions d'après Jean Frederic Osterwald* (Neuchatel: Delachaux et Niestlé, 1947).

5. *Vollständiger Timotheus Verinus* (1718). With his *Unschuldigen Nachrichten von alten und neueren theologischen Sachen* (begun 1701), Löscher initiated the first theological journal in Germany. See also F. Blanckmeister, *Der Prophet von Kursachsen, Valentin Ernst Löscher* (Dresden: F. Sturm & Company, 1920); Hans Martin Rotermund, *Orthodoxie und Pietismus, Valentin Ernst Löschers "Timotheus Verinus," in der Auseinandersetzung mit der Schule August Hermann Franckes* (Berlin: Evangelische Verlagsanstalt, 1959 [1948]).

Lange (1670–1744)[6] takes first place; next to him one should also mention Johann Anastasius Freylinghausen (1670–1739)[7] and J. J. Rambach (1693–1735).[8]

More significant was the new approach which was undertaken in Württemberg on the basis of a thoroughgoing Pietistic Biblicism (Johannes Albrecht Bengel [1687–1752] and his students).[9]

c. Supranaturalism. It is important to note how the developments were differentiated in the course of the 18th century. On the one hand, Pietism was devoting itself more and more to opposing the Enlightenment and less to Orthodoxy, which had scarcely any influence anymore. On the other hand, it becomes clear that the road from Pietism to the Enlightenment can be a very short one in some instances: the Theological Faculty of Halle, established as a bastion of Pietism, was led on by Sigismund Jakob Baumgarten (1706–1757) and his students to a form of supranaturalism which was both pietistic in mood and enlightened.[10] Since Pietism was interested in the practice of piety, this already given subjective element could easily be turned into a generally positive evaluation of subjectivity; the ties between the Church and natural theology, already long established in Orthodoxy, could also become a link between the pious subject and the naturally enlightened one, that is, between Pietism and the Enlightenment. Christian Wolff's (1679–1754) philosophy served here in a variety of ways as a bridge-builder, while in Swabia Leibniz's (1646–1716) philosophy achieved a similar effect: the thought that the divine original monad had established the whole universe as an organic totality became for F. C. Oetinger (1702–1782) (next to Bengel's influence) the point of departure for a theosophy which was ultimately rooted in the idea of organism, and which went its own unusual way between Pietism and the Enlightenment.[11]

Under the circumstances mentioned, the Enlightenment developed within theology and the Church partially in opposition to the Orthodoxy which it so

---

6. *Antibarbarus Orthodoxiae* (1709ff.); *Oeconomia salutis* (1728 and often). See also R. Dannenbaum, *Joachim Lange als Wortführer des Halleschen Pietismus gegen die Orthodoxie* (Göttingen dissertation, 1952).

7. *Grundlegung der Theologie* (1703; Halle: 1767).

8. *Institutiones hermeneuticae sacrae* (1727; Jena: 1764[8]); *Christliche Sittenlehre* (1736).

9. Bengel's influence was focussed largely through his *Gnomon Novi Testamenti* (1752 and often; *New Testament Word Studies*, tr. C. T. Lewis and M. R. Vincent [Grand Rapids: Kregel, 1971 (repr. of 1964 ed.)]) and his *Erklärte Offenbarung Johannis* (1740 and often; Stuttgart: J. C. Erhard, 1758[3]). In his method he was influenced by the Dutchmen who thought in terms of salvation-history, particularly the student of Cocceius, Vitringa, whom Joachim Lange brought to his attention. See J. C. F. Burk, *A Memoir of the Life and Writings of John Albert Bengel*, tr. R. Gladding (1842); K. Hermann, *J. A. Bengel, der Klosterpräzeptor von Denkendorf . . .* (Stuttgart: Calwer Verlagsverein, 1937).

10. *Ev. Glaubenslehre* (ed. posth. by J. S. Semler [1759ff.]). His student, Semler, wrote an enthusiastic assessment of him (*Ehrengedächtnis . . .* [1758]).

11. Oetinger, *Theologia ex idea vitae* (!) *deducta* (1765). Otherwise mostly sermons. For a selection of his writings, Otto Herpel, ed., *Friedrich Christoph Oetinger, Die heilige Philosophie* (Munich: Kaiser, 1923); K. A. Auberlen, *Die Theosophie Christoph Friedrich Oetingers nach ihren Grundzügen* (Berlin: Evang. Verlagsanstalt, 1849); Elisabeth Zinn, *Die Theologie des F. C. Oetinger* (*Beiträge zur Förderung christlicher Theologie*, I, 36, H. 3; Gütersloh: Evangelischer Verlag "Der Rufer," 1932).

deeply despised, partly in opposition to Pietism (cf. the controversy around C. Wolff in Halle which led to his leaving and continuing his work in Reformed Marburg), and partly in a rational translation of the very same Pietism. S. J. Baumgarten, whom we have already mentioned, can be looked upon as one of the early proponents of supranaturalistic Rationalism in a very moderate form. He was followed immediately by the editor of his *Evangelischen Glaubenslehre*, Johann Salomo Semler (1725–91), with his *Versuch einer freien theologischen Lehrart* (1777), fluctuating between the moralism of his own approach and historical positivism which he did not want to give up—like so many others in that age (e.g., Franz Buddeus [1667–1729],[12] Christoph M. Pfaff [1686–1760],[13] and Johann Lorenz von Mosheim [1694–1755][14]): as a historical religion, Christianity requires tradition (e.g., of the canon), but the tradition must be interpreted as the essence of God's accommodation to our still underdeveloped reason.[15] In Semler we see the problem with which his contemporary, Lessing (1729–81), would try to deal with very different breadth and depth[16]—reason and history, reason and revelation! It has remained on the agenda up to today, although the forms have certainly changed. Lessing's own solution, most clearly seen in his *Erziehung des Menschengeschlechts* (*Education of the Human Race*), connects them to each other in the concept of anticipation which is always taking place in education—he could conceive of the idea of development and thereby integrated the legacy of "salvation-historical" thinking into the Enlightenment.

---

12. *Institutiones theologiae dogmaticae* (1723; Francofurti et lipsiae: 1741); *Institutiones theologiae moralis* (1721); *Hist. eccl. Veteris Test.* (1715ff.); A. F. Stolzenburg, *Die Theologie des Joh. Fr. Buddeus und des Chr. Matth. Pfaff; ein Beitrag zur Geschichte der Aufklärung in Deutschland* (Berlin: Trowitzsch & Sohn, 1926). This was salvation-history theology on a rational basis.

13. *Institutio theologiae dogmaticae et moralis* (1719). See also Stolzenburg, *op. cit.*

14. His significance is primarily in the area of church history, which he begins in the Bible, just as did Buddeus and many others (Mosheim in the New Testament and Buddeus in the Old Testament). Dogmatic work: *Vorlesungen über den Beweis der Wahrheit und Göttlichkeit der christlichen Religion*, G. Winkler, ed. (1782ff.). See also K. Heussi, *Johann Lorenz Mosheim; ein Beitrag zur Kirchengeschichte des 18. Jahrhunderts* (Tübingen: J. C. B. Mohr, 1906).

15. The ambiguity in Semler—positivism in the realm of the Church, Rationalism in the area of theology—which is somewhat reminiscent of Hobbes, emerged especially in his approval of Wöllner's Religious Edict in Prussia; see K. Aner, *Die Theologie der Lessingszeit* (Haale/Saale: M. Niemeyer, 1929), pp. 107ff. (reissued Hildesheim: Geo. Olma, 1964). Paul Gastrow, *Johann Salomo Semler in seiner Bedeutung für die Theologie mit besonderer Berücksichtigung seines Streites mit G. E. Lessing* (Giessen: A. Töpelmann, 1905). Heinrich Hoffmann, *Die Theologie Semlers* (Leipzig: Dieterich, 1905). L. Zscharnack, *Lessing und Semler* (1905; n.l.).

16. See H. Thielicke, *Offenbarung, Vernunft und Existenz; Studien zur Religionsphilosophie Lessings* (3rd exp. ed.; Gütersloh: C. Bertelsmann, 1957 [g1936]); M. Haug, *Entwicklung und Offenbarung bei Lessing* (Gütersloh: Bertelsmann, 1928); E. Kretzschmar, *Lessing und die Aufklärung; Eine Darstellung der religions- u. geschichtsphilosophischen Anschauungen des Dichters mit besonderer Berücksichtigung seiner Philosophischen Hauptschrift, "Die Erziehung des Menschengeschlechts"* (Leipzig: B. Richter, 1905); G. Schwarz, *G. E. Lessing als Theologe* (1854; n.l.); K. Barth, *Protestant Theology in the Nineteenth Century; Its Background and History*, tr. B. Cozens and J. Bowden (London: S.C.M., 1972 [g1947]), pp. 234ff.

d. Neology. Rationalism, when it is dealt with in the context of dogmatics, is generally called Neology.[17] The work of leading neologists such as August Friedrich Wilhelm Sack (1703–86)[18] or the Abbot J. F. W. Jerusalem (1709–89)[19] or even J. J. Spalding (1714–1804)[20]—all three of them not specialists in theology but men of the Church!—or of specializing dogmaticians such as Johann Gottlieb Töllner (1724–74)[21] or Abraham Wilhelm Teller (1734–1804)[22] had no great effect upon the dogmatic labors of the following ages. In addition, for an acute critic like Lessing all of these men are seen as being grouped with the "Orthodox" (i.e., the Supranaturalists) because all of them are actually apologists, regardless of how critical they are toward their own traditions, or how energetically they adopt new positions (often through reviving Socinian thoughts) in regard to traditional Christology, eucharistic doctrine, or even the doctrine of predestination. They are willing to sacrifice the outer aspects of the Orthodox system in order to save the citadel of supranatural revelation. The neologists of the 18th century were not yet rationalists in the same sense as later the Weimar General Superintendent Johann Friedrich Röhr (1777–1848) or Julius August Ludwig Wegscheider of Halle (1771–1849) would be;[23] so-called vulgar rationalism may be viewed as evidence of weariness and an echo of what had been.

The accomplishment of Neology was that its proponents really faced the historical criticism of the Bible and the relativism of the general understanding of the world and tried to express dogmatically what they felt was possible in view of the known facts and the existing world understanding. Whoever reads these dogmatic works today, as dusty as they appear to be, will be not so much surprised about their critical approach as at the way in which ultimately the inner substance of their faith is so obviously still intact even though they themselves have scarcely any understanding of it. This dogmatics did not fully sell out Christian discourse to the man of that age—because it was not able to! In addition, it is by no means the case that Rationalism, as much as it held unlimited sway as the form of thought, was equally dominant in the area of religious behavior. Even the neologists were not blind to the practical character of Christian living, and they too

---

17. The comprehensive book by K. Aner, *Theologie der Lessingszeit . . .* , deals basically with Neology.

18. *Verteidigter Glaube der Christen* (1748ff.).

19. Jerusalem, like Sack, is as a dogmatician basically an apologist. See his *Betrachtungen über die vornehmsten Wahrheiten der christlichen Religion* (many editions since 1768); *Fortgesetzte Betrachtungen über die vornehmsten Wahrheiten der Religion* (1772); a third section in outline form is extant, published in 1792 posthumously as a part of the *Nachgelassenen Schriften*. Jerusalem's son was more famous; his death provided the impetus for Goethe's *Werther*. The problem of suicide was a major preoccupation of the late Enlightenment, remarkably enough.

20. Against Pietism, *Gedanken über den Wert der Gefühle im Christentum* (1761); ET: *Thoughts on the Value of Feelings in Religion* (1827); *Vertraute Briefe, die Religion betreffend* (1784) (at first anonymous); *Religion, eine Angelegenheit des Menschen* (1796).

21. *Theologische Untersuchungen* (1773ff.).

22. *Lehrbuch des christlichen Glaubens* (1764); P. Gabriel, *Die Theologie W. A. Tellers* (Giessen: A. Töpelmann, 1914).

23. J. F. Röhr, *Briefe über den Rationalismus* (Aachen: Frosch, 1913); J. A. L. Wegscheider, *Institutiones theologiae christ. dogmaticae* (1815); a Kantian approach.

could on occasion firmly emphasize that religion was "a matter of the heart"—
the humanity to which they committed themselves is something broader than just
reason, so that just as in the case of Orthodoxy, here too subjective emotionalism
is linked with objective rationalism as an equivalent. This is probably the chief
explanation for the fact that the notorious havoc which the "churchly" Enlightenment wrought, for example in the forms of public worship, never resulted in
total destruction. We also notice in viewing the late period that the vitality which
accompanied so many insights in new things, for instance in the area of history,
was followed by a remarkable kind of weariness. In spite of all its efforts, the
churchly Enlightenment was not able to cope with the deepest problems of life
and death. Death itself, which their gravestones reveal as having been understood
in a Greek fashion, was not robbed of its puzzling nature by means of interpreting
it as immortality rather than resurrection.

e. Reaction Against Rationalism. We may therefore understand the series of
occurrences at the end of the 18th century, when an anticipatory form of Romanticism began to excite the spirit: readers responded to such a radical and
inscrutable critic of the Enlightenment as Johann Georg Hamann (1730–88);[24] the
young Goethe seeks contact with such outright "Pietists" as Heinrich Jung-Still-
ing (1740–1817) or Johann Caspar Lavater (1741–1801)[25]; Friedrich Heinrich Jacobi (1743–1819) and also Johann Gottfried Herder (1744–1803), as much as they
belong to the Enlightenment, began to see entirely new aspects of reality;[26] and
a man like Thomas Wizenmann (1759–87),[27] heir of Swabian Biblicism in the
sense of Bengel and Philipp Matthäus Hahn (1739–90),[28] could confront the most
famous personalities of the age with a position totally negating the Enlightenment.

---

24. In regard to what now follows, we refer to W. Lütgert, *Die Religion des deutschen
Idealismus und ihr Ende* (4 vols.; Gütersloh: Bertelsmann, 1923–30), a work which contains
many provocative impulses which have not yet been fully researched; see also E. Hirsch,
op. cit., and K. Barth, *Protestant Theology in the Nineteenth Century . . .*; Hamann's *Sämtliche Werke*, ed. J. Nadler (Vienna: Thomas-Morus Presse im Verlag Herder, 1949). [Cf. in
English, Ronald Gregor Smith, *J. G. Hamann 1730–1788, a study in Christian Existence,
with selections from his writings* (New York: Harper, 1960)—TR.] The most important study
is R. Unger, *Hamann und die Aufklärung; Studien zur Vorgeschichte des romantischen Geistes
im 18. Jahrhundert* (repr. Tübingen: M. Niemeyer, 1963 [g1925²]) with comprehensive materials. See also F. Lieb, *Glaube und Offenbarung bei J. G. Hamann* (Munich: Kaiser, 1926);
F. Thomas, *Die Hauptprobleme der Religionsphilosophie bei J. G. Hamann* (1929; n.l.);
F. Thomas, *Hamanns Berkehrung* (1933; n.l.); James O'Flaherty, *Unity and Language: A
Study in the Philosophy of Johann George Hamann* (Chapel Hill, N.C.: University of North
Carolina, 1952).
25. See *Dichtung und Wahrheit* by Goethe, especially Books 14, 16, 19, in various
standard German editions. ET: *Truth and Poetry: From My Own Life*, tr. A. J. W. Morrison
(*Standard Library Edition*, II) (London: George Bell & Sons, 1874), pp. 1ff., 62ff., 130ff.
26. See especially W. Lütgert, *op. cit.*, II.
27. Wizenmann, *Göttliche Entwicklung des Satans* (!) *durch das Menschengeschlecht*
(1782); *Die Resultate der Jacobi'schen und Mendelsohn'schen Philosophie* (1786); *Die Geschichte Jesu nach dem Matthäusevangelium* (1789); Alexander Freiherr von der Goltz,
*Thomas Wizenmann, der Freund F. H. Jacobi's, in Mittheilungen aus seinem Briefwechsel
und Handschriftl. Nachlasse wie nach Zeugnissen von Zeitgenossen* (2 vols.; Gotha: Osna-
brück, 1859).
28. See J. Rössle, *Leben und Theologie des Ph. M. Hahn* (Bonn dissertation, 1929).

The Age of the Enlightenment, toward its conclusion stirred up by both the French Revolution and the Napoleonic Wars, found an opponent of great intellectual power in a new Pietism which was the predecessor of the later revival movements.

f. Kant. The Enlightenment's most powerful opponent emerged, however, from its own ranks: Immanuel Kant (1724–1804).[29] He was the one who exposed the concealed "dogmatism" of the rationalist system (as he found it most clearly in Hume) and by laying a new epistemological foundation made clear that "pure" reason is by its very nature limited to the objects of possible experience and if it crosses over this boundary will become unavoidably entangled in antinomies. Further, he demonstrated that "God" can only appear as a postulate of practical reason, but then in such a way that the certainty which is given here is of another quality entirely than that possible in the realm of pure reason; Kant approaches what we would today call the "existential." On the basis of this insight he could then come to exciting conclusions in the area of anthropology: he was the only philosopher who dared to speak of the "radical evil,"[30] even though in the context of the philosophical thesis that the principle of good would win out over the evil. Since Kant, Rationalism as the conceptual structure of theology has been outmoded and replaced by an Ethicism, to be sure an extremely abstract one, which would very strongly influence dogmatic work thereafter.

The basic lines along which future dogmatic labors would run were already drawn toward the end of the Enlightened century: Ethicism, the emotional aspect of Romanticism, and the Irrationalism anticipated by Hamann could all become dominant. All three of these lines are, without also denying the Enlightenment, closer to Pietism than to it. It was a "Herrnhuter of a higher order" who gave the new century its most effective impulses: Friedrich Daniel Schleiermacher. However, from the very beginning his work was in tense contact with post-Kantian "German Idealism," which radicalized Kant and thus provided the stuff for a new kind of theological speculation based upon the "idea," which we associate with the names Hegel and Schelling.

B. DOGMATICS IN THE 19TH CENTURY

a. The Relationship of the 19th Century to the Enlightenment. In his book *Protestant Theology in the 19th Century*[31] Karl Barth begins with a "prehistory"

---

29. W. Lütgert's discussion, *op. cit.*, I, 8ff., is probably too simple. A different approach is found in K. Barth, *op. cit.*, pp. 266ff.

We cannot provide listings of the Kant literature here; every philosophy textbook provides selective bibliographies. The *Works* are quoted here according to the German edition of Cassirer (11 vols., 1912–23), unless English editions are available.

30. *Religion within the Limits of Reason Alone*, tr. T. M. Greene and H. H. Hudson (New York: Harper, 1960), pp. 15ff.

31. The book appeared in 1947, was based upon an older manuscript, and remained incomplete: ET 1972 (see p. 131, n. 16).

which outlines the theology of the 18th century. This is intended to demonstrate that the 19th century stands theologically on the shoulders of the 18th.

Most of the leading theologians of the 19th century would have shared this opinion only with very great reservations. There were certainly "Rationalists" in the 19th century, men like Röhr, Wegscheider, and Bretschneider (1776–1848)— and in the Church perhaps more than elsewhere. But they were looked upon as the representatives of what needed to be overcome or was in fact already passé.

Dogmatics in the 19th century applied its best energies to the conquering of Rationalism. However, the 18th century was by no means just the century of Rationalism. Therefore, this victory could be both the establishment of a connection and the continuation of the work already done.

The reception of what had already been done was unavoidable. The decision which the emergence of historical criticism signified could not be reversed in the 19th century. This was as impossible as it was to replace simply the general world view which nourished the Enlightenment with another one.

Thus an important advance decision was made for dogmatics: it would not be able to bring about a simple restoration of the whole Orthodox system (although attempts were made to do this). Wherever it began, it remained under the influence of the autonomous self-understanding which it shared with the Enlightenment. Romanticism, which provided the broad context for most of the effective approaches now, was intellectually autonomistic.

Dogmatics would only have had the character of a radically new beginning if it had been joined by a true reformation. But there was no trace of that. All of the new beginnings are relative in nature. To put it schematically: it is true that the dogmatics of the 19th century appealed to those movements which had shattered Rationalism, especially to Kant's philosophy, to Hegel's and Schelling's reworking of the Kantian approach, and to Romanticism, which arose toward the end of the 18th century and to which the revival movement is related. However, all of these movements were directed against Rationalism but not against the spirit of the Enlightenment.

b. Schleiermacher, 1768 – 1834. Retrospectively, the dogmatics of the 19th century can be understood essentially as the direct, indirect, or negatively re-

---

Other discussions of the theology of the 19th century: Horst Stephan, *Geschichte der [neueren] evangelischen Theologie seit dem deutschen Idealismus* (1937; Berlin: A. Töpelmann, 1938, 1960); E. Hirsch, *op. cit.*, vol. IV (1952), vol. V (1954); F. Kattenbusch, *Die deutsche evangelische Theologie seit Schleiermacher; ihre Leistungen, ihre Schäden* (previously *Von Schleiermacher zu Ritschl*) (Giessen: A. Töpelmann, 1924, 1934, 1936); F. H. R. Frank, *Geschichte und Kritik der neueren Theologie insbes. d. systemat., seit Schleiermacher* (Leipzig: A. Deichert Nachf., 1898); Erich Schaeder, *Theozentrische Theologie; eine Untersuchung zur dogmatischen Prinzipienlehre* (Leipsig: Werner Scholl, 1916 [g1925³]).

On dogmatics outside the German-language area little is to be found in the above-named works. Useful, but only for the latter part of the 19th century, J. K. Mozley, *Some Tendencies in British Theology from the publication of Lux Mundi to the present day* (London: S.P.C.K., 1951); and earlier, W. Vollrath, *Theologie der Gegenwart in Grossbritannien* (Gütersloh: Bertelsmann, 1928).

ceived influence of the theology of Friedrich Daniel Schleiermacher,[32] one of the most powerful personalities in all of church history, in some ways comparable with Augustine. In his mighty new synthesis he summarized what he had himself experienced as the inherited intellectual movement and did so in such a way that even his opponent could not avoid having the lines of his own thinking prescribed by Schleiermacher. Schleiermacher's influence so overshadowed that of those who were seen as his equals in his own time, chiefly the theological Hegelians like Philipp Konrad Marheineke (1780–1846) and Karl Daub (1765–1836), that since 1840 they have been largely forgotten.

Schleiermacher's family came originally from Hesse; his grandfather was involved in the unusual fanaticism of the "Ronsdorf Sect";[33] the family migrated to Silesia and was close to the *Brüdergemeine* (of the Moravian Brethren) to which Schleiermacher was indebted not only for his education but also, in spite of his resistance, for permanent elements of his nature. The young student, for whom Pietism had been transformed into Ethicism, encountered an Enlightenment in Halle which was no longer so certain of itself; Herder and F. H. Jacobi were already involved in attacking it. Soon he also encountered the writings of Kantian criticism. These two great streams battled for the allegiance of the young Schleiermacher but neither was able to win him over completely. Spinoza's influence upon him was greater through the years than either of these; Wehrung describes his position well as "Idealism with a Spinozan attitude."[34] He endeavors

---

32. His *Works* appeared in Berlin in 36 vols. from 1834 to 1864. A selected edition by O. Braun and J. Bauer appeared in 1910ff.

His *Der christliche Glaube* (2 vols.; Berlin: G. Reimer, 1861) appeared after its 2nd edition (1838) in the series *Bibl. theol. Klassiker* published by Perthes, new editions now reprinted by Walter de Gruyter, Berlin. Citations here will be according to the American edition, a reprint of *The Christian Faith*, tr. Mackintosh and Stewart (1928; New York: Harper, 1963), and referred to as *ChrF*.

R. Otto published the *Reden über die Religion* in their original form, with critical notes, in 1899 (orig. 1799); ET: *On Religion, Addresses to its Cultured Critics*, tr. Terrence N. Tice (Richmond, Virginia: John Knox Press, 1968 [g1799, 1899]).

Major edition of the correspondence edited by Ludwig Jonas and Wilhelm Dilthey, *Aus Schleiermachers Leben* (4 vols.; Berlin: G. Reimer, 1860–63); ET: vols. I and II (1860).

W. Dilthey, *Das Leben Schleiermachers* (1870; 2nd ed.). H. Mulert, ed. (1922), vols. 13 and 14 of the *Gesammelte Schriften* (Leipzig: Teubner, 1914–58); and M. Redeker, ed. (2 vols.; Göttingen: Vandenhoeck & Ruprecht, 1970). G. Wehrung, *Schleiermacher in der Zeit seines Werdens* (Gütersloh: C. Bertelsmann, 1927); J. Wendland, *Die religiöse Entwicklung Schleiermachers* (Tübingen: Mohr, 1915); Hermann Süskind, *Der Einfluss Schellings auf die Entwicklung von Schleiermacher's System* (Tübingen: Mohr, 1909); O. Piper, *Das religiöse Erlebnis (Studie zu den Reden)* (1920; n.l.); Emil Brunner, *Die Mystik und das Wort* (Tübingen: Mohr, 1924); Joachim Wach, *Das Verstehen; Grundzüge einer Geschichte der hermeneutischen Theorie im 19. Jahrhundert* (Tübingen: J. C. B. Mohr, 1926; repr. Hildesheim: Georg Olms Verlagsbuchhandlung, 1966 [g1926]); W. Loew, *Das Grundproblem der Ethik Schleiermachers, in seiner Beziehung zu Kants Ethik* (Berlin: Reuther & Reichard, 1914); Felix Flückiger, *Philosophie und Theologie bei Schleiermacher* (Zollikon: Evangelischer Verlag, 1947); further bibliography there.

33. See M. Goebel, *Geschichte des christlichen Lebens in der rheinischwestfälischen evangelischen Kirche*, III (1860).

34. Wehrung, *op. cit.*, p. 70.

to integrate knowledge and being conceptually, and very early the thrust of his thinking is directed toward the "universal," in that the finite spirit finds its completion in the emotional perception of this universal. It is not astonishing that this Spinozan Idealist found his way into early Romanticism during his Berlin period, for the Spinozan element of his idealistic approach was open to the aesthetic. The aesthetic form of self-perfection—the absolutized feeling replacing the supernatural, which was now no longer recognized, making feelings the means to approaching "God"—was encountered by him so overwhelmingly, particularly in his contacts with the Schlegels and Henriette Herz, that any possible critique fell by the wayside and the radicalism of the Kantian ethos, never fully developed anyway, became inconsequential. One could say that Schleiermacher, like Augustine before him, had passed through the intellectual realms of the world out of which he came. But there is a difference: whereas Augustine experienced a conversion, Schleiermacher went through a development. The first great document of this development, aside from a few less important pieces, were his "Discourses on Religion, Directed to her Cultured Despisers" (1799). These were a literarily powerful apology for religion, the document of a discovery which Schleiermacher then never forsook: the discovery of the independence of the religious over against reason as well as over against the ethical—the demonstration of a unique category of religion: the "feeling and intuition of the universal!" Kantian religious ethicism was finally given up at this point, and the Enlightenment subordination of the religious to the norms of reason was also done away with. A new approach to ultimate values was opened up. By uttering the phrase "feeling and intuition," as endlessly variable as it was, Schleiermacher in the year 1799 established the theme for the various approaches to theology in the new century. The objective, eternal, pure Being does not reveal itself to objectivizing reason, nor to active ethical endeavors, but only to the feeling which lives in submission to sensitivity, and this feeling is a totally embracing behavior, the subjective reflection of the only objective extant. Basically, it would appear that even the Enlightenment was still "Orthodox" in that it tried rationally to come to terms with what is authentically there, the "thing per se." And even Kant was also (as many would have thought) "Orthodox" in that he, after closing the perception of the "thing per se" to pure reason, then opened it for practical reason. This was new: there was nothing at all outside of subjective impressions, beyond feelings! Indeed, that was a new solution to things. Therefore neither transcendence nor critical transcendentalism was necessary: there is a direct approach to the eternal available and it reveals itself solely within temporality.

Schleiermacher's approach, meant both in terms of the philosophy and the apology of religion, had immense consequences for dogmatics. He himself turned to dogmatics slowly and with hesitation, starting at the foundation of his religious philosophy and doctrine of being. Essentially, his doctrine of being is a philosophy of identity; it had to be, based upon his approach. General being and special or individual being (culminating in the feeling of absolute dependency) are one. In that the subject experiences itself to be absolutely dependent, it senses itself as being touched and conditioned by a trans-subjective essence, and it is one with it. Thus, for Schleiermacher the "Feeling of absolute dependence," that is, the consciousness of God, is nothing other than the true freedom of man, the foundation for man's genuine self-activity.

Schleiermacher delineated his dogmatics within the pattern of his broadly general concept of religion. The reason for the existence of a *Christian* theology is the circumstance that the "religious self-consciousness" will at some point in its development require "fellowship," will become the Church, both in an irregular flow and in a definite and limited way.[35] This is then the reason that theology is a "positive" science, dealing with genuine givens, and that dogmatics can continue to be counted a part of historical theology in a broad sense.[36] Schleiermacher finds his link to tradition on the basis of his concept of religion, a very important step. But before he can let dogmatics come to the fore, he sets up a "philosophical theology" which begins with "the general concept of the pious or believing community"[37] and then is divided into apologetics and polemics. Only insight into the general will render the uniqueness of Christianity a reasoned foundation and make possible the separation of the essential from the perverted.

Up until now we have been discussing the preconditions under which Schleiermacher's momentous systematic structure, *The Christian Faith* (1821), stands. They are the foundations, but not the building. The philosopher of religion, who gained his fame with his "Discourses on *Religion*," can now speak knowledgeably about Christianity in 1821, building upon the aforementioned foundation, and within the context of apologetics. He speaks of Christianity in such a way that in it (as the "monotheistic faith, belonging to the teleological type of religion") everything is related to "the redemption accomplished through Jesus of Nazareth" (par. 11 of *The Christian Faith*). Christocentrically, this is Christianity! Yet the rediscovery of Christocentricity does not belie its foundation in the concept of the universal, for the Redeemer is what he is "through the constant power of his consciousness of God, which was the actual being of God in him" (par. 94 of *The Christian Faith*). His special being is in fact a unique kind of consciousness! If this statement is true of Jesus Christ—and it was pre-formed long before in the development of the young Schleiermacher—then it is consequentially true in the total realm of Christian statements. *The Christian Faith*, in the whole of its tightly knit structure,[38] speaks of *consciousness*—but based upon

---

35. Schleiermacher, *ChrF*, 6, Thesis, I, p. 26 (a part of the lemmata of the ethic).

36. *Brief Outline on the Study of Theology*, tr. T. N. Tice (Richmond: John Knox Press, 1966 [g1811, 1935]); see pars. 97 and 195ff. under the significant title, "The historical knowledge of the contemporary condition of Christianity." "Philosophical theology" is somewhat different (see the next note).

37. *Brief Outline* . . . , par. 33. In par. 29 Schleiermacher states that studies of theology could begin with philosophical theology if this "were properly developed as a discipline." At the time, however, only various sections could be lifted "fragmentarily" from historical theology, and only if the study of ethics had gone before. Schleiermacher understands ethics as "the Science of the Principles of History" (*loc. cit.*).

38. *The Christian Faith* (which Schleiermacher then proceeds to call a "dogmatics" without any reservations, just as he had done in the *Brief Outline* . . .) is divided, after the foundational section with its lemmata taken from ethics (the conception of the Church), the philosophy of religion (the diversities of religious communions in general), apologetics (peculiar essence of Christianity), and methodological considerations, into two major parts: In the first part the "religious self-consciousness" is developed, as it is "always both presup-

the ontology which the author has presupposed (and this should never be forgotten), this consciousness encompasses nothing less than being itself. By means of this potent synthesis, Schleiermacher does away with the "ugly wide chasm" which had once tortured Lessing so much. History, the location of consciousness as it proceeds along its way, is *ipso facto* the location of being, of the being of God, in whom all being is gathered together into a unity.

It is true that Schleiermacher discovered anew the Christ-orientation of the Christian faith. He felt that he was the rediscoverer of authentic Christianity (and his students felt this even more emphatically, above all J. August W. Neander [1789–1850]), and he had made this discovery within the presuppositions created by historical criticism and the changed view of the world and within the framework of orderly scientific statements. If his fundamental thesis is true, that of the unity of being and consciousness in religion, then everything he says is true. The question which we can only raise here is this: Can God, the real God, be understood as the Being which manifests itself in consciousness—this is the question of the foundations of Schleiermacher's conception.

Even if our portrayal is no more than a broad outline, we would be remiss if we did not make clear that the rediscoverer of Christology was also the rediscoverer of the Church. For him, the Church was not an institution for the encouragement of morals or religion, as it usually was in the Enlightenment, but rather it was a fellowship which was founded in the Spirit. Of course, he meant by "Spirit" the "Common spirit" which obtains in all Christian pious consciousness (being as consciousness!) and makes it active or receptive from situation to situation. Just as the basic act of religion is essentially independent, the Church is also similarly independent: Schleiermacher makes Scripture subordinate to it, he undertakes to analyze its practice in its independence and its relation to the world—he is the founder of the discipline of Practical Theology,[39] and he assumes his own place in it both as a preacher and as a zealous and resolute church politician. In his high estimation of the practical and churchly side of things, Schleiermacher proved more than anywhere else that he really had remained obligated to the "Reformed School."

---

posed by and contained in every Christian Religious Affection." Regarding the relationship of God to the world, the themes of creation and preservation must be discussed, in the same context the divine attributes of eternity, omnipresence, omnipotence, and omniscience, and in regard to the "constitution of the world" its "original perfection" and that of man himself. In the second part, "the facts of the religious self-consciousness" are developed, as they are "determined by antithesis." On the one hand, there is the consciousness of sin and the corresponding constitution of the world, and then, in view of God's attributes, the discussion of God's holiness, his being just and merciful. On the other hand, the "consciousness of grace" is also developed here: this is the place for Christology and also Soteriology; from the viewpoint of the world, the themes of the Church, election, the Holy Spirit, the Church's relationship to the world (here too the doctrine of the sacraments!), and finally the consummation of the Church are discussed. It is significant that what in fact are three sections are structurally two sections: the essence of Christianity as a whole, with two fundamentally differing aspects—sin and grace—stands under the dominant concept of contradiction or contrast (*ChrF*, I, pp. v-viii).

39. His *Praktische Theologie*, J. Frerichs, ed. (1850 posth.), *Sämtliche Werke* (30 vols.; Berlin: G. Reimer, 1835–64), vol. 13.

When we move on from Schleiermacher, the way could go in very different directions. His concept of religion could be expanded pietistically under the influence of the revival movement. His philosophy of identity could be so modified that between the Christian consciousness of a convert and that historical being proclaimed in the Bible a close relationship would be conceived. This is what happened in the Erlangen School, under the influence of Schelling (1775–1854). Schleiermacher's Christocentricity and his rediscovery of the Church, set free from his own presuppositions, and projected into the framework of later, historicizing Romanticism, could indicate the route to a "repristination" of Orthodox doctrine. That aspect of his ecclesiology dominated by the concept of Community could inspire church renewal and separationist movements, which was what happened in the case of Alexandre Vinet (1797–1847);[40] or the very same concept of Community can, alternatively, be bound up with his emphasis upon the practical and be used to help develop the church union which Schleiermacher so strongly encouraged and then to assign the Church its place within the changing structures of society as was done, for example, by C. I. Nitzsch (1787–1868) or G. C. Friedrich Lücke (1791–1855). In short, either the more strongly "scientific" and speculative aspect of his approach or the more traditional one, emphasizing the importance of both history and the Church, could move into the foreground.

c. The Hegelians. Before we briefly treat those directions of dogmatics which are to be understood as derived from Schleiermacher, we should once more point out that at first the major significance of the Berlin theologian was not generally acknowledged. Aside from the effects of Rationalism which were just beginning to be really felt, the strongest opposition came from the school of Georg Wilhelm Hegel (1770–1831), who was Schleiermacher's philosophical colleague and opponent in Berlin from 1818 on. Hegel, too, was a philosopher of identity. However, neither consciousness nor history, in spite of the emphasis upon identity, could gain in his thinking the measure of unique dignity which they had in Schleiermacher. The unity of the knower and the known, ultimately a religious act for Schleiermacher, is given in the spirit for Hegel; the way is the dialectical process of intellectual movement from thesis to the necessary antithesis and then on to synthesis. This then corresponds precisely to the process of the identical object of this movement: history, which bears the knowing spirit in its very essence, proceeds according to the same laws and in the same circular movements as does thought. It was very easy then for the historical, in the dialectic of its movement, to become the form of the absolute universal, projected upon the historical, which

---

40. H. Korth, *Das Verständnis der Kirche bei A. Vinet* (Göttingen dissertation, microcopy, 1950); English editions of Vinet: *Gospel Studies*, tr. R. Baird (New York: M. W. Dodd, 1849); *History of French Literature in the 18th Century*, tr. J. Byrd (Edinburgh: T. & T. Clark, 1854); *Homiletics, or, the Theory of Preaching*, tr. T. H. Skinner (New York: Ivison, Blakeman & Taylor, 1880); *Pastoral Theology, or the Theory of the Evangelical Ministry*, tr. T. Summers (Nashville: M. E. Church, 1893); *Outlines of Theology* (London: Strahan, 1865); original *Works* appearing in Lausanne since 1897, edited by E. Staehelin since 1944. P. Bridel, *Alexandre Vinet; sa personne et ses idées* (Paris: Editions de la "cause," 1924); E. Seillière, *Christianisme et romantisme; Alexander Vinet, historien de la pensée française; Survi d'un appendice sur Henri Frédéric Amiel* (Paris: Payot, 1925); C. Paira, *Staat und Kirche bei Alexandre Vinet* (Gotha: Leopold Klotz Verlag, 1922).

is what happened in Ferdinand Christian Baur (1792–1860) and even more so in David Friedrich Strauss (1808–1874) ("The idea does not delight in pouring its fullness into one single example"). Similarly, the special character of the story of Christ could become a mere exemplary specialness, perhaps no more than a phase in the general course of history! On the other hand, it was equally easy to regard the great triad of knowing and the known as a reflection of the divine Trinity and to erect a speculative theology on the basis of Hegel which was true to his view that in his philosophy the essence of theology was preserved more validly than in theology itself! The first option, that of the "Hegelian left wing," led via the *Leben Jesu* (*Life of Jesus*) of David Friedrich Strauss to the first great trauma which the dogmatics of the 19th century was to experience, a challenge which seemed to be derived from history but which in fact resulted from philosophy. The second option, that of the "Hegelian right wing," led Philipp Marheineke (1780–1846), Schleiermacher's theological colleague in Berlin, to work out his system[41] and above all Karl Daub (1765–1836) to his daring theological speculations.[42] Compared to both groups, Schleiermacher and his followers appear to be naive and unintellectual, just as they were orthodox and reactionary in the eyes of the rationalists.

d. Mediatory Theology. Schleiermacher's followers pursued their master's line most exactly where they developed what is called *Vermittlungstheologie* (Mediatory Theology) in their dogmatics. We mention here especially Carl Immanuel Nitzsch (1787–1868),[43] who was active in Bonn and Berlin as a theologian of the [Prussian Church] Union and who was important both as a dogmatician and as the creator of a major system of practical theology; August Twesten (1789–1876);[44] and Alexander Schweizer (1808–88)[45] of Zürich, who proceeds

---

41. Marheineke established his fame primarily with his work in the area of symbolics. But see also *Grundlehren der christlichen Dogmatik* (Berlin: Dümmler, 1819); *Die Bedeutung der Hegelschen Philosophie in der christlichen Theologie* (1842; n.l.); *Zur Kritik der Schellingschen Offenbarungsphilosophie* (1943; n.l.); A. Weber, *Le système dogmatique de Marheineke* (1857; n.l.).

42. *Einleitung in das Studium der Theologie* (1810); above all, *Judas Ischarioth oder das Böse im Verhältnis zum Guten* (1816ff.; n.l.); *Philosophische und theologische Vorlesungen*, P. K. Marheineke and T. W. Dittenberger, ed. (Berlin: Dunker & Humboldt, 1838–44).

43. *System der christlichen Lehre* (1828; Bonn: Adolph Marcus, 1844); ET: *System of Christian Doctrine*, tr. R. Montgomery and J. Hennen (Edinburgh: T. & T. Clark, 1849); *Praktische Theologie* (1847ff.; n.l.); Willibald Beyschlag, *Carl Immanuel Nitzsch, Eine Lichtgestalt der neueren deutsch-evangelischen Kirchengeschichte* (Berlin: Rauh, 1872).

44. *Vorlesungen über die Dogmatik der evangelischen lutherischen Kirche* (2 vols., 1826–37; Hamburg: F. Perth, 1838⁴). Twesten was the originator of the well-known distinction between the formal and material principles of Protestantism.

45. Schweizer differentiated sharply between historical and systematic-contemporary dogmatics. For the former he contributed little with his *Glaubenslehre der evangelischen reformierten Kirche, dargestellt aus den Quellen belegt* (2 vols.; Zürich: Orell, Füssli, 1847); but for the latter he made an essential contribution with *Die protestantischen Centraldogmen in ihrer Entwicklung innerhalb der reformirten Kirche*, II (2 vols., 1854–56, n.p.)— although by now it is outdated. His own system, *Die Christliche Glaubenslehre nach protestantischen Grundsätzen* (2 vols.; Leipzig: Hirzel, 1877), follows rigidly along Schleiermacher's lines. His position in the Zürich controversy about the call extended to David Friedrich Strauss is also important.

more speculatively than the other two. The "mediation" which they actually attempted intended to overcome the dominant Rationalism including the rationalistic thinking of the Hegelian left by applying Schleiermacher's synthesis of consciousness and being in such a way that the biblical and ancient dogmatic statements would be understood in a new way, thus insuring that both reason and tradition would be equally satisfied. Karl von Hase of Jena (1800–90),[46] less dependent upon Schleiermacher, developed his own kind of mediatory theology in an independent continuation of Idealism. Even Richard Rothe (1799–1867)[47] must be mentioned here; he certainly is not a follower of Schleiermacher, but, after a powerful encounter with revivalist theology, he became the creator of his own speculative system which is related to the late Schelling. Nevertheless, his famous statement that revelation was manifestation and inspiration in a unity does remind one of Schleiermacher's fundamental idea, and it is significant for him as well as for Schleiermacher that both develop what they mean by dogmatics in their ethics, even though the way they do it is very different. In contrast to him, Johann Heinrich August Ebrard (1818–88)[48] returns completely to Schleiermacher's approach as he formulated a theology of consciousness strongly influenced by the fact that he was Reformed.

The proponents of "Mediatory Theology" were all influenced by the revival movement. However, Schleiermacher's Christian religious consciousness, based upon the piety of Romanticism, looked different from that of the theologians between 1820 and 1850. The clearest influence of the theology of the revival

---

46. Hase's *Ideale und Irrtümer (Jugenderinnerungen)* (1872; repr. Leipzig: Brockhaus, 1973) is one of the most delightful documents of the early 19th century (however, they didn't appear until 1872!). The fame of this theological heir of the Age of Goethe rested primarily upon his work in the area of church history, to which his *Hutterus redivivus oder Dogmatik der evangelischen-Lutherischen Kirche, ein Dogmatisches Repertorium für Studierende* (Leipzig: Breitkopf & Härtel, 1868[11]) belongs. Of his dogmatic work, the more popular *Gnosis oder protestantisch-evangelische Glaubenslehre für die Gebildeten in der Gemeinde* (3 vols., 1827–29; Leipzig: Breitkopf und Härtel, 1869–1870[2]) was more influential than the more scientific *Evangelisch-protestantische Dogmatik* (1826; Leipzig: Breitkopf & Härtel, 1860[5]). He also had a considerable effect as a controversial theologian; see his *Handbuch der protestantischen Polemik gegen die römisch-katholische Kirche* (Leipzig: Breitkopf und Härtel, 1862); ET: *Handbook to the Controversy with Rome*, tr. A. W. Streane (2 vols.; London: Religious Tract Society, 1906–09). The truly worthy descendant of this deeply traditional (but not liberal) "Liberal," General von Hase, died in 1944 as a victim of Hitler's revenge for the 20th of July plot.
47. His chief work was the *Theologische Ethik* (3 vols., 1845–48[1]), later expanded into a monumental work (5 vols., repr. ed. by H. J. Holtzmann; Wittenburg: Zimmermann, 1867–71[2]). He also wrote *Zur Dogmatik* (1863[1]; Gotha: F. A. Perthes, 1869[2]); *Dogmatik, Aus dessen handschriftlichem Nachlasse,* ed. Daniel Schenkel (3 vols.; Heidelberg: J. C. B. Mohr, 1870).
Biographies were written by A. Hausrath, *Richard Rothe und seine Freunde* (2 vols.; Berlin: G. Grote, 1902–06); F. Nippold, *Richard Rothe, ein Christliches Lebensbild auf Grund der Briefe Rothe's* (Wittenberg: H. Koelling, 1873–77). This speculative ethicist sees as the goal of the Church's development its eventual absorption into the good state—in this he was not far from Hegel!
48. *Christliche Dogmatik* (2 vols.; Königsberg: August Wilhelm Unzer, 1818–88).

movement can be observed in August Tholuck (1799–1877)[49] whose own impact cannot be overestimated. It is significant that Tholuck's single major contribution to dogmatics dealt with the understanding of sin. In both contact and tension with his position, his colleague in Halle, Julius Müller (1801–78),[50] also a proponent of *Vermittlungstheologie*, worked on the same theme but in a very speculative sense. Isaac August Dorner (1809–84)[51] is another who cannot refute the indirect influence of the great renewal movement upon him.

The revival movement not only influenced Mediatory Theology, but also gave the major impetus to its later counterpart, the Theology of Repristination. It was essentially restricted to Lutheranism, and its development can only be understood in association with the Erlangen theology, which eventually became confessional theology, although its point of departure was quite a different one.

    e. The Erlangen School. The leader of this school was Johann Christian Konrad Hofmann (1810–77),[52] who had become associated with the circle of the

---

49. The *Gesammelte Werke* in 11 vols. appeared from 1862 to 1873; special mention should be given to his *Lehre von der Sünde und vom Versöhner, oder die wahre Weihe des Zweiflers* (1823; repr. Gotha: F. A. Perthes, 1862[8]), a characteristic document of the revival movement. He is critical toward the Orthodox tradition; he deals with it under the heading "Vorgeschichte des Rationalismus" (Pre-History of Rationalism) in *Das kirchliche Leben des 17. Jahrhunderts, Vorgeschichte des Rationalismus*, 2,1, 2,2 (Berlin: Wiegand & Grieben, 1861ff.). He also wrote a very positive presentation of the *Lebenszeugen der lutherischen Kirche, aus allen Ständen vor und während der Zeit des dreissigjährigen Krieges* (Berlin: Wiegandt & Griehen, 1859), and contributed significantly to the editing of Calvin by publishing the last edition of the *Institutes* and the commentaries on the New Testament and on Psalms. His student, Martin Kähler, left him a notable memorial in his biography, *August Tholuck, geb. den 30. März 1799, heimgegangen den 10. Juni 1877; Ein Lebensabriss* . . . (Halle: Fricke's Verlag, 1877); see also Kähler's article in *RE*, 3rd ed., XIX, 695ff.

50. *The Christian Doctrine of Sin*, tr. W. Urwick (2 vols.; Edinburgh: T. & T. Clark, 1885). It is of some importance that Müller could not present the doctrine of sin without a doctrine of freedom. He belonged to the Halle Circle around A. Tholuck. His statements on *Die evangelische Union* (1854) were also important.

51. *A System of Christian Doctrine*, tr. A. Cave and J. S. Banks (4 vols.; Edinburgh: T. & T. Clark, 1880–82); *A History of Protestant Theology; Particularly in Germany*, tr. G. Robson and S. Taylor (2 vols.; Edinburgh: T. & T. Clark, 1871); *History of the Development of the Doctrine of the Person of Christ*, tr. W. L. Alexander and D. W. Simon (5 vols.; Edinburgh: T. & T. Clark, 1872–82).
Thematically, Dorner is close to Schelling and Hegel.

52. Next to Hofmann's voluminous commentaries, which are still important today, see his *Weissagung und Erfullung im Alten und Neuen Testament* (2 vols.; Nördlingen: C. H. Beck'schen Buchhandlung, 1841); and *Der Schriftbeweis* (3 vols.; Nördlingen: C. H. Beck'schen Buchhandlung, 1852, 2nd ed. 1857). In contrast to the other representatives of a conservative theology, Hofmann was politically liberal.
Gottfried Thomasius, *Das Wiedererwachen des evangelischen Lebens in der lutherischen Kirche Bayerns* (Erlangen: 1867); Johann Haussleiter, *Grundlinien der Theologie J. Chr. K. v. Hofmanns* (*Quellenschriften zur Geschichte des Protestantismus*, Heft 11; Leipzig: A. Deichert Nachf., 1910); G. Weth, *Die Heilsgeschichte, ihr universeller und ihr individueller Sinn in der offenbarungs-geschichtlicher Theologie des 19. Jahrhunderts* (München: Kaiser, 1931); E. W. Wendebourg, *Die heilsgeschichtliche Theologie J. Chr. K. von Hofmanns* . . . (Dissertation, 1953).

revival movement under the influence of the Reformed Christian Krafft (1784–1845). The Erlangen School is characterized primarily by its new understanding of history—"*Heilsgeschichte*" (salvation-history)—in which the effects of the old salvation-historical theology are brought together with the speculative ideas of Schelling (1775–1854). The personal faith of the expositor of the Bible (as the document of salvation-history) provides the basis for understanding; in this faith, salvation-history is being continued. Methodologically Hofmann is right in line with Schleiermacher when he makes the famous statement that "I as a Christian am the real matter of my science as a theologian."[53] The unmistakable churchly aspect in Hofmann is then intensified among the other members of the Erlangen School: the experience of rebirth, which all Erlangen thinkers view regressively to its origin and progressively to its goal, not only is essential for the individual, but the individual can only receive it through the ministry of the Community as the "Community of Christ" (Hofmann[54]). Therefore, the theology of the experience of rebirth is not accidentally but substantially theology oriented to the Church. This brings back the Orthodox doctrinal tradition, and the Erlangen School does in fact become more consciously and confessionally Lutheran. This can be recognized in F. H. Reinhold von Frank (1827–94),[55] Adolf von Harless (1806–79),[56] Gottfried Thomasius (1802–75),[57] and Theodosius Harnack (1817–89).[58]

    f. Confessional Theology. Actual repristinational theology is distinct from that of the Erlangen School in that it does not establish its connection to church tradition by means of the subjective experience of rebirth, but directly. In some ways it is a companion movement to the political restorationism of the time (which also results from Romanticism, is nourished by Hegel and certainly by Schelling,

---

53. *Der Schriftbeweis* (1852), I, 10.
54. *Ibid.*, p. 17.
55. *System der christlichen Gewissheit* (2 vols.; Erlangen: A. Deichert, 1870–73); ET: *System of the Christian Certainty*, tr. M. J. Evans (Edinburgh: T. & T. Clark, 1886); *System der christlichen Wahrheit* (2 vols.; Erlangen: A. Deichert, 1878–80); *System der christlichen Sittlichkeit* (2 vols.; Erlangen: A. Deichert, 1884–87); *Geschichte und Kritik der neueren Theologie insbesonders der systematischen, seit Schleiermacher* (Leipzig: A. Deichert Nachf., 1898).
56. *Christliche Ethik* (Stuttgart: S. G. Liesching, 1842–45); ET: *System of Christian Ethics*, tr. A. W. Morrison (Edinburgh: T. & T. Clark, 1887); *Theologische Enzyklopädie und Methodologie vom Standpunkt der protestantischen Kirche* (Nürnberg: Schrag, 1837); *Kirche und Amt nach lutherischer Lehre in grundbelegenden Sätzen mit Luther's Zeugnissen zusammengestellt* (Stuttgart: S. Liesching, 1853); T. Heckel, *Adolf v. Harless, Theologie und Kirchenpolitik eines lutherischen Bischofs in Bayern* (Munich: Kaiser, 1933).
57. *Christi Person und Werk; Darstellung der evangelisch-lutherischen Dogmatik vom Mittelpunkt der Christologie aus* (4 vols.; Erlangen: T. Bläsing, 1856–62); *Die christliche Dogmengeschichte als Entwickelungsgeschichte des Lehrbegriffs* (2 vols.; Erlangen, 1874–76; 2nd ed., Leipzig: N. Bonwetsch and R. Seeberg, 1886–88); *Das Wiedererwachen des evangelischen Lebens in der lutherischen Kirche Bayerns* (Erlangen: 1867).
58. *Luthers Theologie, mit besonderer Beziehung auf seine Versöhnungs- und Erlösungslehre* (2 vols.; Amsterdam: Rodopi, 1862, 1927, 1969), very pointedly against Ritschl; *Praktische Theologie* (Erlangen: Deichert, 1877–78, Erste Abtheilung); *Die Kirche, ihr Amt, ihr Regiment* (1862; Gütersloh: C. Bertelsmann, 1947).

and has passed through critical Idealism). This similarity is evidenced in the way this theology rejects the individual in principle and emphasizes instead the importance of the objective, institutional, historical powers and elements. Remaining in the terminology we have been using, this theology does not move from consciousness directly to objective being (as does Schleiermacher) nor indirectly-regressively (as with the Erlangen School), but goes the opposite direction: the objective—understood as the whole breadth of the romantic synthesis of history and contemporaneity, of state and nation, of institution and living organism, establishes the subjective; the general and universal establishes the special and individual. Here the Church is really an institution above all else, and it is therefore no accident that the disagreement of this group with the Erlangen School was around the understanding of the Church. Erlangen's thought was based upon the believing community, and this theology was based upon churchly office. The most powerful and comprehensible personality in this group was August Vilmar (1800–60).[59] We might also mention Ernst Wilhelm Hengstenberg (1802–69), originally from Pietistic Reformed circles and then via Biblicism to a Lutheranism opposed to the Union,[60] and from his circle Friedrich A. Philippi (1809-82) who

---

59. *Die Theologie der Tatsachen wider die Theologie der Rhetorik; Bekenntnis und Abwehr* (Marburg: S. G. Liesching/Stuttgart, 1864³; Berlin: Christlicher Zeitschriftenverlag, 1947; Darmstadt: Wissenschaftliche Buchgesellschaft, 1968⁵); *Dogmatik; Akademische Vorlesungen*, ed. W. Piderit (Gütersloh: C. Bertelsmann, 1937²); *Die Lehre vom geistlichen Amt*, ed. W. Piderit (1870); *Theologische Moral*, ed. C. Israel (Gütersloh: C. Bertelsmann, 1871). See also W. Hopf, *August Vilmar, ein Lebens- und Zeitbild* (2 vols.; Marburg: N. G. Elwertsche Verlag, 1913); W. Maurer, *Aufklärung, Idealismus und Restauration; Studien zur Kirchen- und Geistesgeschichte in besonderer Beziehung auf Kurhessen* (2 vols., 1780–1850; Giessen: Töpelmann, 1930); M. Wollenweber, *Theologie und Politik bei A.F.C. Vilmar*, in *Forschungen zur Geschichte und Lehre des Protestantismus* (Reihe 3, Bd. 1; München: C. Kaiser [später Lempp], 1930); B. Schlunk, *Amt und Gemeinde im theologischen Denken Vilmar's* (München: Kaiser, 1947); K. Ramge, *Vilmars Bedeutung für die Kirche in der Gegenwart* (Essen: Lichtweg-Verlag [Kleine theologische Handbucherei, 7], 1941).
The controversy about Church and Office resulted in a plethora of polemical writings and programmatic statements. Next to the work by Vilmar given above and Theodosius Harnack's treatise (see p. 144, n. 58), we mention: Wilhelm Löhe, *Drei Bücher von der Kirche; den Freunden der lutherischen Kirche zur Überlegung und Besprechung dargeboten* (Stuttgart: Liesching, 1845; 1st ed. 1833; 3rd ed. reissued 1947; repr. Darmstadt: Wissenschaftliche Buchgesellschaft, 1969); ET: *Three Books concerning the Church, offered to friends of the Lutheran Church for consideration and discussion*, tr. E. T. Horn (Reading, PA: Pilger Publishing House, 1908); also, *Three Books about the Church*, tr. and ed. J. S. Scharf (Philadelphia: Fortress Press, 1969); F. Delitzsch, *Vier Bücher von der Kirche; Seitenstück zu Löhes 3 Büchern von der Kirche* (Dresden: Raumann, 1847); A. Harless, *Kirche und Amt nach lutherischer Lehre* . . . (1853); T. Kliefoth, *Liturgische Abhandlungen (Acht Bücher von der Kirche)* (8 vols.; Schwerin: Stiller, 1854); K. Lechler, *Die neutestamentliche Lehre vom heiligen Amte in ihren Grundzügen dargestellt und auf die bestehenden Rechtsverhältnisse der evangelisch-lutherischen Kirche in Deutschland angewendet* (Stuttgart: J. F. Steinkopf, 1857); J. Stahl, *Die Kirchenverfassung nach Lehre und Recht der Protestanten* (Erlangen: 1862; 2nd ed. Frankfurt am Main: Minerva, 1965); H. Fagerberg, *Bekenntnis, Kirche und Amt in der Deutschen Konfessionellen Theologie des 19. Jahrhunderts* (Uppsala: Lundequistska Bokhandeln, 1952); E. Wolf, ed., *Kirche und Amt*, I (1938), II (1941).
60. Hengstenberg did not produce a material dogmatic work. But his *Christology of*

wrote a many-volumed dogmatics which attained neither the breadth nor the power of Vilmar's work.[61] In the long run, confessional Lutheranism in Germany was characterized more by the elements of the Erlangen School or of the great men of the Church such as T. Kliefoth (1810–95)[62] or Gerhard Uhlhorn (1826–1901) or finally Hermann Bezzel (1861–1917), whereas Lutheranism in Scandinavia was partially under the influence of the Tübingen Pietist Johann Tobias Beck (1804–78).[63]

Around 1870 all of the groups just mentioned were more or less rigidly locked into their contrary positions. We might say that they did not have anything to say to each other anymore. For a long time those voices which belonged to none of these groups and which rejected their common presuppositions remained unheard; we are referring here to the voice of Sören Kierkegaard (1813–55), who defended the concept of the particular which can only be grasped in the existential act against Hegel's concept of the universal,[64] or the voice of Hermann Friedrich

---

the Old Testament and a Commentary on the Messianic Predictions, tr. T. Meyer and J. Martin (4 vols.; Grand Rapids: Kregel, 1956 [1872–78 reprint] [g1829]), and his History of the Kingdom of God under the Old Testament (2 vols.; Edinburgh: T. & T. Clark, 1871 [g1854]) belong to the history of the theology of salvation-history. Here, Hengstenberg was as little independent as he was otherwise in his theology. But his influence was still great; he made his journal, the Evangelische Kirchenzeitung, into one of the most powerful organs of theological, ecclesiastical, and political restorationism.

61. Kirchliche Glaubenslehre (1854ff., 3rd ed. edited by F. Philippi; 7 vols. in 10; Gütersloh: Bertelsmann, 1870–90).

62. Kliefoth, like both Hengstenberg and Philippi an opponent of Hofmann, used the concept "organism" in his thinking on the Church, a term which was widespread at that time and originated in Romanticism; see his Liturgische Abhandlungen; Acht Bücher von der Kirche . . . (1854). His significance rests, aside from church politics, in his consolidation of the position of confessional Lutheranism against the Union, particularly in the area of liturgics.

63. Beck is one of the chief representatives of the group of theologians in the 19th century who connected Biblicism with a historico-theological speculation while completely avoiding any relationship to the traditional dogmatic materials. His dominant thought was that of the transcendent and yet already present Kingdom of God which thus required no human effort, including no missions! Of his contemporaries, only Gottfried Menken can be compared to him. The major works of Beck include Einleitung in das System der christlichen Lehre (Stuttgart: J. F. Steinkopf, 1838, 1870²); Die christliche Lehrwissenschaft nach den biblischen Urkunden (Stuttgart: J. F. Steinkopf, 1841, 1875²); Vorlesungen über Christliche Glaubenslehre, ed. J. Lindenmeyer (Stuttgart: J. F. Steinkopf, 1886–87). It is notable that Beck's work has been evaluated by both C. von Weizsäcker in his Worte der Erinnerung (1879) and Adolf Schlatter, Becks theologische Arbeit, in Christus und Christentum (Beiträge zur Förderung christlicher Theologie, 8,4; Gütersloh: Bertelsmann, 1904). Barth's treatment of him is also important (op. cit.). On Menken, see Gottfried Menken, Schriften (7 vols. in 3; Bremen: J. G. Heysem, 1858); C. H. Gildemeister, Leben und Wirken des Dr. Gottfried Menken; Weiland Pastor Primarius zu St. Martin in Bremen (Bremen: Müller, 1861). Beck's influence upon Scandinavia is still felt today, especially in Finland.

64. Kierkegaard, like the very different Kohlbrügge, is one of the fathers of contemporary theology and one of the great aliens to the theology of the 19th century. He is also one of the major sources of contemporary philosophy (the concept of existence!). Both German and French Kierkegaard research has had to make do with translations (see J. A. Wahl, Études Kierkegaardiennes [Paris: Vrin, 1967³]; in German, Werke, tr. and ed. H. Gottsched and C. Schrempf [12 vols.; Jena: Diederichs, 1913–25]; revision since 1952;

Kohlbrügge (1803–75),[65] who developed an interpretation of the Reformation's *sola gratia* (grace alone) which was completely unromantic, excluding every possibility of grace being won by man, as well as the voices of his students Johannes Wichelhaus (1819–58)[66] and E. Böhl (1836–1903).[67] In the meantime, bourgeois man had conquered the world and began to develop a new and powerful sense of his cultural mission (although from the very beginning the clear-thinking Jakob Burckhardt doubted that mission). Central Europe was about to set as its goal a

---

in English, tr. Lowrie, Drue, Swenson & Swenson [Princeton: Princeton University Press, 1936–46, and with the American Scandinavian Foundation]). The Jena edition is generally regarded as inadequate. Since 1952 a new revision, supervised by E. Hirsch, has been appearing.

The most important literature on Kierkegaard: E. Hirsch, *Kierkegaardstudien* (Gütersloh: Bertelsmann, 1933); E. Geismar, *Sören Kierkegaard, Seine Lebensentwicklung und seine Wirksamkeit als Schriftsteller*, tr. E. Krüger (Göttingen: Vandenhoeck & Ruprecht, 1929); see also in English: *Lectures on the Religious Thought of Sören Kierkegaard* (Minneapolis: Augsburg, 1937); W. Ruttenbeck, *Sören Kierkegaard, der christliche Denker und sein Werk* (Berlin and Frankfurt/Oder: Trowitzsch & Sohn, 1929); A. Gilg, *Sören Kierkegaard* (Munich: Kaiser, 1926); F. A. Voigt, *Sören Kierkegaard, im Kampfe mit der Romantik, der Theologie und der Kirche* (Berlin: Furche, 1928); Hermann Diem, *Die Existenzdialektik von Sören Kierkegaard* (Zollikon: Evangelischer Verlag, 1950); ET: *Kierkegaard's Dialectic of Existence*, tr. Harold Knight (Edinburgh: Oliver & Boyd, 1959); H. Höffding, *Sören Kierkegaard als Philosoph*, tr. by A. Dorner and C. Schrempf into German (1892; Stuttgart: F. Frommann, 1896); R. Hoffmann, *Kierkegaard et la certitude religieuse* (Geneve: Libraire J.-H. Jeheber, 1907); G. Niedermeyer, *Sören Kierkegaard und die Romantik* (1910; n.l.); Torsten Bohlin, *Kierkegaards dogmatische Anschauung, in ihrem geschichtlichen Zusammenhang*, tr. I. Meyer-Lüne (Gütersloh: C. Bertelsmann, 1927); Erich Przywara, *Das Geheimnis Kierkegaards* (Munich and Berlin: R. Oldenbourg, 1929); F. C. Fischer, *Die Nullpunkt-Existenz, dargestellt an der Lebensform Sören Kierkegaards* (Munich: Beck, 1933); for further bibliographies see Ruttenbeck, or Wahl. It is important to note that Kierkegaard has received a great deal of attention from Catholic theology, especially T. Haecker.

65. There is no complete edition of Kohlbrügge's works, which were of a great variety; most of them are no longer available. His theological position can be most easily reviewed in his *Erläuternde und befestigende Fragen und Antworten zu dem Heidelberger Catechismus* (Elberfeld: 1846) and his *Betrachtung über das erste Kapitel des Evangeliums nach Matthäus* (1844); *Das siebente Kapitel des Römerbriefes in ausführlicher Umschreibung* (*Biblische Studien*, Nr. 28, 1839; Neukirchen: Neukirchener Verlag, 1960) (based on a sermon on Romans 7:14 preached in 1833); *Das Alte Testament nach seinem wahren Sinn gewürdigt aus den Schriften der Evangelisten und Apostel, "Wozu das Alte Testament?"* (Elberfeld: 1846); and his 20 sermons from the year 1846, *Zwanzig Predigten im Jahre 1846 gehalten* (Halle: 1857, 1925[3]), to which a brief biography is appended.

J. van Lonkhuizen, *H. F. Kohlbrügge en zijn Prediking, in de lijst van zijn tijd* (Wageningen: Drukkerij "Vada," 1905); H. Klugkist-Hesse, *H. Fr. Kohlbrügge* (Wuppertal: Muller, 1935); T. Stiasny, *Die Theologie Kohlbrügges* (Düsseldorf: Branger, 1935); W. Kreck, *Die Lehre von der Heiligung bei H. F. Kohlbrügge* (München: Kaiser, 1936); J. Loss, *De Theologie van Kohlbrügge* (1948; n.l.); E. Wendel, *Kohlbrügges Verständnis der Kirche im Zusammenhang der Entwicklung seiner Theologie* (Göttingen dissertation, 1951).

66. Next to his exegetical works see especially his *Die Lehre der heiligen Schrift vom Worte Gottes, vom Wesen und Werken Gottes, vom Menschen und Gesetz Gottes*, biographical introduction by A. Zahn (3rd ed. 1892).

67. Böhl systematized Kohlbrügge's conception (*Dogmatik, Darstellung der christlicher Glaubenslehre auf reformirt-kirchlicher Grundlage* [Amsterdam: Scheffer, 1887]) and relieved it of some of its tension, especially in his monograph against A. Ritschl, *Von der Rechtfertigung durch den Glauben* (1899). Very few of his students shared Kohlbrügge's critique of the Reformers.

humanist and secular sense of community, building upon the foundation of bourgeois expansion and in Germany with the added foundation of political power. The conviction behind all this, if not expressed still undeniably present, was that the real problems were about to arise and that neither money nor power would help to solve them, but rather that ethical standards of value were needed. In the midst of this great and tragic epoch of bourgeois self-justification, two totally contradictory theological works appear: Albrecht Ritschl's *Christliche Lehre von der Rechtfertigung und Versöhnung (The Christian Doctrine of Justification and Reconciliation)*[68] and Martin Kähler's *Die Wissenschaft der christlichen Lehre vom evangelischen Grundartikel aus* (The Science of Christian Doctrine based upon the Fundamental Evangelical Article).[69] Two great and very different works which both were based upon the doctrine of justification! Two works which from two different points of view seek to get back directly to Luther! Both Ritschl and Kähler may be regarded as the most important representatives of a new theology which sought to encounter the confusing and murky problems of the age dogmatically.

> *g. Ritschl and His School.* Albrecht Ritschl (1822–89) was originally a his-

---

68. Preceding this was Ritschl's *Die Entstehung der altkatholischen Kirche, Eine Kirchen- und dogmengeschichtliche Monographie* (Bonn: A. Marcus, 1850). His major work was *Die christliche Lehre von der Rechtfertigung und der Versöhnung* (3 vols.; Bonn: A. Marcus, 1888–93³: vol. I, *A Critical History of the Christian Doctrine of Justification and Reconciliation*, tr. J. S. Black [Edinburgh: Edmonston & Douglas, 1872]; vol. III, *The Christian Doctrine of Justification and Reconciliation; the Positive Development of the Doctrine*, tr. H. R. Mackintosh and A. B. Macaulay [New York: Scribner's, 1900; Clifton, N.J.: Reference Book Publishers, 1966 (g1888–89³)]). This work offers a foundation in the history of dogma, including primarily a sharp critique of Anselm's doctrine of reconciliation and a strong endorsement of Abelard's; vol. II provides his biblical basis, the section least read today; vol. III is his dogmatic presentation, in reality a complete dogmatics. Ritschl provided a summary of his system in his book "Instruction in the Christian Religion," in *Three Essays*, tr. P. Hefner (Philadelphia: Fortress Press, 1972 [g1886]), which together with the lecture "Die christliche Vollkommenheit," was republished in a critical edition by C. Fabricius (1924). His rejection of natural theology was defended in "Theology and Metaphysics," in *Three Essays*, tr. P. Hefner (Philadelphia: Fortress Press, 1972 [g1881]) (his most vehement opponent was Otto Pfleiderer, *Die Ritschlsche Theologie* [1891; n.l.]). Ritschl's *Geschichte des Pietismus* (3 vols.; Bonn: A. Marcus, 1880–86; Berlin: W. de Gruyter, 1966) is arbitrary and generally unfair.
    G. Ecke, *Die theologische Schule Albrecht Ritschls* (Berlin: Reuther & Reichard, 1897, 1904); W. Herrmann, *Der evangelische Glaube und die Theologie Albrecht Ritschls* (Marburg: Elwert, 1890); G. Wobbermin, *Schleiermacher und Ritschl in ihrer Bedeutung für die heutige theologische Lage und Aufgabe* (Tübingen: J. C. B. Mohr, 1927).
    69. Erlangen: Deichert, 1883¹, 1905³; repr. of 3rd ed. (Neukirchen: Verlag des Erziehungsvereins, 1966). Kähler's most important study for the later issues was *The So-Called Historical Jesus and the Historic, Biblical Christ*, tr. C. E. Braaten (Philadelphia: Fortress Press, 1964 [g1896, 1953, 1961]). Otherwise and important his *Dogmatische Zeitfragen, Alte und Neue Ausführungen zur Wissenschaft der christlichen Lehre* (Leipzig: Deichert, 1898ff.), which contains very comprehensive and important discussions on the questions affecting the Bible and on the doctrine of reconciliation.
    Anna Kähler, ed., *Theologe und Christ, Erinnerungen und Bekenntnisse von Martin Kähler* (Berlin: Furche, 1926); Otto Zänker, *Grundlinien der Theologie Martin Kähler (Beiträge zur Förderung christlicher Theologie*, 18, 5; Gütersloh: Bertelsmann, 1914); Heinrich Petran, *Die Menschheitsbedeutung Christi bei Martin Kähler* (Gütersloh: Bertelsmann, 1931), with further bibliographies.

torian of the early Church and a part of the school of Ferdinand Christian Baur (1792–1860), from which he soon separated himself as he became a systematician who devoted himself more and more to a new understanding of Kant, under the influence of Hermann Lotze (1817–81) in Göttingen. As the first great theologian who generally received the central concepts of Kant, he shared Kant's total rejection of all theological metaphysics, that is, every attempt to establish religion out of the realm of nature, or based on anything already given, and simultaneously he accepted the decisive interconnectedness of Christianity (religion) with morality—to put it in a more modern fashion, an exclusive relationship of religion to what is not given, not directly perceivable. He felt that he had at this point grasped Luther's true intent: the Reformer's rejection of all forms of speculation, the exclusive relationship of faith not to what is natural but to the person, and the relationship of purely personal justification to the moral deed. The question must be asked whether this understanding of Luther is correct. Nonetheless, it was dominant for decades and resulted in the judgment that Kant was "the philosopher of Protestantism." When, with Ritschl, everything which is related to being is set aside and replaced with the purely personal and ethical, then traditional Christology is also destroyed. The conclusion that Christ is the Son of God could only be a "value judgment," to use the term reminiscent of Lotze, and the old concept of "nature" (the two natures!) had to be given up. Something else which had to be given up was the objective understanding of reconciliation (like that of Anselm); in fact, Ritschl propounded the thesis that reconciliation was nothing other than "successfully conceived" justification:[70] justification is the forgiveness of sins, that is, the effective removal of the consciousness of sinning, quite aside from the moral condition of the sinner (synthetic judgment!), and the mistrust which accompanies it. Reconciliation is the activation of trust and free involvement in the Kingdom of God as the Kingdom of the good. It is clear that Ritschl demonstrated to his age, which doubted profoundly the validity of theological speculation, that it was possible to envisage a modern and unspeculative Christianity which left all intrinsic elements aside and could make itself heard in a progressively scientific world, and could even show the way to productive actions for those who would hear. Thus Ritschl became the trailblazer of "Cultural Protestantism." He has receded somewhat behind those who took up his ideas and led them further, that is, behind Wilhelm Herrmann (1846–1922) who pushed the already present personalistic aspects of Ritschl's theology very near the boundaries of "existential" thought.[71] Herrmann's most influential students, Rudolf Bultmann (1884–1976)

---

70. *The Christian Doctrine of Justification and Reconciliation . . .* , III, 83, thesis 3.
71. *The Communion of the Christian with God*, tr. J. S. Stanyon, 2nd Eng. ed. edited by R. W. Stewart (New York: G. P. Putnam's Sons, 1906 [g1886]); *Ethik* (Tübingen and Leipzig: J. C. B. Mohr, 1901¹, 1913⁵); *Die Religion im Verhältnis zum Welterkennen und zur Sittlichkeit; Eine Grundlegung der Systematische Theologie* (Halle: Niemeyer, 1879); *Offenbarung und Wunder* (Giessen: A. Töpelmann, 1908); *Systematic Theology*, tr. Micklem and Saunders (London: G. Allen & Unwin, 1927 [g1925]).
Rudolf Hermann, *Christentum und Geschichte bei Wilhelm Herrmann* (Göttingen dissertation, 1914; Lucka: S.-A. Berger, 1913; Leipzig: Deichert, 1914); F. W. Schmidt, *Wilhelm Herrmann, ein Bekenntnis zu seiner Theologie* (Tübingen: Mohr, 1922); W. Schütz, *Das Grundgefüge der Herrmannschen Theologie; ihre Entwicklung und ihre geschichtlichen Wurzeln* (Berlin: E. Ebering, 1926).

and Karl Barth (1886–1968), are very different from each other and from their teachers, but they still cannot be understood without Herrmann and thus without Ritschl. If it is permitted to credit later "dialectical theology" with having overcome "Cultural Protestantism," then we must add that the intellectual weapons used (we are thinking of Bultmann's Existentialism and of Barth's rejection of natural theology) were taken in part from the arsenal out of which "Cultural Protestantism" also came.

   h. Kähler and His Students. Martin Kähler (1835–1912) differed from Ritschl by virtue of his deep personal roots in German Idealism and in the thinking of Goethe. Thus he could not make "nature" into the opposite of Christianity, as Ritschl had done. Where Ritschl retreats to ethics, Kähler looks upon apologetics as necessary. The reason was that for him the understanding of what is Christian (what is being sought in apologetics and needs to be protected from all misunderstandings) possesses its own category as a presupposition: the category of the superhistorical which encounters us in history, in the person of Jesus Christ who for Kähler was not the object of our value judgment but the divine self-revelation. Kähler therefore cannot join Ritschl in turning everything which has to do with existence into ethics, although he certainly places the moral elements, on the side of man, in the center—the conscience! In Kähler's work we see an independent theological understanding of being emerging, a historical-personal understanding, which does not mean that the historicity of revelation is absorbed into personal relationship. Thus Kähler's true significance for later generations of theology is to be sought in his understanding of history, in the unusual and certainly difficult concept of the superhistorical as well as in his idea that the New Testament, as the "documentation of the preaching which establishes the Church," proclaims a Christ who is inseparable from the testimony of the believing community but who legitimizes himself in it as the "historical Christ."[72] Of the students of Martin Kähler, it was Karl Heim (1874–1958)[73] in particular who developed further the

---

   72. See *The So-Called Historical Jesus* . . . (1964) (which was intended as an apologetic writing) and *Dogmatische Zeitfragen*, I (2nd ed. 1907).
   73. *Das Weltbild der Zukunft; Eine Auseinandersetzung Zwischen Philosophie, Naturwissenschaft, und Theologie* (Berlin: Schwetschke & Sohn, 1904); *Das Gewissheitsproblem in der systematischen Theologie bis zu Schleiermacher* (Leipzig: Hinrich, 1911); *Leitfaden der Dogmatik, zum Gebrauch bei akademischen Vorlesungen* (Halle: Niemeyer, 1912, 1935); *Glaubensgewissheit, eine Untersuchung der Lebensfrage der Religion* (1916; Leipzig: Hinrichs, 1923[3]; Berlin: Evangelische Verlagsanstalt, 1949[4])—his fundamental work!; *Der evangelische Glaube und das Denken der Gegenwart* (6 vols.; Hamburg: Furche Verlag, 1931–57): ET of various volumes: I, *God Transcendent*, tr. E. P. Dickie (New York: Scribner's, 1936); III, *Jesus, The World's Perfecter: The Atonement and the Renewal of the World*, tr. E. P. Dickie (Philadelphia: Muhlenberg Press, 1961); V, *The Transformation of the Scientific World View*, tr. W. A. Whitehouse (London: S.C.M. Press, 1953); VI, *The World: Its Creation and Consummation*, tr. R. Smith (London: S.C.M., 1962); *Glaube und Leben; gesammelte Aufsätze und Vorträge* (Berlin: Furche, 1926).
   Theology's self-encapsulation over against natural science was proclaimed really by Ritschl, mightily opposed by Kähler, and transformed by Heim into the very opposite, for Heim understood natural science with a depth shared by no other scientist of the modern age. Of course, he was somewhat hindered by his own methodology.
   W. Ruttenbeck, *Die apologetisch-theologische Methode Karl Heims* (Leipzig: A. Deichert, 1925).

epistemology of the master from Halle and, with his critical analysis of the world view of modern natural science in its relationship to the Christian view of the world, created a work which, along Kähler's lines, replaced older apologetics with a new kind of eristic which plunges into the depths of ontology and epistemology. Next to Kähler we would also mention the Greifswald theologian who shared his approach and was influenced by him, Hermann Cremer (1834–1903).[74] Cremer did not leave a completed dogmatics behind but in his writings, particularly in his exposition of the Pauline doctrine of justification, and in his Greifswald activity made that city into a bastion of a theology "which believed in revelation," which as such fundamentally differed from Cultural Protestantism. Kähler's own students, aside from Karl Heim, are more to be found among the exegetes—we think here of Julius Schniewind (1883–1948)—or if they were dogmaticians excelled more in the area of historical studies, as especially with Hans Emil Weber (1882–1950).[75] Thematically close to Kähler but individual in their systems were Erich Schaeder and Wilhelm Lütgert (1867–1938).[76]

Martin Kähler's dogmatic work made Scripture into a central problem again, more so than did Ritschl, with the result that the problem of "faith and history" was brought to the foreground with an urgency unparalleled since Lessing. As a chronological and thematic part of the context, we would consider two dogmatic systems which are both based upon exegesis and which continue to be a concern of contemporary dogmatics. We turn now to the very contradictory positions of Adolf Schlatter and the "History of Religions School" (*religionsgeschichtliche Schule*).

---

74. *Die paulinische Rechtfertigungslehre, im Zusammenhange ihrer geschichtlichen Voraussetzungen* (Gütersloh: C. Bertelsmann, 1899, 1910); *Dogmatische Prinzipienlehre*, in Zöckler, *Handbuch der theologischen Wissenschaften* . . . (Munich: Beck, 1889–90), III, 49–201; *Glaube, Schrift und heilige Geschichte* (Gütersloh: Bertelsmann, 1896); *Die christliche Lehre von den Eigenschaften Gottes* (*Beiträge zur Förderung christlicher Theologie*, 1, 4; Gütersloh: Bertelsmann, 1897, 1917²); *A Reply to Harnack on the Essence of Christianity*, tr. B. Pick (New York and London: Funk & Wagnalls, 1903 [g1902³]). Also, of course, Cremer-Kögel, *Biblico-Theological Lexicon of New Testament Greek*, tr. W. Urwich (New York: Charles Scribner's Sons, 1895⁴ [g1923]).

M. Kähler, *Wie Hermann Cremer wurde* (*Beiträge zur Förderung christlicher Theologie*, 8, 1; Gütersloh: C. Bertelsmann, 1904); Ernst Cremer, *Hermann Cremer; Ein Lebensund Charakterbild* (Gütersloh: Bertelsmann, 1912); Adolf Schlatter, *Die Entstehung der Beiträge zur Förderung christlicher Theologie und ihr Zusammenhang mit meiner theologischen Arbeit* (Gütersloh: Bertelsmann, 1920 [g1929]).

75. *Reformation, Orthodoxie, Rationalismus* (2 vols. in 3; Gütersloh: C. Bertelsmann, 1937–51; repr. Darmstadt: Wissenschaftliche Buchgesellschaft, 1966); *Historisch-kritische Schriftforschung und Bibelglaube* (Gütersloh: C. Bertelsmann, 1914); *Das Geisteserbe der Gegenwart und die Theologie* (Leipzig: Deichert, 1925); *"Eschatologie" und "Mystik" im Neuen Testament, ein Versuch* (*Beiträge zur Förderung christlicher Theologie*, 2nd ser., vol. 20; Gütersloh: C. Bertelsmann, 1930); *Die Beziehungen von Römer 1-3 zur Missionspraxis des Paulus* (*Beiträge zur Förderung christlicher Theologie*, 9, 4; Gütersloh: C. Bertelsmann, 1905) (Greifswald dissertation); *Das Problem der Heilsgeschichte nach Römer 9–11* (Leipzig: Deichert, 1911).

76. *Die Religion des deutschen Idealismus und ihr Ende* (4 vols.; Gütersloh: Bertelsmann, 1923–30); *Die Liebe im Neuen Testament; ein Beitrag zur Geschichte des Urchristentums* (Leipzig: Deichert, 1905); *Schöpfung und Offenbarung; eine Theologie der ersten Artikels* (Gütersloh: Bertelsmann, 1934).

i. Schlatter. Adolf Schlatter (1852–1939)[77] was influenced by Johann Tobias Beck, by Franz von Baader (1765–1841), and by his colleague in Greifswald, Hermann Cremer, but he was in fact no one's student. His *Christliches Dogma* and his other dogmatic works are an independent and unusual development. In his book on the work of philosophy since Descartes (*Die philosophische Arbeit seit Descartes*), which is still highly recommended today, he makes very clear why he could not be anyone's student: the dominant way of doing philosophy since Descartes (which has not gone unopposed—Herder attacked it strongly) goes back to the dialectical distinction between subject and object, between the knowing element (*res cogitans*) and the external element (*res extensa*), between thought and extension, between consciousness and being, and this separation is then overcome dialectically or remains a standing dualism. It is Schlatter's conclusion that this approach, which theology had accepted in so many ways, is wrong, because the philosophical thinking here is not soberly realistic but rather artificially divisive and connective or identifying, and the theological thinking does not deal seriously with the reality of the Creator. This is the primary concern of the dogmatician Schlatter. He is not at all concerned about the charge that he is doing either metaphysics or natural theology. He is much more horrified at the fact that both theology and the Church by going another direction have lost their own place in reality, that God is no longer the absolute First in contrast to the human subject, and that justification (here accusation is directed initially to the Reformers[78]) has been made into an inward affair in such a way that it no longer corresponds to the New Testament. Schlatter the dogmatician really did not have any students who followed him directly. But his questions are still alive today and cannot be forgotten.

j. The History of Religions School. The History of Religions School began with exegesis; at its inception it set about a process of "levelling" the contents of the biblical realm of statements. It had been the purpose of literary criticism to find methodologically the point at which the unmistakable uniqueness of Christianity, especially of the figure of the "historical Jesus," would become clear, having removed all the overlaying strata that concealed it. The Historians of Religion, without scorning literary criticism, were not even interested in this unique element any more, especially after Albert Schweitzer (1875–1965)[79] in his "his-

---

77. *Das christliche Dogma* (Stuttgart: Calwer Verlag, 1923[2] [g1911]); *Die christliche Ethik* (Stuttgart: Calwer Verlag, 1961[4] [g1914]); *Die philosophische Arbeit seit Descartes; ihr ethischer und religiöser Ertrag* (Stuttgart: Calwer Verlag, 1959[4] [g1906]). We cannot list the numerous exegetical works but special mention is given to *Luthers Deutung des Römerbriefs* (*Beiträge zur Förderung christlicher Theologie*, 1st ser., 21, 7; Gütersloh: Bertelsmann, 1917); *Der Dienst des Christen in der älteren Dogmatik* (Gütersloh: C. Bertelsmann, 1897 [g1904]).

78. *Luthers Deutung des Römerbriefs*, and *Der Dienst des Christen in der älteren Dogmatik*.

79. Schweitzer's influence upon dogmatics was not direct. His history of the research of the Life of Jesus, *The Quest of the Historical Jesus*, tr. W. Montgomery (London: A. and C. Black, 1910; London: Adam & Black, 1954[3]; New York: Macmillan, 1960 [g1906]); *Geschichte der Leben-Jesu-Forschung* (Tübingen: J. C. B. Mohr [Paul Siebeck], 1951[6] [g1913]

tory of the study of the Life of Jesus" had revealed the dubiousness of such a quest for a Jesus who would correspond to our ideas of him. The Historians of Religion found in the Bible or in the figure Jesus not what was close and understandable to us but primarily what was alien, what was dependent upon or analogous to the world of ancient religion, itself something we could scarcely assimilate. The first reaction was one of profound shock. It was so profound that the first systematician of the school, Ernst Troeltsch (1865–1923),[80] who in many ways was obligated to Ritschl, finally integrated "Christianity" into the development of European culture and felt that he could only demonstrate the "absolute character"[81] of Christianity by means of the application of philosophical criteria; he maintained the point of view, with a fair degree of perceivable skepticism, that this was what was at stake anyway! Rudolf Otto (1869–1937), on the other hand, although he certainly was aware of the alien element, developed in his book *The*

---

had the effect of an earthquake for both theological Liberalism, whose historical basis was destroyed by it, and for conservative theology for which it raised the very disquieting question of the meaning of eschatology in the New Testament. Schweitzer's *The Mysticism of Paul the Apostle*, tr. W. Montgomery (New York: Henry Holt & Co., 1931 [g1930]) confronted dogmatics with questions which still have not been answered. He developed his systematic position in the form of a philosophy of culture, "Decay and Restoration of Civilization," in *The Philosophy of Civilization*, tr. C. T. Campion (London: Black, 1932, 1946, 1951, 1955 [g1923¹, 1925²]); and "Civilization and Ethics," in *The Philosophy of Civilization*, tr. C. T. Campion (London: Black, 1932, 1946, 1951, 1955 [g1924]).

Martin Werner attempted to draw the theological consequences with his fundamental view of "consequent eschatology" in his *Das Weltanschauungsproblem bei Karl Barth und Albert Schweitzer; Eine Auseinandersetzung* (München: C. H. Beck, 1924); *Albert Schweitzer und das freie Christentum* (1924; n.l.); *The Formation of Christian Dogma; an Historical Study of its Problem*, tr. S. G. F. Brandon (New York: Harper, 1957 [g1941]).

Franz Overbeck had already drawn attention to the eschatological character of primitive Christianity which made the unity of Christianity and culture impossible; see his *Ueber die Christlichkeit unserer heutigen Theologie* (Darmstadt: Wissenschaftliche Buchgesellschaft, 1963³ [g1873]); *Christentum und Kultur; Gedanken und Anmerkungen zur modernen Theologie* (Basel: Benno Schwabe, 1919; Darmstadt: Wissenschaftliche Buchgesellschaft, 1963); *Selbstbekenntnisse* (Basel: B. Schwabe, 1941 posth. with an important introduction by E. Vischer, ed.).

See also K. Barth, "Unsettled Questions for Theology Today," in *Theology and Church, Shorter Writings 1920–1928*, tr. L. P. Smith (London: S.C.M., 1962), pp. 1–73.

It was well known that Overbeck was a friend of Friedrich Nietzsche (correspondence edited by R. Oehler and C. A. Bernoulli, 1916). He formulated the problem of history in its most extreme and acute form.

80. *Gesammelte Schriften* (4 vols.; Tübingen: J. C. B. Mohr, 1912–25; Aalen: Scientia, 1961–66); especially *The Social Teaching of the Christian Churches*, tr. O. Wyon (2 vols.; New York: Macmillan, 1931 [g1912]) (this work is vol. 1 of the *Gesammelte Schriften*); *Der Historismus und seine Probleme* (1922), now vol. III of the *Gesammelte Schriften*; *Glaubenslehre; nach Heidelberger Vorlesungen aus den Jahren 1911 & 1912*, ed. Gertrud Baronness von le Fort (München and Leipzig: Duncker & Humboldt, 1925) (Heidelberg lectures based upon the notes of Gertrud Baronness von Le Fort, who later became famous as a Catholic authoress). Later in his career, Troeltsch, like his friend Max Weber, turned to a positivistic-ethical pessimism.

W. Köhler, *Ernst Troeltsch* (Tübingen: J. C. B. Mohr, 1938, 1941); Marianne Weber, *Max Weber; ein Lebensbild* (Tübingen: Mohr, 1926).

81. *The Absoluteness of Christianity and the History of Religions*, tr. D. Reid (Richmond: John Knox, 1971 [g1902]).

Idea of the Holy[82] the unique character of Christian proclamation in an impressive way. Basically following Schleiermacher's approach and leaving the first and highest concern of Cultural Protestantism aside, he revealed the independent category of the "numinous" in that he designated God "the completely Other" (using the neuter form!). Later on, the Form-Critical School, also building upon exegesis, took up thoughts of Herrmann and Kähler by seriously interpreting the New Testament witness as the witness of the believing Community and by teaching that the Old Testament witness is to be understood in its kerygmatic character. The results for dogmatics are the subject of passionate discussions today: the issue is whether the theological quest can penetrate beyond the Christ of the "kerygma" or beyond the *pro nobis* ("for us" character of the Gospel), or must remain with the insights about the "significance" of Jesus. The problem here addressed is that of the hermeneutics represented by Rudolf Bultmann (1884–1976).

C. ON CONTEMPORARY DOGMATICS

a. The Collapse of the Theology of the 19th Century. As far as the German-speaking countries are concerned, the theology of the 19th century ended with the end of the First World War, which was a deeper break than the Thirty Years' War had been. However, it would be an oversimplification to relate this coincidence of a historical event and a theological development to the profound shock which the year 1918 produced for the world of the white man.[83] The question we must ask is why these critical events could and did affect theology as they did.

The reason is to be sought in the realm of the fundamental problem of dogmatics itself. The theology of the 19th century as represented by most of its proponents was generally a "bourgeois" matter, in spite of all the differences and contradictions. It was broadly the theological form of that which defined the dominant self-understanding. That was the reason for its consolidation of the philosophy of identity, or at least its correlation of being and consciousness. And that also explains its Ethicism and its Historicism, which grew out of Romanticism. This evaluation cannot be generalized sight unseen. But it still holds true if we remain aware of the fact that there were potent counter-movements (Kierkegaard, Kohlbrügge, finally Overbeck), and that it was scarcely theology's intention to be

---

82. *The Idea of the Holy*, tr. J. W. Harvey (London: Oxford University Press, 1946⁴ [g1923]); *Naturalism and Religion*, tr. J. A. and M. D. Thomson (New York: G. P. Putnam's Sons, 1907, 1913 [g1904, 1929³]); *The Philosophy of Religion, based on Kant and Fries*, tr. E. B. Dicker (London: Williams & Norgate Ltd., 1931 [g1909]); *Religious Essays; a supplement to 'The Idea of the Holy'*, tr. B. Lunn (London: Oxford University Press, 1931 [g1923]); *India's Religion of Grace and Christianity Compared and Contrasted*, tr. F. H. Foster (New York: Macmillan, 1930 [g1930]).

83. See W. Koepp, *Die gegenwärtige Geisteslage und die dialektische Theologie* (Tübingen: Mohr, 1930); and as a counterpart see what Karl Holl writes about the Thirty Years' War in "Die Bedeutung der grossen Kriege, usw.," *Gesammelte Aufsätze zur Kirchengeschichte* (3 vols.; Tübingen: J. C. B. Mohr [Paul Siebeck], 1928–48; Darmstadt: Wissenschaftliche Buchgesellschaft, 1948–65), III, 302ff. The effects of the wars of liberation (Holl, *op. cit.*, pp. 347ff.) would be more likely to offer a fair comparison.

merely the outer form of the dominant self-understanding and thus to adapt God to man. The Christendom of the Church, which corresponded to this theology, was in general still stronger than this expression of the dominant self-understanding: in the connection of "throne and altar" as in bourgeois liberalism and in privatized late Pietism. The emerging and fateful issue of the age, the social problem, which Thomas Chalmers (1780–1847) and Johann Hinrich Wichern (1808–81) still looked upon as a problem of the Christian Community and its place in society, became under these circumstances either a purely political problem or the problem of the conscientious attitude of the individual; as such it was not really forgotten by theology, but only in this form did it emerge in theology.

The First World War sealed the downfall of the kind of humanity with which both theology and the Church in the 19th century were so closely identified—a downfall which alert observers had sensed approaching. The consequences were not the development of a new self-understanding, except in a very limited and restricted sense, but instead the collapse in the ideology of the "Third Reich," often only dimly sensed and totally concealed for many; it was only at the end of the Second World War that this collapse was totally obvious. The decision which theology had to make, and often did not know it had to do so, was whether it was going to adapt itself again to a new self-understanding or was going to seek out the Word of God in face of every self-understanding.

b. Early Dialectical Theology. The beginnings of a new theology are not found in the area of "regular dogmatics," but rather completely outside the academic sphere; they are found in the work of theologians laboring in the congregational ministry. Karl Barth (1886–1968), whose commentary on Romans breached the walls in 1919;[84] Friedrich Gogarten (1887–1967), whose controversy with Idealism took place independent of Barth;[85] Emil Brunner (1884–1966), who gradually moved from thinking in a way strongly determined by the philosophy of religion to the "dialectical" theology of that time[86]—all of these men were parish

---

84. *The Epistle to the Romans*, tr. E. C. Hoskyns (London: Oxford University Press, 1933–65 [g1919, 1920]).

85. *Die religiöse Entscheidung* (Jena: E. Diederichs, 1921); *Von Glauben und Offenbarung* (Jena: E. Diederichs, 1923); *Illusionen; eine Auseinandersetzung mit dem Kulturidealismus* (Jena: E. Diederichs, 1926); *Theologische Tradition und theologische Arbeit; Geistesgeschichte oder Theologie?* (Leipzig: Hinrich, 1927); especially, *Ich glaube an den dreieinigen Gott; eine Untersuchung über Glauben und Geschichte* (Jena: Diederichs, 1926).

86. Regarding the concept "dialectic" see A. Sannwald, *Der Begriff der Dialektik und die Anthropologie; eine Untersuchung über das Ich-Verständnis in der Philosophie des deutschen Idealismus und seiner Antipoden* (München: Kaiser, 1931).

"Dialectical" language can essentially be understood to mean the following:

a. Dialogic language, that is, language which does not presuppose an "I" and its object of knowledge but rather is based upon an "I" and another "I" (even if only intellectually conceived) who are each confronted by the varying aspects of the object;

b. Paradoxical language, that is, language in which two or more aspects of the object persist in their oppositeness and interrelatedness without any possibility of coming to a conceptual, synthetic unification;

c. Existential language, that is, language in which the "I" and the object both stand in the same comprehensive relationship which itself cannot be reduced to a simple and unambiguous formula;

d. Conceptual-analytical language, that is, language in which the duality or plurality

pastors. All of them were products of "modern" theology: Gogarten was a student of Troeltsch, both Barth and Bultmann were students of Wilhelm Herrmann. They had had very little contact with the 19th-century Pietism of the revival movement which potentially could have been a counter-movement—we think of the Blumhardts,[87] of Johann Tobias Beck's theology of the Kingdom of God, of Kohlbrügge's Pietistic roots, and those of the very different Abraham Kuyper (1837–1920).[88] The question which moved this new theology, which drove it to Scripture with new questions and led it to listen in a new way to the Reformers,[89] was apparently a questionable simplification, compared particularly to the grand conceptions of the past century: it was the question about the content of the proclamation which is validly addressed to real man. The answer which this the-

---

of possible aspects of an object are dealt with so long that eventually a synthesis emerges, as, e.g., with Abelard.

Dialectical theology fluctuates between the various possibilities, usually avoiding d., without making a final decision.

87. Johann Christoph (1805–80), and his son Christoph Friedrich (1842–1919)—TR.

88. See especially T. L. Haitjema, "Abraham Kuyper und die Theologie des holländischen Neu-Calvinismus," ZZ (1931), pp. 331–54; "Der Kampf des holländischen Neu-Calvinismus gegen die dialektische Theologie," Theologische Aufsätze Karl Barth zum 50. Geburtstag, ed. E. Wolf (Munich: Kaiser, 1936), pp. 571–89.

Books by Kuyper himself: De Gemeene Gratie, in Weierschop en Kunst (Amst-Pretoria: Boekhandel v. Höveker & Wormser, 1902ff.; Kampen: J. H. Kok, 1920); E voto Dordraceno; Toelichting op den Heidelbergschen Catechismus (Amsterdam: J. A. Wormer [Boekhandel v. Höveker & Wormser], 1893); Het Calvinisme; oorsprong en waarborg onzer constitutioneele vrijheden (Amsterdam: B. van der Land, 1874); Encyclopedia of Sacred Theology, tr. J. H. DeVries (New York: C. Scribner's Sons, 1898); see also Principles of Sacred Theology, tr. J. H. DeVries (Grand Rapids: Eerdmans, 1954).

Julius Stahl definitely influenced Kuyper, via Groen van Prinsterer, and in some ways Kuyper is also similar to A. Vilmar, although there was no direct relationship between them.

See W. Kolfhaus, Dr. Abraham Kuyper, 1837–1920; ein Lebensbericht (Elberfeld: Buchhandlung des Erziehungsvereins, 1924); J. R. Slotemaker de Bruine, Abraham Kuyper oder Staatsmann und Christ (Berlin: Acker-Verlag, 1932); P. A. Diepenhort, Abraham Kuyper (1931; n.l.); S. J. Ridderbos, De theologische cultuurbeschouwing van Abraham Kuyper (1947; n.l.); E. E. Rosenboom, Die Idee einer christlichen Universität im theologischen Denken von Abraham Kuyper (Göttingen dissertation, 1950); A. A. van Ruler, Kuyper's Idee eener Christelijke cultuur (1938; n.l.); A. A. van Ruler, "Kuyper's leer van de gemeene gratie," in De Gereformeerde Kerk (Oct. 7–Dec. 15, 1937). For a comprehensive and still very usable dogmatics based upon Kuyper's position see H. Bavinck, Gereformeerde Dogmatiek (4 vols., 1895ff.; Kampen: J. H. Kok, 1906): vol. II, The Doctrine of God, tr. and ed. W. Hendriksen (Grand Rapids: Eerdmans, 1951); Our Reasonable Faith (Grand Rapids: Eerdmans, 1956) (a compendium of the four vols.); and also G. Vellenga, Christelijke Dogmatiek (1919; n.l.).

Newer Dutch theology and philosophy inspired by Kuyper is best expressed in H. Dooyeweerd, A New Critique of Theoretical Thought, tr. D. H. Freeman and W. S. Young (4 vols.; Amsterdam: H. J. Paris; Philadelphia: Presbyterian and Reformed Publishing, 1953–58); and D. T. H. Vollenhoven, Die Noodzakelijkheid eener Christelijke Logica (1932; n.l.). Kuyperian theology became progressively hostile toward Barth; see from the dogmatic side G. C. Berkouwer, Karl Barth (Kampen: J. H. Kok, 1936).

89. Both the Munich German-language edition of Luther and the Munich selection of Calvin (Opera Selecta, ed. P. Barth and W. Niesel [München: Kaiser, 1926–36]) are direct results of this new theology; this is also true of the new edition of Theodosius Harnack's Luther's Theologie; mit besonderer Beziehung auf seine Versöhnungs- und Erlösungslehre (2 vols.; Amsterdam: Rodopi [1862, 1927], 1969).

ology thought it could perceive was more unified in its negative aspects than in its positive ones; it was commonly agreed that theology could not continue along the path of the 19th century, which was at first generally rejected. It was also agreed that theology and the Church should seek only the Word of God and would find their freedom and their obligation only there; from the very beginning, however, there were differences of position in regard to the issues which had been raised in the history of dogma. There was the unmistakable tendency of Barth (very obvious in the second edition of *Romans*) to lean toward dialectical Platonism, the response to which in Gogarten was an early agreement with certain aspects of the existential philosophy then emerging,[90] and Bultmann was totally committed to this philosophy from the point he entered into the theological movement. Thus various directions appeared which still did not conceal their common background. Their concrete activities in regard to the social situation were also marked by contradictions: at the beginning Barth tended toward a Platonizing eschatologism which made every practical decision relative over against God's own Word, whereas Gogarten especially always saw concrete decisions against the background of the given orders (which were certainly relative); this led him to renew the doctrine of law and Gospel. Later decisions and divisions were already being anticipated.

At first the new theology, generally termed "dialectic,"[91] was more a question than a positive new concept, was more united in what it negated than in what it agreed to. And then it had its crisis when, first, it became necessary for it to formulate its own legitimate dogmatics, and secondly, when in Germany it faced the concrete ecclesiastical problem which resulted from the encounter with the ideology of the Third Reich and its Christian supporters. Since 1927, the year in which Karl Barth's incomplete *Die Christliche Dogmatik im Entwurf; Die Lehre vom Worte Gottes* (*Christian Dogmatics; An Outline*), vol. I (Munich: Kaiser, 1927) appeared, the situation has been characterized by this crisis.

"Dialectical" theology had made a similar selection from the broad array of traditional theological and especially dogmatic thought, as did the theology of the Reformation in its first phases. This new theology had its specific points of departure: Luther, Calvin (but not Melanchthon or Zwingli), or Kierkegaard, to a degree Kohlbrügge, Christoph Blumhardt, Franz Overbeck (1837–1905), philosophically Plato (but not Aristotle), Nietzsche, Martin Heidegger (1889–1976),

---

90. It cannot be overlooked that Gogarten is close to E. Grisebach (*Gegenwart; ein kritische Ethik* [Halle: Niemeyer, 1928]); Bultmann was linked to Martin Heidegger at a very early point (major writings: *Being and Time*, tr. J. Macquarrie and E. Robinson [New York: Harper, 1962 (g1926)]; "What is Metaphysics," in *Existence and Being*, tr. R. F. C. Hull and O. Crick [Chicago: H. Regnery Co., 1949 (g1951)]; *Holzwege* [Frankfurt: V. Klostermann, 1950]).

For years M. Heidegger was one of the publishers of the journal, *Theologische Rundschau*.

K. Jaspers, *Philosophy*, tr. E. B. Ashton (3 vols.; Chicago: University of Chicago Press, 1969–71 [g1956]); K. Jaspers, *Rechenschaft und Ausblick; Reden und Aufsätze* (München: R. Piper, 1951, 1958). See also H. Eklund, *Theologie der Entscheidung; Zur Analyse und Kritik der "existentiellen" Denkweise* (Uppsala: A.-b. Lundequistska bokhandeln, 1937).

91. Since 1930 the term has been less frequent.

or Ferdinand Ebner, as well as their opposite Schleiermacher (see Brunner's rigorous book in 1924), or "the" Pietism or "the" Idealism, less often Ritschl but probably Harnack (whose book on Marcion [1921] was emphatically mentioned by Barth in the preface to the second edition of *Romans* [1922]!). A thoroughgoing reworking of the theological tradition, which no new generation can evade, could not immediately take place. But with time it became absolutely necessary for this new theology to express dogmatically what it had already been saying in a pre-dogmatic way—although in the most radical enactment of what is fundamentally dogmatics!

c. The Orientation of the New Theology in Its Environment. The first thing necessary was orientation in the theological environment. And it became clear that within this environment, which had evolved out of the 19th century, dogmatic work had not been inactive. There was a "Luther Renaissance" going on with Karl Holl as its master.[92] A Calvin Renaissance was beginning to appear.[93] And there were prominent proponents of all the dogmatic schools of the 19th century who by no means were prepared to regard themselves as passé and leave the field of battle to this untested new theology. At this time, too, new and significant statements emerged from the direction of the old Schleiermacher position,[94] and from "Mediatory Theology"[95] and Kähler's school[96]; Harnack, a member of the Ritschl group, wrote his book on Marcion at this time.[97] And then we have not

---

92. K. Holl, *Gesammelte Aufsätze . . .* , vols. I and III; E. Wolf, "Luther's Erbe," *EvTheol* (1946), pp. 82ff.

93. We think of the edition of Calvin by Barth and Niesel, and of Niesel's book, *Calvin's Lehre vom Abendmahl* (Munich: Kaiser Verlag, 1935² [g1930]); or of A. Göhler, *Calvin's Lehre von der Heiligung; dargestellt auf Grund der Institutio, exegetischer und homiletischer Schriften* (Munich: Kaiser, 1934); also Niesel, *The Theology of Calvin*, tr. H. Knight (Philadelphia: Westminster Press, 1956 [g1938]); or P. Brunner, *Vom Glauben bei Calvin* (Tübingen: J. C. B. Mohr [Paul Siebeck], 1925) should be mentioned here.

94. G. Wobbermin, *Systematische Theologie nach religionspsychologischer Methode*, vol. I, *Die Religionspsychologische Methode in Religionswissenschaft und Theologie* (Leipzig: J. C. Hinrichs, 1913); vol. II, *The Nature of Religion*, tr. T. Menzel and D. S. Robinson (New York: Thomas Y. Crowell, 1933); vol. III, *Wesen und Wahrheit des Christentums* (Leipzig: Hinrichs, 1925, 1926); G. Wobbermin, *Richtlinien evangelischer Theologie; zur Überwindung der gegenwärtigen Krisis* (Göttingen: Vandenhoeck & Ruprecht, 1929); *Das Wort Gottes und der evangelische Glaube* (Göttingen: Vandenhoeck & Ruprecht, 1933²).

95. Reinhold Seeberg, *Christliche Dogmatik* (Erlangen and Leipzig: Deichert, 1924–25).

96. Karl Heim, *Der evangelische Glaube . . .*; H. E. Weber, *Das Geisteserbe der Gegenwart; und die Theologie* (Leipzig: Deichert, 1925); even Paul Althaus in his *Grundriss der Dogmatik* (2 vols.; Gütersloh: Bertelsmann, 1927, 1932, 1947) belongs in a broader sense to this group.

97. *Marcion; das Evangelium vom fremden Gott* (Leipzig: J. C. Hinrichs, 1921); see also Barth, *The Epistle to the Romans . . .* , pp. 13ff. The Ritschl school produced, aside from the notes on Herrmann's *Systematic Theology . . .* , Martin Rade's *Glaubenslehre* (3 vols.; Gotha: Leopold Klotz, 1924–27); and Horst Stephan, *Glaubenslehre; der evangelische Glaube und sein Weltverständnis* (Giessen: A. Töpelmann, 1921).

even spoken of the situation in Scandinavia or the English-speaking world,[98] both of which devoted very little attention to the "dialecticians,"[99] in contrast to Holland where there was agreement and disagreement from the beginning.[100] In addition, historical studies went on apace; exegesis moved from the methods of the History of Religions School over to form criticism,[101] and Adolf Schlatter wrote during this period one great commentary after another, scarcely affected by the new theology. Certainly it was clear that the young theological generation in both Germany and Switzerland viewed the ongoing activity of what they thought to be "old" with skepticism and met the new theology, which was still rather vague, with high expectations and often genuine enthusiasm; this was equally true of much of the pastorate in many areas. The monthly journal entitled *Zwischen den Zeiten* (Between the Times, *ZZ*), which in its name was a self-evaluation of the new theology, was for many the one place where the essentials of theology were being dealt with. Roman Catholic theology, with its alert interest in everything, turned its attention to "dialectical" theology. This theology, and this was essential, neither could nor wanted to evade orienting itself to its worldwide setting, and this orientation led to varying results. It was its most obstinate toward theological liberalism as a dogmatic position, and this latter movement is scarcely heard from anymore.[102] But were there not positive relationships to the Luther Renaissance, after having energetically penetrated back through to Luther, and even such relationships to confessional theology as with Vilmar, for example?[103] And were there not among the advocates of the new theology heirs of Kähler, such as Dietrich Bonhoeffer,[104] or heirs of Rudolf Hermann like Hans Joachim

---

98. Anders Nygren, *Agape and Eros*, tr. P. S. Watson (London: S.P.C.K., 1953; Philadelphia: Westminster Press, 1953); Gustav Aulén, "Das christliche Gottesbild," in *Vergangenheit und Gegenwart*, tr. G. Jonsson (Gütersloh: Bertelsmann, 1930).

99. Regarding English theology see the overview in John Kenneth Mozley, *Some Tendencies in British Theology, from the publication of Lux Mundi to the present day* (London: S.P.C.K., 1951) and L. E. Elliot-Bynns, *The Development of English Theology in the later nineteenth century* (London and New York: Longmans, Green, 1952).

100. See p. 156, n.88. T. L. Haitjema and K. H. Miskotte spoke out early in favor of Karl Barth; the most intense opposition came especially from the "gereformeerde" grouping, most sharply in K. Schilder, more moderately in G. C. Berkouwer.

101. The work of Albrecht Alt and Martin Noth was fundamental for the Old Testament, the works of K. L. Schmidt, Martin Dibelius, and Rudolf Bultmann for the New Testament.

102. Still we should note that Martin Rade in his *Glaubenslehre* . . . carried on a continuous and quiet controversy with his former colleague Karl Barth, and then especially Theodor Siegfried, *Das Wort und die Existenz; eine Auseinandersetzung mit der dialektischen Theologie* (3 vols.; Gotha: L. Klotz, 1930ff.), initiated a rigorous dispute with Barth, Gogarten, and Bultmann.

103. Representatives of the camp of confessional Lutheranism were especially Georg Merz, co-publisher of *Zwischen den Zeiten*, R. Karwehl, and W. Holsten. In the opposite direction, H. Schlier moved from Gogarten and Bultmann to Vilmar, and then even beyond him.

104. Especially, *Act and Being*, tr. B. Noble (London: Collins, 1962 [g1931]); *The Cost of Discipleship*, tr. R. H. Fuller (New York: Macmillan, 1959 [g1937]); *Ethics*, ed. E. Bethge, tr. N. H. Smith (New York: Macmillan, 1955 [g1949, posthumously]); *Letters and Papers from Prison*, ed. E. Bethge, tr. R. H. Fuller (New York: Macmillan, 1972 [g1951]).

Iwand,[105] or even the heir of the labors of the History of Religions School and of form criticism, Rudolf Bultmann? To be sure, there were critics who thought that a "new Orthodoxy" was on the upswing in this new theology. But that was certainly not what Bultmann was about, and Gogarten's interpretation of Luther was not the "Orthodox" one; even Barth, whose method might most easily encourage this assumption, soon demonstrated that his position was materially different.[106] Another person entering the discussion, not that new but now coming into his prime, was Paul Tillich (1886–1965), a student of Karl Holl and friend of Emmanuel Hirsch, seriously concerned about a careful theological epistemology and about ontology.[107] Thus, by about the year 1933 the situation in dogmatics no longer revealed the sharp contours of the period around 1921, and the new theology had developed from a mere troublemaker to a serious but more careful partner in dialogue.

d. The Dogmatic Tradition. The new theology was forced to deal with the dogmatic tradition in its full breadth. It was Karl Barth's special accomplishment to have tackled this task with energy; he replaced his *Christliche Dogmatik im Entwurf* (1927) (*Christian Dogmatics; an Outline*) five years later with his monumental *Church Dogmatics* (1932–70), and not in vain. One senses from volume to volume that the Church aspect of this dogmatics is not meant as an ornamental epithet but rather implies the painstaking investigation of the total dogmatic task of the Church, including that of the early Church and the European Middle Ages. Barth continued to learn from the ongoing controversy with Roman Catholicism which arose early, and he has not remained without echo among the Catholics; his most incisive critique has been produced by the Catholic scholar Hans Urs von Balthasar.[108] Barth's attempt to understand dogmatically the 18th and 19th

---

105. H. J. Iwand, *Rechtfertigungslehre und Christusglaube; eine Untersuchung zur Systematik der Rechtfertigungslehre Luthers in ihren Anfängen* (Munich: Kaiser, 1966³ [g1930]); *Glaubensgerchtigkeit nach Luthers Lehre* (Munich: Kaiser, 1951², 1959 [g1937]). Rudolf Hermann was a student of Carl Stange who published the first volume of his Dogmatics in 1927; he moved away from Mediatory Theology, remained distant from dialectic theology, and in his *Studien zur Theologie Luthers*, I (Gütersloh: Bertelsmann, 1928), contributed much to a new understanding of the Reformer.
106. This can be seen particularly clearly in Barth's critique of traditional doctrines of God (*CD*, II,1), and of the whole traditional teaching on predestination (II,2).
107. *Religiöse Verwirklichung* (Berlin: Furche Verlag, 1929); *Protestantisches Prinzip und proletarische Situation* (1931; n.l.); *Kairos; zur Geisteslage und Geisteswendung* (2 vols.; Darmstadt: O. Reichl, 1926–29), especially vol. II, *Der Protestantismus als gestaltendes Prinzip*; *The Protestant Era*, tr. J. L. Adams (Chicago: University of Chicago Press, 1948 [GT 1950]); *Systematic Theology* (2 vols.; Chicago: University of Chicago Press, 1951–57 [GT 1955ff.]).
108. We could not begin to provide anything approaching a comprehensive list of the literature dealing with dialectical theology. Much can be found in A. Keller, *Karl Barth and Christian Unity; the influence of the Barthian movement upon the Churches of the World*, tr. M. Manrodt with W. Petersmann, rev. A. J. Macdonald (New York: The Macmillan Co., 1933 [g1932]).
Catholic works: J. Ries, *Die natürliche Gotteserkenntnis in der Theologie der Krisis*

centuries as the embodiment of Church phenomenona is impressively documented in his incomplete *Geschichte der Theologie* (*History of Theology* [1947]). However, Barth's intensive investigation of tradition does not mean his uncritical acknowledgment of all that had gone before. Just as with Gogarten and Bultmann, the chasm which separates contemporary theology from the past is sensed very deeply, so much so that, with the exception of Gogarten's appeal to Luther, the only step which appears possible is to return to the New Testament, and this can only be done by applying certain hermeneutical principles.

e. The Church Struggle and the Barmen Declaration. The result of the German *Kirchenkampf* (Church Struggle), together with the total European crisis caused or signalized by the Third Reich, was to actualize on the level of concrete action what had been going on at the level of theological reflection. First of all, the situation engendered by this struggle led to the final break within the ranks of "dialectical" theology which had long been building up.[109] Secondly, the struggle was forcing the Church to confess its faith in a new and very concrete way, which in effect meant that the Church was being forced to perform the fundamental dogmatic act which is prior and superior to all forms of dogmatic reflection. This resulted in making the long simmering problem of the "natural" knowledge of God into an issue of immediate urgency. During the struggle, new fronts arose, although they were already implied, for example, in the controversy between Karl Barth and Emil Brunner.[110] At the same time theologians were gathering in the Church who would not normally have come together theologically. We are reminded of the way in which genuinely disparate theologians worked side by side without giving up their own positions—a Neo-Lutheran like Hans Asmussen,[111]

(1939; n.l.); J. C. Groot, *Karl Barth en het theologisch kenprobleem* (1946; n.l.); Jérôme Hamer, *Karl Barth*, tr. D. M. Maruca (Westminster, Md.: Newman Press, 1962 [g1949]).

In his book *The Theology of Karl Barth*, tr. J. Drury (New York: Holt, Rinehart & Winston, 1971), Hans Urs von Balthasar tries to identify a concealed ontology in Barth and to prove that the *analogia entis* (analogy of being), which Barth combats so intensively, is implicit in his own system.

109. See the last issue of *Zwischen den Zeiten* (1933), and on the other side, Friedrich Gogarten, *Gericht oder Skepsis; eine Streitschrift gegen Karl Barth* (Jena: E. Diederichs, 1937).

110. See especially E. Brunner's essay "Nature and Grace" and Karl Barth's reply, "No!", both in *Natural Theology*, tr. P. Fraenkel (London: G. Bles, 1946 [also University Microfilms, Ann Arbor, Michigan, 1965]); Peter Barth, *Das Problem der natürlichen Theologie bei Calvin* (*Theologische Existenz heute*, 18; Munich: Kaiser Verlag, 1935); G. Gloede, *Theologia naturalis bei Calvin* (Stuttgart: W. Kohlhammer, 1935); E. Brunner, *Dogmatics*, I; *Justice and the Social Order*, tr. M. Hottinger (New York: Harper, 1945); *Revelation and Reason; The Christian Doctrine of Faith and Knowledge*, tr. O. Wyon (Philadelphia: Westminster, 1946); *Man in Revolt; a Christian Anthropology*, tr. O. Wyon (Philadelphia: Westminster, 1947); R. Bultmann, "The Question of Natural Revelation," in *Essays Philosophical and Theological*, tr. J. C. G. Greig (New York: Macmillan, 1955), pp. 90–118.

111. Asmussen is one of the chief authors of the Barmen Declaration. The direction of his later work can already be recognized in his *Die Offenbarung und das Amt* (Munich: Kaiser, 1932¹, 1934²); it is always the conceptual approach of Vilmar which motivates Asmussen. See his *Warum noch Lutherische Kirche?; ein Gespräch mit dem augsburgischen Bekenntnis* (Darmstadt: Wissenschaftliche Buchgesellschaft, 1969 [1949¹]); *Maria, die Mutter Gottes* (Stuttgart: Evangelisches Verlagswerk, 1950).

students of Kähler like Julius Schniewind or Hans Emil Weber, a student of Herrmann like H. von Soden, and then associates and friends of Karl Barth like Heinrich Vogel[112] or Ernst Wolf.[113] They shared the very concrete experience that it is not dogmatics which surpasses and supports the Church, but the opposite, the Church which comes before dogmatics! The Barmen Declaration, which is in essence dogma and yet did not abrogate any part of traditional dogma, became the symbol both of division and of unity.[114]

Dogmatic work being done outside the German-language area was (and is) characterized by the elements which emerged most clearly in the German Church Struggle. When, after 1940, the Netherlands, Norway, and Denmark were catapulted into the same kind of struggle as that of the Church in Germany, these churches found points of contact in the German Church Struggle for their decisions. In the Netherlands, the struggle resulted in the disappearance of the older directions, to the degree that in 1949 the General Synod was able to accept an explicit new confession which did not do away with their tradition but which said old things in a new way and was capable of reception by the representatives of opposite directions.[115] The Luther research in Scandinavia, which had been pursuing its own very original routes, had a recognizable effect on the decisions in Norway and Denmark.[116] We must also think of the French Church, which, though not large in numbers, made similar decisions to those of the other threatened churches in the work of men like Pierre Maury or Roland de Pury.[117] The unavoidable problem of Israel confronted all of the churches, a problem which had never been thoroughly thought through in traditional theology.[118] And just as unavoidably America's cultural Protestantism in this period, which did not have

---

112. Heinrich Vogel, after writing numerous smaller treatises and after the first volume of his *Christologie* (München: C. Kaiser, 1949), has presented us a complete dogmatic system in his *Gott in Christo; ein Erkenntnisgang durch die Grundprobleme der Dogmatik* (Berlin: Lettner, 1952).

113. Aside from his work in church history, we mention Ernst Wolf's systematic writings, E. Wolf and H. E. Weber, *Begegnung* (1942; n.l.); " 'Natürliches Gesetz' und 'Gesetz Christi'," in *EvTheol* (1935); most of the essays in *Peregrinatio, Studien zur reformatorischen Theologie und zum Kirchenproblem* (2 vols.; Munich: C. Kaiser, 1954–65).

114. German text in K. D. Schmidt, *Die Bekenntnisse und grundsätzlichen Äusserungen zur Kirchenfrage der Jahre 1933/1934/1935* (Göttingen: Vandenhoeck & Ruprecht, 1935); and in W. Niesel, *Bekenntnisschriften und Kirchenordnungen der nach Gottes Wort reformierten Kirche* (Zürich: Evangelische Verlag, 1938³); as well as in the Minutes of the Barmen Synod, *Vorträge und Entschliessungen der Bekenntnis-synode der Deutschen Evangelischen Kirche*, ed. Karl Immer (Wuppertal/Barmen: E. Müller, 1934 [English text of the Declaration in the *Book of Confessions* of the United Presbyterian Church in the U.S.A.]).

115. H. Berkhof, ed., *Fundamenten & Perspektiven von Belijden; Lebendiges Bekenntnis; die "Grundlagen und Perspektiven des Bekennens" der Generalsynode der Niederländischen Reformierten Kirche von 1949*, tr. Otto Weber (Neukirchen: Neukirchener Verlag, 1959).

116. Detailed report by H. H. Schrey, "Die Lutherrenaissance in der neueren schwedischen Theologie," in *Theologische Literaturzeitung* (1949), pp. 513ff.

117. Roland de Pury wrote an excellent dogmatics for non-theologians, *Présence de l'Eternité; Conférences sur des sujets très variés, Avant-propos de W. A. Visser 't Hooft* (Neuchatel: Delachaux et Niestlé, 1943 [GT 1958]).

118. See especially Karl Barth, *CD*, II,2 and III,3, and Erik Peterson, *Die Kirche aus Juden und Heiden* (Salzburg: A. Pustet, 1933).

to undertake the struggle directly, had to cope with the question of its own justification. Next to Reinhold Niebuhr (1892–1971)[119] there was Paul Tillich,[120]
driven by the Third Reich to America, and Otto Piper, who is still active at
Princeton.[121]

f. Opposing Positions Since 1945. We will have to say that the special circumstances of the German Church Struggle are the source of the complicated
situation in which dogmatic work has found itself since 1945, especially in Germany. Dogmatically viewed, there were three movements in the Church Struggle,
either with each other, next to each other, or opposed to each other: one group
consisting of neo-confessionalists which grew out of the new confession, one
"existentialist" grouping devoted to the theological question of human self-understanding, and finally a third group of those who associated or identified with
Barth. These three movements went their various ways at the end of World War
II, as it became clear that the basis of common practical confession simply was
not enough to provide the Church a true mutuality of action beyond the *status
confessionis* (stance or status of confession of faith). The situation was quite
different outside of Germany: Scandinavia persisted in the direction it was going;[122]
the development which started during the war in Holland continued, marked by
both strength and tension; the theology of England and that of Scotland reveal no
new and decisive developments, leaving aside the considerable influence of both
Barth and Brunner in Scotland which had already been there before 1945. American confessional Lutheranism, originally Scandinavian and German in its roots,
exercised strong influence in other lands, but it did not produce anything which
could be called new or different.[123] Unfortunately the vital development of the
Ecumenical Movement has not been fruitful in the area of dogmatics, although
there have been some initial attempts—we are reminded of the theses on the
"theocracy of proclamation" developed by Barth and Nygren at Bossey in 1947.
     In what follows we shall limit ourselves to essentially German-language
developments, although it is questionable whether they have the significance which
we usually assign to them in this country.

g. Lutheran Confessional Theology. Neo-confessional Lutheran theology was
directly or indirectly influenced by the last phases of the Erlangen School (Ludwig
Ihmels)[124] and by the Luther-Renaissance in the sense of Karl Holl, and even by

---

119. *Nature and Destiny of Man* (New York: C. Scribner's Sons, 1941–43); *Faith
and History* (1950 [GT 1951]); *Christian Realism and Political Problems* (New York: Scribner's, 1953).
     120. For Tillich's newer works, see p. 160, n.107.
     121. O. Piper wrote a two-volume ethic before he left Germany, *Die Grundlagen der
evangelischen Ethik* (Gütersloh: Bertelsmann, 1928–30).
     122. See p. 162, n.116.
     123. See the widely read *Christian Dogmatics* (3 vols.; St. Louis: Concordia, 1950–53
[g1946]), written by F. Pieper, and the work of E. F. W. Walther, *The Proper Distinction
between Law and Gospel*, tr. and ed. W. H. T. Dan (St. Louis: Concordia, 1929 [g1901]);
these works reveal the thinking of the Missouri Synod.
     124. Ludwig Ihmels, *Centralfragen der Dogmatik in der Gegenwart* (Leipzig:
A. Deichert, 1910[1], 1918[3], 1921[4]).

"dialectical theology." However, it was now limited to the Lutheran Church. With the appearance of Paul Althaus' *Die christliche Wahrheit*[125] and Werner Elert's *Der Christliche Glaube* (already published during the war),[126] as well as the ethical systems of both Elert and Helmut Thielicke,[127] this theological movement developed in a positive fashion its rejection of Barth by a strong exposition of the doctrine of law and Gospel,[128] and by clearly negating Barth's critique of natural theology.[129] In this process, Althaus represents a milder approach, and Elert the more extreme position. In another direction, there is a certain tendency toward the Una-Sancta Movement in W. Stählin,[130] Hans Asmussen,[131] and Max Lackmann,[132] with the result that the basic position of the Reformation itself is put in question. Thus, neo-confessional theology presents anything but a unified picture, and this is just as true of the other groups.

h. Barth. Up until the height of the Church Struggle it was still marginally possible to neutralize the earthly and historical aspect in theology in the name of the insoluble contradiction between time and eternity. But Barth, at the height of the Church Struggle, energetically destroyed this possibility in his writings *Rechtfertigung und Recht* (1938) (justification and justice), and *Evangelium und Gesetz* (1936) (Gospel and law). In the meantime, Barth completed the majority of his *Church Dogmatics*. They are characterized by the dominant aspect of the uncon-

---

125. P. Althaus, *Die christliche Wahrheit* (2 vols.; Gütersloh: Bertelsmann, 1949, 1952²); his *Die letzten Dinge* had its 5th edition in 1949 (. . . *Lehrbuch der Eschatologie* [Gütersloh: Bertelsmann]). On Althaus' philosophy of history see H. W. Schmidt, *Zeit und Ewigkeit; die letzten Voraussetzungen der dialektischen Theologie* (Gütersloh: C. Bertelsmann, 1927); here Althaus is assigned to dialectical theology.

126. W. Elert, *Der Kampf um das Christentum; Geschichte der Beziehungen zwischen dem evangelischen Christentum in Deutschland und dem allgemeinen Denken seit Schleiermacher und Hegel* (Munich: C. H. Beck, 1921); *An Outline of Christian Doctrine*, tr. C. M. Jacobs (Philadelphia: The United Lutheran Publication House, 1927); *The Structure of Lutheranism*, tr. Walter A. Hansen (2 vols.; St. Louis: Concordia, 1962 [g1931, 1958]); *Der Christliche Glaube; Grundlinien der lutherischen Dogmatik* (Berlin: Furche Verlag, 1941²); *The Christian Ethos*, tr. Carl J. Schindler (Philadelphia: Muhlenberg Press, 1957 [g1949]).

127. Helmut Thielicke, *Theological Ethics*, tr. and ed. W. H. Lazareth (3 vols.; Philadelphia: Fortress Press, 1966– [g1958–68]); *Theologie der Anfechtung* (Tübingen: J. C. B. Mohr, 1949); *Fragen des Christentums an die moderne Welt* (Tübingen: J. C. B. Mohr, 1947); *Der Glaube der Christenheit* (Göttingen: Vandenhoeck & Ruprecht, 1947, 1949, 1965⁵).

128. For the most extreme formulation see H. Thielicke, *Die evangelische Kirche und die Politik; ethisch-politischer Traktat über einige Zeitfragen* (Stuttgart: Evangelisches Verlagswerk, 1953); and W. Künneth, *Politik zwischen Dämon und Gott; eine christliche Ethik des Politischen* (Berlin: Lutherisches Verlagshaus, 1954).

129. See p. 161, n. 10.

130. W. Stählin, *"Allein"—Recht und Gefahr einer polemischen Formel* (Stuttgart: Evangelisches Verlagswerk, 1950).

131. *Maria, die Mutter Gottes.* . . .

132. *Vom Geheimnis der Schöpfung; die Geschichte der Exegese von Römer 1,18–23; 2,14–16, und Acta 14,15–17; 17,22–29, vom 2. Jahrhundert bis zum Beginn der Orthodoxie* (Stuttgart: Evangelisches Verlagswerk, 1952); *Sola fide; eine exegetische Studie über Jakobus 2 zur reformatorischen Rechtfertigungslehre* (Gütersloh: Bertelsmann, 1949). See also P. Althaus, *Die lutherische Rechtfertigungslehre und ihre heutigen Kritiker* (Berlin: Evangelischer Verlags-Anstalt, 1951), p. 15.

ditional prevalence of the Gospel over all shadows and darkness, of grace over sin, of the "in Christ" which is penetrating everything everywhere—so much so that he has been accused of "Christomonism." He has not moved from being a theologian of "diastasis" to one of "synthesis," but he certainly has become an inexhaustible proponent of the synthesis which happens in Christ, and thus in a way completely different from earlier he is now prepared to take seriously the "horizontal" in contrast to the strictly "vertical," the historical in contrast to the "primeval history" which appeared in 1927 as nothing more than the "break-through" and was not capable of expansion. Based upon salvation-history, all history is now viewed in a new way; based upon Christ, all men are now viewed in a new way; based upon the Bible, all literature is now viewed in a new way—in a certain sense, a theological realism in a Christological mold is being established here, founded upon the interpretation of Anselm, itself a theological program, which he published in 1931. Even within the intimate circle of his associates, such as with Heinrich Vogel, Barth has encountered opposition to this conception. In the case of Emil Brunner, who in the meantime published the two first volumes of his *Dogmatics*,[133] the old battle has been renewed along a much broader front. We even find in Bonhoeffer's writings, published since his death, the objection that Barth is guilty of "revelational positivism."[134]

i. Bultmann. Rudolf Bultmann would probably take Bonhoeffer's objection and intensify it. Bultmann himself, who as a New Testament researcher did not produce a dogmatic system, for more than a decade excited the theological and ecclesiastical world more than almost any of the dogmaticians; the reason was his hermeneutical thesis, which is thus a dogmatic one, and which is implied with the term "demythologization." This thesis was first made public in 1941 but was really already there in its essence in 1926.[135] It is in fact a systematic concept which can best be understood when we remember that Bultmann was a student of Wilhelm Herrmann (and in this regard remained more consequential than Barth) who then appropriated in an original fashion the existential philosophy of Martin Heidegger,[136] although Karl Jaspers has recently argued that his interpretation is correct.[137] What is really at stake is Bultmann's concern that theological state-

---

133. Vol. I (1946); II (1950); ET: 1950ff.

134. D. Bonhoeffer, *Letters and Papers* . . . , pp. 144, 171.

135. The essay, "What Does It Mean To Speak of God?," in *Faith and Understanding*, I, tr. L. P. Smith (London: S.C.M., 1969 [g1954]), pp. 53ff., clearly reveals this approach, and his book *Jesus and the Word*, tr. L. P. Smith and E. Huntress (New York: Scribner's, 1934), also discloses very clearly both the historical basis and the hermeneutical principles.
The most important statements in response to Bultmann's theses are found in H. W. Bartsch, ed., *Kerygma and Myth*, tr. R. H. Fuller (2 vols.; London: S.P.C.K., 1953–62).

136. Aside from Heidegger, Bultmann was certainly also influenced by Wilhelm Dilthey and his friend, Count Yorck von Wartenburg. A good introduction to recent philosophy is found in F. Heinemann, *Neue Wege in der Philosophie, Geist, Leben, Existenz; eine Einführung in Philosophie der Gegenwart* (Leipzig: Quelle & Meyer, 1929). See also F. Ebner, *Das Wort und die pneumatologischen Realitäten* (Innsbruck: Brenner Verlag, 1921).

137. K. Jaspers, "Wahrheit und Unheil der Bultmannschen Entmythologisierung," in *Schweizerische Theologische Umschau* (1953), pp. 74ff.

ments, although they have a historical point of departure, are to be stripped of all ontic baggage and thrust completely into the secularized world; only then will they be acknowledged in their real uniqueness. This uniqueness consists of their being statements about the desecularization of human existence which happens in the grasping of justification. This total aspect is not far from Gogarten's great work after the war,[138] while Barth left his earlier reserve behind in regard to Bultmann and started an open attack.[139]

The situation of evangelical dogmatics displays all the marks of profound confusion and none of the marks of an emerging consensus. It is not farfetched to presume that we are catching up today, on a very different level, with a good deal that the 19th century left for us. The view that in such a situation the dogmatic monograph is more relevant than a total system cannot be rejected lightly. In any event, such a system can only be intended to provide some orientation within the total confusion and to do this in receptivity to the voices of the Fathers. It will be difficult for a fundamentally new solution to emerge from the intention to discover such a solution!

The situation of evangelical dogmatics is also a problem in that the newer developments within the Roman Catholic Church[140] have not been met with anything like convergent responses, and the theological dialogue of some years ago has been almost completely broken off.[141] It may be an additional problem that Roman Catholic dogmatics have just begun to work through the tasks created by the creation of new dogmas. On the other side, limited possibilities of conversation with representatives of the orthodox dogmatics of the Eastern Church have begun to arise.[142]

---

138. *Die Verkündigung Jesu Christi; Grundlagen und Aufgabe* (Heidelberg: Lambert Schneider, 1948; Tübingen: J. C. B. Mohr, 1965); *Die Kirche in der Welt* (Heidelberg: L. Schneider, 1948); *Der Mensch zwischen Gott und Welt* (Stuttgart: Friedrich Vorwerk, 1956); *Demythologizing and History*, tr. N. H. Smith (London: SCM, 1955); *Despair and Hope for Our Time*, tr. T. Wieser (Philadelphia: Pilgrim Press, 1970).

139. "Rudolf Bultmann—An Attempt to Understand Him," in H. W. Bartsch, ed., *Kerygma and Myth*, tr. R. H. Fuller (London: S.P.C.K., 1962), pp. 83–132.

140. See the encyclicals *Mystici corporis* (1943) and *Humani generis* (1950), and the constitution *Munificentissimus Deus* (dogma of Mary) (1950).

141. The best publication was E. Wolf and H. E. Weber, *Begegnung* (1942; n.l.). The most up-to-date position is found in L. Ott, *Fundamentals of Catholic Dogma*, ed. J. Bastible, tr. P. Lynch (St. Louis: Herder, 1960 [g1952⁴]). Michael Schmaus, *Katholische Dogmatik* (5 vols.; München: M. Hueber, 1948ff.).

N. B. Otto Weber was writing before the convening of Vatican II—TR.

142. See the journal *Evangelische Theologie*, Nr. 7/8 (1952), and the publication of the German Church Foreign Office (*Kirchliches Aussenamt*), *Kirche und Kosmos* (1951).

PART THREE

The Self-disclosure of God

VII. Revelation and the Knowledge of God

A. REVELATION

1. THE DOGMATIC POSITION OF THE DOCTRINE OF REVELATION

a. Revelation, the Knowledge of God, Self-knowledge. The unique aspect of theology is, to use Ernst Fuchs' phrase, that it is always derived from the "truth" whereas philosophy "is seeking" the truth.[1] However, the "truth" from which theology derives is not the discovered actuality of being but rather the self-disclosure, the "revelation" of God. The reason for this is not primarily that our "reason" meets its limitations in confrontation with the ultimate (as Kant thought) but rather that we, the way we are, are opposed to the truth (Rom. 1:25; 3:4; Eph. 4:25). It is not the absence of light which defines our condition, but the fact that we loved "darkness" more than light (John 3:19). "Truth" and "revelation," then, are not to be understood so much noetically as factually and existentially.

These simple preparatory considerations already raise both methodological and material questions. They concern principally the problem of whether it is appropriate to begin with revelation or whether it would not first be proper to discuss, in an introductory fashion, what we just alluded to. When we spoke about the "event" of "revelation," we seemed to be using a category of understanding which needs to be investigated more closely before we talk about revelation itself. And when we spoke of its "existential character," it seems that this means that it is necessary to conduct a preliminary discussion about existence as such. Since the event envisaged here is one that concerns man and is historical, and the existence understood here is certainly ours, the methodological question can be put very precisely: is it proper method to talk about revelation without previously dealing with man, his historicity and his existence?

Whoever answers this negatively does not necessarily need then to propound a "natural" knowledge of God or a "general" revelation.[2] The introductory

---

1. E. Fuchs, *Was ist Theologie?* p. 7 (1953; n.l.).
2. Karl Barth, too, can admit that man can know what "revelations" are, but he emphasizes that "revelation in the Christian sense of the term" can be visible "only at the edge, only as a frontier, only as a question" ("The Christian Understanding of Revelation,"

discussion of historicity and existence necessitated by such a negative answer can take two different routes. It can either begin with the "natural" pre-understanding in order then to show how this is radicalized, surpassed, or corrected by the reality of revelation. Or it can assume from the very outset that revelation exists, and then deal noetically with man and his "existence in faith" (Bultmann), perhaps with a view to the fact that revelation is not given to us in any other form than the witness of men to men. In this case, we would be proceeding not from the question of revelation but of the knowledge of God, and this we would be dealing with in its correlation to man's knowledge of self.[3]

Three concepts result from the context of our considerations, and they need to be set in relation to one another: revelation, the knowledge of God, and self-knowledge (or self-understanding). It must be conceded that none of these concepts can be grasped without the other: revelation always has to do with the knowledge of God, and the knowledge of God always relates to self-knowledge, and the same is true in reverse order.

b. The Order of Precedence and the Order of Knowledge. We might conceivably integrate these three concepts into one. Self-knowledge would then be at its core the knowledge of God, and this in turn would be revelation. This would be the approach of consistent mysticism, which thinks it finds the divine in the depths of the self. In this case, we cannot really talk about actual "revelation." For the voice that the mystic believes he hears in the depths of his self is certainly not the voice of someone else. And the "God" whom he knows is not in fact his opposite. Thus mysticism can be, in extreme instances, "atheistic," as demonstrated by Buddhism. The "God" of which it speaks is nothing more than a duplication of man's own self.

Christian discussion of God always implies him who is in no sense identical with man. Therefore, when we talk about revelation in a Christian sense, we are always talking about the self-disclosure of the One who is utterly and completely Other, outside us and confronting us.

If this is so, then the order of precedence—revelation, knowledge of God, self-knowledge—is unassailable. But this does not necessarily mean that the order of knowing must be the same. The decision on this point is made more difficult by the fact that apparently we are not dealing here with a distinct series but with a complex intermixture. We cannot speak of revelation per se without talking simultaneously about the knowledge of God, and similarly, we could not speak of the knowledge of God per se without talking about self-knowledge. We would abandon the human standpoint if we wanted to divide here what is given to us

---

in *Against the Stream; Shorter Post-War Writings, 1946–52,* tr. S. Godman, ed. R. G. Smith [London: S.C.M., 1954], pp. 205, 207 [however, my translation—TR]). And Rudolf Bultmann, who rejects "natural theology," can still say, "Every man knows what revelation and life, grace and forgiveness are, because he knows death" (*ZThK* [1930], pp. 351ff.).

3. The second approach can appeal to Calvin, who, along the lines of Augustine, sees the whole sum of our wisdom in the knowledge of God and our self-knowledge in their mutual correlation (*Institutes,* I, i), but he insists that the knowledge of God is prior (*Institutes,* I, xv, 1 and the conclusion of I, i, 3).

only in an undivided, but clearly distinguishable, form. The question we must deal with, then, is whether we will deal first of all with revelation, as God's activity, or with the knowledge of God, as man's activity—all of this within the indivisibility of the issues which is already established.

Our answer must incline to the first of these possibilities. What may be said about the essence of human knowledge of God has its roots in what is seen to be the essence of God's self-disclosure to us. The doctrine of the knowledge which is explicated in theology is always related to the doctrine of the deed which establishes all theology. Theological epistemology is not a special section of general epistemology but is in principle already theology itself, that is, talk about God. If we were to deal first with the doctrine of the knowledge of God, we could well fall prey to the danger of setting up a general doctrine of epistemology with a special relationship to the unique object "God." In the course of such an endeavor, it would become clear that the actual development of the knowledge of God would make revelation "necessary." This would mean that the "necessity" of revelation would have been deduced constructively (even if it is a regressive construction)—very possibly after having tried out all the other possibilities! In actual fact, though, the knowledge of God always derives from revelation which has happened in reality, and it is thus more sensible to proceed in the same order.[4]

The objection could now be raised that it would be a contradiction of the situation of man before God to begin theological considerations any place else than "below"; it could appear to be an attempt at a "theology of glory" (*theologia gloriae*) if we speak first of revelation, that is, of God's activity, and then of the knowledge of God (and self-knowledge), that is, of man's activity. This objection would be well-made if we were talking not about revelation but the pure being of God, that is, about something absolutely and intrinsically "objective." This was the commonest approach of Scholasticism, and the accusation of being a theology of glory is especially directed against it for this very reason. But when we speak of God's revelation, then we mean the gift (how could it be different in Christian theology?) in which God grants to us the possibility of knowing him. We could turn the question around and ask if the attempt to proceed from the knowledge of God, as a given, to revelation is not actually more subject to the judgment of being a theology of glory. In any event, it corresponds to the situation of man as the created receiver when we speak first of the gift from which we derive our knowledge, that is, of revelation. But then everything depends upon what we mean by "revelation."

2. REVELATION AS THE SELF-DISCLOSURE OF GOD

a. The Concept of Revelation as a Uniquely Theological Concept. The concept of revelation belongs to the language of theological concepts. Its origin is never-

---

4. A model example of regressive construction of the necessity of revelation is to be found in the first chapters of Calvin's *Institutes*. Since Calvin starts with the knowledge of God, he cannot avoid developing in outline a general theological doctrine of epistemology, including his doctrine of the "seed of religion" (*semen religionis*), only then to conclude (I, v, 11ff., pp. 63ff.) that all other possibilities fail, and "it remains for God himself to give witness of himself from heaven" (I, v, 13, p. 68).

theless biblical.[5] But the circumstance that there are four New Testament terms for it which are not all synonymous in meaning shows clearly that theology has created a comprehensive concept itself. The fact that the concept of revelation belongs to the language of theology is also seen in the circumstance that for centuries it was not accorded any particularly high regard. To be sure, the precision with which the Vulgate also uses the terms *revelare* and *revelatio* as the translation of *apokalyptein* and *apokalypsis* reveals a certain terminological acuteness. But on the other hand, neither the theology of the early Church nor that of the Middle Ages reveals any special interest in the clarification of the concept of revelation—it does not belong to the fundamental concepts of dogmatic systems. This is still true of the theology of the Reformers. The concept of revelation does not emerge until the period of Orthodoxy and then only gradually. It then becomes a decisive problem in the theology of the Enlightenment and is partially restored or regained in the 19th century. In general we can say that the concept of revelation is primarily a concern of modern dogmatics. And we must add that the concept has become more important in direct proportion to the way in which the thing meant by it has become more doubtful. While God (as man understood him) became more and more the problematic object of a human discovery, the ground of meaning for the world, the significance of the concept of revelation (as long as it was not actually equated with this discovery) was that it served as a last reminder of the divinity of God, as a last bastion which theology laboriously defended, even against strong powers of opposition within its own realm. To put it succinctly: the concept of revelation has become the evidence for the fact that theology no longer derives its life from the reality of revelation.

What we have just stated could give us cause to be very careful with the concept of revelation.[6] However, we may not overlook the fact that today's theology still functions within the same framework as that of the 18th or 19th century. It is not at all true of our structure of reality that there is room in it for "revelation." "Revelation" is no longer an automatically accepted thing, but rather

---

5. See in Kittel, *TDNT*, the following articles: *apokalyptein*, III, 563-92; *dēloun*, II, 61f.; *gnōrizein*, I, 718 within the article on *gnōsis*, pp. 689–719; in Cremer, *apokalyptō*, pp. 342f., *gnōrizō*, pp. 677ff., and *phaneroō*, p. 566. Hannelis Schulte, *Der Begriff der Offenbarung im Neuen Testament* (*Beiträge zur evangelischen Theologie*, 13; Munich: Kaiser, 1949). Rudolf Bultmann's impressive essay, "The Concept of Revelation in the New Testament" (in *Existence and Faith*, tr. S. M. Ogden [London: Hodder & Stoughton, 1961 [g1929], pp. 58-91), borders on systematic-theological interpretation (see also "The Concept of the Word of God in the New Testament," in *Faith and Understanding*, I, . . ., pp. 286-312). F. Büchsel, *Die Offenbarung Gottes* (Gütersloh: C. Bertelsmann, 1938); W. von Loewenich, *Was heisst Offenbarung? Gottes Wort und menschliche Rede im Alten und Neuen Testament* (Berlin: Furche Verlag, 1938).

6. Schleiermacher, in a postscript to chapter 10 of *The Christian Faith*, regarded the concept of revelation as merely a traditional concept, and nothing more. He complained about the ambiguity of the traditional term. His own interpretation does go a bit further when he (purely phenomenologically) only wants to see "revelation" where "not a single moment but a whole existence" "is determined" by "divine communication." This view, coming directly before the strongly Christocentric chapter 11 of *The Christian Faith*, could be developed further. But Schleiermacher did not do that.

something which has become questionable. It remains to be seen whether this ought to be regarded as a deficit or a benefit.

b. Revelation as Act. The term "revelation" means first of all and in every instance an actual event. Regardless of the New Testament term, be it *apokalyptein* with the idea of the removal of veiling, or *phaneroun* with the emergence of what had been concealed, or *dēloun* as the pronouncement of what had been unknown, or *gnōrizein* as the communication of what otherwise is unavailable,[7] all of these terms refer to something which is actually given, and not to something conditional. And the event character is emphasized by the fact that the act must have an actor. There is no support for the idea that "revelation" could be another word for the human "discovery" of the ultimate. Nowhere is "revelation" simply "the state of being revealed." In the one place where *phaneroun* is used and thus revelation could be thought to be a condition, Romans 1:19, the actor and the act are stated so that the meaning is clearly established.[8] As actual event, revelation has a thoroughly temporal nature: it is not happening all the time but at a specific time; and it is not a constantly open possibility, rather its possibility can only be recognized in that it actually happens.

c. Revelation as God's Act. Secondly, revelation is in essence God's act. God is in essence the Revealer. Nothing like that can be asserted about any man. In fact, man is not even able to reveal what is concealed within himself (1 John 3:2; Col. 3:4; Rom. 8:19; 1 Cor. 14:25); who man is before God will not be revealed until the future. This applies to man's status as God's child, but it is also generally true; in God's judgment, on his day, God will judge "the secrets of man" (Rom. 2:16). If, then, revealing is exclusively God's act, it is God's activity when Jesus Christ reveals (e.g., Matt. 11:27) or when the Spirit works as the mediator of revelation (esp. 1 Cor. 2:10ff.). If, in view of such statements, we reject the idea of an apotheosis of the creaturely (that is, of Jesus Christ or of the Spirit), then we have here already the presuppositions for the Church's doctrine of the Trinity: God is the Revealer, but the Revealer is the Father together with the Son and the Spirit!

d. The Content of Revelation. Our first two answers to the query about the nature of revelation were so obvious that they could scarcely become seriously controversial; now, however, we will begin to encounter difficulties. Our third question must ask "what" it is that is revealed. One part of the answer seems to be quite obvious: whatever is revealed is something which would have remained concealed and unreachable without revelation. But what can this possibly be? We will have to start a bit farther back.

---

7. *dēloun* can occasionally have this meaning in regard to God's "eschatological revelational" act, similar to both *apokalyptein* and *phaneroun*; see also Bultmann's article on *dēloun* in Kittel, *TDNT,* II, 61f. regarding 1 Cor. 3:13.

8. ". . . because God has shown it to them (*ephanerōsen*)" (v. 19b). We must emphasize here that the actor, according to many texts in the New Testament, is the Spirit. Most clearly: 1 Cor. 2:6ff.

There is no doubt that in the New Testament "what" is revealed is the *mystērion:* the mystery (or mysteries) of the Kingdom of God (Mark 4:11 par.), the mystery of the Will of God (Eph. 1:9) and of his decrees regarding the Gentiles (Col. 1:27) and Israel (Rom. 11:25), the mystery that is Christ (Col. 1:27; 2:2; Eph. 3:3, 4), the mystery per se (Rom. 16:25), which then is nothing other than the mystery of the Gospel (Eph. 6:19). The revealed mystery is the theme of the hymnic confession (1 Tim. 3:16), and again it is nothing other than the One who was "revealed in the flesh." Revelation is the making known of the mystery.

e. Revelation and Reason. But what does this mean? It is possible that "what" is revealed could at some time be "something" which is "beyond" our reason; more precisely: something which lies beyond the sphere which our reason can perceive. Then revelation would be the pronouncement of knowledge of a "supernatural" type of origin. The mystery which is disclosed to us in revelation would be formally analogous to those mysteries which science has in its immediate purview and is constantly endeavoring to penetrate with each new discovery or insight. The difference would be that we would assert about this particular mystery that it is of such a type that it will absolutely never be penetrated by reason. What reasons can be given for that? Philosophy would not be capable of viewing certain things as absolutely beyond the realm of rational comprehension—of course, everything will depend here upon the definition of reason. However, theology, too, will not be able to delimit the theme of revelation regionally or quantitatively—to do so would be to ban the object of revelation from the realm of reason and thus to assign to reason in its area autonomy, a quality which nothing created can possess before God! No, the "boundary" which separates the mystery of revelation from reason cannot be an "inter-categorial" boundary.[9] If we are to speak of the "supra-rationality" of revelation, then we can only mean that revelation precludes an autonomous reason as well as any other form of human access. But the reason for this is not that revelation's content is something beyond the realm of reason but rather that it is something intrinsically different from what reason could ever be.

But what then is reason? In German, the word for "reason" (*Vernunft*) derives from the word "to perceive" (*vernehmen*), as often has been emphasized. However, the dominant linguistic usage is determined less by the German term than by the Latin or, better, the Greek root (Lat. *ratio,* Gk. *noēsis, noēma*). Both the Latin word, whose root goes back to "to count," and the Greek stem, which refers back to the *nous* which is active in man, signify a human capability, which is based upon a metaphysical capacity. "Rational" man asserts his control of himself and his world in that he activates this capacity. Human existence, according to the view of ancient Greece, is fulfilled in *theōria* (contemplation, intellectual perception).[10] In the process, both man and his world can certainly be understood as a realm in which mysteries are at work; the important thing is the

---

9. With the use of the term "inter-categorial" we are following Karl Heim.
10. See R. Bultmann, "The Concept of Revelation in the New Testament," *op. cit.,* p. 66.

rational mastering of oneself, or as we say today, the realization of one's "authenticity." "Reason" is the way in which man understands himself as master of himself and of his world. It was with "reason" in this sense, and only in this sense, that Luther did battle.[11] For reason understood this way is the epitome of the fact that man is ultimately his own god. Reason could be understood in another way: it could be "perceiving" reason, and then it would not be a matter of an autonomous self but rather of the organ by means of which the self implements its co-humanity, opens itself to the claims of its Thou, instead of wanting to master its reality independently (which means that it must master its Thou and make it into an It).[12]

Revelation, or "what is revealed," does not necessarily have to be something "beyond" the realm of reason. A glance at the first pages of the Bible will show this: how little tension there is there between God's talking and man's receiving! And biblical hope demonstrates this as well: "we shall see him as he is" (1 John 3:2) and ". . . they shall all know me" (Jer. 31:34 in context)! Here we have revelation and reason in perfected unity.

f. Revelation as Salvation-Event. If the object of revelation does not necessarily reside "beyond" the realm of reason, then we must still ask, "beyond" what is revelation actually? For revelation certainly does mean the making known of what was unknown, the unveiling of what otherwise would not be revealed. What is it then which is doing the veiling, which is hindering the being made known? Since revelation is directed toward man, we will have to look for the cause of the veiling, for the obstacle, in man himself. Revelation reverses his problem, breaks through his self-isolation. Revelation is salvific activity.

It is certainly and without reservation true that God "dwells in unapproachable light" (1 Tim. 6:16). Man's error consists of the fact that, although he can perceive God's "invisible nature, namely his eternal power and deity," still he does not "honor him as God or give thanks to him" (Rom. 1:20, 21). For man, in all of his religious and ethical endeavors, construes God's invisibility and divine glory either as God's availability which man can make use of, or God's unapproachability by means of which he can comfort himself or which he penetrates with his own actions. But man, by presuming to make use of God's invisibility and unapproachability, his divinity, testifies to his own obstructedness toward God. God's revelation is a saving activity because it penetrates the closed state of man, and thus it is also the revelation of divine wrath (Rom. 1:18ff.). The mystery of the "righteousness of God" (Rom. 1:17) could not be revealed (Rom. 1:17; 3:21) without simultaneously revealing God's "No" to man's godlessness and unrighteousness.

Now it is clearer what the object of revelation is. If it is God's saving activity for man, then it would be expected that it would not primarily be the impartation of exceedingly relevant portions of knowledge. It is not the information that God

---

11. See W. Link, *Das Ringen Luthers um die Freiheit der Theologie von der Philosophie,* ed. E. Wolf and M. Mezger (München: Kaiser, 1955² [g1940]).

12. We are grateful to F. Gogarten above all for his constant insistence upon another way of understanding reason. We are following him in part in our own terminology.

is our God which breaks through our insular natures, but rather the reality in which he comes to us and remains with us. Or to put it differently, "Revelation is an occurrence that abolishes death, not a doctrine that death does not exist."[13] The "content" of revelation is God's own existence for man. Let us remember what we said about mystery: it is not God's existence per se which is the mystery, but rather God's behavior toward man, God's will (Eph. 1:9) which breaks through the barriers of the law (Col. 1:27—the Gentiles!), and this mystery is named "Christ" (Eph. 3:4; Col. 1:27; 2:2). The "content" of revelation is simultaneously its donor; it is God himself, God himself as the one who turns to man, who realizes his saving will for man (his "righteousness") and thus realizes his own honor. "Thus revelation consists in nothing other than the fact of Jesus Christ."[14] Paul can designate the revelation which made him into an apostle in this way, "he . . . who called me through his grace, was pleased to reveal his Son to me" (Gal. 1:15-16), and this in turn is what Paul means by the "revelation of Jesus Christ" (Gal. 1:12). Thus the basic instruction of the believing Community is "to learn Christ" (Eph. 4:20). God's turning to man has a name and it is Jesus Christ! In him all the promises of God are "Yes and Amen" (2 Cor. 1:20), and he is the basis of the decision whether man will persist in death or come to life (2 Cor. 2:15f.; John 3:18).

God's revelation is saving activity. As such, it reveals what it is that man lacks by meeting that lack, what it is that man needs, because it meets that need. Bultmann pointed out correctly[15] that the supranaturalism of the older concept of revelation (revelation as supernatural communication of knowledge) was based upon a specific self-understanding of man which implied that man could achieve authenticity through knowledge. He demonstrated the same thing in regard to the concept of revelation of "romantic-idealistic speculation" which ultimately resulted in the identification of the irrational with the creative. If we generalize Bultmann, we could say that the traditional understanding of revelation (Bultmann also discusses Liberalism and the cultural Protestantism related to it) was mistaken in that revelation is somehow understood as the overcoming of man's limits: the limit of lack of knowledge, of the inaccessibility of the immortal depths of man's being and of the world, of the inadequacy of moral achievement, and so on. But in the way these limits are overcome in "revelation," man finds himself again, or rather the "picture" of what he thinks he is or ought to be. Is then the limitation of man his actual problem? In this regard Bultmann seems to be in agreement with the positions which he so tellingly rejects; the actual "limitation" which he feels the New Testament postulates for man is death, and revelation is then the gift of life.[16] But does not the New Testament derive death from sin (Rom. 6:23), which is not a limit or boundary, but the trespassing of a boundary? Is not revelation, when it destroys the insularity of man in his self-glorification, actually his liberation precisely because it shows him where his limitations are?

Man's deep need, which is brought to light by God's revelation, is his in-

---

13. R. Bultmann, "The Concept of Revelation in the New Testament," *op. cit.*, p. 72.
14. R. Bultmann, *op. cit.*, p. 75.
15. R. Bultmann, *op. cit.*, pp. 66ff.
16. *Ibid.*, pp. 71ff.

sularity. If man were not so wrapped up in himself, in his self-glorification and obstinacy, in his worldly corruption and his mastery of the world, in his pride and remorse—in his sin—he would be living with his Creator and in subordination to him. We only know ourselves as those who are totally wrapped up in ourselves, to whom God reveals himself, and we only know that this is possible because God, in turning to us, opens us up. We can only recognize our "original state" in the newly given possibility of God's encounter with us as lost creatures, when he gives himself to us, and that means that this is solely an eschatological possibility.

g. *Historicity of Revelation.* If God's revelation as saving activity is God's self-revelation, if it takes place in that God discloses himself to us in Jesus Christ and thereby opens us up to him, then we are saying that revelation is to be understood in a "personal" sense. God does not reveal "something"; he reveals himself. However, he does not reveal himself in an extra-dimensional fashion, but in a historical reality, which we must view from two aspects. The fact that he is the one who is disclosing himself in history places his historical activity in a vertical aspect. He does not become a calculable component of history or of development; he is always himself in every moment of history. But the fact that he really discloses himself in history places his revelation in a horizontal aspect. He does not merely touch this history, rather he acts in it and distinguishes his history from other history and qualifies it. His self-disclosure in Jesus of Nazareth qualifies the history which leads up to Jesus of Nazareth, the history of the old covenant, just as the subsequent history which is defined by what actually happened in Jesus of Nazareth qualifies the history of the Church. Without this central point, the history of Jesus of Nazareth, the old covenant would not be the covenant as such, but the history of the religion of Israel and Judah, and the history of the Church would not be the history of the Church which testifies to Jesus Christ, but rather the history of Christianity in competition with other religions. Based upon this central point, both the preparatory witness to revelation of Israel and the consequent witness of the Church are recognized to be the witness to revelation.

h. *Is Revelation Content?* If we see things this way, then we will firmly hold to the "personal character" of God's self-disclosure, but we will be careful about falling into a kind of personalism which empties history. We can now understand that God in disclosing himself does so as "such and such a One," as the Creator, as the Lord, as the Benevolent One, as the one who qualifies himself in a specific way. And that means that God, in disclosing himself, also discloses "something" to us! It would never be possible to deduce God from the "something," the sum of these contents. If in God's self-disclosure his will, his nature, his behavior and relationship to us and to created reality are revealed, in short, his divine being as a specific kind of being, we can then never turn the process around and reconstruct God's being-for-us out of these component parts of his self-disclosure.

But God's self-disclosure of himself as "being-for-us" is in fact the revelation of what he is really like, and he himself made his true being known to us in this particular way. To put it in a better way: because God did not disclose himself as an idea but as a man, as the specific man Jesus Christ, we may and should talk about this as "contents," based upon his self-disclosure, because he has made himself into such "contents" for man.

Do we still need to sound a warning that the last statement should not be understood as though revelation, at least secondarily, could be the making known of eternal knowledge? This misunderstanding could only arise if one were to forget that God does in fact make himself into "contents" but is never mere contents along with other and similar contents—he is the Lord. We can never talk about him other than before him as those who are addressed by him, who respond to him—but who know who this One is who desires our answer! When we are allowed to talk about him on the basis of his self-disclosure, we are encountered by his self-disclosure in our talk. That means that our perception, reception, and response to revelation are all to be understood on the basis of God's act toward us alone. This is the point where we encounter the meaning of the doctrine of the Holy Spirit.

The question of the "contents" of revelation thrusts us back to the question of the Giver of revelation: God discloses himself. But this does not mean that there is a simple identity here: God discloses himself in that he discloses himself as such and such a One, as concrete, as One who can be expressed in our words. God in his revelation—this is God as he himself.

Our consideration of the concept of revelation has been up until now burdened by a certain formalism. We have been speaking of revelation as an event, of the "subject," "object," and "contents" of revelation. But the question of the form of revelation, which is only implied by the concept of event, has not been touched upon up to now. How does God disclose himself? The only possible answer is that God discloses himself in his Word. It will be appropriate to deal with the question of this Word in a separate section. The additional question of "general" revelation, which needs to be dealt with, will be treated later when we discuss the nature of the knowledge of God.

B. THE WORD OF GOD

1. THE WORD AS EVENT

a. The Word as Address. When we say revelation, we mean that God discloses himself to man who has closed himself off to God. God is the subject. And he is also the object, the contents. But in that he discloses himself and makes himself into the object of his own deed, he reveals himself as "such and such a One," as God in a specific relation and a specific self-qualification. God's self-disclosure is not empty; it is historical, concrete, personal. This leads us to the further statement that God discloses himself in the Word. The Word is *the* form of God's self-disclosure. We could perhaps put it more comprehensively and say that the Word is the "essential form," in order to make clear that this form absolutely cannot be separated from the essence of revelation (it is well known that in John 1:1 the Word and God are equated, but it is done in such a way that in John 1:2 it becomes clear that this is not an ontological but a dynamic identification). Under these circumstances it is fitting to develop the Christian understanding of revelation as the Doctrine of the Word, as Karl Barth treated the theme in his "Prolegomena" (*CD*, I,1 and I,2).

The statement that the Word is *the* form of God's self-disclosure is not meant phenomenologically. As is well known, the Bible exhibits various forms of the human experience of God: vision, theophany, dream, audition, ecstatic excitement, miracle.[17] But what makes these various experiences into forms of the personal consciousness of God? All of them are ambiguous, certainly not restricted to the revelation witnessed to in Scripture, and even in Scripture are certainly not always regarded as forms of the personal experience of God (there are miracles worked by the Anti-Christ, dreams presented by false prophets, etc.). Apparently all of them are to be submitted to some other criterion, although that does not mean that they are to be underestimated.

When we speak of the Word of God as the form of the self-disclosure of God, then we understand this to mean that God discloses himself to man in that he addresses him. The way in which he addresses him is not our concern yet. It can happen in very amazing ways (think of Judg. 3:20). It can also occur that the "Word" is not heard but rather "seen" (Amos 1:1; Mic. 1:1; Isa. 2:1). The decisive thing is that our discussion now is not at the level of phenomena but rather at the level of the criterion of all phenomena. And this criterion consists of the fact that God reveals himself in address.

b. Greek and Biblical Understanding of the Word. How then shall we understand the concept of the Word of God?

It should be agreed without detailed argumentation that the Old Testament concept of the "Word of Yahweh" or the "Word of God,"[18] which dominates the New Testament, must be understood in a way completely different from the Greek concept of the Logos. However, the latter concept has been so dominant in theological thought that it is indispensable that we deal with it briefly.[19]

In general, Logos means for Greek thought the "meaning" of the "existent" as it "shows itself" (as W. Bröcker puts it in regard to Aristotle). Every existing being has its own Logos, and it intends that this Logos be apprehended by a knowing spirit. Thus, this Logos does not have the character of the temporal or of an event: it "is," and it is recognized, but it does not happen. Therefore it is impossible for the Logos to be "address," "summons," "claim," or "encouragement." Logos can, of course, also mean "speech," but this speech is only the making known of what has been recognized, but not the claim which desires

---

17. Older dogmatics tended to deal with these phenomena under the theme of "special revelation" (*revelatio specialis*). See H. Bavinck, *Gereformeerde Dogmatiek* (1895), I, 244ff. See also, ET: *Our Reasonable Faith* (Grand Rapids: Eerdmans, 1956), a compendium of the 4 vols.

18. Oskar Grether, *Name und Wort Gottes im Alten Testament* (Giessen: A. Töpelmann, 1934).

19. See the article on *logos* in Kittel, *TDNT* (written by Hermann Kleinknecht, W. Bröcker, and Rudolf Bultmann), IV, 69-143, with the literature listed there. See also W. Nestle, *Vom Mythos zum Logos; die Selbstentfaltung des griechischen Denkens von Homer bis auf die Scholastik und Sokrates* (Stuttgart: Kröner, 1942; Aalen: Scientia Verlag, 1966).

or motivates decision. Logos can also be an element of religious expression, but then it is subordinated to absolute being and its law. Thus it was possible for Logos to become simply the rule of reason which obtains in all the world, as it was understood in the Hellenistic period.

It will be obvious that Christian speculation since Origen has found much to nourish itself in the basic elements of the Greek concept of Logos. But it should be just as obvious that this Logos-concept cannot mold the Christian, that is, the Old and New Testament understanding of the Word. If "Word of God" is understood in accordance with the Greek concept of Logos, then it would be the divine fullness of being as fullness of meaning, as it is revealed to man (for instance, in a miraculous event of communication). The Word would then be a passive substance which we would have to receive rationally and intellectually, or suprarationally and pneumatically, or perhaps in some kind of ecstatic experience, and then it would be our property. In terms of the Greek understanding of the Logos I am free, since it is meaning per se which demonstrates itself; I can receive it in my own process of rational knowledge, or I can not. If I do not, then I am being foolish. But my existence is not at stake. Both the rationality and the timelessness of the Logos are corollaries to my (limited) power over the Logos as I grasp it.

In contrast to this, the Word of God in the biblical sense is in principle a decision, the divine decision made about me which demands of me a decision. It is the Word of the Lord—not the word of a despot to a slave, but the address of the Creator to his creation. As a word of decision, the Word of God is unconditionally temporal: it "is," in that it "happens." It always has the special time into which it is spoken; it is not "absolute" in the sense of timelessness.

Since this is so, there is no alternative to the Word of God in a kind of regression to the "meaning" concealed in God, or in a discussion about a meaning which is in the Word but which can be perceived beyond it. It remains true that God has his mystery, indeed, that he is this mystery. But this mystery is not the object of some special speculation which bypasses the Word; rather the mystery is only honored when God's Word is heard. Thus, the Word of God as God's Word has the character of relatedness, but it cannot be relativized by means of this relatedness. It fixes the hearer where he stands and makes both his Yes and his No into an unconditional Yes or No, to life or death.

c. I and Thou in the Word-event. The Word of God stands between I and Thou. It is never an It which could be mastered by an I, which receptive reason could appropriate.

It is the Word of the divine I in the most extremely exclusive sense. It never becomes the possession of man. It always stands in exclusive contrast to man's own word (Jer. 23:18; 1 Cor. 2:4, 5; 2 Cor. 2:17; 4:2; 1 Thess. 2:4). Man cannot say God's Word to himself; in relationship to the Word, man is always the hearer. We can see how intimately related God and the Word are when we remember how in the Old Testament the Word can be hypostatized (Jer. 23:29; Isa. 40:8; 55:10, 11; Deut. 30:11f.). It is the Word which is "God once more," God in his self-disclosure, God in his address. The hypostatizing of the Word does not exclude the actual concrete monotheism of the Old Testament message, rather it is the most extreme proclamation of it. If we ascribe to the Word what belongs to God alone, then we are saying that God in his very being is the one who addresses man. This is how far the Old Testament goes, and it points toward the One in whom God himself addresses us as person, not just in the form of words but in the form of the Word become flesh. All of our language about the personal nature of the Word of God receives its substance from this One. The speaking divine I is recognized in the Word become flesh as the One who is truly personal and historical, and therefore definitely never just an idea. In the Word become flesh this I is really recognizable as the subject, which it is by its very nature and therefore was and will be.

However, the Word is always the Word to a Thou. It endows the existence of the creature as creature. Even the word of judgment is the Word of the Creator, for it is the address of God which takes the man by his word who says No, holds him to his No, and thus to his death and destruction. As God's property, which it remains, it goes into the mouth, the ear, into the perception and witness of man. Yes, it can be made into an idol (Jer. 8:8), its "nearness" (Deut. 30:14) can be misinterpreted as easy accessibility, it can be so totally misunderstood that it deteriorates into magic.[20] Man can, instead of being called by this Word, try to force the Word. This possibility of misuse is only given, however, because God's Word really dwells among men. In the form of the *Torah,* of the *Debarim* (the Words), the tradition of the covenants, it dwells with the chosen people; it dwells with the prophets upon the foundation of the election of Israel; but as such it is never insured against being misunderstood; it is never unequivocally proven to be the Word of God in opposition to any other words or thoughts whatever. The Word remains the Word in that the man receiving it continues to hear and to obey, and there is no instance beyond this to which he can turn—neither experience nor history itself. Here again we assert that the fact that the Old Testament so unmistakably testifies to the reality of the Word among men is a reference to the One in whom the Word of God is so present, as the Word of God in person, in a specific, historical man, God's elect, that in him it is no longer an alien Word, like that of the prophets, which is obediently heard, passed on, and testified to. Here, he comes to us in his total authenticity so that this Man no longer just receives and proclaims, but is the Word of God.

In this One, toward which the Old Testament witness points and is proceeding, the personal nature of the Word of God is revealed in both directions. God in person—man in person! Here the Word of God is fulfilled as "encouragement and claim"; it is totally the Word of *God* and totally God's Word with *men.*

This brings us to the original form of the Word of God, which provides the foundation for every other form:[21] the event, which is the source of all meaning and content in every other event of the Word of God—as used to be frequently written, the *Verbum Dei* (Word of God).

---

20. See Gottfried Quell, *Wahre und falsche Propheten; Versuch einer Interpretation* (Gütersloh: C. Bertelsmann, 1952).

21. Here we are following Karl Barth's doctrine of the "threefold form of the Word of God" (*CD*, I,1).

d. The Word as an Act of Revelation. The event of the Word of God! The Word of God also takes the form of the biblical witness, as we shall still discuss, and the form of the Church's proclamation. That we ascribe to the scriptural witness or ecclesiastical proclamation the character of a qualified event is not due to the scriptural witness as such (as though there were some kind of supranatural quality) nor due to the Church's proclamation as such (as though it were its religious power), but alone to the original event of the Word which happened and is happening. Based exclusively on this event, the reservation *"ubi et quando visum est Deo"* ("where and when it pleaseth God" [Augsburg Confession, V]) is not valid, but rather very definitely *"illic et tunc . . ."* (there and then).[22] This Word, in its original event, is as such the "Word of Life" (Phil. 2:16; 1 John 1:1; John 1:4; Acts 5:20). This Word works rebirth (1 Pet. 1:23; James 1:18; John 1:13). For this Word is God himself in his self-disclosure: it is the Father who reveals himself in the incarnate Son by the power of the Spirit. We can never speak directly enough about the Word of God in this form, for all the indirectness and problematics of our talk about every other form of the Word of God are only possible as they derive from this central point of orientation. It is indeed true that we "have" this original "form" of the Word in no other way than as the witness of the witnesses and in the proclamation of the Church which takes up this witness. However, this form of the Word is not exhausted or totally comprehended in the witness. That the witness has any power at all and finds faith is based upon the absolute and overruling power of the One witnessed to in contrast to that witness.

e. The Impossibility of Noetic Certainty. It is assuredly true that everything depends upon the preeminence of the original Word, but in spite of that, we cannot be speaking of any securing of that Word in a way which would be analogous to worldly possibilities of establishing certainty. The only possible guarantor of this original Word is the One who reveals himself in it, his own decision then producing decisions for him.

There have been three major attempts made to certify the credibility of this original Word, the revelation-event as such, by means other than the trustworthiness of the God who speaks himself. One attempt sought to establish the trustworthiness of the original Word by appealing to the concrete authority of the Church.[23] The guarantee which makes the proclaimed and scriptural Word credible, that is, secures the original Word as it is manifested in these, is provided by a holy institution located within the sphere of our experience, a Church authorized once and for all by Christ. This Church replaces the God who discloses himself in the Word for the believer and it becomes the "prolonged Christ" (*Christus prolongatus*). It claims the unimpeachable authority, which the Word only possesses, for itself, and there is no other authority superior to it which has not been absorbed by it. The final fixation of this view is found in the dogma of Vatican

---

22. See K. Barth, *loc. cit.*, p. 133.
23. Augustine's famous sentence, so frequently appealed to by Catholic theologians in defense of their position, "I should not believe the gospel except as moved by the authority of the Catholic Church" (*Against the Epistle of Manichaeus Called Fundamental* [*NPNF*, IV, 131]), already points in this direction.

Council I. It cannot be doubted that the authority which the Roman Church claims to have, by means of which it integrates the credibility of the original Word with its own authority, has been able to give many people today a strong sense of security. The price paid for this, however, is the levelling of the independent credibility of God in his Word to that of the Church, and this means ultimately the self-apotheosis of the Church.[24] Wherever this happens, we lose completely the genuine human freedom which derives from God's self-disclosure alone.

The second attempt to secure the credibility of the original Word of God in some other way than through the self-authentication of the God who discloses himself is the approach taken by Protestant Orthodoxy, in opposition to the Roman Catholic principle of tradition. The certification of the Word-event is sought in the supernatural infallibility of the biblical Word. This means that the supernatural production of the Word of Scripture is exclusively synonymous with revelation. Just as in the Roman Church and theology the Word as event is subsumed into the Word of the Church, this happens in the Protestant realm with the Bible. The result is that the Bible is made the object of a similar apotheosis as that of the Church in the Roman world. This tendency can be seen anew and in a more extreme form in modern Fundamentalism: faith in God in Christ becomes faith in the infallibility of the Bible (naturally, the two are identified with each other, but the latter absorbs the former in practice). Thus the witness of Scripture becomes a witness without a central point of orientation. And for this very reason, the Bible loses its living authority (Late Orthodoxy and the beginning Enlightenment show this happening all too clearly), and finally it is put aside in favor of rational knowledge. The Bible has its authority in truth because it is the witness to the Word that has happened. If, instead of this, its authority is to be based upon some quality which the Bible possesses itself, then the Word as event, which was supposed to be secured in the process, shifts into the shadow of the Word of witness.

The third attempt to secure the credibility of the event of the Word of God is that of modern Protestant theology. It tends to seek this security in the area of history. The Word of God as event is in its very essence historical. Would it not then seem very logical to guarantee the factuality of the revelational act by means of historical certification? If the Church in its "dogmatism" has often perverted the original state of "Christianity" (those who take this approach often equate God's self-disclosure in the Word-event with this original state of Christianity), if indeed there are superfluous "layers" within the biblical documents themselves, then we can use the tools of historical-critical research to peel them off, and original Christianity will explain itself! Where this happens, we no longer are dealing with secondary additions but with the authentic thing itself! Basically, the historical-critical work of the last two centuries has always contained an open or concealed tendency to gain security, not the securing of traditional Christianity but of the authentic thing behind it all. Usually there is a value judgment involved: they are persuaded that what was historically first was substantially purest, and

---

24. Regarding the principle of tradition which is naturally the issue here, see pp. 275ff.

that is what ought to be accorded the predicate "revelation." But is this possible? In spite of the honesty of the search for the historical, are they not in fact producing new dogma, the dogma which states that history in its original stages or at its highest points is revelation? Is not pure and original religion (the "religion of Jesus") being confused here with God's self-disclosure? And regarding the results, was not Nietzsche then right when he said that the product of such a query was in the long run "the purest, most transparent, scarcely visible form in the brain of the contemporary vulgar liberal theologian"?[25] Ever since Martin Kähler, with an apologetic intention, radically contested the possibility of finding another "historical Jesus" behind the Jesus witnessed to in Scripture,[26] and ever since Albert Schweitzer and the History of Religions and Form-Critical Schools have made the commensurability of the "historical" Jesus with our "religious" ideas doubtful, it is in fact no longer possible to take the approach to securing the Word which is advocated in this third solution. What can be historically "secured" is not the Word of God as event but rather historical facts. The revelation of God has taken place in history. But it does not derive from history and cannot be authenticated as revelation on the basis of history. Neither apologetic, conservative maximal historicism nor liberal minimal historicism can alter this. The "theology of facts"[27] is not the historical interpretation of historical facts, although to be sure it does not exist without facts!

Not everything about these three briefly sketched approaches to securing the Word of God as event is wrong. It is not wrong for the Roman Catholic approach to remind us that the original Word of God does encounter us in an obligatory fashion in the Word of the Church. It is wrong when the Word of the Church absorbs into itself the dignity of this original Word. It is wrong to attempt to secure the revelation in such a way that the Church is in fact the one secured. It is not wrong of the old Protestant view that it makes the Word of Scripture superior to the Word of Proclamation and reminds us that we do not have the Word-event in any other form than through the Word of the biblical witnesses. It is wrong, though, that this Word of the witnesses carries its qualification within itself instead of being simply the word of witnesses which then can claim our hearing, but cannot have its own apotheosis. It is wrong that ultimately here too an attempt is made to provide ultimate security, and this then directs faith in the wrong direction: it depends upon a supernatural fact rather than on God who supports faith. It is not wrong, in the third approach, that reference is made to the historicity of the Word-event. But it is wrong to understand God's self-disclosure as the meaning or deepest depth of a historical fact. The whole view is

---

25. "Thoughts Out of Season," Part II, *On the Use and Abuse of History*, tr. A. Collins (New York: The Liberal Arts Press, 1949 [g1922]), p. 58.

26. Kähler's *The So-Called Historical Jesus and the Historic, Biblical Christ*, tr. C. E. Braaten (Philadelphia: Fortress Press, 1964 [g1896, 1953, 1961]), corresponds to Schweitzer's studies in *The Mystery of the Kingdom of God; the Secret of Jesus' Messiahship and Passion*, tr. W. Lowrie (New York: Macmillan, 1950 [g1901¹, 1929², 1956³]); *Geschichte der Leben-Jesu-Forschung* (Tübingen: J. C. B. Mohr [Paul Siebeck], 1951⁶ [g1913]).

27. A. Vilmar, *Die Theologie der Tatsachen wider die Theologie der Rhetorik: Bekenntnis und Abwehr* (Marburg: S. G. Liesching/Stuttgart, 1864³; Berlin: Christlicher Zeitschriftenverlag, 1947; Darmstadt: Wissenschaftliche Buchgesellschaft, 1968⁵).

wrong that faith could gain certainty at the point where the historian is secure in his facts.

The Word of God as event, which grants authority both to the biblical witnesses and to the Church's proclamation, cannot be demonstrated as credible by the use of any other criterion. The thing which conditions everything else cannot be itself the object of conditions. There is therefore no argumentation which could prevent unbelief from being really unbelief, just as alternately faith is not based upon argumentations. But argumentation cannot deprive faith of its strength, for it is certainly not built upon nothing but upon the self-disclosure, which happened and is happening in the Word, of the One who alone is not conditioned or defined, who "upholds the universe by the word of his power" (Heb. 1:3).

2. THE WORD WITNESSED TO

God's "own Word"—as Zwingli put it—is the Word as event. "To say revelation is to say, 'The Word became flesh.' "[28] God's self-disclosure is historical. It has all the ambiguity and liability to confusion which is typical of everything historical. It would not be self-disclosure to us if this were not the case. But it is not given to us in any other way than in the Word of the witnesses. This is the second form of the Word of God, the Holy Scriptures as divine word (*verbum divinum,* as distinct from *Verbum*).

a. The Question of Historical Testimony. A first and obvious issue to be considered is the question as to whether the Word-event shares with all other historical events the necessity of historical testimony for those who come in later generations. This historical testimony has no significance in and of itself. No one would conceive of assigning the Bible its own significance next to the Word-event. What special feature does it then have other than the undebated fact that it is the only source for the historical event which the Church calls revelation? The assertion of the Church that the Holy Scriptures are also the Word of God seems virtually to imply that there is an insufficiency in the historical revelation-event.

b. The Word Witnessed to as Manifestation of the Presence of the Event. In point of fact, the Church's confession of Scripture as the Word of God means simultaneously a rejection of any historistic "revelational positivism." The salvation-event, the Word of God as Word which has happened, has indeed taken place once and for all (1 Pet. 3:18; Heb. 9:7, 26, 27, 28; 10:2), but it has not thereby become just posterity. Just as Yahweh's covenant with Israel never grows old, but is always contemporary in cultic celebration, priestly Torah, and prophetic address, so also the New Testament salvation-event is never just in the past but made present in the reality of the Church, in the reality of baptism and the Lord's Supper, in anamnesis and kerygmatic proclamation, as well as in the pneumatic word of the prophets. Our growing understanding, based upon the application of

---

28. K. Barth, *CD*, I,1, p. 134.

the form-critical method, that the biblical documents were part of Israel's worship and of the New Testament Church's worship to a much greater degree than was supposed earlier, demonstrates that in the Old Testament and New Testament covenant Community the past was constantly being made present. Jesus Christ was not just "yesterday" for the New Testament Community, but "the same yesterday and today and for ever" (Heb. 13:8). The presence of the Word-event does not remove its validity as being once and for all but is the form in which this is manifested. For the Word as event wants to become believed Word, Word confessed before the world. It is not enough for a small circle of initiates to receive the communication "that" Jesus Christ is the Lord, rather the lordship of the *kyrios* should become the confession of all men (Phil. 2:11). Faith is an inseparable part of the salvation-event.[29]

The witness which Holy Scripture contains is essentially the proclamation of what has happened once and for all so that it will be accepted and believed as the event which is once and for all.

c. Witness and Event. In order to interpret this, we must bear in mind that the biblical witness really is dealing with what has happened. The greatness of the biblical witness is its relationship to God's work which has actually occurred. This works out in the Old Testament in that the covenant, the election of Israel, the history of Yahweh with his people is always the foundation for whatever is being done in the present, or being thought or hoped. This is even more so in the New Testament: neither the eschatological expectation nor the present existence of the Community can be separated from what has happened in Jesus Christ. There is no imperative which is not rooted in this indicative,[30] no future tense which does not carry this past tense in it. Thus the biblical witness is always a report, the making known of history which has happened. Whoever endeavors to set aside this element will end up with unsupported Christian "ideology," and the "emergence" of such a "Christianity" or kerygma with no reasons or causes would be a more incomprehensible miracle than all those whose incomprehensibility is so strongly emphasized today. In addition, such a Christian ideology would be something which we would have to realize out of ourselves, cultically or ethically. It would be a Christian program or a Christian world view. The docetism which inheres in this approach would unavoidably transform itself, as docetism always does, into some higher or lower form of works-salvation. No, this is the prior and fundamental aspect of the biblical records, that they speak of God's deeds which are our presupposition in every case; they are the given because they are the gift.

d. Witness for the Present. On the other hand, we must not forget that the event to which the biblical witnesses testify is not some very important element of past reality but rather God's final work, and therefore the work which is valid

---

29. R. Bultmann, "The Concept of Revelation in the New Testament," *op. cit.*, pp. 78ff.
30. For the concordance between New Testament ethics and Christology see K. Barth, *CD*, IV,1, pp. 188ff.

for today. The presence of the Word witnessed to is therefore a result of the present validity of what has already happened. It is also the result of the fact that the Word as event cannot be discovered like a piece of the past awaiting attention; it is Word, and as God's Word it is directed toward our faith. The special feature of the Word witnessed to, then, is that on the one hand it is valid today and on the other it makes known what is valid for faith. If this is true, then this Word cannot be merely a report.

e. The Concept of Original Documents. The weightier concept of original documentation is also not enough. Ludwig Ihmels[31] found two elements of truth in it. First of all, that "the Scriptures belong to the process of revelation"—the document is to be distinguished from the report of what happened in that "it is itself an integrative component of the event." Ihmels finds secondly that the concept of document expresses "that we are dealing in it with a thoroughly reliable communication of knowledge about the fact concerned." Nevertheless, he finds the concept insufficient because Scripture is not always related directly to the "processes of revelation," but quite often indirectly, and because Scripture is not to be confused with a "set of lifeless minutes" but is rather "a living witness." We agree with this.

f. What Is a Witness? Scripture does not just offer us what could be neutral documentation of the Word-event, but rather it is the kind of witness in which the person witnessing has a qualified relationship to what he is making known. Being an "eyewitness" does not solely suffice to make one a witness (1 John 1:1–3; John 21:24; 1 Cor. 9:1; 15:8). There were many "eyewitnesses" to what Jesus did who did not become "witnesses" in the qualified sense of the word, Jews and Romans. There were also eyewitnesses to God's covenant with Israel who were outsiders, neighboring peoples and major powers. If we had the reports of such eyewitnesses, they could be of considerable significance for historical reasons. But they would certainly not be a witness.

The general biblical usage[32] regarding the terms "witness" as persons and "witness" as testimony is taken from the judicial sphere. This implies immediately that the witness is someone who is summoned or interrogated—the situation is a part of the act of witnessing and of the testimony. One is not a witness per se, but rather one is summoned to become a witness.

Certainly the initial qualification of a witness is based upon what he has seen and heard. But we find in the biblical concept of the witness and his testimony (as early as in Deutero-Isaiah [Isa. 43:10, 12; 44:8]) that the content of what is seen and heard is not restricted to the realm of the objective and immediately available to perception. The biblical witness makes not only something but someone known. In Deutero-Isaiah, speaking of Israel, it says "You are my witnesses," and then the concept of witness is tied up with the concept of servant (Isa. 43:10).

---

31. L. Ihmels, *Centralfragen der Dogmatik in der Gegenwart* (Leipzig: A. Deichert, [1910¹, 1918³], 1921⁴), pp. 69ff.

32. See Hermann Strathmann's article on *martys* in Kittel, *TDNT*, IV, 474–514, and the literature listed there.

In the Johannine literature, the term *martyrein* (to witness) has a decisively personal focus, as an answer to the self-testimony of Jesus (see John 8:12ff.; 18:37)! Certainly there are facts here which are witnessed to. But in the facts it is he himself! Therefore, the function of the witness in the Bible is to make his personal confession of the One who is being witnessed to. The theme of his testimony excludes all neutrality. The witness is moving from one decision to another. The question about what people thought of Jesus (Mark 8:27) was neutral. However, the second question, "Who do you say that I am," ends all neutrality. And it is this question which calls forth witness. It is always a qualified statement, a statement that in the very act qualifies the witness himself (the witness becomes the "martyr"[33]).

We can observe to what degree the concept of witness can be restricted to customary factuality by looking at the concept of "false witnesses" in Matthew 26:60. In terms of pure "factuality," what these witnesses state is probably relevant, even in the view of the Evangelists (see also John 2:19ff.; Acts 6:14). But these "witnesses" testify to "something," not to him. They speak with the wrong orientation. This is approximately related to what we could term the witness of the demonic: the Messianic predicates which according to Mark (Mark 1:24; 3:11; 5:7) come out of the mouths of those with demon possession are in the Evangelist's eyes "correct," but their correctness makes neither the demonic personalities nor the power speaking through them into witnesses. Judas Iscariot does not return to the circle of the disciples when he declares that the one he betrayed is innocent (Matt. 27:4), nor does Pilate become a witness when he asserts that the one whom he is condemning to death is innocent (e.g., Luke 23:14; John 18:38; 19:4). The most accurate contents will not make the one into a witness who disseminates them, without disclosing the person of the One about whom he is speaking in reality.

Paul found the witness authority of the apostle expressly established in the "seeing" of the Resurrected One (1 Cor. 9:1; 15:8), and the reality of the Resurrected One is unmistakably present behind the Johannine understanding of "witness." The resurrection is distinct from everything else that went before it by the fact that it has no other witnesses than those called to be its witnesses. In the resurrection event, the factual side is identical with the One who makes himself known to his own, and it is completely separated from any kind of accessibility outside of the witness. This certainly does not mean that it was an event which took place within the witnesses. It does mean that history happens here in absolute unconditionalness—history which cannot be derived from any other happening, history which cannot be coordinated with other history, history whose happening is only recognizable in itself and not based on other happenings, and that means recognizable in the Word of the witnesses which make it known. If this history were merely an inner process in the witnesses, then it would only be past, but it would also not have happened as this history. If it—an absurd thought—were one event among others, an episode or the initiation of an epoch, then it was not this

---

33. See Hans Graf von Campenhausen, *Die Idee des Martyriums in der Alten Kirche* (1936; Göttingen: Vandenhoeck & Ruprecht, 1964²).

history but rather a truly remarkable miracle. But if it was the initiation of a new reality (that of the *eschaton*) and thus the removal of the basic condition of our world as it otherwise exists, then as such it cannot be perceived in any other way than in the Word of the witnesses and can only be perceived by the one who submits to this Word. This means that this history, together with the authority of the witnesses, is decisive for the constitution of the world and of our life. If they were "false witnesses," then we must state in the same breath that our kerygma and our faith are empty and without content (1 Cor. 15:12ff.). Thus the Apostle as the witness to the Resurrected One is the exemplary form of the witness who does not communicate "something" to us but rather the witness in whose word the decision is made about us and on the basis of whose word our decision for death or life is made.

This is the unique thing about the Word witnessed to: it makes the Word-event known to us as valid for today in such a way that our behavior toward this making-known not only can be the means of our own decision, it is the irrevocable decision. Since this is true, the Word witnessed to is God's Word.

g. Scriptural Witness. We have been given the Word of the called witnesses in no other form than in the form of the written tradition. It is not an isolated thing but the human word which has been preserved and shaped by the hand of the Church which has passed it on. It is not protected from becoming the "letter" (2 Cor. 3:6ff.). Even the New Testament can become "letter," something in our hands, a program which we appropriate, a law among laws. The Word witnessed to is not the Word by virtue of the religious powers of the witnesses (which could only result in "letters"), but by virtue of the confrontation of the witnesses with the Word-event which is made known in their testimony. The authority of the witnesses consists of their having no independent authority and not wanting to have any (see 2 Cor. 3:4, 5 in the context of vv. 6ff.).

However, all of his concern about the "letter" did not hinder Paul from seeing the written character of the Word witnessed to as something positive, and this should be just as true of us. The Word witnessed to of the New Testament witnesses became "Scripture" in undeniable analogy to the scriptural character of the Old Testament witness. This is what is meant in the New Testament when it speaks of the "writings" (*graphē*). The scriptural character of the Old Testament witness—the witness to God's covenant with Israel, the witness to the expectation, pointing forward in time, as it stands unfulfilled—is clearly to be understood in the following way: the Word spoken then, related to a valid event, was not merely bound to one individual moment, but was grasped as the Word which will remain valid and true (this can be clearly observed in Isa. 8:16 or Jer. 36). The witness is true, and therefore it will be true later; it is true and therefore it is true not just for the first hearer but for every hearer. In this setting the concept of original documents, which we set aside as being inadequate, is still important; a text like Isaiah 8:1-3 shows how the scriptural character signifies both public availability and legally binding force. In that the New Testament became a "scripture," it was understood that the new covenant was not bound to the *kairos* but possessed lasting validity. Now, every new witness must let itself be measured by the recognized witness, acknowledged in its validity, and accepted by the Church—the canonical witness. "It is upon the written nature of the canon, upon its character as *scriptura sacra*, that its autonomy and independence hang, and therefore its free power towards the Church, and therefore the living nature of the succession."[34]

3. THE PROCLAIMED WORD

a. Preaching and the Word of Scripture. The Word-event implies the Word witnessed to because it is not a past Word, but rather because its having happened once and for all conditions its lasting validity.

The Word witnessed to necessitates then the proclaimed Word in each situation because the validity made known in it is acknowledged in the believing Community, and it in turn makes it known, proclaims it to the world.

"Logos" also means preaching (see especially 1 Cor. 1:18; 14:36; Heb. 13:7; 2 Tim. 4:2; 1 Tim. 5:17; 1 Thess. 1:8 and also Acts 8:4 and 11:19). It is clear that both the process and the contents of preaching are meant. There was no thought given to a substantive difference between the Apostolic Word and the proclamation conducted by other Christians. We never come across the idea that the Apostolic Word was merely to be repeated, but rather it is clearly presupposed that this Word is continually present in new and vital formulations.

Now, a question could emerge with new emphasis which we already dealt with[35] when we asked if it was not prejudicial to the finality of the Word-event if the Church were to assert of the empowered witness to that Word that it also were the Word of God. We found that the understanding of the scriptural witness as the Word of God decisively negates any historical "revelational positivism" in view of the Word that has happened. Now the same question could be raised again in regard to the relationship between the Word witnessed to and the Word proclaimed. If Scripture is the Word of God, then how can preaching be the "Word of God" next to it? Is it not in the best of cases no more than an "exposition" of Scripture which does not produce anything essentially new? Would it not be more proper to replace the human word of the sermon in the worship service with the pure Word of God in Scripture, unmodified by any human opinion—the Scripture reading? It seems that here, with regard to the Word of Scripture, revelational positivism is asserting itself again in its assumption that the Word of God as Scripture is a given in the sense of accessibly and concretely present. If this is so, then we would have to ask why there should be any gathering for worship at all; it would be enough to read the available Word of God alone at home—it would probably suffice just to have it around! The sacral Word would be intrinsically revelational in its power, it would be theophorous, and we would be facing in reality a positivism which Jeremiah already rejected (Jer. 8:8) and which Paul certainly meant when he spoke so positively of Scripture but viewed the letter as a fatal power (2 Cor. 3:6ff.).

The Church's proclamation, although it is certainly an endangered affair,

---

34. K. Barth, *CD*, I,1, p. 117.
35. See above, p. 185.

does not in truth prejudice the validity of the Word of Scripture. Rather, the validity of the scriptural Word requires the "living voice of the Gospel" (*viva vox evangelii*). For this validity is not an intrinsic validity but rather the living validity within the living Community and through it for the world. It is therefore right when Heinrich Bullinger in the Second Helvetic Confession (1566) formulated the famous statement, "The Preaching of the Word of God is the Word of God," and then explains, "when this Word of God is now preached in the church by preachers lawfully called, we believe [!] that the very Word of God is proclaimed, and received by the faith; and that neither any other Word of God is to be invented nor is to be expected from heaven."[36] In this, Bullinger is really a "Biblicist"! It is also interesting to note that the Reformed who were known as "Biblicists" generally had no interest in Scripture lections, and that they certainly did not hold to the doctrine of the "efficaciousness" (*efficacia*) of Scripture before and after its use (*ante et extra usum*).[37] The Scripture of and in itself—to speak in such a fashion means to misunderstand the Scripture, no longer to understand it as witness!

b. The Source of the Preacher's Qualification. It is quite obvious that the Church's proclamation will much more clearly be human words than the witness of the prophets and apostles. How then can the notoriously fallible and changeable word of man be God's infallible and eternal Word? The biblical witnesses are set apart by their qualification as witnesses, by their special position in the history which is defined by the Word-event, and their Word has been acknowledged by the Church as "canonic." What then is the source of the qualifications of all those who stand up to preach today? How can the Community be certain that the Word proclaimed to it is not the product of independent or arbitrary opinions, but is the empowered and valid Word of God directed to it?

c. Punctualism. One possible way of dealing with this issue would be with a kind of "theological punctualism." This view would maintain that the Church's proclamation can only be regarded as God's Word in that the miracle constantly takes place which makes the proclamation into the Word of God anew. It cannot of course be figured out whether or not this miracle really is taking place; it is fundamentally and completely dependent upon the quality of the sermon and of the preacher. If this idea is followed through, then it is not only unimportant

---

36. The first sentence quoted is in the margin, the rest in the text; see Niesel, *Bekenntnisschriften und Kirchenordnungen der nach Gottes Wort reformierten Kirche* (Zurich: Evangelischer Verlag, 1938³, p. 223; Schaff, III, 237; *Book of Confessions*, United Presbyterian Church, par. 5.004. It scarcely requires mentioning that, at this point, Bullinger does agree with Luther, who consistently understands "Word of God" to mean preaching (cf. P. Schempp, "Luthers Stellung zur Heiligen Schrift," in *Theologische Entwürfe (Theologische Bücherei*, 50), ed. R. Widmann (Munich: Kaiser, 1973 [g1929]). Luther's statement in *Against Hans Wurst* (1541) is frequently cited in which he says that the right preacher should not ask for forgiveness of guilt after preaching but in the full confidence of the prophets should say, "God himself has said this" (AE, XLI, 216).

37. The problem broke out in the Rahtmannian Controversy of 1621–28. (See Schaff-Herzog, III, 1995.) See below, pp. 284f. See also K. Barth, *CD*, I,1, p. 124.

whether a sermon is executed carefully and understandably, but also whether it is true to Scripture or heretical. If there is no relationship at all between the character of human words which is horizontally recognizable and the miracle of verbalization which is vertical, "happens from above," then the human word as such becomes totally unimportant. If that is true, then it is also of little interest to know what relationship this human word has to Scripture, and in turn, what it has to do with the Word-event. The *kairos* in which the Word of God "happens" "each time," ultimately has nothing to do with the Word which happened once and for all. But then this word, which is happening today, is separated from Christ and fully emptied. Nothing remains except the pure and miraculous illumination which penetrates through history, and this is not something for which we should make our appeal to the Holy Spirit. It appears then that no Church could exist for such a fanaticism bound up with the *kairos*—at best it would be little more than the accidental public forum in which the miracle of illumination took place. We are in the midst of a radical docetism. Theology has never fallen totally prey to this view. Dialectical theology in the 1920s came close to it while fending off false ecclesiological or Pietistic Positivism, but it quickly left this vicinity again.[38] It is not seriously contested that there is some kind of continuous relationship between the human word heard in proclamation and its qualification as God's Word. But there are differences of opinion in regard to how this relationship is to be construed.

Whereas in the view just sketched the proclaiming person is actually made into an unimportant factor, a neutral medium, or even the showplace of an immediate and present Word-event, one could also attempt to go in the opposite direction and seek the appropriateness of the sermon as God's Word in the personal qualities of the preacher. This can be done in a number of ways.

d. Theologia regenitorum—Theology of the Regenerate? One way would be the so-called *theologia regenitorum*, once a frequent approach of Pietism in justifiable opposition to the objectivism then often found in the understanding of the sermon. Regeneration is then the act which empowers the preacher, be he theologian or not, so that the human word he speaks is as such God's Word. There certainly is no need today to overemphasize the warning which emanates from the term "regeneration." Yet, this is not the way we can establish the qualification of human words as the Word of God. For the Word of God is never identical with a quality found in a person. Regeneration is the effect of the heard and believed Word (1 Pet. 1:23). But it is not the cause of the verbal power of man. Regenerate man is what he is by virtue of what he has received and not by virtue of some quality which now resides in him.

---

38. As late as 1950, Jérôme Hamer, in *Karl Barth,* tr. D. M. Maruca (Westminster, Md.: Newman Press, 1962 [g1949]), termed his position *Occasionalisme théologique.* And then in 1952, M. P. van Dijk in his work, *Existentie en Genade; grondedachten en samenhangen in de Kirchliche Dogmatik von Karl Barth* (Franeker: T. Wever, 1952), assigned Barth's theology to "Existentialism" in a fashion similar to Hamer. Both of these books are as unpersuasive in this regard as is C. Van Til in his *The New Modernism* (Philadelphia: Presbyterian & Reformed, 1947).

e. Ordination. Another way we could consider would be to ask whether the continuum by virtue of which human words could be qualified as the Word of God could be sought in the ordination of the preacher, in his function as the bearer of office. There is a clear relationship between this view and that of the theology of the regenerate. In both instances, the preacher is enabled by means of a religious quality residing in him to speak the Word of God. But the distinction is just as clear. In the first case, the theology of regeneration, this quality is something in every believer; in the second case it is found only in those who possess an ecclesiastical qualification. Thus, the first view tends to integrate "office" into the Community, perhaps by appealing to Luther's doctrine of the "priesthood of all believers,"[39] whereas the second approach distinguishes very sharply, even antithetically, between the "office" and the Community, especially in August Vilmar.[40] This is not the place to discuss the nature of ordination.[41] Even the question whether ordination is the reception of charisma or the delegation to ministry on the basis of the acknowledgment of charisma already present must be left aside at the moment. But even if the first interpretation were true (only 1 Tim. 4:14 would support it), we would still have to conclude that ordination does not create any inherent quality in man, by means of which his words would necessarily contain the facility of being God's Word. Otherwise the human word would not simply be placed in the service of the Word of God but would ultimately have control over the Word of God. We would again have a case of fanaticism, as we did with the kairology mentioned first and the theology of regeneration, only now it would be the "theology of glory" (*theologia gloriae*) which would lead man to prejudice the glory of Christ in his Word.[42] In addition, wherever this view is successfully established, the sermon is shifted to the background or generally devalued in favor of the administration of the sacraments and

---

39. See the highly instructive study by Hans Storck, *Das Allgemeine Priestertum bei Luther (Theologische Existenz heute,* N.S. 37; München: Kaiser, 1953).

40. See Barbara Schlunk, *Amt und Gemeinde im theologischen Denken Vilmars* (München: Kaiser, 1947).

41. Vilmar looked upon ordination as a sacramental act (*Dogmatik, Akademische Vorlesungen,* ed. W. Piderit [Gütersloh: C. Bertelsmann, 1874, 1937[2]]); T. Kliefoth sees it as a personal consecration (*Liturgische Abhandlungen* [8 vols.; Schwerin: Stiller, 1854], I, 404); Höfling views it as an act of benediction (*Grundsätze evangelisch-lutherischer Kirchenverfassung* [Erlangen: T. Bläsing, 1853[3]], p. 94); whereas Luther found the essence of the matter in the concept of calling (*vocatio*) (Storck, *op. cit.,* pp. 36ff.). Calvin emphasizes the laying on of hands, which he can occasionally term a sacrament in the broader, Augustinian sense of the term, this in his definition of what is legal and orderly ordination (*Institutes,* IV, xix, 31, pp. 1478f.; xiv, 20, pp. 1296f.); otherwise he regards it as a rite which arose under the law and which was properly carried over, but which has no "efficacy or virtue in itself" (Calvin, *The Acts of the Apostles,* tr. J. W. Fraser and W. J. G. McDonald [2 vols.; Grand Rapids: Eerdmans, 1965–66], I, 163 [on Acts 6:6]; see also I, 355 [on Acts 13:3]).

42. Barbara Schlunk, *op. cit.,* p. 69, agrees with Martha Wollenweber (*Theologie und Politik bei A. F. C. Vilmar,* in *Forschungen zur Geschichte und Lehre des Protestantismus,* Reihe 3, Bd. 1 [München: C. Kaiser (später Lempp), 1930], p. 46) "that a critique of Vilmar's concept of office would not take place so much in favor of the rights of the community as in view of the glory of Christ."

the power of the keys.[43] Both the latter and former possibilities are especially present in the Roman Catholic Church, in which not the sermon (which is essentially the application of moral theology or is understood as mystagogy) is the "Word of God," but rather the hierarchical pastoral doctrinal decisions (if the term will be allowed) or the doctrinal or moral decrees promulgated in the shadow of this hierarchical-pastoral authority.[44]

A special quality of the preacher cannot as such be the basis for asserting that his sermon is the Word of God. But one thing has been correctly seen both by the theology of regeneration and by this emphasis upon ordination: the presupposition for man's word being God's Word can only be God's own work. If we view regeneration in this fashion, then this important perspective is receiving its proper emphasis, and this is just as true of ordination. What is wrong in both conceptions is that the ever new act of God is replaced by an attribute possessed by man.

f. The Community as Bearer of the Authority of Preaching. God's Word is the word of man if and to the degree that it is based upon God's Word—the word of the sermon, if and to the degree that it stands in the "succession"[45] of the Word witnessed to, the Word of Scripture, and thus in a serving relationship to the Word-event. The individual, however, only stands in this succession as a member of the Community. The presupposition for the Word-character of the proclamation which takes place today is the calling of the Community and the calling of the individual into the Community.

If the Community were a society of the like-minded, those who "had appropriated" the Word witnessed to, then the word which would be heard in it and through it would be merely the expression of its own convictions or sentiments. The Word witnessed to would then be a matter of the past, already completed, available to us as history, which we could appropriate as an intellectual property. The Word-event would also be a past matter to which the Word of witness would be subordinated in much the same fashion that historical witnesses are part of a past event, as sources or documents. Only when the Community has the present Christ in its midst, that is, being proclaimed, is it the bearer of the valid Word, and then it is not talking about what is only past, but what is contemporary and present.

The "succession" in which the Community stands with its proclamation is therefore not identical with its subjective willingness to be in the discipleship of Christ; rather, it is "objectively" enabled by the Lord, whose witnesses were the prophets and apostles, in that he is present in the Community according to his promise. His presence is, however, presence in the Holy Spirit. That means it is

---

43. Barbara Schlunk, *op. cit.*, p. 34, regarding Vilmar. It ought to be easy to see how much Vilmar's position exercises influence today.

44. The inflation of ecclesiastical "statements" and "pronouncements" which overwhelm us today indicates a tendency in this direction in contemporary Protestantism. Do we have less confidence that the preaching of a village pastor could also be the "Word"?

45. See K. Barth, *CD*, I,1, pp. 106ff. Succession as the "empowered" vicariate of Jesus Christ!

the kind of presence which does not do away with the essential distance "from the Lord" in which the Community exists (2 Cor. 5:6) nor with the basic necessity of faith (which "sees" nothing—2 Cor. 5:7); rather, it presupposes these. If the presence of Christ meant his discoverable presence, then there would be no need of either faith or the contemporary witness. The Lord of the Community is, however, in principle not inherently in it but rather absolutely over it, and it is this his absolute superiority—the eschatological superiority which qualifies the existence of the Community here and now as "not yet"—which results in the fact that the Word of the Community, the Word of those in the Community to whom the ministry of this Word is entrusted, can never be anything other than a serving Word, a Word looking forward to his lordship. And that then means that, in light of the present Christ, the Community is dependent upon the Word of witnesses for its proclamation, and its Word is as reliably true and valid as it is prepared to renounce any autonomous validity of its Word. It is not the mere repetition of the Word witnessed to. But it is its obedient reiteration!

If this is true, then the proclamation of the Church is always a risk. It does not bear its character as the Word of God in itself and possesses no other security which would guarantee this character. It can always be false proclamation. It is constantly subject to the error, the deterioration, the emptiness, the autonomousness of the human. It must always be a risk; otherwise we could not avoid becoming involved in a homiletical, sacramental, or liturgical synergism which would militate against the lordship of Jesus Christ and that means against the freedom of the Spirit. But—as a risk, it may really be undertaken! For it takes place in view of the certainty of the promise which supports the Church, in view of the certainty of the Spirit, in view of the infallibility of the Lord who in his freedom is always above all of our ecclesiastical possibilities and impossibilities but still does not withdraw from us but wants to be present with us "always, till the close of the age." Seen from the perspective of man, preaching is a risk which ought not to be attempted. But from within the reality of the promise, this risk is the only possibility which is given to us, and the uncertainty of its success is the only guarantor that it will bear fruit.

C. THE KNOWLEDGE OF GOD

1. THE KNOWLEDGE OF GOD AND FAITH

a. Revelation and the Knowledge of God. When we were speaking of "revelation" and of "God's Word," our content could not be anything which also could be the result of our own abstract thought based on our human knowledge.

Nevertheless, we talked about "revelation" and about the "Word of God."[46] For, on the one hand, God's activity in which he discloses himself to us is not merely the "object" of our knowledge of God, but that which makes it possible. God, in making himself into the object of our knowing, is always the One who

---

46. See pp. 170ff.

acts. He not only makes himself into the object of our knowing, but in the same act he makes us into those who know him. In that he discloses himself to us, he opens us up for himself and for one another. But on the other hand, God's self-disclosure is by no means correlative to our knowledge of God, rather it surpasses all our perceiving and understanding. For God encounters us in his self-disclosure as the Lord in freedom. His activity in us is absolutely primary, so that our behavior toward him can only be obedience and never the mere realization of a correlation. He makes us into his partners. And in doing so he reveals himself as the Creator. He is the absolutely Highest Being in that he becomes involved with us, the Absolute Other precisely where he initiates fellowship with us.

Under these circumstances the knowledge of God as an act of man is never the "subjective" side of an "objective" activity of God with man. It is response. And it takes place not in an act of freely motivated contemplation, but in an act of responsibility. We do not confront God in his self-disclosure as those who could appropriate any kind of "object," but as those upon whom God's act of divine revelation has laid its claim.

b. *"Knowledge" in Biblical Usage.* This is seen in the biblical usage of the terms *gnōsis, epignōsis,* and *ginōskein.*[47] Rudolf Bultmann has rightly taught us to understand the biblical concept of knowledge as being concrete, personal, and unspeculative. The Hebrew verb *yada'* can, as is well known, also be used for the act of marital community (in Gen. 4:1 and then often elsewhere), that original human partnership which in both the Old and New Testaments reflects the relationship between the covenant God and his covenant Community. Regardless of how this usage is explained,[48] it can certainly not be assumed that a term like *yada'* would have the meaning of abstract, theoretical, or speculative knowledge.[49]

This is equally true of the profane understanding of objects: The Old Testament offers virtually nothing which leads to a metaphysics or a doctrine of ideas or anything similar. "Knowing" is both objective and personal simultaneously; it takes place in confrontation with the object. The fact that this is also true of the profane realm is based upon the relationship to God. This is the actual reason that the Old Testament provides such minimal material for speculation. And here, in the encounter, partnership, and covenant character of the relationship with God, are the roots of the very concrete relationship of Old Testament man to his environment. This environment is a creation of the covenant God, and therefore it does not require speculative analysis, but simply living understanding.

Knowing is ultimately always acknowledging. The Old Testament certainly

---

47. See the excellent article by R. Bultmann on *ginōskein,* etc. in Kittel, *TDNT,* I, 689–719.

48. Ludwig Köhler, *Lexicon in Veteris Testamenti Libros* (Leiden: E. J. Brill; Grand Rapids: Eerdmans, 1951 [Supplement, 1958]), p. 365.

49. Rudolf Bultmann, in Kittel, *TDNT,* I, 697, speaking generally: "The concept of knowledge in the Old Testament is not determined by the idea that the reality of what is known is most purely grasped when personal elements are obliterated between the subject and object of knowledge, and knowledge is reduced to contemplation from without. On the contrary, the Old Testament both perceives and asserts the significance and claim of the knowing subject."

does not assert that the sons of Eli (1 Sam. 2:12) did not know anything about Yahweh; in spite of that, it says that they did not *know* him, which means that they refused to grant him concrete acknowledgment. A similar judgment is spoken over all of Israel (Isa. 1:3; Jer. 2:8; 9:2), and again it is certain that noetic shortcomings are not meant. Conversely, the admonition, "Know that Yahweh is God" (Deut. 4:39; 8:5; 29:5; Ps. 46:11; Isa. 43:10), does not have primarily noetic meaning, and we would have to understand Deuteronomy 11:2, Isaiah 41:20, Hosea 11:3, and Micah 6:5 in a similar fashion. Israel "possesses" the knowledge of Yahweh only "in its exercise or actualization."[50] Thus in Hosea 6:6 the knowledge of God is paired with the love of God, and in Hosea 4:1 the people are accused of not having this knowledge (see also Jer. 5:1ff.). If we understand the knowledge of God as concrete acknowledgment, then we also understand that in Hosea 2:22 and Jeremiah 31:34 it is the object of eschatological promise.

Just as in the Old Testament knowing God means to participate in partnership with him and to acknowledge him as the covenant God, Yahweh's own "knowing" means the establishment and maintenance of this partnership. In Amos 3:2 it bears almost the meaning of "election," and it bears a similar meaning in Hosea 13:5, Exodus 33:23, and Isaiah 43:1 (although the terminology is different).

It is quite clear: Knowing is the experience of the I-Thou relationship, from Yahweh to Israel and from Israel to God.

This decisive aspect then returns to view in the New Testament. "If one loves God, one is known by him" (1 Cor. 8:3); those who have known God are actually those whom God has known (Gal. 4:9); that "the Lord knows those who are his" (2 Tim. 2:19) means that he lovingly and caringly seeks them out just as the good shepherd (John 10:14) knows his own and is known to his own. The mystical sound of such statements (which must include 1 Cor. 13:12) should not conceal the fact that the Old Testament foundation is definitive here: knowledge as the act of those in a relationship, as an event in a partnership which cannot be reversed but which is initiated by God.

It certainly cannot be denied that Gnostic speculation about God and the world made a strong impact upon the Christian churches from very early on (this is presupposed in the case of 1 Corinthians). It is also clear that Paul and certainly the Johannine writings adapt themselves to gnostically colored language usage. But this very fact reveals that they were not thinking gnostically in substance. We point again to 1 Corinthians 8:1ff. and Galatians 4:9 and then to the detailed references in Bultmann.[51] If "truth" for the New Testament witnesses were the same thing that it was for the Greeks and for Gnosticism, that is, the unconcealed ground of being, then "knowledge" in Romans 2:20 and in Hebrews 10:26 (*gnōsis* and *epignōsis*) would of course be essentially speculative, abstract, and impersonal. But this is the false presupposition. Truth is concrete; according to John 14:6 it is personal, and therefore knowledge is in fact nothing other than the knowledge of Jesus Christ (see, e.g., 2 Cor. 4:6; John 10:38; 14:9), nothing other than faith

---

50. R. Bultmann, *op. cit.*, p. 697.
51. *Op. cit.*, pp. 708ff.

itself (see, e.g., John 12:44, 45). In the New Testament too, perhaps more so than ever, knowledge has a practical orientation. It is not an end in itself, but rather it leads to concrete behavior in the Community (this distinguishes it clearly from Gnosticism; see Rom. 15:14; Phil. 1:9ff., and very instructively Col. 1:9ff. in context).

At this point we can summarize as follows: in biblical usage, which evidences a strong convergency here in spite of all the variety of expression, the knowledge of God is response to God's loving "knowledge" of man, and therefore it is essentially acknowledgment, knowledge which is binding, not creative in itself, not striving for some ultimate depths, but perceiving God's activity. It is concrete, personal in its process, and therefore to be conceived of together with faith, love, and obedience. The central point of orientation of all this is God's covenant activity. The concreteness of the knowledge of God is based upon the fact that God has acted concretely. Therefore the knowledge of God in the Old Testament is related to the preparatory covenant activity which is characteristic of the old covenant and which delimits it; in the New Testament it is related to God's act in Jesus Christ by which God has established the "new covenant."

c. The Knowledge of God as Fellowship with God. We could express what we have said until now in the following fashion: the knowledge of God is not the noetic reception of "something," but the relationship and behavior which involves all of man, which takes place between the individual "I" (or "we") of knowing man and the Thou of a loving and knowing God. The basis for this is that God in his behavior toward us has established this relationship. The knowledge of God is fellowship with God.

It is not, then, the private property of an esoteric group. The theme of proclamation is the truth of "God-for-us" which is made available for all men in Christ. And this proclamation reveals that the knowledge of God is supposed to be disclosed to all. It even proclaims that it has long been intended for all. God is not situated in ontological inaccessibility. Rather, what can be known about God is available to man since God has revealed it to man (Rom. 1:19). His invisible nature can really be seen (Rom. 1:20) as the object of knowledge. There is no mention anywhere of a speculative possibility which needs to be realized. Rather, we read of God who is proclaimed to all men because he is near to all men, is essential to the life of all men, is the Lord of all men, and thus claims honor and thanksgiving from all men. But, man denies him this honor and thanksgiving, especially in his speculative endeavors, and thus he is without excuse. It is not man's failure to perform a speculative act which makes him unpardonable, it is his failure to respond in the concrete way necessary to God's concrete behavior toward him! Thus, man's downfall is at the point of the fellowship with God offered to him, which he in guilt rejects. And that means that he does not know God. The same man who never can evade God for one moment is still *atheos* (without God [Eph. 2:12]); he lives in darkness (e.g., Eph. 5:8; Col. 1:13) and in falsehood (Rom. 3:4). None of this signifies the ontic absence of fellowship, light, and truth, but rather the break or chasm which defines the existence of man to whom the Word is proclaimed. The unrealized knowledge of God is not a noetic deficiency, and the presence of the knowledge of God is not a noetic advantage.

Everything noetic is just one element in a totality, in a life or death relationship, in functioning or broken fellowship, in faith or in unbelief. The Bible knows nothing of a God who is contrasted with a neutral, relationless man, for whom God might possibly become an object of interest at some time.

d. *Fellowship and Boundary*. The essence of the knowledge of God is fellowship with God, but this does not mean that man in this fellowship would be in a "direct" relationship to God. In the encounter which God enables man to have with himself, God remains totally GOD. "No one has ever seen God" (John 1:18)! The encounter in which God opens himself to us really reveals his concealedness. This is even true of the theophanies which we find in the Old Testament. We never find a description of God, especially not in Ezekiel 1–2 where, in careful theological clarification of the theophany, every statement which appears to be descriptive is then deprived of its binding nature by the word "like" or "likeness" (see Ezek. 1:5, 10, 13, etc.). A direct encounter with God would mean death (Ex. 33:20ff.; Isa. 6:5). Instead, it is the essential characteristic of the encounter with man which God makes possible that he does it in an indirect fashion: he reveals his "name," he shows his "countenance," he proclaims his "wisdom." And all this indirectness leads up to the one Mediator in whom God is completely among us and yet beyond our grasp. This is stated most clearly in Matthew 11:25ff. It is also clear there that the indirectness of God is a good and benevolent boundary.

Fellowship with God is thus not a mystical mixture of our souls with God, not a muddying of the boundary—were this so, then it would not be God whom we would know! Fellowship with God takes place in grateful and obedient response to the Word given to us, in faith which answers the faithfulness of God. Thus it always persists within the boundaries of man; there is no reaching out to the stars, no daring plunges to the abyss, no attempt to get beyond ourselves, but also no dour grumbling about our being limited within our boundaries—instead, there is a thankful living "under" God. That is therefore life "with God" because God in the Mediator has disclosed himself to us where we really are, and because God has spoken to us as we really are.

2. The Question of the Natural Knowledge of God

a. *The Problem*. We described the knowledge of God as an act of encounter, of fellowship, and of faith. It is not contested in the Christian Church and theology that such knowledge of God results from God's own revelation.

However, in view of the passionate controversies of the last decades,[52] we

---

52. H. Engelland, *Die Gewissheit um Gott und der neuere Biblizismus* (Munich: Kaiser, 1933); C. Stange, "Natürliche Theologie," *ZsysTh*, XII; F. Brunstäd, *Allgemeine Offenbarung; zum Streit um die "Natürliche Theologie"* (Halle [Saale]: M. Niemeyer, 1935); P. Althaus, "Uroffenbarung," *Luthertum* (1935; 46. Jahrgang), pp. 4–32; G. Heinzelmann, "Uroffenbarung?" *Theologische Studien und Kritiken*, 106, Nr. 6; K. Binder, *Das Problem der natürlichen Theologie innerhalb der Frage nach Transzendenz und Existenz* (Heidelberg: Theological dissertation, 1935); Wilhelm Link, "Anknüpfung," *ThR* (1935); P. Barth, "Das Problem der natürlichen Theologie bei Calvin" (*Theologische Existenz heute*, Nr. 18; Mu-

must raise the question whether we are not allowed a certain provisional, preparatory, perhaps even figurative knowledge of God which we perceive outside of the encounter with the Word-event which is proclaimed and testified to us or to the reality which is given to us. This kind of knowledge of God, to use the customary terminology, would be called "natural"—a distinction which in principle is derived from the Middle Ages during which they differentiated between what is "natural" and what is of "grace."

The perception referred to for such a "natural" knowledge of God could be of varying types. It could be regarded as an "apprehension," an "intuition," or a sense of "encounter," or it could take the form of rational or contemplative speculation. The areas within which such manifold perceptions could arise also differ from one another: it can be the experience of the events and order of nature, the experience of history, the personal challenge of the ethical "ought," or of some ultimate "value," and it can be the ultimate and most daring possibility of our thought. It always has to do with the perception of an ultimate, as does all religion everywhere, particularly in regard to the way in which the existence of being desires to be understood in the realm of thought.

The question which is the issue here does not fully deal with the theological position in regard to this ultimate or these ultimates, except as it touches upon the question of the knowledge of God. Should not these ultimates, these final values and conditions of being, at least reflect the reality of God himself, the God who reveals himself in the Word? Would it not then be fitting that we speak of a "general revelation" (*revelatio generalis*) next to and obviously theologically subordinate to "special revelation" (*revelatio specialis*)? Many of the Orthodox dogmaticians proceeded in this fashion.[53] Should it not then be possible to build a natural theology upon the foundation of such a natural or general revelation, although, of course, as a preface to revelatory theology? This, too, was attempted by Orthodox theologians.[54] And even if natural theology is not held to be possible

---

nich: Kaiser Verlag, 1935); F. Traub, "Zur Frage der natürlichen Theologie," *ZsysTh,* XIII (1936), Heft 1, pp. 34–53; K. Leese, *Natürliche Religion und christlicher Glaube; eine theologische Neuorientierung* (Berlin: Junker & Dunnhaupt, 1936); V. Glondys, "Das Gewissen als Erkenntnisquelle," *ZsysTh,* XIII (1936), Heft 4, pp. 652–81; A. Bairactaris, "Natürliche Theologie," *ZsysTh,* XIV (1937), Heft 1, pp. 40–62; R. Paulus, "Natur als Offenbarung?" *ZThK,* N.F. 18 (1937), pp. 34–56; H. Schlier, "Die Erkenntnis Gottes bei den Heiden," *EvTheol* (1933); J. C. V. van Bemmel, *Deus absconditus* (Hoorn: Edecea, 1937); A. Titius, *Natur und Gott; ein Vorsuch zur Verständigung zwischen Naturwissenschaft und Theologie* (Göttingen: Vandenhoeck & Ruprecht, 1931[2]); J. Leimesmeier, "Unsere Erkenntnis Gottes und die Analogia entis nach der Lehre des Franz Suarez," *Theologische Quartalschrift* (1941); G. Gloede, *Theologia naturalis bei Calvin* (Stuttgart: W. Kohlhammer, 1935).

53. Of the Lutherans we would especially mention Abraham Calovius, Andreas Quenstedt, and David Hollaz, who all expressed themselves in this fashion; Johann Gerhard preceded all of them. There is frequent mention of "natural religion" (*religio naturalis*) among the Reformed. Both the innate and the acquired natural knowledge of God are asserted. See Heppe-Bizer, pp. 1ff.

54. Natural theology is dealt with very early in special textbooks. Thus we find it in Heinrich Alsted, *Theologia naturalis* (Hanover: C. Eyfridi, 1615), who names seven natural dogmas: God is to be loved above all things; one is to live with integrity; one shall desire for another nothing which one does not desire for oneself; one is to receive what is one's due;

for various reasons, particularly because of its unavoidable inherent rationalistic tendency, should it not be still possible to construe the perception of such ultimates as an entity (perhaps summarized with the term "primitive" or "original revelation"[55]) to which the Gospel relates itself? Thus there would be a (pretheological) "natural" knowledge of God which would discursively be ranked as prior to the knowledge of God derived from the Gospel.

b. The Assertion of a Natural Knowledge of God. For the Roman Catholic Church, the question has been answered in a positive way ever since the First Vatican Council. "The same Holy Mother Church holds and teaches that God, the beginning and end of all things, can be known with certitude by the natural light of human reason from created things. . . ."[56] And in the "Oath Against the Errors of Modernism," the Catholic clergyman confesses, "And first, I profess that God, the beginning and end of all things, can be known and thus can also be demonstrated by the natural light of reason, 'by the things that are made' [Rom. 1:20], that is, by the visible works of creation, as the cause of the effects."[57] In principle, then, the Roman Church has preserved the medieval position, especially that of the Thomist High Middle Ages, and thereby rejected all of the more or less skeptical views which were brought up by radical Nominalism (with its sharp distinction between reason and revelation) and later by Jansenism (with its equally sharp distinction between nature and grace). We must add that the Thomist Middle Ages officially endorsed by the First Vatican Council could appeal to authoritative spokesmen of the early Church, beginning with the Apologists.[58]

The cloud of witnesses who endorse a positive evaluation of "natural theology," of course, extends across a broad stretch of the evangelical Church. Calvin has been appealed to as one of the chief witnesses;[59] it is debatable how

---

no one is to be harmed; that which benefits the community more than the individual is the greater good. Here both the Stoic and natural law influences are very clear. Some of the formulations agree exactly with the Institutes of the *Corpus Juris Civilis,* Book I, Article I. For the Lutheran view see St. Klotz, *Pneumatica sive theologia naturalis* (1640); B. Cellarius, *Epitome theologiae philosophicae seu naturalis* (1651).

55. Thus in Paul Althaus, *Die christliche Wahrheit* (2 vols.; Gütersloh: Bertelsmann, 1949 [1952²]), pp. 45ff.

56. Denzinger, p. 443 (par. 1785). See also on this Hans Urs von Balthasar, *The Theology of Karl Barth,* tr. J. Drury (New York: Holt, Rinehart & Winston, 1971), pp. 245ff., and the further literature cited there. It is clearly demonstrated how carefully serious Roman Catholic theology attempts to integrate the natural knowledge of God into the larger and comprehensive context of divine activity and grace. See also Gottlieb Söhngen, "Analogia fidei," *Catholica* (1934), Hefte 3f.

57. Denzinger, pp. 549f. (par. 2145).

58. See pp. 75ff.

59. Günther Gloede, *op. cit.*; Jean-Daniel Fischer, *Le problème de la théologie naturelle étudié d'après Calvin* (Strasbourg dissertation, 1936); P. Barth, "Das Problem der natürlichen Theologie bei Calvin" (*Theologische Existenz heute,* 18; Munich: Kaiser Verlag, 1935); Peter Brunner, "Allgemeine und besondere Offenbarung in Calvins Institutio," *EvTheol* (1934), pp. 189ff.; Pierre Maury, "La Théologie naturelle d'après Calvin," *Bulletin de la Societe de l'Histoire du Protestantisme française* (1935), pp. 267ff.; François Wendel, *Calvin, the origins and development of his religious thought,* tr. P. Mairiet (New York: Harper & Row, 1963), pp. 160ff.

justified that is, but there is some cause for it. Luther has also been named,[60] and there is also reason for it. Only in the case of the young Melanchthon has the attempt been made to ascertain an exception to the rule;[61] this is certainly not possible for the later Melanchthon. The whole problem was not a major theme of any of the Reformers. For all of them it was more a matter of scholastic tradition. Among the Reformed confessional statements there are at least two which indicate the relative importance which was attached to this matter here and there: the French Confession of Faith of 1559[62] and the Westminster Confession of Faith.[63] Most of the spokesmen for Orthodoxy either spoke directly of general revelation (especially in Late Orthodoxy) or meant what this concept implies.[64] The term "natural theology" is also broadly used.[65] When we turn to Orthodoxy, it is no longer possible to say that the issue was not a matter of emphasis. Whereas with the Reformers every knowledge question was directly bound up with the fundamental issue of soteriology, in Orthodoxy the problem of knowledge becomes a separate and independent issue, and the dominant intellectualism is accompanied by factual and often conscious dependence of theology upon certain logical and epistemological conceptions (usually derived from Aristotle), which in turn clearly contain a natural theology. We have already shown[66] how Orthodoxy really encouraged the development of its own opponent in its very midst,

---

60. R. Seeberg, *Lehrbuch der Dogmengeschichte* (4 vols.; Graz: Akademische Druck- und Verlagsanstalt, 1953), IV/1, pp. 174f. (this passage not in ET), with a citation of Luther, *Galatians* (AE, vol. XXVI), pp. 399f.; *Jonah* (AE, vol. XIX), pp. 53f.; *Genesis* (AE, vol. III), pp. 116f. Link delineates the framework of the problem in his *Das Ringen Luthers um die Freiheit der Theologie von der Philosophie* (Munich: Kaiser, 1940, 1955 [2nd ed. edited by E. Wolf and M. Mezger]). In the *Heidelberg Disputations* (XXff.), Luther connects wisdom and law ([AE, vol. XXXI], pp. 52f.). This reveals the dialectic within which his judgment on the issue moves.

61. Hans Engelland, *Die Gewissheit um Gott* . . . (1933), refers to the statement in the *Loci* of 1521, "The reality of God, the wrath of God, and the mercy of God are spiritual things, and therefore cannot be known by the flesh" (*LCC*, XIX, 90). He finds (p. 66) that the young Melanchthon thought through "Luther's doctrine of sin to the final conclusion."

62. Article 2 (after the article dealing with the nature of God): "As such this God reveals himself to men; firstly, in his works, in their creation, as well as in their preservation and control. Secondly and more clearly (!) in his Word . . ." (Schaff, III, 360). It is remarkable that the wording in the shorter edition of 1559 (later set aside; *Confession de Foy, CR*, IX, 739ff.), which is presumed to be either Calvin's or the Geneva Council's proposal for the Confession, is completely different. On the other hand, the Belgic Confession (Schaff, pp. 383ff.) follows the recognized French text.

63. Art. I, 1: "Although the light of nature, and the works of creation and providence, do so far manifest the goodness, wisdom, and power of God, as to leave men inexcusable; yet are they not sufficient to give that knowledge of God, and of his will, which is necessary unto Salvation . . ." (Schaff, III, 600). This text is closer to Calvin's statements in the *Institutes,* I, i-v, than is the French Confession of Faith.

64. For an overview of Lutheran dogmaticians, see H. Schmid, *The Doctrinal Theology of the Evangelical Lutheran Church, Verified from the Original Sources,* tr. C. A. Hay and H. E. Jacobs (Philadelphia: Lutheran Publication Society, 1889), cited as Schmid, pp. 25ff.; for the Reformed, see Heinrich Heppe, *Reformed Dogmatics, Set Out and Illustrated from the Sources,* rev. and ed. Ernst Bizer, tr. G. T. Thomson (London: Allen & Unwin Ltd., 1950), cited as Heppe-Bizer, pp. 1ff.

65. See pp. 200f., nn. 53 and 54.

66. See pp. 115ff.

Rationalism. What in Orthodoxy was the pattern and initial preparation for thought gradually became in Rationalism, under the domination of a new philosophy, an independent criterion applied to theology and its contents.

    c. Criticism Since Kant. The philosophy of Kant was the first to deal natural theology a blow. Kant's criticism of the traditional proofs of the existence of God, which formed the center and were the model for natural theology, was only the consequence of his critical definition of "pure" reason. He ascribed to pure reason the capacity to form judgments solely in the realm of that which is available to our view, and he proved that it would lead to intellectual contradictions if this limit were trespassed. It should be emphasized strongly that this criticism was derived from a philosophical conception. At first, theology paid little attention to this critique. Although the direction of movement was changing, theology was really beginning to become thoroughly speculative, because in the Idealism of Hegel and Schelling a power was emerging which pulled theology within its scope. Then too, Kant, who had rejected all proofs of God critically, still went on to develop his own proof for the existence of God, the so-called moral proof.[67] And his emphatic and well-founded reminder that this proof, totally within the scope of practical reason, did not contain any theoretical or speculative information, but would only demonstrate itself in the process of ethical activity, could not prevent the further development of a theology of natural moral experience along the lines of his thought. In any event, the first effective theological attempt to exclude natural theology, that of Albrecht Ritschl,[68] was in practice moving upon this basis. This was connected to the clear tendency to regard everything "natural" as irrelevant religiously, to leave it without reservations and without theological interest to the natural sciences and instead of it to discuss God solely in the context of the moral life. This is the way which Wilhelm Herrmann (1846–1922) pursued further. We see in both Ritschl and Herrmann that the exclusion of nature from the realm of theological interest had profound results within the area of what once was called special revelation, especially in Christology. For Ritschl, Christological statements were reduced to an ethically determined "value judgment," and for Herrmann they were only related to the "inner life" of Jesus as the location of revelation. Therefore it ought not to be surprising that the dogmaticians of that period who came out of Biblicism, especially Martin Kähler, Adolf Schlatter, and more recently, Paul Althaus,[69] show a tendency, sometimes cautiously (Kähler), sometimes radically (Schlatter), sometimes critically, not to restrict the

---

    67. Kant, *The Critique of Judgement*, tr. J. C. Meredith, *GBWW*, vol. XLII, pars. 87ff. Similarly already in *The Critique of Practical Reason*, tr. T. K. Abbott, *GBWW*, XLII, 344f.
    68. According to Ritschl (*The Christian Doctrine of Justification and Reconciliation*, tr. Mackintosh and Macaulay [New York: Scribner's, 1900; repr. Clifton, N. J.: Reference Book Publishers, 1966]), "whenever religion appears, it is subject to the presupposition that man opposes himself, as spirit, to surrounding nature, and to human society acting on him through the media of nature . . ." (p. 207). This leads to the result that "we never exercise religious cognition in merely explaining nature by a First Cause, but always and only in explaining the independence of the human spirit over against nature" (p. 208).
    69. See the summary in Hans Engelland, *Die Gewissheit um Gott und der neuere Biblizismus* (Munich: Kaiser, 1933).

knowledge of God exclusively to the realm of inwardness and the ethical. As a result, they end up speaking of a preparatory stage to the knowledge of God based upon the Bible, a stage established upon the perception of self and the world. The very emphatic stress placed upon general revelation and common grace in Kuyper and his associates[70] is also a result of their opposition to ethicism.

d. The Contemporary View of the Problem. It would false if we were to regard the contemporary discussion of this matter solely as a continuation of the debate up to now. We would also accomplish nothing if we sought to explain the well-known and strong opposition of both Barth[71] and Bultmann[72] to natural theology by pointing out that they are students of Wilhelm Herrmann. It is not without significance that Barth's rejection of natural theology does not imply the dismissal of nature from the realm of theological thought. We need only to look at the spiritualistic elements in Emil Brunner's Christology (for example, his position on the problem of the Virgin Birth) in order to see that Barth in opposing him emphasizes the natural much more strongly ("natural" claimed on the basis of the Word of God and also destined to be viewed in such a way), whereas Brunner in his opposition to Barth actually defends natural theology.[73] And if it is said that Karl Heim, together with Barth, was the most outspoken opponent of natural theology, it certainly does not mean that Heim had banned nature from the realm of theological thought.

The contemporary problem can be described in the following way: the point of departure is, as Emil Brunner concedes in his controversy with Karl Barth,[74] that "the proclamation of the Church has not two sources and norms, such as *e.g.* revelation *and* reason or the Word of God *and* history, and that ecclesiastical or Christian action has not two norms, such as *e.g.* commandments *and* 'Ordinances.'" The struggle against this 'and' is the struggle of Elijah on Mount Carmel

---

70. See especially Abraham Kuyper, *De gemeene gratie,* in *Weierschop en Kunst* (Amst-Pretoria: Boekhandel von Höveker & Wormser, 1902ff.; Kampen: J. H. Kok, 1920); and H. Bavinck, *Gereformeerde Dogmatiek* (4 vols., 1895ff.; Kampen: J. H. Kok, 1906), I, 219ff. See also *Our Reasonable Faith* (Grand Rapids: Eerdmans, 1956) (a compendium of the 4 vols.); and G. Vellenga, *Christelijke Dogmatiek* (1918; n.l.), I, 58ff.

It is within the Kuyperian approach that H. Dooyeweerd developed his imposing system in *A New Critique of Theoretical Thought,* tr. D. H. Freeman and W. S. Young (4 vols.; Amsterdam: H. J. Paris; Philadelphia: Presbyterian and Reformed Publishing, 1953–58), which is a "philosophy of the concept of law."

71. Speaking against E. Brunner in "No!", in (E. Brunner), *Natural Theology,* tr. P. Fraenkel (London: G. Bles, 1946); *CD,* I, 2, pp. 303ff. and, above all, II,1, pp. 63ff.; *The Knowledge of God and the Service of God According to the Teaching of the Reformation* (The Gifford Lectures, 1937–38), tr. J. L. M. Haire and I. Henderson (London: Hodder & Stoughton), pp. 3ff.

72. "The Question of Natural Revelation," in *Essays Philosophical and Theological,* tr. J. C. G. Greig (New York: Macmillan, 1955); pp. 90ff.

73. "Nature and Grace," in (E. Brunner), *Natural Theology,* tr. P. Fraenkel (London: G. Bles, 1946; also University Microfilms, Ann Arbor, Michigan, 1965); *Revelation and Reason; the Christian Doctrine of Faith and Knowledge,* tr. O. Wyon (Philadelphia: Westminster, 1946); *Dogmatics,* I, 132ff., and often.

74. "Nature and Grace," *loc. cit.,* p. 18.

against the halting between two opinions and therefore it is the struggle for the glory of the true God."[75] This was the common starting point for all of the theologians who were concerned with the Theology of the Word.[76] It is also agreed that theology "can not, knowing what its responsibility is towards the First Commandment, fail to speak, in its discussion of revelation, *also* of reason and experience, of history and creaturely existence, and certainly also of nationhood, customs and the state."[77] The question, however, is whether these things which legitimately come after the "also" and are then discussed possess their own revelational quality, if only a provisional one. Barth clearly emphasized that he was placing this question in view of a special situation which would not always be there. "Calvin could have been ten times as detailed and emphatic in dealing with the 'seed of religion' in the pagans than he actually was in the *Institutes,* I, 1–5, but we can be quite certain nonetheless that there would never be any kind of reversal between the 'below' of nature and the 'above' of grace, or predestination, of the Word of God and of the Holy Spirit and of faith."[78] But Barth thinks that this is not something we can be so sure of in the theology since 1700. Instead, a general reversal does arise. What the Reformers mentioned marginally becomes now a major theme, and the Word of God is then subjected to the criterion holding sway in this theme. Ultimately, the Word of God becomes the final coronation of "nature," providing everything else with a kind of religious halo; and this state of "nature" is where man senses himself to be, regardless of how honestly he may feel confronted by the Word. This is the situation within which the questioning of the admissibility of natural theology was undertaken so earnestly; this earnestness was something other than scholastic passion and led in the first thesis of the Barmen Declaration[79] to something other than a scholastic formulation. This should never be misconstrued, trivialized, or, as Max Lackmann has recently done, virtually pushed aside.[80] However, the question may fairly be asked whether the modernistic abuse which has become so common since around 1700 should make every other possible use of this matter illegitimate. We must ask whether there are not arguments which favor the assertion of a natural knowledge of God, of a general revelation, or of a primitive revelation, arguments which

---

75. On this see again K. Barth, "No!," *loc. cit.*, pp. 78ff.

76. When P. Althaus in *DchrWahrheit,* I, 72, positions Original Revelation and the Revelation of Christ next to each other, but does not want to do this with Original Revelation and the Revelation of the Word, but rather wants to "conceive of them as one," then even his references to the Bible, which first "truly illumines" Original Revelation, are not sufficient to demonstrate why such an identification should not lead to any other result than the view of the Word as the profound meaning of existence.

77. Thus Karl Barth in his lecture "Das erste Gebot als theologisches Axiom," ZZ (1933), pp. 297ff., which already makes all the elements of his later position quite clear.

78. Karl Barth, *op. cit.*, pp. 310ff.

79. "Jesus Christ, as he is attested for us in Holy Scripture, is the one Word of God which we have to hear and which we have to trust and obey in life and in death" (*Book of Confessions,* par. 8.11).

80. Max Lackmann, *Vom Geheimnis der Schöpfung; die Geschichte der Exegese von Römer 1,18–23; 2,14–16, und Acta 14,15–17; 17,22–29, vom 2. Jahrhundert bis zum Beginn der Orthodoxie* (Stuttgart: Evangelisches Verlagswerk, 1952).

are not done away with because of the abuses which have arisen. Dogmatic thinking must deal with such questions, and when we regard the positions and counterpositions within the contemporary theological camps, it is an absolute necessity that it be done—not at a distance from the present situation but not limited by it either.

The view of the natural knowledge of God has three very differing aspects related to its particular setting.

1) **The Apologetic Aspect.** This view is developed in the controversy with non-Christians, with so-called atheists, for example. Many Christian apologists think that there is only one way to meet such people, and that is in the disguise of the philosopher of religion. Since "reason" is accepted as the mutual basis for understanding and communication, the attempt is made on this basis to prove, not the "truth of Christianity," but possibly the existence of God, or the existence of an unsearchable ultimate in reality, and thus demonstrate the impossibility of nihilism or of theoretical atheism. The legacy of antiquity is very obvious here. The argumentation used also goes back to antiquity. The thing that is theological here is the idea that the Christian concern with regard to a person who does not even recognize what every pagan knows and admits must, as its first goal, try to convince him of at least the pagan possibilities or help him to begin to sense them himself. With the means of rational argumentation, the situation should be restored which primitive Christian proclamation was able to count on as a given. Then real Christian proclamation can begin. Under these circumstances, this proclamation is naturally the continuation of what was possibly already accepted within the realm of paganism. To put it differently, this proclamation is certainly the rejection of pagan existence, but done in such a way that the deepest, concealed truth of this existence will now be truly revealed.

2) **"Theology of the First Article."** The view that a natural knowledge of God is possible becomes an issue for apologetic-dogmatic thought under the rubric of a so-called theology of the first article.[81] To phrase it negatively, it is generally assumed that the statements of the "second" and "third" articles cannot be even partially known by means of the most profound perception of our selves or of the reality around us. Positively put: the ultimates which we discover when we penetrate deeply into ourselves or into the reality which surrounds and defines us are manifestations of the Creator. This whole idea complex is built upon the presupposition that the knowledge of God not only can be different in degree, but that it is virtually quantitatively divisible. A knowledge of the Creator, be it only provisional, vague, and very rudimentary, is still possible without the correlative knowledge of God the Redeemer and God the Holy Spirit. Thus this view incorporates a special understanding of the doctrine of the Trinity: the knowledge, at least, of the three ways that God exists is divisible. This can be done if the Trinity is not seen as a theoretical superstructure which, as something not present

---

81. This is then the subtitle of Wilhelm Lütgert's book *Schöpfung und Offenbarung; eine Theologie des ersten Artikels* (Gütersloh: Bertelsmann, 1934).

in experience,[82] does not deserve theological treatment and therefore is banished to the appendix of a dogmatic system. Moreover, it is obviously assumed here that the ultimates to which both the deity concepts of pagan religions and the concepts of philosophy are related (law of nature, ultimate of history = fate, moral law, conscience) are in some minimal sense identical with the God who is the Father of Jesus Christ. Wherever we encounter in ourselves and in the reality which surrounds and defines us, meaning, existence, and moral sense, there we are meeting God, even if in a concealed way! If this presupposition were lacking, this second approach would not be possible.

3) **The Problem of Continuity.** The acknowledgment of a natural knowledge of God has the function within theological thought of asserting that there is a continuity, if only very indirect, between God's gracious activity and the reality of nature. According to this thinking, reality cannot be regarded as empty and meaningless outside the bounds of special revelation. This consideration easily follows on that of the first article: God is truly not just the Creator of those who believe, but of the world. And thus the world cannot be absolutely meaningless, regardless of how perverted it may be in its sin. This can then lead to other and very important questions. God reveals himself in the man Jesus Christ; either this man only appeared to be a man and revelation was then itself just an appearance, or this man Jesus Christ really was a man, certainly without sin—and then we must conclude, it appears, that human existence, human nature as such, possesses a passive capacity for revelation. This in turn cannot be asserted if everything is meaningless before and outside of revelation (from the perspective of revelation). Therefore, there must be a continuity between "nature" and "grace." We could argue analogously that in the act of revelation in Jesus Christ, God enters history, and therefore history as such must possess a capacity, even though concealed, for being the place where the divine activity of grace can happen. Or, the proclamation of the Word-event happens in rational speech, regardless of its special features, and theology is only able to perform its task toward proclamation by means of rational speech. And it cannot be denied that "natural" reason is at least the formal organ of Christian discourse, and thus our "natural" reason as such must necessarily possess a certain passive capacity (disregarding at this point the perversion which sin would produce) for being the organ of this discourse which expresses the revelation of God and for being then the hearer's organ for the reception of such discourse. From various sides, the same question is really being raised: is there in man, in history, in reason, or, summarily, in "nature" itself a capacity or disposition (even if concealed) for the event of grace? If there is, then there is this continuity which is expressed by the view of the natural knowledge of God. If there is not, then we must conclude either (1) that sin has

---

82. Thus Schleiermacher, *ChrF,* pars. 170ff. The doctrine of the Trinity in "its ecclesiastical formulation" is "not a direct statement about Christian self-consciousness, but rather the connection of several of them" (Thesis of par. 170). Other writers who place this doctrine at the conclusion of their systems include Horst Stephan, *Glaubenslehre, der evangelische Glaube und sein Weltverständnis* (Giessen: A. Töpelmann, 1921); W. Herrmann, Theodor Häring, O. Kirn, and more recently Paul Althaus, *op. cit.,* II, 511ff.

totally depraved the "nature" of man, that it has become his "nature" or "substance" (this would be the "Flaccian" heresy[83]), or (2) that nature, totally aside from sin, possesses ontologically absolutely no passive capacity for God's gracious activity; that means then there is an unbridgeable chasm between creation and reconciliation, and we find ourselves located here in Gnostic or Marcionitic Dualism.[84] It is clear that we are dealing here with fundamental theological questions of great significance. Their answers will have a bearing on issues far beyond the scope of our theme in this section.

e. The Affirmation of the Creation in the Salvation-Event. The problem of continuity will come up again later, because it is of such broad significance.[85] Nevertheless, we may presuppose here that both the proclamation and the doctrine of the Church exclude dualism in every form (the early dogmaticians like to call it Manichaeism) as well as monism. But what is the Church's actual reason for refusing to think either monistically or (more important here) dualistically? What is the source of the Church's knowledge of the proclamation of this continuity which not even sin could erase? And how can a disposition, a passive appropriateness of the creature for the reception of revelation be deduced? How can we know that our reason is not just a "whore," which it is supposed to be according to Martin Luther (although he does not mean that this is all it is), but that it is also permitted to perceive the Word of God? What is the source of our knowledge that man is destined to be the hearer? Do we know all of this through our observation of ourselves and the world surrounding us? And can we then demonstrate it? To put it another way: do we need the concept of natural knowledge of God in order to avoid falling into dualism? Is it not possible that our attempt to establish this continuity, appropriateness, and capacity for perception based upon ourselves could miss the continuity, appropriateness, and capacity for perception which have already been established, the result being that we would see a "problem" at the point where God had founded a fact, and we would find a dualism (which we would seek to overcome by means of intellectual effort) where God already established a unity? This would certainly be true if we were to turn to the assertion that this continuity, appropriateness, and capacity for perception were established in Jesus Christ and made effective in us by the Holy

---

83. The Formula of Concord also postulates a continuity between man before the Fall and after the Fall (see the *Solid Repetition and Epitome,* I, especially *Solid Repetition and Declaration,* I, 34 [Jacobs, p. 545]). A trace of the doctrine of the natural knowledge of God is found in the setting of the doctrine of free will (*Solid Repetition and Declaration,* II, 9 [Jacobs, p. 553]). In order not to lose ultimate continuity in view of the fact of the inexorability of sin, Calvin uses the concept of a double nature, following Augustine: "Therefore we declare that man is corrupted through natural vitiation, but a vitiation that did not flow from nature" (*Institutes,* II, i, 11, p. 254). Indeed, he discovers, "in man's conversion what belongs to his primal nature remains entire" (*op. cit.,* p. 297). See also *CR,* LI, 163.

84. Erich Foerster, writing in *Christliche Welt* (1921), Nr. 45, dealt with Karl Barth under the title "Marcionitic Christianity." See K. Barth himself in his foreword to the second edition of *The Epistle to the Romans,* tr. E. C. Hoskyns (London: Oxford University Press, 1933–65), pp. 13f.

85. See below, Part Six, XIV, pp. 580ff.

Spirit. And there we have the central point of the statement which can be made in our context.

If we look at it in this way, we may conclude that the continuity at stake here is not present in ourselves or in any creaturely process known to us. The fact that Jesus Christ is a man is certainly the revelation of an "ultimate"—but not of a possibility or a capacity in or of man, rather of the fact that God has held onto and holds onto man, while man is lost in himself, because in his totality he exists in "hostility" toward God. Thus the incarnation of Jesus Christ is indeed the announcement of the divine Yes to man, but to man in this One Man alone. If we do not look at this One Man alone, there is no other line which would lead us from man as he is or understands himself or might develop himself to this One Man. The continuity which is given here is only to be seen as God enacts it. And it is God's enactment which causes its existence. Every self-evaluation we produce which included this continuity would be false speculation. When we start with ourselves, we can only conceive of this continuity as a continuation of our lines into infinity. And it is the very opposite which is true: the continuity which God establishes is in truth his constant faithfulness to us.

It can be said analogously that God, in entering into our real human history, demonstrates that this our history is not an empty process. But we must immediately add that this only becomes clear in and through his activity in our history. We could not say that our history possessed an appropriate capacity for this activity before he had actually acted in it. The same is true of "nature," without which there is no history.

We come to similar conclusions from another direction. It is in fact true that human perception perceives the Word of God, that "in the sight of God" the witnesses to Jesus Christ "by the open statement of the truth . . . commend [themselves] to every man's conscience" (2 Cor. 4:2). Here too there is continuity and appropriateness of identity. The human conscience can be the place where the truth is made known. But again we must say that this occurrence cannot be deduced from the most profound analysis of human perception or of human conscience, or be prepared for by the training of the conscience separate from the message. No human activity including the most careful apologetics can change the fact that "the god of this world [!] has blinded the minds of the unbelievers" (2 Cor. 4:4). Instead, the creative readiness of our conscience and our mind is revealed in the new act of creation, done by the One ". . . who said, 'Let light shine out of darkness . . .' " (2 Cor. 4:6)! That man is neither stone nor wood but has ears to hear, a mind to grasp, a conscience to be open to truth is not based upon some "revelational powers" residing in man himself but results from the free readiness of God which he has not taken away from man. By virtue of God's readiness, man is really not stone or wood, not because we evaluate ourselves in this fashion but because God makes us so.

Let us summarize: There is, yes, a continuity, a passive appropriateness of identity, a capacity to receive on the part of man. But we cannot speak of any of these apart from the divine act in which God established this continuity, this appropriateness, this capacity. In view of this divine act, that is, in view of the divine self-disclosure in Jesus Christ, which has reached us effectively in the Holy

Spirit, we now in fact must speak of them. Yet we do so not in the sense of an interpretation of ourselves, of history, or of nature, which we would produce, but rather by virtue of the claim, the enlisting, and (thus) the affirmation which God in his activity has imparted to our humanity, our history, and our world.

This leads then to two insights which we need to discuss in more detail. First of all, regarding the reality of the continuity we were discussing, we conclude that for theological reasons there can be no idea of an ontological remoteness between man and God or an ontological closedness of God toward man. Secondly, in regard to the fact that this continuity is in Jesus Christ and not in our grasp of ourselves or our world, we conclude that for theological reasons we cannot speak of a knowledge of God arising out of our understanding of ourselves or our world.

1) **No Ontological Remoteness Between God and Man.** "He is not far from each one of us" (Acts 17:27). This is the testimony of the Bible not only in the few passages which usually are appealed to in arguing for natural theology. It is noticeable that there is really little evidence of a "noetic" problem of God in the whole Bible. The fact that God "is" does not seem to require proof for a single one of the biblical witnesses. It is equally beyond doubt that he has to do with man and his world. The problem of "God," if we may use the phrase at all, is not a noetic problem in the whole of the Bible.

Under these circumstances, one cannot ascribe a special significance to the much discussed proof texts for a natural theology, particularly Romans 1:18–2:16, Acts 17:16ff., and Acts 14:15–18. They do not depart from the context of the total witness of Scripture, especially when we count the Old Testament as a part of this total witness. The Bible never says that God as such has nothing to do with man, or that man as such has nothing to do with God. As a whole, the Bible testifies to the very opposite. This helps us to understand why the passages just mentioned are all so "indicative" in an unusual way: they are not discussing "something" which will have to be proven with a great deal of rhetoric, rather they are speaking of a fact.

What is remarkable is that all of the passages mentioned deal with the heathen. Thus, there is also no ontological remoteness to God on the part of the heathen. This is unusual enough when we remember that Paul certainly knew the philosophizing of the pagan world well enough to know that they definitely had a noetic God-problem. But he does not even touch upon that in Romans 1–2, nor does Acts ever mention philosophical atheism; even the mention of the Epicureans fails to state that they did not think much of the gods. The heathen are taken not in their theories about God but rather in their factual relationship to God. And this simply exists. It exists the way that the Yahwist (Gen. 10) relates all of the nations known to him to Yahweh, in the way the prophets address themselves to their total pagan environment in their oracles to the nations (although the question whether these nations would have understood such language is not discussed), in the way in which the Old Testament expectation includes the judgment of all nations. There is no nation which could escape the living God to whom witness is given in and through Israel. This is the basis for the understanding of Romans 1–2 especially. The appearance of Stoic terminology does not change this at all.

Romans 1–2 and the Acts passages are an element of proclamation, like the sayings about the nations in the prophets. This is the real reason why the language here is so unusually indicative and unproblematic. None of these passages concludes that man, who is not and cannot be without God, therefore could effectively know God, in the sense of the proclamation being given. Romans 1–2 as a whole stands under the title "For the wrath of God is revealed . . ." (Rom. 1:18), which clearly corresponds to Romans 1:17 and 3:21. But God's wrath consists precisely in his not remaining ontologically remote from man but rather that he acts with man (Rom. 1:24ff.). This judicial act of God does not meet man in the form of incomprehensible fate, for it meets man who is both guilty and inexcusable because he has received God's proclamation. Man's guilt does not consist of his being noetically backward. Man's knowledge is spoken of very directly and indicatively: "For what can be known of God is plain to them" (Rom. 1:19); "Ever since the creation of the world his invisible nature . . . has been clearly perceived in the things that have been made" (Rom. 1:20). There is no trace here that God could be disclosed by means of evidences or that his existence might perhaps be suspected by man! What God has given to be known *is* known. In view of this noetically unproblematical situation, it is all the more important that man has refused to give God the honor and the thanks, which means that he has not dealt with God as God (Rom. 1:21). This means that man in reality denies God and reverses everything. It is not man's insufficiency which subjects him to the wrath of God, it is his guilt. He is guilty toward the God who is near, not a God who is ontologically removed. This is how the proclamation of the Gospel confronts man.

Romans 2:14–16 also stands under the sign of the revelation of wrath and the inexcusability of man (cf. 2:1), applied to both man under the law and man outside of the law. But how is the heathen guilty together with the Jew? This question is the problem from 2:12 to 2:16. Again, it is a fact which accuses the Gentiles with the Jews: the Gentiles "show that what the law requires is written on their hearts, while their conscience also bears witness. . . ." But when is this to be shown? According to verse 16, it is on the day of judgment! Paul considers what it is that will become plain before the judgment of God, the "secrets of men," and he refers to "his" Gospel, that is, to his proclamation, and states that God's judgment will happen "by Jesus Christ." Regardless of how this complex passage is to be interpreted in detail, one thing is clear: Paul evidences no awareness of the Gentiles being ontologically remote from God. The work of the law also takes place in the Gentile, just as he can in fact do "by nature" what the law requires. But the demonstration of this is not the object of human speculation (as, for instance, in the sense of natural law) but rather the object of divine judgment "by Jesus Christ" "according to my Gospel." Paul is obviously not thinking dualistically. But the "secrets," which are already there, are not to be exposed until God's judgmental act!

Acts 17:16ff. and 23ff., the original model of early Christian apologetic discourse, show even more concretely perhaps than the Romans passages how any idea of man's being ontologically remote from God is totally lacking (this is also true of Acts 14:15–18). The quotation in 17:28 reveals this with almost terrifying clarity. The man addressed here is not free of God. Even in his religion, which may be pagan, he is not free of God. Just as man cannot live and move (we think back to Rom. 1) without in fact having to do with God, he cannot conduct his religion without in fact dealing with God. The problematic altar to an unknown God becomes the impulse for the proclamation of the Creator, which then moves on to the announcement of the Judge (just as in Rom. 1 and 2). Unquestionably there are direct lines from Acts 17 to the apologetics which have given birth to all of the natural theology in the Christian Church. But the aspects which are important in our context are the same here: the complete absence of any consideration of an ontological remoteness of God to man or man to God, and the proclamatory character of what is said about the nearness of God which is really being asserted.

   2) No Preparatory "Natural Theology." The very biblical passages which testify to the lack of any ontological remoteness toward God in man or ontological remoteness toward man in God show that both the guilt and the need of man are not in the noetic sphere. Thus they close off the possibility of proceeding from the demonstration of man's noetic possibilities to anything nearly akin to the biblical knowledge of God, not even preliminary and preparatory knowledge.

   We are not saying that our attempts, seen noetically, must necessarily end in skepticism. The biblical witnesses say nothing of that either. We are capable of finding out some ultimates. The religion, mythology, and philosophy of all ages and peoples have shown that. We will look at this more carefully later when we deal with the so-called proofs of the existence of God. Man will come across "God" somewhere or other. But the important thing is that in his search for "God" man reaches beyond himself, to his deepest depth or his highest height. He does this speculatively and practically, in that he deifies the ultimates he has found and ends up with gods, or "fate," or "providence," or "the Good, True, and Beautiful," or even "the Nordic race," and so on. Each time the deity which he conceives or practically influences is the epitome of his own goals (even though they are his highly indirect goals, as Ludwig Feuerbach clearly saw), the epitome of a "beyond" which is really only our "beyond," the last patron for our existence,[86] in which we surpass ourselves and the ultimates which illumine us, and in which we find our security. This brings us to the concept of "idols." It is not a necessary characteristic of "idols" that the ideas which we connect with them are wrong or "snatched out of the air" (it is possible to make the God witnessed to in Scripture into an "idol"). An "idol" results when the "deity" becomes man's guarantor, the protector of his political order, his spiritual and intellectual values, his longing, and his need to analyze the world. There is no debating the fact that man always has been able to accomplish or tolerate extremes for the sake of his "gods." There is therefore no cause for a general "moral" condem-

---

86. R. Bultmann, "The Question of Natural Revelation," *op. cit.*: Man "twists his negative knowledge [which according to Bultmann is given in his "knowledge about his existence"] into a positive knowledge" (pp. 115 and 114).

nation of "natural" religion. The frequent and blustering contempt of paganism in the name of what are supposed to be higher insights or better morals can often betray that those doing so have made their "Christianity" into a fully valid replacement for that paganism.

The question we are dealing with, though, is whether there is reason and possibility in Christian theology to speak in even a provisional fashion of a natural knowledge of God. Can we take a positive distillation of what paganism says or thinks about the divine and make it into an "annex" of Christian discourse? This would mean that we were dealing with a parallel to the problem of Galatians. There the question was whether a person had to become an Israelite first in order to become a Christian (circumcision!), and here the question would be whether the way to become a Christian or understand the Christian message would not at least be made easier if man could first be made receptive for the insights which the pagan also possesses. It is also the question of defining the proper place of "talk about Christianity." To assert a natural knowledge of God means to assign to such talk as a point of departure the positive significance of pre-Christian or extra-Christian discourse or knowledge about God. Of course, this is done in such a way that then "authentic" Christian discourse not only continues and expands upon what it finds already present, but it also corrects it, perhaps even radically.

f. Irrelevant Arguments Against Natural Theology. One cannot counter such an undertaking with the assertion that what is outside the Christian sphere does not concern Christian theology. For God is also "the God of Gentiles" (Rom. 3:29): in the one man Jesus Christ, God revealed himself as the God of all mankind. The extreme particularism of Christian talk about God (Christ alone!) defines its extreme universalism. To put it differently, the God about whom Christian proclamation and theology speak, is the Creator and Lord of all the world. Too exclusive a Christian particularism, which believed it was not supposed to deal with what is beyond the pale of Christianity, is not based upon "Christ alone" but upon the relatively special nature of its "Christian" experiences and thoughts.

Such thinking cannot be dealt with by asserting that philosophy since the end of the Enlightenment has viewed natural theology with the skepticism or rejection established by Kant, radicalized by Feuerbach's late Hegelianism, maintained by Positivism, and even upheld by modern existential philosophy. The opposition of philosophy is generally not directed against every assertion of the existence of ultimates in reality. But more important, it is certainly significant for the theological view of things when philosophy does not believe it can demonstrate a continuity between man and God (to the extent that this really happens). Very clearly, the dominant thought here is that of a world contained in itself (the world of nature or of history or of the human self), in which human reason extended into infinity is nothing other than itself or what is homogenous to it. If this is the dominant thought, then theology could well have good reason to oppose this skepticism on the basis of its own insights, or at least to refuse to enter into any kind of alliance with this kind of skepticism. If, on the one hand, theology, for substantial reasons, is not able to ally itself with the metaphysics of being or with speculative idealism, it has reasons just as substantial never to make skepticism into its sworn deputy. For the continuity which theology certainly can speak of is not the same continuity which the metaphysics of being or idealism claims, and alternately, the insight into discontinuity, which theology also knows of, should not be confused with skepticism.

Thirdly, the attempt to develop a natural knowledge of God is not effectively met by the judgment of Ritschl and most of his followers that theology in principle never deals with anything other than personal morals, and thus every kind of "metaphysics" is far from theology. This judgment is nourished by Kant's proclamation of the primacy of practical reason and by Kant's thesis that religion has to do exclusively and necessarily with morality. Since, in the Ritschl school, the revelation in Jesus Christ consists of Jesus' making the Kingdom of God, that is, God's purpose for the world, conform to his own will, God's self-disclosure here is identical with the highest perfection of man. This then means that God's entry into complete human and historical reality, into human nature, is set aside and thus theology loses every possibility of dealing with the continuity between God and man, God and history, even God and "nature," which is established as God's free act in Jesus Christ. Fundamentally we are dealing here with the dualism between human existence and moral responsibility. But this is not a genuine dualism, but rather a duality residing within the context of human possibilities. Since Ritschl's theology remains consistently within the human sphere (both as existence and as responsibility!), it naturally has no reason to develop a "metaphysics" which goes beyond the limits of the personal and moral realm. In reality, of course, there is a concealed natural theology working uninhibitedly in this conception, which is the systematically structured interrelationship between morality, religion, and revelation.

g. The Gospel's Opposition. Opposition to natural theology can be based neither upon the religious self-sufficiency of Christendom, nor upon epistemological skepticism, nor upon Christian ethicism or personalism, but rather only upon the Gospel. It is the good news proclaimed in the Gospel that God has made man into his partner. This is good news because God himself has established this fellowship with man in Jesus Christ. God has disclosed himself as the Creator who does not let his creation go, as the Reconciler and Redeemer who frees his creature from the fallenness of his sin and makes him into a brother of the "new Adam" (Rom. 5:12ff.; 1 Cor. 15:21, 22, 45). Thus, God's act in Jesus Christ is indirectly the affirmation of man because it is the divine Yes to this man. But it is not to be understood as man's self-confirmation. This is true, too, in a noetic sense: there is no knowledge of God derived from our selfhood which could prepare the way for the proclamation of the Word which happened in Jesus Christ or provide the presupposition for the answer we give in faith to this proclamation. Rather, in the free act of God all of the "works" which result from our selfhood, including our knowledge, are judged as false.

These summarizing theses require further explanation at a few important points.

1) Natural Theology as the Abrogation of the Goodness of God. Everything depends upon the fact that our egoistic and thus sinful attempt to find God in the depths or heights of the reality at our disposal is judged in the very same divine act in which God's indirect affirmation (indirect because it exists in and is revealed by Jesus Christ) of our humanity has taken place. It is because God, in this indirectness, has affirmed us and strengthened the continuity with us that it is meaningless for us still to try to reach for the stars. At this as at every other point, sin is the rejection of the goodness of God.

2) **The Essence of Falsehood.** It cannot be stated that man in his sinful selfhood would not know anything about God at all. "God"—equated with man's ultimates or presumed in their unrecognizable depths—is the theme of man's religion, of his genuine and his secularized mythology, of his philosophy of religion and of his practical-religious and practical-ethical activity. It also cannot be said that the expressions of knowledge which result from all this must necessarily always be irrelevant or wrong. There are innumerable people who state that God exists. Because this thesis is "natural," that is, spoken outside of the Word of God, we cannot respond by saying "No, God is not." Even propositions like the "transcendence" of God, or that God is "Creator," or "Ruler of the world," or "omnipotent," can all be arrived at via a "natural" route. All of these statements are not irrelevant per se. But as such, they are also not true. For in every instance they are elements of the way in which man, in his sinful selfhood, understands himself, his world, and its ultimates. Even when he conceives of transcendence, it is a transcendence which he is postulating, stretching beyond his limits. The "God" whom he thinks up is always the god who is subject to him, the god who results when man expands himself into infinity. This is also true of mysticism, even where it is the mysticism of grace. The god who is arrived at "naturally," thought, postulated, and proven by man, is the extremity of the world of this man. Thus he is always the guarantor of this world, even if this only is effective under certain cultic conditions; possibly he also guarantees this world against other deities who threaten the world of man. In the light of Christian proclamation, however, the man who understands himself, his world, and his "God" in this fashion, is not true, and thus everything is untrue which he may say about God, as intrinsically relevant as it may be. Since man still talks about the light while being in the darkness in which the Word of God finds him, since he still talks about truth while being in the lie at which the Word of God catches him, and since in his own way he "knows" this truth, he is "without excuse" (Rom. 1:20). The falsity of his speech is not that it has no basis or contents, but that it is perverted.

3) **The Impossibility of Our Distinguishing Between Creatureliness and Sin.** When "natural man," "who does not receive the gifts of the Spirit of God," to whom everything spiritual is "folly" which "he is not able to understand" (1 Cor. 2:14)—when such a man is able to make valid statements about God, it could seem to be the task of Christian theology to illuminate these valid statements from the perspective of the "truth" and to refute what is not valid from the same point of view. But this is precisely what is impossible. It would be possible if the abyss which separates the valid from the true had a bottom so that it could be filled in, or if there were a bridge over it. But that is not the case. For these valid

statements are not true because man is not true, because as a sinner he is completely separated from God and oriented against God, although he is surrounded by God. The truth of God cannot be dealt with the way perfectly valid statements are dealt with when compared to less valid ones.

Of course, one could say that the well-known fact that man "knows" God is based ultimately upon his being a creature. This would mean then that the creaturely element of man must be especially distinguished from that part of man which is perverted by sin. (This is the point in the debate, particularly between Brunner and Barth, where the question of the natural knowledge of God is connected to the question of the image of God.[87]) But how can any human being really distinguish between creatureliness and sin? No one would conceive of simply relating the two to each other in a dialectical fashion.[88] But no one could presume to separate here what God alone has separated (Rom. 8:3, 4). Created man is not the deepest basis of man as we know him, now covered over with layers of sin. Man is totally a sinner. Only in Christ is he also totally justified. Thus, his creatureliness is not an object of analysis but rather of faith. Any attempt to grasp analytically man's creatureliness and the relationship to God which is supposed to be inherent in it, as we observe in Wilhelm Lütgert and as must be undertaken as a postulate of every natural theology in order to come up with a receiver for general revelation, means nothing less than the theologian's endeavor to arrive by means of concepts at what God has already completed in the act of reconciliation. Analytical means can in reality arrive at neither sin nor creatureliness.

4) The Qualitative Distinction Between "Natural" and Christian Knowledge of God. We have already described[89] the knowledge of God as concrete, personal, unspeculative, as encounter between the knowing (and electing) I of God and the (answering) Thou of man, and to this degree we have related the knowledge of God and fellowship with God to one another. It will be agreed by everyone that the natural knowledge of God, assuming for a moment that there is such a thing, would not be the knowing of God in the sense in which we would understand it in the interpretation of the biblical witness. There are no theologians who would regard the natural knowledge of God as sufficient knowledge.[90] No one is willing to ascribe more to it than the function of preparation, in the best of cases.

---

87. Cf. on this question Part Six, pp. 533ff. and the bibliography there.

88. E. Hirsch, *Schöpfung und Sünde in der natürlich-geschichtlichen Wirklichkeit des einzelnen Menschen: Versuch einer Grundlegung christlicher Lebensweisung* (Tübingen: J. C. B. Mohr [Paul Siebeck], 1931).

89. See pp. 195ff.

90. Herman Bavinck, *op. cit.*, I, 231ff., who himself advocates the doctrine of general revelation, cites regarding the insufficiency of it, Augustine, *On the Trinity*, XIII, 12 (*NPNF*, III, 173f.); *The City of God*, XII, 20 (*NPNF*, II, 239ff.); *The Usefulness of Belief*, X, 24 (*LCC*, VI, 310f.); *Confessions*, V, v, 7 (*NPNF*, I, 80f.); further, Thomas Aquinas, *STh*, I,i,1, vol. 1, p. 1 (*respondeo*), *Summa contra Gentiles*, I,iv, etc. The orthodox theologians also emphasized the insufficiency of general revelation (material cited in Schmid and Heppe-Bizer). This is also true of those contemporary dogmaticians who in some way or another have advocated a natural theology.

But how are we to understand this preparatory function? Wherever the concept of special revelation has resulted in an understanding of the knowledge of God as rational insight into supranatural truths—as was done all through the Middle Ages and again in the period of Orthodoxy—there it is possible to understand the preparatory function of the natural knowledge of God as a gradual affair: it initiates that knowledge which special revelation then completes. The question is then, wherever this happens, is not in reality Christian knowledge conceived of according to the model of natural knowledge? We must answer this question positively. Perhaps one of the most dangerous effects of natural theology is to be seen here, in that wherever it is allowed, the essence of Christian knowledge as a whole is understood as though it consisted of rational, or meditative, or intuitive insights into general truths. We would even have to ask whether or not this misunderstanding of Christian knowledge, which was already being developed by the early Apologists, was not in fact the overt or concealed reason for a Christian natural theology.

As a matter of fact, there is, after everything is said and done, not a gradual, but rather a qualitative distinction between the "natural" knowledge of God by men (which, e.g., Calvin does not usually call *cognitio* but rather *notitia*) and the biblical understanding of the knowledge of God; there is, analogously, a qualitative distinction between what we regard as an accurate statement and the truth itself. How then can one be said to prepare the way for the other?

This qualitative distinction is rooted in both the subject and the object. In the "subject," the knowledge (*notitia*) of God which man has this side of God's self-disclosure is a work of his selfhood and self-assertion which has fallen prey to sin. In true knowledge of God (*cognitio Dei*), man must sacrifice his selfhood with the result that God discloses himself to man as the Lord who gives himself to man. Thus it is correct of Luther to see the natural knowledge of God as the opposite to the theology of the cross (*Heidelberg Disputations,* 19, 20).[91] In regard to the "object," the natural knowledge of God meant by Christian theology has, in fact, begun with the ultimates which can be perceived in nature, history, human thought, and moral consciousness. It is characteristic that the issue is always the "meaning" or the "origin" in the realms of perception: the first mover, or the last laws in nature, the power of fate, or the power of retribution in history—the issues which fill in the last holes in the otherwise closed structures of our thought, the moral law which renders authority to our moral consciousness. To put it in New Testament terms, it is a matter of the "elemental spirits of the universe" (Gal. 4:3, 9; Col. 2:8, 20), whose reality is not being contested but which never appear as the preparation for the knowledge of God which takes place in faith. They are rather its opposite which is now conquered, and thus they are never the deepest and most profound of all levels over which the real knowledge of God is layered. We may note that the Old Testament's relationship to nature is confirmed in the New Testament and its eschatological view is shifted to a new direction in the process. It is remarkable, though, that the Old Testament often refers to the regularity and the sublimity of natural events, but it never reflects about the

---

91. AE, XXXI, 40, 52f.

"meaning" of them. There is no concept of a historical event which is understandable in itself, where God's activity with man and man's before God are distinguished in what might be called a linear fashion. Thus there is no foundation for any reflection upon the depths of history and its meaning. The reason for this is that here, other than with the Greeks, there is no interest in ultimates, but rather in the fact that the Creator and his creature have something to do with one another. And that means that such ultimates never come into view. In the New Testament, they do emerge (as the "elemental spirits of the universe"), but in so doing, their divine qualities are contested. That all natural theology which has been received by Christian theology does relate to such ultimates reveals that what is at stake here is the search for something other than the creation in the depths and heights of creatureliness. Man, when he is not confronted with God's "claim and address," is not able to act in any other fashion. But it must be recognized that this approach does not produce something which is just essentially less than the true knowledge of God by the creature, but rather its qualitative opposite.[92]

There remain two problems which we have not discussed in the present context: the whole area of the doctrine of creation, which was only implied here,[93] and the problem of the Old Testament witness, that is, the knowledge of God granted to man in the old covenant.[94] The thesis that the knowledge of God found in the old covenant is the still concealed knowledge of God in Christ, enclosed in the as yet unfulfilled law, forms the necessary presupposition of what we have stated here.

3. APPENDIX: REGARDING THE PROOFS OF THE EXISTENCE OF GOD

We shall now briefly discuss the so-called proofs of the existence of God as a model of a carefully structured natural theology. This is especially appropriate in our context since the so-called proofs of God in their classical form reveal that the argumentation for the existence of God is based upon the ultimates already given in one's view of the world.

The proofs of God are all derived from philosophy. However, they were already received by theology as early as the age of the Fathers,[95] and in the Middle Ages they were broadly integrated into dogmatics.[96] Protestant Orthodoxy did not reject the proofs, although they ascribed less significance to them than

---

92. In this subsection we have decided not to enter into a detailed discussion of the literature, since it has already grown disproportionately large. We have also not dealt with those points which have been thoroughly handled in the literature already.

93. See pp. 461ff.

94. See pp. 287ff.

95. Diodore of Tarsus (d. c. 390) adopted the cosmological proof; John of Damascus (c. 675–c. 749) also used it in his *Exposition of the Orthodox Faith*, I, 3 (*NPNF*, IX, 2f.).

96. See especially Thomas Aquinas, *STh*, I,ii,2 and 3, vol. I, pp. 12–14; for further examples, see below. See also G. Grunwald, *Geschichte der Gottesbeweise im Mittelalter bis zum Ausgang der Hochscholastik* (Münster: Aschendorff, 1907).

did Scholasticism. Some Reformed used them especially to combat atheism.[97] And there were dogmaticians who distinguished between implanted natural knowledge (*cognitio naturalis*) and acquired natural knowledge (between *insita* and *acquisita*), and they listed the proofs of God in the latter category. The theology of the Enlightenment ascribed great importance to the proofs of God, as would be expected. Kant's sharp critique of them only gradually began to have its effect upon theology. Nevertheless, during the 19th century the proofs of God progressively disappeared from evangelical theology, whereas Roman Catholic theology continued to maintain the demonstrability of the existence of God as a dogma[98]—as we see asserted in the wording of the Anti-Modernist Oath (1910).[99]

a. The Cosmological Proof. The cosmological proof deserves to be mentioned first. It can be traced back to Aristotle[100] and is also found in other writers of antiquity, as, for example, Cicero.[101] In the Middle Ages, it was further developed both by Anselm[102] and by Thomas.[103] The latter lists five ways of proof, of which we shall deal with the first four. First (according to Thomas, the most certain way): all movement is in a process of transition from potency to act (*potentia* to *actus*); everything which we encounter as an act is derived from another mover or power, which in turn is an act derived from another power behind it. This process, which we must conceive of in a backward direction and which requires our using a causal pattern of thought, must necessarily lead back to a Prime Mover which cannot be reduced to another power, and thus is solely act or actor (this is Aristotle's *prōton kinoun* = First Mover or Unmoved Mover). Thus we arrive at the existence of God. The *second* way is based upon the concept of efficient cause: everything in reality goes back to such a cause in a long chain of cause and effect relationships. However, this series of efficient causes cannot be infinite, but rather at its end there must be one efficient cause which is not itself the effect of a cause. If such a cause did not exist, we would have to deduce that nothing could be caused. This first efficient cause is God. The *third* way uses the distinction between possible and necessary existence. Everything subject to

---

97. Hugo Grotius, *De veritate religionis christianae* (1662), pp. 4ff., proves, in order to demonstrate that "religion is not an inane thing," his basic proposition "that something numinous exists." See also *The Truth of the Christian Religion,* tr. J. Clarke (London: J. & P. Knopton, 1729; Dove, 1827); not available to TR.

98. J. Mausbach, *Dasein und Wesen Gottes* (2 vols.; Münster: Aschendorff, 1929–30).

99. See the *motu proprio* "Sacrorum Antistitum": ". . . can be certainly known and thus can also be demonstrated . . ." (Denzinger, pp. 549f. [par. 2145]).

100. Pseudo-Aristotle, *On the Cosmos,* tr. D. J. Furley (*Loeb Classical Library*; Cambridge, Mass.: Harvard University Press, 1955), VI. 385ff.

101. Cicero, *Tusculan Disputations,* tr. J. E. King (*LCL;* Cambridge: Harvard University Press, 1950), I, xxviii, pp. 78–83; "De Divinatione," in *De Senectute, De Amicitia, De Divinatione,* tr. W. A. Falconer (New York: Putnam's Sons, 1934), II, 76.

102. "Monologium," I–VII, *St. Anselm,* tr. S. W. Deane (La Salle, Ill.: Open Court Publishing, 1962), pp. 37–52; the rest of the writing is dominated by the cosmological proof, whose inner relationship to the ontological proof becomes very obvious; Migne, *PL,* CLVIII, 141ff.

103. *STh,* I,ii,3, vol. I, pp. 13f. and cf. *Summa contra Gentiles,* I, xiii, *On the Truth of the Catholic Faith,* tr. A. C. Pegis *et al.* (5 vols.; Garden City: Doubleday, 1955), I, 85–96.

the process of change and decay (that is, our present reality) is fundamentally mere possible existence: it could exist, but it could also not exist. Everything which is mere possible existence has entered at some point in time into existence, if it is genuinely real. This is, however, not based upon possible existence, but ultimately upon necessary existence. Necessary existence is not identical with an infinite series of necessary beings, but rather all necessary beings go back to one necessary existence, which is God. If this were not so, there would be no convincing reason for not regarding all reality as mere possible existence (Thomas does not treat the alternative choice, which is that there could be behind the infinite series of possible existence another infinite series of necessary existence, that is, the pantheistic approach which is very close to this kind of consideration). If this third way is already colored by Neo-Platonic metaphysics of being, then the *fourth* way is totally dominated by it: in all things there are degrees of excellence. In every realm of being then, whatever has the highest degree is the cause of everything of lower degree; for—here Aristotle is called in as a witness—whatever is to a higher degree true is to the same degree "being" or "existence." Thus, in order for the lower levels of existence to exist at all, there must be a highest level which comprehends everything and causes all reality to be. In principle, this fourth "way" makes the ontological basis clear, upon which all the other "ways" function: the highest being, which is also necessary being, is also the ultimate cause and the first mover. The hierarchy of existence is rooted in one, pure being.

b. The Teleological Proof. The teleological ("physico-theological") proof, in distinction from the cosmological, does not depart from the mere existence of the cosmos, but from the way in which the cosmos exists (*Sosein* rather than *Dasein*).[104] This way of existence, as experience teaches us, is defined by the comprehensive dominance of a purposefulness which holds sway everywhere, that is, a *telos*. This type of functioning toward set ends or purposes is to be postulated even for irrational beings, according to Thomas and others, beings which are not even conscious of their obeying such a *telos*. On this basis, the proof is very simple: if a *telos* is at work even where a subjective *telos* is excluded by definition, then all of reality must be conditioned by a *telos* which is not in things, not in rational man, but rather which is rooted in the ultimate origin of this reality. This proof is less rigid than the cosmological. That is because it is more strongly related to human experience and is less conceptual and abstract. It is therefore also more generally illuminating. It can be found very widely in the writings of antiquity, although not always in the form of a proof, especially in Cicero,[105] and then frequently in the Church Fathers, who appeal to Psalm 104:24. Tertullian[106] is a

---

104. In *STh,* I,ii,3, vol. I, p. 14, Thomas calls it the fifth way, and thus combines the existence and the way of existence of reality.

105. *De Natura Deorum,* tr. H. Rackman (*LCL;* New York: G. P. Putnam's Sons, 1933), II, xxxvii, 93–95, pp. 213ff.

106. *Five Books in Reply to Marcion* (*ANCL,* XVIII, p. 323, ll. 159ff.; p. 356, ll. 347ff.).

witness to it, and so is Augustine.[107] The proof's structure is not causal, as with the cosmological proof, but rather based upon analogy: just as we observe purposefulness in the details around us, and thus conclude that there is a cause, we must also conclude that there is a cause for the whole universe, since purposefulness can be universally ascertained. It is a part of the analogical character of the proof that it represents a function of the "feeling about the world" (*Weltgefühl*); the Enlightenment (at least superficially) evidenced most clearly an optimistic world feeling and therefore was most devoted to the teleological proof. It is equally clear that any weakening of such a world optimism would ultimately have to have its effect upon the proof of God which is rooted in it. The necessity of a theodicy is connected to the teleological proof, and the function of the theodicy is to demonstrate that any dysteleology is only apparently present.[108] It is a process of truly absorbing drama to see how the Enlightenment struggled with its concept of God in view of the theodicy problem, particularly when confronted quite concretely with the earthquake in Lisbon in 1755.[109] The collapse of the optimistic world feeling was one of the causes for both the emergence of the revival movement and the development of modern agnosticism.

c. The Ontological Proof. The third proof of God is fully independent of all the fluctuations of world experience and world feeling, and it is the most daring of them all: the ontological proof. Whereas we found traces of ontology in the cosmological proof, here the doctrine of being is solely dominant. Anselm has produced its classical formulation.[110] God is "that than which nothing greater can be conceived." If this is said to a man, even if he is a fool, then that than which nothing greater can be conceived is extant in his intelligence. In regard to the One about whom nothing greater can be conceived, however, it is postulated that it cannot exist solely in intelligence. For if it were solely a matter of intellect, then we must conclude that it is possible to conceive of a reality or of things which are greater than it. Therefore, that than which nothing greater can be conceived must be both intellect and reality. To put it more simply: even if everything could be conceived of as mere thought, it is impossible to conceive of God as a mere thought without conceiving of his real existence. On the other hand, man cannot conceive of anything which would be higher than God, for with such a thought man would raise himself above the Creator and depart from his creatureliness! "God cannot be conceived of as not existing."[111] When we look at Anselm's

---

107. *Confessions*, X, ch. 6 (*NPNF*, I, 144f.); *The City of God*, VIII, 6 (*NPNF*, II, 148f.).

108. The most impressive document on theodicy up to the present day is Leibniz' work, *Theodicy, essays on the goodness of God, the freedom of man, and the origin of evil*, tr. E. M. Huggard (London: Routledge & Kegan Paul, 1952 [g1710]). See also F. Billicsich, *Das Problem der Theodizee im philosophischen Denken des Abendlandes*, vol. I (Innsbruck/Wiess/München: Tyrolin Verlag, 1936).

109. See the central section of Book I, Goethe's *Dichtung und Wahrheit*, Books I-IV, ed. C. A. Buchheim (Boston: D. C. Heath & Co., 1894), p. 29.

110. "Proslogium," II-IV, *St. Anselm . . .* , pp. 7-10; see also K. Barth, *Fides quaerens intellectum; Anselm's Proof of the Existence of God in the Context of his Theological Scheme*, tr. I. W. Robertson (Richmond: John Knox, 1960).

111. K. Barth, *op. cit.*, pp. 100ff.

proof, we can ask whether or not it can be or should be developed alongside of or apart from revelation which has taken place and which has been perceived.[112] We could regard what Anselm says about this as a confession at the noetic level. In any event, it was a novelty when Descartes[113] sought to use the proof to demonstrate that the self-certainty of the knower which resides in the concept of God actually guarantees the existence of the thing being proven. It is significant that for Descartes the "ontological" proof of God is connected with the proof for the existence of the soul. The situation is different with Spinoza,[114] who conceived of God as the unity of thought and extension and in his pantheistic view rejected the idea that anything negative could be asserted of God; similarly Leibniz[115] understood God as his own cause (*causa sui*) and thus conceived of the non-existence of God as a logical contradiction. Hegel too, who takes up the ontological proof against Kant's critique of it,[116] understands the concept of the absolute as the concept of its existence.

Very early, Anselm's proof was contested by his opponent, Count Gaunilo (11th cent.). Thomas too, who was close to Anselm in many ways, rejected the ontological proof.[117] He takes what Anselm says as a proof in the sense of a logically illuminating argumentation outside the realm of revelation. But something is lacking for a genuine proof: it is not true that everyone recognizes that God is one than which nothing greater can be conceived. Therefore, what is proven here cannot possess general validity. But even if that were not so, Anselm's presupposition (that than which nothing greater can be conceived) would result merely in the existence as intellectually apprehended. In order to prove that God also exists in reality, one would have to assume first that in reality there exists something than which nothing greater can be conceived. And this is precisely what is denied by those who reject the existence of God. Fundamentally then, Thomas simply proves that Anselm's proof is not a proof at all outside of the reality of revelation.

Kant initiated his critique of the proofs of God from another direction,[118] and we must turn to it before we deal with the last two proofs. Kant has demonstrated that both the cosmological and the teleological proof in reality presuppose the ontological proof. Even if the presupposition is accepted (Kant contests it) that a Prime Mover or a World Cause which sets its purpose can be shown to

---

112. Karl Barth denies this but seems to me to underestimate the bracketing function of Platonism.

113. René Descartes, *Discourse on Method*, tr. L. J. Lafleur (*Little Library of Liberal Arts*, 19; New York: Liberal Arts Press, 1950), Part IV, pp. 20ff. (and in the French edition ed. by E. Gilson, his scholasticizing commentary on pp. 347ff.), and *Meditations*, tr. L. J. Lafleur (*Little Library of Liberal Arts*, 29; New York: Liberal Arts Press, 1951), Meditation III, pp. 20ff., and V, pp. 56ff.

114. *Ethics*, Proposition XI, in *The Chief Works of Benedict De Spinoza*, tr. R. H. M. Elwes (2 vols.; New York: Dover Publications, 1955), II, 51–54.

115. Leibniz, *Monadology and Other Philosophical Essays*, tr. P. Schrecker and A. M. Schrecker (Indianapolis and New York: Bobbs-Merrill, 1965), ch. 45, p. 155, *passim*.

116. *Die Encyclopädie der philosophischen Wissenschaften im Grundriss*, pars. 64 and 76 (Jubiläumsausgabe; Stuttgart: Fromann, 1927), VI, 68f. and 77f.

117. *STh*, I,ii,1, especially Reply to Objection 2, vol. I, p. 12.

118. Kant, *Critique of Pure Reason*, tr. J. M. D. Meiklejohn (*GBWW*, XLII, 177ff.).

be conceptually necessary, this by no means results in "the absolute necessity of a thing,"[119] that is, the existence of God as proven to be a conceptual necessity. If I conclude by means of logical deduction that there must be a God, I have not hereby proved that he does in fact exist. This proposition is only true under one presupposition and that is the assumption that what has been proven to be necessary must then necessarily exist. And that is what the ontological proof asserts! According to Kant, this is wrong! For being is "not a real predicate," but rather "merely the positing of a thing, or of certain determinations in it."[120] The concept of one hundred dollars contains no more than one hundred real dollars; nevertheless there is a fundamental difference between the concept and the real dollars. We must find these counter-arguments very flat. They certainly do not touch Anselm when he does not argue outside the faith at all. But Kant correctly pointed out one thing: all proofs of God which appear within natural theology contain a leap. They leap from the assumed necessity of something to its reality, from the intellect to the substance. And this leap is what we are really concerned with. It is what is really at stake in another matter as well: if whatever "must" exist on the basis of compelling proof does not in reality actually exist, then obviously all of our thinking is a rotating of our reason around itself! If at its highest point, regarding the thought of God, the leap from necessary existence to existence cannot be made persuasive, then our thinking as a whole has no convincing relationship to reality.

d. The Moral Proof. It is, however, questionable whether Kant was able to maintain the boldness of his critical position. He certainly deprived the three traditional proofs of God of their persuasive power. But then he proceeded to set up his own proof of God, the so-called moral proof.[121] This proof is based upon a conceptually and empirically insoluble contradiction: moral action is such according to "the law of morality, regarded as worthiness to be happy";[122] but on the other hand, "happiness" as the result of moral action is not discoverable by us in the reality in which we live. "Consequently we must assume a moral world cause (a world mover), in accordance with the moral law, in order to arrive at a final purpose for ourselves; and to the degree that the latter is necessary, to that degree and for the same reason we should assume the former: that is, that there is a God."[123]

Let us put it in other words: first, the fact that we should do certain things forces itself into view together with the "categorical imperative." Secondly, the reality in which we act morally does not seem to be so arranged that moral activity would produce either happiness or success. This leads, thirdly, to the conclusion that apparently the structure of our reality and the moral givens are

---

119. *Op. cit.*, p. 180.
120. *Op. cit.*, p. 181.
121. Kant, *Critique of Judgement*, tr. J. C. Meredith (*GBWW*, XLII, 593). See also *Critique of Practical Reason*, tr. Thomas Kingsmill Abbott (*GBWW*, XLII, 344f.).
122. Kant, *Critique of Judgement*, tr. J. C. Meredith (*GBWW*, XLII, 595).
123. Kant, *Critique of Judgement*, tr. J. C. Meredith (*GBWW*, XLII, 595 [my translation—TR]).

not in harmony with one another; otherwise, "the good people would do well," as they say. If then, fourthly, moral activity is not simply to be persisted at in isolation from the empirical structure of reality, there must be a power which has established the world purpose which we regard as good and which is presupposed in every moral act, and which carries out that purpose (in the Kingdom of God, as Kant expresses it). Now, Kant makes every effort to demonstrate that this proof, in contrast to all the others, does not claim to possess theoretical truth but rather is valid "merely for the practical employment of our reason."[124] That does not alter the fact, though, that here—on another level, but with no less urgency— the same thought pattern is used as in the other proofs of God. If moral activity and reality are not to be hopelessly disparate, then there must be a moral world mover, and therefore he does exist. The proof of God here has no other function than it otherwise does: the unknown entity whose existence is to be proven is ultimately the one without whose existence the proof would never have been undertaken.

e. The Proof e consensu gentium = from the Consensus of All Peoples. In order to complete the picture we mention lastly the proof *e consensu gentium.* It is based upon the fact that there is something like the recognition of the numinous in all nations, even among those totally without culture, as was noted with astonishment in the days of antiquity. By way of this fact, by means of a proof by probability, the conclusion is drawn that an idea which is present among all peoples, for the most part without any reference to one another and independent of their level of civilization, must be valid as a kind of original given. This proof, which we find as early as Cicero[125] and which was advocated in the early Church by Lactantius, (c. 240-c. 320)[126] received little attention during the period of Scholasticism (it seemed to lack the abstract precision they liked), but was taken up again by Calvin,[127] and generally thereafter. Among contemporary writers, Martin Kähler[128] held this proof to be the only "religious" one, in contrast to the more theoretically conceived proofs. In point of fact, the advantage of this proof may be that it is basically not a proof at all. The concept of God is as little a necessary result of this approach as the rising of the sun in the east is proven *e consensu gentium.* We have to know about God from some other source in order to find in the consensus of all peoples more than a consensus in error.

---

124. *Op. cit.*, pp. 604ff.
125. Cicero, *De Natura Deorum*, tr. H. Rackham (*LCL*; New York: G. P. Putnam's Sons, 1933), I, xvi, 43, p. 45; *Tusculan Disputations*, tr. J. E. King (*LCL*; Cambridge: Harvard University Press, 1950), I, xiii, 30, p. 37.
126. *The Divine Institutes,* Book III, 10 (*FC,* XLIX [1964], 185–87).
127. *Institutes,* I, iii, pp. 43–47, with an express appeal to Cicero and a rejection of contemporary and Renaissance "Atheism"; see J. Bohatec, *Bude und Calvin; Studien zur Gedankenwelt des französischen Frühhumanismus* (Graz: H. Böhlaus Nachf., 1950), pp. 149ff. in regard to Calvin's *De Scandalis Quibus Hodie Plerique Absterrentur Nonnulli Etiam Alienantur a Pura Evangelii Doctrina* (1550) (*CR,* VIII, 9f.).
128. *Die Wissenschaft der christlichen Lehre vom evangelischen Grundartikel aus* (Erlangen: Deichert, 1883¹, 1905³; repr. of 3rd ed. Neukirchen: Verlag des Erziehungsvereins, 1966), par. 177; H. Engelland, *Die Gewissheit um Gott und der neuere Biblizismus* (Munich: Kaiser, 1933), p. 25.

f. Evaluation of the Proofs of God. There is little else to be said about the proofs of God than what can be said about the problem of the natural knowledge of God. But there are two characteristics which are particularly clear here, and there is a third point to make which leads beyond the limits of the problem of natural theology.

1) **No Proof for the God Who Discloses Himself in the Word.** It is obvious that all proofs of God accomplish no more than to lead up to ultimates which are located within the realm of reality which we can perceive. These ultimates can be termed the prime mover, the efficient first cause, the act which is not potency, the being which is highest and establishes everything else, the world cause which establishes its purpose, the one than which nothing higher can be conceived, and moral world mover, the meaningful substance of all religious ideas. But to the degree that something is intended to be proven here outside of the Word which has happened, which is witnessed to, which is proclaimed and heard, this proof will certainly not arrive at the One who discloses himself in the Word.

2) **The Secularization of God.** It may be said of all proofs of God (with the possible exception of Anselm's) that the reality available to us, our "world," as the existing, purposefully ordered, meaningful, moral, or religious world, is the secure entity upon the basis of which the proof is developed. In comparison, God is the insecure, uncertain entity which has to be proven. Reason is also certain; God is uncertain and requires proof. Since the "world" of man—in reality it is the ultimate upon which he founds his self-understanding—is his point of departure, then God, whenever he is the result of a proof of God, belongs to this "world" himself and is the extreme ultimate which defines all other ultimates. And since reason is the means of the proof, then God, whenever he emerges as the result, is subject himself to reason; as a logical product, he is a logical God. The living God, who bears his life and the law of his actions within himself, cannot be the result of any proof of God. This is in principle also true of the proof *e consensu gentium,* which does not avoid the variety of religious conceptions initially, but in its results arrives at their ultimate and abstract "meaning."

3) **The Positive Meaning of the Proofs of God: God as Guarantor.** In the final analysis the proofs of God do not really prove the existence of God but rather the absolute necessity of a guarantor for our "world." This is the most important thing to be observed at this point.

The cosmological proof intends to be the consequent application of the cause and effect pattern: what is must have a cause, an origin, a reason. What is intended here in reality? To be sure, many proponents of this proof have nothing else in mind than the disciplined application of the thought pattern which they need in order to cope with reality intellectually, up to its final consequences. Yet ultimately, it is the question of the reason or source, the question of the non-accidence of reality which is in the background, the question which today is usually combined with the question of "meaning." It is more than doubtful whether the existence of such a reason for the world can be proven at all. The proof attempted does demonstrate, however, that all our endeavors to ascertain reality are suspended in nothingness if there "is" not such a reason for the world. The cosmological proof of God seeks to demonstrate this reason based upon the existence of reality. This means that it proceeds in precisely the reverse fashion. For it is not possible to seek seriously the reason or ground of the world if it is not already assumed that the world is grounded, or reasonably established. The question about the ground or reason for the world (= God) in its scientific form is in fact the thesis that reality must have a ground and reason, and the idea of God is nothing other than the unavoidable dominant of this thesis, already anticipated in its presuppositions. God, as he is proven here, is in truth the guarantor for the world's being reasonably grounded, not accidental, not merely the conglomeration of arbitrarily realized possibilities. In contrast to this thesis, Christian proclamation is the message of the Creator. But the Creator is the exact opposite of the World Guarantor. The Creator upholds the world, but as its Lord. He is not its ultimate.

The teleological proof is based upon the view that perceivable reality is purposefully ordered. This view is fundamentally a "faith" proposition. The purposefulness of the world order can certainly not be convincingly proven. We already discussed the undeniable proximity of the theodicy problem to the teleological proof. In all truth, the situation is such that not the purposeful order of the universe proves the existence of God, but rather the existence of God is necessary if we do not want to have our own thinking that we are located within a meaningful reality totally confounded. Since, however, the teleological proof of God seeks to prove the existence of a world mover who gives purpose to everything on the basis of the purposefulness of the world order, it does in fact presuppose that in this world order there is no guarantee for its purposeful functioning. Thus the proof is a case of *petitio principii*, "begging the question," as is every proof of God. Here again, only the necessity of a guarantor is proven; with the term "God," a dominant factor for the presupposed ultimate "world order" is in reality set up. The proof is thus in fact a thesis of human world- and self-understanding. The Word of Christian proclamation in regard to this thesis is the message of God's providence. But this is not a guarantee. For the God who exercises providence is the free Lord of reality and only in this freedom does he address himself to this reality.

We may come to a similar position on the moral proof of God, which we shall deal with at this point. It too postulates a guarantor, although, to be sure, in Kant it is located alone in the realm of practical reason which itself has prime priority. If God does not exist, then the world falls apart: What should be and what is cannot be joined together. The real existence of a moral world mover cannot be objectively proven, even according to Kant. What is proven is that doubting man, "if he wants to think morally consequently," "*must adopt* the assumption of this proposition as a maxim of his practical reason."[129] The necessity of a guarantor for the moral world order is proven, but not his existence. The moral proof of God is again a thesis, this time the thesis of the indestructibility and universality of the moral. If there is no appropriate existence for the guarantor

---

129. Kant, *Critique of Judgement,* tr. J. C. Meredith (*GBWW,* XLII, 595, n. 1).

of this indestructibility and universality (which according to Kant cannot be perceived outside of moral behavior—we would say today that it can only be grasped "existentially"), then the moral world order is nothing other than the self-projection of ethical man into infinity. Then, in turn, the autonomous authority of the moral, its genuine character of "should" and "ought," cannot be maintained any longer, when the protective intellectual walls of morals and moral traditions have given in. Christian proclamation confronts this thesis of the moral world order, including its postulated God, with the message of the Kingdom of God. This is not the kingdom of realized good but rather the lordship of the will of God which asserts itself against evil—and that is the end of our ethical self-understanding in the revelation of the righteousness of God.

The ontological proof is subject to a similar evaluation to those already given. Even in Anselm's formulation it seeks to overcome a dilemma: if we can postulate of the ultimate statements of man (even if they do not derive from man himself) no more than an intellectual existence but not necessarily real existence, then there is no totally certain bridge between intellect and reality at all. Thus, even if it is a misunderstanding, it is not a total misinterpretation when Spinoza, Leibniz, and Descartes, each in his own way, take up the ontological proof. It clearly assists them in preventing the separation of the conscious and the extended factors (in Descartes), of thought and extension (in Spinoza), and of subject and object (generally in Leibniz) by introducing the idea of God. And it is even more significant that, after Kant's critical rejection, Hegel returned to the same solution. In truth, the "necessity" of a guaranteeing instance is obvious. Our thinking loses its ultimate validity if God does not "exist" *in re* (substantively). But for most of the proponents of the ontological proof, "God" is the code-word for "faith" in the validity of our thought, for the self-certainty of reason. The answer of Christian proclamation to this self-certainty is the message of Jesus Christ as the truth which does not confirm our truths but rather catches us in our lie in the midst of our truths and then liberates us from this lie. For what imprisons our reason is the very self-certainty which is then found in the ontological proof of God as it usually is presented.

Our last considerations have shown that the so-called proofs of God can be seen as disguised and erroneous theological propositions. It is the message of the Creator, of the Maintainer, of the Commander of the world, of the Truth, which reveals all our truths in their wrongness and corrects them, and which expresses itself in the proofs of God as long as they are no longer proofs a priori but rather statements based upon the self-disclosure of the living God which has already happened. They are thus understood not as elements of a natural theology but rather as elements of a living theology developed from the Word. In this fashion, the "proof" *e consensu gentium* gains its own significance. For God is also the God of the heathens—but he is not the meaning behind their idols.

VIII. The Authority of Scripture and the Understanding of Scripture

A. "THEOPNEUSTY"[1]

1. THE HOLY SPIRIT AND THE BIBLICAL WITNESSES

a. Word and Spirit. We spoke of the Word of God happened, witnessed to, and proclaimed. The Word happened, as we hoped to make clear, is given to us in no other form than in the Word witnessed to; the proclaimed Word in turn is based upon the Word witnessed to. Thus the Word witnessed to has a significance of a special kind. One of the results of this has been that the authority of the Word witnessed to, that is, the scriptural Word, has been a special concern of dogmatics; in fact, there has been a frequent danger that the preoccupation with the Word witnessed to might lead to the neglect of the Word happened and proclaimed.

The doctrine of Holy Scripture occupied the center of attention primarily in the dogmatics of the Reformation and post-Reformation period. At first, neither Reformation nor Orthodox dogmatics produced essentially new conceptions in this area.[2] But the traditional thinking became involved in a new movement. The reason for this was that the authority of the Church on the one hand and the significance of the "inner word" on the other hand became central problems. The doctrine of Scripture became for Protestantism the bastion against both the Roman Church and Spiritualism. In regard to both, the issue was the relationship of the Word (as the scriptural witness) and the Spirit. The Roman Church claimed and still claims today that in the word of the churchly teaching office ipso facto the Spirit is speaking. This results in the principle of tradition and the doctrine of the infallibility of the doctrinal decisions of the pope. Scripture appears then as one, and certainly the most important element of the churchly tradition. But

---

1. Apparently in order to avoid confusion with the various doctrines of inspiration which he will criticize, Professor Weber entitled this section in German "Theopneustie," making a noun out of the adjective which appears only in 2 Tim. 3:16 (see Kittel, *TDNT*, VI, 453–55). Although the English term "Theopneusty" is found only in a few reference works, I have elected to translate Professor Weber's term throughout as "theopneusty," in order to make his distinctions as clear as possible—TR.

2. One new and influential development was the doctrine of the internal testimony of the Holy Spirit; see pp. 240ff.

the Church is responsible for its exposition in its ultimately infallible decisions. This then means that *next* to the authority of Scripture there is the authority of the Church, because both Spirit and Word appear in practice next to each other, in spite of their mutual interconnection; both Spirit and Word appear in the Word of Scripture and in the Word of the Church which is the bearer of the Spirit in a concrete sense, and as such is equipped with direct authority. The Spiritualism of both Italian and German roots, influenced in part by the Renaissance and in part strongly by mysticism, shares one thing in common despite all of its variety, and that is that the "Spirit" (the divine movement and illumination which takes place in the human subject) also appears next to Scripture; in fact, Scripture is regarded as dead letters without the additional movement of the Spirit in the subject.

Under these circumstances it is easy to understand that the relationship of Spirit and Word became a dominant factor in evangelical dogmatics. But the real reason for this is not to be sought in the polemical situation but rather in the substance of the matter. If we may formulate provisionally[3] that God, who discloses himself to us in Jesus Christ his Son, is present with us in the Holy Spirit, and when we remember that the presence of God is none other than his presence in his Word witnessed to through Scripture, then it is clear that the relationship between Spirit and Word is decisive. The witness of the biblical witnesses is what it is by virtue of the work of the Spirit, and only through this work can it be recognized as what it is. The former refers then to what we call in the theological tradition the doctrine of inspiration, and the latter refers to the doctrine of the internal testimony of the Holy Spirit.

b. Origin of the Doctrine of Inspiration. The concept of inspiration became current in Latin theological terminology at least in part because the Greek term *theopneustos* (inspired by God) found in 2 Timothy 3:16, a text early regarded as particularly significant in this regard, was translated in the Vulgate with *"divinitus inspirata"* (divinely inspired). The term "inspiration" only suggests, however, the actual working of the Holy Spirit. The New Testament speaks often and expressly of such a working. Paul designates his apostolic ministry emphatically as *diakonia tou pneumatos* (ministry of the spirit, 2 Cor. 3:6, 8), his witness as a witness effected by the Spirit (2 Cor. 4:13; Rom. 15:19), the word of the prophets as pneumatic word (1 Cor. 14 *passim*), the effectiveness of apostolic proclamation as the work of the Spirit (1 Thess. 1:5, 6; also 1 Cor. 2:5 in context—not to mention the well-known texts 2 Pet. 1:21; Matt. 22:43; Acts 1:10; 4:2 or even Mic. 3:8; Ezek. 11:5; Isa. 48:16; 61:1!).

It must be remembered that the idea of inspiration already had its own history when it was taken over by theology, and that it was illuminated by views which had long been developed in late Judaism. It was primarily the valuable service of H. Cremer to point this out.[4] He demonstrated that the view of inspiration which was later adopted by the Church was not so much derived from

---

3. See the doctrine of the Trinity, pp. 349–96.
4. Schaff-Herzog, VI, 12–17.

Palestinian synagogal sources, but rather from Hellenistic Judaism.[5] It was a Hellenistic approach which understood the Old Testament witnesses as "prophets" in the sense that the human mind *(nous)* became passive in them and was set aside, as it were, for the act of witness. The biblical writers are understood here as ecstatics, a view which could be traced back to Plato.[6] This purely enthusiastic view is found primarily in the apologetic literature, in Justin,[7] more emphatically in Athenagoras,[8] and also in Theophilus.[9] It experienced a setback in Montanism in that the Church became highly critical of the pure ecstasy characteristic of that movement. But the view of inspiration which dominated the following periods continued to be Hellenistic—Cremer terms it "mechanical" in contrast to the earlier "ecstatic" view. There is no more talk of the setting aside of consciousness. In this regard, the churchly theology approaches the Jewish-Palestinian view more closely which, like Hellenistic Judaism, places its central emphasis upon the work of God or of the Spirit through the biblical witnesses, but which never speaks of the setting aside of consciousness. Nonetheless, the Church's theology in its rejection of contemporary ecstaticism saw Scripture all the more emphatically as the book authorized by the Spirit and thus miraculous in and of itself. The idea emerges very early, and is especially influential in Augustine, that the Scripture is the result of the Spirit's dictation,[10] so that the Evangelists were in effect only his hands. The frequent expression of later times that the writers were nothing other than the pen of the Spirit was already used by Gregory the Great.[11]

We can see in the theologians of the early Church their endeavor to understand the Bible purely as the manifestation of the revelation of God. However, the Hellenistic origin of their thoughts results generally in their expressing this endeavor solely in terms of the "supranatural." The biblical writers were thus the object of a miraculous procedure which could only be imagined as the setting aside of their own activity, if not of their consciousness, and thus in principle the setting aside of their character as true witnesses. In accordance with this, the difference between the Word happened and the Word witnessed to becomes blurred. But precisely at the place where that happens, the Word witnessed to becomes essentially a further and equally significant revelation following that of the Word happened, and wherever this is assumed, it is difficult in the long run to deny that the biblical revelation should be followed by a revelation in the Church, which in turn confirms and certifies the original revelation.

---

5. See also J. Delitzsch, *De inspiratione scripturae sacrae quid statuerint patres apostolici et apologetae secundi saeculi* (Leipzig: Lorentz, 1872).

6. See *Ion* in *Plato: Phaedrus, Ion, Gorgias, and Symposium with passages from the Republic and Laws*, tr. Lane Cooper (London: Oxford University Press, 1938), 534b, pp. 83f.

7. "The First Apology," *Justin Martyr and Athenagoras (ANCL*, II, Ch. XXXVI, p. 38); "Hortatory Address," *Justin Martyr and Athenagoras (ANCL*, Ch. VIII, p. 294).

8. *Embassy for the Christians* (*Ancient Christian Writers*, No. 23), tr. J. H. Crehan (Westminster, Md.: Newman, 1956), pp. 39ff.

9. *The Three Books of Theophilus of Antioch to Autolycus*, Book II, 9 (*ANCL*, III, 74).

10. Augustine, *The Harmony of the Gospels*, I, chs. 35, 34 (*NPNF*, VI, 99–101); similarly Irenaeus, *Against Heresies*, II, xxvii, 2 (*ANCL*, V, 220).

11. Migne, *PL*, LXXV, 517.

c. Medieval View of Inspiration. Since the Middle Ages up through the period of High Scholasticism accepts the Church as the obvious guarantor of the Bible, it can be understood that in this period the idea of inspiration is carefully passed along but is not a particularly vital concern. Even the detailed doctrine of Scripture with which Thomas begins his doctrine of the free gift of grace[12] is no exception (although in another regard, that of salvation-history, this doctrine states more than one would be likely to expect).

It was only at a time in which the authority of the Church came into question, in the late Middle Ages, that the doctrine of Scripture became virulent again.[13] It was able to do so because the concept of "Scripture alone" *(sola scriptura)* was not formally encroached upon in the High Middle Ages.[14] The actual reason for the resurgence of the doctrine was the nominalistic orientation of late medieval Christendom, which on the one hand led to an expansion of the Church's claim to doctrinal authority which was hitherto unknown, and on the other hand, in contrast to that, led to the attempt to establish the Bible as an independent authority over against ecclesiastical arbitrariness—but again, the Bible was looked upon here as a positivistically applicable thing. Therefore, in the conciliar circles and even more so in the oppositional groups like that of Wycliffe (c. 1329–84), they resorted back to the ancient church doctrine of inspiration with new energy, they repeatedly spoke of the biblical authors with the terms "hand," "pen," even the term "amanuensis" so frequently used later, and also "secretaries of the Holy Spirit," calling the Scriptures the *Chirographum Dei* (handwriting of God). The clearest form of this development is found in the late medieval principle of Scripture of Gabriel Biel (c. 1420–95) and already in William of Occam (c. 1300–c. 1349)—what emerges is what Kropatscheck calls "the religion of the book."[15]

d. Reformation and Orthodoxy. The Reformers arrived at the principle of *sola scriptura* (Scripture alone) from a completely different perspective than that of the theologians of the late Middle Ages, not from the point of view of formal authority, but rather of Scripture's contents. In the same way and for the same reasons that theology is dependent upon the incarnation of God, it is also dependent upon the external word. Based upon its contents, however, the Reformers arrive at differentiation within the contents of Scripture: for Luther it is based upon the concept of law and Gospel, for Calvin upon the aspect of threats and

---

12. *gratiis gratis datis* = "gratuitous graces" (*STh*, II,ii,171ff., vol. 2, pp. 1889ff., "Of Prophecy," etc.).

13. See F. Kropatscheck, *Das Schriftprinzip der lutherischen Kirche, geschichtliche und dogmatische Untersuchungen* (Leipzig: A. Deichert, 1904), I—"Die Vorgeschichte; Das Erbe des Mittelalters" (unfortunately the only volume of this valuable work to appear).

14. Kropatscheck, p. 439, appeals to Thomas, "sacred doctrine . . ." "properly uses the authority of the canonical Scriptures as an incontrovertible truth . . . ," and the authority of the "doctors of the church" is used as "merely as probable" (*STh*, I,i,8, Reply to Objection 2, vol. I, p. 6). Thomas appeals here to Augustine, *Letters of St. Augustine*, Letter LXXXII (*NPNF*, I, 349–61).

15. *Op. cit.*, pp. 444f.

promises.[16] Thus Luther made his well-known critical statements about the Epistle of James and the Revelation, so that R. Seeberg, judging on the basis of Occam's or Biel's thinking, terms Luther's view of Scripture as virtually "heretical."[17] The new contentual approach, incidentally, prevented neither Luther[18] nor any of the other Reformers from continuing to hold the traditional medieval position on the general view of inspiration as they had received it. This then made it possible for Orthodoxy, without sensing any break with the Reformation, to expand the traditional doctrine into the doctrine of *verbal* inspiration. It was not really creating a novelty: we find statements pointing in this direction as early as Clement of Alexandria (c. 150–c. 215)[19] and Origen (c. 185–c. 254)[20] and then in Jerome (c. 342–420),[21] and since the view of inspiration had long been developing the tendency to secure the totality of Scripture in its supranatural particularity, further since the whole approach remained essentially unchanged in its contents (with the exception of the Reformation), the doctrine of verbal inspiration had been anticipated and prepared for a long time. Matthias Flacius Illyricus (1520–75) had already drawn the broad conclusion that inspiration included the Hebrew vocalization,[22] and both Johann Buxtorf (1564–1629) and even more emphatically the Formula Consensus Helvetica of 1675[23] went further in this direction. The dogmaticians even attempted to describe the procedure of inspiration and distinguished between the "impulse to write," the "suggestion of the matter," and "the suggestion of the words" as three sequential acts of the Spirit. Thus, in the Age of Orthodoxy the early Church and late medieval doctrine of inspiration was thought through to its conclusion and made into the authoritative teaching of the Church.

e. The Supranaturalism of the Old Doctrine of Inspiration. The concept of inspiration is a theological means of interpretation. The biblical text does not use this concept; in a biblical sense it is more proper to speak of "theopneusty." The concept of inspiration emphasizes chiefly and generally secondary aspects, as a

---

16. *Institutes*, III, ii, 7.29.30, pp. 549–51, 575f.; see also Calvin's Sermon on Genesis 22 (*CR*, XXIII, 690), and his Sermon on Genesis 15, "Sur la Justification" (*CR*, XXIII, 757).

17. Reinhold Seeberg, *Textbook of the History of Doctrines*, tr. C. E. Hay (2 vols. in 1; Grand Rapids: Baker Book House, 1952–58), II, 301, n. 2.

18. See, e.g., R. Seeberg, *op. cit.*, pp. 296ff., and K. Thimme, *Luthers Stellung zur Heiligen Schrift* (1903; n.l.); H. Preuss, *Die Entwicklung des Schriftprinzips bei Luther bis zur Leipziger Disputation* (1901; n.l.); Paul Schempp, "Luther's Stellung zur Heiligen Schrift," in R. Widman, ed., *Theologische Entwürfe* (*Theologische Bücherei*, 50; Munich: Kaiser, 1973 [1929]).

19. *The Exhortation to the Heathen* (*ANF*, II, ix, p. 196).

20. *Commentary on the Psalms*, regarding v. 1:4 (Migne, *PG*, XII, 1081).

21. "The individual sayings, syllables, phonetic markings, and punctuation in divine scripture are filled with meanings" (Migne, *PL*, XXVI, 481, cited by H. Bavinck, *Gereformeerde Dogmatiek* [Kampen: J. H. Kok, 1895, 1906], I, 308). See also *Our Reasonable Faith* (Grand Rapids: Eerdmans, 1956) (a compendium of the 4 vols.).

22. *Clavis Scripturae Sacrae* (1567; Frankfurt: 1719), II, 646f., as cited in E. Hirsch, *Hilfsbuch zum Studium der Dogmatik* (Berlin: Walter de Gruyter, 1937, 1958, 1964), p. 314.

23. Articles I–III; E. F. K. Müller, *Bekenntnisschriften der reformierten Kirche . . .* (Leipzig: Deichert, 1903), pp. 862ff.; this was directed against Louis Cappel the Younger.

result of the influence of both Jewish and Hellenistic ideas, and it neglects the primary aspects. (1) It orients itself essentially to a procedure which the Bible is not totally silent about (we think of Isa. 6, Jer. 1:9, or Ezek. 3:2) but for the most part does not deal with. (2) It is then seeking to designate for the Bible a supranatural source but still one whose effect can be regarded as analogous to all other literary activities, which means that the character of the Bible as human witness is made secondary. Thus (3) it proceeds to set aside the individual participation of the biblical witnesses as much as possible, by viewing them as the mere hands, as amanuenses, as secretaries, as pens, even as musical instruments for the Spirit (a view already found in the Apologist Athenagoras[24]). In all of this, the concept of inspiration (4) serves the effort to ascribe to the Bible a tangible quality, inherently present in it, automatically given by its origin and means of development; that is, the certainty granted to us in faith in Christ is replaced by a security which is found in the tangible realm—"verbal-inspiredness" is Karl Barth's term, who otherwise rightly tries to distill its legitimate sides from the doctrine of verbal inspiration.[25] This whole conception appropriates a type of neutrality in regard to the contents of the Bible, and this in turn leads one to assume that the Holy Spirit can hardly have been correctly understood here.

f. The Meaning of the Doctrine of "Theopneusty." The doctrine of inspiration as we have come to know it has sought to preserve and to secure the mystery which the Community has experienced in Scripture through the centuries. It seeks to express that in our perception of the scriptural Word we are in fact perceiving the "address and claim" of God. It cannot be accused of ascribing too much to God and too little to man: there is no theology which can ascribe too much to God, if it is doing something proper. Thus, under no circumstances can we proceed to replace the doctrine of inspiration with a view of the religious genius of the biblical authors; the old doctrine of inspiration would be absolutely right in its rejection of such a position.[26] If we had to choose in our theological view of Scripture to speak either of God alone or of the witnesses alone, then our choice would be clear. But we do not in fact have to make such a choice. The worthiness of the biblical Word does not consist of its not being real human words but instead the divine Word which miraculously sets aside the human word in its humanity and historicity; no, its worthiness is to be found in the fact that God's Word in the Bible takes the form of human words which are abbreviated in their reality by absolutely nothing. If human authorship were simply to be replaced by the Spirit's authorship, then everything would proceed quite "naturally," except that the originator of this "natural" literature would be "supernatural."[27] But the real

---

24. *Op. cit.*, p. 39: "as a flautist might play upon his flute"!

25. *CD*, I,2, pp. 514ff. Barth speaks of a "secularization" of the concept of revelation, which was a result of the early Church's doctrine of inspiration (p. 519).

26. Kierkegaard wrote an essay in 1847 entitled "Of the Difference between a Genius and an Apostle," in *The Present Age*, tr. A. Dru and W. Lowrie (Oxford: Oxford University Press, 1940). This essay remains of the greatest significance for every consideration of our theme.

27. H. Bavinck, *op. cit.*, I (1895), 352, can go so far as to speak of a "deistic" character of certain views of inspiration.

miracle of the Bible is that here man's word is God's Word without ceasing to be completely man's word.

The doctrine of inspiration understands Scripture on the basis of the work of the Holy Spirit in and on man. This results in two basic aspects: first ("objectively"), that the work of the Spirit is God's own work and thus also Christ's own work, and nevertheless—as the subjective "reality" and "possibility" of revelation[28]—possesses the special reality which is appropriate to it; yet, secondly, that the work of the Spirit ("subjectively") is related to the work of man (to faith, to witness, to obedience) neither exclusively nor complementarily, but in a divinely unpredictable fashion.

We may remark on the first or "objective" aspect, that if we may view the word of qualified witnesses as the word empowered by the Spirit of God, then this means that the work by which the Spirit glorifies the Lord (John 16:14) witnesses to him (John 15:26) in such a way that the certainty of being "children of God" emerges (Rom. 8:16), takes place concretely through the word of the witnesses. This testifying word is therefore not the impartation of information, but the granting of salvation. It encounters us totally as God turns totally to us in this word. How this is to be understood in view of the difference between the Old and New Testament will have to be discussed below.[29] What is important here is the recognition that the word of the witnesses is to be regarded as the work of the Spirit in the sense that it is the word of salvation.[30] Since salvation reality is an event, the Word witnessed to is an instrument of the Holy Spirit because it makes this event real and effective for us. The result is (seen "objectively") that the scriptural Word has its special quality by virtue of its special and substantial relationship to the salvation-event, to God's history with man.

Regarding the other side (the "subjective" view): if the work of God in the biblical witnesses is a work of the Holy Spirit, then this means that the witnesses themselves are at work. It is a mechanistic or ecstatic misunderstanding of the Holy Spirit to view him as a kind of competitor to human action. He is not the mechanical "cause" of human behavior and activity; rather, he is the one who liberates us so that we can act. Therefore the faith effected by the Spirit is in fact our faith, the sanctification effected by the Spirit is ours, the Word effected by the Spirit is human words. It would be possible for the Spirit to be related to human being and activity exclusively, or complementarily, or supportively, if he were within the same "dimension" with human being or activity. Then he would be the power which functioned as the cause of human activity (which then as the

---

29. See below, pp. 278ff.

29. See below, pp. 287ff.

30. See the Heidelberg Catechism, Question 65: "Since, then, we are made partakers of Christ and all his benefits by faith only, whence comes this faith?" Answer: "The Holy Ghost works it in our hearts by the preaching of the Holy Gospel, and confirms it by the use of the holy Sacraments" (Schaff, II, 328). Also Luther, *Against the Heavenly Prophets:* "In this Word the Spirit comes and gives faith where and to whom he wills" (AE, XL, 149). In our context, the important thing is not the—highly significant—predestinarian reservation, which is made with reference to the work of the Spirit and which finds its best-known expression in the Augsburg Confession, Art. V ("when and where it pleaseth God"), but rather the fact that the Word is the gift of salvation.

thing caused would necessarily be nothing more than an effect), or which corresponded complementarily to man in his being and activity (which would result in a pantheistic understanding of the Spirit), or which assisted man in a supportive way (which would have to result in total synergism). In every event, the Spirit would not be the "Third Person of the Trinity," but rather something "divine" within the realm of what we can conceive and calculate. He would be something miraculous, but not God's wonderful miracle. The difference which obtains between the Holy Spirit and all human activity is a qualitative one. The more decisively we conceive of it, the less likely we will be to fall prey to the danger of quantifying it positively or negatively and transforming it into an inner-dimensional difference. This means in regard to the biblical witnesses that if it is God's work in the Holy Spirit which is happening through them, then that by no means implies that their humanity is excluded nor that it is being given a kind of divine coronation. They remain human beings where they are, in their time, subject to the effects of their world view; they remain the representatives of their various theologies (which neither need nor are capable of dogmatic harmonizations); they have their special place within the history of mankind and within the history of God with man; they speak and write their own language; they appear in their own names or, pseudonymously or anonymously, without them; they discover literary traditions and leave others behind them; they are subject to others working through their writings after them, or they are themselves the reworkers of traditions they have received; in every way, "nothing human is alien to them." What is special about them is not to be sought in the realm of the comparable or analogous.

When we summarize these last two points together (the "objective" and the "subjective"), we may conclude in regard to the essence of "theopneusty": Scripture as the compilation of the Word witnessed to is "breathed through by God," that is, it is God's gift and work in the Holy Spirit, because Scripture as the unabbreviated word of man is the Word in which God confronts us unequivocally, for life or for death, because he presents himself to us in it. Therefore our decision about the witness of Scripture, as it meets us in proclamation, is simultaneously our decision for or against God. Decision! The judgment about the historical, religious-historical, or linguistic "contents," about the beauty or lack of beauty of the form, about the theology of an author, and so on, is not the decision. The decision is made in light of the Word which is perceived in the words of the biblical witnesses, by virtue of the relationships of these words to the Word happened. This can be a polar relationship: the "decision" of a Christian to have his child circumcised according to Genesis 17 could be, according to Galatians 5:2, a decision against the Word happened, and the "decision" to do without certain kinds of meat in accordance with Leviticus 11 would also be such a one. The decision with which the Word witnessed to confronts us is related directly to the position of the witness within God's history with man. It is substantially the decision made possible for us in Christ and revealed to us through the Holy Spirit in Scripture, the decision for the One who became flesh, who is the middle and the turning point of the Word witnessed to.

Based upon the points presented here, the "theopneusty" of Scripture must be seen in its material relationship to the salvation-event and in its personal relationship to the person who is receiving its testimony. Scripture is empowered by the event toward which it refers and is related in the variety of its witness, and Scripture is ordained itself to be an event which is to take place within the listening community. It is effective (the context of 2 Tim. 3:16 refers to this) because the Word of God is effective (Heb. 4:12f.).

    g. The "Theopneusty" of Scripture in Its Unity and Totality. It appears that the Word of Scripture is not just one word, but rather the word of numerous witnesses. These are so different among themselves that the search for "contradictions" in the Bible, particularly since the Enlightenment, could become such a customary as well as comfortable endeavor. Can we apply what we have said about the meaning of "theopneusty"—and what in the familiar and basic text 2 Timothy 3:16 is only related to the Old Testament—to the whole of the Bible? This was what the doctrine of verbal inspiration sought to insure, encompassing the most remote verse and the single word. In doing so, it was proceeding with a certain degree of security, for the excluding of certain parts of the whole Bible would naturally mean that the totality of Scripture would be subject to human arbitrariness. Moreover, the doctrine of the verbal inspiration of the Bible was not understood as a historical, organic whole ordered around a central point, but rather as a purely quantitative totality. Thus it was necessary to interpret texts which obviously did not say the same things in the same way everywhere in Scripture with the help of hermeneutical methods which were frequently quite complex, especially the method of the manifold meanings of a Scripture text (a method which often was unconsciously applied). To put it briefly, it was only able to save the quantity of the whole by losing sight of the qualitative unity of Scripture. The supportive thesis of "real inspiration" was not able to provide any real help. Its intent was to recognize as inspired the content expressed and not the literal expression itself. But we must remember that the contradictions in Scripture are not restricted to questions of expression. There is even less help to be anticipated from Schleiermacher's view of so-called personal inspiration,[31] according to which the inspiration applies to the total activity of the witnesses (for Schleiermacher, only those in the New Testament), that is, the Apostles, and thus the written Word participates only in a total condition which is found in specific persons. Here, the variety of Scripture is traced back to the differences of the various personalities involved. We must say that, in comparison to the doctrine of real inspiration, which relativizes the written Word in relationship to the thought contents, or to the doctrine of personal inspiration, which relativizes in relationship to the personality, the doctrine of verbal inspiration has the advantage because it maintains in its own fashion the challenge to our concrete decision which the witness makes as it encounters us in certain words and statements and in no other way.

    However, the fact that the Word witnessed to is only really witness, really empowered, really capable of calling forth decision by virtue of its relationship to the Word happened, is neglected here, and instead of it, the Word witnessed to is made into a second Word-event. The miracle of the supranatural origin of

---

31. Schleiermacher, *ChrF*, §§128ff.

the biblical Word occupies a position next to the divine wonder of the Word happened. The Word witnessed to thereby loses its own profile; the Bible may then be compared to a box containing identical balls, out of which one may take whichever one desired.

"Theopneusty" must be understood in a vital fashion, even "organically," if the totality of the biblical witness is to remain in view.[32] Perhaps it would be better to say that it must grant the individual statement its special place within the totality of the biblical witness. It is only in this sense that we may speak of the "theopneusty" of the whole of the Bible.

If we then maintain the view that the individual statement possesses authority, "theopneusty," in its relationship to the totality and thus to the central point of the Bible, then we are deprived of any foundation for a security connected with the biblical statement in and of itself. But we were able to see that there never has been that kind of security in reality. Faith has never depended upon its holding on to some biblical statement or other, without any distinctions, without any relationship to the central point of the Bible. This can be clarified in a very primitive fashion when we remember that there are statements within the totality of Scripture which formally contradict faith. The sentence "There is no God" (Ps. 14:1; 53:1) is also in the Bible. We can conceive of no heresy or absurdity which could not be "proven" through senseless compilations of biblical statements. But this is not the way that faith has ever dealt with the Bible. Yet that means that faith has never had a purely mechanically effective and directly tangible grip on the concrete reality of the biblical statements, but rather it has always had to inquire about the relationship of the single statements to the whole. Since we cannot distill this whole, this unity, this factor which defines everything else out of the Bible as a kind of substratum, but rather can only perceive it in the statements, this means that we can only receive God's address to us in obedient hearing and in receptive perception of the Word being spoken to us. And this means then that when we persist in remaining attentive to the Word which constantly addresses itself to our ears and consciences, then we penetrate through it and beyond to the One and All.

h. The Differentiation of the Scriptural Witness and "Theopneusty." If we understand "theopneusty" in such a way that the authority of the word of witnesses rests in its substantive relationship to the Word-event, then we are in a position to ascertain the points of view for evaluating the differentiations of the biblical witness.

First of all, we are reminded that in the Bible we by no means find only statements which lay claim to be authoritative. Certainly there are such statements, and we could say that they are the clearest form of the word of witness— they are the prophetic and apostolic statements which directly claim to be authoritative. We think of the prophetic visions of calling which reveal that the prophet is only the possessor of authority when the Word of Yahweh comes to him. We are reminded that the "Word of Yahweh" clearly separates itself from

---

32. H. Bavinck, *op. cit.*, I (1895), 348.

the perhaps ecstatic words of the "false" prophets (as in Jer. 23:27f.; 29; Mic. 3:5ff.; 2 Tim. 3:14ff. and 2 Pet. 1:19–21 refer to the same situation). We remember that the prophet of Yahweh is silent if he does not receive Yahweh's word (Ezek. 3:22ff.) or must wait patiently until he discloses himself (Hab. 2:1ff.), just as the prophet can then be overwhelmed by this word and unable to resist it (Jer. 6:11; 20:7). It is of the essence of the profound drama of Old Testament prophecy that here are men who are emphatically themselves and yet energetically reject the assumption that the word they are speaking is their own affair. Here something of the mystery of "theopneusty" becomes perceptible, which appears in the Old Testament statements as the mystery of the spirit of Yahweh (see 1 Kings 18:12 in very tangible form or Mic. 3:8 or Ex. 11:5 or even Isa. 42:1, 5). Much of what we encounter in Paul's testimony corresponds to the picture of the Old Testament prophets. Paul, too, knows of the irresistibility of the commission (cf. 1 Cor. 9:16 with Jer. 20:9), the establishment of the commission in his calling (Gal. 1:1ff. and 1 Cor. 9:1), the authority which has been granted him thereby (1 Cor. 5:3 in context; 2 Cor. 10:1–6, etc.). He even emphasizes carefully the distinction between his own "words" and the Word of the Lord, a distinction which remained in the background with the prophets (1 Cor. 7:6, 10, 12, 25); he distinguishes tradition (1 Cor. 15:3) and what he has received (1 Cor. 11:23) from "his" Gospel (Rom. 2:16; 16:25) or "our" Gospel (2 Cor. 4:3; 1 Thess. 1:5), without asserting that one could not state of both that they were "God's Gospel" (1 Thess. 2:2, 8) or the "Gospel of Christ" (1 Thess. 3:2 and often). It is precisely because the Word is received Word for the Apostle that he must carefully distinguish between the various forms of reception; he apparently wants to insure that there is no confusing the authority of his Word with his personal authority.

We said that there are statements in the Bible which claim to have direct authority. But it would be foolish to assert that the Bible contained only such statements. The problem for the Jewish-Palestinian tradition was primarily concentrated upon the authorization of the hagiographs, especially the Psalms. Here we seldom have anything like a reflection of Torah-instruction, seldom the reflection of a prophetic word. Normally we have here the word of hymns which appears without any claim to authority, or of national songs of lamentation, or individual laments, or calls of distress or of thanksgiving—the forms are well known. The Word is spoken of, for instance, in the praise of the law (Ps. 19:8 and Ps. 119). But where is the Word here? In order to maintain its grasp upon the authorized Word, the synagogue developed the concept that the Psalms (and the other recognized hagiographs) were the work of prophets, and this idea is expressly received in the New Testament (e.g., Acts 2:30; Matt. 27:35) and apparently assumed in the general designation of the Old Testament as "The Law and the Prophets." The churchly tradition has generally followed along this line. But we cannot deny that there are statements all through the Bible which are nothing other than personal expressions—we think of the "confessions" of Jeremiah, of the numerous personal reports which are to be found in the New Testament epistles, of the forced self-defense of Paul, for example, in 2 Corinthians. How is the Word of God to be perceived here? In the laments of the Psalms, in the confessions of Jeremiah, or in the hymns, God is not the one speaking, but the one spoken to. And we think of Job, the one spoken to under such struggle, doubt, and incomprehension. No one would conceive that he were hearing God's word directly in Jeremiah 20:14ff.; here rather the despairing word of man is heard, foolish, struggling against God, and requiring his forgiveness! Such statements must be a constant stumbling block for a rigid concept of inspiration. And in reference to preaching, for which a great deal is at stake at this point, this means that such texts cannot be dealt with lightly, and there is an immense number of them to cope with. But what if, instead of proceeding on the basis of a rigidly held immanent inspiredness of all biblical texts, we endeavor to find the relationship of such texts to the totality and thus to the middle of the Bible, going along point for point, inquiring, perhaps even seeking answers in vain? Is not then the hymn the real reaction of the election of Israel and thus the word of witness? Does not then every lament point to the one who was accused, and every word of liberation spoken from the condition of the accused point to the One in whom God has liberated us? Is it not the greatness of the Bible that in its very form it is not exclusively "Word" but also always "answer"? And does not this circumstance demonstrate that God's Word does not hover somewhere above man but rather has become man, "flesh"?

At this point we will only suggest another profound differentiation of the biblical Word: it is the difference between the Old Testament and New Testament witness, the noticeable difference between law and Gospel (both within the New Testament as already in the Old), between claim and address, the difference then between promise and fulfillment. But we must deal with all of these themes in greater detail elsewhere.[33] If the Bible were a book without a middle point, then the differences implied here would be nothing less than the contrast between two "religious" total systems, and thus both the New and the Old Testaments would become ununderstandable. We shall have to consider the fact that this middle point is also the turning point, that is, that it is not a concept so much as an event. But we must say this much already: it is only in relationship to this middle point and turning point that the Bible has unity, only in this relationship do the message of law and of Gospel gain their meaning, only from this middle point is the promise recognizable as promise. And here again, nothing can be gained with a rigid concept of inspiration. On the contrary, it must make the incredibly tense movement to which the Bible testifies necessarily obscure and thus block the way to the understanding of the Bible.

Finally, we should refer to a differentiation of another kind altogether. It is well known that the Bible contains not just statements which deal directly with man's relationship to God and God's activity toward man. It also contains a wealth of statements about the state of the world and of man, reports about various "profane" historical events, statements about "nature," which all could make it difficult for contemporary man to get into the Bible. It has become virtually a truism that the Bible is not a textbook of secular history or of biology. This could be taken to mean that the statements we are now referring to would have nothing to do at all with the real substance of the Bible and thus could be excised without difficulty. But that is not the case. This can be seen in the struc-

33. See pp. 287ff.

ture of the creation accounts. The "world view" of both the first and the second creation accounts is obviously that of a specific historical situation and has a recognizable relationship to the Babylonian tradition especially. But the way in which the accounts are designed does not derive directly from these given circumstances, but rather from a definite kerygmatic view. The same can be said of the historical approach of the Deuteronomist. We do not gain the "pure" kerygma of such textual groups merely by the excision of the world-view elements. We do not gain it either by turning to the ancient view, also espoused by Thomas Aquinas,[34] that the biblical authors were exercising condescension in that they adhered to the simple and unanalyzed thought forms and imagery of their day. There is, to be sure, something to this view. The Old Testament's understanding of nature precludes any thrusting out beyond the boundaries of what was then commonly accepted. The Old Testament does not seek to provide explanations for everything or to give reasons based upon the ultimate givens, but rather it remains within the structures of unanalytical thought. However, the reason for this is that the Old Testament does not look for God in the depths of the given but rather in his lordship over the given, and thus it does not tend toward penetrating the depths. And that is an essential characteristic of the biblical message. We cannot begin with a static truth and then assume that the Bible translates it condescendingly into an unanalytic view. Rather, it is part and parcel of the theology of the Bible that it only thinks in the realm which is implied in the idea of a condescending accommodation. And that means that we do not have in the many world-view statements of the Bible, which we cannot accept, an element which can be replaced or set aside, but rather we have before us here the *historical* form of the witness. We are not intended to accept the historical form but the witness itself, but this witness in its historical form, which we must interpret. We can also not simply accept the witness as it stands and without interpretation, but we must understand it in its relationship to the "central point" of the Bible.

The three forms mentioned in which the biblical statements reveal that they may be differentiated are easily recognized even by one not scientifically trained. A view of inspiration which ignored the concrete aspects of the historical situation of the biblical statement and of its author would be unacceptable on the basis of the simple observations which we first brought up. It would certainly not be able to cope with the results of the most painstaking historical research. But these are not the problems which are at stake here. It will have to suffice for us that the differences in the various biblical testimonies, which are obvious to everyone, are only capable of harmony with the proposition of "theopneusty" when we remember that this proposition is stating nothing other than this: the word of the witnesses has its authorization and its orientation point in the Word happened, the Word-event.

2. THE INTERNAL TESTIMONY OF THE HOLY SPIRIT

a. The Nondemonstrability of the Word. The proposition of the "theopneusty" of the Holy Scriptures states that the origin, measure, and point of ori-

---

34. "Condescension," *STh*, I,lxx,1, Reply to Objection 3, vol. I, p. 347.

entation of the Word witnessed to is the Word happened. However, this Word happened is not available to us independently. Formally, we have here a cyclical argumentation. The fact that the Word witnessed to, the scriptural Word, is the Word of God by virtue of its relationship to the Word happened is not objectively provable. That means that we do not have a self-evident criterion which would make this proposition illuminating to everyone. Even a static doctrine of verbal inspiration does not possess such a criterion. The history of the problem demonstrates this assertion: even the proponents of a static doctrine of verbal inspiration, and particularly they, have felt that they could not do without the citation of external criteria. That is, they have supported the absolute uniqueness of Scripture with quite secular arguments: they have cited the great antiquity of Scripture, the undamaged condition of its textual tradition, and so on, thinking that such theses could support their central thesis of the purely pneumatic origins of Scripture. However, as this support became gradually more and more indispensable in Orthodoxy, it was proven that the basic thesis (the verbal inspiration of the Bible) was not really believed in, but rather looked upon as one proposition among others by virtue of its certification from other sources. Thus it was a theorem which was as strong as the weakest of its necessary supports. The frequent attempts today to demonstrate that at least the Gospels are, in general, historically reliable reports of the historical salvation-event would be significant in our context if they were intended to assert historical reliability as a criterion for the authoritative validity of the scriptural Word. This would mean that the relationship of the Word witnessed to to the Word happened would be understood in analogy to that of a historical document to the historical event which it intends to cover. But this would in fact be a shifting of the problem because the historical contents can only be termed "Word-event" not by virtue of themselves but by virtue of their Word-character, that is, their character as a revelational event. This approach certainly does not do away with the "horrible broad chasm" which Lessing saw opening up; the question as to how any kind of historical fact, regardless of its reliable testimony, should be final revelation, is not solved here.

There is no general criterion for measuring the Word witnessed to as God's Word. There is also no general criterion which would serve to demonstrate the Word-character of the Word happened. If there were such a criterion, this would mean that revelation could be recognized through that which was not revelation.

Therefore, God's Word can only be recognized through God's Word. The circular argument we initially mentioned is unavoidable.

b. The Doctrine of the Testimony of the Spirit. Nevertheless, faith can certainly state how it comes to its perception of the Word witnessed to as the Word happened, that is, of both as God's Word. It can do so only within its own sphere of expression: it can only witness to what has already been witnessed to; it cannot take up a position outside of the witness it perceives, and certainly not above that witness. It can only state that and how it has perceived the testimony which created it, that is, which made faith to begin with, the testimony which broke through all the contradictions. And this cannot be done by merely absolutizing the "experience" had with the Word of witness. Rather, the "experience" is understood upon the basis of the testimony which has been perceived. God is the

One at work in the Holy Spirit, not only when the Word is heard, but also in the fact that this Word calls forth response from us. This is what is meant when, since Calvin, we have spoken of the internal or arcane testimony of the Holy Spirit.[35]

It is no more than a historical question whether Calvin meant to name, in his reference to the inward or secret testimony of the Holy Spirit, another instance next and in addition to the contentual "self-authentication" of Scripture. Paul Althaus has pointed out the danger of thinking along these lines,[36] and we must admit that Calvin occasionally moves close to the edges of this tempting and "enthusiastic" possibility. But it is just as certain that he withstood the temptation. The controversy with Spiritualism revealed that he referred back to Scripture upon the basis of the testimony. It is only in my hearing the witness of the Holy Spirit that I know that God is speaking to me in Scripture; yet only in Scripture do I experience what God's address to me is: the evidence of Scripture and the evidence of the Spirit are "identical,"[37] and thus the circular conclusion just arrived at is again unavoidable. The testimony of the Spirit can never be an independent criterion over against the self-evident Scriptures.[38]

The doctrine of the inward testimony of the Holy Spirit in both its detailed form and in the central position which Calvin ascribed to it is the only really new development which Reformation theology produced in regard to the establishment of the authority of Scripture. For his explication, Calvin does not appeal to the

---

35. *Institutes*, I, vii, especially Sections 4 and 5 (pp. 78ff.). The basic thesis is that "credibility of doctrine is not established until we are persuaded beyond doubt that God is its Author. Thus, the highest proof of Scripture derives in general from the fact that God in person speaks in it." If our consciences are then to proceed in the best possible way, they must see that "we ought to seek our conviction in a higher place than human reasons, judgments, or conjectures, that is, in the secret testimony of the Spirit." This testimony is more "excellent than all reason. For as God alone is a fit witness of himself in his Word, so also the Word will not find acceptance in men's hearts before it is sealed by the inward testimony of the Spirit. The same Spirit, therefore, who has spoken through the mouths of the prophets must penetrate into our hearts to persuade us that they faithfully proclaimed what had been divinely commanded" (thus far Section 4, pp. 78f.). Therefore: ". . . those whom the Holy Spirit has inwardly taught truly rest upon Scripture, and that Scripture indeed is self-authenticated; hence, it is not right to subject it to proof and reasoning" (Section 5, p. 80). The origin of the doctrine of the testimony of the Spirit should probably be sought in Luther (see *WA*, 30, II, 688).

36. P. Althaus, *Die Prinzipien der deutschen reformierten Dogmatik im Zeitalter der aristotelischen Scholastik* (Leipzig: Deichert, 1914; Darmstadt: Wissenschaftliche Buchgesellschaft, 1967), p. 211.

37. P. Althaus, *op. cit.*, p. 212.

38. Cf. Calvin, *Institutes*, I, vii, 2, at the conclusion (p. 76). On the relationship of the self-evidence of Scripture to the contingency of Scripture see, above all, K. Heim, *Das Gewissheitsproblem in der systematischen Theologie* (Leipzig: Hinrich, 1911), pp. 256ff., and then *passim*.

On Calvin, see especially S. P. Dee, *Het geloofsbegrip van Calvijn* (Kampen: J. H. Kok, 1918), pp. 114ff. and W. Krusche, *Das Wirken des Heiligen Geistes nach Calvin* (Göttingen: Vandenhoeck & Ruprecht, 1957).

On the whole problem, see O. Ritschl, *Dogmengeschichte des Protestantismus* (4 vols.; Leipzig: Hinrichs, 1908–27), I, 62ff. and Richard Rothe, *Zur Dogmatik* (Gotha: F. A. Perthes, 1863[1], 1869[2]), pp. 140ff.

Church Fathers (contrary to his general custom). The doctrine of the testimony of the Spirit makes clear that the Reformation doctrine of Scripture has its ultimate roots in a new encounter with the Scriptures, with God in the Scriptures. From a certain point of view, David Friedrich Strauss is certainly right when he terms the doctrine of the testimony of the Holy Spirit the "Achilles' heel of the Protestant system."[39] For it asserts nothing less than that there is no "objective" guaranteeing of the authority of Scripture, which results then in the situation that Protestant theology is defenseless when its "scriptural principle" is attacked. It did consider it possible to defend human faith in the Bible, but it had to leave the proving of divine faith alone with the One who testifies to himself in the Word of Scripture.[40]

The meaning and scope of the doctrine of the testimony of the Spirit depends upon our understanding the Spirit as God's spirit, as the Spirit of Christ, as the Holy Spirit.

c. *"Subject" and "Object."* In order to make clear what is meant by this, we must consider the following.

The doctrine of the inward testimony of the Holy Spirit, at least in the form in which it was taken over by Orthodoxy, was then connected with the traditional concept of verbal inspiration.[41] We were constrained to make clear that this doctrinal form, which was developed very long ago, was dealt with critically by the Reformation, and was renewed and expanded by Orthodoxy, suffers from a kind of supranaturalism which cannot be accepted. The Spirit of God here is an objectively overwhelming power, and it causes the Holy Scriptures to emerge directly as literature set aside from all other literature and thus recognizable in their character as supranatural. If the doctrine of the testimony of the Spirit is built into this system, then the testimony is transformed into the subjective affirmation of what is objectively already present.

Thus we must ask whether there is not a decisive error built into this whole

---

39. *Die Christliche Glaubenslehre, in ihrer geschichtlichen Entwicklung und in Kampfe mit der modernen Wissenschaft dargestellt* (2 vols.; Tübingen: C. F. Osiander, 1840–41), I, 136.

40. See K. Barth, *CD*, I,2, p. 537: The "Protestant Church and doctrine" must be willing to face the question about who it is who is testifying to the divinity of the scriptural testimony, "because there at its weakest point, where it can only acknowledge and confess, it has all its indestructible strength." See also R. Rothe, *op. cit.*, pp. 152ff., and Theo Preiss, *Das innere Zeugnis des Heiligen Geistes* (*Theologische Studien*, Nr. 21; Zollikon: Evangelischer Verlag, 1947).

41. It is not possible to affirm that Calvin himself was responsible for this. The careful research done by W. Krusche (see note 38 on p. 242) clearly indicates that one "cannot make Calvin into the father of the old Protestant doctrine of inspiration" (*op. cit.*, p. 197). This against O. Ritschl, *op. cit.*, I, 63ff.; Reinhold Seeberg, *op. cit.*, II, 395f. (in German, IV, 566ff.), and R. H. Grützmacher, *Wort und Geist; eine historische und dogmatische Untersuchung zum Gnadenmittel des Wortes* (Leipzig: A. Deichert, 1902), p. 76. On the whole theme in Calvin see the dissertation by D. J. de Groot, *Calvijns opvatting over de inspiratie der Heilige Schrift* (Zutphen: N. V. Nauta, 1931). The opposing view: J. A. Cramer, *De Heilige Schrift bij Calvin* (Utrecht: A. Oosthoek, 1926) (here Calvin is called "the father of scientific biblical criticism"!).

construction. Is this really the decisive hallmark of the Bible: that it is, objectively, a book which represents a unique situation in terms of its literary genesis and its literary character? Or is not the uniqueness of Scripture that it proclaims in a unique way (as the Word witnessed to) a theme which is absolutely incomparable: God for man, that is, God in Christ? And is this theme in some way "objective" the way other themes are "objective"? If this were so, then we would have to approach the Bible the way we do any other book. The important thing would then be whether or not "something" about this book or in this book would persuade us. We would encounter the objective Bible in our subjectivity. To put it more sharply: this Bible, containing revelation in itself or of itself, would be encountered by us as we ourselves, as those who were prepared to be persuaded, or not prepared to be persuaded. Now if we do become persuaded, one of two things will have happened: either the given object will be transformed into a subjective insight, or we will have given the necessary affirmation to what was objectively given through our subjective decision, perhaps assisted by the Holy Spirit. But what is the situation if what we called "objective" up to now, were by its very essence also and simultaneously "subjective"? That is, what is the situation if the theme which moves the Bible and to which the Bible testifies were essentially this, that God in Jesus Christ is our God? What would be the situation if the Bible, instead of being the communication of all kinds of things, were essentially reaching out to us? Then it would no longer be possible to regard it as an "objective" supranatural book, laden with potential revelation; in this extreme "objectivity," really beyond the limits of what the word means, in this reaching out of the Creator to his creature, the Bible is necessarily "subjective." As the proclamation of this reaching out of the Creator to his creature, the Bible intends that the creature will respond. To put it another way, if the Bible is the Word of God witnessed to, then the answer in regard to this Word is not something secondary or independent, but rather the second work of the very freedom of God which is testified to for us in Scripture. Or to put it even another way and more pointedly, if the testimony of the biblical witness is the work of God's freedom and that means of the Holy Spirit, then the response to it is also the work of the freedom of God. Both Word and response stand in the same divine freedom. Both Word and response are pneumatic.

The "testimony" of the Spirit encounters us in the testimony of the witnesses. But it really encounters us in this witness. In God's Spirit, who enters into analogy to "our" spirit (1 Cor. 2:11) and who gives witness "with" our spirit (Rom. 8:16), the polarity of object and subject is overcome.

Therefore, the testimony of the Spirit cannot compete with the witness of Scripture, as though Scripture were only God's Word to the degree that it "speaks to us." It has been said that the testimony of the Spirit states nothing "genetically," that is, about the origin of the scriptural witness.[42] This is certainly true when we understand the term "genetic" in the sense of the doctrine of inspiration in the 17th century. The testimony of the Spirit does not tell us that the Bible is

---

42. R. Rothe, *op. cit.*, p. 154; A. Twesten, *Vorlesungen über die Dogmatik der evangelischen lutherischen Kirche* (2 vols.; Hamburg: F. Perth, 1826–37 [1838⁴]), I, 433.

a supranatural book. But this testimony does tell us that the witness of the witnesses is not that of a random group of individuals seeking to gain our assent. Here the personal address of God confronts us, defining this witness and also relativizing it. Whoever perceives this witness is not led thereby to acknowledge the supranatural development or uniqueness of Scripture, but certainly to the humble and obedient expectation that the witness to the address and claim of God will confront him even in places and in ways where he perceives neither at the present time.

The doctrine of the inward testimony of the Holy Spirit announces the discovery that the authority of Scripture can be secured neither objectively (in the sense of the classical doctrine of inspiration) nor subjectively (in the sense of our own experience), but rather that we will only be persuaded of it when God the Holy Spirit, God in his freedom as the One who effects both our freedom and our bondage, reaches out to us through the scriptural Word. The *theopneustia* of Scripture is not a passive characteristic of Scripture but rather a vital saving activity.[43]

d. The Testimony of the Spirit According to the New Testament. In speaking of a "discovery" we must add that the Reformation doctrine only rediscovered what the New Testament itself states.[44] Theo Preiss points out with good reason that the *pneuma* in the New Testament is understood "forensically." "The Spirit is primarily a witness."[45] This is clearly attested to in Matthew 10:18ff., in the old hymn in 1 Timothy 3:16 ("vindicated in the Spirit"), and above all in Romans 8:16, or 1 Corinthians 6:11 and John 14:26; 26:13ff. What this definitely does not mean is that the believer is directed to observe his own condition which is supposed to confirm for him that the Word does apply authoritatively to him. What it does mean is that a "witness" appears who states what we, left by ourselves, could never express. We are not removed from the picture; however, certainty is not the result of what we experience but results from our perception of the testimony.

e. The Testimony of the Spirit Not a "Miracle of Certification." After all that has been said, we shall have to reject completely any attempt at replacing or expanding the old Protestant doctrine of inspiration, which connected the emer-

---

43. In the Augsburg Confession, Article V, we find the well-known statement, "For by the Word and Sacraments, as by instruments, the Holy Spirit is given: who worketh faith, *where and when it pleaseth God*, in those that hear the Gospel . . ." (Schaff, III, 10). The Heidelberg Catechism says essentially the same thing in the answer to Question 65. Both of these texts are dealing with the other side of the question we are discussing, in that they are emphasizing that the Spirit is not given without the Word. We are emphasizing here that the Word is not recognized as God's Word without the Spirit. The one conditions the other. It is significant that in the Augsburg Confession, in the Heidelberg Catechism, and in Calvin's doctrine of the testimony of the Holy Spirit, the mystery of election is highlighted: God's freedom in his Word and in the effect of his Word!

44. See T. Preiss, *op. cit.*

45. *Ibid.*, p. 20.

gence of Scripture with a miracle,[46] with a view in which the testimony of the Spirit now appears as a "miracle of certification" and thus becomes the decisive factor for us in the question of the authority of Scripture. The testimony of the Spirit lacks unambiguity just as it did after the Pentecost event, according to Acts 2:12f. We do not arrive here at a criterion which can be rendered illuminating for everyone. As far as the Bible is concerned, nothing essential can be "proven"[47] where there is no faith. But the believer is not in a position of possessing a "criterion" by virtue of the testimony of the Spirit, a criterion which would exclude any struggle or were beyond temptation. Otherwise faith would not be faith. When confronted with the testimony of the Spirit, we are certainly not given the possibility of making our decision based upon our autonomy. But we are placed in that decision which is there when we hear God's decision being attested to for us, which is the decision God has prepared for us and requires of us—and that is decision which no tangible criterion can remove or make easier for us.

f. The Re-establishment of the Original Situation. The doctrine of the testimony of the Spirit does not connect miracles with Scripture. Rather, it is the pronouncement of the profound wonder which has happened again and again upon the hearing of Scripture and which is the source of the Community's life.

In our initial encounter with it, we experience Scripture as an extremely varied collection of reports: reports about a Word given and then responded to in one way or another. A report has accomplished its purpose when it has been integrated into the total mass of our knowledge. It does not require "faith" in the sense of the Christian faith. It demands rather that degree of acknowledgment it deserves according to the criteria available for its evaluation. It does not command us to do anything. It certainly does not command us to give ourselves personally to it. This is something which can only happen in relationship to a person.

But what really happens in our encounter with Scripture is that it is not a mere report which reaches us, but rather a testimony which encounters us, the Word, and in this Word the person of Jesus Christ. And it happens—where and when it pleases God—so that we will note that it is not some random message coming toward us but the message which directly concerns us; it is not something in the past, as significant as that may have been, which is the thing reported, but rather we ourselves are at stake here. Briefly put, what happens is that the Bible in its witness makes us "contemporary" with Christ, as we might put it using Kierkegaard's terms. We cannot evade this encounter. A report can be passed over as uninteresting, and this happens again and again when the Bible is treated as a report or a collection of ideas. But when what we are talking about happens, then we are placed in the original situation in which there is no question of interest or disinterest but only of Yes or No. Wherever that happens, Lessing's profoundly

---

46. M. Kähler, *Dogmatische Zeitfragen; Alte u. neue Ausführungen zur Wissenschaft der christlichen Lehre* (3 vols.; Leipzig: Deichert, 1898ff., 1907²), states: "The historical-critical research of the Bible irrevocably destroys the prejudgment that in the Bible miraculous letters guarantee the revelation" (p. 206).

47. Calvin, *Institutes*, I, vii, 4, p. 79: "Yet they who strive to build up firm faith in Scripture through disputation are doing things backwards."

avoided "horrible broad chasm" is bridged, but not in that Jesus ceases to be "yesterday" (Heb. 13:8) but rather in that I cease to cling desperately to my own "today." That is the work of the Holy Spirit.

The testimony of the Spirit prepares for us the specific and original situation in which we are to encounter the Bible. As long as the Bible is a report or collection of thought for us, we can then maintain a partial relationship to it. That means, we can extract critically this or that section from a historical point of view; we can regard this or that part, possibly a great deal of it, as aesthetically unimpressive; we can observe with the eyes of the historian of religion and see a variety of phenomena of highly varying degrees of importance—but in that we do all that, we are not summoned to a qualified Yes or No which directly affects us. If the Bible confronts us as the Word, then the result is either faith or vexation—the encounter results in the kind of thing which happened when the Word of Jesus, of the Apostles and Prophets, had been spoken. The Word become flesh brought the crisis into the world (John 3:18, 19, 36), and this crisis (or judgment) also takes place in the work of the Spirit (John 16:8ff.). The Apostle, whose word is not Yes and No (2 Cor. 1:18), becomes in his word the fragrance of life to life for some, and the fragrance of death to death for others (2 Cor. 2:16). The establishment of the situation in which our genuine, our "existential" Yes or No happens is the work of the Spirit in and through Scripture.

Nonetheless, the specific situation in which the Word makes my Yes or No possible, in which it encounters me as judgment or grace, is not ambivalent. Yes and No, judgment and grace are not a possibility which balances out the scales, rather they are two sides of the reality of God "for us" which is disclosed to me in the Word which encounters me.

g. The Testimony of the Spirit and the Church. In the last sections we have constantly used the word "I." We have stated that this has not implied the subjectivity which in fact is there. But we must state that this "I" is not the individual person. The testimony of the Spirit is perceived by me as an "I" to the degree that I hear it through the Community or in the Community. We are not talking here about private spiritual experiences. Private existence is not specific existence. My decision develops because it is prepared for me in the work of the Spirit in and through the proclamation of the Community. The fact that this decision does not develop in response to a Yes and No but rather to an unambiguous Yes—even though this unambiguity is not always a matter of experience—is something the Community testifies to for me. The Bible could stand as a report or as a collection of thoughts without the Community. But as the Word which persuades us, it is solely the "Book of the Churches."[48] Calvin developed his doctrine of the testimony of the Holy Spirit in opposition to the thesis that the Church alone guaranteed the authority of Scripture.[49] This was completely correct: there is no sense in which the Church has power over Scripture. But the power of Scripture does not confront us abstractly but in the Church, not in individual isolation in

---

48. M. Kähler, *op. cit.*, I, 2nd ed., pp. 85ff., in reference to Luther.
49. *Institutes*, I, vii, 1–3, pp. 74–78.

which the I remains without a Thou and thus cannot really be a genuine I. This brings us to the threshold of a broad problem to which the next section will address itself.

B. HOLY SCRIPTURE AND THE CHURCH

1. THE CANON

a. The Authority of the Church as the Exercise of Obedience. Holy Scripture does not confront us in an unmediated fashion. It could well happen that a person would come upon the Bible without having experienced any mediation he was aware of. But this possibility is based upon the mediating labors of the Church. We would not have the Bible without the Church. Just as certainly as the Bible is "the book of humanity," to use Martin Kähler's terms,[50] and just as certainly as its history has become a part of history and mankind and cannot be separated from it anymore, it is also certain that this history has its central and constant point in the effect of Scripture "upon the Church."[51]

The question to be dealt with, then, is the undeniably close relationship between Holy Scripture and the Church—what kind of relationship is it?

We may assume, on the one hand, that the Church has always been the bearer of the Word witnessed to, and that on the other hand it has always been receiving it. Yes, it can also be assumed that the Church on the one hand has laid claim to authority and that on the other it cannot understand this authority as being separate from the Scriptures.

We shall deal with the way in which the Church receives the Word witnessed to when we discuss the Orthodox doctrine of the "attributes of sacred Scripture" *(affectiones Scripturae sacrae).*[52]

Here we shall turn to the question of the sense in which the Church has a claim to authority in its presentation of Scripture.

Reformation theology dealt with this question, above all in the controversy with Johannes Cochlaeus (1479–1552)[53] and Johann Eck (1486–1543),[54] particularly in terms of the question whether it was true that the authority of the Church was what effected faith in the Gospel. Roman polemics appealed particularly to Augustine's statement, "I should not believe the gospel except as moved by the authority of the Catholic Church."[55] The opposing question is simple: who will guarantee for me that Scripture is God's Word and that it will not deceive me? Does not Scripture require some kind of tangible authority which will stand for

---

50. *Op. cit.*, I, 2nd ed., pp. 219ff.
51. *Ibid.*, pp. 266ff.
52. See pp. 263ff.
53. *De authoritate ecclesiae et scripturae LL., duo* (1524); *De Canonicae scripturae et Catholicae Ecclesiae Autoritate, ad Henricum Bullingerum* (1543); this latter writing refers to Heinrich Bullinger's *De scripturae sanctae authoritate* (1538); see also P. Barth and W. Niesel, eds., *Calvini Opera* (1926–36), sel. III, 65.
54. *Enchiridion locorum communium adv. Lutherum* (1532).
55. *Against the Epistle of Manichaeus Called Fundamental* (*NPNF*, IV, 131).

it?[56] This was the question to which Calvin responded with his doctrine of the testimony of the Spirit.[57] But that was not the only answer. Calvin first refers to Ephesians 2:20: The Church is founded upon the foundation of the prophets and apostles, and "if the teaching of the prophets and apostles is the foundation, this must have had authority before the church began to exist."[58] Calvin finds that Augustine's statement only intends to say that unbelievers are impressed by the unanimity of the Church's testimony, but later, when they believe, they no longer are dealing just with men but with God's own witness, which Augustine says quite clearly in the same writing.[59] Here Calvin speaks for all of the Reformers.[60]

Of the Orthodox, J. Wolleb formulated it particularly well: "The witness of the church is first in time; that of the Holy Spirit is first in nature and efficacy. We believe the church, but we do not believe on account of the church; the Holy Spirit must be believed on account of himself. The witness of the church shows the 'what'; that of the Holy Spirit, the 'why.' The church gives reasons; the Holy Spirit convinces. The witness of the church offers opinion; that of the Scripture, knowledge and assured faith."[61]

If we set aside the circumstance, which has little bearing here, that the voices from Calvin's side (including Wolleb) ascribe somewhat "more" to the empirical Church than does Luther, we can see a common thrust here. The Church is not able to establish the trustworthiness of Bible nor to certify it because it itself is dependent upon the Bible for its own establishment and certification. The Reformation view of Scripture excludes any authority of the Church next to or even over Scripture. Scripture authenticates itself,[62] because God authenticates it through his Spirit.

It will now be quite clear that with the Reformation view of the self-authentication of Scripture a totally new understanding of the Church itself emerges. The Church is not understood primarily as the divinely established teaching institution but rather as the place of proclamation. This does not exclude the institutional side of the Church.[63] But it does exclude the view that the Church is the

---

56. See M. Schmaus, *Katholische Dogmatik* (5 vols.; München: M. Hueber, 1948ff.), p. 92: "The Scripture as the Word of God written and guaranteed through the Church."

57. *Institutes*, I, vii, 4f., pp. 74ff.

58. *Institutes*, I, vii, 2, p. 75.

59. Augustine, *op. cit.*, pp. 135f.

60. Regarding Luther see P. Althaus, *Die christliche Wahrheit* (2 vols.; Gütersloh: Bertelsmann, 1947), I, 197, with reference to Luther's discussion of the Sermon on the Mount (Matt. 7:15ff.): "Beware of false prophets"; "Therefore God must say to you in your heart, This is God's Word, or otherwise it is uncertain" (*WA*, 30, III, 260); also on *Galatians* (Gal. 1:9; AE, XXVI, 56f.).

61. *Christianae theologiae Compendium* (1626), ET in *Reformed Dogmatics*, ed. and tr. J. W. Beardslee III (New York: Oxford University Press, 1965), p. 33.

62. *Institutes*, I, vii, 5, p. 80.

63. The widespread view that the Church is to be understood either as an institution ("salvation institution" or "institution for grace") or as a fellowship does not correspond to the New Testament view, especially not to the description of the Church as "Body." Unfortunately E. Brunner (*The Misunderstanding of the Church*, tr. H. Knight [Philadelphia: Westminster, 1953]) scarcely led us beyond the traditional polarities, but simply identified "body" and "communion of persons" (a better ET would be "personal fellowship"; *op. cit.*, p. 74—TR) and contrasted them to the concept of institution. The Church as the body of Christ is characterized, however, both by an event nature and the nature of constancy.

distributor and administrator of a supranatural treasury of salvation which is given over to it for its sacral disposition, with the Scripture belonging to this treasury of salvation.

b. The Empowered Presentation of the Scriptures by the Church. In spite of all this, it is still true that the Scriptures are presented to us by the Church. And this is not meant in the sense that the Church is merely the mediator of the Bible which would be available even if it were not present. Rather, the Church is the bearer of the proclaimed Word,[64] and—this is the special theme to be dealt with here—the Church made the decision about which writings belong to the canon of Holy Scripture. In both of these functions the Church is unquestionably exercising authority. In the canon it is not just offering certain writings as possible texts for readings and sermons, but it is determining that these writings are authoritative. How can it do that? In making such authoritative statements does it not demonstrate that it is the instance which really informs us that the Scriptures are authoritative and how they are authoritative, in spite of the whole Reformation critique discussed?

We have here indeed a "circle." If it is true that the Church understands itself in its total existence on the basis of Scripture, then it is also true (1) that the Scriptures in question are none other than the ones canonically determined by the Church, and (2) that the authority of these Scriptures is only believed in within the Church.

This "circle" rests upon another one which then surrounds it: the ground of faith is God's self-disclosure, but God's self-disclosure is only acknowledged and recognized in faith. Faith possesses no inherent and objective ground, but only the one which again is only recognized in faith. All attempts to break out of this circle are doomed to failure. If the proposition of the correlation between faith and the Word is true, then there is no way to establish faith aside from the perceived Word or to establish the perceived Word outside of the process of perception which happens in faith. Since, however, faith is an event within the Church, the correlation between faith and Word results unavoidably in the "circle" which we alluded to above.

But this correlation does not imply that it is faith which first makes the Word into the Word. On the contrary, it implies that it is the Word which makes faith into faith. Within the correlation the principle remains valid that faith comes from hearing (Rom. 10:17). Luther's famous statement that "trust and faith of the heart alone makes both, God and idols,"[65] is certainly not meant to imply that God were a product of our trusting and believing.

In accordance with this, we state that this "circle" cannot be broken through at any place, but it can be thought through in the reverse direction. It is correct that the scriptural Word is only recognizable by us as God's Word upon the basis of proclamation, that is, only in the Church. But it is not true that the Church and proclamation make the scriptural Word into the Word itself. The reverse is

---

64. See above, pp. 190ff.
65. *Larger Catechism*, Explanation of the First Commandment (*WA*, 30, I, 133).

true: without the Word of God witnessed to in Scripture and witnessing to itself, the Church for its part would have absolutely no authority and faith would have no foundation at all.

To be sure, the Church occupies a prior position to faith. The Church does not result from the coming together of believers. Rather, faith results from the Church, the Community proclaiming the Word. Its proclamatory function is purely instrumental. It is not based upon itself nor effective by its own strengths or merits. But as an instrument it is not only the tool through which the Holy Spirit is given, "where and when it pleases God" (Augsburg Confession, Art. V), it is also the tool of the Spirit itself and thus of Christ himself.[66] Because and to the degree that the Church's proclamation continually expresses anew the Word witnessed to (the Scriptures) by virtue of its commission, which means in the power of the Holy Spirit, it is absolutely prior to faith. The result then is that the special and unchangeable position of the Church consists of its being open to the testimony of the scriptural Word. In no sense is it autonomous, not even in the sense that at one time the "deposit of faith" *(depositum fidei)* was committed to it, including the Scriptures, and now it is supposed to administer it, to be sure, assisted by the Spirit. The Church has exactly as much authority as its exercises obedience.

c. The Character of the Scriptural Canon. Here we must turn our attention to the problem of the canon.

The word "canon" itself points to the fact[67] that in establishing a canon, the Church acknowledged the existence of a factor which confronts it, its activity, and its speech with unconditional authority. The concept of "canon" implies something obligatory, something bindingly established by someone else. If it is used in relationship to the decrees issued by synods—this usage later led to the concept of canonic law—then it refers to those things which are no longer left at one's arbitrary disposal. The application of the term to the now completed collection of New Testament writings expressed the fact that these writings, and no others, contained what was authoritative. In this case, however, the Church is not the body which makes the decision about recognition directly, as with the canons of ecclesiastical law or liturgy. Here its decision is simultaneously its acknowledgment of something which it is receiving from an authority over it.

We cannot say, of course, that these Scriptures, thus acknowledged, would have insured, "by virtue of the fact that they were canonic," "that they could later be also acknowledged and proclaimed."[68] There were in broad regions of

---

66. Heidelberg Catechism, Question 54: "That out of the whole human race, from the beginning to the end of the world, the Son of God, by his Spirit and Word, gathers, defends, and preserves for himself unto everlasting life, a chosen communion . . ." (Schaff, III, 324f.); the corresponding section in Luther is in his explanation of the Third Article, in the *Larger Catechism* (*WA*, 30, I, 190).

67. See the article by H. W. Beyer in Kittel, *TDNT*, III, 598ff. We find the term in the New Testament only in Paul (Gal. 6:16; 2 Cor. 10:13ff.; in some manuscripts also in Phil. 3:16). In Paul, it does not refer to writings. Its meaning is "standard" (Gal. 6:16) or "apportioned limits" (2 Cor. 10:13ff.).

68. K. Barth, *CD*, I,2, pp. 473ff.

the early Church many scruples about certain scriptural writings—in the East it was the Book of Revelation and in the West Hebrews which were particularly controversial. Beginning with the second century and ending with the fourth (the Easter Festival Letter of Athanasius, c. 296–373,[69] the Synods of Hippo Rhegius[70] and of Carthage,[71] and the letter of Innocent of Rome to Exuperius[72]), the Church "by authoritative decision set aside these scruples and thereby made these Scriptures canonical for large parts of Christendom."[73] But it did not freely decide what ought to be. Rather, it made its decision with bound hands and upon the basis of the criteria of apostolicity and ecumenicity, that is, what preceded that decision, and what according to its convictions had long been acknowledged as authoritative. The canonic decision of the Church is essentially its confession of the norm already given it, of the standard by which it was prepared to let itself be measured.

d. The Meaning of the Canonic Decision. The process of establishing the canon is illuminated by the fact that it took place in a period that saw the rise of the episcopal office, an office which gradually assumed authoritarian forms. The influential men in the so-called early Catholic Church certainly were not lacking in ecclesiastical self-awareness. Therefore, it is all the more important that they did not weaken the counter-authority, which the canon was, did not try to incorporate it into their own authority which was so virulent at the very same time in the major dogmatic decisions being made, but rather they let it stand. There must have been a mighty power in these Scriptures whose canonicity the Church established, if the Church, so confident of its present claim to authority and possession of truth, acknowledged these Scriptures as its valid source of guidance.

The canon is an expression of the fact that the Church is only in reference backward actually the Church.

In establishing the canon, the early Church was referring back to the witness of the Apostles. Whether or not it made the right decisions from a literary-historical point of view can be put aside here. It is certain that it was convinced that apostolic authority rested in those Scriptures which were finally canonized. The controversies on the canon revolved around the well-known cases where the question of apostolicity was in doubt. In linking itself to the canon, the Church was stating that any given time it wanted to be no other Church than that of the Apostles. The canon guaranteed tangible apostolic succession.

It must now be pointed out that the New Testament witness as set forth in the twenty-seven books of the canon has itself a double back-reference. First, it

---

69. Migne, *PG*, XXVI, 1176.

70. Denzinger, pp. 39f. (par. 92).

71. J. D. Mansi, *Sacrorum Conciliorum Nova et Amplissima Collectio* (31 vols.; Florence, 1759–98; Graz: Akademische Druck- u. Verlagsanstalt, 1960–62); see also C. J. Hefele, *A History of the Christian Councils, from the original documents*, tr. H. N. Oxenham (5 vols.; Edinburgh: T. & T. Clark, 1896), II, 400.

72. Letter of Innocent I (401–17) to Exuperius, Bishop of Toulouse, Feb. 20, 405 (Denzinger, p. 42 [par. 96]).

73. W. G. Kümmel, "Notwendigkeit und Grenze des neutestamentlichen Kanons," *ZThK* (1950), p. 302, in a debate with K. Barth.

presupposes the authority of the Old Testament. The Old Testament canon ("the Scripture," "the law and the prophets," "Moses and the prophets") became the prototype of the New Testament. This was still a matter of debate in the primitive Christian period. The synagogue did not make its final decision until around 100 A.D., and this decision differed significantly in content from what the Septuagint offered in the realm of Hellenistic Judaism, although the early Church took this latter decision over completely in spite of the protests of Jerome. But all of that does not alter the fact that the New Testament witnesses refer back to an Old Testament "Scripture" which in general was available to them.[74] For a long time the honorary title "Scriptures" was reserved for the Old Testament. The Community of the age of salvation accepted the traditional books, under a new basic aspect but with a backward reference which was undebated.

Secondly and primarily, the New Testament witnesses refer back to the salvation-event, to the "Word happened." None of them sees himself as a champion of his own ideas. They are all dealing with the event of the resurrection, of the cross, of the words and work of Jesus. "In the oldest communities of Christians there is an authority next to, and unconsciously much higher than, the law and the prophets. . . . This new 'canon' is Jesus Christ."[75] Their relationship to this event is not that of the historian but that of the witness. As Jews they were well aware of what is implied by the juridical function of the witness. But they also knew that their own witness, precisely because it was not a "new Word" next to that to which they were testifying, participated in the valid authority of that to which they were testifying (Luke 10:16; 1 Thess. 4:15, as well as the general formula *logos tou kyriou*, the word of the Lord). They also knew that the Lord himself speaks in the Spirit (2 Cor. 3:17 also contains this thought), and the pneumatic prophetic word held for them as much authority as an important testimony as did the traditional Word of the Lord (see John 14:26; 15:27; and 16:8ff: the Word effected by the Spirit is authoritative; the Spirit works what the Lord works). Thus, the way in which this backward reference is accomplished becomes a differentiated procedure in which rational memory, teaching transmission, pneumatic word, ecstatic hearing (2 Cor. 12:9!), integration of tradition into the special situation of proclamation and of Community life at any given time and place, and theological reflection on the kerygma all appear in a variety of ways together and alongside one another. But it cannot be doubted that the New Testament witnesses are in essence to be identified with their historical and kerygmatic backward reference to the Christ-event, as they express themselves in the "Gospel" and "Apostolicity" of the developing canon and in the unified duality of worship usage (Epistle and Gospel) which is still current in many churches up to today. In receiving the canon, the Church not only acknowledged the fact that it only is the Church by virtue of its hearing of the witness of the "first witnesses," but it also ranked their Word as being always and everywhere superior to it. We would

---

74. In 1 Cor. 2:9 Paul cites, using the customary formula for such citations, an apocryphal writing, according to Origen, the Ezra Apocalypse.

75. A. Jülicher-E. Fascher, *Einleitung in das Neue Testament* (7th ed., 1931), p. 457; ET: *An Introduction to the New Testament*, tr. J. P. Ward (London: Smith, Elder & Co., 1904 [from the 3rd and 4th German eds.]).

agree with Martin Kähler that this Word is "the charter for the Church's preaching as Church-establishing preaching"[76] which the Church recognized and acknowledged as valid with its canonic decision—but it is the charter for "church-establishing preaching" which is new at every place and time in history. Therefore, Paul Althaus is right when he finds the "exclusive significance" of "the original witness" given "with the genuine historicity of Jesus and of the activity of God in him."[77]

The existence of the canon is a symbol of the fact that the Church never exists just as it is at a specific time, nor merely in its power or weakness, wisdom or foolishness, but rather that the Church is what it is in this "backward reference." To that extent the canonic decision is as much a decisive as a merely declaratory act. However, this declaration was an act of ecclesiastical responsibility and thus a risk—although those involved scarcely would have sensed this. For the Church rendered its own authority to the authority of the recognized Scriptures which it received and which preceded it.

e. Open or Closed Canon? In view of what has just been said, we must now ask whether the canon is necessarily closed, whether the decisions made in the process of canonic establishment are necessarily unrevisable.

The question requires a limitation. Naturally it cannot imply that the Church would have reason to "canonize" some writing or another, regardless of how significant it were, which had been produced within it in dependence upon the biblical witness. It is well known that Luther said on occasion that Melanchthon's *Loci* of 1521 "deserve not only to be immortalized, but even canonized."[78] But he could not have meant with this that the scriptural canon be expanded. When Paul Althaus concludes that "Church writings" could be "inspired by the Holy Spirit,"[79] this by no means leads to the result that the canon would be extended to include such writings, even if their significance in the actual life of the Church were much greater than, say, that of the Epistle of Jude.

If the question of open or closed canon is to be dealt with at all, then it can only be done from the point of view that the canon has been and is viewed by the Church as its historically given "counterpart," and that the Word witnessed to in the canon is a witness which is distinctive and distinguishable from its own proclaimed Word.

Based upon this understanding, it is then easy to assert as a pure hypothesis that if primitive Christian testimonies were to become available to us now which were proven to be in content an element of the witness which is superior to the Church, even though unknown until now, this would result in an expansion of the canon. In regard to the newer manuscript discoveries[80] or of the so-called agrapha,[81] there is no immediate occasion to discuss this point.

---

76. M. Kähler, *op. cit.*, I, 2nd ed., p. 23 and often.
77. P. Althaus, *op. cit.*, I, 178ff.
78. In *The Bondage of the Will* (AE, XXXIII, 16).
79. *Op. cit.*, I, 190.
80. We are thinking especially of the London Papyrus Egerton (see *Theologische Blätter* [1936], cols. 34ff.; F. W. Schmidt and Joachim Jeremias).
81. See Joachim Jeremias, *Unknown Sayings of Jesus*, tr. Reginald H. Fuller (2nd Eng. ed.; London: S.P.C.K., 1964).

The opposite question, whether the scriptural canon is the Church's prior witness in its totality and under all circumstances, or whether there could not be a reduction of it under certain conditions, cannot be put aside in view of both the past and the present. To answer it will mean that we shall have to discuss the problem of the canon in a more detailed fashion than was necessary in the points covered up to now.

It is remarkable that impulses toward a reduction of the canon emanated from the "Church of the Word": The Reformation, for the first time in centuries, dealt with the canon not as a fundamentally closed and inalterable entity. This happened in remembrance of the early Church problems which are best known from the three groups of Scriptures in Eusebius,[82] but the Reformation thinkers were also impressed by the objections raised by Jerome (c. 342–420) and Rufinus (c. 345–410) against the validity of the Old Testament Apocrypha;[83] they were also directly influenced by Erasmus (c. 1466–1536),[84] who was joined by Cajetan (1469–1534);[85] however, they were primarily influenced by their own proclamation.

The exclusion of the Old Testament Apocrypha from the canon is common to all Reformers.[86] The Reformation decided for the Palestinian canon of the Old Testament over against the Hellenistic. Today we are scarcely aware of this decisive line, drawn more sharply on the Reformed than on the Lutheran side but fundamentally common to both. For the sixteenth century it meant a break with more than a thousand years of almost uncontested canon tradition.

But as is well known, the New Testament canon was not beyond debate. Luther's position on James, Hebrews, Jude, and the Apocalypse is well known from his introductions to the various books[87] and was the reason that these four

---

82. *Ecclesiastical History*, III, 25 (*FC*, XIX, 178–80). The "homologoumena" are the four Gospels, Acts, Paul's Epistles (including Hebrews), 1 John and 1 Peter, and possibly the Apocalypse. The "antilegoumena" are the rest of the so-called Catholic Epistles. Spurious *(nothoi)* among others are the Acts of Paul, the Shepherd of Hermas, and possibly also the Apocalypse (which Eusebius thus lists twice because he is registering opposing views here).

83. On this, see Calvin, "Acts of the Council of Trent, With the Antidote," in *Tracts and Treatises in Defense of the Reformed Faith*, tr. H. Beveridge (Grand Rapids: Eerdmans, 1958), III, 70f.

84. K. A. Meissinger, *Erasmus von Rotterdam* (2nd ed. Berlin: A. Nauck, 1948), p. 189; R. Stählin, "Erasmus," *RE*, 3rd ed., V, 439; Hebrews is not by Paul, James could scarcely be apostolic; Ephesians is Pauline in thought but not in style.

85. Hebrews, James, Jude, and 2 and 3 John do not belong to the canon in the full sense, but 2 Peter does; see the article by T. Kolde in *SH*, II, 338f., and Jülicher-Fascher, *op. cit.*, p. 542.

86. According to the Septuagint, the canon included Judith, Tobias, the Books of Maccabees, Jesus Sirach, and the Wisdom of Solomon. The Palestinian canon was supported by Jerome (Migne, *PL*, XXVIII, 1242).

87. See the prefaces to the books of the Bible in the German edition translated by Luther (AE, vol. XXXV). The famous statement about James is found at the conclusion of the introduction to the New Testament. In contrast to the major books of the New Testament (John, Romans, Galatians, Ephesians, 1 Peter), ". . . that show you Christ and teach you all that is necessary and salvatory for you to know . . . ," ". . . St. James' epistle is really an epistle of straw . . . for it has nothing of the nature of the Gospel about it" (*Preface to the New Testament* [AE, XXXV, 362]). Similar statements are found in the preface to James and Jude (German originals in *WA Deutsche Bibel*, 6; also in W. Heinsius, ed., *Luthers Vorreden zur Heiligen Schrift* [Munich: Kaiser, 1934]).

books appeared in the September Testament of 1522 without numbers, thus out-side of the series. We find other voices speaking against the full canonicity of these writings in early Lutheranism. In Duke Christoph of Württemberg's Confes-sion of 1561, the French Reformed are virtually accused of regarding James, Jude, and the Apocalypse as canonic in the French Confession of Faith of 1559 (Art. 3).[88] Martin Chemnitz (1522–86), appealing to early Church positions, rejected not only Eusebius' "antilegomena," but also Hebrews and the Apocalypse, together with the Old Testament Apocrypha.[89] Johann Gerhard (1582–1637) did not dis-tinguish between canonic and apocryphal scriptures but rather in a broad thematic scheme between the New Testament books of the first order and of the second order.[90] A writer as late as Andreas Quenstedt (1617–88) distinguishes between proto-canonic and deutero-canonic writings,[91] while David Hollaz (1648–1713) finally drops the distinction as being irrelevant.[92]

On the Reformed side a much greater restraint is evident quite early. It has, of course, frequently been pointed out that Calvin's strange silence about the Apocalypse must have been for reasons similar to Luther's, which at first were strong and then later weaker.[93] Calvin also agrees with many of his contempo-raries that Hebrews is not Pauline. He is skeptical toward 2 Peter and looks upon it as at most a work of a disciple of Peter, under his tutelage.[94] But he draws virtually no conclusions regarding canonicity. Neither Zwingli's reservations re-garding the Apocalypse, nor Oecolampadius' (1482–1531) clear restraint toward the "antilegoumena" echoing Erasmus, nor even the sharper utterances of Wolf-gang Musculus (1497–1563)[95] left any traces in later dogmatics. Especially Lu-ther's rejection of James was criticized very early from the Reformed side.[96]

We face the important fact that in the sixteenth century the Church of "tradition" fundamentally and finally established the canon of Scripture,[97] while

---

88. O. Ritschl, *Dogmengeschichte des Protestantismus* (4 vols.; Leipzig: Hinrichs, 1908–27), p. 131.

89. Martin Chemnitz, *Examination of the Council of Trent*, tr. F. Kramer (St. Louis: Concordia, 1971–   ), I, 185–87.

90. *Loci communes theologici* (1610ff.), ed. F. R. Frank (1885ff.), I, Chs. 9 and 10.

91. *Theologia didactico-polemica* (Wittenberg: 1685, 1691), p. 235.

92. *Examen theologicum acroaticum* (1707, 1750), p. 131.

93. Compare the two different prefaces of 1522 and 1530; the latter brings an inter-pretation of the book along the lines of Church history or history of heresies.

94. Calvin, *The Epistle of Paul the Apostle to the Hebrews and the First and Second Epistles of St. Peter*, tr. W. B. Johnston (Grand Rapids: Eerdmans, 1963), p. 325.

95. *Loci communes* (1564), p. 175: "The judgment of the ancients gives cause for me to be less strict with those books than with the other Scriptures. Caution is necessary lest we should subject ourselves to false authority" (ET by J. Man [London, 1563], not available to TR). Thus in A. Schweizer, *Glaubenslehre der evangelischen reformierten Kirche, dar-gestellt und aus den Quellen belegt* (2 vols.; Zurich: Orell, Füssli, 1847), I, 215.

96. Zürich Confession of 1545, in E. F. K. Müller, *Bekenntnisschriften der Refor-mierten Kirche . . .* (Leipzig: Deichert, 1903), p. 155; Calvin, *Commentaries on the Catholic Epistles*, tr. J. Owen (Grand Rapids: Eerdmans, 1948), p. 276—the preface to James; newer translation: *A Harmony of the Gospels, Matthew, Mark, and Luke (III), and the Epistles of James and Jude*, tr. A. W. Morrison (Grand Rapids: Eerdmans, 1972), p. 259.

97. The decision on the canon is formed alongside the decision of ranking Scripture and Tradition together as of equal importance (Council of Trent, Session IV [Denzinger, pp. 244–46 (pars. 783–86)]).

conversely the Church of the "Word" dealt with the canon as an open entity, but then was generally satisfied with its factual state. The only consequence then of the Reformation objections was in fact the devaluation of the Old Testament Apocrypha. For the New Testament, they were only a passing episode. It was then Johann Salomo Semler (1725–91) who raised the canonic problem anew, but now from a completely different perspective.[98] Thus the Reformation did not effect much more than raising anew the issue of the possibility and admissibility of a change in the canon.

To define our position, we have to proceed from the fact that the formation of the canon goes back to decisions of the Church. According to Reformation doctrine, these are subject to reexamination. To absolutize the limits of the canon would be to absolutize an element of tradition.

f. No Fundamental Derivation of the Canon. If the decisions on the canon are to be reexamined, then we must ask, According to what criteria? The otherwise valid and general principle that the Church's doctrinal decisions are to be tested by Scripture would not seem at first glance to be applicable for the canon. But no other conclusion is possible: the Scriptures which belong to the canon can only be recognized on the basis of these Scriptures themselves. The French Confession of Faith teaches in its fourth article,[99] so very sharply criticized by Althaus,[100] that the knowledge of the canonic character of the Scriptures and thus the sure rule of our faith does not result so much from the unanimous thinking of the Church, but rather "by the testimony and inward illumination of the Holy Spirit, which enables us to distinguish them from other ecclesiastical books upon which, however useful, we cannot found any article of faith." In doing so, this Confession can only mean substantially that the canonicity of canonic books logically precedes the ecclesiastical establishment of this canonicity. They *are* canonical and demonstrate themselves as the precedent witness over the Church through the testimony of the Holy Spirit. The testimony of the Holy Spirit can only be that which manifests itself in Scripture itself. It is not distinct from the self-authentication of Scripture. This was the view of Luther,[101] who was already showing traces of what later would become the doctrine of the inward testimony of the Holy Spirit. All of this, however, thrusts us back to Scripture itself when we ask, What is canonical?

---

98. *Abhandlung von der freien Untersuchung des Kanons*, ed. H. Scheible (Gütersloh: Mohr, 1967). According to Semler, the canon belongs to the realm of "public religion" as established by the Church and thus has no definitive function for "private religion." It has a legal, but not a religious significance. See also Hermann Strathmann, "Die Krisis des Kanons der Kirche," *Theologische Blätter* (1941), cols. 295ff., and the general presentations by E. Hirsch and K. Aner.

99. Schaff, III, 361f. In spite of its dependence upon the French Confession, the Belgic Confession is somewhat more careful in Article V; see Schaff, pp. 386f.

100. *DchrWahrheit*, I, 189f.

101. R. Seeberg, *Lehrbuch der Dogmengeschichte* (4 vols.; Graz: Akademische Druck- und Verlagsanstalt, 1953), IV/1, 418, quotes Luther: "Whoever bears the testimony of the Holy Spirit in himself will be confirmed, with regard to the Gospel, that it is indeed the Gospel" (*WA*, 30, II, 688, not in ET of Seeberg).

The formation of the canon in the early Church parallels our thinking in that only occasionally does a theological program become visible in it. Certain motives begin to emerge in the Muratorian Canon:[102] to be canonical, a writing must be demonstrated to be apostolic and intended for the whole Church. It cannot be strictly proven that the canon, as Harnack thought,[103] was a carefully planned measure intended to secure the unity of the Church which was jeopardized by the arbitrary canonic selection made by Marcion. Eusebius is still really reporting on what is current; this is the only way to explain why he names the Apocalypse twice under different rubrics. Of course, there were very early attempts made to demonstrate the structural necessity of certain parts of the canon. Irenaeus[104] tried to give reasons for the Gospels' being four in number. But in general, there is no dogmatic reflection upon the given state of the canon. The canon simply developed, and it was only those writings which did not find unanimous agreement (and which were probably only known to certain regions of the Church initially) which finally required a decision in the fourth century. It is true to the course of the canon's history to say, as has frequently been done, that the necessity of its form cannot be proven abstractly. By its very essence, the canon is more a fact than the realization of a theological concept.

g. Criterion of Originality. But certainly this fact can be seen in definite criteria which it itself reveals. Although the formation of the canon did not proceed according to a plan, it was by the same token not an arbitrary or capricious act. The decisive criterion throughout is seen to be apostolicity (the Church faced the issue of canonization only in regard to the New Testament, since it accepted the Old Testament). For the New Testament, canonical meant apostolic. The concept "apostolic" was understood in a slightly expanded sense: it included the apostolic disciples like Mark and Luke. The strong effect of the apostolicity criterion can be seen in the complicated history of the canonization of Hebrews, which was accepted as the view gained general recognition that it was written by Paul.

The criterion of apostolicity expresses what we have stated above about the precedence of the biblical witness over the witness of the Church. The formation of the canon proclaimed that the Church did not understand itself to be autonomous. The canon calls the Church back to its origins. Thus, without curtailing

---

102. W. G. Kümmel, *loc. cit.*, pp. 288f. The text of the Muratorian Canon can be found in E. Preuschen, *Analecta, Kürzere Texte zur Geschichte der Alten Kirche und des Kanons* (2 vols.; Tübingen: J. C. B. Mohr, 1909–10), II, 27ff., and in *Rouët de Journel, Enchiridion Patristicum*, Nr. 268 (see also *Oxford Dictionary of the Christian Church*, p. 934).

103. A. von Harnack, *History of Dogma*, tr. N. Buchanan *et al.* (7 vols.; London: Williams & Norgate, 1896), II, 38ff. Harnack himself admits on p. 45 that only conjectures can be made; further, *The Origin of the New Testament*, vol. 6 in *New Testament Studies*, tr. J. R. Wilkerson (London: Williams & Norgate, 1925), pp. 30ff.; *Marcion; das Evangelium vom fremden Gott* (Leipzig: J. C. Hinrichs, 1921), *passim*. For a critique, see W. G. Kümmel, *loc. cit.,* pp. 285ff.

104. Irenaeus, *Against Heresies*, III, xi, 8 (*ANCL*, V, 293). There could not have been more nor less than four Gospels. This is, incidentally, the first time we see Ezek. 1:5 (cf. Acts 4:7) applied speculatively to the four Gospels (lion, steer, man, eagle).

any of the essentials we can understand the criterion of apostolicity as the criterion of originality. Those Scriptures are canonic which express the origin of the Church, which in turn requires acknowledgment at all times. And even penetrating criticism cannot deny to the early Church the recognition that it "brilliantly discharged its task."[105] It possessed a singularly confident eye for what was original in the profusion of Scriptures handed down. This is all the more important since many, even decisive elements of the writings it canonized were not theologically current in the Church; it continued to preserve the Pauline writings, although Paul had become progressively inaccessible to it. The Church did not edit Paul's texts at those places where its own theories were disputed by him. We find, for example, no substantially significant variants for Galatians 2:11ff., although here the predominant view of the unity of the Apostles and the rapidly growing conception that Peter had the prior rank were both refuted in plain language. One does not need to share the tendencies of Theodor Zahn, which are not altogether free of a perverted conservativism, in his fundamental work on the history of the canon,[106] in order to come to the conclusion that, generally seen, the early Church well knew how much careful faithfulness it owed the originals, which were in fact prior to it.

The early Church identified originality with apostolicity and viewed the latter in a literarily objectified form. When the Reformers turned their attention from the formal and objective aspects of the matter to the question of the content of proclamation, they prepared the way for a deepening and broadening of the substance of the apostolic criterion, which on literary terms was still generally accepted.[107] This could then lead to a material criterion for canonicity: Luther's much discussed "What inculcates Christ."[108]

h. Criterion of Coherence. This then leads to the assertion of another criterion alongside that of originality: the proper Scriptures state, show, and promote basically the same thing. They all agree with one another. Scriptures which do not accord with this criterion, which we shall call the criterion of coherence, cannot be original and thus cannot be apostolic. According to Luther, this cri-

---

105. Jülicher-Fascher, *op. cit.*, p. 503: "In fact the tact with which the Early Church acted in the production of the New Testament is in general admirable; it performed its task brilliantly." Similarly M. Dibelius, *Geschichte der urchristlichen Literatur* (Theologische Bücherei, 58; Munich: Kaiser, 1975), p. 12.

106. *Geschichte des neutestamentlichen Kanons* (2 vols.; Erlangen: Deichert, 1888–92). Regarding Zahn's major thesis, according to which the canon was generally authoritative by 100 A.D., see A. Harnack, *Das Neue Testament um das Jahr 200* (Freiburg: Mohr, 1889). A newer work, J. Leipoldt, *Geschichte des neutestamentlichen Kanons* (Leipzig: Hinrichs, 1907–08).

107. In the "Preface to the Epistles of St. James and St. Jude" we read, "Whatever does not teach Christ is not [yet] apostolic, even though St. Peter or St. Paul does the teaching. Again, what preaches Christ is apostolic, even if it be Judas, Annas, Pilate or Herod who does the preaching" (AE, XXXV, 396). Here the material postulate of originality is fully dominant.

108. In the "Preface" just cited: "All the genuine sacred books agree in this, that all of them preach and inculcate Christ. And that is the true test by which to judge all books, when we see whether or not they inculcate Christ" (AE, XXXV, 396).

terion did not contradict the Old Testament,[109] in that law and Gospel are also related to one another. If the Old Testament is a "law book,"[110] then the New is a "book of grace" and they belong together. Luther was not blind to the fact that the Old Testament is not just a "law book," nor the New Testament just a "book of grace." This distinction applies to the major thrust of each. On the Reformed side, but we could also mention Melanchthon here,[111] the thought was then expanded that in the Old and New Testaments there is the same "economy," the same "covenant," but in different "dispensations."[112] Thus it is easier to subsume the Old Testament under the criterion of coherence. Conversely, Luther was not able to reconcile either James or Hebrews with this criterion, and one gets the impression that Calvin, together with Luther, Zwingli, and Oecolampadius, was so reserved toward the Apocalypse because it provided so many impulses for the "enthusiasts" and thus seemed to endanger the unity of the scriptural witness as the proclaimed witness.

If the Reformation, as we have seen, made use of new approaches for the formulation of criteria for canonicity, then it must be added that Orthodoxy did not continue this development. The initial emphasis upon the substance of the criterion of originality gave way very soon to a return to historicizing objectivity. Both Martin Chemnitz[113] and even more so Johann Gerhard[114] wrote treatments of the historical origins of the biblical writings and thus approached what later was to become the discipline of "Introduction to the Old or the New Testament." What we have called the criterion of coherence also underwent a certain transformation. If the canonic Holy Scriptures are equipped with the passive property of inspiredness, then there is in principle an agreement of all their statements. Then the Reformation principle that Scripture interprets itself leads, when it is dehistoricized and deprived of its relationship to proclamation, to the view that the Scriptures contain one total doctrine, more or less passively residing in the work. This is generally truer of Lutheran High and Late Orthodoxy than of Reformed Orthodoxy. The latter possessed in its federal theology, to the extent that it was able to assert itself, a schematic which made it possible to understand the agreement of scriptural contents, already presupposed, in a salvation-historical fashion and thus to see them in a kind of movement. Thus its exegesis remained more strongly in tension and in movement.

i. The Criterion of Originality in Question. It was necessary to discuss the criteria of canonicity in order to arrive at the elements of the modern position on

---

109. See the "Preface to the Old Testament" (AE, XXXV, 235–51).

110. *Ibid.*, pp. 236f., "a book of laws."

111. See the section "The Difference Between the Old and New Testaments . . . ," in the *Loci* of 1521 (*LCC*, XIX, 120ff.) but primarily in the third edition of 1543–59 (*CR*, XXI, 800f.); Stupperich, II/2, pp. 440ff.

112. For more detail see below, pp. 287ff. Fundamental for this was Calvin, *Institutes*, II, ix–xi, pp. 423–64.

113. Martin Chemnitz, *op. cit.*, pp. 49ff.

114. *Op. cit.*, I, Chs. VIff.—incidentally, this is a rich storehouse of contemporary scriptural erudition, from both the Evangelical and Roman sides!

the problem of the canon. This problem was initiated with Johann Salomo Semler and leads up to the contemporary development of this issue.

There are two facts which are virtually uncontested in modern theology. First of all, the criterion of originality is broadly untenable to the degree that it is to be understood in a historicizing manner, that is, that it means that only the Scriptures actually written by the prophets and the apostles are validly canonical. The extent of the material that is authentic in a literary-historical sense can be judged very differently. But it is no longer disputed that there are in the canonical Scriptures other elements of tradition in profusion alongside the prophetic and apostolic material. Secondly, the share of the Church both in the development of the canonical Scriptures and in their acknowledgment as canonical is incomparably greater than was earlier assumed. The historical and as such the clearly delimitable priority of the (prophetic and) apostolic writings in relationship to the Community can no longer be reasonably maintained. This is also true of the acknowledged authentic apostolic parts of the New Testament insofar as Paul refers to traditions already passed on to himself (e.g., 1 Cor. 11:23ff.) or takes over and cites already extant material, particularly liturgical materials (e.g., Phil. 2:6ff.).

These two facts now necessitate a fresh consideration of the traditional criterion of originality.

j. The Criterion of Coherence in Question. The criterion of coherence also requires new consideration; it was already used by some of the Reformers with some degree of criticism.

Newer exegesis, which does not presuppose the agreement of all biblical writings but rather investigates the individual statements, the writings, and the writers against the background of their various thought structures and proclamation, has found within the canonical Scriptures many more gaps, leaps, and contradictions than someone like Luther could have suspected. None of the Reformers would have viewed as acutely as does, for example, Ernst Käsemann the difference, even contradiction, between 2 Peter and the rest of the New Testament.[115] But matters are not left with just a sharper examination of the Eusebian "antilegoumena." The Lukan writings are the object today of vigorous attack in some quarters,[116] relating not only to their quasi-apostolic origins but also to their contents. In the process, F. C. Baur's reservations are driven to their extreme

---

115. "Eine Apologie der urchristlichen Eschatologie," *ZThK* (1952), pp. 272–96. Käsemann raises the canonic problem directly when he asks at the end of his article (p. 296): "What is the state of a canon in which 2 Peter has its place as the clearest witness to Early Catholicism?"

116. P. Vielhauer, "Der 'Paulinismus' der Apostelgeschichte," *EvTheol* (1950/51), pp. 1–15 and Götz Harbsmeier, "Unsere Predigt im Spiegel der Apostelgeschichte," *EvTheol* (1950/51), pp. 352–68; Wilhelm Anderson, "Die Autorität des apostolischen Zeugnisse," *EvTheol* (1952/53), pp. 467ff. (against Vielhauer and Harbsmeier); Hermann Diem, *Das Problem des Schriftkanons* (*Theologische Studien*, Heft 32; Zollikon: Evangelischer Verlag, 1952); Hermann Diem, "Die Einheit der Schrift," *EvTheol* (1953), pp. 385–405; H. Conzelmann, *Die Mitte der Zeit; Studien zur Theologie des Lukas* (Tübingen: J. C. B. Mohr [Paul Siebeck], 1954).

consequences. Even within the Pauline writings great chasms are being opened up. The Pastorals appear as documents of developing Early Catholicism (like the Lukan writings and 2 Peter), and between the chief Pauline letters on the one hand and Ephesians and Colossians on the other strong differences are claimed (in spite of general agreement on their common elements), and to a certain extent are made convincing. The results of exegesis may never be taken to be final. But even with the most cautious judgment of exegetical labors and their own great self-critique, the fact remains that the criterion of coherence can no longer be assumed to be fulfilled.[117]

It is remarkable that the impact of all the factors stated has led hardly anyone to demand that the canon be newly formulated. The first reason for this is probably the fact that historical research, which has been the source of the major insights involved in the contemporary discussion of the problem, does not work with the category of a binding canon, because it is *historical* research. It sees the individual writings and interprets them as source material about the primitive and early history of Christianity. It views the canon as a historically developed collection without any obligatory force.[118] The theological problem of the canon first became visible in historical research since this research again began to see itself as a theological discipline.[119] Secondly, the virtual lack of any desire to alter the canon can be traced back to the circumstance that very broadly speaking a "canon within the canon" has been predominant in dogmatics, consciously or unconsciously. Thus, even in the area of dogmatics the problem of the canon has only become acute again in recent times.[120]

It should be clear that the questioning of the canon which results from historical-critical exegesis relates less to the Reformation position than to the

---

117. The criterion of coherence is basically the theme of Ernst Käsemann's lecture, "Begründet der neutestamentliche Kanon die Einheit der Kirche?" *EvTheol* (1951/52), pp. 13–21. Also in Käsemann, ed., *Das Neue Testament als Kanon; Dokumentation und Kritische Analyse zur gegenwärtigen Diskussion* (Göttingen: Vandenhoeck & Ruprecht, 1970). For a positive response, see R. Bultmann, *Theology of the New Testament*, tr. K. Grobel, (2 vols.; New York: Scribner's, 1951–55), II, 142. See again E. Käsemann, "Zum Thema der Nichtobjektivierbarkeit," *EvTheol* (1952/53), pp. 455–66, and especially: "Whoever asserts the identity of the Gospel with the canon condemns Christianity to syncretism or to the hopeless controversy of the confessions" (p. 462). It should be expressly stated that E. Käsemann never suggests that the extant canon be altered. What he is concerned about is that one not have God "tangibly enslaved in the New Testament canon" (*EvTheol* [1951/52], p. 20).

118. This is the line to be found in, e.g., H. J. Holtzmann, *Lehrbuch der historisch-kritischen Einleitung in das Neue Testament* (2nd ed.; Freiburg: J. C. B. Mohr [Paul Siebeck]; 1886² [g1892³]), p. 186, and W. Wrede, *Ueber Aufgabe und Methode der sogenannten neutestamentlichen Theologie* (Göttingen: Vandenhoeck & Ruprecht, 1897), p. 11: "Whoever . . . views the concept of the canon as fixed submits himself to the authority of the bishops and theologians of those (scil. Early Church) centuries. Whoever does not acknowledge this authority in other things . . . acts consistently when he questions it here." Cited in W. G. Kümmel, *op. cit.*, p. 279.

119. It must be stressed that the contemporary statements of men like E. Käsemann and P. Vielhauer are made from quite different standpoints than those of Holtzmann or even of Wrede.

120. See especially K. Barth, *CD*, I,2, pp. 473ff. and 597ff.; and Paul Althaus, *op. cit.*, I, 178ff.

historicizing and objectifying approach of some parts of Orthodoxy. The Reformation reveals impulses toward understanding the criterion of originality in a contentual way, that is, in terms of the canonic Scriptures' actual proximity in contents to the substance to which they witness. The Reformation also indicates a tendency toward dealing with the criterion of coherence in a critical way. If we were to begin again with the Reformation and proceed on the presupposition that the canon is "open" in principle in that it received its limits through the Church's fixing them, the question could now be raised as to whether we ought not seriously to consider an alteration in the canon.[121]

k. The Factual Closedness of the Canon. While it can certainly be affirmed in principle that a change would be possible, the question raised should probably be negated in point of fact, because a change of the canon, at least under the current circumstances, would shift the meaning of the canon in a most dangerous way. My arguments for this closing assertion will form the conclusion of this section.

1) **The Contingency of the Canon.** We have understood the canon as the authoritative instance set up as criterion for the Church in its life and work. That there is this authoritative instance and that it has this actual form can only be explained historically. There was the fact of the apostolic preaching and the Church's tradition which took it up, responded to it, carried it further, and even developed it further. Then there was the fact of the Scriptures which were left to us essentially by the first Christian century, or were affirmed by that Church in the case of the Old Testament writings. Then finally, there was the fact of the canonic formation done by the Church which in turn is related back to the facts of the primitive Christian writings and the accepted and affirmed Old Testament. The historical contingency of the canon, or better, of the Scriptures assembled in it, corresponds to the contingency of the salvation-event to which these Scriptures bear witness.

2) **The Canon and Proclamation.** In the canon the Church has recognized and acknowledged these Scriptures as the authoritative instance set before it. What is the function of this instance, then? The early Church sought, at first, and this as early as the second century, to distinguish between those Scriptures which were to be read in the worship assemblies (canonic), and those which were not. In doing this, the Church, it would appear, followed a distinction already practiced in the synagogue. In customary practice, then, the reading would have been associated with the sermon. Later the view became dominant that the canonic Scriptures were those upon which theological doctrine is to be based. This is the authoritative view of the Council of Trent, and it results in the mention of tradition, which under these circumstances certainly is worthy of mention (even if not

---

121. Of course, in this case we would have to bear in mind that every change could only take place as "an action of the Church, i.e., in the form of an orderly and responsible decision by an ecclesiastical body capable of tackling it" (K. Barth, *CD*, I,2, p. 478).

in the sense of Trent), alongside of Scripture,[122] and then later in the ruling that the standard interpretation of Scripture is the business of the Church, that is, of the Church's teaching office.[123] Doctrine thus becomes the doctrinaire self-interpretation of the Church. The criterion of coherence, of which we spoke, need not cause the Roman Church any concern. The teaching office of the Church takes care of the concordance of all doctrinal statements. In contrast, the Reformation is primarily concerned about preaching, and from that point of view one must agree with Hermann Diem when he understands the canon as the "text for proclamation."[124] But what is to be proclaimed is Christ and not doctrinal propositions. The "text for proclamation," the canon, refers beyond itself, not to the Church but to its Lord, and to him in his historicity, which cannot be separated from the witness of Scripture.

3) **No Ideational Coherence of the Canon.** If the canon is understood as the "text for proclamation" and this is the proclamation of Christ (even in the highly indirect form of the proclamation of the law), then the canonic materials cannot be subjected to an ideational criterion of coherence, conceived of as a basic principle. The ideational unity of Scripture could only be the unity of "objective" doctrine. We would then be obligated to be obedient to this in the sense of submission. And such obedience, according to the common conviction of the Reformation, would not be faith. The obedience of faith should be rendered to the canonic Scriptures in their character as the witness of faith. This witness, however, is not ideationally coherent. We are not in possession of a rationally manageable criterion in order either to prove the ideational lack of all contradictions in the canon, or conversely to remove Scriptures from the canon if the aforesaid proof cannot be brought. The gaps within canonized Scripture, as they are revealed today, are as a whole insignificant compared to the differences between the Old and New Testaments, yet these did not lead Luther to question the canonicity of the Old Testament in the Church. The only one who seriously pursued that course was Marcion, because he resolutely made his theological thesis into the authoritative criterion. Only where this happens can the criterion of coherence be used as a criterion for the elimination of the Scriptures. But wherever that does happen, our hearing of the message addressed to us is replaced by the autonomous monologue of the theologian or of the Church. This would have been the case if Luther had used his rule, "What promotes Christ," in order to eliminate writings, that is, if he had continued consistently along the path already paved in the September Testament when he left series numbers off Hebrews, James, Jude, and the Apocalypse. But he did not do that. Otherwise his "What promotes Christ" would have inexorably become a theological theory, justification would have become the correct doctrine of justification, either Pauline or

---

122. Leonhard Hutter, e.g., discusses in Loc. I of his widely used *Compendium* (1610), alongside of Sacred Scripture, the symbols, and he means by that the contents of the Book of Concord of 1580!

123. Denzinger, *Sources*, p. 245.

124. Hermann Diem, *Das Problem des Schriftkanons* (*Theologische Studien*, Heft 32; Zollikon: Evangelischer Verlag, 1952), p. 12.

developed from the Pauline doctrine, and Scripture would only have been authoritative to the degree that it accorded with this imposed doctrine, even though the doctrine was regarded as being substantially "biblical." At that, Docetism would have moved in, for the predominant thought would have stepped into the place of permanently incalculable history. The canon which would be the result of a process of reduction dictated by a fundamental concept would be single-minded in content, free of contradictions, but also without any history. It is striking that Luther's "canon within the canon," that is, his list of the "true and noblest books of the New Testament,"[125] is explained with his thesis that it would be possible to do without the works of Christ but not without his preaching.[126] Therefore, that core canon contains only the fourth of the Gospels, and of Paul only Romans, Galatians, and Ephesians, but not 1 Corinthians, which apparently has much more relationship to history. The production of such an ideationally closed canon would result structurally in the same kind of thing as the fixing of the canon at Trent, only from the other direction. In both cases the Church is in possession of tangible truth which confirms the canon—the canon would no longer be in the strict sense the summary of the external word, but rather the double of Church doctrine. Proclamation would then have to die out or become the mere application of standing doctrine to certain processes in life. But it would no longer "promote Christ" but rather the Church's own concerns.[127]

4) **Historical Coherence.** Although the criterion of coherence does not provide a basis for the elimination of certain writings due to their failure to fit into a given context, it nevertheless contains an uncontested and significant concept. This becomes evident when we see the unity of Scripture, as the Word witnessed to, grounded solely in the unity of the Word happened. There is a material priority of the Word happened over the Word witnessed to, and of the Word witnessed to over the Word proclaimed, and noetically the reverse order is also relevant: moving from the proclaimed Word in which the Word witnessed to encounters us, up to the Word happened which is the substance of the witness. The unity of Scripture is based in the unity of God in his revelation. But this unity of God is precisely not the permanence of a thought but rather "personal" unity. Therefore this unity is revealed solely in the "person" of Jesus Christ. He is the "central point of Scripture." Leading up to him—noetically, based upon him—the Old Testament is "Holy Scripture." Otherwise it, too, would be "deadly" letters. In this sense we can say that the unity of Scripture is historical. Its coherence consists then only of the relationship of the scriptural witness to the salvation-event. This is not to

---

125. This list is found in the "September Testament" as an appendix to the "Preface to the New Testament," but it did not appear after 1534 (AE, XXXV, 316f.).

126. "If I had to do without one or the other—either the works or the preaching of Christ—I would rather do without the works than without his preaching. . . . Now John writes very little about the works of Christ, but very much about his preaching, while the other evangelists write much about his works and little about his preaching. Therefore, John's Gospel is the one, fine, true, and chief Gospel, and is far, far to be preferred over the other three and placed high above them" (AE, XXXV, 362).

127. See especially on this Hermann Diem, "Die Einheit der Schrift," *EvTheol* (1953), pp. 398ff.

say that the historical course of the history of the witness would have its dominant correlative in the historically calculable course of the salvation-event. Such a view, which is the view of "salvation-historical" theology in many of its proponents, would make the salvation-event into the super-elevated correlative of history, and the history of the witness and of the human response to God's activity would lose its human and earthly character. No, we do not possess a "principle" of historical development. But through the biblical witness we are confronted with the "central point" of this witness. This "center" is only made visible to us through the witness, and is not an entity of its own which can be set off. And yet, it is not the witness itself, but rather its basis. Just as this "center" is totally independent and unpredictable, the witness is human and earthly. But we must add to this humanity and earthliness that this witness also has its special historical relationship to the "center," and this is the sole reason for its being recognized as a witness. The scriptural witness, under these circumstances, is infinitely varied in its relationship to this "center" and that means in its character as a witness. A possible result is that under certain conditions we can no longer say of certain writings, based upon the presuppositions of our own knowledge capability, why they should have borne any witness character, as indirect as it may have been. Thus we cannot preach about such texts; practically they do not belong for us to the canon. But we should remember, on the one hand, that such difficult texts may make a relevant contribution to our understanding of the history of the witness, as a human and earthly history, in the total context of the witness (this would be true, for example, of Paul's travel plans in Romans). And on the other hand, it is simply a fact that texts which "do not say anything" during one period of the history of the Church—for example, the Apocalypse in the setting of the Reformation—will be understood in another period (who would want to excise the Apocalypse from the canon today?). Thus there is again and again a "canon within the canon."[128] And yet the Church would abdicate its responsibility if it wanted to canonize this "canon within the canon." What would have happened if the early Church, for which Paul was no longer directly understandable and which knew the theology of justification only in the form of the theology of incarnation, for which therefore the Pauline Epistles did not belong to the "canon within the canon," had therefore rejected this literature because it did not coincide with its then valid criterion of coherence? Apparently there was another criterion at work then which we have not dealt with: the criterion of fidelity. And this would no doubt also be a criterion of the Church.

5) **The Meaning of the Criterion of Originality.** If the criterion of coherence ultimately results in the unity of Scripture, understood as historical and personal, and in principle not tangible, then all that remains at this point in our discussion is the criterion of originality. And we have it only in the sense which Martin Kähler gave it: the Scriptures contain the "charter for the preaching that establishes the Church."[129] The counterpart which the Church and its theology see

---

128. Hermann Diem, *Das Problem des Schriftkanons*, p. 20.
129. *Op. cit.*, p. 23.

confronting them at every point in time is their factual origin, and this origin is represented by the canon, which is closed in fact, though not in principle. The significance of the canon is based solely upon the factually emerging priority. To change the canon, which is possible in principle, would mean one of two things. If the criterion of originality is understood in an objectifying, highly literal fashion, then it would mean that the new and shorter canon would certainly contain the historical originals. Or, if the criterion of coherence is understood in an objectifying sense, it would mean that the resulting new canon would offer the one, noncontradictory, relevant truth. In the first instance, (a) the fact would be ignored that what is most primitive (earliest in time) is not necessarily the most original in substance; (b) the fact that even in the most primitive (earliest in time) witness, Word and Response cannot conceivably be separated from one another; (c) most importantly, the fact that the Church with such a solemn identification of the most primitive contents would opt ecclesiastically for certain results of scientific-historical research. In doing this, the Church would make further research totally impossible, something which it does not do with the present canon, unless it wanted to embark upon the impossible route of constantly reestablishing the canon at short intervals. In the second instance, the results would be worse. The newly conceived canon would be the epitome of objectively tangible, single-minded doctrine, once and for all made clear and authoritatively defined as such. That means that a new formulation of the canon based upon the criterion of coherence would result in the introduction of the very understanding of the canon held by the Council of Trent. In its discourse with Scripture, the Church would engage in a monologue: it would not hear anything which it had not already said. "The canon remains the way it is! Its vulnerable openness, the permanent questionableness of its limits means that it testifies to its true evangelical meaning, against all reliance upon the formal way in which a writing belongs to the canon. . . ."[130]

l. The Vulnerability of the Canon. The Church possesses no unambiguously tangible means to prevent its own abuse of the canon. Indeed, it cannot even objectively defend itself against the mutilation of the canon which E. Käsemann has demonstrated to be possible.[131] In particular, it cannot demonstrate to the Roman Church statistically, so to speak, that it is in error when it de facto prolongs what was initially manifest in the New Testament as "early Catholicism"— regardless of how important that was. Its "weapons" are neither the canon understood statically and objectively nor indeed the canon in the sense of Marcionitic abbreviation. Its only weapon is proclamation. And this is a sharp weapon. This sharpness is demonstrated toward the Church itself, and only to the extent that the Church obediently faces this sharpness will it experience it directed toward others. The truth which the Church is to proclaim is not found in the most cor-

---

130. *Op. cit.*, I, 193.
131. "Begründet der neutestamentliche Kanon die Einheit der Kirche?" *EvTheol* (1951/52), pp. 13ff.

rectly formulated of propositions but in the Person of Jesus Christ. The witnesses assembled in the canon are to be examined upon the basis of this truth. Here every witness has its own voice, and it is the theologically essential task of exegesis to insist that each of these unique voices be heard in its distinctness from the others and in its relationship to the others. It is not the business of theology to opt for the one witness over the other, not even for Paul against James,[132] but rather the question which constantly keeps theology in motion is this one: to what extent is the one voice to be heard, the voice which is the sole concern of the Church, in and through the special and distinctive voices, in their mutual movement and their movement toward the hearer. The Church never has the voice directly "nailed down." Even the ideationally most closed canon, one containing only the most primitive of historical elements, would manifest the Word happened only and always in the form of human witness, and that means also in the form of human response, bound to place, time, and circumstances. Thus the Church never escapes from this question. But the reason for this is that it lives out of the response already given "in, with and under" the human witness. The canon does not provide it any security. The Word alone grants certainty to it, the Word which the Spirit confirms in it.

2. THE PROPERTIES OF SACRED SCRIPTURE

Orthodox dogmatics generally offers a doctrinal complex under the theme of the "properties of sacred Scripture" (*affectiones* or *proprietates Scripturae sacrae*). The statements of the dogmaticians are highly varied in their structure but materially they converge. In essence they are concerned with ascribing to Scripture the characteristics of "authority" (*auctoritas*, and with it "necessity"—*necessitas*), "sufficiency" (*sufficientia*), "perspicuity" (*perspicuitas*), and "efficacy" (*efficacia*).

For Orthodoxy, these attributes are directly connected to the doctrine of inspiration. This is due to the nature of the matter. However, the weaknesses of Orthodox doctrine make themselves felt here anew in that the objectively understood inspiredness of Scripture becomes the source from which objective properties are derived. If we understand inspiration to mean that the Word witnessed to expresses in power the Word happened, then the "characteristics" of Scripture will automatically be understood as the way in which Scripture has this effect. This effect is primarily located in the Church. For this reason we have placed the doctrine of properties here. Properly understood, it states what the Church "has" in the Bible, why it lives out of the Bible, and why the sole lordship of the Word is made manifest in the Church through the Bible.[133]

---

132. Georg Eichholz, *Jakobus und Paulus; ein Beitrag zum Problem des Kanons* (*Theologische Existenz heute*, N.F. Nr. 39; Munich: Kaiser Verlag, 1953).

133. "The holy Christian Church, whose only head is Christ, is born out of the Word of God; it remains in it, and does not hear the voice of a stranger"—thus the famous first thesis of the Ten Conclusions of Berne, A.D. 1528 (see Schaff, III, 210, in German and Latin; here, my translation—TR).

i. AUTHORITY

a. The Special Character of Biblical Authority. The thesis that the Holy Scriptures possess authority, necessary and irreplaceable authority, is found at the head of virtually every list of properties in Orthodox doctrine.

It would be best for us immediately to ask what kind of authority is meant here.[134] Wherever there is authority, the usual meaning is that there is a superior order to which an inferior order corresponds. The correlative to authority is obedience. This relationship between upper and lower orders is only found in interpersonal relationships. The question then is, How much power does the claim to be able to require submission actually render the bearer of authority. It could be said that wherever this question appears, authority is basically shaken. For real authority has the character of being unquestioned, self-evident. But this is a false idea. The "authority" of a robber chieftain can be unquestioned by the members of his band, yet it is not really authority. The question of the source of authority cannot be avoided. It can be answered in very different ways. The source can be sought in the factual exercise of force or at least in the constant possibility of exercising it. But then every tyrant and highwayman would have authority. Therefore, the attempt has repeatedly been made to understand authority in the following way: either a common element is posited between the upper and lower partners in an authority relationship, or the submitting partner possesses a criterion in himself which leads him to look upon the superior partner as one who has received his authority by virtue of this criterion, that is, by virtue of something already present in the submitting partner. This common element, in the first instance, can be, for example, the public welfare. It can also be sought in the idea of God. The factor within the submitting partner which is supposed to serve as the reason for the superior authority can be sought in the fact that man is essentially a political or social animal, or that he delegates his personal sovereignty to others for the sake of his own survival. In the realm of culture, it can consist of the fact that man by virtue of his own reason acknowledges other men to be bearers of a superior reason (the same reason).

The authority of Scripture in the Church and its proclamation in the word differs from all other authority in that, first, it has no character of force like that of, for example, the state or also in a more limited sense that of the father's authority, and that, secondly, it is not based upon its establishment or confirmation through human reason.[135] That means that this authority is "spiritual." It does not mechanically overwhelm us, nor is it derived from us, not even indirectly (by virtue of its being acknowledged by our reason). It is only "objective" in that it is "subjective."[136] It is heteronomous in that it is simultaneously autonomous.

---

134. Instructive passages are found in K. Barth, *CD*, I,2, pp. 538ff. and H. Bavinck, *Gereformeerde Dogmatiek* (4 vols.; Kampen: J. H. Kok, 1906), I, 376ff. or *Our Reasonable Faith* (Grand Rapids: Eerdmans, 1956) (a compendium of the 4 vols.).

135. See especially H. Bavinck, *op. cit.*

136. There is no objective certainty of the authority of Scripture if God as its author does not place it in our heart; there is equally no subjective certainty without a formal concept of this authority in us, if God through the Holy Spirit does not illuminate and persuade us inwardly (Voetius, *Selectae disputationes, theologicae,* in *Reformed Dogmatics,* ed. and tr. J. W. Beardslee III [New York: Oxford University Press, 1965], V, 307–16).

b. Normative, Causative, and Historical Authority. Orthodoxy expressed this at least in part in that it distinguished between the causative and normative authority of Scripture (*causativa* and *normativa*).[137] Causative authority consists in Scripture's generating of divine faith. This authority asserts itself in that in and through it faith arises. Orthodoxy in general asks how this actually happens, and the regular response is to refer to the testimony of the Spirit.[138] Although the Orthodox attributed many miraculous things to Scripture, in this decisive point it was not a miracle book which produced its causative power out of itself. When a part of Reformed Orthodoxy spoke of the historical (or authentic) authority alongside of the normative authority, which is yet to be discussed, then there were reasons for this in the general Orthodox doctrine of inspiration, but also there were motives based upon hermeneutical considerations. What the Scriptures say about the godless has naturally only historical and certainly not normative authority. Some of the Orthodox, for example, Gijsbert Voetius, stretched the boundaries of these merely historical statements even further (Voetius was thinking, for example, of Job and his friends[139]). It is clear that the thesis of historical authority, while set within the context of the assumed doctrine of inspiration, which cannot be reasserted now, maintained an awareness that the Scriptures "can and may not be understood as a book of laws full of articles," and that "revelation, as it is recorded in Scripture, is an historical and organic whole."[140]

For all of the Orthodox, however, the emphasis was placed upon the normative authority, which often was further explained by the term "juridical authority" (*auctoritas judicialis* or *judiciaria*). What that means was expressed by the first sentence in the Formula of Concord (which was beyond all suspicion of alleged "Reformed Biblicism"): "We believe, confess and teach that the only rule and norm, according to which all dogmas and all doctors ought to be esteemed and judged, is no other whatever than the prophetic and apostolic writings both of the Old and of the New Testament. . . ."[141] The Reformed confessional documents, the French Confession of Faith (1559),[142] the Belgic Confession (1561 and 1619),[143] and the Second Helvetic Confession (1566),[144] all begin with solemn announcements of the sole authority of Scripture, which signifies that this was not an inner-Protestant point of difference. Orthodox theology proceeded along the lines pointed out in the confessional documents, with the one reservation that in Lutheranism the authority of the Reformation fathers and confessional state-

---

137. Thus David Hollaz, *Examen theologicum acroaticum*, in Schmid, p. 61.
138. See above, pp. 240ff. Regarding authority see especially J. Gerhard, *Loci communes theologici*, ed. F. R. Frank (1885ff.), I, iii, 136, p. 26, with literal echoes of Calvin, *Institutes*, I, vii, 4, p. 79 (God alone a fit and authentic witness!). See the materials in Schmid, p. 55, and Heppe-Bizer, pp. 22ff., which are all in general agreement in this regard.
139. *Op. cit.*, V, 307–16; see also Bavinck, *op. cit.*, p. 372.
140. H. Bavinck, *op. cit.*, pp. 372f. (translated from Weber's German translation of the Dutch original).
141. Schaff, III, 93f.
142. Schaff, *op. cit.*, articles 3–5, pp. 360–62; the normative authority is the theme of article 5.
143. *Ibid.*, articles 3–7, pp. 384–89, here especially article 7.
144. *Ibid.*, articles 1–2, pp. 237–40; ET in *The Book of Confessions*, United Presbyterian Church in the U.S.A. (1966f.), 5.001–5.015.

ments[145] is ascribed what is certainly a secondary but still recognizably an important position as the so-called *norma normata* ("authoritative norm").

What is then meant by the "Protestant Principle of Scripture"? It is very clear that every other norm outside of Scripture is here excluded. The Evangelical Church only exists where this exclusiveness of the biblical witness is dominant. And that means that the Church is not essentially its own ruler nor understands itself to be autonomous; only for this reason and in this reason is the Church free.

Nonetheless, the concept of norms must be further explored from various directions.

1) The Lordship of Christ and the Authority of Scripture. Obviously it was not the intent of either the Reformers or the Orthodox to encroach upon the personal (!) lordship of Christ over his Church in their assertion of the normativity of Scripture. The government in and over the Church is God's government, exercised in Jesus Christ, in whom God has turned himself to man and accepted him in gracious and liberating lordship, and realized through the Holy Spirit, in whom this gracious liberating lordship becomes a reality in us.[146] God's rule cannot be assumed by someone else. The Reformers had experienced the Church in the form in which God's rule was manifested in the self-rule of the Church and its dominion over the world, and in fact God's rule seemed to be absorbed and suppressed in the process; therefore, the Reformation intended to turn away from this presumptuous kind of autonomy. Since tradition, as it was dogmatically understood in Session IV of the Council of Trent,[147] was virtually the epitome of this autonomy of the Church, particularly in view of the fact that the Church's formulated claim to be the only interpreter of Scripture was organically connected to tradition,[148] this turning away of the Church from its presumptuous autonomy meant primarily the rejection of the principle of tradition and of the interpretational monopoly of the Church. This is what the thesis of the sole normative authority of Scripture seeks to express. But does it accomplish this? Would it not have been more logical, when facing a Church which rules itself,[149] to appeal directly to Christ and to the Holy Spirit? In what way is the authority of Scripture concretely the authority of the Lord of the Church?

In answering we shall repeat what has already been said.[150] Scripture is authoritative because and in that it witnesses to God as the One who has called his Community in his own actions, in the freedom of his historical activity. Thus he has laid once and for all the "cornerstone" upon which the Church is built

---

145. The Formula of Concord (Schaff, *loc. cit.*) reveals this. A line in a popular hymn like "God's Word and Luther's doctrine. . . ." fortunately found no Reformed parallels in regard to Calvin.

146. Wherever the attempt has been made to separate or oppose theocracy, christocracy, and pneumatocracy to each other, there has been at least potentially a misunderstanding of the Church's doctrine of the Trinity at work.

147. See below, pp. 277ff.

148. Denzinger, *Sources*, pp. 245f., and especially p. 303 (par. 995).

149. K. Barth, *CD*, I,2, pp. 575f.

150. See pp. 228ff.

(1 Cor. 3:10, 11; Eph. 2:20; 2 Tim. 2:19). If the Church's existence were rooted in some kind of human thought, then it would be illogical to suppose that new and ongoing thoughts could not be joined to the original ones. If it had its origin or its center in an "absolute" God, far from space, time, and history, then these earlier documents of a religious relationship to this center would need to be expanded upon by further ones. But the Church is rooted in God's activity, in God's covenant, in the history of God with man, and it only knows about God by viewing this history, that is, by regarding the incomprehensible contingency of his acts. Every attempt to absorb the scriptural witness into the Church's statements encroaches upon the freedom of God's gracious activity, upon the free power and contingency of his self-disclosure, and ultimately results in the making of the given Word into an ontic ultimate which is always at our disposal. Wherever God's character as our opposite, the Other, is set aside or even weakened, God is placed at our disposal sacrally or rationally or emotionally—and vice versa. The contingent witness is part of the contingency of revelation. The authority of Scripture is an expression of the authority of God.

2) No Authority on the Basis of Inherent Characteristics. The Scripture has authority as long as it is open for the authority of the Lord of the Church. This is what the Orthodox doctrine of inspiration sought to express. But it failed at one decisive point. Since it understood inspiration as an essentially supernatural way of creating Scripture, the writings were open toward God at the very moment they were coming into being, but now they are characterized by a static, supernatural quality.[151] Where this consideration was maintained, the authority of Scripture had to become a passive potency and the norms passive entities. But where this happens, the fact is overlooked that the Holy Spirit was not just the Lord of Scripture in the past, but always is. And where that is overlooked, a kind of over-exaggerated rationalism moves in. Since Scripture contains the truth in an available form in itself, it then only requires rational examination in order to discover and to unfold this available truth. Then, however, it is a very secondary issue whether this discovering and unfolding is more the business of the Church, or of theology, or finally of individual rational thinking. Normative authority becomes then a characteristic waiting to be made use of. Then the decision of the Church made upon the basis of Scripture becomes a matter of the riskless application of scriptural statements, perhaps using the method of proof-texting or the concordance method. After Scripture's genesis has been dehistoricized, its application is also dehistoricized. We need only to look at Late Orthodoxy to see that we are not caricaturing here.

To be sure, within the given setting the Reformed Orthodox theologians developed careful distinctions which indicate to us that both the exegetical and the dogmatic faculties remained alert. Gijsbert Voetius attempted to work out carefully within inspired Scripture what then really was normative about it. Certainly not the word of the godless! And not the private expressions of the pious!

---

151. Cf. the Rahtmannian Controversy, and below, pp. 284ff.

Rather, solely the words of God himself—as long as they were not extraordinary mandates, as in the command to sacrifice Isaac—and the commissioned words of those persons speaking prophetically or apostolically.[152] The result in Voetius and many others was a quantitative delimitation of the truly authentic statements. This does not touch upon the most difficult issue of all: the question whether normative authority is to be directly ascribed to the rules of the Old Testament. For the areas of ceremonial and juridical law, this is generally denied. But this most immediate problem (which was always borne in mind by the Orthodoxy of both Protestant confessions) ought to have made clear that a quantitative delimitation was not going to be enough. If it is true that the Scriptures in essence remain open toward the Word they testify to and thus toward the Holy Spirit, then this means that the normative authority of Scripture does not provide us any security (the way a judge is "covered" by the law), but rather gives us guidance toward asking the right questions and indicates the way to the true answer, to which it testifies but which it does not possess tangibly. This limitation is not a weakness but a strength of Scripture.

3) **Living Authority.** Based upon what we have said here, the normative authority of Scripture can only be understood as living authority. The "norming norm" *(norma normans)* which we encounter here is not "ready to hand" in any sense. The Reformers and their contemporaries experienced this in innumerable religious discussions and disputations, and their Roman opponents never tired of pointing out what kind of confusion the "scriptural principle" had engendered in fact, or at least had not prevented. It was seen that the authority of Sacred Scripture binds the Church but does not release it from its responsibility.[153] The Reformed synods with their constantly repeated question whether the extant confession really was in full agreement with Scripture indicate that the Reformed Church did understand this. A passive authority of Scripture would have paralyzed the Synods—and it did, as the synodal futility of the Late Orthodox age reveals. At first the Lutheran side also had those who recognized that the Church has the "right and privilege of judging."[154] This was no longer the thesis of Martin Luther, almost forgotten today, "That a Christian Assembly or Congregation Has the Right and Power to Judge All Teaching. . . ."[155] For Martin Chemnitz, "the" Church is no longer the congregation but rather the ordained ministry—obedience to ecclesiastical office had already become the third note of the Church

---

152. Voetius, *op. cit.*, I, 265–75; Heppe-Bizer, pp. 26f.
153. K. G. Steck refers in his essay, "Der 'locus de synodis' in der lutherischen Dogmatik," in *Theologische Aufsätze Karl Barth zum 50. Geburtstag*, ed. E. Wolf (Munich: Kaiser, 1936), p. 346, to David Hollaz's thought that synods were not really necessary since Scripture was enough "in any event," and a large number of congregated people was not necessarily required (David Hollaz, *Examen theologicum acroaticum* [1701, ed. of 1741], pp. 1320f.). This is related to the purely objective view of Scripture which was propounded by Late Orthodoxy.
154. Martin Chemnitz, *op. cit.*, p. 211.
155. AE, XXXIX, 305ff.

next to the proclamation of the Word and the administration of the sacraments.[156] But nonetheless, it was still recognized that in matters of doctrine (dependent upon the principal judgment of normative Scripture) the Church, and that means the ecclesiastical ministry (!), must function as a "ministerial" or "inferior judge."[157] And indeed, the Church is not removed from the area of decision-making once it has been determined that the decision is not its own to make. On the contrary, it is precisely because the Church sees in Scripture a living authority confronting it that it must decide again and again. The Church does not possess a "paper pope." What has been given to it is the certainty that Scripture will assert itself anew as the decisive witness, because it has been affirming and is the affirming witness; it will assert itself even against the Church and against every form of human autonomy. In this sense the thesis of the normative authority of Scripture is an indispensable factor of Evangelical dogmatics.

ii. SUFFICIENCY

a. The Meaning of the Thesis of Sufficiency. In Orthodoxy, the corresponding assertion to that of the sole authority of Scripture is that Scripture suffices unto salvation and for the right knowledge of God in his activity *(sufficientia)*. There are many other statements related to this, most of them interpretive. In many dogmaticians we read that perfection is ascribed to Scripture, meaning that it provides us everything which is necessary for the attainment of salvation, fully and perfectly.[158] Some then add that in addition to this essential perfection there is also the undiminished or integral perfection which means that the biblical books in their condition and present state are also perfectly preserved and have been protected from all falsification.[159] This is again a historical objectification, corresponding to the supernaturalism of primarily Late Orthodoxy. Together with the emphasis upon sufficiency we also find the concept of "necessity,"[160] which is in part explained in a completely rational fashion. The Scriptures were neces-

---

156. Thus in Melanchthon; see Herrlinger, *Theologie Melanchthons, in ihrer geschichtlichen Entwicklung und im Zusammenhange mit der Lehrgeschichte und Culturbewegung der Reformation* (Gotha: Perthes, 1879); David Chytraeus, *Katechismus* (Wittenberg: 1555), in J. M. Reu, *Quellen zur Geschichte des kirchlichen Unterrichts in der evangelischen Kirche Deutschlands zwischen 1530 und 1600* (4 vols. in 9; Gütersloh: Bertelsmann, 1904–35), I,3,2,1, p. 310; T. Heshusius, according to Hackenschmidt in Schaff-Herzog, V, 255f.; also the Regensburger Buch, *CR*, V, 526f.

157. Johann Gerhard, *op. cit.*, I, xxii, 467; ed. F. R. Frank (1885ff.), I, 207. Similarly, Andreas Quenstedt: in contrast to the solely decisive judgment of God the Church has merely the task of interpretation, declaration, announcement, or application to certain persons and things *(Theologica didactico-polemica* (1685), I, 4, 2, 15; in the folio edition of 1691, I, 150). We should note that interpretation is a right of every individual here *(op. cit.*, p. 137).

158. Johann Gerhard, *op. cit.*, I, xviii, 367; ed. F. R. Frank (1885ff.), I, 157.

159. David Hollaz, in Schmid, p. 74 (the first thing mentioned in the list; Hollaz is speaking here rationalistically, of the perfection of Scripture). See further J. H. Heidegger, *Medulla theologiae* (1696), II, 24. Cited in Heppe-Bizer, pp. 28f. In Heppe, it is emphasized that older Reformed theology "thought differently."

160. Especially with the Reformed; see Heppe-Bizer, pp. 30ff.

sary for the preservation of the Church, not just for its "well-being" *(bene esse)* but for its very being *(esse)*.[161] Of course, God could have set things up differently—there is no absolute necessity here. But the way in which he actually desired the Church to be is such that it cannot exist without the Scriptures (necessity based upon the hypothesis of arrangement[162]).

The essential thing about all of these Orthodox theses is that the Church, because it lives on the basis of the Word of God, fundamentally requires Scripture as the witness to this Word (the "necessity"), and it has neither the right nor the need to assert its own Word as authoritative next to the Word witnessed to ("perfection" and "sufficiency"). This means that since the Church is dependent upon the external Word as the witness to the One who is in essence other than we are *(extra nos)*, it should be grateful for the fact that this outward witness has been given, and it should be satisfied with this witness. All its riches consist of its being permitted to hear, and its own speech can respond to these riches thankfully. What it then says in this freedom can never be placed at the same level as what it has been given to hear. Any freedom which would empower the Church to speak its own words of authority would not be Christian freedom.

b. The Rejection of the Principle of Tradition, Not of Tradition. In this setting the thesis of the sufficiency of Scripture is directed straight at the principle of tradition solemnly formulated at Trent.[163] It is equally directed against every inner-Protestant attempt to place the Church's own statements or those of any pious person alongside the voice of Scripture as authoritative, and to ground Scripture upon the Church's own speech.

It probably should not be necessary to mention that the "Church of the Word" is not opposing tradition when it speaks out against the principle of tradition. There have been many in the Evangelical camp who have believed in the apostolic authorship of the so-called Apostles' Creed without accepting the principle of tradition in the process. In fact, the churchly tradition was of much more importance to the Reformers and the Orthodox than would usually be assumed.[164] This was partly due to the fact that the fathers were appealed to in support for their views (we think of Augustine), and partly to the necessity of dealing with

---

161. See A. Polanus von Polansdorf (or Polan), *Syntagma theologiae christianae* (1624 and 1625), I, 35, cited in Heppe-Bizer, p. 32.

162. Polanus, *loc. cit.*

163. Denzinger, *Sources*, p. 244 (par. 783): the Synod perceives that "this truth and instruction are contained in the written books and in the unwritten traditions, which have been received by the apostles from the mouth of Christ Himself, or from the apostles themselves, at the dictation of the Holy Spirit, have come down even to us, transmitted as it were from hand to hand. . . ." The Synod then "holds in veneration with an equal affection of piety and reverence all the books of the Old and of the New Testament . . . and also the traditions themselves, those that appertain both to faith and to morals, as having been dictated either by Christ's own word of mouth, or by the Holy Spirit, and preserved in the Catholic Church by a continuous succession."

164. See especially O. Ritschl, *Dogmengeschichte des Protestantismus* (4 vols.; Leipzig: Hinrichs, 1908–27), I, 193ff. For later periods see H. Leube, *Calvinismus und Luthertum, im Zeitalter der Orthodoxie*, I (Leipzig: Deichert, 1928; repr. Aalen: Scientia Verlag, 1966).

the traditional proofs introduced by their opponents. Works like Calvin's *Institutes* or Johann Gerhard's *Loci communes theologici* are veritable gold mines of patristic and patrological learning. It was Johann Gerhard who really introduced the term "patrology" into theological terminology.[165] The Church of the Gospel did not understand itself as being something new, but rather as being the old Church rightly understood. The tendency which we can observe today of not thinking back beyond 1517 is un-Evangelical, because it is unchurchly.

The thesis of the sufficiency of Scripture raises the problem of the *principle* of tradition.[166] For the problem is not that there is tradition, nor that later tradition is quite logically and to a certain degree dependent upon earlier tradition. The question is precisely framed when we ask if Scripture in principle is sufficient or not.

It is, therefore, one thing to refer to the existence of extrabiblical traditions, even to emphasize their worth, and another thing to ascribe to them fundamentally an autonomous authority alongside of Scripture.[167]

c. Oral Tradition in the Earliest Church. The existence of oral tradition goes without saying. Jülicher-Fascher's thesis that early Christianity was from the outset a "book religion" is to be agreed with,[168] in that the Old Testament was accepted from the beginning. But it is equally uncontested that we have no written legacy from Jesus, and thus certain that the first witnesses felt called to oral proclamation. The relatively few written records from them impress us as being occasional literature, often based upon oral traditions or even expressly referring to them (1 Cor. 11:2, 23; 15:1ff.; 1 Thess. 4:1; 2 Thess. 3:6; Rom. 6:17; 1 Cor. 3:10; Gal. 1:6ff.; 2 Cor. 11:4; Phil. 4:9; Col. 2:6). In 2 Thessalonians 2:15 the *paradosis* (tradition) is said to be taught to them by word or epistle. In the Pastorals, the *parathēkē* is already presupposed as an established entity (the "deposit," or "what is entrusted"; see 1 Tim. 6:20; 2 Tim. 1:12, 14), just as is the "teaching" (whether or not this signifies such a profound break in contrast to 1 Cor. 11:2, 23 as is often stated today can be left aside here). In any event, there is an oral tradition before the written fixing of the New Testament witness and also alongside the fixed witness, naturally. The oldest Church Fathers assume this, especially Irenaeus.[169] The old community was a many-sided missions move-

---

165. See W. Koch, *Lexicon für Theologie und Kirche*, ed. M. Buchherger (10 vols.; Freiburg im Breisgau: Herder & Co., 1930–38), IV, 420.

166. According to Michael Schmaus, *Katholische Dogmatik* (5 vols.; München: M. Hueber, 1948ff.), p. 114, the Scriptures contain "the Word which the Holy Spirit presents to it for proclamation not in an exhaustive or exclusive fashion. Next to it there is the tradition, the orally passed on tradition."

167. M. Schmaus, *op. cit.*, p. 116: "The objective tradition in the narrower sense is an independent source of faith, of equal value with Scripture." This is a statement to be accepted by faith. A more recent treatment of the problem is O. Cullmann, *La Tradition, Problème Exégétique, historique et théologique* (Paris: Delachaux et Niestlé, 1953); GT: *Die Tradition als exegetisches, historisches und theologisches Problem*, tr. P. Schönenberger (Zurich: Zwingli Verlag, 1954).

168. A. Jülicher and E. Fascher, *Einleitung in das Neue Testament* (7th ed., 1931); ET: *An Introduction to the New Testament*, tr. J. P. Ward (London: Smith, Elder & Co., 1904) (from the 3rd and 4th German eds.).

169. Irenaeus, *Against Heresies*, III, iii, 1 (*ANCL*, V, 261f.).

ment, and cannot possibly be reinterpreted as an institution for the production of literature which would be authoritative for the future—the eschatological expectations of the early Church were enough of an obstacle to such a tendency. The Community did have a drive toward the written conservation of its faith. But it lived to proclaim, not to preserve itself in writing.

Nevertheless, this uncontested fact has always been confronted quite properly with the fact that we are not in a position to grasp the oral proclamation in any other form than in the written witness. This consideration is initially noetic in nature. How are we to find out what the essential and original elements are in the virtually incomprehensible confusion of what we find in "tradition," without holding solely to the Word fixed in writing?[170] However, this consideration is also material in nature. The bearers of the original tradition, known or anonymous to us, are, as "eyewitnesses"[171] or by virtue of their vicinity to the first witnesses, qualitatively distinct from the later receivers of tradition. The early Church was aware of the fact that it was encountering a genuine counterpart in this written witness. The qualitative priority of the original witness (even if we only encounter it indirectly at the margins of the New Testament canon) is the reason for its noetic priority.

d. The Principle of Tradition and Ecclesiology. If it is doubtless so that there was in the early Christian age and beyond oral tradition next to the original witness fixed in written form, then the question which becomes decisive is this: Did the Church as the bearer of this tradition and the preserver of this legacy possess in itself the static and tangible continuity which would be necessary if one were to assert that this tradition may claim its own authoritative validity next to Scripture up to our present day? It simply cannot be denied that the Church has suffered profound changes going back to its very earliest times.[172] Whoever asserts that tradition is authoritative next to Scripture must assume that the Church has constantly preserved the traditional material without altering it. If the Church is what Adam Möhler postulates as "the Son of God himself, everlastingly manifesting himself among men in a human form, perpetually renovated, and eternally young—the permanent incarnation of the same . . . ,"[173] then this assumption is assured. But then one would have to add that this kind of Church would basically

---

170. Even M. Schmaus (*op. cit.,* p. 114) finds that the concept of tradition "has not been fully clarified up to the present day."

171. See Markus Barth, *Der Augenzeuge; eine Untersuchung über die Wahrnehmung des Menschensohnes durch die Apostel* (Zollikon: Evangelischer Verlag, 1946), in spite of methodological reservations.

172. Protestant polemics have referred with a degree of aptness to Cyprian's statement, "For custom without truth is the antiquity of error" (Letter 74 [*FC,* LI, 292]), or to Tertullian's phrase, "Our Lord Christ has surnamed Himself Truth, not Custom" (*On the Veiling of Virgins,* Ch. I [*ANCL,* XVIII, 154]). The antiquity of a tradition does not prove anything.

173. *Symbolism; or Exposition of the doctrinal differences between Catholics and Protestants as evidenced by their symbolical writings,* tr. J. B. Robertson (London: Gibbings & Co., 1906⁵ [g1924¹¹⁻¹²]), II, 6. See also M. Schmaus, *op. cit.,* p. 111: the Church is Christ living on!

not have needed the tradition, nor in fact the Scriptures. For why should the "Christ living on" *(Christus prolongatus)* necessarily require the human and historical witness? Why should he not rather constantly produce it himself? Should one not at least say that the Church, if it is the "Christ living on," is involved in an ongoing discourse with itself in its dealing with Scripture and tradition?

The Roman Catholic Church has in fact come to a self-understanding which raises the question whether the principle of tradition has not been transformed into the principle of the sole authority of the teaching office of the Church.

The first and really classical formulation of what can be termed tradition next to Scripture is that of Vincent of Lerins (d. before 450),[174] and significantly it is found in a writing which was in effect directed against Augustine. Man as pious, churchly, baptized man does not live from receiving alone but also from his own activity. And that means when applied to Scripture that, certainly, it is "sufficient" *(cum . . . sufficiat . . .)*. But something must also happen on the side of the hearer. The power to work effectively against the wealth of errors is something Scripture in and of itself does not possess (just as grace does not accomplish all things as free grace). Instead another means is required so that the "interpretations of the prophets and apostles may be guided along lines according to the norm[!] of the ecclesiastical and catholic sense." Thus, in the Catholic Church every effort must be expended, so that "we might hold to what has been believed everywhere, at all times, and by everyone." The standards, then, of universality, antiquity, and consensus are the issue here. That has been the general opinion for centuries—soteriologically it corresponds to Semi-Pelagianism. But when in this way the common consciousness which has developed in history assumes a position next to Scripture,[175] who then is to decide what is really authoritative in the wealth of what this common consciousness has produced? The only, and really only possible, answer was more anticipated than stated at Trent: the reference to the sole right of interpretation of the Church, that is, of the teaching office,[176] in regard to Scripture must of necessity then be applied to the highly varying contents which emerge as tradition. This approach was not perfected until the idea that the Church was the "Christ living on," the *Christus prolongatus*, was able to assert itself, based in part, as Barth has shown,[177] upon the idealistic and romantic views of Adam Möhler. Then, the First Vatican Council with its proclamation of the infallibility of the pope took the step which had been anticipated and prepared since Trent. The teaching office becomes the "epistemological principle of the genuine tradition."[178] And the Marian dogma of 1950 has shown that the old standard, "what has been believed everywhere, at all times, and by all people," can be applied very generously.[179]

---

174. Migne, *PL*, L, 639 (*Commonitorium* 2, around 434).

175. Möhler, *op. cit.*, II, 35ff. Tradition is "the peculiar Christian sense existing in the Church, and transmitted by ecclesiastical education. . . . Tradition is the living word, perpetuated in the hearts of believers." The vicinity to Schleiermacher is very obvious.

176. Denzinger, *Sources*, pp. 245f. (par. 786), and p. 303 (par. 985) above all.

177. *CD*, I,2, pp. 560ff.

178. M. Schmaus, *op. cit.*, p. 122.

179. See the Apostolic Constitution, "Munificentissimus Deus," of November 1, 1950 (Denzinger, *Sources*, pp. 647f.).

The principle of tradition must by inner necessity result in the ascription to the Church of its own and independent spiritual authority. As "Christ living on" or as the institution which concretely contains the Spirit, it is able to preserve the tradition, to recognize and to fix what is valid in it, and to provide the obligatory interpretation of Scripture. It is no longer dependent upon its constantly hearing the Word anew, but rather by virtue of its possession of the Spirit or of its unity with the Risen Lord it now can appear as its own spokesman. It is clear that it is no longer possible to speak here of the sufficiency of Scripture. Roman Catholicism, moreover, has shown in its post-Vatican I phase that basically there is no longer any sufficiency of tradition. Rather, the Church itself, "in its lively teaching office, is the direct and nearest source of faith and of the science of faith,"[180] whereas Scripture and tradition in contrast represent the "distant rule of faith."[181] That means that the Word of the Church is what is directly authoritative. While the Church does refer back to Scripture and tradition, it does so in such a way that the Church's teaching office alone states what Scripture really says and what tradition is truly valid.

e. The Protestant Analogy to the Principle of Tradition: Schleiermacher. There is a similar transformation of the Church from the listening Community into the tangible proprietor of the Spirit in broad sections of recent Protestantism. The very theologian who discovered the Church, so to speak, for the 19th century, Schleiermacher, understood the Holy Spirit in a logical continuation of his whole approach as the "common spirit" "of the Christian fellowship as a moral personality."[182] There is something "divine" in the Church, "something we call accordingly the Being of God in it";[183] "the Christian Church is one through this one Spirit in the same way that a nation is one through the national character common to and identical in all."[184] It is then said of this Church Community which is defined by its common Spirit that in its relationship to Christ and to the Spirit, "it is ever self-identical,"[185] whereas in its relationship to the "world" it is constantly in a state of change. Into this context then Schleiermacher puts his doctrine of the Holy Scripture.[186] The decisive thing is not that Schleiermacher consciously turns away from tradition[187] by placing this doctrine in the doctrine of the Church. That had happened on occasion before Schleiermacher, for example, in the Scotch Confession of Faith of 1560,[188] and repeated most recently within the Reformed circle.[189] Orthodox theology not only mentions Scripture at

---

180. M. Schmaus, *op. cit.*, p. 85.
181. *Ibid.*, p. 86.
182. Schleiermacher, *ChrF*, §116, 3, II, p. 535, and *passim*.
183. Schleiermacher, *ChrF*, §116, 3, II, p. 535.
184. Schleiermacher, *ChrF*, §121, 2, II, p. 563.
185. Schleiermacher, *ChrF*, §126, Thesis, II, p. 582.
186. Schleiermacher, *ChrF*, §128, 1, II, p. 591, at the beginning.
187. Schleiermacher, *ChrF*, §128ff., pp. 591ff.
188. Article 19; compare Schaff, III, 464.
189. H. Berkhof, ed., *Fundamenten en Perspektieven van Belijden Lebendiges Bekenntnis; die "Grundlagen und Perspektiven des Bekennens" der Generalsynode der Niederländischen Reformierten Kirche von 1949*, tr. Otto Weber (Neukirchen: Neukirchener Verlag, 1959), Art. VI,2 and X,1, p. 12 and pp. 15ff.

the beginning of its presentations but returns to it again when treating of the means of salvation. The important thing is that Schleiermacher makes the validity of Scripture dependent upon faith. He is of course quite right when he asserts that the New Testament Scriptures are "such a preaching come down to us" and to that degree faith "springs from them too," but this is not "connected" to the doctrine of Scripture which is already drafted.[190] Just as suspicious as the word "too" in the sentence just mentioned are the methodological reasons given for the discussion of Scripture solely in the context of the Church. "Hence throughout the whole of the foregoing exposition of faith we have assumed no more than faith itself, present in a feeling of need (in whatever source that feeling may have originated), and Scripture we have adduced only as expressing the same faith in detail."[191] Admittedly, Schleiermacher does not find fault "totally" with the traditionally dominant method. But he does not want it to appear that a doctrine "belongs to Christianity because it is contained in Scripture, whereas in point of fact it is only contained in Scripture because it belongs to Christianity."[192] Thus Scripture becomes in fact the (not even sole) principle of the "self-identification" of the Church.[193] It is true, on the one hand, that "no age" has been "without its own originality in Christian thinking," and on the other hand that only that "can be regarded as a pure product of the Christian Spirit" which can be shown to be "in harmony with the original products" (the reference is to the New Testament).[194] It can scarcely be ignored that what is happening here is the same thing as what happened in the Roman Catholicism of the 19th century: the Church finds itself again in Scripture. It is not a long road from this position to the principle of tradition. Ultimately, there is no need to speak any more of the sufficiency of Scripture, as we have discussed above, as the "constitutive" and "critical" effect of Scripture upon Christian doctrine.

f. The Scripture as Sufficient Gift, Not as Doctrinal Law. The Orthodox thesis of the sufficiency of Scripture is directed against the self-sufficiency of the Church. It does not gain its truly Evangelical meaning until it is understood as a reference to the bond and obligatory nature which develop out of the gift of Scripture. If the Scriptures are understood as a legal norm, then this must mean that in so doing they are placed at the disposal of the Church. The more rigidly the literal sense per se is taken as authoritative, the more this understanding tempts one to place the "application" of Scripture within the scope of the Church's free power, or to orient it according to tradition, or to adapt it to the religious needs of a specific situation. The "Scripture alone" *(sola scriptura)* principle is an expression of "grace alone" *(sola gratia)*. If this is true, then Scripture is only what it is supposed to be for the Church when it is understood as alive, as the factor which empowers proclamation, as the gift in which the absolute gift meets us, that is, the liberating and thus binding event of the Word.

---

190. Schleiermacher, *ChrF*, §128, 2, II, p. 593.
191. Schleiermacher, *ChrF*, §128, 3, II, p. 593, at the beginning.
192. Schleiermacher, *ChrF*, §128, 3, II, p. 593, middle.
193. Schleiermacher, *ChrF*, §128, 3, II, p. 594, at the end; my translation of *sich-selbst-Gleichens*—TR.
194. Schleiermacher, *ChrF*, §129, 2, II, p. 596.

iii. PERSPICUITY

a. The Thesis. Does this gift truly meet us? Orthodox doctrine answers this question with a double Yes. It asserts the understandability or perspicuity of Scripture, which exists for everyone, and thus (as developed in Late Orthodoxy) the direct efficacy of Scripture (the *perspicuitas* and *efficacia*). We shall begin with the first of these theses.

Orthodoxy states—we shall take Andreas Quenstedt as its witness[195]—that, in those things which must be believed for salvation, the Holy Scriptures are clear and understandable both from the intention of God as the Author and from the very power of the words so that it is not impinged upon by any foreign or extraneous light but rather can be understood in whatever idiom in which it is read, by the use of proper and expert scholarship. We do not intend to give here a detailed exposition of this thesis. The example of Quenstedt shows on the one hand the supernaturalism of the dominant view of Scripture and on the other the concealed rationalism of the method. Since in Scripture what was previously concealed in God has now been revealed, man is able to recognize what he needs for salvation with his own intelligence, by virtue of his natural equipment. What is much more important is what is meant in the context of this system.

b. The Openness of Scripture for Everyone. The first thing meant is that the approach to Scripture is not dependent upon the obligatory interpretation provided by the Church. The Bible is not a secret book which can only be decoded by those who have been initiated. Even in regard to the texts which are admitted to be "dark," there is no exclusive power of interpretation assigned to the Church. Instead, the principle propounded is that the "dark" texts are to be understood in the light of the "bright" ones—a principle which not only accords with the primitive Reformation stance that "Scripture interprets itself,"[196] but which is also found in Thomas Aquinas (which Quenstedt pointedly mentions[197]). The perspicuity of Scripture makes it possible for "every Christian to deal with Scripture without tutelage."[198] Thus the Bible is the bastion of what one could call "Christian independence." When the Reformation made it ecclesiastically possible for individuals to grapple with the Bible, it was taking a risk from the point of view of Church "order."[199] This was clearly revealed by the "enthusiasts," and the inner-Protestant differences have clearly shown that the Roman criticism was not entirely wrong when it pointed out that the release of biblical exposition

---

195. *Theologia didactico-polemica* (Wittenberg: 1685, 1691), p. 117; similarly Calovius, *Systema locorum theologicorum* (1655–77), p. 467.

196. See Luther, *WA*, VII, 97ff.; K. Holl, *Gesammelte Aufsätze zur Kirchengeschichte* (3 vols.; Tübingen: J. C. B. Mohr [Paul Siebeck], 1928–48; Darmstadt: Wissenschaftliche Buchgesellschaft, 1948–65), I, 559.

197. *STh*, I,i,9, Reply to Objection 2, vol. I, p. 6; I,i,10, Reply to Objection 1, vol. I, p. 7.

198. Martin Kähler, *Dogmatische Zeitfragen; Alte und Neue Ausführungen zur Wissenschaft der christlichen Lehre* (3 vols.; Leipzig: Deichert, 1907²), I, 62.

199. See Luther's laying of the "second wall" in his writing "To the Christian Nobility . . ." (AE, XLIV, 133ff.).

would destroy the unity of the Church. Nevertheless the Reformation generally remained committed to its decision. It would have denied the free power of the grace of God if it had done otherwise. At this point it becomes clear whether the Church has more trust in the witness given to it or more trust in itself. The regulation of biblical activity can only develop out of the concern of the Church that the Bible is too weak, or that it is too strong.

c. *"Ordered Perspicuity."* The second aspect meant by the thesis of the perspicuity of Scripture is that in and with the Bible a witness is addressed to us to which there is also a profane approach, in a manner of speaking. This insight was bracketed for the Orthodox within their supernaturalism. But these brackets are no longer present. Scripture encounters us in our profanity. That means it encounters us as a really historical book which is destined in its particular component parts to be understood under certain, contingent presuppositions. Scripture participates in the condescension of God in his revelation, and it is the documentation of it.

But with this condescension, with this fact that the witness of Scripture encounters us within our history, there is also an impediment to our understanding which is given. For Scripture does not express general and universal things, but rather concrete and temporal things, and thus things which are in the past for us. The Bible does not speak our language. It does not assume our spatial and temporal environment nor our world view. It would not even be historical if it were not for this very glaring distance between us and it, a distance with which we shall have to deal below.[200] The Orthodox expressed this distance by viewing perspicuity not as something absolute but rather conditional. It did not apply to the geographical, historical, and other scientific statements of Scripture, for which scientific insights were necessary, and it did apply to Scripture only to the degree that someone could translate it from the original languages or was able to read such a translation. There are thus presuppositions of a purely factual nature which have to be fulfilled—and therefore Hollaz speaks of "ordered perspicuity" *(perspicuitas ordinata)*. This is the point at which theology gains direct significance for the hearer or reader of the scriptural Word. It does not produce the perspicuity of Scripture, but it does serve in Scripture's impact upon the Community.

d. *Perspicuity and the Decision of Faith.* If we agree that the Scriptures clearly offer what is necessary for salvation without necessitating the mediation of the Church, this still cannot mean that such hearing or reading which resulted in the specific decision of Yes or No would take place solely on the basis of the perspicuity of Scripture and the knowledge gained from it. This is not something which can be done without. Whoever denies the simple availability of Scripture denies logically the simple humanity of Jesus Christ. But it is not enough, qualitatively not enough. Our knowledge of the man Jesus is not the knowledge of Christ. In the witness of Scripture God's mystery is made known as the mystery revealed in God's activity. But the revealed mystery has not become the mystery

---

200. See below, pp. 308ff.

then placed at our disposal. God's self-disclosure is not "present" in the scriptural Word, but rather it is witnessed to there. It remains at the disposal of God. What is the relationship of this statement to the thesis of perspicuity?

Late Lutheran Orthodoxy tended to deal with the problem by stating that a part of the effective demonstration of the perspicuity of Scripture was that the reader was to be a "pious reader" *(pius lector)*; there was otherwise an "obscurity" present in the "contemplating subject"[201] which did not prove that there was any "obscurity" in the "object contemplated" (i.e., in Scripture) but which did make the clarity or perspicuity of Scripture ineffective for such a subject.

The opinion was that a part of the effectiveness of the perspicuity of Scripture was a certain subjective disposition, even the renunciation of prejudices,[202] but above all the invocation of God, the Father of light, as Hollaz expresses it. The Lutheran dogmaticians of the Orthodox period are in fact seeking to do their best in placing the conditions for the effectiveness of perspicuity within the scope of man's accomplishments, partially because of their doctrine of free will, but primarily so that the unconditional priority of the scriptural witness (as the external word) would not be lost in view of this subjective condition. This did not hinder them from seeing that the internal sense of Scripture is only made knowable through the illumination provided by the Holy Spirit.[203] This point was placed at the center from the beginning by the Reformed. Even though they worked with special exegetical zeal, the fundamental principle was upheld that both private and public interpretation require the "calling." That means that Scripture only discloses itself to the faithful.[204]

e. The Subject-Object Pattern in the Orthodox View. These considerations do show that the Orthodox by no means passed over the final problem with which Scripture confronts us. But it did shift the problem with its view that on the one hand there was the clear "objective" Scripture and on the other the "subjective" reader, who was understood with these or those characteristics. But we never find ourselves in our relationship to Scripture as autonomous subjects who are supposed to take a position in regard to this objective factor, the biblical message, in its autonomy. From the outset, we are directly addressed. And yet, truly, we only experience our being addressed in the process of our responding, in the concrete Yes or No.

The peculiar subject-object pattern with which Orthodoxy tried to master the problem being discussed is particularly demonstrated at one point. Orthodox

---

201. Quenstedt, *op. cit.*, p. 118 (Schmid, p. 83). Quenstedt, incidentally, appeals to the communion controversy. The heretics and heterodox exhibited such an obscurity as contemplating subjects, and the result was that the fully clear meaning of the communion words was distorted and not understood, because the naughty Reformed followed "the counsel and dictation of blind reason" (*op. cit.*, p. 124 [Schmid, *loc. cit.*]).

202. See Hollaz, *op. cit.*, p. 149, in Schmid, pp. 82f. Also A. Quenstedt, *op. cit.*, p. 118 (Schmid, p. 83).

203. Calovius, *op. cit.*, p. 657, in Schmid, p. 84.

204. These considerations based upon the Leiden Synopsis (1624 and 1652), pp. 54f. The idea that only the faithful can be the proper readers of Scripture is also found in Quenstedt, *op. cit.*, p. 137, in the thesis (Schmid, p. 86).

discussions about the perspicuity of Scripture seldom refer to the fact that the Word of Scripture customarily confronts us in proclamation or in relationship to it. We are not isolated readers facing a voiceless text, which is passively, patiently waiting there for us, but rather we are those who are addressed by the text and thus those who have been placed before a decision. Our perceiving is really our own. But when we do indeed perceive, then a power has been effective in us which does not derive from us—the "objective" encounters us in our "subjectivity" in such a way that we then cease to be "subjective."

iv. EFFICACY

In these last remarks we have moved into the area of the last thesis which Orthodoxy propounded in regard to the properties of Sacred Scripture. It was not until Late Orthodoxy, primarily until Abraham Calovius (1612–86), that the efficacy of Scripture was spoken of. Reformed Orthodoxy, too, dealt with it, although the thesis of efficacy was fundamentally directed against "Reformed" tendencies within Lutheran Orthodoxy.[205]

a. The Rahtmannian Controversy. The impulse for the development of the doctrine under discussion here was the controversy which revolved around the Danzig pastor Hermann Rahtmann (d. 1628).[206] He was an Orthodox who had become tired of mere Orthodoxy and came under the influence of Johann Arndt (1555–1621), and perhaps also under the possible and indirect influence of Schwenckfeldianism, which was still vital in the east—his opponents accused him of this. Apparently, though, he had no Reformed contacts. In 1621[207] he advanced the thesis that the Scriptures offer only an outward announcement of the Word of God but do not themselves cause that special illumination which leads to conversion. That effect is the sole work of the Holy Spirit, which is always new in relationship to Scripture. Rahtmann's illustrative picture is of Scripture as an axe which is only effective when an arm wields it. Rahtmann's Orthodox contemporaries saw in this view a new outburst of the distinction, long regarded as heterodox, between the outer and the inner Word of God, and most of them rejected Rahtmann's thesis. Of the theological faculties which the Danzig Council queried,

---

205. Calovius: "That the Sacred Scriptures are living and efficacious, and a means of illumination, conversion, and salvation, prepared and vivified by Divine power" (*Systema locorum theologicorum* [1655], I, 478, in H. Schmid, *op. cit.*, p. 90). See also the information on Ludwig Crocius (*Syntagma theol.* [1636]—before Calovius!) and Peter von Mastricht (*Theoretico-practica Theologia* [1699]) in Heppe-Bizer, pp. 21f. An especially differentiated and profitable presentation of the position of Lutheran Orthodoxy is found in Andreas Quenstedt, *op. cit.*, pp. 169ff. (Schmid, pp. 505f.).

206. O. Ritschl, *op. cit.*, IV, 158ff.; R. H. Grützmacher, *Wort und Geist, eine historische und dogmatische Untersuchung zum Gnadenmittel des Wortes* (Leipzig: A. Deichert, 1902), pp. 220f.; and his article in Schaff-Herzog, IX, 382f.; Engelhardt, *Zeitschrift für historische Theologie* (1854), pp. 43ff.; J. G. Walch, *Historische und theologische Einleitung in die Religionsstreitigkeiten der evangelisch-lutherischen Kirchen* (Jena: Meyer, 1730–39), I, cap. IV, 9, pp. 524ff. and IV, cap. IV, 17–21, pp. 577ff.

207. His chief writing: "Jesu Christi . . . Gnadenreich" (1621). The title is reminiscent of Federal Theology, to which Rahtmann was related in that he too was a chiliast.

Wittenberg, Königsberg, Jena, and Helmstedt all took positions against Rahtmann; only Rostock did not find anything essential to complain of.[208]

The Orthodox opponents of Rahtmann asserted against him the thesis that
the Word of God is not only active in use (i.e., during proper reading, preaching,
and hearing) but also when not in use. To be sure, Quenstedt protests against the
obvious misunderstanding that the Scriptures should be seen as something which
works magically.[209] The primary intention at first was simply to emphasize the
union of Scripture and Spirit using the sharpest conceptual means. Wherever
Scripture is, there is the Spirit; he is nowhere else, but here he really is and
therefore is effective. One can well presume that the actual concern behind all of
this was the desire to rule out synergism.[210] It is not the special disposition of
man, even if caused by the Spirit, which makes Scripture into the Word of God,
but rather it is that Word by virtue of divine authority. Everything found on the
side of the reader or hearer is in contrast to this primary aspect strictly secondary.
Nevertheless, K. Barth is certainly right when he concludes that Rahtmann's
opponents wanted "more than that," and that "in this more" they cannot be
followed.[211] A marginal concept which could be understood only as such becomes
totally unacceptable when it is made into a central contentual statement. This is
the case, for example, when Quenstedt concludes, "Whether the Word be read
or not, whether it be heard and believed or not, yet the efficacy of its spiritual
effects is always intrinsically inherent in it by the divine arrangement and communication, nor does this divine efficacy only come to it when it is used."[212] Or
when he contests that Scripture is an instrument which requires "a new motive
or elevating power" in order to produce its effect.[213] Here, in spite of all the
careful reservations and limitations of which Quenstedt is a master, what can only
be conceived of as a promise given to faith becomes something ontically and
tangibly present. The only limitation given is in Quenstedt's distinction between
the "primary act" (the "operating power") and the "secondary act" ("effi-
ciency" in the sense of Eph. 1:19): Scripture is the cause of faith, but does not
cause it automatically.

b. The Positive Meaning of the Doctrine of Efficacy. This short excursion into
the controversies of Orthodox doctrine was necessary because they reveal, even

---

208. The written findings against Rahtmann were printed in 1626 ("Censuren und
Bedenken von Theologischen Facultäten und Doctoren . . .").

209. *Op. cit.*, pp. 169f.

210. Rahtmann had basically understood Scripture as the sum of words and sentences, and reconceived their essential relationship to proclamation as something which was
added to them. This indicates that he pursues the objectification of Scripture in a very
different way (resulting quantitatively in a much narrower result), but he is actually making
Scripture into a thing. This way of dealing with Scripture always corresponds correlatively
with synergism. Incidentally it was Calixtus of all people who accused Orthodox doctrine
of synergism (he appeals to J. Hülsemann) (see Quenstedt, *op. cit.*, pp. 170f. [Schmid, *op.
cit.*, pp. 505ff.]).

211. *CD*, I,1, p. 124.

212. Quenstedt, *op. cit.*, p. 170 (Schmid, p. 510).

213. *Op. cit.*, p. 171 (Schmid, p. 511). Almost more massively, David Hollaz, *op. cit.*,
p. 992, in Schmid, p. 511.

if under rather confusing circumstances,[214] the problem which arises when we seek to appropriate the thesis of the efficacy of Scripture for our own use. This thesis is reminiscent both in language and in content of Hebrews 4:12, which in the Vulgate is translated in such a way that the "discourse" of God *(sermo)* is "living" and "effective" *(efficax)*. Calvin finds quite rightly that this text is by no means to be applied only to the believing;[215] the efficacy is not only present where "one's own will" intervenes, but everywhere. The meaning of the text leads up to the insight, "that as soon as it [the Word] has sounded in our ears our consciences are cited in accusation before the judgment-seat of God." Calvin refers here (as do many after him) to John 16:8. Precisely because the Word (or, as Calvin adds for clarification, the "preaching") is worked by the Spirit and empowered by him, it cannot fall to the earth without effect. And this is true (here Quenstedt agrees with Calvin[216]) not only of the law but also of the Gospel, according to 2 Corinthians 2:16; 10:4. However, for Calvin all of this is related to the preached Word (Rom. 10:8), and not to some kind of internal Word (!). Of course the efficacy of the Word is not based upon what the preacher does. It is based upon the Spirit's "bringing forth his power in the Word that is preached."

If we judge properly, then Calvin, long before the controversies just discussed broke out in the area of Lutheran Orthodoxy, had stated what must be said in this matter. The thesis of the efficacy of the Word, as Calvin establishes it in his Hebrews commentary of 1549, implies the superiority of what is being proclaimed over the Word of proclamation itself. We do not make the Word effective, neither with our scriptural scholarship, nor with our evangelistic forcefulness, nor with the passion of our faith. We also do not make it ineffective with the hardness of our resistance nor the carelessness of our failing to hear. The authoritative validity of the Word is not derived from us. But it also does not carry this authoritative validity within itself. Rather, it has it because it is the Word of witness, as human word, empowered by the Holy Spirit—and thus it is placed at our disposal! That this Word places us in the specific situation of decision is the work of the Spirit. In this work the One at work is the one who is the source of life for the Word of witness, the scriptural Word, and to this One the Word must always be related. In relationship to the Word witnessed to there is no place for our co-working. Christ, through the Spirit, is the One at work in this Word and through it. He is not identical with the Word witnessed to. His being is not exhausted in it. This is what Hermann Rahtmann began to grasp. But he is not partially in this Word in order then to apply the other part in the Spirit's work or even to be dependent upon our own emotional or personal movements. He makes himself known through the Word, and thus it is as efficacious as it is alive (Heb. 4:12).

---

214. The position of the Danish theologian, J. R. Brochmand, who was very important in Late Lutheran Orthodoxy, seems very ambiguous, so much so that even O. Ritschl, *op. cit.,* pp. 163f., cannot interpret him clearly.

215. Calvin, *The Epistle of Paul the Apostle to the Hebrews and the First and Second Epistles of St. Peter,* tr. W. B. Johnston (Grand Rapids: Eerdmans, 1963), pp. 51ff.

216. Quenstedt, *op. cit.,* p. 170 (Schmid, pp. 503f.).

C. THE OLD AND NEW TESTAMENTS

The considerations which we set forth in connection with the Orthodox doctrine of the attributes of Sacred Scripture had led us up to the threshold of the hermeneutic question which is so burning an issue today. Dogmatics finds itself here at the most sensitive point in its relationship to exegesis. This relationship, however, has always been double-sided. On the one hand, dogmatics has always been dependent upon exegesis if it wanted to be something other than the philosophy of religion. It can never be dogmatics' intention that exegesis become "dogmatic" in a perverted sense, but rather it will place the greatest stress upon the biblical texts' being interpreted as they are. On the other hand, dogmatics must constantly confront exegesis with the question whether it is not actually being "dogmatic" in this sense. Since the exegete does not approach his texts with a totally blank mind, the possibility is always there that his mandated "understanding" will be defined by the way he "understands" himself. And there the dogmatician has the task of querying the exegete about the conceptual appropriateness of his method of "understanding." If a dogmatics which thought itself to be independent of or even superior to exegesis is in fact a philosophy of religion, then exegesis which is uninterested in dogmatics could become mere philology or, what is more acute today, also a philosophy of religion in the disguise of its methodology. Thus, dogmatics cannot renounce its participation in the fundamental issues of exegesis. Otherwise it would deny that exegesis is a theological science and it itself, dogmatics, is a labor which is bound to the Scriptures.

a. The Point of Departure in Our Query. Of all the questions which concern both exegesis and dogmatics equally, the relationship of the two halves of the Bible appears as a particularly complicated one. Therefore we are going to devote a special section to it. This corresponds to the approach frequently adopted by the Reformers.[217] The Reformers were well aware of the tensions within the Bible, more so than the Middle Ages. For the Middle Ages, on the one hand, in making the Church of Jesus Christ into a sacral realm with the legalisms pertaining to it, had basically opted for an Old Testament which was separated from the New; on the other hand, in its doctrine of the manifold meanings of Scripture[218] it had a tool which made it possible to interpret the tensions away. Since the Reformation rejected both of these possibilities, the relationship of the two Testaments became a problem again. In this way the Reformation became the source of a new way of defining this relationship.

For our thought the point of departure is definitely the New Testament. It cannot be contested that the New Testament understands it proclamation upon the basis of the Old Testament. It is equally incontestable that the way in which

---

217. Luther, *Against the Heavenly Prophets* (AE, XL, 144ff.); *How Christians Should Regard Moses* (AE, XXXV, 161–74); Melanchthon's section on the discrimination of the Old and New Testaments in the various versions of the *Loci,* e.g., in *LCC,* XIX, 120ff.; Calvin, primarily in the *Institutes,* II, ix-xi, pp. 423–64 (a section with a particularly complicated genesis). See also Luther's "Preface to the Old Testament," first in 1523.

218. See below, pp. 319ff.

the message witnessed to in the New Testament is understood defines the position of the Old Testament. In addition, we only have the Old Testament through the mediation and reception which is made known in the New Testament. There is no other approach to the Old Testament for us than the way paved by the proclamation of the New.[219]

b. Classification in the Sense of the Science of Religion. Since the period of the Enlightenment, the New Testament has essentially been looked upon as the document for the institution of the Christian religion. In general this was connected with the conviction that "Christianity" is the "highest," "noblest," or "most progressive" religion. Even the "absoluteness" of "Christianity" was generally maintained. The theology of the 18th and of the 19th centuries was very sure of its being Christian.

Viewed from this assured "Christian" position, the Old Testament then appears as the document of another very high religion, but one that has been surpassed by Christianity. One can, of course, admit that "even" the Old Testament anticipated or even paved the way for this or that Christian insight, and it can even be asserted further that primitive Christianity still was covered with many Old Testament "layers," which is clearly demonstrated by the innumerable Old Testament citations in the New Testament.

As long as we look at this matter in this fashion, then it is really of no consequence whether the observer of the Old Testament, so happily certain of his Christianity, rejects it as outdated or accepts it as the preparatory stage for Christianity. It is also possible for both points of view to be united, as in Adolf von Harnack, for example. At one time, he averred, it was necessary for the Old Testament to be retained since without it Christendom would have been without any traditions or totally fallen prey to Hellenization; but today this necessity is no longer given; rather it is the actual task of Christendom to free itself from the Old Testament,[220] since its retention today can only be viewed as "the result of a religious and ecclesiastical paralysis." In general the position adopted, based upon the factors presented here, was one of historical-noetic acknowledgment of the Old Testament;[221] it was not possible to understand Christianity without its Old Testament preconditions. This had little to do substantially with an acknowledgment of the Old Testament for the Church's proclamation. Otherwise it would

---

219. A. Alt, J. Begrich, G. von Rad, *Führung zum Christentum durch das Alte Testament* (Leipzig: Dörffling & Franke, 1934); J. Hempel, *Gott und Mensch im Alten Testament, Studie zur Geschichte der Frömmigkeit* (2nd ed.; Stuttgart: Kohlhammer, 1936).

220. Adolf von Harnack, *Marcion; das Evangelium vom fremden Gott* (Leipzig: J. C. Hinrichs, 1921).

221. See Ernst Troeltsch, *Glaubenslehre; nach Heidelberger Vorlesungen aus den Jahren 1911 & 1912* (Munich and Leipzig: Duncker & Humboldt, 1925), p. 97: "The recognition of Christianity as the highest divine revelation includes the acknowledgment of the religion of Israel as the preparatory stage and presupposition of this revelation, for without it Christianity cannot be understood, and it requires the constant connection with its rich Old Testament background" (Dictation; see also "Glaube und Ethos der hebräischen Propheten," *Gesammelte Schriften* [4 vols.; Tübingen: J. C. B. Mohr, 1912–25; repr. Aalen: Scientia, 1961–66], IV, 34ff.).

be necessary, for reasons of understanding, to acknowledge the late Jewish literature and a rather broad scope of Hellenistic documents as well. One thing can be said from the perspective of the Church, though. The Old Testament's "clarity, power, and greatness, flowing into the Christian world of ideas, will never want to be missed."[222] This recommendation of the Old Testament seemed all the less dangerous since theology, as long as it moved within the limits of a general concept of religion, could only ascribe to the New Testament a conditional significance, open to future and "further development."

If the New Testament is understood as a religious document and only as such, then there is no real reason for the Old Testament to have any authority at all. Of course, the authority of the New Testament, too, is then unnecessary. It also has in essence only historical significance, and the "spirit" which makes itself known in it would not be understood as alive if further development and adaptation to the new historical situation were not to be expected of it.

The basic view described here rests upon a peculiar kind of security. This kind of piety, that is, of Christian behavior, was not seriously opposed or threatened for those who propounded this view. Schleiermacher's "common spirit" was regarded as something tangibly identifiable. Just as Schleiermacher's scriptural understanding was in fact derived from the "faith" already there, the Church, too, in its dealings with Scripture was always involved in a discussion with a partner which could only tell it what this faith was stating. That means that an Absolute Other as counterpart was completely out of the picture. Even the document about the origins could only discuss the origin of what was present, mark off the historical beginning of the line upon which they were now moving. Thus a theology which went this path was progressively more open to the understanding of the historical and the contingent (for which Schleiermacher still had a sense) as the expression of the supra-historical or, better, the ahistorical, which means the expression of ideas.

Wherever this counterpart disappears, people may still be convinced that they "understand" the New Testament—as the beginning of the line in which they find themselves. But the Old Testament has no authoritative role to play at all anymore. Schleiermacher's own view shows that clearly enough.[223] But where this has happened, then in truth the New Testament also has been profoundly misunderstood. Basically, it only is "valid" because and to the extent that it states an idea, and the idea meant is that of those reading it. It becomes clear here that the devaluation of the Old Testament based upon religio-scientific grounds in fact presupposes a certain ecclesiastical position, one which in unavoidable logic must deliver the New Testament ultimately to the same fate as the Old.

    c. Classification in the Sense of Salvation-history. Neither the 18th nor certainly the 19th century in its theological view of the Old Testament was shaped solely or even predominantly by concepts derived from the science of religion.

---

222. E. Troeltsch, *op. cit.*, p. 99.
223. Schleiermacher, *ChrF*, §132, Thesis, II, p. 608; also Paul Althaus, *op. cit.*, I, 229.

The conceptual approaches of "salvation-history" *(Heilsgeschichte)* are probably more notable, particularly as they were expressed in Hofmann's great and very influential design.[224] The Old and New Testaments were seen here in their mutual relationship along the customary lines of "prophecy" and "fulfillment," and Hofmann developed a new understanding of this pattern in that he did not see mere statements or single writings as "prophecy" but understood the entire Old Testament event to be such. This pattern was long connected to the idea of a series of "stages" of revelation or of salvation-history, which Paul Althaus in our day has taken up again when he speaks of the "stages of the history of faith."[225] This is not the place for a more detailed discussion of the relationship between "prophecy" or "promise" and "fulfillment."[226] Nonetheless, there could be a view of the term "promise" in which the Old Testament were simply absorbed by the New. Put simply, this means that "promise" would merely be the statement that something was going to come, and it is both confirmed and done away with at the moment where what was promised has come. Certainly this was not the opinion of the salvation-historical theology of the 19th century. In spite of that, since this theology so frequently, and especially in Hofmann, incorporates the idea that I can find "the faith according to which I interpret Scripture" nowhere else than "in myself,"[227] then Scripture in this view can never prove anything else but what is "derived from the personal experience of the Christian."[228] For our understanding of Scripture this leads to the result that the Old Testament is the expression of the preformation of the faith found in the Christian. This must then lead to a tendency in which the Old Testament no longer has its own and unique significance. An Old Testament absorbed into the New Testament, or even into the condition of the given Christian faith, would not be a relevant element of the Bible anymore, and it would then be more sensible to stick to the New Testament directly and exclusively.

d. Polarity as a Methodological Approach. Up until now, we have dealt only with those views of the relationship between the Old and the New Testament which seek to place both in the same line. This procedure, which we shall later adopt under other presuppositions, has demonstrated that it is at least difficult to show why the Church should retain the Old Testament. If it is not more than the historical preparation for or anticipation of the New Testament and its message, then it would appear to be dispensable if not damaging for the Church.

The methodological consideration we would propose here would be whether the reverse approach might not lead to clear insights. What could be asked would be whether the permanent significance of the Old Testament were not in the fact that it expresses its own unique message, but a message which is so structured

---

224. Johann C. von Hofmann, *Weissagung und Erfüllung im Alten und Neuen Testament* (2 vols.; Nördlingen: C. H. Beck'schen Buchhandlung, 1841); *Der Schriftbeweis* (3 vols.; Nördlingen: C. H. Beck'schen Buchhandlung, 1852, 2nd ed. 1857).
225. Althaus, *op. cit.*, I, 234.
226. See below, pp. 304ff.
227. Hofmann, *Der Schriftbeweis*, I, 9.
228. *Ibid.*, p. 28.

that the New Testament proclamation could not be what it is without it. Put differently, if the Old Testament, in a sense still to be discussed, is saying "the same thing," then perhaps its significance would be in the fact that it says this "same thing" differently than does the New Testament, and yet in such a qualified way that the New Testament in the long run could not be understood and accepted without the different message of the Old Testament.

e. The Linear Treatment of the Old Testament in the New. A look at the New Testament itself shows that the message proclaimed there is related to the Old Testament message in a very differentiated and disparate way.

On the one hand, the New Testament constantly refers to and relies upon the Old Testament. As R. Bultmann has shown,[229] the prophecy proof, which is the definitive theological proof in the New Testament, is developed partially along the lines of Old Testament-Jewish tradition (the New Testament proclaims the final age expected in the Old Testament), and partially along the lines of Hellenistic-Stoic argumentation according to which the Old (Testament) in its totality is expressing the New and Real in a concealed form, so that now it can be revealed and disclosed by the Real (allegory). Every Bible reader knows texts demonstrating this. John's "it is they that bear witness to me" (John 5:39) and Paul's "For all the promises of God find their Yes in him" (2 Cor. 1:20) harmonize. According to W. G. Kümmel,[230] this is true of Jesus' proclamation and apparently also of Paul's, who bases his doctrine of justification through faith upon the Old Testament. The righteousness revealed by God is "manifested apart from law, although the law and the prophets bear witness to it . . ." (Rom. 3:21). Abraham is the father of all believers (Rom. 4:12). The Epistle to the Hebrews sees a "cloud of witnesses" emerging (Heb. 12:1), and the whole letter testifies to the comprehensive way this is meant. Every user of the Nestle text can gain an optical impression of the concentration of the Old Testament in the New.

f. Polar Antithesis in the New Testament. On the other hand, New Testament proclamation is related to the Old Testament with a peculiar kind of freedom. Jesus' "But I say unto you" in Matthew 5:22, 28, 32, 34, 39 is directed immediately against regulations in the Torah, which just previously (Matt. 5:17) had been spoken of as expressly unabolishable. In Luke 9:55, Jesus asks, referring to Elijah's actions, "Do you not know what manner of spirit you are of?"[231] Even Jesus' behavior toward the Sabbath and the dietary law, although on the face of it directed against the casuistics of the synagogue, still has its thrust against the law itself, and in Matthew 12:3-7 this is done with appeal to the Old Testament! Paul does not veer from this way when in the question of the laws of cleanliness he does not fear to disagree with Peter (Gal. 2:11ff.). His judgment of circumcision

---

229. R. Bultmann, "Prophecy and Fulfilment" (1949), in *Essays Philosophical and Theological*, tr. J. C. G. Greig (New York: Macmillan, 1955), pp. 182ff.
230. W. G. Kümmel, *Promise and Fulfillment, the eschatological message of Jesus,* tr. D. M. Barton (Naperville, Ill.: A. R. Allenson, 1957).
231. The RSV consigns this text to the margins as a textual emendation—TR.

is probably even more emphatic: for to whoever has himself circumcised Christ will be of no advantage (Gal. 5:2); the preaching of circumcision would destroy the scandal of the cross (Gal. 5:11). These are concrete high points at which the whole proclamation of the Apostle to the Gentiles culminates. One can only properly judge the importance of this proclamation when one remembers that Paul does not see the law as a kind of codex of norms, whose application would be left up to the preferences of the observer. When the born Jew said "God" or "The Lord," then the law was always meant too. New concepts would never have been capable of breaking the power of the law, which was greater than all questions placed to it. Freedom from the law, as preached by Paul and others, did not rest upon an altered religious "view," but rather upon the certainty that in Jesus Christ the law had found its goal and end (Rom. 10:4). And this can only mean that in Jesus Christ God himself, the God witnessed to in the Old Testament(!), has made a decision which excludes the law as a way to salvation, has established an order which replaces the order of the law (according to Paul it was not original anyway—Gal. 3:19; Rom. 5:20) in a new reality (see especially 2 Cor. 3:4ff.).

In terms of its central ideas, the New Testament reveals profound contradictions in its treatment of the Old. The decisive criterion which appears behind all of the conceptual matters is the act of God in Jesus Christ proclaimed in the Gospel, and in this act the New Testament witnesses without exception see the One at work who is proclaimed by the Old Testament. Thus, the Yes and the No grow out of the same roots. But the Yes and the No both remain. The Old Testament is the epitome of promise, and it is the epitome of the law. The fulfilled promise, however, frees from the law.

The salvation-event witnessed to in the New Testament is itself the dividing line between the Old and the New Testament. If we want to begin methodically asking the Old Testament what its unique message is, then we will not primarily be seeking out intellectual concepts as our answers. The Old Testament, to the extent that the New does distance itself from it at all, is not made up of various concepts, but rather is the epitome of authoritative validity which is based upon facts, ultimately upon one fact. It does not want to propagate ideas, nor assert "meanings," but make events known. The message of the Old Testament can only be understood upon the basis of this event, this specific history. The Old Testament does not interpret this history. It proclaims it as authoritatively valid. When Late Judaism called the entire Pentateuch the Torah, it was on the right path in terms of its contents.[232]

We shall have to see the unique element of the Old Testament in the uniqueness of the history which it witnesses to as being authoritatively valid. What is then authoritatively valid about it?

---

232. See H. J. Kraus, "Gesetz und Geschichte; zum Geschichtsbild des Deuteronomisten," *EvTheol* (1951/52), pp. 415–28, and my remarks about "Law and History" in my *Bibelkunde des Alten Testaments* (Berlin: Furche Verlag, 1935–48), vol. I.

g. The Testimony to the Creator. The most obvious first answer could be, The Old Testament witnesses to God as the Creator. In fact, this must be emphasized, since the New Testament does not present the witness to the Creator as an independent element of its own kerygma but rather receives it as a part of the Old Testament. Wherever in Christendom the Old Testament with its own message has been separated from the New and no longer seen with its own message, there Christendom has become a host of esoterics for whom the world was something alien. This was the case with Marcion. It is ultimately the situation with those modern theologians who view the New Testament and its message essentially from the aspect of the "desecularization" of the relationship to God and then obviously must seek to make the Creator into the intentional origin. In a certain sense, this was also true of some proponents of the salvation-historical view, for whom the Old Testament had no message of its own to communicate. It was not able then to prevent the enclosure of what is Christian in its own, pious, inner world. The Old Testament has its own "theme" in the proclamation of God as the Creator, and it must lead to a distortion of the New Testament understanding of Christian existence if the Old Testament theme is not properly heard.

h. Creation and Covenant. The proclamation of the Creator as we find it in the Old Testament is not oriented toward some passive origin out of which reality somehow emanates or which fulfills reality with meaning, but rather toward the One who as Creator is the Lord, and as Lord is the Creator. Therefore, there is no interchangeability between Creator and creature in the Old Testament. And this means primarily that there is absolutely nothing there of the mysticism which seeks "God" in man and wants to find a correlative of the origin in the depths of creaturely existence. Man, as he is and in a specific way, is mere creature. And this means that he stands before his Creator in absolute irreplaceableness. There is nothing "creative" about him—the Old Testament sees him in a fundamentally different way than does the Greek world. God and man are placed in a strict pattern of opposites, as confronting counterparts. God is the "Holy One," and man only participates in this holiness in that God admits man into his own realm. But this is meant in such a way that there is no trace of a static difference nor of a rigid distance between God and man. Martin Buber is right when he sees (in the context of his "principle of dialogue"[233]) the greatness of the Old Testament (he means, in Israel's act!) in the "approachableness . . . of God."[234] The totally and unchangeably Other is personal, moving, alive.

The Old Testament could only make the Creator known because it was coming from the encounter in which the Creator had disclosed himself as the Other and yet the One who turns to man and allows himself to be approached and addressed by man. That means that the faith in God the Creator is, in the Old Testament, faith in the One who elects Israel and who has established his covenant with Israel. "Before Israel recognized God, the Creator of the world, it recognized God as its Lord. He is not our Lord because He can be recognized

---

233. See H. J. Kraus, "Gespräch mit Martin Buber," *EvTheol* (1952–53), p. 64.
234. M. Buber, *Chassidische Bücher; die Erzählungen der Chassidim* (Zürich: Manesse Verlag, 1927), p. XI.

from nature as the Framer of the World, but rather because He reveals himself
to us as our Lord, next to whom there can be no other, and therefore he must be
the Lord of all the worlds."[235] It is in fact the case that the concept of God the
Creator is rooted in the message of the covenant.[236] Thus in the Old Testament
this is never generalized speech but always an element of highly concrete proclamation. God's relationship to man is, according to the Old Testament, certainly
not limited to Israel (the tendency to such limitation is opposed by Amos 9:7,
Deut. 7:7f., Ex. 19:5b, and then certainly the "universalism" of the creation
traditions). But it has its central point, its point of orientation, in this Israel,
whom alone Yahweh has "known" (Amos 3:2). The God of Israel is the Lord of
the world. This is the actual reason that the Old Testament never really can deal
in thoughts or abstract concepts. The primary issue is always this incomprehensible election by Yahweh, unmotivated by Israel, often disavowed by it, thrust
aside and trod upon again and again. If the Old Testament is universalistic, and
that is in fact so, then it is such from a particular central point. The uniqueness
of the Old Testament is not "ethical monotheism," which in truth never was the
center of the Old Testament and as abstract monotheism never was attained, nor
the faith in the Creator as such, nor the doubtless profound view of man, nor even
the "super-terrestrial" character of God, nor the relationship to history. Everything which could be mentioned in detail is rooted in this one thing: the relationship which Yahweh in his goodness and freedom establishes with this nation. The
essential problem of the Old Testament is the problem of Israel.

i. Covenant and Law. This is also true of the law. In none of its varying
forms is it the epitome of abstract norms, but rather it belongs to the reality of
the covenant and has its cultic place in the "covenant renewal festival" of the
amphictyony.[237] It is not something like the application of general norms to this
special people, but is the expression of the fact that this "nation" which has its
national substance solely in its relationship to God is Yahweh's people. There are
only a few elements in which this law is materially different from other legal
codes. Its importance is not to be sought in its ethical or juridical form but in its
connection with the covenant.

In mentioning the "law" we have touched upon the point which especially
characterizes the Old Testament for Luther and many others. The Old Testament
is for Luther "a law book," just as the New Testament is "a Gospel or book of
grace."[238] Luther did not want to overlook the fact that this book is also full of
promise. But he first of all deals with it as law. If what is meant by this is that the

---

235. Emil Brunner, "Die Bedeutung des Alten Testaments für unseren Glauben,"
ZZ (1930), p. 37.
236. K. Barth, *CD*, III,1, passim.
237. H. J. Kraus, *Worship in Israel, A Cultic History of the Old Testament*, tr. Geof-
frey Buswell (Richmond: John Knox Press, 1966), pp. 55ff.; Albrecht Alt, "Die Ursprünge
des israelitischen Rechts," *Sitzungsberichte der Sächsischen Akademie der Wissenschaften,
Philologisch-historische Klasse* (Leipzig: S. Hirzel, 1934); S. Mowinckel, *Psalmenstudien*
(2 vols.; Amsterdam: P. Schippers, 1961); Gerhard von Rad, *The Problem of the Hexateuch
and Other Essays*, tr. E. W. Trueman Dicken (Edinburgh: Oliver & Boyd, 1966).
238. "Preface to the Old Testament" (AE, XXXV, 236f.).

law precedes the Gospel historically in the experience of perceiving man, so that this law is done away with in the Gospel, then we would have to reply that this view accords neither with the New Testament (Rom. 5:20; Gal. 3:19ff.) nor, seen properly, with the contemporary view of the Old.[239] Barth's much discussed thesis according to which the law is to be understood as "the form of the Gospel"[240]— a thesis which should not be turned around methodologicaly nor temporally, just as Luther's intended order of law and Gospel may not be turned around—accords more with the predominant exegetical view today than does Luther's basic thesis. It has its New Testament base in Romans 4, and as far as the Old Testament is concerned, it cannot be denied that commandment, law, and justice are all related back to the covenant, which is praised as the great and fundamental act of blessing.

The law characterizes life in the covenant as life in obedience and thus as historical life. The fundamental "I am" of the decalogue[241] is inseparable from the corresponding "Thou shalt" of the commandments. If the "I am" were isolated, then Yahweh would no longer be acknowledged as the Lord who commands in his grace, nor the covenant as the gift which obligates; the covenant with Yahweh would have become Israel's own possession and would thus have been broken. If the "Thou shalt" were isolated, then the commandments would have become abstract statements of norms which would be subject to ethical investigation. Everything depends upon "I am." Historically we see that in Israel both the social and legal order deteriorated when Yahweh was made into an idol or his sole lordship was denied in practice. But this "I am" is never separate from the "Thou shalt." The prophets, as defenders of the pure "I am" of the God of Israel, were as such attackers of the legal, moral, and social decay in Israel.

The "law" (in point of fact a term containing many highly differing concepts) is based upon promise[242] and leads to promise. Remaining in the law is remaining in the realm of salvation. "You shall therefore keep my statutes and ordinances, by doing which a man shall live" (Lev. 18:5 and based upon it, Rom. 10:5—at this point Paul heard the voice of "righteousness out of the law"—and there are numerous parallels for it). This then led to the idea of a closed circle: whoever keeps the law remains in the covenant, and whoever remains in the covenant must necessarily have success and fulfillment in life, because God is on his side. This could be applied to the nation, but (above all in the later periods)

---

239. ". . . the assertion that the Old Testament contains more law than Gospel is harder to establish today than in Luther's day, for the commandments' function of grounding salvation stands much more in the foreground for us today . . ." (G. von Rad, review of F. Baumgärtel, *Verheissung*, in *EvTheol* [1953], p. 410).

240. See II,2, p. 509; see also, in general, *CD*, II,2, pp. 492ff., and "Gospel and Law," *God, Grace and Gospel* (*Scottish Journal of Theology*, Occasional Papers, No. 8), tr. J. S. McNab (Edinburgh: Oliver & Boyd, 1959). Edmund Schlink, *Gesetz und Evangelium, ein Beitrag zum lutherischen Verständnis der 2. Barmen These* (Munich: Kaiser, 1937); Helmut Thielicke, *Theologische Ethik* (3 vols. in 4; Tübingen: J. C. B. Mohr [Paul Siebeck], 1951), I, 188ff.

241. F. Baumgärtel, *Verheissung; zur Frage des evangelischen Verständnisses des Alten Testaments* (Gütersloh: Bertelsmann, 1952), p. 19, says of this "I am Jahweh" that it is the "basic promise."

242. Again, F. Baumgärtel when he calls the first words of the decalogue the "basic promise."

also to the individual who understands himself as such. But is it really in harmony with the original intent of the Old Testament message to make remaining in the covenant morally and conditionally dependent upon remaining in the law?

j. The Unfulfilled Law. Nevertheless, there is that kind of thinking. And the reason it was there was that the covenant, understood as a fact, never was a tangible and concrete given, but (in its one-sided establishment as the Old Testament sees it: *"My* covenant . . ."!) constantly summoned its human-historical partner to decision. The covenant was never just a part of Israel's past but also always a constant part of its future. Eschatology was connected with the covenant. And the commandment was also connected with the covenant. Both were oriented toward the future. In the Old Testament there is no directing man to introspection nor to an ontic "beyond," but only the direction forward. It does not interpret, it does not provide the meaning of the event, it draws man as the covenant partner into the history which is open toward the future solely because it was founded in the past. This also meant that the covenant was quite concretely unfulfilled. And nothing was more natural than that the man living in this as yet unfulfilled covenant, open toward the future, would attempt to grasp what was before him in his own hands. Then he desired what Paul called "righteousness out of the law," the righteousness of which he could boast not as the one to whom it was given, but as the one who possessed it. He was permitted to live in the covenant, but he lived on the basis of his own "fulfillment," which really was none at all. He was permitted to become "righteous" for the covenant, but he lived on the basis of his own "righteousness" (Rom. 10:3). This was the actual course of Israel's history. The reason it was possible was that the covenant was in fact as yet unfulfilled and thus the law, too, was unfulfilled.

The Old Testament, thus, presents itself as the document of the unfulfilled law incorporated into the unfulfilled covenant. This covenant does not presuppose a human partner which is appropriate to it. However, it calls to this partner. God desires to achieve his rights in man. And Israel—as a whole, excluding Isaiah's remnant and excluding the few who said and did differently—refuses God this right. Israel opposes the covenant itself and therewith its own destiny, which God had never given up (see Rom. 3:1ff.). It opposes in that it breaks the covenant and usurps it. And in doing both it is the primitive image of man in his relationship to God.

k. The Limits of the Old Testament. It may have been noticed that in the last sections of our discussion we have gradually drawn more upon the New Testament. It is in fact true that we can only understand the unfulfilledness which characterizes the Old Testament on the basis of the New Testament message.

It is broadly customary to find the limits, the "not-yet," yes, even the "failure" of the Old Testament relationship to God in the fact that it was bound to what is worldly and historical. Thus R. Bultmann attempted to show in the concept of the covenant, of the royal lordship of God and of the people of God, that a "miscarriage" was unavoidable because the integration of these concepts into a people as an "empirical and historical entity" necessarily must lead to the identification of what is not identifiable. The intention is to understand God in a "transcendent" way, but this does not happen "in the radically transcendent and eschatological sense." And this then corresponds to the notorious impossibility of what is meant being realized in history.[243] Paul Althaus speaks of the "national-particularistic," "empiricistic," and "legalistic" "connection," from which by "the leading of God" faith is to be directed "toward the Gospel."[244] Such thoughts can scarcely appeal to Paul. For him, historical-empirical Israel had a permanent significance, even though his missionary proclamation led him out of it (see primarily Rom. 9–11). Moreover, one should probably distinguish between the particularity established in the covenant and a particularism such as Israel usurped in a "fleshly" way, between the given law and a nomism developed by man himself, between God's coming Kingdom and the human illusion of a worldly ideal kingdom. It is not the limitation which is part and parcel of the uniqueness of the Old Testament which is distorted, which results in "failure," but rather the absolutizing of the limitation as Israel does this in seeking its "own righteousness." In that this happens—in the Old Testament[245]—the unique opening toward the future which can be observed in the Old Testament from the very beginning (the promise of land!) is closed off by man. The Old Testament is, under these circumstances, not only the document of the covenant but also the document of man's distortion of the covenant, not just the testimony to the deity of Yahweh but the testimony to the transformation of Yahweh into an idol by the people of Israel. It is the document of the Israel which thanks in jubilation and dedication, and of the Israel which boasts of itself. That partner of the divine covenant who would be "right" in this covenant is only suggested in a vague outline in the Old Testament. He is suggested in the "miserable ones," the suffering, the servant of God in Deutero-Isaiah. The result of this, however, is not that the covenant did not exist, was not proclaimed, was not renewed constantly as a present reality. The reality of the covenant, the promise, is more powerful than the covenant partner. It has its own set of priorities. And this is the reason that Israel does not merely err, but, as the New Testament generally puts it, is guilty.[246] It does not commit the error of lacking superterrestriality or "desecularization" in its understanding of the relationship to God; it is guilty of self-glorification, of usurpation, of the rejection of God. And the New Testament does not bring a new insight, but a new reality which is the end and the fulfillment in one.

l. Christ, "the End of the Law." The end and goal of the law is not the new understanding of being which develops in us in relationship to the New Testament. It is even less the "religion" of the New Testament or that of Christendom. The latter indicates very similar contradictions to those manifested in the Old

---

243. R. Bultmann, *loc. cit.*, pp. 191ff., 205f.
244. Althaus, *op. cit.*, I, 229ff.
245. In my small paper "Jahwe, der Gott, und Jahwe, der Götze" (1933), I have tried to suggest what tensions are present here.
246. In his essay "Verheissung und Erfüllung," *EvTheol* (1952/53), pp. 34ff., W. Zimmerli also took a position in regard to Bultmann's theses (*op. cit.*, pp. 55ff.), and expressed his assumption that Bultmann was being guided by a view of the New and thus of the Old Testament in which "historicity," as the thing which was to be overcome, threatened to disappear.

Testament and "fails" to the same extent that the "religion" of Old Testament
man in fact "failed." The goal and end of the law is Christ (Rom. 10:4), not as
the new possibility for our own way of understanding ourselves or to arrange our
relationship to God, but rather as the new reality. How should this be
understood?[247]

1) **The Truth of the Law.** Jesus reveals the law as what it really is: God's
claim upon us ourselves, as the God who gives himself to us. The distortion of
which we spoke was based upon the shifting of the covenant in order to hallow
and insure religiously the national community, of God into the guarantor of man
or of the people, and of the law into the assurance of success in life. Wherever
this happens, the relationship to the world becomes the standard of the relationship to God, and man's activity becomes his self-insurance. God is bound to man
and the law becomes the essential summary of all the conditions by which this
happens. And wherever this view is dominant, man's relationship to God is in
order as long as he formally and quantitatively "fulfills" everything which is
required of him. But this is the distortion of the law. For the law does not produce
God's covenant activity and is not established in order to provide security for
man. Rather, in the law what happens concretely is what happens in the covenant
itself: God, Israel's God, reaches out to man himself. God accepts his partner in
just the same way he gives himself. The direction of the law is self-sacrifice, not
personal security. This is how Jesus functioned under the law, as the one who
was "born under the law" (Gal. 4:4). And this is what he taught when he returned
to the Old Testament's love commandment, which the synagogue also knew, but
as a norm for performance (Matt. 22:34ff.). The law is "radical" not because it
is intended to "shock" man radically, but because God gives himself radically to
man.[248] In obeying absolutely, Jesus asserts the validity of the law.

2) **Enduring the Broken Law.** In his actions Jesus confirmed and fulfilled
God's covenant Yes, directed to Israel and in Israel to all men, in that he perse-
vered to the very end with man who had rebelled against God, with Israel which
rejected him. In doing that, he took the No of the law spoken over man who had
broken the covenant upon himself. Jesus manifested that the law is "holy," that
the commandment is "holy, right, and good," by taking the expulsion of the
disobedient upon himself, by enduring the "curse" (Gal. 3:13), and by experiencing the "condemnation" (Rom. 8:3). It is his obedience, his total commitment
to the will of the Father, which brings him to the cross, that is, to the place of the
covenant-breaker. The law expels the man who breaks it into nothingness. And
into this nothingness Jesus goes. He accepts the baptism of John so that, accord-

247. See R. Bultmann, "Christ the End of the Law" (1940), in *Essays Philosophical
and Theological . . .*, pp. 36ff., partially in debate with Paul Althaus, *Paulus und Luther
über den Menschen* (Gütersloh: C. Bertelsmann, 1938, 1951², 1958³, 1963⁴); G. Bornkamm,
Das Ende des Gesetzes (Beiträge zur Evangelischen Theologie, 16; Munich: Kaiser, 1952);
also vol. I, *Gesammelte Aufsätze* (Munich: Kaiser, 1968). Partially in *Early Christian Experience*, tr. P. L. Hammer (New York: Harper & Row, 1969).
248. See a little differently R. Bultmann, *op. cit.*, p. 40, n. 2.

ing to Matthew, "all righteousness" be fulfilled (Matt. 3:13ff.). He assembles the publicans and the public law-breakers around himself, and he goes to the sick, to the people who were regarded as outcasts. He has no home, no power. Everything which seeks to distort the law is rejected by him, including and especially the worldly understanding of the Messianic dignity. He is the fulfiller of the law in that he is completely in the will of the Father and therefore completely with man, up to utter abandonment by God (Mark 15:34).

3) **The Fulfillment.** Jesus Christ is the person in whom God's covenant finds its real partner, and he is simultaneously the one in whom this covenant itself is fulfilled. God's Yes to man and the responding, obedient Yes of man both reach their goal here. God's will comes into its own. And thus responding man, this One as the "first-born among many brethren" (Rom. 8:29), comes into his own. Since this has happened, all man's efforts, those of Israel and of all other men, to establish his own "righteousness" are finally judged as wrong. This is also the end of the cult, which had consistently made clear that Israel as such had not remained in the covenant, even though it was definitely set up to preserve Israel's life in the covenant as something ongoing and ever new (see especially the Epistle to the Hebrews). The new covenant is the fulfillment of the old. And thus it surpasses it. But it does not invalidate the old, but really makes it valid in the first place.

4) **Goal and End.** Romans 10:4 in context asserts primarily that Christ is the goal, the already established point of reference of the law. Not knowing the righteousness of God, the Israelites, in their attempt to establish their own righteousness, "did not submit to God's righteousness" (Rom. 10:3). "For Christ is the end of the law, that every one who has faith may be justified" (v. 4). One could put it a bit generally: Israel missed the "meaning" of the law, which is Christ. But we will have to conclude that this condition does not fully appear until Israel rejects its Messiah. In doing so, it rejected the meaning and goal of its own law, and the fulfillment of the covenant. Israel had made the law into the basis for its own works, into a path to salvation which was placed at man's disposal, but the law really led up to Christ (Gal. 3:24) and was really ordained to keep Israel open for the activity of its Lord. Israel's own path to salvation has reached its irrevocable conclusion. In that sense it is definitely true that Christ is the end of the law. He is not the end of the covenant. He is not the end of God's will toward the covenant partner. But he is the end of the law understood as man's possibility. Since the proclamation of the Gospel, it is impossible for man to continue doing what he was in fact doing before. Nomism is past, because the law has come to its goal.

m. The Law—in Christ Our Past. The way in which the law has reached its goal is none other than in the person and work of Jesus Christ. We could not have set an end for the law. Just as our high-handed managing of the law foundered in Jesus Christ, our high-handed contempt of the law also foundered because of him. We are not liberated in order to be no one's slaves (Rom. 6:16ff.). That would be what the freedom from the law precisely is not. Legalism would be unbelief in Christ. But any antinomism claiming to be Christian would be just as much unbelief. It would fail to see that we are free from the law "solely in Christ." This "in Christ" may never be understood to mean "within the Christian religion," or "within the Christian realm of thought." In such a religion or realm of thought we would have to rely completely on ourselves, and that would be the very thing which put us under the "law," falsely understood as an element of our own capabilities.

The result is that the law has not passed away temporally, as though a new epoch of religious possibilities had been initiated. The law is past as a sphere of power for those who are "in Christ" because it is fulfilled. But this fulfillment can only be recognized when the law remains in view as the polar counterpart to the Gospel. No one can understand the person and work of Jesus without knowing of the law. And if the Gospel were proclaimed without the voice of the law being heard, of the "good" but fatal law for us as its trespassers, then the Gospel would become the mere announcement that sin is not so bad after all since God has become known as the forgiving father in the meantime. This would make grace "cheap," as Dietrich Bonhoeffer often put it, and the Gospel would not be the saving word in what is otherwise a hopeless situation, but rather a piece of information which really could not help anyone. In Christ the "law" is our past— but this past "has not simply been obliterated, but is present as something which is continually to be conquered"; this is "a fact which holds good not just for the individual but analogously for history too, where indeed no stage is reached in which the proclamation of forgiving grace could die away."[249]

n. The Covenant with Israel and the Church of Jesus Christ. The "law" has just appeared to be something which in some sense does concern us. But we said earlier that the Old Testament law was strictly integrated into the covenant of God with Israel. What do we then have to do with the law?

First of all, we would not have the Old Testament with its "law" without the Christ-event, without its being accepted in the primitive community. We receive the "law" including the Old Testament solely in the light of the fulfillment which has taken place. We Gentile Christians do not in fact have a direct relationship "according to the flesh" to the law and to the Old Testament. This can under certain circumstances make it more difficult for us to understand the Old Testament. Martin Buber, for example, can teach us how a man of Israel sees many things differently than we are accustomed to seeing them.[250] But it is an element of the New Testament message that Christ is the end of the law and that only he who believes in him will be just. We can have from the outset no Israelite relationship to the Old Testament, and thus we cannot want to try to understand this book in an Israelite way. Only in Christ do we have a relationship to the Old Testament, to the law, and to Israel! The Messiah of Israel makes us into the

---

249. R. Bultmann, *op. cit.*, pp. 64f.
250. See H. J. Kraus, "Gespräch mit Martin Buber," *EvTheol* (1952), pp. 59ff., and the literature cited there.

"proper Israel, conceived by the Spirit and trusting its God" (Luther). But, conversely, whoever believes in Jesus Christ also believes in the Messiah of Israel. The Community of the new covenant is, for Paul, like the wild olive branch engrafted into the genuine olive tree (contrary to nature!). It is not the self-assured bearer of a new epoch but, as far as it is concerned, it is the modest appendix of the old people of God which has rejected its Messiah but which cannot shatter God's faithfulness. Our relationship to the Old Testament is identical to our relationship to Israel, and this in turn is identical with our relationship to the Christ of Israel, who as such is the Lord of the world.

If what we have just stated is so, then by inner necessity a two-sided relationship of the New Testament Community to the Old Testament results. Up until now, we were basing our discussion upon the question of what the unique message of the Old Testament was. This message can be expressed in one sentence: It proclaimed the one, unique, incomparable, and unaccompanied Creator as the covenant Lord of Israel. As such he is the giver of the law. This Israel is in single and significant figures but not in its totality the responding partner of the covenant, the thankful receiver of the law. This resulted in a polar relationship of the Old Testament to the New, and of the New to the Old. But unquestionably there is also a linear relationship in the New Testament: the Old Testament is the epitome of promise. How can we maintain both a polar and a linear relationship at the same time?

o. Christ and Time. We will only be able to formulate an answer if we make a few anticipatory Christological remarks. The reason for this is that we do not receive the Old Testament directly, but only through the mediation of the Christ-event.

Jesus Christ has really entered into our human history. But he is this still in unity with the Father, as the eternal Son. He is both, indissolubly and totally. He is the historical person and he is the one who belongs completely to the Father. He has his time, and there is a "before" and an "after" to it. And in free, divine grace, he is superior to time, independent of our earthly "before" and "after." He is present because he is historical, and he is future because he is the one present. He who has gone into time has not ceased being the Lord of time.

p. Christ, the Turning Point Between the Old and New Covenants. From the point of view that Jesus Christ has his time, his time as an element of the time given to man but in such a way that "in, with, and under" this time he does not cease being the Lord of time but confirms this lordship in his condescension— from that point of view we can say that the Old Testament is before Christ. This is not to state banally that from a temporal view the Old Testament was already there before Christ was. That is true of all history before Christ's birth.[251] What

---

251. K. Barth, *CD*, I,2, p. 70: "It is not this time [before Christ's birth] as such that is the pre-time to fulfilled time, but a time within this time, namely, the time of a definite history that takes place in it." It should be noted that our thinking at this point is indebted for its decisive elements to Barth's development of the theme, "The Time of Revelation" (*op. cit.*, pp. 45–121).

is meant is that the Old Testament, in relationship to the salvation-event, represents the specific "pre-time." But no more than *pre*-time. We would end up with a docetic Christology, which would fail to see God's real condescension to real humanity and would rob the salvation-event of its event character, if this simple "before" did not exist for us, which then should be termed the "not-yet" of that event. The Old Testament deals with the time of the as yet immature heirs (Gal. 4:1–3), the "time" before the "fullness of time" (Gal. 4:4). It is the document of the old covenant (thus in 2 Cor. 3:14 where we see that "the reading of the old covenant" is spoken of), which has reached its goal as the old covenant. It is the document of the "time of expectation,"[252] which as such has come to its conclusion. It is therefore, to say the least, imprudent to speak of a "Witness to Christ of the Old Testament," as Wilhelm Vischer does.[253] Such language tends to call forth docetic views and to overlook the specific "not-yet" nature of the Old Testament. If the situation were other, then the New Testament, too, would be the making known of a supratemporal idea. But in reality the New Testament is the witness to the Word become flesh, to the Son now sent in the "fullness of time," to the event which cannot be dissolved into an idea. There is therefore no linear connection between the Old and New Testament which could be read as such directly. The Old Testament states its message. We have already pointed out that the hearing of this message is absolutely necessary in order to receive the New Testament. But that does not imply that the Old Testament is in effect saying the same thing as the New. To say that Judaism in rejecting its Messiah has misunderstood the Old Testament is not subject to proof by the Old Testament alone; that is a proposition which is given with the New Testament proclamation of Christ. To be sure, Acts reports that the people in Berea "examined the scriptures daily to see if these things were so" (Acts 17:11)—meaning the Old Testament. But the people of Berea could only become involved in such an investigation after having heard the preaching about Jesus Christ. The Scriptures of the Old Testament would never produce what was proclaimed if that sermon were lacking.

Jesus Christ, as the historical Jesus, as the one who enters our time at his time, is the turning point which stands between the Old and the New Testaments.

q. Christ, the Center of All of Scripture. Jesus Christ in his unity with the Father, by virtue of which he made our time into his time, is at the same time the center of all of Scripture. He did not become the Son—"the only child of the eternal Father"—rather, he is the Son. What this means in detail will be discussed in our section on the Doctrine of the Trinity.[254] The decisive point is that God in encountering us in Jesus Christ is really God himself in that encounter. That means that the Father is not without the Son, just as he is not without the Spirit. Whoever believes in the One in whom we encounter, not something divine next to God, but God himself, God himself in incomprehensible self-distinction, God

---

252. Thus K. Barth, *CD*, I,2, pp. 70ff.
253. *The Witness of the Old Testament to Christ*, tr. A. B. Crabtree (London: Lutterworth, 1949 [g1934–42]).
254. See below, pp. 349ff.

himself in his activity not only in man but also through man and those before God—whoever believes so cannot do other than to regard John 8:58 ("Before Abraham was, I am"), or the Johannine prologue, or the beginning of the Epistle to the Hebrews, or the Christ Hymn in Phillippians 2:6ff. as a necessary and indispensable element of the proclamation which is the source of faith. The concept of "pre-existence" which is implied here can obviously and easily be taken mythologically, and it is difficult to decide whether that has not already influenced the way in which the New Testament witnesses expressed themselves. It would be mythological in substance if the "pre" were meant in terms of temporality, if the purely theological "already before" appeared in the sense of the temporal "always has been," so that the Son would be regarded as the participant at every time in the divinity of a deity at every time. The quality of "every time" is not eternity. The "before" of the being of God, the triune God, is categorically incalculable with the "before" and "after" of our concept of time, and also with the "fixed now" *(nunc stans)* and the "eternal now" *(nunc aeternum)* of mysticism. It is the divine "before," which means that it is qualitatively prior to time in the sense of lordship, of gracious freedom. It is the "before" which is made known in God's activity and only then, and it consists of the fact that God, when he acts in time, never acts out of time and is never enslaved in time. The "pre-existence" of the Son implies that the One who encounters in time historically is not of time himself and not bound to time.

It is only possible to speak of the preexistence of the Son under the terms just described when we speak simultaneously of his historicity, and vice versa. Every separation would result necessarily in seeing the humanity or the deity of Jesus Christ in isolation. It is certain that we may state that in Jesus Christ God himself meets us, the God who spoke to the fathers in the old covenant (Heb. 1:1), the Lord of the covenant, the God of Israel. With the same degree of certainty we must say that we hear the voice of this God in the historical Jesus Christ, and we only hear it in the Word of the Old Testament because we hear it there. The covenant God of Israel is the Father of Jesus Christ, one with the Son and the Holy Spirit in his eternity. When Abraham believed the One who "calls into existence the things that do not exist" (Rom. 4:17), then he believed ipso facto in "him that raised from the dead Jesus our Lord" (Rom. 4:24). When Abraham's existence as a believer was directed toward the future, toward the reception of the promise, it was in point of fact directed toward the "day" of the Son, and with the reception of the promise he "saw" this day (John 8:56). These are statements which do not ruminate on the religion or consciousness of Abraham, but rather reflect on the One who gave the promise and brought the fulfillment. And the situation is similar when it is said of Isaiah (John 12:41) that he saw the glory of the Son. That which is before Christ is not without Christ, if it is God who is at work. But in spite of that, it is before Christ. The Old Testament leads up to the historical "day" in the course of a history which with all of its unique features still can be compared with other histories. But in that the Old Testament lives from the covenant, to the degree that it does in its broad scope of statements, in that it is issuing from God's activity, it is coming from the One whom Calvin called the "truth" *(veritas)*[255]—the Old Testament has its origin in the One toward whom it is moving.

Based upon the given presuppositions it is now possible to ask about the significance of those descriptions of the relationship between the Old and New Testaments which see them as linear rather than polar. Basically we are concerned here with the "promise" (or "prophecy") and "fulfillment" pattern, and with the "typological" interpretation.

r. Promise and Fulfillment. The pattern of promise (prophecy) and fulfillment is a traditional component of theological work with the Bible. In the New Testament itself, the "proof of prophecy" is predominant. In the fourth book of Irenaeus' *Against Heresies*, which is fundamental for the later "salvation-historical" theology (designated thus since the 19th century; *heilsgeschichtliche Theologie*), the prophetic proof, connected with the typological interpretation, is expanded into a major system. The line then leads through Augustine and his medieval followers up to the theology of the Reformation, within which Melanchthon worked out the concept of promise *(promissio)*, whereas Calvin accents more the "unity of the covenant" and the many-sided aspects of its "government" *(administratio)*, and Luther proceeds more typologically.[256] In Orthodox dogmatics, the fulfilling of the Old Testament promises is regularly applied as an important argument for the dominant doctrine of inspiration. But the most emphatically systematized approach to the relationship of the Old and New Testaments, Federal Theology, does not build primarily upon the prophetic proof. It is not until the salvation-historical theology of the revival movement, especially in Hofmann, that the prophecy-fulfillment pattern becomes dominant.

Both of the terms used are New Testament terms. One would expect that they would appear as a conceptual couplet, for we are certainly accustomed to using them that way. Nevertheless, there is no statement which says, quite exactly, that a promise was fulfilled. The nearest thing to this proposition would be statements of Paul which speak of the "guaranteeing" or "confirming" of the promise (Rom. 4:16; 15:8). Usually, though, it is said of the promise that it is received (e.g., Gal. 3:14, 18, 22; Eph. 3:6; also Heb. 6:12, 15; 11:13, 39: the promise is given, is received, and with it the substance of the promise). It is, so to speak, on the way and as the coming promise is received. We could say that it is already en route to the people for whom it was intended. Sometimes it is compared with an "inheritance" (e.g., Gal. 3:29), and one does not "fulfill" an inheritance, but rather comes into it. It already has its content, its worth, its "fullness." In the New Testament usage, less in Paul (although see Col. 1:25 and indirectly Rom. 8:4) and more in the Synoptics and elsewhere, it is the "Scriptures" or the "Scripture" or the "Word" or "that which was said through the prophets" or even Jesus' own words (John 18:9, 32) which are fulfilled. The Old Testament as an aggregate of "words" needed to be fulfilled, and it found its fulfillment according

---

255. *Institutes*, II, xi, 4, pp. 453f.
256. See H. H. Wolf, *Die Einheit des Bundes, Das Verhältnis von Altem und Neuem Testament bei Calvin* (Halle dissertation [1942, 2nd ed. 1958]; Neukirchen: Buchhandlung des Erziehungsvereins, 1958).

to the New Testament prophecy proof. The correlative to "fulfillment" then, from the New Testament view, is not "promise" and scarcely "prophecy" (very seldom in regard to the Old Testament, but compare Matt. 13:14), but the Word spoken at each given time, or the Scriptures. The Word and Scripture announce what is going to happen in the future; the promise, on the other hand, is the event which is already approaching. That means that the statements of the Old Testament would be empty without their fulfillment; they would be a content waiting for its form, a vessel waiting to be filled. This is not true of the promise. It is waiting for the heirs.

It is now easy to state why the "fulfillment" does not make the "words," the "shadows" (Heb. 10:1; Col. 2:17), the "Scripture" of the Old Testament superfluous, as we considered it a hypothetical possibility above.[257] There is little more to be said about the promise here. If the Old Testament is promise, then this promise is in the One whom the father has made his heir, and for his "co-heirs." But all of the other "words," yes, even the ritual law, which is so much of a shadow according to Hebrews and Colossians, now have received their true substance in Christ. And that means that the Old Testament, which we read forward, so to speak, in our discussion of the polar relationship to the New Testament, can, may, and should be read backward on the basis of its own kerygma. Using once more Calvin's term, the Old Testament does not bear its "truth" *(veritas)* in itself. As the essence of truth for us, the Old Testament becomes "true" "in Christ," on the basis of the New Testament. This happens in such a way that any rigid adherence to what is unfulfilled, to the "shadows" and thus to Old Testament religion as it stands, would be tantamount to missing the actual truth of the Old Testament itself. If the Old Testament is understood in the light of its truth, then it does not become outmoded, but rather an element of the Christian kerygma.

This truth is then the standard for our evaluation of the Old Testament. We have already seen that the Old Testament itself reflects the struggle between covenant faithfulness and covenant usurpation. But what actually belongs to the covenant cannot be determined with an evaluation which adheres solely to the Old Testament. There are certainly many forces in the Old Testament which oppose autonomous piety, the national, cultic, and scribal usurpation of the covenant. But these forces remain somewhat ambiguous within the framework of the Old Testament. As a model instance we need only look at the "true" and the "false" prophets. To be sure, Jeremiah was right in point of fact against the cultic prophet Hananiah, since Jerusalem really was conquered and Jehoiakim did not return home (see Jer. 28). But the question is still open whether or not it would have been politically possible to save Jerusalem in one last tremendous effort of all their energies, and aside from that, next to Jeremiah's expectation of a "new covenant" (Jer. 31:31ff.), there is also that of Ezekiel and Trito-Isaiah, as well as of Haggai and Zechariah, which all pave the way for a new temple cult; within the history witnessed to by the Old Testament, these were the ones who ultimately were proven right, without of course implying that Hananiah was also right all

---

257. See above, pp. 290ff.

along. The picture remains self-contradictory, full of tension, and does not allow us to play Jeremiah off against Ezekiel. The Old Testament's expectation of the future, which is our first concern in this context, proceeds in part along the lines of the prolongation of the unfulfilled law. The anticipated great intervention of God will finally give Israel the power, the concrete victory which corresponds to the pattern of fulfillment of the law equalling success in life. The essence of this anticipation is the powerful Messiah, publicly acknowledged as the executor of Israel's carnal claims. It was with this kind of Messianic thinking that Jesus Christ collided. On the other hand, in the midst of the Old Testament another expectation emerges which is oriented to the one who is poor, meek, submissive, and who does not have power on his side, does not exercise violence, shows no outward victory, although Yahweh does not forsake him. No one can even attempt to resolve this tension within the Old Testament. The only resolution is provided in the proclamation of the One who, as the Crucified, was not the Defeated, but rather is the Resurrected One, who has been demonstrated to be the Lord *(kyrios)*. In the light of this One, we can no longer say that he failed in terms of a carnal, national, victorious Messiah ideal; rather the Messiah ideal itself, which could appeal to the Old Testament for its roots, failed as a result of this One. We also cannot say that he represents the final point in that unusual series of suffering obedient ones which we encounter in the Old Testament, but rather he establishes in his death and resurrection the justice of all those suffering, miserable, accused persons, who were not able to justify themselves, the justice which the priest (or the cultic prophet) promised them in the name of God.

If we can say that Christ—not Christianity—is the fulfillment of the Old Testament Word, of the "Scriptures," then he is in this fulfillment simultaneously the One who grants truth to that Word, to those Scriptures. The relationship which is thereby established has a very differentiated character. The various statements of the Old Testament are partially related to the Christ-event in a linear, preparatory fashion, partially in polarity, and we are not able to make a quantitative division in the one or the other direction. Only in regard to the individual statement can we raise the question of how it is to be understood in terms of this truth, which is not at our disposal. Much of the Old Testament seems to be really indifferent in this aspect, for example, the wealth of historical references and information. But it is these references which demonstrate that the Old Testament is truly reporting a real history, and history always has its broad and unspecific accoutrements. Otherwise it would be a chain of ideas. The crucial thing is that in the midst of this history that remarkable mirror becomes visible in which the light which shines in the New Testament is reflected. Old theology found such "mirrors" chiefly in the so-called Messianic prophecies, and in general they were not wrong in doing so. But they did tend to take these statements out of their historical settings and thus did not adequately distinguish between the mirror function of these utterances and the subjective "opinion" of the writer. The mirror function only results when these statements are related to the message of Christ. Perhaps today we would devote as much attention to those figures and appearances in which the unusual thrust forward is recognizable, as we find them in the Old Testament. We will consider the unusual significance of the poor, of the suffering and the accused, and the fact that the circle in which obedience to the law and fulfillment of life are connected to each other is by no means a closed one. With Hebrews 11 we will pay attention to the "believers" of the old covenant. In short, wherever the Old Testament unmistakably reveals "gaps" and "breaks," we shall perceive its openness for what is coming. We only do this in that we can recognize such "gaps" and "breaks" from the perspective of the One who is coming as being anticipations, reflections of the promise. Finally, we are referred back to the fundamental fact which we have already dealt with, to the establishment of the covenant in Yahweh's free activity, who does not find his partner waiting for him, but creates his partner. From this point of view, Hofmann's thesis that the whole Old Testament history is "prophecy" gains new meaning for us.

s. Typological Interpretation. The observational pattern of promise and fulfillment, which we have been discussing in seeking to clarify its meaning and limits, leads over then to a more comprehensive way of dealing with the Old Testament: the "typological." In that we must say that those statements in the Old Testament which point beyond themselves in such an unusual way really are referring ultimately to the one foundation of the institution of the covenant established solely in Yahweh's freedom, we are directed not so much to details but rather to the totality and the fundamentality of the old covenant. And then the decisive question is what we have to do with that covenant. The focus of our consideration is not the continuity of the "history of faith," which we can perceive in this or that fashion, nor the references from some statements and figures to the new covenant, but rather the covenant itself. Federal Theology once made a theological system out of this consideration. We cannot follow it there, when we remember that we are not given a comprehensive historico-theological scheme within which we could assign every event to its proper place in the historical and suprahistorical course of the divine decrees. We are made careful by the fact that the historical theology of the covenant decisions was capable of easy transformation into the historical philosophy of religious phases. And we must also bear in mind that every comprehensive system, by virtue of the "power of the system," can close our ears very easily to the Word which we are supposed to hear continually. We cannot figure out God's ways with Israel after the fact, nor God's history with mankind for that matter. But we can hear the kerygma of the Old Testament regarding the covenant, which is rooted in Yahweh's free decision and maintained in him, together with the highly contradictory response to it in obedience and disobedience, faithfulness and rejection, gratitude and usurpation, reception and self-righteousness, worship of God and worship of idols. None of that is "New Testament." But does it not all lead up to the New Testament, both in the Yes and the No, in the linear and the polar connection? Do we not recognize in the message of the Old Testament, in the Word it states, and in the history it relates as the proclaimed activity of God, a "prefiguration"[258] of "the New Testament Christ-event," including the human response which it has found? Doubt-

---

258. See Gerhard von Rad, "Typologische Auslegung des Alten Testaments," *EvTheol* (1952/53), p. 33.

less there is in this statement a "surpassing" of what the "historical self-understanding" of the Old Testament texts themselves would produce.[259] And also, doubtless, such knowledge will be of necessity fragmentary. We can find no hermeneutical method which by virtue of the basic insights already inherent in it would lead us with adequate certainty to the establishment of the "typos" of the Old Testament.[260] But this does not mean that we must wait for something "to occur to us."[261] The inquiry into the relationship of the Old Testament word to the New Testament salvation-event is not an arbitrary endeavor; with our faith in the One who as the Messiah of Israel is the Lord of the Community and the Savior of the world, this inquiry is completely relevant and unavoidable in the realm of the Church and its theology. It takes place, like every theological inquiry, certainly not without prayer.[262] For, like all theology, it stands under the "freedom of the Holy Spirit."[263] But prayer does not free us from sober labor, not even from sober historical-critical work. And the freedom of the Holy Spirit does not consist of freedom from the Word or next to the Word; rather it is given to us through our hearing of the Word.

D. THE PROBLEM OF SCRIPTURAL INTERPRETATION

1. THE POINTS OF DEPARTURE OF THE PROBLEM

a. Exegesis and Dogmatics. Dogmatics is the interpretation of the Word of God as the Church hears it in Holy Scripture. This hearing is a human act. The Scriptures in which the Church hears the Word are historical documents. The Church itself, which hears and proclaims, proclaims and hears, is a historical entity. This historicity is not accidental, not merely outward, not just the form, so that we could conceive or grasp the substance, the inwardness, the contents without this historicity. For the Word of God did not accidentally or as mere form take on "flesh," but rather it "became flesh." It does not surpass its historicity, but rather it claims history, defines and fulfills it. Historicity itself is as such not the Word. The Word of God is not as such history, but has become it. The event of the Word takes place within history in the form of election: not "history per se"

---

259. *Ibid.*, p. 31.

260. G. von Rad (*ibid.*, p. 33) finds that "the application of this typological interpretation" can "no longer be hermeneutically regulated," but rather happens "in the freedom of the Holy Spirit." Similarly, H. W. Wolff ("Der grosse Jesreeltag [Hosea 2:1–3] . . . ," *EvTheol* [1952/53], p. 78) has opposed the domination of hermeneutical method, following the lines of a statement by Luther. Against this F. Baumgärtel speaks out (" 'Ohne Schüssel vor der Tür Gottes'?" *EvTheol* (1953), pp. 413–44. But in the same number of *EvTheol* von Rad raises the objection to Baumgärtel that in his own method, which he uses in his book *Verheissung* . . . (1952), he succumbs to a spiritualism which is theologically not acceptable (*EvTheol* [1953], pp. 406ff.). This debate is not yet over and indicates the problems of hermeneutics very clearly.

261. F. Baumgärtel, *EvTheol* (1953), p. 416.

262. H. W. Wolff, *loc. cit.*, p. 78.

263. See n. 260 above; Gerhard von Rad.

but rather the special history which we encounter in the biblical witness is the history which both bears the Word and is borne by the Word, without ceasing to be real history. The Church cannot debate the uniqueness of this history as made known in Scripture. It can only explain what it means when it acknowledges it.

Within the division of labors of theology, exegesis has the special task of insuring that the historicity of the Word heard in the Scriptures is taken seriously in its totality, while it is dogmatics' task to see that the Word expressed in history and heard in Scripture is always understood as the one Word of God, beyond man's power of control. These two mutually condition each other, since God's Word is only heard in the historical perception of the historical Word of Scripture and the Word of Scripture conversely only claims obedience as God's Word.

The problem area in which exegesis and dogmatics meet is that of biblical hermeneutics.[264] The crucial thing is that hermeneutics really be a junction. It can only be meaningful when both areas of labor with their special tasks are taken seriously in their totality. For each of these special tasks is nothing more than a special view of the one thing, in all its inner tension. Dogmatics would devolve into speculation if it did not always keep the exegetical view in mind. Exegesis would become philology or philosophy of religion if it did not always consider the view of dogmatics. Both are dealing with Scripture, and both are theology.

b. The Possibility of a Special Biblical Hermeneutic. This leads to the first question. Usually it is placed today in this form: Can and should there be a specifically theological ("biblical") hermeneutics? Karl Barth answers the question in the negative,[265] in that, according to Barth, the "human word" appears in the scriptural Word "in its normal significance and function," so that, more precisely, the "Biblical hermeneutic does not get subsumed within general hermeneutics, but rather the general is subsumed in Biblical hermeneutics."[266] Coming from the opposite direction, Rudolf Bultmann also answers the question in the negative: "The interpretation of biblical writings is not subject to conditions different from those applying to all other kinds of literature."[267]

The rejection of a special biblical or theological hermeneutic has good grounds in that it would separate the Bible from the rest of literature and assign it to a special kind of existence. The Bible does not possess a special quality which sets it off. It would lose its public character if one wanted to deny its "profane" approachableness or even wanted methodically to block it.

---

264. See Karl Holl, "Luthers Bedeutung für den Fortschritt der Auslegungskunst," *Gesammelte Aufsätze zur Kirchengeschichte* (3 vols.; Tübingen: J. C. B. Mohr [Paul Siebeck], 1932[6] and Darmstadt: Wissenschaftliche Buchgesellschaft, 1948–65), I; T. Heckel, *Exegese und Metaphysik bei Richard Rothe* (Munich: Kaiser, 1928); K. A. von Schwartz, *Die theologische Hermeneutik des Matthias Flacius* (Erlangen dissertation, 1933); K. von Hofmann, *Interpreting the Bible*, tr. Christian Press (Minneapolis: Augsburg, 1959 [g1880]); E. Fuchs, *Hermeneutik* (Tübingen: J. C. B. Mohr, 1970[4] [g1954]).

265. *CD*, I,2, p. 466.

266. *CD*, I,2, pp. 463ff. and 722ff.

267. "The Problem of Hermeneutics," in *Essays Philosophical and Theological* . . ., p. 256.

c. Barth's Position. However, the rejection of a special biblical hermeneutic could not imply that the exposition of Scripture would cease to be a theological question. As suggested, this is certainly not the case with Karl Barth. He wants to have his "hermeneutical principles" "dictated by Holy Scripture,"[268] and everything that can be said about "hearing and understanding and expounding" can in his view only be queried "when we presuppose that that which is described or intended by the word of man is the revelation of God. . . ." When Barth then rejects a "special Biblical hermeneutics" (as did Schleiermacher, incidentally[269]), this means that the human act of perception (hearing, understanding, expounding) is only a genuinely human and creaturely act when it perceives in Scripture what Scripture wants to witness to. The important thing is not that in this act there are some special presuppositions in man or that a special method is followed, but rather that this act is directed toward what is decisive in Scripture itself, or better, that this act derives from what is uniquely special in Scripture. "An understanding of the biblical words from their immanent linguistic and factual context, instead of from what they say and what we hear them say in this context" would not be "an historical understanding of the Bible,"[270] because it would be attending to the creature and not to the Creator, to the witness as a human communication and not to what was intended in this witness.

Barth concludes then that only the kind of understanding which corresponds to what the Bible is all about is hermeneutically unobjectionable. He even concludes that only in the human word of the Bible does the human word appear "in its normal significance and function."[271] This is as much as to say that the human word is as a creaturely thing destined to bear witness to the revelation. The scriptural Word denotes "the future of every human word!"[272] It is obviously not necessary to explain that with such propositions hermeneutics is moved into the light of theology. Thus Barth can then delimit his already mentioned statement about the nonexistence of a special biblical hermeneutic in that he says, "For the sake of better general hermeneutics it must therefore dare to be this special hermeneutics."[273]

d. Bultmann's Position. Bultmann's reverse view proceeds from the historicity of the biblical witness, which is to say, from its accessibility. This accessibility is "conditioned" according to the principles of general hermeneutics, as they have been developed since Wilhelm Dilthey,[274] to the degree that "understanding"

---

268. *CD*, I,2, p. 466.

269. See Joachim Wach, *Das Verstehen; Grundzüge einer Geschichte der hermeneutischen Theorie im 19. Jahrhundert* (3 vols.; Tübingen: J. C. B. Mohr, 1926–33; repr. Hildesheim: G. Olms Verlagsbuchhandlung, 1966), I, 121. Wach concludes that Schleiermacher here was only continuing the line of S. J. Baumgarten's school.

270. *CD*, I,2, p. 466.

271. *CD*, I,2, p. 466.

272. *CD*, I,2, p. 472 and similarly p. 724.

273. *CD*, I,2, p. 472.

274. "Die Entstehung der Hermeneutik," *Gesammelte Schriften* (15 vols.; Leipzig: Teubner, 1914–58), V, 317ff. See also Bultmann, *op. cit.*, pp. 234–61 ("The Problem of Hermeneutics").

is only possible under the presupposition of a "relationship between author and expositor."[275] Formerly the expression frequently employed for this presupposition was the concept of congeniality. Existential philosophy has replaced the concept of congeniality with that of the "prior understanding." Understanding presupposes that the person expressing himself is interpreting himself in his statement, is making an "existential" known, and that the one hearing is capable of interpreting himself in the light of this existential. The decisive thing about this thought is found, as we shall show later, in Luther.[276] If understanding presupposes a pre-understanding, then the old question of the "religious *a priori*" emerges again, in greatly modified form. It is necessary for Bultmann to support his subsuming of Scripture understanding under general hermeneutics with the thesis that "the comprehension of records about events as the action of God presupposes a prior understanding of what may . . . be termed the action of God,"[277] and then he further asserts that man could "very well be aware who God is, namely, in the inquiry about him."[278] The question of God, then, if the understanding of the biblical Scriptures is supposed to be a human possibility at all, is a part of the human constitution. The important thing then is to discover the place where this question intrudes into consciousness, since it is already given as an "existential." The hearing of the biblical Word then effects a "correction" of the "notion it brings with it," but this is only possible if the "basic intention" already present "coincides with the intention of the answer given in the New Testament."[279]

The question which must be asked here is whether or not something is being asserted here which cannot be said *a priori*, in the process of discussing the possibility of understanding. It is highly questionable whether the question of God is really inherent in man at all.[280] But even if this were accepted for the moment, it would be all the more questionable whether the biblical witness was merely the "correction" of coinciding basic intentions. Does it not rather destroy our basic intention? Luther, in one of his last utterances,[281] referred in his own way to the necessity of a "pre-understanding." Virgil can only be understood by an experienced farmer, and Cicero only by one who has spent many years in an excellent political system, and Scripture can only be properly understood by someone who has ruled the Church for a hundred years with the prophets. Hence the enormity of the miracle represented by John the Baptist, Christ, and the Apostles. And Luther concludes that one does not possess the divine *Aeneid* but only its traces, which we "bow down and honor." "We are beggars: that is true." Luther apparently did not want to express the coinciding of basic intentions but rather the incalculable superiority of the scriptural Word over all understanding. In a certain sense we will agree with Bultmann that we are asking about "the reality of human existence," when "the inquiry about God and the manifestation of God" are

---

275. Thus Bultmann, *op. cit.*, p. 240.
276. See next paragraph.
277. Bultmann, *op. cit.*, p. 257.
278. *Ibid.*
279. *Op. cit.*, p. 258.
280. Does not Bultmann here revert back to apologetics?
281. *WA*, V, 168.

designated as the "objects of interpretation."[282] But to the extent that "God's revelation" is transformed from the "goal" of our interpretation into a heard answer, it is transformed from a corrective confirmation of our own question into its very abrogation. We cannot tell ourselves "the truth of our existence," not even in the form of a question and therefore not in the most radical indirectness. Our own question in its basic intention will never coincide with God's answer.

e. Our Position. Of course we approach the interpretation of biblical texts with a pre-understanding. We are expecting something. To that extent we are in the same situation in regard to Scripture that we are, by comparison, in regard to Plato. Since we find in the biblical texts human witness and thus human self-interpretation, we certainly will be able to hear something in the process of the pre-understanding and by applying the appropriate method to the text. "We" means here everyone who approaches the text. However, in the course of this hearing, reading, and interpreting—and this is not something which we have brought with us!—it can become clear to us that what we are encountering here is not at all what we expected in our consciousness. Instead, an unexpected and foreign communication is reaching us here: the communication of the revelation of God in the man Jesus of Nazareth. Wherever this happens, we are hearing an answer which then produces our question. Now we are the ones who are not supposed to ask but rather to respond, to be responsible. Whoever has heard God's Word in Scripture can no longer place his questions the way he has until then. The answer places the question. It is not merely a correction. It is not until now, in the hearing of the answer, which turns out to be not the answer to our question and not the fulfillment of our expectations, that we can say what Rudolf Bultmann wanted to say at the very beginning. Now Augustine's statement, "Thou hast formed us for thyself," can be taken up.[283] For this statement, taken in advance, is still a description of the human possibilities which then are shattered by the truth of God and thus do not steer us toward the "truth of our existence." This statement is only meaningful as a response to God's address.

Both Barth and Bultmann place biblical hermeneutics under the definitive power of an overarching judgment. For Barth this judgment is that the understanding of Scripture is based upon the revelation which is witnessed to in it and which is destined for man. For Bultmann it is that the understanding of Scripture rests upon man's own unique question about God.

If we were then to assume that the question about God is there the way Bultmann assumes, we would have to ask why it receives the answer in the Bible which only then makes it into the existentially decisive question. This question cannot be answered generally or in terms of principles, but solely in the form of a confession of faith. Our decision is prepared for us here.

This confession is Barth's point of departure. Bultmann moves toward it.

282. Bultmann, *op. cit.*, p. 259.
283. Bultmann, *op. cit.*, p. 257. See also H. Traub, *Anmerkungen und Fragen zur neutestamentlichen Hermeneutik und zum Problem der Entmythologisierung* (Neukirchen: Neukirchener Verlag, 1952), pp. 15f.

But can one move toward it without in fact coming from it? Can one describe the human understanding of the biblical writings on the basis of general hermeneutical categories, without already knowing that man will be drawn into a decision in regard to this witness, a decision which cannot be derived from general categories? And is not that decision-relatedness based on what the biblical Scriptures are testifying to? Of course, one can approach the biblical writings as a complex of religious statements using general categories. For the Bible is a historical and human book, whose uniqueness is not found in its tangible form or in what can objectively be construed about it. To understand these same writings as witness, as witness to the Word, is only "possible" on the basis of the Bible itself.

   f. Methodological Consequences of a Specific Understanding of the Bible. We must then say, after these considerations, that there is indeed a specific understanding of the Bible which does not apply to other writings. We must repeat that this proposition cannot be generally explained. It is merely another way of speaking of our confession of the Word of God. Thus this proposition cannot be made into a method. If we wanted to take faith's own certainty, that certainty which both supports and issues from faith, the certainty that we are hearing in this book the Word of God, and transform it into a method, then we would be assuming that we can be equipped by certain rules to hear the Word of God. We would have captured the Word methodologically. We would have made it into our own possibility. And that is not possible, for the Word is solely God's own possibility.
   Nevertheless this certainty of faith does not remain without its influence upon method. It deprives methodology of all self-security. The methods predominant up to now, the method of the manifold meanings of Scripture and the fundamentally different historical-critical method, have their roots in philosophy. This does not imply anything as such in regard to their applicability to the Bible. Every method, however, is a way in which man gains control of his world—in this case, the world of history which is represented in the symbols and reports of history. In every method there is therefore a tension between the structure of the control process and the sphere of reality toward which it is directed. The more rigidly a method is thought out, the more it is marked by the idea that reality can be subsumed under one conceptual pattern. This has its special effect in the method of understanding historical documents in that the judgment as to what is historically "possible" or not is established in advance, and thus is not derived from the sources but from a world view. In a similar fashion, other judgments can attain the rank of assumed axioms. As long as Idealism and Romanticism dominated the method of literary understanding, it was, for example, predetermined that all statements of "followers" could never have the standing of "original" statements. In such methodological predecisions, the philosophy which conditions the method is expressing itself directly. They are the expression of the "self-understanding" with which the "methodical" student approaches his "object." The result is that he deals with his texts without any readiness on his part to hear, but primarily with the expectation that he will find infinitely numerous variations of what is already anticipated. And this attitude is impossible for the one who has heard in the Bible what was absolutely unexpected. This perception will not lead him to confuse the literary categories which can be precisely iden-

tified, for example, to regard something as a "historical account" which is not that at all and perhaps was never intended to be. But he loses his secure "world-view" position from which he knew in advance what was awaiting him. The method becomes for him a mere means which sharpens his eye and ear for what he is prepared to perceive without defenses, without his own point of view. What he does know with certainty, and it is qualitatively different from the certainty of world-view positions, is this: I have heard here a Word which confronts me, reaches out to me, binds me, and releases me. And this certainty will constantly place the self-understanding he brings with him in question and thus also reduce the method he employs constantly to a mere means. In his sober labors on the human and historical witness before him, he will never be able to forget that this witness has made Jesus Christ known to him. Since he does not carry Jesus Christ as it were "at his disposal" in himself, it will be impossible for him to insert that witness where he cannot perceive it himself. But he will query every human and historical testimony in the Bible about its relationship to this witness; and just as he has no "Christological method" at his disposal, he will certainly not invest any other method with the right to be heard before the witness, which he has once perceived. Methodologically this means that in the relationship to the Bible there is an unconditional preponderance of the Word of witness over against all securities brought along or established in advance. Here the control process of the interpreter is shifted to the Word which is to be interpreted. And that means that in biblical hermeneutics what happens is what ought probably to happen in all methodologies of understanding. Here, hearing rules over speaking, perceiving over perception—and in perception!

2. THE RELATEDNESS OF THE TEXT

Our first question dealt with the problem whether and in which sense there could be a special biblical hermeneutic. In discussing this problem, we had to ask, on the one hand, about the "basic matter" of the Scriptures, and on the other, about the possibility of there being a generally given "pre-understanding." There is no hermeneutic which could exclusively remain with the text. The question about what is "behind" the text is identical with the question about my purpose in investigating the text. And this question cannot be separated from the other one— who am I, the interpreter, in actuality? For "understanding" is certainly a human act in the course of which I am also "understanding" myself. The text then, in other words, can only be understood within a specific set of relationships. It refers beyond itself in both directions. It says "something," and it says this "something" for someone.

a. The Text in Its Contexts. When we examine it more closely, this relatedness of the text begins to sort itself out. First of all, this text is not something absolutely singular which must be taken seriously in that capacity; rather, it stands in a direct literary relationship to other texts by the same author, of the same literary genre or form, or that are brought together historically, as the canon. The task of understanding is not completed when the single text is perceived, but it requires that the single text be received in the context of the various totalities within which the text meets me. These totalities are not simply the quantitative sum of single texts, but are their own mental and literary entities. It was Schleiermacher's accomplishment[284] to have assigned to the relationship of the part and the whole in general hermeneutics the role that it deserves. The substantive theological question which is raised here concerns the kind of whole within which the single text is to be investigated for its special characteristics. Is it the totality of an idea, or of history, or of a person? This question then leads to the next one: What defines the quantitative totality of the biblical Scriptures as a qualitative unity? "What" does "the Bible" say?

b. The "What" of the Text's Statements. With that, we are at our second point. We might say that the text refers backward beyond itself. It says "something." This "something" can again be regarded as the relatively special character of the self-manifestation of the author, in the language of the 19th century, his "doctrinal concept," or "religion," or "piety." But no one can fail to see that the biblical writers are not just expressing themselves; they are stating an event which is in itself historically differentiated. Since the emergence of form-critical exegesis, this has been seen all the more clearly, so much so that the individual side of the writer has progressively lost all its interest. The biblical authors are now understood predominantly as the bearers of a tradition already formed before them, as the proclaimers of a kerygma.[285] They move into the Community, and they express what is common to the entire Community. They do not express what in their view was history—history as something which happened objectively in the past and which we only encounter in the form of individual reports and individual "evaluations"; rather they express kerygmatic history or historically oriented kerygma.

c. The Hearing Subject. Thirdly, it has always been observed that understanding also has its presuppositions in the knowing subject. One of these was also reason. It was not without cause that theology at a very early date adopted the interpretive rules of Aristotle,[286] and the art of interpretation was seen in connection with logic, dialectics, and rhetoric. But reason is only able to comprehend what is homogenous. If Scripture is supposed to be the manifestation of a "mystery," then it requires an organ of perception which can hear it or a qualification which can enable one to perceive it. This has always been regarded in the Church as the work of the Holy Spirit. Then the issue was how this was understood: as the Spirit expressing itself in the charismatic gift of the individual in the Community, or as the extraordinary possession of the Gnostic which ele-

---

284. In the "Akademiereden über Hermeneutik," *Sämtliche Werke* (30 vols.; Berlin: G. Reimer, 1835–64), III, iii, 344ff.; see also Joachim Wach, *op. cit.*, I, 98ff.; Wach shows that Schleiermacher relates to Friedrich Ast in the point under discussion here (pp. 31f.).

285. The expression was introduced by Martin Kähler. For a critique, see now Fritz Buri, "Entmythologisierung oder Entkerygmatisierung der Theologie," in H. W. Bartsch, ed., *Kerygma und Mythos* (Hamburg: Herbert Reich—Evangelischer Verlag), II, 85–101.

286. E. von Dobschütz, "Interpretation," in *Encyclopaedia of Religion and Ethics*, ed. J. Hastings (New York: Scribner's, 1940), VII, 390–95.

vated him over the rest of the Community, or as a power possessed by a hierarchically structured Church as institution, working through its teaching office. If the Spirit was understood gnostically or hierarchically and institutionally, then the view arose that the initiate or office-bearer or the Church which stands in the teaching tradition could perceive the actual message behind the letters and could even put aside the literal message as being something "fleshly." This is the actual origin of the doctrine of the manifold meanings of Scripture, which in the East (primarily in Alexandria) was developed along the lines of Gnosticism, and in the West (supremely in Augustine[287]) more along the lines of the institutional Church. In contrast, the Reformation declared that the "literal meaning" was the primary one, and that means that it understood the Church and every one of its members as primarily perceivers and denied it both the possibility and the right to its own authoritative voice. It conceived of the Word of Scripture and the Spirit definitely as one, and just as definitely it interpreted Scripture in terms of its middle point, which is Christ. This was not merely a conclusion, but rather it was an intentional unity. For Orthodoxy, the Scriptures were caused by the Spirit in a tangible and concretely identifiable way, that is, the Spirit was captured within the scriptural Word.[288] This resulted in the possibility of a rational interpretation of the supranatural Word of Scripture, which was, so to speak, inherently and ontically God's Word. And that was the point at which modern Protestantism moved in, as it elevated reason, or later "religious congeniality" or "religious aptitude," to the subjective point of departure for interpretation.

The history of hermeneutics is identical with the history of the understanding of these three factors which we have discussed. The method of hermeneutics has always consisted of the relating to one another of these three factors in a certain way. This triad, the statement (the text in the broadest sense) and the thing stated and the perceiving subject, is of course present outside of the Bible. It is basic to every hermeneutical consideration.

d. The General Problem of Biblical Hermeneutics. The problem of biblical hermeneutics emerges, to put it generally at first, from the Church's conviction that the text, which as such is a product of the past, is a statement of what is valid and authoritative for me today. The text is the preaching text, and that is the way Augustine saw it, whose hermeneutics provides the transition to homiletics, the Reformation saw it this way too, and this is the way it is seen today.[289] Dogmatics deals with the text and with hermeneutics with a constant view to proclamation. This then places the problem of history squarely before it. If the Bible is "the preaching text," if it contains it, then this means that the "thing being talked about" in the text directly concerns us. How can that be understood?

287. The standard work is Augustine's *On Christian Doctrine*, Books I–III (*NPNF*, II, 522–73).

288. See above, pp. 232ff.

289. E. Fuchs, *op. cit.*, pp. 47ff., discusses Rudolf Bultmann under the appropriate title, "Der Text und die Predigt" (The Text and the Sermon). See also Hermann Diem, *Grundfragen der biblischen Hermeneutik* (*Theologische Existenz heute*, N.F. 24; Munich: Kaiser, 1950).

It could, first of all, be understood to mean that Scripture is a source for the knowledge of history which has objectively happened. Then the text would show me a piece of the past which is completed. Whoever asserted that "I" would be personally affected by this past could only mean that "I," too, am subject to the consequences of this past event. But this is not something which can be preached about. The consequences of the completed past do not encounter me at the core of my being.

It could, then, be understood to mean that the Scripture is the source not only of knowledge of "facts" but primarily of ideas, of religious and ethical behavioral modes. These, too, would be concluded past events. But it would affect me as long as there is a never ending continuum of the idea and of that which is religious which comprehends and surpasses all cultures and peoples. In addition, we would then say that "I" am placed in a special way in the "tradition" of the ideas and behavioral modes which are expressed in the Bible. We will not deal with the question here whether this continuum and this tradition exist. It is clear that proceeding from this presupposition it is possible to give a religious address, but not hold a sermon. Such ideas and behavioral modes may be related to ours or excite them, but are certainly not something which is capable of proclamation. As ideas and behavioral modes they do not unavoidably concern us.

e. The Word and Existence. We could now continue by saying that the "thing said" in the biblical texts, their "substance," concerns us in the core of our being, unavoidably, if and because this "substance" is the Word of God. This proposition would correspond to the total course of our discussion up to now.[290] The question to be asked here is what this means for the exposition and understanding of Scripture. How can human understanding and expositing of Scripture take place today, here, under the intellectual presuppositions which we have, from the viewpoint that this text from the past confronts us as the statement of the Word of God which affects us directly? The statement, "Scripture witnesses to the Word of God," is indirectly identical with the statement, "It confronts us with its witness unconditionally, irrefutably in our existence." We said that these two statements were identical indirectly. For they cannot be read in reverse order: if something confronts me unconditionally and irrefutably in my existence, then that is not an unambiguous criterion for its being a witness to the Word of God. Identity says much more: because and to the extent that the Scripture witnesses to the Word of God, it encounters me in my existence by virtue of its very nature.

However, the "thing said" in the biblical texts is not given to us directly. The Word of God encounters us in human words alone. We are forbidden to identify directly this human word as being the Word of God; this we dealt with earlier.[291] We are forbidden the thought that the Word of God is located somewhere in the depths of the human words, perhaps at the point where they may appear to us to be especially original, wise, or pious. Finally, we are forbidden

---

290. See above, pp. 178ff.
291. See above, pp. 185ff.

the idea that the Word of God happens every time this human word is perceived, as though the human word could only become God's Word at any given time and place. In this latter view, the experience we have is emphasized one-sidedly and the witness character of the human words is pushed aside. All of this has already been said above, in our discussion of what we mean by the Word of God.[292]

The indirectness remains. We stated above that the way in which the word of witness encounters us is existentially unconditional and unavoidable by virtue of the Word of God which addresses us in it. The indirectness is heightened and clarified in that this way of encounter is not a direct influence in the exposition of Scripture. The type of encounter which people like to call "existential" is essentially removed from all human efforts; interpretation, however, is a human effort.

f. The Question of the Continuum. The question then is whether in the context of this indirectness there is an access to Scripture which is open to human efforts. To put it differently: is there a mediatory factor which comprehends all of the three factors discussed above (the text, the "substance," and the interpreter)? There can be no understanding without such a mediatory factor, such a "continuum." Thus we are asking if there is another element aside from these three which are all tightly related to one another and which relates them all to each other. Since the text is always a product of the past, its "substance" is at least not tangibly available, and the interpreter is in the present, this other element we are looking for would be formally characterized by its capacity to connect or integrate past and present. This sought-for continuum would then be the sphere within which it would be possible to engage in exegesis.

If such a "continuum" is a necessary presupposition of both understanding and exegesis, it also contains its own greatest dangers within itself. For it would be very easy to regard such a "continuum" as an autonomous factor in contrast to the witness of Scripture. This can be seen in a very illuminating way in the situation where "reason" is looked upon as the "continuum." The "substance" of Scripture is rational, the text must be explained in terms of what is rational, and the bearer of reason is then the interpreter. This was how the hermeneutics of the Enlightenment saw the situation, and in our context it is irrelevant whether they meant "reason" in a spiritualistic or historical sense.[293] Since "reason" in the Enlightenment sense was basically man's self-perception, the "continuum" reason was nothing other than the establishment of man's lordship over Scripture and its "substance," man as he perceives himself and gains control over himself and his world. "Reason" here was "decreeing" reason and not "perceiving" reason, to use the term which Wilhelm Kamlah emphasized so strongly. However, an attitude of hearing toward Scripture is not only jeopardized where reason is the continuum. On the contrary, where the Holy Spirit is seen as the continuum,

---

292. See above, pp. 190ff.
293. See G. Gloege, *Mythologie und Luthertum, Recht und Grenze der Entmytholo-gisierung* (Göttingen: Vandenhoeck & Ruprecht, 1963³ [g1952]), pp. 141ff.

the human possession of the Spirit could replace the divine freedom of the Spirit and in a similar fashion assume the role of an autonomous factor. This happened very early in the history of the Church. And wherever the Church as moved and empowered by the Spirit was seen as the continuum, it then could become an autonomous factor as an entity which both understands and controls itself.

As certainly as a continuum is necessary, as little can this continuum independently obstruct hearing rather than making perception possible. The Reformers' struggle against the Roman Church and the "Enthusiasts" was of direct hermeneutical significance. It is directed in both cases against autonomy and in open confession of the Scripture which proclaims its "substance" itself and in this self-manifestation is qualitatively prior to the knowing interpreter. The Reformation's "principle of Scripture" is by no means the denial of a "continuum" for understanding. The Reformers do not deny the Holy Spirit, nor the Church, nor the significance of doctrine, nor even the significance of perceiving reason. But they are certainly in opposition to every attempt of the knowing subject to see the continuum of understanding as something available to him or at his disposal. One could also say that the Reformation's "principle of Scripture" is the confession of the divine freedom of the Holy Spirit and of the lordship of Jesus Christ in his Church which is made known in the Holy Spirit. The "continuum" of understanding, or if one will, the "hermeneutical principle," is not for the Reformers a factor next to or even over Scripture, but rather it reveals its potency in Scripture.

3. THE SENSE OF SCRIPTURE

The traditional ecclesiastical doctrine of scriptural exposition has for its pivot the concept of the "sense" (*sensus,* "the meaning of Scripture"). This refers to the way, within a tacitly assumed continuum, one can come to understand "something" as it is "there." The concept "way of understanding" would be appropriate if it were not commonly understood subjectively in our setting; the "sense" could be at most interpreted as the "way of understanding" which Scripture itself reveals.

a. The Meaning of the Continuum for the "Sense" of Scripture. The turbulent history of the views of the "sense" of Scripture reveals clearly that every view propounded here has by no means been molded by Scripture alone, but that other factors were dominant, that the "continuum" played a major role.

This is particularly obvious in the doctrine of the manifold meanings of Scripture. The well-known fact that the method used here, that of allegory, was already worked out in Greek antiquity, in Stoicism, and in Hellenistic (and partially in Palestinian) Judaism, could as such be unimportant. There is no more an originally Christian method of exposition than there is an originally Christian language. What is more important is that the allegorical method was summoned up whenever texts were to be dealt with which were considered "abhorrent" in their literal sense. The standard for that had to be derived from some kind of evaluative factors. The most decisive thing is that the actual practice of biblical exegesis along the lines of the manifold meanings of Scripture was based fundamentally upon definite theological points of view.[294] In the Christian Gnostics, allegory was dominated by their devaluation of the literal sense, and thus allegory had to appear as the only true exposition since it resolved the historical and earthly aspects into the suprahistorical and supra-earthly. Origen, who presented the first Christian hermeneutics in the fourth book of his chief work, had assigned "so to speak the flesh of Scripture" to the "simple man" who would be "edified" by it; those who "had ascended a certain way" would be able to grasp the "soul" of the Bible, while the "spiritual law" would only edify the "perfect man."[295] The Platonic trichotomy of body-soul-spirit is transferred to the Church and results in the assertion that only pneumatics can grasp the full meaning of Scripture, which of course for Origen is only the "shadow of future riches." The threefold meaning of Scripture, as Origen teaches it, presupposes the Spirit, the possession of "the perfect one," as the dominant continuum. Since Origen in his hermeneutics as in his Christology does not totally give up history, he does give "the simpler spirits" an opportunity for understanding, which though not perfect is not false. But in doing so he advocated an understanding of the Church as the continuum which later, under other circumstances, would put the hierarchy, which is what the pneumatics had become, in possession of doctrinal authority. We find thus in the great Alexandrian the essential elements of the view which would later connect the exegesis of Scripture to the Church.

Nevertheless, it cannot be contested that also the Antiochians, the passionate opponents of Alexandrian hermeneutics, and the proponents of what they called "history" (but not in our contemporary sense), based their exclusive emphasis on the "historical" meaning of Scripture on the conclusive reference to a continuum. This continuum was "history," what since the 19th century has been called "salvation-history," the divine "economy" within which the Old Testament has its place and which historically finds its final realization in the historical Jesus, who was as the Perfect One the Son of God, and as the Son of God the Perfect One. Here a specific understanding of history and a specific understanding of the Church are at work. Since the Church, at the decisive point, is ethically understood, the Scriptures are then interpreted ethically, even though the "historical" sense predominates. In Origen, the essence of Scripture was the "mystery" which was only disclosed to the "perfect," and with the Antiochians this essence is noetically available to everyone but it is a perfection which can only be attained in practice within the Church. We do not need to make a judgment here. If it were done, it could praise the great exegetical accomplishments of men like Theodore of Mopsuestia (c. 350–428), Theodoret of Cyrrhus (c. 393–c. 458), or Diodore of Tarsus (d. c. 390), but it would have to add that the ethicization of the Church, of Christology, and thus of the understanding of Scripture would ultimately have to result in the abrogation of history, just as did the open tendency of the Alexandrians to discount history. What interests us here, however, is the finding that

---

294. Gerhard Ebeling, *Evangelische Evangelienauslegung, Eine Untersuchung zu Luthers Hermeneutik* (Darmstadt: Wissenschaftliche Buchgesellschaft, 1962 [1942]), pp. 110ff.
295. *De principiis*, IV, 11 (*ANCL*, X, 300–301); one must read the whole context.

the doctrine of the predominantly "historical" sense of Scripture was just as much subject to a presupposed continuum as was the doctrine of the threefold meaning of Scripture.

b. The Church as the Dominant Factor. Ultimately the doctrine of the four-fold meaning of Scripture was victor in the West, and it prevailed—even if not uncontested—for a thousand years. It is first found in John Cassian (c. 360–435),[296] the founder of Semi-Pelagianism, but he was influenced by Augustine and is closer to him than to Pelagius. The view which comes to the fore in John Cassian is related to oriental theology, particularly to John Chrysostom (c. 347–407), but we will have to agree with Gerhard Ebeling that its real roots are to be sought in the transition in the basic approach to hermeneutics which Augustine imple-mented. The great African, in open and typical European single-mindedness, car-ried out what was no more than initiated in Origen: the relationship of the Scriptures' statements to the Church as the Body of Christ. This corresponds to the development in which the mystery became the sacrament and the dialectical relation of "sign" *(signum)* and "matter" *(res)* defines exegesis. "Sacrament" can virtually mean "allegory."[297] The continuum which connects both "sign" and "matter" in Scripture, and also connects the interpreter to both, is the Church. Ebeling shows[298] that in this respect Augustine agrees with the *Liber regularum* (Book of Rules) of the Donatist Tyconius (d. c. 400). The Middle Ages then per-fected the doctrine as its leading theologians completed Cassian's work. The fourfold meaning of Scripture is then defined as the literal or historical sense, the allegorical sense, the moral sense, and the anagogical sense.[299] What this means and the great context in which it is located can best be shown by turning to the fine exposition provided by Thomas Aquinas.[300] He regards the literal sense as foundational. But in good Augustinian fashion he adds that in theology not just the single voices have their significance but also the "matter" implied by the words has its own special meaning. The meaning of the "matter" expressed by the "voices" *(voces)* is the "spiritual sense." Thus, what in the "old law" was

---

296. See E. von Dobschütz, "Vom vierfachen Schriftsinn," in *Harnack Ehrung, Festgabe für D. Dr. A. von Harnack . . . zum siebzigsten Geburtstag* (Tübingen: J. C. B. Mohr, 1921), p. 2.

297. Ebeling, *op. cit.*, p. 120.

298. *Ibid.*, pp. 124f. For the text of the *Liber regularum* see F. C. Burkitt, *The Book of Rules of Tyconius, Texts and Studies III* (Cambridge: University Press, 1894; repr. Nen-deln/Liechtenstein: Kraus, 1967); see also Gerhard Strauss, *Schriftgebrauch, Schriftausle-gung und Schriftbeweis bei Augustin* (Tübingen: J. C. B. Mohr, 1959).

299. This was expressed in the Middle Ages with this little verse:
Littera gesta docet, quid credas allegoria,
Moralis quid agas, quo tendas anagogia.
(The letter shows us what God and our fathers did;
The allegory shows us where our faith is hid;
The moral meaning gives us rules of daily life;
The anagogy shows us where we end our strife.)
See R. M. Grant, *A Short History of the Interpretation of the Bible* (London: A. & C. Black, rev. ed. 1965), p. 95—TR.

300. *STh*, I,i,10, vol. I, p. 7.

referring to the coming "new law" would be the subject of allegorical exposition. Again, what in the new law was a "sign" of what we ourselves should do would be interpreted morally, and that finally which refers to eternal glory would be understood in the anagogical sense. The fourfold meaning of "signify" (*signi-ficare*) which is found in Scripture would correspond to the fourfold interpretation. However, the spiritual exegesis (the allegorical, moral, and anagogical senses) corresponds to the three consecutive forms of the Church for which Scripture is intended and into which it is to be interpreted. It is remarkable that according to Thomas an argumental proof can only be derived from the literal sense; he appeals to Augustine for this.[301] It is therefore no contradiction of Thomas when the Franciscan Nicholas of Lyra (c. 1270–1340), whom he influenced hermeneutically anyway, and then in his footsteps Paul of Burgos[302] insisted primarily upon the literal sense while still acknowledging the doctrine of the fourfold meaning of Scripture. They advocated that any exegesis going beyond the literal sense be undertaken with the greatest care. We see here that sober Jewish exegesis was wielding its influence, at least upon the Old Testament, particularly that of Rashi (Rabbi Solomon ben Isaac, 1040–1105).

c. The Analogy of Faith—analogia fidei. The Church, however, was not just the major point of reference toward which the Scriptures were interpreted. What was more important, it provided the criterion for measuring the accuracy of any exegesis. The concept of the "analogy of faith," taken from Romans 12:6 (in an incorrect interpretation of the phrase "in proportion to our faith"), was gen-erally used to assert that both exposition and proclamation should orient them-selves to the "rule of faith" (*regula fidei*). Augustine clearly espouses this requirement,[303] and it was progressively expanded in the period thereafter, so that finally, at Trent, the Holy Mother Church's monopoly on biblical interpretation was canonized.[304] This orientation factor, this presupposed continuum, then be-comes the dominant factor. Thus the process which began basically with Origen reaches its conclusion.

d. The New Approach of the Reformers. The Reformation did not begin by rejecting the doctrine of the fourfold meaning of Scripture nor even the especially controversial allegorical interpretation. From an early point in time, allegory re-cedes clearly in Luther, and he does expressly reject it several times, but as such

---

301. *Ibid.*; see also Augustine, *Letters of St. Augustine*, XCIII, viii, 24 (*NPNF,* I, 391).

302. See Ebeling, *op. cit.*, pp. 130ff. The *Postillae perpetuae* of Nicholas of Lyra (his biblical commentary) and his *Moralitates* (partially allegorical) are usually found in the various editions together with the early medieval *glossa ordinaria*. Luther used Lyra and "after initial contempt" came to esteem him highly (Ebeling, *op. cit.*, p. 154, n. 163).

303. *On Christian Doctrine*, III, ii, 2 (*NPNF,* II, 556f.); on the whole context see G. Heinrici, art. "Hermeneutik," *RE,* VII, 718ff.

304. Session IV (1546) (Denzinger, *Sources,* pp. 244–46 [pars. 783–86]), as well as the Profession of Faith of the Council of Trent (1565), pp. 302–304 (esp. par. 995).

it is never fully given up.[305] Calvin turned away from allegory more sharply,[306] not only as a matter of principle but also in the practical work of the exegete. Nevertheless, it is quite clear that Calvin's judgment is very much like that of the Antiochenes, and that with them he shares the "salvation-history" pattern. The new element which the Reformation brought was at first the discovery of another basic factor for the orientation of Scripture, which was "Christ alone" (solus Christus). If the Scriptures were understood as leading up to Christ and deriving from Christ, then the doctrine of the manifold meanings of Scripture must necessarily lose the significance it had had. It was impossible for it to continue to mean that the Church itself could become the knowing co-speaker of the biblical Word being heard. The "analogy of faith" had to be transformed from a manageable criterion into an obligatory binding to the gift which was received in faith. In the lectures on Romans, Luther had interpreted it "passively."[307] If the gift testified to in Scripture was "Christ alone," then the interpreter was necessarily referred to Scripture itself in order to gain his understanding of it—"scripture is its own interpreter."[308] This resulted in the abrogation of the Church's autonomous power of interpretation, of the possession of the Spirit claimed by the "Enthusiasts," and certainly of the special claim of illuminated reason, which was beginning to be heard in Humanism; incidentally, it is notable that this happened in such a way that Erasmus, for example, began to allegorize extensively.

e. Spirit and Letter in Luther. The question which suggests itself at this point is whether the Reformers with their principle that Scripture interprets itself did not wrongly oversimplify the problem of exegesis. In its history, in which we dealt only with the most important developments, the "sense" of Scripture revealed that exposition always presupposes some kind of orienting factor, which is both the source and the goal of understanding. It could just appear to be true that the Reformers, in opposition to all human and ecclesiastical willfulness which made their "orienting factors" accessible to their control, had exaggerated their counterthesis. Can one really say that Scripture interprets itself?

Reformation exegesis reveals that it, too, deals with a factor with which it sees the Bible confronted. If we were to state simply that this factor was the "Christ alone" which was already mentioned, then it would only be half true.

---

305. Luther's excursus, "Concerning Allegories," in the late Genesis lectures (AE, II, 150ff.) is very cautious. Luther recounts that he formerly was an enthusiastic allegorizer, under the influence of Origen and Jerome, as well as of Augustine. But then he turned away from this. He condemns all allegories ". . . that are fabricated by one's own intellect and ingenuity, without the authority of Scripture" (op. cit., p. 151), but not those "made to agree with the analogy of faith," which means that they are subject to Scripture's own authority.

306. "We must, however, entirely reject the allegories of Origen, and of others like him, which Satan, with the deepest subtlety, has endeavoured to introduce into the Church, for the purpose of rendering the doctrine of the Scripture ambiguous and destitute of all certainty and firmness" (Calvin, *Commentaries on the Book of Genesis*, tr. J. King [Grand Rapids: Eerdmans, 1948], I, 114).

307. *Romans* (12:7) (AE, XXV, 446).

308. Luther, *WA*, 7, p. 97; see also K. Holl, *op. cit.*, I, 559, n. 4.

For Christ is the "matter" of the Bible. It is, of course, accurate to say that for the Evangelical view, the "matter" of the Bible is in fact also the "factor" by which the Bible is supposed to be measured. But then the question must be raised, what binds us to this "matter," and that throws us back to the question of the "factor" or of the "continuum." The answer which the Reformers gave, severally derived from their various theological conceptions, can be formulated with the terminology we have been using up until now in this way: If the "substance" or "matter" of Scripture is God's revelation, God's Word, Christ alone, then this "matter" itself becomes the "continuum" in that God turns to us in Christ, that is, that he makes his turning to us effective at any time and place through the Holy Spirit. For that reason, the Reformers can insist so energetically upon the "literal" sense of Scripture, since they are confident that Scripture in its literalness, in the indissolubly manifold contingency of its human statements, is the "matter," the Word of God, and states it to us with spiritual necessity and power.

This is seen in Luther in the remarkable interrelating of what amounts to a twofold sense of Scripture. According to his view, the literal sense is virtually accompanied by the tropological sense.[309] He does not mean that the literal sense needs to be expanded through a spiritual interpretation, but rather that it is already "spiritual" since the Word of God comes to us through it and the Spirit of God works in us through it. More precisely, because the Scriptures are to be related to Christ and are derived from him, they say simultaneously (the tropological sense) what the new life in faith is. Luther is concerned to maintain the unity of the two senses. "What bothered Luther was not that there was a spiritual meaning behind the literal, or a present significance behind the historical, but rather the fact that the spiritual relationship to the present only established the *historical distance* again was unbearable to him. What he was concerned about was not the conflict between reason and the Word of God, but rather the conflict between the Word of God and existence."[310] Luther's Christology is clearly dominant here. For him, the historical uniqueness is comprehended and defined by the divine presence. We "have" the "present Christ" in no other form than in the concealment of the One become flesh, but we "have" him thus in spiritual reality. This reminds us of Luther's idea that in communion, by virtue of the sacramental union, there is a synecdochic relationship between the "matter" and the "sign." For his view of Scripture, the parallel formulation is characteristic that the scriptural letter is the "spiritual letter" *(litera spiritualis)*.[311] Luther wants to assert then that the literary Word is not in itself empty and dependent upon the additional work of the Spirit, but that the work of the Spirit has already been given to it to the extent that it expresses God's Word and means Christ. But we cannot recognize this character of Scripture in any other way than through the Spirit who makes itself known through Scripture.[312]

---

309. See G. Gloege, *op. cit.*, pp. 67ff.
310. Ebeling, *op. cit.*, pp. 197ff. (my italics).
311. G. Gloege, *op. cit.*, p. 70; Gloege refers to the fact that in this issue Luther had Jacobus Faber (Lefèvre d'Étaples, Stapulensis) as a model.
312. See R. H. Grützmacher, *Wort und Geist; eine historische und dogmatische Untersuchung zum Gnadenmittel des Wortes* (Leipzig: A. Deichert, 1902), pp. 41f.

All of this means that, according to Luther, the relationship to both the present and to existence is given with Scripture. And this means in turn that the Scriptures are understood from the very onset in relationship to preaching. It is in preaching that the interrelationship of the "matter" of Scripture, of the textual word and of the listening person, is accomplished. To use the terminology we have developed, preaching is the "continuum," the orienting factor for the understanding and interpretation of Scripture. To be sure, it is not a static "continuum," and it is not an "orienting instance" placed at our disposal. For as the preached Word it is bound to the scriptural Word. Although the Word is God's Word, preaching can remain without any effect. That is a part of God's concealment in the world. But it also stands under the promise that it will be an instrument, not only in that the Spirit is "given," as the Augsburg Confession states (Article V), but also in that he shares himself through this instrument. It is only from the viewpoint of preaching that we can understand that Luther dealt with the distinction (and relationship) of law and Gospel as a "hermeneutic axiom."[313]

f. Lutheran Orthodoxy. Lutheran Orthodoxy separated more and more Luther's doctrine of the "sense" of Scripture from preaching. Wherever this happened, Luther's concept of the firm mutual relationship of Word and Spirit necessarily became objectified.[314] We see this tendency both in the Orthodox doctrine of inspiration and in the Rahtmannian Controversy.[315] The Word empowered by the Spirit and demonstrating its power in proclamation becomes the supernatural Word. The application of this Word to the reader or the hearer now becomes a problem of its own. The hearing subject confronts the supernatural object of the Scripture, and a chasm is opened up which then is sought to be bridged, the attempts sometimes being more "objectivistic," sometimes more "subjectivistic."

g. Calvin. Just as Luther's understanding of Scripture cannot be separated from his Christology, so we find the corresponding situation with Calvin. His sober exegesis, in comparison to Luther much more strictly adherent to the literal sense, seems to be related to his Christology which seeks to maintain the full historical genuineness of the human nature of Christ. It is only necessary to compare Luther's lectures on Genesis with Calvin's Commentary in order to gain a strong impression of how human, even "rational," Calvin proceeds in relation to Luther's daring but exegetically not always conclusive combinations. We see this constantly. What gave Calvin, whom some have wanted to make the father

---

313. See G. Gloege, *op. cit.*, pp. 37ff., and Hermann Diem, "Karl Barth's Kritik am deutschen Luthertum," ed. P. Schempp, *Evangelische Selbstprüfung* (Beiträge und Berichte von der gemeinsamen Arbeitstagung der kirchlich-theologischen Sozietät in Württemberg und der Gesellschaft für Evangelische Theologie, Sektion Süddeutschland; Stuttgart: W. Kohlhammer, 1947), pp. 91ff.

314. Whether or not Luther in his Christology, which was strongly influenced by his opposition to Zwingli, and in the corresponding doctrine of Scripture did in fact pave the way for this objectification cannot be discussed here.

315 See above, pp. 284f.

of the Orthodox doctrine of inspiration,[316] the courage for such earthy, historically oriented exegesis? Of course, Calvin shared the traditional doctrine of inspiration, without being in any sense original on that point. In complete agreement
with Luther,[317] he fought against the divorce of Spirit and Word. But in spite of
his doctrine of inspiration, he distinguishes between the effect which the (read
and preached) Word is able to exercise as such, and the effect which is produced
by the work of the Spirit through the Word.[318] Certainly there is no lack of
statements in this direction in both Luther and in Lutheran Orthodoxy.[319] But in
Calvin they are anchored in the totality of his theology. The external Word is only
effective where God's election reveals itself as actual calling. In his Christology,
it is true, Calvin did teach the "communicating of properties" *(communicatio
idiomatum)*, but at the same time he contested that the second person of the
Trinity was totally encompassed in the man Jesus of Nazareth. This is the so-
called "extra-Calvinisticum" which developed out of the medieval tradition.[320] In
accordance with this, for Calvin the Holy Spirit is present and at work in the
Word but in such a way that the Spirit remains strictly divine and free and the
Word thus remains strictly historical. Here is the basis for his sober exegesis,
which dealt with the "genuine sense," the "letters," and the views of the writers
manifest in them; this exegesis, of course, always leads up to the question of the
doctrine which reaches us through the Word which is historically understood.[321]

Calvin's intention is different from Luther's, in spite of all the common
elements in their approaches which can be observed. Luther wants to establish
the authoritative validity of the Word for us in the Word itself through the Spirit,
and the danger is that he will limit the divinity and the freedom of the Spirit.
Calvin is concerned, on the other hand, with the divine freedom of the Spirit, in
the Word but also over against the Word.[322] Therefore Calvin understood the

---

316. See above, pp. 243ff., and R. H. Grützmacher, *op. cit.*, p. 122.
317. R. H. Grützmacher, *op. cit.*, pp. 123ff.
318. *Institutes*, III, ii, 33, p. 580: ". . . without the illumination of the Holy Spirit,
the Word can do nothing." See also R. H. Grützmacher, *op. cit.*, pp. 127ff.
319. See Abraham Calovius, who distinguishes between the external sense, which
by chance might be grasped by someone not reborn, and the internal sense, which can be
grasped solely through the Spirit (see *Systema locorum theologicorum*, I, 657, cited in
Schmid, p. 84).
320. See the *Institutes*, II, xiv and II, xiii, 4 at the end, pp. 482–93 and 481.
321. Calvin's exegetical method has been researched, aside from the problem of the
old covenant with which H. H. Wolf dealt (*Die Einheit des Bundes, Das Verhältnis vom
Altem und Neuem Testament bei Calvin* [Halle dissertation (1942; 2nd ed. 1958)]), only by
Paul Kertz in Germany, in his Göttingen dissertation, *Calvin's Verständnis der Heiligen
Schrift* (1939). The author was killed during the war and could not complete the final revision
of his work. For important material and a good evaluation of the literature, see W. Krusche,
Das Wirken des Heiligen Geistes nach Calvin (Göttingen: Vandenhoeck & Ruprecht, 1957
[1953—Heidelberg dissertation]).
322. Commenting on Rom. 10:14, Calvin says that preaching is "the normal mode"
and "the ordinary dispensation." Paul "had no desire to prescribe a law to His grace"
(Calvin, *The Epistles of Paul the Apostle to the Romans and to the Thessalonians*, tr.
R. Mackenzie [Grand Rapids: Eerdmans, 1961], p. 231). But see the other emphasis in the
Institutes, III, ii, 6, pp. 548f. We can see that for Luther, just before his struggle against the
Enthusiasts, there was an even more radical possibility of speaking of the Spirit without the
Word (*WA*, 7, 546, in Grützmacher, *op. cit.*, p. 10). Much sharper than both of these
Reformers was Bucer (see Grützmacher, *op. cit.*, pp. 116ff.).

earthly historicity of the Word much more keenly than Luther, but on the other hand he expected from this earthly-historical Word as such nothing else than earthly-historical effects.[323] In Calvin, this approach to Scripture parallels his approach to the historicity of revelation: God uses it, we are bound to it, but God does not bind himself unconditionally but remains the Lord of his revelation. Thus Calvin is subject to the opposite danger to Luther's: the danger that his concern about the divine freedom of the Spirit could prevent the Word from attaining its full authoritative validity. But he saw this danger and was able to resist it.[324]

Let us now try to summarize the results of the doctrine of the meaning of Scripture.

1) **No Manifold Meanings of Scripture.** It is not possible to hold a systematic doctrine of the manifold meanings of Scripture. It would contain the assertion that behind the earthly-historical meaning of the text there would be a further ("spiritual") meaning. It would only be possible to comprehend that meaning by means of some kind of illumination, which would not result from hearing the historical Word and thus not from God's unique and historical self-disclosure. "Spirit" and "Word" would then be divorced from one another, and the "Spirit" would become the "spiritual talent" of the individual in the Church or perhaps of the Church as a whole. Moreover, the one who thought he could exposit the "spiritual" or "mystical" meaning of Scripture because of the possession of the Holy Spirit or perhaps in referral to the Spirit's possession of the Church would really "know" in advance what was waiting for him in Scripture. "Allegory" kills open hearing because the factor by virtue of which hearing is possible at all—the Church, the possession of the Spirit—is understood in an autonomous way. The next consequence is that the concrete understanding of Scripture is surrendered to chaos.

2) **The Literal Sense as the Meaning "Within" the Totality of Scripture.** The Reformation returned quite properly to the literal sense, within the implied limits and certain reservations, which are clearly observable in Luther. This is the meaning which is understood as the one which we are able to perceive in the utmost impartiality of hearing. However, the Reformation left the next generations, and us, with the question of how we are to understand this literal sense. The Reformers knew very well, without being influenced by the exegetical work that preceded them, that the literal sense is its own problem. This problem is first of all a literary one. For example, the text can be meant parabolically or allegorically (in terms of the latter we would apply it to certain texts which the Reformers regarded as historical reports, for instance, John 2:1ff. or Matt. 8:23ff.). The text has its "rationally" recognizable form and can be understood within this "form" relevantly. But the problem goes further. If the literal sense of the text cannot be isolated but only grasped within the recognizable literary genre, then we must ask if we are not then referred to the author, to his opinion, his view, his witness.

---

323. See Calvin on Rom. 10:16, *op. cit.*, p. 232. It should be noted that Calvin's Commentary on Romans, in spite of occasional polemics, was strongly influenced by Bucer's exposition, which appeared in 1536.

324. See especially *Institutes*, IV, i, 5, pp. 1016–20.

Reformation exegesis, led by Calvin, took that step. But it then accordingly had to see that not every biblical author is simply stating what every other one is. This results, in Bucer, Calvin, Flacius, and others, in the first steps toward a "literary" criticism which initiates with the question of the author. But further, can the author be so isolated? If the authors are not all saying the same thing, then must not their variety of witnesses be related to some totality, in faithfulness to the principle that Scripture interprets itself? And is not the result (as "literal" sense, or "genuine" sense, or "historical" sense) that the essential meaning of every text is its meaning within the Scriptures? If that is so, then the old problem reasserts itself whether or not the analogy of faith must not be called upon to find out the "meaning of Scripture" of a specific text. This question was answered in the positive by all the Reformers and the Orthodox in their own ways, but its dangers had to become apparent whenever this faith was understood as a tangible body of doctrine.[325] The problem of a literal meaning of Scripture which is to be interpreted in a variety of directions still remains.

3) **Reformation Hermeneutics as the Deprivation of Security.** We have now reached the two germinal issues at which the "legacy" of the Reformation view of Scripture and hermeneutics became the source of new problems. First of all, in emphasizing and liberating the literal sense, the Reformation actually liberated the understanding of the Bible. But it also deprived this understanding of the protection which all biblical interpretation had possessed up until then. This had to happen. The Bible must be free. What had protected and bound interpretation up to then was the continuum which was at work in it. The Reformation did not place understanding outside of every continuum. But it did not accept a continuum of understanding which was at man's "disposal." If preaching was the orienting factor within which understanding could become possible, then preaching itself was bound to the Word and was only "Word" itself to the extent it was so bound. If the Spirit was to be prayed to for all understanding of the Word, because without it no appropriate understanding of the "letters" was possible, then this Spirit was not a possession but the Spirit which makes itself manifest in the Word, which is received in hearing and must be received anew again and again (in this, Calvin and Luther were in complete agreement). If preaching by its very essence is the preaching of Christ, if the Spirit is the Spirit of Christ, and if ultimately "God-in-Christ" is the "continuum" of understanding, then there is certainly no factor given here which is at anyone's disposal. Was not the necessary result then that the individual was the only one upon whom the reality of the biblical Word had its effect or did not have its effect? Was it not ultimately left up to the individual alone? Neither the Reformers nor the Orthodox were of the opinion

---

325. Luther, in his *Confession Concerning Christ's Supper* (1528), understands the "analogy of faith" in the following way: ". . . all the words of Christ must foster faith and love, and be in accord with faith" (AE, XXXVII, 262). We can see here again, based upon proclamation, a "canon within the canon" or a "canon for our understanding." Some of the later figures return without hesitation to the "rule of faith" as the summary of what is witnessed to in Scripture, for example, Johann Gerhard, *Loci communes theologici*, I, 532; ed. F. R. Frank (1885ff.), I, 238.

that the individual should have the kind of unique capability of judgment which the Church did not possess. In this situation, the Orthodox reverted back again to the authority of the Church, that is, of dogma and doctrine. But dogma could no longer be in the Evangelical Church what it had once been in the sacral institutional Church of Roman Catholicism. The Reformed, with their unbalanced variety of confessional statements and their initial tendency to examine continually every confession in the light of Scripture, saw this more clearly than did the Lutherans.[326] This was part of the reason for seeking out the Church systematically in Scripture, since the Church could not be conceived of as a counterpart to Scripture. That was the approach of "salvation-historical" theology, particularly Federal Theology, which wanted to make Scripture as a whole historically understandable, with the actual result or corollary that here thinking from the perspective of the Community remained alive. In any event, it remained the case that the removal of a tangible continuum could subject exegesis to the insight or lack of insight of the individual.

4) **The Perceiving Person as a Problem.** This brings us up to the second element which as a part of the hermeneutical legacy of the Reformation was likely to produce new problems. The Reformers saw very clearly that the "matter" expressed in the "letters" of Scripture was directly related to the perceiving person, the perceiving Community. This is what Luther meant with his phrase "the tropological sense." This is what Calvin wanted to express with his emphasis upon the accommodation of God which takes place in Scripture. This is what both the Reformers and the Orthodox had in mind when they used the important concept of "application." The Reformers did not understand God in and of himself but always as God with us *(Deus apud nos)*, nor did they understand Christ in and of himself but always as "for me" and "for us" *(pro me, pro nobis)*, and thus they always conceived of the word of the Spirit together directly with the Word-event. Therefore, the perceiving person is not for them a second and independent factor next to the Word or in contradistinction from the Word, but rather he is essentially posited with it.[327] He was not understood as a subject, which then encounters the "object" of the Word and work of God. The election made manifest in the Word makes man into God's partner. Thus, Reformation anthropology is firmly related to Christology. But, when man was once so understood, then it was possible for him, under other conditions in the history of ideas, to become the subject over against the object of the Word. This was anticipated in the 17th century in the way in which "application" became an independent motive, as well as through Covenant Theology. If "application" was an independent issue, even a special homiletical effort, then the "Word" had thereby become an object which needed to be applied to the subject. In Federal Theology the whole historically systematized process of salvation became God's activity toward man as the "other" partner, and this dual polarity was easily liable to become a

---

326. See K. Barth, "The Desirability and Possibility of a General Reformed Confession of Faith," in *Theology and Church*, tr. L. P. Smith (London: S.C.M., 1962), pp. 112ff.
    327. See H. J. Iwand, "Wider den Missbrauch des 'pro me' als methodisches Prinzip in der Theologie," *EvTheol* (1954), pp. 120–25.

subject-object relationship, something Federal Theology did not intend but which was strongly expanded in the early Enlightenment.

4. MODERN HISTORICAL THINKING AND EXISTENTIAL INTERPRETATION

In referring to the problems which the hermeneutical legacy of the Reformation would create as soon as the Christological (and thus the pneumatological) center was departed from, we have already alluded to the decisive changes which have affected the interpretation of the Bible since the beginning of the Enlightenment.

a. The New Understanding of History. We found that the Reformation emphasized the literal sense. In this virtually all of Protestant exegesis has followed it. Nevertheless, since about the 18th century the literal sense has clearly become the historical sense, and this then in the sense of a new understanding of history in general. For man, history is something to be mastered, like every other area of knowledge. In the act of understanding, man steps out of the stream of events and makes it into his object and then classifies this object in relationship to himself. This means that history *a priori* is regarded as an object which in its basic structure corresponds to the basic structure of knowing man. The broad science of history reveals to man nothing more than the infinite variability of the human itself. Thus it relativizes all history. What has developed in the course of history possesses as such no authoritative validity. The factor by which everything is relativized is the "truth" perceived by means of "reason." That this truth can be found in "the accidental truths of history" is something which Lessing considered impossible. At most, in the course of history "true things" could be said and as the result of history the knowledge of the "truth" could be expanded. Only with Hegel's new approach was the conceptual possibility then given of understanding history itself as the unfolding of the "absolute." But no moment in history as such could make the "absolute" known, since its self-explication is moving ahead toward its completion.[328]

Under the presuppositions of this view of history, the orienting factor toward which the text was interpreted in its historical sense was man in his reason. The historical sense thus gave insight into an incredible variety of human possibilities. This insight could lead directly up to the great and "eternal" thought of great men, but their "greatness" or "eternity" was already contained in "reason" itself. This insight could function more indirectly, in that the text was understood as a source for historical knowledge. The evaluation of this history then took place according to the "reason" which already had established the proper accents. Ultimately there was nothing which could really surprise the interpreter, because nothing absolutely new could ever confront him. History contained merely the variations of man's possibilities, and the biblical text was a part of that history. And if, in spite of this, the text did say something absolutely surprising or unpre-

---

328. See Helmut Thielicke, *Geschichte und Existenz; Grundlegung einer evangelischen Geschichtstheologie* (Gütersloh: C. Bertelsmann, 1935).

dictable, then this was to be "explained rationally," or critically excised. Historical criticism during the Enlightenment was primarily criticism of the contents with the goal of doing away with what was irrational, either by not having it present or by regarding it as secondary. More and more the idea of development assisted in overcoming the alternatives. It became conceivable that the irrational was only relatively irrational and could be regarded as an earlier historical stage on the way to the more rational. It was even thought that what was evidently irrational could have been the disguise of the rational based upon the accommodation of the divine Educator of man, and in this sense even "myth" could be interpreted.[329] Thus in the Late Enlightenment, understanding became more tolerant toward the variety of forms of expression because of its concepts of development and accommodation, although it still maintained that the rational was divine. The idea was still dominant that the rational interpreter could encounter in any text something great and convincing, and also first stages leading up to them or disguises of them, but in no text could he encounter something really new. The text was not the external Word in the Reformation sense at all; it could be at most the outer side of a rational thought or content which was already known.

b. *Hegel's Influence.* The 19th century produced much more refined possibilities of interpretation. These were the result less of the viewpoint of the historical sense than of a new relationship established between the individual and history. For most of the theologians of the Enlightenment, reason was a constant available to man. Since Hegel, on the other hand, the "absolute," the "idea," is involved in a process of constant change and thus the course of history and man who is understanding it are drawn into the idea's changes. The continuum is no longer man in the way he perceives himself, but rather man as he is touched and transcended in his selfhood by the Idea. Now a moving and subjective entity corresponds to what up until now was viewed as the movable object or the biblical text. Everything is history. From here a direct pathway leads to Historicism: man not only views a certain object of his knowledge historically, he views himself that way. History is the category of a relativization which comprehends everything. When Hegel's faith in the absolute was dropped, the only thing left was the all-encompassing historicization of everything.

Although Hegel's questioning of a constant reason (which was much more influential than Kant's criticism) could have made the understanding of biblical texts easier in a formal sense, it only refined the methods in fact. Kierkegaard discovered the reason for this in his own way. Hegel sees at the very point where the dialectics of existence happen, at the "I," a point of indifference.

c. *Schleiermacher and Schelling.* In spite of Hegel, in the 19th century the influence of Schleiermacher and Schelling was greater upon the understanding of

---

329. See C. Hartlich and W. Sachs, *Der Ursprung des Mythosbegriffs in der modernen Bibelwissenschaft* (Tübingen: J. C. B. Mohr [Paul Siebeck], 1952), pp. 20ff., with regard to J. G. Eichhorn and P. J. Gabler.

the Bible, not so much in the historical-critical method but in the actual interpretation of given biblical texts. Schleiermacher's thesis was that the texts express the faith. They are signs of that history which leads up to faith. In theology, primarily in Hofmann, this is the result of the philosophy of Schelling. It is not "reason" or "the" idea which is decisive, but conditions of consciousness. If the biblical text is being understood in its historical sense, then this means that it is grasped as the expression of a state of consciousness or as the self-manifestation of Christian existence as a historical entity. The relationship to the text moves from being "rational" to being aesthetic-religious.

d. Historicism. Nevertheless, the process ended in Historicism. For the aesthetic relationship to history is caught up in the subject-object pattern—only here the subject is understood differently than in the Enlightenment. Does the biblical text say anything to *us*? Does it have *something* to say to us? Both of these questions had to be answered in the negative by Historicism. What is past can only have said something past to beings that existed in the past. In the sense of Historicism it was possible to discover historically-critically what was said and to whom. But in our empty present we stand deaf before voiceless texts. Even if the texts say something about past religion or piety, that does not mean that they say something to us.

We have only given a general outline of the hermeneutical approaches of the 18th and 19th centuries. Joachim Wach has written a detailed study of part of the 18th and most of the 19th century.[330] The problems of contemporary theology, which will concern us now in greater detail, are in part a continuation but more predominantly the attempted overcoming of what could be called the results of these two centuries.

The questions in contemporary hermeneutics revolve primarily around the problem of existential interpretation, as it is propounded by Rudolf Bultmann.

e. The Location of the Contemporary Question. The first thing we must do is define the location at which the problem has arisen and needs to be dealt with. In continuation of what was offered above, the following should be said:

1) The Historical-critical Method. The historical-critical study of Scripture, which developed out of the Enlightenment, dominates the field with its methods and results. In general its rights have not been contested.[331] Conversely, the

---

330. Joachim Wach, *op. cit.* For biblical hermeneutics vol. I (1926) and vol. II (1929) are important.

331. Exceptions are, among others, Erwin Reisner, *Offenbarungsglaube und historische Wissenschaft* (Berlin: Haus und Schule, 1947); Helmut Echternach, *Es stehet geschrieben; Eine Untersuchung über die Grenzen der Theologie und die Autorität des Wortes* (Berlin: Furche, 1937); Hans Asmussen, *Gesetz und Evangelium; das Verhalten der Kirche gegenüber Volk und Staat, als Vorbereitung auf die Weltkirchenkonferenz von Amsterdam, 1948* (Stuttgart: Kreuz, 1947). On this and the whole problem, see Gerhard Ebeling, "Die Bedeutung der historisch-kritischen Methode für die protestantische Theologie und Kirche," *ZThK* (1950), pp. 1–46.

connection of this discipline with the conceptual presuppositions of Rationalism and even more so of Liberalism has been attacked from a variety of directions.[332] Whether this connection is a necessary one, or whether the historical-critical studies do not really fit more into the setting of the Reformation doctrine of justification,[333] or of the Christian self-understanding in general as being radically "historical"[334] is all an open question. That element of the tradition of the last centuries which has been maintained by the representatives of existential interpretation is the general thesis that I am only capable of understanding what is not in irrevocable contradiction to my world view and thus to my self-understanding. That means that they also adhere to the presupposition that everything historical represents only the wealth of human possibilities. The biblical text forms no exception to this. What is seen in a fully new way is the human "self-understanding" as such and the "possibilities" of human interpretation of existence as such. If the existential interpretation both surpasses and overcomes the tradition which has been dominant since the Enlightenment, then it does so by radicalizing this tradition.[335]

2) **The Subject-Object Polarity.** Historical-critical study of Scripture is fundamentally an element of that movement which ended in Historicism and for many still does. Historicism in turn belongs together with Positivism. This latter factor, understood as general intellectual movement, has taken two highly contradictory forms of expression in theology. The "positive" theology of the 19th and early 20th centuries emphasized the "objectivity" of the salvation-event and its supernaturality in its struggle against the "immanentism" of its "liberal" opponents. In its view, the biblical text, which of course was fundamentally open for historical-critical study, was in its essence a credible witness to an "objective fact of salvation" which as such formed an exception to all the rest of history. "Liberal" theology of that period, conversely, adhered to the equally "objective" "story of Jesus," which was regarded, however, as being basically coordinable with the rest of history. Its salvation value consisted of the degree to which Jesus had spoken to man the liberating word. The emphasis then was upon what "modern man" could do with the Word and being of Jesus and with all the other biblical "personalities" whose own testimonies were directed beyond their time. The "objective" was calling out to the "subjective." This process could also be observed in "positive" theology, in that in the subjective attitude of faith the objective fact of faith attained its goal. What both directions shared was this self-enclosed polarity between object and subject. Within this polarity one could emphasize either the object or the subject more strongly, but the polarity as such remained and relegated the "object" to the past and the "subject" to itself. Man remained, together with history, in the realm of what is his and controlled by him.

---

332. Those which have been most influential up to today were the critical positions of Martin Kähler and Albert Schweitzer.

333. Thus Gerhard Ebeling, *loc. cit.*, pp. 41ff.

334. Thus F. Gogarten, *Demythologizing and History,* tr. N. H. Smith (London: S.C.M., 1955).

335. This is not meant as a criticism but as an ascertainment of facts.

e. The Intention and Terminology of "Existential Interpretation." Existential interpretation is the attempt at an exegesis which would break through the rigid polarity of object and subject.[336] That means that this interpretation wants to break the stranglehold of Positivism and remove the futility of Historicism. It derives its terminology from the philosophy of Martin Heidegger which, ". . . in every assertion it makes, . . . is opposed to the subject-object thinking which has achieved practically unquestioned dominance since the awakening of rationalism in the seventeenth century."[337] The concept "existential" is derived from this philosophy.[338] "Existentials" are for Heidegger "the characters of being of existence," that is, the way in which existence interprets itself as such. As "characters" they are subsumed under existence, but they are not themselves "existentiell." "Existentiell" interpretation would be one in the direct encounteredness of existence; "existential" interpretation is one in which a self-interpreting existence meets a self-interpreting existence.

There is no reason to object to the theological usage of philosophical terminology. We must concede to the proponents of existential interpretation that they use Heidegger's terminology for theological reasons.[339] But the question to be asked is what these reasons are and whether or not these reasons could not compel one to take another way.

f. Bultmann's Original Thesis. The main theological thesis, out of which everything else has grown, was formulated by Bultmann in 1925 in his essay, "What Does it Mean to Speak of God?"[340] We cannot talk "about" God; this objectification would be both idiocy and sin because it would fail to see that God has a claim upon us. We also cannot talk about God objectively in such a way that we assume there is a divine correlation to our own experiences and thoughts. We can only talk about God in that we talk about our own "existence," in which we know that "we are being addressed by God." The existence we mean is the one in which we "accept" the "must" which encounters us from God in his claim upon us. But we can "only believe" in this our own existence. Our "free act" takes place then "in faith," not protected by "objective" givens, maintained solely by the "grace of the forgiveness of sins."

Although the concept of the "existential" is not yet present here, it is clear why Bultmann's thinking could move toward it. The concept of "existence" does break through the rigid correlation of object and subject. In my "believed in" existence I am completely myself, but in such a way that I must accept a "must." To use Gogarten's language, in faith I am "historical," in that I am "responsible."

---

336. F. Gogarten, *op. cit.*, pp. 48ff. and often.

337. *Ibid.*, pp. 58f.

338. Martin Heidegger, *Being and Time*, tr. J. Macquarrie and E. Robinson (New York: Harper, 1962), pp. 69ff.

339. Karl Jaspers has raised the question whether Bultmann has understood Heidegger correctly ("Wahrheit und Unheil der Bultmannschen Entmythologisierung," *Schweizerische Theologische Umschau* [1953], p. 79).

340. Now in *Faith and Understanding*, tr. L. P. Smith (London: S.C.M. Press, 1969), I, 53–65.

And in this historicity-responsibility pattern the brass ring of Historicism is broken through and object and subject no longer are in polarity toward each other.

This is the new opportunity which confronts me in the New Testament. It confronts me not in a salvation objectivity per se but rather as an interpretation of existence which is derived from persons, thus in the form of "existentials." This interpretation of existence confronts the interpreter in his own self-interpretation (existentially). Only the one who "understands" himself—but everyone does that!—can understand the existentials in which another person interprets his own existence. And only the one who asks about God, which again everyone does, can understand the possibility of existence which is made known to him in the testimony of the New Testament witnesses.[341]

g. Bultmann's Basic Thesis and Christology. At this point a question must be raised whose answer will condition everything which now follows. It is certainly true that we cannot speak of God as though he were an object in the world. Certainly man, when he talks about God, is talking unavoidably about God's claim which concerns his existence and thus about himself. But why is this so? From what source do we know that God is not our object? Could he not be our highest and most comprehensive idea or the source of our absolute feeling of dependency and thus an intentional object? Heidegger's concept of the structural analysis of existence produces the nonobjectivity of God all the less since Heidegger himself completely rules out the question of God. Why should it not be possible for God to be object, or better, why is it not possible for me to speak of God in any other way except in that I respond to him?

There is no other answer to this question than this, because God has revealed himself as the one who is not God in himself *(Deus apud se)* but in essence God in relation to us *(Deus erga nos)*. Or put differently, because God in his self-disclosure is essentially the God of man. And this means that the nonobjectivity of God is not a postulate but rather the interpretive repetition of the Word which is Jesus Christ. We cannot polarize God and man against each other because God does not meet us "objectively," nor in some depths of our "subjectivity," but in the person and the work of the man Jesus of Nazareth. And he does not do this in such a way that God is to be sought somewhere as the meaning behind this person and work, but rather that he "is" completely himself in this person and this work.

God's "Being" in Jesus Christ is the reason that the subject-object pattern is not usable in reference to God. But it is God's being in this man, and not the reverse. Man is affirmed and confirmed solely by the fact that God in this one man is the God of man. The reality of God in Christ is the first point of anthropology.

How then "is" God in Christ? In anticipation of our discussion of Christology we could say this. God is not in Christ like one substance in another, thus not in ontic tangibility and distinctiveness. He is also not in Christ as a "meaning"

---

341. See on this chiefly Bultmann's lecture "The Problem of Hermeneutics," in *Essays Philosophical and Theological . . .*, especially pp. 256ff., and his conclusion in "Entmythologisierung und Existenz-Philosophie," in H. W. Bartsch, ed., *Kerygma und Mythos*, (5 vols.; Hamburg: Herbert Reich—Evangelischer Verlag, 1952), II, 191ff.

can be in an event, thus in ontological relationship. He "is" in Christ in the only way that accords with his being, which cannot be classified within any realm of being. That means, he is not "objectively" in Christ, not in some kind of available and controllable form, but rather as revealed-being, in that we do not reach out to him but he reaches out to us. We encounter him in that Christ encounters us; we hear him, in that we hear Christ. We cannot penetrate "behind" Christ (into the realm of the exposed majesty of God, or *nuda majestas Dei*). We cannot go beyond him. We possess no criterion by virtue of which we could say, Here is God, there is the man Jesus. To be sure, we can make distinctions. But we distinguish after the fact, after we have submitted to the encounter with Jesus Christ. We are not dealing here with a deified man nor with a humanized God; we have to do with God as he addresses us. Wherever we hear his address, there we have been "known," and then in turn "we know." There is no knowing outside of obedient hearing.

h. The Kerygma. The term kerygma expresses this indissoluble union of knowing and obeying. It implies that the salvation-event does not confront us as a fact in itself (today we say, as a *brutum factum* or insensible fact), but always as fact in proclamation. This does not mean that there is no "fact of Christ." But it does mean that the separation of this "Christ fact" from the kerygma is not possible. This is what Kähler meant methodologically in regard to the results of the investigation of the life of Jesus. And in this sense Albert Schweitzer confirmed his findings. But Kähler himself went beyond the methodological and saw that it was substantially impossible to tear apart Christ and the apostolic proclamation. We shall have to phrase that more pointedly. The meaning of the kerygma is directed toward the awakening of faith and obedience. If the "object" of the kerygma were available outside of this claim in a purely historical way, then we would thus be enabled to have an uninvolved "objective" knowledge of it. To that degree we would not need to "hear" nor to "obey," but we could merely "ascertain." Now it is undeniable that the kerygma really is related to an event and this event could be "ascertained" by any historian with a modicum of impartiality. But what is said to us in the kerygma is not something quantitatively more than what a historian could come up with (perhaps the meaning of his conclusions or their significance for us). It is qualitatively something completely different: it is the Word which lays claim to us and in regard to which we are prohibited from resorting back to the historical conclusions because we would be evading that claim in doing so.

Under these circumstances it is appropriate for existential interpretation to place the kerygma in the middle. But it is questionable whether the kerygma is reasonably dealt with as an "existential." For "witness" and "existential" are two different things. The "existential" of someone else only raises a claim on me on the same level as I am; a call is sounded here which carries my answer as possible future in itself. The "witness" which is heard in the kerygma is absolutely prior to me. It is not superior to me the way that a fact is superior to what I make of it. That kind of superiority is within the one dimension and it can be turned around into the opposite situation. This "witness" makes nothing less than God known to me in his condescension which calls forth my response, God as the one who confirms his claim in his gift. The witness refers to what Bultmann calls the "act of God."[342] But then it is certainly not possible finally to equate this "act of God," which is prior and superior to the kerygma and through it to me, with the kerygma,[343] or to think that the "new creation" established by God's act is nothing other than a "new understanding of existence." If that were so, then the kerygma would exist out of itself and would be intended to "open our eyes to ourselves,"[344] that is, to correct the possibility of our existence before God which is falsely formulated as the question. The real goal of the kerygma is not faith in the kerygma itself but faith in Christ. For the kerygma is not the salvation-event, but rather Jesus Christ in person.[345]

i. Does Existential Interpretation Overcome the Subject-Object Pattern? Existential interpretation is supposed to break through the subject-object pattern. The reason that this pattern is not applicable to God is based upon revelation and thus upon the being of God. God does not have to do with man accidentally or additionally but as a matter of his very essence. The only guarantee we have that we can know God is in the fact that he in Jesus Christ has already known us. Christology essentially precedes anthropology.[346] Existential interpretation reverses this sequence. It gains its concept of the existential from a philosophical analysis of the existence of man, indeed, of man without regard to his relationship to God.[347] It makes the existential way of understanding into the rectification of our self-understanding, evoked by the salvation-event, to be sure. In the process, the salvation-event becomes the dimensionless, punctual source of a new self-

---

342. "The New Testament speaks and faith knows of an act of God through which man becomes capable of self-commitment, capable of faith and love, of his authentic life" ("New Testament and Mythology," in H. W. Bartsch, ed., *Kerygma and Myth . . . ,* I, 33).

343. R. Bultmann, *loc. cit.,* pp. 44ff., in regard to the resurrection.

344. R. Bultmann in his essay "On the Question of Christology," in *Faith and Understanding,* I, 140: Proclamation "brings nothing into our life as a new entity. It only opens our eyes to ourselves—though not, of course, for the purpose of self-observation. The hearing is an event in our historical living and becomes an act of decision for this or for that."

345. Gunther Bornkamm correctly countered to Bultmann that in his theology Jesus Christ has become "mere salvation fact." A little later on, Bornkamm interprets this to mean "punctual fact of salvation," and thus Jesus ceases "to be a person" (*Mythos und Evangelium* [*Theologische Existenz heute,* 26; Munich: Kaiser, 1953], p. 18).

346. See below, pp. 556ff.

347. F. K. Schumann has contended against Bultmann ("Can the Event of Jesus Christ Be Demythologized?" in H. W. Bartsch, ed., *Kerygma and Myth . . . ,* I, 186) that "a pure analysis of existence involves an anterior existential decision (viz., that it is possible to analyse the Being of man without taking into account his relation to God). . . ." Bultmann responded ("Entmythologisierung und Existenz-Philosophie," in H. W. Bartsch, ed., *Kerygma und Mythos . . . ,* II, 193ff.) that this was a correct statement. It was not possible to incorporate the man-God relationship, which only "can be an event in the concrete encounter of man with God" (p. 194), into a pure analysis of existence. Otherwise faith in God becomes something which would be "at our disposal." That is certainly true. Nevertheless, can such a thing as a neutral analysis of existence be imagined, even if it only investigates structures? Is there a third factor aside from the view "man before God," and the view "man in himself"? And won't the latter view be dependent upon whether one is proceeding upon the basis of the former view or not?

understanding. The kerygma, which is understood as the interpretation of human existence, is placed in the position which belongs to Christ, in the consistent realization of the basic approach and under the influence of historical skepticism (which is thus virtually legitimatized theologically). In reality, though, the kerygma is only the way in which Christ encounters us, exercising his decision over us and thus calling forth our decision. At that the foundation has been departed from upon which the kerygma rests, that the object-subject pattern is wrong. For this foundation is God's being in the man Christ. If this essential element of faith is dissolved into the possibility of a new understanding of being, then in point of fact, and in spite of every contrary intention, the "subject" is placed in the foreground at the expense of the "object." That means that the subject-object pattern is still in effect, with new presuppositions. In that event, the existential interpretation does not accomplish what it seeks to do.

The method of existential interpretation has found its most well-known application in the problem of "demythologization." Usually the reverse view is predominant: it is "demythologization," regarded as necessary, which first summons existential interpretation into action. But the actual order is the reverse. Long before the appearance of his well-known essay "The New Testament and Mythology" in 1941, Bultmann had designed the hermeneutics which he applied to the problem then raised.[348]

The extended discussion of the problem Bultmann has raised does not belong within the framework of this study.[349] We are concerned here only with the

---

348. This essay was probably directly the result of the book by Bultmann's student, Wilhelm Kamlah, which appeared one year earlier (*Christentum und Selbstbehauptung, historische und philosophische Untersuchungen zur Entstehung des Christentums und zu Augustins "Bürgerschaft Gottes"* [Frankfurt/Main: Klostermann, 1940], 2nd, thoroughly revised version under the title *Christentum und Geschichtlichkeit; Untersuchungen zur Entstehung des Christentums und zu Augustins "Bürgerschaft Gottes"* [Stuttgart: W. Kohlhammer, 1951]). Kamlah had, very "undialectically" as Bultmann put it, interpreted "commitment" as "the true understanding of being," and explained that "faith" was a fundamental structure of our natural being (pp. 326, 321). Thus Kamlah had pursued the anthropological approach of his Marburg teacher to its conclusion, to its undialectical and uneschatological dissolution. Now Bultmann wanted to show that this approach was not possible. By the use of "demythologization" he wanted to insure that the kerygma is in fact unavoidable for the new self-understanding. Thus his actual tendency is the opposite to what is usually supposed about him in church circles.

349. Rudolf Bultmann, "New Testament and Mythology," in H. W. Bartsch, ed., *Kerygma and Myth; A Theological Debate*, tr. R. H. Fuller (2 vols.; London: S.P.C.K., 1953–62), pp. 1–44. Most of the important essays are in this collection, although the German originals contain more than were translated in the English edition; see *Kerygma und Mythos*, I-V (Hamburg: Herbert Reich—Evangelischer Verlag, 1951ff.). Useful bibliographies are found in both English volumes, German in vol. II, pp. 209ff. In addition, see Helmut Traub, *Anmerkungen und Fragen zur neutestamentlichen Hermeneutik und zum Problem der Entmythologisierung* (Neukirchen: Neukirchener Verlag, 1952); F. Gogarten, *Demythologizing and History*, tr. N. H. Smith (London: S.C.M., 1955 [g1952]); G. Gloege, *Mythologie und Luthertum; Recht und Grenze der Entmythologisierung* (Göttingen: Vandenhoeck & Ruprecht, 1952, 1963³); E. Buess, *Die Geschichte des mythischen Erkennens; wider sein Missverständnis in der "Entmythologisierung"* (Munich: Kaiser, 1953); G. Bornkamm, R. Bultmann, F. K. Schumann, *Die christliche Hoffnung und das Problem der Entmytholo-*

results of this program for the question of the exegesis of Scripture. Bultmann's writings will be assumed to be already known for our discussion.

j. Bultmann's Reasons for Demythologization. Bultmann proceeds on the thesis that the "world view of the New Testament" is "mythical."[350] Accordingly, the "presentation of the salvation event" is integrated into this "mythical world-view." That means that the forms of expression and the world of ideas of the New Testament writers are "mythological." "Mythology is the use of imagery to express the otherworldly in terms of this world and the divine in terms of human life, the other side in terms of this side."[351] Bultmann retained this definition against the objection of Julius Schniewind.[352] More recently it has become controversial again,[353] at least in regard to its application to the New Testament. It is more important for us that the definition itself contains the concepts "unworldly" and "worldly." These concepts are not meant cosmologically but rather in terms of existentialist philosophy. What is "unworldly" is beyond our control, "the worldly" is at our disposal or can be demonstrated. This definition is important in what follows.

Bultmann cites three reasons which make a "demythologizing" interpretation necessary.

First: The mythical "worldview" has passed away and one cannot expect of modern man that he would accept it.[354] If we were to say to modern man the kerygma cloaked in "mythological" forms without translation, he would be offended by things which were no offense to the man of the first century. That would mean that we were actually concealing the real offense[355] and instead of it requiring of man that he perform the pious act of intellectual sacrifice.[356]

---

gisierung (Stuttgart: Evangelisches Verlagshaus, 1954); Karl Barth, "Rudolf Bultmann—An Attempt to Understand Him," in H. W. Bartsch, ed., *Kerygma and Myth . . .*, II, 83–132; Wilhelm Kamlah, *Der Mensch in der Profanität; Versuch einer Kritik des Profanen durch vernehmende Vernunft* (Stuttgart: Kohlhammer, 1949); G. Backhaus, *Kerygma und Mythos bei David Friedrich Strauss und Rudolf Bultmann* (Mainz dissertation, 1951; Hamburg: H. Reich, 1956).

350. Bultmann, *loc. cit.*, I, 1.

351. *Ibid.*, p. 10, n. 2.

352. Julius Schniewind, "A Reply to Bultmann," in H. W. Bartsch, ed., *op. cit.*, I, 47: "By 'mythological' we mean the expression of unobservable realities in terms of observable phenomena." Bultmann's response, "A Reply to the Theses of J. Schniewind," is in *ibid.*, p. 122.

353. See E. Buess, *op. cit.*, pp. 23ff. and, above all, pp. 189ff. Buess's thesis is that the biblical kerygma stands in an essential discontinuity with myth. Thus every mythological utterance can only be in the most pointed tension with what it means. "The boundary between kerygma and mythology in the New Testament was a battle field" (p. 23).

354. Bultmann, "New Testament and Mythology," in H. W. Bartsch, ed., *Kerygma and Myth . . .*, I, 3–4: terms like "untenable" and "obsolete" have made misunderstandings possible, since many readers do not share the terminology which dominates here.

355. Especially clear in Bultmann, "Zum Problem der Entmythologisierung," in H. W. Bartsch, ed., *Kerygma und Mythos . . .*, II, 187f.

356. Bultmann, "New Testament and Mythology," in H. W. Bartsch, ed., *Kerygma and Myth . . .*, I, 4.

What is asserted is the factual impossibility of sharing the world view which we find in the New Testament, and from this is then deduced the necessity of freeing the New Testament kerygma from this world view through translation. Bultmann expressly rejects a separation by "subtraction" or "selection."[357]

Second: "Myth" is by definition an "objectifying" statement.[358] It makes the "other-worldly" (beyond our disposal, nonobjective) appear as "this-worldly." Thus it contradicts from its very inception the understanding of being which Bultmann champions. Here the approach derived from Heidegger has its direct effect. Simultaneously this philosophy contains the existential-analytical presupposition for methodically separating the kerygma from the "objectifying image-content" of the statement.

Third: "Demythologization" is "the demand of faith itself."[359] "For faith demands the liberation from bondage to any world-view, which conceives of objectifying thought, be it the thinking of myth or the thinking of science." Yes, "radical demythologization" is the "consequent realization" of "the Pauline-Lutheran doctrine of justification without the law alone through faith"! This it is because it deprives faith "of every false security," because the man "who wants to believe in God as his God" "is put in the air, as it were." Faith is solely dependent upon the unprovable truth of the proclaimed Word. Here, "demythologization" broadens out to become what it fundamentally is: de-objectification. It is characteristic that in the last sentences partially quoted, in which Bultmann spoke his last public word up until now on the matter, the name of Jesus Christ is not mentioned. Faith is dependent upon the Word. But the Word becomes dimensionless.

k. The "Event of Redemption" According to Bultmann. Of course, what Bultmann then develops under the title "The Event of Redemption," as an analysis of the Christian understanding of existence, is neither dimensionless nor impersonal.[360] He maintains that the person of Jesus Christ is not a "surviving trace of mythology," and as "the agent of God's presence and activity, the mediator of his reconciliation of the world unto himself, [he] is a real figure of history. Similarly the word of God is not some mysterious oracle, but a sober, factual account of a human life, of Jesus of Nazareth, possessing saving efficacy for man."[361] Nevertheless, this significance is logically understood in accordance with the fundamental principle of existentialist interpretation so that the cross (which as such is historical) manifests its meaningfulness as an "eschatological" event in that we as believers in our own day and time win our freedom in our "everyday life," in the "willing acceptance of sufferings" which opens us up to the future—that is, the liberating eschaton.[362] And the resurrection is nothing other than the "escha-

---

357. *Ibid.*, I, 9, 12ff.
358. *Ibid.*, I, 10.
359. R. Bultmann, "Die Rede vom Handeln Gottes," in H. W. Bartsch, ed., *Kerygma und Mythos . . .*, II, 207f.
360. Bultmann, "New Testament and Mythology," in H. W. Bartsch, ed., *Kerygma and Myth . . .*, I, 22ff.
361. *Ibid.*, p. 44.
362. *Ibid.*, pp. 36f.

tological fact" in which "faith in the saving efficacy of the cross" receives its meaning.[363] This all can only be interpreted in one way. For Bultmann the "act" of God is not the establishment of a valid relationship to man which unconditionally and always precedes our understanding. It is, rather, the mere point of orientation which protects faith's own new understanding of self and of existence against being something autonomous. But this protection itself does not exist at all if God's "act" does not really in and of itself—and outside of all conceivable possibilities of ordering it—establish the new order between God and man. If this is not stated before everything else, then the de-objectification becomes, contrary to every intention, in effect subjectification, and that would thrust us back into the subject-object pattern which was supposed to be overcome.

l. "For Us" = pro nobis, and "outside of Us" = extra nos. The "mythological" world from which Bultmann and his friends would like to free the New Testament kerygma consists, as we heard, in the fact that here "the other-worldly, the divine is expressed in terms of this world, of human life, the other side in terms of this side." One may agree or disagree with this definition. One thing can scarcely be doubted: it excludes the existence of God in a specific historical person so far as God is not absolutely distinguished from everything "divine" and this one man absolutely from everything "human." This is what Bultmann apparently wants to accomplish with his concept of the eschatological. Appealing directly to what he calls "eschatological phenomena," he concludes his fundamental essay with the sentence, "the transcendence of God is not as in myth reduced to immanence. Instead, we have the *paradox of a transcendent God present and active in history:* 'The Word became flesh.' "[364] Now the concept of the eschatological used here is very easily misunderstood.[365] In the combination "eschatological event" he means that *nun* (now) which implies "that the 'supra-temporal reality' becomes an event [for me] only by virtue of an encounter in time."[366] One can only understand Bultmann's concept of the eschatological on the basis of Heidegger's understanding of time. He knows nothing of the "fulness of time." But this is quite apparently the basic position of the New Testament. If, in using Bultmann's terminology, we understand the event of the incarnation of God as an "eschatological" event, then we do not mean that something is happening here which might take place in a myth. There is not something divine here which is being transformed or disguised. What is happening here is beyond the adequate expression of any language and yet is the central point of all events. God, in being totally God and remaining so, is acting in history through one man and through history for us and thus in us. If this, too, is supposed to be "myth,"

---

363. *Ibid.*, p. 41.
364. *Ibid.*, p. 44 (italics added).
365. Julius Schniewind had already pointed to this and considered that in Bultmann "the eschatological nature" of the Christ-event was "confused with timelessness" ("A Reply to Bultmann," in *ibid.*, I, 75). Bultmann answered this ("A Reply to the Theses of J. Schniewind," in *ibid.*, I, 113ff.) without changing his position.
366. Bultmann in his answer to J. Schniewind (*ibid.*, I, 115). Note: "Supra-temporal reality" is R. H. Fuller's translation of the German term "timelessness," and in the German Bultmann says "for me," not "for each particular individual"—TR.

then there can be no "demythologizing." That the Word, which Bultmann correctly emphasizes strongly, is the validly authoritative Word is certainly not provable, but it also does not depend upon the decision character of the Word as such but rather consists in the fact that the Word is and has become flesh. To be sure, the Word makes known the "for me, for us" of the Gospel. But as an act of God in our history, it is materially first of all the manifestation of the fact that God is "other than we are" *(extra nos)* and puts into effect his new order with us.[367]

   m. "Incarnation" and Resurrection. The incarnation (if the "mythological" word may be allowed) is certainly not an event in the sense in which the Battle of Issus was an event. The question here is whether the completely different quality of what we are dealing with means that the incarnation was not an event at all. It is certainly not so if it is mythologically understood as something like the appearance of "a divine essence" in a person. However, as the confessional act to man of the God who remains Lord, taking place in Jesus Christ (the Crucified!), it cannot be made into a non-event because it does not fit into the series of "events" which otherwise occur in the passage of time. The same thing is to be said of the resurrection. It may be said that Bultmann himself has developed a "canon within the canon" in that he distinguishes between Paul and John (whom he has abbreviated too much, in my view) on the one side and the Synoptics on the other.[368] Having done so, it is then significant that Bultmann, after so frequently building on 2 Corinthians 5:16 in order to justify his own disinterest in the history of Jesus,[369] then finds his preferred Paul adopting "a dangerous procedure" when he lists the resurrection witnesses in 1 Corinthians 15:3–8.[370] This is apparently because Paul is guilty here of "mythologizing objectification." But one might well ask if that is really what is happening. The peculiar "in accordance with the scriptures" in 1 Corinthians 15:3 and 4 refers to another dimension. One thing is certain, and that is that Paul looked upon the resurrection as a fact. Not as a "miraculous proof"[371] but as the fact in which the age of salvation has broken through. We can integrate the resurrection into the course of coordinate history and into the coordinate understanding of being as little as we can the incarnation.[372] But this quality of total otherness does not mean that the resur-

---

367. Bultmann answers Julius Schniewind that he thinks "that my emphasis on our relation to Christ as one of encounter gives full weight to the idea of extra nos" *(ibid.)*. Must not the accent be placed in the reverse fashion?

368. See his *Theology of the New Testament*, tr. K. Grobel (2 vols.; New York: Scribner's, 1951–55), in which there is an unusual reduction of Paul's theology to anthropology. In my opinion, this portrayal of Paul, as persuasive as it is, is not quite satisfactory.

369. See *Faith and Understanding*, I, 132. In opposition to this, E. Hirsch, "Antwort an Rudolf Bultmann," *ZsysTh*, IV (1927), 631–61.

370. Bultmann, "New Testament and Mythology," in H. W. Bartsch, ed., *Kerygma and Myth . . .*, I, 39.

371. *Ibid.*, p. 40.

372. C. Hartlich and W. Sachs ("Kritische Prüfung der Haupteinwände Barths gegen Bultmann," in H. W. Bartsch, ed., *Kerygma und Mythos . . .*, II, 115ff.) polemicize against Barth's question: "Why should it not have happened? . . . There may have been events which happen far more really in time than the kind of things Bultmann's scientific historian can prove" *(CD*, III,2, p. 446). They find that Barth is making judgments of reality in this

rection was not an event, but rather that it was the salvation-event which breaks through, abrogates but also accepts our passing time, and what it was, it is for faith. The resurrection cannot be reduced to the "Easter faith," as Bultmann does; it is rather the origin of this faith, recognizable only in this faith, but recognized in it to be absolutely superior and prior to it. Again we could say, it is "an eschatological event." But only when we understand that term to include the character of God's confessional act toward man and thus the character of the event which is unconditionally valid, prior, and outside of ourselves (extra nos).

 n. Christ, the End of Myth. "Demythologization" cannot mean that God's act of confession toward man in Jesus Christ as an event should be relegated to the figurative. We must assert the precise opposite: in that God in Jesus Christ has entered into history and broken through the process of coordinate events, an actual "demything" of the world has taken place for the New Testament. The New Testament, as Rudolf Bultmann says with a certain justification, has a mythical world view. But he does not say clearly enough that the New Testament along the whole line is involved in a bitter struggle with this mythical world, with the power of the myth which locked man into his many-storied world. Christ is the end of the myth. That means, he is the end of that world view of man in which man seeks to attain some kind of "beyond" which he senses is there,[373] and in doing so fails to find this very beyond. The New Testament envisages the power of the mythical forces as "real." It speaks of these powers in terms of the overbearing might which they have over man. Nowhere is the "mythological" language of the New Testament more concrete than in those very texts which are documents of the struggle with the myth (think of Rom. 8:38f., or 1 Cor. 8:5f., or Col. 2:18; 2:16ff.). The mythical powers are not overcome through enlightenment. That was the method adopted by Greek philosophy, and it is remarkable that the New Testament did not make use of the Stoic methods of illuminating "demythologization." The fact that the powers have lost their captivating power over man is based upon the resurrection of Jesus Christ (see, e.g., Eph. 1:20ff.), upon the love of God as action (Rom. 8:37), upon the "exaltation" of the One obedient unto death (Phil. 2:9ff.). The salvation-event is the end of the power of the myth. But it is the concealed end. For the resurrection is not an epiphany before the "world." The power of suffering still holds sway (Rom. 8:36; Col. 1:24 and often), by no means do all knees bow and all tongues evoke the praise of the *kyrios* (Phil. 2:11), and the Son is still not the king of a concrete kingdom (John 18:37). To speak of the salvation-event in view of the power of the mythical forces is to spite them in the name of the One who is the Crucified and Resurrected. The Church, deriving from him and moving toward him, wins thereby its freedom, the freedom

---

context without providing adequate reasons for them. This is true. But are there any "reasons" which would make it possible to say that the resurrection was "possible"? Is there any other criterion than the witness given to us, in its very "historical" questionableness? If it were possible methodologically to educe the resurrection, then it would be placed under a given criterion. Paul knows only one: Scripture (1 Cor. 15:3, 4). And this is not a demonstrable nor logically "adequate" criterion.

373. On this, see below, pp. 473f.; 487f.

from the world's anxiety which no myth can provide, but also the unique freedom to exist in the world and thus to use its language without any special reflection. "All are yours, and you are Christ's" (1 Cor. 3:22f.)—this applies to the language of the Community, both then and now.

o. The Freedom of Proclamation. The question of "demythologization" is a question of the freedom of the Community.

The Community has the freedom of language. In the New Testament itself, the modes of expression are highly mixed. Their common element is not in terms of their concepts or their language. None of these modes of expression had its own power. That Paul can make himself a "slave" of both Jews and Gentiles is his freedom, and that is based upon his being "under the law of Christ" (1 Cor. 9:21). Proclamation has always been "translation" at the same time. And it is that today. Translation is a dangerous affair; it can become betrayal.[374] But it may happen in freedom. This freedom is none other than the real freedom in the Holy Spirit (2 Cor. 3:17).

The Community has the freedom not to have to determine the success of its speaking. If it were an institution for the propagation of an idea, then everything would depend upon its getting this idea accepted. But it testifies in the kerygma to the person of Jesus Christ. It cannot expect that this testimony will be "understood" by everyone. It cannot enforce an encounter between the One whom it witnesses to and the people hearing this witness. It is not conducting theurgy with the Word. And therefore it is sober in what it says. It cannot expect that pathos would make this encounter happen. The Community serves with its speaking. And that also means that it can and should speak carefully, but it does not have a method in order to make its kerygma "really talk." If Bultmann points out correctly that the mythical world view of another time is no longer present, then we must add that there has never been a world view in which the incarnation, the death, and resurrection of Jesus Christ for us and reconciling us would have appeared to be possible, and there will never be such a one. Certainly in the primitive Christian period there was a convenient language nearby which the New Testament authors used with what seems to have been unthinking freedom. But the next periods of time reveal that this nearby language, those of late Judaism, Gnosticism, of the Mysteries, and even of Stoicism, could become a threat by virtue of their own autonomous power. Today's proclamation cannot reach back to nearby language in this way. In its freedom it can speak the language of existentialist philosophy, but in the freedom which insists on speaking not "according to the human recipients" but "according to God's speaking," as Luther puts it.

The Community has freedom over against the human self-understanding but also freedom for it. As we said above, the continuum of understanding has been man, since the Enlightenment. He cannot be it! For he does not understand himself until he is addressed. But on the other hand, since God in Jesus Christ is the God-man, there may be in the Community no anxiety about the "self-understanding," no defensive attitude toward "anthropology"—and thus no fear

---

374. See above, pp. 25ff.

of Bultmann in regard to his thinking, in spite of all carefulness in dealing with it!

Bultmann's great accomplishment (not to mention here his uncontested and superlative service as an exegete) is that he has focussed so sharply on the problem of the subject-object pattern. His limitation is that he remains a prisoner of the philosophy which decisively helped him to solve the problem and thus to work out his method. He understands this philosophy formally and structurally. But in his thinking it has caused material shifts of great scope. One of its special effects, next to the influences which Wilhelm Herrmann and others once exercised upon him, has been that he tries to gain his Christological statements out of his anthropology, and thus he makes his anthropology into his criterion. His anthropology, his understanding of history and time, lead him to oppose "objectivity" with an actualism which then evokes, as we pointed out above,[375] the "timelessness" of God as a corollary. In this way he must eventually arrive at opposition to the objectivism he rejects rightly with existentially interpreted and actual "subjectivity." He thereby fails to carry out his original intention.

Theology must learn from Bultmann that it must grasp the freedom of language given to it in the form of service. The hermeneutical problem merges into the homiletical. The most carefully maintained relationship of exegesis to proclamation can obviously not alter the fact that the Bible must always remain open for a purely secular interpretation. Holy Scripture is not a "miracle word." Theological labor in the exegesis of the Bible is already derived from hearing and takes place in readiness to hear. Thus it has no demonstrable security supporting it. It lives from the witness of Christ,[376] and it can only fulfill its task when it investigates every text with the question, How does it relate to the witness to Jesus Christ? It will ask the text. It will not know in advance that it is going to respond. It can, in sober consideration, come to the conclusion that a text has a polar or contrapuntal relationship to the message of Christ. It will not impose a Christology upon the text, and certainly not an anthropology.

---

375. See p. 341.

376. When Bultmann thinks that "radical demythologization" is nothing other than the "logical realization" of the Pauline-Lutheran doctrine of justification "in the area of knowledge," then we would respond that the Pauline-Lutheran (and why just "Lutheran"?) doctrine of justification is an explanation of faith in Christ. Certainly, its nondemonstrability accords with faith in Christ (theology of the cross = *theologia crucis*). But it is not to be understood as though the believer were, "so to speak, left in mid-air." In that event, the Antinomists would have been right. See also G. Gloege, *op. cit.*, *passim*, and for the problem mentioned here, pp. 103ff. Also K. Barth, "Rudolf Bultmann—An Attempt to Understand Him," in H. W. Bartsch, ed., *Kerygma and Myth*, II, 83–132; and H. J. Iwand, "Wider der Missbrauch des 'pro me' als methodisches Prinzip in der Theologie," *EvTheol* (1954), pp. 120–25.

PART FOUR

The Triune God

IX. The Doctrine of the Trinity

A. THE PROBLEM AND THE APPROACH OF THE DOCTRINE OF THE TRINITY

1. THE PLACE OF THE DOCTRINE OF THE TRINITY IN DOGMATICS

a. A General Doctrine of God or the Doctrine of the Trinity? We were speaking in the preceding section of the knowledge of God. It was demonstrated to be concrete, personal, historical, unspeculative, and practical. We would not have been able to reach this result by means of general reflection. A more generally oriented reflection would come up with the opposite results, that is, general and (in terms of contents) abstract results. We were only able to understand the knowledge of God as we did because God himself discloses and has disclosed himself as a person: in Jesus Christ through the Holy Spirit.[1]

Our consideration of the nature of the knowledge of God necessarily had to include some statements about the "object" of this knowledge. Every section of dogmatics includes in its own way and from its point of view the whole of dogmatics within itself, since every dogmatic statement has in view the unity and the totality of God's revelation.[2] "Ontically" and in terms of substance, revelation unconditionally precedes knowledge. This is not due to general epistemological reasons, but because the revelation of God is not only the object but also the foundation of our knowledge. In relation to it we are not independent subjects. In spite of that, we took the "noetically" conditioned approach and sequence, but we did so for reasons of greater clarity of presentation. This procedure is sensible if it becomes clear in the course of it that the "noetic" only comes into view from the perspective of the "ontic" side.

But "Who is God?" Who is the One with whom we obviously were dealing in the last chapter in its special aspect and question?

---

1. See L. Kopler, *Die Lehre von Gott dem Einen und Dreieinigen* (Linz: Katholischer Pressverein, 1933); F. K. Schumann, "Die Einheit der drei Artikel des christlichen Glaubens," in *Um Kirche und Lehre; Gesammelte Aufsätze und Vorträge* (Stuttgart: Kohlhammer, 1936), pp. 225–45; N. Söderblom, *Vater, Sohn, und Geist, unter den heiligen Dreiheiten und vor der religiösen Denkweise der Gegenwart* (Tübingen: J. C. B. Mohr, 1909, 1912).

2. For this reason, Karl Barth has provided in his "Prolegomena" (*CD*, I,1 and I,2) a "Doctrine of the Word of God" which contains a complete dogmatics.

There is an old and widespread tradition[3] according to which we now would be supposed to discuss God's "being" and "attributes." It cannot be said right off that it would be absolutely wrong to proceed in that fashion. The order of the various dogmatic propositions would only be a decisive matter if dogmatics were a system. Nonetheless, there is the question whether or not a certain sequence could not necessarily be bound up with certain previous decisions about their content. And this is definitely the case when the Doctrine of the Being and Attributes of God is treated before the Doctrine of the Trinity. To be sure, in such a case the discussion of the Trinity later can clarify what was always presupposed in the earlier discussion of the Doctrine of God's Being and Attributes.[4] But it is also easily possible that first a "general" doctrine of God is developed and then in the Doctrine of the Trinity the special Christian doctrine of God is brought out.

A "general" doctrine of God is especially dangerous because for centuries this has been one of the most sensitive places for the intrusion of thought patterns of pagan origin and structure. It was particularly Neo-Platonism which developed a strong influence in this area. Even Orthodoxy regarded this view of God with, at least in part, astonishing alacrity as Christian or interpreted it in a Christian fashion. But it should be clear that the second commandment is a theological axiom just like the first one.[5] In our doctrine of God's being and attributes, everything then will depend upon our really talking about the God who encounters us in the biblical witness. This God, however, is the One who discloses himself to us as the Father in the Son through the Holy Spirit. He is the God whose unity, life, and revelation are expressed by the Doctrine of the Trinity in reflection and interpretation.

b. Implicit or Explicit Doctrine of the Trinity. There is no Christian doctrine of God's being and attributes which would not imply some kind of trinitarian theological conception. No dogmatics can seriously evade the fact that the Christian proclamation deals with God in Christ. Therefore there is scarcely a dogmatics which does not attempt to discuss how it is possible to speak of the deity of Jesus Christ or of the Holy Spirit and how such language is related to the unity of God which is also proclaimed by Christendom. Let us suppose that a dogmatics would discuss God's being and attributes without first and simultaneously speak-

---

3. Of the contemporary works I will mention here only that of Paul Althaus, *Die christliche Wahrheit* (2 vols.; Gütersloh: C. Bertelsmann, 1949). F. A. B. Nitzsch, *Lehrbuch der evangelischen Dogmatik*, 3rd ed. ed. by H. Stephan (Tübingen: J. C. B. Mohr, 1912[3]), begins his "special dogmatics" with anthropology, follows it then with "theology" in the more limited sense, and places the Doctrine of the Trinity at the conclusion of that (pp. 474ff.). E. Brunner, *Dogmatics*, I, 205ff., places the Doctrine of the Trinity at the conclusion of the Doctrine of the Name and Nature of God and before the Doctrine of the Attributes of God (pp. 241f.). Similarly R. Seeberg, *Christliche Dogmatik* (Erlangen and Leipzig: Deichert, 1924), I, 366ff., who speaks first of God as Personality and then of the Trinity.

4. In the *Institutes*, I, x, 2, pp. 97f., Calvin gives a brief doctrine of God's attributes and then discusses the Doctrine of the Trinity in detail in I, xiii (pp. 120ff.). C. I. Nitzsch, *System der christlichen Lehre* (Bonn: Adolph Marcus, 1829 [g1844[5]], p. 188; ET: *System of Christian Doctrine*, tr. R. Montgomery and J. Hennen (Edinburgh: T. & T. Clark, 1849), also proceeds very carefully, dealing with the attributes first, and then referring back to them very clearly later (p. 188).

5. K. Barth, "Das erste Gebote als theologisches Axiom," *ZZ* (1933), pp. 297ff.

ing of Jesus Christ and the Holy Spirit. Obviously such a dogmatics would first of all speak of "God per se" in order then to express and interpret "God in Christ." In opposition to such a discussion of "God per se" we would first raise all the well-known objections which the Reformers raised. "God per se" is either the God invented by the "theology of glory" (*theologia gloriae*), the God of that man who has departed from the only place at which God encounters him in truth. Or it really is God, but in that inscrutable majesty which he, in his grace, prevents from swallowing us. Then we would ask how, on the basis of such a "God per se" discussion, "God in Christ" could even be expressed at all. The more abstractly and transcendentally the previous concept of God is formulated, the less actual room will be left for "God in Christ" or "God in the Holy Spirit." And even if the dogmatician makes a serious attempt to hold his general doctrine of God's attributes open for a new and second statement, he will still not be able to avoid proceeding in such a way that he retroactively applies his previous, general concept of God, which was gained by abstracting it from Christ, to Christ and to the Holy Spirit. But the "who and what" of God has already been said. "God was in Christ"[6] can only be stated now in that certain divine characteristics, attributes, predicates are ascribed to Christ or to the Holy Spirit. But that means that in Jesus Christ and in the Holy Spirit it is no longer God himself who encounters us,[7] but something divine, regardless how many superlatives are used to ornament this divine something. This then reveals that any general doctrine of God which consciously and expressly sets aside the Doctrine of the Trinity, Christology, and Pneumatology at first, implies a very definite decision on the basic trinitarian, Christological, and pneumatological question, a decision which in some way is either "subordinationist" or (at least) "modalistic." Moreover, the Trinity doctrine cannot be avoided by simply failing to deal with it at all.[8]

But if the question of the Trinity is implicitly posed in every discussion of God's being and attributes in a Christian dogmatics, then it is advisable to start with it quite explicitly. That is done most conveniently at the head of the detailed discussion about the "object" of Christian knowledge.[9] The widespread objection

---

6. The phrase is in 2 Cor. 5:19. It is used here as an abbreviated concept. In 2 Cor. 5:19, "God was in Christ" may never be separated from the "reconciling the world to himself" which is so intimately connected to it.

7. This is the way W. Elert puts it; he correctly places the Doctrine of the Trinity at the head of his doctrine of "God himself" (*Der christliche Glaube; Grundlinien der lutherischen Dogmatik* [Berlin: Furche Verlag, 1940, 1941²], pp. 239ff.).

8. J. Schniewind relates, in his controversy with R. Bultmann, a statement of W. Herrmann in the year 1906: " 'It is wrong to say that Jesus is God, for that implies that we already know what God is. It implies that Jesus is merely *theios,* a divine being. We really ought to say that God is Jesus. Jesus is the very presence of God, the divine Being himself.' Herrmann reminded us of the original meaning of *homoousios*—of one, not of like, substance" (J. Schniewind, "A Reply to Bultmann," in H. W. Bartsch, ed., *Kerygma and Myth, a Theological Debate,* tr. R. H. Fuller [2 vols.; London: S.P.C.K., 1953], I, 50).

9. We agree here with K. Barth and W. Elert chiefly, among all evangelical contemporaries. K. Barth appeals to Peter Lombard and to the *Breviloquium* of Bonaventure (*CD,* I,1, p. 345). His approach is rather unique in that he places the Doctrine of the Trinity before the Doctrine of Holy Scripture. Of the Catholic contemporaries we would name especially Michael Schmaus, who entitles the first volume of his Catholic dogmatics "God the Three in One" (*Katholische Dogmatik* [5 vols.; München: M. Hueber, 1948ff.]).

that the Doctrine of the Trinity is "speculative"[10] and that it may not be placed at the beginning in order to secure dogmatics against speculation, is wrong. It is precisely the Doctrine of the Trinity which can help to guard dogmatics from speculation. But we shall have to return to this point.[11]

c. The Doctrine of the Trinity at the Conclusion? In a number of newer works (since Schleiermacher), the Doctrine of the Trinity has been shifted to the end of dogmatics.[12] Some have referred to the comprehensive character of the Doctrine of the Trinity,[13] others have characterized this Doctrine as speculative[14] or at least as an "ultimate point of theological reflection."[15] After all that has already been said, such an approach must appear as unadvisable even if the dogmatics in question should have implicitly presupposed a "correct" Doctrine of the Trinity in its Christology. The systematically most illuminating reason for this concluding position (better, supplementary position) of the Doctrine of the Trinity was given by Schleiermacher. He said that the Doctrine of the Trinity was "as ecclesiastically framed" "not an immediate utterance concerning the Christian self-consciousness, but only a combination of several such utterances."[16] It is clear that the Doctrine of the Trinity is not really conceivable as the content of the "Christian self-consciousness." But this would seem to speak in favor of the doctrine. It is the clearest expression of the fact that dogmatics is not concerned primarily with the "Christian self-consciousness" but with the self-disclosure of God which absolutely precedes all knowledge.

d. The Triadic Structure of Dogmatics. Finally, it must be noted that not a few more recent theologians, following perhaps the example of Calvin's *Institutes,*[17] take the creed as the pattern for the whole of their "special" dogmatics.[18]

---

10. Nitzsch-Stephan remark that the proponents of the "speculative Trinity of being" place the Doctrine of the Trinity before the Doctrine of God's Attributes because in their view this is the only way to avoid having "the Trinitarian statements appear as a later supplement to the already complete definition of the being of God" (*op. cit.*, p. 475). Aside from K. Daub and P. Marheineke he also mentions F. Frank and A. von Oettingen. Then he says, "This reason for such an arrangement is not valid for us." That can be taken as a conclusion.

11. See pp. 368ff.

12. Especially T. Haering, but his *The Christian Faith, a System of Dogmatics,* tr. J. Dickie and G. Ferries (London and New York: Hodder and Stoughton, 1913 [g1912]), is arranged according to the three articles of the creed; see also O. Kirn, W. Herrmann, H. Stephan (in his *Grundriss,* but his revision of Nitzsch, *op. cit.*, is not so), and most recently, Paul Althaus, *op. cit.*, pp. 511ff.; also Althaus, *Grundriss der Dogmatik* (2 vols.; Gütersloh: C. Bertelsmann, 1947 [g1932]), II, 135ff.

13. H. Stephan and O. Kirn; also P. Althaus.

14. Schleiermacher, *ChrF,* §172, II, p. 747.

15. P. Althaus, *DchrWahrheit,* II, 511.

16. Schleiermacher, *ChrF,* §170, Thesis, II, p. 738.

17. Calvin divides the Apostles' Creed into four articles, which explains the division of the last version of the *Institutes* into four books.

18. For example, T. Haering, already mentioned, and further, M. Rade, M. Reischle, even H. Martensen, and Alexander Schweizer, *Glaubenslehre der evangelisch-reformierten Kirche, dargestellt und aus den Quellen belegt* (2 vols.; Zürich: Orell, Füssli, 1844, 1847).

This accords with the comprehensive position of the Doctrine of the Trinity. Thus there are only a few works in which the outline does not reveal at least the suggestion of a triadic pattern. However, such a total structure of a dogmatics cannot replace the special discussion of the Doctrine of the Trinity. The three articles of the creed are not referring to three special objects, each with its special faith ("Theology of the First Article . . ."[19]), but rather to the one God, whom the one faith, responding to his self-disclosure, confesses.

2. THE UNITY OF GOD

a. The Monotheistic Thesis. "There is no God but one"—this is "knowledge" which Paul (1 Cor. 8:4ff.) assumes is already present in his readers. This confession of the one God permeates the whole New Testament. When the question is asked about the commandment which is "the first of all," Jesus answers with the reference to Deuteronomy 6:4f.: "Hear, O Israel: The Lord our God, the Lord is one" (Mark 12:29). He responds to the so-called rich young ruler, who addresses him "Good Teacher," with the rather sharp statement, "No one is good but God alone" (Mark 10:18). As in 1 Corinthians, Paul also speaks in Romans 3:30 of the unity of the (justifying) God and does so with a formula which reads like a reference to a confession of faith: "since there is one God." This confession then takes on hymnodic form in Ephesians 4:6 and 1 Timothy 2:5, and it is presupposed as a formula in James 2:19.[20] God is the One, and the Only One.

Primitive Christendom with its confession of the one God proceeded along the path of Judaism and especially of the Old Testament. From the Old Testament it received this "Hear, Israel" (Deut. 6:4f.) which as a component part of the "shema Israel" became the confession of Late Judaism, like the first commandment of the decalogue with its blunt exclusion of all "other Gods" based upon Yahweh's act of deliverance. ". . . the Lord is God; there is no other" (1 Kings 8:60)—that could be a summary of especially the message of the prophets (see 2 Kings 19:15, 19; Deut. 4:35; Jer. 2:11). Deutero-Isaiah proclaimed more pointedly than the others the uniqueness of Yahweh and the nothingness of the gods. "I am the Lord, that is my name; my glory I give to no other, nor my praise to graven images" (Isa. 42:8). There is no need of lengthy proofs that the Bible testifies to God as the One.[21] It would then seem very logical to speak of a biblical monotheism and to designate "Christianity" as a "monotheistic faith"—following Schleiermacher's classical example.[22] Nevertheless, nothing is gained for dog-

---

19. This is the subtitle of the book by W. Lütgert, *Schöpfung und Offenbarung; eine Theologie des ersten Artikels* (Gütersloh: Bertelsmann, 1934).

20. On the formula *eis theos,* see the book by Erik Peterson with that title, *eis theos; epigraphische formgeschichtliche und religionsgeschichtliche Untersuchungen* (Göttingen: Vandenhoeck & Ruprecht, 1926).

21. See W. Eichrodt, *Theology of the Old Testament*, tr. J. A. Baker (2 vols.; London: S.C.M., 1961–67 [g1933, 1948, 1961]), I, 220ff.; O. Weber, *Jahwe, der Gott, und Jahwe, der Götze* (1933; n.l.).

22. Schleiermacher, *ChrF,* §11, Thesis, I, p. 52. With his "definition" of Christianity Schleiermacher refers back to the thesis of par. 8 (p. 34) in which he describes the monotheistic "forms of piety" as those "in which all religious affections express the dependence of everything finite upon one Supreme and Infinite Being." They occupy, as he then seeks to prove in an exhaustive religious-philosophical argument, "the highest level."

matics with the mere concept of monotheism. Instead, we would have to assert that this concept is more apt to lead to a misunderstanding of the Christian kerygma.

b. The Problems of Monotheism. Of course, even Schleiermacher saw clearly that the concept of monotheism in itself is inadequate.[23] He who nevertheless employs it always does so upon the basis of a general concept of religion and then attempts to develop the special nature of the Christian as a unique thing within the broad realm of religion. We must ask whether the thing which is to be developed here, "the peculiarly Christian element," is not already placed in question by this procedure. If the result of phenomenological or apologetic efforts[24] is that Christianity is the highest of all religions, including the monotheistic, then that means that the exclusiveness of God's revelation in Jesus Christ is at least put in question. Moreover, when one compares "Christianity" with later Judaism and Islam, the question must be asked whether these religions do not represent a "purer" form of monotheism than Christianity appears to do. In any event, they both claim to be so, and it is not an accident that their contempt is directed against what they regard as the antithesis to their understanding of an abstract, absolutely transcendent "God is God." And that antithesis is the Christian assertion of the "deity" of Jesus Christ. It is undeniable that monotheism has a strong and certainly impressive tendency toward the "absolute" and the abstract. God's existence per se seems to be put in question at the moment that his real being with us is asserted. In accordance with that, the Christian Church is accused of polytheism when its dares to state that Jesus Christ and the Holy Spirit do not merely participate in God but are themselves deity. God, as he himself, must remain absolutely beyond his revelation. His lordship and reality in his revelation contradict the monotheistic idea of God. Finally, we must ask whether those concepts derived from Greek antiquity, like that of the highest being, also do not conceptually exclude the reality of God in his revelation. If they, in point of fact, even refer to the pantheism of Xenophanes, so that these concepts are to be interpreted in the sense of an all-comprehensive absolute immanence of the divine, then they make revelation ideationally inconceivable.

In contrast to abstract monotheism, the biblical witness is decisively oriented to God's concrete self-disclosure. The Bible does not offer any speculation about God but bears witness to the acts of God. These acts of God have, as concrete events, an equally concrete setting and place, and God himself makes himself into the partner of the man whom he has called into his covenant. He is

---

23. Schleiermacher, *ChrF,* §11, Thesis, I, p. 52, continues, as is well known, by saying that Christianity is distinguished from other teleological monotheistic faiths "by the fact that in it everything is related to the redemption accomplished by Jesus of Nazareth."

24. Schleiermacher finds (*op. cit.,* p. 34) that the Jewish "communion" shows "by its limitation of the love of Jehovah to the race of Abraham a lingering affinity with Fetishism," and monotheism had fully developed only after the Exile. Islam, on the other hand, "with its passionate character and the strongly sensuous content of its ideas betrays a certain inclination towards Polytheism." Christianity on the contrary, by its avoidance of both these wrong paths, asserts itself "as the purest form of Monotheism which has appeared in history."

himself in this personal encounter, in the covenant which he establishes. Whoever considers the unconditional concreteness of God's self-disclosure will grasp why the Old Testament does not reveal the merest trace of pantheism, but does leave the impression, particularly in the later literary strata, that here "henotheism" or "monolatry" has by no means been overcome. The unity of Yahweh is his uniqueness for Israel. He is the one God in that he is the Only One for this people. One might well ask whether the first commandment of the decalogue, as Deutero-Isaiah certainly would have interpreted it, expresses the fundamental and abstract nonexistence of the "other gods" or rather the very concrete assertion that they ought not to be. When we speak of the "nonexistence" of the other gods, then this means primarily their nonexistence for Israel. There is still a trace of similar thinking in the New Testament. In dealing with the question of eating food offered to idols, Paul began with a powerful repetition of the confession to the one God (1 Cor. 8). Whatever else may appear as "gods" and "lords" is merely mentioned (1 Cor. 8:5). But in the course of his discussion, this same Paul can say, "I imply that what pagans sacrifice they offer to demons and not to God" (1 Cor. 10:20). The whole dark region beyond God in his self-disclosure, although it can certainly be called the realm of "nothingness,"[25] is not ontically a nothing. It is beyond God's self-disclosure, and thus here also nothingness rules in all ontic "reality"! This is good Old Testament thinking. The text just referred to points back to Deuteronomy 32:17 and Psalm 106:37. From the point of view of "strict" monotheism, Paul's statement would call forth as many misgivings as all the many henotheistic statements of the Old Testament.[26]

c. The Significance of the Hypostases. The concreteness of the Old Testament witness to God is seen most clearly in the fact that God has a name in the Old Testament. This name, to be sure, bears a mystery within itself (Ex. 3:14; Judg. 13:18), and its revelation is simultaneously its concealment (Ex. 3). But the fact that God has a name makes very clear that he is not one who exists above all nameable things, but rather he is "that one," "this one and no other." His unity and uniqueness do not exclude the fact that his name is distinguished from all those whose names are not supposed to be mentioned in Israel. In the Old Testament the name becomes virtually a "hypostasis." To call upon Yahweh means to call upon his name (e.g., Gen. 4:26; 12:8; 13:4; 21:33; etc.). The holiness of Yahweh is the holiness of his name (Ex. 20:7; Lev. 20:3; 22:2; 24:16; Deut. 5:11; Ps. 111:9; 145:21; Jer. 34:16—but see also Matt. 6:9 and Luke 11:2!). Yahweh is praised in that his name is praised (1 Chron. 16:10; 29:13; Ps. 7:18; 34:4; 48:11; etc.). If God desires to be present in the temple, then that means that he wishes to have his name reside there or be intoned over this building (2 Sam. 7:13, 26; 1 Kings 5:19; 8:19; 2 Kings 21:4; 2 Chron. 6:20; 33:4, 7; Neh. 1:9; Jer. 7:11; etc.). If he gives help, then he does so through his name (Ps. 54:3; 124:8—but see also,

---

25. Thus K. Barth, especially in *CD*, III,3.

26. Christian missionaries in China earlier had to deal with the important question whether they should use a Chinese term for "God" which was of polytheistic origin, or one which had clearly pantheistic accents. A third option was not available. Based upon our considerations, the polytheistic term in this difficult situation would be preferred.

e.g., Acts 3:16). It can truly astonish no one that theology has been motivated for centuries[27] by the remarkable importance of the name of God in the Bible to various dogmatic considerations, not all of them relevant. Is it still a "strict" monotheism when the name can in this way be a "hypostasis"? Our answer must be negative if we mean by "strict" monotheism the view of a God who is not only the sole and unique God, but also isolated because he is withdrawn into an abstractness far from this world. But of course the hypostatized "name" does not designate a being "next" to God. God in his revelation and God himself are to be grasped as a unity much more than could be the case in any abstract monotheism.[28] What holds for the "name" can also be said of the "countenance" or "face" of God. If Yahweh himself is the holy one who inspires fear, then so is his "countenance" (Gen. 3:8; 32:31). If the man who prays seeks Yahweh, he is seeking his "face" (2 Sam. 21:1; Ps. 24:6; 27:8; 105:4; Hos. 5:15; 2 Chron. 7:14). To restore a disturbed relationship to Yahweh means to "entreat or soothe his countenance" (Ex. 32:11; 1 Sam. 12:12; Jer. 26:19, original text). If Yahweh moves out before Israel, then that means that his "face" is moving ahead (Ex. 33:14f.). It should be added that the New Testament follows the Old Testament in this usage (Matt. 18:10; Acts 3:20; 1 Cor. 13:12; Heb. 9:24; 2 Thess. 1:9; Acts 6:16; 20:11; 12:4), and in regard to the "name" of Jesus makes similar statements to those made in the Old Testament about the name of Yahweh (see especially Acts 3:16; 10:43; Phil. 2:10; Col. 3:17; etc.).

But the circle can be broadened considerably. Just like God's "name" and "face," the Word of God is also (according to both the Old Testament and the New) a hypostasis (e.g., Ps. 107:20; 119:74, 81, 114; 130:5; 138:4; Isa. 40:8; 66:2; John 1:1ff.; 17:17; 1 Cor. 1:18; Phil. 2:16; 1 Pet. 1:23, 25; 1 John 1:1; Heb. 1:3; 4:12; 11:3; Acts 19:13). The Word is not communication about God but rather God's own communication of himself, an effective reality, mightily created by God's own Godhead. And it is no different with the *kabod* of Yahweh in the Old Testament and the *doxa* in the New (= glory) (e.g., Ex. 33:18; Isa. 6:3, Ps. 57:12; Ex. 16:10; 29:43; 40:34f.; Lev. 9:6, 23; Num. 4:10; 17:7; 20:6; etc.; in the New Testament: Mark 8:38; Matt. 16:27; Luke 2:9, 14; 9:26; John 1:14; 2:11; 17:5, 24; Acts 7:2; Rom. 1:23; 6:4; 11:36; 16:27; Gal. 1:5; Phil. 4:20; 2 Tim. 4:18;

---

27. The strongest influence was wielded by Dionysius the Pseudo-Areopagite (c. 500), in his "On the Divine Names and the Mystical Theology," in *Translations of Christian Literature,* Series 1, Greek Texts, tr. C. E. Rolt (London: S.P.C.K., 1920, and New York: Macmillan, 1920); and then, partially influenced by him, Thomas Aquinas, *STh,* I, xiii, vol. I, pp. 59ff.: "The Names of God." The Doctrine of the Names of God is a regular part of Orthodox writings (see below, pp. 415ff.). For the exegetical side, see F. Giesebrecht, *Die alttestamentliche Schätzung des Gottesnamens und ihre religionsgeschichtliche Grundlage* (Königsberg: Thomas & Oppermann, 1901); J. Böhmer, *Das biblische 'Im Namen'* (Giessen: J. Ricker, 1898); O. Grether, *Name und Wort Gottes im Alten Testament* (Giessen: A. Töpelmann, 1934); W. Heitmüller, *Im Namen Jesu; eine sprach- und religionsgeschichtliche Untersuchung zum Neuen Testament* (Göttingen: Vandenhoeck & Ruprecht, 1903).
28. "The 'Name' of God covers both the revealed Nature of God and His revealing action" (E. Brunner, *Dogmatics,* I, 120).

Eph. 3:21; 1 Tim. 1:17; 2 Cor. 4:4, 6; Eph. 1:6, 12, 14, 17; 1 Tim. 1:11; Heb. 1:3).[29]
The same can be said, in a somewhat special fashion of course, of the *mal'ak*
(angel) of Yahweh, who not seldom appears in alternation with Yahweh (Gen. 16:7;
21:17; 22:11; 31:11ff.; also Gen. 18; Ex. 3:2ff.; Num. 22:22ff.; Judg. 2:1, 4; 6:11ff.;
13:3ff.). Finally, we refer to the peculiar hypostatization of the "wisdom" of God
in Proverbs 8 and Job 28.[30] What is the significance of all this? Obviously at least
this much, that we can only apply the term monotheism to the biblical witness
with very clear reservations. A self-differentiation of God takes place which is in
the highest degree remarkable. He remains completely God, and yet he is, to use
Barth's phrase, "in the form of something He Himself is not, to be *God a second
time.*"[31]

   d. Revelational Monotheism. Up until now we have been only in the forecourt of the actual scandal which the Bible presents to any abstract monotheism,
the scandal which is central to the Bible and to which everything we have been
discussing up to now has been referring in its own way. We recall those passages
in the New Testament which express the confession to the One God hymnodically.
In 1 Corinthians 8:6, the statement, "Yet for us there is one God, the Father,"
is immediately followed by "and one Lord, Jesus Christ." Is that not blasphemy?
And this out of the mouth of one who lives in the Old Testament! Or 1 Timothy 2:5,
where next to "For there is one God" the companion phrase "and there is one
mediator between God and men" is heard in almost a rhythmic fashion! Or Ephesians 4:5, where the praise of the "one Lord" even precedes that of the "one
God" (v. 6)! The *kyrios* title itself! Whether Paul was influenced to a greater or
lesser degree by the Hellenistic environment, he could not have been unaware
for a moment that he was ascribing a name to the Crucified One here which
expressed the sacred tetragrammaton! And then, above all, those remarkable passages in which quite unguardedly the deity of Jesus Christ is spoken of—there
are not many of them, it is true, and they are partially contested both in their
texts and their interpretation. But they still provide the hardest provocations because they are jubilant expressions of praise of both the divine mystery and of
the divine self-disclosure at the same time (1 Tim. 3:16, which even in the original
reading belongs here; Rom. 9:5; Acts 20:28; Tit. 2:13; the quotation in Heb. 1:8,
and the Johannine passages: John 1:1ff.; 20:28 at the head of the list!). But also
in regard to the Spirit: 2 Corinthians 3:17 or 1 Corinthians 2:9ff. or Acts 5:3, 9 or
even 1 Corinthians 12:4ff. or 2 Corinthians 13:13! One only needs to read these
passages (not yet to speak of Matt. 28:19) with the eyes of Late Judaism in order
to recognize the enormity of these utterances.

---

   29. See H. Kittel, *Die Herrlichkeit Gottes; Studien zur Geschichte und Wesen eines
neutestamentlichen Begriffs (Beihefte zür Zeitschrift für Neutestamentliche Wissenschaft,* 16;
Giessen: Töpelmann, 1934); J. Schneider; *Doxa; eine bedeutungsgeschichtliche Studie* (Gütersloh: Bertelsmann, 1932); and the article "*doxa,*" in Kittel, *TDNT,* II, 233–53.
   30. See H. J. Kraus, *Die Verkündigung der Weisheit; eine Auslegung des Kapitels
Sprüche 8 (Biblische Studien,* Heft 2; Neukirchen: Verlag des Erziehungsvereins, 1951).
   31. *CD,* I,1, p. 363.

But what is more alarming is that these testimonies, contrary to all theories of development, do not become less concentrated as biblical monotheism becomes progressively clearer, and as the message of the one, only, unique God is sounded with growing boldness. Rather, they attain their proper force in the New Testament whose confession of the unity of God we mentioned at the very beginning of our discussion. There is only one reason for this amazing phenomenon. The biblical witnesses did not believe that they were encroaching in any way upon the unity of God with what is called their "hypostatizing" in religious-historical terms, or with their confession of the divine dignity of Jesus Christ and of the Holy Spirit. On the contrary, in their witness they meant the one God as the Lord who concretely discloses himself in his selfhood. Obviously they understood the uniqueness of God with extreme sharpness. The "one God" excludes every second or third one. They did not understand God as a plurality in himself nor as One who united a variety of essences within himself and thereby became an additive being. They also did not proceed from an abstract generic concept of "God" under which all kinds of divine things could then be subsumed. On the contrary, the biblical witness makes three things clear. The one God is not a solitary God. He is not a lifeless God. He is not a God who is wrapped up in himself. He is not a solitary God: Certainly he does not tolerate any god or deity or divinity next to himself in his uniqueness and exclusiveness, but still in an incomprehensible way he is "himself once again" in relationship to himself and in the form of his revelation. He is not a dead God: The Bible never develops a concept of God, knows neither an absolute idea nor the absolute spirit, but knows God in his work, the work which is truly God's emergence out of himself but in such a way that in this emerging God remains himself totally. He is not a God wrapped up in himself: To be sure, he resides "in the high and holy place" (Isa. 57:15), "in unapproachable light" (1 Tim. 6:16); in his concealment, however, he unveils himself; he is not accessible, but he goes—as he himself—toward man, not as the "God who is eternally coming," but as the One who discloses himself in concrete encounter!

e. The Meaning of the Monotheistic Statement. God's unity is his uniqueness in his concrete self-qualification and self-predication. We could also say that it is his unity with himself in his revelation. Or to use Karl Barth's language: it is his unity in his ever concrete existence as Lord.[32]

1) This means first of all that worship, service, and obedience are due to God alone. In view of the Old Testament that means that we find nowhere a trace of the independent worship of the Name, or the Countenance, or the Word, or the "Glory" of Yahweh. All of these "hypostases" are essentially characterized by the fact that they are not independently subject to worship, but rather, Yahweh is present in them. Old Testament monotheism expresses itself most vividly not in resistance to foreign gods but rather in the struggle against the idolization

---

32. *CD*, I,1, p. 351 and *passim*.

of Yahweh himself, which goes on throughout the entire Old Testament.[33] This would be happening if the manifold forms in which he is present himself were to be worshiped as individual deities. "It is not the form that reveals, speaks, comforts, works, helps, but God in the form."[34] Thus, Paul is in complete harmony with the Old Testament witness when he rejects the worship of angels which was arising out of the background of Judaizing Gnosticism (Col. 2:18). We may therefore add, in full awareness of the major leap which we are making here, that any independent and special "religious devotion to Jesus" or to "the Spirit" would not be the acknowledgment of the deity of Jesus Christ or of the Holy Spirit, but rather would be idolatry. In the same way, any independent "religious devotion to the First Article" would be the negation of the concrete lordship of the Father which is praised in the First Article.

2) God is this One God as the Lord who deals with us. His unity is "monarchy" (*monarchia*)[35]—in this the Monarchians in the early Church were right. But the lordship of God has a twofold meaning. It means that God in his activity and in his emergence out of concealment remains he himself. And it means conversely that he is only he himself in point of fact in this his emergence out of his concealment and in his activity. We can thus only speak of his freedom in such a way that we speak simultaneously of the reality of his very own work, and we can speak of the reality of this work only in such a way that his freedom is emphasized and praised. He never becomes the mere object of man. But he is the subject in such a way that he makes himself into the "object" of human knowing. He encounters the creature in his exclusiveness. But he gives himself to his creature. His lordship (even in the Old Testament) is turning to man, saving, acts of love. The exclusiveness of God in his lordship is the exclusiveness of his love, of his "jealousy" (second commandment). Therefore, Christian talk about God can never be such that he is placed in rigid opposition to the "world," but also never be in such a way that something in the "world" is proclaimed as the symbol, expression of power, effluence, or manifestation of God. Herein lies the permanent significance of the second commandment, which is fulfilled in Christ precisely because in him the lordship of God comes to us in its total exclusiveness and its total reality of grace.

3) God is, as the One and the Only One, the God whom we may and should trust solely and completely. God's unity is only to be declared in the joyful news (the Gospel). God's oneness implies that we, wherever he reveals himself to us, are really encountering him himself and thus we do not have to fear that something else, something concealed in God, could say No to us when we have heard the

---

33. To name a few examples, we are reminded of Jeremiah's protest (Jer. 26 and 7) against the idolization of the temple, of Ex. 32 in relationship to 1 Kings 12:25ff., of Num. 21:8ff. in relationship to 2 Kings 18:4, and of Jeremiah's scorn of those who boast of their possession of the Torah (Jer. 8:8).

34. *CD*, I,1, p. 369.

35. See Dionysius of Rome, who calls the "monarchy" or "one power" "the most sacred teaching of the Church of God" (Denzinger, *Sources*, p. 23 [par. 48]); *CD*, I,1, p. 401.

Yes in the revelation.[36] God's uniqueness means that in the act of his turning to us we are freed from all the power of those forces which he negates. Wherever God says Yes, there is no other power alongside of God which can say an effective No.

4) God is the One and the Unique as the God who discloses himself to us really, validly, and as he who stands over against us. If God were the ultimate, unnameable, and nameless Absolute in the sense of abstract monotheism, then he would be known in the way an abstraction can be known. We would have to proceed from the basis of the reality we can perceive and then inquire about the ultimates in it which we cannot perceive, about its ground, meaning, or origin, which would then be found to be the ultimate guarantee or ultimate question itself or the crisis of the existing order. The more deeply the inquiring spirit penetrated given reality, the closer it would come to the sought-for ultimate. One layer after another of what is apparently real and valid would have to be peeled off, and in the course of this progressive discovery of the ultimate as it radiated more and more clearly through the layers, it would finally be "revealed" in an ultimate spurt of the most daring speculation or shattering excitement or profoundest self-renunciation. "Revelation" would be then in truth discovery, and the process of this discovery would always be of a mystical structure. We would find in the final ground what corresponded to the ultimate depths of ourselves. We would be hearing finally the echo of our own voice. We would not meet something outside of us and over against us. No real "Thou" would free us from our "I-Isolation." The conclusion of the "discovery" of God in all its fundamentally different ways is man himself, who "has his God" somehow (in thought, sensitivity, in ethical action, or in mystical reflection)—and man is therefore totally alone. Atheism is the other side of abstract monotheism. It appears when man awakens from his lonely dreams and either voluntarily accedes to his isolation, to the fact that he is not addressed by anyone outside himself, or cynically and resignedly accepts it in the paralysis of his metaphysical powers. The God who discloses himself to us in Jesus Christ through the Holy Spirit is, on the contrary, truly our counterpart, our opposite, but he is this in that he simultaneously is with us, as he himself. He does not make himself into the objection of our deduction. He liberates us from the necessity, otherwise so difficult to get rid of, of penetrating from concrete revelation through the postulates of the philosophy of history up to the "general." He challenges us. When he tells us his own name, he calls us "by name" (Isa. 43:1). In that he becomes a Thou to us, he makes us into an "I," which may answer him. In that he encounters us as a person, he summons us to be persons.[37]

---

36. A. Schlatter, *Das christliche Dogma* (Stuttgart: Calwer Verlag [g1911, 1923²]), p. 380: "The statements which confess the Trinity have the purpose of showing that our connection to Jesus provides us our relationship to God, and this is equally true of the Spirit."

37. E. Brunner, *Dogmatics*, I, 140: "It is not the personal Being of God which is 'anthropomorphic' but, conversely, the personal being of man is a 'theomorphism.' " P. 140: "Human personal existence is the existence which is called into existence by God."

3. The Approach of the Doctrine of the Trinity

a. God's Revelation and God's "Being." We have tried to sketch the outlines of what could be called "biblical" monotheism. The biblical doctrine of God is characterized by a very strong tension. The concreteness of God's self-disclosure could, it seems, place the unity of God in question—at least insofar as we do not make this concreteness into the basis of an abstract construction.[38] God's unity, on the other hand, could reduce the concreteness of revelation to pseudo-concreteness, to the degree that we understand it really as unity, uniqueness, and solitariness and not as the differentiated generic term "God." In both instances, the situation would be that we could not really count upon God in his revelation. We would have to proceed from the God who discloses himself and ask backward or upward about the God who stands behind this self-disclosure. God in his revelation would not be God himself. The ecclesiastical Doctrine of the Trinity— this much can be said now—is de facto (even if this was not always what those who formulated it were aware of) and in the form of a theological interpretation the assertion of the certainty which is absolutely essential for the Christian faith: the certainty that God is as he reveals himself to be. This very provisional definition of the Doctrine of the Trinity indicates that it is not a matter of daring speculation but rather of the resistance to all arbitrary flights of speculation or mysticism. In its intention, the doctrine of the triune God is directed toward the obedient sustaining of the claim which allows us no appeal to a superior court.[39]

b. The Unity of Father and Son. The Doctrine of the Trinity arose out of Christology. To be sure, it is of vital significance for the interpretation of the Old Testament too. But it never would have developed on the basis of the Old Testament alone. It would have remained, together with everything else which the Old Testament states, in the "shadows" (Col. 2:17; Heb. 10:1). In the "Lord who is the Spirit" (2 Cor. 3:18) the "cover" has been taken away, and now everything which we already observed in the Old Testament can shine forth in a new light.

Jesus Christ is called the Son of God in the New Testament in all of the various levels of its witness—in the Synoptics, in John, in Paul, and in Acts. It certainly should be borne in mind that this designation has certain analogies, for example in the predication of the king in the Old Testament (see Ps. 2:7; Acts 13:33; Heb. 1:5; 3:6), and also refers back in its own way to the Father-Son relationship between Yahweh and Israel (see Hos. 11:1; Matt. 2:15; further, Deut. 32:6; Isa. 63:16). The analogies from the history of religion are certainly well known enough. In regard to the Old Testament, however, one may not forget that (1) the predication of the king is fundamentally and in a specific sense "messianic," and (2) that on the other hand the relationship between Yahweh and Israel also and more frequently appears as a marriage covenant and that this relationship does

---

38. The treatment of the names of God in dogmatics has easily fallen prey since the Areopagite to the temptation to make the names into the mere expression of something unnameable and abstract.

39. To show this is one of the chief aims of Gogarten's book *Ich glaube an den dreieinigen Gott; eine Untersuchung über Glauben und Geschichte* (Jena: Diederichs, 1926).

recur in the New Testament—but ecclesiologically, not Christologically. (3) In regard to the rest of the analogies, it is quite clear that none of the New Testament witnesses had any idea of a family of gods. "The" Son, "The Only-Begotten" has the uniqueness and soleness of the Father himself. In accordance with that, it can be said of him, "For in him the whole fulness of deity dwells bodily" (Col. 2:9), and at a few places even the predicate "God" is used. In contrast to the New Testament witness to the "Son," everything which we found in the Old Testament was really only heralding, preparation, and promise. That this is so is demonstrated by the fact that the "hypostases" which we found witnessed to in the Old Testament are all ascribed to the Son of God in the New Testament. If he is the "Lord" (which was the confession of the primitive Church according to the wording of the "maranatha" [1 Cor. 1:8; 2 Cor. 1:14, and similarly in 1 Cor. 5:5; Phil. 1:6; 1 Thess. 5:2]), if he is the "Son" unqualifiedly, if he is "God" or the fullness of deity dwells in him bodily, then we cannot be astonished when his "name," his "countenance," his "glory" are ascribed all the same things which are said of Yahweh's name, countenance, and glory in the Old Testament.[40] Along the same lines, Jesus Christ is prayed to (1 Thess. 3:11 together with the Father; 1 Cor. 16:22; Acts 7:58ff., and probably 2 Cor. 12:8ff. too), and the apostolic blessing usually names the Father and the Son together. We need not go into the Johannine statements which in their special way bring everything together: what kinds of statements are these that Jesus Christ is the light of the world, the truth, the life, that he is not subject to the bounds of time (John 8:56ff.; 17:5), and that the theophanies of the Old Testament reveal him (John 12:41 referring to Isa. 6)! What does it mean, finally, when, outside of the Johannine witness, participation in the dignity and work of the Creator is ascribed to him (1 Cor. 8:6; Col. 1:16f.; Heb. 1:2)! To summarize, we must say that what we find everywhere is not something about a hypostatic manifestation which God fills with his presence, but that God himself is "there," acting, carrying out the final and eschatological decision.

   c. *Unity, Not Identity.* It is just as clear, however, that the New Testament in none of its statements asserts an identity between the Father and the Son. The Son is really the Son, and his sonship consists of his obedience toward the Father (John 4:34 and especially John 5:19f. after 5:18). This nonidentity is expressed not only in regard to the event of "incarnation," but also in regard to the One who was "sent" (e.g., Gal. 4:4; Rom. 8:3; and Mark 12:6). The early Christian hymn which Paul quotes in Philippians 2:5ff. (regardless of how profound the

---

   40. On the name, see above, p. 355; in the New Testament, see especially Acts 3:16; 4:12, 30; 10:43; Matt. 18:20; John 1:12; 2:23; 3:18; 1 John 5:13; 3:23; and John 14:13f.; 15:16; 16:23ff. On "countenance" or "face": while "presence of the Lord" in Acts 3:20 (RSV 3:19) clearly means the Father, we find the same phrase in 2 Thess. 1:9 in equally clear reference to the Son who (1:10) will come on his "day"; see also 2 Cor. 4:6. On "glory": as the New Testament, following the Old, speaks clearly of the *doxa* of the Father (e.g., Rom. 6:4; Acts 7:55; Luke 2:14), it speaks just as clearly of the "glory" of Jesus Christ (see the expressly deific designation "Lord of glory" in 1 Cor. 2:8 which has played a major role in the history of Christology; further Titus 2:13; 1 Pet. 4:13; 5:1; Mark 13:26; John 1:14; 2:11; etc.).

influence of Gnostic elements may have been[41]) directs our view back from the self-emptying and humiliation to the being of Jesus Christ in God's form (*morphē*; 2:6) and uses the predicate "equality with God" (*isa theō;* see also John 5:18). In the light of such statements we may not conclude that the New Testament is merely ascribing to Jesus various divine predicates, or finds in or around him something divine, or elevates him to the sphere of God. All of that would be the express revocation of the glory of God, the dissolution of the unity, uniqueness, and soleness of God and the apotheosis of man. If we nevertheless attempt another interpretation, then we must presuppose that here God in his revelation is truly himself "once more" while maintaining completely the unity of God and, in fact, for the sake of this unity. This leads us up to the problem of the origins of the Church's Doctrine of the Trinity.

The Church's Doctrine of the Trinity has its basis, its point of departure, and its object in revelation.[42] It cannot seek to explain revelation. Its sole task can be to interpret revelation on the basis of its being an event and of that event itself.[43] This interpretation is a human undertaking, which as such has its history, is subject to the process of change, and requires ongoing work at every point in time. The goal of interpretation rests in the Revealer alone, but in such a way that we can only seek out the Revealer in his revelation exclusively, in his being revealed and his revealing himself.

d. The Spirit. It is the biblical testimony and thus the common proclamation of Christendom that God's self-disclosure in Jesus Christ is his self-disclosure for us only in the Holy Spirit. The fact that Jesus is Lord can only be uttered through him (1 Cor. 12:3). The Holy Spirit bears witness to our spirit (or with our Spirit) that we are God's children (Rom. 8:16). The question which is now raised and which cannot be evaded is whether the Spirit, whom God "has sent into our hearts" (according to Gal. 4:6), is a power or a substance or some kind of being next to God? Is what here is asserted something "divine," a middle being? Or is God himself truly with us and at work in us in the Holy Spirit too? Can someone other than God himself open us to God and grant us freedom? If someone else

---

41. See E. Käsemann, "Kritische Analyse von Phil. 2, 5-11," *ZThK* (1950), pp. 313–60.

42. ". . . we do not mean that revelation is the ground of the Trinity, . . . of course, we say that revelation is the ground of the doctrine of the Trinity . . ." (Karl Barth, *CD,* I,1, p. 358). The route which Barth wants to take is that of "an analysis of the concept of revelation" (*ibid.* and often). The "conceptuality" of the Doctrine of the Trinity which is introduced with this (but not only here) has been much criticized. In my opinion, not justifiably. Dogmatics is always going to be conceptual. If one objects that the Doctrine of the Trinity must, as a product of theological reflection, be distinguished from those elements of dogmatics which have to do directly with proclamation (thus, e.g., E. Brunner, *Dogmatics,* I, 236ff. and 205), then our considerations should have demonstrated that at its very core the Doctrine of the Trinity is concerned with the decisive issues of proclamation and the faith.

43. Calvin, *Institutes,* I, xiii, 3, p. 124: "If they call a foreign word one that cannot be shown to stand written syllable by syllable in Scripture, they are indeed imposing upon us an unjust law which condemns all interpretation not patched together out of the fabric of Scripture."

were at work here than God himself, would we not then ultimately be cast back upon our own piety? It ought to be understandable that the problem which led to the Doctrine of the Trinity first arose in connection with Christology and only then with pneumatology. But it is also easy to see that this second and final step had to be taken very soon. One can say that the "Second Article" has always been the crucial issue in the whole problem of Trinitarian theology, but still the "Third Article" reveals most clearly whether a Trinitarian theological concept is on the right path, one which is fruitful for the interpretation of revelation.

4. ON THE ORIGIN OF THE DOCTRINE OF THE TRINITY

a. Triadic Statements in the New Testament. It is the testimony of Scripture itself which raises the problem which the Church's Doctrine of the Trinity[44] has sought to solve by means of interpretation. In our discussion up to now we have intentionally disregarded the fact that the New Testament in a number of places contains expressions which can be spoken of as triadic or even as Trinitarian. For the Doctrine of the Trinity is not based only or even primarily on these passages. It is the interpretation of the total testimony of the New Testament in its actual essence. But now the time has come to name those passages which indicate that within the New Testament itself the steps had been taken whose necessity we have attempted to imply without referring to these texts until now. The most well-known passage is the baptismal command in Matthew 28:19: ". . . baptizing them in the name of the Father and of the Son and of the Holy Spirit. . . ." Regardless of how this text is interpreted in detail, it shows on the one hand, as an established formula, the threeness in which God our Lord is and acts toward us. On the other hand, it is related to baptism, which, according to Ephesians 4:5, is "one" baptism, provides participation in the total new covenant of God, and takes place "in" or "into" one name. The One in whose name one is baptized is the One who is established as Lord over the one being baptized (see Acts 2:38; 8:16; 10:48). He who is baptized does not have three Lords but one Lord. The threeness does not abrogate the oneness, but is rather its form. It can hardly be contested that this formula is not only triadic, but is Trinitarian. It is not unrelated to doctrine (28:19a), but it is primarily related to an act of the Church, to a "sacrament," and thus this demonstrates that the roots of the Doctrine of the Trinity by no means go back solely to the realm of mere reflection.[45] The passage which can best be compared with Matthew 28:19, 2 Corinthians 13:13, is not a doctrinal

---

44. On the origins see especially F. Loofs, *Leitfaden zum Studium der Dogmengeschichte*, pub. K. Aland (Tübingen: M. Niemeyer, 1950, 1959[6], 1968[7]); Adolf von Harnack, *History of Dogma*, tr. N. Buchanan (7 vols.; London: Williams & Norgate, 1896–99); Reinhold Seeberg, *Textbook of the History of Doctrines*, tr. C. E. Hay (2 vols. in 1; Grand Rapids: Baker Book House, 1952–58), particularly vol. I.

45. On this passage see especially J. Schniewind, *Das Evangelium nach Matthäus*, *Neues Testament Deutsch* (Göttingen: Vandenhoeck & Ruprecht, 1936 [g1950[4]], 1964; Otto Michel, "Der Abschluss des Matthäusevangeliums; Ein Beitrag zur Geschichte der Osterbotschaft," *EvTheol* (1950/51), pp. 16–26. On the relationship between triadic confessional formulae and baptism, see especially O. Cullmann, *The Earliest Christian Confessions*, tr. J. K. S. Reid (London: Lutterworth, 1949 [f1948[2]]), pp. 43ff.

formula but clearly bears "liturgical" marks. In terms of content, Paul clearly does not imply with the threeness of this triadic blessing that there are three entities alongside one another, but a unity. Aside from these passages, which express most clearly what is presupposed in a variety of other statements, we would mention primarily Ephesians 4:4–6 and 1 Peter 1:2 and more distantly 1 Corinthians 12:4ff., Romans 5:5, 8, 2 Thessalonians 2:13, 1 Corinthians 6:11, 2 Corinthians 1:21f., Galatians 4:6, Romans 8:3, 4, 8, 9, 11, 16f. and Titus 3:4–6. These will suffice for the present. They show adequately that there is certainly no lack in the New Testament of statements which provide both reason and foundation for the Doctrine of the Trinity.

b. Triadic Confessional Formulae. In the subapostolic and early Catholic Church such three-part (triadic) confessional formulae were situated ("*Sitz im Leben*") primarily in the setting of baptism (baptismal creeds). The *Didache,* which is generally acknowledged to be very ancient, prescribes (in unmistakable dependence upon Matt. 28:19) baptism in the name of the Father, the Son, and the Holy Spirit (7:1). It is probably more significant that we have in the "Romanum," the Roman baptismal creed, a detailed three-part confession about the middle of the 2nd century. The investigations of the earlier stages of this confession have led to the hypothesis that in Rome and Egypt (dependent upon Rome) there was an even older and shorter three-part creed.[46] The confessional formula which Clement presupposes (and expands) in Rome in the 1st century is also three-part in its basic structure (1 Clem. 46:6), and there are similar formulae documented in the 2nd century and at the turn of the 3rd in Irenaeus, Tertullian, and Hippolytus.[47] It should also be mentioned here that in Tertullian, in his book against Praxeas, we encounter what is clearly a theology of the Trinity in his dogmatic and apologetic discussion. It was Tertullian who introduced the term "Trinity" into dogmatics, as well as the terms "substance" and "person" (*substantia* and *persona*).

c. Subordinationism and Modalism. Although, as we have shown, there was certainly a very old tradition which could lead up to a Doctrine of the Trinity, it must nevertheless be stated that the early Church and its theology were first

---

46. See especially H. Lietzmann, *A History of the Early Church,* tr. B. L. Woolf (4 vols. in 2; London: Lutterworth, 1961 [g1936]), II, 109ff.; the further bibliography is there.

47. August Hahn, *Bibliothek der Symbole und Glaubensregeln der Alten Kirche* (Breslau: E. Morgenstern, 1897³; repr. Hildesheim: G. Olms, 1962), pp. 6–8, 9–11; Lietzmann, *op. cit.,* pp. 114ff., and his article, "Symbolstudien," *ZNW* (1922ff.).

Basic to the whole study of the symbols is F. Kattenbusch, *Das apostolische Symbol, seine Entstehung, sein geschichtlicher Sinn, seine ursprüngliche Stellung im Kultus und in der Theologie der Kirche* (2 vols.; Leipzig: J. C. Hinrichs, 1894–1900; repr. Hildesheim: Georg Olms, 1962); Adolf von Harnack, *Geschichte der altchristlichen Literatur bis Eusebius* (2 vols. in 4; Leipzig: Hinrichs, 1893–1904, 1958).

Convenient: H. Lietzmann, *Symbole der alten Kirche* (*Kleine Texte,* Nr. 17, 18; Bonn: A. Marcus & E. Weber, 1914, 1906) (materials for the use of theological lectures and studies [Cambridge: 1906–26] but not translated).

motivated by the emergence of heretical views to develop an express and explicit Trinitarian theology and to establish fundamental Trinitarian dogma. The heresies against which the oldest Trinitarian dogmas were directed were essentially Christological in nature. It is necessary to describe them briefly, particularly because they provide the basic forms for much later conceptions.[48]

In the 2nd and 3rd centuries we see the Church's theology preoccupied with the question as to how the Church's proclamation of Jesus as the Lord and the Son of God could be harmonized with the unity of God. This question became all the more necessary and important as the Apologists viewed "monotheism" as the core of their proclamation which they had transmuted into philosophy with such certainty of victory. The intellectual tools which the theologians used were taken mainly from philosophy, and the contradiction which soon emerged can to a certain degree be understood as the reflection of the contradiction between Platonism and Stoicism, whereby the undercurrent of Gnosticism favored and influenced Platonism the more strongly.

In this unusually complicated process there are primarily two extreme attempts at a solution which we can recognize. They are called customarily "Subordinationism" and "Modalism." Neither of these attempts was ever propounded in a unified fashion, nor is the boundary between them and what might be called orthodoxy then always clear. As is usually the case, one was tempted to oppose the one extreme by calling upon the assistance of the other one, or to accuse one's opponent of the opposite of one's own position.

Subordinationism appeared in an extreme variety of forms. In its first advocates it is seen as the contestant against early forms of Logos-Christology, as we find it based upon New Testament statements, especially in Ignatius and Justin Martyr, and then broadly developed later in Origen. Whether Gnostic elements are found in this first great Christological concept of the Church's theology,[49] or whether an aversion to learned speculation was dominant, the fact was that learned men appeared who identified as the special and unique feature of Jesus that the Holy Spirit had been given to him at baptism and through its work Jesus was enabled to do remarkable deeds (his *dynameis*, or power) and to lead a perfect life. This form of Subordinationism is also called "dynamist" because of its emphasis upon this "power." The essential thing about Jesus here is not God himself but something which issues forth from God. Jesus thus enters the stream of the Old Testament men of God, even though he was the most perfect of them. This was the view advanced by Theodotus the Cobbler, first of all in Byzantium and then in Rome. He was followed by Theodotus the Money-changer and later by Artemon, also in Rome. The teaching of Bishop Beryllos of Bostra, in the Orient, was not decisively different. The fact that all of these men (who all belong to the end of the 2nd and the beginning of the 3rd century) had their predecessors is

---

48. The Reformation confessional documents (Augsburg Confession, Article I; Belgic Confession, Article IX; Second Helvetic Confession, Articles III and XI) and the Orthodox dogmaticians deal with the early Church heretics almost as contemporaries. There is in fact something like the permanency of heresy. And of course the Reformation had to deal with anti-Trinitarian groups from very early.

49. Thus Harnack, *History of Dogma . . . ,* III, 9.

seen primarily in the older Christology which can be derived from the *Shepherd of Hermas*.

The Christology of Paul of Samosata, Metropolitan of Antioch (deposed in 268, overthrown then in 272), exhibits another face, but has the same character. He takes up the idea of the Logos which had been dominant in the East. But for him the Logos, like the Spirit or "wisdom" (*sophia*), is merely an attribute of God. God is a single and unique *prosōpon* (face, countenance, presence), and therefore nothing can appear in Jesus except the attributive Logos. This in turn became possible because Jesus was a sinless person, who overcame sin. On the basis of this perfection God gave him the Logos (in baptism) and elevated him thereby to the highest dignity within the world.

The situation becomes a good deal more complicated in a third form of Subordinationism, the one which became so famous because of Arius. Arius (c. 250–c. 336) was a student of Lucian of Antioch, who in turn went back to Origen but also is to be seen in connection with Paul of Samosata. Like Origen, Lucian and Arius acknowledge a pre-existent Logos which is not an attribute of God. Instead, there is, aside from the so-called inner Logos of God (as an attribute), the Logos as the first and highest creation of God, and this Logos appeared in Jesus of Nazareth. It was not placed in him but replaced his soul. It is easy to understand that the disciples of Lucian (who, in addition, was crowned with the glory of martyrdom) could have the impression (and leave it) that they had reconciled the mystery of Christendom with speculative reason without harming the mystery in any way. But what kind of being was it that was at work in Jesus of Nazareth? Quite clearly, a "semi-deific" being,[50] a "created God."[51] It was not God himself, but something divine, and the more this divine element was praised, the clearer it became that they had surrendered what they were so assiduously trying to protect, the unity of God. God had become the highest point of a manifold divine, undoubtedly a thought which was found in the final extension of Gnosticism.

We interrupt our consideration of the meaning of the Subordinationist position in order to look at its actual adversary, which at first glance said what no Subordinationist could bring himself to say: that in Jesus Christ God himself meets us, and not something merely divine. Modalism agrees with its opponent from the other extreme in that it, too, insists unconditionally upon the "monarchy" (*monarchia*) of God. It is also in agreement with the earliest proponents of Dynamism in its rejection or low estimation of the Logos-Christology. But for different reasons. Its intention, again in a variety of forms, is to solve the secret of the self-disclosure of God by making the one God (they usually say simply, the Father) into the subject of revelation, and they see in Jesus Christ and in the Holy Spirit only various modes, various ways of appearing, of one and the same God. Clearly, modalism can be so stated that it accords with the universally held Christian faith as it is expressed classically in the first sentence of the so-called Second Letter of Clement: "We ought to think of Jesus Christ as we do of God" (2 Clem. 1:1).

---

50. F. Loofs, in Schaff-Herzog, VII, 170f.
51. Harnack, *op. cit.*, IV, 5.

Were not all of the errors of the Subordinationists thoroughly swept away here and all the fancies and the intellectual myths avoided which so easily could associate with the Logos-Christology? It is not at all surprising that Modalism was for decades the official doctrine in Rome, where they had to conduct a particularly difficult struggle against Subordinationism. Nevertheless, we must ask what this doctrine really produces when it becomes concrete. Its earliest exponent (Noetus of Smyrna) may have been thinking of a kind of self-transformation of the Father into the Son. Accordingly, the Father would have been born, would have suffered (thus the sarcastic term "Patripassianism" in Tertullian and many other later figures), and would have ascended to heaven again. However, this rather crude form appears to have been overcome as early as Praxeas, against whom Tertullian fought so rigorously. The purest form was attained by Sabellius (based in Rome and strongly influencing the East), for whom the whole movement is then named. He places the possibility of sonship in the Father and calls God *huiopatōr* ("Son-Father"). In the course of salvation-history (in that day's terminology: in the developing of God's *oikonomia* = economy), this God assumes three different forms: that *prosōpon* (face, countenance, presence) of the Father "as Creator and Law-Giver," of the Son "as Redeemer," and of the Spirit as "Giver and Sustainer of Life."[52] Unmistakably there are ideas which are fundamental here which were developed in Stoicism in order to reconcile the variety of the gods with philosophical monotheism. All of the many gods simply appear as the different *prosōpa* (masks, forms of representation) of the one divine *ousia* (substance). But this very terminology reveals that Modalism, contrary to all appearances, was actually occupied in seeking God's being behind God's revelation. Was not God according to this view the concealed "silence" as Ignatius had already defined him,[53] the "hidden Fourth,"[54] which is unfolded in the three successive *prosōpa* historically and which is capable of further development?

d. The Church Doctrine of the Trinity and Its Soteriological Significance. The extreme views mentioned were, in their fully developed form, always an issue of minorities, although most influential ones. There are broad tendencies, however, which go far beyond those forms which can be theologically defined, but which generally correspond to these extremes, and theologians could be subject to such tendencies without rightfully being ascribed to the one or the other extreme. Origen, for instance, would have tended toward Subordinationism, based upon the slant of his influence, although his own doctrine of the Logos certainly avoided its concepts. Conversely, one of the associates of the later so influential Athanasius, Marcellus of Ancyra (d. c. 374), is clearly shaped by Modalism, albeit in a strongly modified form. In the same way, the group which came to the fore as Orthodoxy later could not quite deny having a light modalistic bent.

---

52. Harnack, *op. cit.*, III, 85.
53. The Son is the "Word issuing from the silence" (Ignatius, *Letter to the Magnesians* 8:2, tr. C. C. Richardson [*LCC*, I, 96]); for further comment, see Walter Bauer, *Die Briefe des Ignatius von Antiochien und der Polykarpbrief (Handbuch zum Neuen Testament)* (Tübingen: J. C. B. Mohr, 1920).
54. K. Barth, *CD*, I,1, p. 439.

It must suffice for us to refer to the extreme solutions and to the breadth of their historical connections. We can and must leave aside the issue of the human unpleasantness which burdened the controversies of these decades, and the degree to which political power factors influenced the Church's decisions—for example, in the cause of Paul of Samosata and even more so during the Arian struggle later on.[55] But in conclusion and by way of summary we must ask what was at stake in terms of substance in these battles.

Our presentation up to now should have made clear that the struggle was not solely a matter of theological reflection divorced from proclamation, but rather that the issue went to the very core of proclamation. It was the question of the truth of revelation and simultaneously of the proper message of salvation. "Inevitably—as we must realize, if we are to understand the strictness with which it must be combated by the Church—all anti-Trinitarianism falls into the dilemma of denying either the revelation of God or the unity of God."[56] The first temptation became more strongly but not exclusively acute in Subordinationism. It was, according to this view, not God but something from God or something divine which appeared in Jesus Christ. The second temptation appeared in Modalism, but not only there. God is the divine *ousia* (substance) which is concealed behind all of the special self-representations of God, but he is never totally he himself in his salvation-historical self-presentation; he is always involved in his self-presentation in salvation-history. Now wherever the reality of revelation is questioned, as in Subordinationism, there against every intention the unity of God disintegrates into an immanent plurality of the divine, and above all, the difference between the Creator and the creature is imposed upon God himself. In the case of Modalism, any disputing of the genuine unity of God is accompanied by the disintegration of the reality of his revelation. God is not then he himself "once more" in his revelation; he is revealing a form which is to be strictly distinguished from him.[57]

The significance of these controversies can be gauged by their effect upon soteriology. The view of redemption which apparently accords with Subordinationism would be one in which man would be expected to embark upon a path of virtue, presumably like Jesus of Nazareth, in order then to attain to the gift of salvation. In the whole system, man is seen in continuity with God, as the system has the Creator and the creature come together at the peak of the great pyramid. And thus man must orient himself to this continuity, and then he will be able to share in salvation. Modalism, on the other hand, implies a view of redemption which intends the transformation of man, a transformation effected through the sacral power which God releases in his various self-representations and has then placed in readiness in the Church. When the unambiguity of the concept of rev-

---

55. See on this H. Berkhof, *Kirche und Kaiser, eine Untersuchung der Entstehung der byzantinischen und der theokratischen Staatsauffassung im 4. Jahrhundert*, tr. G. W. Locher (from Dutch) (Zollikon: Evangelischer Verlag, 1947).

56. K. Barth, *CD*, I,1, p. 404.

57. Harnack, *op. cit.*, III, 62, shows that the two extremes could in fact touch each other. Thus Hippolytus accuses Bishop Callixtus of Rome that he was fluctuating between Sabellius and Theodotus. If the Incarnate One was not strictly conceived of as God himself, then in fact Modalism had to shift over into Subordinationism.

elation is given up, then the unambiguity of the understanding of salvation is also lost.

e. The Meaning of the Church Doctrine of the Trinity. The Church Doctrine of the Trinity is in its essence the attempt to preserve as one the unity and the revelation of God dogmatically. It is (1) directed against the attempt to assume that there is a gradation of the divine within God, and it is (2) opposed to any attempt to understand revelation only as the differentiated and unreal self-representation of God who silently remains behind it. It repeats that God discloses himself in threefold revelation as totally himself each way, and it confesses that he is as he reveals himself to be without thereby jeopardizing his unity. This means that it teaches the Three-in-Oneness of God, God as the Triune God. In its classical form, it does this with the concepts of Hellenistic thought, with concepts which certainly could not maintain their clarity and unambiguity for all times, and thus—as Augustine already saw—requires new formulations. At a time in which Greek speculation or Syrian Nomism was threatening to smother proclamation, this doctrine was able, using the concepts of that time, to overcome those elements of the self-understanding of man then current which were perverting the message of Christ.[58] In contrast to a theology which ascribed to God's deity and his honor a being distinct from God himself, it testified to the deity of God in this its form. In contrast to a theology which distinguished between God in his revelation and God himself and then speculated on it, this doctrine opposed speculation by using the forms of speculative thought.

On the other side of the issue, it was an easy thing for this speculative kind of thinking to gain its own authority within "Orthodox" Trinitarian theology, and thus the Church's acknowledged doctrine became itself the basis for speculation which departed from its scriptural orientation. Melanchthon's famous warning in his Introduction to the *Loci* of 1521 is very appropriate in reference to such errors, "We do better to adore the mysteries of Deity than to investigate them,"[59] a warning which Calvin adopts (without referring to the Doctrine of the Trinity).[60] Nonetheless, such good Reformation reserve prevented neither Melanchthon nor Calvin from renewing the position of the early Church in battling the anti-Trinitarianism of the 16th century (Servetus and the Socinians). What they encountered in their anti-Trinitarian contemporaries was only superficially based upon the Reformation understanding of the Bible but was in fact an outgrowth of the biblical understanding developed by Renaissance philosophy and Humanist legalistic ethics.[61]

---

58. The conceptual language was subjected also to many alterations in the course of the Arian disputes (see below).

59. *LCC,* XIX, 21; Stupperich, II/1, p. 6, which in this context is also applied to the Doctrine of the Trinity. Melanchthon later develops this much more broadly.

60. *Institutes,* I, v, 9, pp. 61f. Calvin is also rather careful in his treatment of the Doctrine of the Trinity; see the *Institutes,* I, xiii, 5, pp. 125–28 and the well-known disputes with Pierre Caroli.

61. See F. Trechsel, *Die protestantischen Antitrinitarier vor Faustus Socinius* (2 vols.; Heidelberg: Winter, 1839–44); for the older literature, see the relevant articles in Schaff-Herzog, especially Servetus, Ochino, Gentile, and Blandrata. Further, P. Tschackert, *Die*

B. FORM AND CONTENT OF THE CHURCH DOCTRINE OF THE TRINITY

1. On the Conceptual Setting of the Doctrine of the Trinity

a. The Necessity and Limits of Interpretation. The Church Doctrine of the Trinity—whether that of the early Church or its development in Augustine or John of Damascus or in the Latin Middle Ages or in its reception in Old Protestant Dogmatics which was scarcely modified from the earlier tradition—derives neither the term "Trinity"[62] nor its component forms (*ousia,* essence, substance, *hypostasis, prosōpon,* person, subsistence, as well as the frequently discussed *homoousios,* consubstantial) from the Bible. This is reason to be careful. It has also been the cause for objections since very early. Nevertheless, the Doctrine of the Trinity is virtually the classical example of a "dogma," in that it interprets the testimony of Scripture, to repeat Calvin's phrase which we have already cited. It is not to be evaluated on the basis of whether it can be found "syllable by syllable" in Scripture (Calvin) but solely in terms of its correct interpretation of the revelation of God testified to in Scripture.[63]

"Interpretation" of the scriptural witness consists, to use Barth's frequently quoted phrase, of the fact that theology or the Church "says with other words the same thing" as Scripture. Accordingly, to be legitimate, the Doctrine of the Trinity is to be measured by Scripture. It does not produce new knowledge for us. It helps us to appropriate the knowledge made known in Scripture by means of interpretation, and it helps us to counter false or erroneous appropriation. For a Doctrine of the Trinity to arise, it must have become clear that the biblical

---

Entstehung der lutherischen und der reformierten Kirchenlehre, samt ihren inner-protestantischen Gegensätzen (Göttingen: Vandenhoeck & Ruprecht, 1910), pp. 460f.; H. E. Weber, *Reformation, Orthodoxie, und Rationalismus* (2 vols. in 3; Gütersloh: C. Bertelsmann, 1937–51). On Servetus a newer work, E. Wolf, "Deus omniformis," in *Theologische Aufsätze Karl Barth zum 50. Geburtstag* (Munich: Kaiser, 1936), pp. 443ff. On the Italians see the major monograph by Dello Cantimore, *Eretici italiani del Cinquecento* (Firenze: G. C. Sansoni, 1937, 1949); GT: *Italienische Haeretiker der Spätrenaissance,* tr. W. Kaegi (Basel: B. Schwabe, 1949).

62. The Greek usage of *trias* was subject to misunderstanding; the Latin *trinitas* is first rendered in German as *Dreifaltigkeit* ("threefoldness"). This is Luther's choice, although he regards the word as "very bad German" (*WA,* 46, 436) and would prefer to say, "*ein gedrits*" ("a threeness"). Unquestionably, *Dreifaltigkeit* corresponds more to the ambiguous Greek term *trias.* For the German problematic, see the standard German dictionaries, especially Grimm.

63. Luther responds to the objection, raised with good reasons by Eck and Cochlaeus and substantially admitted by Luther, that the Trinity is not mentioned as such in Scripture by saying that his adversaries are seeking to aver that the matter is not sufficiently clear and firm in Scripture, which makes them "vocabulists." Erasmus adopted the same position in regard to the question of original sin. But in fact the substance of the Doctrine of the Trinity was clearly witnessed to in Scripture, and ". . . we must retain the substance, we can put in any terms which we want . . ." (*WA,* 39, II, 305); Paul Drews, *Disputationen Dr. Martin Luthers in der Zeit 1535–45 an der Universität Wittenberg . . .* (Göttingen: Vandenhoeck & Ruprecht, 1895), pp. 799ff.; see also E. Hirsch, *Hilfsbuch zum Studium der Dogmatik, Die Dogmatik der Reformatoren und der altevangelischen Lehrer quellenmässig belegt und verdeutscht* (Berlin: Walter de Gruyter, 1958, 1964), pp. 19ff.

witness necessitates an interpretation in a specific direction, and then secondly there must have been a motive in the Church which led to the development of this interpretation. This motive was the appearance of false teaching.

The "other" words of which interpretation makes use are, like all our human words, fundamentally "unbaptized." They are derived from this or that "natural" self-understanding, this or that philosophy, ultimately from this or that mythology. They do not bring their interpretive function along with them; they must receive it always in the process, and it is derived from the substance of revelation itself. The source of these terms is left to theology. It must only be sure that the terms it uses can be made serviceable for the task of interpretation. Really "serviceable"! There is no doubt that the terms used in theology have a strong tendency toward assuming domination. Even the most useful terms can in the course of conceptual analysis and synthesis concentrate themselves into a conceptual system or intellectual mythology which is something completely other than interpretation. The Church Doctrine of the Trinity has not evaded this fate by any means. We can then understand that Calvin quotes Hilary and agrees with him when he does not conceal the fact that in the Doctrine of the Trinity we "deal with unlawful matters . . . speak unutterable words . . . trespass on forbidden ground," and when he excuses himself for introducing truths "in human terms."[64] If it were not for heresy, declares Calvin, all of these "invented names" could remain buried.[65] And he find himself confirmed in this opinion by Augustine.[66] The service function of the Trinitarian interpretation implies that not it but the triune God is the "object" of faith, and from that perspective the beginning of the so-called Athanasian Creed must be viewed as at least easily misunderstood with its "Whosoever would be saved."[67] It certainly gives pause when Johann Gerhard (1582–1637) declares that without the knowledge of the Doctrine of the Trinity, no one could be saved.[68] Statements of that kind can be the expression of a hybris of dogmatics which is then usually closely followed by secularization.

b. The "Vestiges of the Trinity"—Augustine and the Middle Ages. Our caution in regard to the terminology of Trinitarian theology must be all the greater since it early contributed to the attempts to find certain "vestiges of the Trinity" (*vestigia Trinitatis*) in the realm of nature, of the human psyche, and elsewhere, and since this terminology has more recently been positively received by speculative philosophy, a reception which is problematic in itself and which is related to the doctrine of the vestiges.

---

64. *On the Trinity,* II, 2 (*NPNF,* 2nd series, IX, 52); Calvin, *Institutes,* I, xiii, 5, p. 127.

65. Calvin, *loc. cit.*

66. See n. 20 (*LCC,* XX, 127).

67. Calvin's position on the Athanasian Creed was at least at times negative; see Herminjard, *Correspondance des Réformateurs dans les pays de langue française* (9 vols.; Geneva: H. Georg, 1866–97; repr. Nieuwkoop: B. Degraaf, 1965), IV, Letter 610, pp. 185ff. At being summoned to sign the "three symbols," Calvin is supposed to have answered, "We subscribe to faith in God alone, and not in Athanasius, whose symbol the true church will never approve." See also Letters 611, 614, 616 in Herminjard, *op. cit.,* IV, 187ff., 195ff., 198ff.

68. *Loci theologici,* III, 209; ed. F. R. Frank (1885ff.), I, 383ff.

The doctrine of the vestiges of the Trinity found its most impressive form in Augustine's "On the Trinity," where this problem virtually dominates from the conclusion of the eighth book on. The ninth to the eleventh books are devoted exclusively to the vestiges of the Trinity, and in other writings Augustine likes to refer to this point.[69] The most important "traces" of the Trinity within created reality are found within man himself. Man cannot exist intellectually at all unless he first of all knows about himself and about things (memory), secondly makes himself objectively aware of himself and of things (intellect), and thirdly voluntarily confirms what he has become aware of and relates it back to himself (will).[70] In a similar fashion, Augustine distinguishes the basic powers of the soul as spirit (*mens*), self-knowledge (*notitia*), and self-love (*amor*).[71] It was particularly influential that Augustine saw in every act of love a vestige of the Trinity, to the extent that he that loves, and that which is loved, and love itself as the event which binds them together are all connected to one another ("*amans, et quod amatur, et amor*").[72] Similarly, Peter Lombard[73] and Thomas Aquinas[74] among others, and of the Reformers Melanchthon and some of his students[75] all believed that they were able to find such vestiges. The contexts in which this happens are very different. In Augustine,[76] Thomas Aquinas,[77] and of the Early Orthodox Bartholomew Keckermann,[78] it is clear that it is not mere terminological aids which are being sought, that is, they are not simply trying to show that also in the reality of creation there is "threeness in oneness" and "oneness in threeness." Rather, a connecting line is consciously supposed to be drawn between man as reasonable creature and the triune God. Man, as he is and not only at the point where he hears the Word, is "the image of God" by virtue of his capacity for the contemplation of the eternal. Therefore and conversely, the being of God can be recognized as it were as a reflection in the character of man's intellectual being. There is no doubt that this is a "genuine *analogia entis*, with traces of the Trinitarian Creator-God in what exists as such."[79] It is obvious that Platonizing thoughts (the

---

69. See *The City of God*, XI, 24–28 (*NPNF*, II, 218–22); *Confessions*, XIII, xi, 12 (*NPNF*, I, 193f.).

70. *On the Trinity*, X, especially xi, 17ff. (*NPNF*, III, 142f.).

71. *Op. cit.*, IX, 4 (*NPNF*, III, 127f.).

72. *On the Trinity*, VIII, x, 14 (*NPNF*, III, 124).

73. *Sentences*, I, dist. 3, c, 1.

74. *STh*, I, xlv, vol. I, pp. 238f., and especially I, xciii, 6, vol. I, pp. 473f.; recognizably influenced by Augustine. But it should be noted that Thomas, *STh*, I, xxxii, 1, vol. I, pp. 168–70, contests the natural knowability of the Trinity; the dissimilarity of the Trinity to everything which is naturally discernible is greater than the similarity.

75. See the third edition of the *Loci* (*CR*, XXI, 615; Stupperich, II/1, pp. 183f.); the "somnium Philippi" (dream of Philip) is taken over primarily by C. Pezel and Georg Sohnius; M. Hafenreffer and Johann Gerhard repeat almost verbatim the careful wording of Thomas Aquinas; see also Schmid, pp. 135–37; in rejection of this, Calvin, *Institutes*, I, xiii, 18, pp. 142f.

76. Especially instructive, *On the Trinity*, XII, iv, 4 (*NPNF*, III, 156); XV, vii, 11 (*NPNF*, III, 205ff.); and XV, xxi, 40 (*NPNF*, III, 221).

77. *STh*, I, xciii, 6, vol. I, pp. 473f.

78. *Systema Sacrosanctae Theologiae* (Geneva: 1611), pp. 20ff., in Heppe-Bizer, pp. 106–108.

79. K. Barth, *CD*, I,1, p. 384.

soul as the mirror of God) are in the background; epistemology and ontology mutually interact, and the Doctrine of the Trinity is fitted into the framework of an already given ontology. The terms used make their autonomous significance known!

   c. The Vestiges of the Trinity: the 19th Century. This is all the more true of the Trinitarian speculation of the 19th century which developed from the roots of idealistic philosophy. In Hegel, what Augustine once regarded as a vestige of the Trinity has been endlessly magnified and become the essence of the Trinity. God is the Absolute; "the Absolute is the Spirit,"[80] and God exists as Spirit within the dialectic of thesis, antithesis, and synthesis, i.e., "God, who represents Being in-and-of-itself, eternally produces Himself in the form of His Son, distinguishes Himself from Himself, and is the absolute act of judgment or differentiation."[81] But "what He then distinguishes from Himself does not take on the form of something which is other than Himself; but, on the contrary, what is thus distinguished is nothing more or less than that from which it has been distinguished. God is Spirit. . . ."[82]

   Hegel's Absolute is not rigid but flexible within itself, that is, (in the "Son") as the absolute establishment of the word and (in the "Spirit") as the absolute unity of God with this established world. The guiding intention of Schelling (in his last phase of development) was to reconcile faith and knowledge, revelation and reason. He felt he had attained this goal in that he posited in God, both from the viewpoint of reason and that of revelation, three "potencies"—indefinite, definite, and self-defining being. These three "potencies" appear in revelation to the extent that they are revealed in the threenesses which are found in much of ancient mythology, but then fully in Christianity as the "truth of paganism."[83] What one could call "immanent," inner-divine Trinity is thus a postulate of reason in Schelling, and again the vestige has become the essence of the Trinity!

   It cannot be doubted, of course, that the constructions of idealistic and romantic philosophy would not have been possible without the Church Doctrine of the Trinity already there as a given. Nonetheless, Hegel encouraged the development of a speculative theology of the Trinity within dogmatics. In this connection we would mention, aside from Daub and Marheineke, especially Richard

---

   80. *System der Philosophie,* vols. 8–10 in *Sämtliche Werke,* pub. H. Glochner (26 vols. in 24; Stuttgart: Fromann, 1927–40, 1958–64), III, par. 384.
   81. Hegel, *Lectures on the Philosophy of Religion,* tr. E. B. Speirs and J. B. Sanderson (New York: Humanities Press, 1962), III, 12.
   82. *Ibid.* It should be noted here that Lessing already derived the Doctrine of the Trinity from God's self-conception (*The Education of the Human Race,* tr. F. W. Robertson, in *Literary and Philosophical Essays* [New York: P. F. Collier, 1920], par. 73, p. 211). Philosophical speculation on the Trinity was pre-formed as early as Jakob Böhme; see *Die hochteure Pforte von göttlicher Beschaulichkeit* (1620), ch. 3, ed. W. Goeters (Berlin: Furche-Verlag, 1924), p. 48.
   83. *Philosophie der Mythologie 1842,* Book I in *Werke,* ed. M. Schröter (München: Beck, 1956–60 [g1928]), V, 257ff.; *Philosophie der Offenbarung,* Book III, *Werke,* ed. M. Schröter (München: Beck, 1927–28), I, 395ff.

Rothe,[84] then Ernst Sartorius,[85] who has been held to be orthodox, and then, with an especially impressive system, Isaak August Dorner.[86]

In general we are tempted to assert, *vestigia terrent* (vestiges are frightening), in the double sense. The doctrine of the vestiges of the Trinity developed on the basis of Platonic or Neo-Platonic ontology and was thus fundamentally predisposed to emancipate itself as an ontology and in the process to become the embodiment of a philosophy or theology of being which was based not on the Creator, but on the creature—although it certainly contains clear reflections of Christian proclamation.

d. homoousios, ousia. Since we have seen that terms have the potential capacity to become autonomous entities, we have good reasons to discuss briefly the central concepts of the classical doctrinal development in terms of the history of doctrine and then to inquire in what sense these concepts are usable as tools for interpretation.

A part of the traditional terminology of the Doctrine of the Trinity has been taken from the Bible. In both the Creed of Nicaea (325) and the Nicaeno-Constantinopolitan Creed (451)[87] we find at the beginning of the decisive Second Article the belief in the *kyrios* (Lord) Jesus Christ, the *huios tou theou* (Son of God), and the *monogenēs* (only-begotten). As they are understood in the two creeds, these are statements not only about the Incarnate One but also about the "subject" of the Incarnation, or as it was frequently put later, about the divine "nature" of Christ. The detailed explanations which follow and to which we shall turn first are then in fact nothing other than an interpretation of the biblical predicates mentioned in view of the heresies which had arisen (in the earlier Creed of Nicaea they are named, in the Nicaeno-Constantinopolitan Creed they remain in the background).

The biblical terms mentioned (to which then the Nicaeno-Constantinopolitan Creed adds the special predicates of the Spirit) declare, first of all, a definite relationship between the Father and the Son. Basically, the further discussion is devoted to this theme. Putting it somewhat oversimply, we could say that the whole thing has the purpose of interpreting what "the Son of God" could mean. Since both Subordinationism (the exclusive concern of the Creed of Nicaea but still a part of the debate in the Nicaeno-Constantinopolitan Creed) of Arius' type

---

84. *Theologische Ethik,* repr. ed. by H. J. Holtzmann (5 vols.; Wittenberg: Zimmermann, 1869² [g1845–48¹]), I, 104ff.

85. *The Doctrine of Divine Love; or Outlines of the Moral Theology of the Evangelical Church,* tr. S. Taylor (Edinburgh: T. & T. Clark, 1884 [g1840–51]).

86. *A System of Christian Doctrine,* tr. A. Cave and J. S. Banks (4 vols.; Edinburgh: T. & T. Clark, 1880–82 [g1879]), I, 412ff. As in Sartorius, the Trinity is to be developed from the basic idea that God is love (see also Augustine). This necessarily entails an eternal self-differentiation and self-reunification on the part of God.

87. The texts with helpful comments can be found in H. Bettenson, *Documents of the Christian Church* (New York and London: Oxford University Press, 1947), pp. 36f., with further bibliographical citations. For a similar discussion in German, with complete critical apparatus, see *BekSchr: The Nicaenum,* p. xiii; *Nicaeno-Constantinopolitanum,* pp. 26f.; the literary problems and further bibliography are also discussed.

and Modalism understood the Sonship of God in a figurative sense, the symbols of the 4th century were endeavoring primarily to emphasize the literal actuality of sonship, that is, to combat any understanding of the Son as being only a creature or as a form of appearance.

The term which gradually came to the foreground was the much-discussed word "*homoousios*" (of one substance) which was placed by the commission in the Creed of Nicaea and then also in the Nicaeno-Constantinopolitan Creed. This term has a very complicated history which should be discussed here.

The fundamental idea is naturally the concept of the divine *ousia* (substance). We find it only in a rather colorless sense in the New Testament ("property" in Luke 15:12). The more so is it then rooted in philosophical Greek. It can have the meaning of the Latin *essentia* or of *natura* or *substantia*. In all of these instances it has a content which does not exclude a participation of other entities. Therefore, the term *ousia tou patros* ("substance of the Father" in the Creed of Nicaea) by no means implies that it could not also be applied to a nondeific but merely "divine" being. This then explains why the term *homoousios* as used by Paul of Samosata came to mean the very opposite of what it meant in the Creed of Nicaea for the right wing of the Council and what it meant in general in the Nicaeno-Constantinopolitan Creed. In Paul it is related precisely to the subordinated Logos which participates in God's Logos.[88] Thus it is understandable that the term *homoousios* receded rapidly in the controversies which followed Nicaea, even in Athanasius.[89] Even the obviously ambiguous concept *ousia* was consciously excluded at a point where they were looking for a conciliatory approach, as in the second formula of Sirmium.[90] Conversely, there were notable theologians in the East who preferred the concept *homoiousios tōi patri* ("of like substance with the Father") to *homoousios* because it seemed to them to have been better thought through. Around 360 it could even appear as the longed-for unifying formula, which expressed both the unity and the differences equally.[91] It was primarily Athanasius' accomplishment to give the term *homoousios* the meaning "of one substance" instead of "of like substance." But this meaning was not generally established until the adherents of Athanasius came to the point of regarding the concept of the *treis hypostaseis* (three hypostases) as acceptable—a development which we have yet to discuss.

For a Christian doctrine of God, the term *ousia* is only applicable when it is translated as "true nature" (*Eigentlichkeit*) in the sense that it excludes its transference to something which is not God himself. But this means that the term has another meaning entirely. It would virtually have to be rendered as "Godhead": "The essence of God is the godhead of God."[92] Only on such an as-

---

88. Lietzmann, *A History of the Early Church*, tr. B. L. Woolf (4 vols. in 2; London: Lutterworth Press, 1961), III, 99–102.

89. *Ibid.*, p. 197.

90. For the text, see R. Seeberg, *op. cit.*, I, 223f.; further, Lietzmann, *op. cit.*, pp. 218f.; see also the fourth Formula of Sirmium (358), in Seeberg, *op. cit.*, pp. 224f. (both formulae are cited in the German original from Hans, *Bibliothek der Symbole*, pars. 161, 163).

91. Even Hilary of Poitiers was impressed by the term *homoiousios*, as his book *De Synodis* reveals (see Seeberg, *op. cit.*, pp. 255f., and Lietzmann, *op. cit.*, p. 258).

92. K. Barth, *CD*, I,1, p. 401.

sumption is the term *homoousios* appropriate for the task of interpretation. It does not imply participation in the divine substance. It states that in Jesus Christ no other than God himself is dealing with us, God himself as the one who in this his self-disclosure is he himself "once more," he himself in eternity.

One more important restriction is necessary if the concept *ousia* is to be usable in a Christian doctrine of God. We must exclude the option of understanding the term as a kind of general or summary concept which comprehended the Father, the Son, and the Spirit as concrete "person" in itself. This requirement was not met by the Cappadocians especially. For example, they compared the *ousia* of God with the *ousia* of "man," which was possessed in the same way by, say, both Peter and John.[93] Obviously this would lead directly to Tritheism. Thus it was right that this danger was countered, especially on the foundation of Augustine's theology and with meticulous care in the formulations of the Athanasian Creed.[94] Even better is the formulation by Andreas Quenstedt, "The divine essence itself is that pertaining to God, by which God is what He is."[95]

e. hypostasis, persona, relatio. But with this unity in the true nature, this "unity of essence" of the Father, the Son, and the Spirit, we are seeing only one side of what the classical doctrine is saying. The Son is Son, the Spirit of God is Spirit, as certainly as the Father is Father. The unity is a living unity. In order to define this living unity the formulaters of the early Church's Doctrine of the Trinity finally agreed in the course of the controversies of the 4th century on the fundamental concept, *mia ousia treis hypostaseis* (one essence three hypostases). The term *hypostasis* was no more unambiguous than was *homoousios*. But in contrast to the latter, this term does occur in the New Testament,[96] and in one text (Heb. 1:3) it bears the meaning "nature" which later remained dominant for a long time. There is scarcely a distinction at that point between it and *ousia*. Therefore, in the 4th century the terms are frequently used interchangeably. However, Arius,[97] who found that the Son and the Spirit were both not equal with the Father, still spoke of the Father, Son, and Spirit as "three hypostases" and saw in this formulation the opposing concept to what he regarded as the "Manichaeism" of *homoousios*. Accordingly, the term was first regarded with suspicion by the "orthodox," while in the East even non-Arians insisted upon it (especially the Cappadocians later). They felt that only with this term could Modalism be avoided and Christian thought be protected from the loss of every reference to the reality of the salvation-event in history, which was a danger in the

---

93. See Seeberg, *op. cit.*, pp. 227ff.; references there.

94. The Athanasian Creed: "The Father uncreate, the Son uncreate, and the Holy Ghost uncreate." This is also true of the predicates "incomprehensible" and "eternal." "And yet they are not three eternals but one eternal. As also there are not three uncreateds, nor three incomprehensibles, but one uncreated and one incomprehensible." See also Schaff, II, 66f.

95. *Theologia didactico-polemica* (Wittenberg: 1685), P. I., C. 9, sect. 1, Thesis 11, cited in Schmid, p. 152; see also K. Barth, *CD*, I,1, pp. 401f.

96. 2 Cor. 9:4; 11:17; Heb. 1:3; 3:14; and Heb. 11:1 where it means "assurance."

97. See Adolf von Harnack, *op. cit.*, IV, 14ff.; Seeberg, *op. cit.*, pp. 202ff.; Lietzmann, *op. cit.*, III, 109f.

term *homoousios* with its ambiguity in popular piety. When Arius spoke of the "three hypostases," the only possible meaning was that of three "essences," and that was indeed a most questionable formulation. The Latins had a poor linguistic grasp of the term. They translated *hypostasis* with *substantia* and introduced a tritheistic element in the process. Ever since Tertullian they had spoken of *personae,* but not of *substantiae,* and this corresponded to the widespread term used in Greek, *prosōpon.* But this term, too, had its problems. *prosōpon, persona* could also mean "mask" or "role" in a drama, and in that instance Sabellianism was an obvious danger—as if God simply revealed himself in various "masks" or forms of appearance! There was no expression which was totally satisfactory. In the course of the controversy it became the general conviction that both the oneness and threeness of God, the oneness in threeness and the threeness in oneness, had to be expressed. But all the concepts failed. Augustine expressed himself clearly on this point.[98]

Later theologians found it necessary to interpret the term "person." It was especially of great consequence that Thomas,[99] following along Augustine's path materially, defined "person" on the one hand with Boethius (c. 480–c. 524) as "an individual substance of a rational nature," but on the other hand chiefly used the formula, "a divine person signifies a relation as subsisting."[100] He wants to understand "person" as a concrete, really existing relation of God to himself. Thus, the Augsburg Confession understood "person" as something "which properly exists,"[101] and Calvin, who could be very scornful of the popular ideas of "person,"[102] defines the term, again clearly borrowing from Augustine and Thomas, as "a 'subsistence' in God's essence," and thus sharply distinguished from "essence."[103] With the term "subsistence" doubtless a good approach has been found, particularly when we add to it the early Church's interpretation of *hypostasis* as *tropos hyparxeōs* (mode of existence).[104] The most appropriate translation which then results is "mode of being" or "mode of existence." This interpretation is all the more to be preferred today in view of the fact that since the emergence of the modern concept of personality the decisive characteristic of "person" is self-consciousness and self-determination. That is totally useless for the Doctrine of the Trinity, since in this case it is necessary that the concept of

---

98. *On the Trinity,* VII, iv, 7ff. (*NPNF,* III, 109ff.); and V, 9 (*NPNF,* III, 92): "The answer, however, is given, three 'persons,' not that it might be spoken, but that it might not be left unspoken."

99. *STh,* I, xxix, 1, vol. I, pp. 155f. The suggestion that *hypostasis* could be replaced with *subsistentia* had already been made around 360 by the rhetor Victorinus Afer in his writings against Arius; see Harnack, *op. cit.*, IV, 120f. However, the reference to Victorinus Afer is not given in the ET; see Adolf von Harnack, *Lehrbuch der Dogmengeschichte; Die Entwicklung des kirchlichen Dogmas* (Darmstadt: Wissenschaftliche Buchgesellschaft, 1964 [repr.]), II, 297—TR. W. Elert, *Der christliche Glaube, Grundlinien der lutherischen Dogmatik* (Berlin: Furche Verlag, 1940), p. 269.

100. *STh,* I, xxix, 4, vol. I, p. 159.

101. Article I: "Person" is "not a part or quality in another, but that which properly subsists" (Schaff, III, 7).

102. See the sarcastic phrase "three marmosets" in *CR,* XLVII, 473.

103. *Institutes,* I, xiii, 6, p. 128.

104. As was done as early as the Cappadocians.

person be applied equally to the one essence (not just each "person" of the Holy Trinity would be "personality" but the whole Trinity itself would have to be that).[105]

Our review of the terminology of the Doctrine of the Trinity should have made one thing clear: all of the formulae are only approximate attempts to express a mystery which will never be completely comprehended by our thought processes. Basically they are molded more by what they are seeking to oppose than by what they are seeking to assert. It is quite correct "that the understanding of the hypostatic Trinity of God out of his Ousia is denied to us."[106] Of course, this can and may not prevent us from stating what must be said. We can perhaps summarize the "meaning" of the "classical" Doctrine of the Trinity by saying that the issue here is that God, as he himself, in the true nature of his existence as God, lives, acts, and rules from all eternity and thus in his revelation in three-in-oneness. "And the Catholic Faith is this, That we worship one God in Trinity and Trinity in Unity; Neither confounding the Persons, nor dividing the substance."[107]

2. THE SALVATION EVENT AND THE DOCTRINE OF THE TRINITY

a. God's Revelation and God's "Being." The Doctrine of the Trinity, like all theology, is derived from the self-disclosure of God which is made manifest as real in faith. It can be nothing other than the interpretation of the "salvation-event" proceeding *a posteriori*. This point of departure cannot be used by it as the basis for speculation seeking God beyond his self-disclosure. It remains permanently bound to this its point of departure. In fact, its basic thesis is that God's "being" is not to be sought somewhere beyond his revelation, but that God's self-disclosure in Jesus Christ through the Holy Spirit, God's being-for-us, is his true nature. God is who he reveals himself to be to us. His condescension is his essence. In his establishing relationship to us in his self-disclosure, he makes it known that he exists essentially in relationship. In his revelation he does not give us something we are to know, which were only derived from him, but rather he gives himself in his gracious lordship.

This then means, from the other direction, that if God discloses himself to us as the Father, the Son, and the Holy Spirit, then he, the one Lord, has not become something in this self-disclosure which he "had not been before." Rather, in the eternal antecedence to his activity with us he is as he reveals himself to us. He reveals himself as the One in Three, and he is this One in Three. This is the meaning of the well-known phrase of Barth according to which God is in his revelation "antecedently in himself."[108]

The Doctrine of the Trinity underlines this "antecedently in himself." But it does this in order to underline the authority of revelation, the finality of the

---

105. "Mode of being"—especially now in Barth, *passim*, but also in Harnack, *op. cit.*, IV, 120 [where *Seinsweise* is rendered as "manner of existence"—TR].

106. W. Elert, *op. cit.*, p. 271.

107. The Athanasian Creed (Schaff, II, 66).

108. *CD*, I,1, pp. 441, 457, 513, 417, 425f.

"salvation-event." This "antecedence" can therefore not be fitted into our time patterns. Certainly the Nicaeno-Constantinopolitan Creed confesses the Son as "begotten before all ages." But this formulation, which echoes Colossians 1:26, Ephesians 3:9, and Jude 25 and which corresponds to John 17:24, Ephesians 1:4, and 1 Peter 1:20 ("before the foundation of the world"; see also John 17:5), can be interpreted in no other way than in terms of the unconditional priority of God toward all time,[109] of God's eternity, of his lordship over time and in time.[110]

   b. The Regressive Posing of the Question. If it is true that the Doctrine of the Trinity interprets the revelation-event, then the frequently used regressive method for its establishment is justified. We name as an example Calvin, who proceeds on the basis of the deity of the Son and of the Spirit and then discusses the Trinity.[111] The establishment and development of the Doctrine of the Trinity is based then on the question, Who is the one who encounters us as Lord in Jesus Christ and in the Holy Spirit.

   This cannot mean, however, that the Son and the Spirit are merely the form of the Father which emerges into the light in the salvation-event (that would be Modalism). Similarly, it cannot mean that the Father and his work should be thought of as somehow absorbed by that of the Son and of the Spirit. To be sure, the one who "sees" the Son "sees" the Father (John 14:9), and no one knows the Father aside from the Son and "any one to whom the Son chooses to reveal him" (Matt. 11:27). But it is also true that "no one knows the Son except the Father" (*ibid.*), and that the Revealer can do nothing of himself (John 5:19, 20, 30). When we speak of the deity of the Son and of the Spirit, then we mean none other than that of the Father, but not such a deity as would be absorbed by the Godhead of the Father or would absorb it. This is the very mystery which the Doctrine of the Trinity expresses, that in the Son and in the Spirit God himself meets us, in each special "mode of being," without in any sense encroaching upon the oneness of God nor the specialness of the "mode of being" of the Father. This is indicated in the biblical witness chiefly in the fact that God is not directly "our" Father, but rather indirectly the Father of the Son (see Rom. 15:6; 2 Cor. 1:3; 11:31; Eph. 1:3; Col. 1:3 and the passages in which Jesus asserts that his relationship to the Father is absolutely unique, e.g., Matt. 7:21; 15:13; 18:35; 20:23; 26:29, 39 and above all the Johannine statements, most pointedly John 20:17). In accordance with this, the childhood of the believer is designated by Paul as an adoptive relationship (Rom. 8:15, 23; Gal. 4:5; see also Eph. 1:5 and Rom. 8:4). The early Church symbols, when they speak of God as the Father, mean the Father of the Son.[112]

---

109. See pp. 455ff.

110. The first systematically reflected discussion of the problem of time is found in Augustine, especially the *Confessions,* XI, 13ff. (*NPNF,* I, 167ff.). The Doctrine of the Trinity had to lead to the consideration of time because the eternity of the Trinity cannot be conceived of as mere pre-temporality.

111. *Institutes,* I, xiii, 7ff., pp. 129ff.

112. See also the Heidelberg Catechism, Question 33: "Why is he called God's *only-begotten Son,* since we also are the children of God? Because Christ alone is the eternal natural Son of God; but we are children of God by adoption through grace for his sake" (Schaff, III, 318).

c. "God Was in Christ." The theological issue of the Trinity developed, as we have shown, from the biblical witness to Christ. If the "predicates of dignity" of Jesus—"Son of God," "Lord," and in some passages even "God"—are understood as true statements, they would have to be offensive to every sort of abstract monotheistic thought, and they have always been that. Therefore they would have to be interpreted in a nonrealistic way or, since such an interpretation would clearly not be faithful to the New Testament, they would provide a reason to develop a new theological formulation of monotheism. In the process, the concrete and vital form of monotheism actually witnessed to in the Old Testament[113] has always been in the background and often in the foreground.

The predicates mentioned have their own history and context of ideas as human statements. Both are open to historical research, and it would place the historicity of revelation in doubt if "dogmatically" the possibility and necessity of historical study were to be questioned. The results in this area which have been arrived at up to now have not been uniform.[114] However, they provide a wealth of possible and a number of very probable analogies, particularly in Late Judaism and Hellenism, which up to a point enable us to understand the Christological terminology and context of ideas of the New Testament historically.

However, the terminology and context of ideas of the New Testament witnesses should not be confused with the "matter" which they are expressing. Whoever identified this "matter" totally with the context of ideas in which it is made known to us would replace the "salvation-event" with the inner movements of thinking people, who in turn would then cease to be regarded validly as witnesses. At the same time, it would make this context of ideas itself incomprehensible, since doubtless it is to be derived from an event which was understood by none of its bearers as a part of his inwardness but which for all of them was given absolutely, outside of themselves. Conversely, this "matter" cannot be separated in its pure form from the terminology and context of ideas of the witnesses. It is not a substratum and not a timeless "truth."

The New Testament witnesses are proceeding upon the basis of the event of the person and work of Jesus Christ. Their conceptions and terms, derived from such a variety of backgrounds, find their unity and their content solely in that event.

In the person and the work of Jesus Christ, according to their message, God himself disclosed himself, and did so in such a way that the walled insularity of man, his enslavement to the powers and forces, has been utterly broken through "from outside." Jesus did not assume the highest height above the highest possibilities of man in his walled-in insularity. He broke away that insularity and enslavement with all of their ostensible possibilities. His self-disclosure is both

---

113. See pp. 353ff.

114. Above all, W. Bousset, *Kyrios Christos, a History of the Belief in Christ from the Beginnings of Christianity to Irenaeus,* tr. J. E. Steely (Nashville: Abingdon Press, 1970 [g1935⁴]); G. P. Wetter, *"Der Sohn Gottes," eine Untersuchung über den Charakter und die Tendenz des Johannes-Evangeliums* . . . (Göttingen: Vandenhoeck & Ruprecht, 1916); D. A. Frövig, *Der Kyriosglaube des Neuen Testaments, und das Messiasbewusstsein Jesu* (Gütersloh: C. Bertelsmann, 1928); the article *"kyrios"* in Kittel, *TDNT,* III, 1039ff. with a wealth of bibliographical references.

reconciliation and redemption. This event did not take place primarily in the pronouncement of a new way to live rightly. Such a pronouncement (as "law") would have not been the disintegration of that walled-off insularity. Rather, it took place in the life, death, and resurrection of the man Jesus of Nazareth. And he is not essentially a "divine man" who accomplishes within the world of insular man something which astonishes man and thus simply heightens his insular closedness. He is the bringer of the Kingdom of God in that he became the neighbor, "fellow man" to the ordinary man, his fellow man to the very point that he took upon himself the sin, the closedness of this man to his creator, and thereby the total failure of his life upon himself, and endured the No of God against this sin to the extreme of death itself. This endurance up to the ultimate and inconceivable conclusion, up to the death which man could not bear, contains within itself the advance reference to the event of the resurrection in which he leaves death behind him, as he had overcome its actual nature in dying. As this crucified and resurrected One, he made himself known to and let himself be appropriated by his own, those few and contemptible who had surrounded him, and he made them into his witnesses.

This is approximately the way that one can describe the provenance of the New Testament witnesses. Only in light of such a description can we relevantly grasp that they proclaimed him—regardless of the content of the ideas—as "Lord," as "the Christ," as "the Son of God," yes, even as "God." If they were using terms which otherwise were in use, then these concepts were ripped out of their pagan foundations just as the concept of "Christ" was ripped out of the foundations of Late Jewish Messianic dogmatics current at that time. These terms were nothing other than the reflection of the self-manifestation of the One whom they designated with such terms, and from him alone they received their contents and their qualification. The decisive thing is that they connected these concepts with the proclamation of the Crucified One. They apparently never considered the cross as prejudicial to the deity of Jesus—so far from it that John characterized it as "glorifying" or "being lifted up" (John 12:23; 13:31f.; especially John 3:14; 8:28; 12:34). None other than the Son of God could accomplish the redemption of those who were under the law (Gal. 4:4f.), none other could endure the No of God than he.[115] God's work took place here. Here alone, in this person and this work, God revealed himself to man, God himself, the one God, and in doing so he confirmed and fulfilled the whole history of the covenant which had gone before, and he brought the Kingdom near. Thus, at the end point to which God has led men the beginning which he established becomes visible. God has acted, and yet, it is God over against God! God does not remove the sin of man with a declarative statement. He acts. He "sends" the Son (Gal. 4:4) "in the likeness of sinful flesh" (Rom. 8:3). "For our sake he made him to be sin who knew no

---

115. See especially A. Schlatter, *Jesu Gottheit und das Kreuz* (Gütersloh: C. Bertelsmann, 1913² [g1901]). While the Christology of Greek early Church theology reveals a clear tendency to see Christ's Sonship and the lordship of Jesus Christ more or less exclusively on the basis of the incarnation and the resurrection, it was Anselm of Canterbury (*Cur Deus homo?*) who developed the approach to a Christology structured around the cross-event.

sin . . ." (2 Cor. 5:21), and the curse is carried out on him, "having become a curse for us" (Gal. 3:13). The Son's taking upon himself the curse of death "for us," "in our place," is the activity of God's love for us (Rom. 5:8). But this activity takes place over against God, for it is his own Creator claim upon man which has been violated, and the sin for which he is "delivered up" is the sin which is charged against us by God. Regardless of the way in which the biblical witness to the reconciliation may be understood in detail, the issue at stake is the relationship between God and man, which becomes fundamentally new here. In the middle of the abyss which is totally opened and totally bridged does not stand one of us, but God for us, Jesus Christ. Who else could establish peace between God and us than God himself? Who else could be "our peace" (Eph. 2:14), and oppose every breach with the new order? "To be" the righteousness of God is granted to us through none other than this One through whom God acts (2 Cor. 5:21). However it is viewed, it is God himself at work on both sides, God over against himself, and yet in such a way that he is as God completely with man and stands in man's place.

If the work of reconciliation is essentially God's act before God for us and thus God's activity in and with us, then we can understand that the New Testament witnesses require that faith in the Son of God which is solely directed toward God.[116] They do this certainly not thinking that this would mean that God would be deprived of what is due him but rather apparently in the sense that God himself receives in "faith in Christ" the response which corresponds to his work in Christ. We see the same correspondence when we read that Christ is termed the "likeness of God" (2 Cor. 4:4; 3:18; Col. 1:15), both in the sense of a predicate of dignity and in the sense that he is in truth what created man had been promised and received (Col. 3:10; see also Eph. 4:24). The two-sidedness of reconciliation is reflected here, as well as the two-sidedness of every Christology. If God himself is acting in Christ, if Christ is God's likeness, then, finally, it is understandable that the judgment too, God's eschatological work, appears in the New Testament as the work of Christ (see the formula, "the day of Christ Jesus" [Phil. 1:6; further 2 Cor. 5:10; Rom. 14:10; 2 Tim. 4:8; Acts 17:31; Rom. 2:16; John 5:22ff.]), just as God's "kingdom" is designated the "kingdom" of Christ in some passages (Col. 1:13; Eph. 5:5; 2 Tim. 4:1, 18; Heb. 1:8; 2 Pet. 1:11; John 18:36, but also Matt. 13:41; 16:28; 20:21; Luke 22:29f.; 23:42).[117]

It should have been made clear by now that here there is one vast thematic which permeates all of the various strata of the New Testament tradition. God acts over against God, God as God acts over against man, and both of these belong together. For this reason it cannot really be surprising that in John's Gospel as at the beginning of the First Epistle of John this double aspect assumes the

---

116. See especially the Pauline formula *pistis* (*Iēsou*) *Christou* (faith in Jesus Christ) in Rom. 3:22, 26; Gal. 2:16, 20; 3:22; Eph. 3:12; Phil. 3:9 and related expressions in Eph. 1:15 (*en* = in); Col. 1:4 (*en*); 1 Tim. 3:13 (*en*); 2 Tim. 3:15 (*en*); Philem. 5 (*pros* = toward); further Acts 3:16; 20:21; 24:24; 26:18; James 2:1 (!); Acts 2:13; 14:12. *pisteuein* (to believe) is frequently connected to the dative (e.g., John 6:30; 8:31; etc.) but more frequently with *eis* (in) (in reference to Jesus [Matt. 18:16; John 1:12; 3:16, 18; 4:39, and often in John]; but also in Paul [Phil. 1:29; Gal. 2:16]).

117. See also the previous note.

thought-through form in which it has most strongly stimulated Church doctrine. But we must remember that John is materially saying nothing other than what we have already seen in Paul, for example; consider 1 Corinthians 8:6, 2 Corinthians 5:19, Colossians 2:3, 9, and above all 1:11ff. What is of chief importance for our discussion is the fact that the "pre-existence" of the Son is worked out in a particularly clear fashion in John (1:11ff.; 8:58; 17:5, 24; also 3:13). The One in whom God is present and at work, over against himself and over against man, is not a creature who at some time or other appeared, but he stands at the side of the Creator, he has come from God (John 13:3), has been equipped with power by God (John 3:35; 13:3; Matt. 28:18; 11:27), is sent as he who is the Son "before in himself" (thus even Mark 12:1ff.; further Rom. 8:3; Gal. 4:4; and next to John 1:1ff. especially Heb. 1:1ff.).[118]

In that the New Testament states what happened, is happening, and will happen in Jesus Christ, its witness presses forward with an inherent necessity to the ultimate and most profound utterances. The formula which could summarize it all is that of the *monogenēs huios* (only-begotten son [John 1:14; 3:16; 1 John 4:9, more pointedly, John 1:18]), which was then taken over in the creeds. Here Karl Barth is certainly right when he says, "the statement about the *pre-existence* of Jesus Christ is only an explication of the statement about his existence as the Revealer and Reconciler, as of the God who acts on us and for us in time," and also "the statement about his existence is only an explication of the statement about his pre-existence."[119] We shall have to be careful that we do not mythologize the concept of pre-existence by absorbing it into our time pattern. It would then cease to be a proposition of faith and, in complete contradiction to the meaning of the message of the New Testament, it would tempt us to evade speculatively the claim of the person of Jesus Christ. But we shall also have to be very

---

118. Rudolf Bultmann presents in his essay "The Christological Confession of the World Council of Churches" (in *Essays Philosophical and Theological*, tr. J. C. G. Greig [New York: Macmillan, 1955 (g1952)], pp. 273ff.), an analysis of the New Testament which at many points agrees with our discussion above. He summarizes his interpretation: "The formula 'Christ is God' is false in every sense in which God is understood as an entity which can be objectivized, whether it is understood in an Arian or Nicene, an Orthodox or a Liberal sense. It is correct, if 'God' is understood here as the event of God's acting" (p. 287). A few pages earlier, the decisive question is found to be, "whether and how far the titles at any time intend to tell us something about the nature of Jesus—how far they describe him, so to speak, objectifying him in his being in himself, or whether and how far they speak of him in his significance for man, for faith? . . . Does he help me because he is God's Son, or is he the Son of God because he helps me?" (p. 280).

The sentence just cited should demonstrate that Bultmann's alternatives are genuine ones. Nonobjectifiability cannot mean subjectivity. It cannot be objected against the early Church Christology and Doctrine of the Trinity that they neglected the "for me" aspect in an objectifying fashion. On the other hand, they did in fact regard the "before" aspect of the deity of Christ, as a result of their metaphysics, to be a given which could be understood in isolation. That meant that they dehistoricized the figure of Jesus. Therefore it must be the task of a new re-working of the Doctrine of the Trinity to understand this doctrine really as the interpretation of the historical self-disclosure of God. Thus Bultmann's last cited sentence should be altered to read: "He demonstrates to us that He is God in that he helps us; in that he does that, he shows himself to us as God."

119. *CD*, I,1, p. 488.

careful that we not eliminate the concept of pre-existence. This would be just as much a contradiction to the New Testament witness, for we would then postulate the appearance of a being derived from God in place of God's activity on us, or we would dissolve Jesus' work into some kind of general conceptuality, using historical and philosophical speculation. This concept states that God, "before in himself," is none other than the One who acts on us, for us, over against himself, as the One who discloses himself to us in Jesus Christ.

d. *"The Lord Is the Spirit."* In regard to the biblical testimony to the Holy Spirit the same is to be said hermeneutically as was said about Christology. Moreover, there is a close contentual relationship: the Spirit is the one through whom the Incarnate One is received (Matt. 1:18, 20; Luke 1:35), with whom he was equipped in baptism (Mark. 1:10 and pars.), and who is given to him for his work "not by measure" (John 3:34). On the other hand, it is the Spirit whom he gives unto his own (John 20:22 and the Paraclete-passages [John 14:16, 26; 15:26f.; 16:7ff.], while in 1 John 3:24; 4:13 and generally in Paul "God" is the giver). Finally, the Spirit himself is *ho kyrios* (the Lord) (2 Cor. 3:17), and he is called the "Spirit of Christ" (Rom. 8:9), or just as he is called the "Spirit of God" he is also the "Spirit of his Son" (Gal. 4:6).

It is of the greatest importance for our understanding of the biblical statements about the Holy Spirit that the pouring out of the Spirit upon the whole covenant Community is an eschatological expectation of the Old Testament (Joel 3:1; Ezek. 36:27; Isa. 44:3) and as such is taken up in the New Testament and looked upon as fulfilled (see especially Acts 2:17 as well as the concept of the guarantee [2 Cor. 1:22; Eph. 1:14], or of the seal [Eph. 1:13; 4:30]). The reception of the Holy Spirit makes the Community into the Community of salvation, and makes the individual its member. The Community of salvation, however, is the Community of Christ, and in accordance with that, the work of the Spirit consists of his constantly disclosing to the Community and its members the reality of Jesus Christ and in it the reality of the Father. The Spirit is an eschatological gift, in that he effects the freedom which is established in Jesus Christ.

Can we then assert the deity of the Holy Spirit as is done by the whole Church tradition, with the exception of the Macedonians?

The Bible does not make such a statement in so many words. It does state that God is *pneuma* (Spirit; John 4:24), just as we read in 2 Corinthians 3:17, "Now the Lord is the Spirit." If a unity is present here, then the emphasis is more upon "God" and upon the "Lord." But nothing more is said in both passages than an indissoluble unity. Further, in both the Old and the New Testaments, the Spirit is called the "Spirit of God" (already in Gen. 1:2; 41:38; 1 Sam. 10:10; more frequently of course "Spirit of Yahweh," e.g., Gen. 6:3; Judg. 3:10; 11:29; 14:6, 19; 1 Sam. 10:6, etc.; "Spirit of God": see Matt. 3:16; 12:28; Rom. 8:9, 11, 14; 1 Cor. 2:11, 12, 14; 6:11; 7:40; 2 Cor. 3:3; Eph. 4:30; 1 Pet. 4:14). Taken as it stands, this could still refer to a gift which God imparts. The Spirit is not directly called "Holy Spirit" in the Old Testament; Psalm 51:11 means literally, "Spirit of thy holiness" (like Rom. 1:4), and only in the Septuagint do we find the translation "thy holy Spirit"; the situation is similar in Isaiah 63:10–11. In the New Testament, however, this designation is a constant term. The meaning goes somewhat beyond the term "Spirit of God." For holiness is an attribute of the Spirit in quite another sense than as it is given to believers (who are called "saints" solely because they are "sanctified," e.g., 1 Cor. 1:2). The Spirit himself is the one who "sanctifies" (2 Thess. 2:13; 1 Pet. 1:2), which means, to place within the realm of God's salvation and disposition. The Spirit, then, does not receive its holiness, it has it. In accordance with this, we read in 1 Corinthians 2:10 that the Spirit "searches everything, even the depths of God," and that it alone "comprehends the thoughts of God" (v. 11). This passage goes far beyond the understanding of the Spirit as a gift of God. The Spirit is not merely a gift, it belongs to the very nature of God. Therefore, the blasphemy of the Spirit is an unforgivable sin (Mark 3:29, pars.). The Spirit has even a higher dignity than Jesus in his humiliation.[120] Along these lines, the lie against the Holy Spirit is looked upon as a lie against God (Acts 5:3–4). When we look at what the Spirit does, we see the same thing again. It intervenes for the believer who is always subject to weakness in his prayer (Rom. 8:26); it is the Paraclete (John 14–16); it is the quickener (2 Cor. 3:6; 1 Cor. 15:46; John 6:63; see also Ezek. 37); it is the giver of freedom (the freedom which can only be given by God, which leads beyond the old covenant with God [2 Cor. 3:17]), and its service is ranked accordingly as being of higher glory than that of the letter of the law, which God also gave (2 Cor. 3:7ff.)! The Spirit cannot be understood merely as a gift or a power or some other effect which emanates from God.

The Spirit is simultaneously a gift, however, and as such he enters into an inner-world and inner-human relationship. This is indicated not only by the Old Testament statements in which the Spirit often enough comes over man as absolutely incalculable, absolutely alien, but on the other hand, is in and with man as gift (Ps. 51:10–12; 143:10). The gift of the Spirit, always based upon God's freedom, is for that very reason a validly authoritative event. Whereas in the old covenant this always applied to the individual who was specially called, the "pouring out" or "sending" of the Spirit means in the new covenant the establishment of the eschatological community, whose members are all impelled by the Spirit (Rom 8:14; "Spirit of Christ" [8:9]). Through the reception of the Spirit,[121] revelation becomes "subjective reality" and thus "possibility."[122] But this means, as the New Testament shows, that the Holy Spirit is God's reality not only for man but also in him, especially in that he corresponds to the human spirit. He "bears witness with our spirit that we are children of God" (Rom. 8:16). The reality of the Holy Spirit, and it alone, qualifies us as "spirit" which is called and responsible to give answer. Paul can go so far as to assert (1 Cor. 2:11) an analogy:

---

120. At least according to the Q-version of the logion (Matt. 12:32). On this, see A. Schlatter, *Der Evangelist Matthäus, seine Sprache, sein Ziel, seine Selbständigkeit* (Stuttgart: Calwer Verlag, 1959 [1929]), p. 409, and R. Bultmann, *The History of the Synoptic Tradition*, tr. J. Marsh (New York: 1963¹, 1968²), p. 131, for further possible explanations.

121. The "pouring out" of the Spirit (see Ezek. 39:29; Joel 3:1; Acts 2:17f.; 2:33), its "sending" (Luke 24:49; Gal. 4:6; 1 Pet. 1:12; John 14:26; 15:26; 16:7), its "being given" (Ezek. 36:26f.; Luke 11:13; John 14:16; 2 Cor. 1:22) or its "reception" (Acts 8:16; 10:44; Rom. 8:15; Acts 8:15; 10:47; 19:2; 1 Cor. 2:12) is an eschatological event, in a certain (derived) analogy to the "incarnation" or "sending" of the Son.

122. K. Barth, *CD*, I,2, pp. 203ff. and *passim*.

"For what person knows a man's thoughts except the spirit of the man which is in him? So also no one comprehends the thoughts of God except the Spirit of God." In accordance with that, the "fruit" of the Spirit consists very realistically of certain ways of behavior in man (Gal. 5:22f.). We find the same kind of agreement when in Philippians 1:27 "in one spirit" and "with one mind" stand directly next to each other. If we can only speak of the deity of Jesus Christ on the basis of the fact that he has completely identified with us up to and including the ultimate act, that he has appeared "in the likeness of sinful flesh" (Rom. 8:3), then we can only speak of the deity of the Holy Spirit because he is given and granted to us, he has become reality in the Community and thus in its members. And conversely, just as we cannot proceed upward from the human reality of Jesus Christ toward his deity, but rather experience in that reality the condescension of God, similarly in regard to the Holy Spirit we cannot think upward from his human reality to his deity, but we perceive in this his inner-human reality the incomprehensible self-emptying of God. At this point we are dealing with what must be decisive in the context of the Doctrine of the Trinity. The Spirit, whom we can certainly call the sustaining and motivating reality of the Christian life, is not a super-elevated human spirit, and Christian existence is not the noble exaltation of human existence as such. The Spirit is also not merely a gift of God which we could have "at our disposal," but he belongs to the reality of God himself, is God's own Spirit and to that degree is God "once more God himself." The reality of Christian existence lies beyond itself and surpasses qualititatively and infinitely what is found in the realm of our self-understanding and our activity.

The work of the Son like the work of the Spirit is God's own work. After everything that we have said until now about the unity of God, this can mean nothing else than that God himself is at work in the Son as in the Holy Spirit. The way, however, that he is at work is such that on the one hand he is himself the one working, and on the other hand he is "once more himself" in his activity. The Bible never asserts that there is a simple identity between the Father and the Son, the Father and the Spirit, or the Spirit and the Son.[123] Although it clearly emphasizes the deity of both the Son and the Spirit, that is, the unity of the being of the Son and of the Spirit with the being of the Father and of their work with the work of the Father, it also makes a distinction which is quite as clear. The Son is not the Father, but he is sent by him and subject to him. The Spirit is not the Father, but is given by him as well as by the Son (Acts 2:33; Gal. 4:6; Rom. 8:9; John 15:26; 16:7 in comparison to 14:26). Having ascertained that this unity and distinctiveness are both a part of the New Testament statement, then we can no longer be surprised when the same New Testament uses triadic formulae without hesitation, which merely demonstrates that what we have come to see in the individual statements very early found expression in liturgical and dogmatic forms. In terms of the actual issue at stake, the Church's Doctrine of the Trinity was not an innovation.

---

123. There is not an identification in 2 Cor. 3:17. The formula "Now the Lord is the Spirit" is followed immediately by the other formula of v. 17b, and in v. 18 the phrase *apo kyriou pneumatos* should probably be translated, "from the Lord of the Spirit" (RSV: "from the Lord who is the Spirit").

e. The Doctrine of the "Economic" Trinity. In our discussion we have proceeded from the revelation-event. The Trinity is doubtlessly a "revelational Trinity"—we would have known nothing of it if God had not revealed himself as the One in a threefold way.

However, the noetic side of the revelation reality is not revelation reality itself. To make here an equation, as many dogmaticians have tried ever since Johann August Urlsperger's[124] very original attempt, means either to do without the certainty, which is unconditionally a part of faith that in God's revelation God himself in his eternity is at work, that is, in his lordship over time and in time, and that is a regression into early Church Modalism. Or it means the introduction (as we find in Urlsperger) of a theosophy, which to be sure is meant in terms of redemptive history, but which implies that God's Trinitarian revelation is only a transitional phase and that God's unity, in terms of his temporal activity, is dissolved into a redemptive-historical plurality. It is true that the early Church Doctrine of the Trinity often appears "ontologically" to such a degree that, in contrast to it, the reality of revelation as history stands in danger of completely disappearing. But it is ill-advised to try to counter this ontological problem by replacing it with a developmental concept applied to God. Whether the "being" is understood fundamentally as passive or active being (the latter is the case in the developmental pattern) is not decisive at this point. What is decisive is that we truly understand God's "being" as the being *of God,* based purely upon his revelation, and thus as unity in living activity and as living activity in unity.

We would abandon the basis upon which alone theology is possible if we wanted to distinguish between God's revelation and God's being, that is, if we pursued the idea that God could be someone other than the One who reveals himself. What would be the source of our knowledge? But of course, we must distinguish between our knowledge of revelation and revelation itself. We cannot stop at the "revelational Trinity." Revelation itself, which in its happening constantly surpasses our knowledge, requires of us that we always understand our knowledge as a secondary factor in contrast to the incomparable primary factor of revelation. On the basis of these two points, that God's revelation and God's being are not to be separated, and that our knowledge of revelation must constantly experience that it is being directed beyond its own limits, the attempt to conceive of the Trinity as restricted to revelation ("revelational Trinity," "economical Trinity," in contrast to "Trinity in essence") must be rejected. Conversely, we will have to state that because God himself, God in his "essence," is the Triune One, therefore he is that in his revelation, and thus his revelation is living and personal; moreover, because God is the Triune in his revelation, he is also that in our knowledge of this revelation. Noetically we can begin with the latter statement. But the "noetic" order is the reverse of the "ontological" sequence of priorities: our knowledge is methodically the first naturally, but materially it is absolutely the last.

---

124. J. A. Urlsperger (1728–1806), especially his *Kurzgefasstes System meines Vortrages von Gottes Dreieinigkeit* (1777). See also on this M. Kähler, *Die Wissenschaft der christlichen Lehre vom evangelischen Grundartikel aus* (Erlangen: Deichert, 1905³), pp. 325ff. In general we note a mild Sabellianism in many theologians of the 19th century.

3. TRIPLICITY, ONENESS, TRINITY

a. The True Nature of God in His Revelation. In what we have discussed up to now it should have become clear that God's revelation is not inauthentic, but authentic activity; it is the activity which accords with God's true and authentic being. God is in his true nature "his own counterpart" and likewise is a unity, and therefore his work is the work of the Creator, the work of the Reconciler, the work of the One who sanctifies us. Although his work is not the emanation of a necessity which controls him, it is the work of his true nature itself and thus of the necessity which is established in him and through him.[125]

b. Being and Work. We could say what we have just said differently and would approach more closely the actual substance of what must be dealt with here. God, in his eternal, that is, godly readiness, did not become first the Creator, the Reconciler, our Sanctifier, but he is all that in his true nature and his eternity. His work cannot be separated from his nature. He has destined himself in his essence, in his true nature, for this his work. But that means that God as the One is always himself and thus he is always turned toward a counterpart. He is he himself in that he does not exist for himself alone but rather for himself in his distinction from himself. And that means, as Augustine very rightly saw, that God is love. He is not merely the One who acts toward his creation in the revelation of his love; rather he is in himself love (1 John 4:16). It is because God is love in this his true nature that he, the Father of the eternal Son, destines himself to be the Creator of his creation, that he, the eternal Son of the Father and in him the Father himself, destines himself to be the Reconciler of lost creation, that he, the eternal Spirit and in him the Father and the Son, destines himself to be the One who places the lost and reconciled creation into his own holy reality and thus liberates it to be its own created true nature. The work of salvation as the work of divine self-destining is not alien to the essence of God but rather accords with it.

If we may understand it thus, it is then clear that it is not a conceptual construction but rather that this profound relationship between God's being and God's work requires that his unity always be conceived of in a threeness and

---

125. This is the bracket which joins the Doctrine of the Trinity with the Doctrine of Predestination. The latter doctrine deals primarily with God's "counsels," his decree or decrees (thus its discussion often follows that of the Trinity in dogmatics, especially in the Reformed tradition; see, e.g., J. Wolleb, *Compendium theologiae Christianae,* in *Reformed Dogmatics,* ed. and tr. J. W. Beardslee III [New York: Oxford University Press, 1965 (g1935)], and Heppe-Bizer, pp. 133ff.). The fact that we may speak of a special decree of God is based solely on God's decision having its object in the reality which is distinct from him. Since this reality which is distinct from God is only established in God's decree, this decree is to be distinguished from the essence of God only terminologically ("A decree of God is an internal act of the divine will, by which he determines, from eternity, freely, with absolute certainty, those matters which shall happen in time" [Wolleb, *op. cit.,* p. 47; in Heppe-Bizer, p. 137]). The Doctrine of Predestination has been connected with the Doctrine of the Trinity in our day most impressively by Karl Barth, who has thought it through to its boldest consequences (*CD,* I,1–II,2).

God's threeness always in his unity.[126] That means, using the language of the Athanasian Creed, "neither confounding the Persons, nor dividing the substance."[127]

From this point of view we shall now discuss the development of the Doctrine of the Trinity, which the Church's theology has certainly often done under completely other points of view, that is, speculative ones, in terms of its results.

c. Unity in Triplicity. We proceed on the basis of the more obvious considerations about the unity in triplicity. It is fundamentally expressed in the term *homoousios,* the concept of *consubstantiality (consubstantialitas).* This concept is legitimate if it intends to state interpretively that the special and unusual modes of being in God are together one in the real divine nature. This insight has been secured by dogmatics against misunderstandings from various directions.

1) **Living Unity.** This unity in triplicity, and triplicity in unity, can only be conceived of as living. Later early Church theology, and following on it both Scholastic and Protestant-Orthodox Theology, developed the thesis of the *perichōrēsis* (lit. "a proceeding around"; Latin *circumincessio*; in English circum-incession = "intimate interpenetration), in use since John of Damascus,[128] in order to express this insight. Basically what is said here is that the triplicity never encroaches upon the unity of God, not even where Scripture speaks of an activity of one of God's modes of beings alone, but also that this unity is not to be thought of in a rigid fashion. This term belongs in a special way to the tools of interpretation which, according to Hilary, "strain the poor resources of our language to express thoughts too great for words."[129] Who ever sought to deal with them in any other way than solely as marginal terms would be embarking upon the route of intellectual mythology, which is certainly forbidden. But as a purely marginal term, this concept may refer to something which certainly must be said, "not to express what it is, but only not to be silent. . . ."[130]

2) **The Relations.** The unity of God in triplicity, and his triplicity in unity, cannot (without detriment to the perichoresis) be conceived of in an unordered form. This would not only be true if we thought of the unity as a total absence of all distinctions (a kind of "uniformity"), but also if we wanted to ignore the way in which the biblical witness speaks of an order of priority in God. The terms Father, Son, and Spirit would become meaningless if a difference in rank were not expressed in them. It is not the Son who makes the Father into the Father,

---

126. Calvin quotes Gregory of Nazianzus: "No sooner do I conceive of the One than I am illuminated by the Splendor of the Three; no sooner do I distinguish Them than I am carried back to the One" (*Oration on Holy Baptism,* Orations XL and XLI [*NPNF,* 2nd series, VII, 375]; *Institutes,* I, xiii, 17, p. 141).

127. *Quicunque vult* (v. 4); we have already dealt with the terminology critically.

128. *Exposition of the Orthodox Faith,* I, viii (*NPNF,* IX, 6–11).

129. *On the Trinity,* II, 2 (*NPNF,* 2nd ser., IX, 52); Calvin, *Institutes,* I, xiii, 5, p. 127.

130. Calvin, *Institutes,* I, xiii, 5, p. 127; see also Augustine, *On the Trinity,* VII, iv, 7 (*NPNF,* III, 109ff.).

but the Father makes the Son into the Son and "sends" him. The Spirit does not make the Son into the Son (although he certainly accompanies the man Jesus of Nazareth as the witness, and is even set over him[131]), or even the Father into the Father—rather, the reverse is true. This difference in rank (and the term itself is pure marginal terminology) was expressed by the older theology in a variety of ways. In doing so, it was pursuing a precarious path. On the one side it had to guard against the idea of uniformity, and on the other the obvious idea of a temporal sequence of the three modes of being or the idea of tritheism. The narrow path which remained did not permit more than the purest of marginal concepts again. The best expression of what could be said here was the Doctrine of Relations, which first appeared in Tertullian but was fully developed by Augustine. It is his most important contribution to the development of the Doctrine of the Trinity. The significant thing here is the effort to express the fact that each of the unique modes of being of God has its uniqueness in its relation to each of the others. The Father is Father in relation to the Son and vice versa, etc.[132] This insures, first of all (and this was Augustine's first concern), that the modes of being not be misunderstood in their relationship to the being of God as being comparable to the relationship between accidents and the substance. Secondly, tritheism is ruled out. Thirdly, the noninterchangeability of the three modes of being is expressed (the Father is as the Father not also the Son, etc.). And finally, this doctrine maintains that Father, Son, and Spirit, although they are not to be conceived of in analogy to our concepts, are still not unreal concepts. In detail, the relations are as follows: of the Father, paternity toward the Son; of the Son, sonship toward the Father; and of the Spirit, procession or passive spiration toward the Son and the Father.[133] Here again we must warn against every attempt to give more content to these formal and delimiting concepts. To fill these terms would mean to empty them, because it could only happen in a speculative or mythologizing way. When the dogmatic tradition has spoken, in the development of the Doctrine of Relations, of the Son's "generation" (*generatio*) by the Father and of the Spirit's "spiration" (*spiratio*) by the Father and the Son and has seen this as the "internal work" (*opus ad intra*) of the triune God, then these were all safeguarding statements which cannot possibly be filled with ideational contents. We find the same kind of safeguarding when the statement was made that the order of priorities of the three modes of being of God, which is established in the Doctrine of Relations, were not to be construed as a factual dependence of the one upon the other, but applied only to the "mode of subsisting" (*modus subsistendi*).

---

131. See especially Mark 1:10 and pars.; John 3:34; Rom. 1:4; Mark 3:28–30 and in reference to that Matt. 12:32.

132. *On the Trinity*, V, v, 6 (*NPNF*, III, 89).

133. Especially Thomas, *STh*, I, xxx, 2, vol. I, pp. 161f., who in good Augustinian fashion sees in the relations the essence of the divine persons. Protestant Orthodoxy follows tradition here completely. Karl Barth points out (*CD*, I,1, pp. 419f.) that this is also true of both Calvin (*Institutes*, I, xiii, 6, p. 128) and Luther ("Last Words of David" [*AE*, XV, 302f.]). Calvin also likes to speak of "beginning" (*principium*), "wisdom" (*sapientia*), and "virtue" (*virtus*) (see *The Catechism of the Church of Geneva, 1545* [*LCC*, XXII, 93, and *Institutes*, I, xiii, 18, pp. 142f.]).

3) The "filioque" Clause. There was one consequence of the Doctrine of Relations, or better, of the whole Augustinian-European concept of the Doctrine of the Trinity, which was of particular importance in that it resulted in an emendation of the old text of the Nicaeno-Constantinopolitan Creed: the European thesis that the Spirit proceeds from the Father *and from the Son* (*ex Patre filioque*).[134] It is not difficult to find the biblical basis for the proceeding (*processio*) of the Spirit from the Son also. In John 15:26; 16:7ff. the "sending" of the Spirit (of the Paraclete) through the Son "from the Father" is spoken of; in Galatians 4:6 the Pneuma is called "the Spirit of his Son"; in Romans 8:9 he is called both "the Spirit of God" and "the Spirit of Christ," and in Luke 24:29 it is the sending of the Spirit through the Son which is being considered. Obviously the theologians of the Eastern Church, who looked upon the *filioque* clause as heretical innovation,[135] did not overlook these scriptural arguments. They did not dispute that the Holy Spirit, within redemptive history, also proceeded from the Son. But they denied that what was true "economically" was also true "immanently." And this is the only point of their denial; their whole Doctrine of the Trinity would disintegrate if they expanded their opposition further. Europe saw in this quite properly a serious inconsistency, and one must agree with Karl Barth that with this inconsistency there is a breakdown at an essential point in what is the center of the Doctrine of the Trinity. It is not only the fact that "God is there for man" is based in the being of God, but also in the "intradivine, two-sided communion of the Spirit, which proceeds from the Father and from the Son, is founded the fact that in revelation there is a communion, in which . . . man is also there for God."[136] If this existence of man for God is given in the Holy Spirit as something derived from God, then the thesis that the Spirit "in an intradivine way" proceeds solely from the Father means the exclusion of the Son from that existence of man for God and this leads to the view of man from the "point of view of Creator and Creature," which results unmistakably in a tendency to mysticism which then appears in the Eastern Church.[137]

4) opus ad extra = Outward-directed Work. God's unity in triplicity is not solely an "inward" unity, so to speak, but it is also a unity in God's work regarding the creature. This proposition is a direct consequence of the basic thrust of the whole Doctrine of the Trinity. To contest it fundamentally could lead to

---

134. For the fundamental thesis, see especially Augustine, *On the Trinity,* V, xiv, 15 (*NPNF,* III, 94f.). In terms of the material concept, European theology including Protestant Orthodoxy has generally followed the Augustinian view. The Roman Church, in its compromise attempts with Byzantium, the Council of Florence of 1439, offered the formula, ". . . the Holy Spirit proceeds from the Father through the Son . . ." (Denzinger, *Sources,* p. 219, par. 691), but with only short-lived success. The history of the incorporation of the *filioque* clause into the text of the Nicaeno-Constantinopolitan Creed does not belong here.

135. See H. Ehrenberg, ed., *Oestliches Christentum, Dokumente* (2 vols.; München: C. H. Beck, 1923–25), I, 156f. (A. St. Chomjakow), and II, 307ff. (L. P. Karsawin).

136. Karl Barth, *CD,* I,1, p. 550.

137. Karl Barth, with whom we are in agreement here, refers in *CD,* I,1, pp. 550f., to the necessary reservations in judgment here, after he, in his *Christliche Dogmatik im Entwurf* (Munich: Kaiser, 1927), p. 213, had spoken only with question marks on the matter.

Modalism (unity inwardly, triplicity in redemptive history). If then, in material dependence upon Augustine, the proposition has been formulated and become a normal part of the dogmatic tradition that "the work of the Holy Trinity is indivisible outwardly," then something necessary has in fact been articulated. The indivisibility of the inward work is in accordance with the same indivisibility of the outward work. That means that we never have to do with the Father without having to do simultaneously and in the same event with the Son and the Spirit. We know nothing of the Spirit without knowing thereby of the Father and of the Son. The biblical reason for this has always been seen in the fact that Scripture ascribes the creation, which is the peculiar work of the Father, to the Son too (John 1:1ff.; Heb. 1:2; Col. 1:16) and also to the Spirit (Gen. 1:2), that it predicates of the Father the peculiar work of the Son, reconciliation and redemption (e.g., 2 Cor. 5:19ff.), and also of the Spirit (cf., e.g., Eph. 2:16 with 2:18), and that it speaks of sanctification with reference to the Father (e.g., 1 Thess. 5:23), to the Son (e.g., John 17:19; Eph. 5:26; Heb. 10:10), as well as to the Spirit himself (2 Thess. 2:13; 1 Pet. 1:2). It is only when we constantly keep the unity of God in his work in view that we can avoid an isolated "theology of the first article," or an isolated "Christocentrism," or an isolated "Spiritualization" of theology.[138] It can be said that at this point the Doctrine of the Trinity gains its most direct relationship to "piety." It is in any event not difficult to grasp that when the Doctrine of the Trinity falls apart or retreats in the consciousness of the Community, then piety becomes one-sided and, measured by the liveliness and the wealth of the biblical witness, is impoverished. It becomes a "piety of providence," and stumbles over the serious overburdening of the isolated belief in the Creator which is then its basis (we can experience this today). It becomes a purely inward "piety of Jesus," and loses sight of the world and of the Kingdom of God, ultimately succumbing to inwardness for its own sake. It becomes also "a spiritual attitude" which has no foundation and perishes as a result of its own lack of substance. Early theology, in dealing with the very necessary proposition which is our theme here, formulated an equally necessary reservation along the lines of Augustine:[139] this proposition is only true "for preserving the distinction and order of persons. " We shall now discuss this reservation.

d. Triplicity in Unity. In placing special emphasis upon the unity of God in triplicity, we have spoken of this unity as a living, ordered unity, present in the work of God. It is virtually a truism that, conversely, the other requirement of the Athanasian Creed, that the "persons" not be confounded, deserved and found attention in the development of the Doctrine of the Trinity. God is, as the Father, the Son, and the Holy Spirit, not individually different but in all of them God himself, the same. Nevertheless, he is distinct in each, each distinct in his mode of being. The creation is the work of the Father, not "without" the Son and the Spirit, but it is not the peculiar work of the Son or of the Spirit. The crucifixion

---

138. In regard to Calvin, it is instructive to read Paul Jacobs, *Prädestination und Verantwortlichkeit bei Calvin* (Neukirchen: Buchhandlung des Erziehungsvereins, 1937).
139. *On the Trinity,* I, iv, 7 (*NPNF,* III, 20).

is certainly the Father's work and will, but neither the Father nor the Spirit was crucified for us. The Father, the Son, the Spirit is each he himself. If we have in mind everything which we said about the unity of God in his triplicity, then we may and we must accord the same attentiveness to the triplicity in this unity: the triplicity in unity of the being of God and the triplicity in unity of his work. Again the noetic way is "from below to above." What actually encounters us in the reality of the saving activity of God is the "over-againstness" of the Son and the Father, the distinctiveness of the Spirit and Son; it is the peculiar work severally of the Father, the Son, and the Spirit. But this severally peculiar work makes it possible for us, speaking again in purely marginal terms for which we have no ideational contents outside of revelation, to talk about the peculiar "being" and about the peculiar "characteristics" of the Father, the Son, and the Spirit.

e. *The Doctrine of Appropriations.* Theology has attempted to do this with its Doctrine of "Appropriations" (*appropriationes*). Both in the Middle Ages and in Orthodoxy, it proceeded on the basis of the triplicity of the one work of God, and then ascribed certain characteristics of God to each of the "persons" in a special but not in an exclusive way. One of the most well-known appropriations is that of God the Father having omnipotence, the Son having omniscience (Logos!), and the Spirit having omnibenevolence. Similarly, Calvin, following the lines of the Middle Ages, ascribes to God the "beginning," to the Son the "wisdom," and to the Spirit the "power."[140] The iridescent variety of the various theologians' formulations indicates that the attempts themselves were of greater theological significance than the results. More important than these considerations was the most frequent appropriation, which then became broadly accepted, particularly, for example, in catechetical literature: the special but not exclusive designation of the Father as the Creator, of the Son as the Redeemer (Reconciler), and of the Spirit as our Sanctifier.[141]

f. *Creation, Redemption, Sanctification.* It would be advisable to deal briefly with the latter form of the Doctrine of Appropriations at this point. It is obvious that the revelation-event is in view here. It is equally obvious how especially this element of the Doctrine of Trinity adheres to the scriptural witness. And it is similarly clear that, in terms of the appropriations, the scriptural witness is very distinct and straightforward in regard to the Father, which is then true of the dogmatic statements which follow; for the Son they are less clear, and for the Spirit even more manifold, so that, as we pointed out, at this juncture Calvin

---

140. *Institutes,* I, xiii, 18, pp. 142f.; Calvin, *The Catechism of the Church of Geneva, 1545 (LCC,* XXII, 93).

141. This is Luther's approach in his catechisms. It is similar in the Heidelberg Catechism with its orientation to the "we" or "our" of the Community (Answer 24). Calvin's division of the *Institutes* is also well known, as it follows the creed in dealing in Book I with "The Knowledge of God the Creator," in Book II with "The Knowledge of God the Redeemer . . ." (continuing in good Trinitarian fashion with "in Christ"), then to be sure the Third Article (according to Calvin's count) with a divergent title, "The Way in which we receive the Grace of Christ," which deals with the Holy Spirit. We shall deal with Karl Barth's Doctrine of Appropriations, which departs broadly from the tradition, below.

departs from the initial systematic approach he took (in the title of Book III). The decreasing clarity and unambiguity of the possible statements here is related to the "order of the persons" (*ordo personarum*). If it is quite properly correct that the Father is the first, the "fountainhead of deity" (*fons deitatis*), the "initiator" (*principium*), then it can also be understood that his work, to the degree that it can be spoken of in terms of appropriations, emerges more clearly than that of the other two modes of being, in whose unique works the work of the Father or the Son is always co-revealed, by appropriation. If we may say on the basis of the biblical witness that the work of Creation is a work of the Son and of the Spirit, then it cannot be denied that according to the same biblical witness the work of the Father happens "through" the Son (Col. 1:16; John 1:3; Heb. 1:2), and is only the Son's work to that extent. We may then continue that this work happens "in" the Spirit and only to that extent can be called his work too. But it cannot be said of the special work, which is appropriated to the Son, the work of reconciliation and redemption,[142] that it is done by the Son through the Father. Instead, it is the Father here who acts through the Son, in the Spirit. There is no simple equivalency here, but the very order of priority which we have already dealt with.

This is above all true when we ask about the work which is appropriate to the Spirit. Is it sanctification, as is usually stated first? However, that is just as much the work of the Father and of the Son, as we have stated. Is it redemption, as Barth has expressed it? As far as the biblical formulations are concerned, that is unmistakably appropriated to the Son,[143] and through him to the Father. Perhaps Calvin was correct in entitling the Third Book of the *Institutes* in a way

---

142. While Barth correctly conceives of "revelation" and "reconciliation" together (although here, too, distinctions must be made in interpretation), he seeks to distinguish "redemption" (*apolytrōsis, sōtēria*) from both of them, with particular regard to the eschatological character which doubtless is a part of it (*CD*, I,1, p. 468). Thus he calls the Son the Reconciler, by appropriation, and the Holy Spirit the Redeemer (*passim*). Even if we bear in mind that no statement regarding the appropriations can have exclusive character, we must still ask whether one can speak even in this relative sense of the Holy Spirit as "God the Redeemer." It is to be admitted that "redemption" in the New Testament has eschatological meaning. But eschatologically it is also the work of the Son to the extent that he introduces the Kingdom. On the other hand, the New Testament generally appropriates redemption to the Son and the Father. *Apolytrōsis* is only indirectly appropriated to the Spirit in one text (Rom. 8:23), where the *huiothesia* (adoption) is that ascribed to us by the Spirit (Rom. 8:15, 16). *Sōtēria* (salvation), along with *sōzein* (to save) and *sōtērios* (saving), is only appropriated to the Spirit to the extent that "salvation" is connected with faith and with baptism (e.g., 1 Pet. 3:21) or the Gospel is "the power of God for salvation" (Rom. 1:16). This is also where the connection of "salvation" with prayer belongs (e.g., Rom. 10:1), as well as with confession (Rom. 10:10) or even with penitence (2 Cor. 7:10). But the Spirit is never called *sōtēr* (savior) in the New Testament. Thus, the work of the Spirit consists, by appropriation, of opening man to the work of the Father in the Son, making man into a man for God because God is for man. This work is still best formulated with the old concept of "sanctification."

143. See n. 142 above. In his exposition of the Heidelberg Catechism, *The Heidelberg Catechism for Today*, tr. S. C. Guthrie, Jr. (Richmond: John Knox Press, 1964), Karl Barth did not contradict this approach which speaks of God the Son as the Redeemer and of the Spirit as the worker of sanctification (see *op. cit.*, pp. 55f.).

which departed from the tradition.[144] Is there any other work of the Holy Spirit than this one, that he makes the work of the Father in the Son our own, makes us receptive for it, and thus preserves freedom and hope? It should have become clear that the Doctrine of Appropriations is a reflection of the "order of persons" (*ordo personarum*). As a matter of fact, it cannot imply more than this, that God's work, in accordance with his being, realizes the lordship of the Father through the lordship of the Son in the lordship of the Spirit. If the Son is in truth the Son, then he does no other work than that of the Father; if the Spirit proceeds in truth from the Father and from the Son, then his work is nothing other than that of the Son and of the Father in his special way, corresponding to his own mystery. Therefore, the Doctrine of Appropriations refers back to the mystery which does not cease to be a mystery when it has been revealed, the mystery of the unfathomable and inexhaustible unity and triplicity of God.

---

144. See p. 394, n. 140.

X. God's Essence and Attributes

A. GOD IN HIS REVELATION

1. GOD'S REVELATION AND GOD'S MYSTERY

a. The Traditional Doctrine of God. We are discussing the question, "What is God like," after our presentation of the Doctrine of the Trinity, for the reasons already given.[1] Indeed, we discuss this question in the context of the Doctrine of the Triune God itself. If it is correct that we are speaking of God himself when we speak of him as the Three in One, then it is impossible to develop the doctrine of God's "essence," his "reality," and his "attributes" on the basis of some kind of God per se, a genus "God" or even of the Father alone.[2]

There is a broadly held view that in the whole "problem of God as such" there is agreement both within the Christian Church and between it and European thought. To put it simply, there is more or less a consensus in regard to "God," but the special feature of "Christianity" is that Jesus Christ and the Holy Spirit, in addition, so to speak, have been ascribed divine dignity. Or even more crudely: The problems are not related to the "First Article," about whose essential contents even non-Christians (say, post-Christian Judaism or Islam or even religious philosophy) would make statements similar to those of the Church's theology. The problem areas, the sources of controversy, are to be found in the Second and Third Articles. Theology has tended to encourage this view by developing its "general doctrine of God" to a great extent out of a general concept of God.

The doctrine of God in the early Church, in the Middle Ages, and in Orthodoxy is a curious mixture of Greek, especially Neo-Platonic, and biblical ideas. Since the Reformation showed little interest in the traditional doctrine of God, it survived the fiery ordeal of the Reformation's reworking of all tradition far more unscathed than was really good. For this reason, Protestant Orthodoxy on the

---

1. See above, pp. 349ff.
2. Basically, the Cappadocians had already begun to understand the divine *ousia* (substance) as a generic term, without following through on this understanding. In the Middle Ages, Gilbert de la Porrée, in a logical development of the concept of a divinity *(divinitas)* really distinct from God came close to tritheism, while the adherents of Hesychasm in the medieval Eastern Church attempted to establish an absolute and general mysticism of God by the use of a similar idea. See Karl Barth, *CD*, II,1, pp. 331f.

whole maintained the traditional mixture of non-Christian and biblical statements. Or, to put it better, the European world-consciousness, which found in a certain understanding of the essence (*essentia*) of God its ultimate point, was more or less taken over by Orthodoxy too. The result of this was that the profound change of this world-consciousness and of the world view which was introduced in the modern age of necessity involved the concept of God which was a part of it. As far back as Rationalism and from another point of departure as Schleiermacher, dogmatics has endeavored to harmonize its own understanding of God with the constant change of world-consciousness and world views. Only seldom has it simply given up the traditional composite concept in favor of the new world view. Normally it has remained in its traditional duplicity (or dichotomy), except that both components have received new illumination. This whole endeavor has intended to move in the direction of modern man, but in point of fact it has made little impression upon him. The sole result was that some kind of God idea remains as the ultimate point of the world-consciousness in general, and the objections of both Feuerbach and Nietzsche, who perceived that in this concept of God man was only expressing himself, were only grasped by smaller groups of people. Today, this world-consciousness itself has been shaken, and the world view is involved in a process of change whose conclusion cannot be predicted. In accordance with that, the traditional idea of God is beginning to dissolve into nothingness. In regard to the "God" of European consciousness, Nietzsche was right: "All gods are dead." For faith, this means that a clarification of the situation has occurred, and contemporary theology is presently occupied with the separation of the original Christian statement about God from all of the general religious ideas which have clustered about it.

b. Is the Predication of God Possible? Can we even ask, "What is God like?" The answer cannot be formulated in any other way than, God is "such and such" or "this and that." Where could the predicating terms come from which might be used here? Is not God incomparable? Psalm 40:5 says, "None can compare with thee,"[3] and there are many other biblical statements of the same import. Is there anything which has a similarity to God, or which can be placed in analogy to him? Must not all the predicates which would be possible here necessarily be taken from the realm of our human capacity to conceptualize? Or at least from our "world," from the epitome of the reality available to us (that is, of creation), including the values which impress themselves upon us? Where else should they come from? Certainly one could follow Paul Tillich in saying that since all predicates are, so to speak, "symbols," it is impossible for them to say about God what they mean in speaking of created reality. Let us assume that this were so. Where could we find the criterion for distinguishing here between what is inauthentic and authentic?

c. Tautology? We could then ask if, under these circumstances, we have any other choice than to repeat with early "dialectical" theology that God is God.

---

3. See Ps. 35:10; Jer. 10:6; 49:19; 50:44 and of course the Second Commandment.

God is similar only to himself. But even here, we would be on shaky ground. The statement, "God is God," could, first, declare our renunciation of every predicate, resulting then in a pure tautology. It would then be empty.[4] But are we so certain about the subject concept in that tautological proposition? Would we not, secondly, have to consider that even our word "God" is really our word, molded by a special history and unavoidably associated with these or those contents or sentiments? Would it not then be safer, thirdly, to say "God is the non-existent (the *mē on*)," that is, that about which we can make no statement, not even that God is "God," or that he "is"?

d. God per se Is Without a Predicate. All of these questions must necessarily arise if we wanted to talk about God per se, God in himself. It is indeed true that one can only be silent about God per se, and in such silence honor the ultimate which may dawn in the deepest depths of our beings like a diffuse light. But it is just as true that faith does talk about God. How does it do this? Talk about God always has logically the form of a predicated judgment. It says "something" about God. Where does this something come from which we are predicating in such talk? What is the source of the "subject" which we are predicating in this fashion? How do we know that our predicates really correspond to this subject? This is not just a question for meditation. Two things are at stake here: faith's own modesty, that is, its knowledge about its radical dependence upon its being a receiver, and the certainty of faith which lives by the fact that it is response to God's reality for us.

e. God's Self-predication. How then can "predicated judgments" about God be uttered? This question cannot be answered on the basis of general principles, nor on the basis of general doctrines of God derived from them. In fact, we cannot utter such judgments at all. We do not have any predicates for God at our disposal. We would deny our creatureliness if we wanted to produce such predicates, and we deny it a thousand times over in that we do it nevertheless. We can do nothing other than to accept the fact that God has predicated himself. There would be no Church, no faith, and no theology if this self-predication of God were not true, if he in the act of revelation had not carried out this his eternal self-predication toward us temporally.

"God is God"—when we say that in our own strength, it is an empty tautology. But it is in fact true that "God is God," for God is himself once more as the Father, the Son, and the Spirit. That is the "eternal" self-predication of God. God is in himself not lonely, not relationless, nor lacking in attributes. We do not predicate God, but God predicates himself in eternity.

That he does this has been made known to us by him, in that he has disclosed himself to us. Revelation is, as his self-disclosure, the manifestation of his essence.

---

4. Carl Immanuel Nitzsch, *System der christlichen Lehre* (Bonn: Adolph Marcus, 1844[5] [g1851[6]]), p. 143; ET: *System of Christian Doctrine*, tr. R. Montgomery and J. Hennen (Edinburgh: T. & T. Clark, 1849).

f. Interpreting Predicates! We are not inferring that it is possible to deduce the essence and attributes of God from his revelation. That would mean again that we were taking his revelation figuratively and seeking the actual God somewhere in the background. At most, we can merely interpret how God reveals himself to us. However, this interpretation is both allowed us and required of us. For God in his revelation has entered into our reality, and intellectual reality, even logic, is a part of this reality. But, in the same way that God in his revelation enters into creaturely reality without being exhausted in it, he also enters into our logic without being exhausted in it.

g. God's Self-bestowal and God's Being. We have now reached the decisive point in our argumentation. All of the Church's doctrine of God is founded upon the revelation which has taken place and which is taking place. But revelation, as certainly as it is an absolute event as God's action, is for that reason not qualified by the things which we otherwise associate with "event." And, although God certainly makes himself into the "object" of revelation, yet revelation is not the transformation of God into an object comparable to other objects. God bestows himself completely to us; however, he is in this self-bestowal completely himself.

1) **God Turns Completely to Us.** This means for every doctrine of God that it does not deal with God per se, God's "naked essence," but rather with God as the One who has given himself completely to us, God "over against us." This proposition is not meant epistemologically. It does not imply that we are only able to draw conclusions in the setting of "possible experience." It would be virtually impossible to describe the realm of "possible experience" in relationship to God. Such a delimitation could well be the expression of man's closedness in himself. No, our proposition is meant theologically: all talk about God per se would be nothing less than the denial of the revelation or the attempted ascent above it (into pure reality, in comparison to which revelation would be figurative or inauthentic reality). But that would be a "theology of glory" *(theologia gloriae)*, our exiting from the creaturely existence in which the creature lives by every word that proceeds out of the mouth of God (Matt. 4:4; Deut. 8:3).[5]

It was the protest against the "theology of glory" imbedded in medieval metaphysics of being which led the Reformers to warn against all speculation about God as such; instead of that they wanted to structure the doctrine of God solely as the theological form of the witness to "God toward us" *(Deus erga nos)*. "I know of no other God than the one who became man, and I will have no other

---

5. Kant's critique of natural theology assumes great significance, in light of the revelation which has happened and is happening, in that it is the manifestation of a self-limiting philosophy. The fact that it itself really did not have that significance yet is demonstrated by the further development of Idealistic philosophy beyond Kant. This self-limitation became the foundation for a speculation arising from the autonomous movement of the ego, which left all medieval "theology of glory" *(theologia gloriae)* in the shadows by comparison. And conversely, could not man's autonomous insistence upon a knowledge of God within the sphere of his "possible experience" not be virtually exchangeable with a "theology of glory" since it, too, would imply a self-absolutizing of the creature?

one," is what Luther stated in opposition to John Oecolampadius (1482–1531) at Marburg.[6] This was nothing other than the effect of his doctrine of God as "God incarnate" *(Deus incarnatus)* in contrast to "pure God" *(Deus nudus)*. We find both the young Melanchthon and Calvin taking this approach. Calvin developed the contrast between "God as such" *(Deus apud se)* and "God toward us" *(Deus erga nos)*, of which we just spoke,[7] and he can formulate that the task of theology "is not for us to attempt with bold curiosity to penetrate to the investigation of his essence, which we ought more to adore than meticulously to search out, but for us to contemplate him in his works. . . . "[8] He thus agrees with Melanchthon's famous proposition almost literally that "We do better to adore the mysteries of Deity than to investigate them."[9] Statements of this kind are all necessary warnings against a theology which begins with the hybris of reason and must then end in the hybris of despair.

2) **God Remains Completely He Himself in His Turning to Us!** This is what is unfathomable, that God does not show us a mask, but his own countenance, that he does not encounter us anonymously but in his name. His condescension is not his transition into figurativeness but is his true reality. "God is Love!" And that means that we are helped solely by him in his revelation, in that he remains himself in his condescension! His condescension is not his renunciation of his deity. Yet as his condescension it is also his total concealment. The revealed God is the concealed God. When he became man, God did not cease being God. The incarnation is not his transformation into a human being. The declaration of his name does not make it possible for us to give him any name we like. His entry into the realm of our knowledge does not make him subject to reason. His entry into our history does not coordinate him with our history. He is "God toward us" *(Deus erga nos)*, but not "God according to us" *(Deus secundum nos)*. God's revelation is the manifestation of his deity; it is the only effective relegation of the creature to its genuine creatureliness. But it is both of these: the *revelation* of God and the revelation of *God*; establishment of genuine creatureliness and establishment of the unabbreviated creatureliness of the creature! It is the revelation of the love and the freedom of God, and in both of his honor.[10]

---

6. W. Köhler, *Das Marburger Religionsgespräch* (1529) (*Schriften des Vereins für Reformationsgeschichte*, 48, 1; Leipzig: M. Heinsius Nachfolge, 1929), p. 27.

7. *Institutes*, I, x, 2, pp. 97f.

8. *Ibid.*, I, v, 9, p. 62.

9. *Loci* of 1521 (*LCC*, XIX, 21); Stupperich, II/1, p. 6.

10. At this point we are touching upon a controversial topic within Evangelical theology. According to a frequently expressed view, the tendency of Lutheran theology is toward a concept of God which is centered around his "condescension"; in contrast, Reformed theology emphasizes the "transcendence," the "glory," and the freedom of God. To put it differently, Lutheran theology is concerned about the reality, validity, and finality of revelation, and Reformed theology about its divinity. We cannot see any genuine contradiction here, certainly not one which should lead to the breaking of Christian fellowship, so long as Lutheran theology does not make of the condescension of God his availability and Reformed theology does not make God's glory into his arbitrariness, so long as the Lutheran doctrine of condescension does not encroach upon the glory and freedom of God, and the Reformed emphasis upon God's freedom upon the validity of his revelation. An

h. God's Turning to Us and His Freedom According to the Biblical Witness.
The biblical witness repeatedly shows that God makes his deity, his freedom, his
own existence known where he reveals himself, that thus in revelation God is the
Concealed One. We think of the revelation of the name in Exodus 3:14. Usually
the name of a deity places its understandableness, its capacity to be invoked, its
transition into a certain degree of availability in the hands of the worshipper. But
this is precisely what the Old Testament does not mean. The revealed name is
explained with the well-known phrase, "I am that I am"—the covenant God is
the Constant One, but he is constant in himself, and the revelation of his name
is not his surrender of himself. This becomes even clearer in the passage which
is materially a parallel, Exodus 33:19 (34:5ff.). Yahweh intends to proclaim the
name Yahweh before Moses in the theophany, *"for I will be gracious to whom I
will be gracious, and will show mercy on whom I will show mercy."* Doubtless
the theophany, for all of its "numinous" fearfulness (33:20–23), is an act of
Yahweh's gracious turning of himself to man. But the "name" which Yahweh
himself wants to proclaim makes known here as well as in 3:14 both the bestowal
and the freedom of the One who is speaking here. The same basic theme is found
in the other revelation-events which the Old Testament relates—for instance, the
Moses theophany (Ex. 3:5); the Sinai revelation (especially Ex. 19:12, 13, 16), the
Isaiah theophany (Isa. 6:3, 4, 5). In the Old Testament concept of the "Holy One
of Israel" both are incorporated into each other: Yahweh's existence for himself
and his existence for Israel.[11] The New Testament does not do away with this
tension as it was already present, but reveals it in its actual profundity. In view
of the self-disclosure of God in the Son, it maintains that God "dwells in unapproachable light" (1 Tim. 6:16). Coupled with the authority to address God as
"Our Father" (Matt. 6:9; Rom. 8:15; Gal. 4:6) is the certainty that he is "in
heaven." The God very near is the God who is very far away! And where was
this revealed more clearly than in the Crucified One in whom both God's love and
God's concealment are completely present? Here it becomes finally clear that
God's deity as freedom, majesty, yes, as wrath and judgment, is made known at
the very point where it is present as love, as grace, as God's turning to us. This
then makes it possible for us to understand that Jesus Christ can be called the
"mystery" of God among the Gentiles (Col. 1:27) or simply "the mystery of
God," although the New Testament certainly knows of the revelation of this
mystery (Rom. 11:25; 16:25; 1 Cor. 4:1; 15:51; Eph. 1:9; 3:3, 4, 9; 6:19; Col.
1:26f.; 2:2; 4:3; 1 Tim. 3:16; Matt. 13:11 pars.).

---

abstractly constructed contradiction between condescension and the freedom of God would
as such destroy the Christian understanding of revelation, according to which God in his
freedom turns to the creature and in his turning to the creature is free. The polarity between
immanence and transcendence is totally unusable for any understanding of the Christian
concept of God; this is not a fitting approach for understanding either the differences in
Reformation theology nor those within Orthodoxy.

11. To see how deeply both were still sensed in late post-biblical Judaism, see the
hymn "Melek elyon," which finds an impressive translation in Rudolf Otto, *Das Heilige*
(Breslau: Trewendt & Granier, 1927[16]), pp. 233ff.; ET: *The Idea of the Holy*, tr. J. W. Harvey
(London: Oxford University Press, 1946[4] [1923]). Otto's book is of course worthy of mention
in more than one regard; however, we do not espouse his position here.

2. FREEDOM AND LOVE

Dogmatics has sensed the tension we are speaking of for centuries and attempted to express it.

a. The Dogmatic Interpretation of the Tension: 1) **The Duality of the Predicates.** First of all, we should consider the circumstance that Evangelical dogmatics in general has set up two lists of "attributes" of God. This will be discussed in detail further on.[12] What is important here is that the tension we are trying to grasp becomes visible in the duplicity of the groups of statements. The Reformed distinguish between "communicable attributes" and "incommunicable attributes" (*attributa communicabilia et attributa incommunicabilia*). Even a Lutheran Orthodox like Johann Gerhard (1582–1637) makes the corresponding distinction between *akoinōnēta* and *koinōnēta* (uncommunicated and communicated).[13] Lutheran Orthodoxy preferred to make the distinction between "relative attributes" and "absolute attributes" (*attributa relativa et absoluta*).[14] Especially the latter distinction is based upon the difference between "God per se" and "God toward us" and asserts that the attributes of "God per se" can be named. As we shall show, this is not possible. To the extent that the first distinction, apparently more carefully formulated, is based upon the same polarity, it is not acceptable in that form. For the issue at stake here is not that polarity, but rather the fact that God who is free in his revelation and in his freedom is the One who reveals himself. Regardless of that, the Orthodox did in any event envision a duality of statements here, and the theology of the 19th century broadly followed in their footsteps.[15] In our context we will have to correct the older distinctions in that we speak on the one hand of the "attributes" of God as the One who loves and on the other of the "attributes" of God as the One who is free, as the Holy One, or to use Karl Barth's phrases, "The Perfections of the Divine Loving" and the "Perfections of the Divine Freedom."[16] It is this duality as such which should be kept in view, and we may look upon it as a reflection of the duality in revelation itself: revelation is the condescension of the One who is free in his deity.

2) **Deus absconditus, Deus revelatus=God Hidden, God Revealed.** Next we should refer to Luther's well-known distinction between "God hidden" and "God

---

12. See below, pp. 420ff.

13. Johann Gerhard, *Loci communes theologici*, ed. F. Frank (1885), I, 296ff.

14. Schmid, pp. 120f. and 127.

15. See R. A. Lipsius ("metaphysical" and "psychological" attributes), T. Haering (attributes of the holy love and those of the absolute personality of God), H. Stephan (the love and holiness of God). Even the important (and yet to be discussed) monograph by H. Cremer, *Die christliche Lehre von den Eigenschaften Gottes (Beiträge zur Förderung christlicher Theologie*, 1, 4; Gütersloh: Bertelsmann, 1897, 1917²), takes this approach (love and holiness of God). Karl Barth, who in *CD*, II,1, pp. 340f. introduces other forms of differentiation, refers to the fact that this procedure is also followed by Roman Catholic dogmaticians like J. M. Scheeben, B. Bartmann, and F. Diekamp.

16. *CD*, II,1, pp. 351ff. and 440ff.

revealed."[17] This distinction has become somewhat ambiguous because of its prehistory in Scholasticism (the concept of the *potentia Dei absoluta*, or absolute power of God). Could God do something other than what he in actual fact does? Peter Lombard (c. 1100–60)[18] attempted to answer this question, and he noted that to answer it negatively and in abstraction would be to force God into our human "sense." What then actually happened would not be derived from God's freedom but would proceed out of a necessity which was binding upon God himself. Thomas also came to this conclusion.[19] It is acknowledged here that God's activity as he does it is free or, better, godly activity and that God cannot be obligated to his creation to act in the way that he does. Since neither Peter Lombard nor Thomas wanted to doubt the validity of God's activity, we must then say that here both the condescension and freedom of God are preserved as much as possible (in the terminology here in use). In Nominalism, the duplicity was shifted in such a way that the freedom of God was separated from the validity of his activity; the "absolute power of God" *(potentia absoluta Dei)* became the "extraordinary power" *(potentia extraordinaria)* next to the "ordinary power" *(potentia ordinata)*. Initially miracles were being thought of here. Later, however, the concept of "absolute power" was integrated into the concept of God itself, implying that God could even do everything differently than he is doing it. His factual activity is contingent in the sense that he simply does this and not its opposite out of his arbitrariness, or as is now said, as the "God beyond law" *(Deus exlex)*. God's freedom is placed so far above the reality of his revelation that it encroaches upon the latter in its validity and finality. Finally, there is a duality incorporated into God which must rob faith of all its certainty. Luther then emerged from the Nominalist tradition which we have just described. And

---

17. See especially Theodosius Harnack, *Luthers Theologie mit besonderer Beziehung auf seine Versöhnungs- und Erlösungslehre* (2 vols.; Amsterdam: Rodopi, 1862 [g1927²], 1969), I, 94ff.; Karl Holl, *Gesammelte Aufsätze zur Kirchengeschichte* (3 vols.; Tübingen: J. C. B. Mohr [Paul Siebeck] [g1923]; Darmstadt: Wissenschaftliche Buchgesellschaft, 1948–65), I, 38ff. Further, Reinhold Seeberg, *Lehrbuch der Dogmengeschichte* (4 vols.; Graz: Akademische Druck- und Verlagsanstalt, 1953), IV/1, 178ff. (this section is not in the ET by C. E. Hay); Erich Seeberg, *Luthers Theologie, Motive und Ideen, I, Die Gottesanschauung* (Göttingen: Vandenhoeck & Ruprecht, 1929); and E. Seeberg, *Luthers Theologie in ihren Grundzügen* (Stuttgart: W. Kohlhammer, 1950²), pp. 60ff. Monographs: F. Kattenbusch, "Deus absconditus bei Luther" (originally in *Festgabe für D. Dr. Julius Kaftan, . . . zu seinem 70. Geburtstag*, 30 Sept., 1918); F. Blanke, *Der verborgene Gott bei Luther* (Berlin: Furche Verlag, 1928); Gustav Aulén, "Das christliche Gottesbild," in *Vergangenheit und Gegenwart*, tr. G. Jonsson (Gütersloh: Bertelsmann, 1930), pp. 226ff.

18. *Sententiarum Libri Quattuor*, in *Opera*, ed. Franciscans at Quaracchi (4 vols.; Ad Claras Aquas: Quaracchi, 1882–89 and in 2 vols., 1916), I, Dist. 43 (I in the 1916 ed.), pp. 263ff.

19. *STh*, I, xxv, 5, vol. I, pp. 139–41. Similarly Bonaventure, *The Works of Bonaventure: Cardinal, Seraphic Doctor, and Saint*, tr. Jose de Vinck (Paterson, N.J.: St. Anthony Guild Press, vol. II [1963], The Breviloquium), I, Ch. 7, pp. 56f. On Duns Scotus, see R. Seeberg, *Die Theologie des Johannes Duns Scotus* (Leipzig: Dieterich, J. Weicher, 1900), pp. 155ff.; on William of Occam see S. U. Zuidema, *De philosophie van Occam un zijn Commentar op de Sentenzien* (2 vols.; Hilversum: Schipper, 1936), pp. 448ff.; and R. Seeberg, *Textbook of the History of Doctrines*, tr. C. E. Hay (2 vols. in 1; Grand Rapids: Baker Book House, 1952–58), II, 147ff.; and the article in Schaff-Herzog, VIII, 215–20.

there is an unmistakable influence of it upon the way in which he carries out the distinction between "God hidden," which he can on occasion even call "God absolute" *(Deus absolutus)*,[20] and "God revealed." But it would not be proper to look for his intentions at this point. First of all, his thinking in general proceeds in a completely different manner from that of the Nominalists. He does not want to orient faith to the "absolute God" and his "naked majesty" *(nuda majestas)*, but to the "revealed God," who is none other than the "incarnate God." It is only there that faith can find certainty, whereas speculation about "the pure" or "naked God" *(Deus nudus)* can only result in despair. But on the other hand, Luther wants to show that God as "God revealed" is not thereby calculable. The concept of "God hidden" has its particular location in the Doctrine of Predestination, as is well known, and it is, when interpreted positively, a marginal concept which is to protect us from taking the revealed will of God as a fact in itself. To do that would be to adopt Erasmus' approach, which regards the scriptural statements about "general" grace as manifestations of the grace which has been delivered to the free will of man, a grace which one only needs to make use of. No, Luther wants to say that God, as "God revealed," is merely the aspect of the actual being of God which is turned toward us, which has entered into our human existence. It is true that his statements, especially in *The Bondage of the Will*, occasionally leave the impression that Luther is almost speaking of two Gods or of a dual will of God. Later he avoided this, and it becomes clear in the lectures on Genesis that he really meant the one God and the one divine will in revelation. "From an unrevealed God I will become a revealed God. Nevertheless, I will remain the same God."[21] If we may understand Luther this way, it is basically the mystery of God in revelation which he wants to emphasize, the freedom of God in condescension. It is sufficient for us here to ascertain that the duplicity in the fundamental statements is present both in Thomas (and others) and in Luther, who puts it in a better, but more misunderstandable way.

3) **Condescension and Mystery in Calvin.** Finally, it may be noted that Calvin, who follows Scholasticism in his terminology more strongly than does Luther, supports materially a similar duplicity to that of Luther. His discussion of the being of God, exactly as in Luther, is conditioned by a fundamental rejection of speculation about "God in himself" *(Deus apud se)*.[22] In his revelation, God is "God toward us" *(Deus erga nos)*; he is love. It is significant that Calvin, in describing the being of God (toward us!), appeals to Exodus 34:6, ". . . merciful and gracious, slow to anger, and abounding in steadfast love and faithfulness. . . ."[23] There are innumerable other statements by the Genevan Reformer which

---

20. For example, in the powerful exposition of Ps. 51:2 (AE, vol. XII), where he speaks of the "absolute God," and "to think about God [absolutely], as he is in himself" (p. 312); his "absolute power" (p. 313); but see p. 352: "This God is not a vague God, like the God whom the Turks worship. He is a God revealed. . . ."

21. AE, V, 45 (Lectures on *Genesis*, 26:9).

22. See above, p. 401.

23. *Institutes*, I, x, 2, pp. 97–99.

accord with that.[24] God's nature, which he can never forget, is revealed in that he invites us "gently" *(clementer)* to himself.[25] Calvin also teaches the condescension of God—there is no question of that. But there is just as much certainty about the fact that Calvin knows of the mystery of God in his revelation. In order to describe it, he refers to the traditional concept of the "power of God" *(potentia Dei)*, which he obviously does not want to designate as "absolute power" *(potentia absoluta)*. God is not a tyrant. He would not be God if his "lordship" (or empire) would consist of no more than "manifesting absolute power like tyrants!"[26] He is not "God beyond law" *(Deus exlex)*, but his power *(potentia,*

---

24. This is especially impressive in *CR*, XXVIII, 501ff., on Deut. 29. See also E. Doumergue, *Jean Calvin, les hommes et les choses de son temps* (7 vols.; Lausanne: G. Bridel, 1899–1927), vol. IV (*La pensée religieuse de Calvin* [1910]), pp. 85ff., with further material there.

25. Calvin, *Commentaries on the Book of the Prophet Jeremiah*, tr. J. Owen (5 vols.; Grand Rapids: Eerdmans, 1950), I, 47: "Yet he never forgets his own nature, and kindly invites . . ." to himself.

26. *CR*, XXXIV, 222 (Sermons on Job). Since Calvin, because of his Doctrine of Predestination, is still occasionally accused of propounding a doctrine of God which he does not in fact espouse, we shall deal with the crucial issue briefly here. A. Ritschl (in "Geschichtliche Studien zur christliche Lehre von Gott," in *Gesammelte Aufsätze* [2 vols.; Freiburg and Leipzig: J. C. B. Mohr, 1893–1896], II, 94ff.) asserted that in Calvin's doctrine of God the Scotist element had really never been overcome. This is partially true. But one should not equate Duns Scotus with the Nominalism that came later. Calvin clearly rejects that. He energetically rejected the most famous formula of Nominalism, the concept of "God beyond law" *(Deus exlex)* (e.g., *Institutes*, III, xxiii, 2, pp. 949f., esp. n. 6)—incidentally, in contrast to Luther, who preserved the concept but interpreted it in his own sense (the Sermon on Exodus 9 [*WA*, XVI, 132ff., esp. 140ff.]). Similarly, he constantly opposed the traditional concept of "absolute power" *(potentia absoluta)*, again in contrast to Luther. He can say that one makes God into "an idol, a dead thing," when one separates his power and his righteousness (*CR*, XXXIV, 222). When "the sophists babble" about "that absolute will," they are dividing his righteousness from his power "by an impious and profane distinction" (*Institutes*, I, xvii, 2, p. 214). It is virtually blasphemy "to speak of an absolute power as if it were arbitrary" (Sermon on 1 Tim. 2:13–15 [*CR*, LIII, 221]). For God's "nature" is just, and whoever conceives of a power of God without righteousness is asserting "that God renounces His essence and that He is no longer God" (*CR*, XXXIII, 372). When Job (Job 23:1ff.) speaks of an "absolute power of God," this is blasphemy (*CR*, XXXIII, 372). We could assemble a large number of such statements. They can all be summarized by saying that there is both "symmetry" and "consensus" *(symmetria et consensus* [*De Aeterne Dei Praedestinatione* (1552) (*CR*, VIII, 361)])* between God's power and his righteousness. Nonetheless, if God is "beyond the law" *(exlex)*, this means that he follows no other law than his own (*De Aeterne* . . . [*CR*, VIII, 361]). One cannot say that God is *subject* to this law, for "all laws proceed from His will" (Sermon on 1 Tim. 2:13–15 [*CR*, LIII, 221]). God's will is therefore "the rule of righteousness" (*The Epistles of Paul the Apostle to the Romans and to the Thessalonians*, tr. R. Mackenzie [Grand Rapids: Eerdmans, 1961], p. 162 [Rom. 8:7] and pp. 204f. [Rom. 9:15f.]). And this will is to be sure not opposed to revealed law, but it is certainly higher than that law. There is a "righteousness of God which is unknown to us" (J. Bohatec, "Calvins Vorsehungslehre," in *Calvinstudien, Festschrift zum 400. Geburtstage Johann Calvins [*"Elberfelder Calvinstudien"*]* [Leipzig: R. Haupt, 1909], p. 401). There is a "secret will of God" *(arcana Dei voluntas)* which is distinguished from that "will" "to which voluntary obedience corresponds" (*Institutes*, III, xx, 43, p. 906). There is a higher, concealed righteousness of God to which not even the angels measure up (*Institutes*, III, xiv, 16, p. 783). For obvious reasons, Calvin developed many variations on this theme in his sermons on Job. But this righteousness of God which is still concealed to

puissance) is indissolubly interconnected with his righteousness. To be sure, with a righteousness which we are not capable of analyzing, which is also higher than the righteousness revealed in the law, higher even than the righteousness which the angels are able to satisfy. We find therefore in Calvin, too, a double view, which is our concern here, but it is protected against a dichotomization of the will or of the essence of God which would have to rob faith of its certainty.

To summarize what we have discussed in this section, we come to the following results:

First of all, we conclude that God (the triune God!) is in his very essence "in" self-bestowal. He does not encounter us merely in his turning to his creatures, but according to his essence he is God-in-self-bestowal. He is love.

Secondly, we conclude that God as the One who turns to us in this his self-bestowal does not cease in his love to be he himself. His love is therefore not disposability or a kind of divine nature-necessity, but is to be understood as a divine act. It would be just another way of saying the same thing if we put it, his love is as his divine love holy according to its essence.

God is then in his essence, his reality, holy, free, sovereign love. In its shortest form, this is "the Christian concept of God."

To say that God is love does not imply that he is the "good principle" in the world, the positive ground of the world, or the guarantor of our existence. He is not a postulate, but a divine reality. He is love in wondrous miracle. For God in his very essence is "wonderful" (Judg. 13:18). One can only speak of his love with astonishment: "See what love the Father has given us, that we should be called children of God" (1 John 3:1). His love is not automatic, but free love. It is neither an idea, nor a postulate, nor a given, but it is a gift, it is an act, it is the penetration of our closedness and our lovelessness, our hostility to grace and our self-imprisonment.

God's freedom, in turn, is none other than the freedom made known in his love. It is thus not arbitrariness which would place in question his love, and the validity and finality of his revelation. It is not "absolute power" *(potentia absoluta)*. It is indeed his freedom for us. It does not consist of God's holding himself away from us and even against us. It is the freedom in which God gives himself to his creatures.

Thus, God's love is qualified by God's freedom as a real gift. It is thereby

---

us is not derived from a will of God which was in opposition to the will revealed in the law. There are not "two wills in God" (*Institutes*, I, xviii, 3, pp. 232–35; III, xxiv, 17, pp. 985–87). God's will is manifold solely "to our perception"—but at one time we will recognize the unity of God's will, "to recognize how wonderfully he wills what at the moment seems to be against his will" (*ibid.*, p. 986). Whoever knows Calvin's dislike of paradoxical formulations (and appreciates it) will understand the pressure under which he attempts here to say what is inexpressible. When we review the whole process of his thought, then he is certainly no Nominalist. At the decisive point he would rather tend to agree with Thomas. But, in contrast to Thomas, Calvin does not possess the terminological possibility to solve the puzzle intellectually (he cannot possess it). He finally ends up at the point of eschatological expectation: he is not resigned because of the puzzle of the mystery of God, but he is waiting for its disclosure.

qualified noetically as the love which is not subject to the law of consistency,[27] as *agapē* in the original sense.[28]

On the other hand, God's love qualifies his freedom as divine, as freedom turned toward the creature, as freedom which incomprehensibly does not consist of the possibility that God could be "different" (he cannot be the devil, he cannot be wicked), but rather of the fact that purely of his own essence, unconditioned by anything else, with no regard to the quality of the object toward which he turns, God is and acts the way he is and acts.

B. THE KNOWLEDGE OF THE ATTRIBUTES OF GOD

1. THE MEANING OF STATEMENTS ABOUT THE ATTRIBUTES OF GOD

a. The Nameless God. "It will always alienate the faith of the Church to hear how the Platonism of the Greek Fathers struggled with the question and how Scholasticism exhausted itself with the same issue, whether God should be ascribed attributes."[29] H. Cremer's statement is certainly illuminating when we remember that every sermon makes statements about God and thus assigns to God in some kind of sense "attributes." If we also remember that Christian discourse about man does not speak of man "in himself" but "before God," then we must conclude that every mention of man in a sermon includes some kind of statements about "the attributes" of God. It can also be said of theology that from the beginning to the end it is talk about God and can scarcely avoid expressing something "contentual" about God, thereby stating "attributes."

Nevertheless, there is a serious problem here. We have already looked at it above[30] from a particular point of view, and now we must discuss it again in a broader sense.

First of all, the problem is raised in the setting of aesthetic religion. If "God" essentially is the epitome of deepest sensibilities and if one presupposes that the ultimate is only accessible to the dark urges of the heart, then it is impossible to say anything about the attributes of such an ultimate. We must then remain at the position of Goethe's well-known rejection, which is an integral part of the secret religion of modern man.[31]

---

27. It was the special merit of H. Cremer to have worked this out in exhaustive detail in his work, *Die christliche Lehre von den Eigenschaften Gottes* (*Beiträge zur Förderung christlicher Theologie*, 1, 4; Gütersloh: Bertelsmann, 1897, 1917²).

28. See A. Nygren, *Agape and Eros*, tr. P. S. Watson (London: S.P.C.K., 1953 [g1930]), pp. 61ff.

29. H. Cremer, *op. cit.*, p. 10.

30. See above, pp. 398ff.

31. Who dare name Him?
And who avow:
"I believe in Him"?
Who feels and would
Have hardihood
To say: "I don't believe in Him"?
The All-Enfolder,

But the problem also arises where, in an apparent reversal, the issue at stake is the deity of God. It was certainly not an emotional self-projection of the I into the universe which led Plato to say, "For God is without quality or attributes, neither alone nor in the form of man."[32] How can anything at all be said about the Being of all beings, which is the theme here, without speaking anthropomorphically and thus encroaching upon the absoluteness of God? It is not without interest that the basic thrust of this Plato citation recurs at one place in Justin Martyr.[33] Considerations of this kind concerned the Fathers, chiefly the Greek Fathers, and also Scholasticism, particularly in its Nominalistic branch. Nonetheless, even Thomas, apparently under great stress, tried to deal with them.[34] As we have already seen, the metaphysics of being must ultimately lead to an impasse which it is incapable of resolving with its own resources.

b. In Deum non cadit accidens=In God Nothing Happens Accidentally. This problem can also arise under certain circumstances when we are speaking of God in his revelation. There the question is not whether attributes of one kind or another can be stated as being of God, but whether they really can be ascribed to him in truth. What is the idea of "attributes" supposed to mean in the first

---

The All-Upholder,
Enfolds, upholds He not
You, me, Himself?
Do not the heavens over-arch us yonder?
Does not the earth lie firm beneath?
Do not eternal stars rise friendly
Looking down upon us?
Look I not, eye in eye, on you,
And do not all things throng
Toward your head and heart,
Weaving in mystery eternal,
Invisible, visible, near to you?
Fill up your heart with it, great though it is,
And when you're wholly in the feeling, in its bliss,
Name it then as you will,
Name it Happiness! Heart! Love! God!
I have no name for that!
Feeling is all in all;
Name is but sound and smoke,
Beclouding Heaven's glow.

Johann Wolfgang von Goethe, *Faust*, Part One, "Martha's Garden," tr. G. M. Priest, in *GBWW, Goethe*, XLVII, 84.

The religion of Eros in the sense of A. Nygren's well-known formulation has never been described more marvelously. It scarcely needs to be said that this term cannot be regarded as expressing what is "the religion of Goethe." For newer studies of the theme, see G. Schaeder, *Gott und Welt, Drei Kapitel Goethescher Weltanschauung* (Hameln: Seifert, 1947), and E. Busch, *Goethes Religion; die Faust-Dichtung in christlicher Sicht* (Tübingen: Furche, 1949).

32. *Republic*, I, 509 [apparently an incorrect citation (n.l.)—TR].

33. "The Second Apology," *Justin Martyr and Athenagoras* (*ANCL*, II, Ch. VI, p. 76).

34. One would have to read the first 26 questions totally in order to be able to observe this in detail. But it can be seen most clearly in *STh*, I, xiii, vol. I, pp. 59–72.

place? In the European tradition, the proposition has regularly been followed as formulated by Augustine,[35] "In God nothing happens accidentally." The reasoning is quite simple. Every accidental event is something changeable, and moreover, the being to which it is ascribed could be conceived of abstractly without the accidental aspect. But God is "immutable," and the attributes spoken of as his cannot abstractly be conceived of as not a part of him (God is no longer God if he is no longer omnipotent). Thus, there are no "attributes" of God in the sense of accidental aspects (accidentia). Rather, every attribute expresses his being: "Whatever is said of God worthily is not quality but essence."[36] In regard to God, then, one can speak solely of the characteristics of being (proprietates, or properties).

c. God's simplicitas=Simplicity and the Attributes. But is God not always everything in one? Does not his "simplicity" exclude any actual discourse (i.e., to discuss something as though it actually exists) about properties? Do not all "attributes" unavoidably coalesce in one in him? Can I, for example, speak of God in such a way that a distinction between his righteousness and his mercy is even uttered? Does this not then mean the commission of an inadmissible humanization of God?

d. How Then Could Older Theology Speak of the Attributes? Now, neither Scholasticism nor Protestant Orthodoxy was blind to the fact that the Bible mentions a wealth of "attributes," and they sought to utilize statements of this kind dogmatically. It was only possible to find a way of connecting this intention with the aforesaid carefulness in regard to the reality of such statements by ascribing to God "in himself" one "essence" (essentia) alone and relating the "attributes" either to his relationship to the creatures or viewing them generally as the way in which man expresses conceptually his experience of God.

e. The Attributes' Relationship to Creation. An early Church Christo-pagan skeptic, Arnobius (d. c. 330), said, "Whatever you say about God, whatever you conceive in the silence of your mind, passes over and is corrupted into human applications nor can it have the mark of a meaning of its own because it is expressed in our own words and words designed for human affairs."[37] That may be understood in the sense of the absolute concept of being which excludes any statement of attributes even as a statement. Even earlier, Irenaeus points in the direction which we just designated as the earliest and dominant one.[38] But Thomas is chiefly to be cited here, according to whom "these names express God, so far as our intellects know Him." Our "intellect," however, since it knows God "from creatures," "knows Him as far as creatures represent Him."[39] Therefore, God

---

35. The standard citation here is *On the Trinity*, V, v, 6 (*NPNF*, III, 89).
36. *The City of God*, VIII, 6 (*NPNF*, II, 148f.).
37. Arnobius, *The Case Against the Pagans*, tr. G. E. McCracken (*ANW*, VII, Book III, 19, p. 207).
38. Irenaeus, *Against Heresies*, II, xiii, 9 (*ANCL*, V, 159).
39. *STh*, I, xii, 2, vol. I, p. 61.

in himself is unconditionally "simple" *(simplex)* and to that extent without actual attributes.[40] Protestant Orthodox theologians followed Thomas in this, as for example Polanus (1561–1610)[41] or even more explicitly Quenstedt (1617–1688).[42] In spite of attempts to break out of the restrictions thus established—God in himself is united and simple, but has properties outwardly, in relationship to the creatures, properties which merely express this relationship—most of the Orthodox adhered to the middle position defined by Thomas, and modern theology has generally followed them in this.[43] The attributes of God are not his actual and authentic being, but are its reflection in the relationship to the creature!

f. Attributes as Relational Definitions on the Part of Man. It is not surprising that there have been dogmaticians who meant by the attributes of God not God's relationship to the creature, but the opposite, the relationship of our consciousness of God to God. And unmistakably, this approach is prepared for in Scholastic thinking when we remember how there our "intellect" is the place at which the "properties" or the "names" of God come into view in their relationship to the "creature." But to understand the attributes of God ultimately as purely intellectual products was not typical of Thomas but rather of William of Occam (c. 1300–c. 1349). Along these lines we later discover Schleiermacher making a statement like this, "All attributes which *we ascribe* to God are to be taken as denoting *not* something special *in God*, but only something special in the manner in which the feeling of absolute dependence is *to be related* to Him."[44]

There is one common aspect to both of the approaches under discussion. It is the confidence with which the human intellect is ascribed the capacity to express something meaningful about God on the basis of the foundation which is recognized as given in any situation. The meaningfulness of these statements (all of which are relative, based upon a relation) is founded in both approaches upon a presupposed analogy. In Thomas it is what we call today the "analogia entis"

---

40. The clearest passage is *STh*, I, xiii, 4, vol. I, pp. 62f. Our "intellect" recognizes God from the "creatures" and forms, in order to grasp God, "conceptions" which are proportional to the perfections communicated by God to the creatures. These "pre-exist in God unitedly and simply," but they are received in the creatures "divided and multiplied." There is clearly an inadequacy between the "simplicity" of God and the "multiplicity" of the attributes which the creatures perceive. It is, nevertheless, bridged by the fact that the "perfections" of the creature are derived from God. See J. Gredt, *Die aristotelisch-thomistische Philosophie Elementa Philosophiae Aristotelico-Thomisticae* (2 vols.; Freiburg: Herder, 1937, 1958 [g1935]), II, 189.

41. The distinction of the attributes of God's being does not take place "in reality" *(realiter)* but "rationally" or "as the mode," "they are our conception and comprehension" (*Syntagma theologiae christianae* [1610]), p. 902.

42. "For if we want to speak properly and accurately, God does not possess properties, but His essence is pure and most simple . . ." (*Theologia didactico-polemico* [1685, 1691], I, viii, 2, pp. 296f.).

43. Karl Barth, who devotes an especially penetrating discussion to this theme in *CD*, II,1, pp. 327ff., quotes C. I. Nitzsch, "The idea of God discloses its quality only as the movements and changes of self- and world-consciousness give occasion" (*System der christlichen Lehre* [Bonn: Adolph Marcus, 1844[5] (g1851[6])], p. 149; ET: *System of Christian Doctrine*, tr. R. Montgomery and J. Hennen [Edinburgh: T. & T. Clark, 1849]).

44. Schleiermacher, *ChrF*, §50, Thesis, I, p. 194.

(analogy of being). In Schleiermacher it is what we could call an "analogia religiosa" (analogy of religion): there are definite divine attributes which "correspond" to the "different moments of the religious self-consciousness."[45]

What appeared to be an act of human modesty, an attempt to avoid making any kind of anthropomorphic statements, is in truth the emanation of a very definite human claim!

It is significant that in the presentation of the complex discussion of the possibility of making statements about God's attributes, we have regularly been referred to the relationship of God (in general) to the creature (in general), but virtually never to God's self-disclosure in Jesus Christ. If we then set aside revelation, except for "natural revelation," for a moment, is it not completely understandable that in that case the question can arise whether God, who is supposed to be the One who makes himself known in "nature," in the "creature," who is disclosed out of "nature" in fact, could have any "attributes" at all? Is it possible to deduce *a priori*, without having heard a name already, that God has a name? As long as one maintains such a position, is it not necessary for every statement on the attributes to remain entirely subjective? Must not every attempt to express God's attributes *a priori* and deductively lead unavoidably into nothingness? Must not the relativity of the statements on the attributes be regarded as unreal and inauthentic as long as God's true being-in-relationship is neglected?

g. The Three Ways of the Areopagite. If further proof were needed that this is so, then it could be gotten from the most famous attempt to arrive at statements about God's attributes by proceeding from the creature: the theory of the "three ways" which was originally propounded by Dionysius the Pseudo-Areopagite (c. 500)[46] and broadly followed in the Middle Ages, even by Thomas.[47]

In order to make an inference from things to the attributes of God, one must first of all, in pursuance of the "affirmative way" *(via affirmativa)*, or "way of causality" *(causalitatis)*, "include in our statement about God, as the cause of all things, everything which the things contain as perfections."[48] Secondly, one must exclude all the imperfections of the creature from him *(via negativa* =negative way). And thirdly, one must consider that he, as the cause, is infinitely superior to all created things *(via eminentiae* =the prominent or eminent way). In this fashion we arrive at statements about God in which we raise to infinity the perfections we can identify. (The order of the "ways" varies in the various dogmaticians.) The conception of the "three ways" *(triplex via)* clearly reveals its origins

---

45. *Ibid.*, pp. 190f.

46. "On the Divine Names and the Mystical Theology," in *Translations of Christian Literature, Series 1, Greek Texts*, tr. C. E. Rolt (London: S.P.C.K., and New York: Macmillan, 1920), VII, 3, pp. 151–53; see also Peter Lombard, *Sententiarum Libri Quattuor*, ed. Franciscans of Quaracchi (2 vols.; Ad Claras Aquas: Quaracchi, 1916), I, iii, 1ff., p. 30, who speaks of four "reasons or modes" and does not directly refer to the Areopagite.

47. *STh*, I, xii, 12, vol. I, pp. 58f., without mentioning the Areopagite but in agreement with him materially.

48. In the Commentary by H. M. Christmann, *Summa Theologica [die deutsche Thomas Ausgabe]*, tr. Dominicans and Benedictines of Germany and Austria (Salzburg: Anton Pustet, 1933–), I, 409.

in Neo-Platonism. What is behind it is the idea of an ultimate, which is the origin and the extreme surpassing of concrete reality and is contrasted to this reality in its character of derivation, of relativity and temporality. This idea is diametrically opposed to the faith of Christendom. It considers neither God the Creator nor the self-disclosure of the Creator in Jesus Christ. It is metaphysics of being and founds a mysticism of being which corresponds to such a metaphysics.[49] What can be the theological source of our knowledge that in the heights beyond our heights God could really be found? How could one say in a "Christian" fashion that God is the "cause" of things? What would be the source of our reasoning that the negation of everything which we know to be imperfect in ourselves would really result in the perfection of God? The negation takes place within the same categories as the affirmation. In both instances, God appears as coordinable with reality as we see it, except that the coordination takes place in two different directions. In the case of the Areopagite himself, moreover, the attributes which he finds with the help of the "three ways" are not directly ascribable to God himself, "Whom one can neither understand nor express."[50] And in point of fact, this reservation must be asserted if the "three ways" are to be used. Only in this way does it become clear that we are dealing here with the metaphysics of being and not with theology.

h. Positive Consideration. Now we are to discuss positively in which sense we can speak of God's attributes. The following points can be made in this regard.

1) **The Relatedness to Revelation.** We can speak of God's attributes solely because of his revelation. The tendency which can be observed in history of seeing God's attributes "relatively," that is, in the relation of God to man, is sensible to the extent that it is impossible to ascribe to God any attributes by way of deduction. God's revelation should not be confused with some kind of inferred or postulated discovery of God. God is not the "cause" of reality, but its Creator. And he is revealed to us as the Creator in no other way than as the Word which has become flesh. In this his revelation his self-predication takes place; he manifests himself as the One who functions in relationship. Only from this position is it possible to speak sensibly about the attributes of God.

2) *Divine Attributes!* God's attributes, as they are revealed in his self-disclosure, are veritably attributes of himself. For God did not reveal "something," but himself. This leads to the insight that God's attributes are to be conceived of solely as his attributes, if our thinking is to be qualified theologically. He himself in his self-disclosure makes his "attributes" into what they are. We cannot regard the proposition that God is love as fulfilled in that we analyze the predicate concept "love" to its uttermost point and use our own concepts and experiences in doing this. God is not the highest measure of what we call "love," but the predicate concept is filled solely through the subject concept: *God* is love.

---

49. E. Brunner correctly draws attention to the fact that the "three ways" is basically the method of the mysticism of being (*Dogmatics*, I, 245).

50. "In a manner surpassing speech and knowledge" (Dionysius, the Pseudo-Areopagite, *op. cit.*, p. 51, as translated by John Scotus Erigena [Migne, *PL*, CXXII, 1116]).

He is divine love. And this is the way we deal with all of the concepts. This can be provisionally made plain by turning to the concept of the "omnipotence" of God. This concept is not to be filled by our ascribing to God a kind of extreme superlative of what we call "power." God is not located in the direct prolongation and the surpassing far beyond of what is the highest conceivable or perceivable concept of power for us. His omnipotence has been qualified in Jesus Christ as the penetration of what we have called "power"—it is even his capacity for "impotence," for self-abasement.[51]

This is the sole meaning of the statement that God's attributes are not merely nor primarily a relationship to the creature, much less a divisible relationship of the creature to him, or to the consciousness of him, but are his very essence. This his essence, as we have already seen, is in itself relationship, life, self-bestowal, the otherness of God toward us, love. Now we can add that the attributes of God are the manifestations, in his self-disclosure as the revelation of the triune and living God, of his living and divine reality turned to us.

3) Attributes of Him Who Acts. God's attributes are the hallmarks of his living and divine reality turned toward us, and as such they are his essential attributes in that they are the attributes of his activity. God does not reveal "something," he does not reveal "attributes" (so that we, by summarizing these revealed attributes, could then deduce what kind of God he is); rather, he reveals himself. His being and his activity are not to be divorced from one another. He is never the spectator, never an "idle God" *(deus otiosus)*; all of the statements on the attributes refer to him in "being" and "act."

4) Accommodation. But God's action is condescension. As his own, his self-disclosure is certainly also concealment. He discloses himself to us in such a way that we can recognize this self-disclosure in our limitations, our confusion, and the perversion of our existence. He does not become a thing for us which we can then manage. But incomprehensibly, he makes himself into the object of our knowledge. Therefore, our knowledge is always dependent, non-autonomous, creaturely knowledge. It is knowledge in the acknowledgment of the concealment of God. This is naturally also true of the attributes of God. As we are able to know them, they are to be sure his own attributes, but in such a way that he, in his self-disclosure and thus in the way in which we are permitted to grasp his attributes, "accommodates" himself to us. Our concepts are always placed in question by the reality of the revelation. Of course, we have in these concepts a valid knowledge, so far as they are formed legitimately out of God's self-disclosure. But their validity consists of their always being open-ended in an upward direction, so to speak. They may be compared to Moses, who was only permitted

---

51. Luther's well-known statement: "Nothing is so small but God is still smaller, nothing so large but God is still larger, nothing is so short but God is still shorter. . . . He is an inexpressible being, above and beyond all that can be described and imagined" *(Confession Concerning Christ's Supper* [AE, XXXVII, 228]), may sound mystical. But it is only the conclusion from the major proposition that God is no other than "God incarnate" *(Deus incarnatus)*.

to perceive Yahweh's revelation from behind, concealed in a break in the rocks. The actuality of the knowledge granted to us includes its incompleteness, its provisional character, and thus its limitedness.[52] All God's "accommodation," including the anthropomorphic terms which are present in great numbers in the Bible, refers to the one, real accommodation which takes place in the incarnation of the Word. None of our concepts is *the Word*, but they all stand on the side of the flesh which the Word took on. Not the flesh makes the Word incarnate, but the Word destines the flesh to be the site of incarnation. There is no transformation of the flesh. The flesh does not become the Word. But it is claimed by the Word. In the language of the old Christology, it becomes "human nature" *(natura humana)* in relationship to "divine nature" *(natura divina)*. But the "human nature" does not have its own essentiality in contrast to the "divine nature." As the early Church taught, it is "anhypostatic." When we remember that all statements about attributes are based upon the incarnation of the Word, we shall have to say that our concepts receive their appropriateness for such statements by the very fact that they are used "anhypostatically." We emphasize once more that this does not mean the limitation of the validity of what is made known to us in God's self-disclosure, and this includes the concepts which are used to express this. The "accommodation" of God is not conceptual, but actual in nature. It is the eternal Word which becomes "true man" *(vere homo)*. But our concepts do not of themselves have a relationship to the One who is "true man," but they receive this relationship from him, and they are only meaningful in him. Their limitations only make them valid in this sense.

2. THE NAME OF GOD

a. Etymological Procedure? "The essence of God may be understood both from his names and from his properties."[53] Wolleb's thesis repeats a widespread teaching form which had its relationships to the early Church and Scholastic tradition but was especially developed in Reformed Orthodoxy. It will not be dealt with in detail here. In its Orthodox form, which still was espoused by some in the 19th century,[54] its effect was that statements about the nature of God could be derived from etymology and from the interpretation of the Old Testament names of God given in the Bible. Next to these there are then the direct predicates of God which occur in the Bible. The result is two groups of statements which

---

52. No one has emphasized the "accommodation" as strongly as Calvin. It can be said that his concept of revelation is decisively formed by the idea of accommodation, which then, on the other hand, is a guiding motif of his exegesis. In the Enlightenment the concept of accommodation was then used to establish the subjectivity of every statement about God. The self-accommodation of God in his revelation receded into the background.

53. J. Wolleb, *Compendium theologiae Christianae* (1626), ed. E. Bizer (1935), p. 7, in *Reformed Dogmatics*, ed. and tr. J. W. Beardslee III (New York: Oxford University Press, 1965), p. 37.

54. E.g., E. Böhl, *Dogmatik, Darstellung der christlichen Glaubenslehre auf reformiert-kirchlicher Grundlage* (Amsterdam: Scheffer, 1887), and H. Bavinck, *The Doctrine of God*, ed. and tr. W. Hendriksen (Grand Rapids: Eerdmans, 1951 [g1897]), the latter very carefully.

are usually distinguished from one another so that the names of God appear as the direct expression of his nature, and the biblical predicates as the expression of the attributes of God.

The difference between the early Church and Scholastic doctrine "On the names of God" and that of Protestant Orthodoxy consisted of the fact that the earlier tradition generally bore in mind the problem of the nameability of God which was given through its Neo-Platonic influence,[55] whereas the later tradition sought to derive more biblicistically the "Word" directly from the "words."

For our present purposes, the Scholastic query, which was already discussed, can be set aside.[56] But we must ask now whether the biblicistic procedure is possible. At the outset, it is significant to note that the Old Testament knows avowed names for God, whereas the New Testament does not record the Old Testament ones—even though, as we already noted,[57] in the New and in the Old Testaments the name of God or the name of Jesus Christ has the characteristics of a "hypostasis."

The New Testament, by saying *ho kyrios* (the Lord) instead of "Yahweh," follows the practice of the Septuagint. This is shown by the numerous Old Testament quotations. But *ho kyrios* is not etymologically the translation of "Yahweh." And *ho theos* (God) is etymologically not the same as "Elohim" either. Both of these New Testament terms have their own etymology and history of meaning. We can make the problem here more understandable by referring to the well-known fact that in the Baroque period both in poetical and in theological usage the term "Jehovah" was used in preference to "the Lord" or even "God." Was this not an instance in which the great significance of the Old Testament names of God was properly honored, even in the usage of the Church? In other words, would it not be a good thing if in our churches today we would say, in our sermons for example, "Yahweh," "Elohim," or "El Shaddai"?

It would be possible to make very clear that this is something which we are not permitted to do. The reason is not that a New Testament Biblicism is sweeping away an Old Testament one (because the Old Testament names do not occur in the New). In such an instance, the objection could be raised that the lack of names of God in the New Testament could be the effect of the special circumstances of that time (particularly, the influence of the Septuagint). But instead we will have to conclude that Christian theology, when it talks about the names of God, does not refer to the formal vocabulary of the names of God but rather to their meaning in the total witness of Scripture. From that direction some light may be cast upon the vocabulary itself. But only in that direction! This will be demonstrated by the simple fact that in Exodus 3:14 the "explanation" of Yahweh's name by no means belongs to its (very obscure) etymology, but is a special witness which quite rightly has received the greatest attention in all the centuries of the history of theology. Besides, as we shall now show, the repetition of the vocabulary of the names would have to be wrong.

---

55. The most instructive example is Thomas, *STh*, I, xiii, vol. I, pp. 59–72.
56. See above, pp. 410f.
57. See above, pp. 355f.

b. Yahweh. Let us try first of all to clarify what is actually the issue here. The Old Testament's most important name of God is Yahweh. This is a "proper name," absolutely nontransferable, the name of God as the covenant God, the Lord of Israel and thus of the nations. It is the name which introduces the decalogue. The God who speaks here is "I" in the most pregnant sense of the word,[58] and he makes the one to whom he turns into a "Thou." The fact that one can invoke the God whose name one knows has become virtually a non-essential secondary thought in the Old Testament. Yahweh's nameability, his readiness to let himself "be called upon," is based upon his having called Israel. Yahweh is the free one who in this freedom has chosen Israel to be his partner. And as the covenant God he is faithful, he "is who he is" (Ex. 3:14), "who keeps faith forever" (Ps. 146:6). The name Yahweh provides absolutely no basis for any speculation about being which ignores the event and the history of the covenant.[59]

What can then be derived dogmatically from the name Yahweh? First of all this, that God according to the Old Testament (and thus, as we shall see, certainly according to the New) really has a name. He is not an idea and thereby ultimately nameless. He is the One who acts as a person. He makes himself known, in his self-distinction from everything which is not-God in the concrete sense. He makes himself in his Self known and thus gives to the people, to whom he turns, the possibility of calling upon him. When early theology, in regard to the name of God, raised the problem of God's nameability, it made clear that the fact of the name hindered it from uninhibitedly following through on its Hellenistic assumptions. Secondly, we conclude that God according to the Old Testament (again, too, according to the New) remains himself, remains a mystery in his name. Yahweh's name is a "holy name" (Ps. 103:1; 105:3; 111:9, and frequently), and he himself is the "Holy One of Israel." His name does not become a "thing" in the hands of men. Earlier theology was particularly attentive to this thought. Following chiefly Exodus 3:14, they derived from the name Yahweh the "aseity" of God, his "underived existence."[60] They were surely right in this, if we regard the whole Old and New Testament witness beyond Exodus 3:14 and understand aseity positively rather than negatively. This means that we do not conceive of an abstract transcendence (Yahweh is certainly just as immanent as he is "transcendent"), nor deduce God from the negation of our limits. Instead, the concept of aseity is to express the glory of God who owes nothing to anyone and who in this his *autousia* is the God of man![61] Thirdly, and above all, we can learn from the

---

58. See the frequent "I, Yahweh," especially in the Law of Holiness and Deutero-Isaiah (41:4; 42:8; 43:10, 11; 44:6, etc.); also W. Zimmerli, "Ich bin Yahwe," in W. F. Albright *et al., Geschichte und Altes Testament (Beiträge zur historischen theologie*, 1,6; Tübingen: J. C. B. Mohr [Paul Siebeck], 1953), pp. 179ff.

59. In contrast, the Septuagint does offer such a basis in that it translates Ex. 3:14 with *ho ōn* (the existing one), although of course the Hebrew is also obscure. In its context, the meaning of the passage can only be, I am in myself and thus I am for you, who I am. . . .

60. The Greeks use the concept of *autousia* primarily. In European dogmatics, the *a se esse* of God was first emphatically stressed by Anselm and has been a standing element in dogmatics ever since.

61. Karl Barth, *CD*, II,1, pp. 303ff.

usage of the name Yahweh that statements about God cannot be separated from those about God's covenant. The name Yahweh is historical. It is intimately connected to the various covenant agreements which are reported to us. Yahweh is the covenant God in an absolute sense. He is the One who elects and calls; he is the One who rejects and punishes. He is the One who turns to a partnership, specified by him, chosen by him, done in the concreteness of his activity. Therefore, his name is the guarantor of this self-bestowal in its validity and in its divine freedom. His "aseity" is his free being for elect man. His name is thus not a "denomination" but the form of his "accommodation" and of the claim which he makes and effects in his condescension and his adaptation to man. As the God who acts concretely in the covenant, he is according to the message of the Yahwist the Creator and the Lord of the world (Gen. 2:4ff.) and the Ruler of history. From the central point represented by the covenant, the breadth of the world is brought into view. The covenant is the "internal basis of Creation."[62]

Why then, we must ask, do we not say "Yahweh"? The only possible answer is that the name Yahweh belongs to the old covenant. By the late period of the old covenant, it had receded to the same degree that the covenant itself became something past or future, but no longer actually contemporary.[63] But for completely different reasons, though certainly not lacking in contact to late Jewish tradition of both the Palestinian and Hellenistic types, it does not occur in the New Testament. The new and eternal covenant is accompanied by the new Name, which God has given man for salvation (Acts 4:12). Just as Christ is the goal and thus the "end" of the law, the name Yahweh attains its goal and its "end" in him. It may be significant that Jesus in the New Testament is called "Son of God," but never "Son of Yahweh" or "Son of the Lord," although the latter form would be linguistically conceivable. As the Son of God he is himself "the Lord," and now the Old Testament prerogatives of the name Yahweh are ascribed to his name[64]—in Acts 4:12, Joel 3:5 is obviously sounding through! The name Yahweh belongs as a name to the unfulfilled law, to the promise, to the old covenant. That does not mean that God has now become nameless. It also does not mean that God has changed his name. What it does mean is that in the "name which is above every name" (Phil. 2:9), God has fulfilled what was unfulfilled up to then. God has a name, and this name is Jesus Christ. If the Church still wanted to say "Yahweh" (or perhaps "Jehovah"), then it would be denying what God has done. But this also means that theology will find it impossible to do what it has often tried, which is to derive God's attributes in a kind of spiritual philology from the name Yahweh.

c. Elohim. What then does it mean that the Old Testament does not use just "Yahweh" but also "Elohim" (and the New Testament *theos, kyrios*)? Etymology

---

62. K. Barth, *CD*, III,1, pp. 228ff.
63. We are thinking of the fact that Late Judaism read the holy tetragrammaton as "Adonai" and the Septuagint translated it with *kyrios*.
64. See pp. 356f.

can contribute very little to this issue.[65] There is no doubt that "Elohim" is basically an appellative, a generic name. Its usage is thus in the Old Testament very comprehensive. As is well known, "Elohim" can also be used for the pagan "god" or the alien "gods." Even man in his power can on occasion be called by it (Ex. 4:16; similarly Ps. 45:6; 82:6; see also John 10:34f.). It is not without importance that the Old Testament even applies the generic name to Yahweh. On the one hand, this is confirmed by our discussion of the monolatrous tendencies of the Old Testament witness,[66] which emphasizes the concreteness of the Yahweh-revelation, and on the other hand it refers to the fact that God, in the concrete experience of man, enters into those places where the "gods" can also be present. It is the appellative which stimulates the transition to meditated monotheism, as it is expressed, for example, in Jeremiah 2:11: "gods . . . though they are no gods!" We might put it this way: in that God is experienced as "God," he places himself at the level of the struggle with "god" and the "gods." But it is important that the Old Testament never indicates a tendency to explain the "gods" as a kind of expression of God. They cannot be relativized. They can only be rejected. And that brings us up to the essential thing about the Old Testament usage of the concept "God." "Elohim" is, to be sure, basically a generic term, but this concept receives its total content from Yahweh. He is God. The term which originally was not personal now becomes personal. This concept, which basically was not "appropriate," because it expressed nothing more than "power," is made into an appropriate form of expression for what the Old Testament has to testify to. But this then makes very clear that dogmatic statements cannot be directly derived from "Elohim" and its related terms. The word "Elohim" does not lead us beyond what we were able to recognize in the name Yahweh. The same is true in the New Testament of *ho theos* (god). It is impossible to come up with the most minimal of conclusions based upon the etymology of this word or even of its usage outside of the Bible.

d. Relatedness to History. There is only one special point which can be derived from the name of God as such, and that is the explicit relatedness to the history of God's self-manifestation. This in turn is expressed essentially by the fact that God is not "also" but "actually" the covenant God. Thus, the name of God leads us to a direction of thought which is the exact opposite of that of older theology. They wanted to proceed from the names to a "nature" of God "per se." They did this biblicistically with a kind of theologizing philology or (earlier) speculatively in the form of a deduction which of necessity was directed away from the name toward the nameless. Dogmatics will have to avoid both options as long and to the extent that it has its center in the one Name which God has given us unto salvation.

---

65. For *kyrios*, see W. Graf Baudissin, *Kyrios als Gottesname im Judentum und seine Stelle in der Religionsgeschichte* (4 vols.; Giessen: Töpelmann, 1926–29), III, 1ff.; G. Quell's article in Kittel, *TDNT*, III, 79–89; M. Noth, *Die israelitischen Personennamen im Rahmen der gemeinsemitischen Namengebung* (Stuttgart: Kohlhammer, 1928; repr. Hildesheim: G. Olms, 1966), pp. 111ff.

66. See pp. 354ff.

C. THE LOVING ONE

1. ON THE STRUCTURE OF THE DOCTRINE OF GOD'S ATTRIBUTES

God is he who loves in freedom—"the sovereign love."[67] That is his "essence." But we cannot differentiate between his "essence" and his "attributes" in the sense that God's "attributes" would be something additional which could just as well be lacking. The distinction is solely explanatory in nature. We could put it this way, that whoever speaks about the essence of God is emphasizing that "*God* is thus and thus," and whoever speaks about the "attributes" of God is emphasizing that "God is *thus and thus.*" The doctrine of the attributes must strictly avoid any attempt to understand God as the "coincidence of everything" *(coincidentia omnium)* and thus ultimately as the neutralization of every concrete statement. To be sure, all of God's attributes have their unity and their meaning in God himself. We will never come up with clear statements if we interpret certain designations of attributes separately in the sense which we would attach to them based upon ourselves. But when we firmly remember that God's attributes are the hallmarks of his activity in relation to the creature, then we will have to see at the same time that this activity does not proceed in a straight line and cannot be exhausted by our logic, but reveals the strongest of tensions. We need only to mention the relationship between God's mercy and God's righteousness. Intellectually to incorporate into one concept what appears as paradoxical is not the solution. If, for example, we wanted to merge into one concept God's mercy and his righteousness, in a purely intellectual process, by appealing to the fact that God is one, then the cross would be replaced by an intellectual operation. We ourselves, using pure logic, would have discovered that God as one *can* only be merciful *and* righteous, and in a kind of dialectical game we would arrive at what cannot possibly be conceived of dialectically, but which is true only of the fact of the death and resurrection of Jesus Christ. We scarcely need to mention that we certainly cannot conceive of a mixture of the attributes of God which appear to us to be paradoxical. God is not to be thought of as partially merciful or partially righteous!

    a. "Communicable" and "Incommunicable Attributes." As we stated, Protestant Orthodoxy distinguishes in its Reformed tradition between the "incommunicable attributes" *(attributa incommunicabilia, akoinōnēta)* and "communicable attributes" *(attributa communicabilia, koinōnēta)*, in the Lutheran tradition, wherever the same terminology is not used, between "absolute and relative attributes" *(attributa absoluta et relativa)*, "quiescent and operative" *(quiescentia et operativa)*, "internal and external" *(interna et externa)*. The differentiation as such is already found in Thomas.[68] As an example for the Orthodox distinctions we mention the very careful formulations of the Leiden *Synopsis purioris theolo-*

---

67. G. Aulén, *Das christliche Gottesbild . . .*, p. 399.
68. *STh*, I,xiii,6, 7, 9, vol. I, pp. 65–67, 68f.

giae.[69] It understands the "incommunicable attributes" to be those "which in themselves, according to their own pure understanding, are not communicated to the creatures, but in some way only partially and comparatively." The Synopsis speaks of God's "simplicity" (which includes his "unity" and "immutability") and his "infinity" (i.e., his "eternity" and "immensity"). Speaking of the "communicable attributes" it says, ". . . they are of God in such a way that they may also be communicated to creatures, and they may truly be shared by them, and therefore they are said to be analogous on account of the order which they have from God with respect to God and creatures." The Synopsis includes under this category God's "life," "wisdom," "will," and "power." But these also are "peculiar to God" *(Dei propria)* to the extent that they are "transferred" *(traducta)* from the attributes first named—we would say, to the extent that they are comprehended by the former (e.g., the "will" as "eternal will" or "immutable will").

Based upon the presuppositions we have just discussed, we can now say this: It is certainly correct and necessary to speak of God's attributes in two series of statements, because we must speak of God's aseity and God's condescension, of his freedom and of his love, and all of these in unity. But, nevertheless, we can make neither the problem of the transferability of attributes nor such concepts as absoluteness and relativity into the criterion for our differentiations. It will have to be demonstrated that even God's attributes are not necessarily "incommunicable" in his freedom (which the citations from the Leiden Synopsis already indicated). And we certainly will not accomplish anything with the concept "absolute" in relationship to "relative" when we remember that God's "absoluteness" expresses itself in the very act of his self-disclosure and therefore in his entrance into "relativity." We shall have to be content to speak of God's attributes in his freedom and of God's attributes in his love, or, with Karl Barth, of the "Perfections of the Divine Loving" and of the "Perfections of the Divine Freedom."[70]

b. The Christological Basis of the Unity in Duality. The question which now must be dealt with is how we know at all that God in his freedom and in his love, in his "aseity" and in his condescension, is One, that he is in both he himself? Recourse to the argument that God by his very essence is one and that therefore his attributes could not ultimately be in contradiction is not necessarily convincing. Why should not dualism be right after all? Or, why could it not be that God, although he certainly might be One in his own being, would manifest himself to us as "broken," and could be known by us only in the dialectic of freedom and love, of aseity and condescension? In both of these instances, our knowledge of God would not be truly authentic, and we would ultimately be cast into uncertainty. The refuge of a dialectical construction would lack any point of reference, and without it, it would have to devolve into a mere intellectual game. Moreover, as soon as we came into the situation in which we no longer were regarding God

---

69. *Synopsis purioris theologiae* (1624), quoted according to the 4th ed. of 1652, pp. 65 and 67f. (see also H. Bavinck, ed., *Synopsis purioris theologiae disputationibus ("Leiden Synopsis," 1626 & 1652)* [Lugduni Batavorum: Didericum Donner, 1881]).

70. The term "perfections" is taken from Scholastic terminology.

in a dialectical construction or "from outside," but were confronted by him personally ("existentially")—and how else could one even want to talk about God?—the retreat into dialectical games would be closed off to us. We would not even dare to try to appeal, purely constructively, from the one attribute of God to the other or to "save" ourselves with paradoxical formulations.

It is not upon the basis of some construction that we know God as he himself, that is, that in his freedom and aseity he is our God, that he is the One who loves in his sovereignty. We know this solely in the encounter with Jesus Christ. And we do so not by assuming that Jesus Christ is the concept which makes it possible to reconcile elements which otherwise are disparate. He is not a concept, not the extreme point of indifference, not a postulate, not an "emergency concept," without which we would fall prey to dualism. He is "Immanuel," God with us. And he is that because he is the eternal Son of the Father, because God in eternity, God as the God who eternally lives over against himself, is in Christ he-himself and he-for-us, in One. Aside from Christ, we would end up with Pantheism, in which we made out of "God-for-us" a "God" which was in natural continuity with every existing thing and thus was ultimately the being of all being. Or we would have dualism in that we understood God's freedom, his being-in-himself as a being apart from us, and thus ultimately we would arrive at a world which in essence was godless. Wherever the philosophy of religion reveals an exception to this rule, it is through a secularized remembrance of the person of Jesus Christ. Based upon its own assumptions, it will always understand God either as the absolute spiritual element in contrast or even polarity to reality, which is material in some way, or as the Absolute which as meaning or original ground is the basis for our reality.

The self-disclosure of God in Jesus Christ, as it becomes a reality in us and for us in the Holy Spirit, prevents us from permitting the duality of statements to result in dualism. It requires of us that whenever we speak about God in his love, we speak simultaneously of this same God in his freedom, and vice versa. But it does not free us from the necessity of distinguishing God's love and his freedom. Otherwise we could not express the fact that God's love is something other than a kind of higher natural necessity and his freedom is something other than caprice raised to an absolute degree.

2. THE FATHER

After everything which we have discussed thus far, our concern in the next paragraphs can be solely to ask in regard to God's self-disclosure, How is God the loving God? How is he free, sovereign? How is he Lord? He is, we said, always both. But not in such a way that we are to think of both integrated in each other or dialectically related to one another. Therefore, we must make our differentiations and then abrogate them.

a. "Holy Father." God's love is always concrete: his grace, his mercy, his faithfulness, his patience. This is the statement of the Old Testament creed, which appears at one point even in the form of a self-expression of Yahweh (Ex. 34:6–7 [see also Num. 14:18]; Ps. 103:8; Ps. 86:15). The New Testament does not offer a comparable creed, but it makes the same statement in various forms in a wealth of references.

It would go beyond the limits of a brief textbook if we wanted to interpret dogmatically the various terms mentioned in their biblical sense. There are two factors which are of major significance for us:

1. All of these attributes can be summarized in the one word "Father."

2. They all refer to the Father as the "holy" Father (John 17:11), to the "Father in heaven" (Matt. 6:9), and this implies in turn that these attributes are unavoidably accompanied by others which make it clear that God's righteousness, wisdom, and holiness, as attributes of God in his love, belong to his grace, mercy, faithfulness, and patience, as attributes of the God who is our God.

As the God who loves, in his grace, mercy, faithfulness, and patience, God is our Father. This is not a "designation of an attribute" in the customary sense of the word, but a relational concept. And that is significant. The attributes, "the perfections" of God in his love, all imply together this relationship into which God has entered with man. They are concepts of being in that they are relationship concepts. We will ask, first of all, what it means that God is our Father. Then we will ask what the attributes first mentioned mean in this context, that is, as relational attributes.

b. The Old Testament. There are several places in the Old Testament where it is stated that God is the Father (most strikingly Isa. 63:16 and 64:7f., but see also Deut. 32:6; Jer. 31:9; Mal. 1:6 and more indirectly Deut. 14:1; Hos. 11:1; Ex. 4:22). The polemics of Jeremiah 3:4 indicate that the addressing of Yahweh as "Father" was a part of the national faith. The basic understanding of the Father concept seems to have been derived from the idea of the origin. But the relationship is obviously seen as personal too, since in Jeremiah 3:4, Malachi 1:6, and Isaiah 63:16 and 64:8 Yahweh is addressed as Father. It is in any event a clear protest against a naturalized understanding when Yahweh's fatherhood is sharply contrasted with that of Abraham and Israel in Isaiah 63:16. Nevertheless, we must say that the faith in God the Father is not only seldom manifested in the Old Testament but, more importantly, is set within the same brackets which enclose the whole old covenant. Just as the law here is the unfulfilled law, God's fatherhood is, so to speak, unfulfilled. It is restricted to the people to whom the law is given (and to whom Paul also ascribes "sonship" in Rom. 9:4), and it is concealed like the fulfillment of the law and the reality of election. Israel's sonship is proceeding toward the One whom the New Testament calls "the" Son. In accordance with that, the Son terminology has its high point in the Old Testament in the conceptions surrounding the idea of the Messiah (2 Sam. 7:14; Ps. 2:7; 89:27ff.), and the New Testament also reinterprets Hosea 11:1 messianically (Matt. 2:15). Just as the whole Old Testament is oriented toward what is coming, all of the statements about Yahweh as Father are oriented toward the future.

c. The New Testament. The new thing about the New Testament is not that here God is spoken of as Father for the first time. The idea that Jesus replaced a raging Yahweh with a mild Father-God is wrong on two points. The Old Testament already knows of the Father, and the New Testament really knows the "wrath" of God in all its depth. The new thing about the New Testament is not the information that God is the Father, but rather the realization of the fatherhood of God. And this takes place in the One who is the Son. It happens in the One who redeemed "those who were under the law, so that we might receive adoption as sons" (Gal. 4:5). "We"—this was not said by a pagan born outside of the "commonwealth" of Israel (Eph. 2:12) who thus was not a participant in the anticipatory "sonship" of Romans 9:4, but by the born Israelite, Paul. The law stands in the way of the reality of sonship and thus of the effective knowledge of God's fatherhood. For the law "brings wrath" (Rom. 4:15). Man enslaved by the law cannot know God as Father. He must know him either as a partner in a "I give in order that you give" relationship *(do ut des)*, or he must conceive of God as the wrathful God, if the law has its effect. For the New Testament, God's fatherhood and man's childhood (meaning "saved man" and thus including man outside the old covenant) are the supreme miracle. "See what love the Father has given us, that we should be called children of God; and so we are" (1 John 3:1)! The reality of sonship *(huiothesia* means adoption) and thus the realization of the fatherhood of God for man is identical with the justification which is real in Jesus Christ, the crucified and risen One. God's being as Father is an event in Jesus Christ.

If we can say that God's grace, mercy, faithfulness, and patience are all in various ways statements about God's fatherhood, then we must now continue that God's grace, mercy, faithfulness, and patience are all reality for us in the event Jesus Christ. If Orthodoxy could call these attributes the "communicable attributes," then we would now have to say that in Jesus Christ they are the "communicated attributes" *(attributa communicata)*.

3. GOD'S GRACE

The meaning of what we have just said can be demonstrated with the concept grace. The difficult controversy which is found here points out a corresponding divergency in all of the doctrine of God, in fact, in the basic conception of theology in general.

a. Grace as "Attribute," as Behavior or as Gift? In essence, this is a controversy between Roman Catholic and Evangelical doctrine. According to the former, "grace" *(gratia)* is a gift which proceeds from God, is granted to man by means of the Church and its "means of grace," and thereby becomes effective in him. As such, this gift is subject both to expansion and diminishing. According to the Evangelical position, it is primarily "God's goodwill toward us, or the will of God which has mercy on us."[71] Melanchthon refers to the Hebrew concept *chen*, which would have been better translated "favor" than "grace."[72] Luther, in his well-known poetic rendering of Psalm 130, can conjoin "grace and favor." It is only in God's turning to us, stepping to our side in Jesus Christ and bringing

---

71. Melanchthon, *Loci* of 1521 *(LCC,* XIX, 87); Stupperich, II/1, p. 86.
72. *Ibid.*

us to his side through his Holy Spirit,[73] that grace is also a gift. It is never a "something," but it is in the most definite sense one of God's own attributes; it is his own being for us. Protestant Orthodoxy maintained this position in spite of all the other weakening and shifting of the Reformation's basic thrust. So we can read in the late Orthodox Reformed theologian, J. H. Heidegger (1633–98), that "God's grace is His virtue and perfection, by which He bestows and communicates Himself becomingly on and to the creature beyond all merit belonging to it."[74]

b. The Augustinian Heritage. One might well ask who has the early Church or even the Middle Ages more on his side. The Roman Catholic view can be traced back with certainty to Augustine, who firmly asserts that "a gift, unless it is wholly unearned, is not a gift at all,"[75] but who also views grace freely given as the producer of the process of salvation in man. The Reformers knew well that they could not rely upon the highly valued authority of the great African when it came to their doctrine of grace. The question is, Did they have Scripture behind them?

c. Grace as Act. They would certainly not have had it behind them if they had understood grace as an attribute in the sense of the "timeless kindliness" of God, which one had not properly recognized and had finally come to see through the Gospel.[76] For the proclamation of grace does not abrogate the pronouncement of judgment, of wrath, but belongs together with it. "This act of grace does not, as it might seem, take the place of God's previous judgeship, but is His gracious dealing precisely as the Judge."[77] That means that grace is not, so to speak, a passive attribute of God (which now and then is transposed into action), but it is an event; it is "a single act."[78] Grace is an event-reality, placed in contrast to the equally actual event-reality of "wrath" and the law which cannot be separated from it (Rom. 6:14f.). The interpretation of the New Testament statements confirms the thesis already advanced above, that God's grace, mercy, faithfulness, and patience are an "attribute" of God in that they bear the character of an event. This event is Jesus Christ. In him the Father is present with us; in him God is turned toward us. Thus, in Paul and elsewhere, grace is also designated as "the

---

73. *Ibid.* (*LCC*, XIX, 88); Stupperich, II/1, p. 87: "But the gift of God is the Holy Spirit himself, whom God has poured out into their hearts. . . . Moreover, the works of the Holy Spirit in the hearts of the saints are faith, peace, joy . . . (Gal. 5:22)."

74. Heppe-Bizer, p. 96.

75. *Enchiridion*, CVII (*NPNF*, III, 272).

76. R. Bultmann, *Theology of the New Testament*, tr. K. Grobel (2 vols.; New York: Scribner's, 1951–55), I, 288.

77. *Ibid.*, p. 289.

78. *Ibid.*, p. 289: ". . . a single deed [or, "a unique deed"—TR] which takes effect for everyone who recognizes it as such and acknowledges it (in faith)—'grace' is *God's eschatological deed.*" We shall refer to this shortly.

grace of Jesus Christ,"[79] and according to Acts the Gospel is the "Word of grace" (Acts 14:3; 20:32; see also 20:24). This is the heart of what the Reformers wanted to say. When they understand God's grace as his forgiving "benevolence," they are not thinking of a timeless and passive attribute, but of an attribute of God which is really an event in the person and work of Jesus Christ.

d. Grace as an Act of God in Christ. Therefore, we may not understand grace as an "otherworldly," "objective" attribute of God, which only enters into the "subjective" sphere through additional events. Grace has really "appeared," it is present in an epiphany (Tit. 2:11; see also 3:4), in the epiphany of Jesus Christ. It is not an inner process in God (although we may certainly say that its essence is found in God's eternal love), but an event in relationship to man. When we keep in mind the bodily, historical, and concrete character of this event, we will not be surprised that grace in the New Testament is really "with man," just as Jesus Christ is—and to the extent that he is. If it is God's grace in him, then it is God's grace with us. For this reason, and based upon this foundation, the New Testament can speak of this grace in such a way that it appears as a gift. It can "abound" (Rom. 5:15, 20); it can be what the believer is called to (Gal. 1:6), and from which he is not to fall away (Gal. 5:4); it can take on a special form, as in the person of the Apostle (see Rom. 1:5—plural!; Gal. 2:9; Eph. 3:2, 7, 8); it can even work in the sense of what is otherwise called "charisma" (Eph. 4:7). Grace is not transcendent but "transeunt" (crossing over). It is not, however, separate from the person of the One in whom God has established his act of grace, but, as Paul so often puts it, "in him."[80]

The Roman Catholic Church does not err in its understanding of grace in that it conceives of grace being with and effective in man. But it does so in that it places God at a distance from grace, that is, it does not see grace alone in Jesus Christ, but seeks to place it in analogy with "nature," derived from Christ and mediated by the Church, whereby nature is surpassed and perfected by grace, but is not understood as a completely different category or dimension in contrast to grace. The much discussed Thomist proposition that "grace does not elevate (reduce), but (presupposes and) perfects nature" is theologically untenable only in that it sets grace in a direct analogy to "nature" and deprives it of the character of an event which is founded solely in God himself and is real solely in Jesus Christ. The proposition is not incorrect in a completely different sense, that God assumes the misery of his creature,[81] that he in his patience does not destroy but preserves what he has created. Then it does not express an analogy of nature and

---

79. Here we are thinking chiefly of the liturgical formula, "the grace of our Lord Jesus Christ," which is found in a variety of versions: Rom. 16:20; 1 Cor. 13:13; Gal. 6:18; Phil. 4:23; 1 Thess. 5:28; 2 Thess. 3:18; Philem. 25; Rev. 22:21; and 2 John 3. Is this basically a Pauline phrase? We would also refer to 1 Cor. 1:4; 2 Cor. 8:9; Gal. 1:6; 2 Thess. 1:12; 1 Tim. 1:14; 2 Tim. 1:9; 2:1.

80. For grace as "power," see Bultmann, *op. cit.*, I, 289ff. The concept of the "transeunt" attribute of God is found occasionally in A. Ritschl, "Geschichtliche Studien zur christlichen Lehre von Gott," *Gesammelte Aufsätze* (2 vols.; Freiburg and Leipzig: J. C. B. Mohr, 1893–96), II, 94ff. and *passim*.

81. K. Barth, *CD*, II,1, p. 411.

grace, but would be understood on the basis of the fact that God has established the event of his grace not in destruction but in the new relationship to himself granted to his creature, and thus in confirmation of his otherwise imperceptible creatureliness, in the One who was and is "true man." If one wanted to find a continuum between nature and grace within which one could speak of an "analogy," then it could only be the continuum of divine patience and divine faithfulness, which would certainly not be an ontic one but purely a continuum of grace! But the famous Thomistic thesis is basically not meant in that way!

e. Mercy, Faithfulness, Patience. What holds for God's grace can likewise be said of his mercy, faithfulness, and patience. Each of these predicates expresses in its own way God's love. But they really do it "in their own way." We speak of God's grace because God's love is manifested as the love of One "unconditionally superior to the unconditionally inferior," as the love of the Creator to the creature. We speak of God's mercy because this creature, to which God turns, is "in a position of needy distress and misery."[82] We speak of God's faithfulness to the extent that God's love is disclosed to fallen man, who has broken the covenant, and yet this love places man in his "lost" time under the reality of "fulfilled" time.[83] We speak of God's patience, because God in his love grants to this very creature time and space next to himself, and as the "other" in contrast to him "does not suspend it and destroy as this other but accompanies and sustains it and allows it to develop in freedom."[84] This fourfold statement belongs together, but there is good reason for its being fourfold. God in his love turns to the creature the way he is in reality, and God does not scorn becoming truly involved with this creature, but nevertheless in his love God shows himself to be absolutely superior to all the creature's subjection, need, faithlessness, and even its relative independence.

f. God's Reaction? It is not surprising that a doctrine of God which wants to make its theme God in himself will have little idea of what to do with these attributes. It is clearly the case that these very attributes in which God becomes involved in his creature appear to be abstractly irreconcilable with the immutability of God which is so energetically asserted by that type of theology. For one thing, God is virtually ascribed "affects," we might say "reactions" to another being, the created being. How can such reacting on God's part be harmonized with his immutability, or with the fact that he is also called "the pure act" (*actus purus*—incidentally, this is to a certain extent quite legitimate)? Barth refers to Schleiermacher, who cannot bear the fact that dogmatically mercy is ascribed to God, because it is usually understood as a "state of feeling specially evoked by the sufferings of others and finding outlet in acts of relief,"[85] and who therefore

---

82. K. Barth, *CD*, II,1, p. 408.
83. Our language follows Karl Barth. See also O. Weber, "Die Treue Gottes und die Kontinuität der menschlichen Existenz," special edition of *Evangelische Theologie* for Ernst Wolf (1952), pp. 131ff., and in *Gesammelte Aufsätze* (Neukirchen: Neukirchener Verlag, 1967), I.
84. K. Barth, *CD*, II,1, p. 410.
85. Schleiermacher, *ChrF*, §85, I,1, p. 353; see also par. 83,3, p. 344.

considers this manner of speaking "more appropriate to the language of preaching and poetry." Barth states rightly, "The source of the feeling of sheer dependence has no heart."[86] But then, the absolute Being, the *ens realissimum* (most real being), even the *summum bonum* (supreme good) has no heart. In all these instances it is God per se, God's "sheer essence" *(nuda essentia)*, which is being thought of, and not God in Christ. But if we are talking about God in Christ, then we need hear neither anthropomorphic nor (as here) anthropopathic forms of expression.

4. GOD'S RIGHTEOUSNESS

a. The Righteousness and Love of God. We have just discussed what it means that God is our Father and have presented the predicates which are summarized in this designation of and address to God. But our task is not yet concluded. We must constantly keep in mind that God in his love is he himself. It is only because his love is not something alien to his own essence, but rather is his essence, that our salvation is included in it. Because his grace is *his* grace, it is "salvation" (*sōtērios* [Titus 2:11]).

But if then God in his love is he himself, this means that in that love he is the Righteous One, the Wise, the True, the Holy—he is the Holy Father (John 17:11), the Father in heaven (Matt. 6:9). His love is not powerless or unstable, but in it he is *God*.

If we view God's righteousness, wisdom, truth, and holiness as "perfections" of his love, we are following along the lines of older and newer tradition,[87] but primarily we are thinking in terms of the comprehensive new approach to the theology of God developed by Karl Barth.[88]

---

86. *CD*, II,1, p. 370. On the whole section see E. Brunner, *Dogmatics*, I, 266ff.; and A. Vilmar, *Dogmatik; Akademische Vorlesungen*, ed. W. Piderit (Gütersloh: C. Bertelsmann, 1937² [g1874]), I, 190ff.

87. For Reformed Orthodoxy see the *Leiden Synopsis* of 1652, p. 71, which ascribes God's "good affects" *(affectus boni)* to the "communicable attributes," and lists in one breath "truth, love, goodness, kindness, charity, beneficence, mercy, longsuffering, wrath, hatred, righteousness and holiness." Further, Heppe-Bizer: "God's holiness is manifested generally as perfect kindness and love and as perfect righteousness" (p. 95, a systematizing judgment). Of the Orthodox Lutherans, J. Gerhard mentions both "goodness" and "righteousness" as "imitable attributes" *(attributa imitabilia)* but also as "essentials," common to the whole Trinity (*Loci communes theologici* [1610ff.], ed. F. R. Frank [1885ff.], I, 296), and J. W. Baier speaks of "holiness, justice, truth, goodness" as "positive attributes" (*Compendium Theologiae positivae*, in Schmid, pp. 128f.). Of the newer theologians we mention E. Böhl especially, who regards as attributes of God "in a more narrow sense," meaning "those which reveal God to us as our God," love, righteousness, and holiness (*Dogmatik, Darstellung der christlichen Glaubenslehre auf reformirt-kirchlicher Grundlage* [Amsterdam: Scheffer, 1887], pp. 61ff.).

88. Barth couples God's grace and holiness, his mercy and righteousness, his patience and wisdom. This very impressive structure cannot be explained in a brief overview. Barth certainly did not intend to develop this couplet structure for any other reason than for the sake of theological transparency. An actual division of the attributes of God is not conceivable. Therefore every ordering has the actual intent of making indivisible (yet distinguishable) factors evident. That is also the purpose of our presentation.

How is it possible to regard God's righteousness or his holiness as a "perfection" of his "loving"? How can there be unity here when we would tend to see contradictions or at least extreme tension? In order to answer this question, we shall turn again to one of the attributes already mentioned (just as we tried above to understand God's grace), namely, the righteousness of God. The problems which emerge here are similar to those we find in connection with God's holiness, truth, and wisdom, and if we can arrive at a solution here, then it should be applicable to all the rest.

b. Righteousness as a Compensatory Function? The current understanding of righteousness is best expressed in the *Institutes* of Justinian I (483-565): "Justice is the constant and perpetual wish to render every one his due."[89] The concept of "rendering every one his due" is a watchword which calls forth a response everywhere and has become the epitome of a lofty view of the state. The roots of this concept of righteousness go back both to Greek antiquity and to the Old Testament, in different fashions. For the Greeks, the concept *dikē* (justice) serves as the orientation point for their thinking—*dikē* as that which is established, the norm, which works as the power of compensation; and therefore in its personified form (Dike as the daughter of Zeus and Themis) it is almost "vengeance," which no evildoer can avoid. The *dikē* becomes concrete in the legal system of the *polis* (city-state). Since man, according to the Greek understanding, has his existence in the *polis*, his conformity with the law is simply the foundation of his existence. In the language of philosophy this would mean that righteousness (i.e., conformity to *dikē*) is the way in which man achieves his proper existence (this is the sense of Plato[90]), or it is "virtue" to the extent that man has and expresses in it his inner harmony (so Aristotle[91]). This all leads up to an understanding of righteousness as *habitus* (condition, disposition).[92] If in these terms one wanted to say that God is righteous (or just), this would have to mean that God is the principle of compensation, of retribution. Basically this would mean either that he is the principle of vengeance or he is the guarantor of the legal order found in the *polis* and providing man his existence. In any event, God's righteousness would be something explicitly formal, virtually functional.

c. The Judge. There is in the Old Testament one group of statements which can be compared to a degree with the Greek understanding of righteousness. Here, Yahweh is the righteous Judge (Ps. 7:11; 9:4, etc.). It is even regarded as a work of Yahweh's goodness that he does "requite a man according to his work"

---

89. *The Institutes of Justinian*, tr. Thomas Collett Sandars (London: Longmans, Green & Co., 1888[8], Liber Primus, Tit. I, D. i. 1. 10.), p. 5.
90. Plato, *The Republic*, IV, 443 (*GBWW*, VII, 354f.).
91. *Nicomachean Ethics*, V (*GBWW*, IX, 376ff.).
92. On the whole theme, see the article on *dikē* by Thalheim, in G. Wissowa, *Pauly's Real-Enzyklopädie der classischen Altertumswissenschaften*, ed. W. Knoll (Stuttgart: Metzlersche Buchhandlung, 1912), V, cols. 574–80; W. Jaeger, *Paideia, the Ideals of Greek Culture*, tr. G. Highet (3 vols.; New York: Oxford University Press, 1945), I, 102ff.; and the article on *dikē*, etc. in *TDNT*, II, 178–225 (G. Schrenk).

(Ps. 62:12). We should already note here that the New Testament too, most explicitly in Paul, speaks of God as the righteous Judge (Rom. 2:1–11; see also Matt. 16:27; 2 Cor. 5:10; 2 Thess. 1:6–9; Heb. 6:10; also 2 Tim. 4:8). God does not regard the outward appearance (Rom. 2:11); he does not prefer the mighty and does not cast the poor who has right on his side into misery. There are consequences of this for the earthly judge. According to Deuteronomy, the rule for judicial proceedings is that the judges should "acquit the innocent and condemn the guilty" (one should read it in Greek, according to the Septuagint!). Accordingly, Isaiah accuses the evil judges of acquitting the godless (Isa. 5:23), and this procedure is condemned in Proverbs 17:15. Yahweh himself is the One who will hear the pleas of his people, "vindicating the righteous by rewarding him according to his righteousness" (1 Kings 8:32). We note the blunt contrast to this in a passage like Romans 4:5, where God is called the One "who justifies the ungodly."

d. Distributive Righteousness = justitia distributiva. Were we to define God's righteousness upon the basis of what has been said until now, we would have to say that it consisted in his being the avenger who (as it is put in the *Institutes*) has the "constant and perpetual wish" to ascribe to "every one his due." Righteousness in this sense is called "distributive" righteousness, or "vindicative righteousness" *(justitia vindicatrix)* wherever the misdeed is followed by punishment.

"Modern" readers tend to shudder when they read such ideas. They protest that such views of the righteousness of God are "obsolete," "Old Testament" ideas, which cannot be compatible with Jesus' proclamation of the loving Father. They will certainly admit that on earth there must be judgment, under the law in its "political use" *(usus politicus)*. But they would like to have God stay away from such matters.

There is something decisively wrong about this defensive position, which we will not discuss in greater detail. This position fails to see that just judgment is a beneficial act. It acts as an accomplice in the devaluation of earthly justice, which has contributed a great deal to the disintegration of the West. It does not want to admit that the judge is doing a helping work when he judges. He does this not only when he, along the lines of modern jurisprudence, also considers the human situation surrounding an act and the condition of the doer—this is an extension of the principle of "rendering every one his due"—but also when he functions as the "merciful judge" and blunts the sharpness of the sentence which has been passed.[93]

---

93. Regarding the whole problem of justice which is under discussion here, see E. Brunner, *Justice and the Social Order*, tr. M. Hottinger (New York: Harper, 1945); Jacques Ellul, *The Theological Foundation of Law*, tr. M. Wieser (Garden City, N.Y.: Doubleday, 1960); H. H. Walz, ed., *Gerechte Ordnung, 4 Vorträge* (1948; n.l.); H. Brunotte, ed., *Kirche und Recht; ein vom Rat der evangelischen Kirche veranlasstes Gespräch über die christliche Begründung des Rechts* (Göttingen: Vandenhoeck & Ruprecht, 1950); especially the lectures by E. Wolf and U. Scheuner: Erik Wolf, *Rechtsgedanke und biblische Weisung* (1948; n.l.); H. E. Weber and E. Wolf, *Gerechtigkeit und Freiheit* (*Theologische Existenz heute*, N.F. 18; Munich: Kaiser, 1949); H. Coing, *Die obersten Grundsätze des Rechts; ein Versuch zur Neugründung des Naturrechts* (Heidelberg: L. Schneider, 1947); H. Coing, *Grundzüge der Rechtsphilosophie* (Berlin: W. de Gruyter, 1950); see also the material and good articles in

e. God's Righteousness as Saving Activity. In spite of everything, the aforesaid dislike of the concept of "distributive justice" is not wrong in a certain sense.
It is not wrong if it is not merely the result of a sentimental aversion to the law
but is derived somehow from the insight that it would not be easy biblically to
conceive of God as the high court of judicial appeal. To do so would be to understand him in an exaggerated analogy to the maintenance of this "distributive
justice" which is entrusted to earthly jurisprudence.

In fact, the biblical witness to the righteousness of God does not in essence
follow this course. We can view this from various sides.

1) **Righteousness as Covenant-Conformity.** In the Old Testament God's righteousness has a clear relationship to God's covenant. God is not righteous in and
of himself, but he confirms his righteousness in that he is and acts in conformity
with his covenant. A. Ritschl (with whose opposition to "distributive justice" we
shall have to deal) defines righteousness according to the Old Testament as "the
consistency of God's providence [Leitung zum Heil], validated on the one hand
in the existence of pious and upright adherents to the old covenant, and undertaken on the other hand for the community whose salvation would bring God's
government to completion."[94] Ritschl appeals to, among others, Psalm 31:1, 7,
65:5, 143:11, and 51:14— all of those passages in which Yahweh's righteousness
is understood in the sense of his helping intervention. That presupposes that
Yahweh is not righteous in the sense of abstract retribution but that his righteousness consists of his assuming the burden of his chosen people and thus also the
burden of the individual within that people who is threatened. Because this is so,
Yahweh's righteousness is a source of comfort to the pious member of the old
covenant. Quite clearly, it is not something which God possesses "for himself"
or "in himself"—we have encountered this thought before. Rather, it consists in
the fact that he is "right" in terms of the covenant which he has established and
to the degree that he is and does "right" by man whom he has chosen; it is
"transeunt" righteousness!

2) **Righteousness as the Deliverance of the "Wretched."** Those who place
their confidence in Yahweh's righteousness in the Old Testament are not the
mighty nor those who stand in high public regard, but primarily the "wretched,"
those who are sorely tried, whose right is espoused by no man. The position of
the poor in Old Testament proclamation indicates that the concept of retribution
is not the dominant one. For its result would be that things would "go well" for
the "righteous" and vice versa. The further consequence would be that the poor
and ill would always be marked with the stigma of having committed hidden sin—
otherwise things would go "well" for them, too. The lamentations of the sick and

---

the ecumenical study booklet "Die Treysa-Konferenz 1950" (Geneva: 1950). The newer
debate was stimulated primarily by Karl Barth, *Rechtfertigung und Recht* (Zürich: E.V.Z.
Verlag, 1938, 1970[4]).

94. "Instruction in the Christian Religion," in *Three Essays*, tr. P. Hefner (Philadelphia: Fortress Press, 1972), par. 16, p. 227.

the accused in the Psalms and especially in Job reveal that this retribution pattern was very much a part of the folk culture. But it is just as clear that the Torah, even more so the prophets, and finally the Book of Job all battle against this popular view. The fact that Yahweh is on the side of the poor reveals that, although he is a judge, he is certainly something completely other than a mechanically working principle of retribution.

3) **Eschatological Righteousness.** Therefore, God's righteousness cannot be deduced from our available evidence. It is not a principle which has its automatic effect. This is true of both the individual and the people. For the individual, this can mean that he, like Job, expects God to be his advocate through death and beyond (Job 19:25-27), or like the author of the 73rd Psalm, he has Yahweh as his portion and God as his strength even when his flesh and his heart fail (Ps. 73:26). The righteousness of God is thus seen to be "eschatological." In accordance with that, in the Messianic expectation the realization of righteousness moves into the foreground (Isa. 11:4: "with righteousness he shall judge the poor . . ."; Isa. 9:7: the Messianic ruler governs "with justice and with righteousness"; Jer. 23:5: the Messianic office is the establishment of "justice and righteousness"; 23:6: the Messianic name is "The Lord is our righteousness"). These eschatological expectations are already shifting from the individual to the nation. Just as the helping act of God in the period of the Judges was his "just rule" (Judg. 5:11), in the age of salvation according to Trito-Isaiah his "righteousness" will be revealed (Isa. 56:1). Hosea expects righteousness for the people of the age of salvation as the dowry of its God (Hos. 2:19), and according to Deutero-Isaiah, the acclamation of the new nations will be, "Only in the Lord . . . are righteousness and strength" (Isa. 45:24), just as the Servant of God is there to "bring forth justice to the nations" (Isa. 42:1). The coming King is both "triumphant" and "humble" (Zech. 9:9). His righteousness is virtually the same thing as his salvation—and "salvation" is the same thing as God's righteousness. We can see how much these terms have become interwoven when we remember the translations used by the Septuagint, which often rendered *chesed* (favor, lovingkindness) and *'emeth* (trustworthiness, faithfulness) with *dikaiosynē* (righteousness), and at one point *tsedaqah* (justice) with *eleos* (compassion, mercy), and following the sense of the basic Hebrew text attached attributes to *dikaiosynē* like *sōtērios* (saving), *sōtēr* (savior), and *sōtēria* (salvation).[95]

We are very far here from "distributive justice" or "vindicative justice."

4) **Hidden Righteousness in the Old Testament.** We have seen so far that the Old Testament understands God's righteousness as his conformity to the covenant whose realization is expected in the future. There is one boundary which is never crossed over here: both the nation and the individual expect in connection with Yahweh's eschatological act of judgment that a "righteousness" will emerge which is already present among men but not yet humanly recognized. The pattern of

---

95. G. Schrenk, article on *dikaiosynē*, in *TDNT*, II, 195f.

retribution does persist broadly, in the direct sense of the personal quality of the pleading man or the expectant people. This is seen most clearly in Psalm 73 (vv. 17-20). But it can also be seen in the Job discourses (e.g., 27:2, 6; 13:3). And certainly the expectation of a dreadful judgment over the Gentile nations demonstrates the boundary of which we are speaking here. Yahweh asserts the right of his people with mighty acts of demonstration. Late Jewish Messianic dogmatics even further emphasized this element. And it is this theme which Paul is thinking of when he says of Israel that it does not acknowledge the righteousness of God because it seeks to establish its own (Rom. 10:3). There is no question that we are standing here at the limits of the old covenant. From the perspective of the New Testament we must say about the righteousness of God what we already had to say about his fatherhood. It is concealed in the old covenant, concealed in the unfulfilled law, whose non-fulfillment is expressed in the fact that it is not recognized in its full depth and that the covenant of which it is a part is still hidden under what one can call Israel's "religion." Of course, if we think of Deutero-Isaiah and Trito-Isaiah, then we must say that the Old Testament does reveal other aspects. These other aspects are completely clear in Psalm 51, but also in the statements about the new covenant in Jeremiah 31. The "veil" which is spoken of in 2 Corinthians 3:12ff. was transparent enough that the New Testament message was not merely the surpassing of the Old, but in this regard could appeal to the Old.

5) The "Righteousness of God" in Paul. What then does "righteousness of God" mean in the New Testament? With the exception of Matthew 6:33, James 1:20, and perhaps Matthew 3:15, the concept is limited to Paul. In its Pauline formulation it has been most puzzling to both exegesis and dogmatics in every age. There are places where it certainly means the righteousness which proceeds from God (Rom. 10:3; see also Phil. 3:9). But Romans 3:26 shows that the "righteousness" which proceeds out of God results from his being righteous. "At the present time" God's righteousness is being proven in the sense that he is righteous and justifies those who live in faith in Jesus. Romans 3:5 and 3:21, 22 are to be understood in the same sense. Romans 1:17 should be understood in the same sense where, similar to 3:26, the revelation or unveiling of the righteousness of God is discussed, which happens in the Gospel. But what kind of righteousness is this? It is the kind which is turned toward faith ("from faith to faith"—1:17). And the One in whom this faith is placed is the One who justifies the ungodly (4:5), who does literally the opposite of what is righteousness according to the Old Testament.

f. The Reformation Understanding of the justitia Dei=Righteousness of God. There would be no problem here at all, if the theme in the passages mentioned were the mercy of God. It would be conceivable that the Gospel is a message of grace. But a Gospel which reveals God's righteousness?

The problem here was seen even before Luther.[96] From the dogmatic point of view, it would also be there even if the term "mercy" really were found in 1:17. Then we would have to ask how God could be both merciful and righteous. This question was left open by the Old Testament. It knew something about God's forgiving goodness, and it even knew that God proved his deity in withholding his judgment (Hos. 11:8-9). It pointed in the direction in which the unity of righteousness and mercy as a reality was to be sought, in the direction of the new covenant, of the age of salvation in the sense of Deutero-Isaiah. But according to Paul, it is not until the Gospel that the "revelation" of God's "righteousness" is effected. How can this be stated so? The solution which Augustine offered was that the "righteousness of God" in 1:17 was not an attribute of God but a gift "which is placed in man." This is only half correct, as Romans 3:26 shows (incidentally, this half-truth is exactly the same as the one in Augustine's doctrine of grace). The most significant attempt at a solution of the problem before the Reformation was that of Anselm,[97] who has God's mercy proceed out of his righteousness, in that he regards God's goodness and his "justice" *(aequitas)* as the crown of his righteousness. This thought avoids a weakening of the seriousness of God's righteousness only when *Cur Deus homo* is read with it. For there, God's forgiveness is a truly salvific act because it is based upon the real removal of man's unrighteousness.[98] Luther penetrated even deeper when he[99] learned to contrast what he regarded as the traditional interpretation of the righteousness of God as "formal and active, in which God is just and punishes sinners and the unjust," with what amounts to the fundamental discovery of the Reformation, the concept of "passive righteousness" *(justitia passiva*; a term not used throughout, incidentally), "in which God justifies compassionately by faith." It could be thought that Luther did not go beyond Anselm in this position. But Luther contrasted the righteousness of God to the "righteousness of the law" in a way very different from Anselm's. He taught that it should be regarded as the "righteousness of the Gospel" *(justitia evangelii)*, that is, as the righteousness given in Christ and offered to us. The other Reformers, particularly Calvin, followed Luther in this.[100]

Wherever the Reformation understanding, the righteousness of God in Christ for us, is not dominant, there regularly the attempt is made either to uphold God's righteousness by weakening his mercy or to uphold God's mercy by weakening his righteousness. The former approach (the weakening of mercy) was taken

---

96. See K. Holl, "Die justitia dei in der vorlutherischen Bibelauslegung des Abendlandes," in *Festgabe für Adolf von Harnack* (Tübingen: J. C. B. Mohr, 1921), pp. 73ff.; also in *Gesammelte Aufsätze zur Kirchengeschichte* (3 vols.; Tübingen: J. C. B. Mohr [Paul Siebeck], 1928-48; and Darmstadt: Wissenschaftliche Buchgesellschaft, 1948-65), pp. 171ff. The decisive passage in Luther is the "Preface to the Complete Edition of Luther's Latin Writings" (1545) (AE, XXXIV, 323ff.).

97. "Proslogion," IX-XI, in *St. Anselm*, tr. S. W. Deane (La Salle, Ill.: Open Court Publishing Co., 1962²), pp. 14-19.

98. *Cur Deus homo*, I, 12-24, pp. 203ff.

99. See n. 96. Further, see especially Luther's exposition of Psalm 51 (XII, 303ff. and *passim*; especially I, 329ff. and XIV, 390ff.).

100. See especially *Institutes*, III, xi, 4ff., pp. 728ff. (". . . we are reckoned righteous before God in Christ and apart from ourselves" [p. 729]).

broadly by Scholasticism and here and there in Protestant Orthodoxy.[101] In Scholasticism God's righteousness was brought into harmony with his mercy merely by man's self-assurance that God in his righteousness was the rewarder, the One who gave wages for those works which man could do under the stimulus of infused grace.[102] As for Orthodoxy, God's righteousness (as pure "distributive justice") appears to be satisifed through the "merit of Christ" which is supposed to be objectively conceived of, but it no longer becomes clear to what degree God's righteousness itself bore the work of reconciliation. The other option, that of weakening the righteousness in favor of God's mercy, is found wherever righteousness was understood in the Stoic sense as "equity" (aequitas) and thus robbed of its breadth.[103] This is also found in A. Ritschl, who completely rejected the idea of "distributive righteousness"[104] and merely encouraged the view that God was "the loving Father" "without any further ado."

g. The Cross and the "Righteousness of God." What then is to be said about the concept of "distributive righteousness"? First of all, it is impossible to interpret it out of the biblical witness. The passages we have already cited cannot be deprived of their weight, and there are many more which could be added to

---

101. See the Leiden Synopsis (1652): "Righteousness, which disposes all things justly, both distinguishes rewards to the just and punishment to the wicked, and desires to render retribution, and does so efficaciously" (p. 71). Here obviously God's righteousness is viewed solely as "distributive righteousness" and interpreted in this way. Similarly, in a Lutheran position, A. Quenstedt: "The righteousness of God is the summary and the immutable rightness of the divine will, requiring from the rational creature that which is right and just. And it is even the remunerator by which the good receives rewards and the vindicator by which the evil receives punishment" (*Theologia didactico-polemica* [Wittenberg: 1685]), I, viii, 35, p. 292. In a similar manner A. Vilmar, who does see in the righteousness of God precisely "the other side of His holiness and His love" (*op. cit.*, p. 227), but for fear of apokatastasis will see only in "vindicative justice" the actual meaning of the righteousness of God (*ibid.*, p. 228).

102. See K. Holl, *op. cit.*, pp. 183, 185f.

103. Righteousness as "equity": in Ambrosiaster (see K. Holl, *op. cit.*, pp. 172ff.), in Anselm, and later in the Socinians (see A. Ritschl, "Geschichtliche Studien . . ." [n. 80 on p. 426], pp. 140ff.); to a degree also in J. Gerhard (see H. Cremer, *Die christliche Lehre von den Eigenschaften Gottes* [*Beiträge zur Förderung christlichen Theologie*, 1, 4; Gütersloh: Bertelsmann, 1897, 1917²], p. 48); then, very clearly in Leibniz (see C. I. Nitzsch, *System der christlichen Lehre* [Bonn: Adolph Marcus, 1829, 1844⁵], p. 178; ET: *System of Christian Doctrine*, tr. R. Montgomery and J. Hennen [Edinburgh: T. & T. Clark, 1949]) and in F. Nitzsch, *Lehrbuch der evangelischen Dogmatik*, ed. H. Stephan (Tübingen: J. C. B. Mohr, 1912³), pp. 464ff.—God's righteousness as *epieikeia* (clemency, graciousness), appealing to Aristotle.

104. *Die christliche Lehre von der Rechtfertigung und der Versöhnung* (3 vols.; Bonn: A. Marcus, 1888–89³); ET vol. I: *A Critical History of the Christian Doctrine of Justification and Reconciliation*, tr. J. S. Black (Edinburgh: Edmonston & Douglas, 1872); ET vol. III: *The Christian Doctrine of Justification and Reconciliation, the Positive Development of the Doctrine*, tr. H. R. Mackintosh and A. B. Macaulay (New York: Scribner's, 1900; Clifton, N.J.: Reference Book Publishers, 1966), *passim*; further, "Instruction in the Christian Religion" [p. 431, n. 94], p. 227: the righteousness of God cannot "be distinguished from the grace of God"; also "Geschichtliche Studien zur christlichen Lehre von Gott" [p. 426, n. 80], *passim*.

them.[105] God's righteousness is the righteousness of the judge. Traditional dogmatics cannot be contradicted at this point. New Testament research has confirmed this for Paul in that generally it understands the concept of *dikaiosynē* (righteousness) "forensically."[106] In view of what we have already discussed, this would mean that God is the Merciful One who creates salvation as the Judge, or better, as the One who executes his legal claim. He does not exercise judgment next to his mercy, but he is merciful in that he judges. His righteousness as a saving eschatological act does not remove his opposition to man's *adikia* (unrighteousness), his wrath (Rom. 1:18), but rather is the implementation of this opposition. The godless, as Karl Barth quotes in agreement with H. Cremer, "is not saved from the hand of God, but by His hand, and by His righteous hand."[107] How so? Are we being referred here to nothing more than a conceptual dialectic which unites grace and judgment and ultimately could lead us to take neither of them very seriously? Or are we being led from the point of the "righteousness of God" revealed in Christ to another, concealed righteousness, which would provide man no assurance at all? Certainly neither of these! We are being directed to the revelation of the righteousness of God which took place in the cross of Christ, which certainly may be understood as the "reality which all other judgments upon Israel, the world and mankind can only foreshadow or reflect."[108] In the Crucified One, God's righteousness is in reality both: the sentence of death and the provision of life, the fatal no and the quickening yes. There is where the Righteous One suffers for the unrighteous (1 Pet. 3:18), there is where the One who knew no sin "for our sake . . . [was] made . . . to be sin . . . so that in him we might become the righteousness of God" (2 Cor. 5:21). Whoever recognizes the righteousness of God on the cross will then also see it as "distributive righteousness." But yet in such a way that God, in the very act in which he carries out his No against our sin, establishes his Yes to sinning man. In that God's righteousness as his wrath "against the sin of the whole human race"[109] is carried out upon the Crucified One, God's righteousness attains its goal. It destroys man's *adikia* (unrighteousness) and reveals itself to be God's engagement on man's side *against* sin and *for* the creature. From our perspective, we cannot distinguish between the creature and his sin. But God can make this distinction, in that, to speak with Paul again, "for our sake he made him to be sin who knew no sin," and thus provided us existence in his righteousness. Paul expresses this in Romans 4:25 when he says of Jesus Christ that he "was put to death for our trespasses and raised for our justification." One can only speak of "distributive righteousness" in terms of the "theology of the cross" *(theologia crucis)*, and of the "righteousness of God" granted to us in the act of justification in terms of the "theology

---

105. K. Barth, *CD*, II,1, pp. 392ff., lists Gen. 2:17; Deut. 27:26; Ps. 5:4f.; Ps. 34:16; Matt. 22:13; 21:18f.; 25:11f., 41f.

106. See R. Bultmann, *op. cit.*, I, 271ff. (forensically and eschatologically); G. Schrenk's article in *TDNT*, II, 204ff. See also H. Cremer, *Die paulinische Rechtfertigungslehre im Zusammenhange ihrer geschichtlicher Voraussetzungen* (Gütersloh: C. Bertelsmann, 1899).

107. *CD*, II,1, p. 383; H. Cremer, *op. cit.*, 1917², p. 49.

108. K. Barth, *CD*, II,1, p. 396.

109. Heidelberg Catechism, Answer 37 (Schaff, III, 319); see also Rom. 3:5-6.

of the resurrection" which cannot be separated from the "theology of the cross." In light of this event at the central point of "salvation-history," we can then say that all of the single events which now and again are seen as God's judgments refer to this one event on the cross, and that all of the effective negation of our lawlessness and unrighteousness which happens in the course of protective justice is to be understood on the basis of this one event of resurrection.

Therefore, God's righteousness is to be understood as the conformity of God's being and acting, revealed in Jesus Christ, to the covenant which he has established in love and freedom, as it is carried out as "distributive righteousness," as God's effective negation of sin, and as unrighteousness to Jesus Christ, and as it is authentic and authoritative reality as God's gracious Yes to the sinful and reconciled creature in the resurrected Christ.

h. God's Wisdom, Truth, and Holiness. We have attempted to make clear what can be said about God's righteousness, truth, wisdom, and holiness as attributes in his love by dealing with the first of these concepts. We would come to similar results if we were to apply the same procedure to the other concepts. The concept of the wisdom of God refers us to the "decree" *(decretum)* of God, and thus to predestination, which we are to understand in turn as election in Christ (Eph. 1:4). If we are proceeding from a doctrine of God "in himself" or "per se," then election can only be understood as an "absolute decree" *(decretum absolutum)* and thus as the decision of an "absolute God" *(Deus absolutus)*, and such a view must lead to a misunderstanding of the meaning of the biblical witness. With the concept "truth" we mean God's standing by his word, the validity and finality of his revelation. Again, there is no other way we can speak of this except in terms of Jesus Christ. How should we express God's "veracity" and truth other than in relation to the One who is the Truth. With the term "holiness" of God, we mean God as the "Holy One of Israel," God as the One who elects, loves, and affirms the creature even though he is fully free in regard to the creature; we mean "the unity of His judgment with His grace."[110] And how could we do this except by looking to the One whom the New Testament calls "the Holy One of God" (Mark 1:24; Acts 3:14; Rev. 3:7), and in whom the Father as the Holy Father is present to us?

i. The Wrath of God. However, the concept of the wrath of God does require a brief discussion. It is striking that older dogmatics usually does not deal with the wrath of God as an attribute, or does so only secondarily. The question would be what led to that approach. In regard to the Old Testament, we will have to agree with Eichrodt when he says that ". . . wrath never forms one of the permanent attributes of the God of Israel; it can only be understood as, so to speak, a footnote to the will to fellowship of the covenant God."[111] Similar statements may be made of the New Testament. Of course, God's wrath as an eschatological

---

110. K. Barth, *CD*, II,1, p. 363.
111. W. Eichrodt, *Theology of the Old Testament*, tr. J. A. Baker (2 vols.; London: S.C.M., 1961–67 [g1933, 1948, 1961]), I, 262.

event (1 Thess. 1:10; 5:9; Rom. 2:8; 3:5; 5:9 and based on that Rom. 1:18; 1 Thess. 2:16 and Eph. 2:3) is not different from the righteousness of God which is also an event. But we must ask whether it is not really just one side of God's righteousness as an attribute of his love, and to this we would answer Yes. The wrath of God can only be understood as God's real and effective No to sin. Since sin, for its part, is the rejection of the love of God (the law is a commandment of love!), the wrath of God is nothing other than his love turning against its own rejection. It is not, as Ritschl thought, basically a subjective sensibility in the sinner himself, but is God's own "reaction" to sin,[112] the manifestation of the fact that God remains himself even when his love is rejected. It is the manifestation of the divinity of his love toward "the impossible possibility" of man's rejecting God. Whoever rejects God's "distributive righteousness" must also transform his wrath into something subjective. But whoever sees that God's judgmental righteousness attains its goal and conclusion in Jesus Christ knows, too, that he is saved from the wrath (eschatologically understood, taking place at judgment [Rom. 5:9]). But we must also repeat what John emphasizes: outside of faith, outside of Christ, the wrath of God "rests" (John 3:36; see also John 3:18). The removal of "wrath" is not an intrinsic fact but a fact which points toward proclamation.

D. THE FREE ONE

1. HE WHO IS FREE IN LOVE

a. The Predicates of Majesty in Older Theology. It is quite notable that older theology speaks of the "majesty attributes" of God in much greater detail than it does of the attributes of his love.[113] If the sole reason for this had been that older theology was permeated by the incomparability, glory, majesty, and freedom of God in an especially profound way, then we would heartily approve of it. But we can observe that this same older theology, with a lack of concern which astonishes us, can speak of God in himself in his causal-analogous continuity with the creature. We must then conclude that, at least in a secondary sense, the

---

112. It is not at all wrong of E. Brunner to say that God "reacts" (*Dogmatics*, I, 268). See here p. 427.

113. It is by no means only the Reformed Orthodox who may be cited here as examples. To the degree that Federal Theology gained ground among them they liked to speak (as did Calvin) of God's condescension, his accommodation, even of his non-usage of his godly "power" *(dominium)* (especially J. Cameron, *Opera*, ed. F. Spanheim [Geneva: 1659], p. 42, 1; but in explicit opposition to Gomarian Orthodoxy). The stronger tendency, however, is toward the "attributes of majesty." This is also true of Lutheran Orthodoxy. We cite the section titles of the chapter on "The Divine Attributes in Detail" in J. Gerhard: "Of the spiritual and incorporeal essence of God," "Of the invisibility of the divine essence," "Of the simplicity of the divine essence," "Of the eternity of God," "Of the immutability of God," "Of the immortality of God," "Of the infinity of God," "Of the righteousness of God," "Of the omniscience of God," "Of the omnisapience of God," "On the will and freedom to act of God," "On the truth of God," "On the perfection of God," "On the majesty and glory of God," "On the beatitude of God" *(Loci communes theologici*, ed. F. R. Frank [1885ff.], VIII, Loc. II, vol. I, pp. 299–370).

prevailing emphasis upon the attributes of majesty was based upon the fact that, in the theology of God, they dealt with the concept of God "in himself," whereas in the Christology which they then developed they discussed the concept of "God for us." What remained unclear in this approach was the fact that God is the Absolute in his relation to the creature (in the active relativity in which he gives himself to the creature), and that therefore his "absolute" attributes are only such in relationship. The result then was that it was no longer possible to make clear how in effect God, who had been declared to be Absolute, could also be in any kind of "relationship" at all. For example, they were incapable of understanding that God's omnipotence is also his capacity to be weak, that God's omnipresence is precisely his capacity to be present, and that God's eternity is precisely his openness for time.

b. The Heritage of the Areopagite? The attributes of God usually listed here are especially his *omni*potence, *omni*presence, *omni*science, *in*finite wisdom, his *in*finity (eternity), *in*visibility, and his *im*mutability. It is immediately noticeable that the first concepts reflect the "eminent way" *(via eminentiae)* and the latter concepts the "negative way" *(via negationis)* of the Areopagite. The conceptual component which follows each "omni" or "in" appears as an element of perceivable reality. There appears to be something theologically seductive here. It is very easy to be tempted to find out first of all the available meaning of each of these creaturely concepts in our own reality (e.g., "power" or "knowledge"), in order then through either negation or intensification to penetrate to what is the knowledge of an attribute of God. This then returns us to the reservations which we brought up in our discussion of the threefold way *(via triplex)*.

c. A Biblical Critique. It is significant that the Bible is very sparing in the use of words made with "omni-" or "in-." The term *pantokratōr*, which can be translated "almighty," is found in Paul only once (2 Cor. 6:18) in a quotation using the language of the Septuagint; otherwise we find it only in the Apocalypse. Hebrew has no special word for "almighty." But the Old Testament speaks all the more emphatically of Yahweh's concrete power. It does not speculate about what God can do, but it witnesses to what he in fact does.[114] This is generally true.

d. He Who Is Free in Love. The points to be made in this context can best be clarified by turning to three attributes which all raise the same kind of problems and all reveal the inadequacy of a doctrine of God which seeks to make God "in himself" into its theme; we are speaking here of the doctrine of God's omnipotence, omnipresence, and eternity. The decisive thing will always be whether we are speaking of the "attributes of majesty" in the sense that we are dealing with God's "sheer majesty" *(nuda majestas)* or whether we speak of God's attributes in the freedom which he manifests in his love.

---

114. It is characteristic that Ps. 115:3, which Luther translated, "he can do whatever he pleases," really says, "he does whatever he pleases" (RSV).

2. THE POWER OF GOD

a. The Abstract Concept of Omnipotence. When we abstractly consider the concept of omnipotence, we are combining two conceptual components, that of unlimited capacity and that of unrestricted will. The concept of omnipotence has, so to speak, an outward and an inward dimension. It refers to the unrestricted determination of the self and the unrestricted determination of all that is outside of that self.

Is God to be regarded as omnipotent in this sense? It seems obvious that this question must be answered in the negative. God is not power per se. God "cannot" be wicked. He "cannot" be the devil.[115]

b. Absolute Power=potentia absoluta. We can say that God's omnipotence can be nothing other than *divine* omnipotence. In that we are at the mercy of his omnipotence, we are at his mercy as the Almighty. Talk about his omnipotence is only meaningful when we can say who he is. And this kind of talk has a Christian meaning only when we can say that he is *our* God.

This is expressed in the theological tradition chiefly in the thesis that God's power and his will are to be conceived of as a unity.[116] This implies that God's will is to be conceived of as a righteous will, that is, a will which is in conformity with his covenant. If we maintain this undoubtedly correct rule we shall not be allowed to speculate about possibilities of the divine will and of the power of God which are abstractly conceivable but which are shown to be possibilities alien to God in his revelation, and thus are impossibilities. Of course, we shall also have to maintain that God is free in his Godhead, that is, that his will does not obey any foreign will. To that extent, but only that far, we shall have to accept the concept of "absolute power" as valid. But in the modesty which is appropriate to the faith and thus to theology (as the "knowledge of faith," or *intelligentia fidei*), we shall not make the concept of the "absolute" into a super-god as though God would have revealed himself to be such and such but could also become a God which is totally wrapped up in itself. We certainly will not speculate "whether God can make the past not to have been,"[117] "whether God can do what He does not,"[118] or "whether God can do better than what He does."[119] We shall have to leave those impenetrable parts of God (his "adyta") to God. At most, we shall allow (and this only by way of a marginal concept) that God "can do not only

---

115. In spite of its tendency to abstraction, Orthodoxy realized this, of course. Occasionally there are abstract definitions (e.g., Voetius, I, 405: "Omnipotence is the essential property of God by which he can and does effect all things in one and all"). But there is usually some kind of limitation or reservation expressed (again Voetius: "God's power is the infinite and single strength to do all the things which are in harmony with his essence and attributes"). For this and more, see Heppe-Bizer, p. 99.

116. Especially in Calvin (see p. 406, n. 26). In J. Wolleb we read, "The act or being of anything must not be inferred from the power of God, unless will be joined with power" (*Reformed Dogmatics*, ed. and tr. J. W. Beardslee III [New York: Oxford University Press, 1965], p. 40).

117. Thomas, *STh*, I,xxv,4, vol. I, p. 139.

118. *STh*, I,xxv,5, vol. I, p. 139.

119. *STh*, I,xxv,6, vol. I, p. 141.

what he wants, but more than he wants."[120] We can accept this marginal concept because it expresses the fact that God's power is not exhausted in his will as it is revealed to us. But we can only allow such a statement as a marginal statement because, although God's will certainly is infinitely deeper and more comprehensive than we can recognize it to be *(accommodatio!)*, it is never another will than that which is revealed to us in Jesus Christ. This firm conviction is based upon the truth of the fact that God himself has turned to us and that therefore there is in truth faith.

c. God's Activity as the Doing of the Impossible. On the other hand, that rule will prevent us from binding God's power, which cannot be conceived of without his divine will, to whatever we might regard as "possible." As almighty activity, God's activity is free from what we might regard as consistency. Occasionally we find in late Orthodox Lutheran dogmaticians the formula that God's omnipotence is "the divine attribute by which God can accomplish everything that can possibly be done without implying an imperfection (or a contradiction) in God."[121] Apparently this is intended to oppose the idea of "absolute power." But the terminology used is subject to criticism and clearly paves the way for the Enlightenment. What is then "possible" for God? Older dogmatics had provided itself some safeguards here. That which was "impossible" was not defined by "human knowledge" *(scientia humana)*[122] but by the very nature of God[123] as recognized in Scripture.[124] They therefore distinguish between what is "respectively" and "absolutely" impossible *(impossibile respective et absolute)*.[125] But it is very striking that even in J. Gerhard, whom we have been following chiefly here, the actual "impossible" act, which is also the divinely *possible* act, is not placed at the center of attention, namely, the great paradox which represents what is really divinely logical, "God in Christ," "the Word became flesh." Proceeding from another position, we shall constantly fluctuate between the postulate of a God who can do "anything conceivable" (and contradictions are also conceivable) and who is then certainly not reliable, and the postulate of a God who is bound to the rules of the creaturely processes which he may well have established and thus has no freedom over against our knowledge of these rules. There is one fact which stands between a freedom of God which is totally capricious and a self-imposed binding of God to his own work which ultimately leads to God's predictability and his replacement by an idol conceived by our thoughts; this one fact is the basis for the decision about what is possible and impossible. God really does the impossible: he becomes man, he kills death, he justifies the godless—and based upon that, all of his activity is miraculous. And yet this impossible stands under

---

120. J. Wolleb, *op. cit.*, p. 40.
121. D. Hollaz, *Examen theologicum acroaticum* (1707), p. 272, in Schmid, p. 129.
122. J. Gerhard, *Loci communes theologici* (1610ff.), II, 198, ed. F. R. Frank (1885ff.), I, 35. "Those things which imply a contradiction with regard to human capability and knowledge and which thus cannot take place, should not so quickly be considered by us to imply a contradiction with regard to divine power, rendering them impossible."
123. *Ibid.*, p. 336, with an appeal to Calvin and Polanus.
124. *Ibid.*, p. 335.
125. *Ibid.*

the unusual *dei* (it must) of the Bible (Mark 8:31 pars.; Heb 9:26, etc.), that is, under the completely paradoxical assertion that this impossible is not only possible, but necessary!

    d. God's Omnipotence and the Freedom of the Creature: The Middle Knowledge=scientia media. What is then the relationship between God's omnipotence and the freedom of the creature, particularly of man? The context in which this question emerges is the doctrine of the "knowledge of God" *(scientia Dei)*. This, in turn, is connected to the question of the "will of God." God's power is not power per se but the power of his will, which is in turn united with God's knowledge, which precedes all creaturely being and knowing in that it is both unconditional and all-conditioning. The result was that the question of the freedom of the creature, viewed by all participants in the debate as relative, shifted into the context of the doctrine of the "knowledge of God." The so-called classical medieval doctrine had (influenced in part by Aristotle, and in part by Augustine) distinguished especially between God's knowledge of himself and his knowledge of creaturely reality outside of himself.[126] The former is designated "necessary knowledge" *(scientia necessaria)*, to the extent that God is God with divine necessity, and he cannot be Not-God, or only a possible God or nothing at all. This can also be called "simple knowledge" *(scientia simplex)*. The latter is differentiated again, in that one ascribes to God not only the (conditioning, willing, or voluntarily negating) knowledge of what is actually happening *(scientia visionis,* knowledge of what is seen), but also the knowledge of what is merely possible but which he does not accomplish *(scientia simplicis intelligentiae,* knowledge of simple intelligence). The further development of this doctrinal complex, which Protestant Orthodoxy essentially shares with Scholasticism, does not belong in our presentation here. However, the concept of a *scientia media* (middle knowledge), propounded by the Spanish Jesuit Luis de Molina (1535–1600), became most important and had a broad influence.[127] According to it, God knows not

---

126. See Thomas, *STh*, I, xiv, Articles 2–4: God's knowledge of himself; Articles 5–14: God's knowledge of the creature (vol. I, pp. 72–84).

127. Luis de Molina, *Concordia liberi arbitrii cum gratiae donis* (1588) (Paris: Lethielleux, 1876) (*Beiträge zur Geschichte der Philosophie des Mittelalters*; Münster: Aschendorff, 1935), vol. XXXII. This work is a commentary on a number of places in the *STh* of St. Thomas, especially on I,xiv,13. Molina distinguishes between "mere natural knowledge" ("God's knowledge through which he knows all things through which his divine power extends whether immediately or through the intervention of secondary causes"), "free knowledge" ("by which he knows, absolutely and determinately, according to all the contingent circumstances implied, after a free act of his will, without any hypothesis or condition, what will actually take place in the future, although not in the same way"), and "middle knowledge" ("whereby he has seen in his own essence from the most profound and inscrutable comprehension of every free will which will function according to its innate freedom, whether it be placed in this or that or a limitless order of things"). This is the decisive passage (in the Antwerp edition of 1595, p. 227). For a detailed and more extensive discussion of the Molinist Controversy, see K. Barth, *CD*, II,1, pp. 569ff. For the Thomist position, see A. Stolz's commentary on *STh*, I,xiv,13, in *Die deutsche Thomas Ausgabe*, III, 337ff., and F. Diekamp, *Katholische Dogmatik nach den Grundsätzen des heiligen Thomas* (3 vols.; Münster: Aschendorff, 1930⁶), I, 199, and for a more Molinist position, J. Pohle,

only in the sense of "necessary knowledge" of himself and of the infinite number of possibilities which emanate from his rule, and not only in the sense of "the knowledge of what is seen" of the real which he has ordained for this reality, but he also knows what the creature (man) would possibly do under all conceivable circumstances in its own freedom, if these circumstances were to be present. In this aspect, then, God's knowledge is still undefined—the wealth of possible circumstances is necessarily visible to God and he will in his "vision" *(visio)* ordain what will actually develop in the way of circumstances, but in the midst of it all there is the purely hypothetical possibility of human decision which as such is not posited with God's "knowledge," but of course is known by him in advance, in a vague and purely hypothetical way. What Molina wants is clear. He wants to reserve a place for man's freedom of decision without encroaching upon "grace." As the title of his work reveals, he wants to establish the "concordance" of the two. In the Roman Catholic Church, the question as to whether Molina was right, or whether the passionate opposition presented by the Thomists will carry the day,[128] has not been decided up until now.

e. God and Evil. The entire struggle, conducted with the whole armory of Scholastic concepts, is not what is of greatest importance to us, but the question imbedded in it is. The urgency of the issue is indicated by the fact that Molinist ideas were taken over by Lutheran Orthodoxy as well as by the Reformed in some instances. Apparently they are also close to the position of the Reformed opposition group around Moses Amyraldus (1596–1664) of Saumur.[129] It is in the same context that we may understand Luther's hotly debated distinction between *necessitas consequentiae* ("necessity of consequence") and *necessitas consequentis* ("necessity of the thing consequent"; indirect necessity, because it is conditioned by intermediate causes), as he developed it in *The Bondage of the Will*.[130] Even more so can we understand the customary assertion of mere "permission" on God's side, as we find it so emphatically rejected in Luther,[131] in the

---

Dogmatic Theology, God: His knowability, essence, and attributes, ed. A. Preuss (St. Louis: Herder, 1925), pp. 383ff. Michael Schmaus proceeds very cautiously in *Katholische Dogmatik* (5 vols.; München: M. Hueber, 1948ff.), I, 544ff.

128. Denzinger, p. 314 (par. 1090), n. 3, and pp. 316f. (par. 1097).

129. On the Orthodox versions of "middle knowledge" *(scientia media),* see Karl Barth, *CD,* II,1, pp. 573ff., and Heppe-Bizer, pp. 77ff. In reference to the School of Saumur, see the unpublished Göttingen dissertation of J. Moltmann, *Gnadenwahl und Gnadenbund* (1952).

130. Luther, *The Bondage of the Will* (AE, XXXIII, 38f.). Also Melanchthon, *Loci* (1543); Stupperich, II/1, pp. 231f. Calvin makes a more careful judgment in *Institutes,* I, xvi, 9, pp. 208–10. The doctrine itself is found in Thomas, *STh,* I,xix,3, vol. I, pp. 104f. (absolute necessity or by supposition); further in Bonaventure, *In Sent. I, 47 Comm.,* ed. Quaracchi (1882), I, 840: "necessity of consequence or consequent"; Duns Scotus, *Sententia,* I, xxxix, 5, in *Commentaria Oxoniensia,* ed. Franciscans of Quaracchi (1912ff.), I, 1234; see R. Seeberg, *Die Theologie des Johannes Duns Scotus* (Leipzig: Dieterich, J. Weicher, 1900), p. 159. The doctrine is then used by Erasmus against Luther; see Erasmus, *On the Freedom of the Will,* in *Luther and Erasmus, Free Will and Salvation* (LCC, XVII [Philadelphia: Westminster Press, 1969]).

131. Luther, *On the Bondage of the Will, op. cit.,* esp. pp. 184ff.

younger Melanchthon,[132] and in Calvin.[133] The common factor at work in all of this is the desire to ascribe to the creaturely will some kind of autonomy, be it quite small and relative, and at the same time to avoid what appears to be the unavoidable idea that God, if he does precondition the human will in such an all-encompassing manner, is then made into the source of evil or of sin. It is certainly clear that this question does not arise solely in the realm of dogmatic speculation. It can be heard in the accusing question, "How could God allow that," as well as in the frivolous assertion, "God made me the way I am, and if he is omnipotent then he could have prevented the evil which I have done."

f. Omnipotence, Not Omnicausality. The God of whom we have just been speaking is the *causa causarum* (cause of all causes) in his "power," "will," and ultimately in his "knowledge." God and reality are two (unequal) sides of one great ontic context. Two *unequal* sides! For, in the approach we are discussing here, God is regarded as the One who also knows or knew, conditioning all things, everything which was merely possible but never became reality. But there are still two sides here, for both the cause and the effect are located within the same ontic context, within the same "dimension" or "category." Can it then be surprising that the other, the creaturely side in its conditionedness, should demand its rights too, as that other side? Could not the whole structure be turned around? And would anything be changed at all if God himself were simply struck from the context? Is not a God who preconditions everything not himself totally precon-ditioned? Is not the route from the "cause of all causes" to Deism or even more so to Pantheism incredibly short?

One thing should be clear. If God's omnipotence is nothing other than the all-conditioning "power," "will," and "knowledge" of God, then it is not an attribute of God in his freedom, but is rather the forcing of God into the system of necessary laws as we see or presume them to be. And they are then nothing other than the expression of what God "wills"—better, what he basically "must" will or have wanted to will. In that case, it would be a better thing, at least for pedagogical reasons, to persuade man that he really does have his own fate in his hand, or his God in his fist, as Luther translates Job 12:6. But then the question is if it would not be better to say to man that God is dead and he must go his way alone. The conceptual difficulties which the ontological doctrine of God faces

---

132. Melanchthon, *Annotationes in epistulas Pauli ad Romanos et Corinthios* (1522) (*CR*, II, 50). See also H. Engelland, *Melanchthon, Glauben und Handeln* (Munich: Kaiser, 1931), p. 153. Later Melanchthon expressly acknowledges "the permission" (see Engelland, *op. cit.*, p. 419; further material there).

133. Calvin, *Institutes*, I, xviii, 1, pp. 228–31. The concept of permission is already present in Peter Lombard, *Libri Quattuor Sententiarum*, ed. Franciscans of Quaracchi (Ad Claras Aquas: Quaracchi, 1916), vol. I, I, xlv, 6; otherwise it is broadly evident. In Prot-estant Orthodoxy, the Lutherans, following the course of the older Melanchthon, generally spoke of the "permission" of God; the Reformed did too, although with more hesitation. B. Keckermann's formulation is very careful: God desires the permission itself, but not what is then permitted (that is, evil) (*Systema Sacrosanctae Theologiae* [*Opera*, vol. II (Geneva: 1614)], p. 115). The Orthodox generally distinguished between "effective will" and "per-missive will" (*voluntas efficiens et permittens*).

develop, in the form in which they emerge, as a result of the fact that when we assume an ontological analogy between God and creaturely reality, then we cannot decide in which direction this analogy should be thought out. It can be thought out from the direction of God, as Thomism does, and following him, the majority of Reformed Orthodoxy. Within the given context, that is praiseworthy. But it can also be thought out from the direction of man, as Molina and his Protestant followers basically have done—and that is not absolutely impossible.[134]

g. *"Omnipotence" and Salvation Event.* Nevertheless, all of the theologians with whom we are dealing here are theologians of the Church. And we must not ignore the fact that on both sides, in the cloak of ontological concepts and in the transformation which they engender, something is being conceived of which has to do with the God who is proclaimed in the Church. The "cause of all causes" is and cannot be preached. The two sides of this ontic unity cannot be distinguished from one another except through an act of intellectual violence, in order to insure that God's freedom does not abrogate man's, nor man's freedom abrogate God's. But what is the situation if the power of God over the creature is the power of the triune God? What then, if it is true that all things are made "through" Christ and "for" Christ? Then the "continuum" which stands between God and the word is not an unknown third party, namely Being per se, in which both sides participate although in profoundly different ways. No, the "continuum" is present where it can be stated, "Whom the globe cannot contain, He in Mary's womb hath lain." The unity is manifest where God is "in the flesh," where he accepts and takes up the creature.

h. *Power and Free Grace.* Let us put it another way. God's omnipotence is revealed as God's freedom toward the creature in the Son, who did not mount upward from creatureliness but became man in divine freedom. It is revealed to be at the same time the gracious pardoning of the creature in that the Son, as he became man, truly took on this humanity and endured in it up to the end.

It was in the event of the cross that Calvin saw that the idea of God's "permission" was impossible.[135] For, according to the New Testament witness— remember that unusual *dei* (it must be)[136]—the crucifixion is not a permissive act but rather an act of the free will of God which is gracious in its freedom. On the other side of the matter, the resurrection as the act of God in his freedom is then

---

134. M. Schmaus, *op. cit.*, p. 546, finds that the advantage of Thomism over Molinism is that the former is thinking "more from God's direction."
135. *Institutes*, I, xviii, 3, p. 234: "And indeed, unless Christ had been crucified according to God's will, whence would we have redemption?" At the end of this section, Calvin quotes the beautiful statement of Augustine, ". . . so that in a wonderful and ineffable manner nothing is done without God's will, not even that which is against his will" (*Enchiridion*, XXVI, 100f. [*LCC*, VII, 399f.]).
136. See p. 442.

the ground of human, creaturely freedom.[137] From such a point of orientation it becomes impossible to think that God is a kind of competitor of creaturely freedom . . . in every regard. For one thing, it is now impossible to conceive of God and the creature in a causal and thus ontic-mutual relationship to each other. In this central position and based upon it, God is seen in all of reality to be the absolutely superior Lord. He makes himself into the partner of the creature in that he calls it into existence, in that he establishes his covenant with it, in that he takes it upon himself in all its lostness. But it is not ontologically his equal counterpart. And this leads to the other statement that God, seen in this way, is the Lord who has mercy upon his creation. His freedom is the freedom of his grace, and therefore he is not the envier, but the granter of creaturely freedom. In our context this means, first, that it is impossible to speak of any "synergism," of man's or any creature's cooperating with God. For God is absolutely free in the event of his revelation. He is the Almighty in this event and thus in relationship to it. In this sense we should never speak of some mode of God's behavior which would make him appear to be an uninvolved spectator. This is the reason that one must give relative preference to Thomism over its Molinist (and partially Protestant) opponents. This is also the reason that the idea of God's "permitting" evil cannot be accepted, in the form in which it is usually meant. Evil stands under the mystery of divine freedom and omnipotence. But, secondly, proceeding from the central point of orientation we've established, it is no longer possible to think of God as the omnicausal factor, as the epitome of a closed system of interrelationships within which we are located, or as the One whose honor is impugned when man acts in his space and time in the freedom given to him. For God gives freedom in that he reveals himself as the Almighty. Of course, this freedom is here the "freedom of the children of God," the freedom which is granted and may be experienced in the proclamation of the Word. But this is the freedom for which all creation longs, according to Paul in Romans 8:23. And therefore the proclamation of Christ is always the announcement of freedom!

If we may regard the figure of Jesus Christ as the central point from which we may understand God's omnipotence, then this does not mean that we have been given a key for the deciphering of the mystery. God does not become a manageable object by virtue of his self-disclosure. He reveals himself in his mystery. Faith in Jesus Christ does not mean that we can comprehend the course of the world, or our own personal destiny, or above all the dispositions of God's

---

137. See Karl Barth, *CD*, III,3, pp. 147ff.: "What is the value of all our thought and talk about Christ and His resurrection . . . if in face of the simple demand to acknowledge God as the One who does all in all we are suddenly gripped by anxiety, as though perhaps we were ascribing too much to God and too little to the creature, as though perhaps we were encroaching too far on the particularity and autonomy of creaturely activity and especially on human freedom and responsibility?" (p. 147). ". . . It would be a twofold misunderstanding of the grace of God to try to suppose that the overruling will of God involves a kind of absorption and assimilation of creaturely activity into the divine, and therefore a disintegration and destruction of the creaturely in favour of the divine" (p. 149). Then Barth polemicizes against the "bad Christian habit" of "an anxiety complex towards God," which is derived from an impossible concept of freedom—as though human freedom had to be protected against God!

omnipotence. Here is what happens in this faith: what is otherwise impenetrable for us is opened up at one decisive point. God's omnipotence is shown to us as the omnipotence of his free grace. And that is where it really encounters us, we who in our sin have sought to oppose autonomously God's omnipotence, as ones whose own powers have been penetrated and who thus have been led to freedom. The believer will then honor God's omnipotence in all its unfathomable sovereignty. He will not seek to incorporate it into a system and will make no attempt to rob it of its freedom for the sake of the creature's freedom. But he will not find God's omnipotence to be a dark and threatening fate hanging over him, but rather the gracious omnipotence of the One who has "opened his heart" to us in Jesus Christ.

3. GOD'S PRESENCE

Our conclusion was that from the center of the biblical witness a way was opened to the understanding of the omnipotence of God. This center is not a single point, without dimensions, spaceless and timeless, there for itself alone. It is an event in space and time. For that reason, the understanding of the omnipotence of God did not lead us into the narrowness of a single point, but into concrete reality, in view of the fact that God's Son in truth has become man. Our faith does not enable us to postulate the omnipotent rule of God with his own "eyes." But it does make it possible for us, based upon that center which is its source of life, to place our trust, in the breadth and width of creaturely reality, in the one who has revealed himself in that center as the free, almighty, and gracious Lord. It would be especially appropriate for the Church in our day to submit its theology to the witness of Colossians, Ephesians, and 1 Peter, in which we encounter this breadth which is our theme here.

It is into this breadth that the concepts of the omnipresence and eternity of God lead us, again properly understood only on the basis of the center which we have established. These concepts bespeak God as the One who is free in regard to space and to time. They can do this because God has disclosed himself as the free Lord over space and time in the event of the person of Jesus Christ—which was, to be sure, an event in space and time and yet which broke through both space and time. These concepts, however, lose their meaning and lead up to conceptual difficulties if they are understood in ontological terms.

a. "Omni"presence? What is God's omnipresence *(omnipraesentia, ubiquitas, immensitas, infinitas)*? If, according to ontological theology, God is the Being of all being, then he is ontically present in all existence. For what exists cannot be conceived of without the Being in which and out of which it is.[138] Taken as it

---

138. According to Augustine, God "permeates all things" and is "the very creative substance of the world" (*Letter* 187, 11ff. [*FC*, XXX, 229ff.]). We find the same thought in Scholasticism, for example, in Thomas (*STh*, I,vii,2, vol. I, p. 35), "He is in all things as giving them being, power, and operation." We find similar statements in Orthodoxy. Thus, we read in Andreas Hyperius, "By his essence God is everywhere in all things which are created, heaven, earth and everything in them, which receive their being from God . . ." (*Meth. Theol.* [1568], lib. I, p. 141); see also Augustine, *The City of God*, VII, 30 (*NPNF*, II, 140).

stands, this concept is unquestionably pantheistic.[139] God is not, as the Being of all being, the Creator, and at the same time the creation loses its authentic being in that it is only the ontic realization of God—so to speak, the external surface of being. The Christian doctrine of God certainly does not want to lead up to this concept of "God as nature" *(Deus sive natura)* which is so very close at hand. It wants to uphold God's superiority over all being. It also wants to preserve the mystery. Within the given ontological pattern the attempt can first be made to develop the absolute uniqueness of the "presence of God" by a process of differentiation.[140] But above all, the concept of the "immensity" of God makes it possible to express on the one hand God's presence in everything spatial, and simultaneously on the other hand his independence of space, even his spacelessness. God can be "everywhere" because he is "nowhere," viewed from the limitations of the spatial. He is *ubique et nusquam* (everywhere and nowhere).[141]

b. Spacelessness or the Omnispatiality of God? The dialectic of *ubique et nusquam* (everywhere and nowhere), not to speak of the direct declaration that

---

139. E. Brunner, *Dogmatics*, I, 256: If the omnipresence of God is understood "from the metaphysical and speculative standpoint," then "pantheism is practically inevitable." Similarly, August Vilmar, *Dogmatik; Akademische Vorlesungen*, ed. W. Piderit (Gütersloh: C. Bertelsmann, 1874, 1937[2]), I, 205ff.: "The pantheistic omnipresence is an infusion of God's substance into all being." Vilmar also quotes Sebastian Frank, "God, who is the Is of all things."

140. The most influential differentiation of the concept of "presence" was offered by Occamism, in that it provided Luther in his dispute with Zwingli the possibility of distinguishing between three kinds of presence: "There are three modes of being present in a given place: locally or circumscriptively, definitively, repletively . . ." (*Confession Concerning Christ's Supper* [AE, XXXVII, 215]). Local presence applies to everything which is tangibly space-filling, while "definitive" presence applies to something which is present in a "place," but which penetrates its limits (e.g., angels or demons). The third mode "belongs to God alone"; it is "altogether incomprehensible," and "can be maintained only with faith, in the Word" (p. 216). Zwingli, he later goes on to say, errs in that he cannot "conceive of God's omnipresence except by imagining God as a vast, immense being that fills the world, pervades it and towers over it, just like a sack full of straw, bulging above and below. . . ." But God "is no such extended, long, broad, thick, high, deep being. He is a supernatural, inscrutable being who exists at the same time in every little seed, whole and entire, and yet also in all and above all and outside all created things" (p. 228). The basic differentiation here was "taken from Biel" (R. Seeberg, *Textbook of the History of Doctrines . . .*, II, 326, n. 1).

141. Augustine, *The Confessions*, VI, 4 (*NPNF*, I, 91): "For Thou, O most high and most near, most secret, yet most present, who hast not limbs some larger some smaller, but art wholly everywhere, and nowhere in space. . . ." We find the same thought in great detail in Anselm, "Monologium," XXI, XXII, in *St. Anselm*, tr. S. W. Deane (La Salle, Ill.: Open Court Publishing Company, 1962[2]), pp. 73–82. It is found frequently in Orthodoxy, for example. Thus, e.g., Alsted (*Theologica didactica* [1627], p. 68): "The omnipresence of God is that whereby he comprehends all places and all creatures in the matter of one point [or, as if everything were in one place]. God is not a place but contains all places. God is everywhere and nowhere." The fact that God as the Omnipresent is not "localized" *(illocalis)* is also found in the Leiden Synopsis ([1624], 1652), p. 67. Finally, we cite Schleiermacher: "By the omnipresence of God we understand the absolutely spaceless causality of God which conditions not only all that is spatial, but space itself as well" (Schleiermacher, *ChrF*, §53, Thesis, I, p. 206).

God is spaceless, is not suited for banishing the pantheistic danger. It is even less possible to base any statement about God in his revelation upon it. However the concept "space" is interpreted, it always implies in some sense "distance." And then the statement is true that "Non-spatiality means existence without distance, which means identity."[142] Although it is certainly legitimate to speak of God's "immensity," that is, of his freedom toward every "measurement" (mensura), and it is even more necessary to speak of God's inescapability (as it is done in Ps. 139, in Jer. 23:23f., and Acts 17:27), it is just as impossible to use "immensity" as an empty concept for a god who is not really "there" anywhere, in the actual sense. "There is nowhere where God is not, but He is not nowhere."[143] K. Barth is right when he opposes the old games with "everywhere" and "nowhere" by stating that this is to deal with "the lifeless and loveless God of pure human invention" which is "the ultimate secret of all heathen faiths."[144]

The dogmatic tradition has for the most part devoted itself to a distance-less immanence of God in spatial things, or to an equally distanceless existence of God beyond all space, or to the dialectical interplay of both. The reason for this is that generally dogmatics has attempted to conceive of the omnipresence of God without speaking first of the presence of God, of God's existence as "Thou" existence in his revelation. If one proceeds on the basis of a view of God in general, then it is no longer possible to take fully seriously God's presence in his revelation. When this kind of omnipresence is assumed and anticipated, revelation gains the character of an exception or of something not real. God is "in reality" everywhere and nowhere, but in his revelation he can be known especially easily, so to speak! The "revelation" of the God who is omnipresent in the way implied above can only be his passively being discovered, becoming known. That was not the position represented by older theology, but more modern theology since Schleiermacher has in effect drawn this conclusion.

c. God's Presence. If we want to talk about God's omnipresence, then we must start with his presence. God is not "absolute"; rather, he is divinely free in and for the relationship in which he has involved himself with the creature. Talk about God's omnipresence can therefore only mean that God is God in his presence. The relativization of revelation which occurs here means merely the emphasis of the fact that it is God himself who establishes the relationship present in revelation.

God's self-disclosure is his "encounter" with man. This implies the following: it is not just the case that man, to whom God discloses himself, exists spatially, but it is much more the case that God encounters him in this his spatial existence, in the relatedness and distance which is a part of that spatiality. If it were only true that God's revelation were imparted to spatially existing man, then his discovery of God would be identical with the uncovering of a spaceless principle of his spatiality. It would be the discovery of a point of orientation to which

---

142. K. Barth, *CD*, II,1, p. 468.
143. *Ibid.*, p. 471.
144. *Ibid.*, p. 472.

spatially limited man could retreat, the uncovering of an "infinity" which provided man spiritual release. But all of this does not happen in God's revelation. Man does not break through here into infinity, but God breaks in to the closedness of man, into that isolation which expresses itself in modern man in the curiously unbounded feeling by virtue of which man bears the universe within himself, as it were.[145] In this experience, man does not conceive of God in man's place (and at man's time), but God prepares for man the place he has selected and the time he has established. And this then means that God in his revelation is spatial, in a sense which certainly is not capable of being imagined by us. God discloses himself in the concrete encounter at a definite place and at a definite time.

d. God's Presence and Space. The encounter character of revelation is seen in the Old Testament not only in the fact that there is a great number of holy places. but even more clearly in the fact that "ceremonies" were attached to these places. Israel does not seek the "nearness" of its covenant God in the universe, and not in the inward man, but in the places of his revelation, which were retained in both memory and in the tradition. The place of past revelation became the place at which new revelation was expected. Apparently the meaning of such ideas, which impress us as being "monolatrous," is that they express Yahweh's concreteness. It is significant that the development of (fundamental) "monotheism" did not lead to a cultic practice unconnected to any place. We need only to remind ourselves that it was precisely Deutero-Isaiah, who could best be regarded as a proponent of a developed theology of Yahweh-Monotheism, who places "Zion" at the very center of his message. Even Jeremiah, who was such an acute opponent of God's being bound to the temple, did not contest that Yahweh wants to "dwell" in the temple at Jerusalem (Jer. 7:3), which is called by his name (7:10, 14).

If we look at the New Testament, we see that in the One who is witnessed to and who witnesses to himself the Old Testament as the old and unfulfilled comes to an end, and with that the covenant, which was already announced in the Old Testament but which had remained in "the shadows," is now fulfilled reality. The temple, as the place of the revelation of God, belongs to the unfulfilled law. It is now dropped, to be sure. But the Old Testament had already made an effort to ward off any localization and idolization of God connected to the temple (we think of the prayer in 1 Kings 8, which in this regard is thought through with extreme care, of Jeremiah, and of Isa. 66:1ff.). Moreover, it cannot be said that in the New Testament the temple is done away with in favor of a "purely spiritual worship of God," nor that God's revelation now is without a place and time. The precise opposite is true: God himself is here at a highly definite place. He is "in Christ," in whom "the whole fulness of deity dwells bodily" (Col. 2:9), in whom according to God's pleasure "all the fulness of God" was supposed to dwell (Col. 1:19). "Something greater than the temple is here" (Matt. 12:6)! Here is the One from whose "body" rivers of living water proceed (John 7:38, according to the

---

145. Friedrich Gogarten (*Ich glaube an den dreieinigen Gott; eine Untersuchung über Glauben und Geschichte* [Jena: Diederichs, 1926]) carried this out with regard to time.

most probable exegesis). New Testament proclamation does not imply a spaceless revelation, but rather one which takes place unmistakably in its place (and at its time). This is shown most clearly by the author of Hebrews. He does not oppose the special locale (according to 9:23f. a copy of the true holy place) of the old holy place with the spacelessness of something general. He sees the superiority of Christ, who "once and for all" presents himself as the sacrifice, in his appearing for us not in a copied, earthly holy place, but in the original, heavenly sanctuary before the face of God. It could not be expressed more concretely and spatially. We may also mention that the idea of a "heavenly Jerusalem," which is connected with the concept of a heavenly sanctuary (Heb. 12:22), is found in a similar form in Paul (Gal. 4:26). Perhaps the clearest expression of what is meant here is found in the passage which would seem to be asserting the very opposite, John 4:23–25. The theme here is not the spirituality of God which "fundamentally" would obstruct the local worship of God and would only allow a "spiritual" worship. The text speaks of the "hour" which is coming and is come, of the eschatological moment which "renews" the whole "substance of the Church."[146] It speaks of the *pneuma* (Spirit), of God as the Spirit, and of the worshipper who can only worship "in spirit and in truth" when he does so in the One who is Spirit and Truth. In accordance with that, the Samaritan woman responds directly with the confession of Messianic expectation. And Jesus answers her with the dark and mysterious statement, "I who speak to you am he." "The opposite of Jerusalem and Gerizim and all temples made with hands . . . is not the universe at large . . . but Jesus. And the worship of the Father in spirit and in truth is not the undifferentiated worship of a God undifferentiatedly omnipresent. On the contrary, we have only to glance at the way in which the terms 'spirit' and 'truth' are used elsewhere in St. John's Gospel and we shall see at once that it is worship of God mediated through Jesus as the One who makes everything known to us."[147]

God's revelation is local and spatial because it is an encounter. "God is present"—understood properly, this is not a statement without local reference, without any kind of relationship. It is a Christological statement. But in this his revelation, God is *God*. He is not free of his revelation, but he is free in and for his revelation.

e. God's Freedom in Relation to Space. This then means that God is not bound to the place of his revelation. We do not have him under our control in his revelation. The Old Testament expresses this in its repeated polemics against the idolization of Yahweh in relation to the temple. Words which are stating the sheer truth ("This is the temple of the Lord") can become "deceptive words" (Jer. 7:4, 8). The "deception" is that Yahweh is not acknowledged here as *God*. It is similar to the idolatry of the "golden calf" (Ex. 32), where the real drama was not that Israel had fallen away to "other" gods but that the nation had made Yahweh into a graven image (note 1 Kings 12:28; this is where we see the rela-

---

146. A. Schlatter, *Der Evangelist Johannes* (Stuttgart: Calwer Verlag, 1930[1], 1948[2], 1960[3]), p. 127.

147. K. Barth, *CD*, II,1, p. 481.

tionship between idolatry and "locality"). The Old Testament makes very clear that Yahweh is not a "local god," although he certainly is to be sought and can be found at a specific place. (He is just as little a national God; we are reminded of Amos 9:7.) The "house" which they built for Yahweh in Jerusalem was not able to contain him (1 Kings 8:27), and the house that was to be built later would also not be able to do so (Isa. 66:1). For Yahweh cannot be contained, not even by "heaven and the highest heaven" (1 Kings 8:27). His "dwelling" in the midst of his people is "relative."[148] He takes up his abode there in freedom, and he grants this encounter. But his dwelling is not a "permanent fixture." The same is true of the New Testament, but it is deepened there, because it is fulfilled and thus radicalized. God has prepared for us the fulfilled encounter in Christ, and "in him all the fulness of God" dwells (Col. 1:19), the "whole fulness of deity" (Col. 2:9). But this does not alter the fact that the fulfillment is not tangibly at our disposal in him. God is "there" in him in such a way that God is expected together with him. His "being there" is simultaneously something which has not yet come to pass. Our Lord's prayer is directed to the Father "in heaven." The Son of Man, as much as he indeed is "there," is still the One who will "come" "with the clouds of heaven" (Mark 14:62). And the Community, which certainly is "in Christ," and which knows that where two or three are gathered "in his name" its Lord is present (Matt. 18:20), which is also confident in the promise that he is with it "always, to the close of the age" (Matt. 28:20), is the Church which also knows that he is "coming" (see Phil. 4:5). This Church has its "commonwealth" in "heaven," and "from it we await a Savior, the Lord Jesus Christ" (Phil. 3:20). For as certainly as it knows, on the one hand, that Christ dwells in our hearts (see Eph. 3:17), that he "lives" *in* the believer (Gal. 2:20), it is also certain that he "is not here or there" (Matt. 24:23; Luke 12:21; Mark 13:21), and the Church is to "seek the things that are above, where Christ is, seated at the right hand of God" (Col. 3:1). God's "dwelling" in us is truly "real" but it is also "relative." Any direct, uneschatological, unexpectant "deification" of Jesus Christ would be the very opposite of the praise of God in Christ. For God's reality for us *is* his relationship to us, but that is his own relationship, in the full and unique power of his deity.

f. God's Freedom for Spatial Presence. In his self-disclosure, God is certainly not relative in the sense that we could find him "here," but also "there and there" if we wanted to. He is relative to himself. The fact that he is not "there at hand" in spite of the local relatedness of his revelation, but that he desires to be expected in and over this local relatedness is not ultimately based upon his being something universal, without space and time, but upon the very opposite of that. We could say that he has his own "place." The "place" which the Bible (both Testaments) ascribes to him is "heaven," yes, his "throne." But even "heaven" is not able to contain him (1 Kings 8:27). It has been made by God just as has the earth! Obviously, we cannot comprehend heaven, as the epitome of God's invisible creation. The creation which is available to our observation and analysis is "the

---

148. See K. Barth, *CD*, II,1, p. 480.

earth" in biblical terms, and not heaven; it is the visible, and not the invisible creation. But God is also not identical with his invisible creation; he is Lord over all things created. His lordship as he reveals himself to us in his self-disclosure is not his autocratic absence from his creation but rather his sovereign presence in it. If then we may say, again moving into the realm of the purely marginal concept, that God has "space" which is appropriate to him as his own, this also means that this his space is simultaneously what makes space possible; it is the creative origin of the space which he provides for his creation. To put it more pointedly, we could just about say that God is, in the most original sense of the term, in himself and is himself omnipresent. But we only know of this his omnipresence in himself in his self-disclosure as the One who gives space to creation and yet remains unbounded by all spatial limitation in his own freedom. He is not nonspatial (because in himself he is not without distance, but is alive in his unity and tri-unity), neither in himself nor in his revelation. But he is also not bound to created space. His omnipresence is to be understood as his divine lordship over space.

g. God's Presence as Differently Qualified from Time to Time. We can now say that God's omnipresence is his freedom to be present with his creature in varyingly special ways. His presence cannot be compared with a continuum; it is, rather, contingent. It is not a given, but an event. However, since God in his fulfilled presence in Jesus Christ also has accepted the spatiality of the creature as the Lord and has claimed it for himself, his omnipresence is to be understood from this central point, and to be respected in those terms. It is his presence not only with the creature which desires his presence. It is also his presence with the sinful creature which would like to flee from it. It is not only the presence of his grace but also the presence of his judgment. It has the form of his gracious nearness as well as of his wrathful inescapableness. It is always and in every way qualified by him.

This varying qualification of the presence of God was defined by Peter Lombard and by many after him in both Scholasticism and Orthodoxy in this fashion:[149] first, God is present in all nature or essence in terms of his "presence," "power," and "essence"; secondly, "more excellently, that is dwelling by grace, in holy spirits and souls," and thirdly, "most excellently" in the man Christ, "in whom the fulness of the Godhead dwells bodily." Johann Gerhard objected to the succession of stages in this presentation. He wanted to establish that God in "Christ's assuming human nature" was present "in a singular fashion."[150] The presence of God in the man Jesus Christ cannot be understood on the basis of a "general" omnipresence of God. Instead, God's assumption of even the spatiality of the creature as well as his lordship over this spatiality can only be understood from the "center," which is Jesus Christ. In spite of that, the Latin tradition was saying something necessary here. It expressed the fact that God's omnipresence is his omnipresence in that it takes on the form that he elects. There is no general

---

149. Peter Lombard, *op. cit.*, *Sent.*, I, xxxvii, 1, pp. 229f.
150. Johann Gerhard, *op. cit.*, II, 187, ed. F. R. Frank (1885ff.), I, 329.

principle which qualifies the various events of divine presence. God qualifies himself in each event of his presence.

h. Ubiquity. God's omnipresence is his freedom not only in contrast to
space and its limits but also for space, for each encounter in time and space which
he qualifies, and which he grants to the creature. It is because he is "in heaven,"
because he has his own "place," that he is present with the spatial creature in
his spatiality. In this sense it was correct of both Scholasticism and Orthodoxy
to assert of God that he was omnipresent not only with his "power," not only
with his "excellence," but also with his "being" *(esse).* This is a questionable
statement (it can be understood pantheistically), if it is taken on an ontological
basis. It is correct if we read it on the basis of the "center" which alone provides
us a means for understanding God's omnipresence. The result then is that God
is not only the One at work everywhere, but he is the One who himself is at work
everywhere, that is, his "power" *(potentia)* is his "being" *(esse).* He is not the
cause which leads to an effect; he is the Creator who encounters his creature,
although relatively, still in reality, and he coexists with it. Thus, Orthodoxy was
right when it used the old maxim, "God in his being and presence is here, and
in his omnipresence is everywhere," against the Socinians. They distinguished
between the "essential presence" *(praesentia essentialis)* and the "operative presence" *(praesentia operativa)* of God, and only wanted to relate the latter to God's
presence with the creature, whereas they restricted the former to heaven.[151] In
another regard, the Orthodox were not able to come to agreement about a question which remained a bone of contention between the Lutherans and the Reformed. It is the issue of the "ubiquity" of the ("ascended") body of Christ. At
this point we wish to refer to just one point which could be illuminated somewhat
by the discussion just conducted. The particular aspect we mean is the significance of the ascension of Jesus Christ and the understanding of what it could
mean that Jesus Christ is "sitting at the right hand of God." If we understand the
word "above" in Colossians 3:1 in the sense of God's own "place," which as
God's space "makes space" for all things created, then we will have to say that
Jesus Christ is departed from us in the unity and totality of his being, that we do
in fact have to wait upon him (Phil. 3:20) and do not have him at our disposal—
which the Reformers never tired of emphasizing. However, this Jesus Christ, who
is in the glory of the Father, enthroned at the "place" of the divine "majesty,"

---

151. See especially the refutation by S. Maresius (in *Hydra Socianismi* [1651], I,
479ff.) against Johannes Crell, *De Deo et ejus attributis*, c. 27. The Arminians approached
the Socinian position, too. In that regard see Conrad Vorstius, *Tractatus Theologicus de
Dei, sive de Natura et Attributis Dei* (1610), a book with which both the Reformed and
J. Gerhard (*op. cit.*, pp. 322ff.) were in dispute. Even Johannes Cocceius was reproached
with the claim that he understood God's omnipresence to be merely "the most efficacious
will of God sustaining and governing everything" (see Cocceius, *Opera Omnia* [Amsterdam:
Janssonio-Waesbergios, 1673–75; Boom & Goethals, 1701–02³], Tom. VI, pp. 55–57, and
above all Epistles 169, 170, and 176 [to Alting]). The Cartesians, too, related God's omnipresence to his will (see H. Bavinck, *Gereformeerde Dogmatiek* [4 vols.; Kampen: J. H.
Kok, 1895–1906], II, 134, with literature there; or ET: *The Doctrine of God*, tr. W. Hendriksen
[Grand Rapids: Eerdmans, 1951]).

and who is beyond our control and totally beyond it, is totally present for us.[152] He is not less "there" than "here," but of course he is "here" differently than "there." He is here in the reality which can only be known in anticipation, that is, in pneumatic reality, whereas he is there in the direct reality which God's presence bears within itself.

4. GOD AND TIME

We understood God's omnipotence as God's freedom toward space and as God's freedom for space. In precisely the same way, we shall consider God's eternity as his freedom toward time and for time.

a. Eternity as the Opposite of Temporality? Insofar as dogmatics starts from the position of God in himself, God's eternity results from his "immutability"[153] and from his "infinity."[154] In the first instance there is a strong tendency to conceive of God's eternity in opposition to time. Time contains the categories of "before" and "after," and for it "now" is only the point of transition between the Before and the After. But God is eternal, insofar as his being is the "eternal now" *(nunc aeternum)*, the "permanent now" or "now standing still" *(nunc stans)*.[155] For him, everything which time stretches out is present in an instant.[156] It is not a far step to understanding God's eternity with Schleiermacher as "the absolutely timeless causality of God which conditions not only all that is temporal, but time itself as well."[157] If one emphasizes, as does most of Protestant Orthodoxy, that God's eternity results from his "infinity," then the conclusion will likely be similar to what we mentioned in the case of "immutability." However, the accent here is more upon God's being beyond time. Time is the category of becoming and passing away. But God "abides" (Ps. 102:25–28), and this means in this context that God as the Eternal is before time and after time, just as he is with and over time.

The ontological statements have in common their endeavor to contrast as sharply as possible God's eternity with time. To put it very pointedly, the dominant view is that God cannot be there where the creature is, and cannot be the same way that it is. But in his revelation, in divine freedom and grace, God is at the very place where the creature is. And in his revelation, he is temporal. That

---

152. A very careful discussion in K. Barth, *CD*, II,1, pp. 487ff. Barth's discussion, especially about the omnipresence and eternity of God, which we are following here (along with Cremer and Brunner), has disclosed some completely new aspects of the issue.

153. Especially in Thomas, *STh*, I,x, vol. I, pp. 40–45, *passim*.

154. Predominantly in Protestant Orthodoxy.

155. The concept of the "permanent now" *(nunc permanens)* is found in Boethius, *De Trinitate*, IV, in *Loeb Classical Library*, tr. H. F. Stewart and E. K. Rand (Cambridge, Mass.: Harvard University Press, 1918f.), p. 20, and in a certain sense is taken over by Thomas, *STh*, I,x,2, vol. I, p. 41: Our "apprehension of eternity is caused in us by our apprehending the *now* standing still."

156. Time as "some kind of protraction" (Augustine, *Confessions*, XI, 26 [*NPNF*, I, 172], and especially XI, 29 [*NPNF*, I, 174: "Behold, my life is but a distraction"]).

157. Schleiermacher, *ChrF*, §52, Thesis, I, p. 203.

is the only possible point of departure for us, and we are not then to proceed to shift over to some kind of supertemporality or timelessness. We are to take God "by his Word" and understand his eternity not in opposition to his entry into time but rather as his freedom in and for this temporality.[158]

b. Eternity and Time in a Positive Relationship. In this context it is particularly notable that the biblical concepts which are usually translated by "eternity" or "eternal" are all temporal concepts: *'olam* (eternity,) *'ad* (eternity) in the Old Testament, and *aiōn*, *aiōnios* (age, eternity, eternal) in the New. Of course, *'olam* can also mean simply "antiquity," and *aiōn* in the sense of *aiōn houtos* can become the pregnant formula for time destined to pass away (the power of time). It is definitely true that Scripture "speaks of the eternity of God in the forms of time."[159]

For virtually on every page it speaks of God's activity within time, and at its center we find the witness to the time which has been fulfilled (Gal. 4:4). Thus, it is aware of the Before and After of divine activity, and its picture of "salvation-history" is that of a linear stretch of time,[160] much more than that of the eternal repetition of closed cycles.

c. God's Entry into Time. It would appear to be easy to see that the Christian message in its temporality confronts man in his own temporality and prevents him from trying to flee from his own temporality into the realm of so-called "eternal" truths or the "supertemporal." It is the unavoidable scandal of preaching that it testifies to God in Christ, God in time. Lessing found this to be that "gaping wide chasm" which he did not believe could be crossed over. How then could "contingent truths of history" be "the proof of necessary truths of reason"?[161] And Kant left to rationalistic theology the thought that for man, for whom time is "the form of inner intuition," there is no possibility of making metaphysical statements in a "dogmatic" sense within man's limitations.[162] This scandal can be done away with neither via the historico-philosophical escape from temporality, as Hegel offered it, nor through the romantic escape, in which man penetrates religiously

---

158. Thomas also states that we only attain knowledge of eternity "by means of time" *(per tempus)* in *STh*, I,x,1, vol. I, pp. 40f. But he proceeds from the conceived or experienceable time of the creature and not from God's established time, and thus he really "proceeds from" time itself. It is impossible for him to remain there if he wants to arrive at his concept of eternity as the "immutability" of God over against time.

159. H. Bavinck, *op. cit.*, II, 128.

160. Oscar Cullmann, *Christ and Time*, tr. F. V. Filson (London: S.C.M. Press, 1951[1], 1962[2] rev. [g1946]); this work was devoted to working out this point of view.

161. Lessing, "On the Proof of the Spirit and of Power," in *Lessing's Theological Writings*, tr. H. Chadwick (Stanford: Stanford University Press, 1957 [g1777]), pp. 51–56; on Lessing in general see H. Thielicke, *Offenbarung, Vernunft und Existenz, Studien zur Religionsphilosophie Lessings* (3rd exp. ed.; Gütersloh: Bertelsmann, 1957 [g1947[2] entitled *Vernunft und Offenbarung*]).

162. See especially the "Antinomy of Pure Reason," *Critique of Pure Reason*, tr. J. M. D. Meiklejohn (*GBWW*, XLII, 129ff.).

from the finitude of his existence into the "endlessness" of the "universe."[163] It is just as impossible to overcome the scandal by following Neo-Kantianism, the Philosophy of Value, or Existentialism, and concentrating temporality at the "mathematical point" of ethical or existentiell "decision," thereby breaking out of the limitations of the Before and After. The next possible step would be to propound the theological position that in this "mathematical point" our temporality as such is open for God. God is neither general truth, nor the epitome of our obligations at any given time, nor the goal of our decisions at any time. Rather, he is the One who encounters us. In this encounter, of course, he becomes temporally coexistent with us, and thereby he prevents our breaking out of time into an imagined "eternity," which really is the negative reflection of our imprisonment in time. In the very same encounter in which he blocks off all exits he manifests himself as the Lord over our time, as the One who takes on time (just like space) and lays claim to it. In doing this, he blocks off, just as with the exit into the general, the other exit which regards our temporality in its decisive point to be an ultimate in itself. But this it is not, neither in the sense that in its essence it was God—as perhaps *temps durée* (lasting time) in Bergson's sense,[164] or as the time of decision or also in the sense of all-determining fate[165]—nor in the sense that it would be of itself open for God. What we experience in the encounter which is Jesus Christ and which is prepared for us by the Holy Spirit as an encounter with Christ is this: the very temporality in which we are irrevocably placed is also granted to us, and our closedness, including our imprisonment in time, is broken open—our existence in "lost time" is penetrated.[166] In faith I can say, "My times are in thy hands" (Ps. 31:15). And only in unbelief can I regard time as belonging solely to me.

d. God's Lordship in Time. God, by virtue of the fact that he encounters us in time, qualifies time as his time. He opposes our lost time with his fulfilled time and reveals himself in this as the Creator of time, that is, of the time in which he discloses himself to us. We can now phrase it another way: in the act of temporal encounter which he grants to us, he shows himself to be the Lord who reaches out to us in our temporality. But as the Lord of time he is the Eternal.[167]

---

163. The most impressive attempt is in Schleiermacher's second address, *On Religion; Addresses in Response to its Cultured Critics*, tr. Terrence N. Tice (Richmond, Va.: John Knox Press, 1969 [g1799, 1899]), pp. 156f.

164. H. Bergson, *Time and Free Will; an Essay on the Immediate Data of Consciousness*, tr. F. L. Pogson (New York: Macmillan, 1950).

165. Thus, from his position at the time, Goethe states in "Prometheus": "Was it not/ Almighty Time, and ever-during Fate—/ My lords and thine—that shaped and molded me/ Into the MAN I am?" (tr. T. Martin, in *The Permanent Goethe*, ed. Thomas Mann [New York: The Dial Press, 1953], p. 5).

166. The concept of "lost time" is found frequently in K. Barth (at its clearest see *CD*, III,1, p. 72).

167. On this whole theme I refer to my essay, "Die Treue Gottes und die Kontinuität der menschlichen Existenz," in *EvTheol*, special edition for E. Wolf (1952), pp. 131ff., also in *Gesammelte Aufsätze* (2 vols.; Neukirchen: Neukirchener Verlag, 1967), I. By far the most important theological discussion of the problem of time, which we are only dealing with here in a few of its aspects and in a very brief form, is to be found in K. Barth, *CD*, the detailed exposition in III,2, pp. 437–640.

e. God's Freedom in Regard to Time. From this perspective we can now say much of what the theological tradition has already stated under essentially different aspects. We may never forget that even ontologically structured theology desired to be Christian theology and was. By no means did it have merely an abstract concept of time, designed, so to speak, as a reflection of time itself. It, too, could certainly discuss both time and eternity in such a way that it becomes clear that its God in himself, which is its theme, can really only be envisaged in truth as God for us. How striking it is that Augustine could replace the formalism of the time understanding he inherited with a truly new one, which is inconceivable without Paul![168] And how profoundly Christian is even Boethius' formulation, "Eternity therefore is a perfect possession altogether of an endless life. . . ."[169] Eternity is not empty negation and not the empty "principle" of time. It is filled because it is God's eternity, yes, because God is eternity.[170] Naturally that sentence only bears meaning when one knows who this God is. It is possible to know this, however, because God meets us not as the abrogation, negation, and destruction of time, but as its living Lord. Therefore, the temporal which he has chosen is his time, his determined time, and it is not to be regarded with the constant reservation that eternity places this temporality in question.[171] This time, rather, is to be accepted as the time which God defines, whose lostness he has judged and "healed" in this his definition.[172]

God's lordship over time means, first of all, that our time always derives from him, has been previously qualified by him, because it has been created by him. Our time is not the first of all things. There is no origin which we could think or postulate which is the first of all things. The first of all things is the First One— "I am the first and I am the last; besides me there is no God" (Isa. 44:6; 41:4; Rev. 1:8). We may be able today to conceive of billions of years behind us. But the most daring calculation probing the past lengths of our time will not reach back to the origin itself, but at most the limit furthest back in the time which we can calculate. But God is always the First. He has not *been* the First. He always

---

168. See Augustine, *Confessions*, XI (*NPNF*, I, 163ff.), for centuries the mightiest statement in theology on the problem of time (*sub specie aeternitatis!*, or from the perspective of eternity).

169. Boethius, *De Consolatione Philosophiae*, V, 6 (*Loeb Classical Library* . . . , p. 401); often quoted.

170. Thomas, *STh*, I,x,2, vol. I, p. 41: "Nor is He eternal only, but He is His own eternity." See also J. Gerhard, *op. cit.*, ed. F. R. Frank (1885ff.), I, 311.

171. H. W. Schmidt (in his book *Zeit und Ewigkeit, die letzten Voraussetzungen der dialektischen Theologie* [Gütersloh: C. Bertelsmann, 1927]) placed most vividly to the "dialectical theology" of that day the question whether it was not involved in the devaluation of history, because in that theology the "eternal" was the "only positive thing" (p. 21). He accused this theology of being dominated by the "timeless dialectic of finitude and infinity" (p. 27). This objection has often been made. K. Barth dealt with it in a far more pointed way than any of his critics had done (*CD*, II,1, pp. 631ff.) and has totally demolished it. H. W. Schmidt's own concept of time (*nunc aeternum*, the eternal now, the "uninterrupted new creation of the ever identical now" [p. 229]; eternity as "full temporality" [pp. 293ff.]) is by contrast a curious mixture of Augustine and modern speculation, which could only be corrected if the "middle" which time has received in Jesus Christ were to be caught sight of.

172. K. Barth, *CD*, II,1, p. 629.

precedes temporality. For his eternity, as certainly as it is not timelessness, means his absolute previousness in relation to all time. There is one place in dogmatics where this is of special importance. We speak of God's eternal election of grace, or of the election "before the foundation of the world" (Eph. 1:4). If we understand this unconditional pretemporality of the divine election in direct analogy to our time, then the result must be some kind of ontological determinism. Time is then, so to speak, the carrying out of what God had desired in his pretemporal eternity. But we must remember that in Ephesians 1:4 it says that this election took place "in him" before the foundation of the world. The eternity spoken of here is not empty—neither the potentiality of time nor the "cause" of all temporality. It is the eternity of the One who became man and in whom God always precedes us and awaits us! God's lordship over time does not consist of his having once caused time to be, but of the fact that he always precedes our time. Thus his eternity is "pretemporality!"

God's lordship over time is his gracious lordship. That means, secondly, that God's eternity accompanies time, carries it, and grants it to us. Eternity does not will "to be without time, but causes itself to be accompanied by time."[173] God, as the Eternal, coexists with time. This means for us above all that God not only "has time," but that we too, under God's eternity, are permitted to have our time. It means that our Before and After are one in his eternity: our decision, which happens, should and may happen in this murky period between the Before and the After, is supported and borne by the decision which God, absolutely preceding us and yet accompanying us, made long ago. Here we agree with Barth when he finds that this is the essential thing about the "Christian" and "real" concept of time. In his eternal decision made once and for all in Jesus Christ, God established in him the *simul* (simultaneous) which includes our past and our future. To put it another way, because God in Christ has eternally decided in favor of the one who believes, there is in fact in our life this genuine and valid "turning" which is carried and empowered by God's decision. It is this "turning around" by virtue of which "the past is that from which we are set free by Him, and the future that for which we are set free by Him."[174] If eternity were the empty primal ground of time, then we would be dependent upon ourselves in our decisions—and who could assure us that we were even able to make valid decisions? But God's eternity is eternity for us and with us, in Jesus Christ. Therefore, we do have really and truly a past, a present, and a future.

Thirdly and finally, God's eternity is what time is advancing toward. Time is not infinite. It is not infinite extensively, that is, in its measurable protraction, and it is not infinite intensively. It is indeed the category of decision. But time is not advancing toward nothingness, but toward eternity. It does not peter out; it comes to its goal. For God, who began time, also ends it. He has not just acted previous to time, once and for all in the event of his revelation and following up that anew in his Spirit who gives us faith. He does not just act ever again in time, in letting it be our time, the appointed time for our decision which follows after

173. K. Barth, *CD*, II,1, p. 623.
174. K. Barth, *CD*, II,1, p. 628.

his eternal decision. There is more: he *will* act in time in that he prepares for it his Kingdom as its goal and thus lets it enter into his eternity. As we said, we only have God "present" in expectation, and similarly we must now say that only in the anticipation of his coming work can we take our time as determined by God's eternity previously and accompanied by it. Where this expectation is not present, there may be nothing left for man other than to sink into the dream of a time-eternity and thereby to escape from the temporality, historicity, and decision character of his existence, or to take his being at any time as it is and thus to elevate nothingness into God. Without eschatology, time always lacks direction and goal. However, Christian expectation is not romantically looking out for "the eternally coming God." This would be little different from "the constantly disappearing and never coming 'now' of the pagan concept of time."[175] But Christian expectation is the certainty that "The Lord is at hand" (Phil. 4:5). It is the expectation of the One who has come. Therefore, it is not the expectation of the abrogation of time but of its completion, for God's revealed eternity has qualified it at its midpoint.

---

175. K. Barth, *CD*, II,1, p. 629.

PART FIVE

The Creation

XI. God the Creator

A. FAITH IN GOD THE CREATOR

1. THE NATURE OF FAITH IN THE CREATOR

a. The One Who Works and His Work. When we spoke of God's nature and attributes, we could not speak of God in himself. When we now speak of God's work, we do not do so in the sense that up until now we had come to know a passive God, only potentially capable of activity, and were now turning to his activity. We cannot know God's nature in any other way than through his work. Therefore the doctrine of God's nature and attributes was solely an interpretation of his work from the point of view that it is *God's* work. The doctrine of God's work, in turn, can be nothing other than the doctrine of God from the point of view that God is the One who works. Both belong together.

However, it would not be permissible to extend this integration speculatively in such a way that God's work would appear to be nothing more than the other side of his nature. This work is not an emanation of nature but is an event. It is what God has desired in freedom, that is, it takes place in the execution of the divine decision and ordination. That God is for us this God in the way that he is God does not result from an ontologically expressible necessity;[1] if in terms of a necessity, then we can only think of a necessity which he has ordained in his freedom.[2]

b. Decreta Dei =The Decrees of God. Therefore, there is good reason for the approach used frequently by dogmatics: to speak of God's decrees or decisions

---

1. See R. Rothe, *Theologische Ethik* (5 vols.; Wittenberg: Zimmerman, 1867–71[2]), I, 161: "As God, by virtue of His own absolute causality, is He Himself or God, namely, the absolute spiritual Person, so He becomes as such, as God, with inner necessity again by virtue of His own self-determination, the causality of another which is absolutely united with Him and is of itself external to Him. . . ." Somewhat more pointedly, K. H. W. Schwarz, *Zur Geschichte der neuesten Theologie* (Leipzig: Brockhaus, 1856, 1864[3] rev., 1869[4] rev.), p. 307: "God and world are correlatives which cannot do without each other" (speaking about the speculations of I. H. Fichte).

2. Anselm, in *Cur Deus Homo*, seeks also to demonstrate a necessity for the creation of man. But he does not mean a necessity which would bind God on the basis of a givenness immanent in him by his very nature.

before dealing with his work. On the Reformed side, this is usually done in the development of the doctrine of the "decrees of God"[3] or of its core, the doctrine of predestination,[4] or also the doctrine of God's covenant, before the development of the doctrine of God's work. This is also the approach taken by Karl Barth,[5] as well as by Emil Brunner—but from his own position.[6]

One of the reasons for this has been the desire to make clear that God's work is not a given, but a *gift*, made known to us and granted us from the depth of his nature and will. This factor of "what God already is in Himself" which we are regarding here is also, as we saw, a principal motif of the doctrine of the Trinity, to the extent that there, too, the issue is that God not only reveals himself as Father, Son, and Holy Spirit but is his own eternal counterpart and his eternal unity as he himself and in his own divine liveliness as Father, Son, and Spirit. It is then understandable that the doctrine of the Trinity is usually discussed before the doctrine of God's work by those older dogmaticians, who did not develop a doctrine of the decrees of God.[7]

We shall have to say that the older dogmatics made its major effort in describing God's work really as his own, as the work which is founded exclusively in him.

If this insight is correct, then we are dealing in the doctrine of the creation with nothing other than the doctrine of faith. When we are discussing the creation, we are involved in the interpretation of the work of the one God. The knowledge which is our theme is none other than that which is derived from God's self-disclosure, and it does not exist next to the Word spoken to us, but in it and as a result of it.[8]

We now will clarify the uniqueness of the Christian witness to the Creator by dealing with some of its important aspects.

c. The Witness to the Creator in Its Comprehensiveness. First of all, we establish as our point of departure that the Bible's witness to the creation is not

---

3. Thus, e.g., J. Wolleb, *Compendium Theologiae Christianae*, Chapter III, "On the works of God and the divine decrees in general" (in *Reformed Dogmatics*, ed. and tr. J. W. Beardslee III [New York: Oxford University Press, 1965], pp. 45–49). A schematized development of the "decrees," or better, "an order of the matter of the decrees" is then offered by Theodore Beza in his *Summa totius Christianismi*, reprinted in Heppe-Bizer, pp. 147f. The doctrine of the decrees is common to all of Reformed Orthodoxy.

4. Thus in Zwingli, who in his *Commentarius de vera et falsa religione* (1525) (*CR*, III, 640ff.) presents the doctrine of God in the form of the doctrine of providence and predestination.

5. *CD*, II,2.

6. E. Brunner, *Dogmatics*, I, 303ff.; also, e.g., H. Bavinck, *Gereformeerde Dogmatiek* (4 vols.; Kampen: J. H. Kok, 1906), III, 313ff. or *Our Reasonable Faith* (Grand Rapids: Eerdmans, 1956)—a compendium of the 4 vols.

7. The case with most of the Lutheran Orthodox, but also, e.g., in the Leiden Synopsis, as well as in Calvin, *Institutes*, I, xiii, pp. 120–59.

8. See G. Bornkamm, *Gesetz und Schöpfung, im Neuen Testament* (Tübingen: J. C. B. Mohr, 1934); G. S. Hendry, *God the Creator* (Nashville: Cokesbury, 1938); R. Bultmann, "Der Sinn des christlichen Schöpfungsglaubens," *Zeitschrift für Missionskunde und Religionswissenschaft*, 15.

just a backward look to what is at the beginning, but refers in the same way to the beginning, middle, and end. The account of the creation of the heavens and the earth stands at the beginning of our Bible, and the account of the new heaven and the new earth (Rev. 21:1; see also Isa. 65:17; 66:22; 2 Pet. 3:13) is at the end of the scriptural witness. God is witnessed to in the Bible as the living Creator, not as the worker of something which is past. Thus, the witness to the Creator is connected with the promise or with believing anticipation (see Isa. 40:12ff., 26ff.; Ps. 121:2), just as with the present praise of God (Ps. 8; 19) and with thanksgiving (Ps. 104). The Creator is (according to the second account of creation) Yahweh, the Covenant God, and the first account of creation certainly is not speaking of some God or another, but of Israel's God. Creation and history, as the history of the covenant, are indissolubly intertwined. In the miracle of the election, salvation, and preservation of his people, God shows himself as the Creator. In the New Testament witness to the Creator, which clearly builds upon the foundation of the Old Testament, the unity of creation and reconciliation is especially emphasized. For Paul, the God "who justifies the ungodly" (Rom. 4:5) is also the One "who gives life to the dead and calls into existence the things that do not exist" (Rom. 4:17) and who "raised from the dead Jesus our Lord" (Rom. 4:24). The great, new eschatological work of God is none other than the old work! In other phraseology we have the same thing in 2 Corinthians 4:6: "For it is the God who said, 'Let light shine out of darkness,' who has shone in our hearts to give the light of the knowledge of the glory of God in the face of Christ." And it is only a short step from there to the statement that the one *kyrios* (Lord) is the One "through whom are all things and through whom we exist" (1 Cor. 8:6; see also Col. 1:16). In the language of Hebrews, it is the Son through whom God "created the world" (*aiōnas* = "ages") and who, as the One who "reflects the glory of God and bears the very stamp of his nature," upholds everything "with the word of his power." And this very same Son "made purification for sins" and then "sat down at the right hand of the Majesty on high" (Heb. 1:2–3). The mediator of creation is the Reconciler! From this point, it is only a short step to the prologue to John, whose (probable) Gnostic terminology should not be allowed to keep us from seeing the echoes there of Paul and Hebrews, "All things were made through him, and without him was not anything made that was made" (John 1:3). It cannot be doubted that in the middle of the biblical message, as at the beginning and the end, there stands the witness to the Creator. We are dealing with no other God in the event of reconciliation than we are in the event of creation. The Creator does not stand simply at a temporal beginning, but wherever he is, he is at the beginning.

We would have to ignore the New Testament testimonies and set aside the Old Testament's unmistakable relation to the God of Israel if we wanted to arrive at the view that the Bible was teaching something about a special "Creator-God," or about an ultimate ground of the world, or a principle of the world, or a first cause—in order then to say retroactively that this Creator-God also had something to do with Israel or even with Jesus Christ. It is quite clear that the real order is the reverse of that. The location of the witness to the Creator is the location of revelation. This is the case both in the Old and the New Testaments. This is the position in which we hear the pronouncements which "the heavens" are making or the proclamation of the firmament (Ps. 19:1). We should remember that this very psalm, which begins in such a way, continues with the witness to the law in what was certainly originally an independent psalm (19:7ff.), and Paul follows in the sequence of Romans 1:18ff. and 2:1ff. clearly the same pattern (creation—law). This certainly does not mean that the witness to the Creator is secondary. But it does mean that it is a witness to a God who has absolutely nothing in common with the world-makers of massive and subtle mythology.

  d. Faith in the Creator and Faith in Christ. We come to the same conclusions when we ask what meaning the Church's confession of the Creator has. To be sure, the oldest confession in its original form (Phil. 2:11) was made up of one phrase *(kyrios Iēsous Christos)*. But that does not mean that the Father was passed over in silence. Rather, this confession is made with a view to the confession of the beings in all realms of creation ("in heaven and on earth and under the earth"), which is sounded "to the glory of God the Father" (Phil. 2:10f.). It is not an esoteric mystery which was to be protected from the world by being isolated. It is directed to the broadest possible scope. But this broad scope has its middle in the salvation event, in the person of Jesus Christ. In his analysis of the "earliest Christian confessions," Oscar Cullmann[9] could go so far as to say that ". . . in a Christian confession of faith, faith in God is really a function of faith in Christ."[10] He concludes that the ". . . bipartite formulas owe their existence to the struggle against heathenism (cf. 1 Cor. 8:6; 1 Tim. 2:5; 6:13f.; II Tim. 4:1f.),"[11] and also could lead to the threat of suggesting ". . . the Jewish representation of Christ, to which the doctrine of the whole New Testament runs contrary, that one must set out from faith in God the Father in order to reach faith in Christ."[12] In any event, as Cullmann affirms, ". . . to remain true to the spirit of the confession, every exposition of the Credo must set out from the Christological article."[13] The confession of the Church is fundamentally the confession of Christ. And therefore it is the confession of the Creator.[14]

  The Church confesses the Father of Jesus Christ as the Creator of the heavens and the earth. Therefore, the Heidelberg Catechism[15] certainly interpreted the first article correctly when it, clearly borrowing from Luther's explanation of the second article, confesses, "That the eternal Father of our Lord Jesus Christ, who of nothing made heaven and earth, with all that in them is, who

---

  9. *The Earliest Christian Confessions*, tr. J. K. S. Reid (London: Lutterworth, 1949 [g1943]).
  10. *Ibid.*, p. 39.
  11. *Ibid.*, p. 42.
  12. *Ibid.*, p. 50.
  13. *Ibid.*, p. 52.
  14. Cullmann mentions the bipartite confession of Polycarp, "[those who have] . . . believed in Him who raised up our Lord Jesus Christ from the dead, and gave Him glory" (Polycarp, *Epistle to the Philippians*, Ch. II [*ANF*, I, 33, quoting 1 Pet. 1:21]), and concludes that God "is not confessed as Creator" here (p. 39). Christocentrism is expressed in this remark. We need only to think of the obvious relationship between Rom. 4:24 and Rom. 4:17 and beyond that with Rom. 4:5! The resurrection of Jesus Christ is the self-demonstration of the Creator.
  15. Answer 26 (Schaff, III, 316f.).

likewise upholds and governs the same by his eternal counsel and providence, is for the sake of Christ his Son my God and my Father. . . ." This "personal reference" is not based on personalism but rather on the fact that we are dealing in the creed with God in Christ, even in our confession of the Father, or of the Creator. The "I" of the confession does not change from one article to the next, and the "creed" itself changes just as little. Because that is so, Luther even implies the doctrine of justification in his *Smaller Catechism*, ". . . and all this out of pure paternal, divine goodness and mercy, without any merit or worthiness of mine. . . ."[16] The "I" of the creed is always the same "I," which responds to the "I" of God in Jesus Christ, the "I" of the Church or its members. It is the one faith, belonging to the one God, and it cannot be divided. There is not one trace of a special belief in the Creator in the confession of the Church.

That we may say, "I believe," is not the result of our own "being as persons," but is the result of the fact that the God whom we confess has disclosed himself to us as the "I," as a "person." This is the God we mean when we confess the Creator and creation.

e. Faith in the Creator, Not Explanation of the World. This makes clear that faith is not an endeavor seeking to explain the existence and condition of the world. Therefore the doctrine of God the Creator cannot be an attempt to design a "Christian" cosmogony or cosmology. In view of such an attempt, Luther's explanation of the First Article in the "Brief Explanation" sounds like a radical rejection of the "world"[17]—although of course it is not that. A cosmogony or cosmology would always lead either to a world cause or to a world meaning or a world origin. No one can "believe" in such a thing. Moreover, such a meaning, or origin, or cause of the "world" would inevitably be a component part of the "world"—there would then be a causal or intentional relationship between meaning, origin, cause, and "world." And this relationship would be what is truly authentic, the being with which this polarity could exist. In addition, such a conceived origin or meaning or a presupposed cause would be related to the "world"—causally, or logically, or intentionally—in a "necessary" effect relationship, and would thus possess absolutely no "freedom" in relationship to the world. The assertion of a world cause, a world meaning, or a world origin is unavoidably identical with the assertion that the "world" carries its own meaning in itself, or at least, that both the world and the source of its origin belong together to some common structure of being. However, the living God is the Creator. That means that he neither belongs to the world nor is part of a comprehensive struc-

---

16. Schaff, III, 78. "Personalism" is even stronger in the "Brief Explanation" of 1520 (in *Works of Martin Luther* [Philadelphia Edition; Philadelphia: Muhlenberg, 1943], II, 370ff.), where we find the following sentence in his exposition of the Second Article: "I believe that no one can believe in the Father or come to the Father by his own learning, works or reason, nor by anything that can be named in heaven or on earth, save only in and through Jesus Christ, His only Son—that is, through faith in His name and lordship" (p. 371).

17. "I put my trust in no man on earth, nor in myself. . . . I put my trust in no creature in heaven or on earth. I dare to put my trust only in the one absolute, invisible, incomprehensible God, who made heaven and earth . . ." (*op. cit.*, p. 369).

ture of being which includes him and the world. No, he is the Lord. It is totally impossible to conceive speculatively of the true "existence" of this Lord of the world, who has summoned this world into being by his own power. It is just as impossible to conceive of this world as not being subject to itself alone, to its own meaning, and more precisely, to the "elemental substances" (the *stoicheia*). Speculative thought will never be able to get beyond an origin. It would abrogate itself if it attempted that.[18] The preliminary result for us is that our discourse about God the Creator has nothing to do with a cosmogony, whether it is massively or subtly pagan.

f. Faith in the Creator Not One-sidedly Oriented to the Past. On the other hand, we must say that faith in God the Creator is not identical with the assumption of a pretemporal, primitive, or early temporal creation event. There is no doubt that whoever speaks about the creation is speaking about an event. But faith in God the Creator is not the assumption that sometime "before time" there was a creation event which happened. It does not consist of our saying that "I believe that which is said of God is true; just as I do when I believe what is said about the Turk, the devil or hell"; such faith is "knowledge or observation rather than faith."[19] If the Christian faith implied the assumption of a creation event before all time, then we would have to conclude that all Europeans with few exceptions who shared the Christian "world view" into the 18th century were believers. This view would make faith into a "historical belief" (*fides historica*) and the Gospel into law. It is certainly the proper accenting when in the creed faith is expressed not in creation but in the Creator, and when Luther in the *Smaller Catechism* sees faith in the Creator concentrated on the fact that "God has created me and all that exists."[20] Similarly, the Heidelberg Catechism puts the creation of heaven and earth and its preservation in a relative clause.[21] Apparently it has been generally sensed that faith in the Creator is not the same thing as the pious persuasion that before all times a creation event took place.

g. Faith in the Creator and the Relationship to the World. Our insight that faith in the Creator does not imply an explanation of the world and is not to be equated with the assumption of a past event is not to be connected with the view that faith in the Creator is nothing more than the epitome of a personal relationship with God, perhaps the feeling of absolute dependence or my being encountered directly by the Divine Thou as it discloses itself to me. This misunderstanding is

---

18. According to J. G. Fichte (who speaks for many here), "the assumption of a creation" is "the absolute and fundamental error of all false metaphysics and religious doctrine." "A creation cannot be conceived of in a respectable intellectual fashion at all, . . . and no man has ever thought it out in such a way. Especially in regard to religious doctrine, the positing of a creation is the first criterion of the falsity, and the rejection of such . . . is the first criterion of the truth of this religious doctrine" (*The Way Towards the Blessed Life: or, the Doctrine of Religion*, tr. William Smith [London: Chapman, 1849 (g1806)], p. 191).

19. Luther, *op. cit.*, p. 368.

20. Schaff, III, 78.

21. Answer 26 (*ibid.*, p. 315).

found both in Schleiermacher and even more so in Ritschl,[22] although neither carried it through to its conclusion. Today it is one of those presuppositions which seems to be in the very air we breathe.

We shall say now and then discuss later in greater detail[23] the fact that faith in the Creator and the Christian doctrine of the Creator do deal with the "world" given to us, with the epitome of reality outside of God, and therefore by no means merely with man alone or with his "spirit" or "person" or "existence." Faith in God the Creator is never built upon those realities. Our approach to the "world" is opened for us from "outside" as is our approach to our own selves. It is given to us because God "loved" the world (John 3:16), sent his Son into the world (John 3:17; see also John 10:36; 17:18; 1 John 4:9), made him into the Savior of the world (John 4:42; 1 John 4:14), set him as the light of the world (John 8:12), and conquered "the ruler of this world" through him (John 12:31; 14:30; 16:11; see also 1 John 5:4, 5). Neither in the Johannine nor in the Pauline witness is the "world" *(kosmos)* something lovable. The world "is in the power of the evil one" (1 John 5:19), and in Paul it is virtually the hostile power which opposes God's activity (1 Cor. 1:20, 21, 27, 28; 2:3, 19, etc.). But God has acknowledged this world, in that Jesus Christ came into it (1 Tim. 1:15) and was vindicated in it (1 Tim. 3:16). The revelation and the reconciliation are not only the vanquishing of the world in view of its lostness but also in confirmation of the divine will and power of the Creator. Thus, in two directions faith is open for a relationship to the world. It does not live in derivation from the world. Its life is based neither upon the consideration of the "bright side" nor of the "shadow side" of the world. But faith lives in relationship to the world, because and on the basis of the fact that the Creator "relates himself" to the world. A Christian version of religious anti-worldliness is inconceivable. It would presuppose or imply that the incarnation of the Son of God was not a true incarnation but an appearance, or was not significant as an event of becoming *flesh*.

2. "I BELIEVE THAT GOD HAS CREATED ME . . ."

Our most commonly used Reformation Catechisms, which certainly are not in disagreement on this point, interpret the first article in two different directions. Luther begins with the sentence, "I believe that God has created me and all that exists. . . ."; the Heidelberg Catechism leads up to the statement, "That the eternal Father of our Lord Jesus Christ . . . is . . . my God and my Father." It would be well to investigate each of these interpretations in greater detail.

---

22. For Ritschl it is virtually an axiom that religion appears everywhere "under the condition that man as spirit opposes the nature surrounding him and the society of men which is effective through the means of nature" (*The Christian Doctrine of Justification and Reconciliation; the Positive Development of the Doctrine*, tr. H. R. Mackintosh and A. B. Macaulay [New York: Scribner's, 1900; Clifton, N.J.: Reference Book Publishers, 1966], pp. 218ff.). In light of that we can understand the statement that we never exercise "religious cognition in merely explaining nature by a First Cause, but always and only in explaining the independence of the human spirit over against nature" (*op. cit.*, pp. 218f.).

23. See pp. 486ff.

The first can be summarized, in a first step,[24] in the assertion that I recognize and confess myself to be his creature in faith in God the Father. My createdness is the first thing, then, which is expressed here. What does that mean?

a. The Inconceivability of Createdness. The central idea here is not that God once created my ancestors. Luther did not want to exclude that idea, of course. But neither he nor the Heidelberg Catechism delves into that point in their explanations of the first article. What Luther asserts is my own createdness.

This can be understood when we remember that both the first article itself and its Reformation expositions bear the character of a confession. But it cannot be the extent of the confession that I acknowledge the createdness of the "protoplasm" in pious reflection. That could be an assertion, present in my memory (and influenced by my world view and thus becoming doubtful in terms of today's world view), which as such would not be the direct theme of my faith and my confession. The direct theme of faith and of the confession is God himself. The "I" of the creed can only be the "I" which responds to God himself. Therefore, "I believe that God has created me. . . ."

Nonetheless, it is not possible to understand that "God has created me." Even if the procedure of the creation of my ancestors at one time creates all kinds of difficulties in understanding now, it is something which was accepted by the thought of many generations without great opposition. But that God has created me is something which appears to be fully incomprehensible. After all, we do know where people come from: conception and birth take place, but we can perceive there no act of creation. There are certainly conditions affecting conception and birth, genetic inheritance and milieu which are manifold, often difficult to analyze, and outside my realm of influence. But they are all "creaturely" in nature, they are "immanent." How should I know "myself" to be created by God?

b. The Knowledge of Createdness as Knowledge of the Creator. This knowledge is apparently only possible as knowledge of God. I cannot derive it from any kind of source. I cannot first know somehow that I am created and then, separately from that, perhaps also know the One who has created me. I can only recognize my own createdness because and in that I recognize God as the Creator. The fact that God has created me is only known by me in the knowledge that it is *God* who has created me. Here man does not say something of himself and out of himself, something which he as such a man had perceived. Here man states before God what he is as man from God. Of course, in that the "I" of the Church and of its members is the "subject" of this statement, the statement occurs in "eschatological openness"[25]—we are reminded here of Philippians 2:10–11. The confession of the Creator and of our createdness is as a confession of faith not an esoteric event but, like all confessing, an ongoing and representative act. The

---

24. It should not be forgotten that Luther does not remain standing at his first statement: his view is to "all that exists," too.

25. The expression is from Ernst Käsemann; see his lecture, "Kritische Analyse von Phil. 2:5–11," *ZThK* (1950), pp. 313–60.

Church is speaking for "man," and not just for the people in the "circles of the Church." It does this because God is not just the Creator of those who believe. It is called to proclaim the confession of the Creator—in the (eschatological) expectation that at one time it will be confessed by all.

   c. The Other Side. We can clarify what we mean here by asking what the situation of the person is who does not make this confession of the Creator and of his own createdness.

   d. Man as a Natural Phenomenon. On the one hand, we discover ourselves to be under the dominion of a comprehensive kind of limitation of ourselves, a "conditionedness." The Enlightenment opened up for us the conceptual possibilities which enable us to illuminate much of this limitation and to make the wealth of limiting factors into rationally comprehensible contents of our consciousness. If past ages and supposedly "primitive" groupings of today's human society thought themselves to be restricted by "supernatural" powers, then the "closed system of nature" has replaced that for the modern European. Even if nature is joined by "history" as a second central concept of limiting factors, nothing essential is changed for our consciousness. Under these circumstances, man tends to look upon himself as a product which has necessarily emerged from the transparent or (still) obscure interplay of factors, which fundamentally can be known. These factors are biological and sociological, and even history is seen in analogy to them or as even a component part of them. This self-understanding does not necessarily have to be "materialist" in the sense of a world view. Some of the limiting factors can also be "spiritual" in nature. But in general the dominant impression is that even our intellectual and spiritual state is under the power of such limiting factors. If man is then a product in this fashion, he understands himself as a thing, as an object. The sociological phenomenon of mass-thinking is then partially a presupposition and partially a result of this self-understanding. The existence of man, when he understands himself this way, becomes accordingly functional. In principle, "responsibility" is not possible under these presuppositions. It is replaced by man's functioning, both in the economic and in the political spheres.
   It is also possible to speak of "God" on the basis of this self-understanding. He is then the epitome of all of the limiting and conditioning factors, the all-defining power, or "fate." This thesis is only confirmed by the fact that a variety of mythological ideas are reappearing in new forms (especially astrology), and also in the reverse tendency, that the experience of a negative fate leads to the emergence of a hate of God.

   e. Man as Spirit. It is on the other hand undeniably true that there are numerous people who strongly oppose this self-understanding and world view informed by the idea that everything is pre-conditioned. Newer philosophy is, in general, the leader in this resistance. As long as man understands himself as conditioned, or understands himself in terms of some external thing, he has failed to find his actual and authentic being. Quite clearly the problem is still influential here which affected Kant when he sought something unconditioned in contrast to the omnipotence of "nature." German Idealism found this unconditioned factor in part in Kant's own concept of "what we ought to do," and also in the person of the one who ought, that is, in the "I." Philosophy then recognized that the polarity between nature and spirit was an inadequate point of departure for the description or even the solution of the problem of human life; it then placed the concept of values, of the person, and, above all, of existence in the forefront, and finally took on the character of a guide to living based upon intellectual reflection. In that process, the basic position of German Idealism retreated to the background, and the problem of freedom, of personality, and of responsibility became more and more the crucial issue. Thus philosophy has made itself into the spokesman of man who cannot and will not understand himself in terms of comprehensive conditionedness, but senses that such an approach must lead to the disintegration of human existence. The puzzle of the "person," of the "I," by virtue of which man is man, which scorns both man's dissolution into total conditionedness and any rationalist solution, opposes the self- and world-understanding drafted by this approach of comprehensive conditionedness.

It is also possible to talk about God from this direction. German Idealism did, of course, do this with far fewer inhibitions than modern philosophy. In this instance, "God" is the epitome or the point of reference of man's freedom and authenticity. In speculative thought he becomes, as the "absolute" manifesting itself in the spirit, the abstract postulate which conditions and carries all nature, all "things" as its counterpart, and thus he becomes the principle of existence (as in late classical thought), the ground of the world or the meaning of the world. But it is not very far from there to the idea of the self-negating nothingness, which then is as such the being of all being.

f. The Impossibility of Faith in the Creator via These Two Approaches. God as the Creator cannot be spoken of in the context of the major forms of contemporary human self-understanding. These two forms, however, are only the contemporary form for the human self-understanding which is always there when faith in God the Creator is absent. It is not an overstatement to say that man, when he does not believe in God the Creator, always tends either to see himself as an object, that is, to understand his existence and condition on the basis of the "world," or as an autonomous subject, which means that ultimately he interprets the "world" on the basis of the "I."[26] Bondage to the world and contempt of the world are the most emphatic forms of these two self-understandings. In both of them, however, responsibility is only a problematical possibility. It is quite obvious that man, when he understands himself on the basis of the world, is sure that he is not responsible. But the man who understands the world and

---

26. The call heard often today that man should rid himself of the world (*Entweltlichung*, as the breakthrough of man to his authenticity) is at the very least subject to misunderstanding. It is only legitimate as opposition to bondage to the world, whereas its positive meaning in the sense of faith in God the Creator is only clear if one speaks at the same time of "worldliness."

himself on the basis of his own self is only responsible to himself, if he is logical. He is only responsible to another to the extent that that other is a representation or a transparency for a value or an idea which is either (at least potentially) given in his own self or acknowledged by it. Responsibility for another is basically self-responsibility. Self-responsibility, however, means nothing other than that I am of the persuasion that I have in my own self a "counterpart" to me. This then presupposes the deity of an ultimate within me, or it is an empty concept.

g. The "Beyond." "Religion" also does not overcome our nonknowing of the Creator. For no real "counterpart" encounters us in it.[27] It is idolization, mythologization, the transfiguration of the "world" (deities as bearers of power or as molders of fate, as elements, constellations, etc.) or of the "I" (the conceptual deities, the gods of the philosophers). All of them intend something which is "beyond." The world is not merely a power which exists the way it exists, but it is understood as a domineering power, as a power beyond its own existence and condition, and it is experienced in that way. The individual self is not understood as merely my individual person but as something which transcends itself. This "beyondness" is the same thing as the non-acknowledgment of the "counterpart." Religion is not absurd or senseless; it is the lack of a real counterpart, an essentially Other. It can of course appear in the form of postulating such a counterpart, but this postulated counterpart is in fact something "beyond."

At the entry of the message of the Creator into the world, a real process of de-idolization took place. It was a "real" de-idolization because, according to the biblical sense, it was not a better or higher God, a mightier sort of beyondness, which was the subject of proclamation. No, it was God, "who gives life to the dead and calls into existence the things that do not exist" (Rom. 4:17). The proclamation of the Creator is the proclamation of the risen Jesus Christ (Col. 1 should be compared here chiefly, and then Eph. 1 with it). The powers of beyondness—and their powers are by no means underestimated in either the Old or New Testament[28]—thus lose that empirically protective power which they had possessed for the nations, for a certain community, or for a specific cultural grouping. They had, after all, made it possible for man to "arrange himself," as he understood himself, in the "world" or even in his own being as an individual, as well as in his ethos. Therefore, it is the Christian message, the proclamation of God's divine "counterpartness" as his real being among men, which first reveals man to be really man without a counterpart. All of the surrogates are done away with, and where the Christian message does not result in faith, there obviously its proclaimed de-idolization must either result in enlightenment, or else it causes anxiety at this very result within the Church. This leads the Church to make God again something transcendent, the meaning of the world or the ground

---

27. For the concept of the "counterpart," "the one over against us," see especially H. Thielicke, *Fragen des Christentums an die moderne Welt* (Tübingen: J. C. B. Mohr, 1947), *passim*, and F. Gogarten, *Die Verkündigung Jesu Christi, Grundlagen und Aufgabe* (Heidelberg: Lambert Schneider, 1948; Tübingen: J. C. B. Mohr, 1965).

28. See, e.g., Rom. 8:38f.; Col. 1:16; Eph. 1:21; Gal. 4:3; Col. 2:8f.

of personal being,[29] or it even understands itself, in its existence as the Church or in the grace which it preaches, to be an aspect of beyondness, to be supraworldly.

h. The Opposite or "Counterpart." The essential thing is that this opposite factor shows itself to us. We are not able to postulate such an "opposite" or "counterpart" nor even to define its category in order then to discover that God were this "opposite." In our own self-understanding, we do possess a point of departure for the question of the beyond, or of the transcendent. But the transcendent we seek out is still an element of our "world," the highest level of our conceptual world. But the "opposite" cannot be postulated nor can it be discovered by inquiry. It is only in the event of God's self-disclosure that we experience the fact that there is an opposite for us, that our isolation in the world and in ourselves has been broken through, opened up, and thus the path to the world and to the self has been liberated. Therefore we should not say that God is this "opposite" (the one so long sought . . .), but rather, God confronts us as he himself.

Since we do not possess any category for this "opposite factor," there is no possibility of proving that God is the Creator. Every proof consists of the demonstration that what is to be proven can be integrated into the realm of what has already been proven or the axiomatic structure which presupposes all things provable—without any contradictions. Thus we can only prove things which are created in nature. A provable God would not be the Creator. Rather, the Creator demonstrates himself, and only in that way does he demonstrate that we are creatures. The self-demonstration of God the Creator is his word (see Heb. 11:3). But his word is not information about him, but is his communication of himself. His word is the Word which has become flesh for us. That does not mean that not until the event of the incarnation of the Word did God become the Creator. Reconciliation is not the Creation. But it does mean that the Word which the special and elect people of Israel had already received concretely, but which was still unfulfilled, still concealed in the promise, has been revealed and fulfilled in Jesus Christ, as the Word which made the world. To be sure, the Old Testament Word testifies to the creation. But even this testimony has the character of a shadowy outline.[30] The New Testament, when it witnesses to Jesus Christ the Reconciler as also the Mediator of Creation, is not saying something "new," but it does mention the secret which had been concealed "for ages and generations" (Col. 1:26) as the mystery now "revealed." The fact that there is a "counterpart" for man, that man as such is not surrendered to himself or to the world but has a Creator—this is the mystery which is heralded in the old covenant and realized in the new covenant. The Christian discussion of the Creator cannot then retreat

---

29. The structure of the "Christian world view," when we examine it more closely, is found to be a mixture of Christian, classical, and even some oriental ideas. Its chief characteristic is the fact that God is placed at the pinnacle of a system of being of one kind or another, and is therefore a form of the "beyond."

30. Heb. 10:1 and on that, Calvin, *The Epistle of Paul the Apostle to the Hebrews and the First and Second Epistles of St. Peter*, tr. W. B. Johnston (Grand Rapids: Eerdmans, 1963), pp. 132f.; further Col. 2:17.

to an artificially isolated Old Testament, separated from the new covenant. It can even less avoid the uniqueness and contingency of the self-disclosure of the Creator in the Reconciler and instead of that move into a more general sphere. Neither the Old Testament nor the New speaks of a general knowledge of the Creator.[31] The statement that God the Creator also does his work where he is not acknowledged, and that he offers himself even where he is not wanted, is made from the very center of the New Testament. The doctrine of God the Creator must begin at that central point which is the center of the whole Bible.

But how then can we say that God, in the concrete, personal, contingent encounter which he prepares for us in Jesus Christ, really discloses himself as our Creator and qualifies us as his creatures, "me" as one who is made by him?

i. My "I" Derived from God's "Thou." First of all, in the very fact that God encounters me in his self-disclosure, that is, in his Word, as he himself, as the Thou which frees me from my closedness, I am "I." I am not an "I" as long as my self-understanding is based upon the world, and I "am" in derivation from the world. I am also not an "I" in that I assert myself in my own name over against the world, that is, I absolutize my "I-ness." I am an "I" in that God speaks to me. I am a "person" in that I am a person in the "presence of God" *(persona coram Deo)*. My personhood does not exist intrinsically but only in relationship to another—"The personal being of man" is "a theomorphism."[32] In my encounter with God in his Word I am then "I-based-upon-God," and I am then creature. It is only at this point that the debilitating antithesis between existence based on the world and existence based upon selfhood ends.

j. God's "Thou" in My World. However, secondly, God does not disclose himself to me in some kind of upper world, but in my world. Of course, I do not meet him at the place which I would prefer. Rather, he encounters me where he wants to, at his time and in his place. The world in which he encounters me is thus not my own world, and not its most supreme point, but it is the real world as it is given for me. That means then that God manifests himself in his self-disclosure as the One who disposes freely over this real world and simultaneously as the One for whom this world is not an alien sphere but one which belongs to and pertains to him. He manifests himself as the Creator of the world just as he makes himself known as my Creator. The very same event in which he dethrones the autonomous power of my "I" and the arbitrary might of the world is simultaneously the manifestation of the fact that he wants to affirm, establish, and posit my "I" and the existence of the reality which is given and assigned to me. For his self-disclosure is the only true ratification of human existence, of time and of space, just as he does not disclose himself in an abstract way but in the man Jesus of Nazareth, and not at my time or without time, but at a specific time of his choosing, and not in a place I selected, but at his place.

---

31. On the question here of the natural knowledge of God see pp. 199ff.
32. E. Brunner, *Dogmatics*, I, 140.

k. I and My World. Thirdly, this is coupled with the insight that God establishes and defines my own relationship to this reality in that he encounters "me"
in my given reality. Luther's formulation, "I believe that God has created me and
all that exists," sounds like the reversal of the proper sequence. Should it not
state that God created all things that exists, including me? Luther's statement
makes the correct theological emphasis. Faith is not based upon the creation of
all that exists, but, properly understood, upon my being in fact God's creation.
But things cannot stop there. In that God claims our world, he has also made it
into *our* world. If it is not alien to him, then it should not be so to us. The mass
of conditions and restrictions which we find as our world is not summarized in
God, but it has its Lord in God. Time, which is the channel within which all of
these conditions and restrictions function and thus is also the power of becoming
and decaying, has thereby become our time in that he has accepted and claimed
it. Space, the epitome of the distance within which our life as conditioned being
and state runs its course, is our space because God deals with us in his place and
does not pass over our place. This means, first of all, that all of this is not something alien, perhaps in the Gnostic sense, for the one who believes in God the
Creator, and secondly, that all of this possesses no independent power for the one
who believes in God the Creator. The theme can be neither removal of the world
nor incorporation with the world but only acceptance of the world, that is, existence in the "world," which as existence established by God is free and thus free
from the autonomous power of the creation which is given to man and free to act
in that very creation.

Therefore, in the "new creation" (2 Cor. 5:17) creation itself is revealed.
The two are not identical. But they are related to one another.

l. Creationism and Traducianism. We began with Luther's statement, "I believe that God has created me and all that exists." Before we go on, it would be
well to illumine this proposition from two other sides in greater detail.

We must first ask about the significance of the old problem of the creation
of the human soul which apparently is related to this thesis of Luther's. As is well
known, Scholasticism teaches primarily along the lines of "Creationism": every
individual human soul is God's new and special creation, and it is incorporated
with the physical being in the act of human conception. This view was taught in
the early Church by Clement of Alexandria (c. 150–c. 215),[33] somewhat more
unclearly by Lactantius (c. 240–c. 320),[34] and in an ambiguous mixture with pagan
motifs by Arnobius (d. c. 330).[35] It is a dogma of the Roman Catholic Church,[36]

---

33. H. Karpp, *Probleme altchristlicher Anthropologie; biblische Anthropologie und
philosophische Psychologie bei den Kirchenvätern des dritten Jahrhunderts* (*Beiträge zur
Förderung christlicher Theologie*, 44, 3; Gütersloh: Bertelsmann, 1950), pp. 92ff.
34. *Ibid.*, pp. 132ff.
35. *Ibid.*, pp. 171ff.
36. See the Lateran Council, V, 1512–17 (bull "Apostolici Regiminis"), in Denzinger,
pp. 237ff., par. 738: the soul is "infused" into the body (*infunditur*).
For Thomas Aquinas, see *STh*, I,lxxv and lxxvi, vol. I, pp. 363–82. Man "is not a

and is used, for example, to provide a reason for the position that the freedom of the will is a natural capability. Most of the Reformed Orthodox theologians teach the same view, as they occasionally do follow the medieval tradition,[37] although not in order to assert the natural freedom of the will but rather for reasons, on the one hand, of ontological anthropology (the independence of the soul from the body), and on the other, of "emphasizing more lucidly the dependence of the individually developing soul on God."[38] One would think that this view, accepted by Martin Kähler among the moderns,[39] would have led to the strongest development of the basic concept that the createdness of the self were the central point of the confessional statement of faith about the Creator. However, it is notable that Luther,[40] and following him the predominant part of Lutheran Orthodoxy, takes the opposite point of view. They assert, as Tertullian once did,[41] and by appealing to Augustine[42] in a way which is only partly correct, that the soul like all of man is *ex traduce* (from the roots, transmitted by the parents through generation), that is, Traducianism. The establishment of man's physical nature in the act of conception is coupled with the establishment of man's soul in the same way. Luther, and the Orthodox who followed him, thought that this was the

---

soul only, but something composed of soul and body" (lxxv,4, vol. I, p. 366). In addition, the "intellect" is "the form of the human body" (lxxvi,1, vol. I, pp. 370ff.), and it is united to the "animal body" without means of a "body" (lxxvi,7, vol. I, pp. 380f.). Above all, *STh*, I,cxviii, 2, vol. I, p. 575: "It is therefore heretical to say that the intellectual soul is transmitted with the semen," and cxviii,3, vol. I, p. 576: "souls were not created before bodies, but are created at the same time as they are infused into them." Similarly in Peter Lombard, *Libri Quattuorum Sententiarum*, ed. Franciscans of Quaracchi (2 vols.; Ad Claras Aquas: Quaracchi, 1916), II,xvii,2, vol. I, p. 384: "in creating God infused them, and infusing them he created . . ." (according to Augustine, *De Genesi ad Litteram* [Migne, *PL*, XXXIV, 348f.]) and III,xxxii, vol. I, pp. 473ff.

37. See Wolleb, *op. cit.*, p. 57: "The human soul is not reproduced by transmission of semen, but is put into the body as immediately created by God." Similarly, Polanus (see also Heppe-Bizer, pp. 183f.), Voetius (*ibid.*), and others. It should also be noted that Melanchthon espouses Creationism (*CR*, XIII, 17f.), whereas Calvin (*Institutes*, II,i,7, pp. 249f.) leaves it an open question. Incidentally, he does remark (in contrast to Luther; see below, n. 40) that the whole problem is of no significance for the doctrine of original sin. Nevertheless, he appears to tend toward the Creationist position.

38. F. A. B. Nitzsch, *Lehrbuch der evangelischen Dogmatik*, 3rd ed. H. Stephan (Tübingen: J. C. B. Mohr, 1912), p. 307.

39. M. Kähler, *Die Wissenschaft der christlichen Lehre vom evangelischen Grundartikel aus* (Erlangen: Deichert, 1905), p. 272.

40. Luther, Disputation of July 3, 1545 (*WA*, 39, III, 337ff.), does not want to make this issue into a question of faith and appeals in this to a dogmatic decision made by Augustine—and quite rightly. On the other hand he concludes, in what we might call a nondogmatic expression, that Augustine takes the position "that the soul originates by propagation, just as the body originates from the roots" (*loc. cit.*, p. 350). But he concludes with the very significant statement, "Not in the manner that the father would create the body, but *God*; nevertheless as he makes the body from the seed of the father, so God produces the soul from the seed or by propagation *(ex traduce)*" (*ibid.*). Later (*loc. cit.*, p. 352) there is the reference to original sin (p. 355).

41. See H. Karpp, *op. cit.*, pp. 41ff.

42. See *ibid.*, pp. 243ff., and E. Dinkler, *Die Anthropologie Augustins* (Stuttgart: Kohlhammer, 1934).

easiest way to explain original sin (which then does shift into a curious light, not quite fitting in the broader context of Luther's views).[43]

How could we deal with this? For one thing, we could take the approach which Johann Gerhard (1582–1637) suggested: leave the whole problem to philosophy.[44] It can scarcely be doubted that philosophy, if left with the choice, would probably go in the direction of Traducianism. Although it certainly will sense the mystery character of the individuality of the "I," it will not really be prepared to view the origin of the soul, which is the theme of psychology, in any other way than it does the origin of the physical. Nonetheless we must ask whether or not the old theological debate did not in fact view the whole matter differently. Did it not perhaps note that the "I" which says, "I believe," is not simply the same thing as the human soul which is subject to the work of psychology? Did it not catch sight of an ultimate mystery of man which now and then breaks through even in philosophy? In this regard, are not the proponents of Creationism right in a way which they will scarcely be aware of themselves? Who is then this "I" which says, "I believe"? According to Paul, it is in the actual sense the Holy Spirit (Rom. 8:15; Gal. 4:6; 1 Cor. 12:3). But the Spirit is the One who gives life (2 Cor. 5:17). If we adhere to the thesis that creation is illuminated in the new creation, then we shall have to say at the same time that the Holy Spirit qualifies our "I." What the "I" is, in the sense of theological statement, can only be said on the basis of pneumatology. But, according to Romans 8:16, the Spirit witnesses together with our spirit that we are children of God. That means that in the Holy Spirit and in his work, the creaturely "I" made by God is revealed. The Spirit realizes the will of the Creator. To put it another way, the person who confesses and knows Christ is man in harmony with his destiny, is creaturely man. When more recently Helmut Thielicke has pointed out that "modern man" always understands himself and his relationship to a conceptualized God on the basis of one of the overarching realms of existence (politics, economics, race, nation, etc.), then this means basically that a broader Traducianism is holding sway. And that means in turn that man understands his "I," his "self," solely as the empirical "I," as the "I" which obviously does not say, "I believe." This empirical "I," taken in itself, is the closed, isolated "I," created but in contradiction to its creation, the unreal "I."

m. The "I" in the Community. We could take another approach. We spoke of the "I" and distinguished the believing "I" from the empirical, the "I" which is available to psychology. But is this "I" which says, "I believe," really the individual "I"? Have we not produced an abstraction in our discussion of this "I"? Yes, in fact, we have! The creed is not the statement of the individual or isolated person, closed off in its own egoism, but is the statement of the Community! I cannot say, "I believe that God created me. . . ." without saying in

---

43. Whereas, as we said, Melanchthon tends toward Creationism, M. Chemnitz and J. Gerhard leave the question open (the latter in *Loci communes theologici*, VIII, 18, ed. F. R. Frank (1885ff.), II, 132. Later Orthodoxy teaches in general unanimity Traducianism (reference in Schmid, pp. 175ff. and 257).
44. Johann Gerhard, *loc. cit.*

effect "we believe" instead of "I believe." In the loneliness of my "I," I do not conduct myself as a creature. In that state I am the self-glorifying central point of my egoist world. Createdness is, however, essentially "shared humanity." This is not something I realize as a product of my own self-understanding, although I always fail with this my self-understanding if I do not acknowledge my shared humanity. Shared humanity is the mind-set of the creature who knows of his Creator. For it is the glory of the Creator that he does not exist worlds away from man but wants to be near to man, to his creature, in free grace. The "goodness and loving kindness" of God (Titus 3:4) are the origin of shared humanity. And the place in which God's "humanity" (*humanitas*, which is the Vulgate translation of the Greek *philanthrōpia*, love for mankind, kindness) is revealed is the Community! In the "I believe" which is "we believe," the "I," the self, becomes a genuine "we," not collectively and not just postulated, and this happens there where God's humanity is recognized as the incarnation of the Son of God. That obviously does not mean that man outside the Community could not honestly exercise shared humanity. The Community is only the representation, the advance troops of mankind. In and through it is revealed and realized what otherwise exists as the concealed but not ineffective destiny of man. Christ did not become a "Christian," but a "man." And the new creation which is a reality in him and which therefore can only be recognized in faith, is still the beginning and the breakthrough of the new heaven and the new earth.

3. THE CREATOR, "MY GOD AND MY FATHER"

The Heidelberg Catechism explains the first article with the words, "that the eternal Father of our Lord Jesus Christ, who of nothing made heaven and earth, with all that in them is, who likewise upholds and governs the same by his eternal counsel and providence, is for the sake of Christ His Son my God and my Father. . . ."[45] This is the complementary proposition to Luther's. Whereas Luther looks first at man who confesses the Creator in that he confesses his creatureliness, here we look to God who as our Creator provides us our creatureliness in such a way that he is experienced as our God and our Father.[46]

a. Creation as Grace. In that we now follow the Heidelberg Catechism and place the complementary accent—speaking not of man as creature but of the Creator as our God and Father—we are also taking up the fundamental approach of Karl Barth's doctrine of creation. The creation has its ground in the eternal covenant and its predetermination in the preparation of the place for the realization

---

45. Answer 26 (Schaff, III, 314).
46. The wording of Answer 26 of the Heidelberg Catechism appears to go back to Johann Bader's *Gesprächbüchlein* of 1526 (F. Cohrs, *Die evangelischen Katechismusversuche vor Luthers Enchiridion* [5 vols.; *Monumenta Germaniae paedagogica*; Berlin: A. Hofmann, 1900–07]), and in its second section reveals clearly the influence of Luther's Shorter Form (*WA*, 7, 216)—we shall discuss the second section below. This complementary relationship is not even accidental in terms of the genesis of the formulae.

of this covenant.[47] If the Creator is our Father, the Initiator and Preserver of the covenant, then the creation is not the equivocal inauguration of an event which has many meanings, nor the intrinsically neutral foundation of the variety of human activity, and even less (in the Marcionite sense) the provisional, imperfect, even valueless establishment of something itself without any value. Rather, it is grace.[48]

How does one come to such a conclusion? How can man come to affirm creation at all? This question is certainly more urgent today than the issue of how the world came to be. For we are in danger, as we shall discuss below, of having to face the unmistakable "night side" of the created world so brutally that we will not want to risk even mentioning the "good" creation of God. And it is true that we cannot recognize creation as grace as a result of our analysis of the world, just as we cannot recognize our own createdness through an analysis of our selves. The Heidelberg Catechism certainly does not proceed from the observation of the world. And the biblical accounts (or stories[49]) of creation do not do that either. The God who is spoken of in the first account is the God worshipped in the Old Testament cult and witnessed to in the priestly Torah. The God who acts in the second account is Yahweh, the covenant God of Israel. The One to which both accounts point expectantly is the "Father" of "Jesus Christ,"[50] the God in whom the Community believes. "Creation is understood and apprehended as grace in faith in Jesus Christ,"[51] and only in that way. Creation is grasped as grace in that God encounters us as the Gracious One, as "my God and my Father."

If then I am a responsive creature only in my faith in the Creator, then this means that in the Creator's self-disclosure, without which this faith would not exist, God is the Creator for my benefit, his power is power for my benefit, and his eternity is eternity for my benefit. I am completely "cast" upon him (Ps. 22:10). But he is there for me. My being cast is simultaneously my being secured. The God who has all power over me is my Father. His otherness is superior and divine grace.

b. The Father. The Bible speaks more frequently of God's being the Father than it does of our being his children. It is obvious that the one is implied by the

---

47. According to Barth, in the first Creation account, the Creator is "the external basis of the covenant," and in the second, the covenant is the "internal basis of Creation" (*CD*, III,1).

48. See Barth, *CD*, III,1, pp. 40f.

49. K. Barth adopts the widespread usage of the term "creation saga" and gives careful reasons for his procedure (*CD*, III,1, pp. 81ff.). He especially contrasts quite sharply the saga with the myth—and rightly so. However, if we consider that the contents of the creation accounts really cannot be reduced to or forced into any set of coordinates brought in from outside, it would then probably be more correct to avoid the usage of any over-arching term for them, including the usage of the term "saga." Most likely the old concept of "sacred history" *(historia sacra)* would be the best option because it connects the event and the incoordinability in the clearest way. On the problem of the "mythical," see E. Buess, *Die Geschichte des mythischen Erkennens, wider sein Missverständnis in der "Entmythologisierung"* (Munich: Kaiser, 1953).

50. "The eternal Father of our Lord Jesus Christ . . . for the sake of Christ His Son . . ." (Heidelberg Catechism, Answer 26 [Schaff, III, 315]).

51. K. Barth, *CD*, III,1, pp. 40f.

other. But the greater emphasis is placed upon the former. According to Ephesians
3:15, the Father is the One from whom *every* family in heaven and on earth has
its name. This is a thought which is also echoed in Romans 11:36 and Acts 17:28f.
and in its context does assert that God's fatherly lordship, even though it is only
acknowledged and praised in the Community, is certainly not exhausted in and
through that Community. The Community does not exist for its own sake but for
the world. God's fatherhood unconditionally precedes acknowledged childhood,
and it does not end where it is acknowledged. It is the fatherhood of the Creator
and not a special accent placed upon our self-understanding as creatures. This is
no intrinsic quality which would insure that we are God's children. But it is an
intrinsic quality of God that he is the Father. He is the Father before we are
children. He is the eternal Father of the eternal Son!

We cannot speak of the Creator as Father in any other sense than this.
Because and in that the Creator discloses himself as the Father of Jesus Christ,
he is also our Father in eternal precedence to our being the children of God. The
Creed, when it speaks in the first article of the Father, means the Father of the
Son, and our own creaturely childhood is, according to Romans 8:15, 23, Ephesians 1:5, and Galatians 4:5, adoption, secondary childhood. We do not start out
in some neutral sense as creatures, in order then, by means of an optimistic view
of our created nature or of the meaning of the world we have, to come to the
conclusion that we are "children." Instead, we know the Creator first and solely
in the fact that he encounters us in Christ as the Father.

    c. No Emanation. Therefore, God's fatherhood is not to be understood as
a relationship of origins—for example, in the sense of "emanation." The eternal
origin, the "Father of All" as Goethe glorified him poetically,[52] would not be the

---

52. Especially in "Grenzen der Menschheit" (Limits of Humanity):

Wenn der uralte	(When the age-old
Heilige Vater	(Holy Father
Mit gelassener Hand	(With deliberate hand
Aus rollenden Wolken	(Out of rolling clouds
Segnende Blitze	(The Lightnings of blessing
Ueber die Erde sät	(Sows over the earth,
Küss' ich den letzten	(I kiss the final
Saum seines Kleides,	(Seam of his garment,
Kindliche Schauer	(Childly shudder
Treu in der Brust . . .	(Faithful in my breast . . .
Was unterscheidet	(What distinguishes
Götter von Menschen?	(Gods from men?
Dass viele Wellen	(That many waves
Vor jenen wandeln	(Wander before them,
Ein ewiger Strom:	(An eternal current:
Uns hebt die Welle,	(The wave moves us,
Verschlingt die Welle,	(The wave swallows us,
Und wir versinken.	(And we drown.

Or also in the poem "Vermächtnis" (Legacy):

    Kein Wesen kann zu Nichts zerfallen!
      (No being can deteriorate into nothing!)

Creator, but the core of the world, and the relationship to him would not be that of the child but of derivation from the origin. It would be a nonpersonal relationship, and God would not be our Opposite, but only the "Beyond" encompassing creatorless and thus uncreated total reality.

d. Fatherhood and Love. The fatherhood of the Creator is revealed in his love. As we have already stated, this is the event of God's giving himself to the creature, his involvement for the creature, and his recognition of the creature. But it is never God's flowing over into the creation. To use A. Nygren's terminology, it is not Eros, but Agape.[53] It is the granting of personal fellowship. The creature in the specific sense, the receiver of this love of the Creator, is man. God's love in a specific sense is directed to him. For Jesus Christ is the One who became man. To the extent that we can speak beyond that of God's love—in inadequate terms, it is love for man's sake, and thus it is the readying of the creation assigned to men for man's existence and his childhood.

e. The Freedom of the Child. Finally, our statement that God is "my" God and "my" Father means that he provides me creaturely life, my own being and condition and the being and condition of all other forms of creation which define me, all of this as his gift and as the sphere and enablement of my life derived from him and lived out before him. God is not the abstract object of my psychic or spiritual acts; he encounters me in the man Jesus of Nazareth, in the history which he has prepared, and thus in the midst of the world of "nature" which he has created and rules. Therefore, the creation which is subordinate to me is assigned to me as the creation of God and the child of God. And that means that I may move about in this "world" with the freedom of the child who lives in his Father's house. Under this aspect it is quite relevant that the Heidelberg Catechism (together with many dogmaticians) links our confession of the Creator with that of God's providence.[54] The Creator, who is my God and Father, "can" as the almighty God and "desires" as my merciful Father to be my Provider and

---

> Das Ew'ge regt sich fort in allen
>   (The Eternal continues to move in everything,)
> Am Sein erhalte dich beglückt!
>   (In being maintain thyself most happy!)
> Das Sein ist ewig: denn Gesetze
>   (Being is eternal: for laws)
> Bewahren die lebend'gen Schätze,
>   (Preserve the living treasures,)
> Aus welchen sich das All geschmückt . . ."
>   (From which the universe adorns itself.)

Along the same lines, "Eins und Alles," "Parabase," "Epirrhema," and "Antepirrhema."

53. *Agape and Eros*, tr. P. S. Watson (Philadelphia: Westminster Press, 1953).

54. Heidelberg Catechism, Answer 26: ". . . in whom I so trust as to have no doubt that he will provide me with all things necessary for body and soul; and further, that whatever evil he sends upon me in this vale of tears, he will turn to my good; for he is able to do it, being Almighty God, and willing also, being a faithful Father" (Schaff, III, 315f.).

Helper, too. This means that he will "turn to my benefit" all of the possibilities in the realm of creation subordinate to me, even though they are quite obscure to me. It could not be said that they are all positive possibilities in and of themselves. But faith has trust in the Creator that he has power over all of these possibilities, both the positive and the negative. And it trusts him also for the goodness to turn them into "his benefit," just as he is himself God and Creator "for my benefit."

The question, however, must be dealt with, whether all of this is not unreal. Can we accept without contradiction Karl Barth's speaking of "Creation as Benefit," "Creation as Actualization," and "Creation as Justification"[55]—all of which is also in direct contradiction to what some had expected of him?

f. The Dark Side of Creation. The question could be raised first of all from the ground of experience itself. If it appeared to be "easy" to "believe" in God the Creator in past centuries, this was partially due to a one-sided concentration upon the bright side of creation. It was also due, probably, to man's self-understanding, to a secularized form of former Christian faith. "Brethren, above the starry tent must dwell a loving Father"—Schiller could lyricize in this manner and Beethoven conclude his Ninth Symphony in that spirit. It was the reverberation of the view that this world is the best of all possible worlds.[56] In that context, God appeared as the epitome and the origin of the good meaning of a good world. This optimism has virtually disappeared today. The dominant view of the world today is based upon pessimism, or else it may appear in either a heroic or a resigned form. "The world" is seen chiefly from the perspective of its undeniable dark side, and therefore it appears to be dark, empty, and meaningless. It is then characteristic that in this situation two very different developments emerge in regard to the "question of God." On the one hand, the hollowing out of the world view leads to qualified doubt: there is no idea of God appropriate for this particular world. This is the result of man's becoming accustomed for centuries (particularly in Europe) to think of God as that which is beyond the world. A hollow world can have only nothingness as its Beyond. On the other hand, the tendency can be observed in theology of establishing a covenant with the very skepticism which has produced this hollowed world. It is only when man has thought through this necessary world view to its ultimate consequences that he becomes capable of the decision-making in which faith either happens or does not happen. It is probably clear that man's having reached his end within his world is equated with or integrated with having come to an end before God. Wherever this method is carried out logically, there nothing other can result than either a polar structure of creation and sin,[57] or the idea that God is the point of retreat from a meaningless world, which would definitely mean that God is not the Creator.

---

55. *CD*, III,1, pp. 330–414.

56. It is permissible to say that enlightened Optimism was certainly a secularized belief in a Creator. It was the pessimism which followed which did away with the Christian legacy which was still very influential in the Enlightenment.

57. E. Hirsch, *Schöpfung und Sünde in der natürlich-geschichtlichen Wirklichkeit des einzelnen Menschen* (Tübingen: J. C. B. Mohr [Paul Siebeck], 1931).

One thing should be very clear in this situation. Faith in God the Creator is really only possible as faith in the full sense of the creed and in simultaneous view of all three articles of this creed. It is not possible for us to arrive at God the Creator, the good Creator of a good creation, if we proceed from the viewpoint of the world. To confess today that the creation is "grace," "a good act," "realization," or even "justification," is an act of Christian faith which knows of God's grace, good acts, realization, and justification from God's self-disclosure in Christ. "Optimism," once apparently man's given possibility, is illusion or faith today. "Faith in mankind," either in the universal form of the liberal European's confession, or in the nationally restricted, especially utopian form of what was once the confession of a "German world view," is either an impossibility today or an act of faith. There is no road which leads from a hollowed-out world to God. The miracle is that God's road leads into this hollowed-out world and radically strips it of its meaninglessness.

If God's way is the path of the biblical Christ (the Incarnate, Crucified, and Resurrected One), then it is true that God's "self-manifestation" does not just "surpass" both the bright and dark aspects, but it "confirms" both of them[58] to the degree that God in the man Jesus makes "His own [creation's] twofold determination, its greatness and wretchedness, its infinite dignity and infinite frailty, its hope and its despair, its rejoicing and its sorrow."[59] God has said Yes to this world, to its light and to its shadows. And other than in the name of God, in the name of Jesus Christ, we will not be able to say Yes to both of them. The Yes we then say will still be a Nevertheless in view of the Nevertheless which God has spoken.[60] From this point of view we could only say that our present situation has made it easier for us to distinguish and to separate the confession of faith from man's self-understanding based on the world or his own self.[61]

g. Sin. The objection which we mentioned could come from quite a different direction, one which theologically must be taken much more seriously. We were speaking of the dark side of creation. But is there not a darkness which has nothing to do with creation but is nothing other than the darkness of sin itself? It may well be that creation has its own darkness. Perhaps night, sickness, and death (see Gen. 3:22) all belong to creation. But war, faithlessness, oppression, exploitation, and injustice are certainly not to be ascribed to creation but to perverted creation. In view of these powers, should we not put everything we have to say about creation within brackets? Is it not a past history which has been set aside through the existence of sin, through the "mystery of iniquity" *(mys-*

---

58. K. Barth, *CD*, III,1, pp. 375ff.

59. *Op. cit.*, p. 377.

60. *Op. cit.*, p. 380: "The Nevertheless is already spoken. God has spoken it. This divine Nevertheless is not only permitted but necessary for Christian faith because it is the required and legitimate justification of [existence], the freedom in which man may become and be before God the Creator not only [quiet] but [also] at peace with Him and therefore with the world of His creature. . . ."

61. This is where we would find what could be called the comforting message of the first proposition of the Barmen Declaration.

terium iniquitatis), or is it an eschatological future? It is not our present situation, is it?

Evangelical theology has always taken Anselm's warning very seriously, "There is nothing to be considered which is more ponderous than sin." It is therefore all the more notable that theology never speaks of God the Creator solely in the past tense or solely in the future. To the extent that Evangelical theology has thought about the course of God's history with man, it has never done so by assuming that somewhere there is an epoch of the sole domination of sin. Covenant theology rejects this possibility most clearly. "Salvation-history" is a history of the covenant decisions of God, of the "covenant of nature" *(foedus naturae)* and the "covenant of grace" *(foedus gratiae)*, or of the "covenant of works" *(foedus operum)* and the covenant of grace.[62] Karl Barth's emphatic admonition that theology and proclamation should not take sin as seriously as grace is to that extent well based in the theological tradition. There is no question that Evangelical dogmatics has the testimony of Scripture on its side. For the Bible does not say that God's Creator power has been set aside by sin. Instead, it shows all the way through that God constantly adheres to his creative will, that God acts against sin and establishes his covenant with man. God gives up neither his right as Creator nor fallen man.

h. The Beneficial Act of Creation, Not Grace-Monism. Nevertheless, this insight cannot result in a "monism of grace" on the other side. We said that God's goodness to his creation can be recognized only in faith, and this faith is dependent upon the Christ who was once promised, who has come and is coming. There is no direct knowledge of the Creator goodness of God. We must even say that the Creator is not known in any other way than in the light of reconciliation. But the reconciliation is not the creation, and God is the same God in the work of creation as in the work of reconciliation, but the work of creation is appropriate to the Father, while the work of reconciliation is appropriate to the Son. Thus we cannot let the knowledge of the Creator be absorbed, so to speak, by that of the Reconciler. Reconciliation is not the other side of creation; it is the new work of God. As such it is the confirmation of the Creator's will and of the creative power of God. But it is not identical with it.

The major significance of this is that while the work of creation comprehends everything although it is not generally recognizable, the work of reconciliation is directed toward everything (Col. 1:20), in that its goal is the establishment of the Kingdom of God—but that work is only known, revealed, and realized "in Christ," that is, in the Community. It cannot be said that since the Reconciler is also the Creator, the work of reconciliation comprehends all things created as such. There is a gap here which no measure of theological reflection can bridge. Its most explicit representation can be found in the fact that there is not only an "in Christ" but also an "outside of Christ," which is the situation of the one "who does not obey the Son" and upon whom "the wrath of God rests" (John

---

62. See especially G. Schrenk, *Gottesreich und Bund im älteren Protestantismus, vornehmlich bei Johannes Coccejus* (Gütersloh: C. Bertelsmann, 1923).

3:36). As hard as it is to express it, the proclaimed Word is not just "a fragrance from life to life" but also "a fragrance from death to death" (2 Cor. 2:16). In both of these aspects it is the manifestation of the Creator power of God. For the Creator is also the Judge. Quite clearly the Creator power of God has two aspects. It can also be rejected—in the final rejection of Jesus Christ and thus in the fact of the "impossible possibility" of human rejection of God's election. It is not a fact in and of itself, but rather a decisional fact; it is not to be taken ontically but in a real and Christological way.[63]

B. THE CREATOR OF THE WORLD

1. HEAVEN AND EARTH

a. Personal Statement and World Statement. Faith in God the Creator is not founded upon our reflection about the world, its origin and ultimate goal, but in the self-disclosure of God. However, this takes place in the world and in the pronouncement of his lordship over the world. According to the biblical witness, the Creator is everything other than the nonspatial, timeless, and worldless "origin" of our absolute feeling of dependence. He is not a "Thou" to whom the whole realm of the "It" were unapproachable or of no interest. He does not encounter us in the "personal" (ethical) sphere as such, but in the definite person of Jesus Christ, who is what he is for us not by virtue of his personality[64] but by virtue of the encounter which God permits us to experience in him. Christian proclamation knows of no alternative in the sense that God must encounter us either in the universe or in the personal, psychic, or ethical sphere. He encounters us neither in the universe as such nor in the personal sphere as such, but in the one person of his Son. In Jesus Christ, though, we are dealing with the Creator and Lord of the world.

We began our discussion with the relationship of the Reformation confession to the "I" of the creed, which responds to the "I" of the Creator. But now we must heed the fact that the creed itself does not say, "I believe that God has made *me*," or "that the Father of our Lord Jesus Christ . . . is *my* God and my Father," but rather that it confesses the Father as "the Creator of Heaven and Earth." The thrust of the creed (like that of Gen. 1:1; Rom. 1:20; Col. 1:15, 16; also of Ps. 121:2; 146:6; Job 12:7–9; Acts 17:24) is not the reverse of those Catechism propositions, but certainly not along the lines of a Christian personalism. Rather, the emphasis here is upon the world, because it is upon God. Just as the "opposite" who encounters "me" is at stake here, so also the creative "opposite" of the world is at stake. Theology has to do with the totality of divine creation, with the "world," because it has to do with God, and because God in Jesus Christ stands

---

63. See my lecture, "Die Lehre von der Erwählung und die Verkündigung," in *Die Predigt von der Gnadenwahl* (*Theologische Existenz heute*, 28; Munich: Kaiser, 1951), especially pp. 33ff.

64. See the early Church doctrine of the "anhypostasis" of the human "nature" of Christ.

on the side of creation—not just of man in his personality, but of man within the totality of creation preceding and surrounding him.[65]

b. The Varieties of Creation. The Bible and the creed call this totality "heaven and earth." The Nicene Creed and the Nicaeno-Constantinopolitanum appear merely to want to interpret or liturgically to expand upon this when they speak of "the visible and the invisible." Genesis 1:1 refers to the "visible" heaven, the tent of heaven, and especially the constellations. Yet this visible heaven was not, for the oriental, the object of meditative contemplation but of magical fear and hope; the stars were regarded as deities, as governors of fate. To that degree the interpretation of the Nicaeno-Constantinopolitanum was not taking a new tack since fundamentally "heaven" was regarded as the realm superior to man and controlling man. The Bible constantly works with the "world" as subordinated to man, and "heaven" as set above man. This makes the statement all the weightier that not just the earth is created, but also the heavens, God's "place," the location of the angels. In addition, the unseen world, the world of secrets both good and bad, is not a world opposed to God or opposed to the earth. As Colossians expresses it, "in him all things were created, in heaven and on earth, visible and invisible . . ." (Col. 1:16; apparently the source of the formulation we find later in the Nicaeno-Constantinopolitanum).

c. The Confession of the Creator as Liberation from Anxiety. At this point it becomes completely clear that in the formulations of the creed we are really dealing with a confession and not with a cosmology. At most with regard to the earth, to visible reality (which according to our world view also includes the world of the stars), we could assert cosmologically and cosmogonically that it had its "first cause" in a divine being (see the cosmological proof for the existence of God[66]). Certainly that can never be said about the "heavens," about the invisible world beyond or above, which causes man to fear or encourages him to hope all kinds of things. But it is indeed a confession of faith when we testify to the power of God in view of this whole reality, of the earthly as well as supra-earthly world. In point of fact, this is faith that I reject all my confidence in the (heavenly and earthly) creation and all fear of it in the name of God. This faith is the protest against every kind of autonomous power in those forces which have "power" over man. How often the Old Testament warns against the cult of the stars and against the chthonic deities! And how Israel seems to stand there with empty hands facing this whole world! And then, how this protest against the powers of fate, against the "world rulers of this present darkness" (Eph. 6:12) comes to its fulfillment in the New Testament—in the name of the One in whom the powers of the heaven also are created! This is truly an aspect of the Gospel with which the Bible begins: both in heaven and on earth we have to do with no one other than with God the Creator.

d. The De-deification of the World. The source of faith is that, beyond any

---

65. See pp. 479ff.
66. See pp. 219f.

logical, powerful, or demonic "Beyond," the One encounters us who made heaven and earth, as well as the oppressive and captivating powers, and he holds them in his hand. This is the biblical message, and it cannot be stated without eschatology. It is a comforting confession, because it takes away the believer's fear which otherwise keeps the world in suspense (in both mythological and unmythological forms). At the same time it is a declaration of war against every kind of "absoluteness" within the created world. How could anything other than the Creator, be it in heaven or on earth, be "absolute," autonomous, a power unto itself, "eternal," and "creative"? The deification of creaturely spheres—race or nation or economy or machine or "spirit" or "matter" or society or the state—is only the presupposition of or the reverse side of our fear of these very spheres. The "gods of Europe" with their special creeds and laws and cults are just as much implied here as are the gods of antiquity.

It was out of the proclamation of the createdness and relativity of all things that the development of European science was possible. When the Reformation attacked the last effective attempt to establish a kind of super-nature between God and the world, which it did with its concept of grace which surpassed nature (although the alteration of the world views was not its intent), it prepared the way for the genuine secularization of what is secular and laid the foundations simultaneously for the European Enlightenment.

However, the Reformation thrust was not the most decisive factor for the Enlightenment. It was rather the humanistic thrust which emerged from the mere secularization of the Middle Ages, which led ultimately to the result that what was supposed to be understood as of the world became totally worldly. But it is a fact that "pure" worldliness is not possible without the validity of faith in the Creator. This kind of worldliness requires then either the absolutization of the worldly itself and thereby the denial of the Creator, or the addition of an invented god into the world, that is, in some form of the idea of a god permeating the world. But both of these options mean that the world does not remain truly worldly but moves to replace God or the myth which has been deprived of its meaning.

In such a situation the re-emergence of real myths is certainly possible. We think of the spirit or self-myths of idealistic philosophy, or of the race myth, or of all kinds of national mythologies. We can say that all of these appearances are elements of one very differentiated context. In all of them, the intent is to repeal the de-deification of total reality which happens in the proclamation of the Creator, and they make use of whatever means possible. The self-absolutization of the creature, as it constantly appears in some form or another and becomes an intellectual power on European soil, opens in truth the gates to every kind of demon.

2. THE EVIL ONE

God alone is the Creator. All reality distinguished from him, including its mysterious depths, is creation. This is the liberating content of faith in God the Creator. But one dark question still remains. It is the question of evil. Is evil also God's creation?

a. *"The Enemy."* If one feels unable to accept the existence of an extra-human, personal power of evil, the question is modified but not really ameliorated. In that instance, it must be phrased, Does evil, as our evil, our failure in existence, belong to God's creation? And if not, where does it come from? However, there is no theological reason to reduce the question in this way. To be sure, as Christians we do not believe "in" the devil. The devil is not mentioned in the creed. But we do believe "against" the devil. The whole creed is simultaneously the "renunciation of the devil" *(abrenuntiatio diaboli)*. Yet the power against which faith is faith has its own reality, just as certainly as it does not have its own validity. We cannot ascribe its own region to it. In an ontology it would only find space by being banalized and virtually denied as a power. But the biblical witnesses did experience it as power. The devil appears as the absolute "enemy" in the parable of the weeds and the wheat (Matt. 13:28; cf. 13:39). As the biblically well-versed tempter he encounters Jesus (Matt. 4:1ff.). As the prosecutor he appears before God (Job 1) or before God's messenger (Zech. 3). He is the power whose very being is the lie. When the devil lies, "he speaks according to his own nature" (John 8:44). He "has sinned from the beginning" (1 John 3:8), and prowls around among Christians "like a roaring lion" (1 Pet. 5:8), but of course in such a way that he can transform himself into "an angel of light" (2 Cor. 11:14). The common element in all of these statements is that the Evil One—he is also meant in the Lord's Prayer[67]—is a power. Certainly man's sin cannot be "explained" on the basis of the effectiveness of this power. But it is also true that sin appears as merely one sector of the manifestations of the Evil One's power. For the evil in us has a dangerous analogy in a reality "outside" of us, confronting us, overpowering us, tricking us. It is a reality which manifests itself also in the demonic perversions of human life together, in the powerful way in which things which in and of themselves have meaning can become absolutely repugnant to all meaningfulness.[68] No one can seek to "prove" the existence of the devil. But the believer knows his enemy.

b. *Dualism?* Is then this enemy to be regarded as a creation of God? It would appear that everything resists answering this question affirmatively. Would it not mean that we were building a contradiction into God? Would that not make God into the cause of evil? But if the Evil One is not a creature and certainly is not God himself—then what is he? The answer which Zoroaster once gave and which was then taken up by Manichaeism in its own way, and which was also propounded by both Valentinian Gnosticism and by Marcion, was, he is an evil anti-god.[69] It is the answer of dualism. The theology of the Church has rejected

---

67. See E. Lohmeyer, *"Our Father,"* An Introduction to the Lord's Prayer, tr. J. Bowden (New York: Harper & Row, 1965 [g1946]), pp. 214ff.; also Luther in the *Larger Catechism* (*BekSchr*, p. 689), who thinks primarily of the Evil One and only secondarily of wickedness.

68. See P. Tillich, *Das Dämonische* (Tübingen: J. C. B. Mohr, 1926), and O. Piper, article on "Teufelsglaube, IV. Dogmatische" in *RGG*, 2nd ed., V, cols. 1066–68.

69. Irenaeus, *Against Heresies*, Preface (*ANCL*, V, 1ff.) and A. von Harnack, *Marcion, das Evangelium vom fremden Gott* (Leipzig: J. C. Hinrichs, 1921).

it virtually without exception. God is not God if he has a polar opponent who is in any way comparable to him. And in its rejection of dualism the theology of the Church could appeal to the fact that according to 2 Peter 2:4 par. Jude 6 and the late Jewish tradition taken up there, which ultimately goes back to Genesis 6:1ff., the devil was a fallen angel. The large number of satanological statements in the New Testament, even the designation of the devil as the "god of this world" (2 Cor. 4:4) or as the "ruler of this world" (John 12:21; 14:30; 16:11), were never enough to convince the Church that it should concede to dualism. In itself that is a reference to the power of the faith in the one God, the Creator. Certainly the theology of the Church has been correct in this. Dualism is a projection (in the sense of "beyondness") of the last contradictions in and around us concerning what is divine. And it can only project in such a way because it does not understand the Creator to be the Father of Jesus Christ; it passes over the factual involvement of God for his creation against the Evil One, God's power over the Evil One. Dualism, even when it appears in a Christian setting, is pagan.[70]

c. Difficulties for Christian Doctrine. The theology of the Church has not rid itself of all its difficulties when it has asserted that even the Evil One is somehow a creature of God.[71] On the contrary, in comparison with dualism, it is all the more difficult to avoid impossible conclusions. Probability is definitely not on theology's side here!

If the Evil One is not an anti-God but somehow a "creature," then it is difficult to maintain the fundamental evilness of this One without implicating the goodness of the Creator. And in fact we find frequently enough the attempt to solve the problem by diluting somehow the concept of evil. Usually it is done by

---

70. Gottfried Menken, *Dämonologie* (in *Schriften* [7 vols. in 3; Bremen: J. G. Heysem, 1858], VII, 74), finds that "almost all religions of antiquity are based upon Manichaeism"; the error of the Manichaeans was "not that they believed everything good about a good principle and everything evil about an evil principle, but rather, that they did not grasp that evil is subordinate to good, dependent upon good, and must ultimately glorify the good."

71. According to Canon 7 of the Synod of Braga, 561 A.D. (which was directed against late Priscillianism), the devil was "first a good angel made by God," and his "nature" was a "work of God" (Denzinger, p. 93, par. 237). Again in opposition to dualistic tendencies (e.g., of the Cathari) the "Profession of Faith Prescribed for Durand of Osca and His Waldensian Companions" (1208) states, "We believe that the devil was made evil not through creation but through will" (*ibid.*, p. 168, par. 427). This is valid for all of Catholic theology and also for the Reformation and for Orthodoxy. In Reformation theology Calvin should be noted especially, for he was particularly concerned with Satanology in the context of his doctrine of providence. On the make-up of the devil see the *Institutes*, I, xiv, 16, p. 175: the "malice, which we attribute to his nature, came not from his creation but from his perversion." Even more characteristic is I, xiv, 3, p. 163: The Manichaeans have objected that "it is wrong to ascribe to the good God the creation of any evil thing. This does not in the slightest degree harm the orthodox faith, which does not admit that any evil nature exists in the whole universe. For the depravity and malice both of man and of the devil, or the sins that arise therefrom, do not spring from nature, but rather from the corruption of nature." See Augustine, *Against Julian*, I, v, 16, 17 (*FC*, XXXV, 18ff.) and *Contra Julianum, opus imperfectum*, I, 114 (Migne, *PL*, XLIV, 1124). We of course could think here of Thomas too, in whose direction Calvin is generally moving.

understanding evil as the "privation of good" *(privatio boni)*, so that the character of evil's power is underestimated.[72] Evil and the Evil One thus appear easily to be a mere, and ultimately unreal, negation. However, theology has not been satisfied with this approach. For how can this "deprivation," if it is that, find a place in God's good creation?

The idea that evil itself is the "deprivation of goodness" usually has its parallel in the thought that the Evil One was not created evil but in goodness (which was then depraved by his wickedness).[73] It is again clear that here the dominant thing is the rejection of dualism on the one hand, and the rejection of the idea that God is the author of evil on the other hand.

But then this "privation" itself remains an impenetrable riddle. The statement that the fall of Satan is based on his free will which he had as an angel results, obviously, in nothing more than the emphasizing of the riddle.[74] What is the source of the "thing" "for which" the Evil One is supposed to have decided? Moreover, what kind of concept of free will is this?

Every approach leads nowhere. "The Evil One" cannot be clarified by any intellectual means. He is neither an "absolute" being similar to God, nor the merely abstract epitome of what we call "evil," nor can it be assumed that he became evil by making a free decision for evil. The *mysterium iniquitatis* (mystery of iniquity) remains a mystery.

d. Barth's Doctrine of Nothingness. It still remains a mystery when more recently K. Barth expresses it as "the possibility which God in His creative decision has ignored and despised. . . ."[75] In order to understand Barth's concept, we must bear in mind that for him creation and covenant belong together. There is no "covenant of God with nothingness," and thus God in his rejection and ignoring of nothingness is its "cause" but he has not "created" it.[76] Therefore,

---

72. This thought is found in Augustine, *Enchiridion*, XI (*NPNF*, III, 240); *Confessions*, III, 7 (*NPNF*, I, 63ff.); *The City of God*, XI, 22 (*NPNF*, II, 217); *Soliloquy*, V (*NPNF*, VII, 538f., and often). Further, in John of Damascus, *Exposition of the Orthodox Faith*, II, 4 (*NPNF*, IX, 20f.). Primarily, however, in Thomas Aquinas, especially *STh*, I,xlviii,2, vol. I, pp. 249f.

73. See the Calvin passages cited. The question must then follow which did not concern the Reformers but certainly did the Scholastics: Does then the Evil One (or here, evil) have any reality at all? If God is the Being of all being, this question is unavoidable. Thomas provides the characteristic information that, on the one hand, "no privation is a being, and neither therefore is evil a being"; but on the other hand, one must also say that evil "is" the way blindness "is" in the eye, that is, in the sense of "rational being" (*ens rationis* [*STh*, I,xlviii,2, vol. I, p. 250]). It is quite clear how here ontology leads to a failure to see the character of evil's power.

74. Orthodoxy usually deals with Satanology simply under the general title "On good and bad angels," and ascribes to all the angels the predicate of free will, which was then abused by the fallen angels (see, e.g., the Leiden Synopsis of 1624, p. 125). Often *superbia* (pride) is designated the driving force of the Fall.

75. *CD*, III,1, p. 108.

76. "Nothingness, however, is not created by God, nor is there any covenant with it. Hence it has no perpetuity" (*CD*, III,3, p. 360; see also p. 331).

it has no "being" although it is really present.[77] Its being and its nature consist rather of "the fact 1. that God in His omnipotent grace has negated it, and therefore 2. that it exists only in this relationship to His grace."[78] This thesis clearly shows what Barth is getting at. He replaces an ontology based upon intrinsic being or even upon an intrinsic God with what we could call an ontology of grace. This means then that the only possible point of departure for our thinking about evil is the knowledge of God as the One who in Jesus Christ has entered the scene as the negator of evil. What true evil is does not appear to us in our experience of evil or in the shadow side of reality—in that, Barth is quite right.[79] The Evil One becomes visible in God's activity, who alone can oppose the Evil One and alone has cast him as Nothingness into nothing. It cannot be denied that Barth, in these considerations, has the New Testament witness behind him—even though they are presented in rather abstract detail. For the New Testament speaks of the power of the devil and of the principalities solely from the perspective of their having been deprived of their power.

However, it seems rather doubtful that Barth's doctrine of Nothingness is adequately protected against a Platonizing misunderstanding, which crops up immediately when he says that Nothingness "is" only in its relationship to God's grace. This is certainly true if it is supposed to assert that we do not know the devil noetically in any other way than through the real negation of him by the Creator in Jesus Christ. It would be different if we were to design an ontology based upon this event and would say that Nothingness is the dialectical counterpart or antipode of grace. Barth himself saw this danger in that he brought in a detailed polemic against Schleiermacher.[80] He finds Schleiermacher's interpretations correct when he states that evil is only "correlative to good," but rejects all the more energetically the reversal of that proposition. "Good is only correlative to evil."[81] This can only be understood as Barth's basic attack on the Platonism in Schleiermacher. Of course, this contradiction should be raised at the point of the first thesis, that evil is "in connection with the good." For the situation is that the rejection of evil by the Creator takes place as an event and is never presented as a given. If the event of Jesus Christ alone enables us to comprehend the Creator's relationship to the power of evil, we can then well advance the proposition that the Evil One is solely recognizable as a result of the effective No of the Creator. We will not be able to explain how this creative No really estab-

---

77. "Only God and His creature really and properly are. But nothingness is [we remember, in a specific sense] neither God nor His creature" (*ibid.*, III,3, p. 349). But it "is not simply to be equated with what is not" (p. 349). "From the Christian standpoint, therefore, any concept must be regarded as untenable if it ascribes to nothingness any other existence than in confrontation with God's non-willing. . . . Equally untenable from a Christian standpoint, however, is any conception in which its existence in opposition to the divine non-willing is denied and it is declared to be a mere semblance" (*ibid.*, p. 353).

78. *Ibid.*, III,3, p. 326.

79. The "misconception of nothingness" consists of its being confused with the "negative aspect" of creation (*ibid.*, III,3, pp. 295ff.), which "reminds" us of the "threat and corruption" caused by nothingness (*ibid.*, p. 296); in that negative aspect, the creature "is contiguous to nothingness" (p. 350) but the shadow side is not identical with it.

80. *CD*, III,3, pp. 319ff.

81. *Ibid.*, p. 332.

lishes the existence of this Evil One. Here theology must remain silent. If it wanted to interpret the ontological quality of that No, it would make this No into the basis for speculation rather than simply to repeat the divine as the fearless and alert "No" of faith (1 Pet. 5:8; Eph. 6:10ff.).

We cannot explain how the devil has a place in God's good creation. We can only see him in the light of almighty divine negation, which means that we certainly cannot assign him a third place outside of the Creator and his creation. We can understand him as the disturber, and to resist him and to contend for the reality of created being is a part of the confession of the Creator. "The Bible does not know an unconquerable, almighty, omniscient, omnipresent Satan!"[82]

3. "In the Beginning"—"Out of Nothing"

a. The World Derived from God's Freedom. For our contemporary thought, God is the questionable One. God is the One who must "prove," that is, be proven as the One who fits into the context of our world- and self-knowledge without any inconsequences. The world, in turn, does not seem to necessitate any kind of proof. Or better, it appeared that way until its unquestionableness was revealed to be only an appearance, and some felt that they could only make their way by "rejecting" the world.

For biblical thinking, God is not the One who first has to be established; heaven and earth must be. The fact that God "is" is, in view of his self-disclosure, not a theme for a question placed by the creature. But the fact that the world "is," is a miracle. It "is" because God graciously grants it being, existence, and the kind of existence it has.

This derivation of created reality from the freedom of the divine will is the meaning of the biblical statement that God "made heaven and earth in the beginning," and of the biblically founded dogmatic thesis that this created reality is made "out of nothing" or of "the nothing."

Common to both statements is the fact that we cannot conceive of them in a direct line. We can conceive neither of a beginning nor of a Nothing. If we wanted to arrive at the extreme boundaries of the conceivable, we still could not think of an "In the beginning" which had content nor of a "nothing" which was meaningful. Every beginning which we conceive of is simultaneously an ending. Every nothing which we conceive of is the negation of being, is the code word for the fact that being has become closed or meaningless for us.

b. The Inconceivability of a Sheer Beginning. We said that we cannot conceive of the "beginning" in a direct line. That means that a categorical boundary

---

82. Menken, *op. cit.*, pp. 75f. We might mention here that Luther's view of the devil has been carefully analyzed by H. Obendiek in *Der Teufel bei Martin Luther* (Berlin: Furche Verlag, 1931). Karl Heim, *Jesus the Lord; the Sovereign Authority of Jesus and God's Revelation in Christ*, tr. D. H. van Daalen (Philadelphia: Muhlenberg, 1961), pp. 85–135, develops a detailed Satanology as the background of his Christology, and he builds upon Obendiek.

is set for our thinking in the concept of the "beginning." For, as Kant has shown,[83] we also cannot conceive directly of the world's not having had a beginning. Here we encounter a fundamental conceptual impasse. It will still be there if the contemporary physicists are proven to be right who present illuminating reasons for the assumption that reality as we know it is about five to eight billion years old and we are not able to conceive of energy, mass, space, or time beyond that limit.[84] As important as this theory is, it does not do away with the difficulty laid plain by Kant. As temporal beings, we can only think beyond those imagined limits in a (quasi!) temporal fashion. The purely hypothetical "before" of that first physically conceivable point in time cannot appear to us in any other form than as a "temporal before." This is true even if we understand that "time" cannot be thought of apart from energy and space. In short, our thought becomes unavoidably confused at the concept of a beginning, and Kant is right when he directs man back within the limits of possible "experience," that is, in the realm of his temporality, when he wants to make use of his "pure reason."

c. *Existential Limits*. However, the limits before which we are placed when we deal with the concept of the "beginning" do not include only our thought. We cannot conceive of something absolutely initiating its own existence. We can only comprehend "the accidental" in terms of those conditions within which it happens. Even the modification of causal thinking which modern physics has engendered—a process which is not less significant than the revolution of the European world view which was inaugurated by Copernicus—does not alter the fact that we are only capable of thinking of existence in terms of being conditioned by other existence, even if this conditionedness is not to be seen as rigidly causal but can only be understood as "statistical." Something absolutely new is inconceivable. Therefore, the beginning is a marginal concept which explodes our thinking. If we are not able to conceive of the absolutely new, the beginning, and thus the unconditioned, freedom as such, then this means nothing else than the unavoidable relativity of our thinking. It is oriented toward the conditioned and the relative and is located itself within the circle of conditionedness and relativity. In that, our thinking is an expression of the relativity of our existence. "We think in a circle." "We exist in a circle."[85]

---

83. *The Critique of Pure Reason* ("The Antinomy of Pure Reason, First Conflict of the Transcendental Ideas") (*GBWW*, XLII, 135ff.). The proof that the world has no beginning is deduced from the consideration that the option would be a worldless "void" time before that beginning, in which nothing logically could have come to exist. The reverse proof runs: if I assume the temporal infinity of the world, then an eternity has passed up until my present point in time; since, however, this present point in time is going on, this eternity is constantly increasing, which is conceptually impossible. According to Kant, a similar proof is equally valid for the spatial finitude or infinitude of the world.

84. See C. F. von Weizsäcker, *The History of Nature*, tr. F. D. Wieck (Chicago: University of Chicago Press, 1949, 1951 [g1948]); also his *The World View of Physics*, tr. M. Grene (Chicago: University of Chicago Press, 1952); P. Jordan, *Das Bild der modernen Physik* (Hamburg-Bergedorf: Stromverlag, 1947); G. Howe, *Der Mensch und die Physik; ein Ausschnitt aus der abendländischen Geistesgeschichte* (Wuppertal-Barmen: Jugenddienst Verlag, 1953, 1958³).

85. Dietrich Bonhoeffer, *Creation and Fall; a Theological Interpretation of Genesis 1–3*, tr. J. C. Fletcher (New York; Macmillan, 1959 [g1933]), p. 10.

d. Thinking "in a Circle." Now the point of our thinking is to grasp something valid. That means that within this "circle," we are trying to comprehend something which is not relative but "absolute," not conditioned but unconditioned, even universal. Our thinking would exhaust itself with the research of the mediate, and be satisfied with that, if it were to fail to attempt to gain knowledge of what is absolutely valid.

It still seems to be the simplest approach to regard the "circle" within which we exist and think as itself absolute. This is what relativism does, which, for example, in the racial myth can assume virtually absolutistic, imperialist forms. If there is no truth or righteousness for "everyone," then we shall assert our own truth and our "justice." This is the point of contact between Nietzsche's skepticism and the ideology of nationalism. However, the absolutizing of the "circle," of the relative, is always an arbitrary act—relativism exists in dependence upon the suppressed faith in something "absolute."

The other approach to expressing something absolutely valid is to explain the circle within which we exist, by means of a conceptual postulate, to be transparent or secondary in relationship to another circle which surrounds it and is outside of it. Everything mortal is then "only a parable" and is the outward shell for what in truth does define all things, the idea. Behind the conditioned the unconditioned is concealed, behind the relative the absolute, behind all matter the eternal spirit (which manifests itself in the knowing spirit!). This is the approach so impressively taken by the philosophy of German Idealism.

It is easy to understand that neither Idealism nor of course relativism is capable of thinking of a "beginning" or even prepared to do so. We already spoke of Fichte's protest against the "assumption of a creation."[86] Hegel takes a very careful approach.[87] But Idealism of whatever sort cannot avoid objecting to Christian talk about a beginning. For the concept of a beginning does not just surpass the circle, it explodes it, and the postulated immediacy of the relationship between the knowing human spirit and the eternal divine "origin," which surrounds us or manifests itself in us, is negated. Whoever speaks of a beginning is not talking

---

86. See p. 468.

87. In Hegel, what we have termed the double circle is carried out to perfection. In the process, the two circles are related to one another in a dialectical, polar way. "The reality, which the idea gains as natural liveliness, is therefore a reality of appearance. Appearance, namely, means nothing other than that a reality does exist, but does not have its being in itself immediately, but in its existence is simultaneously posited negatively" (*Sämtliche Werke*, ed. H. Glockner [26 vols. in 24; Stuttgart: Fromann, 1927], XII, 173 [*Aesthetik*, I, ch. 2]). "The world which exists in and of itself is the definite ground of the world of appearance, and is such only to the extent that it itself is the negative moment and thus the totality of all the definitions of its content and of its changes which corresponds to the world of appearance but also comprises its completely opposite side" (P. Hasse, *Hegels Philosophie*, in *Berlin Deutsche Bibliothek* [1917], p. 53, n. 1).

"This second super-sensual world is in this way a distorted world. . . ." (*Sämtliche Werke*, II, 129). "Nature has resulted as the idea in the form of other existence. Since in it the idea as the negative is external to itself, nature is not only relatively external over against this idea (and against the subjective existence of it, the spirit), but this externality comprises the very definition within which it exists as nature" (Hegel, *Die Encyclopädie der philosophischen Wissenschaften im Grundriss* [Jubiläumsausgabe; Stuttgart: Fromann, 1927–] par. 192; also in *Sämtliche Werke*, II, 147).

about eternal originalness but about the Creator! And whoever talks about the Creator is not speaking of the eternal Beyond but of the Absolute Opposite to us. The provocation this creates for Idealism as the most conscious and carefully thought-through form of the human sense of autonomy is found in the fact that the human spirit, which Idealism regards as capable of receiving the Absolute or of reflecting it, is delimited by the emphasis upon a beginning and upon the Creator. It is thrust back into the state of mere createdness and thereby loses its claim to have a direct tie to the Absolute which it calls God. This is the actual reason for the passion with which Fichte's protest was presented.

From our perspective we cannot grasp that there is a beginning. Such a beginning cannot be postulated. The one thing which is valid here is what we similarly found in our discussion of the ontological proof for the existence of God,[88] which is that without the reality of an absolute beginning our thinking has no ultimate validity and our existence no ultimate reason. If there is no breaking into the circle of our relativity from outside, then we are enslaved in it, even if we postulate an absolute which comprehends this relativity. The fact that such postulates are made proves the necessity men feel to know something absolutely valid and to exist in the light of whatever that validity is. The fact that the beginning is rejected proves, in turn, that this thing which man "needs" is in truth a scandal and irritation to him, which he then tries to evade by postulating the Absolute.

e. Eternal Creation? Within theology itself, the "beginning" has frequently been questioned through the raising of the thought of *eternal creation*. The most important proponent of this view was Origen (c. 185–c. 254).[89] He could not imagine that there was a time when God was supposed to have not yet been the Creator. He did concede that our world had a temporal beginning. But if he wanted to maintain the eternal power of the Creator, then he had no alternative than to assert that there must also be an eternal creature, for God is only Creator in his self-communication to the creature. It is clear that here every "beginning" can only be relative in nature. In truth God is himself the beginning in the sense that he communicates his being constantly to the creaturely. His relationship to the creature is not a relationship of freedom, for he can only be who he is when he has the eternal creature before him. But this means that he does in fact become the origin of creation rather than the Creator. And this explains why for Origen and everyone who later thought similarly to him God is no longer actually an "I" who becomes the "Thou" of the creature and is thus encountered "personally." Therefore, some statements in Origen appear to us as early flashes of the kind of thinking which was much later developed in German Idealism—which is not surprising, since Plato is their common origin.

In recent Protestant theology, it was Richard Rothe[90] who expressed thoughts similar to Origen's, here as well as otherwise following along in Hegel's footsteps.

---

88. See pp. 226f.
89. *De Principiis*, III, v (*ANCL*, X, 253–62).
90. *Theologische Ethik* (5 vols.; Wittenberg: Zimmermann, 1867–71²), pars. 39ff.

In that God "defines Himself as the Absolute Person" and thus "thinks the thought of Himself," he posits "in the course of an indestructible logical necessity" "the idea of another being," "that is, a being which is everything which He is not."[91] This "Non-I" of God "is the creature."[92] Since God is essentially the communication of himself, for example, positing himself necessarily once more in polarity to himself, the creation is "a process of becoming the world on the part of God the Spirit,"[93] and this process can only be an "endless" one,[94] which means simultaneously that God's creating must also be thought of as "without a beginning."[95] More clearly than in any other theologian we see here that the concept of eternal creation must result in making the creature into the correlation or complement of God. With regard to Origen, Schleiermacher saw this danger, although he did not decide on the question of whether we can speak of temporal or eternal creation because it "has no bearing on the content of the feeling of absolute dependence."[96]

f. The Discussion of the Beginning and the Faith. We saw that the beginning cannot be postulated. Thomas Aquinas was right when he said that it is "an object of faith" but not "of demonstration or science" that the world has a beginning.[97] It is important that a theologian as strongly influenced by ontological thinking as this one, reflects at a decisive point upon the fact that our discourse about a beginning can be nothing other than our testimony to faith in the Creator.[98] If it were even possible to postulate an absolute beginning, it would not be the beginning which God had established. Only when God's freedom in his turning to the creature, this miracle of God which cannot be conceived of in advance, is believed, can we speak about the absolute beginning.

But of course, it then is possible to express what is meant in substance when we speak of the beginning.

g. "The Creation of the World with Time, in Time." We begin again with the concept that it is in fact inconceivable that there was a time in which God "was not yet" the Creator. This is a fiction. It is not possible to speak of a time before the beginning which is analogous to our time. Augustine was certainly correct when he expressed the famous proposition that the world was created "with time" *(cum tempore).*[99] "Before" time all there is is the Creator and his eternity. But

---

91. *Ibid.*, I, 154.
92. *Ibid.*, I, 161.
93. *Ibid.*, I, 186.
94. *Ibid.*, I, 188.
95. *Ibid.*, I, 192.
96. Schleiermacher, *ChrF*, §41, 2, I, p. 155.
97. *STh*, I,xlvi,2, vol. I, p. 243.
98. Thomas refers back to the unprovableness of the doctrine of the Trinity (*STh*, I,xxxii,1, vol. I, pp. 168–70).
99. *The City of God*, XI, 6 (*NPNF*, II, 208). Time is only present where there is some "movement and transition." In eternity there is no "change." Therefore, there can only be time where there is the creature. Therefore, "assuredly the world was made, not in time, but simultaneously with time." In the "condition" of the world there is simultaneously established a "movement of change" which provides the sole presupposition for the discussion of time.

eternity, as we have already sought to explain,[100] is in reality not something "before," nor "above"; rather, it is the perfection of God which is incommensurable with created time, yet still open to it in the very act of creation as the act which includes and encloses time. When we think about the beginning, we may not forget that God's eternity is his "preparedness" for time.

We can therefore accept the situation that theology, as a human endeavor, can only imagine the beginning in temporal, objective terms, although it is certainly beyond all temporal objectivity. But when Augustine connects this thesis that the world is created with time with the thesis that it is not created "in time," and thus seeks to abrogate the temporality of the beginning for very clear reasons, then we can only answer him that, on the contrary, the creation is truly temporal, because in it the world is established together with time.[101] This thesis is paradoxical, to be sure. But it is no less paradoxical than the other thesis that God's eternity is revealed to us as his freedom from time in time, and it does not imply any more than this: the beginning, unavailable to us and concealed from us, is the invisible place at which our time enters into existence, established by the Creator in eternity and out of his eternity, willed and confirmed by him. Time is not based upon abstract timelessness but upon God's eternity. That means that it has issued forth from the founding act of the Creator, and the beginning is not only the point at which eternity and time divide but also at which they are bound together by the almighty word of the Creator. Time is God's time.

h. The Knowledge of the "Beginning." How can we know that? We must emphasize "we." For "we" do not stand in a continuous relationship to this beginning. The way we are as encountered by the proclamation of the Word, the beginning and the Creation are both sealed off to us because the Creator himself is sealed off or, better, because we close ourselves to the Creator. How should we then know that the Creator nevertheless is not closed to us, that his eternity is not only judgment and destruction but also abrogation and fulfillment of our "lost" time. How could *we* say that God's eternity is his "preparedness" for time? The answer can only be a Christological or soteriological one. Paul said of Jesus Christ in Colossians 1:18 that he is the "beginning" as the "first-born from the dead." And the Johannine witness points in the same direction (1 John 1:1; John 1:1–3). In Colossians 1:18 the view is first of all to the "new creation." Because Christ "in rising again had inaugurated the kingdom of God, He is rightly called the beginning. For we truly begin to exist in the sight of God, when we are

---

100. See pp. 455ff.

101. Augustine, *op. cit.*, and *Confessions*, XI, xxx, 40 (*NPNF*, I, 174), makes the existence of time virtually dependent upon that of the "creature" ("there could be no time without a created being" [*Confessions, loc. cit.*]). Therefore he can say, certainly quite pointedly, that God made the world "without time" *(ibid.)*. In view of this position, his proposition about the world being created not "in" but "with time" is cast into a doubtful shadow. Time is placed so totally on the side of the created and eternity (as that in which there is no "change"!) is contrasted with it so abruptly, that Augustine does approach the view of the timeless beginning, in spite of his polemics against it (*The City of God*, XI, 4 [*NPNF*, II, 206f.]). Barth's polemics are relevant (*CD*, III,1, pp. 69ff.), especially in their climax, "The world is made with time, and therefore in time."

renewed and become new creatures."[102] But clearly Colossians 1:18 refers to the thought in Romans 4:17 where God is testified to in one breath as the One "who gives life to the dead and calls into existence the things that do not exist." That is in turn a statement which is only an anticipation of Romans 4:24, where God is confessed as the One "that raised from the dead Jesus our Lord." In view of the knowledge already discussed that the Creation is only disclosed to us in the "new creation" and thus the Creator reveals himself to us as the Reconciler, we may certainly say that we could not express anything at all about the beginning if God did not encounter us in Christ as he himself.

We need only to ask, then, whether or not we do not also have the right to think, with the Johannine witnesses, in the reverse direction and to say that, just as the Creator encounters us as he himself in the reconciler, the Creation also has its inner basis, its determination, and its meaning in reconciliation and thus in the Reconciler. This question must be answered in the positive. The Creator is none other than the Reconciler who fulfills and will perfect his covenant in Jesus Christ. Then we may certainly say that Christ, the Son, was the eternal Word "from the beginning" (1 John 1:1), that he was "in the beginning" with God (John 1:2), and that everything was made by him (John 1:3). And then we can say with Thomas Aquinas that the "in the beginning" of the first statement of the Bible implies simultaneously "in the Son" (*In principio . . . in Filio*).[103] But Calvin, who otherwise as an exegete of John's Gospel advocates the creation mediation of the Son,[104] explains as a sober exegete of Genesis that it is "altogether frivolous to say that the concept of the beginning points to Christ."[105] But must we not admit that the priestly account in Genesis 1 is looking at Yahweh, the God of Israel, the God of the covenant? It would certainly be empty speculation to say that in Genesis 1 Christ was being thought of directly. Calvin is right in that. But it is not speculation to see, together with Thomas and also with Calvin, that beginning, which is beyond our grasp, as the one established in the Son of God, as the gracious beginning based upon God's eternal Yes to the creature. Then, looking back to Origen, we can say, Yes, God is the Creator in eternity, but to be that he does not require an eternal creature, because God in eternity is turned toward the creature in his Son and is prepared for time.

---

102. Calvin, *The Epistles of Paul the Apostle to the Galatians, Ephesians, Philippians and Colossians*, tr. T. H. L. Parker (Grand Rapids: Eerdmans, 1965), p. 311.

103. *STh*, I,xlvi,3, vol. I, p. 244; against the assertion that the world has no beginning, Thomas interprets this "In the beginning" with the addition "of time." Against dualism he states, "in the beginning, that is, in the Son." Against the view that God used "spiritual creation" as the medium of creation, Thomas says, "In the beginning, that is, before all things." For the second of these three theses he appeals to Ps. 104:24 and to Col. 1:16. In addition, see Augustine, *De Genesi ad Litteram*, I, 1 (Migne, *PL*, XXXIV, 247).

104. "For there are two distinct powers of the Son of God. The first appears in the architecture of the world and in the order of nature. By the second he renews and restores fallen nature" (*The Gospel according to St. John 1-10*, tr. T. H. L. Parker [Grand Rapids: Eerdmans, 1959], pp. 12f.). See also *Institutes*, I, xiii, 8, pp. 130f. and especially *Congrégation sur la divinité de Jésus-Christ* (1558) (*CR*, XLVII, 465ff.).

105. Calvin, *Commentaries on the Book of Genesis*, tr. J. King (Grand Rapids: Eerdmans, 1948), I, 69.

i. The Constant Beginning. If we may view the beginning in this fashion, then it ought already to be clear that it can never become for us a *historical* past. It is beyond our grasp. But not in the sense of the "vulgar concept of time," as though God had once been the Creator and is not that any more. There is no place for a past Creator in Christian proclamation. It is closed to both Deism and Pantheism. It understands God's Creatorhood as the impenetrable act, done once and for all, which manifests itself in the covenant event and presently in its fulfillment, in the Son.

Therefore we cannot speak of the beginning in its relationship to the present reality of the world in causal categories. Causality is related to God's Creatorhood and power of providence in the same way that time is to eternity. On the one hand, the one cannot be measured by the other, and on the other, eternity is open for time. It is thus impossible to regard the Creator as the "first cause" in relationship to the wealth of "second causes"—as though there were a category which would enclose both him and the creature! But it would be possible to say, certainly, that God, who in his freedom determined the existence of the creature and of time and summoned them into being and who became "involved" with the creature in the act of the beginning, comprehends even causality within his eternal freedom. He is not subject to it, but it is subordinate to him.[106] For faith, therefore, causally determined reality cannot be closed off over against the Creator. When scientific research today comes upon phenomena which cannot be understood causally,[107] it has not thereby discovered God's work or even his possibility, but it has dethroned one of the last gods of Europe, the idea of a structure of reality which is a completely closed system. Theology will continue to maintain that "between Creator and creature there is neither a law of motive nor a law of effect nor anything else."[108] Between him and the creature there is only his free act.

j. "Out of Nothing." The concept of creation out of nothing is found in those terms only in the apocryphal 2 Maccabees (7:28), where the mother of the seven martyred sons admonishes the youngest as he approaches his death to look at the heavens and the earth and everything in them and to remember that "God has made them out of nothing" (NEB). In essence, however, Romans 4:17 does not say anything else, and an analogous thought is behind 2 Corinthians 4:6. It is also present in the Hebrew *bara'* (to create), which is used only of God's creative activity and implies no relationship to any already given matter. It is true that our two accounts of creation do not express anything of a "creation out of nothing." But we must remember that it is difficult for Hebrew to express an

---

106. See on the whole problem, K. Barth, *CD*, III,3, pp. 101ff.

107. See especially Pasqual Jordan, *Physics of the 20th Century*, tr. E. Oshry (New York: Philosophical Library, 1944). It ought to be clear that our thinking here also provides the basis for the interpretation of miracles.

108. Dietrich Bonhoeffer, *op. cit.*, p. 14. It is somewhat misunderstandable when Bonhoeffer continues, "Between Creator and creature there is simply nothing: the void," and when he provides his reason, "For freedom happens in and through the void." It sounds as though "the nothing" is really the "privative nothing" (*nihil privativum*), the negative but existing being which Bonhoeffer himself rejects (p. 15).

abstract concept of nothingness, and yet it is certainly made adequately clear that God has in his creative activity neither a partner nor an opponent (as in the Babylonian and other myths), nor even any presuppositions. Just as there is no time before the beginning, there is nothing extant before creation.

This was even emphasized by Orthodoxy by its interpreting this "nothing" as the "negative nothing" *(nihil negativum)*. It sought to prevent the development of complex speculation about the "nothing" derived from the concept of "creation out of nothing," and thus rejected the concept of the "negative nothing" which was close to the Greek *mē on* (non-being) and would have made such speculation possible. Since today the concept of nothingness has moved so much into the foreground and often appears as a corollary of the concept of being, theology has good reason to let things stand with the marginal concept of the "negative nothing," which cannot be analyzed further. God bears the ground and the presuppositions of his creative activity in himself. He does not need the creature, and his activity requires no presupposition outside his own being. Outside of the Creator there is nothing other than the creature. God is the absolutely free Creator—"creation from nothing." He is the absolutely free Reconciler—"the justification of the godless." He is the absolutely free Perfecter—"the resurrection of the dead"!

XII. The Providence of God

A. CREATION AND PROVIDENCE

a. The Past and the Present of the Work of Creation. "To make God a momentary Creator, who once for all finished his work, would be cold and barren."[1] To be sure, when we talk about the Creator, we are also talking about the past, a past of a very unique kind. The concepts "in the beginning" and "out of nothing" point out that God's creative act is absolutely beyond our grasp. And that is the very reason that the concept of the past is not adequate to comprehend them. There is between the past and that which we can grasp intellectually no tangible continuity. We cannot assign a place to the "beginning" and to the summoning of the creature from nothing. Only in the encounter which the Creator provides us with Jesus Christ, in the freedom of his grace revealed there and in the gift of his covenant fulfilled there, can we perceive that he is absolutely free and absolutely gracious, that he is the Unconditioned One. Therefore, creation can never become for us a past event, closed and sealed in itself. For we cannot approach it through a "regress to infinity," but only in the self-disclosure of the Creator, in Jesus Christ through the Holy Spirit, which liberates us to become responsible.

Our present relationship to the Creator, therefore, is not of the same conditioned nature as is our present in relationship to our past (that would be Deism). The Creator did not once set the creaturely reality into operation so that we only had to deal with him through the medium of this past event and its effects. The Creator is rather present as the Lord. He is the One who made "me," and who is "my" God and "my" Father. God grants us our present just as he has prepared our past for us. He is not an "idle God" *(deus otiosus)*.[2]

This means that we may accept the reality given and assigned to us, which conditions our existence and our activity, as not only once "begun" by him but also as presently ruled by him, under his sway, under his "providence." God would not be God if the situation were different. "To deny providence is to deny God."[3]

---

1. Calvin, *Institutes*, I, xvi, 1, p. 197.
2. E.g., Calvin, *Institutes*, I, xvi, 4, pp. 201–03.
3. Johannes Wolleb, *Compendium theologiae Christianae* (1626), in *Reformed Dogmatics*, ed. and tr. J. W. Beardslee III (New York: Oxford University Press, 1965), p. 59.

Thus "faith in creation" contains "faith in providence." But can we also say that God's providence can be equated with the creation, that they are two different sides of the same thing?

This question has been answered affirmatively from two different directions and in very different senses.

b. "*Continued Creation*"=*creatio continuata.* Orthodoxy in many of its proponents spoke of "conservation" (as a work of divine providence) as "continued creation." This means something different depending upon whether one is thinking of "active creation" (the divine act of creating) or "passive creation" (the creatures' being created and their createdness). In the former instance, the dominant idea is that the creaturely reality always needs the activity of its Creator. It exists only because and to the degree that its God grants it constantly its existence.[4] In the latter instance, it is an inherent quality of the creature to continue to exist because of the unique act of creation which summoned it into existence.[5] Only in the former case does the creature continually require the Creator. But we can see that the Orthodox theologians usually connected both of the aspects of creation mentioned with each other, and clearly did so on the basis of the metaphysics of being. God as the Being of all being is necessarily and permanently the origin of the reality which exists. The decisive thing ultimately is whether "conservation" is really understood as the free activity of God which is rooted alone in his grace,[6] or whether it is ontologically necessary. If the latter is even silently assumed, then the concept of "continued creation" amounts to nothing less than the reduction of the concept of creation itself and the transformation of

---

4. Of the Lutheran Orthodox Andreas Quenstedt should be especially mentioned here (*Theologia didactico-polemica* [1685], I, xiii, 14, p. 531 [Schmid, p. 187]): "God preserves all things by the continuance of the action by which he first produced things." The Reformed express themselves frequently in accordance with this. H. Heppe (Heppe-Bizer, p. 251) finds that "the Reformed conception of the doctrine of Providence is characterized in the first instance by the fact that in it the conception of Providence is validated as an element of creation or as the reverse side of it." In any case, the pointed emphasis upon the activity of God is characteristic, based upon Calvin. The concept of the "continuation of creation" is found in Z. Ursinus, *Commentary on the Heidelberg Catechism*, tr. G. W. Williard (Grand Rapids: Eerdmans, 1956), p. 147, and also in this sense in Cocceius, *Summa Theologiae* (1662), XXVIII, 9 ("conservation is . . . quasi the continued creation"), and Ames, *The Marrow of Theology*, ed. and tr. J. D. Eusden (Boston: Pilgrim Press, 1968), I, ix, 18, p. 109, and thus not only in the Orthodox in the more narrow sense like Walaeus (*Loci communes* [1640], p. 292). For further references, see Heppe-Bizer, pp. 251 and 257ff.

5. The matter is stated most clearly in J. Gerhard (*Loci communes theologici*, VI, 6, ed. F. R. Frank [1885ff.], II, 27), although without the use of the term "continuing creation": "According to the definition of Scaliger, conservation is nothing else but a continuation of existence. To be and to be preserved is to be attributed to the same author and principle." The influence of the metaphysic of being here can be demonstrated in the idea that "conservation" is a "continual influx" (*continuus influxus*) without which creaturely things can neither be nor act.

6. K. Barth, *CD*, III,3, pp. 71f., cites a very important and surprising statement (for many) in Thomas, *STh*, I,civ,4, vol. I, p. 514, according to which the "annihilation of things does not pertain to the manifestion of grace." The statement loses some of its importance, however, because Thomas obviously is assuming his own concept of grace whereas Barth transfers it to the evangelical concept.

creation into an ontic relationship of origins. This was Schleiermacher's approach, and others followed him.[7]

c. "Continuing Creation" =creatio continua. More recent theology speaks frequently of a "continuing creation," usually in the sense that we only gain sight of creation in the experience of history as established and guided by God. The formative motif here is in the emphasis upon the current relevance of faith in the Creator. It is quite easy for this approach to neglect all talk of a "beginning" and direct its discourse about the Creator toward a "first thing" *(principium)* without a "beginning" *(initium)*. Seen superficially, the tendency here is rather the reverse of Orthodoxy. Orthodoxy began with the "beginning" and thought of "conservation" as the "continuation" of the work of God which had once been initiated. Today, the position is taken in the here and now, and God is understood as the continual origin of the event. However, the difference is not that great in reality, since in Orthodoxy God is also the "first principle" as the Being of all being, and therefore the "beginning" was merely understood as the beginning of the emergence of existing things out of this Being, which for its part continues to exist.[8]

The concept of "continued" or even "continuing creation" can actually express something which is correct, but which is better expressed with the concept of "the Creator continuing His own work" *(creator opus suum continuans)*. But it is definitely a term which it is inadvisable to use. That is more true today than it was in the days of Orthodoxy, because we are in the particular danger today of cladding *our* "Today" with a dignity which it certainly does not deserve from the perspective of God the Creator. Whereas a few decades ago it was necessary to oppose the displacement of the Creator into the distant past in the constant style of Deism, today it is necessary to reject our coercing God into our contemporaneity which only results in making God into a concept which is at our disposal, and which may be used to illuminate the puzzles of our existence. It can be said that God is the concealed origin or the origin which encounters us in the "Thou" of the other,[9] and this thesis can indeed be understood correctly. However, this thesis does in fact enter into the setting of an ontology for which

---

7. According to Schleiermacher (*ChrF*, §36, 1, I, p. 142), the statement "that God sustains the world" is "precisely similar" to the statement about the creation of the world.

8. Proceeding on the foundation of F. Brunstäd's theology, E. Gerstenmaier could speak of the "continuing creation" in *Die Kirche und die Schöpfung, eine theologische Besinnung zu dem Dienst der Kirche an die Welt* (Berlin: Furche-Verlag, 1938), pp. 70ff. In essence, F. Gogarten did so too, although he firmly maintains that "faith in the creation is not the knowledge of a universal truth of reason or a supra-temporal necessity of being," but "faith in a temporal event" (*Ich glaube an den dreieinigen Gott, eine Untersuchung über Glauben und Geschichte* [Jena: Diederichs, 1926], p. 48); yet he connects faith in creation "to the special situation" (*ibid.*, p. 65) and finds the point of departure for all thinking and argument in "our knowing ourselves to be created" (p. 68). "To believe in God the Creator means . . . to believe that history is God's work" (p. 78). Emil Brunner's treatment of "continuing creation" *(creatio continua)* is not essentially different (*Dogmatics*, II, 33ff., 148). And Karl Barth once spoke in the same fashion (*CD*, I,2, pp. 688ff.) but more lately polemicized against the term quite sharply (*CD*, III,3, pp. 4f., 68ff.).

9. F. Gogarten, *op. cit.*, p. 60: "The content of the faith is . . . the encounter with the concrete Thou as the creature of God."

(not being in itself, but rather) being-over-against-the-other is the element which the Creator and the creature have ontically in common. And there is no other conceivable result than the ontological coordination of Creator and creature, which is in effect the levelling of faith in the Creator. It is because the concept of "continued" or "continuing" creation has an obscuring effect here that it is to be rejected. The danger of Pantheism, which lurks in the background of every metaphysic of being, does not require additional discussion here.[10]

   d. The Difference Between Creation and Providence. Creation and conservation, or creation and providence cannot be identified as one, although certainly the Creator is the Conserver and Ruler. The most illuminating reason for this is the simple fact that God's conserving and ruling activity, his providence, by no means takes place "out of nothingness," but conserves created existence as something already extant and active and thus presupposes it. Both Scholasticism and Orthodoxy were acutely aware of this. They attempted to respect it by distinguishing between God as the "first cause" and the "second causes" within created reality. Regardless of the way one proceeds terminologically, the distinction between creation and providence should be quite clearly obvious. Christian theology in general has never fallen prey to the temptation of assuming the Creator's omnicausality so that the reality of the creature's activity was severely restricted. Conversely, it has never assigned such importance to the creature's own causality that the effectiveness and reality of the Creator were made into nothing more than the initiative past. It has avoided both Pantheism and Deism. In doing so, however, it has confronted in the creature's own capacity to work effectively in the world one of the two great problems of the doctrine of providence. The other great problem is raised by the fact of evil. How is God, in his preserving, accompanying, and ruling the creature (to use K. Barth's expression), to be seen in relationship to the evil which is also the evil in the creature? God's providence must cope not with something neutral, nor with something created good, but with the creature who is resisting God's will. The fact of sin makes our thinking about God's providence fraught with profound tension. If faith states that God's will happens, then it cannot avoid the riddle that God's will does not in fact take place in our lives, and so it can then only speak of God's providence in the petition which is confident of its own fulfillment, "Thy will be done."[11]

   e. The Concrete Import of the Doctrine of Providence. Under these circumstances, the doctrine of providence is not dealing with a problem which is only

---

   10. E. Brunner, who approves of the term "continuing creation," warns of the "pantheistic danger" and states, "The danger-zone has already been entered when Creation and Preservation are identified with one another. For anyone who does not admit the distinction between the creation and the preservation of the created world does not take the fact of creation seriously" (*Dogmatics*, II, 33f.).

   11. In K. Barth this point of view receives too little attention. He first of all develops (*CD*, III,3) the doctrine of providence without any notable attention to sin, and then the doctrine of "nothingness," which follows methodically and thematically upon the doctrine of providence but still is not an element of it. The result of this division in his thinking is that the creature in the sense of providence is not seen clearly enough as a sinner.

found in the realm of intellectual reflection. We stated that our confession of God as the Creator is both a comfort and a declaration of battle, because it amounts to the rejection of the creature's own autonomous powers and denies both the trust of the creature and the fear of it. In the same way, our confession of God in his providence is our rejection of the omnipotence of sin and our testimony to the certainty that God does accomplish his will in spite of myself and the power of all evil, and that he will accomplish it. It is our certainty that God for the sake of Jesus Christ has taken sides for me as his creature against all the assembled powers, including the powers which attack and enslave me. Speculation about God's "providence" *(pronoia)* holding sway in all things does not "cost" anything. But faith in God and in his providence does "cost" something, for it cannot exist at all without the practical knowledge that I am not intended to do the will of the Evil One but rather to do God's will and to pray that his will be done.

f. The Faith in Providence and the Idea of Divine Omnicausality. Accordingly, the doctrine of providence like the doctrine of the creation is to be seen in clear relationship to soteriology. Faith in providence is not "a kind of forecourt, or common foundation, on which the belief of the Christian Church may meet with other concepts of the relationship of what is called 'God' with what is called 'world.' "[12] It is faith in the Creator who does not let himself be dethroned as Creator by all of the creature's own work and by all of sin, nor as the Lord of the Covenant. It is faith in Christ.

It cannot be said that the dogmatic tradition has in every instance dealt properly and adequately with the fact that belief in providence is Christian belief. The main reason for this is that Christian theology from very early was involved in contact and disputation with the Stoic doctrine of providence, the doctrine of "fate" *(anankē).*[13] In addition, the ontological conception, chiefly derived from Aristotle but also to a degree from Neo-Platonism, renders its influence; it asserts that God is the "first cause" of all things that happen. The common and fundamental thought, which was not without its effect on the Church's theology, was that everything happens according to an inviolable law and that God was its cause or epitome. It is immediately clear that God in such a thought is not free. At the most, he could have been free when he set the worlds in motion. But now everything must proceed as he has established it, that is, as he has ordained it to function causally. God is in any event in this deterministic view the ultimate component part of the world structure, but certainly not its Creator. He is what is beyond it, but he is not opposite to it. When Christian theology absorbs such thinking, and when it believes that it can combine it with the ontologically applied

---

12. K. Barth, *CD*, III,3, p. 26.

13. On the Stoic belief in providence, see M. Pohlenz, *Die Stoa, Geschichte einer geistigen Bewegung* (2 vols.; Göttingen: Vandenhoeck & Ruprecht, 1955–59 [g1948]), I, 98ff.; II, 55f. In Thomas Aquinas (*STh*, I,cxvi, vol. I, pp. 566–68; *On the Truth of the Catholic Faith [Summa Contra Gentiles]*, tr. A. C. Pegis *et al.* [5 vols.; Garden City: Doubleday, 1955], III, 93, vol. III, pt. 2, pp. 49f.) "fate," which he affirms conditionally, appears as "the ordering of second causes to effects foreseen by God" (*STh*, I,cxvi, 4, vol. I, p. 568). Thereby only the empty hull of the Stoic concept is left.

concept of God's omnipotence (omnicausality), it becomes enmired in a road leading nowhere. It can certainly never successfully show what such a God is supposed to have to do with the God who discloses himself to us in Jesus Christ.

g. *The Creature's Own Reality.* The difference between the Christian discussion of God's providence and the idea of omnicausality is seen even more clearly when we bear in mind that the Christian doctrine of providence includes the creature's own activity and acknowledges the reality of evil in the realm of the creation.

The creature's own activity can only be dealt with mediately in the context of an ontologically determined doctrine of providence. It then belongs to the circle of "second causes" which all result from the "first cause." But if God's providence consists of his making the creature's own activity mediate, then we have in fact the conditionedness, but never the responsibility of man. In other words, it is man's createdness which is at stake here.

What is the place of evil in the context of a reality which is determined by divine omnicausality? It is quite clear that evil then belongs to caused reality. If it really happens, then God willed it to happen. And if that is true, then evil loses its character as evil or evil is acknowledged as such in the specific instance and in regard to the specific person, but in the process of speculative thought it is built into the total process of the event as a positive element. The "theodicy" idea, which we have thus approached, when it is built upon the presupposition of divine omnicausality, always results in depriving evil of its actual wickedness by explaining it and building it into a conceptual whole. It can only appear to be evil, or be relatively evil, since it is also integrated as the evil in the good, in the purposeful course of the totality of reality.

B. PROVIDENCE AND "FATE"

We have stated that our belief in God the Creator is not deduced from an analysis of our selves nor from the observation of the reality which precedes and surrounds us. Similarly, our belief in God's rule in his providence does not have its roots in observation nor its form in the interpretation of life, of history, or of the course of the world.

However, since the Church lives in the world, its talk about God as the Preserver and Ruler is subject to confusion with an interpretation of life and history, both within and outside of theology. This confusion is all the more possible the more urgently a generation is required to deal with the problem of "fate."

a. *Interpretations of Fate.* The attempt at interpreting events is usually motivated less by a theoretical need than by a felt need of life. "Fate" is experienced, in the riddle of both life and death, in collective or individual experiences, in the connection between our acts and their consequences or conversely in the concealed nature of that connection; it is experienced in the reality of guilt, perhaps in the very knowledge of one's personhood. This experience can be related both to "nature" and to "history," to what is usually regarded as respectable and to what is abhorrent, unexpected, and destructive. There are terms for fate which are in reality nothing more than names for the various kinds of experience mentioned here. We could mention, of the terms offered in J. Konrad's typology, "puzzling fate (Sphinx)" or "coincidence (Tyche)."[14] These terms do not yet include any attempt at an "interpretation." But man reacts to the experience of his incomprehensible conditionedness[15] not only by giving it names but also with the attempt to objectify it by interpreting it. Mythology generally is the first source of a means for doing this (we think of Nemesis, or the Erinyes). It is then followed by philosophy, in the more or less emphatic process of the secularization of mythology. The types suggested by J. Konrad which would be mentioned here include "the necessity of fate (Ananke)," "tragic fate (Moira)," and above all "the order of fate (Pronoia)."[16] All attempts at interpretation are, however, characterized by the fact that they basically want to accomplish more than just objectification. The objectifying itself serves the attempt "to cope with fate," that is, to be able intellectually to master it. Man does not want to be merely the object of the processes which make him happy or disturb him; he would like to participate in them reflectively, he would like to "get behind them." And this, in turn, will serve him in opposing his "fate" by choosing what he has recognized as "meaning." In that he knows what the meaning is, he is elevated beyond the mere facticity of what he experiences. In this fashion, the interpretations of fate and of history become covert or overt redemptive religions. The interpretation of the world which has been most influential, that of the Stoa (from whom we have received the concept of "providence"), belongs in this context. The wise man who knows what is in fact happening is able to be not merely the object of factual happenings but the co-participating subject. Man is "redeemed" in that he opts for the law of the happening, be it known by him or concealed from him. Thus, the knowledge of the "meaning" is customarily accompanied by the corresponding guidelines for life.

   b. Determinism and Indeterminism. The two most influential basic forms of the interpretation of events correspond to the two basic forms of human self-understanding. Determinism corresponds to man's understanding of himself based upon the world, as a highly variable basic form for the interpretation of events. Indeterminism corresponds to the self-understanding based upon an "I" which sets itself apart from the world.[17] In Determinism, the experience of conditionedness is the foundation of the system. In Indeterminism the experience of personhood or of "should-ness" forms the foundation. In more recent times, Determinism appears almost invariably as causal Determinism. On the basis of that world view, it is subject to the same questions which are applicable to the traditional views of a causal structure for all of reality as a closed system. Indeterminism, which was based in the 19th century primarily upon an ontology of the spirit (see German

---

14. Joachim Konrad, *Schicksal und Gott, Untersuchungen zur Philosophie und Theologie der Schicksalserfahrung* (Gütersloh: C. Bertelsmann, 1947), pp. 22ff., 33ff.
   15. See pp. 471ff.
   16. J. Konrad, *op. cit.*, pp. 24ff., 26ff., 31ff.
   17. See also pp. 471ff.

Idealism), has retreated to pure analysis of existence, since the emergence of value philosophy and of phenomenology. These two basic forms of interpretation, both of which can be traced back to antiquity, have not been able to overcome each other. We shall have to say that this will never be possible. Their differences are based upon two differing views of reality, upon differing ways for man to cope with reality and to master it by choosing the interpretation of meaning which has been gained. Since this interpretation of meaning is always derived from a self-understanding, it is always in fact an attempt to surpass given reality with all its riddles by means of the knowledge of an inner reality which is prior and superior to it. What happens is not, in fact, the genuine overcoming of fate, but the illumination of its nature: something *beyond* the world and life is caught sight of.

c. Determinism and Indeterminism in Relation to the Doctrine of Providence. It should not be surprising that Christian proclamation has been enlisted or has gotten itself involved in both of the great directions endeavoring to interpret fate. Proclamation speaks both of freedom and of God's providence, and its unique feature is that it says both. Then, of course, both could be conceived of in relation to the interpretive direction which made either freedom or conditionedness into its systematically dominant thought. In the process, though, theological thought has had to sacrifice its essential content. If it regarded God's providence as the theological formulation for what otherwise is known as omnicausality in the deterministic sense, or if it looked upon the freedom given by God as the theologically knowable legitimation for what otherwise was regarded as freedom, then it has lost sight of its own unique content. It has made God, who is the Opposite to the creature, into the god who is what is beyond given reality, a principle for the explanation of the world. And thus it offers to man another kind of redemption than that which is offered in Jesus Christ. Conversely, such theology ends up enmired in the antinomies and intellectual dead-ends which result from such interpretations of events, so that it sacrifices its own unique tension and its actual "matter" at the same time.

d. The Special Emphasis of Belief in Providence. The Christian belief in providence differs from every other view of the course of the world and of life in that it is derived from the perception of the divine Yes to his creature, that is, from the event of the incarnation, crucifixion, and resurrection of Jesus Christ. The ultimate question which every interpretation of history leaves open, the question about a Yes which encounters us in the midst of the conditionedness of our existence, is already answered for the Christian faith. And that answer is not derived from the events which we experience or participate in, but rather it enters into this event. The god of all interpretations of life is the epitome of a law and is bound to that law. He is a silent, automatic "god." He is not himself free (not even when he is conceived of as the epitome of human freedom in contrast to the course of the world). Since he is the epitome of a lawful course of the world or of the higher determination of man represented in the self, he is enslaved by the very thing he epitomizes. "God" belongs then to the closed structure of what factually happens or to the intellectual meaning which stands over it. This then also means that this "god" can only be disclosed on the basis of what happens, and he bears its character. He is a function of the world viewed either positively or negatively. In contrast to that, the Christian faith is based upon the fact that God has disclosed himself to us as "our" God within our uninterpreted world but not subject to it or derived from it. Belief in providence is not the result of an interpretation of historical developments and does not lead up to any. The believer does not know the "why" and "whence." But he does know God the Creator who comes to meet us, and he hears his call even in the darkness.

e. *God and "Fate."* Going on, this then means that God does not function for faith the way in which "fate" *(fatum)* does for Stoicism.[18] God is neither the law of the world nor coincidence, nor the epitome of either. Rather, in the encounter with the living God, every possibility of believing in fate is destroyed. "Fate" is one of the "elemental substances of the world" *(stoicheia tou kosmou)* whose blinding and destructive power has been destroyed by Christ, as the Christian knows.

God is not located, so to speak, at the basis of the course of human events. That does not mean that history is left to itself or is its own god. But it does mean that God's freedom in his grace is not knowable on the basis of history, even for faith. God is not revealed as the Free nor the Gracious, neither as the Judge nor as the Helper in the course of history itself. History remains, even for faith, ambiguous. It cannot be deduced from history directly whether God is good or evil, whether the "cause" is God or the devil. We only perceive that God really rules in his goodness in all that happens through the Word which comes to us. But this Word does not come to us as a word which enlightens us and solves all the puzzles. It comes to us in the puzzle itself. The realization of the divine Yes to the creature and the manifestation of the lordship of God over it take place in the self-emptying of God, take place in concealment within the No of the cross. God's Yes in Christ, according to Luther's famous sermon for the Second Sunday in Lent (on Matt. 15:21–28), is the "very deep and very concealed [yes]" which "appears to be nothing but no."[19] This means then simultaneously that we cannot experience God's Yes in any other way than in the experience of the No that judges us. It is only in that way that it encounters us really.

Therefore, it is impossible to make a Christian interpretation of the course of history. To be a Christian means rather *to be able to endure the uninterpretability of events*. One could think here, as well as at other points, that the Christian faith with its renunciation of interpretation is very close to Nihilism. But actually the wall between the two, even if it may appear to be very thin, is impenetrable. Between them both stands the living God revealing himself in Christ. Nihilism is

---

18. It was certainly not a good thing that some Orthodox did on occasion equate "fate" with "providence" (e.g., J. Gerhard, *op. cit.*, VI, 13, ed. F. R. Frank [1885ff.], VI, 46) and that J. Konrad, in spite of all kinds of reservations, still can speak of a "Christian fate" *(op. cit.*, pp. 319ff.). We find express rejections of the concept in, among others, Calvin, *Institutes*, I, xvi, 8, pp. 207f., with an appeal to Augustine, *Against Two Letters of the Pelagians*, II, v, 10–II, vi, 12 (*NPNF*, V, 395ff.).

19. J. N. Lenker, ed., *Writings of Martin Luther* [Standard Edition] (Minneapolis: Lutherans in All Lands Company, 1906), XI, 152.

only the linear negation of standing world views, within their own categories. Where others posit being or meaning, it posits the Nothing, or better, "nothing." Faith in God the Creator is not different from every interpretation of the course of events in a linear fashion, but categorically. It does not need the interpretation of event because it lives on the revelation of the grace of God in Jesus Christ, which is unambiguous, even though it is not predictable. It looks in an entirely new direction. It does not ask about the ground of all things, but it answers to the self-disclosure of the One who is good to us in all things, who makes "everything work for good" for us (Rom. 8:28). It is not the course of events which is good, nor its "meaning," but God who is good.

C. GOD'S RULE IN THE WORLD

a. Election and Providence. "We know that in everything God works for good with those who love him, who are called according to his purpose" (Rom. 8:28). We find the whole development of what is meant with the Christian belief in providence summarized in this sentence of Paul.

The position taken here is not located somewhere above our reality, in a place where there are no puzzles and no darkness. We only need to continue reading Romans 8 to see that. The most difficult problems of the doctrine of providence, the "powers," are not neglected here (8:35ff.).

But how can one talk about "knowing" anything in this position? The question could be addressed with the same urgency to the instructions given to the disciples in Matthew 6:25ff.; 10:29–31, or to prophetic statements like Isaiah 45:1–8 or 43:1–7, or to the coronation psalms (47; 93; 96; 97; 99 and to some extent 98). Clearly the issue everywhere is the "everything" of which Paul speaks (and which is inconceivable without Rom. 11:36 or Col. 1:16 or even Eph. 1:11).

This "knowing" is related to those who "love God." They are doubtless the same ones who are the called according to God's "purpose" *(prothesis)*. And what that implies is then explained in Romans 8:29f. The whole mystery of divine election now comes into view. Further, they are apparently the same ones who cannot be separated from the love of God which is revealed in Christ Jesus our Lord, directed to him as the first of many brethren (8:29) and present in him for every believer (8:35, 39).

Belief in providence as it is made known here is clearly rooted in election as the decree of God which is merely preceding (8:29f.; see the number of times the prefix *pro* [before] occurs in these verses!). Election, then, is not the result or the application of providence, but the reverse![20] The first result of this insight is that the man who "knows" something here and about whom one can "know" something does not have an advantage over anyone else. For God's Word of

---

20. This was worked out by K. Barth, whereas Zwingli conversely conceives of predestination together with providence, and Calvin's great design of the doctrine of providence (*Institutes*, I, xvi-xviii) suffers because there is no different reference there to predestination. For Calvin that doctrine belongs not to the doctrine of God but to the "knowledge of God as redeemer."

calling and of the announcement of election confronts man totally apart from any qualifications he might have, in God's absolute freedom and grace. And that leads to a second insight. Because God himself addresses his Yes to this man, that person no longer must deal with the confusion of things both material and spiritual, but only with God, who is both free and powerful in relationship to everything else.

Belief in providence, as it is made known in Romans 8:28, is not the interpretation of the "world," but confession of the One who confronts his creature in free and gracious power. It is because God has demolished the closed circle of conditions in the manifestation of his unconditional pre-decision—that is, it is because he has done so in Jesus Christ as the executor of that decision—that this event becomes the source of our certainty that all things are truly being made serviceable "for the good."

     b. Providence as God's Governance. In everything, faith has to do with God. That is the first insight we gain here. The concept of "providence" does not necessarily express that. It is often based upon the Vulgate text of Genesis 22:8, *Deus providebit* (God will provide). However, although this passage does express something of God's faithfulness to his covenant (which in the context seems to be jeopardized), and does speak about his promise to Abraham's heirs, when we look at the original language, it does not say anything about "providence" in the sense in which Stoicism, its followers, and later Christian theology developed it. It cannot be denied that *pronoia* and *providentia* are both fundamentally not Christian concepts, but rather the product of Greek development,[21] which then was taken over into late Jewish literature,[22] in direct proportion to the weakening in Judaism of the knowledge of the living covenant will of its God. It is significant that the New Testament does not use the term *pronoia* in reference to God but to planning man (Rom. 13:14; Acts 24:2). The terms *prothesis* (purpose [Rom. 8:28; 9:11; Eph. 1:11; 3:11; 2 Tim. 1:9]), *prognōsis* (foreknowledge [Acts 2:23, especially 1 Pet. 1:2]); *proginōskein* (to know beforehand [Rom. 8:29; 11:2; 1 Pet. 1:20]) and *proorizein* (to predestine [Rom. 8:29f.; 1 Cor. 2:7; Eph. 1:5, 11]), to the extent that they designate God's activity, are all clearly related to the doctrine of election. The concept of "providence," which in its usual application is quite alien to biblical language, possesses in its usage outside of the Christian faith such power that Christian theology can only make use of it with the exercise of the

---

21. We find the concept of divine providence as early as Herodotus and in Xenophon, and its philosophical development in Stoicism. For material, see *Stoicorum veterum fragmenta*, ed. J. von Arnim (Stuttgart: Teubner, 1964 [1st ed. 1903–24]). The most well-known sources: Chrysippus, *peri pronoias*, in Giercke, *Chrysippea, Jahrbuch für klassische Philologie*, Supplement XIV (München: Hueber, 1925–27), pp. 691ff.; Cicero, *De natura deorum*, tr. H. Rackham (New York: G. P. Putnam's Sons, 1933), II, xxix–lxi, 73–153, pp. 194–271; Seneca, *On Providence*, tr. J. W. Basore, in *Seneca, Moral Essays* (3 vols.; *Loeb Classical Library*; Cambridge, Mass.: Harvard University Press, 1928, repr. 1958), I, 2–47.

22. Wisd. of Sol. 11:25; 14:3; 17:2; 3 Macc. 4:21; 5:30; 4 Macc. 9:24; 13:18; 17:22, and then especially Philo, *peri pronoia*, in *Stoicorum veterum fragmenta* . . .; see footnote 21 above.

greatest care. This special care must consist, first, of its being conceived of as actual (God's providence is his governing activity), and secondly of considering simultaneously the subject of the activity meant by it, namely, the triune God. It is quite clear that today "providence" is often the coded designation of a god which is not the God proclaimed by the Church, and this is also true of the term "fate." Both of these concepts refer to an ultimate, unknown, silent, and abstract Beyond—this is seen, for instance, in the fact that one cannot pray to either "providence" or "fate."

c. Providence as God's Lordship. The proposition that faith has to do with God in all things needs extra emphasis on the aspect "in all things." The one mystery that God truly encounters us in our world of conditionedness but not out of it contains another mystery: that God shows himself to be really Lord "of everything" in that he took on human "nature," claimed earthly "history" as his, and drew it into his election, in the event of his self-disclosure, and in the event of the covenant. If all things cannot separate us from his love, they are conversely all ordained to work for our "good," that is, for the fulfillment of the goal he has established.

We for our part experience the sinister "autonomy" of all things. It is possible that we experience it today in a much more pressing way than did earlier generations. But Israel also experienced the "raging" of the nations (Ps. 2), and it was apparently only an unimportant ball in their game. The contemporaries of the early Church saw themselves surrounded and threatened every step of the way by various fateful powers, be they earthly, chthonic, or cosmic. "History" was only transparent for an age which, as in the case of the Enlightenment, basically knew very little about it. And "nature," although it reveals itself more and more profoundly to be a "cosmos," has lost much of its mystery in its outward phenomena, such as thunder, lightning, and storms, but in its atomic depths it, too, becomes constantly more sinister. "What is man that thou art mindful of him. . . ?" Faith in God-in-Christ dares, in face of all that, to place its trust in the Word which calls and bears it, and that means that it dares to oppose the non-transparency of both "nature" and "history" with the rationally unprovable thesis that "God the Lord reigns." This is not meant in the sense expressed by Ritschl when he said that "in faith in God's providence" "religious lordship over the world is exercised."[23] "Reigning with him" in the sense of 2 Timothy 2:12 is an expectation—and Ritschl is not thinking of that but is instead giving a religious interpretation of Kant's idea of the freedom of the person toward nature experienced in his moral responsibility. This idea is not the issue here at all. What is the issue is God's rule in the world, which the believer understands to be a rule which benefits us, but which he cannot find in himself but only in the oppositeness of God—and in no other way.

From this position we may now look at some of the thinking of older dogmatics.

---

23. *The Christian Doctrine of Justification and Reconciliation, the Positive Development of the Doctrine,* tr. H. R. Mackintosh and A. B. Macaulay (New York: Scribner's, 1900; Clifton, N.J.: Reference Book Publishers, 1966 [g1895⁴]), p. 617.

d. "General Providence," "Special Providence," "Singular Providence." It may seem to be formalistic hair-splitting when the Orthodox, in dealing with the theme of God's governance, distinguish between "general providence" *(providentia generalis)*, "special providence" *(providentia specialis)*, and occasionally even "singular providence" *(providentia specialissima)*.[24] Where we find this distinction, it is an expression of the consideration that, first of all, God does conserve, accompany, and rule over all of creation in every detail ("general" or "universal providence"), but does so, secondly, in a special way in regard to man as the creature equipped with his own will ("special providence"), and here again in a very unique way in regard to the believer—we could add, as the creature which is opening itself to God's activity. The important thing about this distinction is that its emphasis is directed toward the idea of "singular providence," although it is not often called that. Certainly there was an interest in emphasizing (as the Reformed did especially) that God guides and rules everything, not only in the sense of a general motivation but more in the sense of the directness of his work even through the "medial causes" ("second causes"). God's activity in history (this is the scope of the doctrine of "special providence"), in contrast to every kind of independent capability on man's part, is certainly emphasized strongly. But the most important thing is the believer's certainty, "Nothing can happen to me but what He has foreseen and what is a blessing to me. . . ." Calvin devotes a whole chapter of the *Institutes* to this emphatic application of the doctrine, which makes it quite clear that the doctrine of providence is practically oriented.[25]

What is more important is Orthodoxy's highly developed subdivision of the whole doctrine of providence into "conservation" *(conservatio)*, "concurrence" *(concursus)*, and "governance" *(gubernatio)*, which was frequently placed at the very middle of the argument. More recently, Karl Barth has accepted this approach. The outline is relevant and will be explained in the following paragraphs.

e. Conservation. There are few things so obvious as that the creature "is," and often it is regarded as ontological speculation even to think about it at all. For faith, however, this is by no means a truism. For faith, it is not the creature but God, in and of himself and not necessarily for us, who "is" unquestionably. But then the existence of anything else which is not God, but next to God, is anything but a truism. The very fact that the world "is," that it does not represent an enormous apparition, is for faith a miracle. As is well known, Descartes believed that it was possible to find a guarantee for the objective reality of the

---

24. The distinction between "general providence" (or "universal") and "special providence" is very widespread; Calvin presupposes it in the *Institutes*, I, xvi, 4, pp. 201–03. "Singular providence" is found only once in Calvin (*Institutes*, I, xvii, esp. 6, pp. 218f.), in the context of the broad scope of the doctrine of providence in general, and it was not integrated into the traditional distinctions until much later and then only by a few individuals. On the interpretation of this theme see the article by P. Lobstein on "Providence" in Schaff-Herzog, IX, 306–11 as well as K. Hase, *Hutterus redivivus, oder Dogmatik der evangelischen-lutherischen Kirche, ein dogmatisches Repertorium für Studierende* (Leipzig: Breitkopf & Haertel, 1868[11] [g1845[6]]), p. 151 and elsewhere.

25. *Institutes*, I, xvii, pp. 210–28.

external world in the concept of God alone.[26] But the concept of God can scarcely render this service. Descartes' persuasion about the ontological superiority of the "thinking thing" over the "extended thing" *(res cogitans, res extensa)* shows that his doubt was not radical enough and stopped short at the "thinking thing." But how can I intellectually know that my own thinking has grasped something truly valid? The certainty that I not only can think validly but also have a valid object of my thought does not develop from my thought itself. In fact, it only grows in me as God shows himself to me as the Unconditioned One. And in that it is truly established. To put it another way, this validity, this super-empirical reality of both knowing and of the known, this conviction "that I myself am and that the world around me is," can only be expressed from the basis "that it pleased God to become man."[27] From that basis we can then truly say, ". . . I *may exist*, the world may exist, although it is a reality distinct from God. . . . God in the highest, the triune God, . . . is not arbitrary; He does not grudge existence to this other. He not only does not grudge it him, he not only leaves it to him, he gives it him."[28] We may be certain of reality because we may be certain of God.

Thus the preservation of this reality becomes a constant miracle for us. For the creature is not able to preserve itself. It is constantly threatened with non-existence, with chaos, with ruin. It is constantly in need of its Creator—think of Psalm 104:27ff.—and not in the sense that what exists always refers back to being itself in an ontological fashion, but rather in the theological sense that what exists requires, in order to exist, in reality the constant "service" (*servatio*—recalling a statement by Anselm which K. Barth has brought back to our attention),[29] the constant activity of the Creator who snatches it out of nothingness.

1) **Conservation as an Act of the Faithfulness of God**. If we want to understand the concept of "conservation" in a correct way theologically, then we can only do so by considering the faithfulness of God. Faithfulness is not an ontological term. Being which continuously is the ground of what exists works automatically. From the point of view of ontology, "conservation" is not a miracle, because it is not an event but a process. However, God's faithfulness is the permanence of a deed. God does not allow his creature to fall—that is the miracle of conservation. And this miracle is all the more miraculous because this creature in its authoritative representation, in man, has "let God fall" and "lets" God fall. If it is really true that the whole creation is made for man, and if it is true that this man has closed himself off from God, then the whole creation is subjected to "futility" (Rom. 8:20). It not only exists essentially on the basis of the Creator's negating its non-existence and thus exists on the boundary of nothingness, supported and defended alone by the Creator, but the power of the Evil One has its accomplice in the core of the creature. To speak of "conservation" and "service"

26. Descartes, *Discourse on the Method*, tr. L. J. Lafleur (*Little Library of Liberal Arts*, 19; New York: Liberal Arts Press, 1950), Part IV, pp. 20ff.

27. K. Barth, *Dogmatics in Outline*, tr. G. T. Thomson (London: S.C.M. Press, 1949 [g1947]), p. 53.

28. *Ibid.*, p. 54.

29. Anselm, *De casu diaboli*, 1 (Migne, *PL*, CLVIII, 327).

in this situation can only mean to speak eschatologically, to speak in the direction of the liberation in which the creation will be freed from "its bondage to decay" in favor of "the glorious liberty of the children of God" (Rom. 8:21). Yet this eschatological "service" already casts its light upon us, for the covenant of God with man supremely expresses the fact that God has not delivered the fallen creature, who has closed himself off to God and in his perversion has drawn in all the rest of creation subject to him, over to himself. Even God's anger, to which he "gave up" the creature because of his own self-commitment to perversion (Rom. 1:18ff.), is itself the demonstration that God maintains his claim and his power as Creator. Therefore his anger belongs, as the other pole, to the revelation of his "righteousness," which in turn was not demolished by man's "wickedness" (Rom. 3:5) any more than his faith was destroyed by man's "faithlessness" (Rom. 3:3). This is the real miracle of divine conservation for us—it is nothing other than the miracle of redemption.

f. Concurrence. Older dogmatics, and by no means only Lutheran,[30] used the concept of "concurrence" *(concursus)* to emphasize that the creature itself is situated in a "current," that it does possess spontaneity. With the use of this term, it deals with the question of how God's governance is related to the freedom of the creature. In the age of Orthodoxy it was generally agreed that the creature's work had a relative degree of autonomy; however, Lutheran dogmatics emphasized this autonomy more strongly, while the Reformed underlined more emphatically the relativity of this autonomy and stressed "the absolute priority of the divine over the human activity."[31] Of course, Luther once used (in the *Bondage of the Will*) the old picture of the "beast" *(jumentum)* which wills and goes as its rider wills, be that God or the devil.[32] But Lutheran Orthodoxy here as well

---

30. Orthodoxy in both directions, following the terminology already present in Thomas Aquinas, generally distinguishes between "conservation" and "governance" (e.g., the Heidelberg Catechism, Answer 27 [Schaff, III, 316]); somewhat later, the concept of "concurrence" is interposed between the two traditional concepts. But the matter involved was always present. The issue is the non-rejection of the "secondary causes" which are within the scope of creaturely activity, to which Scholastic thinking devoted much effort, and which is generally present in Protestantism. For Calvin, see *Institutes*, I, xvii, 9, pp. 221f. and I, xviii, pp. 228–37, for the whole question. In the Heidelberg Catechism, see Answer 104: God wants to "govern" us through the "hand" of our parents, etc. J. Wolleb says simply, "The providence of God does not destroy secondary causes, but upholds them" *(Reformed Dogmatics*, ed. and tr. J. W. Beardslee III [New York: Oxford University Press, 1965], p. 59); also there the concepts of "precurrence," "concurrence," and "succurrence" into which the generic term "concurrence" was often divided. Karl Barth, *CD*, III,3, pp. 96ff., speaks of the idea that the doctrine of "concurrence" was "peculiar to Lutheran dogmatics" as a "legend of the history of theology."

31. K. Barth, *CD*, III,3, p. 97.

32. AE, XXXIII, 65. It should be noted here that in the same book, Luther appeals to the pagan concept of fate as a secondary proof (pp. 41f.), and proceeds on the theological assumption ". . . that God foreknows nothing contingently, but that He foresees and purposes and does all things by His immutable, eternal, and infallible will" (p. 37). Calvin's much greater caution is shown by J. Bohatec, "Calvins Vorsehungslehre," *Calvinstudien, Festschrift zum 400. Geburtstage Johann Calvins (Elberfelder Calvinstudien*; Leipzig: R. Haupt, 1909), pp. 339ff. But see also *Institutes*, II, iv, 1, pp. 309f.

as elsewhere did not follow Luther, but took the path of Melanchthon, who allowed the creature much "more" autonomy than Thomas had done before him.[33]

1) The Concept of "Concurrence." The fundamental issue with which the concept of "concurrence" confronts us is imbedded in the term itself. If there is supposed to be a concurrence here between two entities both of which ontologically are subsumed within the realm of being, then obviously there are two results. On the one hand, one's zeal for the seriousness and importance of human responsibility must shift the accent in favor of the activity of the creature and against the activity of God. Then, on the other hand, one's zeal for God's deity, for his absolute superiority over the creature, must lead to the shifting of the accent in the opposite direction, in favor of the divine activity and finally to the striking of any activity on the part of the creature at all. If the question were really posed in this fashion, then only the second option would ultimately be able to carry the day. For of what avail were all the well-meaning talk about human responsibility if this responsibility could really only appear as the robbery of the honor of the Creator? Under this presupposition, even Thomas' compromise could not be accepted, for how could there be any kind of middle line between the Creator and the creature at the same level? Even such important considerations as the idea that the creature did not do evil under alien "co-activity" but due to its own inner "necessity"—considerations which are to be found both in Luther[34] and in Calvin[35]—can only confuse the situation. If we persisted in considering the whole issue from the assumption of a common level joining Creator and creature, we would ultimately have to renounce the doctrine of "concurrence" in order to be strictly logical. We would end up with theomonism, which obviously in its effects would not differ from an atheistic monism—whether omnicausality is asserted with or without God does not make much practical difference.

We have clarified for our purposes in several ways that the assumption of a common level, of a sphere of reality which encloses both the Creator and the creature, cannot be maintained.[36] It cannot be stated either that this insight was unknown to older theology.[37] But usually it proceeds by substracting from God what it adds to man, and vice versa. This happens certainly out of a certain fear of the Pantheism which is a constant danger, and which can place God and man on one line because it does not recognize God as an "Opposite." In fact, it would more easily be possible to go along with the idea of concurrence mentioned than to agree to its pantheistic counterpart (the creature as the expression or the func-

---

33. Thomas Aquinas, *STh*, I,cv, especially Article 5, vol. I, pp. 518f.

34. Luther, *op. cit.*, p. 64: "Now, by 'necessarily' I do not mean 'compulsively'; but the necessity of immutability (as they say) and not of compulsion. That is to say, when a man is without the Spirit of God he does not do evil against his will, as if he were taken by the scruff of the neck and forced to do it . . .; but he does it of his own accord, and with a ready will."

35. *Institutes*, II, iii, 5, pp. 294–96, with the same terminology as Luther; both are probably dependent upon Thomas at this point (*STh*, II–1,cxii,3, vol. I, pp. 1141f.).

36. See pp. 444ff.

37. In regard to Thomas, J. Bernhart can say, "God and man are not in concurrence like two finite causes" (*Summa Theologica*, tr. Bernhart, Kröner [1934], I, 379; n.l.).

tion of the divine!). It was the commendable accomplishment of Karl Barth to have worked out what the real error is, and that is, that in older theology the idea of concurrence was conceived of with a remarkable lack of concern for the Christian meaning of all discourse about God.

2) **Concurrence and Covenant.** It is also possible to understand the idea of concurrence as referring to the fact that God has made himself into man's partner and thus does really encounter man in his created reality. Because God has established his covenant, it is possible to speak seriously of concurrence. In the light of this event it is true that God "inspires them all in every one" (1 Cor. 12:6), that "he is at work in you both to will and to work for his good pleasure" (Phil. 2:13), that he has "wrought for us all our works" as has so often been emphasized (Isa. 26:12). But in the light of this event the miracle is also true that God "accompanies" man's own activity.[38] God is not a stranger for the created being, not an unknown origin, not the silent ground of all; in Jesus Christ he has become the partner to man.

If we want to think Christianly and not along the lines of some interpretation of history or another when we deal with "concurrence," then it will not be possible for a moment to view "concurrence" as an ontic relationship or as its effect. It is impossible to conceive of this "concurrence" in any other way than from the basis of the divine freedom in which God truly has stepped on man's side and has shown himself to be gracious in so doing. Therefore, this partnership can be neither man's participating in God nor a *repartée* between God and man.

3) **The Reformed View.** God is not dependent upon man. This was the proper emphasis of Reformed doctrine with its stress upon the "simultaneous concurrence" *(concursus simultaneus)*, upon the superiority of the will and the work of God in every detail of the creature's willing and working. God is not the highest instance within reality, but the Lord over reality, and man cannot even recognize the partnership which is actually there without experiencing the manifestation of the inseparable lordship of the Creator. If we do away with the ontological brackets, which locked in most of the Orthodox in both camps, then we will have to say that both the "young" Luther and the Reformed were correct in that they saw the unconditional freedom and superiority of God in the partnership he establishes, a freedom which is apart from both our influence and our insight.

But the ontological brackets prevented the Reformed from developing their conception as one based upon God's revelation in Jesus Christ, witnessing to it and praising it. Thus it was not protected against the idea of a divine omnicausality, resting upon the eternal predetermination of every single element of all that happens—and this led to their being accused of Stoicism[39] and finally of Mohammedanism by their opponents.

---

38. This is the interpretation of the doctrine of concurrence in K. Barth, *CD*, III,3, pp. 90ff., following J. Cocceius, *Summa Theologiae* (1662), XXVIII, 25, in *Opera Omnia* (Amsterdam: Jansson-Waesberg, 1673–75; Boom & Goethals, 1701³).

39. This accusation emerges as early as 1552 with Melanchthon in regard to the Bolsec case *(CR, VII, 930)*.

4) **The Lutheran View.** By doing away with the ontological brackets we will also see the intention of Lutheran Orthodoxy in another light. Here again we cannot accept the idea that man should be deprived of what is ascribed to God— just as we could not accept the reverse thesis in Reformed Orthodoxy. When Lutheran Orthodoxy spoke of "concurrence," it was thinking primarily of man's freedom and thus limited the scope of divine "causality," whereby it made use in part of the argumentation of the Jesuits.[40]

What is then the Christian reasoning for the establishment of the freedom of the creature? Certainly it cannot be so formulated that God must be limited in his freedom, his work, and his accomplishments in favor of man's freedom! No, even the relative freedom of the creature is based upon that partnership which God has instituted. If the Reformed Orthodox emphasized that God in Christ is the Lord of the covenant and thus Lord of the creature, then now we must emphasize with the Lutherans that it is God *in Christ*, God in his free turning to man, God on the side of the creature. It is the Reformed theologian, Karl Barth, who finds the divine "succurrence" which the Lutherans emphasized over against the Reformed stress upon the "precurrence" quite understandable in the sense that this does away with the "fear-complex" "that God is a kind of stranger or alien or even enemy to the creature."[41] If this "fear-complex" is done away with, which was in fact the result of a concept of concurrence which made no room for God's covenant partnership in Jesus Christ, then obviously we can and must say that God in the very superiority of his activity does not rob the creature of its freedom but rather grants it to him.

5) **The Creaturely Freedom as Eschaton.** However, if the ontological brackets which limit the idea of concurrence are done away with, then it becomes all the clearer that we can only speak of God's free lordship over the creature and of the relative freedom of the creature in terms of *expectation*: in expectation of the revelation of the "glorious liberty" of the sons of God (Rom. 8:21). And how else should we be able to speak of this mystery? The essence of faith in Christ consists of our confessing today what is coming to us from God now, in full view of all of the human autonomy which has turned into demonry and slavery, and to speak now of the freedom of God in relationship to and in everything which happens, as well as of the freedom of man derived from God and experienced before God.[42] The old doctrine of "concurrence" no more makes us capable of interpreting history than does any other element of the doctrine of providence. But as one form of the confession of Christ, it has its own important meaning.

g. Governance. When we said of both "conservation" and "concurrence" that they were miracles, that is, that they can be conceived of only in view of the

---

40. A. Quenstedt appeals to F. Tolet, S.J. (see K. Barth, *CD*, III,3, p. 145). The doctrine of "middle knowledge," which is applicable here, also belongs broadly to the intellectual armory of Lutheran (but also in part of Reformed) Orthodoxy.

41. K. Barth, *CD*, III,3, p. 146.

42. See O. Weber, *Die christliche Freiheit und der autonome Mensch* (*Theologische Existenz heute*, 16; Munich: Kaiser, 1949).

covenant instituted and realized by God and not deducible from the event itself, we were asserting something which is equally true of the concept of "governance." It is no longer necessary to explain in detail that the Orthodox approach, within its ontological brackets, failed to grasp the incomprehensibility of "governance" and thus prepared the way for the Enlightenment. In that period, "governance" was transformed into a positivistically oriented law of history. In terms of the possibility of clearer theological knowledge, we may be better off today in that not even "general opinion" seems to be convinced that "the world" is moving steadily toward a "good" goal, and doing so by its own power—which is Deism, meaning that the built-in laws given the world by its first cause are now moving it. Therefore it may be easier for us today to distinguish between faith in God who rules the world and the idea of a law for the course of history which is moving upward. It is easier to see today that the certainty that this "world" is not subjected to chaos, to nothingness, and to evil, stands and falls with faith in God in Christ. The responsibility which this insight incurs for Christian proclamation is obviously immeasurable.

1) The Concepts of "Governance," "Permission," "Impeding," "Direction," and "Determination." The first thing which the concept of "governance" means is that God integrates and subordinates the creature he preserves and accompanies with his own work into his own divine decree. This is first of all an acknowledgment of the creature; it may and should participate in God's work. It is not merely the object of this work, nor just a stage of his history, but rather has been enlisted in his service. Its being and condition have meaning, importance, and significance. At the same time, a certain limitation of the creature is expressed. It renders the glorious service given to it solely as the object of divine governance and solely toward the goal, which rests in God's lordship and is thus "good." When the Orthodox in their subdivisions of "governance" spoke of "permission" (*permissio*—a term which certainly is doubtful and which was once criticized by both Luther and Calvin[43]), this can be understood in the prior sense. God grants to the creature participation in his work, directs man's history toward the history of his covenant (although it remains concealed), and makes man's activity into one that serves the realization of his decrees (even the actions of Pontius Pilate and Judas Iscariot!). When the Orthodox in their further interpretations joined the concept of "impeding" (*impeditio*) to that of "permission," we have proof that they did not think that the creature was able in and of itself to accomplish any kind of service to which it was called. Rather, it required divine assistance and activity in order to be able to do what it was permitted to do. And when, moreover, terms like "direction" (*directio*) and "determination" (*determinatio*) were enlisted as further interpretations for "governance," we are instructed that God relates to the work of the creature not just as an expectant spectator but dominantly, in his own superior work.

2) Governance to "the Good." What is then this "good," for which all things "work together" (Rom. 8:28) and which establishes limits for the creature and

---

43. See pp. 443ff.

especially for man as the representative creature, with all of his own wishes, desires, and goals? Certainly the answer will be, this good is God's will and decree itself. Then, apparently, everything depends upon who this God is. If he is nothing other than the epitome of what conditions everything, then this "good" is an empty concept. If he is the epitome of a moral ideal—how much has already been sacrificed to the moral ideals and to the God understood as the epitome of those ideals![44] If God is the essence of something unknown, then all talk of his "governance" is certainly not good news, but another expression for the fact that we have in truth not been able to find any meaning in the course of events. Or to cite Karl Barth, ". . . if God Himself has no form nor face nor history, if in the name God we can only look at the empty framework of a concept of the original being and activity of a chief Monad, then the truth that God rules the world is at bottom a dispensable and superfluous luxury."[45] But where then can we really look—or better, what is the real source of our statement when we are speaking of the worldly rule of God?

Christian talk about God's rule in the world does not speak of "the" meaning of history. "For who has known the mind of the Lord or who has been his counselor?" (Rom. 11:34). There is one point, however, at which for faith a "meaning" in events has become apparent, and that is in the historical institution, preservation, and realization of the covenant. This is the middle point from which they are thinking when the prophets state something akin to the observation of history (for instance, Isa. 10 or Isa. 45 or Jer. 29), or to which Paul is referring in his argument in Romans 9 to 11. The position of such statements is the narrow space of the divine decision about man, which then leads to man's decision itself. The "good" is not a general term but is realized in this very special event, in that special development called Israel, in the very special individual who is named Jesus Christ, and in the uniqueness of the Church. This is scandalous enough, and the temptation has frequently been there to leave this position, perhaps by understanding the specialness as a unique instance of something universal. But the result has always been then that this universal, "the" event or "the" history, was by no means able to communicate what one wanted to know or postulate, which was a "meaning" or a goal.

The unique thing we are discussing, however, although it certainly is not a special instance of the universal, cannot be set apart in such a way that it forms its own closed system which has nothing to do with everything else which happens or could even be considered in separation from everything else. "Salvation-history" is an event in the realm of the "world's" history, in the midst of the totality of creaturely reality. The God who makes himself known and communicates himself in this unique event is the Lord of the world, including the history of the world. This was the common assertion of Deutero-Isaiah, of the Coronation Psalms,[46] of Colossians and Ephesians, and doubtlessly of Paul in Romans 9–11. Therefore it is surely correct when K. Barth, whom we are generally following

---

44. K. Barth, *CD*, III,3, pp. 172–74.
45. *CD*, III,3, p. 191.
46. See H. J. Kraus, *Die Königsherrschaft Gottes im Alten Testament; Untersuchungen zu den Liedern von Jahwes Thronbesteigung* (Tübingen: J. C. B. Mohr, 1951).

here, objects to any isolation of "salvation-history" from the rest of world history
and to any world history which is neutral toward "salvation-history," and even
risks the statement, "There is no such thing as 'profane history' which should be
taken seriously."[47]

What are the results? In any event, this, that we are not to understand
God's rule as a general governance of history toward a general good end, but as
the powerful arrangement of all events toward one event in the midst of history.
This event, however, is not the establishment of a divine tyranny, nor even the
tyranny of an ethical ideal, but rather that God in this event takes mercy on man.
If we said above that the concept of "governance" contains the acknowledgment
of creaturely being and acting, we can now put it more concisely. Because God
finds his own honor in being the God of man chosen in Jesus Christ, because his
righteousness consists of his mobilizing his Being as God for man, the creature's
being claimed for the superior decrees of God is not his entrapment in an alien
event but rather his being allowed to participate in the event which applies to
himself most of all. As the "governor" God is the Merciful.

D. PROVIDENCE AND THE KINGDOM OF GOD

We have reached a point in these last considerations at which it must become
clear that we cannot speak of God's providence without speaking of the Kingdom
of God. Of course it could be said that in everything which was discussed in
regard to "governance," we were in reality discussing the Kingdom of God. For
what is the meaning of "Kingdom of God" if it is not this, that God is King, that
he rules, that he permits his will to happen? What remains to be said is in fact
the resumption of our discussion just past, now from a different perspective.

For it is impossible in dealing with this whole thematic to avoid the reality
of evil.[48] It is certainly one of the strengths of Calvin's doctrine of providence
that here, under Augustine's influence and with constant appeals to him, the
problem of evil activity is clearly seen and dealt with courageously enough to
make radical statements.[49] The basic concept of God's omni-effectuality which
is dominant both in him and in the Reformed Orthodox who follow him, is naturally subjected to a hard test through the existence of evil in the world. It is easy
to understand that, in view of the divine omni-effectuality, Calvin would mediate
the "inferior causes," so that they are not ascribed their own powers. But the
circumstance that these "inferior causes" are not just things but also can be
people and thus are not ethically irrelevant, leads him to make the very emphatic

---

47. *CD*, III,3, p. 184.
48. This is also one difficulty in Barth which he has not overcome. To be sure, his
discussion of "Nothingness" follows directly upon his doctrine of providence and clearly
indicates the relationship in which these problems stand. But within the section on the
doctrine of providence there is scarcely any mention of evil. Thus the problem of the
doctrine of providence is seen in a one-sidedly noetic fashion and the danger arises that the
dynamic of biblical speech on the Kingdom of God is transformed into a dialectic.
49. *Institutes*, I, xviii, pp. 228–37.

admonition not to underestimate such "inferior causes." If someone has done good to me, then I cannot evade the obligation of gratitude in that I look past my benefactor and see God.[50] It could be said that such thinking in Calvin is inconsequent. But what in fact is shown here is that Calvin, while making room for the idea of God's omni-effectuality for the sake of God's honor and freedom and of our certainty in trusting God, does not become a theomonist, but wants to let creaturely activity retain its genuineness and responsibility. This obviously becomes clearest when an activity which breaks one of God's commandments emerges as an "inferior cause." If I can regard a man's deed in accordance with the commandments as still being in line with God's own work and will, then this possibility is canceled when an evil deed is done. At that I become involved in a contradictory situation. I am supposed to accept something from God's hand even though it is against God's commandment, and I am supposed to regard this as based in God's incomprehensible will.[51] Quite obviously this is a paradox. It is the paradox to which passages like Genesis 50:20, Job 1, 1 Kings 22:21ff., Isaiah 10, and 1 Corinthians 5:5 all refer and which emerges most clearly in the passion of our Lord (God "gave up" Jesus [Rom. 8:32]; the Jews "delivered him up" [Acts 3:13]; Judas "delivered him" [Matt. 26:15], and frequently!). Even if we were to set aside the idea of God's omni-effectuality—still, what kind of curious "concurrence" is this in which God is involved? The problem is ineluctable.

K. Heim explained the problem by discussing two opposing total views which are united in tension in the "world view" of faith: the "comprehensive view of God's sole agency" on the one hand, which if left alone would lead to Pantheism, and the "comprehensive view of conflict" (God against the devil) on the other, which if left alone would have to mean the substantial godlessness of the world, its surrender to Satan, in short, complete dualism.[52] Heim seeks to show that both "total views" when taken in their relationship to one another and their insoluble tension result in what could be called the "world view" of faith. This means then that we are not able to resolve the riddle, even in faith, but rather that faith can only live in the tension of the unresolved riddle. In Luther, the riddle is described in such a way that the devil on the one hand is "God's devil" and on the other is his opponent against whom God constantly is in struggle. If this is the case, then there cannot be an intellectual solution of the contradiction, for the very reason of faith itself. But that means then that this intellectual paradox is only the reflection of the factual contradiction which is not yet resolved and which does characterize the situation of faith. It consists of the circumstance that God's will does not yet "get done" in the here and now, and that its not being carried out is in accordance *with* his will in the most incomprehensible manner. The evil will is still there, outside of us and in us. The resistance is still there, outside of us and in us. Or to put it more concisely, God's lordship over the

---

50. On all of this, see *Institutes*, I, xvii, 9, pp. 221f.

51. In the *Institutes*, I, xviii, 3, p. 235, he formulates the paradox (following Augustine, *Enchiridion*, Ch. 100 [*NPNF*, III, 269]) in this way, "so that in a wonderful and ineffable manner nothing is done without God's will, not even that which is against his will."

52. Karl Heim, *op. cit.*, pp. 85ff. and especially pp. 103ff.; following H. Obendiek, *Der Teufel bei Martin Luther* (Berlin: Furche Verlag, 1931).

creature is still concealed, not noetically unknowable, but practically covered over beneath its own contradiction.

a. The Kingdom of God as Event. We must now consider the fact that in both the Old and the New Testaments God's lordship does not assume the form of an objective and tangible given, but rather the form of an *event*. The statement that God "is" and that he "is in such and such a way" does not mean that God is a being or an "existence" but rather that he "is" and "is in such and such a way" in the actual and continual manifestation and communication of himself. We cannot speak of God's providence aside from this knowledge. "God the Lord reigns"—that is not the description of something which exists out there, but rather it is the testimony to an event. This is the reason that we cannot describe the problem of evil and its relationship to God's good and omnipotent will merely in an intellectual paradox, but must also see it "dynamically." Certainly that term is much too weak—it, too, is derived from an ontological category. But in any event it can be said that the "lordship of God" in the Bible can more readily be expressed in the category of event, as inadequate as that is, than in the category of being or existence.

b. Jesus Christ and the Kingdom of God. Jesus Christ is not only the herald, but in his deeds and speech he is the bearer, the bringer of the Kingdom of God. He is, in the broadly used terminology of today, the One in whom the "age of salvation" is inaugurated. That means that in him God's lordship arrives at its historical manifestation—unique in its historicity, not subject to coordination with the rest of history, not historically comprehensible, and not subsumable under the category of history. "The reason the Son of God appeared was to destroy the works of the devil" (1 John 3:8). In and through him God brings his will to pass. That means that God carries out his own claim upon man as the Creator in the reality of his being the Creator for man. His lordship is no tyranny but the establishment of freedom. We could also say that God reveals his "righteousness," his "right," to man in that he gives man a right in free mercy. Justification is the granting of a right (which man had forfeited). It is the realization of the covenant! Thus the claim of evil upon man, which is certainly illegitimate in view of God, is made ineffective. There is no doubt that God's "lordship" and his "righteousness" belong together, and the Gospel is both the message of the "Kingdom of God" and the revelation of the "righteousness of God." The work of Jesus Christ is God's victory over the Evil One and thus the liberation of man. The expulsion of devils (primarily as recorded in Matt. 12:28) and the healing of the sick all belong to this. If we think back to the fundamental contradiction with which Heim dealt, then we can say that God shows himself in Jesus Christ to be the One who alone has right on his side, that is, in Jesus Christ God's sole lordship and sole right is established, and thus the contradiction is resolved.

c. The Concealed Nature of the Kingdom. But—how? The very One who brings God's lordship is struck down, in the unity of his will with that of the Father, in carrying out the sole lordship of God as it is realized in him, by the burden of human sin, by the last self-manifestation of the Evil One in the form of legal righteousness as autonomous righteousness. Put another way, the will of God, which he does, lets him endure up to and including his death among men because God truly makes him "to be sin" and places him where sin belongs, "so that in him we might become the righteousness of God" (2 Cor. 5:21). God's victory in Jesus Christ is in the form of the cross. The resurrection is not a public show of miraculous power but an event which is granted to the disciples and reaches us solely through the word of proclamation.

d. The Kingdom of God as the Overcoming of the Contradiction. We ask once more, How then is the contradiction resolved in Jesus Christ? There can at first be no other answer than this, that it is resolved because and in that this One submitted to God's right up to and unto death and thereby abrogated the illegitimate lordship of the Evil One. In this Crucified One, God's lordship is not only in struggle with the Evil One, it is victorious over the Evil One (see John 12:32f.). In him God's No to evil has arrived at its goal and God's Yes to the creature is reality. Just as this No and Yes belong together, so too the cross and resurrection belong together.

This then opens the way for a further insight. When looking at the work of Jesus we had to speak of the evil which had, so to speak, its fling with him up to the very end. At the same time, we had to speak of God who made this triumph of evil into his victory. What happens here is what is implied everywhere else in the form of a riddle. Here God realizes his will, his lordship in such a way that the Evil One, including everything which belongs to and serves the manifestation of evil, is shown to be the loser, conquered in the last manifestation of his power by God's lordship in Jesus Christ.

None of this is an intrinsic fact which we only were supposed to note, but is a fact leading to decision, or better, a fact in Jesus Christ alone. The victory of Jesus Christ is concealed—behind the cross rises up all that which is expressed in the apocalyptic speeches in the Synoptics, as well as what is stated in 2 Thessalonians 2 or in the Apocalypse of St. John. The shadow of this cross spreads itself out over the remnant "of this age." But the lordship of God concealed in the mystery of the cross is, for the believer who is baptized into Jesus' death and thus participates in his resurrection (Rom. 6; see also Eph. 2), the reality now believed which is for him certainty and the definition of life now "in pneumatic reality" (see Rom. 14:17 and then Gal. 5:22ff.). The believer is not rescued from the chasm of paradox. But in the encroaching (and soon ending) night (Rom. 13:12) he is a "child of the light" and "of the day" (1 Thess. 5:5). In this eschatological present, he looks forward to that unbeholdable moment in which God will be "everything to everyone" (1 Cor. 15:28).

PART SIX

Man

XIII. The Creature

A. THE THEME OF THEOLOGICAL ANTHROPOLOGY

1. "THE KNOWLEDGE OF GOD—THE KNOWLEDGE OF OURSELVES"

a. Theocentrism and Anthropocentrism. "Nearly all the wisdom we possess, that is to say, true and sound wisdom, consists of two parts: the knowledge of God and of ourselves."[1] With these words, Calvin begins his *Institutes*. The wording is that of the edition of 1539, but it is almost identical to that of 1536.[2] In the editions between 1539 and 1554 Calvin accordingly has the first chapter, "The Knowledge of God," followed by a chapter two entitled "The Knowledge of Man," the content of which in the edition of 1559 is used in part to introduce Book Two, "The Knowledge of God the Redeemer."

Calvin is to be agreed with at the decisive point in his now famous formulation: the Christian doctrine of God and the Christian doctrine of man belong together.

Occasionally this view is contrasted with the view that theology is supposed to deal with God and not with man. But no dogmatician would propound that view. It has, however, been expressed as an understandable reaction to the "anthropocentric" theology which dominated most of the 19th century,[3] and it has the apparent advantage of sounding both pious and radical. Now, we shall have to deal with this "anthropocentrism" shortly. But we must not allow ourselves to be so frightened by this specter that we come down too decisively, however sincerely, on the other side. "Theology has to do with God and thus not with man"—that could just as well mean that it has to do with the Creator and not with the creature, with eternity and not with time, with the "absolute" and not with the "relative." And all that would mean is that it has nothing to do with the God to whom Holy Scripture witnesses. For this God has to do with man. That is his honor and glory. And no theology may be permitted to diminish this honor

---

1. Calvin, *Institutes*, I, i, 1, p. 35 (1559); *Christianae Religionis Institutio* (1539) (*CR*, I, 279).

2. *Christianae Religionis Institutio* (1536) (*CR*, I, 27).

3. See E. Schäder, *Theozentrische Theologie; eine Untersuchung zur dogmatischen Prinzipienlehre* (Leipzig: Werner Scholl, 1916), I (g1925³), II (g1928²).

by speaking of an "absolute God" without a partner, thereby missing the fact that God wishes to be *our* God.

    b. "God and the Soul?" It is of course true that the first and the last word of the Bible is not "man." It is also true that the God of whom the Bible testifies is not dependent on man and is not his correlative. Augustine made the well-known saying in the *Soliloquies,* "God and the soul, that is what I desire to know. Nothing more? Nothing whatever."[4] "God and the soul, the soul and its God"— this is not unambiguously Christian speech, and Augustine's formulation is well known to have a Neo-Platonic color to it. The "other-worldliness" of the relationship with God, which can be expressed in the phrase "God and the soul," is alien to the Christian message. It is inevitably accompanied by the idea that God is similar in kind to the "soul" as that side of human existence which is turned toward him. As the "soul" is similar to God, so God is similar to the "soul." The same thing takes place when one replaces "soul" with "I" or "authentic self." In all these instances, God is analogous to the essential thing in man, just as that essentiality is analogous to God. Whenever this kind of thinking is done, it means that the Christian discussion of God the Creator has already been forgotten. And it also means further that man is not taken there in his concrete unity and totality, but is stripped of his reality. There is also a correlation of the "knowledge of God" and the "knowledge of ourselves" (*cognitio Dei et nostri*) which is in fact knowledge neither of God nor of ourselves. Christian talk about man does not understand him as a correlative of God, nor as an effluence of the divine, nor as a being which in its deepest point is identical with God.

    c. The Rightness of Anthropocentrism. But this delimitation must not lead us to overlook the fact that the issue in the Bible and in the message of the Church is really man. If we were to speak about God without speaking about man, it would not in fact be an expression of the self-restraint which is appropriate to the creature, but on the contrary a sign of extreme arrogance. For that would be speaking of "God in himself," and we should then presume to speak of God with no regard to our creatureliness, and that would mean, with no regard to his having come to us. By speaking in such a way, we would occupy a position which does not by any means belong to us.[5] We would then be speaking of a "pure" or "naked God" (*Deus nudus*) and ignoring the "incarnate God" (*Deus incarnatus*). This *super*-human attempt at theology would necessarily prove itself to be inevitably an *in*human theology and result in a proclamation which by-passed the reality of man and thus did the very thing which God as the "incarnate God" did *not* do. Such an inhuman theology would become godless theology.

    Man is a theme of theology, not although, but because God is *the* theme of theology.

    d. Extra-theological Anthropology. But, of course, man is not only a theme of theology. In the modern world, man is a theme of biology, of physiology, of

---

    4. *Soliloquies,* I, 7 (*NPNF,* VII, 539); see also *ibid.,* II, 4 (*NPNF,* VII, 548f.).
    5. See above all Calvin, *Institutes,* I, v, 9, pp. 61f.; I, x, 2, pp. 97f.

medicine, of sociology, and of philosophy, and it is significant that there is today an unmistakable endeavor to synthesize the aspects of these various scientific disciplines and produce a total picture. A few decades ago, man was still regarded chiefly as the agent of scientific endeavors and was not himself questioned. Today he has become the central point of the atomized theme of numerous disciplines and questions of science. Next to philosophy and its related field of pedagogy, both psychology and psychiatry are struggling to produce a "totality" in our understanding of man. Indeed, there are indications that the center of science, which was once located in theology, has now shifted completely to anthropology. Whether this expresses a strong human self-consciousness or rather a profound questioning of humanity can remain a moot point. But unquestionably anthropology is today relevant in a way that was not the case for a long time.[6]

e. The Self-interpretation of Man. Man has always and everywhere been the object of his own reflection. It is inherent in him that he always makes himself somehow into an issue. For he "not only has an existence, but he is related to his existence. He does not lose himself in the immediacy of his existence. He knows that he exists. He is for himself, *sibi*."[7] Man is, regardless of the form, a being which "understands" itself. He is himself in that he can also step out of himself, "project" himself. There is no religion which does not implicitly contain a self-understanding of man. There is no legal system or judicial order in which a self-understanding of man is not the hidden directing force. There is no primitive or developed literature in which the self-projection of man is not going on. There is no art in which man does not make known the way he understands himself. And certainly there is no philosophy which is not a fragmentary or complete systematization of a human self-understanding. It was the special accomplishment of W. Dilthey and K. Jaspers[8] to have focussed our attention more precisely upon

---

6. Arnold Gehlen, *Der Mensch, seine Natur und seine Stellung in der Welt* (Bonn: Athenäum Verlag, 1950[4]); Leopold von Wiese und Kaiserswalden, *Homo sum; Gedanken zur einer zusammenfassenden Anthropologie* (Jena: G. Fischer, 1940); Max Scheler, *On the Eternal in Man*, tr. B. Noble (London: S.C.M., 1960); Karl Jaspers, *Philosophy*, tr. E. B. Ashton (3 vols.; Chicago: University of Chicago Press, 1969–71 [g1932ff.]); B. Groethuysen, *Philosophische Anthropologie*, in *Handbuch der Philosophie*, ed. A. Baeumler and M. Schroeter (Munich: R. Oldenbourgh, n.v. 21, 1928). On the debate, see primarily, *ZThK*, No. 5 (1930), and No. 2 (1931), as well as R. Bultmann, *Faith and Understanding*, I, tr. L. P. Smith (New York: Harper & Row, 1969 [g1933]); E. Schlink, *Der Mensch in der Verkündigung der Kirche* (Munich: C. Kaiser, 1936); E. Brunner, *Man in Revolt, a Christian Anthropology*, tr. O. Wyon (Philadelphia: Westminster Press, 1947 [g1937]); W. Bachmann, *Gottes Ebenbild; Systematischer Entwurf einer christlichen Lehre vom Menschen* (Berlin: Furche-Verlag, 1938); E. Michel, *Der Partner Gottes; Weisungen zum christlichen Selbstverständnis* (Heidelberg: n.p., 1946); K. Barth, *CD*, III,2.
7. Paul Althaus, *Die christliche Wahrheit, Lehrbuch der Dogmatik* (2 vols.; Gütersloh: Bertelsmann, 1949), II, 79.
8. W. Dilthey, *passim*, especially vol. II of *Gesammelte Schriften* (15 vols.; Leipzig: Teubner, 1914–58), which bears the title selected by G. Misch, "Weltanschauung und Analyse des Menschen seit Renaissance und Reformation"; K. Jaspers, *Psychologie der Weltanschauungen* (Berlin: Springer, 1960[5]), and *Man in the Modern Age*, tr. E. and C. Paul (London: Routledge & Kegan Paul, 1933, 1951). Oswald Spengler must also be mentioned in this connection.

the self-interpretation of man found in all kinds of historical expressions, and to have posed the problem of understanding with methodical conciseness.

If we understand the term as broadly as possible, then we must say that man is always involved in some way in pursuing the "knowledge of himself" (*cognitio sui*). He does not seem to need theology for this. Theological anthropology enters a sphere which was already fully occupied, and the proclamation of the Church must expect that its talk about man will not by any means encounter a vacuum. Rather, it will encounter the implicit or explicit "monologue" of its hearers, a vague or well-thought-out self-understanding, one oriented toward a world view or already consolidated into a world view. Such a self-understanding makes itself known primarily in its promulgation of (mostly "moralistic") "truisms."[9]

f. Self-interpretation and World View. The situation is complicated by the fact that there are elements belonging to man's constant pursuit of "self-knowledge" which are thoroughly "ethical" (or at least "moral") and "religious." They are not lacking even in the case of modern, "profane" man, even though he is frequently dealing with surrogate religions like the secular religion of politics. It is in any event normally the case that man does not understand and interpret himself as merely "existing," but as being something which he "ought" to be. He "projects" himself outward to something beyond himself which he then conceives of as meaning or "destiny." A particularly important part of his self-understanding here is how he sees himself in regard to other people, to the structuring of society or community or the "other." This projection of man beyond himself is often accompanied then by the emergence of divinity in the sphere of the self-understanding, very frequently in connection with the sphere of politics in the broadest sense. In short, human self-understanding contains a clear tendency toward totality, toward a "world view," in which it projects itself upon the "world."

g. Man Before God. Now the Christian proclamation has entered the world with the claim that what it has to say is absolutely decisive for man, whoever he may be and whatever may be the self-understanding he has developed. The message of Jesus Christ offers man not additional insights about God, the world, and himself, and its content is not just a modification of man's self-understanding. It is the new foundation of his existence, the conversion of the whole direction of his existence. In the face of it, there is no neutrality, no way of continuing as though nothing had happened. It always leads up to the decision about man.

This means that the proclamation of the triune God, of God in his revelation, is essentially characterized by the fact that it directly and absolutely concerns man. In its light, man's very existence is solely who he is before God. For the Christian message, man simply does not "exist" as a being "in and of itself" apart from his relationship to God. It is the very essence of man to exist *before*

---

9. See on this F. Gogarten, *Die Selbstverständlichkeiten unserer Zeit und der christliche Glaube* (Berlin: Furche Verlag, 1932); the 2nd edition appeared as *Weltanschauung und Glaube* (Berlin: Furche Verlag, 1937).

God. This knowledge is not the result of an analysis of man, of his existence or his self-understanding. Rather, it is the other side of the message that God is the Creator, the Lord of this man. However, this message is not, in turn, just the communication of a doctrinal proposition—it is the proclamation of God himself in his dealing with man.

The fact that man is undeniably man-before-God is based upon the fact that God is God-for-the-creature. This is the significance of the linkage of the "knowledge of God" and "knowledge of self." It is only meaningful if the "knowledge of God" is meant in the full sense which it acquires in Calvin, with whom we began here. That means that it is "knowledge of God the Creator" and "knowledge of God the Redeemer" and as such is "knowledge of Christ" in the Holy Spirit. If God were the highest point of an ontological system, then the "knowledge of God" and the "knowledge of self" could be a correlative conceptual couplet, and we would have to decide then in favor of the noetic priority of the "knowledge of self." For what other way would there be to come to acceptable and responsible knowledge about the highest point of the whole except from the foundation of our own self-knowledge? The priority of the "knowledge of God" asserted by Calvin is only valid when the knowledge of God meant is what it is in the Bible. And in the Bible it is the knowledge which God himself grants us in his revelation in the establishment of fellowship between him and us, in the incarnation and work of Jesus Christ, knowledge which he then makes real in us through his Spirit. Only a theology which starts from God's existence *for us* can be "theocentric" in the Christian sense. But then such a theology can assay to proceed in what is apparently such an "anthropocentric" way as does Calvin in the Geneva Catechism[10] or as does the Heidelberg Catechism, which in its three parts is incontestably discussing man.[11]

2. "THE" MAN

The theme of theological anthropology[12] is man before God. *The* man! The question must be asked, In what way can theology speak of *the* man, of man in an absolute sense?

---

10. Compare the first question in the Geneva Catechism (*LCC*, XXII, 91f.). It begins with the question about "the chief end of human life" and answers that it is that "men should know God." Why? Because (Question 2) "he created us . . . that he might be glorified in us." "Man's supreme good" (Question 3) is found in the glorification of God. The "true and right knowledge of God" (Question 6) is only found where "he is so known, that his own proper honour is done him." God receives honor from us when we put all our trust in him" (Question 7), serve him, "by obeying his will," call on him when in need, and "acknowledge him with both heart and mouth to be the only author of all good things." This leads to the subdivision of the Catechism into sections of faith, command, prayer, and sacraments. We can virtually regard the structure of the Catechism as a commentary on the first proposition of the *Institutes*.

11. See the subdivisions of the Heidelberg Catechism: "Of man's misery." "Of man's redemption," "Of thankfulness" (Schaff, III, 307ff.). These three sections are, however, an exposition of the first question, which shows then that in fact the thought is Christian and theocentric.

12. See G. Kuhlmann, *Theologische Anthropologie im Abriss* (Tübingen: J. C. B. Mohr, 1935); W. Gutbrod, *Die paulinische Anthropologie* (Stuttgart-Berlin: W. Kohlhammer, 1934).

   a. The Basis and Crisis of the Idea of Humanity. Man in an absolute sense
cannot be found empirically. It is certainly possible to describe biologically those
anatomical characteristics which belong to homo sapiens. But it is not possible
to say with certainty whether the manifold variations of the human race are concluded now, and the discoveries of any new day can lead us to shift further back
the boundaries of the groupings of living beings which we ascribe to the species
"man." What we do know is a grouping which is extremely varied in its internal
subdivisions, and whose boundaries in all directions are open. "The" man would
then be everything which can be identified between the oldest discoveries and the
most recently developed types.
   Philosophy also speaks of "the" man, but when it does so, it usually is
looking less at the biological phenomena. It has always emphasized that man is
the being which is gifted with "reason." It can also describe man as the "responsible" being, as the being with a sense of its own personhood, as the being
conscious of itself and transcending itself. It can do as Stoicism did, with far-
reaching historical consequences, and develop the concept of the *genus humanum,*
the "human race," "mankind," and understand this to be the abstract sum of all
living beings equipped with certain qualities. To see this abstract sum in some
way as a community, so that our membership in it binds us to each other and
obligates us for each other, is something it could only do with great effort and by
resorting to religious ideas.
   But it is possible to proceed in the reverse fashion. We can first put the
individual in the center, since he alone truly has knowledge of himself and the
world always has its noetic central point in him. Then, we can conceive of and
carry out the community in a limited way, especially as the community of a
concrete *polis* as in the case of earlier Greek thinking, or of whatever tribe or
nation one might belong to. This view has been revived in recent decades, this
time under the banner of nihilism, and has come to power. And that is a process
which is quite understandable in the "post-Christian" period. Is not "mankind"
a very vague, feeble concept? it is asked. Who is it that obligates a people or a
"race" to renounce its collective drive toward self-assertion for its sake? Is community not primarily the mutual acknowledgment of certain "values"? And are
not these acknowledged "values" infinitely variable? Are there not perhaps nations or races of "high" and others of "lesser" value? And does not this result
in the idea that only the "master race" has full rights, and at the opposite end of
the scale the so-called "subhuman race" appears which is destined for serfdom
or extinction? It is quite possible to arrive at such enormities without fundamentally giving up the assumption that "the" man is a living being equipped with
certain qualities. "The" man is then, of course, the man of a certain race, because
only he possesses those qualities completely. "The" man can be the "super-man,"
on the basis of Nietzsche's assumptions, who is then the man who does in fact
transcend himself. There can be other bases, however, which lead to the factual
or intellectual rejection of the concept of "humanity." To the extent that political
views assume the character of confessions of faith and make themselves absolute,
their opponents can easily become valueless people because they are lacking
either subjective rationality or objective reasonableness. Such people could be

entrusted with nothing other than valueless things in practice, and no one else has in any sense an obligation toward them.

The contemporary crisis of the idea of humanity makes it quite clear that "the" man is by no means an undoubted and given quantity. Is there, apart from vague generalities, anything really in common between Neanderthal man and Goethe? And do we wish to claim that our current phenomenology and analysis of man are really valid for the surviving primitive tribes of central Africa? Are we not, in the best of instances, analyzing the European of a certain social class? Does not our talk about "the" man always represent a violent extrapolation? Do we really even know the essentials about the person closest to us? Is not the very idea of humanity in fact merely the expression of the self-understanding of a specific man, breaking into the concrete situation, be it the man of the late classical period or of the European Enlightenment? All these questions confront any anthropology which claims universal validity. And all of these questions point out that it is only possible to perceive "the" man from the perspective of an opposite who is contrasted to every man.

b. "The" Man in the Bible. The Bible, and with it both Christian proclamation and theology, speaks of "the" man.[13]

The universalism of the biblical picture of man is not derived from any qualities which inhered in all men. Nor is its point of departure the universality of sin (Rom. 3:23 in the context of 1:18–3:20), as might be thought, and as certainly will have to be discussed.

We can best arrive at an understanding of Christian universalism if we note that it is based on the message of the Old Testament which states that the God of Israel is the Creator of "the" man, and therefore he is the God who turns to all men in the anticipated age of salvation. The connection of faith in the Creator and universalism is made most clearly in Deutero-Isaiah. But it is already present in Amos, when he understands the election of Israel as a sovereign act of God who could just as well have elected other peoples (Amos 9:7), and who encounters Israel as the Judge just as he does the other nations (Amos 1–2). Even the Yahwist account of creation is clearly universalistic: Israel's God is the Creator of all men without any restrictions.

The universalism of the Old Testament is characterized by the fact that it is conceived of from a historical midpoint. It is not what could be called the linear similarity of all men which is meant, but the creative power and creative dominion of the *one* God over all of them. But this God is Israel's God, the covenant Lord of the chosen people. "The" man in the exemplary sense is Israel, the people chosen by God, which rejects God but which is not abandoned by him.

It is not otherwise in the New Testament. The Father of Jesus Christ is Israel's God. God's relationship to and attitude toward "the" man does not become a self-evident generality in the new covenant; it is now revealed in its

---

13. See on this especially E. Peterson, *Der Monotheismus als politisches Problem; ein Beitrag zur Geschichte der politischen Theologie im Imperium Romanum* (Leipzig: J. Hegner, 1935). Further, J. Jeremias' article on *anthropos* (*TDNT,* I, 364ff.).

exclusiveness and concentration, for it is identical with God's activity in the one man Jesus Christ, toward whom Israel's history has been proceeding and in whom it ends as the history of "Israel according to the flesh."

   c. *Adam – Christ.* The New Testament in its Adam–Christ typology created a compelling expression for what is to be considered here. "The" man is simultaneously "a" man and vice versa. This applies to the "Adam" of the biblical account of primeval history, and it was not wrong that the Septuagint translated the Hebrew word with both *ho anthrōpos* (man) and with the transliteration *Adam*. This "man" in the Genesis account is in fact a being sui generis. Just as his "proper name" is simultaneously a "generic term," he is both himself and yet in every respect the "type of the one who was to come" (Rom. 5:14). In Romans 5:12ff., Paul is concerned to show that what "Adam" once did happened for "all men," just as what "the one man Jesus Christ" did happened for "all men" (or 5:15, in the same sense, "for many"). In the one man the one pattern of existence is defined, and in the other man the other pattern of existence. "The" man—that is "Adam." And "the" man—that is Christ. In 1 Corinthians 15:21f. and 15:45–49 the relationship is seen in one regard (15:21f.) similarly to Romans 5, most expressively in 15:22: "For as in Adam all die, so also in Christ shall all be made alive." In another regard Paul draws a connection in 15:45–49 between the bodily nature of Adam and the spiritual in the resurrection, but in this instance (and this was already true in the passages already mentioned, but here it is more exclusive) it is done in the sense of the fundamental difference which is present within the analogy. The first Adam was a "living being" (15:45); the last will be a "life-giving spirit." The first was "from the earth" (15:47); the second is "from heaven." We are not concerned here with the origin and the further development of the analogy,[14] but only with the fact that we are dealing here with the idea that "the" man is qualified not just by whatever characteristics he may have, but by the total constitution which God has set in him. The generic concept "man" in the context of the New Testament witness (compare the passages already mentioned with 2 Cor. 4:4; Col. 1:15 and then Col. 3:10; Eph. 4:24 as well as Eph. 1:22; 4:15; 5:23; and Col. 1:18; 2:10, 19) is placed in a most unusual tension between creation, the Fall, and redemption. "The" man is the human being, wherever he is, in his determination through God's work, God's covenant, and God's commandment, but also in his determination rendered by the fact that God takes him by his word in his perversity and yet does not surrender him to it but makes him his own partner.

---

   14. See L. Goppelt, *Typos, die typologische Deutung des Alten Testaments im Neuen* (Gütersloh: Bertelsmann, 1939), pp. 155ff.; J. Jeremias, article on *Adam* in *TDNT*, I, 141–43; Jean Daniélou, *Das Geheimnis vom Kommen des Herrn* (Frankfurt: Joseph Knecht, 1951), pp. 139ff.; and B. Murmelstein, "Adam," in *Wiener Zeitschrift für Kunde des Morgenlandes,* XXXV, 242–75. J. Jeremias finds the typology genetically prepared in Gnostic or at least Gnosticizing ideas, in the idea of the original man as the "ideal man," and in the idea of the *bar nasa,* which Paul following Jesus then adopts (*op. cit.*, p. 143). See now K. Barth, *Christ and Adam; Man and Humanity in Romans 5,* tr. T. A. Smail (New York: Harper, 1957); and *CD,* IV,1, *passim.*

d. "The" Man—The Human Being Before God. The reason that we can speak of *the* man is that God has dealt with man and is still dealing with him. To put it another way, "the" man exists because the One God deals with every man. The unity of mankind is rooted in the unity of God as the living, triune unity in which God discloses himself to man. Because God is a person, "the" man is a person. That means that because God emerges from himself and speaks, man is therefore and therein capable of answering and is the being designed to respond. Since God in his address to man is the One God, it is possible to understand the individual responsibility of each separate man in terms of the responsibility of mankind in general, which then makes any isolation inconceivable. Since God has dealt with man in the *one* man Jesus Christ, therefore it is theologically legitimate to speak of *the* man.

The conception of mankind not as a collective abstract but as a historical unity, as the community of responsibility, and thus the conception of a "world history" and a "world order" first emerged through the Christian Church. With the secularization of Christian proclamation, this conception too has been secularized, and has become a self-evident truism, and subsequently a former truism now placed in question again. "World history," "community of nations," and "world order" are in fact only capable of being grounded in the Christian message and then in fact only possible when the Church recognizes and manifests its universality and unity. The unity of the nations "becomes an event and becomes conscious in the unity of the Church."[15] It must not be forgotten that there is also the bitter fact that finds expression in Genesis 11. And the divine remedy, namely the pouring out of the Spirit upon the representatives of the nations of the world (Acts 2), is an eschatological fact. If this is recognized, and if the statement, "one flock and one shepherd" (John 10:16), will be seen in its strict soteriological relationship, then one will have to be careful not to want to establish arbitrarily now what is eschatological expectation. At the same time, we shall have to guard against regarding the object of our expectation in such a futuristic sense that it contains no claim at all now upon our obedience. The implementation of the proclamation intended to make "all nations" into disciples (Matt. 28:19) is a declaration of war against all national polytheisms and international pantheisms. The nations receive their honor and dignity, but also their relativization and the abrogation of their religious self-importance through the proclamation of the Son of God, who is the King of Israel.[16]

3. THEOLOGICAL ANTHROPOLOGY AND HUMAN SELF-UNDERSTANDING

The question of the way in which the theological doctrine of man relates to all the other anthropologies has been touched upon already a number of times. It now must be the subject of a special discussion from the point of view of the

---

15. Paul Althaus, *DchrWahrheit*, II, 88.
16. See on this K. Barth, *CD*, III,4, pp. 291ff., and on the other side, A. A. van Ruler, *Droom en Gestalte, een Discussie over de theologische Principes in het Vraagstuk van Christendom en Politiek* (Amsterdam: Holland Uitgeversmaatschappij, 1947).

more limited issues raised by the contemporary debate. The question to be dealt with is whether the Christian discussion about man expresses a Christian "self-understanding" of man, or, should that be answered negatively, what then its relationship to the other "self-understandings" currently available will be.

There are two abstractly conceived extreme possibilities which we can easily remove from our thinking at the very beginning.

a. No Unrelated Juxtaposition. First of all, an unrelated juxtaposition of the two factors is certainly inconceivable. For this would only be conceivable if the theological statement about man either were able to leave his self-understanding up to man,[17] or if it were to put it directly aside or negate it. In both cases it would have to be assumed that the man to whom the Christian proclamation applies is absolutely incapable of "understanding" what is said to him about himself. Revelation then would be nothing other than the mechanical overpowering of man. He would be able to encounter revelation only by submitting to it dumbly and unthinkingly, and by being transposed as it were into a totally alien, "sacred" sphere. Revelation then would not touch the sphere of profane humanity; it would be a private sphere into which man could only be mysteriously elevated. Obviously such a view would be Gnostic; its ultimate conclusion would be that the creaturely sphere is essentially alien to God and his self-disclosure, and it would simply ignore the fact that God has revealed himself not above man's reality, but in it (although not from within it), namely, in the man Jesus Christ. To be sure, this self-disclosure of God is without analogy. But its lack of an analogy consists of this very fact that God, while remaining completely himself, encounters us where we are, not above or beyond us. Therefore this man, as he has been reached by the Word of God, as he has been encountered by Jesus Christ, as he has not been despised by Christ, cannot be set aside without giving rise to docetic ideas.

b. No Observable Continuity. Secondly—it is just as inconceivable to attempt to add the Christian discussion of man to whatever other statements about man are contained in the current self-understandings. The human self-understanding as such would remain untouched. It would only be "complemented" or "deepened" by the "Christian" statements in a certain way. The element of truth in this view is found in what we just designated as incorrect above, and that is that the human self-understanding is not erased by revelation. But on the other hand, it should be clear that it does not remain unaffected. The revelation of God

---

17. Karl Barth (*Die christliche Dogmatik im Entwurf* [Munich: Kaiser, 1927], p. 404) once emphasized with a view to exegesis that "we all" were wearing "some kind of spectacles," i.e., we all brought some kind of philosophy with us. F. Gogarten in his review (*ThR* [1929], p. 67) related this sentence to the "underestimation of anthropology" characteristic of Barth at that time. He was right to the extent that Barth declared that the various "spectacles" were necessary (since otherwise we could not see at all) but dealt basically with something which was theologically indifferent. There were many who followed Barth in this treatment of the self-understanding (which expressed itself in the philosophies). He himself has clearly shown in the meantime that he is capable of a completely different kind of anthropology.

is the total redefinition of the man who receives it. The easiest way to express this is again in terms of Christology: that Jesus is the Christ of God does not mean an additional definition of man's being but rather a total definition of man's human existence though Christ's work as the Revealer and Reconciler. Whereas the view described above corresponds to Christological Docetism, we are dealing here with an analogy of Subordinationism; this view or statement, which regards itself as Christian, forms the highest point of convergence between two elements, one of them "natural" and the other "supernatural."

It should be plain that we cannot summarily ignore human self-understanding with our theological anthropology, nor can we base our "Christian" statements upon the current self-understanding of man, whatever it is. The reason for this is to be found in Christology, in the fact that God reveals himself to us in the One who is "true man," and as such can be sought neither apart from man with his self-understanding nor at man's heights or depths. God's revelation in Jesus Christ is rather the ultimate questioning of man and simultaneously his only truly positive affirmation. But in questioning man, it is not, so to speak, his negation within the limits of his own categories, but the rejection of the total pattern of man's existence in all conceivable categories. In turn, as affirmation it is not the linear affirmation of something "in" or "about" man, such as the affirmation of some ultimate kernel of personality or of the spirit or of the soul, but rather the complete affirmation of man-before-God, who is man-coming-from-God. Both in affirmation and in denial this applies in the actual sense to the One who is "true God and true man," and it applies to every other man as the fellow man of Jesus Christ.

c. No Direct Delimitation. The relationship of the Christian view of man to the given self-understandings can, under these circumstances, not have the character of an observable delimitation. Every delimitation would in effect assert indirectly the validity of some part of the human self-understanding. Above all, it would declare that the Christian view of man and the human self-understanding are comparable quantities, because one can only draw lines between such quantities. But this in turn could only mean that the Christian view of man for its part would become a special form of the human self-understanding.

Now, the Christian view of man is doubtless one of the many "views" of men, comparable with them, and indeed in agreement with them in this or that insight. But we must keep in mind that this is also true of the Christian statement about God. Yes, we can add at once that there is no generally illuminating and forceful reason why all of theology should be something other than a "Christian philosophy" (*philosophia christiana*),[18] a philosophy built upon the foundation of revelation. However, the very concept itself shows that revelation has become something here which, in the Christian view, that is, in light of itself, it simply is not.

Of course, it is inherent to the revelation of God in Christ that it can be

---

18. This expression, which Erasmus was particularly fond of, was not avoided by even Calvin (e.g., *Concio Academica* [*Epistola 19 bis*] [*CR*, X/2, 30]).

confused with something else, and there is no generally acceptable criterion which could be used to oppose such confusion. If there were such a criterion, it would not be the revelation of God, and it would not be God's revelation in the man Jesus of Nazareth. What Kierkegaard so emphatically characterized as the "incognito" is there, and it is demonstrated effectively by the fact that revelation can be understood as nonrevelation, merely as a religion, or a doctrine of wisdom, or a cultic event. Wherever this happens, it is even possible to derive essential insights from the failure to grasp the revelation. Jesus can certainly and relevantly be understood as a Rabbi, as a miracle worker, or as a prophet (in every instance, as one of many). He would not really be man if this were not possible. God would not really be God-for-us, God in relationship, if he were not exposed to this relativization, and thus to the risk of either being made into an ideal or being deprived of all deity. This possibility of confusion is part and parcel of the concept both of revelation and of the interpretation of the witness to revelation, which is Christian doctrine.

Indeed, we must go one step further. What the eyes see is not as such necessarily wrong. It was not just the judgment of the Pharisees and scribes or of the excitable crowds, but also of the Evangelists that Jesus was a Rabbi, a miracle worker (with many analogies to the "divine men" of that age), and a prophet. And it is not just a misunderstanding when Christian anthropology is regarded as one view of man among many. When the New Testament calls Christian doctrine *didachē* (teaching) and its activity *didaskein* (to teach), then in fact a degree of comparability with other "teachings" and other "teaching" is presupposed. Christian doctrine is not of the kind which would obviously appear to be sui generis.

d. The Cause of Incomparability. Why then should it be the case that the comparability which we have just conceded ultimately is not given? It can perhaps best be seen if we deal with a Pauline passage which is then related to other passages. In 1 Corinthians 8:3 we find the unusual, rather mystical-sounding statement that if one loves God, "one is known by him." There is a similar statement in Galatians 4:9, and we shall also have to think of 1 Corinthians 13:12 and Philippians 3:12. The "knowledge" of man which is envisaged here clearly does not represent any act of human self-understanding. Of course, this does not prevent the saying from taking the form of a human saying about God and his dealing with man. But the actual point which emerges here is not a self-understanding but rather that "knowing" which God exercises and which according to Amos 3:2 is this loving knowing in which God establishes his covenant.[19] Completely in accordance with that, it is not so decisive that we "apprehend" God in Jesus Christ, as that we are apprehended by him. The act of "knowing" on God's side finds then its human manifestation (which, according to 1 Cor. 8:3, grammatically follows it) in love to God (see Rom. 8:28), which in turn (we think of Rom. 8:35, 39) is based upon the love of God "in Christ Jesus our Lord." One can say that

---

19. For "to know" as the carrying out of fellowship, see above, pp. 198ff., and R. Bultmann, *TDNT,* I, 689ff.

in the love of God, that is, in the commitment and conversion of life to God, man "understands" himself in a way. But in so saying, we must immediately state that this is constantly based upon God's activity in man which does not primarily change man's self-understanding but the whole pattern of his existence, gives his life another direction, and gives him a Lord. This new kind of existence of man, to which Scripture testifies, has its center, its origin, and its goal in the person of Jesus Christ, who alone, as the "first among many brethren," is the new Man (Eph. 2:15; see also Rom. 8:29). This could also be expressed more concisely in the terms of Colossians, which (1:13) says of the Father that he has "delivered us from the dominion of darkness" and "transferred us to the kingdom of his beloved Son." It is quite clear that the issue here is not a new self-understanding, but rather a new *constitution* of man. That means simultaneously that what is conquered here is not a perverted self-understanding but again the literally perverted constitution of our existence. It cannot be denied that this is the real issue in the New Testament proclamation, and it is not enough to say that the "new creature" in the sense of 2 Corinthians 5:17 is the new "understanding of existence."[20]

Thus we exclude the abstractly conceivable possibility that the Christian view of man is merely a reinterpretation of an already given self-understanding. The issue is not a change of our self-understanding but a transformation of our existence. But of course, then the issue is also one of the transformation of self-understanding. The man who is "known" of God cannot know himself in any other way than in the light of this God's "knowledge."

We can explain the connection between the transformation of existence and the transformation of our self-understanding by turning to the New Testament concept of *metanoia* (repentance, conversion). *Metanoia* is more than "a change of mind" or "a change of opinion." For behind this idea lies the Old Testament concept of *shub* (to turn back, to turn around), which does not refer to thinking, meditating, or reflecting, but to the direction and constitution of existence. Conversely, it is significant that the New Testament uses an expression for repentance and conversion which includes "thinking" (or the activity of the mind). When at the announcement of the Kingdom of God a man repents, that is, acknowledges and responds to the conversion of his whole constitution of existence brought about by God, then his "thinking" is changed *also*. In Pauline terms, what happens is a *logizesthai* (considering [Rom. 6:11]) which accords with the decisive *logizesthai* of God (Rom. 4:3 and elsewhere). Insofar as it can be said that *metanoia* is also a way of understanding one's self, it can also be said that the Christian view of man is a certain self-understanding. Since, however, *metanoia* is essentially the implementation of the transformation of man's constitution of existence brought about by God, we must then say that Christian anthropology essentially rests upon something other than a mere alteration of our understanding of our being and to that extent also represents something essentially different from the unfolding of such a process.

---

20. R. Bultmann in a statement made in a discussion in 1949.

e. The Question of the Understandability of the Christian Message. We must now discuss whether and in what sense the Christian doctrine of man (as man before God) can be made understandable to man who already has some kind of prior understanding of himself. If it is possible to arrive at a positive answer here, then the self-understanding which man has is ascribed a positive significance, despite the sharpness of any possible or factual collision.

This question is identical with the other question as to whether it is possible to make a man, in the context of his own self-understanding, aware of his creatureliness and his being a sinner—we would not say the Gospel, which is seldom if ever asserted. We are now confronted with the question which Emil Brunner raised, the issue of the "point of contact."[21] Obviously the question whether man is able to know himself as a creature in and of himself is an element of the problem of so-called natural theology and has already been discussed in that context.[22] Whether man in and of himself can know his own creatureliness and his being as a sinner is not our concern here, but rather whether the Christian message when it is brought to him can be received by him within the context of his self-understanding.

f. Reasons to Deny This. Whoever answers this in the negative can appeal to strong theological reasons for doing so. How should man know his creaturehood and his being as a sinner[23] without knowing God? And how should he know God without knowing Christ? And how should he know Christ other than through the Holy Spirit? Is it not so that according to Paul the "unspiritual" or "natural man" does not "receive" all that is given with the Spirit of God (1 Cor. 2:14)? And can the man "born of the flesh" (John 3:16) somehow escape from the curse of the "flesh"? Who would attempt to establish here a kind of "continuity" between the Spirit of God and human self-understanding?[24]

g. Reasons Against It. Nevertheless, however strong these reasons adduced may be, the reasons which are raised against it are just as weighty. If there is a complete, dual "discontinuity," one might ask, Then how can Paul in the same section we just cited also say that only "the spirit of man" can know "a man's thought," and accordingly (*houtōs*, "so"!) no one has known "the thoughts of God" except the Spirit of God alone (1 Cor. 2:11)? Obviously an analogy is being asserted here. The same Paul can in his apostolic freedom make himself a Jew

---

21. E. Brunner, "Die Frage nach dem 'Anknüpfungspunkt' als Problem der Theologie," *ZZ* (1932), pp. 505ff. On this subject see especially K. Barth, "No!", in E. Brunner, *Natural Theology,* tr. P. Fraenkel (London: G. Bles, 1946 [also University Microfilms, Ann Arbor, Michigan, 1965]), pp. 67–128, *passim* indirectly.

22. See pp. 199ff.

23. The fact that the one kind of knowledge belongs with the other will have to be discussed below, pp. 549ff.

24. E. Brunner, *loc. cit.,* orients everything to the concept of continuity. He concludes that the continuity which expresses itself in the pre-understanding and which is based in man's being as a creature is "in the service" of the "discontinuity" of the Church's activity (p. 511). In his later writings, the concept of the formal "image of God" becomes the kernel of what he means by continuity.

to the Jews and (according to the sense) a Greek to the Greeks (1 Cor. 9:19–23).
Why does he do that if the work of the Spirit and thereby the efficacy of his
message take place contingently, unpredictably, and "perpendicularly from above"?
Why does he strive at all, to the point where he is "accommodating himself" to
men (a free translation of 2 Cor. 5:11)? Why does he notoriously use the language
and the imagery of his contemporaries, even to the extent of the extreme case
recorded in Acts 17 (which is assuredly somewhat complex from the literary point
of view)? Why does he prefer prophecy, which is intelligible and even understandable by the "outsiders and unbelievers," to glossolalia (1 Cor. 14:16, 19, 23, 24,
31)? Does it not belong to the essence of God's self-disclosure that he "accommodates" himself to us (as Calvin repeatedly emphasized)?[25] And otherwise would
not Docetism have to be judged right?

h. *Summary.* No, the first argument outlined above cannot lead to the conclusion that the sovereign power of God in his revelation simply overwhelms the
human self-understanding. The concept of "conscience" alone would be sufficient to make clear that in the event of proclamation (we are thinking of 2 Cor. 4:2)
something also happens on the side of the man who hears. The sovereign power
of God is not just God's freedom *from* man, but it is also his freedom *for* man.
And the freedom of the "Spirit," which "blows where it wills" (John 3:8), does
not mean solely his freedom toward all the criteria of our self-understanding and
self-consciousness, but also his freedom to bear witness to himself in relation to
this self-understanding and self-consciousness. The total differentness of the Spirit
from all human "spirit" should not be confused with a delimitation within the
same category. It cannot be thought of as linear, so to speak, but only as
dimensional.

On the other hand, however, that new constitution of existence and the new
understanding of man which accords with it never has the character of confirmation or elevation of the given self-understanding. We can never in any sense
tell ourselves "the truth" about ourselves, because we exist in "falsehood," in
"darkness," in "sin," and we cannot even say what has just been said because
we would have to "know" the "truth," the "light," and "salvation" in order to
know about that. If the continuum sought by Brunner might be found anywhere,
it certainly could not be found in the sense that we could continue along an
already begun road when God's knowledge of us is shared with us and when
God's revelation is granted to us. The "continuity" here, if there is any at all (we
shall speak to that directly), consists not in both directions, but only in one. With
that, however, the concept of continuity is decisively changed.

i. *The Pneumatological Aspect of the Problem as the Solution.* Just as the
Church's Christology goes "right through the middle" between Docetism and
Subordinationism, we must also "go through the middle" in the issue under discussion. The mystery of the person of Jesus Christ lies in the fact that he is in
truth "true man," although we could not comprehend him as the One who he is

---

25. See above, pp. 414f.

on the basis of his humanity. The mystery in the nature and work of the Holy Spirit, which is at stake here, is that he truly does work in and on man, without his true nature and work being discernible from man's perspective. Whoever denies the genuine humanity in the work of the Spirit is engaging in pneumatological Docetism. Whoever bases the work of the Spirit upon human self-understanding or conceives of it as the elevation or surpassing of that self-understanding, is engaging in pneumatological Subordinationism. The mystery of the Holy Spirit lies as it were midway between these two false approaches. His work in the event of proclamation enlists human hearing and perceiving in a way similar to that in which the total humanity of Jesus Christ is enlisted so that in him God reconciles the world with himself (2 Cor. 5:19).

In the work of the Spirit, therefore, the given human factor is neither eliminated nor questioned in its reality. And the new constitution of existence is seen in a nonlinear fashion to be a new reality sui generis, in contrast to all self-understandings. It appears in the form of a self-understanding. It is not protected against this form's being confused with its essence. On the contrary, it is enlisted for service in this very form. Proclamation has just as much the form of discourse (i.e., the goal-oriented expression of "thoughts") as does the philosophical diatribe for its part, and to the extent that witness belongs to Christian existence and represents a decisive element of the service which is obligatory for the Christian, this "inauthentic" form belongs truly to what is "authentic" and real.

j. Results. Our question was whether man in the context of his self-understanding is capable of apprehending the message of his creatureliness and his being a sinner. We can express the result thus far briefly as follows: Yes, he is able to apprehend the message to the extent that it encounters him in the form of human speech and activity, but he is not able to grasp the content, the new constitution of existence and the old composition of his existence defined by sin. It encounters him "in, with, and under" confusable speech and can be received as such. But it becomes the reality which overcomes and transforms him only in the incomprehensible and incalculable work of the Spirit of God. And where this work happens, the self-understanding of man is not eliminated but penetrated, turned around, brought into a new direction and under a new lordship. Then man recognizes the lie which no analysis of existence could unmask and which is not synonymous with the "failure to attain existence" or "existence in inauthenticity." He then recognizes the darkness as that out of which he comes, and the truth as that out of which he does not exist. In other words, in the experience of the Gospel the law now works its work in him, and in the reception of the Good News he is moved to that *metanoia* (conversion) which comes alone in the heralding of the Kingdom of God. Here, in this decisive event, which is categorically different from all perception of rational discourse, it is not possible to speak of a "continuity," unless it is the concealed continuousness of the preparatory, guiding work of the Spirit of God (in the sense of Augustinian "prevenient grace"). It is at this very point that human existence reaches its true meaning. Man would necessarily not be a creature of God if Augustine's famous statement were not true in this regard, "Thou hast formed us for Thyself, and our hearts are restless till they find rest in Thee."[26] In this sense the often misunderstood saying about the "greatest good" (*summum bonum*) is justified, as it in turn is expressed in Augustine's fundamental proposition, "For me to adhere to God is good," and as Calvin, echoing Augustine, expresses it at the beginning of the Geneva Catechism.[27]

4. THEOLOGICAL ANTHROPOLOGY AND CHRISTIAN EXPERIENCE

a. Putting the Question. Whoever acknowledges that there is a specific theological anthropology will not advance the thought that it can be based directly upon the "natural" self-understanding of man, although there have certainly been indirect attempts at such reasoning since the earliest ages of the Church (the Apologists!).

But does it not seem all the more logical to seek the direct source of a Christian doctrine of man in the "special" Christian experience?

The meaning of experience for Church doctrine has been discussed in many forms for centuries. There has scarcely been an attempt to derive *all* the sections of Church doctrine from Christian experience—even Schleiermacher, for example, makes use of other (speculative) elements to assist him. But it does appear to be a very natural procedure to derive at least our propositions about man from what *men* have experienced or "lived through."

b. On the Origin of the Problem. After classical Reformed theology, led by Calvin, had ascribed to "experience" (*experientia*) a significant role, it was the Englishman William Ames (1576–1633), working in Holland, who under the influence of the empirical philosophy of Petrus Ramus (1515–72)[28] first outlined systematically a theology of experience.[29]

Ames has been described as a forerunner of Schleiermacher.[30] This is true at least in regard to his method, which sees theology as the analysis and description of the spiritual life, of Christian existence. Formally and methodically Schleiermacher's theology does in fact dissolve into anthropology. This is revealed in the classical division of his doctrine of faith. In its first part the "religious consciousness" is developed, "as it constantly is presupposed in every Christian religious emotion and also is always contained in them." In its second section, "the facts of the religious consciousness" are discussed "as they are defined by their antithesis," meaning first of all the antithesis based upon the consciousness of sin and then, "from the other side," that "of the consciousness of grace." We

---

26. Augustine, *Confessions*, I, i, 1 (*NPNF*, I, 45).

27. Calvin, *The Catechism of the Church of Geneva, 1545*, tr. J. K. S. Reid (*LCC*, XXII, 83–139).

28. See especially Paul Lobstein, *Petrus Ramus als Theologe; Ein Beitrag zur Geschichte der protestantischen Theologie* (Strassburg: 1878).

29. See K. Reuter, "William Ames, The Leading Theologian . . . ," in Nethenus, Visscher, and Reuter, *William Ames*, tr. D. Horton (Cambridge: Harvard Divinity School Library, 1965); and O. Ritschl, *Dogmengeschichte des Protestantismus* (4 vols.; Leipzig: Hinrichs, 1908–27), III, 381ff.

30. O. Ritschl, *op. cit.*, pp. 382, 384; K. Reuter, *op. cit.*

see a similar picture in the method of Hofmann. He is a biblical theologian. But he expounds Scripture "according" to faith, which he never finds anywhere else than in himself.[31] The task of theology for him is "neither the description of Christian religious emotional conditions nor the repetition of the contents of the doctrine of Scripture and the doctrine of the Church as these have taken their unique shape in me, nor even the derivation of Christian knowledge from a supreme principle, but the explanation of the simple facts which make the Christian into a Christian and distinguish him from the non-Christian. . . ."[32] Therefore he can conclude that theology is only a "free science" "when I the Christian am my very own material of my science for me the theologian."[33] A line may be drawn from the theologians named leading up to the present day.[34]

c. The Relative Validity of the Reference to Experience. It would not be a refutation of this approach if we were to oppose it with the widespread contemporary idiosyncratic attitude toward all forms of personal experience. There is no theological criterion which could prevent us from saying quite uninhibitedly that there is the "experience" of being a Christian or in being a Christian. It does not mean that an "it" in us believes, nor that the Holy Spirit in us believes, but faith is designated in the New Testament as the faith of this or that person. The New Testament is also by no means sparing with its references to particular stirrings of emotion, of the will, or of the understanding, which belong together with faith or, in other words, which are produced by the Holy Spirit. We refer to one example, Galatians 5:22f. *Our* feelings merit in the light of faith no disparagement compared with *our* knowledge (and "our" Pietism as such is therefore by no means more questionable than "our" Orthodoxy!).

And yet, the Christian view of man is not the analysis of the "Christian" person, and theological anthropology is not dependent upon "Christian" experience as its source or its foundation. We may name the following substantial reasons for this.

1) What Makes "Christian" Experience Christian Is Not Contained in That Experience. We could follow the example of the phenomenology of faith originated by Melanchthon and carried on in Question 21 of the Heidelberg Catechism, and summarize all the various component parts which make up faith, and yet we would not have expressed the essence of faith in that, namely, that it lives out of the faithfulness of God (and for that reason solely it is, again speaking with the

---

31. J. C. K. von Hofmann, *Der Schriftbeweis* (3 vols.; Nördlingen: Beck, 1852), I, 9.

32. *Ibid.*, p. 11.

33. *Ibid.*, p. 10.

34. A particularly characteristic example: G. Wobbermin, *Systematische Theologie nach religionspsychologischer Methode* (3 vols.; Leipzig: Hinrichs, 1913ff.; ET of vol. II, *The Nature of Religion,* tr. T. Menzel and D. S. Robinson [New York: Thomas Y. Crowell, 1933]); and *Richtlinien evangelischer Theologie zur Überwindung der gegenwärtigen Krisis* (Göttingen: Vandenhoeck & Ruprecht, 1929).

Heidelberg Catechism and Melanchthon, a "certain knowledge" and a "hearty trust"). For the same reason, the most comprehensive and the most penetrating analysis of Christian experience or of the Christian self-understanding would never contain that which makes such experience *Christian*. This essential quality is not merely the concealed foundation, but much more the heart of faith or of Christian experience. Whatever one can designate with this concept, it has the character of a response. But this response is not simply the reflection of the Word, on the basis of which it is a response.

2) **Christian Experience Is in Itself Contradictory.** We do not believe on the basis of our experience but in spite of our experience—assuming, of course, that this "in spite of" is seen within our "experience." It was Luther who frequently emphasized that our experience provides "opposition" to our faith.[35] Faith does not exist without being attacked, and in such attacks, experience is sharply opposed to faith. The voice of our own heart is as such not the voice of faith. That "I" am the person in the new constitution of existence is an immediate given of experience just as little as the reverse, that I cannot deduce from experience that "I" am a sinner.[36] This opposition, which certainly exists in Christian experience, can only be understood on the basis of the Word addressed to us, as the opposition of our existence before God.[37]

3) **The Imperceptibility of the "Old" and the "New" Man.** The "new" man is, under these circumstances, by no means identical with a given which we can experience, and accordingly what makes the "old" man *old* is not given in a perceptible way. We may recall to mind here what has already been stated:[38] the new creation in the sense of 2 Corinthians 5:17 is not something which is going on "in" us, just as we cannot discover "in" ourselves that we are "the righteousness of God" in the Crucified One (2 Cor. 5:21). The "new creation" is rather the new order established in Jesus Christ, the new "covenant" (1 Cor. 11:25; 2 Cor. 3:6), the new unity of what had previously been separated (Eph. 2:15). And since this newness exists in the person of Jesus Christ (as the second Adam;

---

35. Here we refer to the study by H. M. Müller, *Erfahrung und Glaube bei Luther* (Leipzig: J. C. Hinrichs, 1929), and Karl Barth's discussion of it, "Bemerkungen zu Hans Michael Müllers Lutherbuch," *ZZ* (1929), pp. 561ff.

36. It is significant that the Heidelberg Catechism, which in many ways is the document of "anthropocentric" theology in the good sense, does not answer the question, "Whence knowest thou thy misery" (Question 3) with a reference to experiences of some kind, but states, "Out of the law of God" (Schaff, III, 308).

37. F. Gogarten finds that the decisive thing about a "religious philosophical" understanding of man is "that man is primarily understood as one who exists outside of the revelation of God, who can be conceived of without having to think of God's revelation at the same time. . . . He is understood therefore in and of himself. . . . To be sure, this is done in a way that he is understood on the basis of his own capacity for establishing a relationship to God. For he is understood as homo religiosus." But in truth, what holds is that "only in the direct association of God and man is God God for us and man man" ("Das Problem einer theologischen Anthropologie," *ZZ* [1929], pp. 497ff.).

38. See pp. 463ff.

see Rom. 5:12ff.; 1 Cor. 15:22, 45ff.), "to put on the new nature" (Eph. 4:24; see also Col. 3:10) means the same thing as to "put on Christ" (Gal. 3:27).

We could summarize by saying that the new man in the original sense is Christ. But he is also the One who is God's "likeness" (2 Cor. 4:4). In Jesus Christ, that is, in the establishment of his lordship over us, we are restored to our creatureliness (Col. 3:10) and sin loses its claim (Rom. 6:12ff.). How would one speak of this "experientially"? The "in Christ," which alone expresses this new constitution of existence, is emphatically "outside of us" (*extra nos*).[39] Now it must, of course, immediately be conceded that this "outside of us" cannot be construed in the sense of metaphysical transcendence. The "new man" is really supposed to be "put on" (Col. 3:10; Eph. 4:24), and in fact, the person baptized has "put him on" (Gal. 3:27); conversely, Paul can without inhibitions use what is fundamentally a Hellenistic-Gnostic idea, the "outer nature" (2 Cor. 4:16; Rom. 7:22; see also Eph. 3:16), apparently because he also does not shy away from the mystical-sounding formula, "Christ who lives in me" (Gal. 2:20). Unquestionably the New Testament message, even where it emphasizes most emphatically the "in Christ," reckons with the full involvement of the believing person. If we could say that the new man is Christ, we must now add that it is the Christ "in" whom the believer exists and who "lives in" the believer. Now everything depends here upon whether the accent is correctly placed. The accent is not upon religious experience but upon the One who gives himself to the believer and makes himself his Lord. He never becomes the innermost ground of being of the believing person: he is, rather, "in" him in that he is "coming to him" simultaneously. What might be called "mysticism" here is always and primarily eschatology.[40] The same Paul who can employ "mystical" concepts in such rich abundance still knows (expressing himself here in Gnostic terms) that he, as one who is "at home in the body," "dwells" "away from the Lord" (2 Cor. 5:6), and he, too, knows those experiences to which faith is opposed and in which he is solely dependent upon the promise of "grace" beyond all experience (2 Cor. 12:1–10, especially 12:9). Experience does not possess its own independent significance.

4) **The Border-line Character of Christian Existence.** This may be seen most clearly in the way in which the New Testament frequently relates faith to birth and death. Faith means to be born anew; faith means to die or to be dead. We might say perhaps that this way of putting things corresponds to and is perhaps rooted in the fact that faith and baptism belong together. This is true at least of John 3:3ff., 1 Peter 1:23, and Romans 6:1ff. We should consider further John 1:12, 1 John 2:29; 4:7; 5:4, 1 Corinthians 15:31, and Colossians 3:3. For our context

---

39. Thus not only Luther in numerous passages, but also Calvin, *Institutes*, III, xi, 4, pp. 728f.

40. On this see A. Schweitzer, *The Mysticism of Paul the Apostle*, tr. W. Montgomery (New York: Henry Holt & Co., 1931 [g1930]); H. E. Weber, *"Eschatologie" und "Mystik" im Neuen Testament* (*Beiträge zur Förderung christlicher Theologie*, 2nd ser., 20; Gütersloh: Bertelsmann, 1930); R. Bultmann, *Theology of the New Testament*, tr. K. Grobel (2 vols.; New York: Scribner's, 1951–55 [g1948]), I, 298ff.

the important thing here is that birth and death are the two experiences which involve man most personally but neither of them can ever be demonstrated, described, or analyzed by man. No one can intellectually grasp his own birth or death. The lesson for us in our context is that the reality of faith and the experience granted to it cannot be an independent object of reflection and thus cannot be the starting point for a theological anthropology. This knowledge is then deepened when we remember that this "dying" or "being dead" is a dying "with Christ," and the new birth is a birth "from above." The reality which is the essence of the derived reality of faith as our faith "is" not transcendent or beyond in the metaphysical sense, but in the strictest sense it is "outside" of our self, that is, not derived from us, nor in us, but solely in the triune God himself, who is, however, our God.

d. The Experience of Sin as a Human Possibility? Now it is not the case that we could only be certain of grace "by hearing," but we can certain of sin "by experience." The reality of sin is something which we can no more discern apart from him whom God "for our sake . . . made . . . to be sin" (2 Cor. 5:21) than we know apart from him the "righteousness of God" which we "are" "in him" (*ibid.*). When the Heidelberg Catechism, as we mentioned above, sees in line with Reformation thinking generally the knowledge of sin effected by the law, it is not referring to the law as we manage it, as we "make it our own," but rather to the law as the "custodian until Christ came" (Gal. 3:24), which has its "end" in Christ (Rom. 10:4). Therefore, repentance is not an autonomous ability of "the" man, but the gift granted together with the proclamation of the Kingdom of God to man.[41] Apart from the Gospel our consciousness of sin is a very suspicious affair. It can virtually be our way of confirming ourselves in our sinfulness. In any event, it is never the consciousness of actual sin, and from the perspective of the Gospel it remains itself sin as long as it is not the result of grace.

5. CREATURE AND SINNER

a. The Problematic of Humanity Today. The "nature of man" (*natura hominis*) could only appear as something unproblematic to a very naive mentality. Even the Enlightenment, in whose circles this naivete was most likely to flourish, was not in its most significant representatives so foolish that it did not sense the unique contradictoriness, fragmented character, and dividedness of the human being. It is affecting to observe that in the very age of the "optimistic" view of man suicide became a much-discussed problem. Today it is considered very "modern" to speak of the "problem" of man. The reasons are known to all. Even the physical survival of mankind has become a "problem," and it could easily be that one day the question whether European-American man is still humanly able to cope with the power of his own domination over nature will decide the other question, whether there will even still be European-American humanity

---

41. Repentance as a gift (Acts 5:31; 11:18), and repentance as the theme of the Good News (Luke 3:18).

or not. It is a bitter truism that man is being placed in question in such a comprehensive way. But it would be very dangerous for theology to make this skepticism and anxiety its allies in a way similar to its reliance upon the consciousness of autonomy in the Enlightenment and the 19th century. Was it really a settled issue that the "Yes" to man of that day, which autonomous man thought he heard in the period of modernity now ending, was God's Yes and therefore a valid Yes? On the other hand, is it a settled issue that today's questioning of man is also derived from God? Could it not be that the "nature of man" is hidden behind this public questioning of man in the same way it once was hidden behind the apparently just as public affirmation of man? Might it not be that the questioning of man today is in the final analysis nothing more than the reaction to that earlier affirmation and shares the same roots, namely, in the presumption that man can understand himself, can affirm or deny himself?

b. Creatureliness and Corrupted Creatureliness. What then does theology mean when it speaks of the "nature of man"—using an interpretive concept which is found only once in the Bible and then only suggested in James 3:7? As we have already considered, it means not man in himself, but man in his relationship to God. It understands this relationship of man to God not as something which is added to his nature, but as the relationship which is given to man with his (first) nature. And that means that it understands man as creature. His nature consists in the fact that he is creature. Whether and in what way this man exists, whose nature is to be creature, whose being is to be for God and from God, is a question which must still be dealt with. But there is no theological anthropology which could begin with any other thesis than this, that man is creature.

But there is also no theological anthropology which could stop with that proposition. For man, although certainly creature by his nature, is nevertheless in conflict with his Creator. His creatureliness has fallen prey to perversion. He is a sinner, that is, he is the creature who is separated from his Creator. He is thus a self-contradictory being, for he is not in fact what he "is" according to the omnipotent will of the Creator.

We can therefore only speak of the nature of man contradictorily, paradoxically. Even Calvin expresses himself in a sharply paradoxical way: man is "corrupted through natural vitiation," but in such a way that "this vitiation did not flow from nature."[42] "Natural man" is not natural man. This is the actual contradiction. In the deepest sense it is also a self-contradiction of man—not as

---

42. *Institutes,* II, i, 11, p. 254. Calvin often uses this paradoxical concept of nature. But it should be noted that nature, e.g. in the two sections of the sentence cited above, has two different meanings. The "first or primal nature," as Calvin also calls it (II, iii, 6, pp. 296–98), is the creature (*creatura*). But in II, i, 11, p. 254, Calvin adds that he wants to designate the "vitiation" as natural, because although it is not a "substantial property" of man, still "it holds all men fast by hereditary right." For this second version of the concept of nature he appeals to Eph. 2:3. See on this also *Institutes,* III, iii, 12, pp. 604f. On the whole theme, see especially T. F. Torrance, *Calvin's Doctrine of Man* (London: Lutterworth Press, 1949, 1952; Grand Rapids: Eerdmans, 1957).

though man stood in contradiction to his own deepest being,[43] but in contradiction to the creatureliness which is granted to man by the Creator, promised him and not denied by the Creator.

c. The Two States. Theological anthropology, especially since Orthodoxy, moves back and forth in the polarity between two states of man, two constitutions of existence: the "state of integrity" (*status integritatis*) and the "state of corruption" (*status corruptionis*). This is an approach which is quite correct as a description of the contradictory situation just alluded to. The only question is, How are the two states to be understood and related to one another?

d. Totally Creature! First of all, let us remind ourselves[44] that according to the biblical witness and the Church's witness following it, man was not just God's creature once upon a time, he *is* that. "Every man is at all times wholly and utterly God's creature."[45] "I believe that God has created me"—that is the confession of the Church not just for itself alone but, like everything it confesses, as a representative of all men. This is also the case with the biblical statements to which E. Schlink refers (Job 10:8, 9, 11; 30:15; 33:6; Ps. 139:13ff., etc.). It is really true that "the fallen man, not just the man of the primal state, is to be thought of as God's creature."[46]

We must then say that every person in some sense is a person before God. "The" man cannot escape from God. The Church therefore can never concede that there is a real godlessness of man. Whatever is said about the power of sin, we cannot attribute to it the power to abolish God for man. Every act of the Church's proclamation takes every man as a creature of God. It is not without reason that the statement in Acts, "In him we live and move and have our being" (Acts 17:28), is one of the biblical passages quoted most frequently by Calvin. God is present and at work with man where man is not in the least conscious of it. He overwhelms him with his gifts (think of Ps. 104), and he confronts him as his Judge (think of the oracles regarding the heathen in the Prophets). God is inescapably near to man. He guides even the heathen nations (see, for example, Isa. 7:18; Amos 9:7). He even makes "the wicked for the day of trouble" (Prov. 16:4). How little all this can be used as a foundation for a natural theology has already been shown.[47] But we should not narrow the worldwide breadth of the biblical view for fear of natural theology.

---

43. When even Calvin speaks frequently of the "remnants" of the "image of God" in man, then this implied quantification of something which Calvin would never have quantified encourages the idea that creatureliness, the nature as creature, is somehow and ultimately somewhere "present" "in" man, and simply layered over by sin. It is impossible to think in this fashion. Not even with reference to Calvin, if we remember that for him the direction in which life is lived is what is decisive, in "rectitude" or in "perversity" and "vitiation."

44. See pp. 463ff.

45. E. Schlink, *op. cit.*, p. 119.

46. *Ibid.*, p. 122.

47. See pp. 199ff.

e. Totally Sinner. However, this very same man who is and remains God's creature, who cannot flee from his Creator, this man is totally sinner. His being as a sinner cannot be quantitatively limited. With good reason the theology and the proclamation of the Church have almost unanimously opposed restricting sin to the body, a tendency to which Greek thinking was prone. The biblical statements about man as sinner give not the slightest cause for such a mitigation of sin's seriousness. It is rather thoroughly to the point when the Augsburg Confession in Article 2 detects sin in the fact that man exists "without the fear of God, without trust in him, and with fleshly appetite"; it sees sin primarily in the center of personality, in the "soul," and only mentions the (indirect) relationship to the physical at the end of the list, using the Augustinian term "concupiscence" (*concupiscentia*). The discussion in Calvin, expressly directed against the Greek misunderstanding, has the very same thrust.[48] If, on the one hand, it is true that we "live and move and have our being" in God, if we then cannot speak of man's ontological godlessness, then it is just as true on the other hand that all "have turned aside" (Rom. 3:12), all are sinners (Rom. 3:23), all stand under the dominion of death (Rom. 5:12), and all—"we," says Ephesians 2:3, "like the rest of all mankind"—are "by nature children of wrath." Speaking of the same Gentiles to whom God according to Romans 1:18ff. or Acts 14:17 had not withheld the witness to himself, Paul can say that they were "without God in the world" (Eph. 2:12).

Man's situation is that God is inescapably near to him and that he still is absolutely opposed to God. That man can make God's inescapability into his accessibility, and thus turn God into an idol, must be taken into consideration here along with the reverse, that he can make his own guilty estrangement from God into a static given and can then behave in an outright godless fashion (we think of Ps. 14 and 53). Both of these belong to man's separation from his Creator.

But how should we envision the relation of these two mutually exclusive states or constitutions of man's existence?

f. Temporal Succession of the Two States? Now we cannot simply speak of a temporal succession of these two constitutions of existence. We saw already in the biblical passages cited that this way is closed. Creatureliness is not spoken of in terms of a man that once existed, but in terms of "the" man. Sin does not prevail in the sense that the Creator has been driven from the battle. Orthodoxy expressed this in the controversy with the views of Flacius (1520–75) in that it denied that original sin was the "substance" of man.[49] It is certainly true that

---

48. *Institutes,* II, i, 8f., pp. 250–53; II, iii, 1, pp. 289f.; but see already Thomas, *STh,* I, lxxxiii, 2, vol. I, p. 419.

49. See especially Article I of the Formula of Concord. The "Solid Declaration" (I, 26) declares that the Flacian view is Manichaean. If original sin were the substance, then it would be "as if Satan had created and formed some kind of evil substance" (I, 27). In truth, however, "all substance is either God Himself or the work and creature of God" (I, 55). All of Orthodoxy judges in a similar way. The only question is whether Flacius understood "substance" in the same way as his opponents (see H. Kropatscheck, *Das Problem theologischer Anthropologie auf dem Weimarer Gespräch 1560 zwischen Matthias Flacius Illyricus und Viktorin Strigel* (Unpublished dissertation; Göttingen: 1943). Otherwise,

man in a very definite sense is *no longer* creature. He is the creature which has fallen away from the Creator, and his creatureliness has become inaccessible to himself. But that does not exclude its reality. To put it conceptually, "corruption" is "corruption from something," it is robbery, theft, destruction, "perversity," "vitiation," and not proper reality.[50] For God is also the Creator of fallen man.[51] And since God is not the Creator of sin, it is true that "Sin, therefore, cannot be man himself."[52]

g. Ontological Integration of the States? The paradox in the fundamental statement about man cannot be dealt with by setting up an order of succession. In some sense there is simultaneity between the two parts of the statement. But if that is so, then it seems that the only possible way to think of both of these ideas in one thought is through the concept of ontological condition. That would mean that sin would be understood in some sense as overshadowing the original "nature" so that it robbed that original state of its purity, perfection, and value, without destroying it completely. If one proceeds in this fashion, the paradox is diluted if not altogether removed.

h. The Medieval Definition of the Relation and Its Results. The classical form of this ontological-conditional integration of creatureliness and sin is the view which consistently forms the basis for Roman Catholic anthropology, which states that through sin "the natural good in man was corrupted, the gracious (good or gifts) were taken away."[53] One can obviously emphasize this in various ways. Thomas, for example, emphasizes the second part: sin is "the privation of original justice"[54]—and in this most of the Protestant theologians follow him. But he can also emphasize the fact that sin by no means utterly abrogated that which is "rational."[55] "In this respect man is naturally corruptible as regards the nature of his matter left to itself, but not as regards the nature of his form."[56] But however the distinctions be drawn in detail, the result in every event is the idea that in sinful man there is some last remnant of his original constitution of exis-

---

see H. E. Weber, *Reformation, Orthodoxie und Rationalismus* (2 vols. in 3; Gütersloh: Bertelsmann, 1937–51; repr. Darmstadt: Wissenschaftliche Buchgesellschaft, 1966), I, 2, p. 7; L. Haikola, *Gesetz und Evangelium bei Matthias Flacius Illyricus; eine Untersuchung zur lutherischen Theologie vor der Konkordienformel* (Lund: C. W. K. Gleerup, 1952), pp. 97ff.

50. Thus the Formula of Concord; similarly Calvin, *Institutes,* II, i, 11, pp. 241f.; III, iii, 12, pp. 604f.

51. Formula of Concord, "Solid Declaration," I, 38, p. 546: ". . . God ever since the fall is the Creator of man."

52. *Ibid.,* I, 45, p. 547.

53. Peter Lombard, *Libri Quattuorum Sententiarum,* ed. Franciscans of Quaracchi (2 vols.; Ad Claras Aquas: Quaracchi, 1916), II, xxv, 8, pp. 432ff. It is not uninteresting to see that Calvin agrees with this in principle. He declares in the *Institutes,* II, ii, 12, pp. 270f. his agreement with the "common opinion" derived from Augustine, "the natural gifts were corrupted in man through sin, but . . . his supernatural gifts were stripped from him." Similarly II, v, 15, pp. 335f., again appealing to Augustine.

54. *STh,* I–II, lxxxii, 1, vol. I, p. 956.

55. *STh,* I–II, lxxxv, 2, vol. II, I, p. 967.

56. *STh,* I–II, lxxxv, 6, vol. I, p. 971.

tence which has remained. In this last remnant, his relationship to his Creator is still present. This last remnant is the core of human existence.[57] Only if one does not deny man this last remnant, can one say at all that he is "capable of sin" (*capax peccati*).[58] And conversely, only if one attributes to him this last remnant is he at all capable of redemption in the passive sense.

One can treat this "last remnant" with very great contempt, and can speak more of the "corruption" than of that which is the concealed object of this "corruption." One can even do as Hans Urs von Balthasar has now done and deprive this last remnant, this "nature," of any inherent comprehensibility and view it purely as that which is not grace,[59] but must still be assumed so that grace is not naturalized. But this remnant is always the point of reference for grace, to which it always connects, no matter how indirectly. This last remnant can also be understood formally (the "image of God" in the formal sense) as does E. Brunner, not varying appreciably here from Thomas Aquinas, which means that this remnant is deprived of every material quality and every value emphasis.[60] In doing so, nothing decisive is altered in the fundamental position. The "last remnant" in man or about man is essentially his nearness to God. The core of his existence as a person is, ontologically, oriented to God.

i. The Question of the Continuum. What has made this position so powerful through the centuries is the indisputable fact that it has provided the categories which make the contradiction of the Christian description of man, his being a creature and sinner at the same time, intellectually tolerable. In particular, it offered the possibility of maintaining the responsibility of man in his sinfulness while referring simultaneously to a continuum which leads from creation to reconciliation.

j. Critique of the Medieval Conception. And yet we cannot take this approach. Without a doubt, it leads inevitably to the consequence that grace is no

---

57. Calvin can say that he does not condemn "those inclinations which God so engraved upon the character of man at his first creation, that they were eradicable *only with humanity itself* . . ." (III, iii, 12, p. 604). Although this is not the major point of emphasis in Calvin's understanding of sin, this is in itself a good Thomist statement.

58. This statement, which accords so much with the intentions of Emil Brunner, is found in Thomas, *STh*, I–II, lxxxv, 2, vol. I, p. 967.

59. H. Urs von Balthasar, *The Theology of Karl Barth,* tr. J. Drury (New York: Holt, Rinehart, Winston, 1971 [g1951]), pp. 219ff. Especially p. 225: "So we must formulate our theological concept of nature by working [primarily] from grace." P. 229: "Insofar as Revelation does take place, it sets nature off from itself as the antechamber that is not, of itself, the grace of participation." How this is meant is then shown on p. 236: "Because he is meant to hear this Word, man is by nature a subject. We must never forget, however, that grace not only presupposes man as subject; but also elevates and completes man in a radical way; it is *in the summons* of grace that man is enabled to become God's partner and elevated to a hearer of God's Word."

60. E. Brunner, "Nature and Grace," in *Natural Theology,* tr. Peter Fraenkel (London: Geofrey Bles—The Centenary Press, 1946 [g1935]), p. 24, and *Man in Revolt . . . ,* pp. 169ff.

longer totally grace. The error is not the raising of the question about the reason for man's continuing responsibility and about that permanent element which makes man human. This question is legitimate and demands an answer. The fateful thing is that this last base of responsibility and this permanent remnant is sought *in* man, that it is the subject of an inquiry dealing with man as such. For it is accompanied by the view that God becomes the source of that remnant, the apex of a great pyramid of being—perhaps deeply concealed in what is unknown. Is the God who must then be spoken of, at least "for the time," really the Father of Jesus Christ? And if he is, why does the person of Jesus Christ play absolutely no role in this whole, imposing ideational structure? Apparently one can say all there is to say in this approach without even mentioning him. But if we take this approach, are we not then really already embarked upon "intellectual work-righteousness,"[61] that is, on the endeavor to think away sin abstractly by means of an ontological analysis of man's condition? Has not this kind of thinking become in reality a component of a comprehensive attempt at self-justification? This was the attempt which saw "elevating grace" (*gratia elevans*) as "inherent grace" (*gratia inhaerens*), as the power which makes the buried and corrupt remnant in man effective again and which helps man to develop this root so that sin gradually is overcome, although of course the final result cannot be predicted. Is not the doctrine of justification of Trent to be seen in a close relationship with this conception of sinful man who still is related to God in this remnant? Trent seems to assume this conception.

   k. The Contradiction in the Light of the Gospel. But from what standpoint is this contrasting opposition, that of creature and sinner at the same time, seen? The distinctive feature of the argumentation we have just been discussing is that it initially ignores Jesus Christ and free grace. But if I ignore the grace proffered me by God in Jesus Christ, then of course I will scarcely be able to do anything else than engage in such an ontological analysis of the various levels of my personality. And why should I not pursue it back to the point that "the" man does have a "good core" which is only layered over by a thousand bad influences but which, under the guidance of and in imitation of Jesus of Nazareth, I can lay bare and make fruitful again. Or, why should I not say in terms of existential philosophy that man has lost his authenticity to an anonymous collective of "man," but can regain it by making a breakthrough toward the future? But it is in this methodical (and not just methodical) neglect of free grace, that is, in this very self-justification, which inevitably must then happen, that the deepest, the religious form of sin is found, the sin in which man wants to be master of himself in his most profound depths, and wants to be master of God with the same profundity. In any event, the Reformers saw it this way, and our attempt to arrive at an understanding of man from their position may not begin with the traditional terminology which they doubtless continued to use but with their new view of grace as the

---

61. K. Barth, "No!", *loc. cit.*, p. 102.

absolutely free goodness and benevolence of God to man which is brought to us in the person of Jesus Christ.[62]

We can only see the reality of man when we hear the Gospel which is directed to this man. If it is really so that man can only be understood as man before God, just as God is truly himself in that he is God for man, then neither creatureliness nor sin can be recognized aside from God's self-disclosure.

l. No "Hamartiocentric Theology." We shall search "within" ourselves for a trace of our creatureliness in vain, without straying into the errors just discussed. But neither can we do as Flacius once did, who consciously opposed the medievally colored anthropology of Melanchthon and his students (above all Victorinus Strigel [1524–69]), and deny or even abbreviate the creatureliness of man for the sake of his sin. In so doing we would be forsaking the scriptural path. Indeed, we must never forget that the witness to our creatureliness is the first and then the last word, and the testimony to our sin is only a second and certainly not an ultimate word. Here, too, we will have to be more careful than was Orthodoxy. T. F. Torrance has accused later Calvinism—and this applies not only to it—of having produced "a doctrine of the fall of man and of human depravity apart from the context of grace, and interpreting grace as God's answer to human depravity. This does violence to the doctrine of total depravity, because, when cast in moralistic and legalistic terms, it does not do justice to the undoubted elements of virtue and good in the unregenerate man, which Calvin himself recognized; and it slanders man's natural gifts, thus, as Calvin said, insulting the Creator."[63] One can state it another way. Where God's grace alone does not, so to speak, surround sin, it becomes nothing more than a reaction, and conversely sin gains its own importance in the polarity to grace which it does not deserve. A "hamartiocentric theology" would in fact fail to grasp what is the worst feature of sin.[64]

m. Christological Understanding of Man. But how can we, without minimizing the seriousness of sin, that is, the importance of grace, speak freely about the creatureliness of man? The reason that we can do it is that the man Jesus Christ is the man for God *and* our fellow man. Our creatureliness is not a matter of the past, because he is not relegated to the past. It is not our own characteristic, not even in some ultimate sense, in that he is our fellow man but not our deepest meaning. But neither is it a kind of objective given towering over us, because he

---

62. Several of the citations above showed that the Reformation presented its view of man broadly in the terminology of Scholasticism. The decisive breakthrough to a new dimension of thought, which was really none other than that of Paul, is their view of "total man," which excludes any analysis of the various levels of man's personality. We find Luther and Calvin in agreement on this. But it only works if one begins with the "total Christ."

63. T. F. Torrance, *op. cit.* (1957 ed.), p. 20.

64. The quotation from Torrance and my remarks follow along the lines developed by K. Barth, *CD*, III,2. It is almost ironical that H. W. Schmidt, to whom the unhappy term "hamartiocentric theology" can apparently be traced, once appeared to want to make Karl Barth, of all people, into the chief proponent of this theology (H. W. Schmidt, *Die Christusfrage; Beitrag zu einer christlichen Geschichtsphilosophie* [Gütersloh: Bertelsmann, 1929]).

has become flesh for us. It is he in whom God keeps faith with us as the Creator and overcomes our unfaithfulness. It is he who as our fellow man is truly man, man before God and man for God.

In the preceding sentences we have accepted the basic thesis which Karl Barth uses as the foundation for his doctrine of man as "the creature." What this means in detail can be shown later in our discussion of the concept of "image of God."[65]

Barth formulates the fundamental anthropological question in the following way: "What is the creaturely nature of man to the extent that, looking to the revealed grace of God and concretely to the man Jesus, we can see in it a continuum unbroken by sin, an essence which even sin does not and cannot change?"[66] The "founding of anthropology on Christology" given here[67] has indeed seldom been attempted in the theological tradition, but it is plainly enough suggested by the "true man" of the early Church Christology, which for its part clearly is derived from the New Testament.

Naturally Barth is fully aware that when he develops his anthropology under the title "The Creature," he is not saying everything that has to be said about anthropology. He is similarly aware that it cannot be a matter of "a simple deduction of anthropology from Christology."[68] This is already indicated by the simple reference to the sinlessness of Jesus. In this approach, sin is by no means passed over, but it is not dealt with thematically. Barth is concerned—and we are reminded here of T. F. Torrance—that sin not be permitted to become the power which would then make of grace nothing more than a reaction to it.

n. The Sinner in the Light of Christology. Nevertheless we must ask, while fully recognizing the rightness of this basic idea, whether Christology itself does not compel us to proceed differently from the very beginning. What does "true man" really mean? May we speak of the incarnation in any other way than in the light of the "theology of the cross" (*theologia crucis*)? What kind of man is this who Jesus became "for us men and our salvation"?[69] Can we speak of this man in any other way than Paul when he says that God "made him to be sin who knew no sin" (2 Cor. 5:21)? It is in the same context that Paul makes the fundamental Christological statement, "God was in Christ" (2 Cor. 5:19). But Luther's addition of the word "and" to the next part of the sentence ("and reconciled the world with himself") is weak, since that clause is connected participially to the former clause in Paul much more closely ("God was in Christ reconciling" or "in Christ God was reconciling"; see the RSV). We could almost say that God was in Christ as the One who reconciles the world with himself, in that he did not count against them (men) their trespasses. . . . Incarnation is understood here completely as reconciliation. But this means that from the Christological view we cannot speak of man as creature in an isolated way; we must speak of creature

---

65. See pp. 558ff.
66. *CD*, III,2, p. 43.
67. *CD*, III,2, p. 44.
68. *CD*, III,2, p. 47.
69. Nicaeno-Constantinopolitanum.

and sinner at the same time. If in Barth the fundamental idea prevails that creation is at the same time the effect and the preparation of the covenant, then we must add that this covenant is for the people *who we are*; it is the covenant which man has broken, which has been revealed in Jesus Christ not just in its constancy based upon God's institution but also in its re-creation for us. If we see it that way, then the result does not necessarily have to be the fateful ambivalence of grace and sin which Barth rightly opposes in his whole doctrine of election and creation. Paul's sharp protest against that ambivalence remains (Rom. 5:15, 16, 20). Reconciliation is "more" than the "restoration" of the "creature." But it is also that.

So, adopting and extending Barth's thesis, we must say, Yes, Jesus Christ is the "man for God," "the Man for other men," "the whole Man," the "Lord of time." He is "true man" in the sense of the fulfilled "creature of God," but he is simultaneously "true man" as the One whom God made into sin for us, whom he made into the object of his holy rejection, indeed, in whom he took this rejection upon himself. In other words, in Jesus Christ our creatureliness is revealed in such a way that at the same time our sin is revealed through him as truly sin. But this must be understood in a double sense. The first sense is that in Jesus Christ our sin appears before God as what has been absolutely, powerfully, and effectively negated. He became the "curse" for us (Gal. 3:13), and in him the divine No, which the law announces, became bloody reality. "My God, my God, why have You forsaken me?" The other sense is that in Jesus Christ our sin is first recognized as what it is for us. For we have put him to death, which he suffers for us. It is the human No against the real God, against grace, which wreaks its havoc upon him to the very extreme. These two senses make up the core of the "theology of the cross," in the light of which it becomes clear that only in "looking to the man Jesus," to use Barth's expression, can we fully appear as what we are before God and thus are in truth: creature and sinner, not in ambivalent polarity, but in a unity which we cannot intellectually dissolve but which God solves in this man Jesus.

B. THE IMAGE OF GOD

1. THE PROBLEM

a. The Use of Terms. The Church doctrine of man as creature has placed the concept of the "image of God" (*imago Dei*) in the center since ancient times.[70] Man is the being created by God "in God's image" and "after His likeness."[71]

---

70. See A. Hoffmann, *Die Lehre von der Gottebenbildlichkeit des Menschen in der neueren protestantischen Theologie und bei Thomas von Aquin,* in *Thomas Divus,* Serie 3, Bd. 19, *Jahrbuch für Philosophie und spekulative Theologie* (Freiburg-Schweiz: Albertinum, 1941); W. Bachmann, *Gottes Ebenbild . . . ; Richard Bruch, Die Gottebenbildlichkeit des Menschen nach den bedeutendsten Scholastikern des 13. Jahrhunderts* (Freiburg dissertation, 1946); J. Ries, *Die natürliche Gotteserkenntnis in der Theologie der Krisis* (1939; n.l.).

71. K. Barth, *CD,* III,1, p. 197, translates Gen. 1:26: "Let us make man in our original, according to our prototype." Gerhard von Rad concludes that one could translate, "as our image" (*Das erste Buch Mose, Genesis, Kapitel 1–12,9* [*Altes Testament Deutsch,* 2; Göttingen: Vandenhoeck & Ruprecht, 1949, 1958], p. 45).

The central place of the idea of the "image of God" in theological anthropology is not based on the frequency of its use in the language of the Bible. It is found in what is assuredly a very important passage in the Priestly account of creation (Gen. 1:26f.), and then twice again in the same tradition within the Pentateuch (Gen. 5:1f. and Gen. 9:6). In addition, it is echoed in Psalm 8:6f. In the New Testament we meet the concept in the direct anthropological sense in James 3:9 and 1 Corinthians 11:7, and it is clearly implied in Ephesians 4:24 and Colossians 3:10. We may also mention, with the necessary reservations, the apocryphal passages Sirach 17:3 and Wisdom 2:23. That is, for the time being, the total summary of all the passages. If dogmatics were only a summarizing restatement of the biblical passages, then one could object to the degree of significance attached to a biblical concept which occurs relatively so seldom.

b. The Function of the Concept. However, there can be no doubt that theology has emphasized the concept of "the image of God" so strongly because in it the distinctiveness of man is understood so expressly in his special relationship to God. The Priestly account of creation has in fact created a concept which expresses the decisive element of the biblical view of man far beyond its purely terminological frequency.

However, it is this very significative meaning attached to the concept of the "image" or "likeness" of God which is one of the reasons for the difficulties which it has always caused theology. Because it is so logical to interpret this concept by using other statements of Scripture, the danger is particularly acute that its own unique message will not be seen properly. And this danger is heightened by the fact that anthropology is one of those places in which theology tends most easily to import thought patterns which are foreign to its actual content but familiar to those doing theology. In short, the dogmatic tradition, made up of such a peculiar mixture of Christian and extra-Christian elements, makes it especially difficult at this point to understand this important concept as it ought to be understood.

c. On the Exegesis of Genesis 1:26f. In our further reflections let us begin with Genesis 1:26f., as is appropriate. We notice at once that the Priestly witness, who elsewhere always stresses the majesty of God, departs here from the usual thrust of his creation account. The plural of the divine decision sharply emphasizes the special character of what is now happening. It is not a solitary God who speaks in this fashion; it is God who in himself or with himself has an opposite— the text is probably referring to the world of angels. Furthermore, that being created according to the "image" of this God is, in turn, not "one of a kind" but "two of a kind" (Gen. 1:27). Yet it is not the biological duality which shows that this being is created after the image of God. That is found in other creatures as well. The Priestly account of creation does not say wherein the similarity of the human being with God does substantially consist. The other biblical passages are silent on this point, too. One thing does become immediately clear, however. As the being created after the image and in the likeness of God, man has something inviolable about himself: neither man nor animal may take man's life (Gen. 9:5), "for God made man in his own image" (Gen. 9:6). James 3:9 continues this line: it is a matter of inward impossibility to praise God with the "tongue" and to curse man with the same "tongue," because man is "made in the likeness of God" (James 3:9). For the other creatures and for his fellow man, man is for God's sake and because of God not a thing but "something" holy (*sacrum*). This is also the background of 1 Corinthians 11:7. But that "holiness" is not inherent in man but resides in the special relationship to himself which God the Creator has granted.

By virtue of this special relationship, man is not only inviolable, but he is equipped with a certain kind of authority over his nonhuman fellow creatures. In Genesis 1:26 man's position of dominance is expressed directly after his description as a being after God's image. His being in the image of God issues in the "call to feudal lordship."[72] It is generally characteristic of the Old Testament that it does not make statements about "nature" and "being" but statements about "the task" or a "relationship." As the being who is like God, man is supposed to do something. Just as God's "nature" is not explained but his acts are recounted, the Priestly witness does not explain the "nature" of man, but his "task."[73]

We have thus seen from two sides what the likeness of the created man to his Creator effects. It endows him with a "gift" and a "task" (*Gabe* and *Aufgabe*).[74] But is everything said at that? Is it possible to express more exactly this special relationship to God which is both the center and the starting point of both statements?

d. "The Image of God" as the Definition of the Whole Man. It is easier to answer this question in the negative than in the positive. Negatively, it would certainly not accord with the sense of the Priestly witness and with the rest of the Old Testament if we wanted to restrict the special relationship between man and his Creator to the soul, as theology generally has done.[75] Of course, when H. Gunkel[76] tried to think essentially of the body, that was a reaction to the traditional view which was just as unjustified. It will surely be correct when we apply the description of man as "the image of God" to the "whole man," and not restrict it to the spiritual side.[77] Even if we follow the example of earlier theology and consider the Yahwist account here too, and in view of Genesis 2:7 see the special nature of man in the "breath of life" breathed into him, we must

---

72. W. Zimmerli, *Das Menschenbild des Alten Testaments* (*Theologische Existenz heute*, 14; Munich: Kaiser, 1949), p. 20.

73. *Ibid.*

74. Gerhard von Rad, *op. cit.*, p. 46. Von Rad emphasizes that the "mandate for dominion" does not belong to "the definition of man's being the image of God." He understands it in this fashion, "Just as earthly monarchs set up statues of themselves as symbols of their claim to authority, in provinces of their realms in which they are not constantly physically present, man too in his image nature is set upon earth as a sign of the dominion of God. He is in fact mandated by God, ordered by God to preserve and impose God's claim of sovereignty upon earth." He quotes the essay by W. Caspari, "Imago Divina," in W. Köpp, ed., *Reinhold Seeberg Festschrift* (Leipzig: A. Deichert, 1929).

75. See pp. 562ff.

76. H. Gunkel, *The Legends of Genesis, the Biblical Saga and History,* tr. W. H. Carruth (New York: Schocken, 1964 [g1922⁵]), *ad loc.*

77. G. von Rad, *op. cit.*, p. 45.

not forget that in the Priestly account the animals also have the "breath of life" in them (Gen. 1:30), just as according to Genesis 2:7 man is "a living being." "Soul" in the Old Testament is not the same thing it was for the Greeks, although it certainly implies the mysterious being which makes for "life" in the specific sense, both in man and in animals (although in Gen. 1:30 and Gen. 2:7 in characteristically different ways: man is a living being, and animals carry it in themselves). To understand the "soul" summarily as the element "in" man through which he is like God would be to run counter to the anthropomorphism of the Old Testament (which is by no means theologically irrelevant). In the Old Testament, God really has a form, and it cannot be rejected out of hand that there is in the background of Genesis 1:26f., "the idea of Yahweh's human form."[78] Gerhard von Rad rightly asks, "Did the great prophets speak in any other way about God?" And he refers to Amos 4:13; 9:1, Isaiah 6:1, etc., and especially to Ezekiel 1:26, a passage which seems to be "a prelude" to Genesis 1:26.[79]

> e. The Positive Meaning of the Concept of the "Image of God." What then should we say positively? First of all, it is of decisive importance that the "image of God" is clearly not a concept of being or quality, but of relationship. Man is what he is in his specific inviolability and position of dominion because of a relationship to God which is neither inherent in him nor a characteristic of him, but which reveals its reality in the mandate which is given to him. The very concept of "being in the image of God" is not altogether unambiguous. It suggests that one should look for the "image" of God in or about man (which is a conceptual reversal of what Gen. 1:26f. says), or better, that the "copy" is made abstractly independent of the "original," which in turn makes the relationship into a static relatedness of being. When we use the concept of the "image of God," we must concentrate solely upon the relationship which it bespeaks. Man is "in the image of God" to the degree that he stands in this relationship. In substance this relation cannot mean anything else than this, that the authenticity of man's being is derived from God. This is significant in two directions. On the one hand, man does not have his humanity in himself; he is what he is solely in and out of his relationship to God. Here he is something which he otherwise is never supposed to be: here he is the bearer of a "function." But on the other hand, he is undeniably more than that. Just as he does not have his humanity within himself, this humanity is maintained and supported in the deity of God, because it is willed and established there. God does not merely tolerate the fact that there are creatures there, which are different from him and exist outside of him. He wants this special creature, which represents all other creatures and is set over all of them as the one he has mandated; he wants this specific creature in its specific oppositeness to all other creatures, this creature which is the op-

---

78. *Ibid,*, p. 46.

79. *Ibid.* In view of the thinking of von Rad presented here, the consideration whether Gen. 1:27 speaks not of the image of Yahweh but of God is theologically insignificant. It would be difficult to document that the Priestly witness with his expression was thinking of the image of divine beings—of angels, for example. The differentiation is meant terminologically (as in Ps. 8:6, too) but not theologically.

posite of the other creatures in a "like" way to the way God is this creature's opposite. This is the creature which is supposed to know him, to thank him, and to praise him (see Rom. 1:21). God conducts his history with this creature. That is the reason that this special creature, this creature in the specific sense,[80] is inviolable, and that an honor is ascribed to him (Ps. 8:6) which is not God's own honor but has its origin there.

We have now reached the point where in the process of a critical review of the dogmatic interpretation of "the image of God" we can see the actual problem which has always been there and which, beyond our exegetical efforts with Genesis 1:26f., requires a solution with regard to the Bible's message in its unity and totality.

f. The Ontological Interpretation of the Concept in Dogmatics. In contrast to the interpretation outlined above of the basic biblical passage, theology has generally regarded the "image of God" as a "something" which man "has" in some way, or has partially or completely lost as a sinner. As early as Plato we find the idea[81] that tangible reality is the visible copy of the real world which is accessible only to thought. For Gnosticism it was naturally an important thought that man has in his soul a spark of that original world, from which it had wandered by mistake into matter.[82] The view was then widespread that the human soul manifests something divine, a *homoiōsis,* a likeness or similarity with deity. Beginning with Irenaeus, Christian theology has developed its doctrine of the "image of God" in the controversy with pagan or Christian-Gnostic thought, and in the process generally appropriated the latter's assumption that the image of God is at least hypothetically present in a tangible way in man. Thus the doctrine concentrates essentially upon the *soul.*[83] To be sure, there are many theologians who also view the body from the perspective of the "image of God." In their own way, the Valentinians did that, in that they related the "image" of Genesis 1:26 to the material side of man. Of the oldest Christian dogmaticians to be mentioned

---

80. Karl Barth, *CD,* III,2 (*passim*), understands man simply as *the* creature. As we see in Barth's discussion of the animals (*CD,* III,4, pp. 348ff.), this is not to be understood exclusively, but inclusively. In view of Rom. 8:19ff., we would conclude that man is the representative creature.

81. See H. Kleinknecht's discussion of the Greek usage of *eikōn* (image) in the article in *TDNT,* II, 388–90, with references in Plato to *Timaeus* 92 c, but also *Phaedrus* 107 c and *Theaetetus* 176 b; see also Calvin, *Institutes,* I, iii, 3, pp. 45–47.

82. Irenaeus describes the doctrines of the Valentinians in the following way: physical man was formed in his material part according to God's "image," and in his spiritual part according to God's "likeness"; the spiritual part is also called the "spirit of life," because it emanated from the spiritual (*Against Heresies,* I, v, 5 [*ANCL,* V, 23]).

83. See A. Struker, *Die Gottebenbildlichkeit des Menschen in der christlichen Literatur der ersten zwei Jahrhunderte* (1913; n.l.); H. Karpp, *Probleme altchristlicher Anthropologie; biblische Anthropologie und philosophische Psychologie bei den Kirchenvätern des dritten Jahrhunderts* (*Beiträge zur Förderung christlicher Theologie,* 44, 3; Gütersloh: Bertelsmann, 1950). On Tertullian, see Karpp, *op. cit.,* pp. 53ff. On the whole theme, M. Schmaus, *Katholische Dogmatik* (5 vols.; München: M. Hueber, II, 1949³⁻⁴), pp. 292ff., and especially H. Cremer's article, "Image of God," in Schaff-Herzog, V, 431f.

in this regard are Tertullian (c. 160–c. 220)[84] and Lactantius (c. 240–c. 320),[85] who in turn were followed by Luther[86] and Calvin,[87] each in turn proceeding from his own starting point. However, the soul was regularly given the priority,[88] and in both Clement and Origen[89] the physical is expressly excluded from any share in the "image of God"—again under the influence of a Gnostically defined dualism. We may add that the preeminence of the soul (whatever that is understood to be) is naturally easy to understand if what we are looking for is the "location" of the "image." The early dogmaticians answered the question as to how the soul was supposed to be the bearer of the "image" in a variety of ways. Tertullian virtually conceives of a similarity of the soul's substance to God.[90] Most direct their attention to reason; this is true of the Alexandrians in particular.[91] Augustine then, in a systematic approach, connected the doctrine of the "image of God" to that of the "vestiges of the Trinity" (*vestigia trinitatis*).[92] If it is really so that the soul is the bearer of the "image of God," and if on the other hand God, the Creator, is none other than the triune God, then the tradition which Augustine accepted and developed that the soul is threefold in nature ("memory," "intellect," and "will," or "love"=*memoria, intellectus, voluntas,* or *amor*) must be as such a "vestige" of the Trinity. Augustine's system exercised a profound influence upon the Middle Ages.[93]

    g. "Image of God" and "Original Righteousness"=justitia originalis. There is, in addition, another line which leads from Augustine through the Middle Ages up to Reformation and Orthodox theology. Augustine was not satisfied with the ontological-psychological interpretation of the "image of God." That was really only of secondary importance to him. What was decisive for him was that this concept of "image of God" implied a relationship between man and God. Man as the "image of God" is man who is found "in order" with God, and who is for that reason in order with himself. Such a man is really sinless. He is not ruled by concupiscence, but in him the will is still in proper order, which means it is subordinate to right knowledge. The Middle Ages then developed the concept of "original righteousness" for this original order between man and God and within man himself.

    The interpretation of the image of God through "original righteousness"

---

84. See H. Karpp, *op. cit.*, pp. 53ff.
85. *Ibid.*, p. 237.
86. E.g., in the *Lectures on Genesis* (1:26) (AE, I, 60f.).
87. *Institutes*, I, xv, 3, pp. 186–89.
88. An exception in a sense was found in the later very speculative doctrine of Andreas Osiander, *An Filius Dei fuerit incarnandus* . . . (1550); see also Calvin, *Institutes*, *loc. cit.*, and the references provided in Barth-Niesel.
89. See H. Karpp, *op. cit.*, pp. 106, 203, 237.
90. *Ibid.*, p. 53.
91. See especially H. Cremer, *loc. cit.*
92. *On the Trinity*, X, esp. chs. 6ff. (*NPNF*, III, 138ff.) and *The City of God*, XI, 26 (*NPNF*, II, 220); see above, pp. 372ff.
93. See especially Thomas Aquinas, *STh*, I,xciii, vol. I, pp. 469–77; I,xlv,7, vol. I, pp. 238f.

gradually excluded all the other interpretations for the course of centuries.[94] This was what led to the result that the doctrine of the image of God became the doctrine of the "primal condition" (*status integritatis*) and went far beyond the interpretation of a single biblical concept. If "original righteousness" were understood as the right relationship of man to God, that is, as existence rooted solely in God, then we could accept this concept as an expansive interpretation of the "image of God." We could appeal, as has continually been done, to Ephesians 4:24 where it says of the "new nature" that it is "created after the likeness of God in true righteousness and holiness." And from there we could also turn to Colossians 3:10. The basic proposition used here, that the essence of the "image of God" is made known to us in its renewal,[95] is certainly indisputable. But what must not happen is that the "original righteousness" or "image of God" becomes a "characteristic," a "disposition" (*habitus*), or any other kind of accidental human quality which can be distinguished from man as he is. We must say it even more pointedly: it is sin for man to want to have "in" himself, under his control, what he can only have in his relationship to God. Or, to put it in the language of the biblical primal history (putting aside the differences of the various traditions there), being *based upon* God, which is what is meant with the concept "image of God," is the exact opposite of being *like* God, which is the content of the tempter's promise (Gen. 3:5). In the same way the "righteousness" which man wants to have as his "own" completely fails to be the righteousness (Rom. 10:3) which is God's and which he grants (Rom. 3:26).

Augustinian theology, therefore, in understanding "original righteousness" as a human characteristic, or in not combatting that understanding (here we would see Augustine himself), has subjected all theological anthropology to serious misunderstandings. These misunderstandings erupted then openly at the place where the critical point of the whole argument is located, which is the question of the relationship of the "image of God" to *sin*.

h. The Sinner—"Image of God"? Here the biblical resources confront us with a highly complicated situation. On the one hand, it is unmistakably clear that even sinful man is designated as created after God's image. The Priestly tradition, which does not offer an account of the fall into sin, but does speak in Genesis 6:11–13 of the comprehensive depravity of the "earth" and does not reckon with a restoration of the creation state after the great flood (Gen. 9:1ff.; compare Gen. 9:2f. with Gen. 1:29), does say in this latter context that man cre-

---

94. The speculation about the three capacities of the soul (see above, pp. 372ff.) was repressed by the doctrine of "original righteousness" as was the ancient view that the "image of God" consisted of the dominion delegated to man (Chrysostom, Cyril of Alexandria, and the Pelagians; see Augustine, "On Grace and Free Will," XIII, 25 [*NPNF,* 1st Series, V, 454]). This last view was then revived in the Reformation period by the Socinians and the Arminians, based upon their common opposition to the doctrine of original sin which was connected with the doctrine of "original righteousness." Calvin follows Augustine (see *Institutes,* I, xv, 4, p. 190, the last sentence).

95. See Calvin, *Institutes,* I, xv, 4, pp. 189f., and then the highly developed methodological development in J. Gerhard, *Loci communes theologici* (1610ff.), VIII, 30ff., ed. F. R. Frank (1885ff.), II, 112ff.

ated after the image of God is inviolable (Gen. 9:6). And what is expressed here in an especially solemn way is already heard in Genesis 5:1f. and also stated in the New Testament in James 3:9 as well as 1 Corinthians 11:7. We have also alluded to Psalm 8:6 already. It cannot be denied that according to such scriptural witnesses, sinful man is and remains "in the image of God." On the other hand, we do not find in the New Testament any direct assertion that man is no longer "the image of God," although we do have the statements about the "new man" as the "image of God," which we already mentioned (Eph. 4:24; Col. 3:10). Apparently this new man is contrasted with an old man, about which those things are not true that are asserted of the new man—we need only to think of Romans 5:12ff. How can man still be "the image of God" if he is "dead," if he has become subject to the "reigning power" of death (Rom. 5:15, 17)? How can the statement that "the" man is the "image of God" be in harmony with the polarity between Adam and Christ? Who is then actually this "new" man who is "put on" (in baptism)? According to Galatians 3:27 and Romans 13:14, this man is Christ, and Christ is for Paul "the image of God" (Col. 1:15; 2 Cor. 4:4); in Philippians 2:6 he is "in the form of God" and "equal with God," and in Hebrews 2:6ff. as well as Ephesians 1:22, Psalm 8 is understood Christologically.

In what sense, then, can we state on good theological grounds that "the" man is the "image of God"? "The" man, who is the "old" man, "dead" in sins and trespasses (Eph. 2:1)? What can the "image of God" mean when it is expressed of the sinner, and yet in other places refers not to him at all but to someone else?

If according to Genesis 1:26f. it is man's destiny in accordance with his created nature that he be completely after God's image and like him, what then remains of him to the degree that he no longer is the "image of God"? And conversely, if the redemption of man is not his improvement and healing but his new creation, what else can be said of such man who requires redemption, who is a sinner, than that he has nothing more in common with the man of creation and thus is no longer the "image of God"? But again, how should this man, if he has absolutely nothing more to do with God, if he is not the "image of God" in some sense, then participate in the newness which Christ has prepared for him? Seen in this fashion, the question of the relationship of the "image of God" to sin is no longer a problem which is restricted to exegesis, but a comprehensive theological issue. As such, it has moved theology profoundly, particularly in the period of transition between the Middle Ages and the Reformation and then again in our present day.

i. Division of the Image of God? Medieval theology found an answer to the question raised here which corresponded completely with the basic pattern of progressive synthesis which it methodically applied. To do this, it made use of a conceptual and exegetical aid which had already been used in the earliest periods, and that was the distinction between *imago—eikōn—tselem* (image) on the one hand and *similitudo—homoiōsis—demuth* (likeness) on the other. The "likeness" concept was regarded as superior here, as it had been by the Valentinians and many others, and it was also that which could be lost, because it had been added to the "nature" of man, and was granted to man as a "superadditive gift" (*donum superadditum*). This "likeness" (*similitudo*) is "original righteousness," the "rectitude" (*rectitudo*) of human life and behavior. In contrast to it, the "image of God" is the lesser element, but it cannot be lost. It belongs to man by nature and can be lost by him as little as his nature can be lost. It is his reason, his possession of a soul, his superiority over the animals. This conceptual distinction, as we said, had already been made in the earliest theology. Irenaeus derived it from Valentinian Gnosticism and reinterpreted it for the use of the Church,[96] and since then it has become a standing element of theological anthropology, namely, in Peter Lombard,[97] and most influentially in Bernard of Clairvaux (1090–1153).[98] However, the fundamental idea is even present where the terminology is different[99] or does not seem to be bound essentially to the idea. Roman Catholic theology to this day usually assumes some kind of distinction in its anthropology, which is then combined in a synthesis. It differentiates between "grace" and "nature" in that it regards "nature" as such as being dependent upon "grace" and capable of it, oriented toward it, and based upon it. This means in regard to the "original righteousness" that it is a "superadditive gift" which is added to human nature or to the "image of God." The medieval doubling of "likeness" and "image" is in general no longer applied. But in substance it persists. Sin has, under these assumptions, the effect of destroying not the "image of God" but the "superadditive gift" which accompanied it, "original righteousness." It is, of course, conceded at once that with its loss, the natural part of man is also "wounded" (*vulneratio in naturalibus*). Robert Bellarmine (1542–1621) has probably formulated this anthropology in its most radical form,[100] and it is certainly justified that Johann Gerhard (1582–1637) presents his whole doctrine of the "image of God" in virtually exclusive controversy with this Jesuit theologian.[101]

The Reformers rejected the traditional doctrine of the twofold image of God both exegetically[102] and then, above all, systematically. For our purposes, the

---

96. See above, pp. 82f., and Ernst Klebba, *Die Anthropologie des heiligen Irenäus* (Münster: 1894 [n.l.]).

97. In the *Sententiarum*, II, xvi, 3: "man therefore is made to the image and likeness of God according to the mind, by which he excels irrational creatures; but to the *image* according to memory, intelligence, and love [Augustine?] and to the *likeness* according to innocence and justice which are naturally in the rational mind. Or, *image* may be considered in the cognition of truth, and *likeness* may be considered in the love of virtue" (ed. Franciscans of Quaracchi [2 vols.; Ad Claras Aquas: Quaracchi, 1916], I, 381).

98. *The Treatise of St. Bernard, Abbot of Clairvaux, Concerning Grace and Free Will*, tr. W. W. Williams (New York: Macmillan, 1920).

99. Thomas Aquinas mentions these concepts only in passing in the *STh*. He concludes that "likeness" can be on the one hand a "preamble" to the "image" and on the other be its "expression and perfection" (I, xciii, 9, vol. I, p. 477). Since the conceptual distinction between "image" and "likeness" is not dogma, many newer Catholic dogmaticians maintain the fluctuating way of dealing with it which we find in Thomas, e.g., Michael Schmaus, *op. cit.*, II, 294, who makes no more than a reference to it.

100. *De gratia primi hominis* (1612), *Opera Omnia* (Paris: Vives, 1870–74; Frankfurt/Main: 1965–), IV, 17f.

101. J. Gerhard, *op. cit.*, Loc. VIII (ed. F. R. Frank [1885ff.], II, 107ff.).

102. Luther in the *Lectures on Genesis* (*WA*, XLII, 46f.). Calvin in his commentary on Genesis and the *Institutes*, I, xv, 3, pp. 186–89; accordingly then throughout all of Orthodoxy. Chief arguments: the double terminology does not recur in Gen. 1:27, it is in the

systematic rejection is of importance. The Reformers reject both the idea of a "superadditive gift" and the corresponding idea of a human state without this gift existing in "pure nature" (*in puris naturalibus*), and they identify the "image of God" with "original righteousness." The result, seen in principle (and with qualifications reserved!), is the thesis that with the Fall, the "image of God" was completely lost. Sin causes not only the removal of any "superadditive gift" but the destruction of the "image of God." The special significance of this for the Reformers is that the sinful man does not possess a "free will" (*liberum arbitrium*), which for Scholasticism was a part of the "natural" dowry of man (definitely still present, although wounded).[103]

j. The Antithesis in the Interpretation. With this short presentation of the antithesis, however, what is required is far from being done. This is all the more true since we could not unreservedly subscribe to the view common to both sides that in the doctrine of the "image" or the "likeness" it is "original righteousness" which is the real issue; we must ask whether this common assumption has adequate exegetical grounds. The conflict concerns the general Christian view of man, and not just the concept of "the image of God." The Catholic view is defined by the fact that man exists on two levels of being which are strictly distinguished from each other but related to each other. "Grace" is originally and essentially something next to and superior to "nature." The "nature" of man is in contrast to "grace" a relatively constant given. It consists of certain characteristics which are usually described by using Aristotelian categories quite strongly. Among these is the freedom of the will. As such it is in no sense full of grace. But it is capable of grace in the passive sense. It is, as it were, the neutral continuum to which the original gift of grace, the Fall, and the new gift of grace leading to perfection all make their contribution. It is not unaffected by all that has contributed to it. In particular, the fall into sin results not only in the loss of the "superadditive gift" but also in the "wounding of man's nature" (*vulneratio in naturalibus*). But it is just a "wounding." The continuum as such remains constant. It is still there even if it is allowed a very small space and if "nature" is understood as formally as H. Urs von Balthasar now does.[104] In terms of its basic motivation, the Reformation position is characterized by the fact that man

---

opposite order in Gen. 5:3, and then, Gen.1:26 is nothing more than the usual kind of Hebrew parallelism. In addition, see H. Bornkamm, ed., *Imago Dei; Festschrift für G. Krüger* (*Beiträge zur theologischen Anthropologie*; Giessen: Töpelmann, 1932).

103. On Luther, see especially the resume in Julius Köstlin, *The Theology of Luther in its Historical Development and Inner Harmony,* tr. C. E. Hay (2 vols.; Philadelphia: Lutheran Publishing Society, 1897), II [pages in ET not available to TR; II, 356ff. in German original, 1885]. On Calvin, the *Institutes,* II, ii and II, iii, pp. 255–309; as well as the penetrating interpretation in T. F. Torrance, *Calvin's Doctrine of Man* (London: Lutterworth Press, 1952; Grand Rapids: Eerdmans, 1957), pp. 35ff. There is an especially pertinent contrast of the Roman Catholic and Evangelical views in H. Bavinck, *Gereformeerde Dogmatiek* (4 vols.; Kampen: J. H. Kok, 1906 [g1895ff.]), II, 508; ET: *The Doctrine of God,* tr. and ed. W. Hendriksen (Grand Rapids: Eerdmans, 1951). An overview of the theme is provided by E. Brunner, *Man in Revolt . . . ,* pp. 542ff.

104. See p. 554.

is judged here not according to the levels of his being but according to the direction in which his whole life is moving. The issue here is the unity and totality of man before God, viewed from the perspective of God's revelational activity. That activity reveals man to be *dead*—at the decisive point and thus as a whole!—and not merely wounded; man's "free will" is revealed to be an "enslaved will" (*servum arbitrium*). Since God works his "good work" in free grace toward us and does not connect to an already given continuum of "man" derived from the creation, this continuum does not interest us.[105] And we thus must judge that man, regardless of the abilities he may have under the patience of God, is absolutely "incapable" of good. That "nature" which Catholic theology looks on as the component factor on which grace or the loss of grace work, is not for Reformation theology a neutral, but has its direction through the total state of man, and that direction is toward evil and away from God.

k. Roman Catholic Questioning of the Reformation Position. Let us begin with the Catholic counter-questions. They are naturally connected in the first place with the biblical evidence. The Bible also calls *sinful* man the creature after God's image. Does not that mean that we have some kind of continuum here? Must not everyone admit that in spite of sin there is still "the" man with his "gifts" (*dotes*)? Can we then think in any other way than on two levels? If we do not, are we not surrendering man in a dualistic way totally to sin and thus disgracing the Creator? The question can be put even more pointedly. If one follows the line of Reformation theology and identifies "original righteousness" and "image of God," then the "nature" of man does seem to be something which as such has something of grace about it. It does not require (in the primal state) "elevating grace" (*gratia elevans; gratia gratum faciens*=grace acting graciously) to come to it; instead, it is itself in the form of grace. The reverse of that is that grace and nature coincide—both in the "primal state" and again as the result of redemption—and that also means that grace becomes natural. In short, Evangelical theology is accused of doing what it itself had always thought it could hold up to Catholic theology: the naturalization of grace. The other objection is easily related to this. In Protestantism, nature is ascribed in truth more than in Catholicism, in that the distinction between nature and grace is levelled at the decisive point. Even the charge of works-righteousness is brought up: "With only the image of God . . . salvation is not under man's control only as long as the . . . concept of legalism can be maintained and no longer, because man cannot accord with the infinite claim of God. But this concept . . . cannot be maintained."[106] These are all important counter-questions. Their summary is given in Hans Urs von Balthasar's basic thesis, "Created beings, of their very nature, are real creatures; but they are not, of their very nature, endowed with divine grace and elevated to a higher order." If, with the Reformers, we assume one image-of-God quality of man, then we have a "naturalizing of grace," and it is against that that

105. Calvin, *Institutes*, II, iii, 6, pp. 296–98.
106. Hermann Volk, *Emil Brunners Lehre von dem Sünder* (1950; n.l.), p. 239.

the Catholic "theological concept of nature" is directed, "which did not include grace as an integral part of human nature." It was therefore the "purpose" of the Catholic Church solely "to preserve the purity of the concept of grace."[107] Therefore, grace is only grace when nature is contrasted with it as non-grace, that is, when there is this view of two levels. This is an objection to the Reformation and the newer Evangelical position which requires us to question anew the existence and nature of the neutral continuum of "nature" which seems to be of such great importance to Catholic theology.

1. The Inconsequence of the Reformed View Itself. The question becomes all the more urgent since both the Reformers and the Orthodox have shared a peculiar reticence in thinking through their understanding of the "image of God" to its final consequences. The only precise consequence of the Reformation understanding would necessarily have to be that the sinner is absolutely no longer "the image of God." "Sin ruins nature."[108] But all of the Reformers, with the single exception of Flacius (1520–75) and possibly Andreas Osiander (1498–1552) whose approach was quite unique anyway, veered away from the extreme consequences. Luther says of the "image of God" that it is "*almost* completely lost" (*paene amissa*),[109] and Calvin can speak of the "relics" of the "image of God."[110] Melanchthon leaves man with the capacity for "civil justice,"[111] and the Orthodox try very hard to find "remnants" of the "image of God" and then to build on that basis a natural theology and morality.[112] It is not surprising, then, that in the 19th century the attempt already anticipated in Orthodoxy to speak of the "image of God" in a double sense after all, to declare that the "image" formally persists

---

107. Hans Urs von Balthasar, *The Theology of Karl Barth,* tr. J. Drury (New York: Holt, Rinehart and Winston, 1971 [g1951]), pp. 220f. Balthasar concludes that there is in Protestantism here a parallel to Monophysitism, which combined into an essential unity what was given in "factual synthesis."

108. *Ibid.,* p. 220.

109. E.g., *Lectures on Genesis* (1:26) (AE, I, 67). Luther concludes that what is left to man is solely "the name and the word 'dominion' as a bare title," but not the "substance." Fallen man does not exercise "dominion" but only "industry and skill" (*ibid.*).

110. *Passim,* but most penetrating in *Institutes,* II, ii, 12ff., pp. 270ff. Calvin goes further than Luther and does not avoid, e.g., the typically Scholastic proposition that "reason," by virtue of which man can distinguish between good and evil, is a "natural gift" and "could not be completely wiped out" (p. 270).

111. Thus in the *Loci Communes* of 1521 (*LCC,* XIX, 26); Stupperich, II/1, p. 12, where it is implied that there is a certain "freedom" "according to human reason." More pointedly in the *Institutes* of 1519 (*CR,* XXI, 50). And then *Der Unterricht der Visitationen* (1528) (*CR,* XXVI, 78); Stupperich, I, p. 252; Augsburg Confession, Article XVIII (Schaff, III, 18f.) and the *Apology,* XVIII, in Jacobs, Ch. VIII, Art. xviii, 70, p. 230, etc. For the later period see H. Engelland, *Melanchthon, Glauben und Handeln* (Munich: Kaiser, 1931), pp. 237ff.

112. Particularly instructive is J. Gerhard, *op. cit.,* VIII, 58f. (ed. F. R. Frank [1885ff.], II, 115f.), who wants to reconstruct the "nature" of the "image of God" from those remnants which still remain ("some kind of knowledge of divine law . . . , testimony of conscience"), and VIII, 136 (Frank, II, 140) where he calls the "dictates of conscience" "portions of the divine image."

and is only lost in the substantial sense, gains ground.[113] The final step in this development, wich systematically completes it and even surpasses the 19th century, is found in Emil Brunner's much discussed differentiation between the "image of God" in the formal sense (the *humanum*) and in its substantial fullness.[114] We might ask whether in all of this the medieval approach, which results in a double image of God, has not been proven to be the stronger, and whether in substance the Reformation position was not in fact corrected by the Reformers with good reason. We should not underestimate the fact that there are differences within the Protestant "camp" on this point. It must especially be remembered that E. Brunner emphatically rejects the view of a double image, although he then does develop a doubleness within the image.

2. The Image of God as Covenant Determination

The question we were dealing with in these last considerations was, In what sense can sinful man be "the image of God"? The statements of Scripture made clear that he is that in some sense. But it was also clear on the basis of Scripture that there is some sense in which he is not that. How shall this dilemma be solved?

a. The Image of God and the Covenant. Any solution must be based upon the insight we have already established that man is what he is not in and of himself, but *before God*. In light of this concept, the idea of "original righteousness" as it has been developed in the theology derived from Augustine must be understood in a new way. In contrast to the medieval view, "righteousness"

---

113. E. Brunner (*op. cit.*, pp. 511ff.) cites primarily A. von Oettingen and Martin Kähler. The former (*Lutherische Dogmatik* [2 vols. in 3; Munich: Beck, 1897–1902], II, 1, pp. 363ff.) speaks of a "formal," i.e. "that which belongs essentially to the form of man's being," which "is . . . impossible to lose and is actually not lost," side of the image of God, which is found in the "spiritually personal nature of man," "to the extent that he not only has the need to grasp the idea of God but also by virtue of the indestructible thirst for freedom and the ineradicable voice of the conscience sees himself as constantly directed toward a divine omnipotence and divine norm of life." But there is no way for man to proceed from that concept to the other, the "material" image of God, which von Oettingen understands to be "original righteousness" or fellowship with God. Martin Kähler (*Die Wissenschaft der christlichen Lehre vom evangelischen Grundartikel aus* [Erlangen: Deichert, 1905³], pp. 269ff.) differentiates "between a similarity which consists as natural tendency in an unlosable definition of form, and its realization and fulfillment with the corresponding contents. . . ." But E. Brunner rejects both of these approaches: both of them reveal too much of the "dual division" of Irenaeus, which he rejects.

114. The most detailed presentation is E. Brunner, *op. cit.*, pp. 91ff. In contrast to Irenaeus, Brunner wants to "recognize that the *humanitas* which sinful man still possesses, and the *iustitia originalis* which he has lost, both spring from the same source" (p. 96). Basing his views on the New Testament, he would replace the terms "image and reflection" with "word and answer" (p. 98). That would mean that the "formal" side of the image is to be understood on the basis of the word—"reason" is the "organ for the reception of the Word" (p. 103). All of this could be accepted if Brunner did not subtly make the relationship of reason to revelation into a created characteristic, which becomes quite clear in his later work, *Revelation and Reason, the Christian Doctrine of Faith and Reason,* tr. O. Wyon (Philadelphia: Westminster Press, 1946 [g1941]). See K. Barth, *CD,* III,2, pp. 128ff.

(*justitia*) interpreted in terms of biblical thought is a relational concept. It is not chiefly an issue of what a person is in himself but what he is in relationship to another. In that we acknowledge the rightness of the ancient tradition and interpret "image of God" as "original righteousness," we do so only by understanding "original righteousness" in turn as "in the presence of God." It is nothing other than the creature's response to God's prior and absolutely superior turning to him. Thus E. Brunner is right to the extent that he describes this "original righteousness" as "an existence in love."[115] We could say just as well that it is an existence in the covenant. It is thus not a possession which inheres in man but is his responsive relationship and behavior.

b. Sin as a Failure of Existence. Sin, in contrast, is the unresponsive behavior of man, his departure from the covenant, his rejection of "original righteousness" and in that its loss. As hybris it is also ingratitude; it is the self-assertion of the creature in which it is not capable of asserting its createdness. It is the refusal of the love of God, or negation of trust in him, and thus it is the unchaining of concupiscence in every form (see the Augsburg Confession, Article 2). As a breach of the covenant it is also a breach of the commandment.

If that is so, then sin cannot be merely a weakening of the created state of man, regardless of how wide-reaching it is. If man no longer is the responding covenant partner of God, if he—as the Middle Ages concedes—no longer is in "original righteousness," then he has not just lost a "superadditive gift" but has perverted the very direction of his existence, and left his "rectitude" (as the Reformers understood it). What kind of help could the most tangible "remnant" of his created "attributes" be, be they his "nature" or his "natural gifts"? To that extent the Reformers did well in speaking quite uninhibitedly of this "remnant" as it became clear to them that man as man-before-God is always "total man" and that his essence consists of the direction and state of his existence, which is appropriate to him. Sinful man is "totally sinner." He is that in the very fact that he is "human"; his "humanity" is his sinfulness.

c. The Sinner Before God. When that judgment has been made, however, not everything has been said. The Reformers and certainly the Orthodox—in opposition to Flacius[116]—did not dilute the seriousness of their doctrine of sin,

---

115. E. Brunner, *Man in Revolt . . .* , p. 104.

116. In the course of the synergistic controversy Matthias Flacius Illyricus advanced the thesis that original sin was the "substance" of man. This formula was directed against Victorinus Strigel in the Weimar Disputations of 1560 and indirectly meant for most of the "Philippists." With his very pointed formulation, which is reminiscent of Luther's concept of the "whole man" (*totus homo*), Flacius wished simply to say that there was no distinction between man in his authentic character and man as the one who acts sinfully. But he used for this the traditional concept of substance, which he interpreted in an Aristotelian way according to his own view (substance not as a static basic nature, distinguishable from both "power" and "strength," but constantly effective in activity). Strigel represented a Platonic view of substance, as Flacius rightly maintained; man affected by original sin can be compared to a magnet which has become nonmagnetic after being treated with onion juice, but which is still a magnet. Both opponents with their adherents failed to recognize adequately that it was the concept of substance itself which was the source of confusion. Nonetheless,

but emphasized it in that they rejected the idea that original sin was the "substance" (*substantia*) of man. We may summarize their intention by saying that man who (quantitatively, so to speak) was nothing other than "totally sinner" (*totus peccator*) would be in truth *not* a "sinner." The fact that we are still sinners, that we did not lose God as our Opposite as a result of our rebellion from God's covenant, that we did not forfeit our own inexcusability (Rom. 1:20)—that is in itself already grace. Naturally we do not mean that sin and grace are something like the two poles of a dialectical relationship.[117] But it is true that our factual existence as sinners, this remarkably disturbed and peculiarly self-contradictory sinfulness in which man is constantly involved, is understood on the basis of the knowledge of grace as an existence in which man is "given up" but not left altogether to himself.

d. God's Faithfulness as the Continuum. God's history with the human creature does not begin with sin. God's grace is not a reaction but his own sovereign work. And God's history does not end with sin. Sin is the opponent against whom God turns. But it cannot prevent God from dealing with man. By virtue of God's activity, man is decisively qualified, for even as a sinner he is the object of God's personal attention. We find no trace in the Bible of any inherent capacity of man to be the object of God's activity. But we find all the more the manifestation of this activity which is then the sole basis for man's qualification, by virtue of which he can be the object of this activity and be called to be a partner in God's covenant.

This is to say, then, that man as a sinner has certainly fallen out of the covenant and out of "original righteousness," but God has not been unfaithful to his will and claim, his promise and affirmation. The faithlessness of man does not cancel out the faithfulness of God (see Rom. 3:3). The faithfulness of God is the "continuum" between the creation and the reconciliation and redemption of man.

e. The "Image of God" and God's Commandment. God's faithfulness toward his own creative will is manifested in his commandment. It is of essential impor-

---

there are tendencies in Flacius to understand man's "substance" as his relationship to God. The Formula of Concord (Art. I) was understood by Flacius in terms of the concept of substance which was predominant then, and for that reason he rejected it quite properly: if original sin had been in this sense the substance of man, then man would have been in his essence a creation of the devil; the devil, however, does not create but destroys. See W. Preger, *Matthias Flacius Illyricus und seine Zeit* (2 vols. in 1; Erlangen: Bläsing, 1859–61); O. Ritschl, *Dogmengeschichte des Protestantismus* (4 vols.; Leipzig: Hinrichs, 1908–27), II, especially pp. 431ff.; H. Kropatscheck, *Das Problem der theologischen Anthropologie auf dem Weimarer Gespräch 1560 zwischen Matthias Flacius Illyricus und Viktorin Strigel* (Unpublished dissertation; Göttingen: 1943); H. E. Weber, *Reformation, Orthodoxie und Rationalismus* (2 vols. in 3; Gütersloh: C. Bertelsmann, 1937–51; repr. Darmstadt: Wissenschaftliche Buchgesellschaft, 1966), I, 2, pp. 327ff. Exhaustive materials in *BekSchr,* on Article I of the Formula of Concord, pp. 770ff. Of the Reformed confessional documents see the "Erklärungsschrift" to the resolutions of the Dillenburg Synod of 1578 (E. F. K. Müller, *Bekenntnisschriften der Reformierten Kirche* . . . [Leipzig: Deichert, 1903], p. 726).

117. See E. Hirsch, *Schöpfung und Sünde in der natürlich-geschichtlichen Wirklichkeit einzelner Menschen* (Tübingen: J. C. B. Mohr [Paul Siebeck], 1931).

tance that in the commandment or the law sinful man is addressed as "the image of God."

This is, first of all, the case in those passages which we already have dealt with. In Genesis 9:6, as well as in James 3:9, and (indirectly) in 1 Corinthians 11:7 we are dealing with God's commandment. In Genesis 9:6 we see that behind the threatened life of man the abiding claim of the Creator is sounded, which every man must respect in every other man. In James 3:9 it is presupposed that the honor of the other person has its advocate in the permanent claim of the Creator. The image of God is ascribed to man in such a way that he is not to seek it in himself but must regard it in the other person. It is the definition of man.

This becomes clearer when we see that there are other statements in which God's commandment is what determines that man is "the image of God." This is perhaps shown most clearly in the theme of the law of holiness: "You shall be holy; for I the Lord your God am holy" (Lev. 19:2). The "righteousness" intended here consists of behavior which is analogous to the behavior of Yahweh. We must remember that the Old Testament law, as we have already seen,[118] is not abstract and general, but an element of the covenant of God. The "holiness" of Yahweh is both his sovereign freedom and his power, as manifested in the covenant with Israel. The commandment is directed toward a behavior which corresponds with covenant destiny, and which responds to the behavior of the covenant God. The situation is not different in the more well-known decalogue. "I am the Lord. . . . You shall . . ." (Ex. 20:2ff.). The commandment can only be understood correctly on the basis of the statement, "I am the Lord." What is clearly intended is behavior which accords with the activity of Yahweh. The benevolent effect of the covenant God results, in the commandment, in the making of those addressed, the elect people, into a people who are in harmony with the covenant. Along these lines we read the two statements of Jesus which refer in two directions from one point and in which, as in the law of holiness and the decalogue, the commandment refers to what is appropriate in relationship to God's behavior. "You therefore must be perfect, as your heavenly Father is perfect" (Matt. 5:48). "Be merciful, even as your Father is merciful" (Luke 6:36). Again, the commandment is itself a second element after a primary element, which is that God is our Father. And again its content is a correspondence in behavior. We can thus state that the commandment manifests that man is determined to be in the "image of God." As man who is affected by God's activity and who is pre-determined to respond to this activity, man is the image of God. And because that is true, I am supposed to respect the image of God in others. Being in the image of God has gained the form of a commandment which is based upon the permanent claim of creation and thus upon the permanent creative faithfulness of God.[119]

Since the commandment is based upon the faithfulness of the Creator, it is a gift, and it is therefore "holy," "just," and "good" (Rom. 7:12). And sin is

---

118. See pp. 293ff.
119. See my essay, "Bemerkungen zur Frage der Imago Dei," *Deutsche Theologie* (1936), pp. 17ff.; E. Schlink, *Der Mensch in der Verkündigung der Kirche* (Munich: C. Kaiser, 1936), p. 189.

certainly nothing other than the rejection of what is good for man, including what is truly useful for him. It cannot alter the fact, however, that this good is there, not as man's possession but as his covenant destiny. In this sense one could say with Karl Barth that the "image of God" "can never cease to be God's work and gift or become a human possession."[120]

f. The "Image of God" as Man's Ongoing Predetermination for Love. Just as God's commandment is based in his covenant will, its determinative content is in the love which responds to God's love. Whoever loves God acts in responsive "analogy" to God's activity (see 1 John 4:19). To put it another way, man is in the "image of God" in his predetermination to be one who loves. But he cannot love God without seeing his "neighbor" as destined to be a co-partner in God's covenant and to love him as such. Being-based-upon-God can never be anything other than being-for-the-other person. We encounter here, from another direction, the twofold relationship which is implicit in the idea of "the image of God." God's relationship to man, established in love and responded to in love, is simultaneously man's predetermination for his fellow man, for the realization of the relationship between man and man in love. How is this meant? Dietrich Bonhoeffer (1906–45) has drawn attention to the fact that in Genesis 1:27 the statement about the image of God is closely connected to the other statement, "Male and female created he them." He would like to regard that as definitive for the understanding of the concept "the image of God": "Man is not alone, he is in duality and it is in this *dependence on the other* that his creatureliness consists."[121] The image of God is then to be understood as an "analogy of relationship" (*analogia relationis*). This interpretation and especially the concept of the "analogy of relationship" were then taken up by Karl Barth.[122] But Emil Brunner also understands "the image of God . . . as a relation."[123] In our context, too, the "analogy of relationship" may be regarded as the essence of what is at stake here. If it is true that God himself is not an isolated God, and if further it is true that he in his Son has seen man as the partner of his covenant in eternity, then it is equally true that man, made for this covenant, and existing solely for this covenant (gaining or losing his life in relationship to it!), therefore stands in relationship to his fellow man, to the other—"the analogy between God and man" is "simply the existence of the I and the thou in confrontation."[124]

Nevertheless, there is one point where it will be difficult to follow both Bonhoeffer and Barth, a point which is quite essential to Barth: the identification of the "image of God" with the sexual duality of man and woman. We will have to agree with Barth that "according to Gen. 1, it is the fact that in the case of man the differentiation of sex is the only differentiation."[125] Yet, as such, this is

---

120. *CD*, III,1, p. 201; but here in regard to the "analogy of relationship" (*analogia relationis*), which we have yet to discuss.

121. D. Bonhoeffer, *Creation and Fall, a theological interpretation of Genesis 1–3,* tr. J. C. Fletcher (New York: Macmillan, 1959), p. 36; italics are mine.

122. *CD*, III,1, pp. 184ff. and especially pp. 195ff.

123. E. Brunner, *Dogmatics,* II, 59f.

124. K. Barth, *CD*, III,1, p. 185.

125. *CD*, III,1, p. 186.

not a special characteristic of man. Again, according to Barth, it is much more the "original and most concrete form" of "the relationship of . . . person to person."[126] The decisive thing is that man in this differentiation is man. It does not constitute his personhood, but his personhood is realized in it, in the "analogy of relationship."[127] It must be added that, aside from perhaps 1 Corinthians 11:7, none of the other biblical witnesses even indirectly refers to the sexual differentiation. When Barth refers correctly to the fact[128] that in the biblical witness marriage is frequently and at decisive points understood as an analogy to God's covenant,[129] then we must counter that this is also true of the relationship between father and son, of the relationship of the mother to her child (Isa. 49:15), and even of that between master and slave or king and nation. But it would not be possible to proceed from these analogies to the view that the distinction and relationship of father and child or even of master and slave or king and nation would be based upon the covenant will of God which is maintained from the creation all the way through to reconciliation and redemption (see Gal. 3:28). This continuum can only be represented by the relationship of opposites and by their mutual responsibility. If this is understood, then we must emphasize all the more strongly that the sphere in which this responsibility asserts itself is primarily that of the relationship between man and woman, as the only human relationship which is based upon a "structural and functional distinction."[130] All the other relationships can be interchanged: the father is also the son, the mother is also the child, and in the differentiated society the "master" can also be the "slave," and the "king" can easily become a component part of the "nation." But the man will never become woman, nor the woman become man. It is an unmistakable trait of the mythological self-exaltation of man that this differentiation is denied as a fundamental and essential one (the androgynous myth). Wherever the goal is the unity of essence rather than community,[131] there this differentiation appears as the element which must be abrogated—and in that instance, even love is self-love, since man's existence in relationship to another is regarded as secondary or even of inferior significance. One can only think in that fashion where God is not "person," not "he-himself-in-relationship." But if God is the covenant God who grants us community and determines us for this community, then that polarity is established

---

126. *CD*, III,1, p. 186 [partially my translation—TR].

127. Here we would have to agree with E. Brunner, *op. cit.*, pp. 63ff.

128. *CD*, III,1, pp. 195f.

129. But always based upon God's covenant—it is primary! This is fully clear in Eph. 5:23ff., but no less so in Hos. 1:2ff.; 2:2f., 16; Jer. 3:1ff.; Ezek. 16 and 23.

130. K. Barth, *CD*, III,4, p. 117.

131. E. Brunner, *Dogmatics*, II, 64: The "myth of androgyny" "is necessarily connected with rational thinking, for which the ultimate and supreme truth is UNITY, just as the fact of the two sexes is necessarily connected with the God who wills community. . . . Androgyny belongs to the thought of Platonism, and sexual polarity to Christian thought." Similarly, K. Barth, *CD*, III,4, pp. 159ff., as also Brunner with reference to N. Berdyaev, *The Destiny of Man* (London: G. Bles, 1954 [g1935]). Barth then refers to the androgynous tendency found in the artistic portrayals of Christ: if they wanted "to lay violent hands" on the form of Christ, then they could at least represent him "honourably . . . in the form of a man" but not as a mixture of male and female traits (p. 161).

between us men, between I and Thou, which takes on its most concrete form in the predermination of man for sexual duality.

g. The "Image of God" as Existence Under Protective Law. Even as a sinner, man is in "the image of God," because God maintains his claim as the Creator, that is, his covenant will. The fact that he does this is witnessed to for us in the commandment.

On the one hand, the commandment is a protective power. It protects "life"—the "life" of sinful man who as such is nevertheless the "image of God" (we think again of Gen. 9:6). The very fact that man is alive at all, that he may exist, although certainly in the face of death and toward death, was understood by Luther as the radiant beam of the Gospel.[132] "Life," even in its purely biological sense, is seen in the Old Testament as a "good thing"—thus the high estimation attached to old age in the old covenant. And the law is, so to speak, the protective wall which is built up around this "life"—"by doing [this] a man shall live" (Lev. 18:5)! What we call the "political use of the law" (*usus politicus legis*) belongs in this context. The law is given for the purpose of maintaining earthly life, which is always life with others, in view of the fact that this life is always "limited."[133] It is a part of the constancy of the covenant will of God that man is supposed to and may live.

h. The "Image of God" Under the Unfulfilled Law. On the other hand, the "law" "before" or "outside of Christ" (*ante* or *extra Christum*) is unfulfilled law. If we could say that it bears the "image of God" within itself in the form of the commandment, the manifestation of the constant faithfulness of God in the form of his claim, then we must now add that this claim is unfulfilled. God maintains his affirmation, but God's Yes is not met with the corresponding Yes of man. This is the "contradiction" within which man lives. He lives on the basis of a Yes which he negates for his part and which becomes in the process a No spoken over man. He is in "the image of God," but he negates what he is because he rejects God. Since, however, the "image of God" in the sense of the "analogy of relationship" is simultaneously the existence in contrast of I and Thou, then necessarily the rejection of the Creator must affect the I-Thou relationship at its very roots.[134] And since, further, it is and remains the destiny of man to carry out his

---

132. Luther on Gen. 3:20 (AE, I, 219f.): "The name which Adam gives his wife is a very pleasing and delightful name. For what is more precious, better, or more delightful than life? . . . It is clear from this passage that after Adam had received the Holy Spirit, he had become marvelously enlightened, and that he believed and also understood the saying concerning the woman's seed who would crush the head of the serpent. Moreover, he wanted to give an outward indication of this faith of his and lend distinction to it by means of his wife's name. . . . By this designation of his wife he gave support to the hope in the future seed. . . ."

133. K. Barth, *passim,* especially *CD,* III,2, pp. 587ff.

134. Because man, although he knew of God, did not praise God as God and did not thank him as God, since man "exchanged" the "honor" of the immortal God for "images resembling mortal man," God "gave them up" and took them by their word in their "exchange," with the result that precisely in the sexual relationship there is dishonor and "exchanging" (Rom. 1:21ff.).

"lordship over the earth" (*dominium terrae*) in relationship to his Creator, his No to the Creator and thus to his own existence must necessarily destroy his relationship to his nonhuman fellow creatures. Instead of being free in relationship to them in his bonds to God, he falls victim to them. Instead of administering over them with the preserving and constructive service of the Creator, he tyrannizes over them. Instead of living with them before God, he destroys them in their own meaning of existence and subjects them to "futility" (Rom. 8:20). Man is a sinner precisely in relationship to what he possesses of dignity and commission in the "image of God." In reality, he can escape neither his fellow man nor his extra-human fellow creation, nor the responsibility he bears in relationship to them. He has remained man—but in such a way that he is in conflict with his own human existence.

The commandment is there for this man—but as much as it is the summons of the Creator, it is also the laying bare of his alienation, of his rejection of God. The commandment is seen to be unfulfilled, not because the "moral powers" of man are inadequate, but rather because the way in which it encounters man is the way of negation. The very man who seriously grapples with the "law" as true man, who "practices works," reveals in his self-pride that he is the one who does not love God and does not love his neighbor. The law can produce no more than the unveiling of this contradiction of human existence. If we can say that in the law the "image of God" encounters us in the form of the commandment, then we must say that with the law the "image of God" also remains the unfulfilled destiny of man.

i. Jesus Christ as "the Image of God." The gulf which the law seems to reveal can only be bridged by God, and it has in fact been bridged by him. The law is the polar reference, necessary in its polarity, to the fact that the law's fulfillment is not within itself. It is therefore more than merely the "should" form of the "image of God." It is simultaneously its precedent—not an ideal, but the promise.[135] The fulfillment of the law and the reality of the "image of God" itself is Jesus Christ. He is the man for God, the man out of God, and the man before God. In him our rejection reaches its end; in him—through him and upon him!—it is judged and set aside by God's grace. Therefore, only in and through him is our real rejection truly visible. Who we are "by nature," who we are as those to whom the law has been given, will never be recognized by anyone outside of the reality of the Crucified One. Sin can truly be recognized by us only on the basis of the execution and the abrogation of God's wrath, the righteousness of God. Everything we have said up to now about our No to what we are destined to be according to God can really only be stated from this point of view. Here, in the person of Jesus Christ, man is the image of God—here, in the One whom God sent "in the likeness of sinful flesh" (Rom. 8:3).

---

135. H. F. Kohlbrügge and his students have unceasingly emphasized this. In Karl Barth, the same thought is put in this fashion: "That the nature of the command of God is spiritual means that it does not confront us as an ideal, whether that of an obligation, that of a permission, or that of a combination of the two, but as the reality fulfilled in the person of Jesus Christ" (*CD*, II,2, p. 606).

Jesus Christ—the image of God! This we find expressed in 2 Corinthians 4:4 and Colossians 1:15, and we find it implied in Ephesians 4:24 and Colossians 3:10, when we remember that the putting on of the "new man" according to Galatians 3:27 is the putting on of Christ. Jesus Christ is the new man, the other Adam in the sense of the Adam-Christ typology (Rom. 5:12ff.; 1 Cor. 15:22f. and 15:45ff.); he is the "first-born of all creation" (Col. 1:15); he is the One in whom the new creation is already reality now (2 Cor. 5:17). And he is all this, not for himself, but as the Firstborn of many brothers (Rom. 8:29), whose "image" (*eikōn*) "we" shall bear just as we have borne the "image" of earthly man (1 Cor. 15:49), yes, in whose "likeness" we shall be transformed "from one degree of glory to another" (2 Cor. 3:18). The new man is Christ alone, but not for himself alone, but as the One "in" whom the believer has his new status, his eschatological form of existence. Just as we came across an analogy with a twofold relationship in Genesis 1:26f., we find the same thing here. Just as Jesus Christ is one with the Father, those are also to be one who are given to him by the Father. If in the one instance "thou art in me and I in thee" (John 17:21) is valid, then "I in them and thou in me" (John 17:23) is valid. We can perceive the same analogy in Ephesians 5:23ff. What the Old Testament says about the covenant with Yahweh and marriage is taken up here, probably under the influence of Gnostic thought.[136] Man is the head of woman in the same way Christ is the head of his Church. The Church is subordinate to Christ, and women should thus be subordinate to their husbands. Men should love their wives, as Christ has loved the Church—the loving lordship of Christ over his Church, his "body," establishes and conditions the relationship between man and woman in the Church! There is a similar thought in 1 Corinthians 11:7, although here there is an explicit reference back to Genesis 1. In relationship to Colossians 1:15–18 (with emphasis upon v. 18) and 1 Corinthians 11:7, Karl Barth developed the thesis that Christ together with the Church is the image of God.[137] This cannot be derived with such precision from these passages, but it is certain that the image of God in Jesus Christ is understood "not in an exclusive but in an inclusive sense,"[138] just as Jesus Christ is never in his uniqueness for-himself-alone. He is who he is "for us," for his Church. "In him" the new man is reality, "in him" man is the image of God because in him God's covenant with man has been realized.

j. Critique of the Reformation View. What can we say on the basis of the discussion here about the problematic which we dealt with in our previous section? In contrast to the Reformation position—man has lost the "image of God"— we shall have to emphasize that it is overgrown with an anthropology which it fundamentally had left far behind. It succumbs to the attempt to find the "image of God" somewhere in or about man, and yet it cannot admit that in or about the sinner there is something of it to be found. This latter insight is certainly true. But the setting itself makes this insight unclear. On the one hand it leads to a

---

136. H. Schlier, *Christus und die Kirche im Epheserbrief* (*Beiträge zur historischen Theologie,* 6; Tübingen: J. C. B. Mohr [Paul Siebeck], 1930).
137. *CD,* III,1, p. 205.
138. *CD,* III,1, p. 204.

weakening in the sense of "almost lost" (*paene amissa*), on the other to a retrogressive step like the dualistic-sounding formulation of someone like Flacius. In contrast, the Reformation approach would best be developed by a doctrine of the image which saw man totally on the basis of his relationship to the Creator and the relationship between I and Thou. Then it would be permissible to admit that there is a "continuum"—to the extent that God in Christ establishes, or better, is this continuum with his eternal decree. In this instance one could speak of a "nature" of man without any encroachment upon the freedom of divine grace, a "nature" which obviously would be based upon grace from God's perspective, but which from man's perspective, since he does not respond to this grace, is subject to the inner contradiction which is found in man's rejection of what is his essence. In short, if the Reformation had fully developed its own conception in this matter, if it had not involuntarily accepted the categories of its counter-position and sought to oppose it within them, it would have become clearer than it does in fact that the Reformation represents a completely new understanding of anthropology.[139]

    k. Critique of the Roman Catholic View. On the basis of this position we can also come to a response to the contemporary Roman Catholic critique. We will not be able to concede that even the most careful distillation of the "pure nature" (*pura naturalia*) will preserve the purity of the proclamation of grace, as such a distillation contrasts grace with another sphere which does not yet stand under grace. The purity of the proclamation of grace is preserved rather in the knowledge that the continuum which stretches all the way from creation is not to be sought in the creature at all, but in the Creator. The proposition, "grace does not just tolerate but perfects nature,"[140] had led in Roman Catholic theology to the assertion that there is not a continuity of divine activity and conditioning, but a direct continuity between the Creator and the creature, so to speak, from "below" to "above," which then leads to the idea of a cooperation of the creature with grace—Mariology is the strongest expression of this view. Sin, about which we cannot remain silent if we speak of the "image of God," is not primarily nor secondarily corruption, but it is primarily the hostility toward grace and as such man's falling short of what he was intended to be, as God defined it and Christ fulfilled it. Every theological interest in "pure nature" (*pura naturalia*) is burdened with the reservation that in it the totality of sin and thus the totality of grace no longer is completely valid—and thus it is no longer valid at all.

---

    139. Particularly important on this is Luther's *The Disputation Concerning Man* (1536) (AE, XXXIV, 137ff.), especially the thesis that Paul in Rom. 3:28 ("we hold that a man is justified by faith apart from works") "briefly sums up the definition of man . . ." (p. 139). See also E. Wolf, "Das Problem des neuen Menschen im Protestantismus," *EvTheol* (1951/52), p. 345 and Torrance, *op. cit.*

    140. More correctly the sentence could read: God's work as the creative work done upon the sinner is the divine presupposition of the work of redemption, toward which the former is leading and from which it is recognized.

XIV. The Sinner

A. THE KNOWLEDGE AND NATURE OF SIN

1. PHENOMENA OF HUMAN EVIL

a. The Dynamic Character of the Contradiction of the Two States. By dealing with the theological doctrine of man under the concept of the "image of God," as we have done until now, we have spoken of the sinner as God's creature, as the one destined by God to be his covenant partner. The doctrine of the "image" could not be spoken of without dealing with the sinfulness of man. When we now speak of man as sinner, this can then only mean that we see man, destined by God's covenant will, in his contradiction to the divine determination.

However, this combined view of creatureliness and sin is not to be understood as though there were here two corresponding ways of viewing man, a kind of dialectical duality.[1] Rather, it is justifiable to speak of two "states" (*status*), the original and that state which is in fact the destruction of the original. The relationship to God is not originally disturbed but is in and of itself "in order," and the destroyed relationship to God is not in some ultimate sense intact, not even in a dialectical connection. We do not speak of these two states as historical conditions which follow upon each other. Instead, we can speak of the one as not abrogated but as the origin which remains present in both the commandment and the promise, which does not weaken the other but is preserved as a state of man. This is not dialectical but is solely Christological in its grounds, and it would be most dangerous to transform the reality of Jesus Christ into a conceptual dialectic. Jesus Christ is not only the promise which stands over the lostness of man in his "corrupt state" (*in statu corruptionis*); he is also the victorious attack of God upon this state, and its conquest. He is not only God's "likeness" in

---

1. "Creation and sin are one and the same, placed under two judgments based upon the relationship of God, one of them requiring the other and the other turning them against each other" (E. Hirsch, *Schöpfung und Sünde in der natürlich-geschichtlichen Wirklichkeit des einzelnen Menschen* [Tübingen: J. C. B. Mohr (Paul Siebeck), 1931], p. 33). E. Schlink (*Der Mensch in der Verkündigung der Kirche* [Munich: C. Kaiser, 1936], p. 127) comments that here "the accusation is not excluded that the devil is made into the creator of man and God into the creator of sin."

eternity (2 Cor. 4:4), the reflection "of the glory of God" and the one who bears "the very stamp of his nature" (Heb. 1:3); he was also sent by God in the fullness of time (Gal. 4:4), he was made into sin for us (2 Cor. 5:21), and he has become the "curse" for us (Gal. 3:13), so that we are "in him" the "righteousness of God" (2 Cor. 5:21). He is not the idea of the constant covenant faithfulness of God but its revealer and bringer. Therefore, if we want to describe correctly the duality of creature and sinner, then we may not view it as a conceptual dialectic but only as a "salvation-historical" polarity, made known in God's activity. Otherwise Christological Docetism would make sin appear to be unreal.

b. *The Knowledge of Sin Based upon Forgiveness.* Sin is our reality "in and of ourselves" (*apud nos*), just as the "image of God" is our reality "outside of ourselves" (*extra nos*). But that does not mean that sin is open to investigation in a tangible sense. Luther maintained the proposition that sin, as original sin, was "so deep a corruption of nature, that no reason can understand it, but it must be believed from the revelation of Scriptures."[2] He therefore calls the Scholastic doctrine of sin "pure errors and obscurations contrary to this article." This proposition, with which we agree, can obviously not mean that the Christian is supposed to "believe in his sin." It is not without significance that in the Apostles' Creed sin only appears in the confession of forgiveness.[3] We only recognize sin through faith in God-in-Christ.[4] We have already discussed why this is so,[5] and thus we can limit ourselves here to a few brief sentences. What sin really is only becomes recognizable to us when God himself has disclosed himself or discloses himself to us. Since, further, sin can only be known as "falling short," as departing from the way, when we know what is the "good," then the knowledge of sin can only occur when we recognize that it is our being in the image of God, and not an ideal which we gradually approach, which is the determination of our life granted to us out of the faithfulness of God. And since, finally, all knowledge presupposes a certain distance from its object, we can only recognize sin in that

---

2. Smalcald Articles, III (Jacobs, pp. 321f.).

3. According to the Nicaeno-Constantinopolitan Creed, "We acknowledge one baptism unto remission of sins."

4. A. Ritschl, speaking for many, objected to the proposition cited from Luther. He also, for his part, asserts that "the Gospel of the forgiveness of sins is actually the ground of knowledge of our sinfulness" (*The Christian Doctrine of Justification and Reconciliation, the Positive Development of the Doctrine*, tr. H. R. Mackintosh and A. B. Macaulay [New York: Scribner's, 1900; repr. Clifton, N.J.: Reference Book Publishers, 1966 (g1895[4])], p. 327). But this is not to be taken to mean "that the fact and the explanation of sin were first made certain by revelation, or that they are an article of faith like other elements of the Christian view as a whole" (p. 328). The fact of sin is "familiar . . . apart from Christianity." The specific Christian element is "the determination of its nature, and the estimate of its compass and its worthlessness," and this results from Christianity's "ideas about God, about the supreme good, of the moral destiny of man, and of redemption."

It is clear that the reduction of theological propositions to what Ritschl elsewhere calls "value judgment" is at work here. Its corollary is that "reason," which Luther regarded as powerless in this matter, gains entry again in the form of the knowledge of the "moral ideal" (p. 328), joined with the significant statement that this "good" "coincides entirely with faith in reconciliation through Christ" (p. 329).

5. See pp. 554ff.

we are distinguished from it and separated from it through God's activity.[6] Sin
does not become an "object" for us until we can understand it through its opposite. The "distance" from sin is repentance, and repentance is a gift (Acts 5:31;
11:18), as the call to repentance is the proclamation of the Gospel (Luke 3:18).
The knowledge of sin is not the knowledge of grace, but it does not exist without
the knowledge of grace (Rom. 2:4).

c. Evil Outside of the Church's Proclamation. Nevertheless, we must turn to
the fact that we do encounter outside of the sphere of revelation a knowledge that
man and his world are by no means "in order," by no means "good," but that
there is this inexplicable reality of evil. In our short overview of the various
intellectual approaches to the problem of evil we will have to bear in mind in part
(e.g., in regard to Kant and German Idealism) that the existence of Christian
proclamation was at least significant in raising the issue. However, we do encounter the issue of evil completely apart from the proclamation of the Church.[7]

d. Dualism. This is most clearly evident in the case of Dualism as we find
it in its developed form in Zoroastrian Parseeism. Zoroaster asserts the world
dominion and world struggle of two hostile deities (Ahura Mazda and Ahriman
or Angra Mainyu) and develops on that basis an ethical and ontological dualism
which affects all realms of reality. Gnosticism is not unrelated to Parseeism,[8] and
Manichaeism is in turn closely related to Gnosticism. Dualistic ideas then had
their influence upon the thinking of the Church. But it is quite clear that within
the Church and on the foundation of the Old and New Testaments a consequent
dualism would have to be regarded as an attack upon the deity of God. Evil as
an independent and anti-divine power—that is certainly a tempting explanation
for the puzzle posed to man in all generations by evil and the wickedness which
it has produced. It opens up the chasm which man senses is there, but which he
senses in such a way that he sees himself confronted by an overwhelming auton-

6. E. Brunner, *Man in Revolt, a Christian Anthropology,* tr. O. Wyon (Philadelphia:
The Westminster Press, 1947 [g1937]), p. 117: the "paradox" of sinful existence "shows
itself in faith as the actual condition of man, which man cannot perceive just because he is
so deeply entangled in it." Julius Müller (*The Christian Doctrine of Sin,* tr. W. Urwick
[Edinburgh: T. & T. Clark, 1885 (g1844²)], II, 188f.) does believe in the possibility of intellectual recognition of evil "in its necessity," but he can only regard the "realization" of evil
as something "according to its essential nature, incomprehensible." To be sure, the idea
here is much different than in Brunner or in our own approach, but it cannot be denied that
even a theologian as clearly speculative as J. Müller has reached his limits at this point.
7. Julius Müller, in the first volume of his *The Christian Doctrine of Sin* (pp. 268–417),
has provided an excellent survey, "Examination of the Principal Theories in Explanation of
Sin." We are not primarily concerned with these, although every theory of explanation of
"sin" naturally implies a certain view of evil. We are more interested in providing a simple
and phenomenological typology of a more general sort. On this whole theme, see H. Bavinck,
Gereformeerde Dogmatiek (4 vols.; Kampen: J. H. Kok, 1906), III, 34ff.; ET: *Our Reasonable Faith* (Grand Rapids: Eerdmans, 1956)—a compendium of the 4 vols.
8. H. Jonas, *The Gnostic Religion; the Message of the Alien God and the Beginnings
of Christianity* (Boston: Beacon Press, 1958) [a reworking in English of the original four-
volume German work published in 1934, vol. I of which is cited here by Weber—TR].

omous power which either leads to man's downfall or from which man escapes by reaching out to a supernatural realm of his own conception. Good and evil are then equally present in the world, an opposition which is projected to the status of an absolute, and man fundamentally bears proportionately less responsibility the more transcendent and absolute this opposition is conceived to be.

e. Evil as Sensuality. The dualistic pattern is also at work where its mythological culmination has been dropped or has become a scarcely perceptible part of the background. This is especially the case where evil is seen to be in the realm of the physical or of sensuality. This view can be connected to mythological dualism, as both Parseeism and Manichaeism indicate. But it can also emerge in what is ultimately a monistic system, as, for example, in Plato. It is quite obvious that in such a view sexuality is seen as the location of evil, whereas in other views it is seen in a highly religious way as the realm of the most pulsing life. Man's submission in the sexual act appears then as the epitome of the soul's enslavement to matter, which is itself regarded as absolute evil. In this view, however, "evil" can also mean merely that which is "inferior," and this then leads the ascetic tendency, which seems to be the most logical consequence, to switch around into its opposite: the realm of the physical and sensual is of so little importance that one's behavior with it is irrelevant. Both older and newer forms of Gnosticism provide examples of both tendencies and thus demonstrate that the reduction of evil to what is ontically tangible does not make evil to be fundamentally an act for which man is responsible. Instead, evil is either wickedness, or a burden, or something inferior, or something irrelevant for man's spirit.

f. Evil as a Defect or Inadequacy. A third form in which "evil" has been intellectually understood is related to what we just mentioned. Evil can be understood as the nonexistent, as the mere "inadequacy" or "privation" (*privatio, carentia*) of good. This concept, already implied in Plato, was propounded by Neo-Platonism, and from there moved into the thinking of the Church Fathers (at least in part, it appears, independently of Neo-Platonism[9]). This was especially true of Augustine who sought to use this approach to combat the idea of the opposing deity of evil, as he knew it from Manichaeism. His point was that there is no ontic autonomy of evil. In this instance, evil is easily conceived of as the shadow which is cast by light and which cannot exist without light. Later on, it was Leibniz (1646–1716) who tried to solve the problem of evil (*malus*, evil as wickedness) in this way. If this approach is pursued further, the result is, as Julius Müller correctly saw, the idea that evil is the effect of the "metaphysical imperfection" which is part of man.[10] For man, there is no light without shadows, and no good without the evil which is attached to it. This can be put much more simply in popular jargon: Man is simply "imperfect," and that is a part of his "nature."

---

9. J. Müller, *op. cit.*, I, 289f.
10. J. Müller, *op. cit.*, I, 268ff., especially p. 286.

g. *Evil as the Dialectical Opposite of Good.* The thought that "human evil exists only as attached to good"[11] "can also take on a directly dialectical form. Evil is then logically and historically necessary, so that good can exist. This was especially the view of Hegel (1770–1831). J. Müller has shown that the basic idea is really very early, even within the Church, "aside from some related ideas in a few Gnostics and in the Pseudo-Clementines, as early as in Lactantius."[12] He quotes a hymn:

"O necessary sin of Adam which was blotted out by the death of Christ. O happy fault, that merited such a redeemer."[13]

It is clear that what is meant here is the subordination of evil to the grace which conquers it, as established in God's decree.[14] In the philosophy which was divorced from Christian thought this aspect undergoes a fundamental change. For Hegel, who must receive special mention here, good is the freedom of the spirit over against the natural, which presupposes in the triad of thesis, antithesis, and synthesis that the natural is what must first be negated; this freedom then emerges in the division from the natural in order to reach its dialectical goal in its reconciliation with it. That division is simultaneously the division of man within himself, "evil" itself, and is then an essential part of the concept of man. "Man must eat of the tree of the knowledge of good and evil; otherwise he is not man, but an animal."[15] Again, Julius Müller rightly interprets that the "necessity of evil" is "wholly conditioned upon and involved in the necessity of good."[16] Evil seems here to be a kind of *agent provocateur* of good. Hegel's view is, in its popular form, by now the general approach of many circles. Evil is a necessary transitional stage of development. This is applied both to the individual and to humanity as a whole with the result that evil is not able to obstruct the optimism of faith in progress and virtually stimulates it as a negative agent.

h. *Kant's View of Evil.* Last in the line of intellectual views of evil we mention that of Kant (1724–1804).[17] Kant's view was praised by theology for its unique profundity as much as it appeared to his philosophical contemporaries to be a betrayal of the intellect. Kant, who sees good solely in the good will, can accordingly see the "ground of evil" solely in a "maxim," that is, in a "rule" which free will ("arbitrary will") makes "for the use" of its "freedom." Thus evil is certainly not based upon some kind of natural given, such as sensuality. But Kant then finds that evil not only takes place in an act of the will, but is based

---

11. Schleiermacher, *ChrF,* §80, 2, I, p. 327.
12. J. Müller, *op. cit.*, I, 366.
13. From the "Exsultet" in the "Easter Vigil," *The English Latin Sacramentary* (New York: Catholic Book Publishing Co., 1966); see J. Müller, *op. cit.*, I, 376 for the original Latin text.
14. See K. Barth, *CD,* III,3, pp. 319ff., regarding Schleiermacher.
15. Hegel, *Lectures on the History of Philosophy,* tr. E. S. Haldane and F. H. Simson (London: Kegan Paul, Trench, Trübner & Co., 1895), III, 9 [my translation—TR]. See J. Müller, *op. cit.*, I, 393, and on the whole theme, K. Barth, *CD,* IV,1, pp. 374ff.
16. J. Müller, *op. cit.*, p. 394.
17. Kant, *Religion within the Limits of Reason Alone,* tr. T. M. Greene and H. H. Hudson (New York: Harper, 1960), pp. 15ff.

upon a "propensity to evil," which must "consist in maxims of the will which are contrary to the law," and therefore is "natural" or "innate," but man is still "responsible for it." This inborn, universally present evil in man is called by Kant "radical" evil.[18] In terms of its origins, it is thoroughly incomprehensible and puzzling—Kant concludes that the biblical statement about the devil expresses this incomprehensibility.[19] But it cannot be said that Kant really maintains the incisive thrust of this insight throughout. The reason for that is to be found in his view of freedom,[20] which on the one hand is supposed to have a power over the "free activity of man" which is analogous to the autonomous causality of nature, and on the other hand as the freedom of the will is supposed to include the capacity to take a position in opposition to the moral law, which is the contents of that freedom. It seems then rather like a death-defying acrobatic feat when Kant, referring admittedly to the theoretical obscurity of the matter,[21] concludes that the "principle of good" by virtue of its "legal claim" upon man conquers the "principle of evil" including its "legal claim" upon man in the "establishment of the Kingdom of God upon earth." The fundamental thesis for Kant's whole position is maintained: "You can, because you should."[22] The "moral law" which is identical with the "principle of good" is simultaneously and in a mysterious way the epitome of freedom, which then for its part is the point from which the "Kingdom of God on earth" is derived. "Radical evil" is not as radical as it would initially appear to be. The reason for this is that Kant stays completely within "mere reason," within the sphere of the self-understanding, and never really comes within sight of sin.[23]

i. Extra-Christian Views of Evil as the Demonstration of Phenomena. Our overview has shown primarily that there are manifold forms and intellectual assessments of the perception of what is opposed to rules, norms, and life itself. All ethics implies ideas about what is to be avoided. Ongoing ethical thought produces further differentiations about what is to be avoided and connects ideas of evil with comprehensive understandings of the world and of self. Evil is some-

---

18. *Ibid.*, pp. 27ff.

19. *Ibid.*, pp. 38f.: "This inconceivability, together with a more accurate specification of the wickedness of our race, the Bible expresses in the historical narrative as follows. It finds a place for evil at the creation of the world, yet not in man, but in a *spirit* of an originally loftier destiny. Thus is the *first* beginning of all evil represented as inconceivable by us . . . ," "but man is represented as having fallen into evil only *through seduction,* and hence as being *not basically* corrupt."

20. J. Müller, *op. cit.*, I, 410ff., with reference to Herbart, *Gespräche über das Böse* (Königsberg: Unzer, 1818), pp. 145f.

21. Kant, *op. cit.*, p. 46.

22. *Ibid.*, p. 46. "For when the moral law commands that we *ought* now to be better men, it follows inevitably that we must *be able* to be better men."

23. E. Brunner, *op. cit.*, does admittedly conclude (p. 125) that Kant contributed more to the solution of the problem than modern theology has done; yet he does not offer a "re-formulation of the Christian truth about sin," but rather a "borderline truth" (p. 127). Since Kant does not speak of sin but of evil, and not of God but of the moral law, his idea of the "radical evil" really only deals with a "manifestation of sin," while he does not recognize the other and "far more dangerous" element, which is "the fact that man does good by his own efforts" (p. 128).

thing which is "well-known" in some way everywhere, a fact universally perceived as puzzling.

But is the view of evil arrived at in this fashion to be regarded as a kind of preliminary insight into the nature of sin?

It would be unwise for us to pursue a radicalizing apologetic and simply respond in the negative without further consideration. Our Christian views are as such subject to exactly the same judgment of the Word as are all other views. It cannot be in the interest of theology or of Christian proclamation to contrast its light as sharply as possible to the "darkness" assumed to be present in the realm of philosophy. This procedure, as a form of the "negative way" (*via negativa*), would be just as much a kind of "natural theology" as our more traditional endeavors to present the Christian views as the perfection of everything that "otherwise" exists. We must also remember that the explicitly Christian views are by no means lacking in points of contact with the non-Christian views briefly described above. Although easily misunderstood, it was still in and of itself a proper statement made by Justin when he said that everything which could be said by any side rightly actually belonged to "us Christians."[24] In regard to sin, it could well be that certain "phenomena"[25] emerged which, in spite of the darkness, would truly be recognizable as phenomena of real sin on the basis of the light of the Word of God. For every man is in fact a sinner. We would expect no more than phenomena if we kept clearly in mind what we already discussed, which was that man is only truly man when he is man-before-God. That means then that the true sinner cannot be seen to be anything other than the one whose sins were borne by Jesus Christ and whose righteousness he has become.

When, however, we have come to see our sinful existence in this way, then it can certainly be the case that dualism reveals to us the phenomenon of the intellectual insolubility of the mystery of sin, that the derivation of evil from sensuality refers us to the problem of the physical, which left to its own devices has in fact fallen from its created purpose. It could be that the views which regard evil as the dialectical counterpart of good demonstrate to us, contrary to their own intent, that due to God's free grace there is in fact no autonomous power nor independence of sin. Kant's idea of the radical evil could draw our attention to the fact that evil is not to be sought in some kind of object outside ourselves but in our selves. The blindness of the "heathen" is not due to the phenomena but rather to the reality of which they are then the phenomena.

This obviously means that the phenomena as such are ambiguous. They are so to such a degree that the very way in which they are seen and interpreted demonstrates sin itself. The knowledge of evil, regardless of how it is gained, always takes place within the presupposition (which sometimes may remain implicit) that man is able somehow to distinguish between himself and evil in his own name. Thus, the question must be raised whether the claim which is implied in such knowledge of evil is not essentially what is seen to be sin in the light of the Gospel and only of the Gospel.

---

24. "The Second Apology," *Justin Martyr and Athenagoras* (ANCL, II, Ch. XIII, p. 83): "Whatever things were rightly said among all men, are the property of us Christians."
25. We use the term "phenomenon" in the sense in which Karl Barth (CD, III,2, pp. 71ff.) speaks of the "Phenomena of the Human."

j. The Limits of the Phenomenological View. Evil as we have come to know it as the object of "natural" perception and reflection is evil understood from the point of view of the world or of the human self. Under these circumstances, evil is either an ontic ultimate (an anti-god or an anti-divine, at least an opposing given, such as the sensual), or it is the dialectical counterpart or the ethical-developmental stage which is not yet good but belongs to it. In any event, evil belongs to total reality, which comprises both good and evil. In the dualistic systems, this leads to the separation of total reality, which is then in essence the battlefield of these opposing elements. In the monistic systems, such as in Hegel, the battle is resolved into a higher, dialectical totality, which then can possibly (as it does in Kant) lead to a secular concept of eschatology.

A corollary of this approach is that there is always a definite something in the world or in man which is evil (in man, it could be his sensuality or his puzzlingly evil will). But man is never in and of himself evil. Since every non-Christian perception of evil does in fact intend to provide redemption from that evil, it must declare that something in or about man or within the world of man and attainable by him is good—this is done quite naturally by dualistic Parseeism. It must be added that man, as totally he himself, is not present at all in the realm of all these forms of perception and reflection.

The result is that in all of these approaches there is a pharisaic kind of thinking at the decisive point. Religious or ethical self-assertion through doing what conforms with the norms, or what is appropriate to life, is as such not evil, but good. It is the realization of the good which is present in the sphere of man. This leads ultimately to the idea which dominates Kant's ethics, that good must be done for the sake of the "good," that is, it is done for the sake of the ultimate freedom, autonomy, and nobility of man. All of this can only be said if the God who made himself into the opponent of evil in Jesus Christ himself is unknown or no longer known. But where this God is unknown, evil will not be recognized as sin. It is then not without importance that in this instance the conclusion of all these high-flown systems is some kind of practical compromise (*modus vivendi*) with what is regarded as evil. This can be seen in later Parseeism, and in Hellenism. It is also illustrated in Augustine's experience with Manichaeism, and it is clearly seen in the post-idealistic morality of the European bourgeoisie—everywhere, a working compromise is reached with the evil which is integrated into the total system of reality.[26]

2. THE LAW AND THE KNOWLEDGE OF SIN

a. The Knowledge of Sin Through the Law. The biblical and Church doctrine is that the knowledge of sin is effected through the law of God.[27]

---

26. See on this the fundamental critique rendered by Kierkegaard when he speaks of the "sickness unto death."

27. See especially Rom. 3:20 and Rom. 4:15; 7:7. Further: the *Apology* of the Augsburg Confession, Ch. II, Art. IV, 103 (Jacobs, pp. 101ff.); Ch. V, Art. XII, 53 (Jacobs, pp. 185ff.); The Smalcald Articles, Part III, ii, "Of the Law" (Jacobs, pp. 322f.); Heidelberg Catechism, Question 3 (Schaff, III, 308); The Second Helvetic Confession, Cap. XII, "De lege Dei" (Schaff, III, 259ff. [ET: *The Book of Confessions* (Publishing Office of the General Assembly of the United Presbyterian Church in the U.S.A., 5.080–5.085)]); The Formula of Concord, Art. VI, "Of the Third Use of the Law" (Schaff, III, 130ff.).

We must ask how this can be meant. This is all the more necessary since the thesis in Paul and in the Reformers is polemical: it is directed against another view of the law, one which is legalistic, works-oriented, and autonomous, and thus is another view of sin. It is only when the law is understood as Paul and the Reformers do that sin can be understood in their sense. The conclusion would then be that the law does not under all circumstances work the knowledge of sin. Apparently it depends upon the way in which God's commandment encounters us in the law.

For example, the law in the rabbinical structure was understood as a codex of ethical admonitions, legal and ritual prescriptions. It was then virtually a question of statistical measurement to determine at which points a person did not fulfill the law. But this failure to fulfill it was a performance failure, not a failure of the person. For the codex was a norm for performance or failure to perform. It was oriented toward "works." "Sin" then was a performance failure which had to be eradicated. It was something which was not to be permitted to continue. But man, in and of himself, thought that he possessed the capacity to perform such "works." And he desired to perform them. He wanted to have the life which the fulfillment of the law promised; he wanted it for himself, and on the basis of his own abilities. In truth, the law did not encounter him in his actual personhood except as the concealed covenant partner toward which it could turn. If the "knowledge of sin" emerged here, then it was not the knowledge of true sin.

However, the law could be seen in a more central fashion. The Rabbinate also possessed the Old Testament and had derived from it the commandment to love. But it is in response to the love commandment that the teacher of the law wants "to justify himself" when he asks, "Who is my neighbor?" (Luke 10:29). Apparently love is also an achievement or performance for him, which man can accomplish on his own. Therefore he must ask in which direction he should go with his love activity. But if love is understood as a work performed by a man who ultimately is intact, then the law as the commandment of love does not work the knowledge of real sin, but at the most the insight into man's greater or lesser imperfection. The fact that love is the very thing which excludes such self-justification is not immediately obvious.

The law could also be sought outside of the "scriptural law" of the Bible— we shall leave open the question as to its legitimacy. One could conclude with Luther and also with Calvin[28] that the core of the decalogue, especially the "rule of charity" (regula caritatis), was also known to the heathen and was able to affect the legal norms in many ways, departing broadly from the Old Testament. It would then be understood in the sense of a "law of nature" (lex naturae) or "natural law" (lex naturalis) as the innermost kernel of the standing legal order or as the criterion to be used in reference to that legal order. Yet in every instance

---

28. For Luther, see the well-known passage in *Against the Heavenly Prophets* (1525) (AE, XL, 96f.); see also Johannes Heckel, *Lex charitatis; eine juristische Untersuchung über das Recht in der Theologie Martin Luthers* (München: Abhandlungen der Bayerischen Akademie der Wissenschaften, 1953). On Calvin, see especially *Institutes*, IV, xx, 16, pp. 1504f.; Johannes Bohatec, *Calvin und das Recht* (Feudingen/Westfalen: Buchdruckerei & Verlagsanstalt GmbH, 1934).

it would not reveal to us our sin, but at most our failure to conform to the legal order, to its kernel or to its meaning. For the law would then be a component part of our world, our experience, or our thought, and it would never be able to convict us of the fact that we are in and of ourselves sinners.

b. The Quality of the Encounter with the Law. What has then happened when the law does provide us the knowledge of sin, when God's command affects us as God's judgment?[29] This is the only way to ask. For the knowledge of sin is only true in the confession of sin.[30] Therefore, we cannot construe which conditions must be met so that the law will produce the knowledge of sin in us; we can only state what has already happened when the law has done this work in us.

1) **God's Law.** One thing that has happened is that the law has encountered us as God's commanding and judging Word. This does not mean that we have now grasped that the law is somehow of divine origin. Such an origin would be for us a fact of the past which never directly concerns us. Rather, it means that the law has become my personal opposite in the same way that God himself is my personal opposite. In this encounter the law is definitely not under my control. It is no longer the content of my ethics or ethos, no longer the object of my reflection, nor the guarantee of my moral existence. The law has truly revealed what the introductory sentence, so important to the Reformed catechisms, states in the biblical decalogue, "And God spoke all these words." The law has overpowered me.

2) **The One Law.** But how does that happen? How could it be that here man does not do what we men always in fact do, that is, to rebel?[31]

The answer must initially be that it has happened in this way because the law has been revealed as God's self-manifestation meeting man as "total man" (*totus homo*). The law which works the knowledge of sin is revealed as the law directed toward one thing and therefore directed toward everything. Law understood in a pluralistic and legalistic way always opens the way for me to the possibility, even the necessity, of ethical reflection, for example, on the question, "Who is my neighbor?" In such thought processes, I preserve my selfhood. When the command meets me, this reflection is then excluded, whether it takes place in the form of casuistics or whatever other form. I lose my "standpoint." Under the unity and totality of the divine command, I am recognized as the person who I really am. In view of the command which makes its demands upon all of me, I am then revealed to be the one who grasps onto himself. The unity and totality of the law is certainly the love commandment, as Jesus (not without reference to

---

29. I am following the terminology of Karl Barth, *CD*, II,2, pp. 733ff.

30. This is especially emphasized by H. Vogel, *Gott in Christo; ein Erkenntnisgang durch die Grundprobleme der Dogmatik* (Berlin: Lettner, 1951), pp. 492ff.

31. H. Vogel, *op. cit.*, p. 499: ". . . the demonic possibility that the result is not really the knowledge of sin, not really the acknowledgment of God's judgment over man, that the result is only open and increased rebellion. . . ."

the rabbinical wisdom) derives it from the law (Matt. 22:37ff.), and as the lawyer in Luke 10:25ff. knows it, and as Paul later makes it into the epitome of the law and its fulfillment (Rom. 13:10) and John calls it the "new commandment" of Jesus (John 13:34f.). But even the love commandment can be understood as something which man should fulfill in and of himself, or as an ethical principle which one is to appropriate. Then love becomes a work, the opposite of self-commitment—it becomes in effect the loveless "evidence of love." And that certainly will not produce the knowledge of sin. Consider the counter-arguments which obstruct the love commandment understood as a principle! "Morally permissible self-love" and the "law of self-preservation" will always have the effect that man, left to himself, will make the customary compromises with the love commandment and justify himself in regard to it. Something must have happened if the love commandment—or the First Commandment in the sense of Luther's explanation in the *Larger Catechism*—is to lead us to the knowledge of sin.

3) The Gracious Will of God in the Law. What must have taken place when the law, in the unity and totality of the claim which it makes on us, does not remain a principle or an idealistic demand, but reveals us to be sinners? It is this, that "in, with, and under" the law, the one gracious will of God encounters us. The law as the manifestation of the covenant will of God, as the law established in God's Yes and not requiring our answering Yes, is God's "judgment" over us. Our No is only seen as No in the encounter with God's Yes. The confession of sin which includes the prayer for forgiveness only becomes a reality where the Gospel is received.[32] "Grace is the secret of the command, and except in the light of this secret it cannot be understood how strong and radical its claim and its decision are; nor can it be known that we are put wholly in the wrong by the command."[33]

At this point we must then say, on the one hand, that the unconditionalness of God's claim, which makes every evasion and every compromise impossible, is only visible where God himself has placed that claim. This means that we recognize the unconditionalness of the command in the One whom God made into sin for us. The death of Jesus Christ is the "act of divine proof," "the miracle whose occurrence alone can decide, and has in fact decided, the truth of the

---

32. When the Heidelberg Catechism in Question 3 (Schaff, III, 308) asks, "Whence knowest thou thy misery?", and then answers, "Out of the Law of God," and when it moreover understands this law solely as the love command and sees in it the awakening of the knowledge that "I am by nature prone to hate God and my neighbor," then we may not overlook the fact that all of this stands under the dominant thesis of Question 1, which speaks of the "only comfort in life and death." The fact that the law does not work penitence without the Gospel is also stated in the *Apology* of the Augsburg Confession: ". . . the preaching of the Law . . . only accuses, only terrifies consciences. . . . It is accordingly necessary that the Gospel be added. . . ." The "adversaries" who "exclude the Gospel of Christ from the preaching of repentance . . ." are to be judged as "blasphemers against Christ" (Ch. III, Art. VI, 136, p. 129). In the *Apology*, Art. IV, we find this blunt statement: "For the Gospel convicts all men, that they are under sin . . ." (Jacobs, Ch. II, Art. IV, 62, p. 94). The same assertion is made with regard to the "preaching of the Gospel" in Ch. V, Art. XII, 29 (Jacobs, p. 181).

33. K. Barth, *CD*, II,2, p. 747.

statement that we are sinners."[34] When especially in Melanchthon and his disciples, penitence (*poenitentia*) is understood as "mortification" (*mortificatio*) and "vivification" (*vivificatio*),[35] then "mortification" is not understood here as a work of the law as such, and certainly not as our (mystical, contemplative, or ascetic) own work, but as the work of the law as it was carried out in Christ. The concept of "mortification" goes back to Romans 6, where we read of the death of Christ as our death (Rom. 6:3, 5, 6, 7, 8 and then the "consider yourselves" in Rom. 6:11 which is analogous to Rom. 4:5, and the following parenesis; similarly Col. 3:3 in relation to 3:5). The law has worked its deadly and judging power in him and through him in "me." All of this means that the wrathful power, the function of law as convicting me, confronting me with my sin and thus with sin in general (there is no other way), is revealed in only one way, and that is in and with the "Word of the Cross."

On the other hand, the law reveals sin in that it achieves its own goal, that is, in that it separates the creature from its sin and unites it with the will of the Creator, who is its life. The law is oriented toward the Yes from which it is derived. In the person of Jesus Christ, the separation of the creature from sin is not only achieved in the death which he suffers for mankind, but also the Yes is established which is the source of the creature's life. He was not only "put to death for our trespasses" but also "raised for our justification" (Rom. 4:25). And that means that it is in forgiveness that sin is first "recognized" as sin—forgiveness and the knowledge of sin can only be understood in connection with each other. Only when we see this are we protected from every kind of false methodism which seeks to leave the grace of God its freedom but would like to put the knowledge of sin and thus repentance within the sphere of man's work, thereby in fact declaring grace to be a reactive equivalent of sin and repentance to be a strained "work," depriving it of its evangelical character.

The doctrine of the knowledge of sin presupposes then a certain view of its nature. If sin, as *sin!*, were recognizable on the basis of what we feel about ourselves, then it would either be a special aspect of our human insufficiency or even our frailty, or it would be our failure to achieve the good, the ideal, which we have conceived of ourselves or experienced as an inner necessity within ourselves. If it could be deduced from the law without further ado, as it presents itself to us naturally, then sin would be our lacking morality or inadequate achievement, or even our failure to take the road determined for us by "God." In every one of these instances the harsh judgments of the Bible remain incomprehensible, like that of Paul, according to whom death is the "wages" of sin (Rom. 6:23; see also James 1:15). On the other hand, Luther's judgment would also be incomprehensible: "Where there is the remission of sins, there are also life and salvation."[36] Why should sin result in death, and why should its remission (not its

---

34. *Ibid.*, p. 836.

35. See P. Sprenger, *Vivificatio nach Paulus und deren Bedeutung und Wert für die evangelische Rechtfertigungslehre* (Leipzig: A. Deichert, 1925); especially important, Heidelberg Catechism, Questions 88–90 (Schaff, III, 339); here the weaknesses of Melanchthon's position are clearly visible.

36. *Smaller Catechism*, Part V (Schaff, III, 91).

actual removal by man's work) effect life and salvation? If "sin" is what we just described, then forgiveness cannot be the chief thing at all. Man must rather devote everything to the overcoming of his insufficiency—or he is satisfied with the insight that the "ideal" is unattainable by its very nature.[37] If sin is essentially wrong performance, then it is certainly an agonizing lack but ultimately the kind of thing with which man must come to terms. Legalism, which is at stake here, must always arrive at this view of sin. Of course, where it emerges in the Church, it is accompanied by fear. It cannot be denied that the predominantly Nominalist doctrine of sin which Luther reacted to had caused great fear (whereas, on the other hand, in the area of the Church in which Calvin appeared, both the Renaissance and Humanism had produced the acceptance of sin, if not its glorification). The basic life anxiety of man becomes, under the influence of Nominalism, the legalistic fear of death. But this anxiety, too, is based upon the view that sin is a lack, a failure to fulfill the norm, for whose fulfillment both "nature" and "grace" are available.

What is then the understanding of the nature of sin which conditions the doctrine of the knowledge of sin which we have presented?

  c. Personal Sin. First, it is quite clear that it is a total understanding of sin. Sin is "personal sin." It is not "something" about man, neither a defect nor an attribute nor an act performed by man. It is the comprehensive qualification of his being, in that it defines his direction. This view accords with the biblical concept of sin. Whether we are looking at the Old Testament *chata'* (to sin), *'awah* (to commit iniquity), or *pasha'* (to transgress), or also *hamartanein* (to miss the mark, err, trespass), sin is always missing the way or virtual failure in regard to the relationship to a specific other person: rebellion (*pasha'*). Sin is as comprehensive as the "image of God" is. Thus every pluralism will fail to grasp the nature of sin. This is true of the "general" anthropological pluralism, which divides man into body and soul or the soul into higher and lower levels. It is equally true of the pluralism concealed in every moralism, which deals with specific actions but leaves the person aside.[38] It is of very great significance that the Bible, on its Old Testament basis, knows of no pluralization of man, although

---

37. In that popularized Idealism gradually made the concept of the eternally unattainable ideal popular, and simultaneously dissolved concrete ethics in favor of that ideal, it contributed significantly to the destruction of the European form of life, more than did the superficial moralism of the Enlightenment which secretly still knew something of the goodness of the divine command.

38. Against this, Luther's well-known statement, "Good and devout works never made a man good and duteous; but a good and religious man does good and religious works. . . . The person must first be good and godly; after that come all the works that are good. Good works proceed logically from a godly and good person" (*The Freedom of a Christian Man,* in Bertrand Lee Wolf, *Reformation Writings of Martin Luther* [London: Lutterworth Press, 1952], I, 371). Along those lines, Calvin: "Accordingly, they have spoken very truly who have taught that favor with God is not obtained by anyone through works, but on the contrary works please him only when the person has previously found favor in his sight" (*Institutes,* III, xiv, 8, pp. 775f.), appealing, incidentally, to the Pseudo-Augustinian writing *De vera et falsa poenitentia,* XV, 30 (Migne, *PL,* XL, 1225), and a statement of Gregory the Great in his *Letter,* IX, 122 (Migne, *PL,* LXXVII, 1053).

there is a differentiation of man.[39] The various physical and spiritual components are nothing other than elements within a movement; one can call the biblical view of man a dynamic view, without reservations. Based upon this total dynamism, Paul can even speak of a "law" of sin and of death (Rom. 8:2).

d. Sin Before God. Secondly, the totality of sin cannot be maintained if sin is not seen in a strict relationship to God. Wherever God is set aside, as is the case in the other religions against which the prophets struggled, the activity of the "person" is also lost. Man is truly himself and is encountered in his totality where God meets him as the One God. On the other hand, this is only true where God really encounters man. It is not true where God is made into an idea and the law then into the epitome of an ideal or a principle. Man can withstand the non-fulfillment of an ideal, or his insufficiency over against a principle, but he cannot withstand the living God! The decisive thing is that sin, as our failure to meet the very intended constitution of our existence, must deal with the living and present God. Sin is not based upon some kind of metaphysical insufficiency of man. The fact that man does not recognize the God who is certainly not "far" (Acts 17:27) is not the result of God's being too difficult a thought for man, or the knowledge of God being an impossible noetic achievement. It is significant that Paul, in Romans 1:18ff., speaks consistently in the indicative: "what can be known of God" is plain to man (1:19). The issue here is not an epistemological problem. The problem is the knower himself who does not truly know what has been absolutely revealed because he refuses to acknowledge it. That is the reason for the inexcusability of man (Rom. 1:20), which is based upon man's refusal to thank and to honor God (1:21). It is certainly true that only through proclamation does man experience that he is sinning against the present God. But this proclamation is not communicating to him any metaphysical novelties, but announces to him—with the wrath of God—that the God whom he has somehow known and yet by no means acknowledged has now turned to him and requires of him his Yes, because God has spoken his Yes (even in the No of his wrath). Certainly blindness is a consequence of sin. But it is blindness in the brightest of days, blindness with eyes that see.

e. Originated Sin =peccatum originans. It was not wrong that theology has attempted from very early on to interpret, using chiefly Genesis 3 and the idea of "originated sin," the character of sin with the use of one single concept. Genesis 3 has always been powerful enough to prevent theology from seeking the character of sin in the realm of "morality," that is, to judge the "fall" as a single trespass against a single law or command or one side of the one moral law. It is quite obvious that such a procedure in regard to Genesis 3 can only lead to the most grotesque of distortions. What happens in that account is, seen morally, almost trivial. The sole source of its importance is in the fact that in this apparently

---

39. See especially W. Eichrodt, *Das Menschenverständnis des Alten Testaments* (Zurich: Zwingli Verlag, 1944), pp. 34f.; and W. Zimmerli, *Das Menschenbild des Alten Testaments* (Munich: Kaiser, 1949), pp. 23f.

trivial matter God and his creature are both completely and comprehensively the issue. Thus, hybris, unbelief, and disobedience emerge as the essential descriptions of the character of this so-called model event. Hybris applies in that the offer of the serpent that man should be "like God" and in this capacity know both good and evil, and be able to decide what is useful and what is detrimental in his own competence, reveals that sin is in fact man's self-elevation and thus his rejection of his creatureliness as an act of his own choosing. Unbelief has been seen in the fact that man, in succumbing to the promises of the serpent, apparently does not trust God, becomes mistrusting of God's goodness, and thus wants to gain control of good and evil, the useful and the detrimental, in effect, the ultimate mystery out of which he lives. Disobedience is really identical with unbelief. The command is the protective limit which surrounds man, and sin is the breaking through of this boundary, which again has its roots in mistrust. It is clear that these three definitions all coalesce with each other. It is just as clear that they all presuppose a certain concept of the opposite of sin, of good, and that can be defined as man living within his created limits and dependent totally upon the goodness of his Creator within those limits. We may then summarize that sin, in that it is the active denial of the goodness of God, is simultaneously resistance against God's good command, and against his dominion as a gracious rule.[40] Under these circumstances, it is essentially negation, so very much so that it catapults the existence of man into the negativity of his denied but not deniable creatureliness, that is, into a literally impossible existence. In this sense, sin is "privation" (*privatio*), as the Orthodox emphasized in following Augustine and most of the Middle Ages—"privation" as man's depriving himself of himself by seeking to rob God of what is his. Sin is thus not something created—for what is created is God's creature—but is solely the denial of what is created. It does not live in and of itself but lives from its robbery of what is not its own. But as denial, sin is paradoxically something "positive," something which does in fact exist, although this is incomprehensible. It is not something nonexistent, but something which lives on the basis of its robbery. It is certainly not something which is not yet good or which is lacking in good, but is its "positive negation."[41] It exists, although it cannot exist. And that is its mystery.

---

40. On sin as hybris see above all Augustine, *Enchiridion,* 45 (*NPNF,* III, 252); *The City of God,* XIV, 13 (*NPNF,* II, 273f.); Thomas, *STh,* II–II,clxii, vol. II, pp. 1854–61 (strongly diluted); Calvin, *Institutes,* II, i, 4, pp. 244–46—but Calvin gives greater emphasis to the interpretations of unfaithfulness and disobedience. More recently, E. Brunner emphasizes hybris (arrogance) strongly (e.g., *Man in Revolt . . . ,* p. 130). On sin as unfaithfulness or unbelief, see Luther, *Lectures on Genesis* (3:1) (AE, I, 147ff. and often); Calvin, *loc. cit.*; J. Gerhard, *Loci communes theologici,* IX, ii, 27, ed. F. R. Frank (1885ff.), II, 147 (with his rejection of the view that pride [*superbia*] was the original sin; Gerhard's controversy with Bellarmine, which is otherwise dominant, also holds sway here).

41. The view that sin is something negative was derived from the Greek (and Gnostic) world and then penetrated the theology of the Church. We think here chiefly of Augustine, especially *The City of God,* XI, 17 (*NPNF,* II, 214); *Enchiridion,* 11–13 (*NPNF,* III, 240f.). Similarly, Peter Lombard, *Sentences,* ed. Franciscans of Quaracchi (Ad Claras Aquas: Quaracchi, 1916), I, 496; Thomas Aquinas, *STh,* I,xlviii,1, vol. I, pp. 245f. Part of Protestant Orthodoxy proceeds then on this basis, stretching from Melanchthon to the early Enlightenment. We find the term "positive negation" in E. Brunner, *op. cit.*, pp. 130ff., who accuses the theology influenced by Augustine of subordinating the person to nature.

Sin is hostility toward the grace of God. To that extent, the Reformation-Orthodox interpretation, which places unbelief (*diffidentia*) in the foreground, is to be agreed with, provided that "faith" is understood as the response which is given to the "faith of God" (*fides Dei*). If we may see the meaning of the law in the claim that we, as those destined to be God's covenant partners, are to let God be our God, then sin consists of our not doing that. This "unbelief" always has two sides. It always consists of our not recognizing God or ourselves. We fail to recognize God in that we are not willing to accept that he is good to us. We fail to recognize ourselves in that we are not willing to accept that we should submit ourselves to him.[42] In doing that, we unavoidably submit to ourselves, and everything we then do, which as such within our limitedness and under the gracious dominion of God would be elements of our basic constitution of existence derived from God and oriented toward him, now assumes the character of "concupiscence" (*concupiscentia*). Augustine's idea that sin is made manifest in the dominion of "concupiscence" is, when taken in isolation, at least misunderstandable. It easily leads to an understanding of sin which seeks to identify areas within our being which are essentially sinful, and its emphasizes to a dangerous degree particularly the area of the erotic, where Augustine thought concupiscence primarily to be present, following in the monastic tradition. Nonetheless, we may not forget that the concept itself is biblical—we think particularly of Romans 7 and James 1:14f., but also of Galatians 5:16, 24—and there it certainly is not restricted to the sphere of the sexual. *Epithymia* is the lusts of the "flesh" (*sarx* [Gal. 5:16, 24; Eph. 2:3; 1 Pet. 2:11; 2 Pet. 2:10, 18; 1 John 2:16]), and in the New Testament the "flesh" is man in his fallenness. Thus the "lusts" can also be of the heart (Rom. 1:24) or even of the "soul" (Rev. 18:14). Therefore, "concupiscence" is in truth the willing fallenness of man in himself in his separation from the Creator.

The description which we have given must appear to be one-sided because it has not dealt yet with sin as single sinful acts. However, the nature of sin cannot be deduced from single sinful acts. Whoever tries that approach will end up reckoning act against act, "good" works against "evil." However, sin is not the collective term for a variety of ignoble deeds, but is the constitution of our existence. We can thus understand why Orthodoxy could raise the question whether sin by its very nature were any kind of "action" (*actio*) at all.[43] It is doubtless true that we cannot understand sin from its active side.

Nevertheless, it is conversely a fundamental misunderstanding to conceive of sin exclusively as "habitual sin" (*peccatum habituale*). For then it is transformed from a state of existence into a passive attribute, for which we are basically not responsible, a "sickness" (*morbus*). In addition, the tendency can then easily develop which speaks of sin so abstractly that the Church proclamation following this view must remain incomprehensible. As the very state of our existence, sin is also and essentially active. "Sins" are the form in which we activate sin as our sin. The more concretely we speak of sins and think about them, the more unavoidably we will be directed back to sin itself, and to ourselves as sinners.

---

42. See K. Barth, *CD*, IV,1, pp. 418ff., *passim*.
43. See Heppe-Bizer, pp. 320ff.

B. ORIGINAL SIN (*peccatum original*)

1. MAN'S EXISTENCE AS SINNER

Since Augustine, the Church's doctrine of sin has had at its center the concept of "original sin," or "inherited sin" (*Erbsünde*). One can virtually say that the Church's anthropology revolves around the two concepts of "image of God" and "original sin."

When we compare it to our discussion up to now, the doctrine of "original sin" goes further in that, first, it seeks the sinful existence of man in the roots of his existence, and secondly thus removes our sinful existence as such from our area of decision, declaring, thirdly, that our sinfulness is a condition of man, or of mankind, in an absolute sense. If we understand sin basically as the rebellion against God's goodness and the distortion of the relationship between the Creator and creature, then the doctrine of "original sin" can only be properly understood when it is seen, not as a given state alone, but in terms of that relationship. If we consider, further, that sin can only be recognized from the perspective of forgiveness, then the doctrine of "original sin" can have only the function of making known man's comprehensive need for grace. This, however, makes it clear that our task is to conduct a critical examination of the traditional doctrine.

a. *"Inherited Sin" and the Biblical View of Man.*[44] The concept of "inherited sin" is a theological interpretation. The question is whether it is an adequate interpretation of the scriptural witness. The biblical complex of statements, to which the doctrine of inherited sin is related, is primarily the following:

1) **The Universality of Sin.** The Bible speaks of sin's universality, comprehending absolutely all men. Just as certainly as the Bible sees sin in its concreteness, it testifies that all men are sinners. "All have turned aside, together they have gone wrong; no one does good, not even one," is the way Paul reads Psalm 14:3 (53:3), and he applies this sentence, which in the Psalter was already directed to the "children of men" (Ps. 14:2; 53:2), with pointed emphasis to both "Jews and Greek," "all men . . . under the power of sin" (Rom. 3:9ff.). And it is a fact that the Bible knows of no area within mankind which is untouched by sin (we think of Gen. 6:5 and Gen. 8:21,[45] of Ps. 143:2; 130:3 and 1 Kings 8:46, of Rom. 11:32 [see Gal. 3:22], 1 John 1:8–10, and many other passages). Man as such is a sinner. The weight of this statement is all the greater since the Bible certainly does not deal in wholesale pessimism. If we consider that the Bible continually relates God's activity with man, it is a grotesque thought that this

---

44. *Peccatum originale* is usually translated into German as *Erbsünde,* a word which emphasizes the "inherited" nature of sin. The English usage, "original sin," does not necessarily carry that connotation. For purposes of clarity, I have translated *Erbsünde* as "inherited sin" so that Prof. Weber's polemic is unambiguous. "Original sin" is always the translation of the Latin phrase—TR.

45. "The same situation which establishes God's penal judgment in the prologue reveals God's grace and concern in the epilogue" (G. von Rad, *Das erste Buch Mose, Kapitel 1–12* [*ATD,* 2; Göttingen: Vandenhoeck & Ruprecht, 1949], p. 100).

activity would seem to be so fruitless. Sin seems to emerge in the most obvious forms at the very place where God's activity is most directly effective—in Israel, and in those who are called within Israel (we think here of the Jacob stories or of David). Man, who becomes God's partner, clearly is absolutely unfit and unwilling to be what he is!

2) **Man as "Flesh."** The sinfulness of man is summarized in the Bible with the general proposition that man is flesh. It is not that he "has" a fleshly "side" to him. The judgment that man is flesh is apparently meant in a comprehensive sense. "Flesh" in a pejorative sense (in contrast to the spirit of Yahweh) is first used in Genesis 6:3 as a designation of man (as he seeks to elevate himself). It basically bears the meaning of the "stuff of earth" and also of "mortality" or the unavoidability of death. This understanding constantly emerges in the Old Testament: all "flesh" is "like grass" (Isa. 40:6), "cursed" is the person who "makes flesh his arm" (Jer. 17:5). Man, who has succumbed to nothingness, does not deserve to have anyone rely upon him. But on the other side of the coin, it is this very man who yearns for his God as a partner in the covenant of Yahweh. "My flesh faints for thee . . ." (Ps. 63:1), even "all flesh" will "bless his holy name" (Ps. 145:21), and God is the "God of all flesh" (Jer. 32:27). If we may summarize at this point, "flesh" is man in his frailty and fallenness as the one whom God has selected to be his partner. Man is "flesh" before God. The New Testament maintains and deepens the Old Testament view. "Flesh" (*sarx*) is virtually hypostatized (see Gal. 5:17; Rom. 8:12). But above all, in Paul "flesh" is not quite equated with *hamartia* (sin; which also frequently appears to be hypostatized), but a very close connection between the two is established. In Romans 8:3 we read of "sinful flesh," and it is the bearer of the "desires" (*epithymia*; Gal. 5:16; see also Eph. 2:3; 1 John 2:16; 2 Pet. 2:10). The "flesh" has its own "mind" (*phronēma*), and that is death (Rom. 8:6) and hostility against God (Rom. 8:7). Since flesh is the absolute characteristic of man (most clearly in John 3:6), man is understood with this term as the one who is completely directed against God, and having succumbed to nothingness. Because he is flesh, he is separated from God and "by nature children of wrath" (Eph. 2:3). It is all the more significant that God sent his Son "in the likeness of sinful flesh" (Rom. 8:3), and that Jesus Christ is come in the flesh (1 John 4:2). In Christ, God has accepted *the* man who is nothing other than "flesh," the sinner, the one who has voluntarily succumbed to nothingness. In this the fleshly nature of man is revealed. Man is the being who is in the wrong in relationship to God.

3) **Original Sinfulness.** In a few biblical passages sin is related to the origin of man. This is primarily true of Romans 5:12ff. as the classical passage for the doctrine of "original sin." Augustine placed this passage at the center of his scriptural argumentation. Since he found the phrase *eph' hō* (inasmuch as, because) at the end of verse 12 translated with *in quo* (in whom), [46] and along with

---

46. The text is that of the Old Latin translation. However, Origen stated in his Commentary on this passage, "All men, who have been or are born in this world, were in the loins of Adam, as if with him up until now in Paradise" (Migne, *PG,* XIV, 1009f.). See also T. Zahn, *Römerbrief* (Leipzig: A. Deichert [1910¹⁻²], 1925³), p. 266, n. 33.

those before him referred this back to Adam, he derived from this passage the thesis that in the "loins" of Adam (see Heb. 7:9f.) all men had originally sinned: "In Adam all have sinned."[47] The translation of *eph' hō* with *in quo* cannot be sustained. If one looks for a nominal solution for *eph' hō*, then the only thing available is *ho thanatos* (death) in Romans 5:12. That would then mean that upon the basis of the sentence of death which has come over all men through the sin of Adam, all men have sinned. Death would not be the "wages" of sin but, as a comprehensive fate, its cause. It is very improbable that Paul would have understood death (in the one instance as everyone's fate, in another as its individual occurrence) equally as both the cause and the effect of sin.[48] The only other option then is to read *eph' hō* without any nominal connection, but, as in Philippians 3:12, with a general reference. Then the phrase could be interpreted as an attraction (as it is in Phil. 3:12), in which case the meaning would be that death has spread to all men "as a result of the fact that" (*epi toutō, hoti*) they had all sinned. Then the coming of death into the world would be the consequence of the sin of one man, its extension to all men the consequence of the fact that all men, once sin was "in the world," had sinned.[49] The other option would be that the phrase *eph' hō* has a relative connection; it would then mean "whereupon" and we could paraphrase it, Through one man sin has come into the world, and through it death, which "thus" has extended to all men, and "thereupon"—on the basis of the intrusion of sin and death—all have sinned.[50] Although this latter exposition has neither linguistic nor material improbabilities against it, the former one deserves a certain preference as the more natural. It is also the one most frequently espoused in more recent exegetical work. In any event, Romans 5:12ff. is a kind of parallel to 1 Corinthians 15:22, "as in Adam all die. . . ." Apparently the Adam-Christ typology in Paul corresponds to the double thesis that in Adam sin came into the world in such a way that all have become sinners, and in Adam death came into the world in such a way that it has now become the fate of all. Between "Adam" and every man there is inclusive unity. Man is man in Adam— or in Christ!

Regardless of how one exposits Romans 5:12ff., sin is certainly here not

---

47. For Augustine's view, see primarily *On Forgiveness of Sins, and Baptism*, II, vii, 14 (*NPNF,* V, 74, and generally in that writing). Further, *On Marriage and Concupiscence*, II, v, 15 (*NPNF,* V, 288f.); and *Opus imperfectum contra Julianum*, II, 17/8 (Migne, *PL,* XLV, 1215).

48. A. Schlatter, *Gottes Gerechtigkeit, ein Kommentar zum Römerbrief* (Stuttgart: Calwer Verlag, 1935, 1959³), p. 187, who does not agree with this exegesis, does point out that the "mortal body" is in Paul also the "body of sin" (we think here chiefly of Rom. 7:24; further, Rom. 8:10f. and Rom. 6:6, 12).

49. Thus Calvin, *The Epistles of Paul the Apostle to the Romans and to the Thessalonians*, tr. R. Mackenzie (Grand Rapids: Eerdmans, 1961), pp. 111f. (Rom. 5:12), "for that all sinned" (Calvin certainly did not intend to weaken the doctrine of inherited sin!), and of the newer expositors, Lietzmann, Jülicher, K. Heim (unpublished lecture), and also Karl Barth ("as to such, which all have sinned . . ." [*Romans*, tr. E. C. Hoskyns (London: Oxford University Press, 1933–65 [g1922²]), pp. 164ff.]).

50. This is the exegesis espoused by A. Schlatter, *op. cit.*, p. 188: God's "punishment" is recognizable in the fact that all sin. More explicitly in T. Zahn, *op. cit.*, p. 265, who paraphrases the *eph' hō* with *et propterea* ("and on that account").

merely an act, but above all a power and as such prior to the sinful act. When one compares the other passages in the Bible, especially the New Testament, it is difficult to conclude that Romans 5:12 says something absolutely unique. This also cannot be said of Psalm 51:5, the second classical passage for the doctrine of inherited sin. The composer of the Psalm has come, in the depth of his repentance, to the recognition of his original existence as a sinner in his sinful activity, and that leads him automatically back to his individual origin; as John 3:6 expresses it, "That which is born of the flesh is flesh." But there is no negative designation here of conception and birth, but the recognition of sin as personal sin.

4) **The Universality of Grace.** It can only be stated that sin is really the sin of all when it is first validly asserted that God is the Creator and Lord of all, and this in turn is revealed in that in Jesus Christ he has accepted all. The universality of the biblical witness to the Creator and the Reconciler is the decisive biblical approach to the thesis that all have sinned and are sinners. This "all" does not connote the sum of all individuals but the totality which is superior to and encloses all individuals: man "in Adam."

b. **The Doctrine of the Church.** The Church's doctrine of "original sin" is basically the theological formulation of the fact that God's work in Jesus Christ applies absolutely to all men, and that man is absolutely in need of this work without restrictions, can contribute to this work neither actively nor receptively, but merely must let it happen to himself.

c. **Augustine's Intention.** The systematic doctrine of "original sin" arose in the European Church. Its counterpart in the East is the Christology which has been developed with extremely precise intellectual finesse. It could well be said that both belong together. At one significant junction of theological controversy, this became apparent. That the Synod of Ephesus in 431 condemned Nestorius together with the Pelagian Celestius[51] was not for theological reasons but does point out the relationship between Nestorian Christology and Pelagianism. In both of them, the freedom of divine grace is not recognized.

Augustine's doctrine of "original sin" was developed in opposition to Pelagius. But like the doctrine of predestination, in which context it belongs, this doctrine is not fundamentally polemical.[52] Augustine is concerned with the concept of "to God alone be the glory" (*soli Deo gloria*) and thus with the question of the certainty of salvation.[53] If the sinner is merely man as he does evil things— by imitating others, or because of a tendency to evil, which would be opposed by a tendency to good—if, therefore, there is "something" in man which is not

---

51. Text in Denzinger, p. 52, pars. 126f.
52. See Harald Diem, "Augustines Interesse in der Predestinationslehre," in E. Wolf, ed., *Theologische Aufsätze, Karl Barth zum 50. Geburtstag* (Munich: Kaiser, 1936), pp. 362ff.
53. Harald Diem, *op. cit.*, p. 365, cites *On the Gift of Perseverance*, VI, 12 (*NPNF*, V, 530): "We live, therefore, more securely if we give up the whole to God, and do not entrust ourselves partly to Him and partly to ourselves. . . ."

touched by sin, if there is a positively oriented "freedom" (*libertas*) for him, then God the Reconciler has not been "given all things" and both God's honor and the certainty of salvation based solely upon God's work in Christ have been encroached upon. The doctrine of the total sinfulness of man is only the reverse side of the witness to the totality of grace. Since this grace is never inactive or ineffective, we note the tendency in Augustine not to conceive of sinfulness in a one-sided conditional way. It is well known that he concludes that through the Fall, the created ability of man not to sin (*posse non peccare*, to be able not to sin) became the inability not to sin (*non posse non peccare*, not to be able not to sin): man must sin. However, this "must" is not a physical constraint, but paradoxically a voluntary "must."[54] Augustine never completely gave up the idea of the "free will" (*liberum arbitrium*). But he cannot conceive of a "free will" which would diminish grace, and it can thus be asserted that herein lies the kernel of his contradiction of both Pelagius and Julian of Eclanum (c. 386–454).

d. *The Anti-Pelagian Theses of Augustine*. For the Pelagians, sin is an individual action, proceeding from natural freedom, which although weakened has still been preserved in the man deciding—it is activity resulting from one's own decision. This means that man is seen as man in himself, certainly in relationship to other persons (*imitatio*) and to God as the lawgiver and judge, but the relationships to God and others are accidental. Augustine cannot view man in that fashion, either in his "original state" or in his sin. For him, sin is essentially "rejection of God" (*carentia Dei*); it is not primarily my individual decisions, but it conditions me in my decision; as a "defect" (*defectus*) it is simultaneously a power. The man who exists in the "rejection of God" lives as such unavoidably in "self-love" (*amor sui*), in "exaltation" (*elatio*), "pride" (*superbia*), and "concupiscence" (*concupiscentia*). And this applies not only to the individual. Augustine, who certainly was his own man in a way rare among theologians, was still a man of the Church and thus had regard for both history and totality. For the very reason that man is man before God, he is in essence not singular. He is totally involved in the "human race" as the "mass of perdition" (*genus humanum, massa perditionis*). Or, he is a member of the Church which mediates "grace" (*gratia*) to him and within which he is the object of "election" (*electio*).

In contrast to the thesis of Pelagius according to which sin is transferred by "imitation" (*imitatio*), Augustine is not satisfied with the reference to the unity of the "human race" in Adam. He attempts rather to make this unity understandable as a genetic unity. The unity of all men in Adam is identical with their genetic descent from him. And at this point Augustine develops the doctrine of inherited sin, which is not merely "original sin" (*peccatum originale*) or the "sin of the

---

54. E. Brunner, *Man in Revolt . . .* , pp. 146ff., concludes with good reason that Augustine has done more than Luther and Calvin to solve the problem of responsibility and total sinfulness. A. Möhler, *Symbolism; or, Exposition of the doctrinal differences between Catholics and Protestants as evidenced by their symbolical writings*, tr. J. B. Robertson (London: Gibbings & Co., 1906⁵ [g1924¹¹⁻¹²]), pp. 103f., would probably except Calvin here.

origin" (*peccatum originis*) but "sin in a certain way hereditary" (*peccatum quo-dammodo haereditarium*).[55]

This concept is explained by Augustine partially with juridical and partly with ethical considerations. According to the juridical argument, Augustine states that Adam's descendants assume the "legal responsibility" or "liability" (*reatus*) which was placed upon their generic father, and to that extent "inherited sin" is both guilt and punishment for guilt once contracted. It can be compared to the financial indebtedness which children take over from their parents as testators. But the descendants of Adam also inherit from generation to generation the effective consequences of sin, especially "concupiscence." Augustine conceives of this in predominantly erotic terms. This then leads to the connection of what we have already described with the thought that procreation, because it is not pure but takes place under the dominion of "concupiscence," is then the medium for the "propagation" of sin.[56] It is clear that sin can then be understood in two very different directions. It can be viewed essentially as the "rejection of God" (*carentia Dei*) which has been overcome in grace (!), or it can appear as an interpersonal, inner-human, and ontological defect, as a given. Doubtless the second possibility has gained the upper hand.

e. Semi-Pelagianism. However, this second possibility had to lead to a weakening of Augustine's approach with almost natural necessity. If sin is hereditary in this sense, is it possible to regard the whole man as absolutely sinful? Does not man receive from his parents and predecessors other endowments? Does he not, as Augustine clearly admitted in his early stage, possess a "free will"? Must one not conclude that some remnant remained unaffected by sin? This line in Augustine had to lead on to Semi-Pelagianism, which then in fact did dominate post-Augustinian theology, chiefly in the Middle Ages. We have already discussed this. If it is true that sin destroyed the "superadditive gift," "original righteousness" (*donum superadditum, justitia originalis*) and thus is a pure defect, but causes only a "vulnerability" in the sphere of the "natural gifts," then man is not totally and fundamentally a sinner as man himself. One must admit that there is an ultimate and unaffected part of him. It is not the ability to do good, that is, to appropriate salvation on one's own, but it is the will to do that (and thus we have the great role which "disposition" or "preparation" play for the reception of salvation in Roman Catholicism). The result is then that in the concept of sin itself there is a corresponding division. Seen formally, it is nothing other than the lack of "original righteousness" which is then remedied in baptism. Seen materially, it is chiefly "concupiscence." As such it remains in the baptized person, but only as "tinder" (*fomes*), which can be the occasion for real sin (what is called *peccatum actuale*), but which cannot harm the one who does not "consent" to it but "courageously" (*viriliter*) battles against it by the "grace" of Christ

---

55. *The Retractions*, I, xii, 5 (*FC*, LX, 53f.).
56. Thus especially in the writing *On Marriage and Concupiscence* (*NPNF*, V, 258–308).

Jesus.[57] It is as though it was not very obvious in terms of "lust" or "desires" that we do not merely do evil but are evil! The accent was completely shifted to "actual sinning" (*peccatum actuale*), at least for the baptized.

f. The Reformation Doctrine. In contrast with the Semi-Pelagianism of the Middle Ages, the Reformers basically resumed the doctrine of Augustine. The most obvious difference from the great African theologian was to be found in the new understanding of the concept "concupiscence," which was separated from the sexual sphere, and in the logically pursued rejection of the "free will." Melanchthon's presentation in the *Apology* is characteristic of the new understanding of the concept "concupiscence."[58] The fact that the contesting of "free will" comes to the fore is related to the reverse situation in the Middle Ages in which free will had become the summary of all the "natural characteristics" which were regarded as wounded and corrupted but still extant. It was chiefly the result of a new understanding of God (even in comparison with Augustine), which was conceived of less in terms of being than in terms of the will.

g. "Inherited Sin" as Fate? The more decidedly the Reformers opposed every kind of Semi-Pelagianism, the more sin appeared to assume the character of a fate which man, who had no "free will" at all, could not escape. Luther and Calvin knew how to bear the intellectual difficulties which resulted, and Reformed Orthodoxy followed in their path, developing obviously a logically conceived deterministic system. Melanchthon and Zwingli (not to speak of Flacius) tried to resolve the tension with diametrically opposed approaches. Melanchthon, who in his *Loci* of 1521 was still the most concise advocate of Luther's position, later expanded what was in effect a semi-Pelagian view, according to which man had retained the capacity of submitting himself to grace (*sese applicare ad gratiam*) or of resisting it.[59] Melanchthon's theological interest at this point was in respon-

---

57. See Thomas, *STh,* I–II,lxxxi, especially Art. 3, vol. I, p. 954; Council of Trent, Session V (June 17, 1546), c. 5 (Denzinger, pp. 247–58, par. 792); Michael Schmaus, *Katholische Dogmatik* (5 vols.; München: M. Hueber, II, 1949³⁻⁴), pp. 402f., draws attention to the fact that at Trent the Augustine General, Girolamo Seripando, devoted a great deal of effort to gaining the acknowledgment from the Council that "concupiscence" was sin "by some kind of rationale" (*aliqua ratione*). He was not successful. See H. Rückert, *Die Rechtfertigungslehre auf dem tridentinischen Konzil* (Bonn: Marcus & Weber, 1925), pp. 217ff.

58. *Apology,* II, 25 (Jacobs, p. 79): "Concupiscence" is not just "a corruption of the qualities of the body, but also, in the higher powers, a vicious turning to carnal things." The German translation (*BekSchr,* p. 152) elucidates further: "an evil desire and tendency, since we with the very best and highest powers, and the light of reason are nevertheless minded and turned against God in a fleshly way." Then, with an appeal to Augustine, Luther's thesis, held by the other Reformers, is defended, that concupiscence is not an adiaphoron but a sin (*Apology,* II, 38f. [Jacobs, pp. 81ff.]). In a similar way, Calvin rejects the assertion that "corruption" is limited to the sensual activity or is just a "tinder." It is situated in the whole of man, and the soul is affected in a decisive way (*Institutes,* II, i, 9, pp. 252f.). We must also consider here that Thomas also (*STh,* I–II,lxxxiii,1, vol. I, pp. 959f.) declared the soul to be the bearer of inherited sin—at decisive points he is still an Augustinian!

59. References in Hans Engelland, *Melanchthon, Glauben und Handeln* (Munich: Kaiser, 1931), pp. 392ff.

sibility, and for its sake he reintroduced "free will" in an indirect form. Zwingli took another approach in that he termed "inherited sin" as "being precedent" (*praest*).[60] With this idea Zwingli, in good Augustinian fashion, meant the concept of "self-love" (*amor sui*). But precisely because he understands "inherited sin" in this sense in a strictly theological way, he then rejects its being directly guilty in nature. It causes damnation because man, rather than following the "law," submits to it and thus becomes guilty. As such, it is not guilt (the special consequences of this are that according to Zwingli there is no damnation of newly born children). A. Ritschl concludes,[61] "If . . . the assumption of an hereditary transmission of sin be maintained at all, it can be understood only in Zwingli's sense." In any event, it will have to be said that Zwingli is not Pelagian in his thought, although with the concept of *praest* (*morbus*, sickness!) he would seem to make the opposite impression. He merely wants to prevent sin's becoming nothing more than fate and losing the character of guilt. To do that, he must understand "inherited sin" solely in its actualized form as guilt.[62] It is questionable whether this is adequate. In any case, it is to Zwingli's credit that he posed the issues of "inherited sin" and guilt in their most emphatic form.

    h. Liability, Debt, Guilt=reatus, debitum, culpa. As Augustine already stated, "inherited sin" establishes "liability" (*reatus*), a condition of objective conviction of guilt. The concept of *reatus* can also be found in the confessional documents.[63] It is based upon the fact that man, as he is, owes God something from the very beginning, a "debt" (*debitum*), namely, "righteousness" (*justitia*).[64] The state in which man finds himself is as such already laden with guilt. Man does not "possess" what he is supposed to have as God's creature, as the one predetermined

---

60. R. Pfister, *Das Problem der Erbsünde bei Zwingli* (Leipzig: M. Heinsius Nachfolge, 1939).

61. *The Christian Doctrine of Justification and Reconciliation, the Positive Development of the Doctrine*, tr. H. R. Mackintosh and A. B. Macaulay (New York: Scribner's, 1900; Clifton, N.J.: Reference Book Publishers, 1966 [g1895⁴]), p. 374.

62. As A. Ritschl emphasizes, the covenant idea is decisive here. The children of Christians (who are the sole point of Zwingli's thought) cannot be damned because of inherent sin as participants in the covenant, because they are located in the covenant and thus in grace; what is damnable is only the violation of the covenant in "practical sinning" (*peccatum actuale*) (A. Ritschl, *op. cit.*, pp. 373f.).

63. In general the confessional documents emphasize that "inherited sin" is sin in the full sense of the word. Thus the Augsburg Confession, Article II: Original sin "is truly sin, condemning and bringing eternal death now also upon all that are not born again by baptism and the Holy Spirit" (Schaff, III, 8). Similarly the French Confession of Faith of 1559: Original sin "is truly sin, sufficient for the condemnation of the whole human race, . . . and . . . God considers it as such" (*ibid.*, p. 366). The Belgic Confession of 1561 agrees with this, using in part the same terminology (Article XV [*ibid.*, p. 400]). The *Apology* speaks of *reatus* (II, 35 [Jacobs, p. 81]; "imputation"), conceiving of it as the "formal aspect" of original sin, whereas the "material aspect" is "concupiscence." We also find in the "Solid Declaration" of the Formula of Concord, I, 9, the formula "culpa seu reatus" (guilt or liability) (Jacobs, p. 541). See also, in the 17th century, the Westminster Confession of Faith of 1647 (Schaff, III, 600ff.); and the Formula Consensus Helvetici, Can. X, in E. F. K. Müller, *op. cit.*, p. 864.

64. *Apology*, II, 28 (Jacobs, p. 80): "the want of the righteousness that is due."

to be in fellowship with God. To that extent, the concept of "liability" is not to be contested.[65] The more difficult question is whether it was helpful to connect the concept of "guilt" (*culpa*) with that of "liability" and to erase virtually every distinction between them. This is exactly what emerging and flourishing Orthodoxy did in general. That meant that the same quality was assigned to "original sin" as to "actual sin." It is only possible to say that "original sin" is or causes "guilt" when "original sin" and "actual sin" are firmly related to each other like "being a sinner" and "committing sin."

i. The "Imputation" of "Original Sin." As a matter of fact, Orthodoxy went to complicated lengths in order to retain the "guilt"-character of original sin. It could not resort back to the idea of "propagation," however it might have been conceived of.[66] Through the process of transferal it was possible to make the facticity of sin understandable, but not the guilt. On the contrary, if the original sin of the individual was based upon "propagation," then it was fate but not "guilt" in the sense of being caused in a responsible way, contrary to the norms. Therefore Orthodoxy opted to base the guilt-character of original sin upon an act of divine "imputation." In and of itself, that was a fruitful idea. The unity of mankind in sin, the unity of every man with the sinner Adam, does not appear here to be ontic, based upon heredity, but rather theological. God has selected man to be his counterpart, and takes all men as the one man, every man as the sinner who is Adam. Moreover, the concept of "imputation" is taken from the context of the doctrine of justification and shifts sin indirectly into that light. Nevertheless, the concept as it is used is the result of a legalizing systematization of the relationship to God. But in our relationship to God the issue is not something being reckoned for or against us, but the acceptance or rejection of a person. The "reckoning" of faith for righteousness consists of the fact that the believer is "just" before God. Conversely, one could only say here that man is as a sinner absolutely not "just" before God. The way that this is then set up juridically can be seen when it is described in greater detail. "Imputation" is understood as "immediate imputation" (the reckoning of Adam's sin and the "liability" it renders to every man) and as "mediate imputation" (the reckoning of effective guilt

---

65. P. Althaus, in complete agreement with E. Brunner, objects here to the "distinction between original sin and actual sin," which is "for us an antiquated form of the correct doctrine of sin." We can only conceive of personal existence in terms of "activity." But it is significant that Althaus immediately weakens his thesis: "I act as a consequence of what I have always been in my fundamental position towards God." This reality is nothing other than another version of the idea of "disposition" (*habitus*), which cannot be completely avoided if I recognize myself before God. In that position, I am not only there in my actions but as I am in and of myself, obviously in my actions but still I myself in my actions. See P. Althaus, *Die christliche Wahrheit, Lehrbuch der Dogmatik* (2 vols.; Gütersloh: Bertelsmann, 1948), II, 122, and E. Brunner, *op. cit.*, pp. 116f., 145ff. To speak of "liability" on the basis of "original sin" is only possible in regard to personal sin when this is always my sin, as little as I commit it voluntarily, seen abstractly.

66. The reader is reminded here of the old antithesis between Creationism and Traducianism. A. Vilmar concludes that it is only possible to speak of "immediate imputation" (*imputatio immediata*) when pre-existence is assumed (*Dogmatik: Akademische Vorlesungen*, ed. W. Piderit [Gütersloh: C. Bertelsmann, 1874 (1937²)], I, 372).

which every man has assumed on the basis of the sinfulness passed on to him, his sinful condition [*habitus*]). The distinction we find in the Reformed Orthodox between "imputed sin" and "inherent sin"[67] results in the same dualism: "inherent sin" is then also imputed.

j. Objections to the Doctrine of "Original Sin." There has been much criticism of the Church's doctrine of "original sin." And there has been no lack of attempts to weaken it (Semi-Pelagianism in the early Church and in the Middle Ages, "Synergism" in the older Melanchthon and certainly in Johann Pfeffinger [1493–1573] and Victorinus Strigel [1524–69]). The self-understanding molded by Humanism opposed it violently—we need only to mention the Socinians and the Remonstrants. The Enlightenment set aside few elements of traditional dogma as self-confidently as it did the doctrine of original sin, which contradicted its view of man totally. The theology which was self-consciously post-Enlightenment, Schleiermacher and Ritschl, made attempts to develop a new basis for what had been conclusively given up in its older form. But all they accomplished was the demonstration that the old was truly past, but not that something new had replaced it. In contemporary theology, the doctrine of original sin is also a *crux,* as this has already become apparent in especially E. Brunner and P. Althaus.

The objections to the Church's doctrine of original sin are, seen as a whole, the expression of a self-understanding which revolves around the concepts freedom, responsibility, and person. The following questions then emerge. First of all, how can sin still be understood as a personal and responsible decision if the "chief sin" (Luther) is not that but a kind of condition which is ascribed to me fully heteronomously? Secondly: How can sin be understood as present deeds (individual or collective) if there is a super-individual and historical once-and-for-all to our existence as sinners? Does not this deprive sin of its actual seriousness?

k. "Original Sin" and Grace. The question must nonetheless be raised whether or not the most serious objection to the Church's doctrine of original sin does not come from another quarter. Is not the curious gloom which attaches to the traditional doctrine of sin irreconcilable with the light, within which the true darkness of man is first recognized? Can we say that the Church's doctrine of hereditary sin still reckons unconditionally with God's grace? Is not the state of existence which we are speaking of when we say "original sin" the one which God has overcome in Jesus Christ? Is it not the case that we can only speak of "original sin" as the sin out of which we have come and which we may look back upon "in Jesus Christ"? Has not the chasm been long closed and is not our horror merely a reflex movement of our gratitude that it is closed? In that it tried to work out as sharply as possible who we are in and of ourselves, did not the Church's doctrine of hereditary sin pay too little attention to the fact that every self-observation of man which sees him solely in and of himself is in fact sin, is "distrust"

---

67. See Heppe-Bizer, pp. 331ff. It is significant that within Reformed Orthodoxy there were objections raised to the concept of "imputation," namely, by the circle related to the Academy at Saumur.

(*diffidentia*)? Should not the doctrine of "original sin" rather be the praise of the One who has established his covenant with man, who is totally undeserving of it?

1. *"Original Sin" and Baptism.* The issue at stake here can be clarified somewhat by turning to the relationship between "hereditary sin" and baptism. This relationship has been central ever since Augustine.[68] According to the doctrine of the Middle Ages and the post-Trent period, hereditary sin is removed in baptism.[69] The "liability" is a "past liability" for the baptized. The Roman Church has, however, not quite maintained this view. Even in the baptized there is a remnant of forgiven hereditary sin, the "tinder" of "concupiscence." This is related to the fact that baptism is regarded as one stage in a process of salvation which has its empirical side. It cannot be "empirically" denied that "concupiscence" is still "there" after baptism. But in fact it is the case that with baptism as the authorized "sign" the "old man" does die ("is drowned"). The judgment is spoken here over man which can only be repeated by the best of doctrines of hereditary sin: "dead in sins and trespasses" and "died with Christ"—but both of these as one judgment! However, here another judgment is spoken over man in the one act: this very person lives in Christ. We will not deal with the question whether this insight may be used to support or contest the baptism of infants. But one thing should be clear: the sin of which theology speaks is that which was borne by Jesus Christ, and our all-encompassing enslavement to it is what he has abrogated for all (even though not all have in faith in him acknowledged that it is abrogated). The doctrine of "original sin" is the doctrine about that particular state of existence from which we are coming in our hearing of the Word of grace.

The Reformers did not contest the thesis that hereditary sin is forgiven in baptism.[70] But in contrast to the medieval doctrine, they asserted that the baptized will have to struggle with sin for the rest of his life. In their eyes, baptism was not one step in a process of salvation, and what remained of hereditary sin did not appear to them as "tinder" but as sin in the real sense, which required then "daily repentance."[71] Baptism has the character of a valid affirmation but not of an ontically effected transformation. Man is always located in precisely the same position in which he was at the moment of his baptism. But this then means more than ever that, protected against every ritualistic or perfectionistic misunderstand-

---

68. The writing *On Forgiveness of Sins, and Baptism* (*NPNF,* V, 15–78) has as its subtitle, "*And on the Baptism of Infants.*"

69. Trent, Session V, Can. 5 (Denzinger, pp. 247f. [par. 792]).

70. See the Augsburg Confession, Article II: Sin brings condemnation and eternal death to those "that are not born again by baptism and the Holy Spirit" (*sic!*) (Schaff, III, 8). See also Calvin, *Institutes,* IV, xv, 10ff., pp. 1311ff.

71. The *Apology* of the Augsburg Confession, II, 35 (Jacobs, p. 81); Luther, *The Babylonian Captivity of the Church* (AE, XXXVI, 69): Baptism, "even with respect to its sign, is not a matter of the moment, but something permanent." Although it takes place at a given time, "the thing it signifies continues until we die, yes, even until we rise on the last day. For as long as we live we are continually doing that which baptism signifies, that is, we die and rise again." See also Calvin, *Institutes,* IV, xv, 10ff., pp. 1311ff. The *Apology* (II, 36 [Jacobs, p. 81]) also refers somewhat inaccurately to Augustine: "Sin is remitted in baptism, not in such a manner that it no longer exists, but so that it is not imputed" (Augustine, *On Marriage and Concupiscence* [*NPNF,* V, 275–XXV, 28).

ing, the doctrine of original sin in terms of baptism is what we are coming from. For the penitence which allowed itself to be confined to the sins "still left" would not be "evangelical penitence."

m. Sin as Personal Sin. Sin as "original sin" is in Christ our past. But it is not something past about us which is then contrasted with a remnant still present. It is our past in an absolute sense. Baptism makes known to us not the dying of something but our dying and our living in Christ. Sin which is so taken care of is in the same sense personal sin (or the sin of the person), as I can say, "it is no longer I who live, but Christ who lives in me" (Gal. 2:20). In Christ I am seen as the "I" who I am—as the "I" which I am in my death, descended from Adam, as a member of mankind for which Christ died, and as the "I" which I am in Christ.

The fact that sin is not something about me but the power which defines my very being is only revealed to me in that it is forgiven.

It is then impossible for me to seek to secure something about me or in me as a reserve maintained over against the superior power of grace. That is the reason that all talk about "free will" is un-Christian.

But in this situation it is just as impossible for me to view myself as an isolated "I" and to deal with my sin as a final and negative activity of my own. I cannot be "in Christ" at all, placed in the sphere of his rule, that is, in his Church, without experiencing by that very fact my solidarity with all men. It is typical of all Pelagianism that it is individualistic. This individualistic trend is all the more evident in the Socinians and the Arminians. In contrast to that it is obvious that Augustine, for whom individualism fundamentally was not that alien, developed his new conception of the nature of the Church with his view of sin— regardless of the questionable aspects of that view.

It should now be possible to develop in a few broad lines the positive aspects of the reality which the Church's doctrine of "original sin" brings to our view.

1) The Doctrine of "Original Sin" Is the Expression of the Fact That Sin Is a Mystery. When we speak of a mystery in theology, then we mean the incomprehensibility of what is revealed. What is revealed is the involvement of God in Jesus Christ for man who is God's enemy (Rom. 5:6ff.). Sin is incomprehensible because it has become the object of divine rejection. It is therefore something incomparably other than the negative quality of individual acts or persons. It is always action, but it is simultaneously the power which is superior to every action. In that it is always our sin, we are its slaves (John 8:34).

This mystery is made manifest in that sin is beyond all explanation. We cannot say how it came into the world. Even the biblical statements which revolve around Genesis 3 do not explain but recount what is inexplicable. We also cannot say how sin began in each of our individual lives. For us, sin is something original. We are able to "understand" the special sinful action as we now and again reconstruct it. But we do not understand on what basis we committed it as our deed. This inexplicability of sin has its reason in the fact that we are not capable of placing ourselves either intellectually or existentially outside of sin. Our sin is transparent only to the One who is its true opponent. We are not its enemies, but God is, the God whose enemies we are in our sin. Therefore, the only way we can know it is when we are "known" by God. We cannot distinguish ourselves from our sin before God. But God distinguishes between us and our sin.

The Church's doctrine of hereditary sin has not resolved the mystery of our sinful existence, the mystery revealed in the death and resurrection of Jesus Christ. But it has interpreted it rationally and thus encroached upon it. If, for example, our sin were the result of biological descent, then it would not be the mystery which the Bible portrays.

2) The Doctrine of "Original Sin" Is the Expression of the Fact That Our Sin Is Personal Sin But Not That Our Person Is Sin. In relationship to sin we are always in a position of decision. We cannot decide whether we are sinners or not. Yet that does not mean that we are sinners in the same way that we are organisms with the structure of vertebrates. We do not realize that structure decisionally. But it also does not mean that we are sinners in such a way that we live under certain local and temporal conditions. All of those, as great as their power can be, are not fundamentally unchangeable. Our sinful being is comparable in its structure solely with our personal being (and it is more than just comparable). It is not a given which has nothing to do with our active decisions, and it not a given which we could actively do away with.

All of this is abhorrent to our "reason," that is, to our autonomous self-understanding. It would not necessarily be abhorrent to our "reason" to assume that there are inherited attributes or defects in the psychic or physical structure of man which prevent us from being truly "good." It would similarly not be abhorrent to reason to assume such inhibiting factors in our environment. But it is abhorrent to it to be expected to admit a sinful being which cannot be conceived of as next to our personal being. Man can first accept that when in the encounter with the Word of God he realizes that his personal being is absolutely responsible and absolutely enslaved by sin—more precisely, when in this encounter man is persuaded that he does not willingly fear nor love God. The experience of man's sin as his very roots is the experience of the believer in view of the proclaimed love of God. As long as the love of God is an abstract concept, then our failure to love will at most be viewed as the omission of an achievement beyond the call of duty and will be compared with the list of our right or less wrong actions. My failure to love and my own personal being become inescapable for me only when the person of God makes me into his Thou.

It also becomes apparent in this event that the evil I do before God I do not do under compulsion. If it were done under compulsion, then it would not be my evil but the evil which happens to me. For some reason I would be incapable of defending myself against the evil attacking me from outside my person. As far as my own person was concerned, I would not be evil. But in the sight of God, who gives himself to me, I am my own person. And there, my evil is revealed as *my* evil, which I commit "necessarily" but without any kind of compulsion. The old thesis that sin, as "hereditary sin," happens not "by compulsion" (*coactio*) but by "necessity" (*necessitas*) is objectively correct.[72] In sinning, "my" will is not opposed to something alien to me but is subject to its own coercion; it does not battle against corruption but is in and of itself corrupt.

If our knowledge that our sin is personal sin were derived from ethical considerations, then it could lead to the radical conclusion that our personhood as such is sin. This would be a view which corresponds to that of Buddhism, and it has its parallels in Christian mysticism. If we view the apparently ineradicable drive in us to assert ourselves for our own sakes as a manifestation or even the chief form of evil, would then salvation not best be found in the self-destruction of the person (mysticism, asceticism, etc.), and in the self's merging into God? It is important that in the Church's proclamation this approach was generally and correctly not taken. Sin is personal sin, inseparable from our being as persons, but our personal being is not sin. For God is a person! He makes us into a Thou in relationship to his creative I, into partners of his covenant. The identification of sin with the person is not a Christian teaching. We remember once more Flacius, this time from another perspective. Sin remains a theft, the perversion of the person, but it is never the being of that person.

3) The Church's Doctrine of "Original Sin" Expresses the Fact That in Our Sin We Have Solidarity with One Another. The reason that sin is personal sin is that it is not only our individual sin. Personhood is not individuality, because God as a person is not God per se but God in relationship. In that we are all placed under the word of reconciliation, we are all sinners, not as the sum of individuals, but as a fellowship.

We have now reached the place where the concept of "hereditary" sin can be examined for its positive meaning. "Original sin" does not mean "hereditary sin," but rather original, primordial sin, sin which is associated with our being fundamentally and which cannot be separated from it. But very early, the parallel idea of an inheritable sin or depravity arose,[73] and this is the concept which has become dominant in German usage (*Erbsünde*; the verb *erben* means "to inherit"—TR).

The concept of a "hereditary sin" is very likely to be misunderstood. The main reason for this is that it creates the impression for us that a biological process

---

72. It is significant that the doctrine of "necessity" originates in the doctrine of grace: grace is received as a divine "necessity" but not under compulsion. This is the intention in Thomas, *STh*, I–II,cxii,3, vol. I, pp. 1141f., and was already so in Augustine, *On Nature and Grace*, XLVI, 54 (*NPNF*, V, 139). Elsewhere, see Luther, *On the Bondage of the Will* (AE, XXXII, 54–56), and, with direct reference to original sin, Calvin, *Institutes*, II, ii, 5, pp. 294–96.

73. Augustine concludes that sin was "in a certain way hereditary" (*The Retractions*, I, xii, 5 [*FC*, LX, pp. 53f.]). Similarly in *Opus imperfectum*, VI, 21 (Migne, *PL*, XLV, 1550). The concept of "hereditary sin" is not foreign to the confessional documents, e.g., Luther, Smalcald Articles, III, i, 3 (Jacobs, p. 321), where he speaks of "hereditary sin" (*peccatum haereditarium*). On the other side, the French Confession of Faith (1559), Art. 10, where we read of sin as a "hereditary evil" (*vice héréditaire*) (Schaff, III, 365); or The Belgic Confession, Art. 15 (Schaff, III, 400). See also Calvin, *Institutes*, II, i, 5, p. 246, "inherited corruption."

is suspected to be the bearer of sin. Sin thus becomes an element of an ontic sphere. It would be inherited in the same way that characteristics are inherited. There is no way to proceed from that position to the biblical (holistic) understanding of sin (before God!). For we know that what is inherited through the genes are certain characteristics and thus certain dispositions of character. But these are then partially "good" and partially "bad" from this point of view. There certainly are "bad" inherited predispositions. Genetic biology and eugenics can report a good deal about them. But they are opposed by the "good" inherited predispositions. And above all, inherited "good" or "bad" predispositions are, in view of all that we have stated, never to be confused with our righteousness or sin before God. Moreover, this approach would lead to the quantification of sin. The one person would be a "hereditary" sinner "more" than the other—a thought which is theologically inconceivable.

It must then be made clear that this was never really intended by the Church's theology. When it speaks of inherited sin, it is thinking of "nature" (natura)[74] and not what we would call heredity or inheritance. What is at stake is the qualified human existence as it is passed on from person to person. Thus Luther can virtually regard "nature" and "personal sin" as identical.[75] If we understand "nature" as man's being before God, which Luther certainly could not deny, then his identification of "nature" and "person" is unobjectionable.[76] What must be objected to is that the being of man in his corrupt "nature" was related essentially or exclusively to the process of man's genesis (whether in the sense of Traducianism or Creationism).

We must be very cautious in our judgments here, more cautious than most recent theology has been. The Bible ascribes fundamental importance to the fact that man is an heir. We think of the so-called genealogical tables, of the integration of history into the "toledoth" (generations), of the significance given to the heirs in the patriarchal accounts and then again in Romans 4 or Galatians 3. In the Bible, man is always an heir also. He has his identity solely in his hereditary relationship to his forefathers. The history of the covenant takes the form of a history of inheritance. From this point of view, we could never ascribe to the inheritance aspect of these events only incidental importance. The doctrine of sin as "inherited sin" has its counterpart in the doctrine of the covenant as a hereditary covenant. The Reformed theologians, who incorporated baptism (which was our point of departure) totally into covenant theology, always could appeal to

---

74. In Thomas, e.g., it is pointedly emphasized that what is corrupted is the "nature" itself (STh, I–II,lxxxi,1, vol. I, pp. 951–53).

75. E.g., WA, LI, 354 ("An die Pfarrherren wider den Wucher zu predigen" [1540]).

76. E. Gerstenmaier, Die Kirche und die Schöpfung; eine theologische Besinnung zu dem Dienst der Kirche an die Welt (Berlin: Furche-Verlag, 1938), sees here "the misfortune of the Reformation doctrine of hereditary sin." His reasoning: "The facts and contents of personhood cannot be comprehended by the concepts of nature." This is an objection which one would then have to direct against Ephesians (Eph. 2:3) and against the entire "two-nature doctrine" in Christology, which in truth reveals only an inadequate endeavor to apply the concept of nature (as though "nature" in the sense of older and newer theology were the same thing which we regard today as the realm of "natural science"). See also K. Barth's defense of the concept of nature in the older theology (CD, I,2, pp. 126ff.).

significant biblical witnesses. But of course, Old Testament man's existence as heir is oriented to the one Heir of the total old covenant. And everything we say about "hereditary sin" can only be directed toward the One who was made sin for us!

Therefore, the true nature of sin cannot be recognized on the basis of biological processes of inheritance nor even in direct relationship to them. Our being "in Adam" is not based upon the purely factual descent, which itself is subject to factual investigation, but upon the fact that we are this man before God who Adam was. It is significant that not one passage in the Bible explains man's sinfulness with reference to biological descent (as we demonstrated, Rom. 5:12 cannot be appealed to here). If we remember that our "nature" is the state of our existence before God, then we will not understand our "nature" as a kind of constant factor which is passed on from generation to generation. The "nature of man" (*natura hominis*) is not a gene! Therefore we must conclude that, first of all, the concept of "hereditary sin" (*peccatum haereditarium*) should not be used to interpret "original sin" (*peccatum originale*), and secondly, that the doctrine of "imputation," developed as a supporting doctrine by Orthodoxy, contained a correct basic thought to the extent that the participation of all men in the "nature of man" ("after the Fall") is based upon our all being in solidarity before God as human beings.

If this is then the basis of our knowledge, then it does become clear that the biological side, including the genetic processes, also belongs to the "everything" which God has comprehended under sin (Gal. 3:22). Then, too, we will grasp that the somewhat altered form of the same thought, namely, that God "has consigned all men to disobedience that he may have mercy upon all" (Rom. 11:32), is the decisive one for our understanding of "original sin." The universality of grace with its Christological basis reveals the universality of sin.

4) The Church's Doctrine of "Original Sin" Expresses the Fact That Man's Solidarity in Sin Also Appears in the Experienceable Fellowship of Man. If otherwise God is the Creator and Lord of all reality, then man's relationship to God cannot be separated from the total reality of his existence. That then means that the broken relationship to God must also destroy the reality of life within which we live. To put it another way, if we are in solidarity as sinners, then we are also in solidarity in the perceivable manifestations of that very solidarity, in all the forms of our life together. This we would have been even if we were to try to retreat into isolation for fear that we could be "tainted." This self-isolation, by which we were attempting to escape sin, would be a vain attempt at self-purification or self-salvation, for we are still in solidarity with one another involuntarily (sin does not stop at the walls of our hermitages, as empirical experience shows). Self-isolation would be doubly foolish.

Sin is a power within our life together. This is what A. Ritschl had in mind especially when he spoke of the "kingdom of sin" and sought to reduce the concept of "original sin" to that.[77] Of course, Ritschl weakened his thought

---

77. A. Ritschl, *op. cit.*, pp. 338ff. Here Ritschl is clearly under the influence of Kant's idea of the Kingdom of God, whose intellectual antithesis is the idea of the kingdom of sin.

partially by viewing "humanity" solely within the alternatives "natural species" or "the sum of all individuals." And thus he did not grasp that there is a historical and sociological mutuality of man which is rooted in the unity man has before God. But he doubtlessly referred with his concept to the fact that we are, as God's image, singly an "I" for the "Thou" and a "Thou" for the "I," and that in our sin it is not only this relationship which is destroyed but that we ourselves are destroyed within that relationship and because of it. Our existence as sinners is also a social existence as sinners. We have all fallen, are all comprehended within sin, and that means that we now are involved in leading each other astray, in our relationships to one another. Our world is the kind of world in which we are certain to incur guilt. This is true of the economic conditions: whoever participates in our economic existence (which we all share) participates in the guilt which develops out of us and out of it. This is also true of the vast sphere of politics, of the world of power and its "order." We cannot escape it. And we always become participants in guilt. This is true even of the sphere of the family and of our private existence (see the second commandment!). As sinners, we are historical and social beings.

2. SIN AS ACT

a. Sin as Condition and Event? The tendency of the older doctrine of "original sin" was to accept sin as a condition. "Actual sin" was then the act which was derived from this condition. This is most clearly seen in Zwingli, who also draws the conclusion that if "original sin," understood as a "disease" (*morbus*) and as already present (*praest*), is something conditional, then it cannot be directly guilt-laden, but only indirectly, namely, as the cause of "actual sin." However, we must remember that the view of "original sin" as a "disease" is by no means restricted to Zwingli.[78]

b. The Evangelical and Roman Catholic Conceptions. If we start from the distinction between condition and act, then it is immediately obvious that much is dependent upon whether we place the accent upon the condition or the act for our understanding of the concrete situation of the Christian. In general, the Evangelical emphasis has been upon the former, and the Roman Catholic upon the latter.

The Roman Catholic looks backward and views sin as "original sin" behind him. It was done away with in baptism. What remains is the "tinder of sin" which

---

78. The *Apology* of the Augsburg Confession also uses this term quite uninhibitedly (II, 14 [*BekSchr*, p. 150 (in the German text, *Jammer* =misery); Jacobs, p. 78 ("diseases")]). Further, see a dogmatician like Leonhard Hutter, who would never be suspected of Zwinglianism, who describes hereditary sin as ". . . a natural disease, an innate infection and fault of all men . . ." (which accords with the Augsburg Confession, Article II [*Compendium locorum theologicorum* (1610), A. Twesten, ed. (Berlin: Hertz, 1855)], VIII, 4, p. 44; ET: *Compend of Lutheran Theology,* tr. H. E. Jacobs and G. F. Speiker [Philadelphia: Lutheran Book Store, 1868]).

does not become relevant until he commits "actual sins." Then all of the concern is directed to this "actual sin." It is subdivided in a variety of ways, but it forms the central point in the practice of the Church, especially the practice of penitence.

In Evangelical doctrine, "actual sin" also appears in the light of "original sin." The basic reason for this is that there is by no means such a profound difference between the two as there is in the Roman Church. Man's sinful activity is always seen from the perspective of man's sinful existence. This is directly related to the Reformation doctrine of justification. Justification is not a process within which baptism is one phase among several, but is rather God's judgment which as such qualifies the total man as both sinner and righteous (*simul peccator et justus*). Thus, it is conceded that in baptism the forgiveness of all sins (!) is affirmed, but what then has happened once in baptism is now decisive for the whole life of the believer. In that case, "hereditary sin" is never just a matter of the past for man; it is past alone in Christ. Thus it is not constantly present as only "tinder" but as a genuine power—but it is a conquered power (and that is something which is not always seen and expressed with the clarity required by Scripture).

If we can then say that in Roman Catholicism the accent rests on sin as act, and in Protestantism upon "hereditary sin," we can understand the differences in their ethics, as they can generally be observed. Roman Catholic ethics is characterized by a remarkable degree of concreteness which does not even shy away from casuistry. Protestant ethics, in contrast, is usually more general in nature, not seldom outright abstract, and as a rule opposed to all casuistry. Roman Catholic ethics is oriented toward the act, and Evangelical toward the person.

c. Sin as "Personal Sin" and "Actual Sin." However, the alternative between condition and act is in reality inappropriate. Accordingly, one must exercise the greatest reserve in dealing with this differentiation between "original sin" and "actual sin."

We have understood sin as personal sin (or the sin of the person). "Original sin" is sin to the degree that it defines me totally. As such, it is not a condition but a relationship, and it is realized in me continually in my relational behavior. My "status" (the constitution of my existence before God) is my "disposition" (*habitus,* the constitution of my existence as I constantly realize it in practice). "Habitual sin" is thus always and simultaneously "actual sin." I am a sinner, and I commit sin. That is the necessary order for that statement, of course. I am not a sinner because I commit sin. In that case, sin would somehow be a matter of my judgment. My person as such would be, seen abstractly, indifferent, in possession of "freedom" to commit sin or not to. But I am not that at all. I am, rather, a sinner in such a way that I, realizing the constitution of my existence, rebel against my Creator in the very direction of my existence. And in that I do this continually, I sin. To put it another way, In that I (actively) am who I am, I do (existentially) what I do. "Original sin," therefore, may be distinguished from "actual sin" in the same way that a person may be distinguished in terms of his being as a person, and the realization of his personal being in activity. This distinction is meant neither temporally (as though I were only a sinner but without the concrete realization of it!) nor really (as though in various relationships I were only the one or the other). The marginal instance of the infant, to whom Paul himself refers in one context (Rom. 9:11), should not lead us to seek in a psychological fashion the "initiation" of "actual sin" in the individual. It is part of the mystery of sin that such an initial point cannot be found (and that is apparently not what Paul is after,[79] but rather he is seeking to emphasize the freedom of God's decision in contrast to man's). It would be a poor idea to connect the practice of infant baptism with the idea that only such infants bore "original sin" (with the corollary possibility of seeking in them an "infant faith"—*fides infantium*). When we baptize an infant, we look upon this human being as a true person, not as a special instance of humanity, and we are thinking of the totality of his existence, stretching through all of the temporal future—just as we, conversely, conceive of the totality of human existence as oriented to the moment of baptism, even if that took place in infancy.

Under these circumstances, we should distinguish not between conditional and actual sin but between sin as the sin of the person and sin as an act, and we shall make this distinction in such a way that we conceive of the two together. All "actual sins" in their plurality and variety are the constant active expression of sin as the sin of the person (and we cannot imagine that active expression not being present). If we see it in this fashion, we will avoid two errors which have been a serious burden to the doctrine and more so to the pastoral care of the Church. First of all, along the lines of the Roman Catholic approach, we will not view "actual sin" in isolation, as a fact which is to be juridically judged, distinct from the person and the sin of the person. Secondly, along the lines of the Evangelical tendency, we will not minimize the concreteness of sinful actions in favor of the existence of the sinner as a person. If we wanted to put things very briefly, we could say that the actualism of Roman Catholicism points toward Nomism while the Evangelical attitude in regard to individual sins could lead to indifferentism.

d. The Application to Pastoral Care. As we implied, this contrast is especially perceptible in the area of pastoral care. Roman Catholic penitential practice is directed exclusively toward "actual sins." The "contrition of the heart" (*contritio cordis*) is related to specific sins; "oral confession" (*confessio oris*) is supposed to include all the actual trespasses which can be remembered; "absolution" (*absolutio*) is then related to these, and the "satisfaction of works" (*satisfactio operis*) opposes evil deeds with what is regarded as good deeds, if only in a subsidiary fashion. The whole process is close to a judicial one, and does belong to the "jurisdictional power" (*potestas jurisdictionis*) of the Church and its clergy.

---

79. The Rabbinate, proceeding from an actual understanding of sin, maintained in part that very small children were sinless (see Strack-Billerbeck, *Kommentar zum Neuen Testament aus Talmud und Midrasch* [München: Beck, 1922–28, 1974⁶], IV, 466ff.). The same view is hidden behind Tertullian's famous objection to infant baptism: "Why does the innocent period of life hasten to the 'remission of sins'?" (*On Baptism* [*ANCL,* XI (vol. I of Tertullian), 253]).

Sin is the single, special act of the will.[80] In contrast with that, Evangelical pastoral care always tends to be oriented toward the person and especially in our present day seems to have become incapable of coming to terms with concrete sin and concrete absolution. The justified concern that law might re-enter the picture, that the various sins could conceal the one sin, and that the concrete word of forgiveness could then be no longer understood as the total divine Yes to total man, results in pastoral care being subject to the misunderstanding that the sin of the person is general sinfulness, so that in effect there is some kind of condition there, and this makes then neither confession, nor forgiveness, nor any special, explicit dealing with personal sin necessary. Thus, seen broadly, the final conclusion of a concept of sin born out of the deepest seriousness is a minimalization of sin and a kind of resigned self-justification—or the shifting of even the serious-minded Protestant from the Church's pastoral care to psychotherapy or the Oxford Movement. If Roman Catholic Nomism can easily become the source of un-Christian anxiety, then Evangelical Personalism can become the origin of an equally un-Christian sense of "security," which must express itself in neuroses, since it is inwardly false.

e. The Equal Weight of All Sins? The dogmatic problem becomes acute with the question as to whether it can be said that all sins are equal to each other. Obviously this question must be answered affirmatively in that all sins are derived from the one sin. It was the formulation of the common persuasion of the Reformation when Calvin declared that "all sin is mortal. For it is rebellion against the will of God, which of necessity provokes God's wrath, and it is a violation of the law, upon which God's judgment is pronounced without exception."[81] In this assertion, to which we would unconditionally ascribe on the basis of our assumptions, and which can appeal both in letter and in meaning to 1 John 3:4; 5:17, there is no distinction at the decisive point between "original sin" and "actual sin." However, the weight of the foundational Reformation insight here becomes clear when we consider that in truth this assertion expresses the comprehensive fullness of forgiveness. It does not just deal with "original sin" at baptism, so that in the course of the ongoing process of justification the single "actual sins" can be dealt with according to their seriousness by means of the penitential sacraments. No, this forgiveness has been granted once and for all and is applied anew in the Word of proclamation—which for the Reformers is the actual "office of the keys"[82]—and then in absolution attested to the individual when needed. In an incomprehensible way the believer does have, in spite of his "actual sin," his sin behind him.[83]

---

80. The idea of the potentially sinful "tinder" is based on the view found even in Thomas, "that sin is in the will as its subject" (*STh*, I–II,lxxiv, vol. 1, p. 919 and lxxi,5, vol. I, pp. 900f.). See the rejection of this thesis in the *Apology* of the Augsburg Confession, II, 43f. (*BekSchr*, pp. 155f. [Jacobs, pp. 82f.]).

81. *Institutes*, II, viii, 59, p. 423.

82. In Luther this is a well-known position, but also in the Augsburg Confession, XXVIII (Schaff, III, 29f. [here Art. VII of Part II]), but also in Calvin, *Institutes*, IV, i, 22, pp. 1035f. and often.

83. See above, pp. 605ff.

If grace is no longer understood as truly God's grace, this can lead to wantonness, to the idea of "cheap grace," to the illusion of the kind of grace which no longer requires discipline of us (Tit. 2:12). However, this corrupt form of a "Protestantism" which fundamentally lacks grace cannot enable us to understand the humble freedom in which the Reformers really lived and proclaimed. They turned their backs on sin, "by the grace of God." And thus "actual sin" can have the frightening importance which accrues when the gift of grace is contemned, but it never bears its own moral weight which could then be balanced out by the equal weight of the "works of satisfaction" (*opera satisfactoria*). Reformation ethics is an ethics of grace, and only on that basis is it an ethics of law, which then can be nothing other than the "custodian" who constantly appears anew to direct us to Christ (Gal. 3:24).

In the confrontation of the sinner, who commits sin, with Christ, his sin then is first demonstrated to be "mortal sin" (*peccatum mortale*), the sin which has brought him death. No one who is "in Christ" can make his sin "approved" by appealing to the pardoning grace which has become an event. He cannot do that because the death of Christ is in fact our death. But conversely, in the confrontation with Jesus Christ, which happens in the word of reconciliation, our sin and with it our total existence, which is now certainly seen to be fundamentally lost, is abolished, gotten out of the way. In place of either our remorseful or resigned concentration upon ourselves and our sin, our life enters into the light of the resurrection. "Actual sin" is thus placed within the freedom and discipline of grace, and actual forgiveness takes place in a constantly new way in the form of the proclamation of grace.

That the Roman Catholic view of "actual sin" does in fact see sin concretely cannot be an objection to it. Rather we should learn from it in this regard. The sin of the person is not general or abstract sin; rather, abstract sin is the kind for which man, in his own concept of "grace" (which is not grace in Jesus Christ!), forgives himself. Our objection would be that the Roman Catholic view of "actual sin" evades Christ. The "one sacrifice of Christ on the cross" is looked back upon in such a way that it appears as a past event, having its effect and being present in the Eucharist, but not really present in the person of the present Christ for us. That being the case, both the understanding and the pastoral treatment of "actual sin" must necessarily shift into a juridical setting: the Church, which distributes grace, decides about the seriousness of sins and about the modalities within which absolution becomes possible. This must necessarily mean that sin is depersonalized.

f. "Mortal and Venial Sin." This is seen most clearly in the distinction between "mortal sins" and "venial sins" (*peccata mortalia et peccata venialia*). It grew out of the penitential practice. And it is anchored dogmatically already in Augustine.[84] In opposition to the Reformation, it was finally dogmatized at Trent.[85]

---

84. E.g., *On the Spirit and the Letter*, XXVIII, 48 (*NPNF,* V, 104); *On Marriage and Concupiscence*, I, xv, 17 (*NPNF,* V, 270f.).

85. See especially Session VI, Decree on Justification, Ch. 11 (Denzinger, pp. 253f. [par. 804]).

It is quite obvious that, according to the dominant view held in regard to man and to interpersonal relationships, one offense is by no means equal to another. Penal law reveals this most clearly, in that its decisive task really is to discover for the variety of crimes the just and appropriate punishment, based upon the seriousness of each offense. It is equally unnecessary to contest that in contrast to the variety of human offenses—ranging from trivial breaches of the law to major crimes—there is also the great number of really good works:[86] a vast wealth reaching from honesty and helpfulness to genuine sacrifice. It was not a good thing to summarize all of these under a superficial understanding of "egoism," along the lines of the old saying that the virtues of the pagans are "splendid faults" (*splendida vitia*).[87] Such a denigration on principle of man's good activity is based upon an always questionable mixture of theological judgment with moral judgment, which must destroy both. No, as a result of God's sustaining grace[88] there are among us men not only "faults" and even "splendid faults" but also "civil virtues" (*virtutes civilis*). They can only redound to the praise of grace. But together with them we also see that our human activity progresses through all possible stages and forms. It is therefore all the less possible to equate generally sin with sin—so long as sin here is understood as human activity toward men. There may be here not only "venial sin" compared with "mortal sin"—which of course belongs to a completely different dimension—but also the many differentiations which both Scholasticism[89] and Orthodoxy[90] developed, in a peculiar mixture of theology and psychology.

g. "But Not Before God" (Rom. 4:2)! The Church's doctrine does not have the right to minimalize the sphere of the "moral." At this point it can as little afford to be skeptical or even cynical as it can elsewhere. It cannot withdraw its interest from moral customs or individual morality, nor from law, nor from any of those powers which manage to preserve this world one way or another as it proceeds toward its conclusion at the last judgment. For the God of which this

---

86. Dietrich Bonhoeffer, in the fragment of his *Ethic* which has come down to us (*Ethics*, ed. E. Bethge, tr. N. H. Smith [New York: Macmillan, 1955]), attempted to re-win the sphere of the "penultimate" for Christian ethics and thus the possibility of "penultimate" good works (see pp. 84ff.).

87. See Augustine, *Against Julian*, IV, Ch. 3, especially 25 and 26 (*FC*, XXXV, 180–86); moreover, and with astonishing sharpness, Melanchthon, *Loci* (*LCC*, XIX, 33); Stupperich, II/1, p. 21; more cautiously, Calvin, *Institutes*, II, iii, 3f., pp. 292–94 (the "virtues" as a work of "grace").

88. Calvin, *Institutes*, II, iii, 3, p. 292: "amid this corruption of nature there is some place for God's grace." "Thus God by his providence bridles perversity of nature" (p. 293). All of this is really already present in Augustine, *op. cit.*, but the accent in Calvin is more clearly placed upon "grace."

89. See especially Thomas, *STh*, I–II, lxxii, vol. I, pp. 902ff., "On the Distinction of Sins."

90. See, e.g., the Leiden Synopsis (H. Bavinck, ed., *Synopsis purioris theologiae disputationibus* [1626 and 1652] [Lugduni Batavorum: Didericum Donner, 1881]), which follows Thomas, or the very developed form in Heppe-Bizer, p. 349, which follows especially J. H. Heidegger, *Corpus Theologiae* (1700), X, 61–71. In contrast with most Reformed, on the Lutheran side the distinction between "mortal sin" and "venial sin" was taken up again (see especially Leonhard Hutter, *op. cit.*, VIII, 22ff., pp. 50ff.).

doctrine speaks is not a cynic, does not hold the world or man in contempt; rather, he is their Creator just as certainly as he is their Judge. But what is not permitted for the Church's doctrine would be the mixing of these aspects. This side the judgment, here among men, all of these distinctions between "good" and "evil" and even between various kinds of "evil" hold true. The Sermon on the Mount speaks, too, of "good" and "evil," "just" and "unjust" (Matt. 5:45), in this sense. And certainly the wisdom literature of the Old Testament is well aware of the differences between good and evil, just and unjust, wise and foolish, which are permitted to exist among men by virtue of God's sustaining grace. And Paul knows that Abraham, "if [he] was justified by works," deserved to "boast" (Rom. 4:2). Paul is also interested in preserving his personal honor (1 Cor. 4:3). But none of this has any standing "before God"—it has no effect upon sin as sin! This is expressed by Paul in Romans 4:2 as well as in 1 Corinthians 4:4—the things which are true among men do not have any authority before God. If we understand "sin" as we did, then we shall see in all of the "sins" which appear within our world this side of the Last Judgment expressions of the one "sin," but we will never moralize them theologically, especially not speaking of them as "mortal sins" and "venial sins" in a theological sense. Paul's thesis that everything which is not of faith is sin (Rom. 14:23) will have to stand. Such a statement cannot be made as a moral judgment. For this thesis encompasses even the "good"[91] which does not proceed out of faith, even the work of love (1 Cor. 13:1) which is not love. Conversely, this thesis leads to the common Roman Catholic and Evangelical view that "unbelievers" are always enslaved in "mortal sin."[92] This is again a morally impossible assertion, and its moralization has produced the aforementioned and fateful mixtures, even in Augustine.[93] If we draw a conclusion, we shall have to say that it is precisely from the perspective of "righteousness by faith" (*justitia fidei*) and the doctrine of sin which is its proper counterpart that we come to the proper respect and freedom in regard to morality which is fitting for the Gospel as the good news.

3. SIN AND DEATH

a. "The Wages of Sin." "The wages of sin is death," says Paul in Romans 6:23. "Sin . . . brings forth death," asserts James (1:15). The doctrine of the Church has always and generally regarded death as the "punishment" for sin, as God's judgment over sinful man.

---

91. Trent objects to the assertion "that in every good work the just one sins at least venially or (what is more intolerable) mortally . . ." (Decree on Justification, Ch. 25 [Denzinger, p. 260, par. 835]). That is an exaggerated formulation of the Reformation doctrine because it includes Trent's own doctrinal concept of sin. It is opposed by the reverse thesis which Calvin formulates, "by faith alone not only we ourselves but our works as well are justified" (*Institutes,* III, xvii, 10, p. 813).

92. When 1 John 5:16f. speaks of a sin "unto death," then it would seem most obvious to think here of Matt. 12:31 and pars., and of Heb. 6:4ff.: implied is the extreme and intellectually insoluble possibility of man's self-rejection through his rejection of the grace granted to him. It is certain that moral offenses are not implied.

93. *Against Julian,* IV, Ch. 3 (*FC,* XXXV, 176ff.).

Now this term "punishment" is not completely clear. The Pauline term, "wages" (*ta opsōnia*), and the expression in James view death simply as the consequence which follows directly upon sin. Death is what unavoidably results from sin. It is implicit in sin—just as life is implicit in the "image of God." We must in fact protect this idea of punishment from any kind of heterogenous conception. Death is not related to sin in the way that a jail sentence is related to the commission of a burglary. Human judicial punishment is a heterogenous sanction. The "punishment" placed by God's judgment upon the sin consists of the sinner's being taken at his word. What is already present within the sin, namely, separation of the creature from the Creator, is now realized. This is the sense in which we should understand the threat in Genesis 2:17. It is the warning of the benevolent Creator, comparable to a mother's warning to her child, "Don't touch the stove or you will burn yourself." Genesis 3:22 certainly leads to this understanding: man, who has now become what he is, would only "gain" with his immortality the infinity of the impossible, namely, existence without the Creator.[94]

According to these considerations, the concept of punishment must be used carefully. Penal punishment, however it is viewed in terms of the theory of punishment, is always the reaction of a given legal order to a partial offense. Its sanction secures the given order as well as dealing with the offense and the offender. But sin is not a partial offense against a standing order, but the comprehensive destruction of the relationship between the Creator and the creature. It is not possible to secure a broken marriage through some kind of institutional sanctions; in the same way, the "punishment" for sin cannot secure the relationship to God, which would be assumed to continue in and of itself, as though the offense had never occurred. Here, "punishment" cannot be what it is within the legal order. Death is what is already contained within sin. In contrast to sin there is only one thing which supersedes it, and that is not the permanence of an order but the miracle of divine covenant faithfulness. And we shall have to see how, proceeding from that basis, even death gains new aspects. Indeed, even "curse" (Gal. 3:10, 13) and "wrath" (Rom. 1:18) as God's personal reaction to sin find their truly appropriate significance from that perspective.

But for now we shall have to say that sin causes death in that it is the alienation of the creature from the Creator, from the "source of life." It receives what it already is.

b. The Death of Man as Person. In what we have said up to now, a specific understanding of death has been assumed. What we have meant is the death which encounters the self. The question could be raised whether death is not an unavoidable component of "nature," of the biologically given make-up of man. Is the "immortality" of man physiologically conceivable? And can then death be the "wages" of sin? Is it not merely the "tribute" which man must pay to his biological existence? It appears that the question is justified. Viewed from the

---

94. See the impressive interpretation in Roland de Pury, *Présence de l'Éternité; Conférences sur des sujets très variés* (Neuchâtel: Delachaux et Niestlé, 1943), pp. 37f., and similarly, Dietrich Bonhoeffer, *Creation and Fall, A Theological Interpretation of Genesis 1-3*, tr. J. C. Fletcher (New York: Macmillan, 1959), pp. 92ff.

biological structure of man, an "immortal" being is unimaginable. For that reason, death could well be understood as something absolutely "natural." There is only life in the biological sense where there is also death.

The remarkable fact is that man always deals with this empirical necessity that he will have to die as something with which he must "come to terms." Even the apparently sober thesis that man as an organism belonging to one group of mammals "simply has to die" is in fact one way he tries to come to terms with death. Death, even though it doubtless can be medically researched, observed thousands of times, and its causes explained pathologically, is a riddle. As a riddle, it is only comparable with the other inexplicable riddle of evil—or with the riddle which manifests itself in both, that of the person himself. Man's relationship to his death is absolutely different from that of any other mortal creature to his. Man must die his own death, and that means that in this death he does not experience a process concluding, a "termination,"[95] but the end for which he exists. Heidegger is right when he characterizes human existence as "existence for death."[96] The riddle of death is thus the riddle of life in its most extreme concrete form. And it is part of the essence of man that he understand himself. Thus man cannot evade death as his own death. The way he deals with it is the way in which he interprets his existence. In every one of the ways, which are not to be discussed here, he does prove that his life is not just an organic process (*bios*) but in some sense "Life" (*zōē*), or at least intended to be that. Man demonstrates, though not always in his behavior in regard to his death or in his opinion of his death, but certainly in the way he lives toward his death, that he is a being who does not merely possess organic life (*bios*) as an "it," but that he *is* as an "I" and that as this "I" he "exists" toward death. The main forms for dealing with death are these. First of all, man can try to make his death unreal in that he removes his true self from it (the immortality of the soul in all its forms). Secondly, he can look upon his death as his own "deed" and thus participate in it actively as a mere experience.[97] Thirdly, he can integrate his death into the "everydayness" of existence, emphasizing "Nobody doubts that one dies" and thus "conceal" his existence toward death.[98] Or fourthly, he can endure his existence with death and toward death, and in this acceptance of death into his life he can live

---

95. M. Heidegger, *Being and Time,* tr. J. Macquarrie and E. Robinson (New York: Harper, 1962 [g1931³]), p. 291.

96. *Ibid.,* p. 278. Heidegger himself knows that his thesis, without the Christian anthropology which he does not affirm in substance, would be difficult to conceive of. It is well known that he was influenced by Kierkegaard. He also says (*ibid.,* p. 494, n. vi): "In its interpretation of 'life', the anthropology worked out in Christian theology—from Paul right up to Calvin's '*meditatio futurae vitae*'—has always kept death in view." See also S. Kierkegaard, *The Concept of Dread,* tr. W. Lowrie (Princeton: Princeton University Press, 1958); Calvin, *Institutes,* III, ix, pp. 712ff., "Meditation on the Future Life," and on that, M. Schulze, *Meditatio futurae vitae, Ihr Begriff und ihre herrschende Stellung im System Calvins* (Leipzig: Dieterich, T. Weicher, 1901) and *Calvins Jenseitschristentum* (1902; n.l.).

97. R. Bultmann, article on *thanatos,* in *TDNT,* III, 7ff., 11ff., in regard to classic Greece and Stoicism.

98. M. Heidegger, *op. cit.,* p. 299.

this life as such in decision and decisiveness.[99] In all of these instances there is at least the intuition that our death has something to do with us as persons, and that it is in the qualified sense "my own death." This is also true of the third approach mentioned, which Heidegger characterizes well by saying that in it one "does not permit us the courage for anxiety in the face of death."[100] But one is not able to change the fact "that one is defined as a being for death, and this is true even if it is not involved in any 'thinking about death' "—the "daily routine of existence" (or "everydayness") is virtually evidence of this.[101]

In regard to this brief review of man's religious and philosophical endeavors to deal with death we could come to a judgment very similar to our conclusion about the corresponding efforts with evil: certainly something of the phenomenon of death becomes visible, of that death which is something other than man's termination or passing.

The question as to the sense in which we are to understand the assertion that our sin is "rewarded" in death, must be dealt with quite apart from the other question, whether physically immortal human life is imaginable. The death which we are concerned with here is the death toward which we are going.

c. God and Death. The death which is "the wages of sin" is not death "per se." To want to speak of death "per se," which would be to neutralize or to objectivize death, would mean that we were seeking to escape from our humanness. This is not possible in reference to "my very own death."

This death, rather, is characterized by the fact that it is the death of the sinner. Not just any death, but this death is the wages of sin. More precisely, this death is death before God, just as our sinful existence is an existence before God.

In order to describe what that means, we must first seek to summarize the biblical view of death in its major elements.

Our point of departure is the universal biblical testimony to the fact that God is the Living God and the One who gives life. The Israelite vows "as the Lord lives" (Judg. 8:19 and often), and Yahweh swears by his own life (Num. 14:21 and often). God and life belong together. The Bible knows of no god of the dead (see Mark 12:27). In the Old Testament, death is not a mythological realm of its own nor a deity assigned to that realm. God is the "fountain of life" (Ps. 36:9), compared to the spring bubbling forth from the rocks, and not to the cistern (Jer. 2:13). He is the Living One (Matt. 16:16; 26:63; John 6:57; Acts 14:15; 1 Thess. 1:9, etc.). All of this means basically one thing, that he is the Creator. Life is therefore incomparably more than biological "existence" or even "being" in the everyday sense. Life is the relationship to the origin which is God himself. Next to the creation accounts, this is seen most impressively in Psalm 104. God's "breath" gives life, creates the creature, and renews the face of the earth; when he withdraws, the creature is surrendered to nothingness (Ps. 104:29f.). Life is

---

99. This would be Heidegger's own guidance for life, without saying anything at all about the possibility of its realization.

100. *Ibid.*, p. 298.

101. *Ibid.*, pp. 298f. [my translation—TR].

thus the absolute opposite of non-existence, because it is life derived from God. Therefore life is "originalness," joy, and power.

Under these circumstances, death is qualitatively that which has nothing to do with God. The Old Testament frequently expresses this by its understanding of the realm of the dead, *sheol,* as the realm of qualified distance from God. The dead do not praise God—that is the decisive thing about their being dead. For the Old Testament, life based upon the covenant means life in the community which praises God. The Old Testament does not contest the fact that the dead "exist somewhere"—they do have their place, and Israel developed ideas about it similar to those of the heathen world surrounding it. But that is not where the accent lies. Whatever the situation of the dead may be, the terrible thing which has happened to them is that they are now excluded from the community of those who praise Yahweh (Ps. 6:5; 30:9; 88:10–12; 115:17; Isa. 38:18f.). Thus the physically alive person who experiences the question of his opponents, "Where is your God?", and finds no answer, the one far from the place of praise and suffering there, can cry out, "As with a deadly wound in my body my adversaries taunt me" (Ps. 42:11). To be isolated from God is death. This is even true where death is personified (we think of the picture of death as the reaper [Jer. 9:20f.]). It is never the god of the dead, but rather the incomprehensible opponent of life derived from God. With death, the relationship to God is destroyed; conversely, the destruction of the relationship to God is death.[102] The moment of death is, so to speak, the boundary beyond which the realm of death, *sheol,* is located, but which conversely penetrates the sphere of life of those still physically existing (Karl Barth refers to Ps. 107).

In the New Testament we find first only a deepening and intensification of what was already commenced in the Old Testament. If we can use the idea of "life lived in the midst of death" (*media vita in morte*) as an apt description of the Old Testament understanding of death, it is certainly appropriate for the New Testament. Here, death is nothing other than distance from God (i.e., the distance of the creature from the near God who is therefore threateningly present!). To put it differently and more precisely, every distance from God is death. As a sinner, man is dead "through the trespasses and sins" (Eph. 2:1; Col. 2:13), the prodigal son "was dead" (Luke 15:24), the commandment which promised life causes "death" in man (Rom. 7:10); the letter of the law "kills" (2 Cor. 3:6, 7). Apparently "death" is the constitution of man's existence. The "mind-set" (*phronēma*) of the "flesh" (*sarx*), that toward which man in his fallen state is in fact directed, is death (Rom. 8:6; see also Rom. 8:13; Gal. 6:8), and in accordance with that, the man who does not love "remains in death" (1 John 3:14). The moment of death, dying itself, can therefore only be the visible consummation of

---

102. On the Old Testament understanding of death see especially W. Eichrodt, *Theology of the Old Testament,* tr. J. A. Baker (London: S.C.M. Press, 1961–67 [g1939]), II, 496f.; Christoph Barth, *Die Errettung vom Tode in den individuellen Klage- und Dankliedern des Alten Testaments* (Zollikon: Evangelischer Verlag, 1947); Gerhard von Rad and Rudolf Bultmann, article on *thanatos,* in *TDNT,* II, 382ff.; A. Bertholet, *Die israelitischen Vorstellungen vom Zustand nach dem Tode* (Tübingen: J. C. B. Mohr, 1914²); also *RGG,* 2nd ed., V, 1195f.

what always had been there anyway. Older theology, which distinguished between "corporal death" (*mors corporalis*), "spiritual death" (*mors spiritualis*), and "eternal death" (*mors aeterna*—which was already made known in spiritual death), was exegetically right to the extent that it understood "spiritual" not as a level of being but as a total aspect of man. "Spiritual death" is man's death before God, who is the life of man. Biological death is therefore specific, death-oriented death, because life has already fallen prey to death. We will, in fact, have to come to terms with an even greater disparity between death and another kind of death. There is not only a life which is already death, but there is also life-bringing death ("For to me to live is Christ, and to die is gain" [Phil. 1:21]). That statement would not have been possible in the Old Testament, for this statement is not concerned with life beyond as such, but with the person of Jesus Christ in whom God is our "beyond."

The moment of death, man's entry into the state of no longer being, the point of junction between the biological end (in which "the wise man dies just like the fool" [Eccl. 2:16], and in which "the fate of the sons of men and the fate of beasts is the same; as the one dies, so dies the other" [Eccl. 3:19]) and the specific death, gains here the character of an effective sign that man, regardless of his state, stands before God. In this moment the decision made in life about life or death is finally ratified, made permanent. Our life, lived in the face of death (as the event of death) and of the judgment which appears in it, is a life lived in decision. But it is only that from the point of view of God's judgment. If our death were something other than a sign of divine judgment, then it could only be the sign of nothingness, and every decision would be made in relationship to nothingness, that is, it would be either senseless or be the form of our own self-assertion or self-destruction. That would mean that we would be in our decisions absolutely without a counterpart. Death as a sign, as the manifestation of nothingness, would necessarily mean the casting of the decision back upon ourselves and that would mean the condemning of our existence to self-centered isolation. Nothingness would then be in very truth the death which kills. Death can only have a revealing, an opening sense, when it confronts us with the living God.

Death as an event is, in any event, the thing which makes our life irrevocable. But if our death were the thing which confronted us with nothingness, then it would not in fact be the basis for the irrevocability of our existence, but of a definite complex of time-consuming processes which quite accidentally made use of us (in our accidentality) as their place or bearers. That would mean that our life were really our life in a very inauthentic way, and the irrevocability of our actions would be nothing more than their vulgar nature as things which once were, and which now are past. But if it is true that our death means nothing less than this, that we "fall into the hands of the living God" (Heb. 10:31), then the irrevocability which it establishes means that we are ourselves responsible in the totality of our actions. Then we are truly "living in the midst of death" (*media vita in morte*). Death is the qualification of our life as our very own life. And the moment of death concludes the possibility of a new decision, and makes every decision already made now final.

d. *Death as the Finalization of Sin*. What does it now mean from this perspective that death is "the wages of sin"? Before we answer, it should be pointed out that there is one aspect of death which could emerge for which this statement would not be true. Death could be the finalization of the irrevocability of the life which had been lived totally from God's life. This possibility, which is only conceivable from the point of view of its realization, is, however, not our possibility according to Christian insight. What becomes irrevocable in our death is the life which failed. Our death is thus nothing other than the final revelation of the fatal fallen state in which it always had been lived. The moment of death is the moment in which the meaning of life is revealed as the meaning which we did not grasp.

Now we can say what it means that death comes from us out of sin, our death out of our sin. It is our final and irrevocable identification with all that we already are. It is the finalization of the "retrogression" in which we find ourselves,[103] which is not just a defect or a lack, but rather that we continue to remain guilty of not giving ourselves to God and our neighbor. The failed existence which is our "life" becomes apparent in death as the end, the fallenness, which corresponds to it. If we want to judge exactly, we will not view dying (the moment of death) as the primary curse laid upon us, but rather death as that which dominates our existence, as the power which characterizes existence for death. We are "dead" before we died, and we would be "dead" even if there were no biological cessation of life.

We must view this same matter from another side. The Bible does not view death as an ontological necessity, but rather as an intervention made by God. It does not know of an independent power of death, hypostatized as the opponent of God.[104] The actual power of death is the power of God in his concealment. That is the power of God which takes us by our word when we say No and which confronts us as the ones who are negating his life. "It is a fearful thing to fall into the hands of the living God" (Heb. 10:31)! Death derives its power from God's No. This even appears in the biological cessation of life to the degree that there we are deprived of our illusory control of ourselves, and the final dishonesty of our own existence is uncovered. Seen in terms of the moment of death, death is the "wages of sin" in that it completes what is the essence of sin, namely, our distance vis-à-vis the God who is present, and it reveals sin's mystery, which is our illusory desire to be autonomous.

We have developed here two fundamental insights. First of all, death characterizes our life and defines it. Secondly, death is the "wages of sin" in that it is already present in sin, is an autogenetic given with it. Death causes death. Therefore, our fear of death, which we can cover up in a thousand ways but which

---

103. This is the term used by Karl Barth, *CD,* III,2, p. 596: "Guilt means retrogression. And retrogression consists in a failure to use our God-given freedom; in a failure to be truly human in our relationships with Him and our fellows; in an inconceivable renunciation of our freedom; in our incredible, inexplicable and impossible choice of the imprisonment of a being in renunciation on both sides; in our incomprehensible lapse into a state of ungodliness and inhumanity."

104. We read that God has power over death in Ps. 90:3, 7ff., Matt. 10:28, and often. The fact that according to Heb. 2:14 this is the power of the devil does not make him into a god of death, in that he had his power as a result of the effective No of God.

is still the driving impulse of our existence as "concern" or "care,"[105] is the characteristic form of our surrender to the slavery we have chosen for ourselves (Heb. 2:15).

e. The Seriousness of Death and the Certainty of Life. Nonetheless, it is certainly clear by now and must be emphasized that everything which we said about death as the "wages" of sin was uttered from the perspective of the victory over death. Death could be simply an unquestioned, unpuzzling, purely positive given element; it could be simply a constant factor of our existence. We could bear it as an animal does—although certainly with momentary resistance, but without any overshadowing of our life based on it, and without any questioning of it. But we do not do that. Certainly there are many people who would like to be able to do that. But man can only evade this concern as the given ontological structure at the cost of his own human existence. Man cannot die as the animals do. And the very desire of such a death, the very thought which imagines it, is a peculiar manifestation, an unavoidable phenomenon, of the fact that in such an instance we still act like humans, in this case by trying to renounce our human existence. Yet the idealistic and spiritualistic endeavor to make death unreal by removing the realm of the soul from it does not truly help us further. Belief in immortality is, of course, an extreme misunderstanding of death, and as such, experienced as the echo of Plato's Phaedo, it is the extreme opponent of the Christian view of death. But its whole impulse is also to dehumanize the undeniable process of death by removing what is genuinely human from it.

Death is only taken in total seriousness where God is taken in total seriousness. In the history of the Christian Church there is a wealth of examples of comforted dying. But there is no legitimate, that is, in accordance with the witness of revelation, "contempt" of death.[106] There is also no coming to terms with death, even along the lines of Heidegger. Death is the enemy (the final enemy [1 Cor. 15:26]). It is the absolute intrusion. And it is quite noticeable that this is expressed much more directly and explicitly in the New Testament than in the Old. This is all the more remarkable because the New Testament, in contrast with virtually all of the Old Testament witness, knows about the overcoming of death. It would seem obvious to ask, Is there not an inner relationship present here, and do not the seriousness of death and the message of life, of the resurrection, belong together?

In terms of the terminology this is apparently not the case. Would not the prospect of the resurrection rob death of its seriousness? And would not the

---

105. As is well known, this is the fundamental concept in M. Heidegger, following Kierkegaard. One characteristic passage: "The being thrust into death reveals itself to existence in a more original and penetrating fashion (than in theoretical knowledge) in the condition of fear. Fear of death is fear of one's very own, unrelated, and unrecoverable ability to be" (M. Heidegger, *op. cit.*, p. 295 [my translation—TR]). And further: "As regards its ontological possibility, dying is grounded in care" (p. 296).

106. See the instructive work by P. Althaus, *Der Friedhof unserer Väter; ein Gang durch die Sterbe- und Ewigkeitslieder der evangelischen Kirche* (Gütersloh: Bertelsmann, 1923²). Above all we think of Luther's statement, "In the midst of life we are surrounded by death," and of Calvin's "Meditation on the future life" (*Institutes*, III, ix, pp. 712ff.).

seriousness of death be greatest where death itself has the last word? In point of fact, neither of these is true (not even the latter: where death has the last word, it is not being taken seriously as death but becomes the conclusion which, in a manner of speaking, belongs to life).

f. Jesus Christ and Death. The inner connection between the seriousness of death and the certainty of life is based not upon intellectual reflection but solely upon the work of Jesus Christ. We do not know what death really is either through our experience of someone else's death nor from the expectation of our own, but only from His death. And we do not know what life really is from the most enthusiastic affirmation of life (which in its strained character always betrays the secret concern and the concealed death) but only through his resurrection.

The death of Jesus Christ is the actual death, the real confrontation of forfeited life with the living God. This death is the "curse" (Gal. 3:13). In this death God's judgment is rendered. This death is the true and fully paid "wages" of sin. For God "made him to be sin" "for our sake" (2 Cor. 5:21). Here man in his identity with his sin is really cast into nothingness—"My God, my God, why hast thou forsaken me?" In this death, God takes death upon himself. Here the No, out of which human death lives, arrives at its goal, at its execution. The cross of Jesus Christ reveals the meaning of death and is the end of all neutralization and all minimalization of death.

The death of Jesus Christ makes plain that death, man's death, really is the result of sin. Death is to be recognized as the sign of the judgment of God at the very point where he bears it whose life is not of death but is of the life of God. He was not subject to death, but he dies. And therefore death reveals its true face here: it is not that death is an end which gives it its power but that it is the end under God's No. There could be a "blessed ending," and there is one. But this "end" is the exact opposite of blessed.

This ending is our ending. If one has died for all, then all have died (2 Cor. 5:14). And not only "all," but every believer (baptized person), according to the contents of Romans 6 and the meaning of Galatians 2:19. Death is "through the law" and thus carried out through the "power" of sin, which is the "sting" of death (1 Cor. 15:56). With the death of Jesus Christ a decision has been made about every man, and faith in Jesus Christ is the acknowledgment of this decision. But that can only mean that the believer accepts this decision as completed and thus completed for him and in him.

g. Death Overcome. If then Christian doctrine only interprets what is given to us in faith, it can only speak of death, as of sin, in the sense that it is death overcome. To take death totally seriously means to understand it as the death which Jesus Christ took upon himself for us. Death has already attained its goal, the goal set for it by God, which was the execution of the divine No—in the One whose obedience (and to that extent, whose authentic life, lived in dependence upon God) was obedience "unto death, even death on a cross" (Phil. 2:8). Because that is so, Paul can conclude the passage about death as the "wages" of sin with a testimony to the "gift" (*charisma*) of God, which consists of "eternal life in Christ Jesus our Lord" (Rom. 6:23). And with that, at the end of Romans 6, he can return to what had already been established at the end of Romans 5, the royal dominion of sin which happens in death is now opposed by the royal power of grace which exercises its reign "through righteousness [as the new constitution of existence established in Christ] to eternal life through Jesus Christ, our Lord" (Rom. 5:21). Where grace reigns, where righteousness has established itself, there death is a matter of the past. In other words, where the "new creation" has taken place (2 Cor. 5:17), there everything "old," including death which is the epitome of the "old," "passed away." Or again, in other words, "Jesus Christ [has] abolished death and brought life and immortality to light through the gospel" (2 Tim. 1:10). Or in Johannine terms, "He who believes in the Son has eternal life" (John 3:36), and "he does not come into judgment, but has passed from death to life" (John 5:24). The absolute eschatological event, that God "will swallow up death forever" (Isa. 25:8), can be designated by Paul as having already taken place in Christ, in the resurrection: "Death is swallowed up in victory" (1 Cor. 15:54), although it certainly still is before us, when projected upon time as the progressive form. Death is the "last enemy," which must still be overcome (1 Cor. 15:24).

If all this is then established, it is finally clear that death—our death as Jesus Christ took it upon himself—is what absolutely is not supposed to be. It has no other power than that of the No, which is the No of the living God. It is what God has revealed to be alien to him. But as the curse which holds sway over man, its power is not unlimited. God himself has taken this curse upon himself in the work of Jesus Christ. Just as he opposed the power of sin with his faithfulness, he has counter-attacked the power of death with the power of his life victoriously. "Life retained the victory. . . !" This is the only way to speak of death in a Christian manner.

Of course, when death is spoken of in this way, it gains another aspect. There are statements in the New Testament witness which view death as deprived of all fear, as a blessed ending. Some of these statements may sound as though Hellenistic thinking had gained sway over Old Testament thinking. This, for example, seems to be the case when Paul can go so far as to say that he has the "desire" to weigh anchor and to be with Christ (Phil. 1:23), that dying would be a gain (Phil. 1:21). Certainly one would think, as Karl Barth suggests,[107] of the not seldom passages in which death is characterized by the use of the singularly placid term, "to fall asleep" (koimasthai [e.g., John 11:11; 1 Cor. 15:6]). There is, according to these passages, a liberated dying, free from the curse. Man's being freed "from unnatural death" obviously means that as "he is freed for eternal life, he is also freed for natural death."[108] The concept of "natural death" implies that in light of the overcoming of the negative power of death which God has made possible, its authentic, original, and thus creative meaning emerges, the meaning that it is a "gracious ending," that ending in which man, now certainly confronted with God, is confronted with life, with his life. This good dying is not understandable to us. For our dying is always in terms of what we can see as that

---

107. *CD,* III,2, pp. 638f.
108. *Ibid.,* p. 638.

other ending, in which the judgment spoken over us in baptism becomes visible, and to that extent it has been rightly termed by Karl Barth the "sign of the judgment of God."[109] Yet faith recognizes in it another sign, so long as it is faith in the One who is not just the sign of this judgment but who bore this judgment for us himself and thereby has opened up to us life, the life which man has, "though he die" (John 11:25).

---

109. *CD,* III,2, pp. 597ff., *passim.*

Index of Subjects

Index of *Termini*

Index of Scripture References

Index of Names

651